Lecture Notes in Compu

Founding Editors

Gerhard Goos
Juris Hartmanis

Editorial Board Members

Elisa Bertino, *Purdue University, West Lafayette, IN, USA*
Wen Gao, *Peking University, Beijing, China*
Bernhard Steffen, *TU Dortmund University, Dortmund, Germany*
Moti Yung, *Columbia University, New York, NY, USA*

The series Lecture Notes in Computer Science (LNCS), including its subseries Lecture Notes in Artificial Intelligence (LNAI) and Lecture Notes in Bioinformatics (LNBI), has established itself as a medium for the publication of new developments in computer science and information technology research, teaching, and education.

LNCS enjoys close cooperation with the computer science R & D community, the series counts many renowned academics among its volume editors and paper authors, and collaborates with prestigious societies. Its mission is to serve this international community by providing an invaluable service, mainly focused on the publication of conference and workshop proceedings and postproceedings. LNCS commenced publication in 1973.

Leonid Reyzin · Douglas Stebila
Editors

Advances in Cryptology – CRYPTO 2024

44th Annual International Cryptology Conference
Santa Barbara, CA, USA, August 18–22, 2024
Proceedings, Part VII

☼ Springer

Editors
Leonid Reyzin
Boston University
Boston, MA, USA

Douglas Stebila
University of Waterloo
Waterloo, ON, Canada

ISSN 0302-9743　　　　　　ISSN 1611-3349 (electronic)
Lecture Notes in Computer Science
ISBN 978-3-031-68393-0　　　ISBN 978-3-031-68394-7 (eBook)
https://doi.org/10.1007/978-3-031-68394-7

© International Association for Cryptologic Research 2024

This work is subject to copyright. All rights are solely and exclusively licensed by the Publisher, whether the whole or part of the material is concerned, specifically the rights of translation, reprinting, reuse of illustrations, recitation, broadcasting, reproduction on microfilms or in any other physical way, and transmission or information storage and retrieval, electronic adaptation, computer software, or by similar or dissimilar methodology now known or hereafter developed.
The use of general descriptive names, registered names, trademarks, service marks, etc. in this publication does not imply, even in the absence of a specific statement, that such names are exempt from the relevant protective laws and regulations and therefore free for general use.
The publisher, the authors and the editors are safe to assume that the advice and information in this book are believed to be true and accurate at the date of publication. Neither the publisher nor the authors or the editors give a warranty, expressed or implied, with respect to the material contained herein or for any errors or omissions that may have been made. The publisher remains neutral with regard to jurisdictional claims in published maps and institutional affiliations.

This Springer imprint is published by the registered company Springer Nature Switzerland AG
The registered company address is: Gewerbestrasse 11, 6330 Cham, Switzerland

If disposing of this product, please recycle the paper.

Preface

The 44th International Cryptology Conference (CRYPTO 2024) was held at the University of California, Santa Barbara, California, USA, from August 18th to August 22nd, 2024. It is an annual conference organized by the International Association for Cryptologic Research (IACR).

A record 526 papers were submitted for presentation at the conference, and 143 were selected. Six pairs of papers and one triple of papers were "soft-merged"; that is, given one speaking slot while remaining separate in the proceedings. To accommodate the record high number of 135 presentations, CRYPTO had three tracks in 2024, for the second time in its history.

To smoothly handle consideration of such a large number of papers, CRYPTO 2024 benefited from the excellent leadership of nine area chairs: Sonia Belaïd, Nir Bitansky, Dario Catalano, Dana Dachman-Soled, Susah Hohenberger, Seny Kamara, Tanja Lange, Mariana Raykova, and Yu Sasaki. Each of them helped manage the reviewing process, lead discussions, and move toward decisions for approximately 60 submissions. Their help was invaluable and we could not have managed without them.

To evaluate the submissions, we selected a program committee of 114 top cryptography researchers from all over the world. This was the largest program committee that CRYPTO has ever had. Each paper was assigned to three program committee members who reviewed it either by themselves or with the help of trusted sub-referees. As a result, we benefited from the expertise of 485 sub-referees. The program committee and the sub-referees, all of whom are named below, generated a staggering 1584 reviews. We thank our program committee members and the sub-referees for the hard work of peer review, which is the bedrock of scientific progress.

The review process was double-blind and confidential. In accordance with the IACR conflict-of-interest policy, the reviewing software we used (HotCRP) kept track of which reviewer had a conflict of interest with which author (for example, by virtue of being a close collaborator or an advisor) and ensured that no paper was assigned a conflicted reviewer.

In order to be considered, submissions had to be anonymous and their length was limited to 30 pages excluding the bibliography and supplementary materials. After the first seven or so weeks of evaluation, the committee chose to continue considering 349 papers; the remaining 177 papers were rejected, including three desk rejects and six withdrawn submissions. This rejection decision was based on three (or, in a few cases, two) reviews, none of which favored acceptance. The papers that remained under consideration were invited to submit a response (rebuttal) to clarifications requested from their reviewers. One paper was withdrawn during this second phase. Each of the 348 remaining papers received at least three reviews. After around three weeks of additional discussions, the committee made the final selection of the 143 papers that appear in these proceedings. For 27 of the papers that were not accepted, the committee flagged them as "revise-and-resubmit", meaning that one (anonymous to the authors) reviewer from

CRYPTO 2024 volunteered to review the paper should the authors resubmit it in the next cycle of IACR General Conferences (Asiacrypt 2024, Eurocrypt 2025, CRYPTO 2025) and request the volunteer reviewer.

We thank all the authors who submitted their papers to CRYPTO 2024. The vast majority of the submissions, including those that were ultimately not selected, were of very high quality, and we are very honored that CRYPTO was the venue that the authors chose for their work. We are additionally grateful to the authors of the accepted papers for the extra work of incorporating the reviewers' feedback and presenting their papers at the conference.

This year the Best Paper Awards were given to Seyoon Ragavan and Vinod Vaikuntanathan for their paper "Space-Efficient and Noise-Robust Quantum Factoring" and Gal Arnon, Alessandro Chiesa, Giacomo Fenzi, and Eylon Yogev for their paper "STIR: Reed–Solomon Proximity Testing with Fewer Queries". The Best Early Career Paper Award went to Quang Dao and Aayush Jain for their paper "Lossy Cryptography from Code-Based Assumptions". These three papers were subsequently invited to be submitted to the IACR Journal of Cryptology.

In addition to the presentations of contributed papers included in these proceedings, the conference also featured an invited talk by Karthikeyan Bhargavan titled "Integrating Formal Verification in Cryptographic Standards and Implementations". The traditional rump session, chaired by Craig Costello and Eysa Lee, took place on Tuesday, August 20th, and featured numerous short talks.

Co-located cryptography workshops were held in the preceding weekend; they included the following five events: "GHTC—Glowing Hot Topics in Cryptography: Has academic cryptography over-promised and under delivered?", "CFAIL—Conference for Failed Approaches and Insightful Losses in Cryptology", "WAC7—Workshop on Attacks in Cryptography 7", "PPML—Privacy-Preserving Machine Learning Workshop", and "SKAW—Symmetric Key Agreement Workshop". We gladly thank Adeline Roux-Langlois for serving as the Affiliated Events Chair and putting together such an enticing program.

For the first time, CRYPTO 2024 included an artifact evaluation process. Authors of accepted papers were invited to submit associated artifacts, such as software or datasets, for archiving alongside their papers; 12 artifacts were submitted. Marc Stevens was the Artifact Chair, and led an artifact evaluation committee of 12 members listed below. In the interactive review process between authors and reviewers, the goal was not just to evaluate artifacts, but also to improve them. Artifacts that passed successfully through the artifact review process were publicly archived by the IACR at https://artifacts.iacr.org/.

We are grateful to the IACR Board of Directors and especially to Kevin McCurley and Kay McKelly for their help with many technical aspects, including reviewing software, technical, web, and A/V support. Our 2023 predecessors, Helena Handschuh and Anna Lysyanskaya, were invaluable sources of wisdom and advice. Last but not least we thank Tancrède Lepoint for serving as our General Chair and making sure the conference went smoothly and attendees had a great experience. Thank you to our industry sponsors for their generous contributions, including early sponsors: Apple, Algorand Foundation, AWS, Google, and TII (gold sponsors); Input Output Global, Meta, and a16z (silver sponsors); and PQShield, NTT Research, CryptoExperts, HEaaN CryptoLab, and IBM (bronze sponsors).

August 2024

Leonid Reyzin
Douglas Stebila

Organization

General Chair

Tancrède Lepoint   Amazon Web Services, USA

Affiliated Events Chair

Adeline Roux-Langlois   CNRS, GREYC, France

Program Co-chairs

Leonid Reyzin   Boston University, USA
Douglas Stebila   University of Waterloo, Canada

Area Chairs

Sonia Belaïd   CryptoExperts, France
Nir Bitansky   Tel Aviv University, Israel
Dario Catalano   University of Catania, Italy
Dana Dachman-Soled   University of Maryland, USA
Susan Hohenberger   Johns Hopkins University, USA
Seny Kamara   Brown University and MongoDB, USA
Tanja Lange   Eindhoven University of Technology,
                               the Netherlands
Mariana Raykova   Google, USA
Yu Sasaki   NTT Laboratories, Japan

Program Committee

Masayuki Abe   NTT Social Informatics Laboratories, Japan
Benny Applebaum   Tel Aviv University, Israel
Gilad Asharov   Bar-Ilan University, Israel
Christian Badertscher   Input Output, Switzerland
Zhenzhen Bao   Tsinghua University, China

James Bartusek	University of California, Berkeley, USA
Jonathan Bootle	IBM Research Europe, Switzerland
Christina Boura	University of Versailles, France
Benedikt Bünz	New York University, USA
Anne Canteaut	Inria, France
David Cash	University of Chicago, USA
Guilhem Castagnos	Université de Bordeaux, France
Wouter Castryck	KU Leuven, Belgium
Yilei Chen	Tsinghua University, China
Arka Rai Choudhuri	NTT Research, USA
Michele Ciampi	University of Edinburgh, UK
Sandro Coretti	IOG, France
Craig Costello	Microsoft Research, USA
Elizabeth Crites	Web3 Foundation, UK
Joan Daemen	Radboud University, the Netherlands
Pratish Datta	NTT Research, USA
Itai Dinur	Ben-Gurion University, Israel
Sebastian Faust	TU Darmstadt, Germany
Luca De Feo	IBM Research Europe, Switzerland
Marc Fischlin	TU Darmstadt, Germany
Cody Freitag	Boston University and Northeastern University, USA
Chaya Ganesh	Indian Institute of Science, Bengaluru, India
Lorenzo Grassi	Ruhr-Universität Bochum, Germany
Jian Guo	Nanyang Technological University, Singapore
Siyao Guo	NYU Shanghai, China
Mohammad Hajiabadi	University of Waterloo, Canada
Lucjan Hanzlik	CISPA Helmholtz Center for Information Security, Germany
Justin Holmgren	NTT Research, USA
Kathrin Hövelmanns	Eindhoven University of Technology, the Netherlands
Yuval Ishai	Technion, Israel
Tibor Jager	University of Wuppertal, Germany
Stanislaw Jarecki	University of California, Irvine, USA
Zhengzhong Jin	MIT, USA
Elif Bilge Kavun	University of Passau, Germany
Dakshita Khurana	University of Illinois Urbana-Champaign, USA
Elena Kirshanova	Technology Innovation Institute, UAE
Karen Klein	ETH Zurich, Switzerland
Markulf Kohlweiss	University of Edinburgh and IOG, UK
Vladimir Kolesnikov	Georgia Institute of Technology, USA

Chelsea Komlo	University of Waterloo, Canada
Russell W. F. Lai	Aalto University, Finland
Gaëtan Leurent	Inria, France
Fukang Liu	Tokyo Institute of Technology, Japan
Qipeng Liu	University of California San Diego, USA
Meicheng Liu	Chinese Academy of Sciences, China
Tianren Liu	Peking University, China
Alex Lombardi	Princeton, USA
Mohammad Mahmoody	University of Virginia, USA
Chloe Martindale	University of Bristol, UK
Takahiro Matsuda	AIST, Japan
Bart Mennink	Radboud University, the Netherlands
Peihan Miao	Brown University, USA
Tarik Moataz	MongoDB, USA
Yusuke Naito	Mitsubishi Electric Corporation, Japan
Khoa Nguyen	University of Wollongong, Australia
Phong Q. Nguyen	Inria and DIENS/PSL, France
Ryo Nishimaki	NTT Social Informatics Laboratories, Japan
Emmanuela Orsini	Bocconi University, Italy
Rafail Ostrovsky	University of California, Los Angeles, USA
Jiaxin Pan	University of Kassel, Germany
Omer Paneth	Tel Aviv University, Israel
Dimitrios Papadopoulos	Hong Kong University of Science and Technology, China
Charalampos Papamanthou	Yale University, USA
Alice Pellet-Mary	CNRS and University of Bordeaux, France
Ludovic Perret	Sorbonne University, France
Giuseppe Persiano	Università di Salerno and Google, Italy
Thomas Peyrin	NTU, Singapore
Benny Pinkas	Aptos Labs and Bar-Ilan University, Israel
Bart Preneel	KU Leuven, Belgium
Willy Quach	Weizmann Institute of Science, Israel
Peter Rindal	Visa, USA
Matthieu Rivain	CryptoExperts, France
Alon Rosen	Bocconi University, Italy and Reichman University, Israel
Yann Rotella	UVSQ, Paris-Saclay University, France
Ron Rothblum	Technion, Israel
Lawrence Roy	Aarhus University, Denmark
Paul Rösler	FAU Erlangen-Nürnberg, Germany
Palash Sarkar	Indian Statistical Institute, India
Phillipp Schoppmann	Google, USA

André Schrottenloher	University of Rennes, Inria, IRISA, France
Peter Schwabe	MPI-SP, Germany and Radboud University, the Netherlands
Sruthi Sekar	University of California, Berkeley, USA
Yaobin Shen	Xiamen University, China
Luisa Siniscalchi	Technical University of Denmark, Denmark
Daniel Slamanig	Universität der Bundeswehr München, Germany
Ling Song	Jinan University, China
Pratik Soni	University of Utah, USA
Nicholas Spooner	University of Warwick, UK and New York University, USA
Tsuyoshi Takagi	University of Tokyo, Japan
Qiang Tang	University of Sydney, Australia
Yosuke Todo	NTT Social Informatics Laboratories, Japan
Dominique Unruh	RWTH Aachen, Germany and University of Tartu, Estonia
Vinod Vaikuntanathan	MIT, USA
Prashant Nalini Vasudevan	National University of Singapore, Singapore
Daniele Venturi	Sapienza University of Rome, Italy
Damien Vergnaud	Sorbonne Université, France
Huaxiong Wang	Nanyang Technological University, Singapore
Qingju Wang	Telecom Paris, Institut Polytechnique de Paris, France
Shiyuan Xu	University of Hong Kong, China
Jiayu Xu	Oregon State University, USA
Sophia Yakoubov	Aarhus University, Denmark
Rupeng Yang	University of Wollongong, Australia
Bo-Yin Yang	Academia Sinica, Taiwan
Kevin Yeo	Google and Columbia University, USA
Arkady Yerukhimovich	George Washington University, USA
Thomas Zacharias	University of Glasgow, UK
Bin Zhang	Institute of Software, Chinese Academy of Sciences, China
Yupeng Zhang	University of Illinois Urbana Champaign, USA
Vassilis Zikas	Purdue University, USA

Additional Reviewers

Kasra Abbaszadeh
Calvin Abou Haidar
Damiano Abram
Anasuya Acharya
Abtin Afshar
Amit Agarwal
Siddharth Agarwal
Ahmet Ramazan Ağırtaş
Shweta Agrawal
Akshima
Navid Alamati
Andreea Alexandru
Nicolas Alhaddad
Miguel Ambrona
Ghous Amjad
Yoshinori Aono
Gal Arnon
Arasu Arun
Nuttapong Attrapadung
Benedikt Auerbach
Renas Bacho
Ruben Baecker
Karim Baghery
Shi Bai
Mirza Ahad Baig
David Balbás
Fabio Banfi
Manuel Barbosa
Gilles Barthe
Carsten Baum
Josh Beal
Agathe Beaugrand
Amit Behera
Christof Beierle
Amos Beimel
James Bell-Clark
Shany Ben-David
Loris Bergerat
Ward Beullens
Rishabh Bhadauria
Raghav Bhaskar
Ritam Bhaumik
Nina Bindel

Suvasree Biswas
Olivier Blazy
Alexander Block
Jan Bobolz
Andrej Bogdanov
Nicolas Bon
Xavier Bonnetain
Carl Bootland
Giacomo Borin
Joppe Bos
Cecilia Boschini
Mariana Botelho da Gama
Alexandre Bouez
Clémence Bouvier
Pedro Branco
Nicholas Brandt
Lennart Braun
Pierre Briaud
Maya Farber Brodsky
Paul Bunn
Jeff Burdges
Fabio Campos
Yibo Cao
Pyrros Chaidos
Anirban Chakrabarthi
Bishwajit Chakraborty
Anirudh Chandramouli
Rohit Chatterjee
Binyi Chen
Caicai Chen
Edward Chen
Hao Chen
Jessica Chen
Jie Chen
Liyan Chen
Long Chen
Megan Chen
Shiyao Chen
Xue Chen
Yu Long Chen
James Hsin-Yu Chiang
Chongwon Cho
Wonseok Choi

Hien Chu
Valerio Cini
Daniel Collins
Jean-Sébastien Coron
Anamaria Costache
Alain Couvreur
Ben Curtis
Jan-Pieter D'Anvers
Paolo D'Arco
Ivan Damgård
Sourav Das
Leo de Castro
Gabrielle De Micheli
Paola de Perthuis
Thomas Debris-Alazard
Mathieu Degré
Cyprien Delpech de Saint Guilhem
Thomas den Hollander
Jean-Christophe Deneuville
Yi Deng
Patrick Derbez
Lalita Devadas
Julien Devevey
Jesus Diaz
Samuel Dittmer
Fangqi Dong
Nico Döttling
Rafael Dowsley
Leo Ducas
Dung Duong
Moumita Dutta
Christoph Egger
Fatima Elsheimy
Reo Eriguchi
Jonathan Eriksen
Andreas Erwig
Daniel Escudero
Zachary Espiritu
Andre Esser
Diego F. Aranha
Pooya Farshim
Prastudy Fauzi
Joël Felderhoff
Hanwen Feng
Matthias Fitzi

Sam Frengley
Eiichiro Fujisaki
Margot Funk
Hiroki Furue
Nicolas Gama
Shang Gao
Rachit Garg
Gayathri Garimella
Joel Gärtner
Adrià Gascón
Robin Geelen
Kai Gellert
Paul Gerhart
Ashrujit Ghoshal
Benedikt Gierlichs
Niv Gilboa
Evangelos Gkoumas
Aarushi Goel
Aron Gohr
Eli Goldin
Xinxin Gong
Jérôme Govinden
Rishab Goyal
Scott Griffy
Aditya Gulati
Sam Gunn
Chun Guo
Qian Guo
Aparna Gupte
Peter Hall
Tobias Handirk
Yonglin Hao
Keisuke Hara
Keitaro Hashimoto
David Heath
Rachelle Heim Boissier
Lena Heimberger
Raphael Heitjohann
Alexandra Henzinger
Minki Hhan
Ryo Hiromasa
Viet Tung Hoang
Alexander Hoover
Akinori Hosoyamada
Xiaolu Hou

Marc Houben
Zihan Hu
Tairong Huang
Yi-Lin Hung
Moritz Huppert
Vincent Hwang
Yasuhiko Ikematsu
Akiko Inoue
Tetsu Iwata
Malika Izabachene
Robin Jadoul
Joseph Jaeger
Vahid Jahandideh
Aayush Jain
Samuel Jaques
Ruta Jawale
Ashwin Jha
Lin Jiao
Daniel Jost
Eliran Kachlon
Fatih Kaleoglu
Chethan Kamath
Ioanna Karantaidou
Shuichi Katsumata
Mahimna Kelkar
Mustafa Khairallah
Hamidreza Khorasgani
Jaehyung Kim
Fuyuki Kitagawa
Michael Klooß
Sebastian Kolby
Dimitris Kolonelos
Ilan Komargodski
Manu Kondapaneni
Yashvanth Kondi
Alexis Korb
Gaurish Korpal
Abhiram Kothapalli
David Kretzler
Ben Kreuter
Simran Kumari
Noboru Kunihiro
Fabien Laguillaumie
Junzuo Lai
Roman Langrehr

Mario Larangeira
Arthur Lazzaretti
Changmin Lee
Keewoo Lee
Charlotte Lefevre
Anthony Leverrier
Baiyu Li
Hanjun Li
Huina Li
Shuaishuai Li
Shun Li
Yanan Li
Mingyu Liang
Xiao Liang
Chengyu Lin
Fuchun Lin
Wei-Kai Lin
Yao-Ting Lin
Eik List
Guozhen Liu
Jiahui Liu
Linsheng Liu
Tianyi Liu
Xiangyu Liu
Yanyi Liu
Zeyu Liu
Chen-Da Liu-Zhang
Patrick Longa
Wen-jie Lu
Yuan Lu
Han Luo
Lin Lyu
Fermi Ma
Lorenzo Magliocco
Rasoul Akhavan Mahdavi
Mohammad Mahzoun
Luciano Maino
Jules Maire
Giulio Malavolta
Mary Maller
Nathan Manohar
Ignacio Manzur
Varun Maram
Mario Marhuenda Beltrán
Erik Mårtensson

Elisaweta Masserova
Loïc Masure
Surya Mathialagan
Alexander May
Noam Mazor
Willi Meier
Matthias Meijers
Kelsey Melissaris
Sanketh Menda
Michael Meyer
Pierre Meyer
Charles Meyer-Hilfiger
Elena Micheli
Kazuhiko Minematsu
Ankit Misra
Ethan Mook
Tal Moran
Tomoyuki Morimae
Tomoki Moriya
Tamer Mour
Pratyay Mukherjee
Marzio Mula
Marta Mularczyk
Michael Naehrig
Mikito Nanashima
Varun Narayanan
Shintaro Narisada
María Naya-Plasencia
Barak Nehoran
Patrick Neumann
Lucien Ng
Jerome Nguyen
Phuong Hoa Nguyen
Ariel Nof
Julian Nowakowski
Adam O'Neill
Miyako Ohkubo
Hiroki Okada
Hiroshi Onuki
Jean-Baptiste Orfila
Maximilian Orlt
Michał Osadnik
Hussien Othman
Elif Özbay Gürler
Tapas Pal

Yanbin Pan
Mahak Pancholi
Christodoulos Pappas
Andrew Park
Aditi Partap
Guillermo Pascual-Perez
Alain Passelegue
Shravani Patil
Sikhar Patranabis
Yevhen Perehuda
Octavio Perez Kempner
Léo Perrin
Thomas Peters
Phuong Pham
Duong Hieu Phan
Federico Pintore
Erik Pohle
Simon Pohmann
Guru Vamsi Policharla
Yuriy Polyakov
Alexander Poremba
Eamonn Postlethwaite
Thomas Prest
Ludo Pulles
Wei Qi
Luowen Qian
Tian Qiu
Justin Raizes
Ninad Rajgopal
Sebastian Ramacher
Lars Ran
Shahram Rasoolzadeh
Divya Ravi
Michael Reichle
Nicolas Resch
Doreen Riepel
Guilherme Rito
Silvia Ritsch
Bhaskar Roberts
Marc Roeschlin
Gyumin Roh
Felix Rohrbach
Yusuke Sakai
Simona Samardjiska
Olga Sanina

Maria Corte-Real Santos
Amirreza Sarencheh
Santanu Sarkar
Sven Schäge
Markus Schofnegger
Peter Scholl
Jacob Schuldt
Mark Schultz-Wu
Nikolaj I. Schwartzbach
Mahdi Sedaghat
Gregor Seiler
Nicolas Sendrier
Joon Young Seo
Srinath Setty
Yannick Seurin
Akash Shah
Zehua Shang
Yixin Shen
Yu Shen
Kazumasa Shinagawa
Ferdinand Sibleyras
Janno Siim
Tjerand Silde
Jaspal Singh
Adam Smith
Yifan Song
Yongsoo Song
Eduardo Soria-Vazquez
Sebastian Spindler
Amber Sprenkels
Akshayaram Srinivasan
Shravan Srinivasan
François-Xavier Standaert
Kruglik Stanislav
Damien Stehlé
Lukas Stennes
Gilad Stern
Christoph Striecks
Yann Strozecki
Takeshi Sugawara
Bing Sun
Ling Sun
Siwei Sun
Yao Sun
Erkan Tairi

Akira Takahashi
Suprita Talnikar
Quan Quan Tan
Khai Hanh Tang
Titouan Tanguy
Samuel Tap
Athina Terzoglou
Cihangir Tezcan
Julian Thomas
Jean-Pierre Tillich
Pratyush Ranjan Tiwari
Ivan Tjuawinata
Kabir Tomer
Junichi Tomida
Ni Trieu
Daniel Tschudi
Ida Tucker
Giannis Tzannetos
Akin Ünal
Neekon Vafa
Barry Van Leeuwen
Wessel van Woerden
Nikhil Vanjani
Karolin Varner
Marloes Venema
Mattia Veroni
Psi Vesely
Zoe Vignes
Ivan Visconti
Hilder Vitor Lima Pereira
Jonas von der Heyden
Benedikt Wagner
Hendrik Waldner
Han Wang
Haoyang Wang
Liping Wang
Mingyuan Wang
Peng Wang
Shichang Wang
Weijie Wang
William Wang
Xiao Wang
Yunhao Wang
Fiona Weber
Yu Wei

Mor Weiss
Daniel Wichs
Ivy K. Y. Woo
David J. Wu
Ke Wu
Yusai Wu
Yu Xia
Zejun Xiang
Zhiye Xie
Jiajun Xin
Shota Yamada
Takashi Yamakawa
Kazuki Yamamura
Tianqi Yang
Yibin Yang
Yiran Yao
Yuping Ye
Eylon Yogev
Yu Yu
Zuoxia Yu
Chen Yuan
Peter Yuen
Arantxa Zapico
Hadas Zeilberger
Runzhi Zeng
Jiaheng Zhang
Jiang Zhang
Liangfeng Zhang
Liu Zhang
Rachel Yun Zhang
Tianyu Zhang
Tina Zhang
Yiding Zhang
Jun Zhao
Yongjun Zhao
Jinwei Zheng
Mingxun Zhou
Yuqing Zhu
Nusa Zidaric

Artifact Chair

Marc Stevens — Centrum Wiskunde & Informatica, the Netherlands

Artifact Evaluation Committee

Maxime Bombar	Centrum Wiskunde & Informatica, the Netherlands
Sofía Celi	Brave, Portugal
Michael Naehrig	Microsoft Research, USA
Thomas Prest	PQShield, France
Lawrence Roy	Aarhus University, Denmark
Simona Samardjiska	Radboud University, the Netherlands
André Schrottenloher	Inria, France
Gregor Seiler	IBM Research Europe, Switzerland
Eran Tromer	Boston University, USA
Aleksei Udovenko	University of Luxembourg, Luxembourg
Wessel van Woerden	Institut de Mathématiques de Bordeaux, France
Floyd Zweydinger	Technology Innovation Institute, UAE

Rump Session Chairs

Craig Costello   Microsoft Research, USA
Eysa Lee   Brown University, USA

Contents – Part VII

Quantum Cryptography

A Modular Approach to Unclonable Cryptography 3
  Prabhanjan Ananth and Amit Behera

Unconditionally Secure Quantum Commitments with Preprocessing 38
  Luowen Qian

Unconditionally Secure Commitments with Quantum Auxiliary Inputs 59
  Tomoyuki Morimae, Barak Nehoran, and Takashi Yamakawa

Quantum Public-Key Encryption with Tamper-Resilient Public Keys
from One-Way Functions 93
  *Fuyuki Kitagawa, Tomoyuki Morimae, Ryo Nishimaki,
  and Takashi Yamakawa*

Robust Quantum Public-Key Encryption with Applications to Quantum
Key Distribution 126
  Giulio Malavolta and Michael Walter

How (not) to Build Quantum PKE in Minicrypt 152
  Longcheng Li, Qian Li, Xingjian Li, and Qipeng Liu

Secret Sharing with Certified Deletion 184
  James Bartusek and Justin Raizes

On Central Primitives for Quantum Cryptography with Classical
Communication 215
  Kai-Min Chung, Eli Goldin, and Matthew Gray

Threshold Cryptography

Adaptively Secure BLS Threshold Signatures from DDH and co-CDH 251
  Sourav Das and Ling Ren

Round-Optimal, Fully Secure Distributed Key Generation 285
  Jonathan Katz

Accountability for Misbehavior in Threshold Decryption via Threshold
Traitor Tracing 317
    Dan Boneh, Aditi Partap, and Lior Rotem

Threshold Encryption with Silent Setup 352
    *Sanjam Garg, Dimitris Kolonelos, Guru-Vamsi Policharla,
and Mingyuan Wang*

Two-Round Threshold Signature from Algebraic One-More Learning
with Errors 387
    Thomas Espitau, Shuichi Katsumata, and Kaoru Takemure

Flood and Submerse: Distributed Key Generation and Robust Threshold
Signature from Lattices 425
    Thomas Espitau, Guilhem Niot, and Thomas Prest

Adaptively Secure 5 Round Threshold Signatures from MLWE/MSIS
and DL with Rewinding 459
    Shuichi Katsumata, Michael Reichle, and Kaoru Takemure

Author Index 493

Quantum Cryptography

A Modular Approach to Unclonable Cryptography

Prabhanjan Ananth[1]($\boxtimes$) and Amit Behera[2]

[1] University of California Santa Barbara, Santa Barbara, USA
prabhanjan@cs.ucsb.edu
[2] Ben-Gurion University, Be'er Sheva, Israel
behera@post.bgu.ac.il

Abstract. We explore a new pathway to designing unclonable cryptographic primitives. We propose a new notion called unclonable puncturable obfuscation (UPO) and study its implications for unclonable cryptography. Using UPO, we present modular (and in some cases, arguably, simple) constructions of many primitives in unclonable cryptography, including, public-key quantum money, quantum copy-protection for many classes of functionalities, unclonable encryption, and single-decryption encryption.

Notably, we obtain the following new results assuming the existence of UPO:
- We show that any cryptographic functionality can be copy-protected as long as it satisfies a notion of security, which we term puncturable security. Prior feasibility results focused on copy-protecting specific cryptographic functionalities.
- We show that copy-protection exists for any class of evasive functions as long as the associated distribution satisfies a preimage-sampleability condition. Prior works demonstrated copy-protection for point functions, which follows as a special case of our result.

We put forward two constructions of UPO. The first construction satisfies two notions of security based on the existence of (post-quantum) sub-exponentially secure indistinguishability obfuscation, injective one-way functions, the quantum hardness of learning with errors, and the two versions of a new conjecture called the simultaneous inner product conjecture. The security of the second construction is based on the existence of unclonable-indistinguishable bit encryption, injective one-way functions, and quantum-state indistinguishability obfuscation.

1 Introduction

Unclonable cryptography leverages the no-cloning principle of quantum mechanics [WZ82,Die82] to build many novel cryptographic notions that are otherwise impossible to achieve classically. This has been an active area of interest since the 1980s [Wie83]. In the past few years, researchers have investigated a dizzying variety of unclonable primitives such as quantum money [AC12,Zha19,

Shm22, LMZ23] and its variants [RS19, BS20, RZ21], quantum one-time programs [BGS13], copy-protection [Aar09, CLLZ21], tokenized signatures [BS16, CLLZ21], unclonable encryption [Got02, BL20] and its variants [KN23], secure software leasing [AL21], single-decryptor encryption [GZ20, CLLZ21], and many more [BKL23, GMR23, JK23].

Establishing the feasibility of unclonable primitives has been quite challenging. The adversarial structure considered in the unclonability setting (i.e., spatially separated and entangled) is quite different from what we typically encounter in the traditional cryptographic setting. This makes it difficult to leverage traditional classical techniques, commonly used in cryptographic proofs, to argue the security of unclonable primitives. As a result, there are two major gaping holes in the area.

- UNSOLVED FOUNDATIONAL QUESTIONS: Despite the explosion of results in the past few years, many fundamental questions in this area remain to be solved. This includes designing public-key quantum money schemes [AC12, Zha19] on well-studied assumptions. Another problem that is open is precisely characterizing the class of functionalities for which quantum copy-protection [Aar09] is possible.
- LACK OF ABSTRACTIONS: Due to the lack of good abstractions, proofs in the area of unclonable cryptography tend to be complex and use sophisticated tools, making the literature less accessible to the broader research community. This makes not only verification of proofs difficult but also makes it harder to use the techniques to obtain new feasibility results.

Overarching Goal of Our Work. We advocate for a modular approach to designing unclonable cryptography. Our goal is to identify an important unclonable cryptographic primitive that would serve as a useful abstraction leading to the design of other unclonable primitives. Ideally, we would like to abstract away all the complex details in the instantiation of this primitive, and it should be relatively easy, even to classical cryptographers, to use this primitive to study unclonability in the context of other cryptographic primitives. We believe that the identification and instantiation of such a primitive will speed up the progress in the design of unclonable primitives.

Indeed, similar explorations in other contexts, such as classical cryptography, have been fruitful. For instance, the discovery of indistinguishability obfuscation [BGI+01, GGH+16] (iO) revolutionized cryptography and led to the resolution of many open problems (for instance: [SW14, GGHR14, BZ17, BPR15]). Hence, there is merit to exploring the possibility of such a primitive in unclonable cryptography, as well.

Thus, we ask the following question:

Is there an "iO-like" primitive for unclonable cryptography?

We seek the pursuit of identifying unclonable primitives that would have a similar impact on unclonable cryptography as iO did on classical cryptography.

1.1 Our Contributions in a Nutshell

In our search for an *"iO-like"* primitive for unclonable cryptography, we propose a new notion called *unclonable puncturable obfuscation* (UPO) and explore its impact on unclonable cryptography.

NEW FEASIBILITY RESULTS. Specifically, using UPO and other well-studied cryptographic tools, we demonstrate the following new results.

- We show that any class of functionalities can be copy-protected as long as they are puncturable (more details in Sect. 1.2).
- We show that a large class of evasive functionalities can be copy-protected.

The above two results not only subsume all the copy-protectable functionalities studied in prior works but also capture new functionalities.

Even for functionalities that have been studied before our work, we get qualitatively new results. For instance, our result shows that **any** puncturable digital signature can be copy-protected whereas the work of [LLQZ22] shows a weaker result that the digital signature of [SW14] can be copy-protected. We get similar conclusions for copy-protection for pseudorandom functions.

IMPLICATION TO UNCLONABLE CRYPTOGRAPHY. Apart from quantum copy-protection, UPO implies many of the foundational unclonable primitives such as public-key quantum money, unclonable encryption, and single-decryptor encryption. *The resulting constructions from UPO are conceptually different compared to the prior works.* Since building unclonable primitives is a daunting task even when relying on exotic computational assumptions, it becomes crucial to venture into alternative approaches. Moreover, this endeavor could potentially yield fresh perspectives on unclonable cryptography.

SIMPLER CONSTRUCTIONS. We believe that some of our constructions are simpler than the prior works, albeit the underlying assumptions are incomparable[1]. The construction of copy-protection for puncturable functionalities yields simpler constructions of copy-protection for pseudorandom functions, studied in [CLLZ21], and copy-protection for signatures, studied in [LLQZ22].

One potential criticism of our work is that our construction of UPO is based on a new conjecture. Specifically, we show that UPO can be based on the existence of post-quantum secure iO, learning with errors and a new conjecture.

However, it is essential to keep in mind the following facts:

- ASSUMPTIONS: If our conjectures are true, then this would mean that we can construct UPO from indistinguishability obfuscation and other standard assumptions. On the other hand, we currently do not know whether the other direction is true, i.e., whether UPO implies post-quantum indistinguishability obfuscation. As a result, it is plausible that UPO could be a weaker

---

[1] We assume UPO whereas the previous works assume post-quantum iO and other well-studied assumptions.

assumption than post-quantum iO! One consequence of this is the construction of public-key quantum money from generic assumptions weaker than post-quantum iO.

If our conjectures are false, by itself, this does not refute the existence of UPO. *We would like to emphasize that there is no reason to believe these conjectures are necessary for the existence of UPO.* Instead, it merely suggests that we need a different approach to investigate the feasibility of UPO.

- PUSHING THE FEASIBILITY LANDSCAPE: Time and time again, in cryptography, we have been forced to invent new assumptions. In numerous instances, these assumptions have unveiled a previously uncharted realm of cryptographic primitives, expanding our understanding beyond what we once deemed feasible. While not all of the computational assumptions have survived the test of time, in some cases[2], the insights gained from their cryptanalysis have helped us to come up with more secure instantiations in the future. In a similar vein, being aggressive with exploring new assumptions could push the boundaries of unclonable cryptography.

We also present another construction of UPO from quantum state iO and unclonable encryption. We discuss this more at the end of Sect. 1.2.

1.2 Our Contributions

Definition. We discuss our results in more detail. Roughly speaking, unclonable puncturable obfuscation (UPO) defined for a class of circuits $\mathfrak{C}$ in P/Poly, consists of two QPT algorithms (Obf, Eval) defined as follows:

- OBFUSCATION ALGORITHM: Obf takes as input a classical circuit $C \in \mathfrak{C}$ and outputs a quantum state ρ_C.
- EVALUATION ALGORITHM: Eval takes as input a quantum state ρ_C, an input x, and outputs a value y.

In terms of correctness, we require $y = C(x)$. To define security, as is typically the case for unclonable primitives, we consider non-local adversaries of the form $(\mathcal{A}, \mathcal{B}, \mathcal{C})$. The security experiment, parameterized by a distribution $\mathcal{D}_\mathcal{X}$, is defined as follows:

- $\mathcal{A}$ (Alice) receives as input a quantum state ρ^* that is generated as follows. $\mathcal{A}$ sends a circuit C to the challenger, who then samples a bit b uniformly at random and samples $(x^\mathcal{B}, x^\mathcal{C})$ from $\mathcal{D}_\mathcal{X}$. If $b = 0$, it sets ρ^* to be the output of Obf on input C, or if $b = 1$, it sets ρ^* to be the output of Obf on G, where G is a punctured circuit that has the same functionality as C on all the points except $x^\mathcal{B}$ and $x^\mathcal{C}$. It is important to note that $\mathcal{A}$ only receives ρ^* and in particular, $x^\mathcal{B}$ and $x^\mathcal{C}$ are hidden from $\mathcal{A}$.
- $\mathcal{A}$ then creates a bipartite state and shares one part with $\mathcal{B}$ (Bob) and the other part with $\mathcal{C}$ (Charlie).

---

[2] Several candidates of post-quantum indistinguishability obfuscation had to be broken before a candidate based on well founded assumptions was proposed [JLS21].

- $\mathcal{B}$ and $\mathcal{C}$ cannot communicate with each other. In the challenge phase, $\mathcal{B}$ receives $x^{\mathcal{B}}$ and $\mathcal{C}$ receives $x^{\mathcal{C}}$. Then, they each output bits $b_{\mathcal{B}}$ and $b_{\mathcal{C}}$.

$(\mathcal{A}, \mathcal{B}, \mathcal{C})$ win if $b_{\mathcal{B}} = b_{\mathcal{C}} = b$. The scheme is secure if they can only win with probability at most 0.5 (ignoring negligible additive factors).

KEYED CIRCUITS. Towards formalizing the notion of puncturing circuits in a way that will be useful for applications, we consider keyed circuit classes in the above definition. Every circuit in a keyed circuit class is of the form $C_k(\cdot)$ for some key k. Any circuit class can be implemented as a keyed circuit class using universal circuits and thus, by considering keyed circuits, we are not compromising on the generality of the above definition.

CHALLENGE DISTRIBUTIONS. We could consider different settings of $\mathcal{D}_{\mathcal{X}}$. In this work, we mainly focus on two settings. In the first setting (referred to as *independent* challenge distribution), sampling $(x^{\mathcal{B}}, x^{\mathcal{C}})$ from $\mathcal{D}_{\mathcal{X}}$ is the same as sampling $x^{\mathcal{B}}$ and $x^{\mathcal{C}}$ uniformly at random (from the input space of C). In the second setting (referred to as *identical* challenge distribution), sampling $(x^{\mathcal{B}}, x^{\mathcal{C}})$ from $\mathcal{D}_{\mathcal{X}}$ is the same as sampling x uniformly at random and setting $x = x^{\mathcal{B}} = x^{\mathcal{C}}$.

GENERALIZED UPO. In the above security experiment, we did not quite specify the behavior of the punctured circuit on the points $x^{\mathcal{B}}$ and $x^{\mathcal{C}}$. There are two ways to formalize and this results in two different definitions; we consider both of them in Sect. 2. In the first (basic) version, the output of the punctured circuit G on the punctured points is set to be $\perp$. This version would be the regular UPO definition. In the second (generalized) version, we allow $\mathcal{A}$ to control the output of the punctured circuit on inputs $x^{\mathcal{B}}$ and $x^{\mathcal{C}}$. For instance, $\mathcal{A}$ can choose and send the circuits $\mu_{\mathcal{B}}$ and $\mu_{\mathcal{C}}$ to the challenger. On input $x^{\mathcal{B}}$ (resp., $x^{\mathcal{C}}$), the challenger programs the punctured circuit G to output $\mu_{\mathcal{B}}(x^{\mathcal{B}})$ (resp., $\mu_{\mathcal{C}}(x^{\mathcal{C}})$). We refer to this version as *generalized UPO*.

Applications. We demonstrate several applications of UPO to unclonable cryptography.

We summarise the applications[3] in Fig. 1. For a broader context of these results, we refer the reader to related works section in the full version.

COPY-PROTECTION FOR PUNCTURABLE CRYPTOGRAPHIC SCHEMES (SEE THE RELEVANT SECTIONS IN THE FULL-VERSION). We consider cryptographic schemes satisfying a property called puncturable security. Informally speaking, puncturable security says the following: given a secret key sk, generated using the scheme, it is possible to puncture the key at a couple of points $x^{\mathcal{B}}$ and $x^{\mathcal{C}}$ such that it is computationally infeasible to use the punctured secret key on $x^{\mathcal{B}}$ and $x^{\mathcal{C}}$. We formally define this in the full version. We show the following:

---

[3] We refer the reader unfamiliar with copy-protection, single-decryptor encryption, or unclonable encryption to the introduction section of [AKL23] for an informal explanation of these primitives.

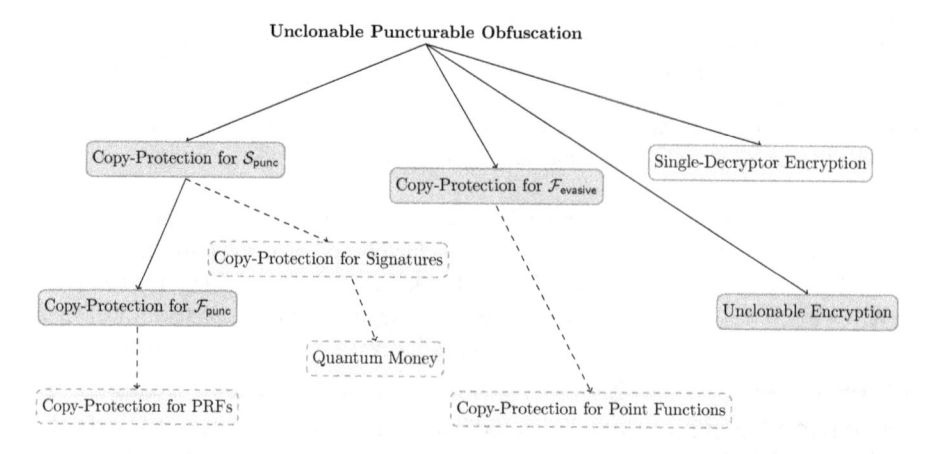

Fig. 1. Applications of Unclonable Puncturable Obfuscation. $\mathcal{S}_{\mathsf{punc}}$ denotes cryptographic schemes satisfying puncturable property. $\mathcal{F}_{\mathsf{punc}}$ denotes cryptographic functionalities satisfying functionalities satisfying puncturable property. $\mathcal{F}_{\mathsf{evasive}}$ denotes functionalities that are evasive with respect to a distribution $\mathcal{D}$ satisfying preimage-sampleability property. The dashed lines denote corollaries of our main results. The blue-filled boxes represent primitives whose feasibility was unknown prior to our work. The red-filled boxes represent primitives for which we get qualitatively different results or from incomparable assumptions when compared to previous works. (Color figure online)

Theorem 1. *Assuming UPO for P/poly, there exists copy-protection for any puncturable cryptographic scheme.*

Prior works [CLLZ21,LLQZ22] aimed at copy-protecting specific cryptographic functionalities whereas we, for the first time, characterize a broad class of cryptographic functionalities that can be copy-protected.

As a corollary, we obtain the following results assuming UPO.

- We show that **any** class of puncturable pseudorandom functions that can be punctured at two points [BW13,BGI14] can be copy-protected. The feasibility result of copy-protecting pseudorandom functions was first established in [CLLZ21]. A point to note here is that in [CLLZ21], given a class of puncturable pseudorandom functions, they transform this into a different class of pseudorandom functions[4] that is still puncturable and then copy-protect the resulting class. On the other hand, we show that *any* class of puncturable pseudorandom functions, which allows for the puncturing of two points, can be copy-protected. Hence, our result is qualitatively different than [CLLZ21].

---

[4] Specifically, they add a transformation to generically make the pseudorandom function extractable.

- We show that **any** digital signature scheme, where the signing key can be punctured at two points, can be copy-protected. Roughly speaking, a digital signature scheme is puncturable at two points if the signing key can be punctured on two messages $m^{\mathcal{B}}$ and $m^{\mathcal{C}}$ such that given the punctured signing key, it is computationally infeasible to produce a signature on one of the punctured messages. Our result rederives and generalizes a recent result by [LLQZ22] who showed how to copy-protect the digital signature scheme of [SW14].

In the technical sections, we first present a simpler result where we copy-protect puncturable functionalities (for more details, see the full-version) and we then extend this result to achieve copy-protection for puncturable cryptographic schemes (for more details, see the full-version).

COPY-PROTECTION FOR EVASIVE FUNCTIONS. We consider a class of evasive functions associated with a distribution $\mathcal{D}$ satisfying a property referred to as preimage-sampleability which is informally defined as follows: there exists a distribution $\mathcal{D}'$ such that sampling an evasive function from $\mathcal{D}$ along with an accepting point (i.e., the output of the function on this point is 1) is computationally indistinguishable from sampling a function from $\mathcal{D}'$ and then modifying this function by injecting a uniformly random point as the accepting point. We show the following.

Theorem 2. *Assuming generalized UPO for P/poly, there exists copy-protection for any class of functions that is evasive with respect to a distribution $\mathcal{D}$ satisfying preimage-sampleability property.*

Unlike Theorem 1, we assume generalized UPO in the above theorem.

As a special case, we obtain copy-protection for point functions. A recent work [CHV23] presented construction of copy-protection for point functions from post-quantum iO and other standard assumptions. Qualitatively, our results are different in the following ways:

- The challenge distribution considered in the security definition of [CHV23] is arguably not a natural one: with probability $\frac{1}{3}$, $\mathcal{B}$ and $\mathcal{C}$ get as input the actual point, with probability $\frac{1}{3}$, $\mathcal{B}$ gets the actual point while $\mathcal{C}$ gets a random value and finally, with probability $\frac{1}{3}$, $\mathcal{B}$ gets a random value while $\mathcal{C}$ gets the actual point. On the other hand, we consider identical challenge distribution; that is, $\mathcal{B}$ and $\mathcal{C}$ both receive the actual point with probability $\frac{1}{2}$ or they both receive a value picked uniformly at random.
- While the result of [CHV23] is restricted to point functions, we show how to copy-protect functions where the number of accepting points is a fixed polynomial.

We clarify that none of the above results on copy-protection contradicts the impossibility result by [AL21] who present a conditional result ruling out the possibility of copy-protecting contrived functionalities.

UNCLONABLE ENCRYPTION. Finally, we show, for the first time, an approach to construct unclonable encryption in the plain model. We give a direct and simple construction of unclonable encryption for bits, see the full version for more details.

Theorem 3. *Assuming generalized UPO for P/poly, there exists a one-time unclonable bit-encryption scheme in the plain model.*

We also obtain a construction of unclonable encryption for arbitrary fixed length messages by first constructing public-key single-decryptor encryption (SDE) with an identical challenge distribution.

Theorem 4. *Assuming generalized UPO for P/poly, post-quantum indistinguishability obfuscation (iO), and post-quantum injective one-way functions, there exists a public-key single-decryptor encryption scheme with security against identical challenge distribution, see the full version for more details.*

[GZ20] showed that SDE with such a challenge distribution implies unclonable encryption. Prior work by [CLLZ21] demonstrated the construction of public-key single-decryptor encryption with security against independent challenge distribution, which is not known to imply unclonable encryption. We, thus, obtain the following corollary.

Corollary 1. *Assuming generalized UPO, post-quantum iO, and post-quantum injective one-way functions[5], there exists a one-time unclonable encryption scheme in the plain model.*

Note that using the compiler of [AK21], we can generically transform a one-time unclonable encryption into a public-key unclonable encryption in the plain model under the same assumptions as above.

We note that this is the first construction of unclonable encryption in the plain model. All the previous works [BL20, AKL+22, AKL23] construct unclonable encryption in the quantum random oracle model. The disadvantage of our construction is that they leverage computational assumptions whereas the previous works [BL20, AKL+22, AKL23] are information-theoretically secure.

Apart from unclonable encryption, single-decryptor encryption also implies public-key quantum money, thereby giving the following corollary.

Corollary 2. *Assuming generalized UPO, post-quantum iO, and post-quantum one-way functions, there exists a public-key quantum money scheme.*

---

[5] Unlike Theorem 4, we do not need injective one-way functions here because the [GZ20] construction of unclonable encryption from single-decryptor encryption only requires selectively secure single-decryptor encryption with the above-mentioned challenge distribution, which we construct in our work using *any* post-quantum one-way functions along with the other assumptions; see the full version for more details.

The construction of quantum money from UPO offers a conceptually different approach to constructing public-key quantum money in comparison with other quantum money schemes such as [Zha19, LMZ23, Zha23].

As an aside, we also present a lifting theorem that lifts a selectively secure single-decryptor encryption into an adaptively secure construction, assuming the existence of post-quantum iO. Such a lifting theorem was not known prior to our work.

Construction. Finally we demonstrate a construction of generalized UPO for all classes of efficiently computable keyed circuits. We show that the same construction is secure with respect to both identical and independent challenge distributions. Specifically, we show the following:

Theorem 5 (Informal). *Suppose $\mathfrak{C}$ consists of polynomial-sized keyed circuits. Assuming the following:*

- *Post-quantum sub-exponentially secure indistinguishability obfuscation for P/poly,*
- *Post-quantum sub-exponentially secure injective one-way functions,*
- *Compute-and-compare obfuscation secure against QPT adversaries and,*
- *Simultaneous inner product conjecture.*

there exists a generalized UPO *with respect to identical $\mathcal{D}_\mathcal{X}$ for $\mathfrak{C}$.*

ON THE SIMULTANEOUS INNER PRODUCT CONJECTURE: There are two different versions of the simultaneous inner product conjecture (Conjecture 1 and Conjecture 2) we rely upon to prove the security of our construction with respect to identical and independent challenge distributions. At a high level, the simultaneous inner product conjecture states that two (possibly entangled) QPT adversaries (i.e., non-local adversaries) should be unsuccessful in distinguishing $(\mathbf{r}, \langle \mathbf{r}, \mathbf{x} \rangle + m)$ versus $(\mathbf{r}, \langle \mathbf{r}, \mathbf{x} \rangle)$, where $\mathbf{r} \xleftarrow{\$} \mathbb{Z}_Q^n, \mathbf{x} \xleftarrow{\$} \mathbb{Z}_Q^n, m \xleftarrow{\$} \mathbb{Z}_Q$ for every prime $Q \geq 1$. Moreover, the adversaries receive as input a bipartite state ρ that could depend on $\mathbf{x}$ with the guarantee that it should be infeasible to recover $\mathbf{x}$. As mentioned above, we consider two different versions of the conjecture. In the first version (*identical*), both the adversaries get the same sample $(\mathbf{r}, \langle \mathbf{r}, \mathbf{x} \rangle)$ or they both get $(\mathbf{r}, \langle \mathbf{r}, \mathbf{x} \rangle + m)$. In the second version (*independent*), the main difference is that $\mathbf{r}$ and $\mathbf{x}$ are sampled independently for both adversaries. Weaker versions of this conjecture have been investigated and proven to be unconditionally true [AKL23, KT22]. We refer the reader to Sect. 3 for a detailed discussion on the conjectures.

COMPOSITION: Another contribution of ours is a composition theorem (see the full version for more details), where we show how to securely compose unclonable puncturable obfuscation with a functionality-preserving compiler. In more detail, we show the following. Suppose UPO is a secure unclonable puncturable obfuscation scheme and let Compiler be a functionality-preserving circuit compiler. We define another scheme UPO' such that the obfuscation algorithm of

UPO', on input a circuit C, first runs the circuit compiler on C to obtain $\widetilde{C}$ and then it runs the obfuscation of UPO on $\widetilde{C}$ and outputs the result. The evaluation process can be similarly defined. We show that the resulting scheme UPO' is secure as long as UPO is secure. Our composition result allows us to compose UPO with other primitives such as different forms of program obfuscation without compromising on security. We use our composition theorem in some of the applications discussed earlier.

1.3 Technical Overview

We give an overview of the techniques behind our construction of UPO and the applications of UPO. We start with applications.

Applications

Copy-Protecting Puncturable Cryptographic Schemes. We begin by exploring methods to copy-protect puncturable pseudorandom functions. Subsequently, we generalize this approach to achieve copy-protection for a broader class of puncturable cryptographic schemes.

CASE STUDY: PUNCTURABLE PSEUDORANDOM FUNCTIONS. Let $\mathcal{F} = \{f_k(\cdot) : \{0,1\}^n \to \{0,1\}^m : k \in \mathcal{K}_\lambda\}$ be a puncturable pseudorandom function (PRF) with λ being the security parameter and $\mathcal{K}_\lambda$ being the key space. To copy-protect $f_k(\cdot)$, we simply obfuscate $f_k(\cdot)$ using an unclonable puncturable obfuscation scheme UPO. To evaluate the copy-protected circuit on an input x, run the evaluation procedure of UPO.

To argue security, let us look at two experiments:

- The first experiment corresponds to the regular copy-protection security experiment. That is, $\mathcal{A}$ receives as input a copy-protected state ρ_{f_k}, which is copy-protection of f_k where k is sampled uniformly at random from the key space. It then creates a bipartite state which is split between $\mathcal{B}$ and $\mathcal{C}$, who are two non-communicating adversaries who can share some entanglement. Then, $\mathcal{B}$ and $\mathcal{C}$ independently receive as input x, which is picked uniformly at random. $(\mathcal{B}, \mathcal{C})$ win if they simultaneously guess $f_k(x)$.
- The second experiment is similar to the first experiment except $\mathcal{A}$ receives as input copy-protection of f_k punctured at the point x, where x is the same input given to both $\mathcal{B}$ and $\mathcal{C}$.

Thanks to the puncturing security of $\mathcal{F}$, the probability that $(\mathcal{B}, \mathcal{C})$ succeeds in the second experiment is negligible in λ. We would like to argue that $(\mathcal{B}, \mathcal{C})$ succeed in the first experiment also with probability negligible in λ. Suppose not, we show that the security of UPO is violated.

Reduction to UPO: The reduction $\mathcal{R}_\mathcal{A}$ samples a uniformly random f_k and forwards it to the challenger of the UPO game. The challenger of the UPO game then generates either an obfuscation of f_k or the punctured circuit f_k punctured at x. The obfuscated state is then sent to $\mathcal{R}_\mathcal{A}$, who in turn forwards this to $\mathcal{A}$ who prepares the bipartite state. The reduction $\mathcal{R}_\mathcal{B}$ (resp., $\mathcal{R}_\mathcal{C}$) then receives as input x which it duly forwards to $\mathcal{B}$ (resp., $\mathcal{C}$). Then, $\mathcal{B}$ and $\mathcal{C}$ each output $y_\mathcal{B}$ and $y_\mathcal{C}$. Then, $\mathcal{R}_\mathcal{B}$ outputs the **bit 0** if $f_k(x) = y_\mathcal{B}$, otherwise it outputs 1. Similarly, $\mathcal{R}_\mathcal{C}$ outputs **bit 0** if $f_k(x) = y_\mathcal{C}$, otherwise it outputs 1. The reason behind boldifying "bit 0" part will be discussed below.

Let us see how well $(\mathcal{R}_\mathcal{A}, \mathcal{R}_\mathcal{B}, \mathcal{R}_\mathcal{C})$ fares in the UPO game.

- *Case 1. Challenge bit is $b = 0$.* In this case, $\mathcal{R}_\mathcal{A}$ receives as input obfuscation of f_k with respect to UPO. Denote p_0 to be the probability that $(\mathcal{R}_\mathcal{B}, \mathcal{R}_\mathcal{C})$ output $(0, 0)$.
- *Case 2. Challenge bit is $b = 1$.* Here, $\mathcal{R}_\mathcal{A}$ receives as input obfuscation of the circuit f_k punctured at x. Similarly, denote p_1 to be the probability that $(\mathcal{R}_\mathcal{B}, \mathcal{R}_\mathcal{C})$ output $(1, 1)$.

From the security of UPO, we have the following: $\frac{p_0+p_1}{2} \leq \frac{1}{2} + \mu(\lambda)$, for some negligible function $\mu(\cdot)$. From the puncturing security of $\mathcal{F}$, $p_1 \geq 1 - \nu(\lambda)$, for some negligible function ν. From this, we can conclude, p_0 is negligible which proves the security of the copy-protection scheme.

Perhaps surprisingly (at least to the authors), we do not know how to make the above reduction work if $\mathcal{R}_\mathcal{B}$ (resp., $\mathcal{R}_\mathcal{C}$) instead output bit 1 in the case when $f_k(x) = y_\mathcal{B}$ (resp., $f_k(x) = y_\mathcal{C}$). This is because we only get an upper bound for p_1 which cannot be directly used to determine an upper bound for p_0.

GENERALIZING TO PUNCTURABLE CRYPTOGRAPHIC SCHEMES. We present two generalizations of the above approach. We first generalize the above approach to handle puncturable circuit classes see the full version for more details. A circuit class $\mathfrak{C}$, equipped with an efficient puncturing algorithm Puncture, is said to be puncturable[6] if given a circuit $C \in \mathfrak{C}$, we can puncture C on a point x to obtain a punctured circuit G such that given a punctured circuit G, it is computationally infeasible to predict $C(x)$. As we can see, puncturable pseudorandom functions are a special case of puncturable circuit classes. The template to copy-protect an arbitrary puncturable circuit class, say $\mathfrak{C}$, is essentially the same as the above template to copy-protect puncturable pseudorandom functions. To copy-protect C, obfuscate C using the scheme UPO. The evaluation process and the proof of security proceed along the same lines as above.

We then generalize this further to handle puncturable[7] cryptographic schemes. We consider an abstraction of a cryptographic scheme consisting of efficient algorithms (Gen, Eval, Puncture, Verify) with the following correctness guarantee: the verification algorithm on input (pk, x, y) outputs 1, where Gen(1^λ) produces the secret key-public key pair (sk, pk) and the value y is the output of

---
[6] We need a slightly more general version than this. Formally, we puncture the circuit at two points (and not one), and then we require the adversary to predict the output of the circuit on one of the points, see the full version for more details.
[7] We again consider a general version where the circuit is punctured at two points.

Eval on input (sk, x). The algorithm Puncture on input (sk, x) outputs a punctured circuit that has the same functionality as $\mathsf{Eval}(\mathsf{sk}, \cdot)$ on all the points except x. The security property roughly states that predicting the output $\mathsf{Eval}(\mathsf{sk}, x)$ given the punctured circuit should be computationally infeasible. The above template of copy-protecting PRFs can similarly be adopted for copy-protecting puncturable cryptographic schemes.

Copy-Protecting Evasive Functions. Using UPO to construct copy-protection for evasive functions turns out to be more challenging. To understand the difficulty, let us compare both the notions below:

- In a UPO scheme, $\mathcal{A}$ gets as input an obfuscation of a circuit C (if the challenge bit is $b = 0$) or a circuit C punctured at two points $x^{\mathcal{B}}$ and $x^{\mathcal{C}}$ (if $b = 1$). In the challenge phase, $\mathcal{B}$ gets $x^{\mathcal{B}}$ and $\mathcal{C}$ gets $x^{\mathcal{C}}$.
- In a copy-protection scheme for evasive functions, $\mathcal{A}$ gets as input copy-protection of C, where C is a circuit implements an evasive function. In the challenge phase, $\mathcal{B}$ gets $x^{\mathcal{B}}$ and $\mathcal{C}$ gets $x^{\mathcal{C}}$, where $(x^{\mathcal{B}}, x^{\mathcal{C}})$ is sampled from an input distribution that depends on the challenge bit b. As example, we can sample $(x^{\mathcal{B}}, x^{\mathcal{C}}) = (x, x)$ as follows: x is sampled uniformly at random (if challenge bit is $b = 0$), otherwise x is sampled uniformly at random from the set of points on which C outputs 1 (if the challenge bit is $b = 1$).

In other words, the distribution from which $\mathcal{A}$ gets its input from depends on the bit b in UPO but the challenges given to $\mathcal{B}$ and $\mathcal{C}$ are sampled from a distribution that does not depend on b. The setting in the case of copy-protection is the opposite: the distribution from which $\mathcal{A}$ gets its input does not depend on b while the challenge distribution depends on b.

PREIMAGE SAMPLEABLE PROPERTY: To handle this discrepancy, we consider a class of evasive functions called preimage sampleable evasive functions. The first condition we require is that there is a distribution $\mathcal{D}$ from which we can efficiently sample a circuit C (representing an evasive function) together with an input x such that $C(x) = 1$. The second condition states that there exists another distribution $\mathcal{D}'$ from which we can sample (C', x'), where x' is sampled uniformly at random and then a punctured circuit C' is sampled conditioned on $C'(x') = 1$, satisfying the following property: the distributions $\mathcal{D}$ and $\mathcal{D}'$ are computationally indistinguishable. The second condition is devised precisely to ensure that we can reduce the security of copy-protection to UPO.

CONSTRUCTION AND PROOF IDEA: But first, let us discuss the construction of copy-protection: to copy-protect a circuit C, compute two layers of obfuscation of C. First, obfuscate C using a post-quantum iO scheme and then obfuscate the resulting circuit using UPO. To argue security, we view the obfuscated state given to $\mathcal{A}$ as follows: first sample C from $\mathcal{D}$ and then do the following: (a) give ρ_C to $\mathcal{A}$ if $b = 0$ and, (b) ρ_C to $\mathcal{A}$ if $b = 1$, where ρ_C is the copy-protected state and b is the challenge bit that is used in the challenge phase. So far, we have not changed the distribution. Now, we will modify (b). We will leverage the above conditions to modify (b) as follows: we will instead jointly sample the circuit and the challenge input from $\mathcal{D}'$. Since $\mathcal{D}$ and $\mathcal{D}'$ are computationally indistinguishable, the adversary will not notice the change. Now, let us examine the modified experiment: if $b = 0$, the adversary receives ρ_C (defined above), where (C, x) is sampled from $\mathcal{D}$ and if $b = 1$, the adversary receives $\rho_{C'}$, where (C', x') is sampled from $\mathcal{D}'$. We can show that this precisely corresponds to the UPO experiment and thus, we can successfully carry out the reduction.

Single-Decryptor Encryption. A natural attempt to construct single-decryptor encryption would be to leverage UPO for puncturable cryptographic schemes. After all, it would seem that identifying a public-key encryption scheme where the decryption key can be punctured at the challenge ciphertexts would be helpful to achieve our desired result. A UPO obfuscation of the decryption algorithm would be the quantum decryption key of the single-decryptor encryption scheme.

Unfortunately, this does not quite work: the reason lies in the challenge distribution of UPO. In this work, we only consider challenge distributions whose marginals correspond to the uniform distribution. On the other hand, the public-key encryption scheme we start with might not have pseudorandom ciphertexts which would in turn make it incompatible with combining it with the UPO scheme as suggested above. Of course, we could have considered more general challenge distributions but the techniques we have developed is limited to achieving challenge distributions with uniform marginals. This suggests that we need to start with a public-key encryption scheme with pseudorandom ciphertexts.

We start with the public-key encryption scheme due to Sahai and Waters [SW14]. The advantage of this scheme is that the ciphertexts are pseudorandom. First, we show that this public-key encryption scheme can be made puncturable. Once we show this, using UPO for puncturable cryptographic schemes (and standard iO tricks), we construct single-decryptor encryption schemes of two flavors:

- First, we consider search security. In this security definition, $\mathcal{B}$ and $\mathcal{C}$ receive ciphertexts of random messages and they win if they are able to predict the messages.
- Next, we consider selective security. In this security definition, $\mathcal{B}$ and $\mathcal{C}$ receive encryptions of one of two messages adversarially chosen and they are supposed to predict which of the two messages was used in the encryption. Moreover, the adversarially chosen messages need to be declared before the security experiment begins and hence, the term selective security. Once we achieve this, we propose a generic lifting theorem to lift SDE security satisfying selective security to full adaptive security, where the challenge messages can be chosen later in the experiment.

Construction of UPO We move on to the construction of UPO.

STARTING POINT: DECOUPLING UNCLONABILITY AND COMPUTATION. We consider the following template to design UPO. To obfuscate a circuit C, we build two components. The first component is an unclonable quantum state that serves the purpose of authentication. The second component is going to aid in the computation of C once the authentication passes. Specifically, given an input x, we first use the unclonable quantum state to authenticate x and then execute the second component on the authenticated tag along with x to get the output $C(x)$.

The purpose of designing the obfuscation scheme this way is two-fold. Firstly, the fact that the first component is an unclonable quantum state means that an adversary cannot create multiple copies of this. And by design, without this state, it is not possible to execute the second component. Secondly, decoupling the unclonability and the computation part allows us to put less burden on the unclonable state, and in particular, only require the first component for authentication. This is in turn allows us to leverage existing classical tools to instantiate the second component.

To implement the above approach, we use a copy-protection scheme for pseudorandom functions [CLLZ21], denoted by CP, and a post-quantum indistinguishability obfuscation scheme, denoted by iO. In the UPO scheme, to obfuscate C, we do the following:

1. Copy-protect a pseudorandom function $f_k(\cdot)$ and,
2. Obfuscate a circuit, with the PRF key k hardcoded in it, that takes as input (x, y) and outputs $C(x)$ if and only if $f_k(x) = y$.

FIRST ISSUE. While syntactically the above template makes sense, when proving security we run into an issue. To invoke the security of CP, we need to argue that the obfuscated circuit does not reveal any information about the PRF key k. This suggests that we need a much stronger object like virtual black box obfuscation instead of iO which is in general known to be impossible [BGI+01]. Taking a closer look, we realize that this issue arose because we wanted to completely decouple the CP part and the iO part.

SECOND ISSUE. Another issue that arises when attempting to work out the proof. At a high level, in the security proof, we reach a hybrid where we need to hardwire the outputs of the PRF on the challenge inputs $x^\mathcal{B}$ and $x^\mathcal{C}$ in the obfuscated circuit (i.e., in bullet 2 above). This creates an obstacle when we need to invoke the security of copy-protection: the outputs of the PRF are only available in the challenge phase (i.e., *after* $\mathcal{A}$ splits) whereas we need to know these outputs in order to generate the input to $\mathcal{A}$.

ADDRESSING THE ABOVE ISSUES. We first address the second issue. We introduce a new security notion of copy-protection for PRFs, referred to as copy-protection with *preponed security*. Roughly speaking, in the preponed security experiment, $\mathcal{A}$ receives the outputs of the PRF on the challenge inputs instead of being delayed until the challenge phase. By design, this stronger security notion solves the second issue.

In order to resolve the first issue, we pull back and only partially decouple the two components. In particular, we tie both the CP and iO parts together by making non-black-box use of the underlying copy-protection scheme. Specifically, we rely upon the scheme by Colandangelo et al. [CLLZ21]. Moreover, we show that Colandangelo et al. [CLLZ21] scheme satisfies preponed security by reducing their security to the security of their single-decryptor encryption construction; our proof follows along the same lines as theirs. Unfortunately, we do not know how to go further. While they did show that their single-decryptor encryption construction can be based on well studied cryptographic assumptions, the type of single-decryptor encryption schemes we need have a different flavor. In more detail, in [CLLZ21], they consider *independent* challenge distribution (i.e., both $\mathcal{B}$ and $\mathcal{C}$ receive ciphertexts where the challenge bit is picked independently), whereas we consider *identical* challenge distribution (i.e., the challenge bit for both $\mathcal{B}$ and $\mathcal{C}$ is identical). We show how to modify their construction to satisfy security with respect to different challenge distributions based on the two different versions of the simultaneous inner product conjecture.

SUMMARY. To summarise, we design UPO for keyed circuit classes in P/poly as follows:

- We show that if the copy-protection scheme of [CLLZ21] satisfies preponed security, UPO for P/poly exists. This step makes heavy use of iO techniques.
- We reduce the task of proving preponed security for the copy-protection scheme of [CLLZ21] to the task of proving that the single-decryptor encryption construction of [CLLZ21] is secure in the identical challenge setting.

2 Unclonable Puncturable Obfuscation: Definition

Next, we present the definition of an unclonable puncturable obfuscation scheme.

Keyed Circuit Class. A class of classical circuits of the form $\mathfrak{C} = \{\mathfrak{C}_\lambda\}_{\lambda \in \mathbb{N}}$ is said to be a keyed circuit class if the following holds: $\mathfrak{C}_\lambda = \{C_k : k \in \mathcal{K}_\lambda\}$, where C_k is a (classical) circuit with input length $n(\lambda)$, output length $m(\lambda)$ and $\mathcal{K} = \{\mathcal{K}_\lambda\}_{\lambda \in \mathbb{N}}$ is the key space. We refer to C_k as a keyed circuit. We note that any circuit class can be represented as a keyed circuit class using universal circuits. We will be interested in the setting when C_k is a polynomial-sized circuit; henceforth, unless specified otherwise, all keyed circuit classes considered in this work will consist only of polynomial-sized circuits. We will also make a simplifying assumption that C_k and $C_{k'}$ have the same size, where $k, k' \in \mathcal{K}_\lambda$.

Syntax. An unclonable puncturable obfuscation (UPO) scheme (Obf, Eval) for a keyed circuit class $\mathfrak{C} = \{\mathfrak{C}_\lambda\}_{\lambda \in \mathbb{N}}$, consists of the following QPT algorithms:

- Obf($1^\lambda, C$): on input a security parameter λ and a keyed circuit $C \in \mathfrak{C}_\lambda$ with input length $n(\lambda)$, it outputs a quantum state ρ_C.
- Eval(ρ_C, x): on input a quantum state ρ_C and an input $x \in \{0,1\}^{n(\lambda)}$, it outputs (ρ'_C, y).

Correctness. An unclonable puncturable obfuscation scheme (Obf, Eval) for a keyed circuit class $\mathfrak{C} = \{\mathfrak{C}_\lambda\}_{\lambda \in \mathbb{N}}$ is δ-correct, if for every $C \in \mathfrak{C}_\lambda$ with input length $n(\lambda)$, and for every $x \in \{0,1\}^{n(\lambda)}$,

$$\Pr\left[C(x) = y \;\Big|\; \begin{array}{c}\rho_C \leftarrow \mathsf{Obf}(1^\lambda, C)\\(\rho'_C, y) \leftarrow \mathsf{Eval}(\rho_C, x)\end{array}\right] \geq \delta$$

If δ is negligibly close to 1 then we say that the scheme is correct (i.e., we omit mentioning δ).

Remark 1. If $(1-\delta)$ is a negligible function in λ, by invoking the almost as good as new lemma [Aar16], we can evaluate ρ'_C on another input x' to get $C(x')$ with probability negligibly close to 1. We can repeat this process polynomially many times and each time, due to the quantum union bound [Gao15], we get the guarantee that the output is correct with probability negligibly close to 1.

2.1 Security

Puncturable Keyed Circuit Class. Consider a keyed circuit class $\mathfrak{C} = \{\mathfrak{C}_\lambda\}_{\lambda \in \mathbb{N}}$, where $\mathfrak{C}_\lambda$ consists of circuits of the form $C_k(\cdot)$, where $k \in \mathcal{K}_\lambda$, the input length of $C_k(\cdot)$ is $n(\lambda)$ and the output length is $m(\lambda)$. We say that $\mathfrak{C}_\lambda$ is said to be puncturable if there exists a deterministic polynomial-time puncturing algorithm Puncture such that the following holds: on input $k \in \{0,1\}^\lambda$, strings $x^\mathcal{B} \in \{0,1\}^{n(\lambda)}, x^\mathcal{C} \in \{0,1\}^{n(\lambda)}$, it outputs a circuit G_{k^*}. Moreover, the following holds: for every $x \in \{0,1\}^{n(\lambda)}$,

$$G_{k^*}(x) = \begin{cases} C_k(x), & x \neq x^\mathcal{B}, x \neq x^\mathcal{C}, \\ \bot, & x \in \{x^\mathcal{B}, x^\mathcal{C}\}. \end{cases}$$

Without loss of generality, we can assume that the size of G_{k^*} is the same as the size of C_k. Note that for every keyed circuit class, there exists a trivial Puncture algorithm. The trivial Puncture algorithm on any input $k, x_1, x_2, \mu_1, \mu_2$, constructs the circuit C_k and then outputs the circuit G that on input x, if $x = x_0$ or x_1 outputs $\bot$, else if $x \notin \{x_1, x_2\}$ outputs $C_k(x)$[8].

Definition 1 (UPO Security). *We say that a pair of QPT algorithms* (Obf, Eval) *for a puncturable keyed circuit class* $\mathfrak{C}$, *associated with puncturing procedure* Puncture, *satisfies* **UPO security** *with respect to a distribution* $\mathcal{D}_\mathcal{X}$ *on* $\{0,1\}^{n(\lambda)} \times \{0,1\}^{n(\lambda)}$ *if for every QPT* $(\mathcal{A}, \mathcal{B}, \mathcal{C})$ *in* UPO.Expt *(see Fig. 2), there exists a negligible function* $\mathsf{negl}(\lambda)$ *such that*

$$\Pr\left[1 \leftarrow \mathsf{UPO.Expt}^{(\mathcal{A},\mathcal{B},\mathcal{C}),\mathcal{D}_\mathcal{X},\mathfrak{C}}(1^\lambda, b) \;:\; b \xleftarrow{\$} \{0,1\}\right] \leq \frac{1}{2} + \mathsf{negl}(\lambda).$$

---

[8] The output circuit G_{k^*} is not of the same size as C_k, but this issue can be resolved by sufficient padding of the circuit class.

$$\underline{\mathsf{UPO.Expt}^{(\mathcal{A},\mathcal{B},\mathcal{C}),\mathcal{D}_\mathcal{X},\mathfrak{C}}\left(1^\lambda, b\right)}:$$

- $\mathcal{A}$ sends k, where $k \in \mathcal{K}_\lambda$, to the challenger Ch.
- Ch samples $(x^\mathcal{B}, x^\mathcal{C}) \leftarrow \mathcal{D}_\mathcal{X}(1^\lambda)$ and generates $G_{k^*} \leftarrow \mathsf{Puncture}(k, x^\mathcal{B}, x^\mathcal{C})$.
- Ch generates ρ_b as follows:
  - $\rho_0 \leftarrow \mathsf{Obf}(1^\lambda, C_k(\cdot))$,
  - $\rho_1 \leftarrow \mathsf{Obf}(1^\lambda, G_{k^*}(\cdot))$

  It sends ρ_b to $\mathcal{A}$.
- Apply $(\mathcal{B}(x^\mathcal{B}, \cdot) \otimes \mathcal{C}(x^\mathcal{C}, \cdot))(\sigma_{\mathbf{B},\mathbf{C}})$ to obtain $(b_\mathbf{B}, b_\mathbf{C})$.
- Output 1 if $b = b_\mathbf{B} = b_\mathbf{C}$.

Fig. 2. Security Experiment

Generalized Security. For most applications, the security definition discussed in Sect. 2.1 suffices, but for a couple of applications, we need a generalized definition as follows. We allow the adversary to choose the outputs of the circuit generated by Puncture on the punctured points. Previously, the circuit generated by the puncturing algorithm was such that on the punctured points, it output $\bot$. Instead, we allow the adversary to decide the values that need to be output on the points that are punctured. We emphasize that the adversary still would not know the punctured points itself until the challenge phase. Formally, the (generalized) puncturing algorithm GenPuncture now takes as input $k \in \mathcal{K}_\lambda$, polynomial-sized circuits $\mu^\mathcal{B} : \{0,1\}^{n(\lambda)} \to \{0,1\}^{m(\lambda)}$, $\mu^\mathcal{C} : \{0,1\}^{n(\lambda)} \to \{0,1\}^{m(\lambda)}$, strings $x^\mathcal{B} \in \{0,1\}^{n(\lambda)}, x^\mathcal{C} \in \{0,1\}^{n(\lambda)}$, if $x^\mathcal{B} \neq x^\mathcal{C}$, it outputs a circuit G_{k^*} such that for every $x \in \{0,1\}^{n(\lambda)}$,

$$G_{k^*}(x) = \begin{cases} C_k(x), & x \neq x^\mathcal{B}, x \neq x^\mathcal{C} \\ \mu_\mathcal{B}(x^\mathcal{B}), & x = x^\mathcal{B} \\ \mu_\mathcal{C}(x^\mathcal{C}), & x = x^\mathcal{C}, \end{cases}$$

else it outputs a circuit G_{k^*} such that for every $x \in \{0,1\}^{n(\lambda)}$,

$$G_{k^*}(x) = \begin{cases} C_k(x), & x \neq x^\mathcal{B} \\ \mu_\mathcal{B}(x^\mathcal{B}), & x = x^\mathcal{B}. \end{cases}$$

As before, we assume that without loss of generality, the size of G_{k^*} is the same as the size of C_k. A keyed circuit class $\mathfrak{C}$ associated with a generalized puncturing algorithm GenPuncture is referred to as a *generalized puncturable keyed circuit class*. Note that for every keyed circuit class $\mathfrak{C} = \{C_k\}_k$, there exists a trivial GenPuncture algorithm, which on any input $k, x_1, x_2, \mu_1, \mu_2$, constructs the circuit C_k and then outputs the circuit G_{k^*}.[9] that on input x, if $x = x_i$ for any $i \in \{0,1\}$, outputs $\mu_i(x_i)$, else if $x \notin \{x_1, x_2\}$ outputs $C_k(x)$.

Definition 2 (Generalized UPO security). *We say that a pair of QPT algorithms* (Obf, Eval) *for a generalized keyed circuit class* $\mathfrak{C} = \{\mathfrak{C}_\lambda\}_{\lambda \in \mathbb{N}}$ *equipped with a puncturing algorithm* GenPuncture, *satisfies* **generalized UPO security** *with respect to a distribution* $\mathcal{D}_\mathcal{X}$ *on* $\{0,1\}^{n(\lambda)} \times \{0,1\}^{n(\lambda)}$ *if the following holds for every QPT* $(\mathcal{A}, \mathcal{B}, \mathcal{C})$ *in* GenUPO.Expt *defined in Fig. 3:*

$$\Pr\left[1 \leftarrow \text{GenUPO.Expt}^{(\mathcal{A},\mathcal{B},\mathcal{C}),\mathcal{D}_\mathcal{X},\mathfrak{C}}\left(1^\lambda, b\right) \;:\; b \xleftarrow{\$} \{0,1\}\right] \leq \frac{1}{2} + \mathsf{negl}(\lambda).$$

GenUPO.Expt$^{(\mathcal{A},\mathcal{B},\mathcal{C}),\mathcal{D}_\mathcal{X},\mathfrak{C}}\left(1^\lambda, b\right)$:

- $\mathcal{A}$ sends $(k, \mu_\mathcal{B}, \mu_\mathcal{C})$, where $k \in \mathcal{K}_\lambda, \mu_\mathcal{B} : \{0,1\}^{n(\lambda)} \rightarrow \{0,1\}^{m(\lambda)}, \mu_\mathcal{C} : \{0,1\}^{n(\lambda)} \rightarrow \{0,1\}^{m(\lambda)}$, to the challenger Ch.
- Ch samples $(x^\mathcal{B}, x^\mathcal{C}) \leftarrow \mathcal{D}_\mathcal{X}(1^\lambda)$ and generates $G_{k^*} \leftarrow$ Puncture$(k, x^\mathcal{B}, x^\mathcal{C}, \mu_\mathcal{B}, \mu_\mathcal{C})$.
- Ch generates ρ_b as follows:
  - $\rho_0 \leftarrow \text{Obf}(1^\lambda, C_k)$,
  - $\rho_1 \leftarrow \text{Obf}(1^\lambda, G_{k^*})$

  It sends ρ_b to $\mathcal{A}$.
- Apply $(\mathcal{B}(x^\mathcal{B}, \cdot) \otimes \mathcal{C}(x^\mathcal{C}, \cdot))(\sigma_{\mathcal{B},\mathcal{C}})$ to obtain $(b_\mathbf{B}, b_\mathbf{C})$.
- Output 1 if $b = b_\mathbf{B} = b_\mathbf{C}$.

Fig. 3. Generalized Security Experiment

Instantiations of $\mathcal{D}_\mathcal{X}$. In the applications, we will be considering the following two distributions:

1. $\mathcal{U}_{\{0,1\}^{2n}}$: the uniform distribution on $\{0,1\}^{2n}$. When the context is clear, we simply refer to this distribution as $\mathcal{U}$.
2. $\mathsf{Id}_\mathcal{U}\{0,1\}^n$: identical distribution on $\{0,1\}^n \times \{0,1\}^n$ with uniform marginals. That is, the sampler for $\mathsf{Id}_\mathcal{U}\{0,1\}^n$ is defined as follows: sample x from $\mathcal{U}_{\{0,1\}^n}$ and output (x,x). When the context is clear, we simply refer to this distribution as $\mathsf{Id}_\mathcal{U}$.

---

[9] As before, the output circuit G_{k^*} may not have the same size as C_k, but this can be resolved by sufficient padding of the complexity class.

3 Conjectures

To show that our construction satisfies the UPO security notions, we rely upon some novel conjectures. Towards understanding our conjectures, consider the following problem: suppose say an adversary $\mathcal{B}$ is given a state $\rho_{\mathbf{x}}$ that is generated using a secret vector $\mathbf{x} \in \mathbb{Z}_Q^n$, where $Q, n \in \mathbb{N}$ and Q is prime. We are given the guarantee that just given $\rho_{\mathbf{x}}$, it should be infeasible to compute $\mathbf{x}$ with inverse polynomial probability over the randomness of sampling $\mathbf{x}$. Now, the goal of $\mathcal{B}$ is to predict $(\mathbf{u}, \langle \mathbf{u}, \mathbf{x} \rangle)$ versus $(\mathbf{u}, \langle \mathbf{u}, \mathbf{x} \rangle + m)$, where $\mathbf{u} \xleftarrow{\$} \mathbb{Z}_Q^n$ and $m \xleftarrow{\$} \mathbb{Z}_Q$. The quantum Goldreich-Levin theorem [AC02, CLLZ21] states that, for the case when $Q = 2$, the probability that $\mathcal{B}$ succeeds is negligibly close to $\frac{1}{2}$. The quantum Goldreich-Levin theorem has been generalized [APV23, STHY23] to the case when Q is large.

We study a generalized version of this problem where there are two non-communicating but entangled parties $\mathcal{B}$ and $\mathcal{C}$ and both are simultaneously participating in the above distinguishing experiment. Depending on the entangled state shared by $\mathcal{B}$ and $\mathcal{C}$ and the distributions from which the samples are generated, we obtain many generalizations. We conjecture that in some of these generalized versions, the prediction probability is close to $\frac{1}{2}$. But first, we will capture all the generalizations by defining the following problem.

$(\mathcal{D}_\mathcal{X}, \mathcal{D}_{\mathsf{Ch}}, \mathcal{D}_{\mathsf{bit}})$-*Simultaneous Inner Product Problem* $((\mathcal{D}_\mathcal{X}, \mathcal{D}_{\mathsf{Ch}}, \mathcal{D}_{\mathsf{bit}})$-simultIP$)$. Let $\mathcal{D}_\mathcal{X}$ be a distribution on $\mathbb{Z}_Q^n \times \mathbb{Z}_Q^n$, $\mathcal{D}_{\mathsf{Ch}}$ be a distribution on $\mathbb{Z}_Q^{n+1} \times \mathbb{Z}_Q^{n+1}$ and finally, let $\mathcal{D}_{\mathsf{bit}}$ be a distribution on $\{0,1\} \times \{0,1\}$, for prime $Q \in \mathbb{N}$. Let $\mathcal{B}'$ and $\mathcal{C}'$ be QPT algorithms. Let $\rho = \{\rho_{\mathbf{x}^\mathcal{B}, \mathbf{x}^\mathcal{C}}\}_{\mathbf{x}^\mathcal{B}, \mathbf{x}^\mathcal{C} \in \mathbb{Z}_Q^n}$ be a set of bipartite states. If $\mathbf{x}^\mathcal{B} = \mathbf{x}^\mathcal{C} = \mathbf{x}$ then we denote $\rho_{\mathbf{x}^\mathcal{B}, \mathbf{x}^\mathcal{C}}$ by $\rho_{\mathbf{x}}$.

Consider the following game.

- Sample $(\mathbf{x}^\mathcal{B}, \mathbf{x}^\mathcal{C}) \leftarrow \mathcal{D}_\mathcal{X}$,
- Sample $((\mathbf{u}^\mathcal{B}, m^\mathcal{B}), (\mathbf{u}^\mathcal{C}, m^\mathcal{C})) \leftarrow \mathcal{D}_{\mathsf{Ch}}$,
- Set $z_0^\mathcal{B} = \langle \mathbf{u}^\mathcal{B}, \mathbf{x}^\mathcal{B} \rangle$, $z_0^\mathcal{C} = \langle \mathbf{u}^\mathcal{C}, \mathbf{x}^\mathcal{C} \rangle$, $z_1^\mathcal{B} = m^\mathcal{B} + \langle \mathbf{u}^\mathcal{B}, \mathbf{x}^\mathcal{B} \rangle$, $z_1^\mathcal{C} = m^\mathcal{C} + \langle \mathbf{u}^\mathcal{C}, \mathbf{x}^\mathcal{C} \rangle$,
- Sample $(b^\mathcal{B}, b^\mathcal{C}) \leftarrow \mathcal{D}_{\mathsf{bit}}$,
- $(\widehat{b}^\mathcal{B}, \widehat{b}^\mathcal{C}) \leftarrow (\mathcal{B}'(\mathbf{u}^\mathcal{B}, z_{b^\mathcal{B}}^\mathcal{B}, \cdot) \otimes \mathcal{C}'(\mathbf{u}^\mathcal{C}, z_{b^\mathcal{C}}^\mathcal{C}, \cdot))(\rho_{\mathbf{x}^\mathcal{B}, \mathbf{x}^\mathcal{C}})$.

We say that $(\mathcal{B}', \mathcal{C}')$ succeeds if $\widehat{b}^\mathcal{B} = b^\mathcal{B}$ and $\widehat{b}^\mathcal{C} = b^\mathcal{C}$.

Our goal is to upper bound the optimal success probability in the above problem. We are primarily interested in the following setting: $\mathcal{D}_{\mathsf{bit}}$ is a distribution on $\{0,1\} \times \{0,1\}$, where (b, b) is sampled with probability $\frac{1}{2}$, for $b \in \{0,1\}$. In this case, we simply refer to the above problem as $(\mathcal{D}_\mathcal{X}, \mathcal{D}_{\mathsf{Ch}})$-simultIP problem.

Conjectures. We state the following conjectures. In the conjectures, we assume that the order of the field is $Q \geq 2^\lambda$. We are interested in the following distributions:

- We define $\mathcal{D}_{\mathsf{Ch}}^{\mathsf{ind}}$ as follows: it samples $\left(\left(\mathbf{u}^{\mathcal{B}},m^{\mathcal{B}}\right),\left(\mathbf{u}^{\mathcal{C}},m^{\mathcal{C}}\right)\right)$, where $\mathbf{u}^{\mathcal{B}} \xleftarrow{\$} \mathbb{Z}_Q^n, \mathbf{u}^{\mathcal{C}} \xleftarrow{\$} \mathbb{Z}_Q^n, m^{\mathcal{B}} \xleftarrow{\$} \mathbb{Z}_Q, m^{\mathcal{C}} \xleftarrow{\$} \mathbb{Z}_Q$. We define $\mathcal{D}_{\mathsf{Ch}}^{\mathsf{id}}$ as follows: it samples $((\mathbf{u},m),(\mathbf{u},m))$, where $\mathbf{u} \xleftarrow{\$} \mathbb{Z}_Q^n, m \xleftarrow{\$} \mathbb{Z}_Q$.
- Similarly, we define $\mathcal{D}_{\mathcal{X}}^{\mathsf{ind}}$ as follows: it samples $\left(\mathbf{x}^{\mathcal{B}},\mathbf{x}^{\mathcal{C}}\right)$, where $\mathbf{x}^{\mathcal{B}} \xleftarrow{\$} \mathbb{Z}_Q^n, \mathbf{x}^{\mathcal{C}} \xleftarrow{\$} \mathbb{Z}_Q^n$. We define $\mathcal{D}_{\mathcal{X}}^{\mathsf{id}}$ as follows: it samples $(\mathbf{x},\mathbf{x})$, where $\mathbf{x} \xleftarrow{\$} \mathbb{Z}_Q^n$.

Conjecture 1 (($\mathcal{D}_{\mathcal{X}}^{\mathsf{id}}, \mathcal{D}_{\mathsf{Ch}}^{\mathsf{id}}$)-simultIP Conjecture). Consider a set of bipartite states $\rho = \{\rho_\mathbf{x}\}_{\mathbf{x}\in\mathbb{Z}_Q^n}$ satisfying the following property: for any two QPT adversaries $\mathcal{B}, \mathcal{C}$,

$$\Pr\left[(\mathbf{x},\mathbf{x}) \leftarrow (\mathcal{B} \otimes \mathcal{C})(\rho_\mathbf{x}) \ : \ (\mathbf{x},\mathbf{x}) \leftarrow \mathcal{D}_{\mathcal{X}}^{\mathsf{id}}\right] \leq \nu(n)$$

for some negligible function $\nu(\lambda)$.

Any QPT non-local solver for the $(\mathcal{D}_{\mathcal{X}}^{\mathsf{id}}, \mathcal{D}_{\mathsf{Ch}}^{\mathsf{id}})$-simultIP problem succeeds with probability at most $\frac{1}{2} + \varepsilon(n)$, where ε is a negligible function.

Conjecture 2 (($\mathcal{D}_{\mathcal{X}}^{\mathsf{ind}}, \mathcal{D}_{\mathsf{Ch}}^{\mathsf{ind}}$)-simultIP Conjecture). Consider a set of bipartite states $\rho = \{\rho_{\mathbf{x}^{\mathcal{B}},\mathbf{x}^{\mathcal{C}}}\}_{\mathbf{x}^{\mathcal{B}},\mathbf{x}^{\mathcal{C}}\in\mathbb{Z}_Q^n}$ satisfying the following property: for any two QPT adversaries $\mathcal{B}, \mathcal{C}$,

$$\Pr\left[(\mathbf{x}^{\mathcal{B}},\mathbf{x}^{\mathcal{C}}) \leftarrow (\mathcal{B} \otimes \mathcal{C})(\rho_{\mathbf{x}^{\mathcal{B}},\mathbf{x}^{\mathcal{C}}}) \ : \ (\mathbf{x}^{\mathcal{B}},\mathbf{x}^{\mathcal{C}}) \leftarrow \mathcal{D}_{\mathcal{X}}^{\mathsf{ind}}\right] \leq \nu(n)$$

for some negligible function $\nu(\lambda)$.

Any QPT non-local solver for the $\mathcal{D}_{\mathsf{Ch}}^{\mathsf{id}}$-simultIP problem succeeds with probability at most $\frac{1}{2} + \varepsilon(n)$, where ε is a negligible function.

3.1 Discussion

Special Cases. Variants of the above conjectures, obtained by modifying the input and challenge distributions, have been proven to be true by considering different flavors of the simultaneous Goldreich-Levin theorem. We mention three such special cases below.

	Field Size	Input distribution	Challenge sample distribution	Challenge bit distribution
[AKL23]	$Q = 2$	$\mathcal{D}_{\mathcal{X}} = \mathcal{D}_{\mathcal{X}}^{\mathsf{id}}$	$\mathcal{D}_{\mathsf{Ch}} = \widetilde{\mathcal{D}}_{\mathsf{Ch}}^{\mathsf{ind}}$	$\mathcal{D}_{\mathsf{bit}} = \mathcal{D}_{\mathsf{bit}}^{\mathsf{ind}}$
[KT22]	$Q \in \{2,3\}$	$\mathcal{D}_{\mathcal{X}} = \mathcal{D}_{\mathcal{X}}^{\mathsf{ind}}$	$\mathcal{D}_{\mathsf{Ch}} = \widetilde{\mathcal{D}}_{\mathsf{Ch}}^{\mathsf{ind}}$	$\mathcal{D}_{\mathsf{bit}} = \mathcal{D}_{\mathsf{bit}}^{\mathsf{ind}}$
[AKY24]	$Q = 2$	$\mathcal{D}_{\mathcal{X}} = \mathcal{D}_{\mathcal{X}}^{\mathsf{id}}$	$\mathcal{D}_{\mathsf{Ch}} = \widetilde{\mathcal{D}}_{\mathsf{Ch}}^{\mathsf{ind}}$	$\mathcal{D}_{\mathsf{bit}} = \mathcal{D}_{\mathsf{bit}}^{\mathsf{id}}$

We define $\widetilde{\mathcal{D}}_{\mathsf{Ch}}^{\mathsf{ind}}$, for the case when $Q = 2$, to be the distribution that samples $((\mathbf{u}^{\mathcal{B}}, 1), (\mathbf{u}^{\mathcal{C}}, 1))$, where $\mathbf{u}^{\mathcal{B}} \xleftarrow{\$} \mathbb{Z}_Q^n$ and $\mathbf{u}^{\mathcal{C}} \xleftarrow{\$} \mathbb{Z}_Q^n$. Note that this is similar to $\mathcal{D}_{\mathsf{Ch}}^{\mathsf{ind}}$ except that $m^{\mathcal{B}}$ and $m^{\mathcal{C}}$ is always set to 1.

Although not explicitly stated, the generic framework of upgrading classical reductions to non-local reductions, introduced in [AKL23], can be leveraged to extend the above result to large values of Q. Finally, the work of [CG23] considers a similar simultaneous Goldreich-Levin theorem as [AKL23] except that Bob's and Charlie's challenge messages consists of multiple Goldreich-Levin samples.

Among all the works so far, [AKY24] (which was subsequent to our work) is the only work that can handle *identical* challenge bit distributions (i.e. $\mathcal{D}_{\mathsf{bit}}^{\mathsf{id}}$) but for the case when $Q = 2$.

Proving our conjecture: Challenges. Unfortunately, it is unclear how to leverage the techniques used in the aforementioned works to prove our conjectures. To understand the difficulties, let us look at each of the two conjectures separately.

Let us start with the $(\mathcal{D}_{\mathcal{X}}^{\mathsf{ind}}, \mathcal{D}_{\mathsf{Ch}}^{\mathsf{ind}})$-simultIP conjecture (Conjecture 2). Recall that this conjecture is defined for large fields (of size $\geq 2^\lambda$). When $Q = 2$, a version of this conjecture was proven in a subsequent work by [AKY24]. Their proof is sensitive to the case that they are dealing with binary fields and their techniques do not seem to readily generalize to the case of large fields.

Proving $(\mathcal{D}_{\mathcal{X}}^{\mathsf{id}}, \mathcal{D}_{\mathsf{Ch}}^{\mathsf{id}})$-simultIP conjecture seems much harder although this is incomparable to the $(\mathcal{D}_{\mathcal{X}}^{\mathsf{ind}}, \mathcal{D}_{\mathsf{Ch}}^{\mathsf{ind}})$-simultIP conjecture. Let us illustrate its difficulty using the example of simultaneous Goldreich-Levin theorem proven in [AKL23,KT22]. They consider the independent setting where both Bob and Charlie receive independent Goldreich-Levin samples (i.e. $\mathcal{D}_{\mathsf{Ch}} = \widetilde{\mathcal{D}}_{\mathsf{Ch}}^{\mathsf{ind}}$ and $\mathcal{D}_{\mathsf{bit}} = \mathcal{D}_{\mathsf{bit}}^{\mathsf{ind}}$). To recall, the quantum Goldreich-Levin extractor (for a single party), as proven by [AC02,CLLZ21], proceeds as follows: it creates a superposition over all the challenge messages, coherently computes the distinguisher on it, applies a phase flip operation, uncomputes and finally, measures the answer in the Fourier basis. In the simultaneous version, we are required to extract from two parties, say, Bob and Charlie, simultaneously. In the independent setting, Bob's extractor and Charlie's extractor can each independently run the (single party) Goldreich-Levin extractor, and the analysis for the single party case smoothly extends to the simultaneous case as well. However, in the identical setting, this approach does not work. This is due to the fact that Bob and Charlie, instead of applying the Fourier basis measurement independently, would have to apply an entangled measurement jointly on their system. Since the two extractors are not allowed to communicate, it is not at all clear if such a measurement operation can be implemented. Another, and perhaps a more serious problem, is that the phase flip operations done by both Bob and Charlie cancel each other out, making the rest of the extraction process useless. Even though these difficulties are in the context of proving the simultaneous Goldreich-Levin theorem in the identical challenge setting, similar issues seem to exist with other non-local approaches to proving the identical simultaneous Goldreich-Levin theorem.

4 Direct Construction

In this section, we construct unclonable puncturable obfuscation for all efficiently computable generalized puncturable keyed circuit classes, with respect to $\mathcal{U}$ and $\mathsf{Id}_{\mathcal{U}}$ challenge distribution (see Sect. 2.1). Henceforth, we assume that any keyed circuit class we consider will consist of circuits that are efficiently computable. We present the construction in three steps.

1. In the first step (Sect. 4.1), we construct a single decryptor encryption (SDE) scheme based on the CLLZ scheme [CLLZ21] (see Fig. 4) and show that it satisfies $\mathcal{D}_{\text{ind-msg}}$-indistinguishability from random anti-piracy (and $\mathcal{D}_{\text{ind-msg}}$-indistinguishability from random anti-piracy respectively) (for more details on the definition, see the full version), based on the conjectures, Conjectures 1 and 2 .
2. In the second step (Sect. 4.2), we define a variant of the security definition considered in [CLLZ21] with respect to two different challenge distributions and prove that the copy-protection construction for PRFs in [CLLZ21] (see Fig. 8) satisfies this security notion, based on the indistinguishability from random anti-piracy guarantees of the SDE scheme considered in the first step.
3. In the third step (Sect. 4.3), we show how to transform the copy-protection scheme obtained from the first step into UPO for a keyed circuit class with respect to the $\mathcal{U}$ and $\mathsf{Id}_\mathcal{U}$ challenge distribution.

4.1 A New Public-Key Single-Decryptor Encryption Scheme

The first step is to construct a SDE scheme of the suitable form. While SDE schemes have been studied [GZ20, CLLZ21], we require a weaker version of security called indistinguishability from random anti-piracy (for more details on the definition, see the full version), which has not been considered in prior works.

Our construction is based on the SDE scheme in [CLLZ21, Section 6.3] which we recall in Fig. 4. From here on, we will refer to it as the CLLZ SDE scheme, given in Fig. 4. Next, we define a family of SDE schemes based on the CLLZ SDE, called CLLZ *post-processing* schemes, as follows.

CLLZ Post-processing Single Decryptor Encryption Scheme: Definition. We call a SDE scheme (Gen, QKeyGen, Enc, Dec) a CLLZ post-processing if there exists polynomial time classical algorithms (EncPostProcess, DecPostProcess), such that DecPostProcess is a deterministic algorithm. For correctness of a CLLZ *post-processing* SDE scheme (see Fig. 5) we require that for every string r, m,

$$c' \leftarrow \mathsf{EncPostProcess}(m, r), m' \leftarrow \mathsf{DecPostProcess}(c', r) \implies m = m'. \quad (1)$$

It is easy to verify that assuming Eq. (1), δ-correctness of the CLLZ SDE implies δ-correctness of a CLLZ *post-processing* SDE for every $\delta \in [0, 1]$.

Construction. We next consider the following CLLZ *post-processing* scheme given in Fig. 6. As mentioned before, we will assume that the message length is at least polynomial in the security parameter. Note that the algorithms (EncPostProcess, DecPostProcess) in Fig. 6 satisfies Eq. (1), and hence if the CLLZ

Tools: post-quantum indistinguishability obfuscation iO.

$\mathsf{Gen}(1^\lambda)$:
1. Sample ℓ_0 uniformly random subspaces $\{A_i\}_{i \in [\ell_0]}$ of dimension $\frac{\lambda}{2}$ from $\mathbb{Z}_2^\lambda$ and for each $i \in [\ell_0]$, sample vectors $s_i, s'_i \xleftarrow{\$} \mathbb{Z}_2^\lambda$, where $\ell_0 = \ell_0(\lambda)$ is a polynomial in λ.
2. Compute $\{R_i^0, R_i^1\}_{i \in \ell_0}$, where for every $i \in [\ell_0]$, $R_i^0 \leftarrow \mathsf{iO}(A_i + s_i)$ and $R_i^1 \leftarrow \mathsf{iO}(A_i^\perp + s'_i)$ are the membership oracles.
3. Output $\mathsf{sk} = \{\{A_{is_i, s'_i}\}_i\}$ and $\mathsf{pk} = \{R_i^0, R_i^1\}_{i \in \ell_0}$

$\mathsf{QKeyGen}(\mathsf{sk})$:
1. Interprete sk as $\{\{A_{is_i, s'_i}\}_i\}$.
2. Output $\rho_{\mathsf{sk}} = \{\{|A_{is_i, s'_i}\rangle\}_i\}$.

$\mathsf{Enc}(\mathsf{pk}, m)$:
1. Interprete $\mathsf{pk} = \{R_i^0, R_i^1\}_{i \in \ell_0}$.
2. Sample $r \xleftarrow{\$} \{0,1\}^n$.
3. Generate $\tilde{Q} \leftarrow \mathsf{iO}(Q_{m,r})$ where $Q_{m,r}$ has $\{R_i^0, R_i^1\}_{i \in \ell_0}$ hardcoded inside, and on input $v_1, \ldots, v_{\ell_0} \in \{0,1\}^{n\ell_0}$, checks if $R_i^{r_i}(v_i) = 1$ for every $i \in [\ell_0]$ and if the check succeeds, outputs m, otherwise output $\perp$.
4. Output $\mathsf{ct} = (r, \tilde{Q})$

$\mathsf{Dec}(\rho_{\mathsf{sk}}, \mathsf{ct})$
1. Interprete $\mathsf{ct} = (r, \tilde{Q})$.
2. For every $i \in [\ell_0]$, if $r_i = 1$ apply $H^{\otimes n}$ on $|A_{is_i, s'_i}\rangle$. Let the resulting state be $|\psi_x\rangle$.
3. Run the circuit $\tilde{Q}$ in superposition on the state $|\psi_x\rangle$ and measure the output register and output the measurement result m.

Fig. 4. The CLLZ single decryptor encryption scheme, see [CLLZ21, Construction 1].

SDE scheme (depicted in Fig. 4) satisfies δ-correctness so does the SDE scheme in Fig. 6. It is also easy to see that DecPostProcess is a determinisitc algorithm. Next, we prove security for the SDE scheme in Fig. 6 based on the simultaneous inner product conjectures.

Remark 2. By the definition of the randomized embedding Embed_Q defined in the algorithm EncPostProcess given in Fig. 6, it is easy to see that the ensemble

$$\{\mathsf{Embed}_Q(m)\}_{m \xleftarrow{\$} \{0,1\}^M} = \{\tilde{m}_Q\}_{\tilde{m}_Q \xleftarrow{\$} \{0,1,\ldots,LM-1\}} \approx_s \{\tilde{m}_Q\}_{\tilde{m}_Q \xleftarrow{\$} \mathbb{Z}_Q},$$

Tools: CLLZ SDE scheme given in Figure 4.

Gen(1^λ): Same as CLLZ.Gen(1^λ).

QKeyGen(sk): Same as CLLZ.QKeyGen(sk).

Enc(pk, m):

1. Sample $r \xleftarrow{\$} \mathbb{Z}_Q^\lambda$, where Q is the smallest prime greater than or equal to $M \cdot 2^\lambda$ with M being the size of the message space, i.e., $M = 2^{|m|}$ and $|m|$ is the bit-size of the message m.
2. Generate $c \leftarrow \mathsf{EncPostProcess}(m, r)$ and generate $c' \leftarrow \mathsf{CLLZ.Enc}(\mathsf{pk}, r)$[10].
3. Output $\mathsf{ct} = (c, c')$.

Dec(ρ_{sk}, ct)

1. Interprete $\mathsf{ct} = (c, c')$.
2. Generate $r \leftarrow \mathsf{CLLZ.Dec}(\rho_{\mathsf{sk}}, c')$.
3. Output $m \leftarrow \mathsf{DecPostProcess}(c, r)$.

Fig. 5. Definition of a CLLZ *post-processing* SDE scheme.

EncPostProcess(m, r):

1. Sample $u \xleftarrow{\$} \mathbb{Z}_Q^\lambda$, where Q is the smallest prime number greater than $2^{|m|+\lambda}$, and $|m|$ is the bit-size of the binary string m.
2. Generate $\tilde{m} \leftarrow \mathsf{Embed}_Q(m)$, where Embed_Q randomly embeds the binary string m in $\mathbb{Z}_Q$, i.e., $\tilde{m}_Q \equiv kM + m_Q$ where $k \xleftarrow{\$} \{0, 1, \ldots, L-1\}$, $M \equiv 2^{|m|}$, $L \equiv \lceil Q/M \rceil$, and m_Q is the canonical embedding of m in $\mathbb{Z}_Q$.
3. Output $u, \tilde{m}_Q + \langle u, r \rangle$, where the addition and inner product uses the product over the field $\mathbb{Z}_Q$.

DecPostProcess(c, r):
1. Interprete c as u, z.
2. Generate $\tilde{m}_Q \leftarrow z + \langle u, r \rangle$.
3. Output m where m is the binary representation of $\tilde{m}_Q \mod M$.

Fig. 6. Construction of a CLLZ *post-processing* SDE scheme.

because $Q - L < M$ by definition of L, and hence, $\frac{Q-L}{Q} < \frac{M}{Q}$ which is at most $\frac{M}{M \cdot 2^\lambda} = \frac{1}{2^\lambda}$, by our choice of Q.

---

[10] We would like to note that the obfuscated circuit may be padded more than what is required in the CLLZ SDE scheme, for the security proofs of the CLLZ *post-processing* SDE.

Theorem 6. *Assuming Conjecture 2, the existence of post-quantum sub-exponentially secure* iO *and one-way functions, and the quantum hardness of Learning-with-errors problem (LWE), the* CLLZ *post-processing* SDE *as defined in Fig. 5 given in Fig. 6 satisfies* $\mathcal{D}_{\text{ind-msg}}$-*indistinguishability from random anti-piracy (for more details on the definition, see the full version).*

Theorem 7. *Assuming Conjecture 1, the existence of post-quantum sub-exponentially secure* iO *and one-way functions, and quantum hardness of Learning-with-errors problem (LWE), the* CLLZ *post-processing* SDE *(as defined in Fig. 5) given in Fig. 6 satisfies* $\mathcal{D}_{\text{identical-cipher}}$-*indistinguishability from random anti-piracy (for more details on the definition, see the full version).*

The proof of Theorems 6 and 7 is given in full version.

4.2 Copy-Protection for PRFs with Preponed Security

We first introduce the definition of *preponed security* in Sect. 4.2 and then we present the constructions of copy-protection in Sect. 4.2.

Definition. We introduce a new security notion for copy-protection called *preponed security*.

Consider a pseudorandom function family $\mathcal{F} = \{\mathcal{F}_\lambda\}_{\lambda \in \mathbb{N}}$, where $\mathcal{F}_\lambda = \{f_k : \{0,1\}^{\ell(\lambda)} \to \{0,1\}^{\kappa(\lambda)} : k \in \{0,1\}^\lambda\}$. Moreover, f_k can be implemented using a polynomial-sized circuit, denoted by C_k.

Definition 3 (Preponed Security). *A copy-protection scheme* CP = (CopyProtect, Eval) *for* $\mathcal{F}$ *(see the full version for the formal definition) satisfies* $\mathcal{D}_\mathcal{X}$-*preponed security if for any QPT* $(\mathcal{A}, \mathcal{B}, \mathcal{C})$, *there exists a negligible function* negl *such that:*

$$\Pr[\text{PreponedExpt}^{(\mathcal{A},\mathcal{B},\mathcal{C}),\mathcal{F},\mathcal{U}}(1^\lambda) = 1] \leq \frac{1}{2} + \text{negl}.$$

where PreponedExpt *is defined in Fig. 7.*

We consider two instantiations of $\mathcal{D}_\mathcal{X}$:

1. $\mathcal{U}$ which is the product of uniformly random distribution on $\{0,1\}^\ell$, meaning $x_1, x_2 \leftarrow \mathcal{U}(1^\lambda)$ where $x_1, x_2 \xleftarrow{\$} \{0,1\}^\ell$ independently.
2. $\text{Id}_\mathcal{U}$ which is the perfectly correlated distribution on $\{0,1\}^\ell$ with uniform marginals, meaning $x, x \leftarrow \text{Id}_\mathcal{U}(1^\lambda)$ where $x \xleftarrow{\$} \{0,1\}^\ell$.

Construction. The CLLZ copy-protection scheme is given in Figs. 8 and 9.

PreponedExpt$^{(\mathcal{A},\mathcal{B},\mathcal{C}),\mathsf{CP},\mathcal{D}_\mathcal{X}}(1^\lambda)$:

1. Ch samples $k \leftarrow \mathsf{KeyGen}(1^\lambda)$, then generates $\rho_{C_k} \leftarrow \mathsf{CopyProtect}(1^\lambda, C_k)$ and sends ρ_{f_k} to $\mathcal{A}$.
2. Ch samples $x^\mathcal{B}, x^\mathcal{C} \leftarrow \mathcal{D}_\mathcal{X}(1^\lambda)$, $b \xleftarrow{\$} \{0,1\}$. Let $y_1^\mathcal{B} = f(x^\mathcal{B}), y_1^\mathcal{C} = f(x^\mathcal{C})$, and $y_0^\mathcal{B} = y_1, y_0^\mathcal{C} = y_2$ where $y_1, y_2 \xleftarrow{\$} \{0,1\}^{\kappa(\lambda)}$. Ch gives $(y_b^\mathcal{B}, y_b^\mathcal{C})$ to Alice.
3. $\mathcal{A}(\rho_{C_k})$ outputs a bipartite state $\sigma_{\mathcal{B},\mathcal{C}}$.
4. Apply $(\mathcal{B}(x^\mathcal{B}, \cdot) \otimes \mathcal{C}(x^\mathcal{C}, \cdot))(\sigma_{\mathcal{B},\mathcal{C}})$ to obtain $(b_\mathbf{B}, b_\mathbf{C})$.
5. Output 1 if $b_\mathbf{B} = b_\mathbf{C} = b$.

Fig. 7. Preponed security experiment for copy-protection of PRFs with respect to the distribution $\mathcal{D}_\mathcal{X}$.

Tools: Punctrable and extractable PRF family $F_1 = (\mathsf{KeyGen}, \mathsf{Eval})$ (represented as $F_1(k, x) = \mathsf{PRF.Eval}(k, \cdot)$) and secondary PRF family F_2, F_3 with some special properties as noted in [CLLZ21]

CopyProtect(K_1):

1. Sample secondary keys K_2, K_3, and $\{\{|A_{is_i,s'_i}\rangle\}_i\}$, and compute the coset state $\{\{|A_{is_i,s'_i}\rangle\}_i\}$.
2. Compute $\tilde{P} \leftarrow i\mathcal{O}(P)$ where P is as given in Figure 9.
3. Output $\rho = (\tilde{P}, \{\{|A_{is_i,s'_i}\rangle\}_i\})$.

Eval(ρ, x):

1. Interprete $\rho = (\tilde{P}, \{\{|A_{is_i,s'_i}\rangle\}_i\})$.
2. Let $x = x_0 \| x_1 \| x_2$, where $x_0 = \ell_0$. For every $i \in [\ell_0]$, if $x_{0,i} = 1$ apply $H^{\otimes n}$ on $|A_{is_i,s'_i}\rangle$. Let the resulting state be $|\psi_x\rangle$.
3. Run the circuit $\tilde{C}$ in superposition on the input registers (X, V) with the initial state $(x, |\psi_x\rangle)$ and measure the output register to get an output y.

Fig. 8. CLLZ copy-protection for PRFs.

Construction of Copy-Protection.

Proposition 1. *Assuming the existence of post-quantum iO, and one-way functions, and if there exists a* **CLLZ** *post-processing* **SDE** *scheme that satisfies* $\mathcal{D}_{\mathsf{ind\text{-}msg}}$*-indistinguishability from random anti-piracy (for more details on the definition, see the full version), then the* **CLLZ** *copy-protection construction*

P:

Hardcoded keys $K_1, K_2, K_3, R_i^0, R_i^1$ for every $i \in [\ell_0]$ On input $x = x_0 \| x_1 \| x_2$ and vectors $v = v_1, \ldots v_{\ell_0}$.

1. If $F_3(K_3, x_1) \oplus x_2 = x_0 \| Q$ and $x_1 = F_2(K_2, x_0 \| Q)$:
   Hidden trigger mode: Treat Q as a classical circuit and output $Q(v)$.
2. Otherwise, check if the following holds: for all $i \in \ell_0$, $R^{x_{0,i}}(v_i) = 1$ (where $x_{0,i}$ is the ith coordinate of x_0).
   Normal mode: If so, output $F_1(K_1, x)$ where $F_1() = \mathsf{PRF.Eval}()$ is the primary pseudorandom function family that is being copy-protected. Otherwise output $\bot$.

Fig. 9. Circuit P in CLLZ copy-protection of PRF.

in [CLLZ21, Section 7.3] (see Fig. 8) satisfies $\mathcal{U}$-preponed security (Definition 3).

Proposition 2. *Assuming the existence of post-quantum* iO, *and one-way functions, and if there exists a* CLLZ *post-processing* SDE *scheme that satisfies* $\mathcal{D}_{\mathsf{identical\text{-}cipher}}$-*indistinguishability from random anti-piracy, (for more details on the definition, see the full version), then the* CLLZ *copy-protection construction in [CLLZ21, Section 7.3] (see Fig. 8) satisfies* $\mathsf{Id}_{\mathcal{U}}$-*preponed security (Definition 3).*

The proofs of Propositions 1 and 2 can be found in full version.

4.3 UPO for Keyed Circuits from Copy-Protection with Preponed Security

Theorem 8. *Assuming Conjecture 2, the existence of post-quantum subexponentially secure* iO *and injective one-way functions, and the quantum hardness of Learning-with-errors problem (LWE), there is a construction of unclonable puncturable obfuscation satisfying* $\mathcal{U}$-*generalized* UPO *security (see Definition 2), for any generalized keyed puncturable circuit class* $\mathfrak{C}$ *in* P/poly, *see Sect. 2.1.*

Proof. The proof follows by combining Lemma 1 and Theorem 10. □

Theorem 9. *Assuming Conjecture 1, the existence of post-quantum subexponentially secure* iO *and injective one-way functions, and the quantum hardness of Learning-with-errors problem (LWE), there is a construction of unclonable puncturable obfuscation satisfying* $\mathsf{Id}_{\mathcal{U}}$-*generalized* UPO *security (see Definition 2), for any generalized keyed puncturable circuit class* $\mathfrak{C}$ *in* P/poly, *see Sect. 2.1.*

Proof. The proof follows by combining Lemma 1 and Theorem 11. □

In the construction given in Fig. 10, the PRF family (KeyGen, Eval) satisfies the requirements as in [CLLZ21] and has input length $n(\lambda)$ and output length m; PRG is a length-doubling injective pseudorandom generator with input length m, which can be constructed based on injective one-way functions.

Tools: PRF family (KeyGen, Eval) with same properties as needed in [CLLZ21], PRG, CLLZ copy-protection scheme (CopyProtect, Eval).

Obf($1^\lambda, W$):

1. Sample a random key $k \leftarrow$ PRF.KeyGen(1^λ).
2. Compute $iO(P), \{\{|A_{is_i, s'_i}\rangle\}_i\} \leftarrow$ CLLZ.CopyProtect(k).
3. Compute $\tilde{C} \leftarrow iO(C)$ where $C = \text{PRG} \cdot iO(P)$.
4. Compute $iO(D)$ where D takes as input x, v, y, and runs C on x, v to get y' and outputs $\perp$ if $y' \neq y$ or $y' = \perp$, else it runs the circuit W on x to output $W(x)$.
5. Output $\rho = (\{\{|A_{is_i, s'_i}\rangle\}_i\}, \tilde{C}, iO(D))$.

Eval(ρ, x)

1. Interprete $\rho = (\{\{|A_{is_i, s'_i}\rangle\}_i\}, \tilde{C}, iO(D))$.
2. Let $x = x_0 \| x_1 \| x_2$, where $x_0 = \ell_0$. For every $i \in [\ell_0]$, if $x_{0,i} = 1$ apply $H^{\otimes n}$ on $|A_{is_i, s'_i}\rangle$. Let the resulting state be $|\psi_x\rangle$.
3. Run the circuit $\tilde{C}$ in superposition on the input registers (X, V) with the initial state $(x, |\psi_x\rangle)$ and then measure the output register to get an output y. Let the resulting state quantum state on register V be σ.
4. Run $iO(D)$ on the registers X, V, Y in superposition where registers X, Y are initialized to classical values x, y and then measure the output register to get an output z. Output z.

Fig. 10. Construction of a UPO scheme.

Lemma 1. *The construction given in Fig. 10 satisfies (1−negl)-UPO correctness for any generalized puncturable keyed circuit class in P/poly for some negligible function* negl.

The proof is given in the full version.

Theorem 10. *Assuming Conjecture 2, post-quantum sub-exponentially secure iO and injective one-way functions, and the quantum hardness of Learning-with-errors problem (LWE), the construction given in Fig. 10 satisfies $\mathcal{U}$-generalized* unclonable puncturable obfuscation security (see Sect. 2.1) for any generalized puncturable keyed circuit class in P/poly.

Proof. The proof follows by combining Lemma 2 and Proposition 1, and Theorem 6. □

Theorem 11. *Assuming Conjecture 1, the existence of post-quantum subexponentially secure* iO *and injective one-way functions, and the quantum hardness of Learning-with-errors problem (LWE), the construction given in Fig. 10 satisfies* $\mathsf{Id}_{\mathcal{U}}$*-generalized unclonable puncturable obfuscation security (see Sect. 2.1) for any generalized puncturable keyed circuit class in* P/poly.

Proof. The proof follows by combining Lemma 3 , Proposition 2, and Theorem 7. □

Lemma 2. *Assuming the existence of post-quantum* iO*, injective one-way functions, and that* CLLZ *copy protection construction for* PRF*s given in Fig. 8, satisfies* $\mathcal{U}$*-preponed security (defined in Definition 3, the construction given in Fig. 10 for* $\mathcal{W}$ *satisfies* $\mathcal{U}$*-generalized* UPO *security guarantee (see Sect. 2.1), for any puncturable keyed circuit class* $\mathcal{W} = \{\{W_s\}_{s \in \mathcal{K}_\lambda}\}_\lambda$ *in* P/poly.

Lemma 3. *Assuming the existence of post-quantum* iO*, injective one-way functions, and that* CLLZ *copy protection construction for* PRF*s given in Fig. 8, satisfies* $\mathsf{Id}_{\mathcal{U}}$*-preponed security (defined in Definition 3), the construction given in Fig. 10 for* $\mathcal{W}$ *satisfies* $\mathsf{Id}_{\mathcal{U}}$*-generalized* UPO *security guarantee (see Sect. 2.1), for any puncturable keyed circuit class* $\mathcal{W} = \{\{W_s\}_{s \in \mathcal{K}_\lambda}\}_\lambda$ *in* P/poly.

The proof of the Lemmas 2 and 3 can be found in the full version.

5 Construction of UPO from Quantum State iO

Recently, Coladangelo and Gunn [CG23] proposed the definition of quantum state indistinguishability obfuscation (qsiO) and presented a candidate construction of qsiO. In this section, we show how to construct UPO from qsiO, assuming unclonable encryption and injective one-way functions. As an intermediate tool, we consider a variant of private-key unclonable encryption introduced in [CG23], called key-testable (private-key) unclonable encryption.

Key-Testable Unclonable Encryption. A key-testable unclonable encryption scheme [CG23] is an unclonable encryption scheme (Gen, Enc, Dec) where, given a ciphertext ρ and a key sk', we can efficiently determine with probability 1 whether ρ was generated using the secret key sk' or not.

Formally, a key-testable private-key unclonable encryption is associated with an additional QPT algorithm Test that takes as input a key $\mathsf{sk} \in \{0,1\}^\lambda$, a quantum ciphertext ρ and outputs a bit b such that for every pair of keys $\mathsf{sk}, \mathsf{sk}' \in \{0,1\}^\lambda$, $\mathsf{sk} \neq \mathsf{sk}'$, a message $m \in \{0,1\}^n$,

$$\Pr\left[b \leftarrow \mathsf{Test}(\mathsf{sk}',\rho) : \begin{matrix}\mathsf{sk} \leftarrow \mathsf{Gen}(1^\lambda),\\ \rho \leftarrow \mathsf{Enc}(\mathsf{sk},m),\\ b=\delta_{\mathsf{sk}}(\mathsf{sk}')\end{matrix}\right] = 1,$$

where δ_{sk} is the function that is 1 at sk and 0 everywhere else, and Enc is the encryption algorithm for the unclonable encryption scheme.

Unclonable Encryption Schemes with Uniform Key-Generation. In addition to the key-testable property, for the purpose of our construction of UPO, we also require that the key generation algorithm of the underlying unclonable encryption scheme samples the secret key uniformly at random from $\{0,1\}^\lambda$. We need this restriction on the key-generation algorithm because, in our construction, the output distribution of the key-generation algorithm determines the challenge distribution $\mathcal{D}_\mathcal{X}$, i.e., the distribution of the point to be punctured.

We next show that given an unclonable encryption scheme, we can generically transform it into another scheme satisfying the above-mentioned restriction.

Theorem 12. *An unclonable encryption scheme* $\mathsf{UE} = (\mathsf{Gen}, \mathsf{Enc}, \mathsf{Dec})$ *can be transformed into another unclonable encryption scheme* $\mathsf{UE}' = (\mathsf{Gen}', \mathsf{Enc}', \mathsf{Dec}')$ *such that the output distribution of* Gen' *is uniform. Moreover,* UE' *supports messages of the same length as* UE.

Proof. Given $\mathsf{UE} = (\mathsf{Gen}, \mathsf{Enc}, \mathsf{Dec})$, we define $\mathsf{UE}' = (\mathsf{Gen}', \mathsf{Enc}', \mathsf{Dec}')$ as follows.

- $\mathsf{Gen}'(1^\lambda)$: Sample $k' \xleftarrow{\$} \{0,1\}^\lambda$, and output k'.
- $\mathsf{Enc}'(k', m)$: Generate $k \leftarrow \mathsf{Gen}(1^\lambda)$, and then generate $\rho \leftarrow \mathsf{Enc}(k, m)$. Output $\rho' = (\rho, k \oplus k')$.
- $\mathsf{Dec}'(k', \rho')$: Interprete $\rho' = (\rho, c)$. Generate $k = k' \oplus c$, and then generate $m \leftarrow \mathsf{Dec}(k, \rho)$. Output m.

Clearly, the correctness of UE' is immediate from the correctness of UE. Furthermore, Gen' satisfies the property mentioned in the theorem.

To argue security, let $(\mathcal{A}, \mathcal{B}, \mathcal{C})$ be an adversary that violates unclonable indistinguishability security of UE' (see the formal definition in the full version). Consider the following reduction $(\mathcal{R}_\mathcal{A}, \mathcal{R}_\mathcal{B}, \mathcal{R}_\mathcal{C})$ that uses $(\mathcal{A}, \mathcal{B}, \mathcal{C})$ to violate the unclonable indistinguishability security of UE.

1. $\mathcal{R}_\mathcal{A}$ runs $\mathcal{A}$ on the security parameter and get backs a message pair (m_0, m_1), which she sends to the challenger Ch.
2. Ch sends a ciphertext ρ.
3. $\mathcal{R}_\mathcal{A}$ samples $r \xleftarrow{\$} \{0,1\}^\lambda$, and feeds $\rho' = (\rho, r)$ to $\mathcal{A}$ who then outputs a bipartite state $\sigma_{(\mathcal{B},\mathcal{C})}$. $\mathcal{R}_\mathcal{A}$ outputs $(r_\mathcal{B}, \sigma_{(\mathcal{B},\mathcal{C})}, r_\mathcal{C})$ where $r_\mathcal{B} = r_\mathcal{C} = r$.
4. $\mathcal{R}_\mathcal{B}$ (respectively, $\mathcal{R}_\mathcal{C}$) on receiving $(r_\mathcal{B}, \sigma_\mathcal{B})$ (respectively, $(r_\mathcal{C}, \sigma_\mathcal{C})$) from $\mathcal{R}_\mathcal{A}$ and a key k from the challenger, runs $\mathcal{B}$ on $(r_\mathcal{B} \oplus k, \sigma_\mathcal{B})$ (respectively, $\mathcal{C}$ on $(r_\mathcal{C} \oplus k, \sigma_\mathcal{C})$), and outputs $\mathcal{B}$'s output (respectively, $\mathcal{C}$'s output).

It follows that the success probability of $(\mathcal{R}_\mathcal{A}, \mathcal{R}_\mathcal{B}, \mathcal{R}_\mathcal{C})$ is the same as that of $(\mathcal{A}, \mathcal{B}, \mathcal{C})$, which completes the proof of the theorem. □

It was shown in [CG23] that assuming qsio, the key testable property can be generically attached to any unclonable encryption scheme that satisfies the above restriction on the key generation algorithm.

Theorem 13 (Adapted from [CG23, Theorem 16]). *If injective one-way functions and qsio exist, then any unclonable bit encryption scheme (with the key generation algorithm outputting a uniformly random key from $\{0,1\}^\lambda$) can be compiled into one with key testing (with the same key generation algorithm).*

For the rest of the section, for any key testable unclonable encryption scheme, we will assume that the Gen algorithm has uniform output distribution. Hence we will use a triplet of algorithms (Enc, Dec, Test) to represent a key testable unclonable encryption scheme and in particular, we omit Gen from the description.

UPO from qsiO. We consider the following tools:

- A key-testable unclonable bit encryption scheme UE = (Enc, Dec, Test).
- Quantum state iO scheme, denoted by qsio = (Obf, Eval).

Theorem 14. *Suppose there exists a key-testable unclonable bit encryption scheme, UE = (Enc, DecTest). Then, any qsio scheme (Obf, Eval) for P/poly is also a UPO scheme satisfying $\mathsf{Id}_\mathcal{U}$-generalized UPO security guarantee (see Sect. 2.1), for any puncturable keyed circuit class $\mathcal{W} = \{\{W_s\}_{s \in \mathcal{K}_\lambda}\}_\lambda$ in P/poly.*

Proof. The correctness is immediate from the correctness of the qsio scheme.

Next, we prove security. Let $(\mathcal{A}, \mathcal{B}, \mathcal{C})$ be a QPT adversary in the generalized UPO security experiment given in Fig. 3 with $\mathcal{D}_\mathcal{X} = \mathsf{Id}_\mathcal{U}$.

Hybrid$_0$: Same as the security experiment given in Fig. 3.

1. $\mathcal{A}$ sends a key $s \in \mathcal{K}_\lambda$ and function μ^{11} to Ch.
2. Ch samples $x^* \xleftarrow{\$} \{0,1\}^{n(\lambda)}$, and a bit $b \xleftarrow{\$} \{0,1\}$.
3. Ch generates $\tilde{\rho}_0 \leftarrow \mathsf{Obf}(1^\lambda, W_s)$, and $\tilde{\rho}_1 \leftarrow \mathsf{Obf}(1^\lambda, W_{s,x^*,\mu})$, where $W_{s,x^*,\mu} \leftarrow \mathsf{GenPuncture}(s, x^*, x^*, \mu, \mu)$.
4. Ch sends $\tilde{\rho}_b$ to $\mathcal{A}$.
5. $\mathcal{A}(\tilde{\rho}_b)$ outputs a bipartite state $\sigma_{\mathcal{B},\mathcal{C}}$.
6. Apply $(\mathcal{B}(x^*, \cdot) \otimes \mathcal{C}(x^*, \cdot))(\sigma_{\mathcal{B},\mathcal{C}})$ to obtain $(b_\mathbf{B}, b_\mathbf{C})$.
7. Output 1 if $b_\mathbf{B} = b_\mathbf{C} = b$.

Hybrid$_1$:

1. $\mathcal{A}$ sends a key $s \in \mathcal{K}_\lambda$ and function μ to Ch.
2. Ch samples $x^* \xleftarrow{\$} \{0,1\}^{n(\lambda)}$, and a bit $b \xleftarrow{\$} \{0,1\}$.
3. Ch generates $\tilde{\rho}_b \leftarrow \mathsf{Obf}(1^\lambda, (C, \rho_b))$ where $\rho_b \leftarrow \mathsf{UE.Enc}(x^*, b)$ and C is the circuit that on input (x, ρ_b), first checks if $\mathsf{UE.Test}(x, \rho_b)$ rejects, in which case, C outputs $W_s(x)$. Else, C runs $d \leftarrow \mathsf{UE.Dec}(x, \rho_b)$ and if $d = 0$ outputs $W_s(x)$ else outputs $\mu(x)$.

---

[11] In the security experiment in Fig. 3, $\mathcal{A}$ sends two functions $\mu_\mathcal{B}, \mu_\mathcal{C}$ but since in this proof, $\mathcal{D}_\mathcal{X} = \mathsf{Id}_\mathcal{U}$, the second function $\mu_\mathcal{C}$ is redundant. Hence, for the sake of the proof, we can assume, without loss of generality, that $\mathcal{A}$ sends a *single* function μ to Ch.

4. Ch sends $\tilde{\rho}_b$ to $\mathcal{A}$.
5. $\mathcal{A}(\tilde{\rho}_b)$ outputs a bipartite state $\sigma_{\mathcal{B},\mathcal{C}}$.
6. Apply $(\mathcal{B}(x^*,\cdot) \otimes \mathcal{C}(x^*,\cdot))(\sigma_{\mathcal{B},\mathcal{C}})$ to obtain $(b_\mathbf{B}, b_\mathbf{C})$.
7. Output 1 if $b_\mathbf{B} = b_\mathbf{C} = b$.

Observe that W_s and (C, ρ_0) are functionally equivalent. Here, (C, ρ_0) represents an implementation of a classical function that maps x to $C(\rho, x)$. Similarly, $W_{s,x^*,\mu}$ and (C, ρ_1) are functionally equivalent. From the security of qsio, it follows that the hybrids Hybrid_0 and Hybrid_1 are computationally indistinguishable.

Next, we give a reduction $(R_\mathcal{A}, R_\mathcal{B}, R_\mathcal{C})$ from Hybrid_1 to the unclonable indistinguishability experiment for UE as follows.

- $R_\mathcal{A}$ sends $(0, 1)$ as the challenge message pair to the challenger.
- Challenger sends a ciphertext ρ.
- $R_\mathcal{A}$ generates (C, ρ) (as described in Hybrid_1), and then computes $\tilde{\rho} \leftarrow \mathsf{Obf}(1^\lambda, (C, \rho))$.
- $R_\mathcal{A}$ feeds $\tilde{\rho}$ to $\mathcal{A}$ and outputs a bipartite state $\sigma_{\mathcal{B},\mathcal{C}}$.
- $R_\mathcal{B}$ (respectively, $R_\mathcal{C}$) on receiving x from the challenger, runs $\mathcal{B}$ (respectively, $\mathcal{C}$) on $\sigma_\mathcal{B}$ (respectively, $\sigma_\mathcal{C}$) and x, and outputs $\mathcal{B}'s$ output (respectively, $\mathcal{C}$'s output).

It follows that the advantage of the QPT adversary $(\mathcal{A}, \mathcal{B}, \mathcal{C})$ in breaking UPO security is within a negligible additive factor of the advantage of the QPT adversary in breaking the unclonable indistinguishability of UE. This completes the proof of generalized UPO security for (Obf, Eval). □

Combining Theorems 12 to 14, we conclude the following.

Corollary 3. *Suppose there exists a post-quantum injective one-way function and an unclonable bit encryption scheme* UE. *Then, any* qsio *scheme* (Obf, Eval) *is also a UPO scheme satisfying* $\mathsf{Id}_\mathcal{U}$*-generalized UPO security guarantee (see Sect. 2.1), for any puncturable keyed circuit class* $\mathcal{W} = \{\{W_s\}_{s \in \mathcal{K}_\lambda}\}_\lambda$ *in* P/poly.

Acknowledgements. A.B. has received funding from the European Union (ERC-2022-COG, ACQUA, 101087742). Views and opinions expressed are, however, those of the author(s) only and do not necessarily reflect those of the European Union or the European Research Council Executive Agency. Neither the European Union nor the granting authority can be held responsible for them.

P.A. is supported in part by the National Science Foundation under Grant No. 2329938 and Grant No. 2341004.

We thank Supartha Podder for discussions during the early stages of the project. We are grateful to the anonymous reviewers of Crypto 2024 for various suggestions to improve the paper and specifically, for suggesting the use of the key-testable unclonable encryption [CG23] in constructing unclonable puncturable obfuscation from quantum state indistinguishability obfuscation.

References

[Aar09] Aaronson, S.: Quantum copy-protection and quantum money. In: 2009 24th Annual IEEE Conference on Computational Complexity, pp. 229–242. IEEE (2009)

[Aar16] Aaronson, S.: The Complexity of Quantum States and Transformations: From Quantum Money to Black Holes (2016). arXiv:1607.05256 [quant-ph]

[AC02] Adcock, M., Cleve, R.: A quantum Goldreich-Levin theorem with cryptographic applications. In: Alt, H., Ferreira, A. (eds.) STACS 2002. LNCS, vol. 2285, pp. 323–334. Springer, Heidelberg (2002). https://doi.org/10.1007/3-540-45841-7_26

[AC12] Aaronson, S., Christiano, P.: Quantum money from hidden subspaces. In: Proceedings of the Forty-Fourth Annual ACM Symposium on Theory of Computing. STOC '12, pp. 41–60. Association for Computing Machinery. New York, New York, USA (2012). ISBN 9781450312455. https://doi.org/10.1145/2213977.2213983

[AK21] Ananth, P., Kaleoglu, F.: Unclonable encryption, revisited. In: Nissim, K., Waters, B. (eds.) TCC 2021. LNCS, vol. 13042, pp. 299–329. Springer, Cham (2021). https://doi.org/10.1007/978-3-030-90459-3_11

[AKL+22] Ananth, P., Kaleoglu, F., Li, X., Liu, Q., Zhandry, M.: On the feasibility of unclonable encryption, and more. In: Dodis, Y., Shrimpton, T. (eds.) CRYPTO 2022. LNCS, vol. 13508, pp. 212–241. Springer, Cham (2022). https://doi.org/10.1007/978-3-031-15979-4_8

[AKL23] Ananth, P., Kaleoglu, F., Liu, Q.: Cloning games: a general framework for unclonable primitives. arXiv preprint arXiv:2302.01874 (2023)

[AKY24] Ananth, P., Kaleoglu, F., Yuen, H.: Simultaneous haar indistinguishability with applications to unclonable cryptography. arXiv preprint arXiv:2405.10274 (2024)

[AL21] Ananth, P., La Placa, R.L.: Secure software leasing. In: Canteaut, A., Standaert, F.-X. (eds.) EUROCRYPT 2021. LNCS, vol. 12697, pp. 501–530. Springer, Cham (2021). https://doi.org/10.1007/978-3-030-77886-6_17

[APV23] Ananth, P., Poremba, A., Vaikuntanathan, V.: Revocable cryptography from learning with errors. In: Rothblum, G., Wee, H. (eds.) TCC 2023. LNCS, vol. 14372, pp. 93–122. Springer, Cham (2023). https://doi.org/10.1007/978-3-031-48624-1_4

[BGI+01] Barak, B., et al.: On the (im)possibility of obfuscating programs. In: Kilian, J. (ed.) CRYPTO 2001. LNCS, vol. 2139, pp. 1–18. Springer, Heidelberg (2001). https://doi.org/10.1007/3-540-44647-8_1

[BGI14] Boyle, E., Goldwasser, S., Ivan, I.: Functional signatures and pseudorandom functions. In: Krawczyk, H. (ed.) PKC 2014. LNCS, vol. 8383, pp. 501–519. Springer, Heidelberg (2014). https://doi.org/10.1007/978-3-642-54631-0_29

[BGS13] Broadbent, A., Gutoski, G., Stebila, D.: Quantum one-time programs. In: Canetti, R., Garay, J.A. (eds.) CRYPTO 2013. LNCS, vol. 8043, pp. 344–360. Springer, Heidelberg (2013). https://doi.org/10.1007/978-3-642-40084-1_20

[BKL23] Broadbent, A., Karvonen, M., Lord, S.: Uncloneable quantum advice. arXiv preprint arXiv:2309.05155 (2023)

[BL20] Broadbent, A., Lord, S.: Uncloneable quantum encryption via oracles. en. In: Schloss Dagstuhl - Leibniz-Zentrum für Informatik (2020). https://doi.org/10.4230/LIPICS.TQC.2020.4, https://drops.dagstuhl.de/opus/volltexte/2020/12063/

[BPR15] Bitansky, N., Paneth, O., Rosen, A.: On the cryptographic hardness of finding a Nash equilibrium. In: 2015 IEEE 56th Annual Symposium on Foundations of Computer Science, pp. 1480–1498. IEEE (2015)

[BS16] Ben-David, S., Sattath, O.: Quantum Tokens for Digital Signatures (2016). https://doi.org/10.48550/ARXIV.1609.09047, https://arxiv.org/abs/1609.09047

[BS20] Behera, A., Sattath, O.: Almost public quantum coins. arXiv preprint arXiv:2002.12438 (2020)

[BW13] Boneh, D., Waters, B.: Constrained pseudorandom functions and their applications. In: Sako, K., Sarkar, P. (eds.) ASIACRYPT 2013. LNCS, vol. 8270, pp. 280–300. Springer, Heidelberg (2013). https://doi.org/10.1007/978-3-642-42045-0_15

[BZ17] Boneh, D., Zhandry, M.: Multiparty key exchange, efficient traitor tracing, and more from indistinguishability obfuscation. Algorithmica **79**, 1233–1285 (2017)

[CG23] Coladangelo, A., Gunn, S.: How to use quantum indistinguishability obfuscation. arXiv preprint arXiv:2311.07794 (2023)

[CHV23] Chevalier, C., Hermouet, P., Vu, Q.-H.: Semi-quantum copy-protection and more. Cryptology ePrint Archive (2023)

[CLLZ21] Coladangelo, A., Liu, J., Liu, Q., Zhandry, M.: Hidden cosets and applications to unclonable cryptography. In: Malkin, T., Peikert, C. (eds.) CRYPTO 2021, Part I. LNCS, vol. 12825, pp. 556–584. Springer, Cham (2021). https://doi.org/10.1007/978-3-030-84242-0_20

[Die82] Dieks, D.G.B.J.: Communication by EPR devices. Phys. Lett. A **92**(6), 271–272 (1982)

[Gao15] Gao, J.: Quantum union bounds for sequential projective measurements. Phys. Rev. A **92**(5), 052331 (2015)

[GGH+16] Garg, S., Gentry, C., Halevi, S., Raykova, M., Sahai, A., Waters, B.: Candidate indistinguishability obfuscation and functional encryption for all circuits. SIAM J. Comput. **45**(3), 882–929 (2016)

[GGHR14] Garg, S., Gentry, C., Halevi, S., Raykova, M.: Two-round secure MPC from indistinguishability obfuscation. In: Lindell, Y. (ed.) TCC 2014. LNCS, vol. 8349, pp. 74–94. Springer, Heidelberg (2014). https://doi.org/10.1007/978-3-642-54242-8_4

[GMR23] Goyal, V., Malavolta, G., Raizes, J.: Unclonable commitments and proofs. Cryptology ePrint Archive (2023)

[Got02] Gottesman, D.: Uncloneable encryption (2002). https://doi.org/10.48550/ARXIV.QUANT-PH/0210062. url: https://arxiv.org/abs/quant-ph/0210062

[GZ20] Georgiou, M., Zhandry, M.: Unclonable decryption keys. IACR Cryptology ePrint Archive https://eprint.iacr.org/2020/877 (2020)

[JK23] Jawale, R., Khurana, D.: Unclonable non-interactive zero-knowledge. arXiv preprint arXiv:2310.07118 (2023)

[JLS21] Jain, A., Lin, H., Sahai, A.: Indistinguishability obfuscation from well-founded assumptions. In: Proceedings of the 53rd Annual ACM SIGACT Symposium on Theory of Computing, pp. 60–73 (2021)

[KN23] Kitagawa, F., Nishimaki, R.: One-out-of-many unclonable cryptography: definitions, constructions, and more. arXiv preprint arXiv:2302.09836 (2023)

[KT22] Kundu, S., Tan, E.Y.-Z.: Device-independent uncloneable encryption. In: arXiv preprint arXiv:2210.01058 (2022)

[LLQZ22] Liu, J., Liu, Q., Qian, L., Zhandry, M.: Collusion resistant copy-protection for watermarkable functionalities. In: Kiltz, E., Vaikuntanathan, V. (eds.) TCC 2022, Part I. Lecture Notes in Computer Science, vol. 13747, pp. 294–323. Springer, Cham (2022). https://doi.org/10.1007/978-3-031-22318-1_11

[LMZ23] Liu, J., Montgomery, H., Zhandry, M.: Another round of breaking and making quantum money: how to not build it from lattices, and more. In: Hazay, C., Stam, M. (eds.) EUROCRYPT 2023. LNCS, vol. 14004, pp. 611–638. Springer, Cham (2023). https://doi.org/10.1007/978-3-031-30545-0_21

[RS19] Radian, R., Sattath, O.: Semi-quantum money. In: Proceedings of the 1st ACM Conference on Advances in Financial Technologies, pp. 132–146 (2019)

[RZ21] Roberts, B., Zhandry, M.: Franchised quantum money. In: Tibouchi, M., Wang, H. (eds.) ASIACRYPT 2021. LNCS, vol. 13090, pp. 549–574. Springer, Cham (2021). https://doi.org/10.1007/978-3-030-92062-3_19

[Shm22] Shmueli, O.: Public-key Quantum money with a classical bank. In: Proceedings of the 54th Annual ACM SIGACT Symposium on Theory of Computing, pp. 790–803 (2022)

[STHY23] Sudo, K., Tezuka, M., Hara, K., Yoshida, Y.: Quantum search-to-decision reduction for the LWE problem. In: El Mrabet, N., De Feo, L., Duquesne, S. (eds.) AFRICACRYPT 2023. LNCS, vol. 14064, pp. 395–413. Springer, Cham (2023). https://doi.org/10.1007/978-3-031-37679-5_17

[SW14] Sahai, A., Waters, B.: How to use indistinguishability obfuscation: deniable encryption, and more. In: Proceedings of the Forty-Sixth Annual ACM Symposium on Theory of Computing, pp. 475–484 (2014)

[Wie83] Wiesner, S.: Conjugate coding. ACM SIGACT News **15**(1), 78–88 (1983)

[WZ82] Wootters, W.K., Zurek, W.H.: A single quantum cannot be cloned. Nature **299**(5886), 802–803 (1982)

[Zha19] Zhandry, M.: Quantum lightning never strikes the same state twice. In: Ishai, Y., Rijmen, V. (eds.) EUROCRYPT 2019. LNCS, vol. , pp. 408–438. Springer, Cham (2019). ISBN 978-3-030-17659-4, https://doi.org/10.1007/978-3-030-17659-4_14

[Zha23] Zhandry, M.: Quantum money from abelian group actions. arXiv preprint arXiv:2307.12120 (2023)

Unconditionally Secure Quantum Commitments with Preprocessing

Luowen Qian[1,2](✉)

[1] Boston University, Boston, USA
`luowen@qcry.pt`
[2] NTT Research, Sunnyvale, USA

Abstract. We demonstrate how to build computationally secure commitment schemes with the aid of quantum auxiliary inputs *without unproven complexity assumptions*. Furthermore, the quantum auxiliary input can be either sampled in uniform exponential time or prepared in at most doubly exponential time, without relying on an external trusted third party. Classically, this remains impossible without first proving $P \neq NP$.

1 Introduction

It has been known since 1990 [IL89,Gol90] that almost all interesting classical cryptographic tasks requires computational security, and furthermore, hardness assumptions that are at least as strong as the existence of one-way functions. Thus realizing these cryptographic tasks unconditionally faces the barrier of "$P \stackrel{?}{=} NP$", a problem that has undergone intense studies by complexity theorists. These cryptographic tasks in particular include constructing a commitment scheme, the feasibility of which is equivalent to the existence of one-way functions.

Auxiliary-input cryptography, studied since the 1990s [OW93], is a non-uniform version of cryptography where every party in the protocol gets access to a copy of some public information that might not be efficiently preparable. This is not to be confused with non-uniform security, which is the default security notion where the adversaries, in addition to running in polynomial time, get some advice at the beginning from an inefficient preprocessing phase or perhaps some residual information from another protocol execution. Following the same proofs, the same barrier of "$P \stackrel{?}{=} NP$" still applies in this more relaxed setting.

Given this difficulty, it is natural to consider constructing *quantum* commitments instead. Recent works have demonstrated that quantum commitments play a similar central role as classical ones, in terms of its tight connections to both quantum cryptography at large [Yan22,BCQ23,BEM+23] and quantum complexity [BEM+23]. While commitments statistically (or information theoretically) secure against both parties are impossible even quantumly [May97,LC97], recent works have demonstrated that computationally secure

© International Association for Cryptologic Research 2024
L. Reyzin and D. Stebila (Eds.): CRYPTO 2024, LNCS 14926, pp. 38–58, 2024.
https://doi.org/10.1007/978-3-031-68394-7_2

ones are possible under complexity assumptions [BCQ23, BEM+23, Bra23] that are evidently milder than $P \neq NP$ [Kre21, AQY22, MY22, KQST23, LMW23]. This line of works suggests that achieving computationally secure quantum cryptography might not be susceptible to the same barriers that apply to classical cryptography.

Nonetheless, it is still reasonable to speculate that any reasonable quantum computational cryptography could face some other barriers. Indeed, all prior quantum computational cryptography still starts by assuming some hardness assumptions, even though they may be weaker than what is needed classically as was shown above.

In this work, we consider a natural quantum non-uniform cryptography notion called quantum auxiliary input, meaning that every party receives copies of the same quantum pure state as input.[1] Therefore, in some sense, this quantum auxiliary information can be thought of as a "cryptographic magic state", extremely similar to magic states that occur in quantum fault tolerance, where a piece of quantum state can augment the computational power of a less powerful circuit family.

Our main theorem, perhaps surprisingly, constructs quantum auxiliary-input commitments without unproven complexity assumptions.

Theorem 1. *There exists a computationally-hiding statistically-binding non-interactive quantum commitment scheme with quantum auxiliary input. Furthermore, the quantum auxiliary input has an exponential-size classical description that can be sampled uniformly in exponential time.*

Our proof builds upon the prior work of Chailloux, Kerenidis, and Rosgen [CKR16] who established the same result assuming the unproven complexity separation that $QIP \not\subseteq QMA$. However, our construction uses a sparse pseudorandom ensemble constructed with a probabilistic method instead of the assumed hardness of a QIP-complete problem.

Despite their similarities, the fundamental nature of this theorem is different since it is unconditional. As a result, there are a few interpretations of this theorem.

1. This is the *first* demonstration of a <u>useful cryptographic task with unconditional inherently-computational security</u> (quantum or classical), meaning that such tasks are impossible with statistical security. Cryptographers are often trained to instinctively assume that computational security protocols rely on

---

[1] There are two different variants of auxiliary-input security considered in the literature: in this work, we focus on the strong variant where the adversary's success probability is small for all but finitely many auxiliary inputs; however, there is also a weaker variant where we only require the adversary's success probability to be small for infinitely many auxiliary inputs [OW93]. Note that classical auxiliary input *weakly* secure quantum commitments can be built assuming $QCZK \not\subseteq BQP$ [BCQ23], classical auxiliary-input (strong) quantum commitment can be built assuming $QCZK \not\subseteq QMA$, and finally standard quantum commitments without auxiliary input can be built assuming various other unproven assumptions.

hardness assumptions, and conversely unconditionally secure protocols are statistically secure. This work, however, reveals that such presumptions are unwarranted, especially in the quantum setting.
2. Theorem 1 also reveals that we should be more cautious about the speculation that quantum computational cryptography still requires making hardness assumptions, and perhaps even reassess its validity and <u>investigate the existence of barriers</u>.
3. This is also arguably a conditional demonstration of <u>quantum computational advantage through cryptography</u>. As discussed, a classical analogue of Theorem 1 would still imply P $\neq$ NP [IL89]. Conversely, this shows that quantum auxiliary-input commitments are feasible even if P = NP and classical (auxiliary-input) commitments are impossible. This is different from traditional conditional quantum computational advantages (such as factoring) where the condition is classical easiness rather than classical hardness of certain problems.

In fact, it is possible to strengthen this classical impossibility above further. As we show in Theorem 2, this is true even if we consider the model where all parties get access to a single (possibly inefficient) sampling oracle, and each sample is private to the requested party. Here we allow access to randomized auxiliary information in order to level the playing field a bit for classical protocols, since a pure quantum state can also implement such randomized samples by taking an appropriate superposition over bitstrings. This model is even stronger than having access to classical auxiliary input, since the oracle could just output that fixed string with probability 1. (Considering every party having access to the same randomized advice can be simply replaced with a fixed classical advice by an averaging argument.) Thus in some sense, our result is even stronger than Raz's result of QIP/qpoly = IP/rpoly = ALL [Raz05] as the power of the quantum advice does not come from the advice being inherently randomized and this randomness being private to each party.

Removing Trust. One might be skeptical of the security since naïvely it appears that the parties need to assume they can trust the quantum auxiliary input given to them. One way to address this concern is to ask the skeptical party to simply inspect the classical description of the magic state and verify that the commitment built with it is secure. This takes at most a doubly exponential time since we can cast it as a **QMA** problem (Proposition 4). Alternatively, we could also ask them to find the lexicographically first magic state that works, which also takes at most doubly exponential time.

In Sect. 4, we show how to achieve computationally secure commitments without any trusted auxiliary inputs through a more efficient preprocessing. Specifically, in the scheme we only need to ask both the committee and the receiver to perform a uniform exponential-time preprocessing phase.

Removing Inefficiency. Complementary to that, we also show how to do commitments in a *completely efficient* setting with a weakly trusted setup in Sect. 3. Specifically, we adapt our construction into a trusted setup model where a trusted third party efficiently generates a few copies of the quantum auxiliary information for every party in the protocol to use before the protocol begins. However, unlike Theorem 1, here the pure state distributed to every party is not deterministic. Furthermore, the scheme could in fact be statistically secure against all parties if the number of copies distributed is restricted.

In comparison, a stronger (in terms of trust) setup model is the secret parameter model [Ps05], where we need to trust the setup to sample two correlated secret strings for each party. While statistically secure classical non-interactive commitments are possible in the secret parameter model, our model appears to be meaningfully weaker than the secret parameter model. In particular, we can again invoke our classical impossibility (Theorem 2) to argue that statistically secure commitments remain impossible in a classical sampling analogue of our model, since an unbounded adversary could always solve any NP problem.

Polynomially Bounded Adversaries are Physical, Probably. A possible concern regarding the claimed "unconditional" nature of this result is that the security relies on the "assumption" that the adversary is polynomially bounded during the execution of the protocol. We address that concern by noting that it is possible to reduce this assumption to physical assumptions. On one hand, physical assumptions and more generally modeling assumptions (the mapping between real world and mathematics) are unavoidable in any form of provably secure cryptography. On the other hand, this suggests a new win-win philosophy, since either we can have secure cryptography or we are able to discover exciting new physics.

More specifically, there is most likely a fundamental physical limit to the density of quantum information before collapsing into a black hole given by the Bekenstein bound (see [Llo00] for an exposition of this). Since any malicious computation must be done in polynomial time, and thus space by the no superluminal signaling principle, it follows from extended Church–Turing thesis (for quantum information tasks) that any polynomial-time physical computation can be described by a polynomial-size quantum circuit. Therefore, we can force adversary to be polynomially bounded by simply limiting the protocol execution time. Even if the adversary could somehow leverage black holes to perform useful computations, we could still monitor the energy density nearby to make sure that this does not happen. We leave further materializing this idea to future work.

Additional Applications. We note that it is possible to use this commitment scheme to further instantiate oblivious transfer (OT) and secure multiparty computations (MPC), as we further detail in Appendix B (see also [BCQ23]). This is in contrast with Kent's statistically secure relativistic commitment scheme [Ken99,Ken12] since (statistical) OT and MPC are known to be impossible even in that quantum relativistic model [Rud02,Col06]. (Another comparison is that our model also does not impose any strict constraints on the physical location of the parties: they simply need to be a polynomial distance away from each other so that the polynomial timing constraints can be satisfied.)

For a more concrete example for MPC, consider the classical Yao's Millionaires' Problem [Yao82], except that now it's a Trillionaires' Problem! This means that two trillionaires want to figure out who is richer without revealing anything else. Also since they are trillionaires, their entire families and businesses are somehow also on the line, so if cheating is detected then chaos would ensue. Furthermore, they also have the world's best cryptanalyst to break any computational hardness assumption should it be necessary and possible, and they are willing to use exponential-time preprocessing as a small sacrifice.

Secure multiparty computations with preprocessing is *the perfect* solution for this problem! They first spend exponential time to set up and during the protocol execution, they ensure that the other party finish in time and no cheating occurs. So if nothing bad occurs, then both of them can be satisfied knowing that their secrets are safe. Additionally, using certified everlasting transfer [BK23], they can achieve everlasting security by having a third party referee, who is trusted to be uninterested in spending exponential resources recovering the input, to certifiably delete the remaining information.

Open Problems. One undesirable feature of our scheme is that there is no good way to get additional copies of the magic state. In the trusted setup model, it is possible to redo the setup every once in a while to preserve statistical security and efficiency, but otherwise generating new copies still takes exponential time, although it is possible to build dedicated hardware to pipeline this process. A natural question is whether we can construct quantum cryptography with quantum auxiliary information that is efficiently clonable or reusable. While there are families of quantum states that is efficiently clonable but cannot be prepared in uniform polynomial time relative to a quantum oracle [NZ24], even having a standard model candidate is open since the quantum oracle there is a cloning oracle. The biggest issue with reusing our schemes is that for each invocation of the commitment scheme, on average $\Theta(\lambda)$ copies of the magic state is transferred to the other party, and there does not appear to be a way to certifiably retrieve these states. Of course, the ultimate goal would be to construct these without inefficient preprocessing or having trusted setup at all.

Concurrent Work. Near the completion of this work, I became aware of a parallel work done by Tomoyuki Morimae, Barak Nehoran, and Takashi Yamakawa [MNY23]. In particular, both works have the same constructions of quantum auxiliary-input commitments (Theorem 1) and statistically secure commitments with a weakly trusted (stateful) setup (Corollary 2 and Proposition 2). They have an additional statistical commitment construction with stateless setup, however, the downside is that this can only be secure given that at most a bounded number of copies is generated. Complementary to the classical impossibility of Theorem 2, they also give an impossibility of classical auxiliary-input (quantum) commitments in a weak setup model. They in addition have the application of quantum auxiliary-input zero-knowledge proofs for NP (with negligible simulation security). They also point out an observation by Fermi Ma that the cube root security loss of Proposition 1 can be improved to square root if we instead augment the [GK92] argument with a matrix Chernoff bound like was done in [LMW23]. This square root loss is also tight even against classical algorithms [DTT10, page 651].

Notably, their work point out that the quantum auxiliary-input commitment cannot be immediately used to construct simulation-secure commitments through the [BCKM21] compiler due to the use of Watrous rewinding in the simulator there. After the discussions with [MNY23], I present the resolution of this in Appendix B by showing how to adapt [BCKM21] to recover ε-simulation security, which still suffices to recover almost all applications of a standard quantum commitment.

2 Quantum Auxiliary-Input Commitment

We formally define non-interactive commitments and handle its subtleties for later applications in Appendix A. To prove our main theorem, we first need the following result on the quantum non-uniform security of pseudorandomness.

Proposition 1 ([CGLQ20a, Liu23]). *For a random function $H : [N] \to [M]$, the best quantum circuit of size S (potentially depending on H) can distinguish its output from a random element from $[M]$ with advantage at most $12 \cdot \sqrt[3]{\frac{S}{N}}$ (averaged over the choice of H).*

While these works consider the more general case where quantum algorithms that could additionally make queries to H, the same proofs also give a polynomial upper bound for standard query-less algorithms. For completeness, we show this precise bound in Appendix C.

In particular, this implies the existence of a good function for which this is true against size $S - 1$, since we can always use an extra bit to make the bias always have the same sign for all H. In other words, for any $(S-1)$-size algorithm A', there is an S-size algorithm A such that

$$\left| \mathop{\mathbb{E}}_{H}\left[\mathop{\mathbb{E}}_{x}[A'(H(x))] - \mathop{\mathbb{E}}_{y}[A'(y)] \right] \right| = \mathop{\mathbb{E}}_{H}\left[\left| \mathop{\mathbb{E}}_{x}[A(H(x))] - \mathop{\mathbb{E}}_{y}[A(y)] \right| \right],$$

where A simply runs A' and XOR its output with the extra advice bit. With some small inverse exponential security loss, we can also use Markov's inequality to argue that even sampling a function uniformly at random would satisfy this with overwhelming probability.

Instantiating the above with $S = 2^\lambda + 1, N = 2^{5\lambda}$ and $M = 2^{6\lambda}$, we get the following corollary, which generalizes the classical (inefficient) sparse pseudorandom ensemble construction of Goldreich and Krawczyk [GK92] to the post-quantum setting[2].

---

[2] The naïve attempt of quantizing [GK92] proof cannot seem to handle quantum advice. For readers familiar with that work, a natural strategy is to use union bound over all quantum algorithms/advice using an ε-net, however, this fails since the size of the ε-net is doubly exponential, and thus eliminating the single exponential concentration we get from Hoeffding's bound.

Corollary 1 (Exponentially secure sparse pseudorandom ensemble).
There exists a pseudorandom ensemble $H : \{0,1\}^{5\lambda} \to \{0,1\}^{6\lambda}$ against all 2^λ-size quantum circuits A with quantum auxiliary information, whose security $|\mathbb{E}_x[A(H(x))] - \mathbb{E}_y[A(y)]| \leq 2^{-\lambda}$ for all $\lambda \geq 11$.

Proof (Proof of Theorem 1). Let $\{H(x)\}_{x \in \{0,1\}^{5\lambda}}$ be the exponentially secure sparse pseudorandom ensemble as above. We first specify the quantum auxiliary input

$$|M_\lambda\rangle := 2^{-5\lambda/2} \sum_{x \in \{0,1\}^{5\lambda}} |x\rangle \otimes |H(x)\rangle,$$

a pure state of 11λ qubits that can be prepared using a circuit of size $\tilde{O}(2^{5\lambda})$.

We now specify the protocol. The sender, to commit to 0, simply sends the second half of $|M_\lambda\rangle$; and to commit to 1, sends the second half of a maximally entangled state

$$|\Psi_\lambda\rangle := 2^{-3\lambda} \sum_{y \in \{0,1\}^{6\lambda}} |y\rangle \otimes |y\rangle;$$

to later decommit, the rest of the state is sent. The receiver, upon receiving the entire state and the bit b can efficiently test by performing a SWAP test between the received state and the correct state of either $|M_\lambda\rangle$ or $|\Psi_\lambda\rangle$. Finally, a λ-fold parallel repetition is applied to this construction, meaning that the committer commits to the same bit λ times in parallel, and the receiver checks that all commitment decommits to the same bit.

For binding, we note that our construction is identical to that of [CKR16, Section 4] except for the choice of two pure states used for the commitments. In our case, since the two reduced density matrices on the commitment register are classical, so the fidelity between them is

$$\left(\sum_y \sqrt{\frac{\Pr[H(x) = y]}{2^{6\lambda}}} \right)^2 \leq 2^{-\lambda} \tag{1}$$

by applying Cauchy–Schwarz on y's in the image of H. The rest follows the same proof as [CKR16, Proposition 4.4], thus we get that our commitment after taking λ-fold parallel repetition is statistical sum binding.

For hiding, the two reduced density matrices given to the hiding adversary exactly corresponds to the security game of the pseudorandom ensemble. Finally taking a parallel repetition also preserves hiding by a standard hybrid argument.

We remark that this construction can be straightfowardly "derandomized" using a (post-quantum) pseudorandom generator, and thus eliminating the inefficiency at the cost of assuming the security of the pseudorandom generator.

In fact, if we are only aiming for a commitment scheme with quantum auxiliary input and do not require the classical description to be computable in exponential time, any non-trivial computationally indistinguishable pair of quantum states suffices. The construction is essentially the same except that the receiver does a SWAP test with the corresponding pure state for decommitments to either bits.

Classical Impossibility. For convenience, we focus on non-interactive statistically-binding commitments for the classical case. This is a fair comparison since such a commitment with classical auxiliary information does exist assuming existence of one-way functions, by applying averaging argument to the first message of Naor commitment [Nao91]. We leave improving this impossibility to future work. The main insight is that having sample access to the oracle suffices to break the security.

Theorem 2. *If there exists a computationally-hiding statistically-binding non-interactive classical commitment scheme where all parties share access to a sampling oracle, then* NP $\not\subseteq$ P/poly.

Proof. For simplicity, we consider that committer and receiver each gets a private sample s, r respectively from the sampling oracle; to commit to bit b, the committer computes a deterministic function $\mathsf{Commit}(s, b) = \tau$ and sends τ to the receiver; to decommit, the committer sends s, b and the receiver computes a deterministic function $\mathsf{Reveal}(s, b, \tau, r) \in \{\top, \bot\}$ indicating accept or reject the revealed bit b. This is without loss of generality since we can always have the oracle give multiple samples per query and pad the oracle with uniform random bits so that the only source of randomness is from the oracle.

Assume NP $\subseteq$ P/poly, we show how to efficiently break the hiding. Let each sample be ℓ bits long. The malicious receiver, on input τ and $(\ell+1)$ independent samples $\vec{r} := r_0, ..., r_\ell$ from the sampling oracle, predicts the commitment is to 0 if there exists s_0 such that $\mathsf{Reveal}(s_0, 0, \tau, r_i) = \top$ for all i, and predicts to 1 otherwise. This is also an NP language since Reveal is efficient and ℓ is polynomial. Then in the case when the committer commits to 0, by completeness with overwhelming probability over τ, $\Pr_r[\mathsf{Reveal}(s_0, 0, \tau, r)]$ is negligibly close to 1, so this receiver always predicts 0 except with negligible probability. On the other hand, when the committer commits to 1, by statistical binding, with overwhelming probability over τ, for every s_0 we have that $\Pr_r[R(s_0, 0, \tau, r)]$ is negligible, and by independence of samples, $\Pr_{\vec{r}}[\forall i : \mathsf{Reveal}(s_0, 0, \tau, r_i)] \leq 2^{-\ell-1}$ for all sufficiently large λ, thus by union bound, $\Pr_{\vec{r}}[\exists s_0 \forall i : \mathsf{Reveal}(s_0, 0, \tau, r_i)] \leq \frac{1}{2}$. This gives a hiding adversary with advantage at least $\frac{1}{2} - \mathsf{negl}$.

Not accounting for implementing the NP oracle, the malicious receiver we construct in this proof uses roughly quadratic space compared to the honest parties. Curiously, this matches the quadratic space lower bound proven for bit commitments in the bounded storage model [GZ19, Section 6] so this suggests that taking multiple samples is likely required for such attacks in general.

3 Commitment in the Unclonable Common Random State Model

The common random string (CRS) model is a commonly considered relaxation of the standard trustless model where the only trust in the setup is that a classical string is uniformly sampled and then published. This model was first proposed in the context of non-interactive zero knowledge (NIZK) [BFM88] since interesting NIZK is impossible in the trustless model.

In this work, we introduce a quantum analogue of the CRS model that we call the unclonable common random state ($|\mathsf{UCRS}\rangle$) model. In the $|\mathsf{UCRS}\rangle$ model, the only trust in the setup is that a random pure state is drawn from a state distribution, and then many copies of that pure state are made available to all parties. Furthermore, there should be a way to efficiently generate any polynomial (but a priori unbounded) number of the common state. We emphasize that unclonability only indicates a lack of the cloning functionality of the common state but the scheme's security does not rely on the common state being unclonable—in fact in this model, any malicious party is allowed to inefficiently process the classical description of the random state before the protocol begins.

Going back to the commitment construction of Theorem 1, we note that the magic state is simply a uniform superposition query on a function H, and even using a random function H is secure except with inverse exponential probability. Therefore, that construction is indeed also secure in the $|\mathsf{UCRS}\rangle$ model, so the only missing piece of the puzzle is to show efficient sampling of the magic state. This is tricky since the classical description requires an exponential size and there are a doubly exponential number of possible states to sample from.

Nevertheless, we show that there is an efficient way to statefully sample these states. To do this, we invoke Zhandry's compressed oracle technique [Zha19].

Lemma 1 ([Zha19]). *There exists a stateful simulation oracle* CStO *that perfectly simulate any number of (quantum) queries to a random function* $H : \{0,1\}^n \to \{0,1\}^m$ *for any* n, m. *Furthermore, the t-th query can be processed in time polynomial in mt, and the state (also called the database) after t queries consists of $(m + n + 1) \cdot t$ qubits.*

Since the simulation is perfect, the commitment constructed in Theorem 1, after replacing H with a truly random function, still works. The simulation is also efficient since both m and t are polynomial in λ. Thus we arrive at the following corollary.

Corollary 2. *There exists a computationally-hiding statistically-binding non-interactive quantum commitment scheme in the $|\mathsf{UCRS}\rangle$ model.*

Interestingly, the hiding of the commitment in fact becomes statistical if at most a polynomial number of states are given out to the adversary, and the proof of this is deferred to Appendix C. Therefore, we get a completely statistically secure commitment if we in addition trust the setup to not generate too many copies of the magic state.

Proposition 2. *Assuming the receiver has at most P copies of the magic state on H, then the commitment scheme of Corollary 2 is $\left(8\sqrt{2} \cdot \sqrt{\frac{P}{N}}\right)$-statistically hiding.*

Another interesting consequence of this is that for our scheme, we cannot trust either party to distribute the magic state. If the receiver chooses the magic state for the committer, then computational hiding can be trivially broken by picking a bad magic state like the all zero state. If the committer chooses the magic state for the receiver, then Proposition 2 shows that this scheme is in fact statistically hiding and thus not statistical binding. In fact, it is not even computationally binding as we show below.

Proposition 3. *Take the commitment scheme from Theorem 1 but instead have the committer choose H as a random function. Then this commitment scheme has computational sum binding error of at least $1 - O(t/\sqrt{N})$ even after taking t-fold parallel repetition using the same random function.*

Proof (Proof sketch). We sketch how to efficiently break sum binding, even if the scheme is repeated t times in parallel. Consider a binding adversary that commits to 0 honestly using the compressed oracle. Certainly by sending the decommitment registers honestly, the receiver would accept 0 with probability 1. We now show how to decommit to 1 with probability $1 - O(t/\sqrt{N})$. First, we measure the x for every magic state (including the ones held by the decommitter are also measured, which is okay since the receiver does not touch those registers when checking decommitment to 1 so they are essentially traced out) and abort if they are not all distinct, which happens with probability at most $O(t^2/N)$ by collision probability. Otherwise, every magic state holds a distinct x. For each fold, the decommitment register contains some x_i: we apply $\mathsf{StdDecomp}_{x_i}$ and search in the database where the entry x_i occurs and send the corresponding image register as decommitment to 1, which is maximally entangled with the corresponding commitment register. To make this into a malicious committer that does not measure the x's held by the receiver, we note that this measurement is only used to conditionally abort the committer, so the success probability of the same adversary except that it never aborts is still $1 - O(t/\sqrt{N})$ by gentle measurement.

4 Eliminating Trust with Preprocessing

We first give a PromiseQMA upper bound on the complexity of verifying the computational insecurity of H up to a constant multiplicative loss. Therefore, we can check if a function H is secure in doubly exponential time, or even exponential time if BQP = QMA. Another consequence is that a $\Sigma_2\mathsf{P}^{\mathsf{QMA}}$ machine can also find the lexicographically smallest H that is secure. Thus we can complete the preprocessing phase from the construction of Theorem 1 in doubly-exponential time, or even exponential time if BQP = QMA.

Proposition 4. *The language L, consisting of all functions H such that the commitment constructed in Theorem 1 using H is insecure, is in PromiseQMA.*

Proof. We prove this by constructing a PromiseQMA verifier. The verifier, on input H (of length $N \log M$) and a witness $|C\rangle$ (a distinguisher quantum circuit of length S which is polynomial in $|H|$), samples a random bit b and runs the universal quantum circuit on either $(|C\rangle, H(x))$ for a random $x \in [N]$ or $(|C\rangle, y)$ for a random $y \in [M]$, and accepts if the universal quantum circuit predicts b correctly. We set completeness to be $\frac{1}{2} + 2^{-\lambda}$ and soundness to be $\frac{1}{2} + 2^{-\lambda-1}$, so the gap is $2^{-\lambda-1}$ which is inverse polynomial in $|H|$.

If the output of H is pseudorandom, then we have that $H \notin L$ as desired. On the other hand, if there exists an S-sized witness for H that distinguishes with advantage higher than $2 \cdot 2^{-\lambda}$, then $H \in L$.

We now give an alternative *unconditional* approach to eliminate trust on the magic state in uniform exponential time, but at the cost of introducing exponential communication between the parties in the preprocessing phase.

Theorem 3. *There exists a computationally-hiding statistically-binding non-interactive quantum commitment scheme with an exponential communication preprocessing phase.*

Proof. We again adapt the commitment from Theorem 1 by adding a preprocessing phase to generate the magic states for both parties. More specifically, the sender samples a random function H on their own, then send the classical description of H to the receiver. Afterwards, they generate multiple copies of the magic state for that function on their own before the protocol begins. (It is important that they generate the quantum magic state on their own to not run into the impossibility of Proposition 3 above.)

Computational hiding is preserved since in this case H is honestly generated, and the proof of Theorem 1 actually suffices to show that the commitment is statistically binding for any H: specifically, the fidelity computed in (1) is bounded by $2^{-\lambda}$ for any H.

Acknowledgements. The author thanks Ran Canetti, William Kretschmer, Qipeng Liu, Daniel Wichs, as well as Tomoyuki Morimae, Barak Nehoran, and Takashi Yamakawa [MNY23] for their invaluable feedback on an earlier draft of this work. Special gratitude is owed to Qipeng Liu for proposing to augment Theorem 1 with compressed oracles (Corollary 2), and Tomoyuki Morimae, Barak Nehoran, and Takashi Yamakawa [MNY23] for their helpful discussions contributing to the development of Appendix B. The author also thanks Yilei Chen and Peihan Miao for their helpful discussions. The work is supported by DARPA under Agreement No. HR00112020023.

A Non-Interactive Quantum Commitments

In this section, we use $x \in S$ as the auxiliary information for a certain set S and implicitly its length $|x|$ as the security parameter. Thus if x is a classical unary string, then it is a standard uniform commitment scheme. In order to prevent degeneracy, we require that S must contain arbitrarily long bitstrings or quantum states: for any integer n, there exists $x \in S$ such that $|x| \geq n$. We refer the readers to [BCQ23] for quantum information and cryptography background.

Definition 1. *A non-interactive commitment scheme is a pair of efficient quantum algorithms* Commit *and* Reveal *where* Commit(x, b) *produces a bipartite state ρ over the commitment register* C *and the decommitment register* D*, and* Reveal(x, ρ) *outputs either the committed bit b' or a rejection symbol $\perp$. Furthermore,* $\Pr[\text{Reveal}(x, \text{Commit}(x, b)) \neq b]$ *is negligible for any $b = 0, 1$ and $x \in S$.*

We say it is computationally (or statistically) hiding if the C *registers of* Commit$(x, 0)$ *and* Commit$(x, 1)$ *are computationally (or statistically, respectively) indistinguishable.*

We say it is statistically (or computationally) sum binding if for any state ρ (over C, D *and a private register* M*) and any possibly inefficient (or efficient, respectively) unitary U not acting on register* C*, $p_0 + p_1 - 1$ is negligible, where p_b is the probability that the receiver accepts bit b. In particular, $p_0 := \Pr[\text{Reveal}(x, \rho_{\text{CD}}) = 0]$ and $p_1 := \Pr[\text{Reveal}(x, (U\rho)_{\text{CD}}) = 1]$.*

Finally, we say it is in canonical form [Yan22], if Reveal *takes the following form:*

1. *Perform a rank-1 projection on* CD *and output 0 if it succeeds.*
2. *Perform another orthogonal rank-1 projection on* CD *and output 1 if it succeeds.*
3. *Output $\perp$.*

Note that here ρ can be arbitrarily inefficient even in the case of computational hiding, which captures the standard non-uniform security notion where the adversary can have potentially a different auxiliary input for every security parameter.

Since statistical sum binding is traditionally unwieldy to use in applications, the work of Ananth, Qian, and Yuen defines an extractor-based binding definition [AQY22, Definition 6] (hereby called extractable binding in order to distinguish), which on a high level states that for any malicious committer, there is an extractor that can extract the committed bit from the receiver's view after the commitment phase in an imperceptible way, as long as the receiver does not touch those registers until the reveal phase. More specifically, it is defined as an indistinguishability between a real experiment and an ideal experiment. The real experiment simply performs the commitment normally and outputs the revealed bit along with the committer's residual state. The ideal experiment is defined as follows: after a normal execution of the commit phase, the extractor is ran on the receiver's view to obtain a trit $b \in \{0, 1, \perp\}$ and a post-measurement view; after the reveal phase, the output is set to the revealed bit b' along with the committer's residual view if $b' \in \{b, \perp\}$, otherwise the output is set to a special symbol $\perp$ indicating extraction failure.

For canonical form commitments, it is known that many variants of binding are equivalent, including statistical sum binding and extractable binding [FUYZ22]. It is unclear how to make commitments constructed in this work into canonical form due to the presence of quantum auxiliary information, so for completeness we show how to extend the equivalence to general non-interactive schemes.

We call a commitment scheme having a projective Reveal if Reveal is a projective measurement on the receiver's view. For example, any post-quantum commitment with a deterministic Reveal algorithm or any canonical-form commitment has a projective Reveal but our schemes do not due to the swap test. Without loss of generality we can always generically make a commitment have a projective Reveal via Stinespring dilation. In particular, we need to purify the Reveal algorithm so that it is a unitary on registers CD and potentially some auxiliary register A (which holds x and potentially some zeroes), followed by a complete measurement on a qutrit in the auxiliary register to obtain the output. Furthermore, we ask the receiver to prepare the auxiliary register A immediately after the commit phase. This change is also imperceptible from the committer's perspective.

We remark that due to a technicality, the equivalence cannot hold without giving the extractor access to A. Consider the following unnatural counterexample, a non-interactive (classical) commitment scheme without a projective Reveal that satisfies sum binding but not extractable binding. To commit to bit b, the committer simply send a mode bit 1 followed by b; and the decommitment message is empty. The Reveal algorithm checks that if the mode bit is 1 then output b, and if the mode bit is 0 then output a random bit. Intuitively this scheme is binding since no matter which mode the malicious committer uses, he cannot later change the bit in any way since the decommitment message is empty; and indeed it is straightforward to see that it satisfies sum binding. However, a malicious committer can cause the extractor to fail since without access to the random bit register later used to sample the output of Reveal, it is impossible for the extractor to predict the bit that would be revealed later.

Theorem 4. *Statistical sum binding is equivalent to extractable binding for any commitment scheme with a projective Reveal, thus we can build an extractable binding commitment scheme from any statistical sum binding commitment scheme (and vice versa).*

Proof. Extractable binding implies sum binding is straightforward: $p_0 + p_1 \leq 1$ in the ideal experiment where the bit is extracted and guaranteed to be correct, thus the indistinguishability between the real and the ideal experiments implies sum binding.

For the other direction, fix any sender where the overall state before executing Reveal is ρ. Without loss of generality we assume ρ is pure by taking the purification into committer's private register. Let $|\rho_0\rangle$ be the state post-selected on the event that $\mathsf{Reveal}(|\rho\rangle) = 0$ and $|\rho_1\rangle$ be the state post-selected on the event that $\mathsf{Reveal}(|\rho\rangle) = 1$, or 0 if such post-selection is not possible. $|\rho_0\rangle$ and $|\rho_1\rangle$ are orthogonal by the fact that Reveal is projective. Consider a canonical-form variant of Reveal where the rank-1 projections are given by $|\rho_0\rangle\langle\rho_0|$ and $|\rho_1\rangle\langle\rho_1|$. We claim that this variant is still sum binding since any sum binding adversary succeeding for this variant would also succeed in breaking sum binding against the original Reveal. Then the result of Fang, Unruh, Yan, and Zhou [FUYZ22] (also in [MY22, Appendix B]) implies that there is an extractor for this modified scheme, in particular, the extractor performs the optimal distinguishing measurement between these two states on registers AC. This extractor also works for the original scheme since the extractor almost perfectly project the state onto either $|\rho_0\rangle$ or $|\rho_1\rangle$ by statistical sum binding and gentle measurement, and the two Reveal algorithms behave identically in the subspace spanned by these states.

B Simulation Security

Simulation security captures the security of a primitive using the real-ideal world paradigm more precisely than the game-based security definitions (which are usually used for hardness assumptions) and is the default security notion in the context of zero knowledge and secure multiparty computations. In this appendix, we discuss how to further augment our commitment scheme following the template of Bartusek, Coladangelo, Khurana, and Ma [BCKM21] so that it satisfies simulation security.

The simulation security for a bit commitment is morally trying to capture the following ideal world: (1) in the commit phase, the committer sends a bit b to the ideal functionality; (2) in the reveal phase, the committer asks the ideal functionality to open and the ideal functionality sends the bit b to the receiver. More specifically, the security against receiver is called equivocality, which states that the commitment can be simulated in a way that b is only determined at the beginning of the reveal phase. The security against committer is called extractability, which states that the commitment can be simulated in a way that b can be extracted from the committer after the commit phase completes.

ε-simulation security for inefficient preprocessing. We first consider augmenting the base protocol (Theorem 1) with simulation security. We note some caveats before proceeding.

The first caveat is that we allow the simulator to take a few copies of the auxiliary input state as additional inputs. Intuitively, this means that a malicious party can come out of the protocol obtaining a few extra copies of the magic state. Indeed, if we look at the construction of Theorem 1, the receiver after an honest interaction gains one copy of the magic state from the committer for each fold of repetition, and there does not seem to be a way for the committer to certifiably retrieve the state back. We believe that this weakening is still meaningful and non-trivial since (1) the magic state is supposed to be public knowledge anyways (everyone should have many copies), and (2) the simulation security still guarantees that the "real" input is hidden from the other party.

The second caveat is that we only achieve ε-simulation security (with quantum auxiliary information $|aux\rangle$), which states that there is an efficient simulator S and some polynomial t such that for every adversary A (that is possibly entangled with the distinguisher) and every ε, the view outputted by $(I \otimes S)(A, |aux\rangle^{\otimes t(1/\varepsilon)})$ is distinguishable from the real view except with advantage no more than ε, where S does not touch the distinguisher's private register. We stress that the protocol itself is independent of ε. Furthermore, this still suffices for almost any game-based application that needs simulation security although with a larger polynomial security loss. To see this, for example, suppose an adversary can break a downstream game-based security with some non-negligible probability p, then we can set our overall simulation error to be $p/2$ to reach a contradiction. On the other hand, to prove a downstream ε-simulation security, we can similarly pick a smaller ε for each fold and invoke hybrid argument.

The main technical ingredient we need is to implement reflection unitary for an arbitrary initial state, which in this case could contain some inefficient auxiliary information. This is proven in the following lemma, which constructs such an algorithm by using a generalized SWAP test.

Lemma 2 (Approximate state reflection). *For any pure state $|\psi\rangle$, let $\mathcal{R}_\psi$ be the unitary channel for unitary $R_\psi := I - 2|\psi\rangle\langle\psi|$. Then there is a uniformly efficient channel $\tilde{\mathcal{R}}$ such that $\tilde{\mathcal{R}}(\cdot, |\psi\rangle\langle\psi|^{\otimes n})$ is $\sqrt[4]{\frac{64}{n+1}}$-close to $\mathcal{R}_\psi$ in diamond norm for all $\psi, n \geq 0$.*

Proof. We describe the algorithm as follows. We denote the registers as $X_0, ..., X_n$ with X_0 being the input register and the rest being initialized to $|\psi\rangle$.

1. Initialize a uniform superposition $|+\rangle_N := \frac{1}{\sqrt{n+1}} \sum_{i=0}^{n} |i\rangle_N$.
2. Controlled on N being $|i\rangle$, swap X_0 and X_i.
3. Controlled on N being $|+\rangle$, apply phase -1.
4. Uncompute step 2.
5. Trace out everything except X_0.

We begin analyzing the algorithm by considering pure state inputs. If the input is $|\psi\rangle$ then phase -1 is correctly applied since steps 2 and 4 do not affect the state. If the input is some orthogonal state $|\phi\rangle$, let $|\phi_i\rangle$ denote the state where X_i is $|\phi\rangle$ and everywhere else is $|\psi\rangle$. Then after step 3, we get the state

$$\frac{1}{\sqrt{n+1}} \sum_{i=0}^{n} |\phi_i\rangle (|i\rangle - 2|+\rangle) = \frac{1}{\sqrt{n+1}} \sum_i |\phi_i\rangle|i\rangle - \frac{2}{n+1} \sum_{i,j} |\phi_i\rangle|j\rangle.$$

Therefore after step 4, we get

$$|\tilde{\phi}\rangle := \left(1 - \frac{2}{\sqrt{n+1}}\right)|\phi_0\rangle|+\rangle - \frac{2}{n+1} \sum_{i \neq j} |\phi_i\rangle|j\rangle.$$

We compare this state with the expected output and get that the overlap

$$(\langle\phi_0|\langle+|)|\tilde{\phi}\rangle = 1 - \frac{2}{\sqrt{n+1}}\left(1 + \frac{n}{n+1}\right) \geq 1 - \frac{4}{\sqrt{n+1}}.$$

By decomposing a general pure state $|x\rangle = \sqrt{p}|\psi\rangle + \sqrt{1-p}|\phi\rangle$ and let $|\psi_n\rangle := |\psi\rangle^{\otimes n}|+\rangle$, we have that

$$(\langle x| R_\psi^\dagger \otimes \langle\psi_n|)|\tilde{x}\rangle \geq 1 - \frac{4}{\sqrt{n+1}} \qquad (2)$$

as well by combining the two cases above. Furthermore, (2) generalizes to a larger entangled pure state by simply applying (2) linearly to the Schmidt decomposition. For diamond norm, it suffices to consider any input state where the overall entangled state is pure (since we can without loss of generality purify the state for the distinguisher), thus we have that the trace distance between $(I \otimes R_\psi) \ket{x} \otimes \ket{\psi_n}$ and $\ket{\tilde{x}}$ is at most

$$\sqrt{1 - \left(1 - \frac{4}{\sqrt{n+1}}\right)^2} \le \sqrt[4]{\frac{64}{n+1}}.$$

This completes the proof since trace distance cannot increase after the operation of tracing out the auxiliary registers holding $\ket{\psi_n}$, which is CPTP.

Theorem 5. *ε-simulation secure commitment schemes with quantum auxiliary input exist. Furthermore, it can be built from any non-interactive extractable-binding computationally-hiding commitment scheme with quantum auxiliary input.*

Proof. This follows the same construction and proof strategy as [BCKM21, AQY22] except for one change. In particular, Watrous rewinding [Wat06] was used for a total of λ times in the equivocal simulator [BCKM21, Section 4.1], which involved applying a unitary $I - 2\ket{0}\bra{0}$ on a certain private register of the simulator's. The purpose of this unitary was to check whether this register returned to all zero state. In our context, this register would be initialized to $\ket{0} \otimes \ket{aux}^{\otimes t}$ instead for a suitably large zero register and some polynomial $t(\lambda)$, and similarly we need to reflect around this state in order for the analysis to go through[3].

We establish ε-equivocality as follows. We first consider a simulator that runs the [BCKM21] equivocal simulator with access to an inefficient reflection oracle: this gives a negligible simulation error, and thus it is at most $\varepsilon/2$ for all sufficiently large λ. We now instantiate this inefficient oracle with Lemma 2 where $n = \lceil 1024(\lambda/\varepsilon)^4 \rceil - 1$ and $\ket{\psi} = \ket{0} \otimes \ket{aux}^{\otimes t}$, then by a standard hybrid argument we arrive that the overall simulation error is at most ε. Furthermore, the number of copies of $\ket{aux}$ used is $O(t(\lambda/\varepsilon)^4)$ which is polynomial.

The rest of the proof follows as [BCKM21] using a similar trick of running the inner simulator with a polynomially smaller error parameter.

Simulation Security in the Unclonable Common Random State Model. We conclude by remarking on the simulation security of the commitment scheme with trusted setup from Corollary 2. First of all, we can still apply the [BCKM21] transformation, but in this case we would get negligible simulation security since

---

[3] One naïve idea to fix this is to ask the simulator to only reflect the zero part and ignore the auxiliary information. However, this does not work since we can calculate and see that such a rewinding algorithm (without any further changes) would not work for an adversary that picks its challenge by measuring the auxiliary information it receives from the simulator.

with access to the compressed database register, the simulator can efficiently test/uncompute the magic state.

However, we note that the argument of Proposition 3 gives an adversary that breaks honest binding when the adversary could control the sampling of the random function using compressed oracles, and thus an analogous argument can show that the commitment of Corollary 2 is in fact already negligibly equivocal even without any further modification to the scheme.

Using similar ideas this commitment is probably also negligibly extractable as well, however, the argument is more complicated since in this case we need to be able to extract any malicious committer (this is unlike the equivocal case where the only freedom a passive but malicious receiver has is to distinguish the views, so it suffices to simply show simulation correctness). We leave formalizing this to future work.

C   Post-quantum Pseudorandomness

We view a quantum query-less circuit with auxiliary input of total size S as an S-qubit input fed to a universal quantum circuit, which itself is independent of the random function H. (Indeed we can without loss of generality even take S to be the number of qubits that actually depend on the function H.)

The first polynomial upper bound for this problem was established by Chung, Guo, Liu, and Qian [CGLQ20a] and was subsequently improved by Liu [Liu23]. We follow the second work in this proof. We first recall a game G in a P-BF-QROM [Liu23] to be the following:

0. A random function $H : [N] \to [M]$ is sampled uniformly at random.
1. The adversary starts by making P (quantum) queries to H, and then we postselect on measuring its first qubit and obtaining 1 (abort if it is not possible). This postselection may affect its residual state as well as the conditional distribution of the random function.
2. The challenger then samples a random classical challenge to the adversary, using T_{samp} queries.
3. The adversary produces a response, using T queries.
4. The challenger outputs a bit indicating accept or reject, using T_{verify} queries.

We say G is $\nu(P, T)$-secure in the P-BF-QROM if any adversary with T queries cannot make the challenger accept with probability higher than ν. In our case, the security game of a pseudorandom ensemble (or PRG) against a query-less adversary corresponds to $T_{samp} = 1$ and $T = T_{verify} = 0$: the challenger flips a random bit and either sends a pseudorandom $H(x)$ (using a single query) or a random y, and asks the adversary to predict the bit.

Similarly, an (S, T) non-uniform quantum adversary plays the same security game, except that in step 1 it can do an arbitrary amount of queries but is not allowed to do post-selection, and its output (to be used later in step 3) is restricted to at most S qubits.

Lemma 3 ([Liu23, Lemma 4], with the coefficient from [CGLQ20b, Proof of Lemma 5.13]). *The PRG game has $\nu(P,T) = \frac{1}{2} + 4\sqrt{2} \cdot \sqrt{\frac{P+T^2}{N}}$ in the P-BF-QROM.*

Theorem 6 ([Liu23, Theorem 5]). *Any game G that has security ν in the P-BF-QROM has security*

$$\delta(S,T) \leq \min_{\gamma > 0}\{\nu(P/\gamma, T) + \gamma\}$$

against (S,T) non-uniform adversaries in QROM, where $P = S(T + T_{verify} + T_{samp})$.

Proof (Proof of Proposition 1). Combining Lemma 3 and Theorem 6, we find that for any non-uniform algorithm A of size S (that potentially depends on H),

$$\left| \mathbb{E}_H \left[\mathbb{E}_x[A(H(x))] - \mathbb{E}_y[A(y)] \right] \right| = 2 \left| \delta(S \cdot 1, 0) - \frac{1}{2} \right|$$

$$\leq 2 \min_{\gamma > 0} \left\{ \sqrt{2^5 \cdot \frac{S}{\gamma N}} + \gamma \right\}$$

$$= 12 \cdot \sqrt[3]{\frac{S}{N}},$$

showing the bound above.

Proof (Proof of Proposition 2). Since each copy of the magic state can be efficiently prepared through a single quantum query to H, any distinguishing adversary is a valid query-less adversary in the P-BF-QROM, and thus we arrive at the proposition by invoking Lemma 3.

References

[AQY22] Ananth, P., Qian, L., Yuen, H.: Cryptography from Pseudorandom Quantum States. In: Advances in Cryptology - CRYPTO 2022, pp. 208–236 (2022). https://doi.org/10.1007/978-3-031-15802-5_8, (cit. on pp. 1, 15, 19)

[BCKM21] Bartusek, J., Coladangelo, A., Khurana, D., Ma, F.: One-way functions imply secure computation in a quantum world. In: Advances in Cryptology - CRYPTO 2021, pp. 467–496 (2021). https://doi.org/10.1007/978-3-030-84242-0_17, (cit. on pp. 5, 6, 17, 19, 20)

[BCQ23] Brakerski, Z., Canetti, R., Qian, L.: On the computational hardness needed for quantum cryptography. In: 14th Innovations in Theoretical Computer Science Conference (ITCS 2023). Vol. 251, pp. 24:1–24:21 (2023). https://doi.org/10.4230/LIPIcs.ITCS.2023.24, (cit. on pp. 1, 2, 4, 15)

[BEM+23] Bostanci, J., Efron, Y., Metger, T., Poremba, A., Qian, L., Yuen, H.: Unitary Complexity and the Uhlmann Transformation Problem (2023). arXiv: 2306.13073, (cit. on p. 1)

[BFM88] Blum, M., Feldman, P., Micali, S.: Non-interactive zero-knowledge and its applications. In: Proceedings of the Twentieth Annual ACM Symposium on Theory of Computing, pp. 103–112 (1988). https://doi.org/10.1145/62212.62222, (cit. on p. 8)

[BK23] Bartusek, J., Khurana, D.: Cryptography with certified deletion. In: Advances in Cryptology - CRYPTO 2023, pp. 192–223 (2023). https://doi.org/10.1007/978-3-031-38554-4_7, (cit. on p. 5)

[Bra23] Brakerski, Z.: Black-Hole Radiation Decoding Is Quantum Cryptography. In: Advances in Cryptology - CRYPTO 2023, pp. 37–65 (2023). https://doi.org/10.1007/978-3-031-38554-4_2, (cit. on p. 1)

[CGLQ20a] Chung, K.-M., Guo, S., Liu, Q., Qian, L.: Tight quantum time-space tradeoffs for function inversion. In: 2020 IEEE 61st Annual Symposium on Foundations of Computer Science (FOCS), pp. 673–684 (2020). https://doi.org/10.1109/FOCS46700.2020.00068, (cit. on pp. 6, 20)

[CGLQ20b] Chung, K.-M., Guo, S., Liu, Q., Qian, L.: Tight Quantum Time-Space Tradeoffs for Function Inversion (2020). arXiv: 2006.05650v2, (cit. on p. 21)

[CKR16] Chailloux, A., Kerenidis, I., Rosgen, B.: Quantum commitments from complexity assumptions. In: Computational Complexity, vol. 25, no. 1, pp. 103–151 (2016). https://doi.org/10.1007/s00037-015-0116-5, (cit. on pp. 2, 7)

[Col06] Colbeck, R.: Quantum And Relativistic Protocols For Secure Multi-Party Computation. PhD thesis. Trinity College, University of Cambridge (2006). arXiv: 0911.3814 (cit. on p. 4)

[DTT10] De, A., Trevisan, L., Tulsiani, M.: Time space tradeoffs for attacks against one-way functions and PRGs. In: Advances in Cryptology - CRYPTO 2010, pp. 649–665 (2010). https://doi.org/10.1007/978-3-642-14623-7_35, (cit. on p. 5)

[FUYZ22] Fang, J., Unruh, D., Yan, J., Zhou, D.: How to base security on the perfect/statistical binding property of quantum bit commitment?" In: 33rd International Symposium on Algorithms and Computation (ISAAC 2022), Vol. 248, pp. 26:1–26:12 (2022). https://doi.org/10.4230/LIPIcs.ISAAC.2022.26, (cit. on pp. 16, 17)

[GK92] Goldreich, O., Krawczyk, H.: Sparse pseudorandom distributions. In: Random Structures & Algorithms, vol. 3, no. 2, pp. 163–174 (1992). https://doi.org/10.1002/rsa.3240030206, (cit. on pp. 5, 6)

[Gol90] Goldreich, O.: A note on computational indistinguishability. In: Information Processing Letters, vol. 34, no. 6, pp. 277–281 (1990). https://doi.org/10.1016/0020-0190(90)90010-U, (cit. on p. 1)

[GZ19] Guan, J., Zhandary, M.: Simple Schemes in the Bounded Storage Model. In: Advances in Cryptology - EUROCRYPT 2019, pp. 500–524 (2019). https://doi.org/10.1007/978-3-030-17659-4_17, (cit. on p. 8)

[IL89] Impagliazzo, R., Luby, M.: One-way functions are essential for complexity based cryptography. In: 30th Annual Symposium on Foundations of Computer Science, pp. 230–235 (1989). https://doi.org/10.1109/SFCS.1989.63483, (cit. on pp. 1, 3)

[Ken12] Kent, A.: Unconditionally Secure Bit Commitment by Transmitting Measurement Outcomes. In: Physical Review Letters, vol. 109, pp. 130501 (2012). https://doi.org/10.1103/PhysRevLett.109.130501, (cit. on p. 4)

[Ken99] Kent, A.: Unconditionally Secure Bit Commitment. In: Physical Review Letters, vol. 83, pp. 1447–1450 (1999). https://doi.org/10.1103/PhysRevLett.83.1447, (cit. on p. 4)

[KQST23] Kretschmer, W., Qian, L., Sinha, M., Tal, A.: Quantum cryptography in algorithmica. In: Proceedings of the 55th Annual ACM Symposium on Theory of Computing, pp. 1589–1602 (2023). https://doi.org/10.1145/3564246.3585225, (cit. on p. 1)

[Kre21] Kretschmer, W.: Quantum pseudorandomness and classical complexity. In: 16th Conference on the Theory of Quantum Computation, Communication and Cryptography (TQC 2021), Vol. 197, pp. 2:1–2:20 (2021). https://doi.org/10.4230/LIPIcs.TQC.2021.2, (cit. on p. 1)

[LC97] Lo, H.-K., Chau, H.F.: Is quantum bit commitment really possible? In: Physical Review Letters, vol. 78, pp. 3410–3413 (1997). https://doi.org/10.1103/PhysRevLett.78.3410, (cit. on p. 1)

[Liu23] Liu, Q.: Non-uniformity and quantum advice in the quantum random oracle model. In: Advances in Cryptology - EUROCRYPT 2023, pp. 117–143 (2023). https://doi.org/10.1007/978-3-031-30545-0_5, (cit. on pp. 6, 20, 21)

[Llo00] Lloyd, S.: Ultimate physical limits to computation. In: Nature, vol. 406, no. 6799, pp. 1047–1054 (2000). https://doi.org/10.1038/35023282, (cit. on p. 4)

[LMW23] Lombardi, A., Ma, F., Wright, J.: A one-query lower bound for unitary synthesis and breaking quantum cryptography (2023). arXiv: 2310.08870 (cit. on pp. 1, 5)

[May97] Mayers, D.: Unconditionally Secure Quantum Bit Commitment is Impossible. In: Physical Review Letters, vol. 78, pp. 3414–3417 (1997). https://doi.org/10.1103/PhysRevLett.78.3414, (cit. on p. 1)

[MNY23] Morimae, T., Nehoran, B., Yamakawa, T.: Unconditionally Secure Commitments with Quantum Auxiliary Inputs (manuscript) (2023) (cit. on pp. 5, 6, 11)

[MY22] Morimae, T., Yamakawa, T.: Quantum commitments and signatures without one-way functions. In: Advances in Cryptology - CRYPTO 2022, pp. 269–295 (2022). https://doi.org/10.1007/978-3-031-15802-5_10, (cit. on pp. 1, 17)

[Nao91] Naor, M.: Bit commitment using pseudorandomness. In: Journal of Cryptology, vol. 4, no. 2, pp. 151–158 (1991). https://doi.org/10.1007/BF00196774, (cit. on p. 8)

[NZ24] Nehoran, B., Zhandry, M.: A computational separation between quantum no-cloning and no-telegraphing. In: 15th Innovations in Theoretical Computer Science Conference (ITCS 2024), Vol. 287, pp. 82:1–82:23 (2024). https://doi.org/10.4230/LIPIcs.ITCS.2024.82, (cit. on p. 5)

[OW93] Ostrovsky, R., Wigderson, A.: One-way functions are essential for nontrivial zero-knowledge. In: The 2nd Israel Symposium on Theory and Computing Systems, pp. 3–17 (1993). https://doi.org/10.1109/ISTCS.1993.253489, (cit. on pp. 1, 2)

[Ps05] Pass, R., Shelat, A.: Unconditional characterizations of non-interactive zero-knowledge. In: Advances in Cryptology - CRYPTO 2005, pp. 118–134 (2005). https://doi.org/10.1007/11535218_8, (cit. on p. 4)

[Raz05] Raz, R.: Quantum information and the PCP theorem. In: 46th Annual IEEE Symposium on Foundations of Computer Science (FOCS'05), pp. 459–468 (2005). https://doi.org/10.1109/SFCS.2005.62, (cit. on p. 3)

[Rud02] Rudolph, T.: The Laws of Physics and Cryptographic Security (2002). arXiv: quant-ph/0202143, (cit. on p. 4)

[Wat06] Watrous, J.: Zero-Knowledge against Quantum Attacks. In: Proceedings of the Thirty-Eighth Annual ACM Symposium on Theory of Computing, pp. 296–305 (2006). https://doi.org/10.1145/1132516.1132560, (cit. on p. 19)

[Yan22] Yan, J.: General Properties of Quantum Bit Commitments (Extended Abstract). In: Advances in Cryptology - ASIACRYPT 2022, pp. 628–657 (2022). https://doi.org/10.1007/978-3-031-22972-5_22, (cit. on pp. 1, 15)

[Yao82] Chi-Chih Yao, A.: Protocols for secure computations. In: 2013 IEEE 54th Annual Symposium on Foundations of Computer Science, pp. 160–164 (1982). https://doi.org/10.1109/SFCS.1982.88, (cit. on p. 4)

[Zha19] Zhandry, M.: How to Record Quantum Queries, and Applications to Quantum Indifferentiability. In: Advances in Cryptology - CRYPTO 2019, pp. 239–268 (2019). https://doi.org/10.1007/978-3-030-26951-7_9, (cit. on p. 9)

Unconditionally Secure Commitments with Quantum Auxiliary Inputs

Tomoyuki Morimae[1(✉)], Barak Nehoran[2], and Takashi Yamakawa[1,3,4]

[1] Yukawa Institute for Theoretical Physics, Kyoto University, Kyoto, Japan
tomoyuki.morimae@yukawa.kyoto-u.ac.jp
[2] Princeton University, Princeton, NJ, USA
bnehoran@princeton.edu
[3] NTT Social Informatics Laboratories, Tokyo, Japan
takashi.yamakawa@ntt.com
[4] NTT Research Center for Theoretical Quantum Information, Atsugi, Japan
https://www.cs.princeton.edu/~bnehoran/
https://sites.google.com/view/takashiyamakawa

Abstract. We show the following unconditional results on quantum commitments in two related yet different models:

1. We revisit the notion of quantum auxiliary-input commitments introduced by Chailloux, Kerenidis, and Rosgen (Comput. Complex. 2016) where both the committer and receiver take the same quantum state, which is determined by the security parameter, as quantum auxiliary inputs. We show that computationally-hiding and statistically-binding quantum auxiliary-input commitments exist unconditionally, i.e., without relying on any unproven assumption, while Chailloux et al. assumed a complexity-theoretic assumption, **QIP** $\not\subseteq$ **QMA**. On the other hand, we observe that achieving both statistical hiding and statistical binding at the same time is impossible even in the quantum auxiliary-input setting. To the best of our knowledge, this is the first example of unconditionally proving computational security of any form of (classical or quantum) commitments for which statistical security is impossible. As intermediate steps toward our construction, we introduce and unconditionally construct post-quantum sparse pseudorandom distributions and quantum auxiliary-input EFI pairs which may be of independent interest.

2. We introduce a new model which we call the common reference quantum state (CRQS) model where both the committer and receiver take the same quantum state that is randomly sampled by an efficient setup algorithm. We unconditionally prove that there exist statistically hiding and statistically binding commitments in the CRQS model, circumventing the impossibility in the plain model.

We also discuss their applications to zero-knowledge proofs, oblivious transfers, and multi-party computations.

1 Introduction

Commitments are one of the most fundamental primitives in cryptography. A committer commits a bit string to a receiver, and later it is opened. The receiver cannot learn the committed message until it is opened (hiding), and the committer cannot change the message once it is committed (binding). It is easy to see that in classical cryptography, it is impossible to achieve both statistical hiding and statistical binding at the same time (i.e., hiding and binding hold against computationally unbounded adversaries).[1] It is likewise well-known that the no-go holds even in quantum cryptography where quantum computing and quantum communication are possible [29,31]. Thus, there has been an extensive body of research on quantum commitments with computational hiding or binding where the computational power of the adversary is assumed to be quantum polynomial-time (QPT) [1,10,13,20,26,27,34,46].

This raises the question of what is the minimal complexity assumption that would imply quantum commitments. In the classical setting, the existence of commitments is known to be equivalent to the existence of one-way functions [19,36]. In the quantum setting, Brakerski, Canetti, and Qian [5] (based on an earlier work by Yan [45]) recently showed that the existence of quantum commitments is equivalent to the existence of *EFI pairs*, which are pairs of two efficiently generatable quantum states that are statistically far but computationally indistinguishable. Some useful quantum cryptographic primitives such as oblivious transfers (OTs) and multiparty computations (MPCs) can be constructed from EFI pairs [1,2,17,34]. Moreover, various quantum cryptographic primitives imply EFI pairs including pseudorandom states generators [24], private-key quantum money with pure banknotes [24,25], one-way states generators with pure output states [25,34], and one-time-secure secret-key encryption [33]. The ultimate goal would be to prove the existence of EFI pairs *unconditionally*, i.e., without relying on any unproven assumption, which would lead to the unconditional existence of commitments (and, consequently, OTs and MPCs).[2]

There has been recent progress in understanding the computational complexity of EFI pairs. For instance, their complexity cannot be captured within traditional complexity classes of classical inputs and outputs [30], and instead requires the study of unitary complexity classes [4]. It is yet unclear, however,

---

[1] Let $\mathsf{Comm}(b,x)$ be the commitment of the bit b with the decommitment x. Because it is statistically hiding, there should be another x' such that $\mathsf{Comm}(b \oplus 1, x') = \mathsf{Comm}(b, x)$. However, then, an unbounded malicious committer can compute x' to break the binding.

[2] One might mistakenly assume that because statistically-secure commitments are impossible, commitments and EFI pairs may not exist unconditionally. However, this is not correct: The unconditional existence (i.e., existence without any assumption) of a cryptographic primitive, and its statistical security (i.e., security against unbounded adversaries), are not the same and should not be confused. Here, we mean the unconditional existence (without relying on an unproven complexity assumption) of commitments that are *computationally* secure (i.e., either hiding or binding is secure only against QPT adversaries).

if known barriers to proving complexity separations from the classical theory may reappear in similar form in the quantum case (though the barriers are not directly implied), or if the distinctive nature of unitary complexity classes allows such results to be within reach of present techniques. In this work, we demonstrate that the complexity assumptions previously thought necessary can in fact be removed from commitments of a special non-standard form: those that take quantum auxiliary inputs.

(Quantum) Auxiliary-Input Commitments. Chailloux, Kerenidis, and Rosgen [7] studied computationally-secure quantum commitments in an *auxiliary-input* setting where the honest committer and receiver can take classical or quantum auxiliary inputs (which are not necessarily efficiently generatable) for executing the protocol.[3] Such auxiliary-input versions of cryptographic primitives have often been studied when we only assume worst-case assumptions that do not imply conventional notions of cryptographic primitives [35,37,42]. The paper [7] obtained feasibility results on classical and quantum auxiliary-input quantum commitments based on some worst-case complexity assumptions. Specifically, they showed that:

- if $\mathbf{QSZK} \not\subseteq \mathbf{QMA}$, then there are classical auxiliary-input quantum commitments (that are statistically binding and computationally hiding), and
- if $\mathbf{QIP} \not\subseteq \mathbf{QMA}$, then there are quantum auxiliary-input commitments[4] (both statistically hiding and computationally binding as well as statistically binding and computationally hiding).

Brakerski, Canetti, and Qian [5] gave an alternative construction of classical auxiliary-input quantum commitments assuming $\mathbf{QCZK} \not\subseteq \mathbf{BQP}$. This is, however, not a viable path to proving the unconditional existence of quantum auxiliary-input commitments, since proving any of these complexity-theoretic separations *unconditionally* seems still out of reach of the current knowledge of complexity theory. In this work, we show, perhaps surprisingly, that such complexity-theoretic assumptions can be removed completely.

1.1 Our Results

Quantum Auxiliary-Input Commitments. We show that quantum auxiliary-input commitments exist *unconditionally*, i,e., without relying on any unproven assumption.

Theorem 1.1. *There exist quantum auxiliary-input commitments that satisfy computational hiding and statistical binding.*

---

[3] Quantum auxiliary inputs are called *quantum advice* in [7]. We use "auxiliary input" and "advice" interchangeably.

[4] When we consider the quantum auxiliary-input setting, we omit "quantum" before "commitments" since it is clear that they must be quantum commitments given that the auxiliary input is quantum.

We stress that the unconditional construction does not mean that our construction satisfies statistical hiding and statistical binding. Rather, we prove that our construction satisfies *computational* hiding and statistical binding without relying on any unproven assumption. Indeed, we show that it is impossible to achieve both statistical hiding and statistical binding simultaneously even in the quantum auxiliary-input setting by extending the impossibility result in the plain model [29,31]. To the best of our knowledge, this is the first example of any form of (classical or quantum) commitments for which statistical security is impossible but computational security is proven unconditionally.

Post-quantum Sparse Pseudorandom Distributions and Quantum Auxiliary-Input EFI. As intermediate steps to show the above theorem, we introduce two new primitives, namely, a post-quantum version of sparse pseudorandom distributions defined in [15] and a quantum auxiliary-input version of EFI pairs,[5] and show their existence unconditionally.

Theorem 1.2. *There exist post-quantum sparse pseudorandom distributions and quantum auxiliary-input EFI pairs.*

A sparse pseudorandom distribution is a (not necessarily efficiently samplable) classical distribution supported by a sparse subset but indistinguishable from the uniform distribution against classical non-uniform polynomial-time distinguishers. Goldreich and Krawczyk [15] showed the existence of such distributions unconditionally. We extend sparse pseudorandom distributions to the post-quantum setting where the distinguishers are QPT with quantum advice, and construct them unconditionally. Quantum auxiliary-input EFI pairs are the same as the EFI pairs except that the two states are not necessarily efficiently generatable. We construct quantum auxiliary-input EFI pairs from post-quantum sparse pseudorandom distributions, which shows the unconditional existence of quantum auxiliary-input EFI pairs. Interestingly, in the classical case, it is not known how to construct (even auxiliary-input) classical commitments from classical sparse pseudorandom distributions.

Application to Zero-Knowledge. As an application of our quantum auxiliary-input commitments, we plug them into Blum's Hamiltonicity protocol [3] to obtain the following theorem.

Theorem 1.3. *There exist zero-knowledge proofs for* **NP** *in the quantum auxiliary-input setting with non-uniform simulation (with quantum advice) and soundness error* $1/2$.

We can also use our quantum auxiliary-input commitments to instantiate the 3-coloring protocol of [16] and the quantum Σ-protocol for **QMA** of [6]. On the other hand, unfortunately, we do not know how to instantiate the construction of OTs of [2] using our quantum auxiliary-input commitments. This is due to the fact that there may not be an efficient way to generate the quantum auxiliary-

---

[5] Quantum auxiliary-input EFI pairs are mentioned in [5] without a formal definition.

input, which prevents us from applying Watrous' rewinding lemma [43] that is used in the security proof in [2].[6]

Commitments in the CRQS Model. Our result on quantum auxiliary-input commitments is theoretically interesting. However, the fact that there is no efficient way to generate the quantum auxiliary input makes it unlikely to have uses in real-world applications. We therefore consider an alternative model that involves only efficiently generatable states. Specifically, we introduce a new notion that we call the *common reference quantum state (CRQS) model*,[7] where an efficient setup algorithm randomly samples a classical key k and then distributes many copies of a (pure) quantum state $|\psi_k\rangle$ associated with the key k. It is a natural quantum analog of the common reference string model in classical cryptography.

At first glance, the CRQS model may look similar to the quantum auxiliary-input setting since in both settings, the committer and receiver receive some quantum state as a resource for executing the protocol. However, the crucial differences are that:

1. quantum auxiliary input may not be efficiently generatable, but a CRQS must be efficiently generated by the setup algorithm, and
2. whereas quantum auxiliary input must be a fixed quantum state that is determined by the security parameter, the CRQS is instead associated with a randomly sampled classical key k that is hidden from the adversary.[8]

Thus, the two settings are incomparable. Nonetheless, we can use a similar idea to construct commitments in the CRQS model unconditionally:

Theorem 1.4. *There exist commitments in the CRQS model that satisfy statistical hiding against adversaries that are given bounded polynomial number of copies of the CRQS $|\psi_k\rangle$ and statistical binding even against adversaries that are given the classical key k.*[9]

---

[6] A knowledgeable reader may wonder why we could prove quantum zero-knowledge even though the original proof in the plain model also uses Watrous' rewinding lemma. This is because we can avoid using Watrous' rewinding lemma in the fully non-uniform simulation setting (see Sect. 1.2).

[7] [14] also introduced a model which they call the CRQS model, but their model is different from ours. In their CRQS model, parties may take arbitrarily entangled quantum states as setup. In our opinion, this is a quantum analog of the correlated randomness model [22] rather than the common reference string model.

[8] Later we will see that this property enables the CRQS model to realize statistically-secure commitments (i.e., both hiding and binding are statistical), a feat which is not possible in the auxiliary-input setting.

[9] The honest receiver requires only a single copy of the CRQS $|\psi_k\rangle$, but we consider hiding security even against a malicious receiver that collects many copies of $|\psi_k\rangle$. Similarly, the honest committer requires only a single copy of the CRQS $|\psi_k\rangle$, but we consider binding security even against a malicious committer that knows the secret key k. These relaxations just make the theorem stronger.

We remark that our scheme in the CRQS model satisfies both statistical hiding and statistical binding simultaneously unlike the case in the quantum auxiliary-input setting, where the hiding is only computational. This is made possible by the assumption that the number of copies of the CRQS given to the hiding adversary (malicious receiver) is bounded. We explain why the no-go result of [29,31] does not extend to this setting in Sect. 1.2. It is worth noting that the no-go result *does* extend to quantum commitments in the (classical) common reference string (CRS) model[10], which demonstrates a fundamental difference between the CRQS and CRS models. More generally, we show that the no-go result extends to the correlated randomness model,[11] if the correlation of the strings sent to the committer and the receiver is too strong or too weak. See the full version of this paper [32] for details.

Applications to OTs and MPCs. As an application of our quantum commitments in the CRQS model, we can plug them into the compiler of [2] to obtain the following theorem:

Theorem 1.5. *There exist maliciously simulation-secure OTs in the CRQS model that is statistically secure against adversaries that are given bounded number of copies of CRQS.*

We note that we can apply the compiler of [2] unlike in the quantum auxiliary-input setting since the CRQS $|\psi_k\rangle$ can be efficiently generated given the classical key k, which can be sampled by the simulator itself.[12] Moreover it is known that OTs imply MPCs for classical functionalities [23] or even for quantum functionalities [12] in a black-box manner. Thus, we believe that similar constructions work in the CRQS model, which would lead to statistically maliciously simulation-secure MPCs in the CRQS model. However, for formally showing them, we have to carefully reexamine these constructions to make sure that they work in the CRQS model as well. This is out of the scope of this work, and we leave it to future work.

1.2 Technical Overview

Post-quantum Sparse Pseudorandom Distributions. We start from recalling the notion of sparse pseudorandom distributions introduced by Goldreich and Krawczyk [15]. We say that a family $\{D_\lambda\}_{\lambda \in \mathbb{N}}$ of distributions D_λ over $\{0,1\}^\lambda$ is a sparse pseudorandom distribution if it satisfies the following:

---

[10] In the CRS model, a bit string x is sampled by the setup algorithm, and the same x is sent to both the committer and receiver.
[11] In the correlated randomness model, a pair of bit strings (x, y) is sampled by the setup algorithm, x is sent to the committer, and y is sent to the receiver.
[12] Note that we allow the simulator to "program" the CRQS similarly to conventional simulation-based security in the classical CRS model. See the full version of this paper [32] for the precise definition of the simulation-based security for OTs in the CRQS model.

Sparseness: The support of D_λ is sparse, i.e., $\frac{|\mathsf{Supp}(D_\lambda)|}{2^\lambda} = \mathsf{negl}(\lambda)$, where $\mathsf{Supp}(D_\lambda)$ denotes the support of D_λ;

Pseudorandomness: A string sampled from D_λ is computationally indistinguishable from a uniformly random λ-bit string against non-uniform *classical* polynomial-time distinguishers.

We stress that D_λ is not assumed to be efficiently samplable. Goldreich and Krawczyk [15] gave an unconditional proof for the existence of sparse pseudorandom distributions. Their proof is based on a simple counting argument where they rely on the fact that the number of possible classical circuits of size s is at most 2^{s^2}.

We consider the post-quantum version of sparse pseudorandom distributions where we require pseudorandomness against non-uniform QPT distinguishers. If we only consider QPT distinguishers with *classical* advice, then a similar counting argument works. However, when we consider QPT distinguishers with *quantum* advice, then such a simple counting argument no longer works since the number of possible s-qubit states is *double exponential* rather than exponential in s even if we consider the ϵ-net with sufficiently small ϵ. Looking ahead, we need pseudorandomness against QPT distinguishers with quantum advice for our construction of quantum auxiliary-input commitments, and thus we first need to resolve this problem.

Our key observation is that we can rely on recent progress on quantum random oracle model with quantum auxiliary-input [8,9,21,28] to resolve the issue. In particular, Liu proved that a length doubling random function $H : \{0,1\}^{\lfloor \lambda/2 \rfloor} \to \{0,1\}^\lambda$ is a PRG against adversaries that take polynomial-size quantum advice ρ_H that depends on H and make polynomially many quantum queries to H, i.e., the adversary cannot distinguish $H(x)$ for uniformly random $x \leftarrow \{0,1\}^{\lfloor \lambda/2 \rfloor}$ from a uniformly random string $y \leftarrow \{0,1\}^\lambda$. In particular, we will only need the result in the setting where the adversary does not make any query to H. By an averaging argument, this implies that for any fixed (possibly unbounded-time) adversary $\mathcal{A}$, there exists H^* such that $H^*(x)$ for uniformly random $x \leftarrow \{0,1\}^{\lfloor \lambda/2 \rfloor}$ is indistinguishable from a uniformly random string $y \leftarrow \{0,1\}^\lambda$ for $\mathcal{A}$ with any polynomial-size quantum advice. In particular, if $\mathcal{A}$ is a quantum universal Turing machine, we can encode any non-uniform QPT computation into the quantum advice of $\mathcal{A}$. Thus, by using the corresponding function H^*, we can see that the distribution of $H^*(x)$ for $x \leftarrow \{0,1\}^{\lfloor \lambda/2 \rfloor}$ is computationally indistinguishable from the uniformly random distribution over $\{0,1\}^\lambda$ against any non-uniform QPT distinguishers with quantum advice. Moreover, it is clear that the distribution is sparse since the size of the support of the distribution is at most $2^{\lfloor \lambda/2 \rfloor}$ whereas the size of the whole space is 2^λ. This means that the distribution is a post-quantum sparse pseudorandom distribution.

Quantum Auxiliary-Input EFI Pairs. Our next step is rather conceptual: We regard post-quantum sparse pseudorandom distributions as giving us an instance of quantum auxiliary-input EFI pairs. Here, quantum auxiliary-input EFI pairs are defined similarly to EFI pairs except that we do not require the states to be efficiently generatable but only require that the states are polynomial-size.[13] That is, they are pairs of two (not necessarily efficiently generatable) quantum states that are statistically far but computationally indistinguishable. If $\{D_\lambda\}_{\lambda \in \mathbb{N}}$ is a post-quantum sparse pseudorandom distribution, then the following two states form a quantum auxiliary-input EFI pair:

$$\xi_{\lambda,0} := \sum_{y \in \{0,1\}^\lambda} D_\lambda(y) |y\rangle \langle y|, \quad \xi_{\lambda,1} := \frac{1}{2^\lambda} \sum_{y \in \{0,1\}^\lambda} |y\rangle \langle y|.$$

Indeed, they are statistically far by the sparseness and computationally indistinguishable by the post-quantum pseudorandomness.

Quantum Auxiliary-Input Commitments. We then convert quantum auxiliary-input EFI pairs into quantum auxiliary-input commitments. In the plain model (where there is no auxiliary input), it is known that EFI pairs imply quantum commitments (and in fact, they are equivalent) as folllows [5]. Let (ξ_0, ξ_1) be an EFI pair. We can assume that the fidelity between ξ_0 and ξ_1 is $\mathsf{negl}(\lambda)$ without loss of generality since otherwise we can exponentially decrease the fidelity by taking many copies of the state. For $b \in \{0,1\}$, let $|\psi_b\rangle$ be a purification of ξ_b over registers X and Y where X is the original register for ξ_b and Y is the register for purification. Then, a quantum commitment scheme is constructed as follows: to commit to a bit b, the committer generates $|\psi_b\rangle$ and sends register X to the receiver as a commitment. In the reveal phase, the committer sends the corresponding purificaton register Y along with the revealed bit b. Then the receiver applies a projective measurement $\{|\psi_b\rangle \langle \psi_b|, I - |\psi_b\rangle \langle \psi_b|\}$ on the state in registers (X, Y) and accepts if the first outcome is obtained, i.e., the state is projected onto $|\psi_b\rangle$. Then the hiding and binding of the protocol follows from computational indistinguishability and statistical farness of the EFI pair, respectively.

Our idea is to apply a similar construction in the quantum auxiliary-input setting. However, it does not directly work. First, if (ξ_0, ξ_1) is a quantum auxiliary-input EFI pair, then $|\psi_b\rangle$ may not be efficiently generatable, and thus the committing procedure may not be efficiently done.[14] To resolve this, we can include $(|\psi_0\rangle, |\psi_1\rangle)$ in the quantum auxiliary input of the commitment scheme so that the committer can make use of it.

The second issue is that the projective measurement $\{|\psi_b\rangle \langle \psi_b|, I - |\psi_b\rangle \langle \psi_b|\}$ may not be efficiently realized because again, $|\psi_b\rangle$ may not be efficiently generatable. To resolve this issue, our idea is to let the receiver perform the SWAP test between the state sent from the committer and another fresh copy of $|\psi_b\rangle$

---

[13] This is equivalent to requiring that the states can be generated by a non-uniform QPT algorithm with quantum advice since any polynomial-size quantum state can be generated by the trivial algorithm that takes the state itself as quantum advice and simply outputs it.

[14] In our particular construction of quantum auxiliary-input EFI pairs, $|\psi_1\rangle$ is efficiently generatable, but $|\psi_0\rangle$ is not. We consider a more general setting where neither of them is efficiently generatable.

given as the receiver's quantum auxiliary input and accept if the test accepts. Note that the SWAP test between two states ρ and σ is accepted with probability $\frac{1+\text{Tr}(\rho\sigma)}{2}$. Thus, the SWAP test by the receiver somewhat checks if the state sent from the committer is close to $|\psi_b\rangle$ or not. However, this is not sufficient: malicious committers who sent other states can be accepted with probability at least $1/2$, which breaks any meaningful notion of binding. Nevertheless, we can amplify this by running the above protocol $m = \omega(\log \lambda)$ times in parallel by including m copies of $(|\psi_0\rangle, |\psi_1\rangle)$ in the quantum auxiliary input. We can expect the binding error to be reduced to $2^{-m} = \mathsf{negl}(\lambda)$ while preserving the hiding property by a standard hybrid argument.

On Definition of Binding. While the proof of computational hiding is straightforward, proving binding is technically not as straightforward as one would expect. In the beginning, it is already unclear how we should define binding in the quantum auxiliary-input setting. The previous work [7] adopted the notion that is often called *sum-binding* and has been traditionally used in many works on quantum commitments [10, 13, 26, 27, 34].[15] Sum-binding requires that after finishing the commit phase, if we let p_b be the probability that the committer can reveal the commitment to b and that is accepted by the receiver for $b \in \{0,1\}$, then we have $p_0 + p_1 \leq 1 + \mathsf{negl}(\lambda)$. While this ensures some nontrivial security, Unruh [41] pointed out that it is not sufficient if we want to use the quantum commitment as a building block of other cryptographic primitives such as zero-knowledge proofs and OTs.[16] For this reason, we adopt an extractor-based definition of binding introduced in [1]. It very roughly requires that there is a possibly inefficient extractor that extracts the committed bit from a commitment. This definition enables us to define a *classical* bit committed in a quantum commitment, which is quite useful in security proofs of other protocols. In Sect. 5, we show that our construction satisfies the extractor-based binding by using an analysis of parallelly repeated SWAP tests [18] along with a similar template to those used in the proof of the extractor-based binding in the plain model [1, 45].

Application to Zero-Knowledge Proofs. To demonstrate applicability of our quantum auxiliary-input commitments, we use them to instantiate Blum's Hamiltonicity protocol [3]. This yields an unconditional construction of computational zero-knowledge proofs for **NP** with soundness error $1/2$ in the quantum auxiliary-input setting, i.e., the honest prover and honest verifier are allowed to take a common quantum auxiliary input. The proof of soundness is straightforward once we assume the extractor-based binding for the commitment: It ensures that we can "extract" the classical committed bits from commitments,

---

[15] To our knowledge, the term "sum-binding" was used in [41] for the first time.
[16] In the plain model (where there is no quantum auxiliary-input), it is known that any (possibly interactive) quantum commitments can be compiled into a non-interactive "canonical form" [45] and sum-binding for canonical form quantum commitments is sufficient for those applications [1, 11, 45]. However, this does not seem to work in the quantum auxiliary-input setting.

after which the analysis is identical to the classical case. Note that we are proving statistical soundness and thus it does not matter that the extractor is inefficient. On the other hand, there is some subtlety in the proof, and actually also in the definition, of the zero-knowledge property. Recall that the standard quantum zero-knowledge property [43] requires that there is a simulator that efficiently simulates the malicious verifier's view by using the same (possibly quantum) auxiliary-input as the verifier. We argue that this is unlikely to hold if we instantiate Blum's protocol using our quantum auxiliary-input commitments. In the protocol, the prover sends commitments to bits derived from the witness of the statement being proven and later reveals some of them. In our quantum auxiliary-input commitment scheme, after sending a commitment and then revealing the committed bit, the receiver gets m copies of state $|\psi_b\rangle$ that is included in the quantum auxiliary input. Since $|\psi_b\rangle$ is not necessarily efficiently generatable, this already gives some "knowledge" to the verifier, i.e., the simulator cannot efficiently simulate $|\psi_b\rangle$. We believe that the above is just a definitional issue: Since the honest prover and receiver use the quantum auxiliary input, it is reasonable to allow the simulator to use them too. In particular, we define the zero-knowledge property by using a *non-uniform* simulator whose quantum auxiliary input can depend on the malicious verifier's quantum auxiliary input.[17] While this is weaker than the conventional definition of zero-knowledge, it still ensures meaningful security, in particular, it implies witness indistinguishability.

Defining the zero-knowledge property as above allows the proof to follow through. Remark that the simulator's quantum advice can include arbitrarily many copies of the quantum auxiliary input of the malicious verifier and the honest prover. This allows the simulator to circumvent the rewinding issue and instead use fresh quantum auxiliary input whenever it runs the prover and verifier.

Commitments in the CRQS Model. Next, we explain how to modify our construction to one in the CRQS model. If we concretely write down our quantum auxiliary-input commitment scheme, its quantum auxiliary-input consists of m copies of $|\psi_0\rangle = \sum_{x \in \{0,1\}^\lambda} |H(x)\rangle |x\rangle |0^\lambda\rangle$ and $|\psi_1\rangle = \sum_{y \in \{0,1\}^{2\lambda}} |y\rangle |y\rangle$ where $H : \{0,1\}^\lambda \to \{0,1\}^{2\lambda}$ is an appropriately chosen function. Since H may not be efficiently computable, the quantum auxiliary input may not be efficiently generatable. However, we observe that we could actually use uniformly random H if we allow the quantum auxiliary input to be randomized. Thus, our idea is to use many copies of $|\psi_0\rangle$ and $|\psi_1\rangle$ for a uniformly random H as a CRQS.[18] Since the CRQS must be efficiently generatable, we have to make sure that H is efficiently computable. While this is not possible if H is a completely random function, it is known that a $2q$-wise independent function is perfectly indistinguishable from

---

[17] In this definition, the simulator is fully non-uniform, i.e., it can take arbitrary polynomial-size quantum auxiliary input. A more conservative definition would be to allow the simulator to only take the quantum auxiliary inputs of the malicious verifier and the honest prover, but we do not know how to prove such a variant.

[18] Though $|\psi_1\rangle$ is efficiently generatable, we include it in the CRQS for the ease of presentation.

a uniformly random function if the function is given as an oracle and the distinguisher is allowed to make at most q quantum queries [47]. Therefore, as long as the number of copies of the CRQS that is given to the adversary is at most t, then we can simulate the random function in quantum polynomial-time by using a $2m(t+1)$-wise independent function, which is computable in polynomial-time for any polynomial t.[19] This is the idea for our construction in the CRQS model. Remarkably, we can achieve statistical hiding instead of computational hiding unlike the quantum auxiliary-input setting. This crucially relies on the fact that the random classical key k is hidden from the adversary, in particular, the malicious receiver (see also the next paragraph). So we can achieve both statistical hiding and statistical binding simultaneously in the CRQS model.

Why the Standard No-Go Does Not Apply in the CRQS Model. In the plain model, it is well-known that it is impossible to simultaneously satisfy both statistical hiding and statistical binding [29,31], and such a result can also be extended to the quantum auxiliary-input setting. However, in the CRQS model, this no-go theorem does not apply.

To see why this is the case, consider an attempt to apply the argument of the no-go theorem to the CRQS model. In the CRQS model, the setup algorithm samples a hidden key $k \leftarrow \mathcal{K}_\lambda$ and sends $|\psi_k\rangle$ to the committer and receiver. Assume that the honest committer wants to commit a bit $b \in \{0,1\}$. On input the CRQS, $|\psi_k\rangle$, the committer generates a state $|\Psi(\psi_k, b)\rangle_{\mathsf{R,C}}$ over two registers R and C, and sends C to the receiver. The receiver's state is then

$$\sigma_b := \frac{1}{|\mathcal{K}_\lambda|} \sum_{k \in \mathcal{K}_\lambda} \mathrm{Tr}_{\mathsf{R}}[|\Psi(\psi_k, b)\rangle \langle \Psi(\psi_k, b)|_{\mathsf{R,C_1}}] \otimes |\psi_k\rangle \langle \psi_k|_{\mathsf{C_2}}. \quad (1)$$

Assume that the commitment scheme satisfies statistical hiding. Then $\mathsf{TD}(\sigma_0, \sigma_1) = \mathsf{negl}(\lambda)$. However, due to Uhlmann's theorem [40], there exists a unitary on the registers that purify σ_b (in this case, the registers $\mathsf{S} \cup \mathsf{R}$ of the setup algorithm and the committer) that transforms the purified version of σ_0

$$\frac{1}{\sqrt{|\mathcal{K}_\lambda|}} \sum_{k \in \mathcal{K}_\lambda} |k\rangle_{\mathsf{S}} \otimes |\Psi(\psi_k, 0)\rangle_{\mathsf{R,C_1}} \otimes |\psi_k\rangle_{\mathsf{C_2}} \quad (2)$$

to a state that is negligibly close to a purified version of σ_1. However, notice that unlike in the plain model, this does not necessarily mean that the unbounded committer can break binding, because the committer does not have access to the register S. In other words, the committer does not have the ability to modify the classical key sampled by the setup algorithm. It is for this reason that the prohibition against statistically binding, statistically hiding commitments fails to hold in this setting.

Applications in the CRQS Model. Finally, we argue applications of our quantum commitments in the CRQS model. We observe that we can simply

---

[19] Note that we should use $2m(t+1)$-wise independent function instead of $2mt$ since we need to also consider one copy of the CRQS that is used by the honest committer.

plug our scheme into the compiler of [2] to obtain an OT in the CRQS model. We remark that we can apply this compiler unlike in the quantum auxiliary-input setting because the CRQS $|\psi_k\rangle$ is efficiently generatable given the classical key k, which can be generated by the simulator itself.

1.3 Concurrent Work

Qian [38] concurrently and independently shows similar results to ours. In particular, he also gives unconditionally secure quantum auxiliary-input commitments and quantum commitments in the CRQS model (with stateful setup) using our terminology. As additional results that are not present in our work, he also discusses how to generate the quantum auxiliary-input by exponential-time pre-processing and shows a barrier for constructing a classical analog.

After exchanging our manuscripts and having some discussions, he came up with an idea of achieving ϵ-simulation security using the compiler of [2]. This is presented in [38, Appendix B].

2 Preliminaries

2.1 Basic Notations

We use standard notations of quantum computing and cryptography. λ is the security parameter. negl is a negligible function. poly is a polynomial. For any set A, $x \leftarrow A$ means that an element x of A is sampled from A uniformly at random. For any algorithm A, $y \leftarrow A(x)$ means that the algorithm A outputs y on input x. For sets $\mathcal{X}$ and $\mathcal{Y}$, $\mathsf{Func}(\mathcal{X}, \mathcal{Y})$ is the set consisting of the all functions from $\mathcal{X}$ to $\mathcal{Y}$. $|\pm\rangle$ means $\frac{1}{\sqrt{2}}(|0\rangle \pm |1\rangle)$. For the notational simplicity, we often omit the normalization factor of quantum states. (For example, we often denote $\frac{1}{\sqrt{2}}(|0\rangle + |1\rangle)$ by $|0\rangle + |1\rangle$.) For any quantum state $\rho_{\mathsf{A},\mathsf{B}}$ over the registers A and B, $\mathrm{Tr}_\mathsf{A}(\rho_{\mathsf{A},\mathsf{B}})$ is the partial trace over the register A. For any quantum states ρ and σ, $F(\rho, \sigma) := \left(\mathrm{Tr}\sqrt{\sqrt{\sigma}\rho\sqrt{\sigma}}\right)^2$ is the fidelity, and $\mathsf{TD}(\rho, \sigma) := \frac{1}{2}\|\rho - \sigma\|_1$ is the trace distance. For a pure state $|\psi\rangle$, we write $\| |\psi\rangle \|$ to mean the Euclidean norm of $|\psi\rangle$. $I := |0\rangle\langle 0| + |1\rangle\langle 1|$ is the two-dimensional identity operator. For simplicity, we often write $I^{\otimes m}$ just as I when the dimension is clear from the context. We write QPT to mean quantum polynomial time. A non-uniform QPT algorithm $\mathcal{A}$ is specified by a family $\{\mathcal{A}_\lambda, \rho_\lambda\}_{\lambda \in \mathbb{N}}$ where $\mathcal{A}_\lambda$ and ρ_λ are a quantum circuit of size $\mathrm{poly}(\lambda)$ and quantum advice of size $\mathrm{poly}(\lambda)$ that are used when the input length is λ, respectively.

2.2 Lemmas

We review several lemmas that are proven in existing works.

It is known that random oracles work as pseudorandom generators (PRGs) against adversaries that make quantum queries and take quantum advice.

Lemma 2.1 ([28]). *Let N, M, T, and S be positive integers. Let $\{\sigma_H\}_H$ be a family of S-qubit states indexed by $H : [N] \to [M]$. For any oracle-aided algorithm $\mathcal{A}$ that makes at most T quantum queries to H, it holds that*

$$\left|\Pr[1 \leftarrow \mathcal{A}^H(\sigma_H, y_0)] - \Pr[1 \leftarrow \mathcal{A}^H(\sigma_H, y_1)]\right| \leq 8\sqrt{2} \cdot \min_{\gamma > 0} \left\{ \left(\frac{S(T+1)}{\gamma N} + \frac{T^2}{N}\right)^{\frac{1}{2}} + \gamma \right\}$$

where $H \leftarrow \mathsf{Func}([N], [M])$, $x \leftarrow [N]$, $y_0 := H(x)$, and $y_1 \leftarrow [M]$.

Corollary 2.1. *Let N, M, and S be positive integers. Let $\{\sigma_H\}_H$ be a family of S-qubit states indexed by $H : [N] \to [M]$. For any algorithm $\mathcal{A}$ that does not make any query, it holds that*

$$\left|\Pr[1 \leftarrow \mathcal{A}(\sigma_H, y_0)] - \Pr[1 \leftarrow \mathcal{A}(\sigma_H, y_1)]\right| \leq 16\sqrt{2} \cdot \left(\frac{S}{N}\right)^{\frac{1}{3}}$$

where $H \leftarrow \mathsf{Func}([N], [M])$, $x \leftarrow [N]$, $y_0 := H(x)$, and $y_1 \leftarrow [M]$.

Proof. Set $T := 0$ and $\gamma := \left(\frac{S}{N}\right)^{\frac{1}{3}}$ in Lemma 2.1. □

It is known that $2q$-wise independent functions are indistinguishable from random functions by at most q quantum queries.

Lemma 2.2 ([47]). *For any sets $\mathcal{X}$ and $\mathcal{Y}$ of classical strings and q-quantum-query algorithm $\mathcal{A}$, we have*

$$\Pr[1 \leftarrow \mathcal{A}^H : H \leftarrow \mathsf{Func}(\mathcal{X}, \mathcal{Y})] = \Pr[1 \leftarrow \mathcal{A}^H : H \leftarrow \mathcal{H}_{2q}]$$

where $\mathcal{H}_{2q}$ is a family of $2q$-wise independent functions from $\mathcal{X}$ to $\mathcal{Y}$.

Lemma 2.3 (rm [18, Lemma 2]). *Let ρ be a quantum state over m registers $\mathsf{A}_1, ..., \mathsf{A}_m$. Let σ be a quantum state over m registers $\mathsf{B}_1, ..., \mathsf{B}_m$. Let us consider the following test.*

1. *For each $i \in [m]$, do the SWAP test[20] between A_i and B_i.*
2. *Accept if all SWAP tests are successful.*

Then the probability that the above test accepts is $\frac{1}{2^m} \sum_{S \subseteq [m]} \mathrm{Tr}[\rho_S \sigma_S]$, where ρ_S is the state obtained by tracing out all A_i of ρ such that $i \notin S$, and σ_S is the state obtained by tracing out all B_i of σ such that $i \notin S$.

Lemma 2.4 ([44, Lemma 31]). *Let $|\psi_0\rangle_{\mathsf{X},\mathsf{Y}}$ and $|\psi_1\rangle_{\mathsf{X},\mathsf{Y}}$ be pure states over registers (X, Y) such that*

$$F(\mathrm{Tr}_\mathsf{Y}(|\psi_0\rangle\langle\psi_0|_{\mathsf{X},\mathsf{Y}}), \mathrm{Tr}_\mathsf{Y}(|\psi_1\rangle\langle\psi_1|_{\mathsf{X},\mathsf{Y}})) = \epsilon.$$

---

[20] The SWAP test for two states ρ_0 and ρ_1 is the following algorithm: On input $|+\rangle\langle+| \otimes \rho_0 \otimes \rho_1$, apply the controlled-SWAP gate so that the first qubit is the controlled qubit, and then measure the first qubit in the Hadamard basis. If the output is $|+\rangle$, the test is successful.

Then there is a projective measurement $\{\Pi_0, \Pi_1, \Pi_\perp := I - \Pi_0 - \Pi_1\}$ over register X such that for each $b \in \{0,1\}$,

$$\left\|(\Pi_{b\mathsf{X}} \otimes I_\mathsf{Y})|\psi_b\rangle_{\mathsf{X},\mathsf{Y}}\right\|^2 \geq 1 - \sqrt{2\epsilon}.$$

Lemma 2.5 ([39, Lemma 4]). *Let ρ and σ be any possibly subnormalized density operators. Then it holds that*

$$\mathsf{TD}(\rho, \sigma) = \max_{\Pi} \mathrm{Tr}(\Pi(\rho - \sigma)) - \frac{\mathrm{Tr}(\rho - \sigma)}{2}$$

where the maximum is taken over all projections Π.

3 Post-quantum Sparse Pseudorandom Distributions

Goldreich and Krawczyk [15] introduced the notion of sparse pseudorandom distributions. A sparse pseudorandom distribution is a distribution supported by a sparse subset but looks uniformly random against non-uniform classical polynomial-time distinguishers. They showed that sparse pseudorandom distributions unconditionally exist. Here, we introduce its *post-quantum* version where the distribution looks uniformly random even against non-uniform QPT distinguishers. Then we show that post-quantum sparse pseudorandom distributions also exist unconditionally.

Definition 3.1 (Post-quantum sparse pseudorandom distributions). *We say that an ensemble $\{D_\lambda\}_{\lambda \in \mathbb{N}}$ of probabilistic distributions where D_λ is a distribution on $\{0,1\}^\lambda$ is a post-quantum sparse pseudorandom distribution if the following hold:*

Sparseness: D_λ *is sparse, i.e.,* $\frac{|\mathsf{supp}(D_\lambda)|}{2^\lambda} = \mathsf{negl}(\lambda)$.
(Non-uniform) post-quantum pseudorandomness: $\{D_\lambda\}_{n \in \mathbb{N}}$ *is computationally indistinguishable from the uniform distribution for non-uniform QPT distinguishers. That is, for any non-uniform QPT distinguisher $\{\mathcal{A}_\lambda, \rho_\lambda\}_{\lambda \in \mathbb{N}}$,*

$$\left|\Pr_{y_\lambda \leftarrow D_\lambda}[\mathcal{A}_\lambda(\rho_\lambda, y_\lambda) = 1] - \Pr_{y'_\lambda \leftarrow \{0,1\}^\lambda}[\mathcal{A}_\lambda(\rho_\lambda, y'_\lambda) = 1]\right| = \mathsf{negl}(\lambda).$$

Theorem 3.1. *There exist post-quantum sparse pseudorandom distributions.*

Proof. For any ensemble $\mathcal{H} := \{H_\lambda\}_{\lambda \in \mathbb{N}}$ of functions $H_\lambda : \{0,1\}^{\lfloor \lambda/2 \rfloor} \to \{0,1\}^\lambda$, let $D_\mathcal{H} := \{D_{\mathcal{H},\lambda}\}_{\lambda \in \mathbb{N}}$ where $D_{\mathcal{H},\lambda}$ is the distribution of $H_\lambda(x)$ for $x \leftarrow \{0,1\}^{\lfloor \lambda/2 \rfloor}$. Since the image size of H_λ is at most $2^{\lfloor \lambda/2 \rfloor}$, $D_\mathcal{H}$ is an ensemble of sparse distributions for all $\mathcal{H}$. For completing the proof, it suffices to prove that there exists $\mathcal{H}$ such that $D_\mathcal{H}$ is pseudorandom. For each $\lambda \in \mathbb{N}$, function $H_\lambda : \{0,1\}^{\lfloor \lambda/2 \rfloor} \to \{0,1\}^\lambda$, and a quantum distinguisher $\mathcal{A}_\lambda$ with quantum advice ρ_λ, let $\mathsf{Adv}[H_\lambda, \mathcal{A}_\lambda, \rho_\lambda]$ be the distinguisher's advantage, i.e.,

$$\mathsf{Adv}[H_\lambda, \mathcal{A}_\lambda, \rho_\lambda] := \left|\Pr_{x_\lambda \leftarrow \{0,1\}^{\lfloor \lambda/2 \rfloor}}[\mathcal{A}_\lambda(\rho_\lambda, H_\lambda(x_\lambda)) = 1] - \Pr_{y_\lambda \leftarrow \{0,1\}^\lambda}[\mathcal{A}_\lambda(\rho_\lambda, y_\lambda) = 1]\right|.$$

For each $\lambda \in \mathbb{N}$, let $\mathcal{S}_\lambda$ be the set consisting of all tuples $(\mathcal{A}_\lambda, \rho_\lambda)$ of a distinguisher and its quantum advice such that the sum of the description size of $\mathcal{A}_\lambda$ (as a bit string) and the length of ρ_λ is at most $2^{\lambda/4}$. For each $\lambda \in \mathbb{N}$, let H_λ^* be the "most pseudorandom" function against distinguishers in $\mathcal{S}_\lambda$, i.e.,

$$H_\lambda^* := \operatorname*{argmin}_{H_\lambda} \max_{(\mathcal{A}_\lambda, \rho_\lambda) \in \mathcal{S}_\lambda} \mathsf{Adv}[H_\lambda, \mathcal{A}_\lambda, \rho_\lambda],$$

where argmin is taken over $H_\lambda \in \mathsf{Func}(\{0,1\}^{\lfloor \lambda/2 \rfloor}, \{0,1\}^\lambda)$ and let

$$\epsilon^*(\lambda) := \max_{(\mathcal{A}_\lambda, \rho_\lambda) \in \mathcal{S}_\lambda} \mathsf{Adv}[H_\lambda^*, \mathcal{A}_\lambda, \rho_\lambda].$$

Below, we prove that $\epsilon^*(\lambda) = \mathsf{negl}(\lambda)$. If this is proven, it is easy to see that $D_{\mathcal{H}^*}$ for $\mathcal{H}^* := \{H_\lambda^*\}_{\lambda \in \mathbb{N}}$ is pseudorandom noting that for any non-uniform QPT distinguisher $\{\mathcal{A}_\lambda, \rho_\lambda\}_{\lambda \in \mathbb{N}}$, we have $(\mathcal{A}_\lambda, \rho_\lambda) \in \mathcal{S}_\lambda$ for sufficiently large λ. Thus, we are left to prove $\epsilon^*(\lambda) = \mathsf{negl}(\lambda)$.

By the definitions of H_λ^* and $\epsilon^*(\lambda)$, for any function $H_\lambda \in \mathsf{Func}(\{0,1\}^{\lfloor \lambda/2 \rfloor}, \{0,1\}^\lambda)$, there is $(\mathcal{A}_{H_\lambda}, \rho_{H_\lambda}) \in \mathcal{S}_\lambda$ such that

$$\mathsf{Adv}[H_\lambda, \mathcal{A}_{H_\lambda}, \rho_{H_\lambda}] \geq \epsilon^*(\lambda). \tag{3}$$

For each λ, we consider an algorithm $\mathcal{B}_\lambda$ and a family $\{\sigma_{H_\lambda}\}_{H_\lambda}$ of quantum advice indexed by functions $H_\lambda : \{0,1\}^{\lfloor \lambda/2 \rfloor} \to \{0,1\}^\lambda$ that tries to break the inequality of Corollary 2.1 for $N = 2^{\lfloor \lambda/2 \rfloor}$ and $M = 2^\lambda$ as follows.[21]

- The advice σ_{H_λ} is defined to be a tuple of $(\mathcal{A}_{H_\lambda}, \rho_{H_\lambda})$ and an additional bit b that takes 0 if $\Pr_{x_\lambda \leftarrow \{0,1\}^{\lfloor \lambda/2 \rfloor}}[\mathcal{A}_\lambda(\rho_\lambda, H_\lambda(x_\lambda)) = 1] - \Pr_{y_\lambda \leftarrow \{0,1\}^\lambda}[\mathcal{A}_\lambda(\rho_\lambda, y_\lambda) = 1] \geq 0$ and otherwise takes 1. Note that the size S of σ_{H_λ} is at most $2^{\lambda/4} + 1$ since $(\mathcal{A}_{H_\lambda}, \rho_{H_\lambda}) \in \mathcal{S}_\lambda$.
- $\mathcal{B}_\lambda$ takes the advice $\sigma_{H_\lambda} = (\mathcal{A}_{H_\lambda}, \rho_{H_\lambda})$ and an input $y \in \{0,1\}^\lambda$, which is $y = H_\lambda(x)$ for $x \leftarrow \{0,1\}^{\lfloor \lambda/2 \rfloor}$ or uniformly sampled from $\{0,1\}^\lambda$, and runs $\mathcal{A}_{H_\lambda}$ on advice ρ_{H_λ} and input y. If $b = 0$, $\mathcal{B}_\lambda$ outputs whatever $\mathcal{A}_{H_\lambda}$ outputs and if $b = 1$, $\mathcal{B}_\lambda$ flips the output of $\mathcal{A}_{H_\lambda}$ and outputs it.

It is easy to see that $\mathcal{B}_\lambda$'s distinguishing advantage between the two cases is

$$\mathop{\mathbb{E}}_{H_\lambda} [\mathsf{Adv}[H_\lambda, \mathcal{A}_{H_\lambda}, \rho_{H_\lambda}]] \geq \epsilon^*(\lambda)$$

where the inequality holds because Eq. (3) holds for all H_λ. On the other hand, Corollary 2.1 implies that the distinguishing advantage is at most $16\sqrt{2}\left(\frac{S}{N}\right)$, which is negligible in λ. This implies that $\epsilon^*(\lambda)$ is negligible in λ. □

Remark 3.1. It was pointed out by Fermi Ma that an alternative conceptually simpler proof of Theorem 3.1 with a better bound is possible using the matrix Chernoff bound based on a similar idea to that used in [30, Section 2.2].

---

[21] We identify $[N]$ (resp. $[M]$) with $\{0,1\}^{\lfloor \lambda/2 \rfloor}$ (resp. $\{0,1\}^\lambda$) in a natural way.

4 Quantum Auxiliary-Input EFI Pairs

Brakerski, Canetti, and Qian [5] introduced the notion of EFI pairs as a pair of two mixed states that are efficiently generatable, statistically far, and computationally indistinguishable. Here, we consider its quantum auxiliary-input version where the efficiently generatable requirement is omitted. We show that post-quantum sparse pseudorandom distributions imply quantum auxiliary-input EFI pairs. From Theorem 3.1, it means that quantum auxiliary-input EFI pairs unconditionally exist.

Definition 4.1 (Quantum auxiliary-input EFI pairs). *A quantum auxiliary-input EFI pair is a family $\{\xi_{\lambda,b}\}_{\lambda \in \mathbb{N}, b \in \{0,1\}}$ of (mixed) states that satisfies the following:*

Polynomial size: For each $b \in \{0,1\}$, $\xi_{\lambda,b}$ is a $\mathrm{poly}(\lambda)$-qubit state.
Statistically far: $\mathsf{TD}(\xi_{\lambda,0}, \xi_{\lambda,1}) = 1 - \mathsf{negl}(\lambda)$.
Computational indistinguishability: $\xi_{\lambda,0}$ and $\xi_{\lambda,1}$ are computationally indistinguishable against non-uniform QPT distinguishers. That is, for any non-uniform QPT distinguisher $\{\mathcal{A}_\lambda, \rho_\lambda\}_{\lambda \in \mathbb{N}}$,

$$|\Pr[\mathcal{A}_\lambda(\rho_\lambda, \xi_{\lambda,0}) = 1] - \Pr[\mathcal{A}_\lambda(\rho_\lambda, \xi_{\lambda,1}) = 1]| = \mathsf{negl}(\lambda).$$

Remark 4.1. In the original definition of EFI pairs in [5], the statistically far property only requires that $\mathsf{TD}(\xi_{\lambda,0}, \xi_{\lambda,1}) = 1/\mathrm{poly}(\lambda)$. However, this can be generically amplified to $1 - \mathsf{negl}(\lambda)$ by parallel repetition while preserving the computational indistinguishability. We note that we can use a hybrid argument to show that parallel repetition preserves computational indistinguishability even though $\xi_{\lambda,b}$ is not efficiently generatable since we require computational indistinguishability against non-uniform distinguishes with quantum advice.

Theorem 4.1. *Quantum auxiliary-input EFI pairs exist.*

Proof. Let $\{D_\lambda\}_{\lambda \in \mathbb{N}}$ be a post-quantum sparse pseudorandom distribution, which exists by Theorem 3.1. We define

$$\xi_{\lambda,0} := \sum_{y \in \{0,1\}^\lambda} D_\lambda(y) |y\rangle \langle y|$$

$$\xi_{\lambda,1} := \sum_{y \in \{0,1\}^\lambda} 2^{-\lambda} |y\rangle \langle y|.$$

They satisfy the polynomial size property since they are λ-qubit states. To see the statistically far property, consider the following unbounded-size distinguisher: Given $\xi_{\lambda,0}$ or $\xi_{\lambda,1}$, measure the state in the computational basis and output 0 if the measurement outcome belongs to $|\mathsf{supp}(D_\lambda)|$ and otherwise outputs 1. We can see that its distinguishing advantage is $1 - \frac{|\mathsf{supp}(D_\lambda)|}{2^\lambda} = 1 - \mathsf{negl}(\lambda)$ by the sparseness of $\{D_\lambda\}_{\lambda \in \mathbb{N}}$. This implies $\mathsf{TD}(\xi_{\lambda,0}, \xi_{\lambda,1}) = 1 - \mathsf{negl}(\lambda)$. Finally, computational indistinguishability immediately follows from post-quantum pseudorandomness of $\{D_\lambda\}_{\lambda \in \mathbb{N}}$. □

5 Quantum Auxiliary-Input Commitments

In this section, we define quantum auxiliary-input commitments following [7], and construct it without relying on any assumption.

5.1 Definition

We define quantum auxiliary-input commitments following [7].

Definition 5.1 (Quantum auxiliary-input commitments [7]). *A (non-interactive) quantum auxiliary-input commitment scheme is given by a tuple of QPT algorithms C (a committer), R (a receiver), and a family $\{|\psi_\lambda\rangle\}_{\lambda \in \mathbb{N}}$ of poly(λ)-qubit states (referred to as quantum auxiliary inputs). The scheme is divided into the following three phases, the quantum auxiliary-input phase, the commit phase, and the reveal phase.*

- **Quantum auxiliary-input phase:** *For the security parameter λ, a single copy of $|\psi_\lambda\rangle$ is sent to C, and a single copy of $|\psi_\lambda\rangle$ is sent to R.*
- **Commit phase:** *C takes a bit $b \in \{0,1\}$ to commit (and $|\psi_\lambda\rangle$ given in the first phase) as input, generates a quantum state on registers C and R, and sends the register C to R.*
- **Reveal phase:** *C sends b and the register R to R. R takes (b, C, R) given by C (and $|\psi_\lambda\rangle$ given in the first phase) as input, and outputs b if it accepts and otherwise outputs $\bot$.*

As correctness, we require that R accepts with probability 1 if the protocol is run honestly.

Below, we define security of quantum auxiliary-input commitments. First, we define hiding and sum-binding following [7].

Definition 5.2 (Hiding). *A quantum auxiliary-input commitment scheme $(C, R, \{|\psi_\lambda\rangle\}_{\lambda \in \mathbb{N}})$ satisfies statistical (resp. computational) hiding if for any non-uniform unbounded-time (resp. QPT) algorithm $\{\mathcal{A}_\lambda, \rho_\lambda\}_{\lambda \in \mathbb{N}}$,*

$$|\Pr[1 \leftarrow \mathcal{A}_\lambda(\rho_\lambda, \mathrm{Tr}_\mathsf{R}(\sigma_{\mathsf{C},\mathsf{R}})) : \sigma_{\mathsf{C},\mathsf{R}} \leftarrow C_\mathsf{com}(|\psi_\lambda\rangle, 0)] - $$
$$\Pr[1 \leftarrow \mathcal{A}_\lambda(\rho_\lambda, \mathrm{Tr}_\mathsf{R}(\sigma_{\mathsf{C},\mathsf{R}})) : \sigma_{\mathsf{C},\mathsf{R}} \leftarrow C_\mathsf{com}(|\psi_\lambda\rangle, 1)]| \leq \mathsf{negl}(\lambda)$$

where C_com is the commit phase of C.

Remark 5.1. In the above definition, we do not explicitly include $|\psi_\lambda\rangle$ as input to $\mathcal{A}_\lambda$. However, it holds even if $\mathcal{A}_\lambda$ is given polynomially many copies of $|\psi_\lambda\rangle$ since they could have been included in the quantum advice ρ_λ.

Definition 5.3 (Sum-binding). *A quantum auxiliary-input commitment scheme $(C, R, \{|\psi_\lambda\rangle\}_{\lambda \in \mathbb{N}})$ satisfies statistical (resp. computational) sum-binding if the following holds. For any pair of non-uniform unbounded-time (resp. QPT) malicious committers C_0^* and C_1^* that take $|\psi_\lambda\rangle$ as a quantum auxiliary input* and work in the same way in the commit phase, if we let p_b to be the probability that R accepts the revealed bit b in the interaction with C_b^* for $b \in \{0, 1\}$, then we have

$$p_0 + p_1 \leq 1 + \mathsf{negl}(\lambda).$$

While the sum-binding is the notion used in the previous work [7], we introduce a stronger definition which we call extractor-based binding inspired by [1]. The motivation of introducing this definition is that it is more suitable for applications like zero-knowledge proofs.

Definition 5.4 (Extractor-based binding). *A quantum auxiliary-input commitment scheme $(C, R, \{|\psi_\lambda\rangle\}_{\lambda \in \mathbb{N}})$ satisfies statistical (computational) extractor-based binding if there is a non-uniform unbounded-time algorithm $\mathcal{E} = \{\mathcal{E}_\lambda\}_{\lambda \in \mathbb{N}}$ (called the extractor) such that for any non-uniform unbounded-time (resp. QPT) malicious committer C^*, $\mathsf{Real}_\lambda^{C^*}$ and $\mathsf{Ideal}_\lambda^{C^*, \mathcal{E}}$ are indistinguishable against non-uniform unbounded-time (resp. QPT) distinguishers where the experiments $\mathsf{Real}_\lambda^{C^*}$ and $\mathsf{Ideal}_\lambda^{C^*, \mathcal{E}}$ are defined as follows.*

- *$\mathsf{Real}_\lambda^{C^*}$: The malicious committer C^* takes $|\psi_\lambda\rangle$ as input, and interacts with the honest receiver R in the commit and reveal phases. Let $b \in \{0, 1, \bot\}$ be the output of R and τ_{C^*} be the final state of C^*. The experiment outputs a tuple (τ_{C^*}, b).*
- *$\mathsf{Ideal}_\lambda^{C^*, \mathcal{E}}$: C^* takes $|\psi_\lambda\rangle$ as input, and runs its commit phase to generate a commitment σ_C where C^* may keep a state that is entangled with σ_C. $\mathcal{E}_\lambda$ takes the register C as input, outputs an extracted bit $b^* \in \{0, 1\}$, and sends a post-execution state on C (that may be different from the original one) to R as a commitment. Then C^* and R run the reveal phase. Let b be the output of R and τ_{C^*} be the final state of C^*. If $b \notin \{\bot, b^*\}$, then the experiment outputs a special symbol $\mathtt{fail}$ and otherwise outputs a tuple (τ_{C^*}, b).*

We can easily see the following lemma.

Lemma 5.1. *Statistical (resp. computational) extractor-based binding implies statistical (resp. computational) sum-binding.*

Proof. Suppose that there are non-uniform unbounded-time (resp. QPT) malicious committers C_0^* and C_1^* that break statistical (resp. computational) sum-binding. This implies that

$$\Pr[b_0 = 0 : (\tau_{C_0^*}, b_0) \leftarrow \mathsf{Real}_\lambda^{C_0^*}] + \Pr[b_1 = 1 : (\tau_{C_1^*}, b_1) \leftarrow \mathsf{Real}_\lambda^{C_1^*}] - 1$$

is non-negligible. Here, C_0^* and C_1^* work in the same way in the commit phase. By statistical (resp. computational) extractor-based binding, the above implies that

$$\Pr[b_0 = 0 : (\tau_{C_0^*}, b_0) \leftarrow \mathsf{Ideal}_\lambda^{C_0^*, \mathcal{E}}] + \Pr[b_1 = 1 : (\tau_{C_1^*}, b_1) \leftarrow \mathsf{Ideal}_\lambda^{C_1^*, \mathcal{E}}] - 1 \quad (4)$$

is non-negligible. However, since C_0^* and C_1^* share the same commit phase and the extracted bit b^* only depends on the commit phase, we clearly have

$$\Pr[b_0 = 0 : (\tau_{C_0^*}, b_0) \leftarrow \mathsf{Ideal}_\lambda^{C_0^*, \mathcal{E}}] + \Pr[b_1 = 1 : (\tau_{C_1^*}, b_1) \leftarrow \mathsf{Ideal}_\lambda^{C_1^*, \mathcal{E}}] \leq 1.$$

This contradicts the fact that Eq. (4) is non-neglibible. Thus, statistical (resp. computational) sum-binding is satisfied. □

5.2 Construction

We show that quantum auxiliary-input commitments can be constructed without any assumption.

Let $\{\xi_{\lambda,b}\}_{\lambda \in \mathbb{N}, b \in \{0,1\}}$ be a quantum auxiliary-input EFI pair, which exists unconditionally. Let $|\psi_{\lambda,b}\rangle_{\mathsf{X},\mathsf{Y}}$ be a purification of $\xi_{\lambda,b}$ such that $\mathrm{Tr}_{\mathsf{Y}}(|\psi_{\lambda,b}\rangle \langle \psi_{\lambda,b}|_{\mathsf{X},\mathsf{Y}}) = \xi_{\lambda,b}$. Then we construct a quantum auxiliary-input commitment scheme as follows where $m = \lambda$.[22]

- **Quantum auxiliary-input phase:** For security parameter $\lambda \in \mathbb{N}$, define the quantum auxiliary input $|\psi_\lambda\rangle := |\psi_{\lambda,0}\rangle^{\otimes m} \otimes |\psi_{\lambda,1}\rangle^{\otimes m}$. One single copy of $|\psi_\lambda\rangle$ is sent to C and the other single copy of $|\psi_\lambda\rangle$ is sent to R.
- **Commit phase:** C takes a bit $b \in \{0, 1\}$ to commit (and the quantum auxiliary input $|\psi_\lambda\rangle$ given in the first phase) as input. C sends the register C of $|\psi_{\lambda,b}\rangle^{\otimes m}_{\mathsf{C},\mathsf{R}}$ to R, where $\mathsf{C} := (\mathsf{X}_1, ..., \mathsf{X}_m)$ and $\mathsf{R} := (\mathsf{Y}_1, ..., \mathsf{Y}_m)$.[23]
- **Reveal phase:** C sends b and the register R to R. In the first phase, R received $|\psi_\lambda\rangle$. R uses only $|\psi_{\lambda,b}\rangle^{\otimes m}_{\mathsf{C}',\mathsf{R}'}$, where $\mathsf{C}' := (\mathsf{X}'_1, ..., \mathsf{X}'_m)$ and $\mathsf{R}' := (\mathsf{Y}'_1, ..., \mathsf{Y}'_m)$. For each $i \in [m]$, R runs the SWAP test between registers $(\mathsf{X}_i, \mathsf{Y}_i)$ and $(\mathsf{X}'_i, \mathsf{Y}'_i)$. If all of the tests accept, R accepts by outputting b and otherwise rejects by outputting $\bot$.

If the protocol is run honestly, the registers $(\mathsf{X}_i, \mathsf{Y}_i)$ and $(\mathsf{X}'_i, \mathsf{Y}'_i)$ take exactly the same state $|\psi_{\lambda,b}\rangle$ for all $i \in [m]$. Thus, R accepts with probability 1 and thus correctness holds.

Theorem 5.1. *The above protocol satisfies computational hiding and statistical extractor-based binding.*

Proof.
Computational hiding. It immediately follows from computational indistinguishability of the quantum auxiliary-input EFI pair.

Statistical Extractor-Based Binding. Since $\mathsf{TD}(\xi_{\lambda,0}, \xi_{\lambda,1}) = 1 - \mathsf{negl}(\lambda)$ we have $F(\xi_{\lambda,0}, \xi_{\lambda,1}) = \mathsf{negl}(\lambda)$. Let $\epsilon := F(\xi_{\lambda,0}, \xi_{\lambda,1})$. Then Lemma 2.4 implies that there is a projective measuremt $\{\Pi_0, \Pi_1, \Pi_\bot = I - \Pi_0 - \Pi_1\}$ on register X such that for each $b \in \{0, 1\}$, it holds that

$$\|(I - \Pi_b)|\psi_{\lambda,b}\rangle\|^2 \leq \sqrt{2\epsilon}. \tag{5}$$

---
[22] In fact, it suffices to set $m = \omega(\log \lambda)$.
[23] Here, the X (Y) register of the ith $|\psi_{\lambda,b}\rangle$ of $|\psi_{\lambda,b}\rangle^{\otimes m}$ is set to X_i (Y_i).

Here, we simply write Π_b to mean $\Pi_{b\mathsf{X}} \otimes I_\mathsf{Y}$ for simplicity.

The extractor $\mathcal{E}_\lambda$ is described as follows: Upon receiving the commitment register $\mathsf{C} = (\mathsf{X}_1, ..., \mathsf{X}_m)$, for each $i \in [m]$, it applies the projective measurement $\{\Pi_0, \Pi_1, \Pi_\perp\}$ on X_i to obtain an outcome $b_i \in \{0, 1, \perp\}$.

- If $|\{i \in [m] : b_i = 0\}| > 2m/3$, it outputs $b^* = 0$.
- If $|\{i \in [m] : b_i = 1\}| > 2m/3$, it outputs $b^* = 1$.
- Otherwise, it outputs $b^* = \perp$.

By using an additional ancilla register E, we can describe the extractor $\mathcal{E}_\lambda$ as a projective measurement $\{\widetilde{\Pi}_0, \widetilde{\Pi}_1, \widetilde{\Pi}_\perp\}$ over registers C and E, i.e., they are defined in such a way that running $\mathcal{E}_\lambda$ on ρ_C is equivalent to applying the projective measurement $\{\widetilde{\Pi}_0, \widetilde{\Pi}_1, \widetilde{\Pi}_\perp\}$ on $\rho_\mathsf{C} \otimes |0...0\rangle\langle 0...0|_\mathsf{E}$ for any state ρ_C.

For $b \in \{0, 1\}$, let P_b be the projector corresponding to the purified verification procedure by the receiver R. That is, it is defined so that R is described as follows: Upon receiving the quantum auxiliary input $|\psi_{\lambda,b}\rangle^{\otimes m}_{\mathsf{Aux}'}$ where $\mathsf{Aux}' := \{\mathsf{X}'_i, \mathsf{Y}'_i\}_{i \in [m]}$ and $(b, \mathsf{C}, \mathsf{R})$ from the committer, R initializes its ancilla register V to $|0...0\rangle_\mathsf{V}$, applies the projective measurement $(P_b, I - P_b)$ on registers $(\mathsf{Aux}', \mathsf{C}, \mathsf{R}, \mathsf{V})$, and accepts (i.e., outputs b) if the measurement outcome is P_b (i.e., the state is projected onto the image of P_b) and otherwise rejects (i.e., outputs $\perp$).

Let C^* be an unbounded-time malicious committer. By using the above notations, we can describe the experiments $\mathsf{Real}^{C^*}_\lambda$ and $\mathsf{Ideal}^{C^*,\mathcal{E}}_\lambda$ in the following form where we highlight the differences in red bold texts:

$\mathsf{Real}^{C^*}_\lambda$:
1. C^* takes the quantum auxiliary input $|\psi_\lambda\rangle$ as input and generates a state $|\phi_b\rangle$ over registers $(\mathsf{C}, \mathsf{R}, \mathsf{W})$ along with a bit $b \in \{0, 1\}$ where W is the internal register of C^*.[24]
2. C^* sends C to R.
3. C^* sends (b, R) to R.
4. R runs the verification in the reveal phase. That is, R takes the quantum auxiliary input $|\psi_{\lambda,b}\rangle^{\otimes m}_{\mathsf{Aux}'}$, $(b, \mathsf{C}, \mathsf{R})$ sent from C^*, and the ancilla qubits $|0...0\rangle_\mathsf{V}$, applies the projective measurement $(P_b, I - P_b)$ on registers $(\mathsf{Aux}', \mathsf{C}, \mathsf{R}, \mathsf{V})$.
5. If R rejects (i.e., the measurement results in projection onto the image of $I - P_b$), b is replaced by $\perp$.
6. The experiment outputs (b, W).

$\mathsf{Ideal}^{C^*,\mathcal{E}}_\lambda$:
1. C^* takes the quantum auxiliary input $|\psi_\lambda\rangle$ as input and generates a state $|\phi_b\rangle$ over registers $(\mathsf{C}, \mathsf{R}, \mathsf{W})$ along with a bit $b \in \{0, 1\}$ where W is the internal register of C^*.

---

[24] It may be possible that C^* generates b after applying some unitary in the reveal phase. However, since it does not receive anything between the commit and reveal phases, we can assume that C^* does not apply any unitary between the two phases without loss of generality.

2. C^* sends C to R.
3. The extractor $\mathcal{E}_\lambda$ prepares the ancilla qubits $|0...0\rangle_\mathsf{E}$, applies the projective measurement $\{\widetilde{\Pi}_0, \widetilde{\Pi}_1, \widetilde{\Pi}_\perp\}$ on registers C and E, lets $b^* \in \{0, 1, \perp\}$ be the outcome, and sends C to R.
4. C^* sends (b, R) to R.
5. R runs the verification in the reveal phase. That is, R takes the quantum auxiliary input $|\psi_{\lambda,b}\rangle_{\mathsf{Aux}'}^{\otimes m}$, $(b, \mathsf{C}, \mathsf{R})$ sent from C^* and $\mathcal{E}$, and the ancilla qubits $|0...0\rangle_\mathsf{V}$, applies the projective measurement $(P_b, I - P_b)$ on registers (Aux', C, R, V).
6. If R accepts (i.e., the measurement results in projection onto the image of P_b) and $b \neq b^*$, the experiment outputs the special symbol fail and halts.
7. If R rejects (i.e., the measurement results in projection onto the image of $I - P_b$), b is replaced by $\perp$.
8. The experiment outputs (b, W).

The rest of the proof is similar to [44, Appendix B] where it is proven that canonical quantum bit commitments satisfy the extractor-based binding property defined in [1]. We define density operators $\rho_\mathsf{real}(b)$ and $\rho_\mathsf{ideal}(b)$ that correspond to the outputs of $\mathsf{Real}_\lambda^{C^*}$ and $\mathsf{Ideal}_\lambda^{C^*, \mathcal{E}}$ conditioned on the bit sent from C^* being b, respectively. That is, we let

$$\rho_\mathsf{real}(b) := \mathrm{Tr}_{\mathsf{Aux}', \mathsf{C}, \mathsf{R}, \mathsf{V}, \mathsf{E}}(P_b |\widetilde{\phi}_b\rangle \langle \widetilde{\phi}_b|) \otimes |b\rangle \langle b| + \mathrm{Tr}_{\mathsf{Aux}', \mathsf{C}, \mathsf{R}, \mathsf{V}, \mathsf{E}}((I - P_b) |\widetilde{\phi}_b\rangle \langle \widetilde{\phi}_b|) \otimes |\perp\rangle \langle \perp|$$

and

$$\rho_\mathsf{ideal}(b) := \mathrm{Tr}_{\mathsf{Aux}', \mathsf{C}, \mathsf{R}, \mathsf{V}, \mathsf{E}}(N_b |\widetilde{\phi}_b\rangle \langle \widetilde{\phi}_b|) \otimes |b\rangle \langle b| + \mathrm{Tr}_{\mathsf{Aux}', \mathsf{C}, \mathsf{R}, \mathsf{V}, \mathsf{E}}(N_\perp |\widetilde{\phi}_b\rangle \langle \widetilde{\phi}_b|) \otimes |\perp\rangle \langle \perp|$$
$$+ \mathrm{Tr}_{\mathsf{Aux}', \mathsf{C}, \mathsf{R}, \mathsf{V}, \mathsf{E}}(N_\mathtt{fail} |\widetilde{\phi}_b\rangle \langle \widetilde{\phi}_b|) \otimes |\mathtt{fail}\rangle \langle \mathtt{fail}|$$

where

$$|\widetilde{\phi}_b\rangle := |\phi_b\rangle_{\mathsf{C}, \mathsf{R}, \mathsf{W}} \otimes |\psi_{\lambda, b}\rangle_{\mathsf{Aux}'}^{\otimes m} \otimes |0...0\rangle_\mathsf{V} \otimes |0...0\rangle_\mathsf{E}$$

and

$$N_b := \widetilde{\Pi}_b P_b \widetilde{\Pi}_b, \quad N_\mathtt{fail} := (I - \widetilde{\Pi}_b) P_b (I - \widetilde{\Pi}_b), \quad N_\perp := I - N_b - N_\mathtt{fail}.$$

We note that $N_\mathtt{fail}$ and $N_\perp$ depend on b, but we omit the dependence for simplicity. Noting that the distribution of b is identical in the both experiments, it suffices to prove

$$\mathsf{TD}(\rho_\mathsf{real}(b), \rho_\mathsf{ideal}(b)) = \mathsf{negl}(\lambda)$$

for $b \in \{0, 1\}$. We show the following lemma.

Lemma 5.2. *For each $b \in \{0, 1\}$, it holds that*

$$\|P_b(I - \widetilde{\Pi}_b) |\widetilde{\phi}_b\rangle\|^2 = \mathsf{negl}(\lambda).$$

Proof of Lemma 5.2. By the definitions of P_b and $|\widetilde{\phi}_b\rangle$, $\|P_b(I - \widetilde{\Pi}_b)|\widetilde{\phi}_b\rangle\|^2$ is the probability that $\rho := \text{Tr}_{W,E}\left((I - \widetilde{\Pi}_b)_{C,E}|\phi_b\rangle_{C,R,W}|0...0\rangle_E\right)$ passes the verification by R with respect to the committed bit b.[25] By Lemma 2.3, it is equal to

$$\frac{1}{2^m}\sum_{S\subseteq[m]}\text{Tr}(\rho_S\sigma_S)$$

where $\sigma := \bigotimes_{i\in[m]}|\psi_{\lambda,b}\rangle\langle\psi_{\lambda,b}|_{X_i,Y_i}$. Here, ρ_S and σ_S are the states obtained by tracing out all (X_i, Y_i) such that $i \notin S$.[26] By the definition of $\widetilde{\Pi}_b$, we can write[27]

$$\rho = \sum_{T\subseteq[m]:|T|\leq 2m/3}\text{Tr}_W \hat{\Pi}_b^{(T)}|\phi_b\rangle\langle\phi_b|\hat{\Pi}_b^{(T)} \tag{6}$$

where

$$\hat{\Pi}_b^{(T)} := \left(\bigotimes_{i\in T}\Pi_{b X_i}\right) \otimes \left(\bigotimes_{i\in[m]\setminus T}(I - \Pi_b)_{X_i}\right).$$

Thus, we have

$$\frac{1}{2^m}\sum_{S\subseteq[m]}\text{Tr}(\rho_S\sigma_S) = \frac{1}{2^m}\sum_{S\subseteq[m]}\sum_{\substack{T\subseteq[m]\\|T|\leq 2m/3}}\text{Tr}\left(\left(\text{Tr}_{(\cdot)_{i\notin S}}\hat{\Pi}_b^{(T)}|\phi_b\rangle\langle\phi_b|\hat{\Pi}_b^{(T)}\right)\left(\bigotimes_{i\in S}|\psi_{\lambda,b}\rangle\langle\psi_{\lambda,b}|_{\cdot,\cdot}\right)\right).$$

For any S and T, we have

$$\text{Tr}\left(\left(\text{Tr}_{(\cdot)_{i\notin S}}\hat{\Pi}_b^{(T)}|\phi_b\rangle\langle\phi_b|\hat{\Pi}_b^{(T)}\right)\left(\bigotimes_{i\in S}|\psi_{\lambda,b}\rangle\langle\psi_{\lambda,b}|_{\cdot,\cdot}\right)\right)$$

$$= \text{Tr}\left((I - \Pi_b)_{(\cdot)_{i\in S\setminus T}}^{\otimes |S\setminus T|}\left(\text{Tr}_{(\cdot)_{i\notin S}}\hat{\Pi}_b^{(T)}|\phi_b\rangle\langle\phi_b|\hat{\Pi}_b^{(T)}\right)(I - \Pi_b)_{(\cdot)_{i\in S\setminus T}}^{\otimes |S\setminus T|}\left(\bigotimes_{i\in S}|\psi_{\lambda,b}\rangle\langle\psi_{\lambda,b}|_{\cdot,\cdot}\right)\right)$$

$$= \text{Tr}\left(\left(\text{Tr}_{(\cdot)_{i\notin S}}\hat{\Pi}_b^{(T)}|\phi_b\rangle\langle\phi_b|\hat{\Pi}_b^{(T)}\right)(I - \Pi_b)_{(\cdot)_{i\in S\setminus T}}^{\otimes |S\setminus T|}\left(\bigotimes_{i\in S}|\psi_{\lambda,b}\rangle\langle\psi_{\lambda,b}|_{\cdot,\cdot}\right)(I - \Pi_b)_{(\cdot)_{i\in S\setminus T}}^{\otimes |S\setminus T|}\right)$$

$$\leq \|\hat{\Pi}_b^{(T)}|\phi_b\rangle\|^2 \cdot \text{Tr}\left((I - \Pi_b)_{(\cdot)_{i\in S\setminus T}}^{\otimes |S\setminus T|}\left(\bigotimes_{i\in S}|\psi_{\lambda,b}\rangle\langle\psi_{\lambda,b}|_{\cdot,\cdot}\right)(I - \Pi_b)_{(\cdot)_{i\in S\setminus T}}^{\otimes |S\setminus T|}\right)$$

---

[25] Precisely speaking, it is not correct because ρ is not a state (it is not normalized). However, we believe the abuse of terminology will not cause any confusion.

[26] Again, ρ_S is not a state because it is not normalized.

[27] The purified extractor is assumed to work as follows. It "coherently measures" $\{\Pi_0, \Pi_1, \Pi_\perp\}$ on each X_i and writes the result $b_1\|...\|b_m$ on an ancilla register. Depending on the value on the ancilla register, 0, 1, or $\perp$ is written in another ancilla register. Finally the second register is measured in the computational basis. If we trace out those two registers, we get Equation (6) as the (sub-normalized) post-measurement state.

$$\leq \left\| \hat{\Pi}_b^{(T)} |\phi_b\rangle \right\|^2 \cdot \left\| (I - \Pi_b) |\psi_{\lambda,b}\rangle \right\|^{2|S\setminus T|}$$

$$\leq \left\| \hat{\Pi}_b^{(T)} |\phi_b\rangle \right\|^2 \cdot (2\epsilon)^{|S\setminus T|}$$

where the first inequality follows from $\mathrm{Tr}_{\{X_i,Y_i\}_{i\notin S},\mathsf{W}} \hat{\Pi}_b^{(T)} |\phi_b\rangle \langle \phi_b| \hat{\Pi}_b^{(T)} \leq \left\| \hat{\Pi}_b^{(T)} |\phi_b\rangle \right\|^2 \cdot I$ and the final inequality follows from Eq. (5).

Thus, for any T such that $|T| \leq 2m/3$, we have

$$\frac{1}{2^m} \sum_{S \subseteq [m]} \mathrm{Tr}\left(\left(\mathrm{Tr}_{\{X_i,Y_i\}_{i\notin S},\mathsf{W}} \hat{\Pi}_b^{(T)} |\phi_b\rangle \langle \phi_b| \hat{\Pi}_b^{(T)}\right) \left(\bigotimes_{i\in S} |\psi_{\lambda,b}\rangle \langle \psi_{\lambda,b}|_{X_i,Y_i}\right)\right)$$

$$\leq \frac{1}{2^m} \sum_{S \subseteq [m]} \left\| \hat{\Pi}_b^{(T)} |\phi_b\rangle \right\|^2 \cdot (2\epsilon)^{|S\setminus T|}$$

$$\leq \left\| \hat{\Pi}_b^{(T)} |\phi_b\rangle \right\|^2 \cdot \frac{1}{2^m} \left(\sum_{S\subseteq[m]:S\subseteq T} 1 + \sum_{S\subseteq[m]:S\not\subseteq T} 2\epsilon \right)$$

$$\leq \left\| \hat{\Pi}_b^{(T)} |\phi_b\rangle \right\|^2 \cdot \left(2^{-m/3} + 2\epsilon \right)$$

where the final inequality follows from $|\{S \subseteq [m] : S \subseteq T\}| = 2^{|T|} \leq 2^{2m/3}$ and $|\{S \subseteq [m] : S \not\subseteq T\}| \leq 2^m$.

Therefore, we have

$$\frac{1}{2^m} \sum_{S \subseteq [m]} \mathrm{Tr}(\rho_S \sigma_S) \leq \sum_{T\subseteq[m]:|T|\leq 2m/3} \left\| \hat{\Pi}_b^{(T)} |\phi_b\rangle \right\|^2 \cdot \left(2^{-m/3} + 2\epsilon\right)$$

$$\leq 2^{-m/3} + 2\epsilon \leq \mathsf{negl}(\lambda)$$

where the final inequality follows from $m = \omega(\log \lambda)$ and $\epsilon = \mathsf{negl}(\lambda)$. This completes the proof of Lemma 5.2. □

We define

$$\tau_{\mathsf{real}}^{(b)} := \mathrm{Tr}_{\mathsf{Aux}',\mathsf{C},\mathsf{R},\mathsf{V},\mathsf{E}}(P_b |\widetilde{\phi}_b\rangle \langle \widetilde{\phi}_b|), \quad \tau_{\mathsf{real}}^{(\bot)} := \mathrm{Tr}_{\mathsf{Aux}',\mathsf{C},\mathsf{R},\mathsf{V},\mathsf{E}}((I-P_b) |\widetilde{\phi}_b\rangle \langle \widetilde{\phi}_b|),$$

$$\tau_{\mathsf{ideal}}^{(b)} := \mathrm{Tr}_{\mathsf{Aux}',\mathsf{C},\mathsf{R},\mathsf{V},\mathsf{E}}(N_b |\widetilde{\phi}_b\rangle \langle \widetilde{\phi}_b|), \quad \tau_{\mathsf{ideal}}^{(\bot)} := \mathrm{Tr}_{\mathsf{Aux}',\mathsf{C},\mathsf{R},\mathsf{V},\mathsf{E}}(N_\bot |\widetilde{\phi}_b\rangle \langle \widetilde{\phi}_b|),$$

$$\tau_{\mathsf{ideal}}^{(\mathtt{fail})} := \mathrm{Tr}_{\mathsf{Aux}',\mathsf{C},\mathsf{R},\mathsf{V},\mathsf{E}}(N_{\mathtt{fail}} |\widetilde{\phi}_b\rangle \langle \widetilde{\phi}_b|)$$

so that we can write

$$\rho_{\mathsf{real}}(b) = \tau_{\mathsf{real}}^{(b)} \otimes |b\rangle\langle b| + \tau_{\mathsf{real}}^{(\bot)} \otimes |\bot\rangle\langle\bot| \qquad (7)$$

and

$$\rho_{\mathsf{ideal}}(b) = \tau_{\mathsf{ideal}}^{(b)} \otimes |b\rangle\langle b| + \tau_{\mathsf{ideal}}^{(\bot)} \otimes |\bot\rangle\langle\bot| + \tau_{\mathsf{ideal}}^{(\mathtt{fail})} \otimes |\mathtt{fail}\rangle\langle\mathtt{fail}|. \qquad (8)$$

Then we use Lemma 5.2 to show the following lemma.

Lemma 5.3. *For each $b \in \{0,1\}$, the following hold:*

1. $\text{Tr}(\tau_{\text{ideal}}^{(\text{fail})}) = \text{negl}(\lambda)$.
2. $\text{TD}(\tau_{\text{real}}^{(b)}, \tau_{\text{ideal}}^{(b)}) = \text{negl}(\lambda)$.
3. $\text{TD}(\tau_{\text{real}}^{(\perp)}, \tau_{\text{ideal}}^{(\perp)}) = \text{negl}(\lambda)$.

Proof of Lemma 5.3.

First item. We have
$$\text{Tr}(\tau_{\text{ideal}}^{(\text{fail})}) = \text{Tr}(N_{\text{fail}} |\widetilde{\phi}_b\rangle \langle\widetilde{\phi}_b|) = \langle\widetilde{\phi}_b| (I - \widetilde{\Pi}_b) P_b (I - \widetilde{\Pi}_b) |\widetilde{\phi}_b\rangle = \| P_b (I - \widetilde{\Pi}_b) |\widetilde{\phi}_b\rangle \|^2 = \text{negl}(\lambda)$$
where the final equality follows from Lemma 5.2.

Second item. We have
$$\text{TD}(\tau_{\text{real}}^{(b)}, \tau_{\text{ideal}}^{(b)}) \leq \text{TD}(P_b |\widetilde{\phi}_b\rangle, P_b \widetilde{\Pi}_b |\widetilde{\phi}_b\rangle)$$
$$= \max_Q \text{Tr}\left(Q\left(P_b |\widetilde{\phi}_b\rangle \langle\widetilde{\phi}_b| P_b - P_b \widetilde{\Pi}_b |\widetilde{\phi}_b\rangle \langle\widetilde{\phi}_b| \widetilde{\Pi}_b P_b\right)\right)$$
$$- \frac{1}{2}\left(\text{Tr}(P_b |\widetilde{\phi}_b\rangle \langle\widetilde{\phi}_b| P_b) - \text{Tr}(P_b \widetilde{\Pi}_b |\widetilde{\phi}_b\rangle \langle\widetilde{\phi}_b| \widetilde{\Pi}_b P_b)\right)$$
$$= \max_Q \left(\| Q P_b |\widetilde{\phi}_b\rangle \|^2 - \| Q P_b \widetilde{\Pi}_b |\widetilde{\phi}_b\rangle \|^2\right) - \frac{1}{2}\left(\| P_b |\widetilde{\phi}_b\rangle \|^2 - \| P_b \widetilde{\Pi}_b |\widetilde{\phi}_b\rangle \|^2\right),$$

where the maximum is taken over all projectors Q on $(\mathsf{W}, \mathsf{Aux}', \mathsf{C}, \mathsf{R}, \mathsf{V}, \mathsf{E})$, the first inequality follows from the monotonicity of the trace norm, and the first equality follows from Lemma 2.5. For any projector Q, we have

$$\left|\| Q P_b |\widetilde{\phi}_b\rangle \|^2 - \| Q P_b \widetilde{\Pi}_b |\widetilde{\phi}_b\rangle \|^2\right| = \left|\| Q P_b (\widetilde{\Pi}_b + (I - \widetilde{\Pi}_b)) |\widetilde{\phi}_b\rangle \|^2 - \| Q P_b \widetilde{\Pi}_b |\widetilde{\phi}_b\rangle \|^2\right|$$
$$= |\langle\widetilde{\phi}_b| (I - \widetilde{\Pi}_b) P_b Q P_b (\widetilde{\Pi}_b + (I - \widetilde{\Pi}_b)) |\widetilde{\phi}_b\rangle + \langle\widetilde{\phi}_b| \widetilde{\Pi}_b P_b Q P_b (I - \widetilde{\Pi}_b) |\widetilde{\phi}_b\rangle|$$
$$\leq \| P_b (I - \widetilde{\Pi}_b) |\widetilde{\phi}_b\rangle \| \cdot \| Q P_b (\widetilde{\Pi}_b + (I - \widetilde{\Pi}_b)) |\widetilde{\phi}_b\rangle \|$$
$$+ \| Q P_b \widetilde{\Pi}_b |\widetilde{\phi}_b\rangle \| \cdot \| P_b (I - \widetilde{\Pi}_b) |\widetilde{\phi}_b\rangle \|$$
$$\leq 2 \| P_b (I - \widetilde{\Pi}_b) |\widetilde{\phi}_b\rangle \| = \text{negl}(\lambda)$$

where the final equality follows from Lemma 5.2. In particular, the above also holds for the case of $Q = I$. Combining the above, we have $\text{TD}(\tau_{\text{real}}^{(b)}, \tau_{\text{ideal}}^{(b)}) = \text{negl}(\lambda)$.

Third item.
$$\text{TD}(\tau_{\text{real}}^{(\perp)}, \tau_{\text{ideal}}^{(\perp)}) = \text{TD}\left(\text{Tr}_{\mathsf{Aux}',\mathsf{C},\mathsf{R},\mathsf{V},\mathsf{E}}((I - P_b) |\widetilde{\phi}_b\rangle \langle\widetilde{\phi}_b|), \text{Tr}_{\mathsf{Aux}',\mathsf{C},\mathsf{R},\mathsf{V},\mathsf{E}}((I - N_b - N_{\text{fail}}) |\widetilde{\phi}_b\rangle \langle\widetilde{\phi}_b|)\right)$$
$$= \text{TD}\left(\text{Tr}_{\mathsf{Aux}',\mathsf{C},\mathsf{R},\mathsf{V},\mathsf{E}}(P_b |\widetilde{\phi}_b\rangle \langle\widetilde{\phi}_b|), \text{Tr}_{\mathsf{Aux}',\mathsf{C},\mathsf{R},\mathsf{V},\mathsf{E}}((N_b + N_{\text{fail}}) |\widetilde{\phi}_b\rangle \langle\widetilde{\phi}_b|)\right)$$
$$\leq \text{TD}\left(\text{Tr}_{\mathsf{Aux}',\mathsf{C},\mathsf{R},\mathsf{V},\mathsf{E}}(P_b |\widetilde{\phi}_b\rangle \langle\widetilde{\phi}_b|), \text{Tr}_{\mathsf{Aux}',\mathsf{C},\mathsf{R},\mathsf{V},\mathsf{E}}(N_b |\widetilde{\phi}_b\rangle \langle\widetilde{\phi}_b|)\right) + \frac{1}{2}\text{Tr}(N_{\text{fail}} |\widetilde{\phi}_b\rangle \langle\widetilde{\phi}_b|)$$
$$= \text{negl}(\lambda)$$

where we have used the triangle inequality in the third line, and the first and second items of this lemma in the final line. This completes the proof of Lemma 5.3. □

By Eqs. (7) and (8), we have

$$\mathsf{TD}(\rho_{\mathsf{real}}(b), \rho_{\mathsf{ideal}}(b)) = \mathsf{TD}(\tau_{\mathsf{real}}^{(b)}, \tau_{\mathsf{real}}^{(b)}) + \mathsf{TD}(\tau_{\mathsf{real}}^{(\bot)}, \tau_{\mathsf{ideal}}^{(\bot)}) + \frac{1}{2}\mathrm{Tr}(\tau_{\mathsf{ideal}}^{(\mathtt{fail})}) = \mathsf{negl}(\lambda)$$

where the final equality follows from Lemma 5.3. This implies statistical binding and completes the proof of Theorem 5.1. □

5.3 Impossibility of Statistical Security

It is easy to prove that achieving both statistical hiding and statistical (sum)-binding is impossible even in the quantum auxiliary-input setting based on the similar impossibility result in the plain model [29,31].

Theorem 5.2. *There do not exist statistically hiding and statistically sum-binding quantum auxiliary-input commitments.*

Proof sketch. Given a quantum auxiliary-input commitment scheme, we can regard the classical description of the quantum auxiliary-input as a classical auxiliary-input if we allow the sender and receiver to be unbounded-time. Since the impossibility of [29,31] is applicable to classical auxiliary-input quantum commitments with unbounded-time sender and receiver, the theorem follows. More concretely, assume that the honest committer generates $|\Psi(\psi_\lambda, b)\rangle_{\mathsf{R,C}}$ over two registers R and C to commit to $b \in \{0,1\}$ given the quantum auxiliary input $|\psi_\lambda\rangle$. Due to the statistical hiding, $\mathrm{Tr}_{\mathsf{R}}(|\Psi(\psi_\lambda, 0)\rangle_{\mathsf{R,C}})$ should be negligibly close to $\mathrm{Tr}_{\mathsf{R}}(|\Psi(\psi_\lambda, 1)\rangle_{\mathsf{R,C}})$. However, it means, from the Uhlmann's theorem, that there exists a unitary U on R that maps $|\Psi(\psi_\lambda, 0)\rangle_{\mathsf{R,C}}$ to a state that is negligibly close to $|\Psi(\psi_\lambda, 1)\rangle_{\mathsf{R,C}}$, which breaks the statistical binding. □

Thus, it is necessary to relax either of hiding or binding to the computational one. In Theorem 5.1, we unconditionally construct a computationally hiding and statistically binding construction. On the other hand, we do not know how to construct statistically hiding and computationally binding one without assuming any assumption. We remark that it is unclear if the flavor conversion theorems in the plain model [10,20,45] work in the quantum auxiliary-input setting.

5.4 Application to Zero-Knowledge Proofs

To demonstrate the applicability of our quantum auxiliary-input commitments, in the full version of this paper [32], we show an application to zero-knowledge proofs. We use quantum auxiliary-input commitments to instantiate Blum's Hamiltonicity protocol [3], yielding an unconditional construction of computational zero-knowledge proofs for **NP** with soundness error $1/2$ in the quantum auxiliary-input setting. See the full version [32] for details.

6 Commitments in the Common Reference Quantum State Model

In this section, we introduce quantum commitments in the common reference quanutm state (CRQS) model and construct them unconditionally. Unlike the quantum auxiliary-input setting, our construction in the CRQS model satisfies both statistical hiding and statistical binding as long as the number of copies of the CRQS given to the malicious receiver is bounded.

6.1 Definition

Definition 6.1 (Quantum commitments in the CRQS model). *A (non-interactive) quantum commitment scheme in the CRQS model is given by a tuple of the setup algorithm* Setup, *committer* C, *and receiver* R, *all of which are uniform QPT algorithms. The scheme is divided into three phases, the setup phase, commit phase, and reveal phase as follows:*

- **Setup phase:** Setup *takes* 1^λ *as input, uniformly samples a classical key* $k \leftarrow \mathcal{K}_\lambda$, *generates two copies of the same pure state* $|\psi_k\rangle$ *and sends one copy each to* C *and* R.
- **Commit phase:** C *takes* $|\psi_k\rangle$ *given by the setup algorithm and a bit* $b \in \{0, 1\}$ *to commit as input, generates a quantum state on registers* C *and* R, *and sends the register* C *to* R.
- **Reveal phase:** C *sends* b *and the register* R *to* R. R *takes* $|\psi_k\rangle$ *given by the setup algorithm and* $(b, \mathsf{C}, \mathsf{R})$ *given by* C *as input, and outputs* b *if it accepts and otherwise outputs* $\perp$.

As correctness, we require that R *accepts with probability* 1 *if the protocol is run honestly.*

Below, we define security of commitments in the CRQS model. For the definition of hiding, even though the honest receiver takes only one copy of the CRQS, we consider hiding against adversaries that take many copies of the CRQS. This is to capture the scenario where an authority distributes many copies of the CRQS and the adversary collects some of them.

Definition 6.2 (t-copy statistical hiding). *A quantum commitment scheme* (Setup, C, R) *in the CQRS model satisfies t-copy statistical hiding if for any non-uniform unbounded-time algorithm* $\mathcal{A}$,

$$\left| \Pr[1 \leftarrow \mathcal{A}(1^\lambda, |\psi_k\rangle^{\otimes t}, \text{Tr}_\mathsf{R}(\sigma_{\mathsf{C},\mathsf{R}})) : k \leftarrow \mathcal{K}_\lambda, \sigma_{\mathsf{C},\mathsf{R}} \leftarrow C_{\mathsf{com}}(|\psi_k\rangle, 0)] - \right.$$
$$\left. \Pr[1 \leftarrow \mathcal{A}(1^\lambda, |\psi_k\rangle^{\otimes t}, \text{Tr}_\mathsf{R}(\sigma_{\mathsf{C},\mathsf{R}})) : k \leftarrow \mathcal{K}_\lambda, \sigma_{\mathsf{C},\mathsf{R}} \leftarrow C_{\mathsf{com}}(|\psi_k\rangle, 1)] \right| \leq \mathsf{negl}(\lambda)$$

where C_{com} *is the commit phase of* C.

Similarly to the quantum auxiliary-input setting, we define two notions of binding, sum-binding and extractor-based binding. We stress that we require those to hold against adversaries who know the classical key k instead of having copies of $|\psi_k\rangle$ unlike the hiding property. This only makes the security stronger.

Definition 6.3 (Statistical sum-binding). *A quantum commitment scheme* (Setup, C, R) *in the CQRS model satisfies statistical sum-binding if the following holds. For any pair of non-uniform unbounded-time malicious committers C_0^* and C_1^* that take the classical key k, which is sampled by the setup algorithm, as input and work in the same way in the commit phase, if we let p_b to be the probability that R accepts the revealed bit b in the interaction with C_b^* for $b \in \{0, 1\}$, then we have*

$$p_0 + p_1 \leq 1 + \mathsf{negl}(\lambda).$$

Definition 6.4 (Extractor-based binding). *A quantum commitment scheme* (Setup, C, R) *in the CQRS model satisfies statistical (computational) extractor-based binding if there is a (uniform) unbounded-time algorithm $\mathcal{E}$ (called the extractor) such that for any non-uniform unbounded-time (resp. QPT) malicious committer C^*, $\mathsf{Real}_\lambda^{C^*}$ and $\mathsf{Ideal}_\lambda^{C^*, \mathcal{E}}$ are indistinguishable against non-uniform unbounded-time (resp. QPT) distinguishers where the experiments $\mathsf{Real}_\lambda^{C^*}$ and $\mathsf{Ideal}_\lambda^{C^*, \mathcal{E}}$ are defined as follows.*

- $\mathsf{Real}_\lambda^{C^*}$: *The experiment chooses $k \leftarrow \mathcal{K}_\lambda$ and sends k and $|\psi_k\rangle$ to C^* and R, respectively. The malicious committer C^* interacts with the honest receiver R in the commit and reveal phases. Let $b \in \{0, 1, \bot\}$ be the output of R and τ_{C^*} be the final state of C^*. The experiment outputs a tuple (τ_{C^*}, b).*
- $\mathsf{Ideal}_\lambda^{C^*, \mathcal{E}}$: *The experiment chooses $k \leftarrow \mathcal{K}_\lambda$ and sends k and $|\psi_k\rangle$ to C^* and R, respectively. The experiment also sends k to the extractor $\mathcal{E}$ The malicious committer C^* runs its commit phase to generate a commitment σ_C where C^* may keep a state that is entangled with σ_C. $\mathcal{E}$ takes the register C, outputs an extracted bit $b^* \in \{0, 1\}$, and sends a post-execution state on C (that may be different from the original one) to R as a commitment. Then C^* and R run the reveal phase. Let b be the output of R and τ_{C^*} be the final state of C^*. If $b \notin \{\bot, b^*\}$, then the experiment outputs a special symbol* `fail` *and otherwise outputs a tuple (τ_{C^*}, b).*

Remark 6.1. Differently from the definition for quantum auxiliary-input commitments, we require the extractor to be *uniform* unbounded-time algorithm that takes the classical key k as input. This is useful for constructing uniform simulators in the applications.

Lemma 6.1. *Statistical (resp. computational) extractor-based binding implies statistical (resp. computational) sum-binding.*

Since the above lemma can be proven similarly to that in the quantum auxiliary-input setting (Lemma 5.1), we omit the proof.

6.2 Construction

We construct a commitment scheme in the CRQS model as follows. Let $m := \lambda^{28}$ and $\mathcal{H}_\lambda := \{H_k : \{0,1\}^\lambda \to \{0,1\}^{2\lambda}\}_{k \in \mathcal{K}_\lambda}$ be a family of $2m(t+1)$-wise independent functions. Then our construction is described below.

---
[28] In fact, it suffices to set $m = \omega(\log \lambda)$.

- **Setup phase:** Setup takes 1^λ as input and does the following. It samples $k \leftarrow \mathcal{K}_\lambda$ and generates $2m$ copies of the following states:[29]

$$|\psi_{k,0}\rangle := \frac{1}{2^{\lambda/2}} \sum_{x \in \{0,1\}^\lambda} |H_k(x)\rangle |x\|0^\lambda\rangle, \quad |\psi_{k,1}\rangle := \frac{1}{2^\lambda} \sum_{y \in \{0,1\}^{2\lambda}} |y\rangle |y\rangle.$$

Then it defines $|\psi_k\rangle := |\psi_{k,0}\rangle^{\otimes m} \otimes |\psi_{k,1}\rangle^{\otimes m}$. A single copy of $|\psi_k\rangle$ is sent to C, and a single copy of $|\psi_k\rangle$ is sent to R.
- **Commit phase:** C takes quantum auxiliary input $|\psi_k\rangle = |\psi_{k,0}\rangle^{\otimes m} \otimes |\psi_{k,1}\rangle^{\otimes m}$ and a bit $b \in \{0,1\}$ to commit as input. For each $i \in [m]$, let X_i and Y_i be the first and second registers of the i-th copy of $|\psi_{k,b}\rangle$, respectively. Set $\mathsf{C} := (\mathsf{X}_1, ..., \mathsf{X}_m)$ and $\mathsf{R} := (\mathsf{Y}_1, ..., \mathsf{Y}_m)$ and sends the register C to R.
- **Reveal phase:** C sends b and the register $\mathsf{R} := (\mathsf{Y}_1, ..., \mathsf{Y}_m)$ to R. For each $i \in [m]$, let X'_i and Y'_i be the first and second registers of the i-th copy of $|\psi_{k,b}\rangle$, respectively. For each $i \in [m]$, R runs the SWAP test between registers $(\mathsf{X}_i, \mathsf{Y}_i)$ and $(\mathsf{X}'_i, \mathsf{Y}'_i)$. If all of the tests accept, R accepts by outputting b and otherwise rejects by outputting $\bot$.

If the protocol is run honestly, the registers $(\mathsf{X}_i, \mathsf{Y}_i)$ and $(\mathsf{X}'_i, \mathsf{Y}'_i)$ take exactly the same state $|\psi_{k,b}\rangle$. Thus, R accepts with probability 1 and thus correctness holds.

Theorem 6.1. *The above protocol satisfies t-copy statistical hiding and statistical extractor-based binding.*

Proof of Theorem 6.1.
t-copy statistical hiding. Note that we can generate $|\psi_{k,0}\rangle$ by a single quantum oracle access to H_k and $|\psi_{k,1}\rangle$ does not depend on H_k. Thus, we can generate $|\psi_k\rangle = |\psi_{k,0}\rangle^{\otimes m} \otimes |\psi_{k,1}\rangle^{\otimes m}$ by m quantum oracle access to H_k. In the t-copy hiding experiment, $(t+1)$ copies of $|\psi_k\rangle$ (including the one used by the honest committer) are used. Since $(t+1)$ copies of $|\psi_k\rangle$ can be generated by $m(t+1)$ quantum oracle access to H_k, and H_k is chosen from a family of $2m(t+1)$-wise independent functions, Lemma 2.2 implies that the adversary's advantage in the t-copy hiding experiment does not change even if we replace H_k with a uniformly random function H. After this replacement, the t-copy statistical hiding is shown by a direct reduction to Corollary 2.1 via a hybrid argument where t copies of the quantum auxiliary input given to the adversary are regarded as σ_H in Corollary 2.1.

---

[29] The state $|\psi_{k,1}\rangle$ does not depend on k, but we use this notation for convenience of the presentation.

Statistical Extractor-Based Binding. Fix k, and for $y \in \{0,1\}^{2\lambda}$, let N_y be the number of $x \in \{0,1\}^\lambda$ such that $H_k(x) = y$. Then we have

$$F(\text{Tr}_\mathsf{Y}(|\psi_{k,0}\rangle\langle\psi_{k,0}|_{\mathsf{X},\mathsf{Y}}), \text{Tr}_\mathsf{Y}(|\psi_{k,1}\rangle\langle\psi_{k,1}|_{\mathsf{X},\mathsf{Y}})) = \left(\sum_{y \in \{0,1\}^{2\lambda}} \sqrt{\frac{N_y}{2^{3\lambda}}}\right)^2$$

$$= \left(\sum_{y \in \mathsf{Im}(H_k)} \sqrt{\frac{N_y}{2^{3\lambda}}}\right)^2$$

$$\leq |\mathsf{Im}(H_k)| \cdot \sum_{y \in \mathsf{Im}(H_k)} \frac{N_y}{2^{3\lambda}}$$

$$\leq \frac{1}{2^\lambda}$$

where $\mathsf{Im}(H_k)$ denotes the image of H_k, the first inequality follows from the Cauchy-Schwarz inequality, and the second inequality follows from $|\mathsf{Im}(H_k)| \leq 2^\lambda$ and $\sum_{y \in \mathsf{Im}(H_k)} N_y = 2^\lambda$. We observe that $\text{Tr}_\mathsf{Y}(|\psi_{k,0}\rangle\langle\psi_{k,0}|)$ and $\text{Tr}_\mathsf{Y}(|\psi_{k,1}\rangle\langle\psi_{k,1}|)$ play the roles of $\xi_{\lambda,0}$ and $\xi_{\lambda,1}$ in the construction in Sect. 5.2 and the only assumption needed for proving statistical extractor-based binding there was $F(\xi_{\lambda,0}, \xi_{\lambda,1}) = \mathsf{negl}(\lambda)$. Thus, the rest of the proof is almost identical to that in the quantum auxiliary-input setting (Theorem 5.1) noting that we can implement the extractor $\mathcal{E}$ by a *uniform* unbounded-time algorithm given k. Thus, we omit the details. □

Impossibility of Unbounded-Copy Security. We have constructed a quantum commitment scheme in the CRQS model that satisfies t-copy statistical hiding and statistical extractor-based binding for any bounded polynomial t. One may wonder if this can be achieved for unbounded polynomials t. Unfortunately, it turns out this is impossible even if we relax the security of binding to the sum-binding against adversaries that receive t copies of the CRQS (instead of receiving the classical key k as in Definition 6.3). See the full version of this paper [32] for a proof of this impossibility.

Circumventing the Impossibility Using Stateful Setup. Interestingly, we can circumvent the above impossibility if we allow the setup algorithm to be stateful.[30] To see this, we first observe that if H_k is replaced with a uniformly random function from $\{0,1\}^\lambda$ to $\{0,1\}^{2\lambda}$ in the construction in Sect. 6.2, then it satisfies t-copy statistical hiding for all polynomials (or even subexponential) t. However, such a modified protocol has inefficient setup algorithm since a random function cannot be computed efficiently. A common solution in such a situation is to use pseudorandom functions, but then the hiding becomes a computational one. This is not useful for our purpose since if we can use pseudorandom functions, we could directly construct computationally hiding and statistically

---
[30] We thank Fermi Ma for suggesting this.

binding quantum commitments in the plain model. Another common method to efficiently simulating a random function is to rely on lazy-sampling, i.e., instead of sampling the whole function at the beginning, we assign the function values only on queried inputs. Recently, Zhandry [48] proposed a technique called the compressed oracle that enables us to perfectly and efficiently simulate a quantumly-accessible random oracle. Thus, if the setup algorithm uses the compressed oracle technique to simulate the random function, we can achieve t-copy statistical hiding for all polynomials t and statistical extractor-based binding simultaneously,[31] at the cost of making the setup algorithm stateful so that it can keep the quantum "database" needed for the simulation of the random oracle.

6.3 Applications of Commitments in the CRQS Model

In the plain model (where there is no CRQS), [2] constructed oblivious transfers (OTs) from any post-quantum classical commitments. [1] observed that the construction works based on any quantum commitments that satisfy a binding property they introduced.[32] Since our definition of the extractor-based binding closely follows the definition of binding in [1], we observe that we can similarly plug our commitments in the CRQS model into the compiler of [2] to obtain a statistically secure oblivious transfer in the CRQS model. Thus, we obtain the following corollary.

Corollary 6.1. *For any polynomial t, there exist t-copy statistically maliciously simulation-secure OTs in the CRQS model.*

For clarity, we describe our definition of OTs in the CRQS model in the full version of the paper [32].

Remark 6.2. One may wonder why the compiler of [2] works in the CRQS model but does not work in the quantum auxiliary-input setting as considered in Sect. 5. Roughly, this is because the CRQS can be efficiently computed given the classical key k, but there is no way to efficiently compute the quantum auxiliary input. The lack of efficient generation of the quantum auxiliary input prevents us from applying Watrous' rewinding lemma [43], which is a crucial tool in the compiler in [2].

Moreover it is known that OTs imply MPCs for classical functionalities [23] or even for quantum functionalities [12] in a black-box manner. Thus, we believe

---

[31] In the stateful setup setting, we have to slightly modify the definition of statistical extractor-based binding since the classical key k no longer appears. We allow the malicious committer and extractor to receive arbitrarily many (possibly exponential number of) copies of the CRQS. The proof still works in this setting essentially in the same way.

[32] Later, Yan [45] showed that any canonical quantum bit commitment scheme satisfies the binding property defined in [1].

that similar constructions work in the CRQS model, which would lead to statistically maliciously simulation-secure MPCs in the CRQS model. However, for formally stating it, we have to carefully reexamine these constructions to make sure that they work in the CRQS model as well. This is out of the scope of this work, and we leave it to future work.

Acknowledgments. We thank Taiga Hiroka for helpful discussions, Qipeng Liu for answering questions regarding [28], and Fermi Ma for many insightful comments including suggestion of an alternative proof of Theorem 3.1 and the idea of using the compressed oracle to achieve unbounded-copy security. We thank Luowen Qian for sharing an early draft of [38] and providing many helpful comments on our earlier draft, especially pointing out flaws in the proofs of Theorems 3.1 and 5.1. This work was done in part while T. Morimae and B. Nehoran were visiting the Simons Institute for the Theory of Computing. This work was done in part while B. Nehoran was visiting the Yukawa Institute for Theoretical Physics. TM is supported by JST CREST JPMJCR23I3, JST Moonshot R&D JPMJMS2061-5-1-1, JST FOREST, MEXT QLEAP, the Grant-in Aid for Transformative Research Areas (A) 21H05183, and the Grant-in-Aid for Scientific Research (A) No.22H00522.

Disclosure of Interests. The authors have no competing interests to declare that are relevant to the content of this article.

References

1. Ananth, P., Qian, L., Yuen, H.: Cryptography from pseudorandom quantum states. In: Dodis, Y., Shrimpton, T. (eds.) CRYPTO 2022. LNCS, vol. 13507, pp. 208–236. Springer, Heidelberg (2022). https://doi.org/10.1007/978-3-031-15802-5_8
2. Bartusek, J., Coladangelo, A., Khurana, D., Ma, F.: One-way functions imply secure computation in a quantum world. In: Malkin, T., Peikert, C. (eds.) CRYPTO 2021. LNCS, vol. 12825, pp. 467–496. Springer, Cham (2021). https://doi.org/10.1007/978-3-030-84242-0_17
3. Blum, M.: How to prove a theorem so no one else can claim it. In: International Congress of Mathematicians, pp. 1444–1451 (1987)
4. Bostanci, J., Efron, Y., Metger, T., Poremba, A., Qian, L., Yuen, H.: Unitary complexity and the uhlmann transformation problem (2023)
5. Brakerski, Z., Canetti, R., Qian, L.: On the computational hardness needed for quantum cryptography. In: ITCS 2023: 14th Innovations in Theoretical Computer Science (2023)
6. Broadbent, A., Grilo, A.B.: QMA-hardness of consistency of local density matrices with applications to quantum zero-knowledge. SIAM J. Comput. **51**(4), 1400–1450 (2022). https://doi.org/10.1137/21m140729x
7. Chailloux, A., Kerenidis, I., Rosgen, B.: Quantum commitments from complexity assumptions. Comput. Complex. **25**(1), 103–151 (2016). https://doi.org/10.1007/s00037-015-0116-5
8. Chung, K.M., Guo, S., Liu, Q., Qian, L.: Tight quantum time-space tradeoffs for function inversion. In: 61st FOCS, pp. 673–684. IEEE Computer Society Press (2020). https://doi.org/10.1109/FOCS46700.2020.00068

9. Chung, K.M., Liao, T.N., Qian, L.: Lower bounds for function inversion with quantum advice. In: Kalai, Y.T., Smith, A.D., Wichs, D. (eds.) ITC 2020, pp. 8:1–8:15. Schloss Dagstuhl (2020). https://doi.org/10.4230/LIPIcs.ITC.2020.8
10. Crépeau, C., Légaré, F., Salvail, L.: How to convert the flavor of a quantum bit commitment. In: Pfitzmann, B. (ed.) EUROCRYPT 2001. LNCS, vol. 2045, pp. 60–77. Springer, Heidelberg (2001). https://doi.org/10.1007/3-540-44987-6_5
11. Dall'Agnol, M., Spooner, N.: On the necessity of collapsing for post-quantum and quantum commitments. In: Fawzi, O., Walter, M. (eds.) 18th Conference on the Theory of Quantum Computation, Communication and Cryptography, TQC 2023, Aveiro, Portugal, 24–28 July 2023. LIPIcs, vol. 266, pp. 2:1–2:23. Schloss Dagstuhl - Leibniz-Zentrum für Informatik (2023). https://doi.org/10.4230/LIPICS.TQC.2023.2
12. Dulek, Y., Grilo, A.B., Jeffery, S., Majenz, C., Schaffner, C.: Secure multi-party quantum computation with a dishonest majority. In: Canteaut, A., Ishai, Y. (eds.) EUROCRYPT 2020. LNCS, vol. 12107, pp. 729–758. Springer, Cham (2020). https://doi.org/10.1007/978-3-030-45727-3_25
13. Dumais, P., Mayers, D., Salvail, L.: Perfectly concealing quantum bit commitment from any quantum one-way permutation. In: Preneel, B. (ed.) EUROCRYPT 2000. LNCS, vol. 1807, pp. 300–315. Springer, Heidelberg (2000). https://doi.org/10.1007/3-540-45539-6_21
14. Dupuis, F., Lamontagne, P., Salvail, L.: Fiat-shamir for proofs lacks a proof even in the presence of shared entanglement. Cryptology ePrint Archive, Paper 2022/435 (2022). https://eprint.iacr.org/2022/435
15. Goldreich, O., Krawczyk, H.: Sparse pseudorandom distributions. Rand. Struct. Algor. **3**(2), 163–174 (1992). https://doi.org/10.1002/RSA.3240030206
16. Goldwasser, S., Micali, S., Rackoff, C.: The knowledge complexity of interactive proof systems. SIAM J. Comput. **18**(1), 186–208 (1989)
17. Grilo, A.B., Lin, H., Song, F., Vaikuntanathan, V.: Oblivious transfer is in MiniQCrypt. In: Canteaut, A., Standaert, F.-X. (eds.) EUROCRYPT 2021. LNCS, vol. 12697, pp. 531–561. Springer, Cham (2021). https://doi.org/10.1007/978-3-030-77886-6_18
18. Harrow, A., Montanaro, A.: Testing product states, quantum merlin-arthur games and tensor optimization. J. ACM (2013)
19. Håstad, J., Impagliazzo, R., Levin, L.A., Luby, M.: A pseudorandom generator from any one-way function. SIAM J. Comput. **28**(4), 1364–1396 (1999). https://doi.org/10.1137/S0097539793244708
20. Hhan, M., Morimae, T., Yamakawa, T.: From the hardness of detecting superpositions to cryptography: Quantum public key encryption and commitments. In: Hazay, C., Stam, M. (eds.) EUROCRYPT 2023, Part I. LNCS, vol. 14004, pp. 639–667. Springer, Heidelberg (2023). https://doi.org/10.1007/978-3-031-30545-0_22
21. Hhan, M., Xagawa, K., Yamakawa, T.: Quantum random oracle model with auxiliary input. In: Galbraith, S.D., Moriai, S. (eds.) ASIACRYPT 2019. LNCS, vol. 11921, pp. 584–614. Springer, Cham (2019). https://doi.org/10.1007/978-3-030-34578-5_21
22. Ishai, Y., Kushilevitz, E., Meldgaard, S., Orlandi, C., Paskin-Cherniavsky, A.: On the power of correlated randomness in secure computation. In: Sahai, A. (ed.) TCC 2013. LNCS, vol. 7785, pp. 600–620. Springer, Heidelberg (2013). https://doi.org/10.1007/978-3-642-36594-2_34

23. Ishai, Y., Prabhakaran, M., Sahai, A.: Founding cryptography on oblivious transfer – efficiently. In: Wagner, D. (ed.) CRYPTO 2008. LNCS, vol. 5157, pp. 572–591. Springer, Heidelberg (2008). https://doi.org/10.1007/978-3-540-85174-5_32
24. Ji, Z., Liu, Y.-K., Song, F.: Pseudorandom quantum states. In: Shacham, H., Boldyreva, A. (eds.) CRYPTO 2018. LNCS, vol. 10993, pp. 126–152. Springer, Cham (2018). https://doi.org/10.1007/978-3-319-96878-0_5
25. Khurana, D., Tomer, K.: Commitments from quantum one-wayness. Cryptology ePrint Archive, Paper 2023/1620 (2023). https://eprint.iacr.org/2023/1620
26. Koshiba, T., Odaira, T.: Statistically-hiding quantum bit commitment from approximable-preimage-size quantum one-way function. In: Childs, A., Mosca, M. (eds.) TQC 2009. LNCS, vol. 5906, pp. 33–46. Springer, Heidelberg (2009). https://doi.org/10.1007/978-3-642-10698-9_4
27. Koshiba, T., Odaira, T.: Non-interactive statistically-hiding quantum bit commitment from any quantum one-way function. arXiv:1102.3441 (2011). https://doi.org/10.48550/ARXIV.1102.3441
28. Liu, Q.: Non-uniformity and quantum advice in the quantum random oracle model. In: Hazay, C., Stam, M. (eds.) EUROCRYPT 2023, Part I. LNCS, vol. 14004, pp. 117–143. Springer, Heidelberg (2023). https://doi.org/10.1007/978-3-031-30545-0_5
29. Lo, H.K., Chau, H.F.: Is quantum bit commitment really possible? Phys. Rev. Lett. (1997)
30. Lombardi, A., Ma, F., Wright, J.: A one-query lower bound for unitary synthesis and breaking quantum cryptography. Cryptology ePrint Archive, Paper 2023/1602 (2023). https://eprint.iacr.org/2023/1602
31. Mayers, D.: Unconditionally secure quantum bit commitment is impossible. Phys. Rev. Lett. **78**, 3414–3417 (1997)
32. Morimae, T., Nehoran, B., Yamakawa, T.: Unconditionally secure commitments with quantum auxiliary inputs. Cryptology ePrint Archive, Paper 2023/1844 (2023). https://eprint.iacr.org/2023/1844
33. Morimae, T., Yamakawa, T.: One-wayness in quantum cryptography. Cryptology ePrint Archive, Paper 2022/1336 (2022). https://eprint.iacr.org/2022/1336
34. Morimae, T., Yamakawa, T.: Quantum commitments and signatures without one-way functions. In: Dodis, Y., Shrimpton, T. (eds.) CRYPTO 2022, Part I. LNCS, vol. 13507, pp. 269–295. Springer, Heidelberg (2022). https://doi.org/10.1007/978-3-031-15802-5_10
35. Nanashima, M.: On basing auxiliary-input cryptography on NP-hardness via non-adaptive black-box reductions. In: Lee, J.R. (ed.) ITCS 2021. LIPIcs, vol. 185, pp. 29:1–29:15 (2021). https://doi.org/10.4230/LIPIcs.ITCS.2021.29
36. Naor, M.: Bit commitment using pseudorandomness. J. Cryptol. 151–158 (1991)
37. Ostrovsky, R., Wigderson, A.: One-way fuctions are essential for non-trivial zero-knowledge. In: Second Israel Symposium on Theory of Computing Systems, ISTCS 1993, Natanya, Israel, 7–9 June 1993, Proceedings, pp. 3–17. IEEE Computer Society (1993). https://doi.org/10.1109/ISTCS.1993.253489
38. Qian, L.: Unconditionally secure quantum commitments with preprocessing (2023). Private communication
39. Rastegin, A.E.: Trace distance from the viewpoint of quantum operation techniques. J. Phys. A: Math. Theor. **40**(31), 9533–9549 (2007). https://doi.org/10.1088/1751-8113/40/31/026
40. Uhlmann, A.: The "transition probability" in the state space of a *-algebra. Rep. Math. Phys. **9**(2), 273–279 (1976)

41. Unruh, D.: Computationally binding quantum commitments. In: Fischlin, M., Coron, J.-S. (eds.) EUROCRYPT 2016. LNCS, vol. 9666, pp. 497–527. Springer, Heidelberg (2016). https://doi.org/10.1007/978-3-662-49896-5_18
42. Vadhan, S.: An unconditional study of computational zero knowledge. SIAM J. Comput. **36**(4), 1160–1214 (2006)
43. Watrous, J.: Zero-knowledge against quantum attacks. SIAM J. Comput. **39**(1), 25–58 (2009)
44. Yan, J.: General properties of quantum bit commitments. Cryptology ePrint Archive, Paper 2020/1488 (2020). https://eprint.iacr.org/2020/1488
45. Yan, J.: General properties of quantum bit commitments (extended abstract). In: Agrawal, S., Lin, D. (eds.) ASIACRYPT 2022, Part IV. LNCS, vol. 13794, pp. 628–657. Springer, Heidelberg (2022). https://doi.org/10.1007/978-3-031-22972-5_22
46. Yan, J., Weng, J., Lin, D., Quan, Y.: Quantum bit commitment with application in quantum zero-knowledge proof (extended abstract). In: Elbassioni, K., Makino, K. (eds.) ISAAC 2015. LNCS, vol. 9472, pp. 555–565. Springer, Heidelberg (2015). https://doi.org/10.1007/978-3-662-48971-0_47
47. Zhandry, M.: Secure identity-based encryption in the quantum random oracle model. In: Safavi-Naini, R., Canetti, R. (eds.) CRYPTO 2012. LNCS, vol. 7417, pp. 758–775. Springer, Heidelberg (2012). https://doi.org/10.1007/978-3-642-32009-5_44
48. Zhandry, M.: New techniques for traitor tracing: size $N^{1/3}$ and more from pairings. In: Micciancio, D., Ristenpart, T. (eds.) CRYPTO 2020. LNCS, vol. 12170, pp. 652–682. Springer, Cham (2020). https://doi.org/10.1007/978-3-030-56784-2_22

Quantum Public-Key Encryption with Tamper-Resilient Public Keys from One-Way Functions

Fuyuki Kitagawa[2,3](✉), Tomoyuki Morimae[1], Ryo Nishimaki[2,3], and Takashi Yamakawa[1,2,3]

[1] Yukawa Institute for Theoretical Physics, Kyoto University, Kyoto, Japan
[2] NTT Social Informatics Laboratories, Tokyo, Japan
fuyuki.kitagawa@ntt.com
[3] NTT Research Center for Theoretical Quantum Information, Atsugi, Japan

Abstract. We construct quantum public-key encryption from one-way functions. In our construction, public keys are quantum, but ciphertexts are classical. Quantum public-key encryption from one-way functions (or weaker primitives such as pseudorandom function-like states) are also proposed in some recent works [Morimae-Yamakawa, eprint:2022/1336; Coladangelo, eprint:2023/282; Barooti-Grilo-Malavolta-Sattath-Vu-Walter, TCC 2023]. However, they have a huge drawback: they are secure only when quantum public keys can be transmitted to the sender (who runs the encryption algorithm) without being tampered with by the adversary, which seems to require unsatisfactory physical setup assumptions such as secure quantum channels. Our construction is free from such a drawback: it guarantees the secrecy of the encrypted messages even if we assume only unauthenticated quantum channels. Thus, the encryption is done with adversarially tampered quantum public keys. Our construction is the first quantum public-key encryption that achieves the goal of classical public-key encryption, namely, to establish secure communication over insecure channels, based only on one-way functions. Moreover, we show a generic compiler to upgrade security against chosen plaintext attacks (CPA security) into security against chosen ciphertext attacks (CCA security) only using one-way functions. As a result, we obtain CCA secure quantum public-key encryption based only on one-way functions.

1 Introduction

1.1 Background

Quantum physics provides several advantages in cryptography. For instance, statistically-secure key exchange, which is impossible in classical cryptography, becomes possible if quantum states are transmitted [BB84]. Additionally, oblivious transfers and multiparty computations are possible only from one-way functions (OWFs) in the quantum world [BCKM21, GLSV21]. Those cryptographic primitives are believed to require stronger structured assumptions in classical cryptography [IR89, GKM+00]. Furthermore, it has been shown that several cryptographic tasks, such as (non-interactive) commitments, digital signatures, secret-key encryption, quantum money, and multiparty computations, are possible based on new primitives such as pseudorandom states generators, pseudorandom function-like states generators, one-way states generators, and EFI, which seem to be weaker than OWFs [JLS18, Kre21, MY22b, AQY22, BCQ23, AGQY22, CX22, MY22a, KQST23].

Quantum Public Key Encryption from OWFs. Despite these developments, it is still an open problem whether public-key encryption (PKE) is possible with only OWFs (or the above weaker primitives) in the quantum world. PKE from OWFs is impossible (in a black-box way) in the classical cryptography [IR90]. However, it could be possible if quantum states are transmitted or local operations are quantum. In fact, some recent works [MY22a, Col23, BGH+23a] independently constructed quantum PKE (QPKE) with quantum public keys based on OWFs or pseudorandom function-like states generators. However, the constructions proposed in those works have a huge drawback as explained below, and thus we still do not have a satisfactory solution to the problem of "QPKE from OWFs".

How to Certify Quantum Public Keys? When we study public key cryptographic primitives, we have to care about how to certify the public keys, that is, how a sender (who encrypts messages) can check if a given public key is a valid public key under which the secrecy of the encrypted messages is guaranteed. When the public keys are classical strings, we can easily certify them using digital signature schemes. However, in the case where the public keys are quantum states, we cannot use digital signature schemes to achieve this goal in general[1], and it is unclear how to certify them.

As stated above, some recent works [MY22a, Col23, BGH+23a] realized QPKE with quantum public keys from OWFs or even weaker assumptions. However, those works did not tackle this quantum public key certification problem very much. In fact, as far as we understand, to use the primitives proposed in those works meaningfully, we need to use secure quantum channels to transmit the quantum public keys so that a sender can use an intact quantum public key. This is a huge drawback since the goal of PKE is to transmit a message *without assuming secure channels*. If the sender can establish a secure channel to obtain the quantum public key, the sender could use it to transmit the message in the first place, and there is no advantage to using the PKE scheme.

QPKE with Tamper-Resilient Quantum Public Keys. One of our goals in this work is to solve this issue and develop a more reasonable notion of QPKE with quantum public keys. Especially, we consider the setting with the following two natural conditions. First, we assume that every quantum state (that is, quantum public keys in this work) is sent via an unauthenticated channel, and thus it can be tampered with by an adversary. If we do not assume secure

---

[1] There is a general impossibility result for signing quantum states [AGM21].

quantum channels, we have to take such a tampering attack into account since authentication generally requires secrecy for quantum channels [BCG+02]. Second, we assume that every classical string is sent via an authenticated channel. This is the same assumption in classical PKE and can be achieved using digital signatures. Note that the security of the constructions proposed in the above works [MY22a, Col23, BGH+23a] is broken in this natural setting. In this work, we tackle whether we can realize QPKE with quantum public keys that provides a security guarantee in this natural setting, especially from OWFs.

1.2 Our Results

We affirmatively answer the above question. We realize the first QPKE scheme based only on OWFs that achieves the goal of classical PKE, which is to establish secure communication over insecure channels. We define the notions of QPKE that can be used in the above setting where unauthenticated quantum channels and classical authenticated channels are available. Then, we propose constructions satisfying the definitions from OWFs. Below, we state each result in detail.

Definitional Work. We redefine the syntax of QPKE. The difference from the previous definitions is that the key generation algorithm outputs a classical verification key together with the secret key. Also, this verification key is given to the encryption algorithm with a quantum public key and a message so that the encryption algorithm can check the validity of the given quantum public key. We require ciphertexts to be classical.[2] We require a QPKE scheme to satisfy the following two basic security notions.

- **Indistinguishability against public key tempering chosen plaintext attacks (IND-pkT-CPA security).** Roughly speaking, it guarantees that indistinguishability holds even if messages are encrypted by a public key tampered with by an adversary. More specifically, it guarantees that no efficient adversary can guess the challenge bit b with a probability significantly better than random guessing given $\mathsf{Enc}(\mathsf{vk},\mathsf{pk}',\mathsf{msg}_b)$, where vk is the correct verification key and $(\mathsf{pk}',\mathsf{msg}_0,\mathsf{msg}_1)$ are generated by the adversary who is given the verification key vk and multiple copies of the correctly generated quantum public keys.[3] IND-pkT-CPA security captures the setting where the classical verification key is sent via a classical authenticated channel. Thus, everyone can obtain the correct verification key. However, a quantum public key is sent via an unauthenticated quantum channel and thus can be tampered with by an adversary.

---

[2] We could also consider QPKE schemes with quantum ciphertexts if we only consider IND-pkT-CPA security. However, it is unclear how we should define IND-pkT-CCA security for such schemes because the decryption oracle cannot check if a given ciphertext is equivalent to the challenge ciphertext. Thus, we focus on schemes with classical ciphertexts in this paper.
[3] The tampered quantum public key pk' can be entangled with the adversary's internal state.

– **Decryption error detectability.** In our setting, an adversary may try to cause a decryption error by tampering with the quantum public key. To address this issue, we introduce a security notion that we call *decryption error detectability*. It roughly guarantees that a legitimate receiver of a ciphertext can notice if the decrypted message is different from the message intended by the sender.

IND-pkT-CPA security considers adversaries that may tamper with quantum public keys but only passively observe ciphertext. For classical PKE, the golden standard security notion is indistinguishability against chosen ciphertext attacks (IND-CCA security) that considers active adversaries that may see decryption results of any (possibly malformed) ciphertexts. Thus, we also define its analog for QPKE. In Sect. 1.3, we discuss its importance in a natural application scenario.

– **Indistinguishability against public key tempering chosen ciphertext attacks (IND-pkT-CCA security).** This is similar to IND-pkT-CPA security except that the adversary is given access to the decryption oracle that returns a decryption result on any ciphertext other than the challenge ciphertext.[4] Moreover, we allow the adversary to learn one-bit information indicating if the challenge ciphertext is decrypted to $\perp$ or not. We note that it is redundant for classical PKE since the challenge ciphertext is always decrypted to the challenge message, which is not $\perp$, by decryption correctness. On the other hand, it may give more power to the adversary for QPKE since if the adversary tempers with the public key that is used to generate the challenge ciphertext, decryption correctness may no longer hold.

IND-pkT-CPA Secure Construction from OWFs. We propose a QPKE scheme satisfying IND-pkT-CPA security from a digital signature scheme that can be constructed from OWFs. Our construction is inspired by the duality between distinguishing and swapping shown by Aaronson, Atia, and Susskind [AAS20] and its cryptographic applications by Hhan, Morimae, and Yamakawa [HMY23]. Our construction has quantum public keys and classical ciphertexts. We also propose a general transformation that adds decryption error detectability. The transformation uses only a digital signature scheme.

Upgrading to IND-pkT-CCA Security. We show a generic compiler that upgrades IND-pkT-CPA security into IND-pkT-CCA security while preserving decryption error detectability only using OWFs. It is worth mentioning that constructing such a generic CPA-to-CCA compiler is a long-standing open problem for classical PKE, and thus we make crucial use of the fact that public keys are quantum for constructing our compiler. By plugging our IND-pkT-CPA secure construction into the compiler, we obtain a QPKE scheme that satisfies IND-pkT-CCA security and decryption error detectability only based on OWFs.

Recyclable Variant. Our above definitions for QPKE assume each quantum public key is used to encrypt only a single message and might be consumed.

---

[4] Recall that ciphertexts are classical in our definition, and thus this is well-defined.

We also introduce a notion of *recyclable QPKE* where the encryption algorithm given a quantum public key outputs a ciphertext together with a classical state that can be used to encrypt a message many times. Then, we show that any standard IND-pkT-CPA (resp. IND-pkT-CCA) secure QPKE scheme with classical ciphertexts can be transformed into a recyclable one with IND-pkT-CPA (resp. IND-pkT-CCA) security while preserving decryption error detectability. The transformation uses only a CPA (resp. CCA) secure classical symmetric key encryption scheme that is implied by OWFs. Thus, by combining the transformation with the above results, we obtain a recyclable IND-pkT-CCA QPKE scheme with decryption error detectability from OWFs.

1.3 Discussion

Pure State Public Keys vs. Mixed State Public Keys. The quantum public keys of our QPKE schemes are mixed states. Some recent works [Col23, BGH+23a] that studied QPKE explicitly require that a quantum public key of QPKE be a pure quantum state. The reason is related to the quantum public key certification problem, which is this work's main focus. Barooti et al. [BGH+23a] claimed that a sender can check the validity of given quantum public keys by using SWAP test if they are pure states, but not if they are mixed states. However, as far as we understand, this claim implicitly requires that at least one intact quantum public key be transmitted via secure quantum channels where an adversary cannot touch it at all[5], which is an unsatisfactory assumption that makes QPKE less valuable. It is unclear how a sender can check the validity of a given quantum public key in the constructions proposed in [BGH+23a] without assuming such secure transmission of intact quantum public keys.

We believe that it is not important whether the quantum public keys are pure states or mixed states, and what is really important is whether a sender can check the validity of given quantum public keys without assuming unsatisfactory setups such as quantum secure channels. Although our QPKE schemes have mixed state quantum public keys, they provide such a validity checking of quantum public keys by a sender without assuming any unsatisfactory setups. In addition, we can easily extend our construction into one with pure state quantum public keys. We provide the variant in the full version.

1.4 Related Works

The possibility that QPKE can be achieved from weaker assumptions was first pointed out by Gottesman [Got], though he did not give any concrete construction. The first concrete construction of QPKE was proposed by Kawachi, Koshiba, Nishimura, and Yamakami [KKNY05]. They formally defined the

---

[5] More precisely, their model seems to require a physical setup assumption that enables a sender to obtain at least one intact quantum public key, such as secure quantum channels or tamper-proof quantum hardware.

notion of QPKE with quantum public keys, and provided a construction satisfying it from a distinguishing problem of two quantum states. Recently, Morimae and Yamakawa [MY22a] pointed out that QPKE defined by [KKNY05] can be achieved from any classical or quantum symmetric key encryption almost trivially. The constructions proposed in these two works have mixed state quantum public keys. Then, subsequent works [Col23,BGH+23b] independently studied the question whether QPKE with pure state quantum public keys can be constructed from OWFs or even weaker assumptions.

The definition of QPKE studied in the above works essentially assume that a sender can obtain intact quantum public keys. As far as we understand, this requires unsatisfactory physical setup assumptions such as secure quantum channels or tamper-proof quantum hardware, regardless of whether the quantum public keys are pure states or mixed states. In our natural setting where an adversary can touch the quantum channel where quantum public keys are sent, the adversary can easily attack the previous constructions by simply replacing the quantum public key on the channel with the one generated by itself that the adversary knows the corresponding secret key. We need to take such adversarial behavior into consideration, unless we assume physical setup assumptions that deliver intact quantum public keys to the sender. Our work is the first one that proposes a QPKE scheme secure in this natural setting assuming only classical authenticated channels that is the same assumption as classical PKE and can be implemented by digital signature schemes. It is unclear if we could solve the problem in the previous constructions by using classical authenticated channels similarly to our work. Below, we review the constructions of QPKE from OWFs proposed in the recent works.

We finally compare Quantum Key Distribution (QKD) [BB84] with our notion of QPKE. QKD also enables us to establish secure communication over an untrusted quantum channel assuming that an authenticated classical channel is available similarly to our QPKE. An advantage of QKD is that it is information theoretically secure and does not need any computational assumption. On the other hand, it has disadvantages that it must be interactive and parties must record secret information for each session. Thus, it is incomparable to the notion of QPKE.

1.5 Concurrent Work

A concurrent and independent work by Malavolta and Walter [MW23] constructs a two-round quantum key exchange protocol from OWFs. Their underlying idea is similar to our IND-pkT-CPA secure construction. Indeed, the technical core of their work is a construction a QPKE scheme that is secure against adversaries that only see one copy of the quantum public key. A nice feature of their scheme is that it satisfies everlasting security. That is, as long as the adversary is quantum polynomial-time when tampering with the public key, it cannot recover any information of the encrypted message even if it has an unbounded computational power later. They also show how to extend the scheme to satisfy security in the many-copy setting at the cost of sacrificing everlasting security. This gives an alternative construction of IND-pkT-CPA secure QPKE scheme from OWFs using our terminology. On the other hand, they do not consider CCA security, and our CPA-to-CCA compiler is unique to this work.

1.6 Open Problems

In our construction, public keys are quantum states. It is an open problem whether QPKE with classical public keys are possible from OWFs. Another interesting open problem is whether we can construct QPKE defined in this work from an even weaker assumption than OWFs such as pseudorandom states generators.

In our model of QPKE, a decryption error may be caused by tampering attacks on the quantum public key. To address this issue, we introduce the security notion we call decryption error detectability that guarantees that a legitimate receiver of a ciphertext can notice if the decrypted message is different from the message intended by the sender. We could consider even stronger variant of decryption error detectability that requires that a sender can notice if a given quantum public key does not provide decryption correctness. It is an open problem to construct a QPKE scheme satisfying such a stronger decryption error detectability.

The notion of IND-pkT-CCA security is defined with respect to a classical decryption oracle. In fact, this is inherent for our proof technique. We leave it open to construct a tamper-resilient QPKE scheme that resists attacks with a quantumly-accessible decryption oracle.

2 Technical Overview

2.1 Definition of QPKE

Syntax. We define QPKE that can be used in the setting where quantum unauthenticated channels and classical authenticated channels are available. To this end, we introduce the following two modifications to the previous definitions.

- The secret key generation algorithm outputs a classical verification key together with the secret key.
- The verification key is given to the encryption algorithm together with a quantum public key and a message so that the encryption algorithm can check the validity of the given quantum public key.

Concretely, in our definition, a QPKE scheme consists of four algorithms (SKGen, PKGen, Enc, Dec). SKGen is a classical secret key generation algorithm that is given the security parameter and outputs a classical secret key sk and a classical verification key vk. PKGen is a quantum public key generation algorithm that takes as input the classical secret key sk and outputs a quantum public key pk. Enc is a quantum encryption algorithm that takes as inputs the classical verification key vk, a quantum public key pk, and a plaintext msg, and outputs a classical ciphertext ct. Finally, Dec is a classical decryption algorithm that takes as input the classical secret key and a ciphertext, and outputs the decryption result.

The above definitions for QPKE assume each quantum public key is used to encrypt only a single message and might be consumed. We also introduce a notion of recyclable QPKE where the encryption algorithm given a quantum public key outputs a ciphertext together with a classical state that can be used to encrypt a message many times. In this overview, we mainly focus on non-recyclable QPKE for simplicity.

IND-pkT-CPA Security. IND-pkT-CPA security roughly guarantees that indistinguishability holds even if messages are encrypted by a public key pk' tampered with by an adversary as long as the encryption is done with the correct verification key vk. Formally, IND-pkT-CPA security is defined using the following security experiment played by an adversary $\mathcal{A}$. The experiment first generates classical secret key and verification key pair $(\mathsf{sk}, \mathsf{vk}) \leftarrow \mathsf{SKGen}(1^\lambda)$ and m copies of the quantum public key $\mathsf{pk}_1, \ldots, \mathsf{pk}_m \leftarrow \mathsf{PKGen}(\mathsf{sk})$. Then, $\mathcal{A}$ is given the classical verification key vk and m quantum public keys $\mathsf{pk}_1, \ldots, \mathsf{pk}_m$, and outputs a tampered quantum public key pk' and a pair of challenge plaintexts $(\mathsf{msg}_0, \mathsf{msg}_1)$. The experiment generates the challenge ciphertext using the adversarially generated quantum public key, that is, $\mathsf{ct}^* \leftarrow \mathsf{Enc}(\mathsf{vk}, \mathsf{pk}', \mathsf{msg}_b)$, where $b \leftarrow \{0, 1\}$. Finally, $\mathcal{A}$ is given ct^* and outputs the guess for b. IND-pkT-CPA security guarantees that any efficient quantum adversary cannot guess b significantly better than random guessing in this experiment.

IND-pkT-CPA security captures the setting where the classical verification key is sent via a classical authenticated channel and thus everyone can obtain correct verification key, but a quantum public key is sent via an unauthenticated quantum channel and thus can be tampered with by an adversary. Especially, it captures an adversary $\mathcal{A}$ who steals a quantum public key pk sent to a user, replace it with a tampered one pk', and try to break the secrecy of a message encrypted by pk'.

To capture wide range of usage scenarios, we give multiple copies of the quantum public keys $\mathsf{pk}_1, \ldots, \mathsf{pk}_m$ to $\mathcal{A}$. We also consider a relaxed security notion where an adversary is given a single quantum public key and denote it as IND-pkT-CPA$^{(1)}$.

Decryption Error Detectability. We also define a security notion related to the correctness notion that we call decryption error detectability. It roughly guarantees that a legitimate receiver of a ciphertext can notice if the decrypted message is different from the message intended by the sender. Such a decryption error could occur frequently in our setting as a result of the tampering attacks on the quantum public key sent via an unauthenticated quantum channel. Note that our definition of QPKE requires a ciphertext of QPKE to be a classical string and we assume all classical information is sent through a classical authenticated channel. Thus, similarly to the verification key, we can assume that ciphertexts can be sent without being tampered.

2.2 IND-PkT-CPA Secure Construction

We provide the technical overview for IND-pkT-CPA secure construction.

Duality Between Distinguishing and Swapping. Our construction is inspired by the duality between distinguishing and swapping shown by Aaronson, Atia, and Susskind [AAS20] and its cryptographic applications by Hhan, Morimae, and Yamakawa [HMY23].[6] We first review their idea. Let $|\psi\rangle$ and $|\phi\rangle$ be orthogonal states. [AAS20] showed that $|\psi\rangle + |\phi\rangle$ and $|\psi\rangle - |\phi\rangle$ are computationally indistinguishable[7] if and only if one cannot efficiently "swap" $|\psi\rangle$ and $|\phi\rangle$ with a non-negligible advantage, i.e., for any efficiently computable unitary U, $|\langle\phi|U|\psi\rangle + \langle\psi|U|\phi\rangle|$ is negligible. Based on the above result, [HMY23] suggested to use $|\psi\rangle + (-1)^b |\phi\rangle$ as an encryption of a plaintext $b \in \{0,1\}$. By the result of [AAS20], its security is reduced to the hardness of swapping $|\psi\rangle$ and $|\phi\rangle$.

Basic One-Time SKE. We can construct one-time SKE scheme with quantum ciphertext using the above duality between distinguishing and swapping as follows. A secret decryption key is (x_0, x_1) for uniformly random bit strings $x_0, x_1 \in \{0,1\}^\lambda$, and the corresponding secret encryption key is

$$|0\rangle|x_0\rangle + |1\rangle|x_1\rangle. \tag{1}$$

Then, when encrypting a plaintext $b \in \{0,1\}$, it transforms the secret encryption key into the ciphertext

$$|0\rangle|x_0\rangle + (-1)^b|1\rangle|x_1\rangle. \tag{2}$$

One-time indistinguishability of this scheme is somewhat obvious because the adversary has no information of x_0 or x_1 besides the ciphertext, but let us analyze it using the idea of [AAS20] to get more insights. Suppose that the above scheme is insecure, i.e., $|0\rangle|x_0\rangle+|1\rangle|x_1\rangle$ and $|0\rangle|x_0\rangle-|1\rangle|x_1\rangle$ are computationally distinguishable with a non-negligible advantage. Then, by the result of [AAS20], there is an efficient unitary U that swaps $|0\rangle|x_0\rangle$ and $|1\rangle|x_1\rangle$ with a non-negligible advantage. By using this unitary, let us consider the following procedure:

1. Given a state $|0\rangle|x_0\rangle \pm |1\rangle|x_1\rangle$, measure it in the computational basis to get $|\alpha\rangle|x_\alpha\rangle$ for random $\alpha \in \{0,1\}$.
2. Apply the unitary U to $|\alpha\rangle|x_\alpha\rangle$ and measure it in the computational basis.

Since U swaps $|0\rangle|x_0\rangle$ and $|1\rangle|x_1\rangle$ with a non-negligible advantage, the probability that the outcome of the second measurement is $|\alpha \oplus 1\rangle|x_{\alpha\oplus 1}\rangle$ is non-negligible. This yields the following observation: If one can efficiently distinguish $|0\rangle|x_0\rangle+|1\rangle|x_1\rangle$ and $|0\rangle|x_0\rangle-|1\rangle|x_1\rangle$, then one can efficiently compute both x_0 and x_1 from $|0\rangle|x_0\rangle \pm |1\rangle|x_1\rangle$. On the other hand, it is easy to show that one

---

[6] In the main body, we do not explicitly use any result of [AAS20, HMY23] though our analysis is similar to theirs.
[7] We often omit normalization factors.

cannot compute both x_0 and x_1 from $|0\rangle|x_0\rangle \pm |1\rangle|x_1\rangle$ with a non-negligible probability by a simple information theoretical argument. Thus, the above argument implies one-time indistinguishability of the above construction.

Extension to IND-pkT-CPA$^{(1)}$ Secure QPKE with Quantum Ciphertext. We show how to extend the above SKE scheme into an IND-pkT-CPA$^{(1)}$ secure QPKE scheme with quantum ciphertext. One natural approach is to use the secret encryption key $|0\rangle|x_0\rangle + |1\rangle|x_1\rangle$ as a quantum public key. However, it does not work since the adversary for IND-pkT-CPA$^{(1)}$ who is given $|0\rangle|x_0\rangle + |1\rangle|x_1\rangle$ as the public key can replace it with $|0\rangle|x'_0\rangle + |1\rangle|x'_1\rangle$ for x'_0, x'_1 of its choice. To fix this issue, we partially authenticate a quantum public key by using classical digital signatures. Concretely, the secret key generation algorithm SKGen generates a signing key and verification key pair (sk, vk) of a digital signature scheme, and use them as the secret key and verification key of the QPKE scheme. Then, public key generation algorithm PKGen takes as input sk and outputs a quantum public key

$$|0\rangle|\sigma(0)\rangle + |1\rangle|\sigma(1)\rangle, \qquad (3)$$

where $\sigma(\alpha)$ is a signature for $\alpha \in \{0,1\}$ by the signing key sk. Here, we assume that the signature scheme has a deterministic signing algorithm. The encryption algorithm Enc that is given vk, a quantum public key, and a plaintext $b \in \{0,1\}$ first coherently verifies using vk the validity of the signatures in the second register of the public key and aborts if the verification rejects. Otherwise, Enc generates the ciphertext by encoding the plaintext b into the phase of the quantum public key as before.

The IND-pkT-CPA$^{(1)}$ security of the construction is analyzed as follows. We assume that the digital signature scheme satisfies strong unforgeability, i.e., given message-signature pairs $(\mathsf{msg}_1, \sigma_1), ..., (\mathsf{msg}_n, \sigma_n)$, no efficient adversary can output $(\mathsf{msg}^*, \sigma^*)$ such that $(\mathsf{msg}^*, \sigma^*) \neq (\mathsf{msg}_i, \sigma_i)$ for all $i \in [n]$.[8] Then, no matter how the adversary who is given a single correctly generated quantum public key tampers with it, if it passes the verification in Enc, the state after passing the verification is negligibly close to a state in the form of

$$c_0|0\rangle|\sigma(0)\rangle|\Psi_0\rangle + c_1|1\rangle|\sigma(1)\rangle|\Psi_1\rangle \qquad (4)$$

with some complex coefficients c_0 and c_1, and some states $|\Psi_0\rangle$ and $|\Psi_1\rangle$ over the adversary's register (except for a negligible probability). The encryption of a plaintext $b \in \{0,1\}$ is to apply Z^b on the first qubit of Eq. (4). The cipertext generated under the tampered public key is therefore

$$c_0|0\rangle|\sigma(0)\rangle|\Psi_0\rangle + (-1)^b c_1|1\rangle|\sigma(1)\rangle|\Psi_1\rangle. \qquad (5)$$

By a slight extension of the analysis of the above SKE scheme, we show that if one can efficiently distinguish $c_0|0\rangle|\sigma(0)\rangle|\Psi_0\rangle + c_1|1\rangle|\sigma(1)\rangle|\Psi_1\rangle$ and

---

[8] At this point, two-time security (where $n = 2$) suffices but we finally need to allow n to be an arbitrary polynomial.

$c_0\,|0\rangle\,|\sigma(0)\rangle\,|\Psi_0\rangle - c_1\,|1\rangle\,|\sigma(1)\rangle\,|\Psi_1\rangle$, then one can efficiently compute both $\sigma(0)$ and $\sigma(1)$. On the other hand, recall that the adversary is only given one copy of the public key $|0\rangle\,|\sigma(0)\rangle + |1\rangle\,|\sigma(1)\rangle$. We can show that it is impossible to compute both $\sigma(0)$ and $\sigma(1)$ from this state by the strong unforgeability as follows. By [BZ13, Lemma 2.1], the probability to output both $\sigma(0)$ and $\sigma(1)$ is only halved even if $|0\rangle\,|\sigma(0)\rangle + |1\rangle\,|\sigma(1)\rangle$ is measured in the computational basis before given to the adversary. After the measurement, the adversary's input collapses to a classical state $|\alpha\rangle\,|\sigma(\alpha)\rangle$ for random $\alpha \in \{0,1\}$, in which case the adversary can output $\sigma(\alpha \oplus 1)$ only with a negligible probability by the strong unforgeability. Combining the above, security of the above scheme under tampered public keys is proven.

Achiving IND-pkT-CPA Security. The above QPKE scheme satisfies IND-pkT-CPA$^{(1)}$ security, but does not satisfy IND-pkT-CPA security where the adversary is given multiple copies of quantum public keys. If the adversary is given two copies of the quantum public key, by measuring each public key in the computational basis, the adversary can learn both $\sigma(0)$ and $\sigma(1)$ with probability $1/2$. In order to extend the scheme into IND-pkT-CPA security, we introduce a classical randomness for each public key generation. Specifically, a public key is

$$(r, |0\rangle\,|\sigma(0,r)\rangle + |1\rangle\,|\sigma(1,r)\rangle) \tag{6}$$

where $r \in \{0,1\}^\lambda$ is chosen uniformly at random for every execution of the public key generation algorithm, and $\sigma(\alpha, r)$ is a signature for $\alpha\|r$.[9] An encryption of a plaintext $b \in \{0,1\}$ is

$$(r, |0\rangle\,|\sigma(0,r)\rangle + (-1)^b\,|1\rangle\,|\sigma(1,r)\rangle). \tag{7}$$

Since each quantum public key uses different r, security of this scheme holds even if the adversary obtains arbitrarily many public keys.

Making Ciphertext Classical. The above constructions has quantum ciphertext, but our definition explicitly requires that a QPKE scheme have a classical cipheretxt. We observe that the ciphertext of the above schemes can be made classical easily. In the IND-pkT-CPA secure construction, the ciphertext contains a quantum state $|0\rangle\,|\sigma(r,0)\rangle + (-1)^b\,|1\rangle\,|\sigma(r,1)\rangle$. Suppose that we measure this state in Hadamard basis and let d be the measurement outcome. Then an easy calculation shows that we have

$$b = d \cdot (0\|\sigma(0,r) \oplus 1\|\sigma(1,r)). \tag{8}$$

Thus, sending (r, d) as a ciphertext is sufficient for the receiver who has the decryption key to recover the plaintext b. Moreover, this variant is at least as secure as the original one with quantum ciphertexts since the Hadamard-basis measurement only loses information of the ciphertext.

Achieving Recyclability. Given that we achieve classical ciphertext property, it is rather straightforward to transform the construction into recyclable one

---

[9] $\alpha\|r$ is the concatenation of two bit strings α and r.

where the encryption algorithm outputs a classical state that can be used to encrypt many plaintexts. The transformation uses standard hybrid encryption technique. Concretely, the encryption algorithm first generates a key K of a SKE scheme, encrypt each bit of K by the above non-recyclable scheme in a bit-by-bit manner, and encrypt the plaintext msg by the symmetric key encryption scheme under the key K. The final ciphertext is $(\mathsf{ct}, \mathsf{ct}_{\mathsf{ske}})$, where ct is the ciphertext of K by the non-recyclable scheme and $\mathsf{ct}_{\mathsf{ske}}$ is the ciphertext of msg by the SKE scheme. The encryption algorithm outputs a classical state (ct, K) together with the ciphertext. The encryptor can reuse the state when it encrypts another message later.[10]

Adding Decryption Error Detectability. So far, we are only concerned with IND-pkTA security. On the other hand, the schemes presented in the previous paragraphs do not satisfy decryption error detectability. (See Definition 4.2 for formal definition.) Fortunately, there is a simple generic conversion that adds decryption error detectability while preserving IND-pkTA security by using digital signatures. The idea is that the encryption algorithm first generates a signature for the message under a signing key generated by itself, encrypts both the original message and signature under the building block scheme, and outputs the ciphertexts along with the verification key for the signature scheme in the clear. Then, the decryption algorithm can verify that the decryption result is correct as long as it is a valid message-signature pair (except for a negligible probability).

2.3 CPA-to-CCA Transformation

We now explain how to transform IND-pkT-CPA secure QPKE scheme into IND-pkT-CCA secure one using OWFs.

Definition of IND-pkT-CCA Security. IND-pkT-CCA security is defined by adding the following two modifications to the security experiment for IND-pkT-CPA security.

- Throughout the experiment, the adversary can get access to the decryption oracle that is given a ciphertext ct and returns $\mathsf{Dec}(\mathsf{sk}, \mathsf{ct})$ if $\mathsf{ct} \ne \mathsf{ct}^*$ and $\bot$ otherwise.
- The adversary is given the 1-bit leakage information that the challenge ciphertext is decrypted to $\bot$ or not.

As discussed in Sect. 1.3, the second modification is needed to support a natural usage scenario of QPKE. For simplicity, we will ignore this second modification for now and proceed the overview as if IND-pkT-CCA security is defined by just adding the decryption oracle to the security experiment for IND-pkT-CPA security.

---

[10] The idea to achieve the recyclability by the hybrid encryption technique was also used in one of the constructions in [BGH+23a].

We also define a weaker variant of IND-pkT-CCA security where the adversary is allowed to make only a single query to the decryption oracle. We denote it as IND-pkT-1CCA security. We consider a relaxed variant of IND-pkT-CCA security and IND-pkT-1CCA security where the adversary is given only a single copy of quantum public key. We denote them as IND-pkT-CCA$^{(1)}$ security and IND-pkT-1CCA$^{(1)}$ security respectively, similarly to IND-pkT-CPA$^{(1)}$ security.

IND-pkT-1CCA from IND-pkT-CPA. In classical cryptography, the CCA security where the number of decryption query is a-priori bounded to q is called q-bounded-CCA security. It is known that any CPA secure classical PKE scheme can be transformed into q-bounded-CCA secure one using only a digital signature scheme [CHH+07]. We show that by using a similar technique, we can transform an IND-pkT-CPA secure QPKE scheme into an IND-pkT-1CCA secure one using only a digital signature scheme.

Boosting 1-Bounded-CCA into Full-Fledged CCA. Classically, it is not known how to boost bounded-CCA security into CCA security without using additional assumption, and as a result, "general transformation from CPA to CCA" is a major open question in classical public key cryptography. Surprisingly, we show that 1-bounded-CCA security can be boosted into CCA security for QPKE assuming only OWFs. More specifically, we show that IND-pkT-1CCA$^{(1)}$ secure QPKE can be transformed into IND-pkT-CCA$^{(1)}$ secure one assuming only OWFs.

The key component in the transformation is tokenized message authentication code (MAC) [BSS21]. Tokenized MAC is a special MAC scheme where we can generate a quantum MAC token using the secret MAC key. The quantum MAC token can be used to generate a valid signature only once. In other words, an adversary who is given a single quantum MAC token cannot generate valid signatures for two different messages. Tokenized MAC can be realized using only OWFs [BSS21].

The high level idea is to design CCA secure scheme so that a public key contains quantum MAC token and an adversary can generate a valid ciphertext only when it consumes the MAC token, which ensures that the adversary can make only one meaningful decryption query and CCA security is reduced to 1-bounded-CCA security. Consider the following construction of a QPKE scheme CCA based on IND-pkT-1CCA$^{(1)}$ secure QPKE scheme 1CCA and tokenized MAC scheme TMAC. The secret key of CCA consists of the secret keys of 1CCA and TMAC, and the verification key of CCA is that of 1CCA. A quantum public key of CCA consists of that of 1CCA and a MAC token of TMAC. The encryption algorithm of CCA first generates a ciphertext 1cca.ct of 1CCA and then generates a signature tmac.σ for the message 1cca.ct by consuming the MAC token contained in the public key. The resulting ciphertext is (1cca.ct, tmac.σ). The decryption algorithm of CCA that is given the ciphertext (1cca.ct, tmac.σ) first checks validity of tmac.σ by using the secret MAC key included in the secret key. If it passes, the decryption algorithm decrypts 1cca.ct by using the secret key of 1CCA.

In the experiment of IND-pkT-CCA$^{(1)}$ security for CCA, we can ensure that an adversary can make at most one decryption query whose result is not $\perp$ by the power of TMAC, as we want. However, the adversary in fact can make one critical query (1cca.ct*, tmac.σ'), where 1cca.ct* is the first component of the challenge ciphertext, which allows the adversary to obtain the challenge bit. This attack is possible due to the fact that the adversary is allowed to tamper the quantum public key.[11] Fortunately, this attack can be prevented by using a digital signature scheme and tying the two components 1cca.ct* and tmac.σ' together. Once this issue is fixed, we can successfully reduce the IND-pkT-CCA$^{(1)}$ security of the construction to the IND-pkT-1CCA$^{(1)}$ security of 1CCA, since now the adversary can make only one non-critical decryption query.

Upgrading IND-pkT-CCA$^{(1)}$ to IND-pkT-CCA. We can easily transform an IND-pkT-CCA$^{(1)}$ secure QPKE scheme into an IND-pkT-CCA secure one. The transformation is somewhat similar to the one from IND-pkT-CPA$^{(1)}$ secure scheme to IND-pkT-CPA secure one. We bundle multiple instances of IND-pkT-CCA$^{(1)}$ secure scheme each of which is labeled by a classical random string. The transformation uses pseudorandom functions and digital signatures both of which are implied by OWFs.

How to Deal with 1-Bit Leakage "The Challenge is Decrypted to $\perp$ or Not". So far, we ignore the fact that our definition of IND-pkT-CCA security allows the adversary to obtain 1-bit leakage information whether the challenge is decrypted to $\perp$ or not. We introduce an intermediate notion between IND-pkT-CPA security and IND-pkT-CCA security that we call IND-pkT-CVA security where the adversary is given the 1-bit leakage information but is not allowed to get access to the decryption oracle. We then show that an IND-pkT-CPA secure QPKE scheme can be transformed into IND-pkT-CVA secure one using the cut-and-choose technique. Moreover, we show that the above construction strategy towards IND-pkT-CCA secure construction works even if the adversaries are given the 1-bit leakage information, if we start with IND-pkT-CVA secure scheme.

Some Remarks. We finally provide some remarks.

Recyclability: Similarly to IND-pkT-CPA secure scheme, we consider recyclable variant for IND-pkT-CCA secure one. We show that a recyclable

---

[11] More specifically, the attack is done as follows. The adversary is given a quantum public key (1cca.pk, token) where 1cca.pk is a public key of 1CCA and token is a MAC token of TMAC. The adversary generates another token token' of TMAC by itself and sends (1cca.pk, token') to the challenger as the tempered public key. Since there is no validity check on the MAC token in the encryption algorithm, this tampered public key is not rejected and the challenge ciphertext (1cca.ct*, tmac.σ*) is generated. Given the challenge ciphertext, the adversary generates a signature tmac.σ' for 1cca.ct* using token contained in the given un-tampered public key and queries (1cca.ct*, tmac.σ') to the decryption oracle. Since tmac.σ' is a valid signature generated using the correct token, this query is successful and the adversary obtains the challenge bit.

IND-pkT-CCA secure QPKE scheme can be constructed from non-recyclable one using the hybrid encryption technique similarly to IND-pkT-CPA secure construction.

Strong decryption error detectability: In the proof of the construction from IND-pkT-1CCA[(1)] secure scheme to IND-pkT-CCA[(1)] secure one, we use the underlying scheme's decryption error detectability. The proof of CCA security is sensitive to decryption errors, and it turns out that decryption error detectability that only provides security guarantee against computationally bounded adversaries is not sufficient for this part. Thus, we introduce statistical variant of decryption error detectability that we call strong decryption error detectability. We also prove that our IND-pkT-CVA secure construction based on the cut-and-choose technique achieves strong decryption error detectability, and the subsequent transformations preserve it.

3 Preliminaries

3.1 Basic Notations

We use the standard notations of quantum computing and cryptography. We use λ as the security parameter. For any set S, $x \leftarrow S$ means that an element x is sampled uniformly at random from the set S. We write negl to mean a negligible function. PPT stands for (classical) probabilistic polynomial-time and QPT stands for quantum polynomial-time. For an algorithm A, $y \leftarrow A(x)$ means that the algorithm A outputs y on input x. For two bit strings x and y, $x\|y$ means the concatenation of them. For simplicity, we sometimes omit the normalization factor of a quantum state. (For example, we write $\frac{1}{\sqrt{2}}(|x_0\rangle + |x_1\rangle)$ just as $|x_0\rangle + |x_1\rangle$.) $I := |0\rangle\langle 0| + |1\rangle\langle 1|$ is the two-dimensional identity operator. For the notational simplicity, we sometimes write $I^{\otimes n}$ just as I when the dimension is clear from the context.

3.2 Digital Signatures

Definition 3.1 (Digital signatures). *A digital signature scheme is a set of algorithms* (Gen, Sign, Ver) *such that*

- Gen(1^λ) → (k, vk) : *It is a PPT algorithm that, on input the security parameter* λ, *outputs a signing key* k *and a verification key* vk.
- Sign(k, msg) → σ : *It is a PPT algorithm that, on input the message* msg *and* k, *outputs a signature* σ.
- Ver(vk, msg, σ) → ⊤/⊥ : *It is a deterministic classical polynomial-time algorithm that, on input* vk, msg, *and* σ, *outputs* ⊤/⊥.

We require the following correctness and strong EUF-CMA security.

Correctness: *For any* msg,

$$\Pr[\top \leftarrow \mathsf{Ver}(\mathsf{vk}, \mathsf{msg}, \sigma) : (k, \mathsf{vk}) \leftarrow \mathsf{Gen}(1^\lambda), \sigma \leftarrow \mathsf{Sign}(k, \mathsf{msg})] \geq 1 - \mathsf{negl}(\lambda). \tag{9}$$

Strong EUF-CMA Security: *For any QPT adversary $\mathcal{A}$ with classical oracle access to the signing oracle $\mathsf{Sign}(k, \cdot)$,*

$$\Pr\left[(\mathsf{msg}^*, \sigma^*) \notin \mathcal{Q} \wedge \top \leftarrow \mathsf{Ver}(\mathsf{vk}, \mathsf{msg}^*, \sigma^*) : \begin{array}{c}(k, \mathsf{vk}) \leftarrow \mathsf{Gen}(1^\lambda) \\ (\mathsf{msg}^*, \sigma^*) \leftarrow \mathcal{A}^{\mathsf{Sign}(k, \cdot)}(\mathsf{vk})\end{array}\right] \leq \mathsf{negl}(\lambda),$$

where $\mathcal{Q}$ is the set of message-signature pairs returned by the signing oracle.

Remark 3.1. Without loss of generality, we can assume that Sign is deterministic. (The random seed used for Sign can be generated by applying a PRF on the message signed, and the key of PRF is appended to the signing key.)

Theorem 3.1 ([Gol04, Sec. 6.5.2]). *Strong EUF-CMA secure digital signatures exist if OWFs exist.*

3.3 Pseudorandom Functions

Definition 3.2 (Pseudorandom functions (PRFs)). *A keyed function $\{\mathsf{PRF}_K : \mathcal{X} \to \mathcal{Y}\}_{K \in \{0,1\}^\lambda}$ that is computable in classical deterministic polynomial-time is a quantum-query secure pseudorandom function if for any QPT adversary $\mathcal{A}$ with quantum access to the evaluation oracle $\mathsf{PRF}_K(\cdot)$,*

$$|\Pr[1 \leftarrow \mathcal{A}^{\mathsf{PRF}_K(\cdot)}(1^\lambda)] - \Pr[1 \leftarrow \mathcal{A}^{H(\cdot)}(1^\lambda)]| \leq \mathsf{negl}(\lambda), \tag{10}$$

where $K \leftarrow \{0,1\}^\lambda$ and $H : \mathcal{X} \to \mathcal{Y}$ is a function chosen uniformly at random.

As we can see, we consider PRFs that is secure even if an adversary can get access to the oracles in superposition, which is called quantum-query secure PRFs. We use the term PRFs to indicate quantum-query secure PRFs in this work.

Theorem 3.2 ([Zha12]). *(Quantum-query secure) PRFs exist if OWFs exist.*

3.4 Symmetric Key Encryption

Definition 3.3 (Symmetric Key Encryption (SKE)). *A (classical) symmetric key encryption (SKE) scheme with message space $\{0,1\}^\ell$ is a set of algorithms $(\mathsf{Enc}, \mathsf{Dec})$ such that*

- $\mathsf{Enc}(K, \mathsf{msg}) \to \mathsf{ct}$: *It is a PPT algorithm that, on input $K \in \{0,1\}^\lambda$ and the message $\mathsf{msg} \in \{0,1\}^\ell$, outputs a ciphertext ct.*
- $\mathsf{Dec}(K, \mathsf{ct}) \to \mathsf{msg}'$: *It is a deterministic classical polynomial-time algorithm that, on input K and ct, outputs msg'.*

We require the following correctness.

Correctness: *For any $\mathsf{msg} \in \{0,1\}^\ell$,*

$$\Pr[\mathsf{msg} \leftarrow \mathsf{Dec}(K, \mathsf{ct}) : K \leftarrow \{0,1\}^\lambda, \mathsf{ct} \leftarrow \mathsf{Enc}(K, \mathsf{msg})] = 1. \tag{11}$$

Definition 3.4 (IND-CPA Security). *For any QPT adversary $\mathcal{A}$ with classical oracle access to the encryption oracle $\mathsf{Enc}(K, \cdot)$,*

$$\Pr\left[b \leftarrow \mathcal{A}(\mathsf{ct}^*, \mathsf{st})^{\mathsf{Enc}(K, \cdot)} : \begin{array}{c} K \leftarrow \{0,1\}^\lambda \\ (\mathsf{msg}_0, \mathsf{msg}_1, \mathsf{st}) \leftarrow \mathcal{A}^{\mathsf{Enc}(K, \cdot)}(1^\lambda) \\ b \leftarrow \{0,1\} \\ \mathsf{ct}^* \leftarrow \mathsf{Enc}(K, \mathsf{msg}_b) \end{array}\right] \leq \frac{1}{2} + \mathsf{negl}(\lambda).$$
(12)

Theorem 3.3 ([GGM86, HILL99]). *IND-CPA secure SKE exists if OWFs exist.*

Definition 3.5 (IND-CCA Security). *For any QPT adversary $\mathcal{A}$ with classical oracle access to the encryption oracle $\mathsf{Enc}(K, \cdot)$,*

$$\Pr\left[b \leftarrow \mathcal{A}(\mathsf{ct}^*, \mathsf{st})^{\mathsf{Enc}(K,\cdot), O_{\mathsf{Dec},2}(\cdot)} : \begin{array}{c} K \leftarrow \{0,1\}^\lambda \\ (\mathsf{msg}_0, \mathsf{msg}_1, \mathsf{st}) \leftarrow \mathcal{A}^{\mathsf{Enc}(K,\cdot), O_{\mathsf{Dec},1}(\cdot)}(1^\lambda) \\ b \leftarrow \{0,1\} \\ \mathsf{ct}^* \leftarrow \mathsf{Enc}(K, \mathsf{msg}_b) \end{array}\right] \leq \frac{1}{2} + \mathsf{negl}(\lambda).$$
(13)

Here, $O_{\mathsf{Dec},1}(\mathsf{ct})$ returns $\mathsf{Dec}(K, \mathsf{ct})$ for any ct. $O_{\mathsf{Dec},2}$ behaves identically to $O_{\mathsf{Dec},1}$ except that $O_{\mathsf{Dec},2}$ returns $\bot$ to the input ct^*.

Theorem 3.4 ([BN08]). *IND-CCA secure SKE exists if OWFs exist.*

3.5 Lemma by Boneh and Zhandry

In this paper, we use the following lemma by Boneh and Zhandry [BZ13].

Lemma 3.1 ([BZ13, Lemma 2.1]). *Let A be a quantum algorithm, and let $\Pr[x]$ be the probability that A outputs x. Let A' be another quantum algorithm obtained from A by pausing A at an arbitrary stage of execution, performing a partial measurement that obtains one of k outcomes, and then resuming A. Let $\Pr'[x]$ be the probability that A' outputs x. Then $\Pr'[x] \geq \Pr[x]/k$.*

4 Definition of QPKE

In this section, we define QPKE.

Definition 4.1 (Quantum Public-Key Encryption (QPKE)). *A quantum public-key encryption scheme with message space $\{0,1\}^\ell$ is a set of algorithms $(\mathsf{SKGen}, \mathsf{PKGen}, \mathsf{Enc}, \mathsf{Dec})$ such that*

- $\mathsf{SKGen}(1^\lambda) \to (\mathsf{sk}, \mathsf{vk})$: *It is a PPT algorithm that, on input the security parameter λ, outputs a classical secret key sk and a classical verification key vk.*
- $\mathsf{PKGen}(\mathsf{sk}) \to \mathsf{pk}$: *It is a QPT algorithm that, on input sk, outputs a quantum public key pk.*
- $\mathsf{Enc}(\mathsf{vk}, \mathsf{pk}, \mathsf{msg}) \to \mathsf{ct}$: *It is a QPT algorithm that, on input vk, pk, and a plaintext $\mathsf{msg} \in \{0,1\}^\ell$, outputs a classical ciphertext ct.*

- Dec(sk, ct) → msg' : *It is a classical deterministic polynomial-time algorithm that, on input* sk *and* ct, *outputs* msg' $\in \{0,1\}^\ell \cup \{\bot\}$.

We require the following correctness and IND-pkTA security.

Correctness: *For any* msg $\in \{0,1\}^\ell$,

$$\Pr\left[\text{msg} \leftarrow \text{Dec}(\text{sk}, \text{ct}) : \begin{array}{l} (\text{sk}, \text{vk}) \leftarrow \text{SKGen}(1^\lambda) \\ \text{pk} \leftarrow \text{PKGen}(\text{sk}) \\ \text{ct} \leftarrow \text{Enc}(\text{vk}, \text{pk}, \text{msg}) \end{array}\right] \geq 1 - \text{negl}(\lambda). \quad (14)$$

IND-pkT-CPA Security: *For any polynomial* m, *and any QPT adversary* $\mathcal{A}$,

$$\Pr\left[b \leftarrow \mathcal{A}(\text{ct}^*, \text{st}) : \begin{array}{l} (\text{sk}, \text{vk}) \leftarrow \text{SKGen}(1^\lambda) \\ \text{pk}_1, ..., \text{pk}_m \leftarrow \text{PKGen}(\text{sk})^{\otimes m} \\ (\text{pk}', \text{msg}_0, \text{msg}_1, \text{st}) \leftarrow \mathcal{A}(\text{vk}, \text{pk}_1, ..., \text{pk}_m) \\ b \leftarrow \{0, 1\} \\ \text{ct}^* \leftarrow \text{Enc}(\text{vk}, \text{pk}', \text{msg}_b) \end{array}\right] \leq \frac{1}{2} + \text{negl}(\lambda).$$

(15)

Here, $\text{pk}_1, ..., \text{pk}_m \leftarrow \text{PKGen}(\text{sk})^{\otimes m}$ *means that* PKGen *is executed* m *times and* pk_i *is the output of the* i*th execution of* PKGen. st *is a quantum internal state of* $\mathcal{A}$, *which can be entangled with* pk'.

As we discussed in Sect. 1.3, the above definition does not require the quantum public key pk to be a pure state.

We also define a security notion related to the correctness notion that we call decryption error detectability.

Definition 4.2 (Decryption error detectability). *We say that a QPKE scheme has decryption error detectability if for any polynomial m, and any QPT adversary $\mathcal{A}$,*

$$\Pr\left[\text{msg}' \neq \bot \wedge \text{msg}' \neq \text{msg} : \begin{array}{l} (\text{sk}, \text{vk}) \leftarrow \text{SKGen}(1^\lambda) \\ \text{pk}_1, ..., \text{pk}_m \leftarrow \text{PKGen}(\text{sk})^{\otimes m} \\ (\text{pk}', \text{msg}) \leftarrow \mathcal{A}(\text{vk}, \text{pk}_1, ..., \text{pk}_m) \\ \text{ct} \leftarrow \text{Enc}(\text{vk}, \text{pk}', \text{msg}) \\ \text{msg}' \leftarrow \text{Dec}(\text{sk}, \text{ct}) \end{array}\right] \leq \text{negl}(\lambda).$$

(16)

It is easy to see that we can generically add decryption error detectability by letting the sender generate a signature for the message under a signing key generated by itself, encrypt the concatenation of the message and signature, and send the ciphertext along with the verification key of the signature to the receiver. The receiver can check that there is no decryption error (except for a negligible probability) if the decryption result is a valid message-signature pair. That is, we have the following theorem.

Theorem 4.1. *If there exist OWFs and a QPKE scheme that satisfies correctness and IND-pkT-CPA security, there exists a QPKE scheme that satisfies correctness, IND-pkT-CPA security, and decryption error detectability.*

We omit the proof since it is straightforward by the construction explained above. Since we have this theorem, we focus on constructing QPKE that satisfies correctness and IND-pkT-CPA security.

5 Construction of QPKE

In this section, we construct a QPKE scheme that satisfies correctness and IND-pkT-CPA security (but not decryption error detectability) from strong EUF-CMA secure digital signatures. The message space of our construction is $\{0,1\}$, but it can be extended to be arbitrarily many bits by parallel repetition. Let (Gen, Sign, Ver) be a strong EUF-CMA secure digital signature scheme with a deterministic Sign algorithm and message space $\{0,1\}^u$ for $u = \omega(\log \lambda)$.

Our construction of QPKE is as follows.

- SKGen(1^λ) → (sk, vk) : Run $(k, \mathsf{vk}) \leftarrow \mathsf{Gen}(1^\lambda)$. Output sk := k. Output vk.
- PKGen(sk) → pk : Parse sk = k. Choose $r \leftarrow \{0,1\}^u$. By running Sign coherently, generate the state

$$|\psi_r\rangle := |0\rangle_\mathbf{A} \otimes |\mathsf{Sign}(k, 0\|r)\rangle_\mathbf{B} + |1\rangle_\mathbf{A} \otimes |\mathsf{Sign}(k, 1\|r)\rangle_\mathbf{B} \qquad (17)$$

  over registers $(\mathbf{A}, \mathbf{B})$. Output pk := $(r, |\psi_r\rangle)$.
- Enc(vk, pk, b) → ct : Parse pk = (r, ρ), where ρ is a quantum state over registers $(\mathbf{A}, \mathbf{B})$. The Enc algorithm consists of the following three steps.
  1. It coherently checks the signature in ρ. In other words, it applies the unitary

  $$U_{r,\mathsf{vk}} |\alpha\rangle_\mathbf{A} |\beta\rangle_\mathbf{B} |0...0\rangle_\mathbf{D} = |\alpha\rangle_\mathbf{A} |\beta\rangle_\mathbf{B} |\mathsf{Ver}(\mathsf{vk}, \alpha\|r, \beta)\rangle_\mathbf{D} \qquad (18)$$

  on $\rho_{\mathbf{A},\mathbf{B}} \otimes |0...0\rangle \langle 0...0|_\mathbf{D}$,[12] and measures the register $\mathbf{D}$ in the computational basis. If the result is $\bot$, it outputs ct := $\bot$ and halts. If the result is $\top$, it goes to the next step.
  2. It applies Z^b on the register $\mathbf{A}$.
  3. It measures all qubits in the registers $(\mathbf{A}, \mathbf{B})$ in the Hadamard basis to get the result d. It outputs ct := (r, d).
- Dec(sk, ct) → b' : Parse sk = k and ct = (r, d). Output

$$b' := d \cdot (0\|\mathsf{Sign}(k, 0\|r) \oplus 1\|\mathsf{Sign}(k, 1\|r)). \qquad (19)$$

Theorem 5.1. *If* (Gen, Sign, Ver) *is a strong EUF-CMA secure digital signature scheme, then the QPKE scheme* (SKGen, PKGen, Enc, Dec) *above is correct and IND-pkT-CPA secure.*

The correctness is straightforward. First, the state over the registers $(\mathbf{A}, \mathbf{B})$ is $|\psi_r\rangle$ if pk was not tampered with and the first step of Enc algorithm got $\top$. Second, in that case, the state becomes

$$|0\rangle |\mathsf{Sign}(k, 0\|r)\rangle + (-1)^b |1\rangle |\mathsf{Sign}(k, 1\|r)\rangle \qquad (20)$$

---
[12] $\mathbf{C}$ is skipped, because $\mathbf{C}$ will be used later.

after the second step of Enc algorithm. Finally, because in that case d obtained in the third step of Enc algorithm satisfies

$$b = d \cdot (0\|\mathsf{Sign}(k,0\|r) \oplus 1\|\mathsf{Sign}(k,1\|r)), \quad (21)$$

we have $b' = b$.

We prove IND-pkT-CPA security in the next section.

6 Proof of IND-PkT-CPA Security

In this section, we show IND-pkT-CPA security of our construction to complete the proof of Theorem 5.1. The outline of the proof is as follows. The security game for the IND-pkT-CPA security of our QPKE (Hybrid 0) is given in Fig. 1. We introduce two more hybrids, Hybrid 1 (Fig. 2) and Hybrid 2 (Fig. 3). Hybrid 1 is the same as Hybrid 0 except that the challenger does not do the Hadamard-basis measurement in the third step of Enc algorithm, and the challenger sends the adversary r and the state over the registers $(\mathbf{A}, \mathbf{B})$. Hybrid 2 is the same as Hybrid 1 except that the adversary outputs two bit strings μ_0, μ_1 and the adversary wins if $\mu_0 = \mathsf{Sign}(k, 0\|r)$ and $\mu_1 = \mathsf{Sign}(k, 1\|r)$. The formal proof is as follows.

Assume that the IND-pkT-CPA security of our construction is broken by a QPT adversary $\mathcal{A}$. It means the QPT adversary $\mathcal{A}$ wins Hybrid 0 with a non-negligible advantage. Then, it is clear that there is another QPT adversary $\mathcal{A}'$ that wins Hybrid 1 with a non-negligible advantage. ($\mathcal{A}'$ has only to do the Hadamard-basis measurement by itself.) From the $\mathcal{A}'$, we can construct a QPT adversary $\mathcal{A}''$ that wins Hybrid 2 with a non-negligible probability by using the idea of [HMY23]. (For details, see Sect. 6.1). Finally, we show in Sect. 6.2 that no QPT adversary can win Hybrid 2 except for a negligible probability. We thus have the contradiction, and therefore our QPKE is IND-pkT-CPA secure.

6.1 From Distinguishing to Outputting Two Signatures

We present the construction of $\mathcal{A}''$. Assume that there exists a QPT adversary $\mathcal{A}'$ and a polynomial p such that

$$|\Pr[1 \leftarrow \mathcal{A}' \mid b=0] - \Pr[1 \leftarrow \mathcal{A}' \mid b=1]| \geq \frac{1}{p(\lambda)} \quad (23)$$

in Hybrid 1 (Fig. 2) for all $\lambda \in I$ with an infinite set I. From the $\mathcal{A}'$, we construct a QPT adversary $\mathcal{A}''$ such that

$$\Pr[(\mathsf{Sign}(k,0\|r), \mathsf{Sign}(k,1\|r)) \leftarrow \mathcal{A}''] \geq \frac{1}{q(\lambda)} \quad (24)$$

in Hybrid 2 (Fig. 3) with a polynomial q for infinitely many λ.

Let $t := (k, \mathsf{vk}, r_1, ..., r_m, r)$, and $\Pr[t]$ be the probability that t is generated in Item 1, Item 2, and Item 4 in the game of Fig. 2. Let Good be the event that

---

Hybrid 0

1. $\mathcal{C}$ runs $(k, \mathsf{vk}) \leftarrow \mathsf{Gen}(1^\lambda)$. $\mathcal{C}$ sends vk to $\mathcal{A}$.
2. $\mathcal{C}$ chooses $r_1, ..., r_m \leftarrow \{0,1\}^u$.
3. $\mathcal{C}$ sends $\{(r_i, |\psi_{r_i}\rangle)\}_{i=1}^m$ to the adversary $\mathcal{A}$, where

$$|\psi_{r_i}\rangle := |0\rangle \otimes |\mathsf{Sign}(k, 0\|r_i)\rangle + |1\rangle \otimes |\mathsf{Sign}(k, 1\|r_i)\rangle. \tag{22}$$

4. $\mathcal{A}$ generates a quantum state over registers $(\mathbf{A}, \mathbf{B}, \mathbf{C})$. $((\mathbf{A}, \mathbf{B})$ corresponds to the quantum part of pk', and $\mathbf{C}$ corresponds to st.) $\mathcal{A}$ sends a bit string r and the registers $(\mathbf{A}, \mathbf{B})$ to $\mathcal{C}$. $\mathcal{A}$ keeps the register $\mathbf{C}$.
5. $\mathcal{C}$ coherently checks the signature in the state sent from $\mathcal{A}$. If the result is $\bot$, it sends $\bot$ to $\mathcal{A}$ and halts. If the result is $\top$, it goes to the next step.
6. $\mathcal{C}$ chooses $b \leftarrow \{0,1\}$. $\mathcal{C}$ applies Z^b on the register $\mathbf{A}$.
7. $\mathcal{C}$ measures all qubits in $(\mathbf{A}, \mathbf{B})$ in the Hadamard basis to get the result d. $\mathcal{C}$ sends (r, d) to $\mathcal{A}$.
8. $\mathcal{A}$ outputs b'. If $b' = b$, $\mathcal{A}$ wins.

Fig. 1. Hybrid 0

Hybrid 1

1.-6. All the same as Figure 1.
7. $\mathcal{C}$ does not do the Hadamard-basis measurement, and $\mathcal{C}$ sends r and registers $(\mathbf{A}, \mathbf{B})$ to $\mathcal{A}$.
8. The same as Figure 1.

Fig. 2. Hybrid 1

Hybrid 2

1.-7. All the same as Figure 2.
8. $\mathcal{A}$ outputs (μ_0, μ_1). If $\mu_0 = \mathsf{Sign}(k, 0\|r)$ and $\mu_1 = \mathsf{Sign}(k, 1\|r)$, $\mathcal{A}$ wins.

Fig. 3. Hybrid 2

$\mathcal{C}$ gets $\top$ in Item 5 in the game of Fig. 2. Let Bad be the event that Good does not occur. Then, from Eq. (23), we have

$$\frac{1}{p(\lambda)} \leq \left| \sum_t \Pr[t] \Pr[\mathsf{Good} \mid t] \Pr[1 \leftarrow \mathcal{A}' \mid t, \mathsf{Good}, b=0] \right. \tag{25}$$
$$\left. + \sum_t \Pr[t] \Pr[\mathsf{Bad} \mid t] \Pr[1 \leftarrow \mathcal{A}' \mid t, \mathsf{Bad}, b=0] \right.$$

$$-\sum_t \Pr[t]\Pr[\mathsf{Good}\mid t]\Pr[1\leftarrow\mathcal{A}'\mid t,\mathsf{Good},b=1] \tag{26}$$

$$-\sum_t \Pr[t]\Pr[\mathsf{Bad}\mid t]\Pr[1\leftarrow\mathcal{A}'\mid t,\mathsf{Bad},b=1]\Big| \tag{27}$$

$$\leq \sum_t \Pr[t]\Pr[\mathsf{Good}\mid t]\Big|\Pr[1\leftarrow\mathcal{A}'\mid t,\mathsf{Good},b=0]-\Pr[1\leftarrow\mathcal{A}'\mid t,\mathsf{Good},b=1]\Big|$$

$$+\sum_t \Pr[t]\Pr[\mathsf{Bad}\mid t]\Big|\Pr[1\leftarrow\mathcal{A}'\mid t,\mathsf{Bad},b=0]-\Pr[1\leftarrow\mathcal{A}'\mid t,\mathsf{Bad},b=1]\Big| \tag{28}$$

$$= \sum_t \Pr[t]\Pr[\mathsf{Good}\mid t]\Big|\Pr[1\leftarrow\mathcal{A}'\mid t,\mathsf{Good},b=0]-\Pr[1\leftarrow\mathcal{A}'\mid t,\mathsf{Good},b=1]\Big| \tag{29}$$

for all $\lambda \in I$, because if Bad occurs, $\mathcal{A}'$ gets only $\bot$ which contains no information about b. (Here, we often abuse notation to just write t to mean the event that t is generated in Item Item 1, Item 2, and Item 4.) Therefore, if we define

$$T_\lambda := \left\{t : \Pr[\mathsf{Good}\mid t]\cdot\Big|\Pr[1\leftarrow\mathcal{A}'\mid t,\mathsf{Good},b=0]-\Pr[1\leftarrow\mathcal{A}'\mid t,\mathsf{Good},b=1]\Big|\geq \frac{1}{2p(\lambda)}\right\}, \tag{30}$$

we have, for all $\lambda \in I$,

$$\Pr[\mathsf{Good}\mid t]\geq \frac{1}{4p(\lambda)} \tag{31}$$

and

$$\Big|\Pr[1\leftarrow\mathcal{A}'\mid t,\mathsf{Good},b=0]-\Pr[1\leftarrow\mathcal{A}'\mid t,\mathsf{Good},b=1]\Big|\geq \frac{1}{2p(\lambda)} \tag{32}$$

for any $t\in T_\lambda$ and $\sum_{t\in T_\lambda}\Pr[t]\geq \frac{1}{2p(\lambda)}$.

Let $\left|\phi_b^{t,good}\right\rangle$ be the state over the registers $(\mathbf{A},\mathbf{B},\mathbf{C})$ immediately before Item 8 of Fig. 2 given that t is generated, Good occurred, and b is chosen in Item 6 of Fig. 2. We can show the following lemma. (Its proof is given later.)

Lemma 6.1. *If* (Gen, Sign, Ver) *is strong EUF-CMA secure, there exists a subset $T'_\lambda \subseteq T_\lambda$ such that the following is satisfied for all $\lambda \in I'$, where $I' := \{\lambda \in I : \lambda \geq \lambda_0\}$ with a certain λ_0.*

- $\sum_{t\in T'_\lambda}\Pr[t]\geq \frac{1}{4p(\lambda)}$.
- *For any $t\in T'_\lambda$, $\left|\phi_b^{t,good}\right\rangle$ is close to a state*

$$\left|\widetilde{\phi}_b^{t,good}\right\rangle := c_0\left|0\right\rangle_\mathbf{A}\left|\mathsf{Sign}(k,0\|r)\right\rangle_\mathbf{B}\left|\Psi_0\right\rangle_\mathbf{C} + (-1)^b c_1\left|1\right\rangle_\mathbf{A}\left|\mathsf{Sign}(k,1\|r)\right\rangle_\mathbf{B}\left|\Psi_1\right\rangle_\mathbf{C} \tag{33}$$

within the trace distance $\frac{1}{p^{10}(\lambda)}$, where c_0 and c_1 are some complex coefficients such that $|c_0|^2+|c_1|^2=1$, and $\left|\Psi_0\right\rangle$ and $\left|\Psi_1\right\rangle$ are some normalized states.

Now let us fix $t \in T'_\lambda$. Also, assume that Good occurred. Because $T'_\lambda \subseteq T_\lambda$, it means that $t \in T_\lambda$. Then, from Eq. (32),

$$\left| \Pr[1 \leftarrow \mathcal{A}' \mid t, \mathsf{Good}, b = 0] - \Pr[1 \leftarrow \mathcal{A}' \mid t, \mathsf{Good}, b = 1] \right| = \Delta \quad (34)$$

for a non-negligible $\Delta \geq \frac{1}{2p(\lambda)}$ for all $\lambda \in I$. Without loss of generality, we can assume that in Item 8 of Fig. 2, $\mathcal{A}'$ applies a unitary V on the state $\left| \phi_b^{t,good} \right\rangle$, and measures the register $\mathbf{A}$ in the computational basis to get $b' \in \{0, 1\}$. By Eq. (34) we have

$$V \left| \phi_0^{t,good} \right\rangle = \sqrt{p} \left| 1 \right\rangle_{\mathbf{A}} \left| \nu_1 \right\rangle_{\mathbf{B,C}} + \sqrt{1-p} \left| 0 \right\rangle_{\mathbf{A}} \left| \nu_0 \right\rangle_{\mathbf{B,C}} \quad (35)$$

$$V \left| \phi_1^{t,good} \right\rangle = \sqrt{1-p+\Delta} \left| 0 \right\rangle_{\mathbf{A}} \left| \xi_0 \right\rangle_{\mathbf{B,C}} + \sqrt{p-\Delta} \left| 1 \right\rangle_{\mathbf{A}} \left| \xi_1 \right\rangle_{\mathbf{B,C}} \quad (36)$$

for some real number p and some normalized states $|\nu_0\rangle, |\nu_1\rangle, |\xi_0\rangle, |\xi_1\rangle$. (This is because any state can be written as $p|1\rangle|\nu_1\rangle + \sqrt{1-p}|0\rangle|\nu_0\rangle$ with some p and normalized states $|\nu_0\rangle, |\nu_1\rangle$, and due to Eq. (34), the coefficients of $|1\rangle|\xi_1\rangle$ has to be $\sqrt{p-\Delta}$.) If we define W as $W := V^\dagger (Z \otimes I) V$, we have

$$\left| \left\langle \tilde{\phi}_b^{t,good} \right| W \left| \tilde{\phi}_b^{t,good} \right\rangle - \left\langle \phi_b^{t,good} \right| W \left| \phi_b^{t,good} \right\rangle \right| \leq \frac{2}{p^{10}(\lambda)} \quad (37)$$

for all $\lambda \in I'$ from Lemma 6.1. Therefore,

$$|c_0^* c_1 \langle 0 | \langle \mathsf{Sign}(k, 0\|r) | \langle \Psi_0 | W | 1 \rangle | \mathsf{Sign}(k, 1\|r) \rangle | \Psi_1 \rangle \quad (38)$$

$$+ c_0 c_1^* \langle 1 | \langle \mathsf{Sign}(k, 1\|r) | \langle \Psi_1 | W | 0 \rangle | \mathsf{Sign}(k, 0\|r) \rangle | \Psi_0 \rangle | \quad (39)$$

$$= \frac{1}{4} |(\langle \tilde{\phi}_0^{t,good} | + \langle \tilde{\phi}_1^{t,good} |) W (|\tilde{\phi}_0^{t,good}\rangle - |\tilde{\phi}_1^{t,good}\rangle) \quad (40)$$

$$+ (\langle \tilde{\phi}_0^{t,good} | - \langle \tilde{\phi}_1^{t,good} |) W (|\tilde{\phi}_0^{t,good}\rangle + |\tilde{\phi}_1^{t,good}\rangle)| \quad (41)$$

$$= \frac{1}{2} \left| \left\langle \tilde{\phi}_0^{t,good} \right| W \left| \tilde{\phi}_0^{t,good} \right\rangle - \left\langle \tilde{\phi}_1^{t,good} \right| W \left| \tilde{\phi}_1^{t,good} \right\rangle \right| \quad (42)$$

$$\geq \frac{1}{2} \left| \left\langle \phi_0^{t,good} \right| W \left| \phi_0^{t,good} \right\rangle - \left\langle \phi_1^{t,good} \right| W \left| \phi_1^{t,good} \right\rangle \right| - \frac{2}{p^{10}(\lambda)} \quad (43)$$

$$= \frac{1}{2} \left| \left(\sqrt{p} \langle 1 | \langle \nu_1 | + \sqrt{1-p} \langle 0 | \langle \nu_0 | \right) \left(-\sqrt{p} |1\rangle |\nu_1\rangle + \sqrt{1-p} |0\rangle |\nu_0\rangle \right) \right.$$
$$\left. - \left(\sqrt{1-p+\Delta} \langle 0 | \langle \xi_0 | + \sqrt{p-\Delta} \langle 1 | \langle \xi_1 | \right) \left(\sqrt{1-p+\Delta} |0\rangle |\xi_0\rangle - \sqrt{p-\Delta} |1\rangle |\xi_1\rangle \right) \right|$$
$$- \frac{2}{p^{10}(\lambda)} \quad (44)$$

$$= \frac{1}{2} \left| -p + (1-p) - (1-p+\Delta) + (p-\Delta) \right| - \frac{2}{p^{10}(\lambda)} \quad (45)$$

$$= \Delta - \frac{2}{p^{10}(\lambda)} \quad (46)$$

$$\geq \frac{1}{2p(\lambda)} - \frac{2}{p^{10}(\lambda)} \quad (47)$$

$$\geq \frac{1}{p(\lambda)} \qquad (48)$$

for all $\lambda \in I'$. Here, Eq. (43) follows from Eq. (37), and Eq. (44) follows from Eq. (35) and (36) and the definition of W. From the triangle inequality and the facts that $|c_0| \leq 1$ and $|c_1| \leq 1$,

$$\frac{1}{p(\lambda)} \leq |c_1| \cdot |\langle 0| \langle \mathsf{Sign}(k,0\|r)| \langle \Psi_0| W |1\rangle |\mathsf{Sign}(k,1\|r)\rangle |\Psi_1\rangle | \qquad (49)$$
$$+ |c_0| \cdot |\langle 1| \langle \mathsf{Sign}(k,1\|r)| \langle \Psi_1| W |0\rangle |\mathsf{Sign}(k,0\|r)\rangle |\Psi_0\rangle | \qquad (50)$$

for all $\lambda \in I'$. Then,

$$\frac{1}{2p(\lambda)} \leq |c_1| \cdot |\langle 0| \langle \mathsf{Sign}(k,0\|r)| \langle \Psi_0| W |1\rangle |\mathsf{Sign}(k,1\|r)\rangle |\Psi_1\rangle | \qquad (51)$$

or

$$\frac{1}{2p(\lambda)} \leq |c_0| \cdot |\langle 1| \langle \mathsf{Sign}(k,1\|r)| \langle \Psi_1| W |0\rangle |\mathsf{Sign}(k,0\|r)\rangle |\Psi_0\rangle | \qquad (52)$$

holds for all $\lambda \in I'$. Assume that the latter holds. (The following proof can be easily modified even if the former holds.) Then

$$\frac{1}{4p^2(\lambda)} \leq |c_0|^2 \cdot |\langle 1| \langle \mathsf{Sign}(k,1\|r)| \langle \Psi_1| W |0\rangle |\mathsf{Sign}(k,0\|r)\rangle |\Psi_0\rangle |^2 \qquad (53)$$
$$\leq |c_0|^2 \cdot \|(I \otimes \langle \mathsf{Sign}(k,1\|r)| \otimes I) W |0\rangle |\mathsf{Sign}(k,0\|r)\rangle |\Psi_0\rangle \|^2 \qquad (54)$$

for all $\lambda \in I'$. With this W, we construct the QPT adversary $\mathcal{A}''$ as is shown in Fig. 4.

$\mathcal{A}''$

1. Simulate $\mathcal{A}'$ in steps 1.–7. of Figure 3. If $\bot$ is sent from $\mathcal{C}$, output $\bot$ and halt.
2. Measure the register **A** in the computational basis. If the result is 1, output $\bot$ and halt. If the result is 0, measure the register **B** of the post-measurement state in the computational basis to get the measurement result μ_0.
3. Apply W on the post-measurement state and measure the register **B** in the computational basis to get the result μ_1.
4. Output (μ_0, μ_1).

Fig. 4. $\mathcal{A}''$

We show that $\mathcal{A}''$ wins the game of Fig. 3 with a non-negligible probability for infinitely many λ. The probability that $t \in T'_\lambda$ and Good occur in Item 1 of

Fig. 4 is at least $\frac{1}{16p^2(\lambda)}$ for all $\lambda \in I'$, because of the following reasons. First, $\sum_{t \in T'_\lambda} \Pr[t] \geq \frac{1}{4p(\lambda)}$ for all $\lambda \in I'$ from Lemma 6.1. Second, because $t \in T'_\lambda$ means $t \in T_\lambda$, $\Pr[\mathsf{Good} \mid t] \geq \frac{1}{4p(\lambda)}$ for all $\lambda \in I$ from Eq. (31).

Assume that $t \in T'_\lambda$ and Good occur. If $\mathcal{A}''$ does the operations in Item 2 and Item 3 on $\left|\tilde{\phi}_b^{t,good}\right\rangle$, the probability that $(\mu_0, \mu_1) = (\mathsf{Sign}(k, 0\|r), \mathsf{Sign}(k, 1\|r))$ is at least $\frac{1}{4p^2(\lambda)}$ for all $\lambda \in I'$ from Eq. (54). From Lemma 6.1, the trace distance between $\left|\phi_b^{t,good}\right\rangle$ and $\left|\tilde{\phi}_b^{t,good}\right\rangle$ is at most $\frac{1}{p^{10}(\lambda)}$ for all $\lambda \in I'$. Therefore, if $\mathcal{A}''$ does the operations in Item 2 and Item 3 on $\left|\phi_b^{t,good}\right\rangle$, the probability that $(\mu_0, \mu_1) = (\mathsf{Sign}(k, 0\|r), \mathsf{Sign}(k, 1\|r))$ is at least $\frac{1}{4p^2(\lambda)} - \frac{1}{p^{10}(\lambda)}$ for all $\lambda \in I'$. Hence, the overall probability that $\mathcal{A}''$ outputs $(\mu_0, \mu_1) = (\mathsf{Sign}(k, 0\|r), \mathsf{Sign}(k, 1\|r))$ is non-negligible for infinitely many λ.

We prove Lemma 6.1 to complete this subsection.

Proof of Lemma 6.1. Fix $t \in T_\lambda$. Immediately before the coherent signature test in Item 5 of Fig. 2, the entire state over the registers $(\mathbf{A}, \mathbf{B}, \mathbf{C})$ is generally written as $\sum_{\alpha,\beta} d_{\alpha,\beta} |\alpha\rangle_\mathbf{A} |\beta\rangle_\mathbf{B} |\Lambda_{\alpha,\beta}\rangle_\mathbf{C}$, where $d_{\alpha,\beta}$ are some complex coefficients such that $\sum_{\alpha,\beta} |d_{\alpha,\beta}|^2 = 1$, and $|\Lambda_{\alpha,\beta}\rangle$ are some normalized states. Define the set

$$S := \{(\alpha, \beta) : \mathsf{Ver}(\mathsf{vk}, \alpha\|r, \beta) = \top \land \beta \neq \mathsf{Sign}(k, \alpha\|r)\}. \tag{55}$$

The (unnormalized) state after obtaining $\top$ in the coherent signature test in Item 5 of Fig. 2 is

$$\begin{aligned}
& d_{0,\mathsf{Sign}(k,0\|r)} |0\rangle_\mathbf{A} |\mathsf{Sign}(k, 0\|r)\rangle_\mathbf{B} |\Lambda_{0,\mathsf{Sign}(k,0\|r)}\rangle_\mathbf{C} \\
& + d_{1,\mathsf{Sign}(k,1\|r)} |1\rangle_\mathbf{A} |\mathsf{Sign}(k, 1\|r)\rangle_\mathbf{B} |\Lambda_{1,\mathsf{Sign}(k,1\|r)}\rangle_\mathbf{C} \\
& + \sum_{(\alpha,\beta) \in S} d_{\alpha,\beta} |\alpha\rangle_\mathbf{A} |\beta\rangle_\mathbf{B} |\Lambda_{\alpha,\beta}\rangle_\mathbf{C}.
\end{aligned} \tag{56}$$

Define

$$T'_\lambda := \left\{ t \in T_\lambda : \sum_{(\alpha,\beta) \in S} |d_{\alpha,\beta}|^2 \leq \frac{1}{4p^{21}(\lambda)} \right\}. \tag{57}$$

If $\sum_{t \in T_\lambda \setminus T'_\lambda} \Pr[t] \geq \frac{1}{4p(\lambda)}$ for infinitely many $\lambda \in I$, it contradicts the strong EUF-CMA security of the digital signature scheme. Therefore, $\sum_{t \in T_\lambda \setminus T'_\lambda} \Pr[t] \leq \frac{1}{4p(\lambda)}$ for all $\lambda \in I'$, where $I' := \{\lambda \in I : \lambda \geq \lambda_0\}$ with a certain λ_0. This means that

$$\sum_{t \in T'_\lambda} \Pr[t] \geq \sum_{t \in T_\lambda} \Pr[t] - \frac{1}{4p(\lambda)} \geq \frac{1}{2p(\lambda)} - \frac{1}{4p(\lambda)} = \frac{1}{4p(\lambda)} \tag{58}$$

for all $\lambda \in I'$.

Moreover, because $t \in T'_\lambda$ means $t \in T_\lambda$, $\Pr[\mathsf{Good} \mid t] \geq \frac{1}{4p(\lambda)}$ for all $\lambda \in I$ from Eq. (31). Therefore, for any $t \in T'_\lambda$,

$$|d_{0,\mathsf{Sign}(k,0\|r)}|^2 + |d_{1,\mathsf{Sign}(k,1\|r)}|^2 + \sum_{(\alpha,\beta) \in S} |d_{\alpha,\beta}|^2 \geq \frac{1}{4p(\lambda)} \tag{59}$$

for all $\lambda \in I$. If we renormalize the state of Eq. (56) and apply Z^b, we have

$$|\phi_b^{t,good}\rangle \tag{60}$$

$$= \frac{d_{0,\mathsf{Sign}(k,0\|r)}}{\sqrt{|d_{0,\mathsf{Sign}(k,0\|r)}|^2 + |d_{1,\mathsf{Sign}(k,1\|r)}|^2 + \sum_{(\alpha,\beta)\in S}|d_{\alpha,\beta}|^2}} |0\rangle_\mathbf{A} |\mathsf{Sign}(k,0\|r)\rangle_\mathbf{B} |\Lambda_{0,\mathsf{Sign}(k,0\|r)}\rangle_\mathbf{C} \tag{61}$$

$$+ (-1)^b \frac{d_{1,\mathsf{Sign}(k,1\|r)}}{\sqrt{|d_{0,\mathsf{Sign}(k,0\|r)}|^2 + |d_{1,\mathsf{Sign}(k,1\|r)}|^2 + \sum_{(\alpha,\beta)\in S}|d_{\alpha,\beta}|^2}} |1\rangle_\mathbf{A} |\mathsf{Sign}(k,1\|r)\rangle_\mathbf{B} |\Lambda_{1,\mathsf{Sign}(k,1\|r)}\rangle_\mathbf{C} \tag{62}$$

$$+ Z^b \frac{\sum_{(\alpha,\beta)\in S} d_{\alpha,\beta}}{\sqrt{|d_{0,\mathsf{Sign}(k,0\|r)}|^2 + |d_{1,\mathsf{Sign}(k,1\|r)}|^2 + \sum_{(\alpha,\beta)\in S}|d_{\alpha,\beta}|^2}} |\alpha\rangle_\mathbf{A} |\beta\rangle_\mathbf{B} |\Lambda_{\alpha,\beta}\rangle_\mathbf{C}. \tag{63}$$

For any $t \in T_\lambda'$, its trace distance to the state

$$\frac{d_{0,\mathsf{Sign}(k,0\|r)}}{\sqrt{|d_{0,\mathsf{Sign}(k,0\|r)}|^2 + |d_{1,\mathsf{Sign}(k,1\|r)}|^2}} |0\rangle_\mathbf{A} |\mathsf{Sign}(k,0\|r)\rangle_\mathbf{B} |\Lambda_{0,\mathsf{Sign}(k,0\|r)}\rangle_\mathbf{C} \tag{64}$$

$$+ (-1)^b \frac{d_{1,\mathsf{Sign}(k,1\|r)}}{\sqrt{|d_{0,\mathsf{Sign}(k,0\|r)}|^2 + |d_{1,\mathsf{Sign}(k,1\|r)}|^2}} |1\rangle_\mathbf{A} |\mathsf{Sign}(k,1\|r)\rangle_\mathbf{B} |\Lambda_{1,\mathsf{Sign}(k,1\|r)}\rangle_\mathbf{C} \tag{65}$$

is less than $\frac{1}{p^{10}(\lambda)}$ for all $\lambda \in I$. □

6.2 No QPT Adversary Can Output Two Signatures

Here we show that no QPT adversary can win Hybrid 2 (Fig. 3) with a non-negligible probability. We first give an intuitive argument for the proof, and them give a precise proof.

Intuitive argument for the proof is as follows. First, note that the probability that all $\{r_i\}_{i=1}^m$ are distinct in Item 3 in Fig. 3 is at least $1 - \mathsf{negl}(\lambda)$. Therefore, we can assume that all $\{r_i\}_{i=1}^m$ are distinct with a negligible loss in the adversary's winning probability. If $r \notin \{r_i\}_{i=1}^m$, it is clear that $\mathcal{A}$ cannot win the game of Fig. 3 except for a negligible probability. The reason is that $\mathcal{A}$ cannot find $\mathsf{Sign}(k,0\|r)$ or $\mathsf{Sign}(k,1\|r)$ except for a negligible probability due to the security of the digital signature scheme. Therefore, we assume that r is equal to one of the $\{r_i\}_{i=1}^m$.

Assume that, in the game of Fig. 3, $\mathcal{C}$ is replaced with $\mathcal{C}'$ who is the same as $\mathcal{C}$ except that it measures the first qubit of $|\psi_r\rangle$ in the computational basis before sending the states in Item 3. Let $s \in \{0,1\}$ be the measurement result. Then, for any QPT adversary $\mathcal{A}$, the probability that $\mathcal{A}$ wins the game of Fig. 3 is negligible. The reason is that $\mathcal{A}$ cannot find $\mathsf{Sign}(k, s \oplus 1\|r)$ except for a negligible probability due to the strong EUF-CMA security of the digital signature scheme. From Lemma 3.1, we therefore have

$$\Pr[(\mathsf{Sign}(k,0\|r), \mathsf{Sign}(k,1\|r)) \leftarrow \mathcal{A} \mid \mathcal{C}] \leq 2\Pr[(\mathsf{Sign}(k,0\|r), \mathsf{Sign}(k,1\|r)) \leftarrow \mathcal{A} \mid \mathcal{C}'] \tag{66}$$

$$\leq \mathsf{negl}(\lambda), \tag{67}$$

where the left-hand-side of Eq. (66) is the probability that $\mathcal{A}$ outputs $(\mathsf{Sign}(k,0\|r), \mathsf{Sign}(k,1\|r))$ with the challenger $\mathcal{C}$, and the right-hand-side is that with the challenger $\mathcal{C}'$.

We give a precise proof below. Let Alg be an algorithm that, on input $(r_1,...,r_m)$, simulates $\mathcal{C}$ and $\mathcal{A}$ in Fig. 3 and outputs (r,μ_0,μ_1). The probability that $\mathcal{A}$ wins in the game of Fig. 3 is

$$\frac{1}{2^{um}} \sum_{r_1,...,r_m} \sum_r \Pr[(r,\mathsf{Sign}(k,0\|r),\mathsf{Sign}(k,1\|r)) \leftarrow \mathsf{Alg}(r_1,...,r_m)] \tag{68}$$

$$= \frac{1}{2^{um}} \sum_{(r_1,...,r_m)\in R} \sum_r \Pr[(r,\mathsf{Sign}(k,0\|r),\mathsf{Sign}(k,1\|r)) \leftarrow \mathsf{Alg}(r_1,...,r_m)] \tag{69}$$

$$+ \frac{1}{2^{um}} \sum_{(r_1,...,r_m)\notin R} \sum_r \Pr[(r,\mathsf{Sign}(k,0\|r),\mathsf{Sign}(k,1\|r)) \leftarrow \mathsf{Alg}(r_1,...,r_m)] \tag{70}$$

$$\leq \frac{1}{2^{um}} \sum_{(r_1,...,r_m)\in R} \sum_r \Pr[(r,\mathsf{Sign}(k,0\|r),\mathsf{Sign}(k,1\|r)) \leftarrow \mathsf{Alg}(r_1,...,r_m)] + \frac{1}{2^{um}} \sum_{(r_1,...,r_m)\notin R} \tag{71}$$

$$\leq \frac{1}{2^{um}} \sum_{(r_1,...,r_m)\in R} \sum_r \Pr[(r,\mathsf{Sign}(k,0\|r),\mathsf{Sign}(k,1\|r)) \leftarrow \mathsf{Alg}(r_1,...,r_m)] + \frac{(m-1)m}{2^u} \tag{72}$$

$$= \frac{1}{2^{um}} \sum_{(r_1,...,r_m)\in R} \sum_{r\in\{r_i\}_{i=1}^m} \Pr[(r,\mathsf{Sign}(k,0\|r),\mathsf{Sign}(k,1\|r)) \leftarrow \mathsf{Alg}(r_1,...,r_m)] \tag{73}$$

$$+ \frac{1}{2^{um}} \sum_{(r_1,...,r_m)\in R} \sum_{r\notin\{r_i\}_{i=1}^m} \Pr[(r,\mathsf{Sign}(k,0\|r),\mathsf{Sign}(k,1\|r)) \leftarrow \mathsf{Alg}(r_1,...,r_m)] + \frac{(m-1)m}{2^u} \tag{74}$$

$$\leq \frac{1}{2^{um}} \sum_{(r_1,...,r_m)\in R} \sum_{r\in\{r_i\}_{i=1}^m} \Pr[(r,\mathsf{Sign}(k,0\|r),\mathsf{Sign}(k,1\|r)) \leftarrow \mathsf{Alg}(r_1,...,r_m)] \tag{75}$$

$$+ \frac{1}{2^{um}} \sum_{(r_1,...,r_m)\in R} \mathsf{negl}(\lambda) + \frac{(m-1)m}{2^u} \tag{76}$$

$$\leq \frac{1}{2^{um}} \sum_{(r_1,...,r_m)\in R} \sum_{r\in\{r_i\}_{i=1}^m} \Pr[(r,\mathsf{Sign}(k,0\|r),\mathsf{Sign}(k,1\|r)) \leftarrow \mathsf{Alg}(r_1,...,r_m)] \tag{77}$$

$$+ \mathsf{negl}(\lambda) + \frac{(m-1)m}{2^u} \tag{78}$$

$$\leq \frac{1}{2^{um}} \sum_{(r_1,...,r_m)\in R} \sum_{r\in\{r_i\}_{i=1}^m} 2\Pr'[(r,\mathsf{Sign}(k,0\|r),\mathsf{Sign}(k,1\|r)) \leftarrow \mathsf{Alg}(r_1,...,r_m)] \tag{79}$$

$$+ \mathsf{negl}(\lambda) + \frac{(m-1)m}{2^u} \tag{80}$$

$$\leq \frac{1}{2^{um}} \sum_{(r_1,...,r_m)\in R} \sum_{r\in\{r_i\}_{i=1}^m} \mathsf{negl}(\lambda) + \mathsf{negl}(\lambda) + \frac{(m-1)m}{2^u} \tag{81}$$

$$\leq \mathsf{negl}(\lambda) + \mathsf{negl}(\lambda) + \frac{(m-1)m}{2^u} \tag{82}$$

$$= \mathsf{negl}(\lambda). \tag{83}$$

Here, $R := \{(r_1,...,r_m) : \text{All of them are distinct}\}$. In Eq. (76), we have used the strong EUF-CMA security of the digital signature scheme. $\Pr'$ is the probability that, in Alg, $\mathcal{C}$ is replaced with $\mathcal{C}'$ who is the same as $\mathcal{C}$ except that it measures the first qubit of $|\psi_r\rangle$ in the computational basis before sending the states in Item 3. Equation (79) comes from Lemma 3.1. Equation (81) is from the strong EUF-CMA security of the digital signature scheme.

7 Chosen Ciphertext Security

We extend IND-pkT-CPA security to the chosen ciphertext setting as follows.

Definition 7.1 (IND-pkT-CCA security). *For any polynomial m, and any QPT adversary $\mathcal{A}$, we have*

$$\Pr\left[b \leftarrow \mathcal{A}^{O_{\mathsf{Dec},2}(\cdot)}(\mathsf{ct}^*, \mathsf{cv}, \mathsf{st}) : \begin{array}{l} (\mathsf{sk}, \mathsf{vk}) \leftarrow \mathsf{SKGen}(1^\lambda) \\ \mathsf{pk}_1, ..., \mathsf{pk}_m \leftarrow \mathsf{PKGen}(\mathsf{sk})^{\otimes m} \\ (\mathsf{pk}', \mathsf{msg}_0, \mathsf{msg}_1, \mathsf{st}) \leftarrow \mathcal{A}^{O_{\mathsf{Dec},1}(\cdot)}(\mathsf{vk}, \mathsf{pk}_1, ..., \mathsf{pk}_m) \\ b \leftarrow \{0,1\} \\ \mathsf{ct}^* \leftarrow \mathsf{Enc}(\mathsf{vk}, \mathsf{pk}', \mathsf{msg}_b) \\ \mathsf{cv} := 0 \text{ if } \mathsf{Dec}(\mathsf{sk}, \mathsf{ct}^*) = \bot \text{ and otherwise } \mathsf{cv} := 1 \end{array}\right] \leq \frac{1}{2} + \mathsf{negl}(\lambda).$$
(84)

Here, $\mathsf{pk}_1, ..., \mathsf{pk}_m \leftarrow \mathsf{PKGen}(\mathsf{sk})^{\otimes m}$ *means that* PKGen *is executed m times and* pk_i *is the output of the ith execution of* PKGen. st *is a quantum internal state of* $\mathcal{A}$*, which can be entangled with* pk'*. Also,* $O_{\mathsf{Dec},1}(\mathsf{ct})$ *returns* $\mathsf{Dec}(\mathsf{sk}, \mathsf{ct})$ *for any* ct. $O_{\mathsf{Dec},2}$ *behaves identically to* $O_{\mathsf{Dec},1}$ *except that* $O_{\mathsf{Dec},2}$ *returns* $\bot$ *to the input* ct^*.

In the full version, we show a generic compiler that upgrades an IND-pkT-CPA secure QPKE scheme to IND-pkt-CCA secure one while preserving decryption error detectability by additionally using OWFs. Combined with our construction of IND-pkT-CPA secure QPKE scheme based on OWFs, we obtain the following theorem.

Theorem 7.1. *If there exist OWFs, then there exists a QPKE scheme that satisfies IND-pkT-CCA security and decryption error detectability.*

Due to space limitation, we omit the proof. Its overview can be found in Sect. 2.3 and the full proof can be found in the full version.

8 Recyclable Variants

In the construction given in Section 5, a quantum public key can be used to encrypt only one message and a sender needs to obtain a new quantum public key whenever it encrypts a message. This is not desirable from practical perspective. In this section, we define recyclable QPKE where a sender only needs to receive one quantum public key to send arbitrarily many messages, and then show how to achieve it.

8.1 Definitions

The definition is similar to QPKE as defined in Definition 4.1 except that the encryption algorithm outputs a classical *recycled* key that can be reused to encrypt messages many times.

Definition 8.1 (Recyclable QPKE). *A recyclable QPKE scheme with message space $\{0,1\}^\ell$ is a set of algorithms* (SKGen, PKGen, Enc, rEnc, Dec) *such that*

- SKGen$(1^\lambda) \to$ (sk, vk) : *It is a PPT algorithm that, on input the security parameter λ, outputs a classical secret key* sk *and a classical verification key* vk.

Quantum Public-Key Encryption with Tamper-Resilient Public Keys   121

- PKGen(sk) → pk : *It is a QPT algorithm that, on input* sk, *outputs a quantum public key* pk.
- Enc(vk, pk, msg) → (ct, rk) : *It is a QPT algorithm that, on input* vk, pk, *and a plaintext* msg $\in \{0,1\}^\ell$, *outputs a classical ciphertext* ct *and classical recycled key* rk.
- rEnc(rk, msg) → ct : *It is a PPT algorithm that, on input* rk *and a plaintext* msg $\in \{0,1\}^\ell$, *outputs a classical ciphertext* ct.
- Dec(sk, ct) → msg' : *It is a classical deterministic polynomial-time algorithm that, on input* sk *and* ct, *outputs* msg' $\in \{0,1\}^\ell \cup \{\bot\}$.

We require the following correctness.

Correctness: *For any* msg, msg' $\in \{0,1\}^\ell$,

$$\Pr\left[\mathsf{msg} \leftarrow \mathsf{Dec}(\mathsf{sk},\mathsf{ct}) \land \mathsf{msg}' \leftarrow \mathsf{Dec}(\mathsf{sk},\mathsf{ct}') : \begin{array}{c}(\mathsf{sk},\mathsf{vk}) \leftarrow \mathsf{SKGen}(1^\lambda)\\ \mathsf{pk} \leftarrow \mathsf{PKGen}(\mathsf{sk})\\ (\mathsf{ct},\mathsf{rk}) \leftarrow \mathsf{Enc}(\mathsf{vk},\mathsf{pk},\mathsf{msg})\\ \mathsf{ct}' \leftarrow \mathsf{rEnc}(\mathsf{rk},\mathsf{msg}')\end{array}\right] \geq 1 - \mathsf{negl}(\lambda).$$
(85)

Definition 8.2 (IND-pkT-CPA Security for Recyclable QPKE). *We require the followings.*

Security Under Quantum Public Keys: *For any polynomial m, and any QPT adversary* $\mathcal{A}$,

$$\Pr\left[b \leftarrow \mathcal{A}^{\mathsf{rEnc}(\mathsf{rk},\cdot)}(\mathsf{ct}^*,\mathsf{st}) : \begin{array}{c}(\mathsf{sk},\mathsf{vk}) \leftarrow \mathsf{SKGen}(1^\lambda)\\ \mathsf{pk}_1,...,\mathsf{pk}_m \leftarrow \mathsf{PKGen}(\mathsf{sk})^{\otimes m}\\ (\mathsf{pk}',\mathsf{msg}_0,\mathsf{msg}_1,\mathsf{st}) \leftarrow \mathcal{A}(\mathsf{vk},\mathsf{pk}_1,...,\mathsf{pk}_m)\\ b \leftarrow \{0,1\}\\ (\mathsf{ct}^*,\mathsf{rk}) \leftarrow \mathsf{Enc}(\mathsf{vk},\mathsf{pk}',\mathsf{msg}_b)\end{array}\right] \leq \frac{1}{2} + \mathsf{negl}(\lambda).$$
(86)

Security Under Recycled Keys: *For any polynomial m, and any QPT adversary* $\mathcal{A}$,

$$\Pr\left[b \leftarrow \mathcal{A}^{\mathsf{rEnc}(\mathsf{rk},\cdot)}(\mathsf{ct}^*,\mathsf{st}') : \begin{array}{c}(\mathsf{sk},\mathsf{vk}) \leftarrow \mathsf{SKGen}(1^\lambda)\\ \mathsf{pk}_1,...,\mathsf{pk}_m \leftarrow \mathsf{PKGen}(\mathsf{sk})^{\otimes m}\\ (\mathsf{pk}',\mathsf{msg},\mathsf{st}) \leftarrow \mathcal{A}(\mathsf{vk},\mathsf{pk}_1,...,\mathsf{pk}_m)\\ (\mathsf{ct}',\mathsf{rk}) \leftarrow \mathsf{Enc}(\mathsf{vk},\mathsf{pk}',\mathsf{msg})\\ (\mathsf{msg}_0,\mathsf{msg}_1,\mathsf{st}') \leftarrow \mathcal{A}^{\mathsf{rEnc}(\mathsf{rk},\cdot)}(\mathsf{ct}',\mathsf{st})\\ b \leftarrow \{0,1\}\\ \mathsf{ct}^* \leftarrow \mathsf{rEnc}(\mathsf{rk},\mathsf{msg}_b)\end{array}\right] \leq \frac{1}{2} + \mathsf{negl}(\lambda).$$
(87)

Here, $\mathsf{pk}_1,...,\mathsf{pk}_m \leftarrow \mathsf{PKGen}(\mathsf{sk})^{\otimes m}$ *means that* PKGen *is executed m times and* pk_i *is the output of the ith execution of* PKGen, $\mathsf{rEnc}(\mathsf{rk},\cdot)$ *means a classically-accessible encryption oracle, and* st *and* st' *are quantum internal states of* $\mathcal{A}$, *which can be entangled with* pk'.

Definition 8.3 (IND-pkT-CCA Security for Recyclable QPKE). *We require the followings.*

122   F. Kitagawa et al.

Security Under Quantum Public Keys: *For any polynomial m, and any QPT adversary $\mathcal{A}$,*

$$\Pr\left[b \leftarrow \mathcal{A}^{\mathsf{rEnc}(\mathsf{rk},\cdot),\mathcal{O}_{\mathsf{Dec},2}(\cdot)}(\mathsf{ct}^*,\mathsf{cv},\mathsf{st}) : \begin{array}{c}(\mathsf{sk},\mathsf{vk}) \leftarrow \mathsf{SKGen}(1^\lambda) \\ \mathsf{pk}_1,\ldots,\mathsf{pk}_m \leftarrow \mathsf{PKGen}(\mathsf{sk})^{\otimes m} \\ (\mathsf{pk}',\mathsf{msg}_0,\mathsf{msg}_1,\mathsf{st}) \leftarrow \mathcal{A}^{\mathcal{O}_{\mathsf{Dec},1}(\cdot)}(\mathsf{vk},\mathsf{pk}_1,\ldots,\mathsf{pk}_m) \\ b \leftarrow \{0,1\} \\ (\mathsf{ct}^*,\mathsf{rk}) \leftarrow \mathsf{Enc}(\mathsf{vk},\mathsf{pk}',\mathsf{msg}_b) \\ \mathsf{cv} := 0 \text{ if } \mathsf{Dec}(\mathsf{sk},\mathsf{ct}^*) = \bot \text{ and otherwise } \mathsf{cv} := 1 \end{array}\right] \leq \frac{1}{2} + \mathsf{negl}(\lambda). \quad (88)$$

Security Under Recycled Keys: *For any polynomial m, and any QPT adversary $\mathcal{A}$,*

$$\Pr\left[b \leftarrow \mathcal{A}^{\mathsf{rEnc}(\mathsf{rk},\cdot),\mathcal{O}_{\mathsf{Dec},2}(\cdot)}(\mathsf{ct}^*,\mathsf{cv},\mathsf{st}') : \begin{array}{c}(\mathsf{sk},\mathsf{vk}) \leftarrow \mathsf{SKGen}(1^\lambda) \\ \mathsf{pk}_1,\ldots,\mathsf{pk}_m \leftarrow \mathsf{PKGen}(\mathsf{sk})^{\otimes m} \\ (\mathsf{pk}',\mathsf{msg},\mathsf{st}) \leftarrow \mathcal{A}^{\mathcal{O}_{\mathsf{Dec},1}(\cdot)}(\mathsf{vk},\mathsf{pk}_1,\ldots,\mathsf{pk}_m) \\ (\mathsf{ct}',\mathsf{rk}) \leftarrow \mathsf{Enc}(\mathsf{vk},\mathsf{pk}',\mathsf{msg}) \\ (\mathsf{msg}_0,\mathsf{msg}_1,\mathsf{st}') \leftarrow \mathcal{A}^{\mathsf{rEnc}(\mathsf{rk},\cdot),\mathcal{O}_{\mathsf{Dec},1}(\cdot)}(\mathsf{ct}',\mathsf{st}) \\ b \leftarrow \{0,1\} \\ \mathsf{ct}^* \leftarrow \mathsf{rEnc}(\mathsf{rk},\mathsf{msg}_b) \\ \mathsf{cv} := 0 \text{ if } \mathsf{Dec}(\mathsf{sk},\mathsf{ct}^*) = \bot \text{ and otherwise } \mathsf{cv} := 1 \end{array}\right] \leq \frac{1}{2} + \mathsf{negl}(\lambda).$$

(89)

Here, $\mathsf{pk}_1,\ldots,\mathsf{pk}_m \leftarrow \mathsf{PKGen}(\mathsf{sk})^{\otimes m}$ *means that* PKGen *is executed m times and pk_i is the output of the ith execution of* PKGen, $\mathsf{rEnc}(\mathsf{rk},\cdot)$ *means a classically-accessible encryption oracle, and* st *and* st' *are quantum internal states of* $\mathcal{A}$, *which can be entangled with* pk'. *Also,* $\mathcal{O}_{\mathsf{Dec},1}(\mathsf{ct})$ *returns* $\mathsf{Dec}(\mathsf{sk},\mathsf{ct})$ *for any* ct. $\mathcal{O}_{\mathsf{Dec},2}$ *behaves identically to* $\mathcal{O}_{\mathsf{Dec},1}$ *except that* $\mathcal{O}_{\mathsf{Dec},2}$ *returns* $\bot$ *to the input* ct^*.

8.2 Construction

We show a generic construction of recyclable QPKE from (non-recyclable) QPKE with classical ciphertexts and SKE via standard hybrid encryption.

Let QPKE = (QPKE.SKGen, QPKE.PKGen, QPKE.Enc, QPKE.Dec) be a (non-recyclable) QPKE scheme with message space $\{0,1\}^\lambda$ and SKE = (SKE.Enc, SKE.Dec) be an SKE scheme with message space $\{0,1\}^\ell$. Then we construct a recyclable QPKE scheme QPKE' = (QPKE'.SKGen, QPKE'.PKGen, QPKE'.Enc, QPKE'.rEnc, QPKE'.Dec) with message space $\{0,1\}^\ell$ as follows:

- QPKE'.SKGen$(1^\lambda) \to (\mathsf{sk}',\mathsf{vk}')$: Run $(\mathsf{sk},\mathsf{vk}) \leftarrow$ QPKE.SKGen(1^λ) and output a secret key $\mathsf{sk}' := \mathsf{sk}$ and verification key $\mathsf{vk}' := \mathsf{vk}$.
- QPKE'.PKGen$(\mathsf{sk}') \to \mathsf{pk}'$: Run $\mathsf{pk} \leftarrow$ QPKE.PKGen(sk) and outputs $\mathsf{pk}' := \mathsf{pk}$.
- QPKE'.Enc$(\mathsf{vk}',\mathsf{pk}',\mathsf{msg}) \to (\mathsf{ct}',\mathsf{rk}')$: Parse $\mathsf{pk}' = \mathsf{pk}$ and $\mathsf{vk}' = \mathsf{vk}$, sample $K \leftarrow \{0,1\}^\lambda$, run $\mathsf{ct} \leftarrow$ QPKE.Enc$(\mathsf{vk},\mathsf{pk},K)$ and $\mathsf{ct}_{\mathsf{ske}} \leftarrow$ SKE.Enc(K,msg), and output a ciphertext $\mathsf{ct}' := (\mathsf{ct},\mathsf{ct}_{\mathsf{ske}})$ and recycled key $\mathsf{rk}' := (K,\mathsf{ct})$.
- QPKE'.rEnc$(\mathsf{rk}',\mathsf{msg}) \to \mathsf{ct}'$: Parse $\mathsf{rk}' = (K,\mathsf{ct})$, run $\mathsf{ct}_{\mathsf{ske}} \leftarrow$ SKE.Enc(K,msg), and output a ciphertext $\mathsf{ct}' := (\mathsf{ct},\mathsf{ct}_{\mathsf{ske}})$.
- QPKE'.Dec$(\mathsf{sk}',\mathsf{ct}') \to \mathsf{msg}'$: Parse $\mathsf{ct}' = (\mathsf{ct},\mathsf{ct}_{\mathsf{ske}})$ and $\mathsf{sk}' = \mathsf{sk}$, run $K' \leftarrow$ QPKE.Dec$(\mathsf{sk},\mathsf{ct})$ and $\mathsf{msg}' \leftarrow$ SKE.Dec$(K',\mathsf{ct}_{\mathsf{ske}})$, and output msg'.

Correctness and Decryption Error Detectability. Correctness of QPKE′ immediately follows from correctness of QPKE and SKE. Also, the decryption error detectability of QPKE′ directly follows from that of QPKE.

IND-pkT-CPA Security and IND-pkT-CCA Security. If QPKE satisfies IND-pkT-CPA (resp. IND-pkT-CCA) security and SKE satisfies IND-CPA (resp. IND-CCA) security, then QPKE′ satisfies IND-pkT-CPA (resp. IND-pkT-CCA) security. The proofs can be done by standard hybrid arguments, thus omitted.

Acknowledgments. TM is supported by JST CREST JPMJCR23I3, JST Moonshot R&D JPMJMS2061-5-1-1, JST FOREST, MEXT QLEAP, the Grant-in-Aid for Scientific Research (B) No. JP19H04066, the Grant-in Aid for Transformative Research Areas (A) 21H05183, and the Grant-in-Aid for Scientific Research (A) No. 22H00522.

References

[AAS20] Aaronson, S., Atia, Y., Susskind, L.: On the hardness of detecting macroscopic superpositions. Electron. Colloquium Comput. Complex. 146 (2020)

[AGM21] Alagic, G., Gagliardoni, T., Majenz, C.: Can you sign a quantum state? Quantum **5**, 603 (2021)

[AGQY22] Ananth, P., Gulati, A., Qian, L., Yuen, H.: Pseudorandom (function-like) quantum state generators: New definitions and applications. In: Kiltz, E., Vaikuntanathan, V. (eds.) TCC 2022, Part I. LNCS, vol. 13747, pp. 237–265. Springer, Heidelberg (2022). https://doi.org/10.1007/978-3-031-22318-1_9

[AQY22] Ananth, P., Qian, L., Yuen, H.: Cryptography from pseudorandom quantum states. In: Dodis, Y., Shrimpton, T. (eds.) CRYPTO 2022, Part I. LNCS, vol. 13507, pp. 208–236. Springer, Heidelberg (2022). https://doi.org/10.1007/978-3-031-15802-5_8

[BB84] Bennett, C.H., Brassard, G.: Quantum cryptography: Public key distribution and coin tossing. In: IEEE International Conference on Computers Systems and Signal Processing, pp. 175–179. IEEE (1984)

[BCG+02] Barnum, H., Crépeau, C., Gottesman, D., Smith, A., Tapp, A.: Authentication of quantum messages. In: 43rd FOCS, pp. 449–458. IEEE Computer Society Press (2002)

[BCKM21] Bartusek, J., Coladangelo, A., Khurana, D., Ma, F.: One-way functions imply secure computation in a quantum world. In: Malkin, T., Peikert, C. (eds.) CRYPTO 2021. LNCS, vol. 12825, pp. 467–496. Springer, Cham (2021). https://doi.org/10.1007/978-3-030-84242-0_17

[BCQ23] Brakerski, Z., Canetti, R., Qian, L.: On the computational hardness needed for quantum cryptography. In: Kalai, Y.T. (ed.) 14th Innovations in Theoretical Computer Science Conference, ITCS 2023, 10–13 January 2023, MIT, Cambridge, Massachusetts, USA. LIPIcs, vol. 251, pp. 24:1–24:21. Schloss Dagstuhl - Leibniz-Zentrum für Informatik (2023)

[BGH+23a] Barooti, K., et al.: Public-key encryption with quantum keys. In: TCC 2023, pp. 198–227 (2023)

[BGH+23b] Barooti, K., et al.: Public-key encryption with quantum keys. IACR Cryptol. ePrint Arch. 877 (2023)

[BN08] Bellare, M., Namprempre, C.: Authenticated encryption: relations among notions and analysis of the generic composition paradigm. J. Cryptol. **21**(4), 469–491 (2008)

[BSS21] Behera, A., Sattath, O., Shinar, U.: Noise-tolerant quantum tokens for MAC. Cryptology ePrint Archive, Report 2021/1353 (2021). https://eprint.iacr.org/2021/1353

[BZ13] Boneh, D., Zhandry, M.: Secure signatures and chosen ciphertext security in a quantum computing world. In: Canetti, R., Garay, J.A. (eds.) CRYPTO 2013, Part II. LNCS, vol. 8043, pp. 361–379. Springer, Heidelberg (2013). https://doi.org/10.1007/978-3-642-40084-1_21

[CHH+07] Cramer, R., et al.: Bounded CCA2-secure encryption. In: Kurosawa, K. (ed.) ASIACRYPT 2007. LNCS, vol. 4833, pp. 502–518. Springer, Heidelberg (2007). https://doi.org/10.1007/978-3-540-76900-2_31

[Col23] Coladangelo, A.: Quantum trapdoor functions from classical one-way functions. Cryptology ePrint Archive, Paper 2023/282 (2023). https://eprint.iacr.org/2023/282

[CX22] Cao, S., Xue, R.: On constructing one-way quantum state generators, and more. Cryptology ePrint Archive, Report 2022/1323 (2022). https://eprint.iacr.org/2022/1323

[GGM86] Goldreich, O., Goldwasser, S., Micali, S.: How to construct random functions. J. ACM **33**(4), 792–807 (1986)

[GKM+00] Gertner, Y., Kannan, S., Malkin, T., Reingold, O., Viswanathan, M.: The relationship between public key encryption and oblivious transfer. In: 41st FOCS, pp. 325–335. IEEE Computer Society Press (2000)

[GLSV21] Grilo, A.B., Lin, H., Song, F., Vaikuntanathan, V.: Oblivious transfer is in MiniQCrypt. In: Canteaut, A., Standaert, F.-X. (eds.) EUROCRYPT 2021. LNCS, vol. 12697, pp. 531–561. Springer, Cham (2021). https://doi.org/10.1007/978-3-030-77886-6_18

[Gol04] Goldreich, O.: Foundations of cryptography: Volume 2, basic applications (2004)

[Got] Gottesman, D.: Quantum public-key cryptography with information-theoretic security. https://www2.perimeterinstitute.ca/personal/dgottesman/Public-key.ppt

[HILL99] Håstad, J., Impagliazzo, R., Levin, L.A., Luby, M.: A pseudorandom generator from any one-way function. SIAM J. Comput. **28**(4), 1364–1396 (1999)

[HMY23] Hhan, M., Morimae, T., Yamakawa, T.: From the hardness of detecting superpositions to cryptography: quantum public key encryption and commitments. In: EUROCRYPT 2023, Part I. LNCS, vol. 14004, pp. 639–667. Springer, Heidelberg (2023). https://doi.org/10.1007/978-3-031-30545-0_22

[IR89] Impagliazzo, R., Rudich, S.: Limits on the provable consequences of one-way permutations. In: 21st ACM STOC, pp. 44–61. ACM Press (1989)

[IR90] Impagliazzo, R., Rudich, S.: Limits on the provable consequences of one-way permutations. In: Goldwasser, S. (ed.) CRYPTO 1988. LNCS, vol. 403, pp. 8–26. Springer, New York (1990). https://doi.org/10.1007/0-387-34799-2_2

[JLS18] Ji, Z., Liu, Y.-K., Song, F.: Pseudorandom quantum states. In: Shacham, H., Boldyreva, A. (eds.) CRYPTO 2018, Part III. LNCS, vol. 10993, pp. 126–152. Springer, Cham (2018). https://doi.org/10.1007/978-3-319-96878-0_5

[KKNY05] Kawachi, A., Koshiba, T., Nishimura, H., Yamakami, T.: Computational indistinguishability between quantum states and its cryptographic application. In: Cramer, R. (ed.) EUROCRYPT 2005. LNCS, vol. 3494, pp. 268–284. Springer, Heidelberg (2005). https://doi.org/10.1007/11426639_16

[KQST23] Kretschmer, W., Qian, L., Sinha, M., Tal, A.: Quantum cryptography in algorithmica. In: Saha, B., Servedio, R.A. (eds.) Proceedings of the 55th Annual ACM Symposium on Theory of Computing, STOC 2023, Orlando, FL, USA, 20–23 June 2023, pp. 1589–1602. ACM (2023)

[Kre21] Kretschmer, W.: Quantum pseudorandomness and classical complexity. In: TQC 2021 (2021)

[MW23] Malavolta, G., Walter, M.: Robust quantum public-key encryption with applications to quantum key distribution (2023)

[MY22a] Morimae, T., Yamakawa, T.: One-wayness in quantum cryptography. Cryptology ePrint Archive, Report 2022/1336 (2022). https://eprint.iacr.org/2022/1336

[MY22b] Morimae, T., Yamakawa, T.: Quantum commitments and signatures without one-way functions. In: Dodis, Y., Shrimpton, T. (eds.) CRYPTO 2022, Part I. LNCS, vol. 13507, pp. 269–295. Springer, Heidelberg (2022). https://doi.org/10.1007/978-3-031-15802-5_10

[Zha12] Zhandry, M.: How to construct quantum random functions. In: 53rd FOCS, pp. 679–687. IEEE Computer Society Press (2012)

Robust Quantum Public-Key Encryption with Applications to Quantum Key Distribution

Giulio Malavolta[1,2(✉)] and Michael Walter[3]

[1] Bocconi University, Milan, Italy
giulio.malavolta@hotmail.it
[2] Max Planck Institute for Security and Privacy, Bochum, Germany
[3] Ruhr-Universität Bochum, Bochum, Germany

Abstract. Quantum key distribution (QKD) allows Alice and Bob to agree on a shared secret key, while communicating over a public (untrusted) quantum channel. Compared to classical key exchange, it has two main advantages: (i) The key is *unconditionally* hidden to the eyes of any attacker, and (ii) its security assumes only the existence of authenticated classical channels which, in practice, can be realized using Minicrypt assumptions, such as the existence of digital signatures. On the flip side, QKD protocols typically require multiple rounds of interactions, whereas classical key exchange can be realized with the minimal amount of two messages using public-key encryption. A long-standing open question is whether QKD requires more rounds of interaction than classical key exchange.

In this work, we propose a two-message QKD protocol that satisfies *everlasting* security, assuming only the existence of quantum-secure one-way functions. That is, the shared key is unconditionally hidden, provided computational assumptions hold during the protocol execution. Our result follows from a new construction of quantum public-key encryption (QPKE) whose security, much like its classical counterpart, only relies on authenticated *classical* channels.

1 Introduction

Quantum key distribution (QKD) [5] enables Alice and Bob to exchange a secret key over a public (untrusted) quantum channel. Compared to classical key exchange, it offers two main advantages: (i) It hides the key *unconditionally* or *information-theoretically* to the eyes of any (possibly unbounded and quantum) attacker, and (ii) it relies only on the existence of authenticated classical channels, which in practice can be instantiated using Minicrypt [13] computational assumptions. The former is plainly impossible to achieve without quantum information, and we also have strong evidence [14] that classical key exchange requires more structured (Cryptomania) computational assumptions.

Over the past decades, QKD has inspired a staggering amount of research, ranging from profound theoretical works [18–20,23] all the way to large-scale experiments [15,17,26]. As such, QKD is one of the most studied topics in the theory of quantum information. Despite the vast literature on the topic, QKD protocols still do not outperform classical key exchange in all aspects: Whereas classical key exchange can be realized using two messages [6], which is optimal, to the best of our knowledge all known QKD protocols require more than two rounds of interaction.

This raises the question of whether more rounds of interaction are really necessary for QKD. Apart from its theoretical importance, there are also practical reasons for addressing this question. Indeed, two-message protocols are particularly desirable for practical scenarios where parties may drop offline during the protocol execution, may want to send their message at a later point in time, or do not want to keep a state across rounds. Arguably, this minimal interaction pattern is the property that makes traditional cryptographic primitives, such as public-key encryption, so useful. However, despite this strong motivation and almost fifty years of intense research, the optimal round complexity of QKD is still an open problem.

1.1 Our Results

In this work we show that two messages are sufficient to build a QKD protocol with everlasting security. Specifically, we prove the following statement:

If quantum-secure one-way functions exist, then there exists two-message everlasting QKD.

Since two messages are clearly necessary for QKD, our protocol achieves the optimal round complexity. Furthermore, only the first message (from Alice to Bob) is quantum, whereas Bob's response is entirely classical. The protocol satisfies the strong notion of *everlasting security*: As long as the attacker runs in quantum polynomial time during the execution of the protocol, the shared key is hidden in an *information-theoretic* sense.

We view our approach as a big departure from the traditional design of QKD protocols [5,9], and it is inspired instead by recent works on cryptography with certified deletion [4] and quantum public-key encryption [3]. Both our protocol and its analysis are entirely elementary and they are simple enough to be fully described in an undergraduate class. For comparison, it took more than ten years for researchers to establish a formal proof of the first QKD protocol [5].

Our main technical ingredient is a new framework for building quantum public-key encryption (QPKE), a cryptographic primitive that allows Alice to sample a public key consisting of a quantum state ρ and a classical string pk. The scheme is *robust*, in the sense that security is guaranteed to hold even if the distinguisher is given pk, and it is allowed to tamper arbitrarily with the quantum state ρ. We present two instances of QPKE:

– (Everlasting Security) In our first scheme, the message m remains *information-theoretically* hidden, provided that the distinguisher was computationally bounded during the execution of the protocol. This property

holds if the distinguisher is given a *single copy* of the public key, which is sufficient to build QKD.
- (Computational Security) In our second scheme, the message m is computationally hidden, i.e., we only require security against a computationally bounded distinguisher. While this is a weaker security notion, the advantage of the scheme is that security holds even if the distinguisher is given *arbitrarily many* copies of the public key.

The fact that the first construction is only secure in a model where we give access to a single copy of the public key is not a coincidence. It is shown [3] that given enough (but polynomially-many) copies of the public key, an unbounded adversary can launch a key-recovery attack. This means that there does not exist any QPKE with everlasting security against a distinguisher that sees arbitrarily-many copies of the public key, and it justifies the need for a weaker security notion (computational security).

Everlasting Security. We point out a subtle difference between the attacker model that we consider in this work, compared to the standard attacker model for QKD. The latter, considered for instance in [24,25], models the attacker as a computationally unbounded quantum channel, that is however not allowed to tamper with the information sent over the *classical channels*. That is, it only assumes the existence of authenticated classical channels, but otherwise does not impose any restriction on the runtime of the distinguisher. On the other hand, in this work we consider – in addition to the existence of authenticated classical channels – an attacker that runs in *quantum polynomial time* during the protocol execution, but it is allowed to be unbounded once the protocol terminates. That is, we prove *everlasting security* in the sense of [21].

While technically different, we argue that for most practical scenarios the two models are in fact equivalent. The assumption of an authenticated classical channel is most often justified by having each party sign their own messages with a digital signature, which would require computational assumptions to hold (at the very least) during the execution of the protocol. In this sense, the mere existence of authenticated classical channels already restricts the attacker to run in quantum polynomial time during the protocol execution (as otherwise it could just break the security of the digital signature).

Finally, it is not hard to show that everlasting security is the *best possible* security notion for QPKE, i.e., there exists a generic attack against any QPKE scheme, if the distinguisher is allowed to run in unbounded time during the execution of the protocol. The attack works even in the presence of authenticated classical channels and succeeds with certainty. For completeness, we report the proof of this fact in Appendix A.

1.2 Concurrent and Related Work

A concurrent work [16] obtains similar results on robust QPKE, where security holds only against a distinguisher that is allowed to tamper arbitrarily with the quantum portion of the public key. Compared to our work, they only consider the setting of *computational* security, whereas we view the scheme with *everlasting* security as the main contribution of our work, which is the one that enables our two-message QKD protocol. Even focusing on the computational settings, our schemes share many similarities but, interestingly, they are not identical. At a technical level, their approach is based on one-time signatures for Wiesner states, whereas our approach can (in retrospect) be thought of as one-time signing the $|+\rangle$ state. On the other hand, [16] presents a scheme where the public key is a pure state and furthermore their schemes achieve the stronger notion of CCA-security, which we do not consider in this work.

Finally, both the present work and [16] can be seen as a follow-up to [3], that formally introduced the notion of QPKE. However, the security definition presented in [3] is in a much weaker adversarial model, where the public keys are distributed via an authenticated *quantum* channel. In contrast, both our work and [16] require only authenticated *classical* channels, which is the same assumption as in traditional PKE.

1.3 Open Problems

Our work leaves open a series of questions, that we hope will inspire further research in this area. For starters, our protocols are described in the presence of perfect (noiseless) quantum channels. Any practical protocol would need to withstand the presence of noise. While theoretically one could simply encode all states using a quantum error correcting code, this may lead to poor concrete efficiency. We leave open the question of investigating variants our non-interactive QKD protocol that are efficient in the presence of noise.

A compelling aspect of standard QKD protocols such as [5] is that all quantum states consists of tensor products of single qubits, whereas our protocols require coherent superpositions of many-qubit states. The former property is desirable, since it allows the experimental realization of the protocol on present-day quantum hardware. We view the problem of constructing a non-interactive QKD protocol in this qubit-by-qubit model as fascinating research direction, and believe that it might require substantially different techniques from the present approach.

1.4 Overview of the Solution

Our main technical contribution is a new recipe to construct QPKE, whose definition we recall next. The syntax of QPKE consists of three algorithms: key generation, encryption, and decryption. The key generation algorithm produces a classical key pair (sk, pk), along with a quantum state ρ. The pair (pk, ρ) makes up the public key. Given this public key, anyone can compute a classical ciphertext ct encrypting a given message m, which can only be decrypted by the owner of the secret key. In terms of security, we require that the message m should be hidden, even if an efficient attacker is allowed to tamper arbitrarily with the quantum state associated with the public key.

To understand the challenge, let us recall that the security of existing quantum PKEs [3] only apply if the (quantum) public key is honestly delivered to the encrypter. In other words, such schemes implicitly assume the presence of authenticated quantum channels. This is in contrast with the standard model for QKD, which requires only authenticated *classical* channels. As discussed before, this model is justified by the fact that it is easy to implement in practice (e.g., by signing all messages), whereas authenticating quantum states is a notoriously difficult problem, and there is evidence that it is in fact not possible in full generality [2].

Fortunately, full authentication of quantum channels is not necessary for constructing quantum PKE: For instance, it is acceptable if some malformed state passes the authentication check, so long as the encryption algorithm results in an "undecryptable" cipher. In this work, we show how to achieve this, assuming the existence of (one-time) digital signatures. In more details, a public key in our scheme consists of a uniform superposition of two valid message-signature pairs

$$\frac{|0, \sigma_0\rangle + |1, \sigma_1\rangle}{\sqrt{2}} \tag{1.1}$$

where σ_b is a valid signature on b, under some verification key vk. Given such state, the encrypter authenticates the states by applying the projection

$$\Pi = \sum_{\sigma \in \Sigma_0} |0, \sigma\rangle\langle 0, \sigma| + \sum_{\sigma \in \Sigma_1} |1, \sigma\rangle\langle 1, \sigma|.$$

where Σ_b is the set of all valid signatures on b. Note that Π can be implemented efficiently given vk by running the verification algorithm coherently, and measuring the bit that denotes acceptance/rejection. If this test passes, the encrypter encodes its message $m \in \{0, 1\}$ by applying a conditional phase flip to the resulting state. In an honest run of the protocol, this results in the state

$$\frac{|0, \sigma_0\rangle + (-1)^m |1, \sigma_1\rangle}{\sqrt{2}}$$

which is efficiently decodable by decrypter, who knows both σ_0 and σ_1, by measuring the state in the corresponding basis. Our analysis boils down to showing that for any state that passes one of the following two events must have occurred:

– The state is identical to the one in Eq. (1.1). In which case, the attacker must have done nothing, and therefore the state was honestly delivered to the encrypter. One can then show that the message m is hidden by appealing to the *distinguishing implies swapping* principle [1,12].
– The state was measured in the computational basis. Note that in this case, the state is in the image of the projector Π, and therefore it will pass the authentication check. However, a phase flip on any basis state only adds a global phase, and therefore has no effect on the ciphertext. Therefore, the message is information-theoretically hidden.

Once we built QPKE, it appears to be an easy exercise to construct a two-message QKD protocol: Alice can sample a public key and send it to Bob, who replies with an encryption of a randomly sampled key $k \in \{0,1\}^\lambda$. However, there is a subtle aspect in the analysis of this protocol, where one needs to ensure that an attacker cannot cause Alice and Bob to agree on *different keys*. Note that this does not follow immediately from the security of the QPKE, which only protects privacy of the plaintext. We once again rely on one-time signatures to (provably) prevent this class of attacks.

1.5 Organization of This Paper

In Sect. 2, we discuss preliminaries in quantum information and cryptography and we prove some useful technical statements. In Sect. 3, we define the notion of QPKE, and we present two constructions (with different tradeoffs) whose security can be reduced to the one-wayness of any post-quantum one-way function. In Sect. 4 we present the formal description and the analysis of our two-message QKD protocol.

2 Preliminaries

Throughout this work, we denote the security parameter by λ. We denote by 1^λ the all-ones string of length λ. We say that a function negl is *negligible* in the security parameter λ if $\mathsf{negl}(\lambda) = \lambda^{\omega(1)}$. For a finite set S, we write $x \leftarrow S$ to denote that x is sampled uniformly at random from S. We write Tr for the trace of a matrix or operator.

2.1 Quantum Information

In this section, we provide some preliminary background on quantum information. For a more in-depth introduction, we refer the reader to [22]. A *register* x consisting of n qubits is given by a Hilbert space $(\mathbb{C}^2)^{\otimes n}$ with name or label x. Given two registers x and y, we write $x \otimes y$ for the composite register, with Hilbert space the tensor product of the individual registers' Hilbert spaces. A *pure quantum state* on register x is a unit vector $|\Psi\rangle_x \in (\mathbb{C}^2)^{\otimes n}$. A *mixed quantum state* on register x is represented by a density operator ρ_x on $(\mathbb{C}^2)^{\otimes n}$, which is a positive semi-definite Hermitian matrix with trace 1. Any pure state $|\Psi\rangle_x$ can also be regarded as a mixed state $\rho_x = |\Psi\rangle_x\langle\Psi|_x$, but there are mixed states that are not pure. In the above, we use subscripts to denote registers, but we often omit these when clear from context. We adopt the convention that

$$\{|0\rangle, |1\rangle\} \text{ and } \left\{\frac{|0\rangle + |1\rangle}{\sqrt{2}}, \frac{|0\rangle - |1\rangle}{\sqrt{2}}\right\}$$

denote the *computational* and the *Hadamard basis* states, respectively.

A *quantum channel* F is a completely-positive trace-preserving (CPTP) map from a register x to a register y. That is, on input any density matrix ρ_x, the operation F produces $F(\rho_x) = \tau_y$, another state on register y, and the same is true when we apply F to the x register of a quantum state ρ_{xz}. For any unitary operator U, meaning $U^\dagger U = UU^\dagger = \mathsf{Id}$, one obtains a quantum channel that maps input states ρ to output states $\tau := U\rho U^\dagger$. The Pauli operators $\mathsf{X}, \mathsf{Y}, \mathsf{Z}$ are 2×2 matrices that are unitary and Hermitian. More specifically:

$$\mathsf{X} = \begin{pmatrix} 0 & 1 \\ 1 & 0 \end{pmatrix}, \quad \mathsf{Y} = \begin{pmatrix} 0 & -i \\ i & 0 \end{pmatrix}, \quad \mathsf{Z} = \begin{pmatrix} 1 & 0 \\ 0 & -1 \end{pmatrix}.$$

A *projector* Π is a Hermitian operator such that $\Pi^2 = \Pi$. A *projective measurement* is given by a collection of projectors $\{\Pi_j\}_j$ such that $\sum_j \Pi_j = \mathsf{Id}$. Given a state ρ, the measurement yields outcome j with probability $p_j = \mathsf{Tr}(\Pi_j \rho)$, upon which the state changes to $\Pi_j \rho \Pi_j / p_j$ (this can be modeled by a quantum channel, but we will not need this). For any two registers x and y, the partial trace Tr_y is the unique channel from $x \otimes y$ to x such that $\mathsf{Tr}_y(\rho_x \otimes \tau_y) = \mathsf{Tr}_y(\tau_y) \rho_x$ for all ρ_x and τ_y.

The *trace distance* between two states ρ and τ, denoted by $\mathsf{Td}(\rho, \tau)$ is defined as

$$\mathsf{Td}(\rho, \tau) = \frac{1}{2}\|\rho - \tau\|_1 = \frac{1}{2}\mathsf{Tr}\left(\sqrt{(\rho - \tau)^\dagger (\rho - \tau)}\right).$$

The operational meaning of the trace distance is that $\frac{1}{2}(1 + \mathsf{Td}(\rho, \tau))$ is the maximal probability that two states ρ and τ can be distinguishdd by any (possibly unbounded) quantum channel or algorithm. If $\tau = |\Phi\rangle\langle\Phi|$ is a pure state, we have the following version of the Fuchs-van de Graaf inequalities:

$$1 - \langle\Phi|\rho|\Phi\rangle \leq \mathsf{Td}(\rho, \tau) \leq \sqrt{1 - \langle\Phi|\rho|\Phi\rangle}. \tag{2.1}$$

Quantum Algorithms. A non-uniform *quantum polynomial-time (QPT) machine* $\{\mathcal{A}_\lambda\}_{\lambda \in \mathbb{N}}$ is a family of polynomial-size quantum machines $\mathcal{A}_\lambda$, where each is initialized with a polynomial-size advice state $|\alpha_\lambda\rangle$. Each $\mathcal{A}_\lambda$ can be described by a CPTP map. A quantum interactive machine is simply a sequence of quantum channels, with designated input, output, and work registers. We say that two probability distributions $\mathcal{X}$ and $\mathcal{Y}$ are *computationally indistinguishable* if there exists a negligible function negl such that for all QPT algorithms $\mathcal{A}_\lambda$ it holds that

$$\left| \Pr\left[1 \leftarrow \mathcal{A}_\lambda(x) : x \leftarrow \mathcal{X}\right] - \Pr\left[1 \leftarrow \mathcal{A}_\lambda(y) : y \leftarrow \mathcal{Y}\right] \right| = \mathsf{negl}(\lambda).$$

We say that they are *statistically indistinguishable* if the same holds for all (possibly unbounded) algorithms.

Distinguishing Implies Swapping. We recall the formal statement of the equivalence between distinguishing states and swapping on the conjugate basis. This was proven in [1] and below we show a rephrased version borrowed from [12]. We actually only state one direction of the implication (the converse is also shown to be true in [1]), since it is the one needed for our purposes.

Theorem 1 (Distinguishing Implies Swapping [1]). *Let $|\Psi\rangle$ and $|\Phi\rangle$ be orthogonal n-qubit states, and suppose that a QPT distinguisher $\mathcal{A}_\lambda$ distinguishes $|\Psi\rangle$ and $|\Phi\rangle$ with advantage δ without using any ancilla qubits. Then, there exists a polynomial-time computable unitary U over n-qubit states such that*

$$\frac{|\langle y|U|x\rangle + \langle x|U|y\rangle|}{2} = \delta \text{ where } |x\rangle = \frac{|\Psi\rangle + |\Phi\rangle}{\sqrt{2}} \text{ and } |y\rangle = \frac{|\Psi\rangle - |\Phi\rangle}{\sqrt{2}}.$$

Moreover, if $\mathcal{A}_\lambda$ does not act on some qubits, then U also does not act on those qubits.

2.2 Information Theory

Recall the definition of the min-entropy of a random variable X as

$$H_\infty(X) = -\log\left(\max_x \Pr[X = x]\right).$$

We recall the definition of average conditional min-entropy in the following.

Definition 1 (Average Conditional Min-Entropy). *Let X be a random-variable supported on a finite set $\mathcal{X}$ and let Z be a (possibly correlated) random variable supported on a finite set $\mathcal{Z}$. The average-conditional min-entropy $\tilde{H}_\infty(X|Z)$ is defined as*

$$\tilde{H}_\infty(X|Z) = -\log\left(\mathbb{E}_z\left[\max_{x\in\mathcal{X}} \Pr[X = x|Z = z]\right]\right).$$

It is shown in [7,8] that the average conditional min-entropy satisfies a *chain rule*, that is

$$\tilde{H}_\infty(X|Z) \geq H_\infty(X) - H_0(Z) \tag{2.2}$$

where $H_0(Z)$ denotes the logarithm of the size of the support of Z. Next, we recall the definition of a seeded randomness extractor.

Definition 2 (Extractor). *A function $\mathsf{Ext} : \{0,1\}^d \times \mathcal{X} \to \{0,1\}^\ell$ is called a seeded strong average-case (k, ε)-extractor, if it holds for all random variables X with support $\mathcal{X}$ and Z defined on some finite support that if $\tilde{H}_\infty(X|Z) \geq k$, then it holds that the statistical distance of the following distributions is a most ε*

$$(\mathsf{seed}, \mathsf{Ext}(\mathsf{seed}, X), Z) \approx_\varepsilon (\mathsf{seed}, U, Z)$$

where $\mathsf{seed} \leftarrow \{0,1\}^d$ and $U \leftarrow \{0,1\}^\ell$.

Recall that a hash function $\mathsf{Hash} : \mathcal{X} \to \mathcal{Y}$ is a universal hash if for all $x \neq x' \in \mathcal{X}$ it holds that

$$\Pr[\mathsf{Hash}(x) = \mathsf{Hash}(x')] \leq \frac{1}{|\mathcal{Y}|}$$

where the probability is taken over the choice of the hash function. It is shown [7, 8] that any universal hash function is an average-case randomness extractor.

Lemma 1 (Leftover Hash Lemma). *Let X be a random-variable supported on a finite set $\mathcal{X}$ and let Z be a (possibly correlated) random variable supported on a finite set $\mathcal{Z}$ such that $\tilde{H}_\infty(X|Z) \geq k$. Let $\mathsf{Hash} : \mathcal{X} \to \{0,1\}^\ell$, where $\ell \leq k - 2\log\left(\frac{1}{\varepsilon}\right)$, be a family of universal hash functions. Then Hash is a seeded strong average-case (k, ε)-extractor.*

2.3 Pseudorandom Functions

We recall the notion of a pseudorandom function [11]. A pseudorandom function (PRF) is a keyed function

$$\mathsf{PRF} : \{0,1\}^\lambda \times \{0,1\}^\lambda \to \{0,1\}^\lambda$$

that is computationally indistinguishable from a truly random function. More precisely, we require that there exists a negligible function negl such that for all QPT $\{\mathcal{A}_\lambda\}$, for all $\lambda \in \mathbb{N}$, it holds that the following distributions are computationally indistinguishable

$$\mathcal{A}_\lambda(1^\lambda)^{\mathsf{PRF}(k,\cdot)} \approx \mathcal{A}_\lambda(1^\lambda)^{f(\cdot)}$$

where $k \leftarrow \{0,1\}^\lambda$ and f is a uniformly-sampled function. It is well-known that quantum-secure PRFs can be built from any one-way function [11].

2.4 One-Time Signatures

We recall the notion of a one-time signature scheme [10].

Definition 3 (One-Time Signature). *A one-time signature (OTS) scheme is defined as a tuple of algorithms* (SGen, Sign, Ver) *such that:*

- (vk, sk) ← SGen(1^λ): *A polynomial-time algorithm which, on input the security parameter 1^λ, outputs two bit strings* vk *and* sk.
- σ ← Sign(sk, m): *A polynomial-time algorithm which, on input the signing key* sk *and a message* m, *outputs signature* σ.
- $\{0,1\}$ ← Ver(vk, m, σ): *A polynomial-time algorithm which, on input the verification key* vk, *a message* m, *and a signature* σ, *returns a bit denoting accept or reject.*

The OTS scheme is *correct* if for all $\lambda \in \mathbb{N}$ and all messages m it holds that

$$\Pr\left[1 = \mathsf{Ver}(\mathsf{vk}, m, \mathsf{Sign}(\mathsf{sk}, m)) : (\mathsf{vk}, \mathsf{sk}) \leftarrow \mathsf{SGen}(1^\lambda)\right] = 1.$$

Next we define the notion of strong existential unforgeability for OTS, which states that one should not be able to produce a different signature (even if on the same message) than the one provided by the signing oracle. It is well-known that strongly unforgeable signatures can be constructed from any one-way function (OWF) [10]. For convenience we define a slightly weaker notion, where the message to be signed is fixed in advance – this notion is clearly implied by the standard one, where the attacker can query the signing oracle adaptively.

Definition 4 (Strong Existential Unforgeability). *We say that an OTS scheme* (SGen, Sign, Ver) *satisfies (quantum-secure) strong existential unforgeability if there exists a negligible function* negl *such that for all QPT* $\{\mathcal{A}_\lambda\}$, *for all $\lambda \in \mathbb{N}$, and for all messages m, it holds that*

$$\Pr\left[1 = \mathsf{Ver}(\mathsf{vk}, m^*, \sigma^*) \text{ and } (m^*, \sigma^*) \neq (m, \sigma) : \begin{array}{l} (\mathsf{vk}, \mathsf{sk}) \leftarrow \mathsf{SGen}(1^\lambda); \\ \sigma \leftarrow \mathsf{Sign}(\mathsf{sk}, m); \\ (m^*, \sigma^*) \leftarrow \mathcal{A}_\lambda(\mathsf{vk}, m, \sigma) \end{array}\right] = \mathsf{negl}(\lambda).$$

Indistinguishability of Signature States. We provide a formal statement and a proof of the indistinguishability of our signature states and the corresponding classical mixture. This proof is inspired by, and closely follows, the work of [12].

Lemma 2. *Let* (SGen, Sign, Ver) *be an OTS scheme that satisfies strong existential unforgeability. Then the following distribution ensambles are computationally indistinguishable*

$$\left\{\frac{|0,\sigma_0\rangle + |1,\sigma_1\rangle}{\sqrt{2}} \frac{\langle 0,\sigma_0| + \langle 1,\sigma_1|}{\sqrt{2}}, (\mathsf{vk}_0, \mathsf{vk}_1)\right\}$$
$$\approx \left\{\frac{|0,\sigma_0\rangle\langle 0,\sigma_0| + |1,\sigma_1\rangle\langle 1,\sigma_1|}{2}, (\mathsf{vk}_0, \mathsf{vk}_1)\right\}$$

where $(\mathsf{vk}_b, \mathsf{sk}_b) \leftarrow \mathsf{SGen}(1^\lambda)$ *and* $\sigma_b \leftarrow \mathsf{Sign}(\mathsf{sk}_b, b)$, *for* $b \in \{0,1\}$.

Proof. By convexity,[1] it suffices to show that no QPT adversary acting on registers v and x can distinguish between the states $|\Psi_0\rangle$ and $|\Psi_1\rangle$ with non-negligible probability, where

$$|\Psi_b\rangle = \sum_{(\mathsf{vk},\mathsf{sk})} \sqrt{D(\mathsf{vk},\mathsf{sk})}|\mathsf{vk},\mathsf{sk}\rangle_\mathsf{s}|\mathsf{vk}\rangle_\mathsf{v} \otimes \frac{|0,\sigma_0\rangle_\mathsf{x} + (-1)^b|1,\sigma_1\rangle_\mathsf{x}}{\sqrt{2}}$$

and we adopt the following convention for the notation:

$\mathsf{sk} = \{\mathsf{sk}_0, \mathsf{sk}_1\}$; $\mathsf{vk} = \{\mathsf{vk}_0, \mathsf{vk}_1\}$; $\sigma_b = \mathsf{Sign}(\mathsf{sk}_b, b)$ and $D(\mathsf{vk},\mathsf{sk}) = \Pr[(\mathsf{vk},\mathsf{sk}) = \mathsf{SGen}(1^\lambda)]$.

Assume towards contradiction that there exists a QPT distinguisher acting on registers v, x, as well as an auxiliary register $|\alpha_\lambda\rangle_\mathsf{a}$ that succeeds with probability δ. Then, by Theorem 1 there exists a polynomial-time computable unitary U such that

$$\frac{1}{2}\left|\begin{matrix}\langle\Psi'_1|_{\mathsf{s},\mathsf{v},\mathsf{x}}\langle\alpha_\lambda|_\mathsf{a}(U_{\mathsf{v},\mathsf{x},\mathsf{a}} \otimes \mathsf{Id}_\mathsf{s})|\Psi'_0\rangle_{\mathsf{s},\mathsf{v},\mathsf{x}}|\alpha_\lambda\rangle_\mathsf{a} \\ +\langle\Psi'_0|_{\mathsf{s},\mathsf{v},\mathsf{x}}\langle\alpha_\lambda|_\mathsf{a}(U_{\mathsf{v},\mathsf{x},\mathsf{a}} \otimes \mathsf{Id}_\mathsf{s})|\Psi'_1\rangle_{\mathsf{s},\mathsf{v},\mathsf{x}}|\alpha_\lambda\rangle_\mathsf{a}\end{matrix}\right| = \delta$$

where

$$|\Psi'_b\rangle = \frac{|\Psi_0\rangle + (-1)^b|\Psi_1\rangle}{\sqrt{2}} = \sum_{(\mathsf{vk},\mathsf{sk})} \sqrt{D(\mathsf{vk},\mathsf{sk})}|\mathsf{vk},\mathsf{sk}\rangle_\mathsf{s}|\mathsf{vk}\rangle_\mathsf{v} \otimes |b,\sigma_b\rangle_\mathsf{x}.$$

Consequently, it must be the case that either

- $\langle\Psi'_1|_{\mathsf{s},\mathsf{v},\mathsf{x}}\langle\alpha_\lambda|_\mathsf{a}(U_{\mathsf{v},\mathsf{x},\mathsf{a}} \otimes \mathsf{Id}_\mathsf{s})|\Psi'_0\rangle_{\mathsf{s},\mathsf{v},\mathsf{x}}|\alpha_\lambda\rangle_\mathsf{a} \geq \delta$, or
- $\langle\Psi'_0|_{\mathsf{s},\mathsf{v},\mathsf{x}}\langle\alpha_\lambda|_\mathsf{a}(U_{\mathsf{v},\mathsf{x},\mathsf{a}} \otimes \mathsf{Id}_\mathsf{s})|\Psi'_1\rangle_{\mathsf{s},\mathsf{v},\mathsf{x}}|\alpha_\lambda\rangle_\mathsf{a} \geq \delta$.

---

[1] Note that the mixed state $\frac{|0,\sigma_0\rangle\langle 0,\sigma_0| + |1,\sigma_1\rangle\langle 1,\sigma_1|}{2}$ is a convex combination of $\frac{|0,\sigma_0\rangle + (-1)^b|1,\sigma_1\rangle}{\sqrt{2}} \frac{\langle 0,\sigma_0| + (-1)^b\langle 1,\sigma_1|}{\sqrt{2}}$ for $b \in \{0,1\}$.

Without loss of generality we assume that the former holds, but the argument works symmetrically also for the latter case. We will show that this leads to a contradiction with a reduction against the one-time unforgeability of OTS. In fact we will consider an even weaker definition where the adversary receives *no signature*.

On input a verification key vk_1 and an advice $|\alpha_\lambda\rangle_\mathsf{a}$ the reduction samples a uniform $(\mathsf{vk}_0, \mathsf{sk}_0) \leftarrow \mathsf{SGen}(1^\lambda)$, and sets $\mathsf{vk} = \{\mathsf{vk}_0, \mathsf{vk}_1\}$. Then it computes $\sigma_0 \leftarrow \mathsf{Sign}(\mathsf{sk}_0, 0)$ and
$$U_{\mathsf{v},\mathsf{x},\mathsf{a}}|\mathsf{vk}\rangle_\mathsf{v}|0,\sigma_0\rangle_\mathsf{x}|\alpha_\lambda\rangle_\mathsf{a}$$
and returns the result of a measurement of the x register in the computational basis.

We now analyze the success probability of the reduction in producing a valid signature, for a fixed key pair $(\mathsf{vk}_1, \mathsf{sk}_1)$. Let us denote by Σ_1 the set of all valid signatures on 1 under vk_1, and by $\sigma_1 = \mathsf{Sign}(\mathsf{sk}_1, 1)$. Then we have that the success probability of the reduction equals

$$\sum_{\sigma_1' \in \Sigma_1} |\Sigma_1| \cdot \|\langle 1, \sigma_1'|_\mathsf{x} U_{\mathsf{v},\mathsf{x},\mathsf{a}}|\mathsf{vk}\rangle_\mathsf{v}|0,\sigma_0\rangle_\mathsf{x}|\alpha_\lambda\rangle_\mathsf{a}\|^2$$

$$\geq \|\langle 1, \sigma_1|_\mathsf{x} U_{\mathsf{v},\mathsf{x},\mathsf{a}}|\mathsf{vk}\rangle_\mathsf{v}|0,\sigma_0\rangle_\mathsf{x}|\alpha_\lambda\rangle_\mathsf{a}\|^2$$

$$\geq |\langle \mathsf{vk}|_\mathsf{v} \langle 1, \sigma_1|_\mathsf{x} \langle \alpha_\lambda|_\mathsf{a} U_{\mathsf{v},\mathsf{x},\mathsf{a}}|\mathsf{vk}\rangle_\mathsf{v}|0,\sigma_0\rangle_\mathsf{x}|\alpha_\lambda\rangle_\mathsf{a}|^2$$

$$= |\langle \mathsf{vk},\mathsf{sk}|_\mathsf{s}\langle \mathsf{vk}|_\mathsf{v}\langle 1, \sigma_1|_\mathsf{x}\langle \alpha_\lambda|_\mathsf{a}(U_{\mathsf{v},\mathsf{x},\mathsf{a}}|\mathsf{vk}\rangle_\mathsf{v} \otimes \mathsf{Id}_\mathsf{s})|\mathsf{vk},\mathsf{sk}\rangle_\mathsf{s}|0,\sigma_0\rangle_\mathsf{x}|\alpha_\lambda\rangle_\mathsf{a}|^2$$

where the second inequality follows from the fact that inserting $\langle \mathsf{vk}|_\mathsf{v}$ and $\langle \alpha_\lambda|_\mathsf{a}$ can only decrease the norm. Now, over the random choice of $(\mathsf{vk}, \mathsf{sk})$ the success probability of the reduction can be lower bounded by

$$\mathbb{E}_{(\mathsf{vk},\mathsf{sk})}\left[|\langle \mathsf{vk},\mathsf{sk}|_\mathsf{s}\langle \mathsf{vk}|_\mathsf{v}\langle 1, \sigma_1|_\mathsf{x}\langle \alpha_\lambda|_\mathsf{a}(U_{\mathsf{v},\mathsf{x},\mathsf{a}}|\mathsf{vk}\rangle_\mathsf{v} \otimes \mathsf{Id}_\mathsf{s})|\mathsf{vk},\mathsf{sk}\rangle_\mathsf{s}|0,\sigma_0\rangle_\mathsf{x}|\alpha_\lambda\rangle_\mathsf{a}|^2\right]$$

$$\geq |\mathbb{E}_{(\mathsf{vk},\mathsf{sk})}[\langle \mathsf{vk},\mathsf{sk}|_\mathsf{s}\langle \mathsf{vk}|_\mathsf{v}\langle 1, \sigma_1|_\mathsf{x}\langle \alpha_\lambda|_\mathsf{a}(U_{\mathsf{v},\mathsf{x},\mathsf{a}}|\mathsf{vk}\rangle_\mathsf{v} \otimes \mathsf{Id}_\mathsf{s})|\mathsf{vk},\mathsf{sk}\rangle_\mathsf{s}|0,\sigma_0\rangle_\mathsf{x}|\alpha_\lambda\rangle_\mathsf{a}]|^2$$

$$\geq \delta$$

where the first inequality follows from Jensen's inequality. This contradicts the unforgeability of OTS and concludes our proof.

3 Quantum Public-Key Encryption

In the following we define and construct the central cryptographic primitive of this work, which we refer to as *quantum-public-key encryption*.

3.1 Definitions

The syntax for this primitive is taken almost in verbatim from [3], although in this work we consider a stronger notion of security. For notational convenience, we define the primitive for encrypting one-bit messages, but it is easy to generalize the notion and the corresponding construction to multiple bits, via the standard bit-by-bit encryption. Security of the multi-bit construction follows by a standard hybrid argument.

Definition 5. (QPKE). *A quantum-public-key encryption (PKE) scheme is defined as a tuple of algorithms (SKGen, PKGen, Enc, Dec) such that:*

- sk ← SKGen(1^λ): *A PPT algorithm which, on input the security parameter 1^λ outputs a secret bit string sk.*
- (ρ, pk) ← PKGen(sk): *A QPT algorithm which, on input the secret key sk, outputs a (possibly mixed) quantum state ρ and a bit strings pk.*
- ct ← Enc(ρ, pk, m): *A QPT algorithm which, on input the public key (ρ, pk) and a message $m \in \{0,1\}$, outputs a ciphertext ct.*
- m ← Dec(sk, ct): *A QPT algorithm which, on input the secret key sk and the ciphertext ct, outputs a message $m \in \{0,1\}$.*

A QPKE scheme (SKGen, PKGen, Enc, Dec) satisfies correctness if for all $\lambda \in \mathbb{N}$ and all $m \in \{0,1\}$ it holds that:

$$\Pr\left[m = \mathsf{Dec}(\mathsf{sk}, \mathsf{ct}) : \mathsf{sk} \leftarrow \mathsf{SKGen}(1^\lambda); (\rho, \mathsf{pk}) \leftarrow \mathsf{PKGen}(\mathsf{sk}); \mathsf{ct} \leftarrow \mathsf{Enc}(\rho, \mathsf{pk}, m)\right] = 1.$$

Everlasting Security. Next, we define the security notion of *everlasting security* for QPKE. Informally, we require that the message is unconditionally hidden from the eyes of an attacker, even if a QPT attacker is allowed to tamper with the public key arbitrarily. However, the attacker is supplied a *single copy* of the public key.

Definition 6 (Everlasting Security). *For a family of QPT algorithms $\{\mathcal{A}_\lambda\}_{\lambda \in \mathbb{N}}$, we define the experiment $\mathsf{Exp}^{\mathcal{A}_\lambda}(1^\lambda, m)$ as follows:*

1. *Sample sk ← SKGen(1^λ) and (ρ, pk) ← PKGen(sk) and send the corresponding public key (ρ, pk) to $\mathcal{A}_\lambda$.*
2. *$\mathcal{A}_\lambda$ returns two quantum registers. The first register is parsed as the modified public-key register, whereas the second register is arbitrary and will be referred to as the adversary's internal register.*
3. *Compute ct by applying the map defined by Enc($\cdot$, pk, m) to the public-key register returned by the adversary in the previous round.*
4. *The output of the experiment is defined to be the joint state of ct and the internal register of the adversary.*

Then we say that a QPKE scheme (SKGen, PKGen, Enc, Dec) satisfies everlasting security *if there exists a negligible function negl such that for all $\lambda \in \mathbb{N}$ and all QPT $\mathcal{A}_\lambda$ it holds that*

$$\mathsf{Td}\left(\mathsf{Exp}^{\mathcal{A}_\lambda}(1^\lambda, 0), \mathsf{Exp}^{\mathcal{A}_\lambda}(1^\lambda, 1)\right) = \mathsf{negl}(\lambda).$$

Let us comment on the definition as stated above. First, we remark that the definition can be easily extended to the case of multi-bit messages, provided that the syntax of the encryption scheme is extended accordingly. We also mention that an alternative definition might also allow the adversary to do some arbitrary post-processing on the output of the experiment. However, our definition is equivalent (and arguably simpler) by the monotonicity of the trace distance.

An important point of our definition (which distinguishes it from prior works) is that the attacker is allowed to modify the quantum states arbitrarily, although it cannot tamper with the classical information (such as pk or ct). This models the presence of *authenticated classical channels*, which are assumed to deliver the classical information faithfully. Note that the same assumption is also present (although somewhat more implicitly) for the standard notion of *classical* PKE, where the encryption algorithm in the CPA/CCA-security experiment is always provided as input the correct public key sampled by the challenger. This restriction is of course necessary, since if the attacker is allowed to choose the public key arbitrarily, then the definition would be impossible to achieve.

Finally, we mention that a stronger definition would allow the adversary to see a polynomial number of copies of the public key, instead of a single one. Unfortunately the work of [3] shows a key recovery attack against any QPKE, if the attacker is given sufficiently many copies of the public key and it is allowed to run in unbounded time. This immediately rules out any QPKE with everlasting security in the presence of polynomial copies of the public key, since an unbounded distinguisher can simply run such key recovery algorithm, and decrypt the challenge ciphertext using the honest decryption algorithm. To overcome this limitation, we define the notion of computational security.

Computational Security. We define the weaker notion of computational security for QPKE, where the message is only required to be kept hidden against computationally bounded adversary. The upshot is that this can hold even if the adversary is given access to multiple copies of the public key. We present a formal definition below.

Definition 7 (Computational Security). *For a family of QPT algorithms $\{\mathcal{A}_\lambda\}_{\lambda \in \mathbb{N}}$, we define the experiment* $\mathsf{Exp}^{\mathcal{A}_\lambda}(1^\lambda, m, n)$ *as follows:*

1. *Sample* sk $\leftarrow$ SKGen(1^λ) *and* $\{(\rho_i, \mathsf{pk}_i) \leftarrow \mathsf{PKGen}(\mathsf{sk})\}_{i=1,\ldots,n}$ *and send the corresponding public keys* (ρ_i, pk_i) *to* $\mathcal{A}_\lambda$.
2. $\mathcal{A}_\lambda$ *returns two quantum registers. The first register is parsed as the modified public-key register, whereas the second register is arbitrary and will be referred to as the adversary's internal register.*
3. *Compute* ct *by applying the map defined by* $\mathsf{Enc}(\cdot, \mathsf{pk}_1, m)$ *to the public-key register returned by the adversary in the previous round.*
4. *The output of the experiment is defined to be the joint state of* ct *and the internal register of the adversary.*

Then we say that a QPKE scheme (SKGen, PKGen, Enc, Dec) *satisfies computational security if there exists a negligible function* negl *such that for all* $\lambda \in \mathbb{N}$, *all polynomials* $n = n(\lambda)$, *and all QPT* $\mathcal{A}_\lambda$ *it holds that the distributions*

$$\mathsf{Exp}^{\mathcal{A}_\lambda}(1^\lambda, 0, n) \approx \mathsf{Exp}^{\mathcal{A}_\lambda}(1^\lambda, 1, n)$$

are computationally indistinguishable.

3.2 Everlasting Secure QPKE

We describe our scheme below. As the only computational ingredient, we assume the existence of a quantum-secure strongly existentially unforgeable one-time signature scheme (SGen, Sign, Ver), see Sect. 2.4. As discussed, this can be constructed from any quantum-secure one-way function.

- SKGen(1^λ):
  - Sample two key pairs $(\mathsf{sk}_0, \mathsf{vk}_0) \leftarrow \mathsf{SGen}(1^\lambda)$ and $(\mathsf{sk}_1, \mathsf{vk}_1) \leftarrow \mathsf{SGen}(1^\lambda)$.
  - Compute $\sigma_0 \leftarrow \mathsf{Sign}(\mathsf{sk}_0, 0)$ and $\sigma_1 \leftarrow \mathsf{Sign}(\mathsf{sk}_1, 1)$.
  - Sample a bit $d_0 \leftarrow \{0, 1\}$.
  - Return $\mathsf{sk} = (\mathsf{vk}_0, \mathsf{vk}_1, \sigma_0, \sigma_1, d_0)$.
- PKGen(sk):
  - Define the state
  $$|\Psi\rangle = \frac{|0, \sigma_0\rangle + (-1)^{d_0}|1, \sigma_1\rangle}{\sqrt{2}}.$$

  This state is efficiently computable by preparing an EPR pair and CNOT-ing the bits of the signatures into an auxiliary register, controlled on the value of the first qubit. The relative phase can be then added by a controlling the application of Z with d_0.
  - Set the quantum part of the public key ρ to be the state $|\Psi\rangle$ and set the classical part of the public key and the classical secret key to pk $= (\mathsf{vk}_0, \mathsf{vk}_1)$.
- Enc(ρ, pk, m):
  - Project ρ onto the subspace of valid signatures of 0 and 1, under vk_0 and vk_1, respectively. More precisely, denote by Σ_0 and Σ_1 the set of accepting signatures on 0 and 1, under vk_0 and vk_1, respectively, and consider the projector
  $$\Pi = \sum_{\sigma \in \Sigma_0} |0, \sigma\rangle\langle 0, \sigma| + \sum_{\sigma \in \Sigma_1} |1, \sigma\rangle\langle 1, \sigma|.$$

  Apply the projective measurement $\{\Pi, \mathsf{Id} - \Pi\}$, and abort the execution (return $\bot$) if the measurement returns the second outcome. Note that this measurement can be implemented efficiently by running the verification algorithm coherently, CNOT-ing the output qubit onto a separate register, and measuring this register.
  - Measure the residual state in the Hadamard basis, to obtain a bit string (d_1, d_2), where we denote by $d_1 \in \{0, 1\}$ the first bit of the measurement outcome and by d_2 the rest.

- Return the following as the classical ciphertext:
$$\mathsf{ct} = (m \oplus d_1, d_2). \tag{3.1}$$

– Dec(sk, ct):
  - Parse $\mathsf{ct} = (\mathsf{ct}_1, \mathsf{ct}_2)$, where $\mathsf{ct}_1 \in \{0,1\}$ is one bit, and return
$$m = d_0 \oplus \mathsf{ct}_1 \oplus \mathsf{ct}_2 \cdot (\sigma_0 \oplus \sigma_1). \tag{3.2}$$

Analysis. We claim that the scheme satisfies correctness. First, observe that the state ρ taken as input by the encryption algorithm is in the image of the projector Π as defined above. Consequently, applying the projective measurement $\{\Pi, \mathsf{Id} - \Pi\}$ returns the outcome associated with Π with certainty and does not change the state. Applying the Hadamard transformation to the state $|\Psi\rangle$ gives

$$H|\Psi\rangle \propto \sum_{d_1, d_2} (-1)^{(d_1,d_2)\cdot(0,\sigma_0)} |d_1, d_2\rangle + (-1)^{d_0 \oplus (d_1,d_2)\cdot(1,\sigma_1)} |d_1, d_2\rangle$$

$$= \sum_{d_1,d_2 \,:\, (d_1,d_2)\cdot(1,\sigma_0 \oplus \sigma_1) = d_0} |d_1, d_2\rangle,$$

omitting overall normalization factors. Therefore, a measurement returns a uniformly random bit string (d_1, d_2) satisfying

$$d_1 \oplus d_2 \cdot (\sigma_0 \oplus \sigma_1) = d_0.$$

Substituting Eq. (3.1) in Eq. (3.2) and using this relation, we obtain

$$d_0 \oplus \mathsf{ct}_1 \oplus \mathsf{ct}_2 \cdot (\sigma_0 \oplus \sigma_1) = d_0 \oplus (m \oplus d_1) \oplus d_2 \cdot (\sigma_0 \oplus \sigma_1) = m,$$

as desired. Next, we show that the scheme satisfies everlasting security.

Theorem 2 (Everlasting security). *If quantum-secure one-way functions exist, then the QPKE (SKGen, PKGen, Enc, Dec) satisfies everlasting security.*

Proof. We proceed by defining a series of hybrid experiments that we show to be indistinguishable from the eyes of any (possibly unbounded) algorithm. For convenience, we define

$$\mathsf{Adv}(i) = \mathsf{Td}\left(\mathsf{Hyb}_i^{A_\lambda}(1^\lambda, 0), \mathsf{Hyb}_i^{A_\lambda}(1^\lambda, 1)\right).$$

– $\mathsf{Hyb}_0^{A_\lambda}(1^\lambda, b)$: This is the original experiment $\mathsf{Exp}^{A_\lambda}(1^\lambda, b)$, as defined in Definition 6.
– $\mathsf{Hyb}_1^{A_\lambda}(1^\lambda, b)$: In this experiment, we modify the PKGen algorithm to measure the state $|\Psi\rangle$ in the computational basis, before outputting ρ.

Since the result sk of the SKGen algorithm is not used in the experiment, we only need to argue that the reduced states of (pk, ρ) are unchanged by this modification. This is indeed the case, since adding a random phase is equivalent to measuring in the computational basis by a standard Pauli Z-twirl argument. Thus the two experiments are identical from the perspective of the adversary and therefore $\mathsf{Adv}(0) = \mathsf{Adv}(1)$.

- $\mathsf{Hyb}_2^{\mathcal{A}_\lambda}(1^\lambda, b)$: In this experiment, we further modify the PKGen algorithm to sample the state ρ as follows. Flip a random coin $c \leftarrow \{0, 1\}$. If $c = 0$ then return $|0, \sigma_0\rangle\langle 0, \sigma_0|$, and otherwise return $|1, \sigma_1\rangle\langle 1, \sigma_1|$.

Observe that the state ρ returned by the modified PKGen algorithm is the classical mixture
$$\rho = \frac{|0, \sigma_0\rangle\langle 0, \sigma_0| + |1, \sigma_1\rangle\langle 1, \sigma_1|}{2}$$
which is identical to the state returned in the previous hybrid. Therefore $\mathsf{Adv}(1) = \mathsf{Adv}(2)$. Next, let us denote by ρ^* the reduced density matrix of the modified public-key register returned by the adversary in step 2 of the experiment. We will assume that the state ρ^* returned by the adversary is such that the encryption algorithm accepts (i.e., does not abort) with non-negligible probability (for otherwise $\mathsf{Adv}(2) = \mathsf{negl}(\lambda)$ and we are done). We can then establish that the state ρ^*, conditioned on the verification succeeding, must be negligibly close in trace distance from the state produced by the PKGen algorithm. More precisely:

Lemma 3. *There exists a negligible function* negl *such that, for any* $c \in \{0, 1\}$ *and for* ρ^* *the state returned by the adversary conditional on the result of the coin toss in the* Gen *algorithm being equal to* c,

$$\mathsf{Td}\left(\frac{\Pi \rho^* \Pi}{\mathsf{Tr}(\Pi \rho^*)}, |c, \sigma_c\rangle\langle c, \sigma_c|\right) = \mathsf{negl}(\lambda).$$

Proof (Proof of Lemma 3). The proof follows by a reduction to the unforgeability of the OTS. Indeed, assume for sake of contradiction that the post-measurement state is non-negligibly far from $|c, \sigma_c\rangle$ in trace distance. By Eq. (2.1), the latter is equivalent to saying that if we measure in the computational basis then the probability of obtaining outcome (c, σ_c) is non-negligibly smaller than 1. Since the post-measurement state is supported on range of Π, it follows that if we measure in the computational basis then we must with non-negligible probability obtain an outcome (z, σ) such that

$$(z, \sigma) \neq (c, \sigma_c) \quad \text{and} \quad \mathsf{Ver}(\mathsf{vk}_z, z, \sigma) = 1,$$

that is, $(z, \sigma) \neq (c, \sigma_c)$ is a valid message-signature pair. As the adversary along with the projective measurement $\{\Pi, I - \Pi\}$ and the standard basis measurement run in quantum polynomial time, and the projective measurement returns Π with non-negligible probability, this contradicts the strong existential unforgeability of the OTS scheme.

We conclude by establishing that the message m is statistically hidden in the last experiment.

Lemma 4. *There exists a negligible function* negl *such that* $\mathsf{Adv}(2) = \mathsf{negl}(\lambda)$.

Proof (Proof of Lemma 4). By Lemma 3, the post-measurement state is negligibly close to the state $|c, \sigma_c\rangle$. As the latter is a pure state and extensions of pure states are always in tensor product, by Uhlmann's theorem it follows that the post-measurement register is negligibly close to being in tensor product with the internal register of the adversary. Thus it suffices to show that the output distribution of the Enc algorithm does not depend on the message m when given as input $|c, \sigma_c\rangle$. To see this, observe that the rotated state in the Hadamard basis is up to overall normalization given by

$$H|c, \sigma_c\rangle \propto \sum_{d'} (-1)^{d' \cdot (c, \sigma_c)} |d'\rangle,$$

and therefore a measurement returns a uniformly random bit string $d' = (d_1, d_2)$. In particular, $\mathsf{ct} = (m \oplus d_1, d_2)$ has the same distribution for $m \in \{0,1\}$. As explained above, it is also negligibly close to being independent from the internal register of the adversary, and thus the claim follows.

By Lemma 4 we have that

$$\mathsf{Adv}(0) = \mathsf{Adv}(1) = \mathsf{Adv}(2) = \mathsf{negl}(\lambda),$$

and this concludes the proof of Theorem 2.

3.3 Computationally Secure QPKE

Our scheme assumes the existence of a quantum-secure strongly existentially unforgeable one-time signature scheme (SGen, Sign, Ver) and a quantum-secure pseudorandom function PRF. Both such building blocks can be constructed assuming any quantum-secure one-way function.

- $\mathsf{SKGen}(1^\lambda)$:
  - Sample a key $k \leftarrow \{0,1\}^\lambda$ and set $\mathsf{sk} = k$.
- $\mathsf{PKGen}(\mathsf{sk})$:
  - Sample two uniform $(r_0, r_1) \leftarrow \{0,1\}^\lambda$ and compute

    $(\mathsf{sk}_0, \mathsf{vk}_0) \leftarrow \mathsf{SGen}(1^\lambda; \mathsf{PRF}(k, r_0))$ and $(\mathsf{sk}_1, \mathsf{vk}_1) \leftarrow \mathsf{SGen}(1^\lambda; \mathsf{PRF}(k, r_1))$.

  - Compute $\sigma_0 \leftarrow \mathsf{Sign}(\mathsf{sk}_0, 0)$ and $\sigma_1 \leftarrow \mathsf{Sign}(\mathsf{sk}_1, 1)$.
  - Define the state
    $$|\Psi\rangle = \frac{|0, \sigma_0\rangle + |1, \sigma_1\rangle}{\sqrt{2}}.$$
    This state is efficiently computable by preparing an EPR pair and CNOT-ing the bits of the signatures into an auxiliary register, controlled on the value of the first qubit.
  - Set the quantum part of the public key ρ to be the state $|\Psi\rangle$ and set the classical part of the public key and the classical secret key to $\mathsf{pk} = (\mathsf{vk}_0, \mathsf{vk}_1, r_0, r_1)$.
- $\mathsf{Enc}(\rho, \mathsf{pk}, m)$:

- Project ρ onto the subspace of valid signatures of 0 and 1, under vk_0 and vk_1, respectively. More precisely, denote by Σ_0 and Σ_1 the set of accepting signatures on 0 and 1, under vk_0 and vk_1, respectively, and consider the projector

$$\Pi = \sum_{\sigma \in \Sigma_0} |0,\sigma\rangle\langle 0,\sigma| + \sum_{\sigma \in \Sigma_1} |1,\sigma\rangle\langle 1,\sigma|.$$

Apply the projective measurement $\{\Pi, \mathsf{Id} - \Pi\}$, and abort the execution (return $\bot$) if the measurement returns the second outcome. Note that this measurement can be implemented efficiently by running the verification algorithm coherently, CNOT-ing the output qubit onto a separate register, and measuring this register.
- Apply the Z^m operator to the first qubit of ρ, classically controlled on the message m.
- Set ct to be the residual state, along with (r_0, r_1).
- Dec(sk, ct):
  - Use the secret key k to recompute

  $$(\mathsf{sk}_0, \mathsf{vk}_0) \leftarrow \mathsf{SGen}(1^\lambda; \mathsf{PRF}(k, r_0)) \quad \text{and} \quad (\mathsf{sk}_1, \mathsf{vk}_1) \leftarrow \mathsf{SGen}(1^\lambda; \mathsf{PRF}(k, r_1)).$$

  along with $\sigma_0 \leftarrow \mathsf{Sign}(\mathsf{sk}_0, 0)$ and $\sigma_1 \leftarrow \mathsf{Sign}(\mathsf{sk}_1, 1)$.
  - Measure the quantum state of ct in the

  $$\left\{ \frac{|0,\sigma_0\rangle + |1,\sigma_1\rangle}{\sqrt{2}}, \frac{|0,\sigma_0\rangle - |1,\sigma_1\rangle}{\sqrt{2}} \right\}$$

  basis. And return the corresponding outcome.

Analysis. To see why the scheme satisfies correctness, first observe that the state $|\Psi\rangle$ as defined in the PKGen algorithm lies in the image of the projector Π. Therefore the projective measurement $\{\Pi, \mathsf{Id} - \Pi\}$ acts as the identity on $|\Psi\rangle$. Then, the state output by the encryption algorithm corresponds to

$$(\mathsf{Z}^m \otimes \mathsf{Id}) \frac{|0,\sigma_0\rangle + |1,\sigma_1\rangle}{\sqrt{2}} = \frac{|0,\sigma_0\rangle + (-1)^m |1,\sigma_1\rangle}{\sqrt{2}}.$$

Therefore, the output of the decryption algorithm equals m with certainty. Next, we show that the scheme is computationally secure.

Theorem 3 (Computational security). *If quantum-secure one-way functions exist, then the QPKE (SKGen, PKGen, Enc, Dec) satisfies computational security.*

Proof. We proceed by defining a series of hybrid experiments that we show to be indistinguishable from the eyes of any QPT algorithm.

- $\mathsf{Hyb}_0^{\mathcal{A}_\lambda}(1^\lambda, b)$: This is the original experiment $\mathsf{Exp}^{\mathcal{A}_\lambda}(1^\lambda, b, n)$, as defined in Definition 7.

- $\mathsf{Hyb}_1^{\mathcal{A}_\lambda}(1^\lambda, b)$: In this experiment, we simulate the output of the PRF by lazy sampling, i.e., every time that the PKGen algorithm is invoked, the experiment sample a uniform tuple $(r_0, r_1, \tilde{r}_0, \tilde{r}_1)$ and uses the latter pair as the randomness for the OTS scheme. To keep things consistent, the experiment maintains a list of all such tuples.

Note that the only difference between these two hybrids is in the way the random coins of the OTS are sampled. Therefore, by the pseudorandomness of PRF, the two hybrids are computationally indistinguishable. Note that, in the second hybrid, different copies of the public key are now independent from each other.

- $\mathsf{Hyb}_2^{\mathcal{A}_\lambda}(1^\lambda, b)$: In this experiment, we further modify the *first invocation* of the PKGen algorithm to sample the state ρ as follows. Flip a random coin $c \leftarrow \{0, 1\}$. If $c = 0$ then return $|0, \sigma_0\rangle\langle 0, \sigma_0|$, and otherwise return $|1, \sigma_1\rangle\langle 1, \sigma_1|$.

Observe that the state ρ returned by the modified PKGen algorithm is the classical mixture

$$\rho = \frac{|0, \sigma_0\rangle\langle 0, \sigma_0| + |1, \sigma_1\rangle\langle 1, \sigma_1|}{2}.$$

By a direct application of Lemma 2, we can conclude that the two hybrids are computationally indistinguishable. At this point, we can appeal to Lemma 3 (in the proof of Theorem 2) to establish that the state ρ^*, as returned by the adversary in the security experiment, must be within negligible trace distance from a basis state. The proof is concluded by noting that the distributions of an encryption of 0 and an encryption of 1 are identical, up to a global phase, if the algorithm is called on input any basis state.

4 Two-Message Quantum Key Distribution

In the following we outline how to use a QPKE scheme (SKGen, PKGen, Enc, Dec) to construct a QKD protocol with a minimal number of two rounds of interaction, as announced in the introduction.

4.1 Definitions

We give a formal definition of quantum key distribution in the everlasting settings, i.e., where an attacker is required to be computationally bounded only during the execution of the protocol. For convenience, we adopt a syntax specific for two-message protocols, but the definitions can be extended to the more general interactive settings canonically.

Definition 8 (Two-Message QKD). *A quantum key distribution (QKD) scheme is defined as a tuple of algorithms (QKDFirst, QKDSecond, QKDDecode) such that:*

- $(\mathsf{msg}, \mu, \mathsf{st}) \leftarrow \mathsf{QKDFirst}(1^\lambda)$: *A QPT algorithm which, on input the security parameter 1^λ outputs a message, consisting of a classical component msg and a (possibly mixed) quantum state μ, and an internal state st.*

- $\{(\mathsf{resp}, \eta, k), \bot\} \leftarrow \mathsf{QKDSecond}(\mathsf{msg}, \mu)$: *A QPT algorithm which, on input the first message* (msg, μ), *outputs a response, consisting of a classical component* resp *and a (possibly mixed) quantum state* η, *along with a key* $k \in \{0,1\}^\lambda$, *or a distinguished symbol* $\bot$, *denoting rejection.*
- $\{k, \bot\} \leftarrow \mathsf{QKDDecode}(\mathsf{st}, \mathsf{resp}, \eta)$: *A QPT algorithm which, on input the internal state* st, *and the response* (resp, η), *returns a key* $k \in \{0,1\}^\lambda$ *or a distinguished symbol* $\bot$, *denoting rejection.*

We say that a QKD scheme (QKDFirst, QKDSecond, QKDDecode) satisfies *correctness* if for all $\lambda \in \mathbb{N}$ it holds that:

$$\Pr\left[\bot = \mathsf{QKDSecond}(\mathsf{msg}, \mu) : (\mathsf{msg}, \mu, \mathsf{st}) \leftarrow \mathsf{QKDFirst}(1^\lambda)\right] = 0$$

and

$$\Pr\left[k = \mathsf{QKDDecode}(\mathsf{st}, \mathsf{resp}, \eta) : \begin{array}{l}(\mathsf{msg}, \mu, \mathsf{st}) \leftarrow \mathsf{QKDFirst}(1^\lambda); \\ (\mathsf{resp}, \eta, k) \leftarrow \mathsf{QKDSecond}(\mathsf{msg}, \mu)\end{array}\right] = 1.$$

Everlasting Security. Next, we define the security notion of *everlasting security* for QKD, which consists of two properties. Privacy requires that the key k should be hidden unconditionally in the presence of an adversary that is computationally bounded during the execution of the protocol. In addition, as standard for QKD, we assume the existence of an authenticated classical channel, which is modeled by not allowing the adversary to tamper with the classical messages. On the other hand, verifiability requires that no computationally bounded adversary should be able to cause Alice and Bob to disagree on the key, without any of them noticing.

Definition 9 (Everlasting Security). *For a family of QPT algorithms* $\{\mathcal{A}_\lambda\}_{\lambda \in \mathbb{N}}$, *we define the experiment* $\mathsf{QKDSec}^{\mathcal{A}_\lambda}(1^\lambda)$ *as follows:*

1. *Sample* $(\mathsf{msg}, \mu, \mathsf{st}) \leftarrow \mathsf{QKDFirst}(1^\lambda)$ *and send the corresponding first message* (msg, μ) *to* $\mathcal{A}_\lambda$.
2. $\mathcal{A}_\lambda$ *returns two quantum registers. The first register is parsed as the modified first message, whereas the second register is arbitrary and will be referred to as the adversary's internal register.*
3. *Compute* $\{(\mathsf{resp}, \eta, k_0), \bot\}$ *by applying the map defined by* $\mathsf{QKDSecond}(\mathsf{msg}, \cdot)$ *to the modified first message register returned by the adversary in the previous round.*
   (a) *If the above message is* $\bot$, *set* $(k_0, k_1) = (\bot, \bot)$ *and conclude the experiment.*
   (b) *Otherwise, return* (resp, η) *to the adversary, along with its internal state.*
4. $\mathcal{A}_\lambda$ *returns once again two quantum registers. The first register is parsed as the modified response, whereas the second register is the adversary's internal register.*
5. *Compute* $\{k_1, \bot\}$ *by applying the map defined by* $\mathsf{QKDDecode}(\mathsf{st}, \mathsf{resp}, \cdot)$ *to the modified response register returned by the adversary in the previous round. If the result is* $\bot$, *then set* $k_1 = \bot$.

6. The output of the experiment is defined to be the internal register of the adversary.

Then we say that a QKD scheme (**QKDFirst, QKDSecond, QKDDecode**) satisfies everlasting security *if the following properties hold.*

- *(Privacy) There exists a negligible function* negl *such that for all* $\lambda \in \mathbb{N}$ *and all QPT* $\mathcal{A}_\lambda$ *it holds that*

$$\mathsf{Td}\left(\left\{\mathsf{QKDSec}^{\mathcal{A}_\lambda}(1^\lambda), k_0, k_1\right\}, \left\{\mathsf{QKDSec}^{\mathcal{A}_\lambda}(1^\lambda), \tilde{k}_0, \tilde{k}_1\right\}\right) = \mathsf{negl}(\lambda)$$

where the variables k_0 *and* k_1 *are defined in the experiment, whereas* $\tilde{k}_b$*, for* $b \in \{0, 1\}$*, is defined as*

$$\begin{cases} \tilde{k}_b = \bot & \text{if } k_b = \bot \\ \tilde{k}_b \leftarrow \{0,1\}^\lambda & \text{otherwise.} \end{cases}$$

- *(Verifiability) There exists a negligible function* negl *such that for all* $\lambda \in \mathbb{N}$ *and all QPT* $\mathcal{A}_\lambda$ *it holds that*

$$\Pr[k_0 \neq k_1 \text{ and } k_1 \neq \bot] = \mathsf{negl}(\lambda)$$

where k_0 *and* k_1 *are defined in the experiment.*

Note that the above definition of verifiability is tight for two message protocols: An adversary can easily cause a disagreement between the keys by doing nothing on the first round, and blocking the second message. In this case k_0 would be a valid key (by correctness), whereas k_1 would be set to $\bot$, since the second message was never delivered.

4.2 Two-Message QKD from QPKE

We are now ready to describe our QKD protocol. Our ingredients are a QPKE scheme (SKGen, PKGen, Enc, Dec) and a OTS scheme (SGen, Sign, Ver), which can be both constructed from one-way functions. Additionally, we will use a universal hash function family

$$\mathsf{Hash} : \{0,1\}^{4\lambda} \to \{0,1\}^\lambda$$

which exist unconditionally. For convenience, we denote by $s(\lambda)$ the size of a signature for a message of size λ. We present the protocol below.

- QKDFirst(1^λ):
  - For all $i = 1, \ldots, 4\lambda + s(4\lambda)$ sample a QPK key pair

  $$\mathsf{sk}_i \leftarrow \mathsf{SKGen}(1^\lambda) \quad \text{and} \quad (\rho_i, \mathsf{pk}_i) \leftarrow \mathsf{PKGen}(\mathsf{sk}_i).$$

  - Set the first message to $\mathsf{msg} = (\mathsf{pk}_1, \ldots, \mathsf{pk}_{4\lambda+s(4\lambda)})$ and $\mu = \rho_1 \otimes \cdots \otimes \rho_{4\lambda+s(4\lambda)}$.

- QKDSecond(msg, μ):
  - Sample a OTS key pair $(\mathsf{vk}, \mathsf{zk}) \leftarrow \mathsf{SGen}(1^\lambda)$, a key $k \leftarrow \{0,1\}^{4\lambda}$, and a universal hash function Hash.
  - Compute $\sigma \leftarrow \mathsf{Sign}(\mathsf{zk}, k)$.
  - For all $i = 1, \ldots, 4\lambda + s(4\lambda)$ compute

  $$\{\mathsf{ct}_i \leftarrow \mathsf{Enc}(\rho_i, \mathsf{pk}_i, k_i)\}_{i \leq 4\lambda} \quad \text{and} \quad \{\mathsf{ct}_i \leftarrow \mathsf{Enc}(\rho_i, \mathsf{pk}_i, \sigma_i)\}_{i > 4\lambda}$$

  where $k = (k_1, \ldots, k_{4\lambda})$ and $\sigma = (\sigma_1, \ldots, \sigma_{s(4\lambda)})$.
  - If any of the encryption procedures fails, return $\perp$.
  - Else, set the response as $\mathsf{resp} = (\mathsf{Hash}, \mathsf{vk}, \mathsf{ct}_1, \ldots, \mathsf{ct}_{4\lambda + s(4\lambda)})$, no quantum state is present.
  - Set the key to $K = \mathsf{Hash}(k)$.
- QKDDecode(st, resp):
  - For all $i = 1, \ldots, 4\lambda + s(4\lambda)$ compute

  $$\{k_i \leftarrow \mathsf{Dec}(\mathsf{sk}_i, \mathsf{ct}_i)\}_{i \leq 4\lambda} \quad \text{and} \quad \{\sigma_i \leftarrow \mathsf{Dec}(\mathsf{sk}_{\lambda+i}, \mathsf{ct}_{\lambda+i})\}_{i > 4\lambda}.$$

  - If $\mathsf{Ver}(\mathsf{vk}, k, \sigma) \neq 1$ return $\perp$.
  - Else, return $K = \mathsf{Hash}(k)$.

Correctness follows immediately from the correctness of the underlying building blocks. Next we prove that the scheme is private and verifiable.

Theorem 4. *If quantum-secure one-way functions exist, then the QKD (QKDFirst, QKDSecond, QKDDecode) satisfies everlasting security (privacy and verifiability).*

Proof. We first show that the scheme satisfies privacy. Let us change the syntax of the experiment to explicitly include the view of the adversary the flag abort $\in \{0,1\}$ that denotes whether the experiment aborted or not in step 5. Then, it suffices to show that the distribution of the keys K_0 (as defined step 3 of the experiment) and K_1 (as defined in step 5 of the experiment) are statistically close to uniform, conditioned on the variables

$$\left\{\mathsf{QKDSec}^{\mathcal{A}_\lambda}(1^\lambda), \mathsf{abort}\right\}.$$

As a first step, we claim that the min-entropy of k is $H_\infty(k) \geq 3\lambda$ in the above view. To show this, we will first consider a modified distribution, where the distinguisher *is not provided* the variable abort. We then define $\mathsf{Hyb}_0^{\mathcal{A}_\lambda}(1^\lambda)$ to be the output of the original experiment $\mathsf{QKDSec}^{\mathcal{A}_\lambda}(1^\lambda)$ as defined in Definition 9. Then for $i = 1, \ldots, 4\lambda + s(4\lambda)$ we define the hybrid $\mathsf{Hyb}_i^{\mathcal{A}_\lambda}(1^\lambda)$ as follows.

- $\mathsf{Hyb}_i^{\mathcal{A}_\lambda}(1^\lambda)$: This is defined as the previous hybrid, except that the i-th ciphertext ct_i is computed as

$$\mathsf{ct}_i \leftarrow \mathsf{Enc}(\rho_i, \mathsf{pk}_i, 0).$$

The statistical indistinguishability of neighbouring outputs follows immediately from the everlasting security of the QPKE scheme, i.e.,

$$\mathsf{Td}\left(\mathsf{Hyb}_{i-1}^{\mathcal{A}_\lambda}(1^\lambda), \mathsf{Hyb}_{i}^{\mathcal{A}_\lambda}(1^\lambda)\right) = \mathsf{negl}(\lambda) \text{ for all } i = 1, \ldots, 4\lambda + s(4\lambda).$$

Note that in the last hybrid $\mathsf{Hyb}_{4\lambda+s(4\lambda)}^{\mathcal{A}_\lambda}(1^\lambda)$ the view of the adversary is formally independent from the key k and therefore k has exactly 4λ bits of entropy. An application of Lemma 1 already shows that K_0 is statistically close to uniform, since its distribution is independent of the event abort.

This is however not the case for K_1, since whether or not $K_1 = \bot$ depends on the event abort. Applying the same argument backwards, we lose only a negligible summand in the entropy of k, and so we can conclude that $H_\infty(k) \geq 4\lambda - 1$ in the original experiment. By Eq. (2.2) (chain rule for average-case min entropy), we have that, conditioned on the event abort, it holds that

$$\tilde{H}_\infty(k|\mathsf{abort}) \geq H_\infty(k) - 2 > 3\lambda$$

since $\mathsf{abort} \in \{0, 1\}$. By Lemma 1, the statistical distance of K_1 from uniform is bounded from above by $\varepsilon = 2^{-\lambda}$ since

$$\tilde{H}_\infty(k|\mathsf{abort}) - 2\log\left(\frac{1}{\varepsilon}\right) \geq 3\lambda - 2\lambda = \lambda = \ell.$$

This shows that both K_0 and K_1 are statistically close to uniform, and concludes the proof of everlasting security.

As for verifiability, let us assume towards contradiction that there exists a QPT adversary that causes a key mismatch $k_0 \neq k_1$ while not causing the decoding algorithm to reject, i.e., $k_1 \neq \bot$. Then it must be the case that the adversary is able to produce a valid message-signature pair (k_1, σ^*) under vk, for a message $k_1 \neq k_0$. Since the adversary runs in quantum polynomial time, this contradicts the unforgeability of the OTS scheme and concludes our proof.

Acknowledgments. The authors would like to thank Khashayar Barooti for many discussion on quantum public key encryption and Takashi Yamakawa for suggesting a proof of Theorem 5. G.M. was partially funded by the European Research Council through an ERC Starting Grant (Grant agreement No. 101077455, ObfusQation), by the German Federal Ministry of Education and Research (BMBF) in the course of the 6GEM research hub under grant number 16KISK038, and by the Deutsche Forschungsgemeinschaft (DFG, German Research Foundation) under Germany's Excellence Strategy - EXC 2092 CASA - 390781972. M.W. acknowledges support by the European Union (ERC, SYMOPTIC, 101040907), by the Deutsche Forschungsgemeinschaft (DFG, German Research Foundation) under Germany's Excellence Strategy - EXC 2092 CASA - 390781972, by the BMBF through project QuBRA, and by the Dutch Research Council (NWO grant OCENW.KLEIN.267). Views and opinions expressed are those of the author(s) only and do not necessarily reflect those of the European Union or the European Research Council Executive Agency. Neither the European Union nor the granting authority can be held responsible for them.

A Impossibility of Unconditionally Secure QPKE

In the following we describe a simple argument that rules out the existence of *unconditionally* secure QPKE, even if the adversary is given access to a single copy of the public key. In more details, we show an adversary that can break the security of any QPKE if it is allowed to be unbounded also *during* the protocol execution.

Theorem 5 (Unconditional Security). *There does not exists an unconditionally secure QPKE.*

Proof. We provide a description of our generic attacker that, running in unbounded time, wins the experiment defined in Definition 6 with certainty. The attacker proceeds as follows.

- On input a state ρ and a bitstring pk, enter the following loop:
  - Sample a secret key $\mathsf{sk}^* \leftarrow \mathsf{SKGen}(1^\lambda)$ uniformly.
  - Run $(\rho^*, \mathsf{pk}^*) \leftarrow \mathsf{PKGen}(\mathsf{sk})$.
  - If $\mathsf{pk}^* = \mathsf{pk}$ exit the loop and return $(\rho^*, \mathsf{pk}^*, \mathsf{sk}^*)$.
  - Else, start over.
- Let $(\rho^*, \mathsf{pk}^*, \mathsf{sk}^*)$ be the tuple output by the above loop. Return ρ^* to the challenger.
- Upon receiving ct, use sk^* to decrypt the message.

To show that the attack always succeeds, it suffices to observe that the internal loop eventually returns a tuple $(\rho^*, \mathsf{pk}^*, \mathsf{sk}^*)$ such that

$$\mathsf{pk}^* = \mathsf{pk} \quad \text{and} \quad (\rho^*, \underbrace{\mathsf{pk}^*}_{=\mathsf{pk}}) = \mathsf{PKGen}(\mathsf{sk}^*)$$

In particular, this means that the algorithm Enc run by the challenger is run on a valid pair (ρ^*, pk). Therefore, by the correctness of QPKE, the secret key sk^* recovers the correct message with certainty.

We point out that the same attack works also against protocol with imperfect correctness. For a protocol where decryption succeeds with probability $1-\varepsilon$, the same attack also succeeds with probability $1-\varepsilon$: Observe that sampling the triple $(\rho, \mathsf{pk}, \mathsf{sk})$ honestly, is identical to sampling a random pk, and then a pair (ρ^*, sk^*) that is consistent with pk (by rejection sampling). This implies that the correctness guarantee also applies to $(\rho^*, \mathsf{pk}, \mathsf{sk}^*)$ as sampled by the attacker. Since $1-\varepsilon$ must be non-negligible, we have an attacker that succeeds with non-negligible probability.

Furthermore, we also mention that a similar attack can be applied against general quantum key agreement protocols. The attack works identically (except for obvious syntactical modifications) even if Bob's message is quantum, and results in the adversary and Bob sharing a key, without Bob noticing any difference, by the correctness of the protocol. However, we also point out that the same attack does not allow the attacker to fool Alice, nor it rules out the fact that Alice could notice that something went wrong.

References

1. Aaronson, S., Atia, Y., Susskind, L.: On the hardness of detecting macroscopic superpositions. Electronic Colloquium on Computational Complexity TR20-146 (2020). https://eccc.weizmann.ac.il/report/2020/146
2. Alagic, G., Gagliardoni, T., Majenz, C.: Can you sign a quantum state? Quantum **5**, 603 (2021). https://doi.org/10.22331/q-2021-12-16-603
3. Barooti, K., et al.: Public-key encryption with quantum keys. CoRR abs/2306.07698 (2023). https://doi.org/10.48550/arXiv.2306.07698
4. Bartusek, J., Khurana, D.: Cryptography with certified deletion. CoRR abs/2207.01754 (2022). https://doi.org/10.48550/arXiv.2207.01754
5. Bennett, C.H., Brassard, G.: Quantum cryptography: public key distribution and coin tossing. In: Proceedings of IEEE International Conference on Computers, Systems, and Signal Processing, India, p. 175 (1984)
6. Diffie, W., Hellman, M.E.: New directions in cryptography. IEEE Trans. Inf. Theory **22**(6), 644–654 (1976). https://doi.org/10.1109/TIT.1976.1055638
7. Dodis, Y., Ostrovsky, R., Reyzin, L., Smith, A.D.: Fuzzy extractors: how to generate strong keys from biometrics and other noisy data. SIAM J. Comput. **38**(1), 97–139 (2008). https://doi.org/10.1137/060651380
8. Dodis, Y., Reyzin, L., Smith, A.: Fuzzy extractors: how to generate strong keys from biometrics and other noisy data. In: Cachin, C., Camenisch, J.L. (eds.) EUROCRYPT 2004. LNCS, vol. 3027, pp. 523–540. Springer, Heidelberg (2004). https://doi.org/10.1007/978-3-540-24676-3_31
9. Ekert, A.K.: Quantum cryptography based on Bell's theorem. Phys. Rev. Lett. **67**(6), 661 (1991)
10. Goldreich, O.: The Foundations of Cryptography - Volume 2: Basic Applications. Cambridge University Press, Cambridge (2004). https://doi.org/10.1017/CBO9780511721656
11. Goldreich, O., Goldwasser, S., Micali, S.: How to construct random functions. J. ACM (JACM) **33**(4), 792–807 (1986)
12. Hhan, M., Morimae, T., Yamakawa, T.: From the hardness of detecting superpositions to cryptography: quantum public key encryption and commitments. IACR Cryptology ePrint Archive, p. 1375 (2022). https://eprint.iacr.org/2022/1375
13. Impagliazzo, R.: A personal view of average-case complexity. In: Proceedings of Structure in Complexity Theory. Tenth Annual IEEE Conference, pp. 134–147. IEEE (1995)
14. Impagliazzo, R., Rudich, S.: Limits on the provable consequences of one-way permutations. In: Johnson, D.S. (ed.) Proceedings of the 21st Annual ACM Symposium on Theory of Computing, 14–17 May 1989, Seattle, Washington, USA, pp. 44–61. ACM (1989). https://doi.org/10.1145/73007.73012
15. Jouguet, P., Kunz-Jacques, S., Leverrier, A., Grangier, P., Diamanti, E.: Experimental demonstration of long-distance continuous-variable quantum key distribution. Nat. Photonics **7**(5), 378–381 (2013)
16. Kitagawa, F., Morimae, T., Nishimaki, R., Yamakawa, T.: Quantum public-key encryption with tamper-resilient public keys from one-way functions. CoRR abs/2304.01800 (2023). https://doi.org/10.48550/arXiv.2304.01800
17. Korzh, B., et al.: Provably secure and practical quantum key distribution over 307 km of optical fibre. Nat. Photonics **9**(3), 163–168 (2015)
18. Lo, H.K., Chau, H.F.: Unconditional security of quantum key distribution over arbitrarily long distances. Science **283**(5410), 2050–2056 (1999)

19. Mayers, D.: Unconditional security in quantum cryptography. J. ACM (JACM) **48**(3), 351–406 (2001)
20. Mayers, D., Yao, A.C.: Quantum cryptography with imperfect apparatus. In: 39th Annual Symposium on Foundations of Computer Science, FOCS 1998, 8–11 November 1998, Palo Alto, California, USA, pp. 503–509. IEEE Computer Society (1998). https://doi.org/10.1109/SFCS.1998.743501
21. Müller-Quade, J., Unruh, D.: Long-term security and universal composability. J. Cryptol. **23**(4), 594–671 (2010). https://doi.org/10.1007/s00145-010-9068-8
22. Nielsen, M.A., Chuang, I.L.: Quantum Computation and Quantum Information (10th Anniversary edition). Cambridge University Press, Cambridge (2016)
23. Renner, R.: Security of quantum key distribution. Int. J. Quantum Inf. **6**(01), 1–127 (2008)
24. Shor, P.W., Preskill, J.: Simple proof of security of the BB84 quantum key distribution protocol. Phys. Rev. Lett. **85**(2), 441 (2000)
25. Tomamichel, M., Leverrier, A.: A largely self-contained and complete security proof for quantum key distribution. Quantum **1**, 14 (2017)
26. Yin, J., et al.: Satellite-based entanglement distribution over 1200 kilometers. Science **356**(6343), 1140–1144 (2017)

How (not) to Build Quantum PKE in Minicrypt

Longcheng Li[1](✉), Qian Li[2], Xingjian Li[3], and Qipeng Liu[4]

[1] State Key Lab of Processors, Institute of Computing Technology, Chinese Academy of Sciences, Beijing, China
`lilongcheng22s@ict.ac.cn`
[2] Shenzhen International Center for Industrial and Applied Mathematics, Shenzhen Research Institute of Big Data, Shenzhen, China
`liqian.ict@gmail.com`
[3] Tsinghua University, Beijing, China
`lxj22@mails.tsinghua.edu.cn`
[4] University of California, San Diego, San Diego, CA, USA
`qipengliu0@gmail.com`

Abstract. The seminal work by Impagliazzo and Rudich (STOC'89) demonstrated the impossibility of constructing classical public key encryption (PKE) from one-way functions (OWF) in a black-box manner. Quantum information has the potential to bypass classical limitations, enabling the realization of seemingly impossible tasks such as quantum money, copy protection for software, and commitment without one-way functions. However, the question remains: can quantum PKE (QPKE) be constructed from quantumly secure OWF?

A recent line of work has shown that it is indeed possible to build QPKE from OWF, but with one caveat. These constructions necessitate public keys being quantum and unclonable, diminishing the practicality of such "public" encryption schemes—public keys cannot be authenticated and reused. In this work, we re-examine the possibility of perfect complete QPKE in the quantum random oracle model (QROM), where OWF exists.

> Our first main result: QPKE with classical public keys, secret keys and ciphertext, does not exist in the QROM, if the key generation only makes classical queries.

Therefore, a necessary condition for constructing such QPKE from OWF is to have the key generation classically "un-simulatable". Previous results (Austrin et al. CRYPTO'22) on the impossibility of QPKE from OWF rely on a seemingly strong conjecture. Our work makes a significant step towards a complete and unconditional quantization of Impagliazzo and Rudich's results.

> Our second main result extends to QPKE with quantum public keys. The second main result: QPKE with quantum public keys, classical secret keys and ciphertext, does not exist in the QROM, if the key generation only makes classical queries and the quantum public key is either pure or "efficiently clonable".

© International Association for Cryptologic Research 2024
L. Reyzin and D. Stebila (Eds.): CRYPTO 2024, LNCS 14926, pp. 152–183, 2024.
https://doi.org/10.1007/978-3-031-68394-7_6

The result is tight due to these existing QPKEs with quantum public keys, classical secret keys, quantum/classical ciphertext and classical-query key generation require the public key to be mixed instead of pure; or require quantum-query key generation, if the public key is pure. Our result further gives evidence on why existing QPKEs lose reusability.

We also explore other sufficient/necessary conditions to build QPKE from OWF. Along the way, we use a new argument based on conditional mutual information and Markov chain to reprove the classical result; leveraging the analog of quantum conditional mutual information and quantum Markov chain by Fawzi and Renner (Communications in Mathematical Physics), we extend it to the quantum case and prove all our results. We believe the techniques used in the work will find many other usefulness in separations in quantum cryptography/complexity.

1 Introduction

Quantum information and computation has the remarkable capability to transform classical impossibility into reality, ranging from breaking classically secure cryptosystems (Shor'a algorithm [26]), realizing classically impossible primitives (quantum money [27], quantum copy-protection [1,3]) to weakening assumptions (quantum key distribution [11], oblivious transfer/multi-party computation [9,16], commitment [4,24])[1].

In the seminal work by Impagliazzo and Rudich [19], they proved that one-way functions (OWFs) were insufficient to imply the existence of public-key encryption (PKE) in a black-box manner. Coined by Impagliazzo [18], the word "Minicrypt" was referred to a world where only one-way functions exist; this word now broadly denotes all cryptographic primitives that are constructible from one-way functions. Thus, their result is now often interpreted as "classical PKE is not in Minicrypt". Given the increasing instances of quantum making classical impossibility feasible, we explore the following question in this work:

Does quantum PKE (with classical plaintext) exist in Minicrypt?

Upon posing the question, ambiguity arises. A general quantum public-key encryption (QPKE) scheme allows everything to be quantum: its interaction with an OWF, both its public key and secret key, as well as ciphertext. Indeed, many efforts have already been made towards understanding different cases.

Classical Keys, Classical Ciphertext. In the work by Austrin, Chung, Chung, Fu, Lin and Mahmoody [6], they initialized the study on the impossibility of quantum key agreement (QKA) in the quantum random oracle model. QKA is a protocol that Alice and Bob can exchange classical messages in many rounds, quantumly query a random oracle, and eventually agree on a classical key. They show that, under a seemingly strong[2] assumption called "polynomial compatibility conjecture", such QKA with perfect completeness does not exist. Since

---

[1] Here, we only cite works that initialized each area.
[2] It seems strong because it implies that the eavesdropper can attack quantum Alice and Bob with only a polynomial number of classical queries.

QPKE with both keys and ciphertext being classical implies a two-round QKA, their conditional impossibility extends to this type of QPKE as well.

The result provides evidence on the negative side: such QPKE does not exist under the polynomial compatibility conjecture. However, not only proving or refuting the conjecture is quite challenging, but also the conjecture (or some form of the conjecture) is necessary. To prove QKA is impossible, one needs to design an eavesdropper that observes the whole transcript, interacts with the random oracle, and guesses a classical key. In a general QKA, both Alice and Bob can make quantum queries to the random oracle; the eavesdropper in the attack by Austrin et al. only makes classical queries. It inherently requires a simulation of a quantum-query algorithm using only classical queries (at least for the QKA functionality). Although not directly comparable, such efficient simulation for decision problems [2] (Aaronson-Ambainis conjecture) is conjectured to exist but the question still remains open until now. Moreover, [6] showed that if the Aaronson-Ambainis conjecture is false, a classical-query eavesdropper is insufficient to break imperfect complete QKA protocols.

In light of these considerations, our focus in this work centers on the following question:

Q1. Can we separate QPKE with classical keys, classical ciphertext from Minicrypt, without any conjecture?

Quantum Public Key, Classical Secret Key and Quantum/Classical Ciphertext. The quantum landscape introduces a paradigm shift. It was first realized by Morimae and Yamakawa [23] that some forms of QPKE with quantum public keys and quantum ciphertext might be constructed from OWFs (or even presumably weaker primitives). Subsequent QPKE schemes were later proposed by Coladangelo [14], Kitagawa et al. [20], Malavolta and Walter [21] and Barooti et al. [8].

On the surface, it seems to give a good answer: QPKE with quantum public keys exists in Minicrypt, showcasing a notable distinction between the quantum and classical world. However, is this demarcation as unequivocal as it seems? Indeed, all the aforementioned constructions share one limitation—they lose one of the most important properties inherent in all classical PKE—reusability. A classical PKE scheme allows a user who possesses a public key to encrypt any polynomial number of messages, by reusing the classical public key. In contrast, public keys in [8,14,20,21,23] are essentially unclonable[3] and not reusable. Although some may argue for the practicality of QPKE with an additional public interface for generating quantum public keys, it introduces additional complexities such as the authentication of quantum keys, leading to increased interactions and other potential challenges.

Thus, our second focus is the question:

---

[3] Although unclonability does not necessarily imply no-reusability, it is an evidence of no-reusability.

Q2. Must reusability be sacrificed in constructing QPKE with quantum public keys from OWFs?

1.1 Our Main Results

We make progress towards these two questions. A table discussing and comparing all existing results and our results is provided on the next page (Table 1). Our first main result establishes an impossibility result on QPKE with classical keys and classical ciphertext in the QROM.

Theorem 1. *QPKE with classical keys and classical ciphertext does not exist in the QROM, if*

1. *It has perfect completeness.*
2. *The key generation algorithm only makes classical queries to the random oracle.*

Unlike the approaches used in [6], our result does not require any conjecture, as the eavesdropper in our attack makes quantum queries. Perfect completeness is a natural property shared by many PKE schemes[4].

Consequently, if QPKE could be constructed in the QROM, one must have the key generation procedure being classical-query "un-simulatable"; meaning the keys can not be computed by an efficient classical-query algorithm. If we believe the Aaronson-Ambainis conjecture [2] (all quantum-query-solvable decision problems can be simulated by classical-query), the theorem suggests that the key generation must be a sampling procedure. Thus, to build QPKE in the QROM, we need to find a search/sampling problem that is only tractable by quantum queries; one such example is the Yamakawa-Zhandry problem [29].

[6] ruled out perfect complete QPKE with classical keys and classical ciphertext in the QROM, if (i) the encryption only makes classical queries, or (ii) both the key generation and decryption makes classical queries, without using the polynomial compatibility conjecture. Our result immediately improves their result (ii). Additionally, both of their impossibility results apply to the case where the oracle access in encryption and decryption procedure is asymmetric. Our result further completes the picture by making both encryption and decryption symmetric (quantum queries).

Another difference in our work is that our eavesdropper makes quantum queries. The capability of leveraging quantum eavesdroppers and conditioning on quantum events in this work, immediately gives us two strengthened versions (Theorem 2 and Theorem 3) of Theorem 1, which work for quantum public keys and quantum ciphertext. These two extensions provide many interesting discussions on the feasibility and impossibility of building QPKE in Minicrypt. [12] also discussed the feasibility of QPKE with quantum ciphertext, with a weaker result and based on the polynomial compatibility conjecture. Thus, we

---

[4] Very recently, Mazor [22] proposed the first perfectly complete "Merkle Puzzle", which was not known for many years.

believe our framework is versatile and has the potential to completely answer these questions. We elaborate on them now.

Our second main result extends the previous theorem to QPKE with quantum public keys and ciphertexts. This scheme is tight to all existing QPKE with quantum public keys and perfect completeness, see Table 2.

Theorem 2 (Subsuming Theorem 1). *QPKE with quantum public key, classical secret key, and classical or quantum ciphertext does not exist in the QROM, if*

1. *It has perfect completeness.*
2. *The key generation algorithm only makes classical queries to the random oracle.*
3. *The quantum public key is either pure or "efficiently clonable".*

At first glance, the theorem may appear unexciting: how can a classical-query key generation produce meaningful quantum public keys? Interestingly, the QPKE constructions in [20,21] have only classical-query key generation procedures. Namely, their public keys are of the form $\frac{1}{\sqrt{2}}(|s_0\rangle + |s_1\rangle)$ of two strings s_0, s_1, which can be computed using only classical queries.

Let us explain the third condition in our result. In QPKE, one needs to guarantee that having multiple copies of a quantum public key, the IND-CPA security still holds. If the public key generation procedure outputs a pure state, in other words the security holds against copies of the same pure state, we call the public key pure. Otherwise, each copy of a quantum public key is a mixed state (a distribution of pure states) and even holding multiple copies from the same distribution does not mean having the same pure states[5]. In the latter case, we require that there exists a query-efficient cloning procedure that can perfectly duplicate the pure state of the quantum public key.

As the schemes in [20,21] have perfect completeness and classical-query key generation, our result essentially says that their public keys must be mixed and can not be cloned. While the absence of perfect cloning does not imply non-reusability, our result provides crucial insights into the feasibility of building QPKE with quantum public keys and reusability from OWFs. Many intriguing open questions will be discussed further at the end of this section.

Our second theorem also is tight to the QPKE scheme by [8,14]. Their scheme has perfect completeness, pure state quantum public keys. Our theorem suggests that their schemes must make quantum queries; which is the case in their construction, as they need to query a pseudorandom function (implied by OWFs in a black-box manner) on an equal superposition.

---

[5] For example, even if having two copies of the same mixed state $\frac{I}{2}$, they can be two different states, like $|0\rangle|1\rangle$.

Table 1. Comparing impossibility results on classical public keys. 'Q' denotes quantum, 'C' denotes classical, 'checkmark' denotes yes, and '⋆' denotes no oracle queries. "RO" stands for "(quantum) random oracle".

	[6]	[6]	[6]	Thm 1	[12]	Thm 3
perfect complete	✓	✓	✓	✓	✓	
ciphertext	C	C	C	C	Q	Q
Gen	Q	Q	C	C	Q	Q
Enc	Q	C	Q	Q	Q	Q
Dec	Q	Q	C	Q	⋆	⋆
conjecture	✓				✓	
oracle	RO	RO	RO	RO	RO	any oracle

Table 2. Comparing our Thm 2 with existing constructions. [20,21] overcame the impossibility by allowing the ciphertext to be mixed; [8,14] overcame the impossibility by allowing the Gen procedure to make quantum queries.

	Thm 2 (Impossibility)	[20,21]	[8,14]
perfect complete	✓	✓	✓
ciphertext	pure or "efficiently clonable"	mixed and unclonable	pure
Gen	C	C	Q

Our next result is on the type of QPKE with classical keys and quantum ciphertext, whose decryption makes no queries to an oracle. The impossibility extends to any oracle model (even quantum oracles), not just the random oracle model.

Theorem 3. *(Imperfect/Perfect) QPKE with classical keys and quantum ciphertext does not exist in any oracle model, if*

1. *The decryption algorithm makes no queries to the oracle.*

Here, an oracle model means an oracle is sampled from a distribution, and the KA is executed under this oracle; both the key generation algorithm, the encryption algorithm and the attacker can have quantum access to the oracle. We remark that in our impossibility result, such QPKE does not need to be perfectly complete. We also note that, our theorem holds in the classical setting; PKE does not exist in any oracle model if the decryption algorithm makes no queries. This does not contradict constructions in the generic group model, as the decryption algorithm is required to make oracle queries.

A recent work by Bouaziz-Ermann, Grilo, Vergnaud and Vu [12] also discusses a similar separation. They proved that, under the polynomial compatibility conjecture, perfect complete QPKE with classical keys and quantum ciphertext does not exist in the QROM, if decryption makes no queries. Our Theorem 3 improves their results in three aspects: we remove the conjecture and the requirement on perfect completeness, and the impossibility works in any oracle model.

Other Results. As we progress towards achieving our main results, our techniques also enable us to establish additional impossibility results on QPKE and QKA as well. These results include

- Separation between pseudorandom quantum states and QKA (Remark 2);
- Impossibility of Merkle-like QKA (more generally, non-interactive QKA) in *any oracle model* (Theorem 5); we emphasize that this result also holds for quantum oracles, e.g., when a black-box unitary is chosen from Haar measure.
- Impossibility of QPKE with a short classical secret key in *any oracle model* (Appendix C in the full version).

We refer interested readers to these sections for more details.

1.2 Open Questions and Discussions

Before the overview of our techniques in the next section, we discuss some open questions and directions. Some discussions may become clearer upon reviewing both the overview and the entirety of the paper.

Remove Perfect Completeness. Our Theorem 1 and Theorem 2 both rely on the underlying QPKE is perfectly complete. Can we remove this condition and make the impossibility result work for any QPKE?

Extending Clonable Keys to Reusable Keys. When quantum public keys are reusable, that means there exists an encryption procedure Enc' that takes two messages m, m' and only one quantum public key pk, and outputs two valid ciphertexts. Since Enc' is not necessarily honest, it seems difficult to convert such assumptions into the setting of a QKA protocol. An intermediate goal is to have Enc "deterministic", which means it takes pk and m, outputs the original pk together with a valid ct—this is a weaker but promising step towards a full understanding of reusability. Another direction is to relax the "clonable" condition to some form of "approximate clonable" in our impossibility result.

Make Key Generation Quantum. Our Theorem 1 and Theorem 2 assume key generation procedure only makes classical queries. The current techniques require addressing some sorts of "heavy queries" made by an encryption procedure. For classical-query key generation, the number of such possible inputs is only polynomial. But it will be less clear how to handle this, when the key generation is fully quantum. Upon resolving this, one can get a full separation between QPKE and OWFs.

The basic idea of our approach is to keep the conditional mutual information (between Alice and Bob, conditioned on quantum Eve) small during the execution of QKA protocols or QPKE schemes. The characterization of quantum states with small CMI provided by Fawzi and Renner [15] (see Theorem 4) plays a major role. To achieve a full separation between QPKE and OWF, the argument has to critically utilize the condition that H is a uniform random function rather than drawn from a general oracle distribution. This is because our separation works in both the quantum and classical setting, but in the full classical KA case, KA exists in the generic group model. Thus, we really need to use the structures of a random oracle. In this work, we show it is possible when key generation only makes classical queries but not clear for quantum-query key generation.

2 Technical Overview

In this section, we shed light on several key ideas used in the work, especially those on how to attack with quantum queries and how to deal with quantum public keys. Our method for handling quantum ciphertext is similar to that in [12] by leveraging the Gentle Measurement Lemma.

Translating QPKE to QKA. Although we focus on the separation between QPKE and OWFs (or the quantum random oracle model), we will mostly study two-round QKA protocols. Say, if we have a QPKE scheme in the QROM (Gen, Enc, Dec), we can easily convert it to a two-round QKA:

Definition 1 (Informal, Two-round QKA). *We define a two-round QKA as follows.*

- *Alice runs* Gen *to produce* pk, sk *and sends* pk *as the first message* m_1 *to Bob. We call Alice's algorithm at this stage* $\mathcal{A}_1$.
- *Bob upon receiving* $m_1 :=$ pk, *it samples a uniformly random key* k. *It computes* ct $\leftarrow$ Enc(pk, k) *and sends* $m_2 :=$ ct *to Alice. We call Bob's algorithm at this stage* $\mathcal{B}$.
- *Alice will then run* Dec(sk, ct) *to retrieve* k. *We call Alice's algorithm at this stage* $\mathcal{A}_2$.

If the QPKE has security against randomly chosen messages, then the underlying QKA is secure. Quantum public keys will make m_1 quantum in the corresponding QKA, quantum ciphertext translates to a quantum m_2 and classical-query Gen makes $\mathcal{A}_1$ classical-query. Thus, we focus on breaking various types of two-round QKA with perfect completeness.

2.1 Recasting the Classical Idea for Merkle-Like KA

The classical proofs [7,19] share one common idea: as long as an eavesdropper Eve learns all the queries that are both used in Alice and Bob's computation, Eve can learn the key[6]. Here we re-interpret the idea for a special case: two-round Merkle-like KA. In this type of KA, m_1, m_2 are generated based on oracle queries and sent simultaneously to the other party (so that m_2 has no dependence on m_1). Furthermore, to recover the shared key, Alice and Bob only need to do local computation on their internal states and the communication, *without making any oracle queries*. This is a strong form of KA, which is not implied by PKE using the aforementioned reduction. We refer to it as Merkle-like because the famous Merkle Puzzles are of this form.

Let us assume for a specific execution of Alice and Bob, the queries made by Alice is the list R_A, her private coins are s_A and similarly R_B, s_B, R_E is the query made by Eve; we define $\text{View}_A = (s_A, R_A)$ as the personal view of Alice, similarly View_B for Bob. A tuple $(\text{View}_A, \text{View}_B, m_1, m_2, H)$ is a possible execution of the KA right after Alice and Bob exchange their messages but have not started working on computing the key. The tuple specifies Alice's random coins and queries, similarly for Bob, communication m_1, m_2 and the oracle H under which the protocol is executed. We say $(\text{View}_A, \text{View}_B)$ is consistent with a transcript (m_1, m_2) if there exists an oracle H, such that $(\text{View}_A, \text{View}_B, m_1, m_2, H)$ has *strictly positive* probability of appearing in some real execution. Similarly, View_A is consistent with (m_1, m_2) if $(\text{View}_A, m_1, m_2, H)$ has non-zero probability for some oracle H.

For a transcript (m_1, m_2), it is always easy to find a pair of Alice's fake $\text{View}'_A = (s'_A, T'_A)$ that is consistent with m_1, m_2. Since we do not care about the actual computation cost, and only the number of queries matters, we can keep sampling oracles until we see a transcript (m_1, m_2). Upon receiving View'_A, we hope that $(\text{View}'_A, \text{View}_B)$ has the same distribution as $(\text{View}_A, \text{View}_B)$; if that is true, based on perfect completeness, any non-zero support in $(\text{View}_A, \text{View}_B)$ should provide us with the agreed key.

Unfortunately, this does not hold true. The overlap in inputs between R_A and R_B leads to a correlation in the distribution $(\text{View}_A, \text{View}_B)$, making it impossible to sample independently. This correlation is the resource for Alice and Bob to compute an agreed key, akin to Merkle Puzzles.

The key insight from [7,19] is to eliminate this correlation, often referred to as "intersection queries". In their attacks, Eve queries the oracle in a manner such that R_E encompasses all the shared knowledge between Alice and Bob. More precisely, for any execution R_A, R_B consistent with (m_1, m_2), it holds that $R_A \cap R_B \subseteq R_E$. Consequently, conditioned on R_E and the transcript, the distribution $(\text{View}_A, \text{View}_B)$ becomes close to a product distribution. Eve can then sample View'_A conditioned on m_1, m_2, R_E, and this fake view will yield the correct key.

---

[6] [13] also gave a proof for the case of perfect completeness. Their proof works even if not all intersection queries are learned.

Finally, [7,19] demonstrate that as long as Eve queries Alice and Bob's "heavy queries" (those with a relatively noticeable probability of being queried), with high probability R_E will contain all intersection queries.

2.2 A Quantization Attempt by Austrin et al.

[6] focuses on the fully general QKA, but here we explain their ideas for the Merkle-like protocols. The first challenge arises when attempting to formally describe an execution for both quantum Alice and Bob. As they can make quantum queries, neither the random coins s_A nor the query list R_A can be explicitly delineated. A quantum algorithm can possess randomness that is impossible to be purified as random coins, and can make quantum superposition queries. An execution right after Alice and Bob exchange messages, is represented by $(\mathsf{View}_A, \mathsf{View}_B, m_1, m_2, H)$ where $\mathsf{View}_A := \rho_A, \mathsf{View}_B := \rho_B$ are the internal quantum states of Alice and Bob.

To quantize the strategy of [7,19], one needs to define "heavy quantum queries" and "quantum intersection queries", and establish some form of independence between Alice and Bob conditioned on transcripts and Eve's knowledge. Austrin et al., leveraged the breakthrough technique ("compressed oracle") by Zhandry [30], defined "heavy quantum queries". On a very high level (without introducing Zhandry's technique), "heavy quantum queries" are classical inputs that have high weights on the oracle, when the oracle is examined under the Fourier basis. Their proposed attack queries all "heavy quantum queries" classically. Under their polynomial compatibility conjecture, they can argue the success of their attacks.

This approach is less ideal in the following aspects. First, even for Merkle-like protocols, the polynomial compatibility conjecture seems necessary. Second, the classical-query Eve has to somehow "simulate" the ability of quantum Alice or quantum Bob. Although such simulation is believed to be true for decision problems [2], this kind of simulation in the QKA setting is both unclear to hold and potentially unnecessary. Finally, establishing independence between two quantum states (quantum Alice and Bob) is challenging to define and can be intricate.

2.3 Step Back—Classical and Quantum Proofs Using Markov Chain

Stepping back, let's reconsider if there are other approaches that are more quantum-friendly: potentially can take advantage of quantum-query Eve. The key insight in [7,19] is, when conditioned on some query list R_E and (m_1, m_2), the distribution $(\mathsf{View}_A, \mathsf{View}_B)$ is a product distribution, meaning Alice and Bob are independent. Based on this, Eve can therefore sample View'_A and they together with the real View_B have the same distribution as $(\mathsf{View}_A, \mathsf{View}_B)$.

Our first contribution is to give an alternative view of the classical proofs for Merkle-like KA. We realize that, in the classical proof, when intersection queries $R_A \cap R_B$ always is in R_E, the conditional mutual information (CMI) between R_A, R_B conditioned on E, m_1, m_2 is 0.

$$I(\text{View}_A : \text{View}_B | (m_1, m_2, R_E)) = 0.$$

There are two seemingly classically equivalent consequences when CMI is 0.

- **Perspective 1.** From Pinsker's inequality, a CMI of 0 immediately implies that View_A and View_B are independent conditioned on (m_1, m_2, R_E). This further implies that we can sample View'_A accordingly.
- **Perspective 2.** Another perspective is that, $\text{View}_B \to (m_1, m_2, R_E) \to \text{View}_A$ forms a Markov chain.

   Three random variables XYZ form a Markov chain if $p_{xyz} = p_{xy} p_{z|y}$. In our case, it says there exists a way to take (m_1, m_2, R_E) as inputs and sample View'_A such that $(\text{View}'_A, \text{View}_B)$ and $(\text{View}_A, \text{View}_B)$ are identically distributed.

The above discussion explains the attacks for Merkle-like protocols, through the lens of CMI.

From this, we propose one candidate quantum attack for Merkle-like QKA:

Quantum Eve: A Framework

- Eve makes some quantum queries and let $\text{View}_E := \rho_E$ be its internal quantum state. It "somehow" makes sure that the CMI between Alice and Bob, conditioned on Eve and the transcript is small enough.

$$I(\text{View}_A : \text{View}_B \mid m_1, m_2, \text{View}_E) < \epsilon.$$

- Use "some quantum analogy" of 1 or 2 above to produce a quantum state $\text{View}'_A := \rho_{A'}$ from ρ_E such that,

$$\text{View}'_A \text{View}_B \approx_{\text{poly}(\epsilon)} \text{View}_A \text{View}_B.$$

There are two questions remain to be answered:

Does there exist a query-efficient Eve's strategy that always makes CMI small? Does there exist a quantum analogy of step 1 or 2?

We answer both of the questions affirmatively.

Decreasing CMI. Assume Alice and Bob each makes at most d queries and $H : [2^n] \to \{0, 1\}$ be any oracle of domain $[2^n]$ and binary range. We show that,

Lemma 1 (Informal). *For any standard two-round QKA right after Alice receives m_2, Eve can run the same Bob t times for some $t \in \{0, 1, \ldots, 2dn/\epsilon\}$ and store all t copies of Bob's internal states, such that the CMI between Alice and Bob conditioned on Eve's register and m_1, m_2 is at most ϵ.*

A couple of things we clarify here. First, why don't we set $t := 2dn/\epsilon$ (the largest value)? This is due to the nature of quantum conditional mutual information. Classically, when we condition on more classical queries, the CMI will never increase. However, quantum entropy and mutual information behave unlike their classical counterparts. Still, we are able to show the existence of such small t. The existence of such t will not make our Eve non-uniform, as t is (inefficiently) computable without making any oracle query.[7]

Second, this strategy works for any oracles. Third, the lemma does not distinguish between whether m_1 is classical or quantum. Even if Bob takes a quantum input, as long as we have access to t copies of the same quantum state, we can run Bob with the same pure state t times and thus the lemma still holds. This fact will be useful for the case of quantum public keys.

Finally, the lemma works for any two-round QKA[8]. As Alice and Bob are asymmetric for general protocols, we do not know how to only simulate Alice's queries and make the CMI small in the general two-round QKA case. We will mention it after finishing the discussion on Merkle-like QKA.

Sampling Fake Alice. When the CMI is small, we need to sample a fake Alice. If the CMI is 0, Hayden et al. [17] showed an approach that can be viewed as a quantum analogy of Perspective 1. However, their approach only works for the case of CMI being exactly 0 and is not robust.

We realize the second interpretation works much better. The work by Fawzi and Renner showed that

Lemma 2 (Approximate Quantum Markov Chain, [15]). *Let X, Y, Z be three quantum registers, and ρ_{XYZ} be the state. If $I(X : Z|Y) < \epsilon$, then there exists a channel $\mathcal{T} : Y \to Y'Z'$ such that*

$$|\rho_{XZ} - \sigma_{XZ'}|_{\mathsf{Tr}} \leq |\rho_{XYZ} - \sigma_{XY'Z'}|_{\mathsf{Tr}} \leq O(\sqrt{\epsilon}),$$

where $\sigma_{XY'Z'}$ is the state from applying $\mathcal{T}$ on the Y register of ρ_{XY}. Furthermore, $\mathcal{T}$ is explicitly (and inefficiently) constructible if knowing the state ρ_{XYZ}.

On a high level, Lemma 1 states that if the CMI $I(X : Z|Y)$ for a tripartite state ρ_{XYZ} is small enough, then we can apply a local channel on Y to generate a state close to the original state in XY. This directly provides us a way to sample a fake Alice. In our case, X is the view of Bob, Z is the view of Alice and Y is the view of Eve and the transcript. Thus, the whole density matrix of ρ_{XYZ} is known by Eve[9]. By applying the lemma, Eve can sample $Z' := \mathsf{View}'_A$ such that $\mathsf{View}'_A \mathsf{View}_B \approx_{O(\sqrt{\epsilon})} \mathsf{View}_A \mathsf{View}_B$; although $\mathcal{T}$ in this case could be inefficient, it makes no queries. This completes the second step of our Eve.

---

[7] One can also guess a uniform t if we do not require finding the key with probability close to 1.
[8] It is a general lemma that works for any two-classical-message quantum interactive protocol. We focus on its application in QKA in this paper.
[9] ρ_{XYZ} in this case, is not the state under a particular oracle, but the mixed state averaged over the distribution of all oracles. Only in this case, Eve knows ρ_{XYZ}.

Combining the approach of making the CMI arbitrarily small with the quantum Markov chain for sampling a fake Alice, our Eve can attack any Merkle-like QKA in any oracle model. We remark that for a general two-round QKA, Lemma 1 and Lemma 2 only cover the part up to receiving the last message m_2. In the next subsection, we will discuss how to handle additional queries made after the last message.

2.4 Ruling Out QPKE with Classical-Query Key Generation

The exact same idea from the previous section also applies to the standard two-round QKA as defined in Definition 1, particularly when $\mathcal{A}_2$ (or the decryption algorithm) makes no queries to the oracle. In this scenario, we let View$_A$ and View$_B$ represent the views of Alice and Bob right after m_1 is received by Alice, and she has not yet begun working on producing the key. When we sample View$'_A$View$_B \approx$ View$_A$View$_B$, since $\mathcal{A}_2$ only applies a local unitary that is independent of the oracle, Eve can perform the same on the fake view and still successfully obtain the key. However, what if $\mathcal{A}_2$ makes queries?

It is not immediately clear whether our CMI-based method works when $\mathcal{A}_1$, $\mathcal{A}_2$, and $\mathcal{B}$ all make classical queries only, as in the case of classical KA instead of QKA. There are two attempts, that one might immediately come out.

- Attempt 1: run $\mathcal{A}_2$ on the fake View$'_A$ using any oracle that is compatible with View$'_A$;
- Attempt 2: run $\mathcal{A}_2$ on the fake View$'_A$ using the real oracle.

Unfortunately, both approaches fail. Consider the following two classical examples for KA.

- Example 1: $\mathcal{A}_1$ does not query and does not send messages, $\mathcal{B}$ sends a random $m_2 = x$ and both Alice and Bob agree on $H(x)$.
  It is easy to see that, even if Eve does not query, $I(\text{View}_A : \text{View}_B | m_2) = 0$ as View$_A$ is empty. Thus, any oracle H' is consistent with a fake View$'_A$ but with overwhelming probability, $H'(x) \neq H(x)$.
- Example 2: $\mathcal{A}_1$ queries $H(0)$ and stores it as y, but does not send messages to $\mathcal{B}$; $\mathcal{B}$ sends a random $m_2 = x$ that is not equal to 0; $\mathcal{A}_2$ queries $H(0)$ again and aborts if $y \neq H(0)$, otherwise the key will be $H(x)$.
  In an honest execution, Alice and Bob will always agree on a key $H(x)$ for some $x \neq 0$ as y is always equal to $H(0)$.
  We claim that $I(\text{View}_A : \text{View}_B | m_2) = 0$ as View$_A$ and View$_B$ have no intersection queries. Let View$'_A$ be the fake view that consists of some y'. A real oracle with overwhelming probability has $H(x) \neq y'$, which fails the second attempt.

Our solution is to combine both Attempt 1 and Attempt 2.

Solution for Simulating $\mathcal{A}_2$ in the Classical Case. Our solution provides an alternative proof for the classical impossibility "PKE is not in Minicrypt" using our CMI-based framework and our solution for simulating $\mathcal{A}_2$ below.

When $\mathcal{A}_1$, $\mathcal{A}_2$, and $\mathcal{B}$ are all classical-query algorithms, we propose the following method to execute a fake $\text{View}'_A = (s'_A, R'_A)$. Here, s'_A represents Alice's random coins, and R'_A represents the query list (a list of input-output pairs).

– Run $\mathcal{A}_2$ on the fake View'_A using the real oracle, except for every $x \in R'_A$, respond with the corresponding image $y \in R'_A$.

In other words, we adjust the real oracle such that it is consistent with R'_A; let's denote this modified oracle as H'.

Why it works? Assume we sample View'_A such that $\text{View}'_A \text{View}_B$ has the same distribution as the real views for Alice and Bob. The fake view View'_A together with the real View_B must be reachable under some oracle (not necessarily the real oracle). Therefore, R'_A and R_B must be consistent. We also know that, since View_B is the real view of Bob under the real oracle H, R_B and H must also be consistent.

Thus, changing the oracle to be consistent with R'_A will only alter its behavior on those $x \notin R_B$. That means, under oracle H', this KA will still have a strictly positive probability to end up with $\text{View}'_A, \text{View}_B, m_1, m_2$. By perfect completeness, when running $\mathcal{A}_2$ on View'_A with oracle H', we must obtain the key held by Bob.

Extending to QPKE with Classical-Query Key Generation. For QKA with $\mathcal{A}_1$ making only classical queries (or QPKE with the key generation making classical queries), we can still run our Eve algorithm such that $I(\text{View}_A : \text{View}_B | (m_0, m_1, E)) < \epsilon$. However, since $\mathcal{B}$ is now quantum, View_B is some quantum state ρ_B and its query list R_B is no longer defined.

We repeat our strategy again: sample View'_A and run $\mathcal{A}_2$ on View'_A with oracle H' as defined above (mostly the real oracle, but made consistent with R'_A). If Bob has low query weights on R'_A, then our attack still works. If the total query weight of Bob on R'_A is 0, changing the real oracle to H' will not change View_B at all. Similarly, if the weight is small, changing the real oracle to H' will only change View_B by a small amount [10]. Thus, we can still argue that $\text{View}'_A, \text{View}_B, m_1, m_2$ are reachable under H' and with perfect completeness, we must recover the key.

What if Bob has a large query weight on some $x \in R'_A$? We imagine a hypothetical Bob, who will first produce View_B, but then keep running itself from the beginning multiple times and randomly measure one of its queries. By doing so, the hypothetical Bob's functionality does not change; the advantage is now the hypothetical Bob has a *classical list* L_B that consists of all its queries with high weights, with a high probability.

If we run our Eve with this hypothetical Bob, View'_A must have R'_A consistent with L_B. Thus, changing the oracle to be consistent with R'_A will only change its behavior on those $x \notin L_B$, or in other words, those x that do not have a large query weight! Then we can use the argument in the previous paragraphs and claim that $\text{View}'_A, \text{View}_B := (\rho_B, L_B), m_1, m_2$ are reachable under H' and with perfect completeness, we can get the key.

Handling Quantum Public Keys. Quantum public keys (or quantum m_1) are handled without additional efforts using our CMI-based Eve. This further demonstrates the versatility and power of our new framework; previous approaches based on classical-query Eve do not extend to this case.

When m_1 is quantum, the challenge arises in how Eve can effectively run multiple copies of Bob on quantum input m_1. In the context of QPKE, the attacker needs access to multiple copies of the quantum m_1. If m_1 is a pure state, it becomes evident that running the same Bob on the same pure state m_1 is feasible, allowing us to minimize the CMI accordingly. Alternatively, if a query-efficient perfect cloner for m_1 exists, multiple runs of the same Bob become possible.

Given that the subsequent analysis relies solely on the capability to run Bob multiple times on input m_1, we can extend our conclusion to rule out perfect complete QPKE with quantum public keys and classical-query key generation under the condition that the quantum public keys are either pure or query-efficiently clonable.

3 Preliminaries

We refer reader to [25] for more details about quantum computing and quantum information. Below, we mention some backgrounds that are heavily used in this work.

3.1 Distance Measures

Let us recall the definition of total variation distance and trace distance.

Definition 2 (Total variation distance). *For two probabilistic distributions D_X, D_Y over the same finite domain $\mathcal{X}$, we define their total variation distance as*

$$TV(D_X, D_Y) = \frac{1}{2} \sum_{x \in \mathcal{X}} |D_X(x) - D_Y(x)|.$$

Definition 3 (Trace distance). *For two quantum states ρ, σ, the trace distance between the two states is*

$$TD(\rho, \sigma) = \frac{1}{2} \text{Tr}\left[\sqrt{(\rho-\sigma)^\dagger(\rho-\sigma)}\right] = \sup_{0 \leq \Lambda \leq I} \text{Tr}[\Lambda(\rho-\sigma)].$$

3.2 Quantum Oracle Model and Random Oracle

A quantum oracle algorithm equipped with access to $H: [2^{n_\lambda}] \to [2^{m_\lambda}]$ is expressed as a series of unitaries: $U_1, U_H, U_2, U_H, \cdots, U_T, U_H, U_{T+1}$. Here, U_i denotes a local unitary acting on the algorithm's internal register. Oracle access to H is defined by a unitary transformation U_H, where $|x, y\rangle$ is transformed to $|x, y + H(x)\rangle$. For an oracle algorithm $\mathcal{A}$, we would use $\mathcal{A}^H$ to denote the algorithm $\mathcal{A}$ has classical access to the oracle H, and $\mathcal{A}^{|H\rangle}$ to denote $\mathcal{A}$ has quantum access to the oracle.

We would also consider the case when the oracle $H\colon [2^{n_\lambda}] \to \{0, 1\}$ is sampled from some distribution of oracles $\mathcal{H}_\lambda$. We would call some primitive in the quantum random oracle model(QROM) if the distribution $\mathcal{H}_\lambda$ is uniformly random over all possible oracles.

3.3 Entropy

Definition 4 (Von Neumann Entropy). *Let $\rho \in \mathbb{C}^{2^n}$ be a quantum state describing a system A. Let $|\phi_1\rangle, |\phi_2\rangle, \cdots, |\phi_{2^n}\rangle$ be the eigenbasis of ρ; ρ is written in this eigenbasis as $\sum_i \eta_i |\phi_i\rangle\langle\phi_i|$.*

Then its Von Neumann Entropy is denoted by $S(\rho)$ (or $S(\mathsf{A})_\rho$),

$$S(\mathsf{A})_\rho = S(\rho) = -\sum_i \eta_i \log(\eta_i).$$

Given a composite quantum system AB having joint state ρ_{AB}, we define the conditional Von Neumann Entropy as $S(\mathsf{A}|\mathsf{B})_\rho$,

$$S(\mathsf{A}|\mathsf{B})_\rho = S(\mathsf{AB})_\rho - S(\mathsf{B})_\rho.$$

Below, we often omit ρ in the definition when the quantum state is clear in the context. For example, $S(\mathsf{A})$ and $I(\mathsf{A} : \mathsf{B})$ instead of $S(\mathsf{A})_\rho$ and $I(\mathsf{A} : \mathsf{B})_\rho$.

Fact 1 ([25]). *Suppose p_k are probabilities, $|k\rangle$ are orthogonal basis of a system A and ρ_k are quantum states for another system B. Then*

$$S\left(\sum_k p_k |k\rangle\langle k| \otimes \rho_k\right) = H(p_k) + \sum_k p_k S(\rho_k)$$

where $H(p_k)$ is the Shannon entropy of distribution p_k.

Fact 2 ([28]). *If ρ_{AB} is a separable state, then $S(\mathsf{A}|\mathsf{B}) \geq 0$.*

Definition 5 (Mutual Information). *Let ρ be a quantum state describing two joint systems A and B. Then the mutual information between the system A and B is denoted by $I(\mathsf{A} : \mathsf{B})$,*

$$I(\mathsf{A} : \mathsf{B}) = S(\mathsf{A}) + S(\mathsf{B}) - S(\mathsf{AB}).$$

Definition 6 (Conditional Mutual Information). *Let ρ be a quantum state describing three joint systems A, B and C. Then the conditional mutual information $I(\mathsf{A} : \mathsf{B}|\mathsf{C})$,*

$$I(\mathsf{A} : \mathsf{B}|\mathsf{C}) = S(\mathsf{AC}) + S(\mathsf{BC}) - S(\mathsf{ABC}) - S(\mathsf{C}).$$

Fact 3 (Chain rule). $I(A_1, A_2, \cdots, A_t : B \mid C) = \sum_{i=1}^{t} I(A_i : B \mid C, A_1, \cdots, A_{i-1})$.

Fact 4. *Let ABC be a composite quantum system. When a unitary is applied on A, it will not change $S(A)$. Similarly, the local unitary on A will not change $I(A : B)$ or $I(A : B|C)$.*

Proof. This directly follows from the definition of $S(A)$ and applying any unitary will not change the spectrum of a density matrix.

The strong subadditivity for (conditional) entropy concludes that both mutual information and conditional mutual information are always non-negative.

Lemma 3 (Strong Subadditivity, [5]). *Given Hilbert spaces A, B, C,*

$$S(AC) + S(AB) \geq S(ABC) + S(C).$$

(The conditional form) Given Hilbert spaces A, B, C, D,

$$S(AC|D) + S(AB|D) \geq S(ABC|D) + S(C|D).$$

3.4 Operational Meaning of Conditional Mutual Information: Approximate Quantum Markov Chain

Fawzi and Renner [15] provided a nice characterization of quantum states for which the conditional mutual information is approximately zero. Intuitively, if $I(A : B \mid E)$ is small, then B can be approximately reconstructed from E.

Theorem 4 ([15], restate of Lemma 2). *For any state ρ_{AEB} over systems AEB, there exists a channel $\mathcal{T} : E \to E \otimes B'$ such that the trace distance between the reconstructed state $\sigma_{A'E'B'} = \mathcal{T}(\rho_{AE})$ and the original state ρ_{AEB} is at most*

$$\sqrt{\ln 2 \cdot I(A : B|E)_\rho}.$$

3.5 Quantum Key Agreement and Quantum Public Key Encryption

In the following, we provide formal definitions of quantum key agreement (QKA) and quantum public key encryption (QPKE) in the oracle model.

Definition 7 (Quantum Key Agreement in the Oracle Model). *Let $\lambda \in \mathbb{Z}_+$ be the security parameter and $\mathcal{H}_\lambda$ be a distribution of oracles. Let $H \leftarrow \mathcal{H}_\lambda$ be a classical oracle, drawn according to $\mathcal{H}_\lambda$.*

A key agreement protocol consists of two parties Alice and Bob, who start with all-zero states and have the ability to apply any quantum operator, get quantum access to H, and send classical messages to each other.

Both Alice and Bob can make at most $\mathsf{poly}(\lambda)$ number of quantum queries to H. Finally, Alice and Bob output classical strings k_A, k_B[10]. We would call the set of classical messages between Alice and Bob, denoted by Π, the transcript of the key exchange protocol.

---
[10] k_A, k_B can be of any length (even exponential in λ). Our impossibility results apply to protocols with any output key length.

A key agreement protocol should satisfy both correctness and security.

Definition 8 (Correctness). *Let k_A, k_B be the keys outputted in the protocol. Then $\Pr[k_A = k_B] \geq 1/q(\lambda)$ for some polynomial $q(\cdot)$, where the probability is taken over the randomness of Alice and Bob's channels, and the random choice of oracle H.*

Definition 9 (Security). *For any eavesdropper Eve that makes at most $\mathsf{poly}(\lambda)$ number of quantum queries to $H \leftarrow \mathcal{H}_\lambda$, eavesdrops classical communication between Alice and Bob and outputs k_E, the probability that $\Pr[k_A = k_E]$ is negligible in λ.*

We are interested in whether there exists a protocol that satisfies both correctness and security in the QROM. It is worth noting that the ability of making quantum queries is essential in our setting; when Alice and Bob can only make polynomially many classical queries, secure key agreement does not exist; i.e., there always exists an eavesdropper making polynomially many classical queries and breaking it [7,19].

We also focus on breaking quantum public key encryption schemes in the oracle model.

Definition 10 (Quantum Public Key Encryption in the Oracle Model). *Let $\lambda \in \mathbb{Z}_+$ be the security parameter and $\mathcal{H}_\lambda$ be a distribution over oracles $H\colon [2^{n_\lambda}] \to \{0,1\}$. Let $H \leftarrow \mathcal{H}_\lambda$ be a classical oracle, a QPKE scheme in the oracle model consists of three algorithms (Gen, Enc, Dec), each of which is allowed to make at most $d(\lambda) = \mathsf{poly}(\lambda)$ quantum queries to H:*

- $\mathsf{Gen}^{|H\rangle}(1^\lambda) \to (\mathsf{pk}, \mathsf{sk})$: *The quantum key generation algorithm that generates a pair of classical public key pk and secret key sk.*
- $\mathsf{Enc}^{|H\rangle}(\mathsf{pk}, m) \to \mathsf{ct}$: *the quantum encryption algorithm that takes a public key pk, the plaintext m, produces the ciphertext ct.*
- $\mathsf{Dec}^{|H\rangle}(\mathsf{sk}, \mathsf{ct}) \to m'$: *the quantum decryption algorithm that takes secret key sk and ciphertext ct and outputs the plaintext m'.*

The algorithms should satisfy the following requirements:

Completeness $\Pr\left[\mathsf{Dec}^{|H\rangle}\left(\mathsf{sk}, \mathsf{Enc}^{|H\rangle}(\mathsf{pk}, m)\right) = m \colon \mathsf{Gen}^{|H\rangle}(1^\lambda) \to (\mathsf{pk}, \mathsf{sk})\right] \geq 1 - \mathsf{negl}(\lambda).$

IND-CPA Security *For any adversary $\mathcal{E}^{|H\rangle}$ that makes $\mathsf{poly}(\lambda)$ queries, for every two plaintexts $m_0 \neq m_1$ chosen by $\mathcal{E}^{|H\rangle}(\mathsf{pk})$, we have*

$$\Pr\left[\mathcal{E}^{|H\rangle}\left(\mathsf{pk}, \mathsf{Enc}^{|H\rangle}(\mathsf{pk}, m_b)\right) = b\right] \leq \frac{1}{2} + \mathsf{negl}(\lambda).$$

Especially in Sect. 6, we will focus on when the key generation algorithm Gen^H is an algorithm with classical access to the oracle H.

It is a folklore result that we can construct a two-round key agreement protocol from a public key encryption scheme as follows:

1. Alice runs $\mathsf{Gen}^{|H\rangle}$ to produce a public key pk and a secret sk, and sends the public key pk as the first message m_1 to Bob. We call Alice's algorithm at this stage $\mathcal{A}_1$.
2. Bob upon receiving pk, it samples a uniformly random classical string k as the key. It computes the ciphertext $\mathsf{ct} \leftarrow \mathsf{Enc}^{|H\rangle}(\mathsf{pk}, k)$ and sends $m_2 := \mathsf{ct}$ to Alice. We call Bob's algorithm at this stage $\mathcal{B}$.
3. Alice will then run $\mathsf{Dec}^{|H\rangle}(\mathsf{sk}, \mathsf{ct})$ to output k', which is her guess of k. We call Alice's algorithm at this stage $\mathcal{A}_2$.

We further notice that the only information required by $\mathcal{A}_2$ from $\mathcal{A}_1$ is the secret key sk. Thus if sk is classical, we can assume without loss of generality that the internal state of $\mathcal{A}_1$ at its termination is a mixed state in the computational basis.

We would also consider the recently proposed QPKE with quantum public key [8,14,20] in Sect. 6. We would only focus on the variant where the protocol is perfect complete, and key generation algorithms can only make classical queries.

Definition 11 (QPKE with quantum public key). *Let $\lambda \in \mathbb{Z}_+$ be the security parameter and $\mathcal{H}_\lambda$ be a distribution over oracles $H: [2^{n_\lambda}] \to \{0,1\}$. Let $H \leftarrow \mathcal{H}_\lambda$ be a classical oracle, a QPKE scheme in the oracle model consists of four algorithms (SKGen, PKGen, Enc, Dec), each of which is allowed to make at most $d(\lambda) = \mathsf{poly}(\lambda)$ queries to H:*

- $\mathsf{SKGen}^H(1^\lambda) \to \mathsf{sk}$: *The secret key generation algorithm that generates a classical secret key sk.*
- $\mathsf{PKGen}^H(\mathsf{sk}) \to \rho_{\mathsf{pk}}$: *The public key generation algorithm that takes the secret key sk and generates a quantum public key ρ_{pk}.*
- $\mathsf{Enc}^{|H\rangle}(\rho_{\mathsf{pk}}, m) \to \mathsf{ct}$: *the quantum encryption algorithm that takes a public key pk, the plaintext m, produces the (possibly quantum) ciphertext ρ_{ct}.*
- $\mathsf{Dec}^{|H\rangle}(\mathsf{sk}, \rho_{\mathsf{ct}}) \to m'$: *the quantum decryption algorithm that takes secret key sk and ciphertext ct and outputs the plaintext m'.*

The algorithms should satisfy the following requirements:

Perfect Completeness

$$\Pr\left[\mathsf{Dec}^{|H\rangle}\left(\mathsf{sk}, \mathsf{Enc}^{|H\rangle}(\rho_{\mathsf{pk}}, m)\right) = m: \mathsf{SKGen}^H(1^\lambda) \to \mathsf{sk}, \mathsf{PKGen}^H(\mathsf{sk}) \to \rho_{\mathsf{pk}}\right] = 1.$$

IND-CPA Security *For any adversary $\mathcal{E}^{|H\rangle}$ that makes $\mathsf{poly}(\lambda)$ queries, given any polynomial copies of public key $\rho_{\mathsf{pk}}^{\otimes t(\lambda)}$, for every two plaintexts $m_0 \neq m_1$ chosen by $\mathcal{E}(\rho_{\mathsf{pk}}^{\otimes t(\lambda)})$, we have*

$$\Pr\left[\mathcal{E}^{|H\rangle}\left(\rho_{\mathsf{pk}}^{\otimes t(\lambda)}, \mathsf{Enc}^{|H\rangle}(\rho_{\mathsf{pk}}, m_b)\right) = b\right] \leq \frac{1}{2} + \mathsf{negl}(\lambda).$$

We call the public key pure if given sk, $\rho_{\mathsf{pk}} \leftarrow \mathsf{PKGen}(\mathsf{sk})$ is a pure state, and call the public key clonable if there is some polynomial query algorithm $\mathcal{D}^{|H\rangle}$ that takes $\rho_{\mathsf{pk}} = \sum p_i |\psi_i\rangle\langle\psi_i|$ in its eigenvector decomposition, and generates the state $\rho' = \sum p_i |\psi_i\rangle\langle\psi_i|^{\otimes t(\lambda)}$ for some polynomial $t(\cdot)$.

Remark 1. *The definition of clonable here might seem odd at first glance, we would give some examples here for further explanations. The public key generation algorithm from [20,21] PKGen(sk) generates a $\rho_{\mathsf{pk}} = (\mathsf{pk}_r, |\psi_r\rangle)$ according to some private coin r of PKGen(sk), where pk_r is a classical string, $|\psi_r\rangle$ is a pure quantum state. Thus our cloning algorithm $\mathcal{D}$ can be seen as given a sample $(\mathsf{pk}_r, |\psi_r\rangle)$, it can generate multiple copies of state $|\psi_r\rangle$.*

4 Helper Lemmas

In this section, we introduce three helper lemmas. Lemma 4 tells how to decrease CMI. Lemma 5 and Lemma 6 claim that classical communication does not increase CMI. Lemma 7 will be used in Sect. 6.

4.1 Repetition Decreases CMI

Definition 12 (Permutation Invariance). *Let $\mathsf{A}_1, \mathsf{A}_2, \mathsf{A}_3, \ldots, \mathsf{A}_t, \mathsf{B}$ be $(t+1)$-partite quantum system. Given the joint state $\rho_{\mathsf{BA}_1\mathsf{A}_2\cdots\mathsf{A}_t}$, we say $A_1, \ldots, A_t$ are permutation invariant, if for any permutation π on $[t]$, we have*

$$\rho_{\mathsf{BA}_1\mathsf{A}_2\cdots\mathsf{A}_t} = \rho_{\mathsf{BA}_{\pi(1)}\mathsf{A}_{\pi(2)}\cdots\mathsf{A}_{\pi(t)}}.$$

Lemma 4. *Let $\mathsf{A}_1, \mathsf{A}_2, \mathsf{A}_3, \ldots, \mathsf{A}_t, \mathsf{B}, \mathsf{C}$ be $(t+2)$-partite quantum system. Suppose the state of the composite system $\rho_{\mathsf{BCA}_1\mathsf{A}_2\cdots\mathsf{A}_t}$ is fully separable. If $\mathsf{A}_1, \mathsf{A}_2, \mathsf{A}_3, \ldots, \mathsf{A}_t$ are permutation invariant, then there is a $0 \leq i \leq t-1$ such that*

$$I(\mathsf{A}_t : \mathsf{B} \mid \mathsf{C}, \mathsf{A}_1, \ldots, \mathsf{A}_i)_\rho \leq S(\mathsf{B})/t.$$

Proof. By the chain rule of conditional mutual information (see Fact 3), we have

$$\sum_{i=1}^{t} I(\mathsf{A}_i : \mathsf{B} \mid \mathsf{C}, \mathsf{A}_1, \ldots, \mathsf{A}_{i-1}) = I(\mathsf{A}_1, \ldots, \mathsf{A}_t : \mathsf{B} \mid \mathsf{C}). \tag{1}$$

Besides,

$$I(\mathsf{A}_1, \ldots, \mathsf{A}_t : \mathsf{B} \mid \mathsf{C}) = S(\mathsf{B} \mid \mathsf{C}) - S(\mathsf{B} \mid \mathsf{C}, \mathsf{A}_1, \ldots, \mathsf{A}_t) \leq S(\mathsf{B} \mid \mathsf{C}) \leq S(\mathsf{B}), \tag{2}$$

where the inequalities are Fact 2 and that $I(\mathsf{B} : \mathsf{C}) = S(\mathsf{B}) - S(\mathsf{B} \mid \mathsf{C})$ is always non-negative. By (1) and (2), there must exist $i \in [t]$ such that $I(\mathsf{A}_i : \mathsf{B} \mid \mathsf{C}, \mathsf{A}_1, \ldots, \mathsf{A}_{i-1}) \leq S(\mathsf{B})/t$. Finally, by the permutation invariance, we have $I(\mathsf{A}_i : \mathsf{B} \mid \mathsf{C}, \mathsf{A}_1, \ldots, \mathsf{A}_{i-1}) = I(\mathsf{A}_t : \mathsf{B} \mid \mathsf{C}, \mathsf{A}_1, \ldots, \mathsf{A}_{i-1})$. Now we finish the proof.

4.2 Classical Communication Does Not Increase CMI

Lemma 5 (Local quantum operation does not increase CMI). *Let ABC be a composite quantum system. After performing a quantum operation M on A, the state of the system becomes $\mathsf{A'B'C'}$. Then $I(\mathsf{A'} : \mathsf{B'}|\mathsf{C'}) \leq I(\mathsf{A} : \mathsf{B}|\mathsf{C})$.*

Proof. We introduce another quantum system D, initialized as zero. The quantum operation M can be treated as first performing a unitary transformation U on AD and then discarding D.

$$\begin{aligned} I(\mathsf{A}:\mathsf{B}|\mathsf{C}) &= I(\mathsf{AD}:\mathsf{B}|\mathsf{C}) \\ &= I(U(\mathsf{AD})U^\dagger : \mathsf{B}|\mathsf{C}) \\ &= I(\mathsf{A'D'}:\mathsf{B'}|\mathsf{C'}) \\ &= S(\mathsf{A'D'}|\mathsf{C'}) - S(\mathsf{A'D'B'}|\mathsf{C'}) + S(\mathsf{B'}|\mathsf{C'}). \end{aligned}$$

By the conditional form of strong sub-additivity (see the condition form of Lemma 3), $S(\mathsf{A'D'}|\mathsf{C'}) - S(\mathsf{A'D'B'}|\mathsf{C'}) \geq S(\mathsf{A'}|\mathsf{C'}) - S(\mathsf{A'B'}|\mathsf{C'})$. Then

$$\begin{aligned} I(\mathsf{A}:\mathsf{B}|\mathsf{C}) &\geq S(\mathsf{A'}|\mathsf{C'}) - S(\mathsf{A'B'}|\mathsf{C'}) + S(\mathsf{B'}|\mathsf{C'}) \\ &= I(\mathsf{A'}:\mathsf{B'}|\mathsf{C'}). \end{aligned}$$

□

Lemma 6 (Sending classical message does not increase CMI). *Let* ABC *be a composite quantum system and* $\mathsf{A} = (\mathsf{W_A}, \mathsf{M_A})$ *where* $\mathsf{W_A}$ *is the working register and* $\mathsf{M_A}$ *is the message register containing a classical state. After* B *and* C *both obtain a copy of* $\mathsf{M_A}$, *the system becomes* A'B'C'. *Then* $I(\mathsf{A'}:\mathsf{B'}|\mathsf{C'}) \leq I(\mathsf{A}:\mathsf{B}|\mathsf{C})$.

The following claim will be used.

Claim 1 (Copying classical state does not change entropy). *Given a system* PQR *where* Q *and* R *contain identical classical states. Then* $S(\mathsf{PQR}) = S(\mathsf{PR}) = S(\mathsf{PQ})$.

Proof. The joint state of PQR can be written as

$$\sum_k p_k \rho_\mathsf{P}^{(k)} \otimes |k\rangle\langle k|_\mathsf{Q} \otimes |k\rangle\langle k|_\mathsf{R}$$

where p_k are probabilities, $\rho_\mathsf{P}^{(k)}$ are quantum states in P, and $|k\rangle$ are computational basis of Q (also R). Then by Fact 1,

$$\begin{aligned} S(\mathsf{PQR}) &= S\left(\sum_k p_k \rho_\mathsf{P}^{(k)} \otimes |k\rangle\langle k|_\mathsf{Q} \otimes |k\rangle\langle k|_\mathsf{R}\right) \\ &= H(p_k) + \sum_k p_k S\left(\rho_\mathsf{P}^{(k)}\right) = S\left(\sum_k p_k \rho_\mathsf{P}^{(k)} \otimes |k\rangle\langle k|_\mathsf{Q}\right) = S(\mathsf{PQ}). \end{aligned}$$

By symmetry, $S(\mathsf{PQR}) = S(\mathsf{PR}) = S(\mathsf{PQ})$.

□

Proof of Lemma 6. Let $\mathsf{B}' = (\mathsf{B}, \mathsf{M_B})$, $\mathsf{C}' = (\mathsf{C}, \mathsf{M_C})$ where $\mathsf{M_B}, \mathsf{M_C}$ are the message registers which contain a copy of $\mathsf{M_A}$. Then

$$I(\mathsf{A}' : \mathsf{B}'|\mathsf{C}')$$
$$= I(\mathsf{W_A}, \mathsf{M_A} : \mathsf{B}, \mathsf{M_B}|\mathsf{C}, \mathsf{M_C})$$
$$= S(\mathsf{W_A}, \mathsf{C}, \mathsf{M_A}, \mathsf{M_C}) + S(\mathsf{B}, \mathsf{C}, \mathsf{M_B}, \mathsf{M_C}) - S(\mathsf{W_A}, \mathsf{B}, \mathsf{C}, \mathsf{M_A}, \mathsf{M_B}, \mathsf{M_C}) - S(\mathsf{C}, \mathsf{M_C}).$$

Since $\mathsf{M_A}, \mathsf{M_B}, \mathsf{M_C}$ contain identical classical states, by Claim 1, we can remove $\mathsf{M_A}, \mathsf{M_B}$ from above equation while keeping each term unchanged. Then

$$I(\mathsf{A}' : \mathsf{B}'|\mathsf{C}') = S(\mathsf{W_A}, \mathsf{C}, \mathsf{M_C}) + S(\mathsf{B}, \mathsf{C}, \mathsf{M_C}) - S(\mathsf{W_A}, \mathsf{B}, \mathsf{C}, \mathsf{M_C}) - S(\mathsf{C}, \mathsf{M_C})$$
$$= I(\mathsf{W_A} : \mathsf{B}|\mathsf{C}, \mathsf{M_C})$$
$$= I(\mathsf{W_A}, \mathsf{M_C} : \mathsf{B}|\mathsf{C}) - I(\mathsf{M_C} : \mathsf{B}|\mathsf{C}).$$

By the non-negativity of $I(\mathsf{M_C} : \mathsf{B}|\mathsf{C})$,

$$I(\mathsf{A}' : \mathsf{B}'|\mathsf{C}') \leq I(\mathsf{W_A}, \mathsf{M_C} : \mathsf{B}|\mathsf{C})$$
$$= S(\mathsf{W_A}, \mathsf{C}, \mathsf{M_C}) + S(\mathsf{B}, \mathsf{C}) - S(\mathsf{W_A}, \mathsf{B}, \mathsf{C}, \mathsf{M_C}) - S(\mathsf{C}).$$

Since $\mathsf{M_A}$ and $\mathsf{M_C}$ are identical classical states, $\mathsf{M_C}$ can be replaced with $\mathsf{M_A}$ by Claim 1. Then

$$I(\mathsf{A}' : \mathsf{B}'|\mathsf{C}') \leq S(\mathsf{W_A}, \mathsf{C}, \mathsf{M_A}) + S(\mathsf{B}, \mathsf{C}) - S(\mathsf{W_A}, \mathsf{B}, \mathsf{C}, \mathsf{M_A}) - S(\mathsf{C})$$
$$= I(\mathsf{W_A}, \mathsf{M_A} : \mathsf{B}|\mathsf{C}) = I(\mathsf{A} : \mathsf{B}|\mathsf{C}).$$

$\square$

4.3 Other Useful Lemmas

We would also need the following lemma.

Lemma 7. *For two classical probabilistic distributions D_X and D_Y over the same domain, if $TV(D_X, D_Y) \leq \epsilon$, we have that*

$$\Pr_{x \leftarrow D_X}[x \notin \mathsf{SUPP}(D_Y)] \leq 2\epsilon.$$

Proof. We use p_x^X, p_x^Y to denote the probability of x drawn from D_X, D_Y respectively.

$$\sum_{x \notin \mathsf{SUPP}(D_Y)} p_x^X \leq \sum_x |p_x^X - p_x^Y| = 2TV(D_X, D_Y) \leq 2\epsilon.$$

$\square$

5 Non-interactive Quantum Key Agreement

We say a QKA is *non-interactive* if all queries are made before communication. Formally,

Definition 13 (Non-interactive Quantum Key Agreement). *A non-interactive key agreement protocol between Alice and Bob consists of the following steps:*

1. *Let $\lambda > 0$ be a security parameter and $H \leftarrow \mathcal{H}_\lambda$.*
2. *Alice and Bob each makes $d_\lambda = \text{poly}(\lambda)$ queries to H.*
3. *Alice and Bob continue an arbitrary number of rounds of classical communication and local quantum operations, but will never make queries to H.*
4. *Eventually, Alice and Bob will output k_A, k_B.*

Theorem 5. *Non-interactive QKA does not exist in any oracle model.*

Proof. Let e_λ denote the number of qubits on which the quantum query unitary U_H acts, i.e., the total length of the input register and the output register. For example, if $H : [2^{n_\lambda}] \to \{0,1\}$ is a random function, then $e_\lambda = n_\lambda + 1$. Let ρ_A^0 and ρ_B^0 denote the states of Alice and Bob respectively right after the query algorithm but before any communication.

First, Eve repeatedly runs the same Alice's query algorithm $t = Cd_\lambda e_\lambda$ times (C is some polynomial determined afterwards) and prepares the state ρ_E^0, which consists of t registers $\mathsf{A}_1^0, \ldots, \mathsf{A}_t^0$ of ρ_A^0's copies. Observing that $\mathsf{A}^0, \mathsf{A}_1^0, \ldots, \mathsf{A}_t^0$ are permutation invariant, by Lemma 4, we have

$$I(\mathsf{A}^0 : \mathsf{B}^0 \mid \mathsf{E}^0) \leq \frac{S(\mathsf{B}^0)}{t+1} \leq \frac{2d_\lambda e_\lambda}{t+1} \leq \frac{1}{2C}.$$

The second inequality is because we can implement the query unitary U_H by a quantum communication process: suppose there are two parties, namely Bob and Oracle; if Bob wants to apply the unitary U_H, then

1. Bob sends its input register and output register, e_λ qubits in total, to Oracle;
2. Oracle applies U_H on these e_λ qubits and then sends them back to Bob.

By subadditivity of entropy, the entropy of Bob can increase by at most $2e_\lambda$ bits through the above quantum communication process. Since B^0 is prepared from a pure state by making d quantum queries, we have that $S(\mathsf{B}^0) \leq 2d_\lambda e_\lambda$.

Let ρ_A^f and ρ_B^f denote the states of Alice and Bob respectively right after finishing the communication but before outputting the key. Since classical communication does not increase CMI (see Lemma 6), we have

$$I(\mathsf{A} : \mathsf{B} \mid \mathsf{E}, \Pi)_{\rho_{ABE}^f} \leq I(\mathsf{A} : \mathsf{B} \mid \mathsf{E})_{\rho_{ABE}^0} \leq \frac{1}{2C}.$$

Finally, Eve applies the channel in Lemma 2 and obtains a fake view $\hat{\mathsf{A}}^f$ of A^f such that the joint state of $\rho_{\hat{A}B}^f$ is $O(1/\sqrt{C})$-close to ρ_{AB}^f. By letting $C = O(1/\epsilon^2)$, Eve can use $\hat{\mathsf{A}}^f$ to generate k_E such that $\Pr[k_B = k_E]$ is ϵ-close to $\Pr[k_A = k_B]$.

Remark 2(a). *Theorem 5 directly implies the separation of pseudorandom quantum states (PRS) and QKA. This is because PRS can be prepared by random queries, and without loss of generality, we can assume all random queries are made at the very beginning before any communication.*
(b). *In the proof of Theorem 5, Eve makes $O(d_\lambda^2 e_\lambda)$ quantum queries. This bound can be improved to $\tilde{O}(d_\lambda^2)$ if Alice and Bob are restricted to making non-adaptive queries (i.e., queries can depend on neither any previous queries nor classical communication) to a random function. The famous Merkle Puzzles and PRS-based protocols are both examples of this non-adaptive case. We refer interested readers to Appendix B in the full version for details.*
(c). *By almost the same proof, Theorem 5 can be extended to include quantum oracles, e.g., Haar random oracles, where the query unitary operator is chosen from some Haar measure.*

We can further notice that the non-interactive requirement can be relaxed to one-sided if we are considering two-round key agreement protocols. That is, Bob can make queries after receiving the first message from Alice, while Alice can only make queries before communication. Viewing the protocol in the model of QPKE, we have the following theorem:

Theorem 6 (Restate of Theorem 3). *For any QPKE scheme with a classical public key and a classical/quantum ciphertext in any oracle model, if it satisfies the following conditions:*

1. *The key generation algorithm makes at most d quantum queries;*
2. *The encryption algorithm makes at most d quantum queries;*
3. *The decryption algorithm makes no queries.*

There exists an adversary Eve that could break the public key encryption scheme with probability $1 - O(\epsilon)$ by making $O(d^2 e/\epsilon^2)$ number of oracle queries.

Proof. In this case, if Eve generates $O(de/\epsilon^2)$ copies of message m_1 and runs Bob $\mathcal{B}(m_1)$ according to the first message m_1, we can see that the permutation invariant condition still holds. Consider the stage before Bob sends the second message, similar to Theorem 5, we have that

$$I(\mathsf{A}:\mathsf{B}\mid \mathsf{E}) \leq \frac{1}{2C} \leq O(\epsilon^2).$$

Thus by applying the channel in Theorem 4 to E, we can obtain a state $\rho_{A'B}$ that is $O(\epsilon)$ close to the state ρ_{AB}. Now Eve receives the message register from Bob and runs the decryption algorithm on A', by the completeness of the protocol we can obtain that

$$\Pr[k_B = k_E] \geq \Pr[k_A = k_B] - O(\epsilon) \geq 1 - O(\epsilon) - \mathsf{negl}(\lambda).$$

□

Note that our impossibility result can be extended to the Classical Communication One Quantum Message Key Agreement (CC1QM-KA) model from [12]. In their security definition, the quantum message channel is unauthenticated, thus it can be modified by the adversary $\mathcal{E}$. As long as the completeness of the original key agreement protocol is $1 - \mathsf{negl}(\lambda)$, we can apply the gentle measurement lemma to ensure that $\Pr[k_A = k_B = k_E] \geq 1 - O(\sqrt{\epsilon})$.

6 Public Key Encryption with a Classical Key Generation

In this section, we devote ourselves to proving black-box separation results for public key encryption schemes with a classical key generation process and one-way functions.

Recall the definitions of QPKE schemes from Sect. 3.5. We will focus on the specific public encryption schemes defined as follows:

Definition 14. *A public key encryption scheme with a classical key generation process, relative to a random oracle $H \leftarrow \mathcal{H}_\lambda$ consists of the following three bounded-query quantum algorithms:*

- $\mathsf{Gen}^H(1^\lambda) \to (\mathsf{pk}, \mathsf{sk})$: *The key generation algorithm that generates a pair of public key pk and secret key sk.*
- $\mathsf{Enc}^{|H\rangle}(\mathsf{pk}, m) \to \mathsf{ct}$: *the encryption algorithm that takes a public key pk, the plaintext m, and the randomness r, produces the ciphertext ct.*
- $\mathsf{Dec}^{|H\rangle}(\mathsf{sk}, \mathsf{ct}) \to m'$: *the decryption algorithm that takes secret key sk and ciphertext ct and outputs the plaintext m'.*

Here we use H to denote the algorithm has classical access to the oracle, and $|H\rangle$ to denote quantum access to the oracle.

The algorithms should satisfy the following requirements:

Perfect Completeness

$$\Pr\left[\mathsf{Dec}^{|H\rangle}\left(\mathsf{sk}, \mathsf{Enc}^{|H\rangle}(\mathsf{pk}, m)\right) = m : \mathsf{Gen}^H(1^\lambda) \to (\mathsf{pk}, \mathsf{sk})\right] = 1.$$

IND-CPA Security *For any QPT adversary $\mathcal{E}^{|H\rangle}$, for every two plaintexts $m_0 \neq m_1$ chosen by $\mathcal{E}^{|H\rangle}(\mathsf{pk})$ we have*

$$\Pr\left[\mathcal{E}^{|H\rangle}\left(\mathsf{pk}, \mathsf{Enc}^{|H\rangle}(\mathsf{pk}, m_b)\right) = b\right] \leq \frac{1}{2} + \mathsf{negl}(\lambda).$$

To prove a black box separation, we would view the public key encryption scheme as a two-round key agreement protocol as described before, and utilize the previous tools from information theory. From the perspective of a key agreement protocol, it could be viewed as a two-stage Alice: before sending the first message, Alice would first make classical queries to the oracle H; And after receiving the message from Bob, it would make quantum queries to the oracle, and output the key they agree on. We denote the first stage as $\mathcal{A}_1$ and the second stage as $\mathcal{A}_2$.

We would use the following lemma from [10].

Lemma 8. *Consider a quantum algorithm $\mathcal{B}$ that makes d queries to an oracle H. Denote the quantum state immediately after t queries to the oracle as*

$$|\psi_t\rangle = \sum_{x,w} \alpha_{x,w,t} |x, w\rangle,$$

where w is the content of the workspace register. Denote the query weight q_x of input x as

$$q_x = \sum_{t=1}^{d} \sum_{w} |\alpha_{x,w,t}|^2.$$

For any oracle $\tilde{H}$, denote $|\phi_d\rangle$ as the final state before measurement obtained by running $\mathcal{B}$ with oracle $\tilde{H}$, we have that

$$\||\psi_d\rangle - |\phi_d\rangle\| \leq 2\sqrt{d \sum_{x:\ \tilde{H}(x) \neq H(x)} q_x}.$$

To define Eve's algorithm, we would first introduce the following algorithm $\mathcal{B}'$ as the modified algorithm of $\mathcal{B}$:

1. On receiving message m_1, first run $\mathcal{B}(m_1)$, and stop before the final output measurement.
2. Repeat the following process $3d^2(\log d + \log(1/\epsilon))$ times: randomly choose $i \leftarrow [d]$, simulate $\mathcal{B}(m_1)$ to its ith query to the oracle, and measure the input register, obtaining output $x \in [2^n]$, and classically query the oracle to obtain $H(x)$.
3. Measure the output register of the first $\mathcal{B}(m_1)$, and obtain key k_B and the second message m_2.

The first part of the the adversary algorithm $\mathcal{E}$ would be generating $O(dn/\epsilon^2)$ copies of m_1, and repeating the $\mathcal{B}'$ algorithm on each of these copies without performing step 3. It records all the query input-output pairs $R_E = \{(x_E, H(x_E))\}$ obtained from step 2 of $\mathcal{B}$.

We denote the heavy weight set W_B of $\mathcal{B}^{|H\rangle}(m_1)$ as $W_B = \{x \colon q_x \geq \epsilon^2/d^2\}$. We have the following lemma:

Lemma 9. *Let In_E be the set of input that is recorded in R_E, we have that*

$$\Pr[W_B \not\subseteq In_E] \leq \epsilon.$$

Proof. For each $x \in W_B$, it would be measured w.p. at least ϵ^2/d^3 at each step 2 $\mathcal{B}'$ performed by $\mathcal{E}$. Thus the probability it is not measured is bounded by

$$\Pr[x \notin In_E] \leq \left(1 - \frac{\epsilon^2}{d^3}\right)^{3d^3 n(\log d + \log(1/\epsilon))/\epsilon^2} \leq \epsilon^3/d^3.$$

Since $\sum_x q_x = d$, we have $|W_B| \leq d^3/\epsilon^2$, thus by a union bound we obtain the desired result.

Since step 2 of $\mathcal{B}'$ would not affect the output of the algorithm, we can equivalently think as the key agreement protocol consists of $\mathcal{A}$ and $\mathcal{B}'$. Note that in this case, $\mathcal{E}$ holds $O(dn/\epsilon^2)$ copies of registers that suffice the permutation invariant condition. Consider the joint state ρ_{ABE} at the stage before $\mathcal{B}'$ performing step 3, by Lemma 4 we have that $I(A : B \mid E) \leq \epsilon^2$. Moreover, applying the channel $\mathcal{T}: E \to E \otimes A'$ from Theorem 4, we can generate a state $\rho_{A'BE}$ such that $TD(\rho_{ABE}, \rho_{A'BE}) \leq \epsilon$.

For the rest of this section, we are only interested in the following registers of A, B, E:

- The classical internal state st_A and oracle query input-output pairs $R_A = \{(x_A, H(x_A))\}$. This assumption can be made since the secret key sk is classical.
- The output register consists of the key k_B and the message m_2 of $\mathcal{B}$.
- The input-output pairs recorded by Eve $R_E = \{(x_E, H(x_E))\}$.

Without specification, we reuse A, B, E for the beyond registers respectively. We denote the measurement in computational basis on these registers as Π_{ABE}, and the measurement outcome distribution as D_{ABE}. Similarly we can define $\Pi_{A'BE}$ and $D_{A'BE}$.

By perfect completeness, any sample $\text{View}_{ABE} = (st_A, R_A, k_B, m_2, R_E) \leftarrow D_{ABE}$ would be a valid execution. That is to say, there is some oracle H' that is consistent with R_A and R_E, and running $\mathcal{A}_2$ on H' would always output $k_A = k_B$. It also implies for any $x \in In_A \cap In_E$, the corresponding input-output pair should also be consistent for R_A and R_E.

Since $TD(\rho_{ABE}, \rho_{A'BE}) \leq \epsilon$, we have that $TV(D_{ABE}, D_{A'BE}) \leq \epsilon$ by the operational meaning of trace distance. By Lemma 7, we have that

$$\Pr_{\text{View}_{A'BE} \leftarrow D_{A'BE}} [\text{View}_{A'BE} \notin \text{SUPP}(D_{ABE})] \leq 2\epsilon.$$

Now we show that if we reprogram the oracle H to make it consistent with $R_{A'} = \{(x_A, H'(x_A))\}$ from the new sample $\text{View}_{A'BE}$, with high probability the algorithm $\mathcal{B}$ is consistent with $\tilde{H}$ and output (k_B, m_2). We define the reprogrammed oracle $\tilde{H}$ as follows:

$$\tilde{H}(x) = \begin{cases} H'(x), & x \in In_A; \\ H(x), & \text{else}. \end{cases}$$

We have the following theorem,

Theorem 7. *For the reprogrammed oracle $\tilde{H}$ defined as beyond, for any quantum algorithm $\mathcal{B}$ making d queries to the oracle*

$$\Pr_{(k_B, m_2) \leftarrow \mathcal{B}^{|\tilde{H}\rangle}(m_1)} \left[(k_B, m_2) \in \text{SUPP}\left(\mathcal{B}^{|\tilde{H}\rangle}(m_1)\right) \,\Big|\, \text{View}_{A'BE} \in \text{SUPP}(D_{ABE}) \right] \geq 1 - O(\epsilon),$$

here we slightly abuse the notation $\mathcal{B}^{|H\rangle}(m_1)$ for the classical output distribution of $\mathcal{B}$.

Proof. Combining Theorem 4 and Lemma 9 we have that

$$\Pr[\mathsf{View}_{A'BE} \in \mathsf{SUPP}(D_{ABE}) \wedge W_B \subseteq In_E]$$
$$\geq 1 - \Pr[\mathsf{View}_{A'BE} \notin \mathsf{SUPP}(D_{ABE})] - \Pr[W_B \nsubseteq In_E]$$
$$\geq 1 - O(\epsilon).$$

Given $\mathsf{View}_{A'BE} \in \mathsf{SUPP}(D_{ABE})$ and $W_B \subseteq In_E$, we apply Lemma 8 and obtain that

$$TV\left(\mathcal{B}^{|\tilde{H}\rangle}(m_1), \mathcal{B}^{|H\rangle}(m_1)\right) \leq 4\||\psi_d\rangle - |\phi_d\rangle\|$$
$$\leq 8\sqrt{d} \sqrt{\sum_{x: \, \tilde{H}(x) \neq H(x)} q_x}$$
$$\leq 8\sqrt{d}\sqrt{d \cdot \frac{\epsilon^2}{d^2}} = O(\epsilon),$$

where the first inequality comes from [10, Theorem 3.1], the second inequality is Lemma 8, and the third inequality is by that $|\{x: \tilde{H}(x) \neq H(x)\}| \leq |In_A| \leq d$. By Lemma 7, we have that

$$\Pr_{(k_B, m_2) \leftarrow \mathcal{B}^{|H\rangle}(m_1)} \left[(k_B, m_2) \in \mathsf{SUPP}\left(\mathcal{B}^{|\tilde{H}\rangle}(m_1)\right) \Big| \mathsf{View}_{A'BE} \in \mathsf{SUPP}(D_{ABE}) \wedge W_B \subseteq In_E\right]$$
$$\geq 1 - O(\epsilon).$$

The final statement can be obtained by a conditional probability formula.

Now we will prove the first main theorem of the section.

Theorem 8. *For any public key encryption scheme in the random oracle model, if it satisfies the following conditions:*

1. *Perfect completeness;*
2. *The key generation algorithm makes at most d classical queries to the oracle;*
3. *The encryption algorithm makes at most d quantum queries to the oracle;*
4. *The decryption algorithm makes at most D quantum queries to the oracle.*

There exists an adversary Eve that could break the public key encryption scheme w.p. $1 - O(\epsilon)$ by making $O(d^4 n(\log d + \log(1/\epsilon))/\epsilon^2 + D)$ queries to the oracle.

Proof. We have already described most of the adversary algorithm $\mathcal{E}$ as we prove the beyond lemmata and theorems. We summarize the algorithm $\mathcal{E}$ as follows: it first generates $O(dn/\epsilon^2)$ copies of m_1, and repeats the $\mathcal{B}'$ algorithm on each of these copies without performing step 3. It applies the channel $\mathcal{T}$ to the register E(including the full workspace) and generates a state $\rho_{A'BE}$. Applying $\Pi_{A'BE}$ to $\rho_{A'BE}$ to obtain a sample $\mathsf{View}_{A'BE} = (st_{A'}, R_{A'}, k_B, m_2, R_E)$. It runs the algorithm $\mathcal{A}_2(m_2)$ on register A' with the reprogrammed oracle $\tilde{H}$, and obtaining the final output $k_E = k_{A'}$.

Now we argue the correctness of the algorithm. Assume that before performing $\Pi_{A'BE}$, we first perform Π_{ABE} on the state ρ_{ABE}. This assumption can be made since $\Pi_{A'BE}$ and Π_{ABE} commute. By perfect completeness of the protocol, we can see that the result View$_{ABE}$ is a valid internal state, compatible with oracle H. Now we discuss the measurement result of $\Pi_{A'BE}$. Note that in this case, the (k_B, m_2, R_E) in View$_{A'BE}$ is the same as in View$_{ABE}$.

Consider the case that View$_{A'BE} \in \mathsf{SUPP}(D_{ABE})$, i.e. View$_{A'BE}$ is a valid execution for some oracle H', we now argue that actually View$_{A'BE}$ is also a valid execution for oracle $\tilde{H}$ with high probability. From the perspective of A', the result $st_{A'}, R_{A'}$ is compatible with $\tilde{H}$, and will output message m_1. From the perspective of $\mathcal{B}^{|H\rangle}(m_1)$, before the measurement on the output register, it can be viewed as a distribution of key-message pairs $\{(k_B, m_2)\}$. Now we imagine we are running the algorithm $\mathcal{B}^{|\tilde{H}\rangle}(m_1)$ instead. By Theorem 7, we can see that with probability $1 - O(\epsilon)$, $(k_B, m_2) \leftarrow \mathcal{B}^{|H\rangle}(m_1)$ would also be in the support of $\mathcal{B}^{|\tilde{H}\rangle}(m_1)$.

Together they imply that View$_{A'BE}$ would be a valid execution for $\mathcal{A}, \mathcal{B}$ under oracle $\tilde{H}$ when $\mathcal{B}$ outputs key k_B. Thus if we run $\mathcal{A}_2(m_2)$ with the reprogrammed oracle $\tilde{H}$, by perfect completeness, it would also output $k'_A = k_B$.

For each run of $\mathcal{B}'$, it would simulate $\mathcal{B}$ for $O(d^2(\log(d) + \log(1/\epsilon)))$ times, and each time it makes at most d queries. For the adversary algorithm $\mathcal{E}$, it would run $\mathcal{B}'$ for $O(dn/\epsilon^2)$ times, giving us the query complexity beyond.

Reviewing our proof beyond, we notice that m_1 may not necessarily be a classical message. As long as $|m_1\rangle$ is a pure state, and we can obtain any polynomial copies of $|m_1\rangle$, the analysis in our proof exactly applies. Recall the IND-CPA Security from Definition 11, if the public key is pure, the adversary algorithm $\mathcal{E}$ can obtain polynomial many copies of $|\mathsf{pk}\rangle$. For any message $m_0 \neq m_1$, we can construct a key agreement for one bit by setting the second message as the ciphertext $\mathsf{ct}_0/\mathsf{ct}_1$ respectively. Thus by running our $\mathcal{E}$ beyond, we can break the IND-CPA security game with advantage $1 - O(\epsilon)$.

Now we show that our attack would still apply when the ciphertext is also quantum. The proof would be similar to the proof beyond. By running the same algorithm $\mathcal{E}$ we obtained the state $\rho_{A'BE}$, we would perform the measurement $\Pi_{A'BE}$, but for the B part we do not include the ciphertext ρ_{m_2} register. We can define $\tilde{H}$ as beyond, and prove the following statements given View$_{A'BE}$ is a valid execution:

1. From the perspective of A', the result $st_{A'}, R_{A'}$ is compatible with $\tilde{H}$, and will output message $|m_1\rangle$. By definition, $R_{A'}$ is compatible with $\tilde{H}$. Since B is not affected by channel $\mathcal{T}$, by uncomputing $\mathcal{B}$ on state $\rho_{A'B}$, we can see that $\mathcal{B}$ would also receive $|m_1\rangle$ from A'. From the observation, we can see that after performing the uncomputation, $TD(\rho_A, \rho_{A'}) = TD(\rho_{A'B}, \rho_{AB}) \leq \epsilon$, thus $st_{A'}, R_{A'}$ is compatible with output $|m_1\rangle$ under oracle $\tilde{H}$ w.p. $1 - \epsilon$.
2. From the perspective of $\mathcal{B}^{|H\rangle}(|m_1\rangle)$, the state before the measurement $\Pi_{A'BE}$ can be written as $\rho_B = \sum_{k_B} p_{k_B} |k_B\rangle\langle k_B| \otimes \rho_{k_B}$. Similarly, we denote the state of $\mathcal{B}^{|\tilde{H}\rangle}(|m_1\rangle)$ as $\sigma_B = \sum_{k_B} p'_{k_B} |k_B\rangle\langle k_B| \otimes \sigma_{k_B}$. In the proof of Theorem 7, when we apply Lemma 8, we can obtain that $TD(\rho_B, \sigma_B) \leq O(\epsilon)$. Now we consider the classical part of ρ_B and σ_B. Since partial trace will not

increase the trace distance, we have for distribution $D_B = \{p_{k_B}\}$ and $D'_B = \{p'_{k_B}\}$, $TV(D_B, D'_B) \leq \epsilon$. Thus for state $\rho'_{AB} = \sum_{k_B} p'_{k_B} |k_B\rangle\langle k_B| \otimes \rho_{k_B}$, $TD(\rho_B, \rho'_B) \leq \epsilon$, and by triangular inequality, $TD(\rho'_B, \sigma_B) \leq 2\epsilon$. Since $TD(\rho'_B, \sigma_B) = \mathbb{E}[TD(\rho_{k_B}, \sigma_{k_B})]$, using Markov inequality, we can see that

$$\Pr_{(\mathsf{sk},k_B) \leftarrow D_{A'B}} [TD(\rho_{k_B}, \sigma_{k_B}) \leq C\epsilon] \geq 1 - \frac{2}{C}.$$

If we take $C = 1/\sqrt{\epsilon}$, we can obtain that w.p. $1 - O(\sqrt{\epsilon})$, $TD(\rho_{k_B}, \sigma_{k_B}) \leq \sqrt{\epsilon}$.

We can see that $|m_1\rangle, \sigma_{k_B}$ would be a valid transcript for $\mathcal{A}, \mathcal{B}$ under oracle $\tilde{H}$. Thus when ρ_{k_B} and σ_{k_B} is $O(\sqrt{\epsilon})$ close, $\mathcal{A}^{\tilde{H}}(\mathsf{sk}, \rho_{k_B})$ will output $k_{A'} = k_B$ with probability $1 - O(\sqrt{\epsilon})$. Thus we obtain the following theorem:

For the clonable public key case $\rho_{m_1} = \sum_i p_i |\psi_i\rangle\langle\psi_i|$, we observe that the output of $\mathcal{B}(\rho_{m_1})$ would be the convex combination of $\mathcal{B}(|\psi_i\rangle)$. Thus by the perfect completeness property of the protocol, each $|\psi_i\rangle$ would also be a valid public key. Further observing that the clonable case is a convex combination of pure public keys, we have the following theorem:

Theorem 9. *For any QPKE scheme with quantum public key in the random oracle model, if it satisfies the following conditions:*

1. *Perfect completeness;*
2. *The public key ρ_{pk} is pure or clonable.*
3. *The key generation algorithm makes at most d classical queries to the oracle;*
4. *The encryption algorithm makes at most d quantum queries to the oracle;*
5. *The decryption algorithm makes at most D quantum queries to the oracle.*

There exists an adversary Eve that could break the public key encryption scheme w.p. $1 - O(\sqrt{\epsilon})$ by making $O(d^4 n(\log d + \log(1/\epsilon))/\epsilon^2 + D)$ queries to the oracle.

This theorem gives a tight characterization of multiple existing QPKE schemes. In [8] and [14], they both provided a QPKE scheme with a pure quantum public key, but their public key generation algorithms need to make quantum queries. Our result shows that the quantum query is necessary for their key agreement scheme. In [20,21], they provided another QPKE scheme where the quantum public key is mixed, but the key generation algorithm can only make classical queries. Our result shows that their key must be mixed and unclonable in a strong sense.

Acknowledgement. Qipeng Liu would like to thank Navid Alamati for bringing up this problem in 2019 while interning at Fujitsu Research of America, and Jan Czajkowski, Takashi Yamakawa and Mark Zhandry for insightful discussions at Princeton during 2019 and 2020. The authors also thank Luowen Qian for pointing out the problem of Merkle-like QKA with Haar-random unitary, which prompted the realization of Theorem 3 applicable to even quantum oracles.

Longcheng Li was supported in part by the National Natural Science Foundation of China Grants No. 62325210, 62272441, 12204489, 62301531, and the Strategic Priority Research Program of Chinese Academy of Sciences Grant No. XDB28000000.

Qian Li's work was supported by the National Natural Science Foundation of China Grants (No. 62002229), and Hetao Shenzhen-Hong Kong Science and Technology Innovation Cooperation Zone Project (No. HZQSWS-KCCYB-2024016).

References

1. Aaronson, S.: Quantum copy-protection and quantum money. In: 2009 24th Annual IEEE Conference on Computational Complexity, pp. 229–242. IEEE (2009)
2. Aaronson, S., Ambainis, A.: The need for structure in quantum speedups. Theory Comput. **10**(1), 133–166 (2014)
3. Aaronson, S., Liu, J., Liu, Q., Zhandry, M., Zhang, R.: New approaches for quantum copy-protection. In: Malkin, T., Peikert, C. (eds.) CRYPTO 2021. LNCS, vol. 12825, pp. 526–555. Springer, Cham (2021). https://doi.org/10.1007/978-3-030-84242-0_19
4. Ananth, P., Qian, L., Yuen, H.: Cryptography from pseudorandom quantum states. In: Dodis, Y., Shrimpton, T. (eds.) CRYPTO 2022. LNCS, vol. 13507, pp. 208–236. Springer, Heidelberg (2022). https://doi.org/10.1007/978-3-031-15802-5_8
5. Araki, H., Lieb, E.H.: Entropy inequalities. Commun. Math. Phys. **18**(2), 160–170 (1970)
6. Austrin, P., Chung, H., Chung, K.M., Fu, S., Lin, Y.T., Mahmoody, M.: On the impossibility of key agreements from quantum random oracles. In: Dodis, Y., Shrimpton, T. (eds.) CRYPTO 2022. LNCS, vol. 13508, pp. 165–194. Springer, Heidelberg (2022). https://doi.org/10.1007/978-3-031-15979-4_6
7. Barak, B., Mahmoody-Ghidary, M.: Merkle puzzles are optimal—an $O(n^2)$-query attack on any key exchange from a random oracle. In: Halevi, S. (ed.) CRYPTO 2009. LNCS, vol. 5677, pp. 374–390. Springer, Heidelberg (2009). https://doi.org/10.1007/978-3-642-03356-8_22
8. Barooti, K., et al.: Public-key encryption with quantum keys. In: Rothblum, G., Wee, H. (eds.) TCC 2023. LNCS, pp. 198–227. Springer, Heidelberg (2023). https://doi.org/10.1007/978-3-031-48624-1_8
9. Bartusek, J., Coladangelo, A., Khurana, D., Ma, F.: On the round complexity of secure quantum computation. In: Malkin, T., Peikert, C. (eds.) CRYPTO 2021. LNCS, vol. 12825, pp. 406–435. Springer, Cham (2021). https://doi.org/10.1007/978-3-030-84242-0_15
10. Bennett, C.H., Bernstein, E., Brassard, G., Vazirani, U.: Strengths and weaknesses of quantum computing. SIAM J. Comput. **26**(5), 1510–1523 (1997)
11. Bennett, C.H., Brassard, G.: Quantum cryptography: public key distribution and coin tossing. Theor. Comput. Sci. **560**, 7–11 (2014). https://doi.org/10.1016/j.tcs.2014.05.025
12. Bouaziz-Ermann, S., Grilo, A.B., Vergnaud, D., Vu, Q.H.: Towards the impossibility of quantum public key encryption with classical keys from one-way functions. arXiv preprint arXiv:2311.03512 (2023)
13. Brakerski, Z., Katz, J., Segev, G., Yerukhimovich, A.: Limits on the power of zero-knowledge proofs in cryptographic constructions. In: Ishai, Y. (ed.) TCC 2011. LNCS, vol. 6597, pp. 559–578. Springer, Heidelberg (2011). https://doi.org/10.1007/978-3-642-19571-6_34
14. Coladangelo, A.: Quantum trapdoor functions from classical one-way functions. arXiv preprint arXiv:2302.12821 (2023)
15. Fawzi, O., Renner, R.: Quantum conditional mutual information and approximate markov chains. Commun. Math. Phys. **340**(2), 575–611 (2015)

16. Grilo, A.B., Lin, H., Song, F., Vaikuntanathan, V.: Oblivious transfer is in MiniQCrypt. In: Canteaut, A., Standaert, F.-X. (eds.) EUROCRYPT 2021. LNCS, vol. 12697, pp. 531–561. Springer, Cham (2021). https://doi.org/10.1007/978-3-030-77886-6_18
17. Hayden, P., Jozsa, R., Petz, D., Winter, A.: Structure of states which satisfy strong subadditivity of quantum entropy with equality. Commun. Math. Phys. **246**, 359–374 (2004)
18. Impagliazzo, R.: A personal view of average-case complexity. In: Proceedings of Structure in Complexity Theory. Tenth Annual IEEE Conference, pp. 134–147. IEEE (1995)
19. Impagliazzo, R., Rudich, S.: Limits on the provable consequences of one-way permutations. In: Proceedings of the Twenty-First Annual ACM Symposium on Theory of Computing, pp. 44–61 (1989)
20. Kitagawa, F., Morimae, T., Nishimaki, R., Yamakawa, T.: Quantum public-key encryption with tamper-resilient public keys from one-way functions. arXiv preprint arXiv:2304.01800 (2023)
21. Malavolta, G., Walter, M.: Robust quantum public-key encryption with applications to quantum key distribution. Cryptology ePrint Archive, Paper 2023/500 (2023). https://eprint.iacr.org/2023/500
22. Mazor, N.: Key-agreement with perfect completeness from random oracles. Cryptology ePrint Archive (2023)
23. Morimae, T., Yamakawa, T.: One-wayness in quantum cryptography. arXiv preprint arXiv:2210.03394 (2022)
24. Morimae, T., Yamakawa, T.: Quantum commitments and signatures without one-way functions. In: Dodis, Y., Shrimpton, T. (eds.) CRYPTO 2022. LNCS, vol. 13507, pp. 269–295. Springer, Heidelberg (2022). https://doi.org/10.1007/978-3-031-15802-5_10
25. Nielsen, M.A., Chuang, I.L.: Quantum Computation and Quantum Information: 10th Anniversary Edition. Cambridge University Press, Cambridge (2010). https://doi.org/10.1017/CBO9780511976667
26. Shor, P.W.: Polynomial-time algorithms for prime factorization and discrete logarithms on a quantum computer. SIAM Rev. **41**(2), 303–332 (1999)
27. Wiesner, S.: Conjugate coding. ACM SIGACT News **15**(1), 78–88 (1983)
28. Wilde, M.M.: From classical to quantum shannon theory. arXiv preprint arXiv:1106.1445 (2011)
29. Yamakawa, T., Zhandry, M.: Verifiable quantum advantage without structure. J. ACM **71**(3), 1–50 (2024)
30. Zhandry, M.: How to record quantum queries, and applications to quantum indifferentiability. In: Boldyreva, A., Micciancio, D. (eds.) CRYPTO 2019. LNCS, vol. 11693, pp. 239–268. Springer, Cham (2019). https://doi.org/10.1007/978-3-030-26951-7_9

Secret Sharing with Certified Deletion

James Bartusek[1](✉) and Justin Raizes[2]

[1] UC Berkeley, Berkeley, USA
james.bartusek@gmail.com
[2] Carnegie Mellon University, Pittsburgh, USA
jraizes@cmu.edu

Abstract. Secret sharing allows a user to split a secret into many shares so that the secret can be recovered if, and only if, an authorized set of shares is collected. Although secret sharing typically does not require any computational hardness assumptions, its security *does* require that an adversary cannot collect an authorized set of shares. Over long periods of time where an adversary can benefit from multiple data breaches, this may become an unrealistic assumption.

We initiate the systematic study of secret sharing *with certified deletion* in order to achieve security *even against an adversary that eventually collects an authorized set of shares*. In secret sharing with certified deletion, a (classical) secret s is split into quantum shares that can be destroyed in a manner verifiable by the dealer.

We put forth two natural definitions of security. **No-signaling security** roughly requires that if multiple non-communicating adversaries delete sufficiently many shares, then their combined view contains negligible information about s, even if the total set of corrupted parties forms an authorized set. **Adaptive security** requires privacy of s against an adversary that can continuously and adaptively corrupt new shares and delete previously-corrupted shares, as long as the total set of corrupted shares minus deleted shares remains unauthorized.

Next, we show that these security definitions are achievable: we show how to construct (i) a secret sharing scheme with no-signaling certified deletion for *any monotone access structure*, and (ii) a *threshold* secret sharing scheme with adaptive certified deletion. Our first construction uses Bartusek and Khurana's (CRYPTO 2023) 2-out-of-2 secret sharing scheme with certified deletion as a building block, while our second construction is built from scratch and requires several new technical ideas. For example, we significantly generalize the "XOR extractor" of Agarwal, Bartusek, Khurana, and Kumar (EUROCRYPT 2023) in order to obtain better seedless extraction from certain quantum sources of entropy, and show how polynomial interpolation can double as a high-rate randomness extractor in our context of threshold sharing with certified deletion.

1 Introduction

Secret sharing [9,17,23] is a foundational cryptographic primitive that allows a dealer to distribute a secret s among n parties so that only certain "authorized" subsets of the parties may recover the secret. A particularly common scenario is (k, n) *threshold* secret sharing, where the dealer splits s into n shares such that any k of the shares can be combined to recover the secret s, but any $k-1$ or fewer shares leak no information about s. However, one can also consider a much more versatile setting, in which the authorized subsets of n are defined by any *monotone access structure* $\mathbb{S}$.[1] Secret sharing schemes are ubiquitous in cryptography, and we refer the reader to Beimel's survey [7] for a broader discussio, including several applications.

A particularly appealing aspect of secret sharing that sets it apart from most other cryptographic primitives is that it *doesn't require computational hardness assumptions*. That is, one can construct secret sharing schemes for arbitrary monotone access structures secure against any computationally unbounded adversary (e.g. [8,17,19]).

However, the security of these schemes still rests on a stringent assumption: over the course of the (potentially unbounded) adversary's operation, it only ever sees an unauthorized set of shares. This may be unacceptable for users sharing particularly sensitive information. Even if an adversary initially may only access a limited number of shares, over time they may be able to corrupt more and more parties, or perhaps more and more shares become compromised independently and are leaked into the public domain. A user who becomes paranoid about this possibility generally has no recourse, and, worse yet, cannot even *detect* if an adversary has obtained access to enough shares to reconstruct their secret.

In this work, we ask whether it is possible to strengthen the standard notion of secret sharing security, and relax the assumption that the adversary only ever corrupts an unauthorized set of parties. In particular:

Is it possible to achieve meaningful secret sharing security against adversaries that may eventually corrupt authorized sets of parties?

Now, if the shares consist of only classical data, then there is no hope of answering the above question in the affirmative. Indeed, once an adversary obtains any share, they can make a copy and store it away. Once they've collected and stored an authorized set, they'll be able to recover the secret due to the correctness of the secret sharing scheme.

Certified Deletion. On the other hand, the *uncertainty principle* of quantum mechanics offers some hope: if shares are encoded into quantum states, then the useful share information may be erased by applying certain destructive measurements. Thus, a user that is worried about an adversary eventually corrupting an authorized set of shares may request and verify that this "deletion" operation is performed on some set of their shares. Now, even if the adversary learns enough shares in the future to constitute an authorized set, the already-deleted shares will remain useless, and there is hope that the user's secret remains private.

---

[1] A set $\mathbb{S}$ of subsets of $[n]$ is monotone if for any subset $S \in \mathbb{S}$, it holds that $S' \in \mathbb{S}$ for all supersets $S' \supset S$.

Indeed, the basic idea of leveraging the uncertainty principle to perform "certified deletion" of private information was first put forth by Broadbent and Islam [11] in the context of one-time-pad encryption, and has since been applied in several contexts throughout cryptography, e.g. [3–5, 14–16, 20]. In fact, Bartusek and Khurana [4] previously constructed a very limited flavor of secret sharing with certified deletion, namely, 2-out-of-2 secret sharing where only one of the two shares admits the possibility the deletion. Their scheme allows a user to split a secret s into a quantum share $|sh_1\rangle$ and a classical share sh_2. If an adversary first obtains and deletes $|sh_1\rangle$, then obtains sh_2, it will still be unable to reconstruct the secret s. One can also view the original one-time-pad encryption with certified deletion scheme of [11] as exactly this flavor of 2-out-of-2 secret sharing with certified deletion, where the quantum share is the ciphertext and the classical share is the secret key. In this work, we show that it is possible to introduce certified deletion guarantees into more versatile and general flavors of secret sharing, addressing several definitional and technical issues along the way.

1.1 Our Results

We formulate two powerful but incomparable notions of certified deletion security for general-purpose secret sharing schemes, and show how to construct a scheme satisfying each definition. One of our key technical tools is a high-rate seedless extractor from certain quantum sources of entropy that significantly generalizes and improves upon the "XOR extractor" of [1].

No-signaling Security. First, we address the shortcomings of [4]'s security definition for 2-out-of-2 secret sharing sketched above, and formulate a natural extension that (i) applies to schemes for *any* monotone access structure, and (ii) allows for the possibility that *any* of the shares may be deleted.

In particular, we model a scenario involving multiple non-communicating adversaries that each individually have access to some unauthorized set of shares. These adversaries may even share entanglement, but may not exchange messages. Now, the user may request that some of its shares are deleted. If the adversaries jointly delete enough shares so that the remaining undeleted shares form an *unauthorized* set, then we combine the views of all the adversaries together, and require that the user's secret remains private even given this joint view. That is, even if a single adversarial entity is eventually able to corrupt up to *all* of the parties, they will still not be able to recover the secret if enough shares have previously been deleted.[2]

We refer to this security notion for secret sharing schemes as *no-signaling security* (see Sect. 4 for a precise definition), emphasizing the fact that shares must be deleted by adversaries that cannot yet pool information about an authorized set of shares, as this would trivially allow for reconstruction of the secret.

---

[2] We remark that this definition also captures adversaries that don't end up corrupting *all* the shares, by imagining that there is a separate component of the adversary that honestly deletes the uncorrupted shares.

Then, in Sect. 5 we show how to combine [4]'s simple 2-out-of-2 secret sharing scheme with any standard secret sharing scheme for monotone access structure $\mathbb{S}$ (e.g. [8,17,19]) in order to obtain a secret sharing scheme for $\mathbb{S}$ with no-signaling security.

Theorem 1 (Informal). *There exists a secret sharing scheme with no-signaling certified deletion security for any monotone access structure $\mathbb{S}$.*

Adaptive Security. Next, we consider a particularly cunning but natural class of adversaries that exhibit the following behavior. Suppose that initially the adversary only obtains access to some unauthorized set of shares. At some point, the user becomes paranoid and requests that some subset of these shares are deleted. The adversary obliges but then continues to corrupt new parties or locate other leaked shares. The adversary may continue to delete some of these shares to appease the user, while continuing to work behind the scenes to mount a long-term attack on the system. However, as long as the set of corrupted parties minus the set of certifiably deleted shares continues to be unauthorized, we can hope that the user's secret remains private from such an adversary.

Unfortunately, the notion of no-signaling security does not capture the behavior of such an *adaptive* adversary. That is, no-signaling security only models adversaries that delete once, and then receive some extra information after this single round of deletion. Thus, we formalize *adaptive security* as an alternative and quite strong notion of certified deletion security for secret sharing schemes (see Sect. 4 for a precise definition).

Protecting against such arbitrarily adaptive adversaries turns out to be a significant challenge. The main technical component of our work realizes a secret sharing scheme with adaptive certified deletion security for the specific case of threshold access structures (Sect. 6).

Theorem 2 (Informal). *There exists a threshold secret sharing scheme with adaptive certified deletion security.*

High-rate Seedless Extractors from Quantum Sources of Entropy. One of our technical building blocks is an improved method for seedless extraction from certain quantum sources of entropy. Roughly, the source of entropy comes from performing a standard basis measurement on a register that is in superposition over a limited number of Fourier basis states.

While seedless extraction from such sources of entropy [1] has been a crucial component in previous realizations of cryptographic primitives with certified deletion [4],[3] the technique had been limited to (i) extracting from qubit registers (i.e. where data is natively represented as superpositions of bitstrings) and (ii) extracting only a single bit of entropy. Here, we generalize these techniques to extract from qu*dit* registers (i.e. where data is natively represented as superpositions of vectors over finite fields), and produce several field elements worth of entropy, vastly improving the rate of extraction. Beyond being interesting in its

---
[3] See discussion therein why *seedless* as opposed to seeded extraction is crucial.

own right, it turns out that these improvements are crucial for showing security our construction of threshold sharing with adaptive certified deletion. Moreover, we show how these high-rate extraction techniques can be applied to extension fields, meaning that we can represent our quantum shares as string of qubits (as opposed to qudits), removing the need for entanglement in our construction. We refer the reader to Sect. 2.3 and Sect. 3 for more details.

2 Technical Overview

Intuitively, certified deletion for secret sharing aims to keep the secret private from an adversary if the total set of undeleted shares they have access to is unauthorized. One could formalize this by considering an adversary who initially receives an unauthorized set of shares and then deletes some of them. If the undeleted shares are still unauthorized when combined with the shares that the adversary did not receive, then we allow the adversary to access these remaining shares. This closely matches the definition of encryption with certified deletion, where the adversary initially receives and deletes a ciphertext $\mathsf{Enc}(k, m)$ encrypting message m using key k, and then later receives the key k.

However, this definition is not meaningful for all access structures. For example, in a k out of n access structure where $k < n/2$, the shares that the adversary does not start with *already* form an authorized set on their own, so it never makes sense to allow the adversary to access all of these shares at once. In this section, we give an overview of two different ways to address this definitional deficiency: no-signaling certified deletion and adaptive certified deletion.

2.1 No-Signaling Certified Deletion

In no-signaling certified deletion, we address this problem by allowing the adversary to delete from multiple sets of shares $P_1, \ldots, P_\ell$. However, if $P_1 \cup \cdots \cup P_\ell$ contains all shares, then the adversary as a whole gets to see every share before it generates any deletion certificates. Thus, to prevent trivial attacks, we do not allow the adversary to communicate across sets. However, the different parts of the adversary may still *share entanglement*. This modification yields the no-signaling certified deletion game $\mathsf{SS\text{-}NSCD}_\mathbb{S}(s)$ for secret s and access structure $\mathbb{S}$ over n parties, which we describe here.

1. The challenger secret-splits s into n shares with access structure $\mathbb{S}$.
2. Each adversary Adv_i is initialized with one register of a shared state $|\psi\rangle$, receives the shares in a set P_i, and produces some set of certificates $\{\mathsf{cert}_j\}_{j \in P_i}$. If Adv_i does not wish to delete share j, then it may set $\mathsf{cert}_j = \bot$.
3. If the total set of shares that have not been deleted is unauthorized, then output the joint view of the adversaries. Otherwise, output $\bot$.

No-signaling certified deletion for secret sharing requires that for every secret pair (s_0, s_1) and every partition $P = (P_1, \ldots, P_\ell)$ of $[n]$, the outputs of $\mathsf{SS\text{-}NSCD}_\mathbb{S}(s_0)$ and $\mathsf{SS\text{-}NSCD}_\mathbb{S}(s_1)$ have negligible trace distance.

Tool: 2-of-2 Secret Sharing with Certified Deletion [4]. Recently, Bartusek and Khurana constructed a variety of primitives with certified deletion. One of these primitives is a secret sharing scheme which splits a secret s into a quantum share $|\mathsf{sh}_1\rangle$ and a classical share sh_2, along with a verification key vk that can be used to test the validity of deletion certificates. Given either one of the shares, the secret is hidden. Furthermore, if an adversary given $|\mathsf{sh}_1\rangle$ performs a destructive measurement that yields a valid deletion certificate, then they will never be able to recover s, even if they later obtain sh_2. Note that in this scheme, only one of the two shares can be deleted.

A Black-Box Compiler. We show how to compile Bartusek and Khurana's 2-of-2 certified deletion scheme together with any classical secret sharing scheme into a secret sharing scheme with no-signaling certified deletion. Notably, the compiled scheme inherits the same access structure as the classical secret sharing scheme. Thus, one can construct secret sharing with no-signaling certified deletion for general access structures by using any classical secret sharing scheme for general access structures, e.g. [2,17].

As a starting point, let us first construct a scheme where only one of the shares can be deleted.

1. Secret split the secret s into a quantum share $|\mathsf{qsh}\rangle$ and a classical share csh using the 2-of-2 secret sharing scheme with certified deletion. This also produces a verification key vk.
2. Split the 2-of-2 classical share csh into classical shares $\mathsf{csh}_1, \ldots, \mathsf{csh}_n$ using the classical secret sharing scheme for $\mathbb{S}$.
3. The verification key is vk and the i'th share is csh_i. The deletable quantum share is $|\mathsf{qsh}\rangle$.

Given the quantum share and any authorized set of classical shares, s can be reconstructed by first recovering csh from the authorized set. On the other hand, any adversary which attempts to delete $|\mathsf{qsh}\rangle$ with only access to an unauthorized set of classical shares has no information about the 2-of-2 classical share csh. Thus if they produce a valid deletion certificate, they will have no information about s even after obtaining the rest of the classical shares, which only reveals csh.

Who Deletes? To finish the compiler, we need to enable certified deletion of *any* share. This can be achieved by adding a step at the beginning of the compiler to create n classical shares $\mathsf{sh}_1, \ldots, \mathsf{sh}_n$ of s with the same access structure $\mathbb{S}$. Then, the splitter can enable certified deletion for each share sh_i by using the prior compiler to produce a set of classical shares $\mathsf{csh}_{i,1}, \ldots, \mathsf{csh}_{i,n}$, a deletable quantum share $|\mathsf{qsh}_i\rangle$, and a verification key vk_i. The i'th share contains the deletable state $|\mathsf{qsh}_i\rangle$, as well as $\{\mathsf{csh}_{j,i}\}_{j \in [n]}$.

Note that anyone holding share i is able to delete sh_i by deleting $|\mathsf{qsh}_i\rangle$, as discussed previously. If sufficiently many shares are deleted, so that the only remaining sh_i form an unauthorized set, then no adversary can learn anything about the secret even after obtaining all of the remaining shares and residual states.

Proof of Security: Guessing Deletions. Although the intuition is straightforward, there is a nuance in the proof of security. When proving security, we wish to replace the deleted 2-of-2 secrets sh_i with empty secrets $\bot$. If we could do so, then security immediately reduces to the security of the classical $\mathbb{S}$-scheme, since only an unauthorized set of sh_i remains. However, it is difficult to determine which of these 2-of-2 secrets sh_i to replace with $\bot$ when preparing the shares.

Since non-local operations commute, we could consider generating the shares for each adversary Adv_i one at a time. For example, supposing Adv_1 operates on the set of shares $P_1 \subset [n]$, the experiment could initialize Adv_1 with uniformly random shares, and then for each $i \in P_1$, reverse-sample the shares $\{\mathsf{csh}_{i,j}\}_{j \in [n] \setminus P_1}$ for the rest of the adversaries to match either sh_i or $\bot$, depending on whether or not Adv_1 deleted share i.

Unfortunately, we cannot continue this strategy for all of the adversaries. It may be the case that the union of Adv_1 and Adv_2's shares $P_1 \cup P_2$ contains an authorized set. Thus, when initializing Adv_2, the challenger must already know whether, for each $i \in P_2$, the i'th share of s should be set to sh_i or $\bot$ (since this will be determined by $\{\mathsf{csh}_{i,j}\}_{j \in P_1 \cup P_2}$). This view is constructed before the adversary decides whether or not to delete share i, so the only way for the challenger to do this is to guess whether the adversary will delete share i or not.

Now, guessing which shares the entire set of adversaries will delete incurs a multiplicative exponential (in n) loss in security. Fortunately, Bartusek and Khurana's 2-of-2 scheme actually satisfies an *inverse exponential* trace distance between the adversary's view of any two secrets, after deletion. Thus, by setting the parameters carefully, we can tolerate this exponential loss from guessing, and show that our scheme for general access structures satisfies negligible security.

2.2 Adaptive Certified Deletion

Intuitively, any definition of certified deletion should allow the adversary to eventually receive an authorized set of shares, as long as they have previously deleted enough shares so that their total set of undeleted shares remains unauthorized. In no-signaling certified deletion, we allowed multiple non-communicating adversaries to delete from different unauthorized sets of shares. That is, when Adv_i generates its set of certificates, it only has access to a single unauthorized set P_i. However, one could also imagine a more demanding setting where, after deleting some shares, the adversary can adaptively corrupt *new shares*, as long as their total set of undeleted shares remains unauthorized. Then, they can continue deleting shares and corrupting new shares as long as this invariant holds. This setting arises naturally when we consider an adversary which covertly compromises shares over a long period of time, while occasionally deleting shares to avoid revealing the extent of the infiltration. We call this notion *adaptive certified deletion*. It is defined using the following adaptive certified deletion game $\mathsf{SS\text{-}ACD}_\mathbb{S}(s)$.

1. The challenger splits the secret s into n shares with access structure $\mathbb{S}$. The adversary starts with an empty corruption set C and an empty deletion set D.

2. For as many rounds as the adversary likes, it gets to see the shares in C and choose whether to corrupt or delete a new share.
   Corrupt a new share. The adversary corrupts a new share i by adding i to C. If $C\backslash D$ is authorized, the experiment immediately outputs $\bot$.
   Delete a share. The adversary outputs a certificate cert for a share i. If cert is valid, add i to D. Otherwise, the experiment immediately outputs $\bot$.
3. When the adversary is done, the experiment outputs its view.

Adaptive certified deletion for secret sharing requires that for every secret pair (s_0, s_1), the outputs of $\mathsf{SS\text{-}ACD}_\mathbb{S}(s_0)$ and $\mathsf{SS\text{-}ACD}_\mathbb{S}(s_1)$ have negligible trace distance. In this work, we focus on the (k, n) threshold access structure, where any set of size $\geq k$ is authorized.

Incomparable Definitions. We have already seen that no-signaling certified deletion does not imply adaptive certified deletion. It is also the case that adaptive certified deletion does not imply no-signaling certified deletion. Consider a two-part no-signaling adversary Adv_1 and Adv_2 with views P_1 and P_2. To change $(\mathsf{Adv}_1, \mathsf{Adv}_2)$ to an adaptive adversary, one would need to come up with a transformation that deletes the same shares as $(\mathsf{Adv}_1, \mathsf{Adv}_2)$, in the same way. However, Adv_1 might not even decide which shares to delete until after they have seen every share in P_1. So, the new adaptive adversary would have to corrupt all of P_1 before it can delete a single share that Adv_1 would. Similarly, it would also have to corrupt all of P_2 before it knows which shares Adv_2 would delete. However, if $P_1 \cup P_2$ is authorized, then the experiment would abort before the new adaptive adversary gets the chance to delete shares for both Adv_1 and Adv_2.

An Attack on the No-Signaling Construction. Unfortunately, the previous construction actually does *not* in general satisfy adaptive certified deletion security. Indeed, observe that the classical parts of each share can never be deleted. Because of this, an adversary could, for any i, obtain k classical shares $\mathsf{csh}_{i,1}, \ldots, \mathsf{csh}_{i,k}$ that reveal csh_i, simply by corrupting and immediately deleting the first k shares one-by-one. Afterwards, the adversary will always have *both* the classical share csh_i and the quantum share $|\mathsf{qsh}_i\rangle$ when it corrupts a new share i, so it can recover the underlying classical share sh_i. Now it can "delete" the i'th share while keeping sh_i in its memory. Eventually, it can collect enough sh_i in order to obtain the secret s.

The core problem with the no-signaling construction is the fact that it encodes the 2-of-2 classical shares csh in a form which can never be deleted. If we were to take a closer look at Bartusek and Khurana's 2-of-2 scheme, we would observe that csh contains a mapping θ of which parts of $|\mathsf{qsh}\rangle$ encode the secret (the "data indices") and which parts contain only dummy information used to verify certificates (the "check indices"). Without θ, there is no way to decode the secret. Unfortunately, in order to encode θ in a deletable form, we seem to be back where we started - we need secret sharing with adaptive certified deletion!

A New Construction. To avoid this pitfall, we take a new approach that allows the parties to reconstruct *without knowledge of the check indices*. This removes the need to encode θ altogether. To achieve this, we begin with Shamir's secret sharing [23], in which the shares are evaluation points of a degree $k-1$ polynomial f where $f(0) = s$. This polynomial is over some finite field $\mathbb{K}$ with at least $n+1$ elements. A useful property of Shamir's secret sharing is that it has good error-correcting properties - in fact, it also forms a Reed-Solomon code, which has the maximum possible error correction [21].

To split a secret s, we start by constructing a polynomial f where $f(0) = s$. Each share contains some number of evaluations of f encoded in the computational basis. These evaluations are mixed with a small number of random Fourier basis states that will aid in verifying deletion certificates. The positions of these checks, along with the value encoded, make up the verification key. An example share and key are illustrated here.

$$\mathsf{sh} = |f(1)\rangle \otimes |f(2)\rangle \otimes \mathsf{QFT}\,|r_1\rangle \otimes |f(4)\rangle \otimes \mathsf{QFT}\,|r_2\rangle \otimes \ldots$$
$$\mathsf{vk} = \quad * \quad\quad\quad * \quad\quad\quad r_1 \quad\quad\quad * \quad\quad\quad r_2 \quad\quad \ldots$$

When reconstructing the secret, these checks are essentially random errors in the polynomial evaluation. By carefully tuning the degree of the polynomial together with the number of evaluations and checks in each share, we can ensure that any k shares contain enough evaluation points to correct the errors from the check positions, but that any $k-1$ shares do not contain enough evaluation points to determine the polynomial. This results in f being determined by slightly more than $k-1$ shares worth of evaluations. Additionally, we slightly increase the degree of the polynomial to account for the limited amount of information that an adversary can retain after deletion. See Sect. 6 for more details.

Share deletion and certificate verification follow the established formula. To delete a share, measure it in the Fourier basis and output the result as the certificate. To verify the certificate, check that it matches the verification key at the check positions.

Proving Adaptive Certified Deletion. Intuitively, we want to show that after the adversary deletes a share, the next share it corrupts gives it no additional information, no matter how many shares the adversary has seen so far. To formalize this, we will show that the adversary cannot distinguish between the real $\mathsf{SS}\text{-}\mathsf{ACD}_{(k,n)}(s)$ experiment and an experiment in which each share is generated uniformly at random and independently of the others. Since the first $k-1$ shares to be corrupted do not yet uniquely determine the polynomial f, they already satisfy this. Thus, we can restrict our attention to modifying the last $n-k+1$ shares to be corrupted.

It will be useful to name the shares in the order they are corrupted or deleted. The a'th share to be corrupted is c_a, and the b'th share to be deleted is share d_b. In the (k,n) threshold case, if c_{k-1+b} is corrupted before d_b is deleted, then $C \backslash D$ has size k and is authorized, so the experiment will abort.

Techniques from BK23. We begin by recalling the techniques introduced in [4] to analyze 2-of-2 secret sharing with certified deletion, along with the construction. These techniques will form the starting point of our proof. To share a single-bit secret $s \in \{0,1\}$, sample random $x, \theta \leftarrow \{0,1\}^\lambda$ and output

$$\mathsf{sh}_1 = H^\theta \ket{x}, \quad \mathsf{sh}_2 = \left(\theta, s \oplus \bigoplus_{i:\theta_i=0} x_i\right), \quad \mathsf{vk} = (x,\theta),$$

where H^θ denotes applying the Hadamard gate H to the i'th register for each $i : \theta_i = 1$. Bartusek and Khurana showed that if an adversary given sh_1 produces a certificate cert such that $\mathsf{cert}_i = x_i$ for every check position $i : \theta_i = 1$, then they cannot distinguish whether $s = 0$ or $s = 1$ even if they later receive sh_2. Their approach has three main steps.

1. First, they delay the dependence of the experiment on s by initializing sh_1 to be the register $\mathcal{X}$ in $\sum_x \ket{x}^\mathcal{X} \otimes \ket{x}^\mathcal{Y}$. Later, the challenger can obtain x by measuring register $\mathcal{Y}$, and use it to derive s.
2. Second, they argue that if the adversary produces a valid deletion certificate, then sh_1 has been "almost entirely deleted", in the sense that the challenger's copy satisfies a checkable predicate with high probability. Intuitively, this predicate shows that the data positions ($\theta_i = 0$) of the challenger's copy have high joint entropy when measured in the computational basis. To show that the predicate holds, they use the fact that the adversary does not have sh_2 in their view, so sh_1 looks uniformly random. This allows a cut-and-choose argument where the locations of the check indices are determined *after* the adversary outputs its deletion certificate.
3. Finally, they show that the challenger derives a bit s that is uniformly random and independent of the adversary's view. This utilizes a result from [1] which shows that XOR is a good seedless extractor for entropy sources that satisfy the aforementioned predicate.

Adapting to Secret Sharing. As a starting point, let us try to adapt these techniques to undetectably change shares to uniformly random. For concreteness, consider the task of switching a share c_{k-1+b} to uniformly random. Although we have not yet outlined the general proof structure, we will eventually need to perform this task. We will use this starting point to gain insights that will help guide the eventual proof structure.

1. The first step is to delay the synthesis of the secret information until after the adversary outputs a deletion certificate. In our case, we will delay creating share c_{k-1+b} until after the adversary produces a valid certificate for share d_b.

   This can be achieved by sampling the first $k-1$ corrupted shares to be uniformly random, then using polynomial interpolation to prepare the rest of the shares. More concretely, consider the first corrupted $k-1$ shares $c_1, \ldots, c_{k-1}$. The challenger will prepare each of these shares c_a using two registers $\mathcal{C}_{c_a}$

and $\mathcal{S}_{c_a}$, then send the share to the adversary in register $\mathcal{S}_{c_a}$. To prepare the j'th position of c_a, the experiment challenger prepares either a uniform superposition $\sum_{x\in\mathbb{K}}|x\rangle^{\mathcal{C}_{c_a,j}}$ or $\sum_{x\in\mathbb{K}}\mathsf{QFT}\,|x\rangle^{\mathcal{C}_{c_a,j}}$, depending on whether j is an evaluation position or a check position. If j is an evaluation position for share c_a, the experiment challenger copies $\mathcal{C}_{c_a,j}$ to $\mathcal{S}_{c_a,j}$ in the computational basis, yielding

$$\propto \sum_{x\in\mathbb{K}} |x\rangle^{\mathcal{S}_{c_a,j}} \otimes |x\rangle^{\mathcal{C}_{c_a,j}},$$

and otherwise it copies $\mathcal{C}_{c_a,j}$ to $\mathcal{S}_{c_a,j}$ in the Fourier basis, yielding

$$\propto \sum_{x\in\mathbb{K}} \mathsf{QFT}\,|x\rangle^{\mathcal{S}_{c_a,j}} \otimes \mathsf{QFT}\,|x\rangle^{\mathcal{C}_{c_a,j}}.$$

Note that the adversary cannot determine which positions are evaluation positions and which are check positions, since each $\mathcal{S}_{c_a,j}$ register looks maximally mixed. Also observe that $\mathcal{C}_{c_a}$ contains a copy of share c_a, and the evaluation positions in the initial $k-1$ $\mathcal{C}_{c_a}$ registers determine the polynomial f. Then, when the adversary requests to corrupt a later share, the challenger computes the evaluation points for that share by performing a polynomial interpolation using its copies of the prior shares. For reasons that will become apparent shortly, we require that share d_b is included when interpolating c_{k-1+b}. The other points may be arbitrary.

The above procedure is actually slightly simplified; since the degree of f is slightly larger than the number of evaluation positions in $k-1$ shares, the first $k-1$ shares do not quite determine f. To remedy this, we will also initialize a small portion of *every* $\mathcal{S}_i$ to be uniformly random, before any interpolation takes place.

2. Next, we will need to show that $\mathcal{C}_{d_b}$, which contains the challenger's copy of share d_b, satisfies the deletion predicate if cert_{d_b} passes verification. This is not hard to show if d_b was generated uniformly at random, but it is not clear what happens if the adversary has some information about where the check positions are in d_b before deleting it. The first $k-1$ shares are uniformly random in the original experiment, so this is not a problem for any share which is deleted before c_k is corrupted. However, later shares depend on earlier shares, potentially leaking information about the check positions. This will be our first barrier to overcome.

3. Finally, we will need to show that interpolating c_{k-1+b} using $\mathcal{C}_{d_b}$ produces a uniformly random value whenever $\mathcal{C}_{d_b}$ satisfies the deletion predicate. In other words, **polynomial interpolation should double as a good randomness extractor from deleted shares**. Fortunately, polynomial interpolation is a matrix multiplication, and we have intuition from the classical setting that linear operations are good randomness extractors. Since a small amount of every share is uniformly random "for free", the extractor needs to produce only slightly less than a full share's worth of evaluations to produce c_{k-1+b}. This is our second technical contribution, which we will revisit in Sect. 2.3.

In step two, we seem to need the evaluation points in d_b to look like the check positions when d_b is deleted, i.e. they should be uniformly random and independent of the rest of the adversary's view. A natural approach to ensure this is to modify the shares to uniformly random round-by-round over a series of hybrid experiments. In hybrid i, the first $k-1+i$ shares to be corrupted are uniformly random. Since d_{i+1} must be deleted before c_{k+i} is corrupted (or else the experiment aborts), d_{i+1} must have been one of the uniformly random shares. Now we can apply the cut-and-choose argument to show that $\mathcal{C}_{d_i}$ satisfies the deletion predicate, thereby satisfying the extractor requirements to change c_{k+i} to be uniformly random and reach hybrid $i+1$. The first $k-1$ shares are already uniformly random, which gives us an opening to begin making modifications in round k.

Unfortunately, the strategy of modifying the shares one-by-one to be uniformly random has a major flaw. In particular, the challenger needs to produce additional polynomial evaluations whenever the adversary wishes to corrupt another share, which it does via interpolation. Recall that in order to claim that c_{k-1+i} is indistinguishable from random, we apply an extractor which uses register $\mathcal{C}_{d_i}$ as its source of entropy. But in order to invoke the security of the extractor, it seems that we cannot allow the challenger to re-use $\mathcal{C}_{d_i}$ when interpolating later points, as this might leak additional information about the source to the adversary.

To get around this issue, we might require that the challenger never uses $\mathcal{C}_{d_i}$ again to interpolate later points. However, the randomness extractor outputs *less* randomness than the size of a share. Intuitively, this occurs because the adversary can avoid fully deleting the source share d_i by guessing the location of a very small number of check positions.[4] Imperfect deletion limits the entropy of the source, which in turn limits the size of the extractor output. Now, since the challenger started with *exactly* enough evaluations to uniquely determine f, if we take away the points in $\mathcal{C}_{d_i}$ then there are no longer enough evaluation points remaining to create the rest of the shares, even given the newly interpolated points.

Predicates First, Replacement Later. Intuitively, the problem outlined above arises from the possibility that the adversary receives additional information about earlier shares from the later ones, since they are all correlated through the definition of the polynomial f. Our first idea to overcome this issue is to prove that the predicate holds for all rounds *before* switching any shares to uniformly random. In particular, we will consider a sequence of hybrid experiments where in the i'th hybrid, the challenger performs the predicate measurement on $\mathcal{C}_{d_i}$

---

[4] One may wonder whether it is possible to instead use coset states for the shares, which provide guarantees of *full* deletion [3]. Unfortunately, coset states induce errors which are the sum of a small number of uniformly random vectors. It is not clear how to correct these errors to reconstruct the secret without prior knowledge of the underlying subspace. However, encoding the subspace brings us back to the original problem of secret sharing with adaptive certified deletion.

after receiving and verifying the corresponding certificate. If the measurement rejects, the experiment immediately aborts and outputs $\bot$.

If we can undetectably reach the last hybrid experiment, then it is possible to undetectably replace every share with uniform randomness by working backwards. In the last hybrid experiment, either the predicate holds on the challenger's copy $\mathcal{C}_{d_{n-k+1}}$ of share d_{n-k+1} or the experiment aborts. In either case, the last share c_n to be corrupted can be undetectably replaced with uniform randomness. Since no further shares are interpolated, we no longer run into the issue of re-using the randomness source $\mathcal{C}_{d_{n-k+1}}$, allowing the challenger to safely complete the experiment. Then, once c_n is uniformly random, the challenger no longer needs to interpolate shares after c_{n-1}, so c_{n-1} can also be replaced with uniform randomness. This argument can be continued until all shares are replaced.

To undetectably transition from hybrid i to hybrid $i+1$, we must show that the predicate measurement returns success with high probability on $\mathcal{C}_{d_{i+1}}$. This is not hard to show for shares which are deleted *before* the k'th share is corrupted, because the deleted shares must be one of the shares which were generated uniformly at random. However, it is not clear how to show for shares which are deleted *after* the k'th share is corrupted, since this seems to require replacing c_k with uniform randomness, which brings us back to our previous problem.

Chaining Deletions via Truncated Experiments. Our second insight is the observation that the result of a measurement made when d_i is deleted *is independent of later operations*. Thus, when arguing about the probability that the predicate measurement accepts on $\mathcal{C}_{d_i}$, it is sufficient to argue about the truncated experiment that ends immediately after the predicate measurement on $\mathcal{C}_{d_i}$. Crucially, the adversary cannot corrupt share c_{k+i} in the truncated experiment without causing the experiment to abort due to $|C\backslash D| \geq k$. Instead, c_{k-1+i} is the last share that can be corrupted. This prevents the catastrophic re-use of $\mathcal{C}_{d_i}$ after share c_{k-1+i} is constructed.

Let us assume that we have already shown that the deletion predicate measurement accepts on $\mathcal{C}_{d_i}$ with high probability; for example, this clearly holds for d_1, which must be corrupted before c_k is corrupted. How likely it is to accept on $\mathcal{C}_{d_{i+1}}$? Say the deletion predicate measurement accepts on $\mathcal{C}_{d_i}$. Then we can invoke the extractor to undetectably replace share c_{k-1+i} with uniform randomness in the truncated game, since no further shares are corrupted before the game ends. We can use similar logic to replace each of the first $k-1+i$ shares to be corrupted in the truncated game. At this point, the adversary has no choice but to delete a uniformly random share as d_{i+1}, so we can apply a cut-and-choose argument to show that the predicate holds with high probability on $\mathcal{C}_{d_{i+1}}$. This argument can be repeated inductively to show that the predicate holds in each of the polynomially many rounds.

Recap of the First Challenge. In summary, the first challenge to address in proving adaptive certified deletion is the possibility of later shares leaking information about prior shares through the re-use of $\mathcal{C}_{d_b}$ in interpolation. This prevents directly replacing each share with uniform randomness. To sidestep this issue, we first argue that every $\mathcal{C}_{d_b}$ is a good source of entropy using a series of games which end after d_b is deleted. Then even if $\mathcal{C}_{d_b}$ is used to interpolate both share c_{k-1+b} and c_{k+b}, we can rely on the entropy from $\mathcal{C}_{d_{b+1}}$ to mask its re-usage when interpolating c_{k+b}.

2.3 High Rate Seedless Extractors from Quantum Sources of Entropy

The final task to finish the proof of adaptive certified deletion security in the previous section is to show that polynomial interpolation is a good randomness extractor for entropy sources formed by deleted shares. Although polynomial interpolation arises quite naturally in our construction, there are additional technical reasons why it would be difficult to design a construction for adaptive certified deletion using existing extractors.

If we were to design a scheme using a *seeded* extractor, as done in [11], then every deletion would need to be independent of the seed to avoid the entropy source depending on the seed. However, as we saw with the no-signaling construction, safely encoding the seed seems to already require secret sharing with adaptive certified deletion. [4] makes use of the seedless XOR extractor developed by [1] to avoid a similar problem. Unfortunately, the XOR extractor produces only a single bit from a relatively large input. In the case of threshold secret sharing, the extractor must use the randomness produced by deleting a single share to extract an output which is only slightly smaller than a full share.

To address this need, we give a new family of seedless randomness extractors for quantum entropy sources with high rate. These constructions have connections to linear error-correcting codes and may be of independent interest.

A Family of Extractors. The input of the extractor is a vector of M elements of a finite field $\mathbb{F}$, and the output is a vector of m elements of $\mathbb{F}$. The source consists of a register $\mathcal{X}$ which may be arbitrarily entangled with a side-information register $\mathcal{A}$. If the register $\mathcal{X}$ is in superposition over Fourier basis vectors with Hamming weight $\leq (M-m)/2$ in $\mathbb{F}$, then we can argue that the output $\mathsf{Extract}(\mathcal{X})$ is uniformly random, even given $\mathcal{A}$.[5]

The extractor family consists of matrices $R \in \mathbb{F}^{m \times M}$ such that every set of m columns of R are linearly independent. In other words, R is a parity check matrix for a linear error-correcting code with distance at least m. An extractor R is applied by coherently multiplying R with the source register $\mathcal{X}$ in the computational basis and writing the result to the output register.

Application to Polynomial Interpolation. This family generalizes both the XOR extractor and polynomial interpolation. The XOR extractor can be represented as the all-ones matrix with one row. Each column is non-zero, so the extractor

---

[5] The Hamming weight over a (potentially non-binary) finite field is being the number of nonzero entries in the vector.

can produce a one-bit output. In the case of polynomial interpolation, we can write the linear interpolation operator for a polynomial f as a matrix R with $\deg(f) + 1$ columns and a number of rows equal to the number of points being interpolated. R is a sub-matrix of a parity check matrix for a Reed-Solomon code, so it falls into the new extractor family. In fact, our result shows that any subset of columns in a polynomial interpolation matrix forms a good randomness extractor for an appropriate randomness source. When interpolating a share c_{k-1+b}, we can write the interpolation matrix as $R = [R_1|R_2]$, where R_2 is applied to d_b and R_1 is applied to the other points x on the polynomial. Then the new share is $c_{k-1+b} = R_1 x + R_2 d_b$. If d_b has satisfies the deletion predicate, then our extractor result shows that $R_2 d_b$ is uniformly random. Thus, the newly interpolated share c_b is also uniformly random.

Removing Entanglement. A downside of using polynomials for secret sharing is that each evaluation point exists in field $\mathbb{F}$ whose size scales with the total number of distinct points that must be defined on the polynomial. For example, $\mathbb{F}$ might be $\mathbb{Z}_p$ for some prime $p > nt$, where t is the number of evaluations per share. Using the approach outlined so far, each check position must be encoded in the Fourier basis over the same field $\mathbb{K}$. However, a logical $\mathbb{Z}_p$-qudit requires $\lceil \log_2(nt+1) \rceil$ qubits, which must all be entangled to produce a Fourier basis element of $\mathbb{Z}_p$.

We show how to remove the entanglement of the construction to only use *single-qubit* states, either in the Hadamard basis or in the computational basis. We modify the construction by setting the field $\mathbb{F}$ to be the binary extension field with $2^{\lceil \log_2(nt+1) \rceil}$ elements, so that each check position consists of $\lceil \log_2(nt+1) \rceil$ qubits. Then, we *individually* set each of these qubits to be a random Hadamard basis element. The other parts of the construction remain the same. Note that computational basis vectors over $\mathbb{F}$ can be encoded as a tuple of computational basis qubits.

Proving the security of this modification requires an expansion of the extractor theorem to allow general finite fields $\mathbb{F}$, which may have p^k elements for some prime p and $k \geq 1$. A Fourier basis element for such a field is obtained by applying the quantum Fourier transform over the additive group of $\mathbb{F}$, which is $\mathbb{Z}_p^k$. In particular, a Fourier basis element of $\mathbb{F}$ consists of k Fourier basis elements of $\mathbb{Z}_p$. In the case where $p = 2$, these are single-qubit Hadamard basis elements.

We emphasize that the *only* change is to modify how Fourier basis elements are defined by allowing general finite fields; both the extractor family and the Hamming weight requirement remain the same (i.e. they are still defined with respect to $\mathbb{F}$, *not* $\mathbb{Z}_p$). To gain intuition about the usefulness of this statement, let us consider its application in our secret-sharing construction. Ideally, an honest deleter would measure each qubit of its share in the Hadamard basis. However, since the dealer can only verify check positions, which each consist of $\lceil \log_2(nt+1) \rceil$ qubits, we can only prove a bound on the Hamming weight of the deleted state over $\lceil \log_2(nt+1) \rceil$-sized chunks, which corresponds to $\mathbb{F}$. This matches the entropy source requirements of the theorem. On the other hand, the polynomial that the secret is encoded in is also over $\mathbb{F}$, so polynomial interpolation must take place over $\mathbb{F}$. This matches the extractor family.

2.4 Open Problems

Although our results significantly strengthen secret sharing to resist new classes of attacks, we have only scratched the surface of an area with many fascinating open problems. We mention a few of them here.

- **Adaptive Certified Deletion for General Access Structures.** Against adaptive attacks, we construct a secret sharing scheme for the special case of threshold access structures. Is it possible to construct one for *general access structures*?
- **Stronger Definitions.** We prove the security of our schemes against *either* "distributed" attacks (i.e. no-signaling security) *or* adaptive attacks. Can we (i) formulate natural security definitions that capture both types of attacks, and (ii) prove the security of secret sharing schemes under such all-encompassing definitions?
- **Public Verification.** The question of publicly verifiable certificates for encryption with certified deletion has seen significant progress recently [3,6,15,18,20]. However, the techniques used seem to require the use of a classical secret to decode the plaintext. For secret sharing with certified deletion, this secret would need to also be encoded in a manner that can be certifiably deleted, as mentioned in Sect. 2.2. Is it possible to construct secret sharing with *publicly verifiable* certificates of deletion?
- **Other Threshold Primitives.** Aside from secret sharing, there are many other primitives which use thresholds or other access structures. For example, in threshold signatures, any k members may non-interactively sign messages under a secret key split between n parties [13]. Is it possible to construct *threshold signatures or other threshold primitives* with certified deletion?
- **High Rate Commitments with Certified Deletion.** A commitment with certified deletion allows the committed message to be certifiably and information-theoretically deleted [4,16]. However, current approaches either work in the random oracle model or require $\Theta(\lambda)$ qubits to commit to a single bit. Our new high-rate extractor (Theorem 3) provides a promising start to reduce the commitment overhead. Unfortunately, the proof technique pioneered by [4] for the plain model requires guessing the committed message, which incurs a security loss that is exponential in the size of the message. Is it possible to overcome this difficulty and construct commitments with certified deletion that have are *not much larger than the committed message*?

3 High-Rate Seedless Quantum Extractors

In this section, we study seedless extraction of large amounts of entropy from a quantum source. The source of entropy comes from applying a quantum Fourier transform to a state which is "almost" a computational basis state. In particular, the source register $\mathcal{X}$ is in superposition over vectors with low Hamming weight, and may be arbitrarily entangled with a register $\mathcal{A}$ that contains side-information about the source. Previously, [1] showed that the XOR function perfectly extracts a single bit of entropy in this setting. However, in order to extract multiple bits of entropy, they resorted to the use of a random oracle. We also remark that the case of *seeded* extraction has been well-studied by, e.g. [10,12,22].

We describe a general class of extractors that produces multiple truly random elements of any finite field $\mathbb{F}$, even conditioned on the side-information register $\mathcal{A}$. In the case where the finite field has order p^k for a prime p, we show that a large amount of entropy is generated even when the quantum Fourier transform is applied by interpreting each element $x \in \mathbb{F}_{p^k}$ as a vector $\mathbf{x} \in \mathbb{F}_p^k$ and applying the transform mod p to each index (as opposed to applying the transform mod p^k directly to the field element). This feature allows the source to be prepared using less entanglement in our eventual application to secret sharing.

Notation. The Hamming weight $h_\mathbb{F}(\mathbf{v})$ of a vector $\mathbf{v} \in \mathbb{F}^M$ over a finite field $\mathbb{F}$ is its number of non-zero positions. We denote vectors $\mathbf{v}$ and matrices $\mathbf{R}$ using bold font. Since we will be working with elements which can be interpreted as elements of two different fields, we use $(\cdot)_\mathbb{F}$ to denote that the contents of the parentheses should be interpreted as elements and operations over $\mathbb{F}$. For example, $(x + y)_\mathbb{F}$ denotes addition of x and y inside the field $\mathbb{F}$. If $\mathbf{x}, \mathbf{y} \in \mathbb{F}^k$, then $(\mathbf{x} + \mathbf{y})_\mathbb{F}$ denotes vector addition. For an extension field $\mathbb{K}$ of $\mathbb{F}$, a scalar $x \in \mathbb{K}$ can also be interpreted as a vector $\mathbf{x} \in \mathbb{F}^k$. In this case, for $x, y \in \mathbb{K}$, $(\mathbf{x} \cdot \mathbf{y})_\mathbb{F}$ produces a scalar in $\mathbb{F}$. If an element can be interpreted as either a vector or a scalar, we bold it depending on the context of the first operation applied; for example, $(xy)_\mathbb{K}$ or $(\mathbf{x} \cdot \mathbf{z})_\mathbb{F}$ for $x \in \mathbb{K}$, $\mathbf{y} \in \mathbb{K}^n$, and $\mathbf{z} \in \mathbb{F}^k$.

Theorem 3. *Let $\mathbb{F}$ be a finite field of order p^k. Let $\mathcal{X} = \mathcal{X}_1, \ldots, \mathcal{X}_M$ be a register containing M $\mathbb{F}$-qudits, and consider any quantum state*

$$|\gamma\rangle^{\mathcal{A},\mathcal{X}} = \sum_{\mathbf{u} \in \mathbb{F}^M : h_\mathbb{F}(\mathbf{u}) < \frac{M-m}{2}} |\psi_\mathbf{u}\rangle^{\mathcal{A}} \otimes |\mathbf{u} + \mathbf{w}\rangle^{\mathcal{X}}$$

for some integer $m \leq M$ and some fixed string $\mathbf{w} \in \mathbb{F}^M$. Let $\mathbf{R} \in \mathbb{F}^{m \times M}$ be a matrix such that every set of m columns of $\mathbf{R}$ are linearly independent.

Let $\rho^{\mathcal{A},\mathcal{Y}}$ be the mixed state that results from the following procedure:

1. *Apply a quantum Fourier transform over $\mathbb{F}$'s additive group $\mathbb{Z}_p^k$ to each register $\mathcal{X}_i$. In other words, interpret $\mathcal{X}_i$ as a sequence of registers $\mathcal{X}_{i,1}, \ldots, \mathcal{X}_{i,k}$ containing $\mathbb{Z}_p$-qudits, then apply a quantum Fourier transform mod p to each $\mathcal{X}_{i,j}$.*
2. *Initialize a fresh register $\mathcal{Y}$, and apply the isometry $|\mathbf{x}\rangle^{\mathcal{X}} \mapsto |\mathbf{x}\rangle^{\mathcal{X}} \otimes |\mathbf{R}\mathbf{x}\rangle^{\mathcal{Y}}$.*
3. *Trace out register $\mathcal{X}$.*

Then

$$\rho^{\mathcal{A},\mathcal{Y}} = \mathsf{Tr}^\mathcal{X}[|\gamma\rangle\langle\gamma|] \otimes \left(\frac{1}{|\mathbb{F}|^m} \sum_{\mathbf{y} \in \mathbb{F}^m} |\mathbf{y}\rangle\langle\mathbf{y}|\right).$$

Remark 1. As an example, consider $\mathbb{F}$ to be the field with 2^n elements. Note that for the source, the Hamming weight is taken over the larger field $\mathbb{F}$, but the quantum Fourier transform is done over the individual qubits, which in this case makes it just a Hadamard gate. The extractor R operates over $\mathbb{F}$ and produces an output in $\mathbb{F}^m$.

Proof. First, we apply the Fourier transform to $|\gamma\rangle$ to obtain

$$\sqrt{|\mathbb{F}|^{-M}} \sum_{\mathbf{u}\in\mathbb{F}^M : h_\mathbb{F}(\mathbf{u})<\frac{M-m}{2}} |\psi_\mathbf{u}\rangle^\mathcal{A} \otimes \sum_{\mathbf{x}\in\mathbb{F}^M} \omega_p^{((\mathbf{u}+\mathbf{w})_\mathbb{F}\cdot\mathbf{x})_{\mathbb{Z}_p}} |\mathbf{x}\rangle^\mathcal{X},$$

where ω_p is a primitive p'th root of unity. Next, after applying the extractor, but before tracing out $\mathcal{X}$, the state becomes

$$\sqrt{|\mathbb{F}|^{-M}} \sum_{\mathbf{x}\in\mathbb{F}^M} \left(\sum_{\mathbf{u}\in\mathbb{F}^M : h_\mathbb{F}(\mathbf{u})<\frac{M-m}{2}} \omega_p^{((\mathbf{u}+\mathbf{w})_\mathbb{F}\cdot\mathbf{x})_{\mathbb{Z}_p}} |\psi_\mathbf{u}\rangle^\mathcal{A} \right) \otimes |\mathbf{x}\rangle^\mathcal{X} \otimes |R\mathbf{x}\rangle^\mathcal{Y} \tag{1}$$

$$:= \sqrt{|\mathbb{F}|^{-M}} \sum_{\mathbf{x}\in\mathbb{F}^M} |\phi_\mathbf{x}\rangle^\mathcal{A} \otimes |\mathbf{x}\rangle^\mathcal{X} \otimes |R\mathbf{x}\rangle^\mathcal{Y}. \tag{2}$$

Since the additive group of $\mathbb{F}$ is $\mathbb{Z}_p^k$, for every $\mathbf{u}, \mathbf{w} \in \mathbb{F}^M$ and $\mathbf{x} \in \mathbb{Z}_p^{kM}$, we have

$$((\mathbf{u}+\mathbf{w})_\mathbb{F} \cdot \mathbf{x})_{\mathbb{Z}_p} = ((\mathbf{u}+\mathbf{w})_{\mathbb{Z}_p^k} \cdot \mathbf{x})_{\mathbb{Z}_p} = ((\mathbf{u}+\mathbf{w}) \cdot \mathbf{x})_{\mathbb{Z}_p}.$$

Tracing out register $\mathcal{X}$ yields

$$\rho^{\mathcal{A},\mathcal{Y}} = |\mathbb{F}|^{-M} \sum_{\mathbf{x}\in\mathbb{F}^M} |\phi_\mathbf{x}\rangle\langle\phi_\mathbf{x}| \otimes |R\mathbf{x}\rangle\langle R\mathbf{x}| \tag{3}$$

$$= |\mathbb{F}|^{-M} \sum_{\substack{\mathbf{y}\in\mathbb{F}^m \\ \mathbf{x}\in\mathbb{F}^M : (R\mathbf{x})_\mathbb{F}=\mathbf{y}}} |\phi_\mathbf{x}\rangle\langle\phi_\mathbf{x}| \otimes |\mathbf{y}\rangle\langle\mathbf{y}| \tag{4}$$

$$= |\mathbb{F}|^{-M} \sum_{\substack{\mathbf{y}\in\mathbb{F}^m \\ \mathbf{x}\in\mathbb{F}^M : (R\mathbf{x})_\mathbb{F}=\mathbf{y}}}$$

$$\left(\sum_{\substack{\mathbf{u}_1,\mathbf{u}_2\in\mathbb{F}^M : \\ h_\mathbb{F}(\mathbf{u}_1), h_\mathbb{F}(\mathbf{u}_2)\leq\frac{M-m}{2}}} \omega_p^{((\mathbf{u}_1+\mathbf{w})\cdot\mathbf{x})_{\mathbb{Z}_p}} \overline{\omega_p^{((\mathbf{u}_2+\mathbf{w})\cdot\mathbf{x})_{\mathbb{Z}_p}}} |\phi_{\mathbf{u}_1}\rangle\langle\phi_{\mathbf{u}_2}| \right) \otimes |\mathbf{y}\rangle\langle\mathbf{y}|$$

$$\tag{5}$$

$$= \sum_{\substack{\mathbf{u}_1,\mathbf{u}_2\in\mathbb{F}^M : \\ h_\mathbb{F}(\mathbf{u}_1), h_\mathbb{F}(\mathbf{u}_2)\leq\frac{M-m}{2}}} |\phi_{\mathbf{u}_1}\rangle\langle\phi_{\mathbf{u}_2}|$$

$$\otimes \left(|\mathbb{F}|^{-M} \sum_{\mathbf{y}\in\mathbb{F}^m} |\mathbf{y}\rangle\langle\mathbf{y}| \sum_{\mathbf{x}\in\mathbb{F}^M : (R\mathbf{x})_\mathbb{F}=\mathbf{y}} \omega_p^{((\mathbf{u}_1+\mathbf{w})\cdot\mathbf{x}-(\mathbf{u}_2+\mathbf{w})\cdot\mathbf{x})_{\mathbb{Z}_p}} \right) \tag{6}$$

$$= \sum_{\substack{\mathbf{u}_1, \mathbf{u}_2 \in \mathbb{F}^M: \\ h_{\mathbb{F}}(\mathbf{u}_1), h_{\mathbb{F}}(\mathbf{u}_2) \leq \frac{M-m}{2}}} |\phi_{\mathbf{u}_1}\rangle \langle \phi_{\mathbf{u}_2}|$$

$$\otimes \left(|\mathbb{F}|^{-M} \sum_{\mathbf{y} \in \mathbb{F}^m} |\mathbf{y}\rangle \langle \mathbf{y}| \sum_{\mathbf{x} \in \mathbb{F}^M : (\mathbf{R}\mathbf{x})_{\mathbb{F}} = \mathbf{y}} \omega_p^{((\mathbf{u}_1 - \mathbf{u}_2) \cdot \mathbf{x})_{\mathbb{Z}_p}} \right). \quad (7)$$

Next, we apply Proposition 1, proven below, to show that every $|\phi_{\mathbf{u}_1}\rangle \langle \phi_{\mathbf{u}_2}|$ term where $\mathbf{u}_1 \neq \mathbf{u}_2$ has coefficient 0. To see this, consider any such $\mathbf{u}_1, \mathbf{u}_2$ and the value $\mathbf{u} = (\mathbf{u}_1 - \mathbf{u}_2)_{\mathbb{Z}_p} = (\mathbf{u}_1 - \mathbf{u}_2)_{\mathbb{F}}$. Condition 1 is satisfied by $\mathbf{u}$ since $\mathbf{u}_1 \neq \mathbf{u}_2$. Condition 2 is satisfied since $h_{\mathbb{F}}(\mathbf{u}) \leq h_{\mathbb{F}}(\mathbf{u}_1) + h_{\mathbb{F}}(\mathbf{u}_2) \leq M - m$, so there are at least m indices of $\mathbf{u}$ which are zero. Finally, condition 3 is satisfied since any m columns of R are linearly independent.

Finally, noting that if $\mathbf{u}_1 = \mathbf{u}_2$, then the coefficient of $|\phi_{\mathbf{u}_1}\rangle \langle \phi_{\mathbf{u}_1}| \otimes |\mathbf{y}\rangle \langle \mathbf{y}|$ is the number of solutions to $(\mathbf{R}\mathbf{x})_{\mathbb{F}} = \mathbf{y}$, which is $|\mathbb{F}|^{M-m}$, we conclude that

$$\rho^{\mathcal{A}, \mathcal{Y}} = \sum_{\mathbf{u} \in \mathbb{F}^M : h_{\mathbb{F}}(\mathbf{u}) \leq \frac{M-m}{2}} |\phi_{\mathbf{u}}\rangle \langle \phi_{\mathbf{u}}| \otimes \left(|\mathbb{F}|^{-m} \sum_{\mathbf{y} \in \mathbb{F}^m} |\mathbf{y}\rangle \langle \mathbf{y}| \right) \quad (8)$$

$$= \mathrm{Tr}^X[|\gamma\rangle \langle \gamma|] \otimes \left(|\mathbb{F}|^{-m} \sum_{\mathbf{y} \in \mathbb{F}^m} |\mathbf{y}\rangle \langle \mathbf{y}| \right). \quad (9)$$

□

Proposition 1. *Let* $\mathbf{u} \in \mathbb{F}^M$ *and* $\mathbf{y} \in \mathbb{F}^m$, *and suppose that*

1. $\mathbf{u}_i \neq 0$ *for some index* i.
2. *There exists a set* $J \subseteq [0, \ldots, M-1]$ *of size* m *such that for every* $j \in J$, $\mathbf{u}_j = 0$.
3. *The submatrix* $\mathbf{R}_J$ *consisting of the columns of* $\mathbf{R}$ *corresponding to* J *has full rank.*

Then

$$\sum_{\mathbf{x} \in \mathbb{F}^M : (\mathbf{R}\mathbf{x})_{\mathbb{F}} = \mathbf{y}} \omega_p^{(\mathbf{u} \cdot \mathbf{x})_{\mathbb{Z}_p}} = 0.$$

Remark 2. We note that in the case that $\mathbb{F} = \mathbb{F}_p$, then the above expression actually holds for any $\mathbf{u} \notin \mathrm{rowspan}(\mathbf{R})$, which follows from a standard argument. The three conditions above do imply that $\mathbf{u} \notin \mathrm{rowspan}(\mathbf{R})$, but are more restrictive. We take advantage of the extra restrictions in order to prove that the expression holds even in the case where $\mathbb{F}$ is an extension field of $\mathbb{F}_p$.

Proof. Our strategy will be to partition the affine subspace $S_{\mathbf{y}} = \{\mathbf{x} \in \mathbb{F}^M : (\mathbf{R}\mathbf{x})_{\mathbb{F}} = \mathbf{y}\}$ into parallel lines, and then claim that the sum over each line is 0.

To begin, define a vector $\mathbf{z} \in \mathbb{F}^M$ so that

- $z_i = 1$,
- $z_j = 0$ for all $j \notin J \cup \{i\}$, and
- $(\mathbf{Rz})_\mathbb{F} = 0^m$,

which is possible because the $m \times m$ submatrix $\mathbf{R}_J$ has full rank. By construction, we have that for any $c \in \mathbb{F}$,

$$(\mathbf{u} \cdot (c\mathbf{z})_\mathbb{F})_{\mathbb{Z}_p} = \left(\mathbf{u}_i \cdot (cz_i)_\mathbb{F} + \sum_{j \in J} \mathbf{u}_j \cdot (cz_j)_\mathbb{F} + \sum_{j \notin J \cup \{i\}} \mathbf{u}_j \cdot (0)_\mathbb{F} \right)_{\mathbb{Z}_p} = (\mathbf{u}_i \cdot \mathbf{c})_{\mathbb{Z}_p}, \tag{10}$$

where note that in the final expression, $\mathbf{u}_i$ and $\mathbf{c}$ are interpreted as vectors in $\mathbb{Z}_p^k$.

Now, fix any $\mathbf{x} \in S_\mathbf{y}$ and $c \in \mathbb{F}$. Then we have that $(\mathbf{x} + c\mathbf{z})_\mathbb{F} \in S_\mathbf{y}$, since $(\mathbf{R}(\mathbf{x}+c\mathbf{z}))_\mathbb{F} = \mathbf{y}+0$. Therefore, we can partition $S_\mathbf{y}$ into one-dimensional cosets (lines) of the form $\{\mathbf{x} + c\mathbf{z}\}_{c \in \mathbb{F}}$.

We now show that the sum over any particular coset is 0, i.e. that for any $\mathbf{x} \in S_\mathbf{y}$,

$$\sum_{c \in \mathbb{F}} \omega_p^{(\mathbf{u} \cdot (\mathbf{x}+c\mathbf{z})_\mathbb{F})_{\mathbb{Z}_p}} = 0.$$

Since the additive group of $\mathbb{F}$ is $\mathbb{Z}_p^k$, by Eq. (10) we have that

$$(\mathbf{u} \cdot (\mathbf{x} + c\mathbf{z})_\mathbb{F})_{\mathbb{Z}_p} = (\mathbf{u} \cdot \mathbf{x} + \mathbf{u} \cdot (c\mathbf{z})_\mathbb{F})_{\mathbb{Z}_p}$$
$$= (\mathbf{u} \cdot \mathbf{x} + \mathbf{u}_i \cdot \mathbf{c})_{\mathbb{Z}_p}$$

We now view $\mathbf{u}_i \in \mathbb{F}$ as a vector $\mathbf{u}_i = u_{i,0}, \ldots, u_{i,k-1} \in \mathbb{Z}_p^k$. In particular, since $\mathbf{u}_i \neq 0$, there exists an index t such that $u_{k,t} \neq 0 \in \mathbb{Z}_p$. By also interpreting $\mathbf{c} \in \mathbb{F}$ as an element of $\mathbb{Z}_p^k$, we can decompose it as $\mathbf{c} = (\mathbf{c}' + c_t \mathbf{e}_t)_{\mathbb{Z}_p}$, where $\mathbf{c}' \in \mathbb{Z}_p^k$ is such that $\mathbf{c}'_t = 0$, where $c_t \in \mathbb{Z}_p$, and where $\mathbf{e_t} \in \mathbb{Z}_p^k$ is the t'th standard basis vector. Therefore

$$(\mathbf{u} \cdot (\mathbf{x} + c\mathbf{z})_\mathbb{F})_{\mathbb{Z}_p} = (\mathbf{u} \cdot \mathbf{x} + \mathbf{u}_i \cdot \mathbf{c}' + u_{i,t} c_t)_{\mathbb{Z}_p}.$$

Since $u_{i,t} \neq 0$ and ω_p is a primitive p'th root of unity, we know that $\omega_p^{u_{i,t}} \neq 1$ is a p'th root of unity. Therefore,

$$\sum_{c \in \mathbb{F}} \omega_p^{(\mathbf{u} \cdot (\mathbf{x}+c\mathbf{z})_\mathbb{F})_{\mathbb{Z}_p}} = \sum_{\mathbf{c}' \in \mathbb{Z}_p^k : \mathbf{c}'_t = 0} \omega_p^{(\mathbf{u} \cdot \mathbf{x} + \mathbf{u}_i \cdot \mathbf{c}')_{\mathbb{Z}_p}} \cdot \sum_{c_t \in \mathbb{Z}_p} \left(\omega_p^{u_{i,t}} \right)^{c_t} \tag{11}$$

$$= \sum_{\mathbf{c}' \in \mathbb{Z}_p^k : \mathbf{c}'_t = 0} \omega_p^{(\mathbf{u} \cdot \mathbf{x} + \mathbf{u}_i \cdot \mathbf{c}')_{\mathbb{Z}_p}} \cdot 0 \tag{12}$$

$$= 0. \tag{13}$$

□

4 Definitions of Secret Sharing with Certified Deletion

A secret sharing scheme with certified deletion augments the syntax of a secret sharing scheme with additional algorithms to delete shares and verify deletion certificates. We define it for general access structures. As described in the full version an access structure $\mathbb{S} \subseteq \mathcal{P}([n])$ for n parties is a monotonic set of sets, i.e. if $S \in \mathbb{S}$ and $S' \supset S$, then $S' \in \mathbb{S}$. Any set of parties $S \in \mathbb{S}$ is authorized to access the secret. A simple example of an access structure is the threshold structure, where any set of at least k parties is authorized to access the secret. We denote this access structure as (k, n).

Definition 1 (Secret Sharing with Certified Deletion). *A secret sharing scheme with certified deletion is specified by a monotone access structure $\mathbb{S}$ over n parties, and consists of four algorithms:*

- $\mathsf{Split}_{\mathbb{S}}(1^\lambda, s)$ *takes in a secret s, and outputs n share registers $\mathcal{S}_1, \ldots, \mathcal{S}_n$ and a verification key* vk.
- $\mathsf{Reconstruct}_{\mathbb{S}}(\{\mathcal{S}_i\}_{i \in P})$ *takes in set of share registers for some $P \subseteq [n]$, and outputs either s or $\bot$.*
- $\mathsf{Delete}_{\mathbb{S}}(\mathcal{S}_i)$ *takes in a share register and outputs a certificate of deletion* cert.
- $\mathsf{Verify}_{\mathbb{S}}(\mathsf{vk}, i, \mathsf{cert})$ *takes in the verification key* vk, *an index i, and a certificate of deletion* cert, *and outputs either $\top$ (indicating accept) or $\bot$ (indicating reject).*

Definition 2 (Correctness of Secret Sharing with Certified Deletion). *A secret sharing scheme with certified deletion must satisfy two correctness properties:*

- **Reconstruction Correctness.** *For all $\lambda \in \mathbb{N}$ and all sets $S \in \mathbb{S}$,*

$$\Pr\left[\mathsf{Reconstruct}_{\mathbb{S}}(\{\mathcal{S}_i\}_{i \in S}) : (\mathcal{S}_1, \ldots, \mathcal{S}_n, \mathsf{vk}) \leftarrow \mathsf{Split}_{\mathbb{S}}(1^\lambda, s)\right] = 1.$$

- **Deletion Correctness.** *For all $\lambda \in \mathbb{N}$ and all $i \in [n]$,*

$$\Pr\left[\mathsf{Verify}_{\mathbb{S}}(\mathsf{vk}, i, \mathsf{cert}) = \top : \begin{array}{l}(\mathcal{S}_1, \ldots, \mathcal{S}_n, \mathsf{vk}) \leftarrow \mathsf{Split}_{\mathbb{S}}(1^\lambda, s) \\ \mathsf{cert} \leftarrow \mathsf{Delete}_{\mathbb{S}}(\mathcal{S}_i)\end{array}\right] = 1.$$

The standard notion of security for secret sharing requires that no set of unauthorized shares $S \notin \mathbb{S}$ reveals any information about the secret (see the full version). We next present our notion of *no-signaling certified deletion security*. Here, the shares are partitioned into unauthorized sets, and different parts of the adversary operate on each partition, potentially deleting some number of shares from each. The different parts of the adversary are allowed to share entanglement, but are not allowed to signal. If the adversaries jointly produce a valid certificate for at least one share from every authorized set, then we require that the joint residual state of *all* of the adversaries contains no (or negligible) information about the secret. Observe that this notion of security is at least as strong as the standard notion of security for secret sharing (if we relax to statistical rather than perfect security). Indeed, if the standard notion does not hold, and thus there is some unauthorized set S that leaks information about the secret, then the adversary would be able to win the certified deletion game by honestly deleting every share except for those in S.

Definition 3 (No-Signaling Certified Deletion Security for Secret Sharing). *Let $P = (P_1, \ldots, P_\ell)$ be a partition of $[n]$, let $|\psi\rangle$ be an ℓ-part state on registers $\mathcal{R}_1, \ldots, \mathcal{R}_\ell$, and let $\mathsf{Adv} = (\mathsf{Adv}_1, \ldots, \mathsf{Adv}_\ell)$ be an ℓ-part adversary. Define the experiment $\mathsf{SS\text{-}NSCD}_\mathbb{S}(1^\lambda, P, |\psi\rangle, \mathsf{Adv}, s)$ as follows:*

1. *Sample $(\mathcal{S}_1, \ldots, \mathcal{S}_n, \mathsf{vk}) \leftarrow \mathsf{Split}_\mathbb{S}(1^\lambda, s)$.*
2. *For each $t \in [\ell]$, run $(\{\mathsf{cert}_i\}_{i \in P_t}, \mathcal{R}'_t) \leftarrow \mathsf{Adv}_t(\{\mathcal{S}_i\}_{i \in P_t}, \mathcal{R}_t)$, where $\mathcal{R}'_t$ is an arbitrary output register.*
3. *If for all $S \in \mathbb{S}$, there exists $i \in S$ such that $\mathsf{Verify}_\mathbb{S}(\mathsf{vk}, i, \mathsf{cert}_i) = \top$, then output $(\mathcal{R}'_1, \ldots, \mathcal{R}'_\ell)$, and otherwise output $\bot$.*

A secret sharing scheme for access structure $\mathbb{S}$ has no-signaling certified deletion security if for any "admissible" partition $P = (P_1, \ldots, P_\ell)$ (i.e. for all $P_t \in P$ and $S \in \mathbb{S}$, $P_t \not\subseteq S$), any ℓ-part state $|\psi\rangle$, any (unbounded) ℓ-part adversary Adv, and any pair of secrets s_0, s_1,

$$\mathsf{TD}[\mathsf{SS\text{-}NSCD}_\mathbb{S}(1^\lambda, P, |\psi\rangle, \mathsf{Adv}, s_0), \mathsf{SS\text{-}NSCD}_\mathbb{S}(1^\lambda, P, |\psi\rangle, \mathsf{Adv}, s_1)] = \mathsf{negl}(\lambda).$$

Next, we present an alternative definition which allows the adversary to start by corrupting some unauthorized set, and then continue to adaptively delete some shares and corrupt new parties, as long as the total set of parties corrupted minus the set of shares deleted is unauthorized. Similarly to the previous definition, adaptive certified deletion for secret sharing subsumes the standard notion of security for secret sharing.

Definition 4 (Adaptive Certified Deletion for Secret Sharing). *Let Adv be an adversary with internal register $\mathcal{R}$ which is initialized to a state $|\psi\rangle$, let $\mathbb{S}$ be an access structure, and let s be a secret. Define the experiment $\mathsf{SS\text{-}ACD}_\mathbb{S}(1^\lambda, |\psi\rangle, \mathsf{Adv}, s)$ as follows:*

1. *Sample $(\mathcal{S}_1, \ldots, \mathcal{S}_n, \mathsf{vk}) \leftarrow \mathsf{Split}_\mathbb{S}(1^\lambda, s)$. Initialize the corruption set $C = \emptyset$ and the deleted set $D = \emptyset$.*
2. *In each round i, the adversary may do one of three things:*
    (a) *End the experiment by outputting a register $\mathcal{R} \leftarrow \mathsf{Adv}(\{\mathcal{S}_j\}_{j \in C}, \mathcal{R})$.*
    (b) *Delete a share by outputting a certificate cert_i, an index $j_i \in [n]$, and register $(\mathsf{cert}_i, j_i, \mathcal{R}) \leftarrow \mathsf{Adv}(\{\mathcal{S}_j\}_{j \in C}, \mathcal{R})$. When the adversary chooses this option, if $\mathsf{Verify}_\mathbb{S}(\mathsf{vk}, j_i, \mathsf{cert}_i)$ outputs $\top$, then add j_i to D. Otherwise, immediately abort the experiment and output $\bot$.*
    (c) *Corrupt a new share by outputting an index $j_i \in [n]$ and register $(j_i, \mathcal{R}) \leftarrow \mathsf{Adv}(\{\mathcal{S}_j\}_{j \in C}, \mathcal{R})$. When the adversary chooses this option, add j_i to C. If $C \setminus D \in \mathbb{S}$, immediately abort the experiment and output $\bot$.*
3. *Output $\mathcal{R}$, unless the experiment has already aborted.*

A secret sharing scheme for access structure $\mathbb{S}$ has adaptive certified deletion security if for any (unbounded) adversary Adv, any state $|\psi\rangle$, and any pair of secrets (s_0, s_1),

$$\mathsf{TD}[\mathsf{SS\text{-}ACD}_{\mathbb{S}}(1^\lambda, |\psi\rangle, \mathsf{Adv}, s_0), \; \mathsf{SS\text{-}ACD}_{\mathbb{S}}(1^\lambda, |\psi\rangle, \mathsf{Adv}, s_1)] = \mathsf{negl}(\lambda)$$

It will also be convenient to establish some notation for the order of the corrupted and deleted shares. Let c_a be the a'th share to be corrupted (i.e. added to C) and let d_b be the b'th share to be deleted (i.e. added to D).

5 Secret Sharing with No-Signaling Certified Deletion

In this section, we'll show how to combine any classical secret sharing scheme $(\mathsf{CSplit}_{\mathbb{S}}, \mathsf{CReconstruct}_{\mathbb{S}})$ (see the full version for the definition) for access structure $\mathbb{S} \in \mathcal{P}([n])$ with a 2-out-of-2 secret sharing scheme with certified deletion $(\mathsf{Split}_{2\text{-}2}, \mathsf{Reconstruct}_{2\text{-}2}, \mathsf{Delete}_{2\text{-}2}, \mathsf{Verify}_{2\text{-}2})$ (see the full version for the definition) in order to obtain a secret sharing scheme for $\mathbb{S}$ that satisfies no-signaling certified deletion security (Definition 3).

$\mathsf{Split}_{\mathbb{S}}(1^\lambda, s)$
- Sample $(\mathsf{sh}_1, \ldots, \mathsf{sh}_n) \leftarrow \mathsf{CSplit}_{\mathbb{S}}(s)$.
- Set $\kappa = \max\{\lambda, n\}^2$, and for each $i \in [n]$, sample $(|\mathsf{qsh}_i\rangle, \mathsf{csh}_i, \mathsf{vk}_i) \leftarrow \mathsf{Split}_{2\text{-}2}(1^\kappa, \mathsf{sh}_i)$.
- For each $i \in [n]$, sample $(\mathsf{csh}_{i,1}, \ldots, \mathsf{csh}_{i,n}) \leftarrow \mathsf{CSplit}_{\mathbb{S}}(\mathsf{csh}_i)$.
- Set $\mathsf{vk} = (\mathsf{vk}_1, \ldots, \mathsf{vk}_n)$, and initialize register $\mathcal{S}_i$ to $|\mathsf{qsh}_i\rangle, \{\mathsf{csh}_{j,i}\}_{j \in [n]}$.

$\mathsf{Reconstruct}_{\mathbb{S}}(\{\mathcal{S}_i\}_{i \in P})$
- Parse each register $\mathcal{S}_i$ as $|\mathsf{qsh}_i\rangle, \{\mathsf{csh}_{j,i}\}_{j \in [n]}$.
- For each $i \in P$, compute $\mathsf{csh}_i \leftarrow \mathsf{CReconstruct}_{\mathbb{S}}(\{\mathsf{csh}_{i,j}\}_{j \in P})$, and output $\bot$ if the result is $\bot$.
- For each $i \in P$, compute $\mathsf{sh}_i \leftarrow \mathsf{Reconstruct}_{2\text{-}2}(|\mathsf{qsh}_i\rangle, \mathsf{csh}_i)$.
- Output $s \leftarrow \mathsf{CReconstruct}_{\mathbb{S}}(\{\mathsf{sh}_i\}_{i \in P})$.

$\mathsf{Delete}_{\mathbb{S}}(\mathcal{S}_i)$
- Parse $\mathcal{S}_i$ as $|\mathsf{qsh}_i\rangle, \{\mathsf{csh}_{j,i}\}_{j \in [n]}$ and output $\mathsf{cert} \leftarrow \mathsf{Delete}_{2\text{-}2}(|\mathsf{qsh}_i\rangle)$.

$\mathsf{Verify}_{\mathbb{S}}(\mathsf{vk}, i, \mathsf{cert})$
- Parse $\mathsf{vk} = (\mathsf{vk}_1, \ldots, \mathsf{vk}_n)$ and output $\mathsf{Verify}_{2\text{-}2}(\mathsf{vk}_i, \mathsf{cert})$.

Fig. 1. Secret sharing with no-signaling certified deletion security for any access structure $\mathbb{S}$.

Theorem 4. *The construction given in Fig. 1 satisfies no-signaling certified deletion security (Definition 3).*

Proof. Let $\mathsf{Adv} = (\mathsf{Adv}_1, \ldots, \mathsf{Adv}_\ell)$ be any ℓ-part adversary that partitions the shares using an admissible partition $P = (P_1, \ldots, P_\ell)$ and is initialized with the ℓ-part state $|\psi\rangle$ on registers $\mathcal{R}_1, \ldots, \mathcal{R}_\ell$. Let s_0, s_1 be any two secrets, and assume for contradiction that

$$\mathsf{TD}[\mathsf{SS}\text{-}\mathsf{NSCD}_\mathbb{S}(1^\lambda, P, |\psi\rangle, \mathsf{Adv}, s_0), \mathsf{SS}\text{-}\mathsf{NSCD}_\mathbb{S}(1^\lambda, P, |\psi\rangle, \mathsf{Adv}, s_1)] = \mathsf{nonnegl}(\lambda).$$

Now, for $s \in \{s_0, s_1\}$, define a hybrid $\mathcal{H}_1(s)$ as follows.

$\underline{\mathcal{H}_1(s)}$

1. Sample $C \leftarrow \mathcal{P}([n])$.
2. Sample $(\mathsf{sh}_1, \ldots, \mathsf{sh}_n) \leftarrow \mathsf{CSplit}_\mathbb{S}(s)$.
3. Set $\kappa = \max\{\lambda, n\}^2$, and for each $i \in [n]$, sample $(|\mathsf{qsh}_i\rangle, \mathsf{csh}_i, \mathsf{vk}_i) \leftarrow \mathsf{Split}_{2\text{-}2}(1^\kappa, \mathsf{sh}_i)$.
4. For each $i \in [n]$, sample $(\mathsf{csh}_{i,1}, \ldots, \mathsf{csh}_{i,n}) \leftarrow \mathsf{CSplit}_\mathbb{S}(\mathsf{csh}_i)$.
5. Set $\mathsf{vk} = (\mathsf{vk}_1, \ldots, \mathsf{vk}_n)$, and initialize register $\mathcal{S}_i$ to $|\mathsf{qsh}_i\rangle, \{\mathsf{csh}_{j,i}\}_{j \in [n]}$.
6. For each $t \in [\ell]$, run $(\{\mathsf{cert}_i\}_{i \in P_t}, \mathcal{R}'_t) \leftarrow \mathsf{Adv}_t(\{\mathcal{S}_i\}_{i \in P_t}, \mathcal{R}_t)$.
7. Let $C^* := \{i : \mathsf{Verify}_{2\text{-}2}(\mathsf{vk}_i, i, \mathsf{cert}_i) = \top\}$. Output $(\mathcal{R}'_1, \ldots, \mathcal{R}'_\ell)$ if $C = C^*$ and $[n] \setminus C^* \notin \mathbb{S}$, and otherwise output $\bot$.

That is, $\mathcal{H}_1(s)$ is the same as $\mathsf{SS}\text{-}\mathsf{NSCD}_\mathbb{S}(1^\lambda, P, |\psi\rangle, \mathsf{Adv}, s)$ except that $\mathcal{H}_1(s)$ makes a uniformly random guess C for the subset of shares for which the adversary produces a valid deletion certificate, and aborts if this guess is incorrect.

Proposition 2. $\mathsf{TD}\left[\mathcal{H}_1(s_0), \mathcal{H}_1(s_1)\right] = \mathsf{nonnegl}(\lambda) \cdot 2^{-n}$.

Proof. This follows directly from the fact that $\mathcal{H}_1(s)$'s guess for C is correct with probability $1/2^n$, and, conditioned on the guess being correct, $\mathcal{H}_1(s)$ is identical to $\mathsf{SS}\text{-}\mathsf{NSCD}_\mathbb{S}(1^\lambda, P, |\psi\rangle, \mathsf{Adv}, s)$. □

Now, for $s \in \{s_0, s_1\}$ and $k \in [0, \ldots, n]$, define a sequence of hybrids $\mathcal{H}_{2,k}(s)$ as follows.

$\underline{\mathcal{H}_{2,k}(s)}$

1. Sample $C \leftarrow \mathcal{P}([n])$.
2. Sample $(\mathsf{sh}_1, \ldots, \mathsf{sh}_n) \leftarrow \mathsf{CSplit}_\mathbb{S}(s)$.
3. Set $\kappa = \max\{\lambda, n\}^2$ and for each $i \in [n]$, if $i \leq k$ and $i \in C$, sample $(|\mathsf{qsh}_i\rangle, \mathsf{csh}_i, \mathsf{vk}_i) \leftarrow \mathsf{Split}_{2\text{-}2}(1^\kappa, \bot)$, and otherwise sample $(|\mathsf{qsh}_i\rangle, \mathsf{csh}_i, \mathsf{vk}_i) \leftarrow \mathsf{Split}_{2\text{-}2}(1^\kappa, \mathsf{sh}_i)$.
4. For each $i \in [n]$, sample $(\mathsf{csh}_{i,1}, \ldots, \mathsf{csh}_{i,n}) \leftarrow \mathsf{CSplit}_\mathbb{S}(\mathsf{csh}_i)$.
5. Set $\mathsf{vk} = (\mathsf{vk}_1, \ldots, \mathsf{vk}_n)$, and initialize register $\mathcal{S}_i$ to $|\mathsf{qsh}_i\rangle, \{\mathsf{csh}_{j,i}\}_{j \in [n]}$.
6. For each $t \in [\ell]$, run $(\{\mathsf{cert}_i\}_{i \in P_t}, \mathcal{R}'_t) \leftarrow \mathsf{Adv}_t(\{\mathcal{S}_i\}_{i \in P_t}, \mathcal{R}_t)$.

7. Let $C^* := \{i : \mathsf{Verify}_{2\text{-}2}(\mathsf{vk}_i, i, \mathsf{cert}_i) = \top\}$. Output $(\mathcal{R}'_1, \ldots, \mathcal{R}'_\ell)$ if $C = C^*$ and $[n] \setminus C^* \notin \mathbb{S}$, and otherwise output $\bot$.

First, note that $\mathcal{H}_1(s_0) = \mathcal{H}_{2,0}(s_0)$ and $\mathcal{H}_1(s_1) = \mathcal{H}_{2,0}(s_1)$. Next, we show the following claim.

Proposition 3. $\mathcal{H}_{2,n}(s_0) \equiv \mathcal{H}_{2,n}(s_1)$.

Proof. In each experiment, if the output is not $\bot$, then we know that $[n] \setminus C$ is an unauthorized set. Moreover, the experiments do not depend on the information $\{\mathsf{sh}_i\}_{i \in C}$. Thus, the claim follows by the perfect privacy of $(\mathsf{CSplit}_\mathbb{S}, \mathsf{CReconstruct}_\mathbb{S})$, which implies that

$$\{\{\mathsf{sh}_i\}_{i \in C \setminus [n]} : (\mathsf{sh}_1, \ldots, \mathsf{sh}_n) \leftarrow \mathsf{CSplit}_\mathbb{S}(s_0)\}$$
$$\equiv \{\{\mathsf{sh}_i\}_{i \in C \setminus [n]} : (\mathsf{sh}_1, \ldots, \mathsf{sh}_n) \leftarrow \mathsf{CSplit}_\mathbb{S}(s_1)\}.$$

$\square$

Finally, we show the following claim.

Proposition 4. *For $s \in \{s_0, s_1\}$ and $k \in [n]$, it holds that* $\mathsf{TD}[\mathcal{H}_{2,k-1}(s), \mathcal{H}_{2,k}(s)] = 2^{-\Omega(\kappa)}$.

Proof. The only difference between these hybrids is that if $k \in C$, we switch sh_k to $\bot$ in the third step. So, suppose that $k \in C$, and consider the following reduction to the certified deletion security (see the full version for the definition) of $(\mathsf{Split}_{2\text{-}2}, \mathsf{Reconstruct}_{2\text{-}2}, \mathsf{Delete}_{2\text{-}2}, \mathsf{Verify}_{2\text{-}2})$. This experiment is parameterized by a bit b which determines which one of two secrets the certified deletion challenger will share.

- The reduction samples $C \leftarrow \mathcal{P}([n])$ and $(\mathsf{sh}_1, \ldots, \mathsf{sh}_n) \leftarrow \mathsf{CSplit}_\mathbb{S}(s)$, and sends $\{\mathsf{sh}_k, \bot\}$ to the challenger.
- The challenger samples $(|\mathsf{qsh}_k\rangle, \mathsf{csh}_k, \mathsf{vk}_k) \leftarrow \mathsf{Split}_{2\text{-}2}(1^\kappa, \mathsf{sh}_k)$ if $b = 0$ or $(|\mathsf{qsh}_k\rangle, \mathsf{csh}_k, \mathsf{vk}_k) \leftarrow \mathsf{Split}_{2\text{-}2}(1^\kappa, \bot)$ if $b = 1$, and sends $|\mathsf{qsh}_k\rangle$ to the reduction.
- For each $i \in [n] \setminus \{k\}$, if $i < k$ and $i \in C$, the reduction samples $(|\mathsf{qsh}_i\rangle, \mathsf{csh}_i, \mathsf{vk}_i) \leftarrow \mathsf{Split}_{2\text{-}2}(1^\kappa, \bot)$, and otherwise samples $(|\mathsf{qsh}_i\rangle, \mathsf{csh}_i, \mathsf{vk}_i) \leftarrow \mathsf{Split}_{2\text{-}2}(1^\kappa, \mathsf{sh}_i)$.
- Let $t^* \in [\ell]$ be such that $k \in P_{t^*}$. For each $i \in [n] \setminus \{k\}$, the reduction samples $(\mathsf{csh}_{i,1}, \ldots, \mathsf{csh}_{i,n}) \leftarrow \mathsf{CSplit}_\mathbb{S}(\mathsf{csh}_i)$. Next, the reduction samples $\{\mathsf{csh}_{k,i}\}_{i \in P_{t^*}} \leftarrow \mathsf{Sim}(P_{t^*})$, where Sim is the simulator guaranteed by the privacy of $(\mathsf{CSplit}_\mathbb{S}, \mathsf{CReconstruct}_\mathbb{S})$.
- For each $i \in P_{t^*}$, initialize register $\mathcal{S}_i$ to $|\mathsf{qsh}_i\rangle, \{\mathsf{csh}_{j,i}\}_{j \in [n]}$.
- The reduction runs $(\{\mathsf{cert}_i\}_{i \in P_{t^*}}, \mathcal{R}'_{t^*}) \leftarrow \mathsf{Adv}_{t^*}(\{\mathcal{S}_i\}_{i \in P_{t^*}}, \mathcal{R}_{t^*})$, and sends cert_k to the challenger.
- The challenger checks whether $\mathsf{Verify}_{2\text{-}2}(\mathsf{vk}_k, \mathsf{cert}_k) = \top$. If so, the challenger returns csh_k, and otherwise the experiment aborts and outputs $\bot$.

– The reduction samples $\{\mathsf{csh}_{k,i}\}_{i\in[n]\setminus P_{t^*}}$ conditioned on the joint distribution of $(\mathsf{csh}_{k,1},\ldots,\mathsf{csh}_{k,n})$ being identical to $\mathsf{CSplit}_\mathbb{S}(\mathsf{csh}_k)$. This is possible due to the guarantee of $\mathsf{Sim}(P_{t^*})$, that is,

$$\{\{\mathsf{csh}_{k,i}\}_{i\in P_{t^*}} : (\mathsf{csh}_{k,1},\ldots,\mathsf{csh}_{k,n}) \leftarrow \mathsf{CSplit}_\mathbb{S}(\mathsf{csh}_k)\}$$
$$\equiv \{\{\mathsf{csh}_{k,i}\}_{i\in P_{t^*}} : \{\mathsf{csh}_{k,i}\}_{i\in P_{t^*}} \leftarrow \mathsf{Sim}(P_{t^*})\}.$$

– For each $i \in [n]\setminus P_{t^*}$, the reduction initializes register $\mathcal{S}_i$ to $|\mathsf{qsh}_i\rangle$, $\{\mathsf{csh}_{j,i}\}_{j\in[n]}$.
– For each $t \in [\ell]\setminus\{t^*\}$, run $(\{\mathsf{cert}_i\}_{i\in P_t}, \mathcal{R}'_t) \leftarrow \mathsf{Adv}_t(\{\mathcal{S}_i\}_{i\in P_t}, \mathcal{R}_t)$.
– Let $C^* := \{i : \mathsf{Verify}_{2\text{-}2}(\mathsf{vk}_i, i, \mathsf{cert}_i) = \top\}$. The reduction outputs $(\mathcal{R}'_1,\ldots,\mathcal{R}'_\ell)$ if $C = C^*$ and $[n]\setminus C^* \notin \mathbb{S}$, and otherwise outputs $\bot$.

Observe that in the case $b = 0$, the output of this experiment is identical to $\mathcal{H}_{2,k-1}(s)$ while if $b = 1$, the output of this experiment is identical to $\mathcal{H}_{2,k}(s)$. Thus, the claim follows from the certified deletion security of $(\mathsf{Split}_{2\text{-}2}, \mathsf{Reconstruct}_{2\text{-}2}, \mathsf{Delete}_{2\text{-}2}, \mathsf{Verify}_{2\text{-}2})$. □

Thus, by combining Proposition 3 and Proposition 4, we have that

$$\mathsf{TD}\left[\mathcal{H}_1(s_0), \mathcal{H}_1(s_1)\right] = 2n \cdot 2^{-\Omega(\kappa)} \leq 2^{-\Omega(\{\max\{\lambda,n\}^2\})}.$$

However, this violates Proposition 2, since

$$2^{-\Omega(\{\max\{\lambda,n\}^2\})} < \mathsf{nonnegl}(\lambda) \cdot 2^{-n},$$

which completes the proof. □

6 Threshold Secret Sharing with Adaptive Certified Deletion

In this section, we show how to construct a secret sharing scheme for threshold access structures that satisfies adaptive certified deletion (Definition 4).

6.1 Construction

Our construction is given in Fig. 3, which uses a set of parameters described in Fig. 2. We provide some intuition about the parameter settings here.

The secret is encoded in a polynomial f of degree p. For security, we need p to be at least as large as the number of points of f that the adversary can learn. At most, the adversary can hold up to $k-1$ intact shares and the residual states of $n-k+1$ deleted shares. Each of the $k-1$ intact shares contains t' evaluations of f. Additionally, the adversary may retain some small amount of information about each of the deleted shares. We upper bound the retained information by a parameter ℓ for each share. This gives the adversary a maximum of

$$(k-1)t' + (n-k+1)\ell$$

> The construction in Figure 3 uses the following parameters.[a]
>
> - Each share consists of t total $\mathbb{K}$-registers, where
>
> $$t = (k+1)r\left(1 + \frac{(n-k+1)\log(\lambda)}{\lambda}\right) + 1$$
>
> - A share is divided into r check indices and $t' = t - r$ data indices, where
>
> $$r = (\lambda + (n-k+1)\log(\lambda))^2$$
>
> - ℓ intuitively represents an upper bound on the amount of information which is not destroyed when an adversary generates a valid deletion certificate for a share.
>
> $$\ell = t\frac{\log(\lambda)}{\sqrt{r}}$$
>
> See the proof of security in the full version for a more precise usage of ℓ.
> - The secret will be encoded in a polynomial of degree
>
> $$p = (k-1)t' + (n-k+1)\ell$$
>
> ---
> [a] The parameters provided here are slightly looser than necessary, to facilitate easier inspection. We present a tighter set of parameters in the full version.

Fig. 2. Parameters for Secret Sharing with Adaptive Certified Deletion

evaluations of f, which becomes the minimum safe setting for p.

Each share will also include a number of "check positions", which contain Fourier basis states that are used for verification of deletion. The number of check positions r and upper bound ℓ are set roughly so that with overwhelming probability, the adversary can retain no more than ℓ evaluations of f when it deletes a share (more precisely, the adversary may retain a *superposition* over potentially different sets of ℓ evaluations). The reader may find it useful to think of ℓ as being the maximum number of unexamined positions in a classical string x when an adversary successfully creates a string y that matches x on r random verification indices. Finally, the total size t of each share is set so that k shares contain less than $(kt - p)/2$ check positions, which is the maximum number of errors that can be corrected in kt evaluations of a polynomial of degree p (see the full version).

Theorem 5. *There exists secret sharing for threshold access structures which satisfies adaptive certified deletion.*

Proof. The construction is given in Fig. 3. Deletion correctness is apparent from inspection of the construction. We prove reconstruction correctness in Lemma 1. See Sect. 2.2 for an overview of the security proof and the full version for more details. □

Parameters: Let $\mathbb{F}_2$ be the binary field and let $\mathbb{K}$ be the field with $2^{\lceil \log_2(nt+1) \rceil}$ elements. See Figure 2 for descriptions and settings of the parameters t, t', r, ℓ, and p.

$\mathsf{Split}_{(k,n)}(1^\lambda, s)$

- Sample a random polynomial f with coefficients in $\mathbb{K}$ and degree p such that $f(0) = s$.
- For each $i \in [n]$:
  1. Sample a random set of indices $J_i \subset [t]$ of size $t' = t - r$.
  2. For each $j \in J_i$, set $|\psi_{i,j}\rangle = |f(it+j)\rangle$. These are the t' data positions.
  3. For each $j \in [t]\setminus J_i$, sample a uniform element $y_{i,j} \leftarrow \mathbb{K}$ and set $|\psi_{i,j}\rangle = H^{\otimes \lceil \log_2(n+1) \rceil} |y_{i,j}\rangle$. These are the r check positions.
  4. Initialize register $\mathcal{S}_i$ to $\bigotimes_{j=1}^{t} |\psi_{i,j}\rangle$.
- Set $\mathsf{vk} = \{J_i, \{y_{i,j}\}_{j\in[t]\setminus J_i}\}_{i\in[n]}$.

$\mathsf{Reconstruct}_{(k,n)}(1^\lambda, \{\mathcal{S}_i\}_{i\in P})$

- If $|P| < k$, output $\bot$. Otherwise, set P' to be any k shares in P.
- For each $i \in P'$, measure $\mathcal{S}_i$ in the computational basis to obtain $y_i = (y_{i,1}, \ldots, y_{i,t}) \in \mathbb{K}^t$.
- Compute $f \leftarrow \mathsf{Correct}_{\mathbb{K},p}(\{(it+j, y_{i,j})\}_{i\in P', j\in[t]})$, as defined in the full version.
- Output $f(0)$.

$\mathsf{Delete}_{(k,n)}(1^\lambda, \mathcal{S}_i)$

- Parse $\mathcal{S}_i$ as a sequence of $t\lceil \log_2(n+1) \rceil$ single qubit registers, measure each qubit register in Hadamard basis and output the result cert.

$\mathsf{Verify}_{(k,n)}(1^\lambda, \mathsf{vk}, i, \mathsf{cert})$

- Parse $\mathsf{vk} = \{J_i, \{y_{i,j}\}_{j\in[t]\setminus J_i}\}_{i\in[n]}$, and parse $\mathsf{cert} \in \mathbb{K}^t$ as a sequence of t elements of $\mathbb{K}$. Output $\top$ if $\mathsf{cert}_j = y_{i,j}$ for every $j \in J_i$, and $\bot$ otherwise.

Fig. 3. Construction for Secret Sharing with Adaptive Certified Deletion

Lemma 1. *The construction in Fig. 3 using parameters from Fig. 2 has reconstruction correctness.*

Proof. The set $\{(it+j, y_{i,j})\}_{i\in P', j\in[t]}$ contains kt pairs which were obtained by measuring k shares. As mentioned in the full version, if all but $e < (kt-p)/2$ of these pairs $(it+j, y_{i,j})$ satisfy $y_{i,j} = f(it+j)$, then $\mathsf{Correct}_{\mathbb{K},p}$ recovers the original polynomial f, where $f(0) = s$. The only points which do not satisfy this are the check positions, of which there are r per share, for a total of kr.

Therefore for correctness, we require that

$$2kr < kt - p \tag{14}$$
$$= kt - (k-1)(t-r) - (n-k+1)\ell \tag{15}$$
$$= t + (k-1)r - (n-k+1)\ell \tag{16}$$

Therefore $t - (n-k+1)\ell > (k+1)r$. Substituting $\ell = t\frac{\log(\lambda)}{\sqrt{r}}$ yields

$$t\left(1 - (n-k+1)\frac{\log(\lambda)}{\sqrt{r}}\right) > (k+1)r \tag{17}$$

$$t > (k+1)r \frac{1}{1 - (n-k+1)\frac{\log(\lambda)}{\sqrt{r}}} \tag{18}$$

$$= (k+1)r \frac{\sqrt{r}}{\sqrt{r} - (n-k+1)\log(\lambda)} \tag{19}$$

$$= (k+1)r \left(1 + \frac{(n-k+1)\log(\lambda)}{\sqrt{r} - (n-k+1)\log(\lambda)}\right) \tag{20}$$

$$= (k+1)r \left(1 + \frac{(n-k+1)\log(\lambda)}{\lambda + (n-k+1)\log(\lambda) - (n-k+1)\log(\lambda)}\right) \tag{21}$$

$$= (k+1)r \left(1 + \frac{(n-k+1)\log(\lambda)}{\lambda}\right) \tag{22}$$

Note that Eq. (18) requires that $\left(1 - (n-k+1)t\frac{\log(\lambda)}{\sqrt{r}}\right) > 0$. Since the number of check positions is $r = (\lambda + (n-k+1)\log(\lambda))^2$, we have

$$1 - (n-k+1)\frac{\log(\lambda)}{\lambda + (n-k+1)\log(\lambda)} > 1 - \frac{(n-k+1)\log(\lambda)}{(n-k+1)\log(\lambda)} = 0 \tag{23}$$

Finally, observe that the choice of parameters in the construction satisfies these constraints. □

Acknowledgements. We thank Orestis Chardouvelis and Dakshita Khurana for collaboration and insightful discussions during the early stages of this research.

References

1. Agarwal, A., Bartusek, J., Khurana, D., Kumar, N.: A new framework for quantum oblivious transfer. In: Hazay, C., Stam, M. (eds.) EUROCRYPT 2023, Part I. LNCS, vol. 14004, pp. 363–394. Springer, Heidelberg (2023). https://doi.org/10.1007/978-3-031-30545-0_13
2. Applebaum, B., Beimel, A., Farràs, O., Nir, O., Peter, N.: Secret-sharing schemes for general and uniform access structures. In: Ishai, Y., Rijmen, V. (eds.) EUROCRYPT 2019, Part III. LNCS, vol. 11478, pp. 441–471. Springer, Heidelberg (2019). https://doi.org/10.1007/978-3-030-17659-4_15

3. Bartusek, J., Goyal, V., Khurana, D., Malavolta, G., Raizes, J., Roberts, B.: Software with certified deletion. In: Eurocrypt 2024 (2024, to appear)
4. Bartusek, J., Khurana, D.: Cryptography with certified deletion. In: Handschuh, H., Lysyanskaya, A. (eds.) CRYPTO 2023, Part V. LNCS, vol. 14085, pp. 192–223. Springer, Heidelberg (2023). https://doi.org/10.1007/978-3-031-38554-4_7
5. Bartusek, J., Khurana, D., Malavolta, G., Poremba, A., Walter, M.: Weakening assumptions for publicly-verifiable deletion. In: Rothblum, G., Wee, H. (eds.) Theory of Cryptography, vol. 14372, pp. 183–197. Springer, Cham (2023). https://doi.org/10.1007/978-3-031-48624-1_7
6. Bartusek, J., Khurana, D., Poremba, A.: Publicly-verifiable deletion via target-collapsing functions. In: Handschuh, H., Lysyanskaya, A. (eds.) CRYPTO 2023, Part V. LNCS, vol. 14085, pp. 99–128. Springer, Heidelberg (2023)
7. Beimel, A.: Secret-sharing schemes: a survey. In: Chee, Y.M., et al. (eds.) IWCC 2011. LNCS, vol. 6639, pp. 11–46. Springer, Heidelberg (2011). https://doi.org/10.1007/978-3-642-20901-7_2
8. Josh Cohen Benaloh and Jerry Leichter: Generalized secret sharing and monotone functions. In: Goldwasser, S. (ed.) CRYPTO'88. LNCS, vol. 403, pp. 27–35. Springer, Heidelberg (1990). https://doi.org/10.1007/0-387-34799-2_3
9. Blakley, G.R.: Safeguarding cryptographic keys. In: 1979 International Workshop on Managing Requirements Knowledge (MARK), pp. 313–318 (1979)
10. Bouman, N.J., Fehr, S.: Sampling in a quantum population, and applications. In: Rabin, T. (ed.) CRYPTO 2010. LNCS, vol. 6223, pp. 724–741. Springer, Heidelberg (2010). https://doi.org/10.1007/978-3-642-14623-7_39
11. Broadbent, A., Islam, R.: Quantum encryption with certified deletion. In: Pass, R., Pietrzak, K. (eds.) TCC 2020. LNCS, vol. 12552, pp. 92–122. Springer, Cham (2020). https://doi.org/10.1007/978-3-030-64381-2_4
12. Damgård, I., Fehr, S., Lunemann, C., Salvail, L., Schaffner, C.: Improving the security of quantum protocols via commit-and-open. In: Halevi, S. (ed.) CRYPTO 2009. LNCS, vol. 5677, pp. 408–427. Springer, Heidelberg (2009)
13. Desmedt, Y., Frankel, Y.: Threshold cryptosystems. In: Brassard, G. (ed.) CRYPTO 1989. LNCS, vol. 435, pp. 307–315. Springer, New York (1990). https://doi.org/10.1007/0-387-34805-0_28
14. Hiroka, T., Kitagawa, F., Morimae, T., Nishimaki, R., Pal, T., Yamakawa, T.: Certified everlasting secure collusion-resistant functional encryption, and more. In: Eurocrypt 2024 (2024, to appear)
15. Hiroka, T., Morimae, T., Nishimaki, R., Yamakawa, T.: Quantum encryption with certified deletion, revisited: public key, attribute-based, and classical communication. In: Tibouchi, M., Wang, H. (eds.) ASIACRYPT 2021, Part I. LNCS, vol. 13090, pp. 606–636. Springer, Cham (2021). https://doi.org/10.1007/978-3-030-92062-3_21
16. Hiroka, T., Morimae, T., Nishimaki, R., Yamakawa, T.: Certified everlasting zero-knowledge proof for QMA. In: Dodis, Y., Shrimpton, T. (eds.) CRYPTO 2022, Part I. LNCS, vol. 13507, pp. 239–268. Springer, Heidelberg (2022). https://doi.org/10.1007/978-3-031-15802-5_9
17. Ito, M., Saito, A., Nishizeki, T.: Secret sharing schemes realizing general access structure. In: Proceedings of the IEEE Global Telecommunication Conference (Globecom'87), pp. 99–102 (1987)
18. Kitagawa, F., Nishimaki, R., Yamakawa, T.: Publicly verifiable deletion from minimal assumptions. In: Rothblum, G.N., Wee, H. (eds.) TCC 2023, Part IV. LNCS, vol. 14372, pp. 228–245. Springer, Cham (2023). https://doi.org/10.1007/978-3-031-48624-1_9

19. Liu, T., Vaikuntanathan, V.: Breaking the circuit-size barrier in secret sharing. In: Proceedings of the 50th Annual ACM SIGACT Symposium on Theory of Computing, STOC 2018, page 699-708, New York, NY, USA, 2018. Association for Computing Machinery (2018)
20. Poremba, A.: Quantum proofs of deletion for learning with errors. In: Tauman Kalai, Y. (ed.) 14th Innovations in Theoretical Computer Science Conference (ITCS 2023), volume 251 of *Leibniz International Proceedings in Informatics (LIPIcs)*, pp. 90:1–90:14, Dagstuhl, Germany (2023). Schloss Dagstuhl – Leibniz-Zentrum für Informatik
21. Reed, I.S., Solomon, G.: Polynomial codes over certain finite fields. J. Soc. Ind. Appl. Math. **8**(2), 300–304 (1960)
22. Renner, R., König, R.: Universally composable privacy amplification against quantum adversaries. In: Kilian, J. (ed.) TCC 2005. LNCS, vol. 3378, pp. 407–425. Springer, Heidelberg (2005). https://doi.org/10.1007/978-3-540-30576-7_22
23. Shamir, A.: How to share a secret. Commun. Assoc. Comput. Mach. **22**(11), 612–613 (1979)

On Central Primitives for Quantum Cryptography with Classical Communication

Kai-Min Chung[1](✉), Eli Goldin[2], and Matthew Gray[3]

[1] Academia Sinica, Taipei, Taiwan
kmchung@iis.sinica.edu.tw
[2] New York University, New York, USA
eli.goldin@nyu.edu
[3] University of Oxford, Oxford, UK
matthew.gray@cs.ox.ac.uk

Abstract. Recent work has introduced the "Quantum-Computation Classical-Communication" (QCCC) (Chung et al.) setting for cryptography. There has been some evidence that One Way Puzzles (OWPuzz) are the natural central cryptographic primitive for this setting (Khurana and Tomer). For a primitive to be considered central it should have several characteristics. It should be well behaved (which for this paper we will think of as having amplification, combiners, and universal constructions); it should be implied by a wide variety of other primitives; and it should be equivalent to some class of useful primitives. We present combiners, correctness and security amplification, and a universal construction for OWPuzz. Our proof of security amplification uses a new and cleaner construction of EFI from OWPuzz (in comparison to the result of Khurana and Tomer) that generalizes to weak OWPuzz and is the most technically involved section of the paper. It was previously known that OWPuzz are implied by other primitives of interest including commitments, symmetric key encryption, one way state generators (OWSG), and therefore pseudorandom states (PRS). However we are able to rule out OWPuzz's equivalence to many of these primitives by showing a black box separation between general OWPuzz and a restricted class of OWPuzz (those with efficient verification, which we call EV − OWPuzz). We then show that EV − OWPuzz are also implied by most of these primitives, which separates them from OWPuzz as well. This separation also separates extending PRS from highly compressing PRS answering an open question of Ananth et al.

1 Introduction

In the realm of cryptography, there is perhaps no primitive more important than one-way functions. A one-way function is an efficiently computable deterministic function which is easy to compute, but hard to invert. Although at first glance the definition seems simple, one-way functions are special for several reasons.

First and foremost, one-way functions are "minimal." If modern cryptography exists in any form, then one-way functions must also exist [HILL99, IL89, Imp95]. Furthermore, pretty much all of these constructions are obvious. Second, one-way functions are "useful." There is a large class of cryptographic primitives (known as Minicrypt) which can all be built from and are equivalent to one-way functions [Imp95]. Included in Minicrypt are symmetric key encryption, pseudorandom generators, and commitment schemes [HILL99, GGM86, Nao91]. Finally, one-way functions are "well-behaved." They satisfy several natural properties [Lev87], and are equivalent to most of their variants [Yao82, IL89]. Due to these three characteristics of one-way functions, one of the most useful things to do when trying to understand a new classical cryptographic primitive is to compare it to a one-way function.

This centrality of one-way functions no longer holds once quantum computation enters the picture. In particular, in the quantum setting, it seems that one-way functions are no longer minimal [Kre21]. In particular, there exists a quantum oracle relative to which one-way functions do not exist, but quantum cryptography (in the form of pseudorandom state generators, quantum bit commitments, and many other primitives) is still possible. Recently, there has been strong evidence in support of a new simple primitive, the EFI pair, being minimal [KT24, BCQ22]. An EFI pair is a pair of efficiently samplable quantum mixed states which are indistinguishable yet statistically far. Furthermore, EFI pairs are also useful. They can be used to build a large number of quantum cryptographic primitives, from quantum bit commitments to secure multiparty computation [BCQ22, AQY22]. Finally, EFI pairs are fairly well-behaved. The security of EFI pairs can be amplified [BQSY23], there exists combiners and universal constructions for EFI pairs [HKNY23], and EFI pairs are also equivalent to some of their variants [HMY23].

In the classical setting, it appears that one-way functions serve as an effective minimal primitive. In the quantum output setting, EFI pairs are a promising candidate for our minimal primitive. A number of recent works have also considered a hybrid setting, primitives where the cryptographic algorithms are quantum, but all communication and outputs are classical [ACC+22, ALY23a, CLM23, KT24]. In the style of [ACC+22], we will refer to this as the quantum computation classical communication (QCCC) setting. An immediate and natural question about this setting is "what is a good central primitive?"

Just like in the fully quantum setting, it is unlikely that one-way functions can be a minimal primitive in the QCCC setting. In particular, there is a barrier to building one-way functions from a QCCC primitive known as the one-way puzzle [KT24, Kre21]. A one-way puzzle consists of an efficient quantum sampler which produces keys and puzzles along with a (possibly inefficient) verification procedure. The one-wayness corresponds to the idea that given a puzzle, it should be hard to find a matching key. Although one-way functions cannot serve as a central QCCC primitive, at first glance one-way puzzles make a fairly good candidate. In particular, one-way puzzles are minimal in the sense that almost all QCCC primitives can be used to build one-way puzzles [KT24].

On the other hand, their well-behavedness and usefulness are less clear. It is known that one-way puzzles can be used to build EFI pairs (and thus everything which follows from EFI pairs) [KT24]. However, as far as the authors are aware, there are no existing constructions of QCCC style primitives from one-way puzzles. The well-behavedness of one-way puzzles is similarly unstudied.

Our Results. In this work, we seek to investigate what primitives can be built from one-way puzzles, as well what useful properties one-way puzzles may or may not satisfy. Whether or not one-way puzzles are adopted as a central primitive in the same manner as one-way functions or EFI pairs is a community matter, but we hope that our results help shed light onto the question. To summarize our results, we show that

1. There exists a robust combiner for one-way puzzles. That is, given two candidate one-way puzzles, there is a way to combine the candidates to get a construction which is secure as long as one of the candidates is secure.
2. There exists a universal construction of a one-way puzzle. That is, a construction which is secure as long as one-way puzzles exist.
3. There exist amplification theorems for one-way puzzles. That is, there is a method to take a one-way puzzle with weakened correctness or security guarantees and transform it into a full one-way puzzle.
4. We show that one-way puzzles can be built from EFID pairs (the QCCC version of EFI pairs).
5. We show that one-way puzzles are equivalent to one-way puzzles whose key is generated uniformly at random, answering an open question of [KT24].

We also consider in detail an important restricted variant of one-way puzzles, which was first introduced under the name "hard quantum planted problem for QCMA," [KNY23], but which we will refer to as efficiently verifiable one-way puzzles. We show the following results about this variant

1. There exists combiners, a universal construction, and amplification theorems for efficiently verifiable one-way puzzles.
2. Most QCCC primitives which can be used to build one-way puzzles can also be used to build efficiently verifiable one-way puzzles, with the notable exception of interactive commitment schemes. In particular, we show explicitly that pseudodeterministic PRGs and non-interactive commitments imply efficiently verifiable one-way puzzles.
3. There exists a quantum oracle relative to which one-way puzzles and pseudorandom states exist but efficiently verifiable one-way puzzles do not.

The last two points here together provide a barrier to building most QCCC primitives from one-way puzzles. Perhaps this means that efficiently verifiable one-way puzzles make a better candidate for centrality. However, if QCCC commitments can be built from one-way puzzles, then it may make sense to treat one-way puzzles as a central primitive on a lower level than efficiently verifiable one-way puzzles. We compare the relationship to the separation between one-way functions and one-way permutations.

In addition to this, since pesudorandom states also exist under the same oracle, our results provide a barrier to building most QCCC primitives from pseudorandom states.

Note that our separation in fact separates efficiently verifiable one-way puzzles from pseudorandom state generators with linear output. But it is not hard to show that pseudorandom state generators with logarithmic output can be used to build efficiently verifiable one-way puzzles. Thus, our final separation also provides a barrier to length reduction for pseudorandom state generators, answering an open question of [ALY23b].

A summary of known relationships between QCCC primitives is included in Fig. 1.

A Better Construction of EFI Pairs from One-Way Puzzles. The most technically demanding of our results is, surprisingly, the amplification theorem for one-way puzzles. It turns out that due to the inefficient nature of verification, most natural techniques fail. The techniques we use to achieve amplification for one-way puzzles can be also be used to construct EFI pairs from one-way puzzles, recreating a result from [KT24]. In addition, our construction has several advantages over the existing construction in the literature.

First, the proof of security for our construction is significantly more straightforward than the existing argument. In particular, the argument does not rely on techniques dealing explicitly with a preimage space (such as leftover hash lemma or Goldreich-Levin), and so more naturally fits with the quantum nature of the primitive. Second, our construction produces an EFI pair even when instantiated with a one-way puzzle with weakened security guarantees. This is the essential reason that this technique is useful for proving amplification.

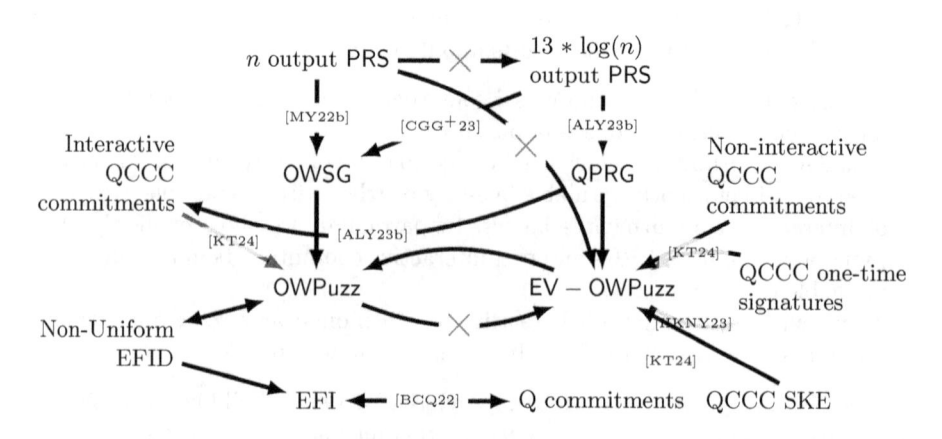

Fig. 1. All implications known about one-way puzzles (OWPuzz) and efficiently verifiable one-way puzzles (EV − OWPuzz).

2 Technical Overview

2.1 A Cleaner Construction of EFI Pairs from Any One-Way Puzzle

In a recent work by Khurana and Tomer [KT24], it was shown that there is a black-box construction of an EFI pair from any one-way puzzle. Since one-way puzzles can be built from one-way state generators, this then shows that if one-way state generators exist, so do EFI pairs (and thus quantum bit commitments).

Since EFI pairs intuitively are a "pseudorandom" primitive while one-way puzzles are a "one-way" primitive, the argument presented in [KT24] is heavily inspired by the classical construction of a pseudorandom generator from any one-way function, first shown in [HILL99].

The key idea behind [HILL99] is to first use the one-way function to construct something called a pseudoentropy generator. A pseudoentropy generator is simply a samplable distribution which is indistinguishable from another (not necessarily samplable) distribution with greater entropy. Then, the pseudoentropy generator is used to construct a non-uniform PRG. That is, a PRG where the construction takes in a short advice string of length $O(\log \lambda)$ depending on the security parameter. This gives out a different PRG candidate for each possible value of the advice string. Applying a PRG combiner to all of these candidates then gives a standard PRG.

[KT24] follows the same overall structure to build an EFI pair from any one-way puzzle. In particular, they show how to build a pseudoentropy generator from any one-way puzzle, and then show how to use a one-way puzzle to build something they refer to as an imbalanced EFID pair. An EFID pair is classical version of an EFI pair. We recall that a non-uniform EFID pair is an EFID pair that takes in a short advice string. An imbalanced EFID pair is a stronger primitive than a non-uniform EFID pair, where there are additional requirements on hiding and/or binding when the primitive is instantiated with incorrect advice. Finally, they show how to use an imbalanced EFID pair to build a standard EFI pair, although this technique requires switching to quantum output.

In this work, we present an alternative construction of EFI pairs from one-way puzzles, with several advantages. The foremost advantage, which is useful for our other results, is that our construction works even when instantiated with weak one-way puzzles. In addition to this, the proof of our construction is significantly simpler, and relies almost entirely on standard classical techniques.

Theorem 1 (Informal Version of Corollary 14). *If there exists a weak one-way puzzle, then there exists an EFI pair.*

The Overall Approach. While [KT24] relies on the techniques of [HILL99] to realize their construction, there have been a number of follow-up works succeeding [HILL99] providing more efficient constructions of PRGs from OWFs [HRV10, VZ12, MP23]. In particular, we observe that the techniques of [VZ12] are particularly "quantum-friendly," much more so than the techniques of [HILL99]. Furthermore, we make the (as far as we are aware) novel observation that the construction of [VZ12] gives a pseudorandom generator even when instantiated with a weak one-way function.

The Failure of Goldreich-Levin for Weak One-Way Puzzles. One key idea underlying [HILL99], as well as most other constructions of PRGs from one-way functions [HRV10, MP23], is to extract $H_{min}(x|f(x)) + O(\log n)$ bits of pseudoentropy from x given $f(x)$. The leftover hash lemma gives the ability to extract $H_{min}(x|f(x)) - O(\log n)$ bits of entropy from x, and Goldreich-Levin provides an extra $O(\log n)$ bits of pseudoentropy [GL89], so these two techniques together can extract a pseudorandom string of length $H_{min}(x|f(x)) + O(\log n)$ from x given $f(x)$.

In particular, the Goldreich-Levin theorem shows that if there is an algorithm distinguishing $\mathsf{Ext}(x)$ from uniform given $f(x)$ with advantage ϵ, then there is an algorithm computing x from $f(x)$ with probability $\mathsf{poly}(\epsilon)$ [GL89]. Since ϵ^2 is negligible for a strong one-way function, so is ϵ, and so these distributions are indistinguishable. However, if f is only a weak one-way function, then we only get a constant bound on the distinguishing advantage, and so the approaches of [HILL99, HRV10, MP23] all break down.

A similar approach, with some technically involved adjustments to handle quantum sampling, is done in [KT24] by using a quantum version of the Goldreich-Levin theorem [AC01]. In particular, [KT24] also relies on using Goldreich-Levin to extract $O(\log n)$ bits from the key k given the puzzle s. But for the same reason as before, this approach does not hold when the sampler is only weakly one-way.

Furthermore, there is a lot of technical care needed when using the leftover hash lemma and Goldreich-Levin on puzzles sampled using quantum randomness [KT24]. This is because the pre-image space of a puzzle is now a distribution over keys instead of a set, and so hashing techniques become significantly more complicated. Luckily, [VZ12] demonstrates a way to construct PRGs from one-way functions without relying on either of these techniques, providing an approach that is both quantum-friendly and applies even with weak security. A figure illustrating their construction is given in Fig. 2.

The Construction of [VZ12]. To build a PRG from a one-way function f, [VZ12] makes the observation that the distribution $(f(x), x)$ satisfies a property which they call KL-hard to sample. In particular, this means that for any sampler $\mathcal{S}$ (which in this case can be thought of as a distributional inverter),

$$KL(f(x), x || f(x), \mathcal{S}(f(x))) \geq \delta$$

for some value of $\delta \geq \frac{1}{\mathsf{poly}(\lambda)}$. Here KL refers to Kullback-Leibler divergence, or "relative entropy." They then adapt the techniques of [HRV10] to build a PRG from a distribution which is KL-hard to sample. Note that this construction requires knowledge of the entropy of the KL-hard to sample distribution. However, for a one-way function, $H(f(x), x) = |x|$ the input length of the one-way function.

For an ϵ one-way function, the KL-hardness parameter is $\delta = -\log \epsilon$. Thus, for a standard one-way function, $\delta = \omega(\log \lambda)$. But the techniques of [HRV10] apply whenever $\delta = \frac{1}{\mathsf{poly}(\lambda)}$, and so the techniques of [VZ12] work just as well for weak one-way functions. Thus, the same construction gives a PRG from any weak one-way functions.

Building a KL-Hard to Sample Distribution from a One-Way Puzzle. The key observation underlying [VZ12] is that KL divergence can only decrease from computation. That is, for any function F,

$$KL(F(X)||F(Y)) \leq KL(X||Y)$$

But the boolean function $F(y,x) = 1$ if and only if $f(x) = y$ is well-defined. So if $\mathcal{S}$ is any sampler,

$$KL(f(x), x || f(x), \mathcal{S}(f(x))) \geq KL(F(f(x), x) || F(f(x), \mathcal{S}(f(x))))$$
$$= KL(1 || Bern(p)) = -\log p$$

where p is the advantage of $\mathcal{S}$ in the one-way function security game. This immediately gives that the distribution $(f(x), x)$ is KL-hard to sample.

We observe that the same exact technique also works for one-way puzzles. In particular, let (Samp, Ver) be a one-way puzzle and let Samp $\to (k, s)$. The equivalent of checking if $f(x) = y$ is simply to run verification. And so

$$KL(s, k || s, \mathcal{S}(k)) \geq KL(\mathsf{Ver}(s, k) || \mathsf{Ver}(s, \mathcal{S}(k))) = KL(Bern(q) || Bern(p))$$

where p is the success probability of $\mathcal{S}$ in the one-way puzzle game and q is the correctness parameter of the one-way puzzle. Although we do not have $KL(Bern(q) || Bern(p)) = -\log p$, when Samp is a weak one-way puzzle, we can still lower bound $KL(s, k || s, \mathcal{S}(k))$ by $\frac{1}{\mathsf{poly}(\lambda)}$. And so (s, k) is KL-hard to sample.

Building a Non-uniform EFID Pair from a KL-Hard to Sample Distribution. Note that the techniques [VZ12] uses to build a PRG from a KL-hard to sample distribution are entirely black box, and so also work in the quantum setting. Thus, applying the same construction to (s, k) produces a pseudorandom distribution D with length $d = |D|$ depending on $H(k, s)$. When building a PRG, the approach [HRV10, VZ12] takes is to argue that D can be sampled by applying some function G to a uniformly random string of length $d' < d$, and so G is a PRG. Here, the randomness of the distribution is quantum, and so this idea will not apply directly. But similar reasoning can be used to show a upper bound on the entropy of D. In particular, we produce such an argument directly and show that $H(D) < d - \mathsf{poly}(\lambda)$. For a visualization of the construction of D, see Fig. 2.

We then observe that any distribution with sufficiently less entropy than its length must have some statistical distance from the uniform distribution. Thus,

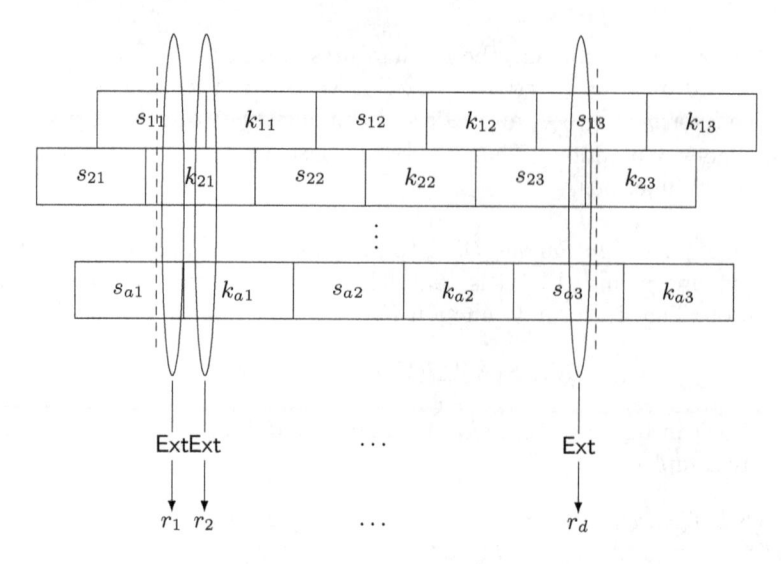

Fig. 2. The construction of [VZ12,HRV10] applied to a one-way puzzle Samp $\to (k,s)$. The idea is that many samples are taken and arranged in a grid. Then, each row is given a random offset, with both sides truncated. Finally, some number of random bits are extracted from each column using a pairwise-independent hash Ext. This produces a pseudorandom string with less than full entropy, and we can repeat to get a non-uniform EFID pair.

the [VZ12] construction applied to a one-way puzzle produces a distribution D which is indistinguishable from uniform but has noticeable statistical distance from uniform. We then use parallel repetition to boost the statistical distance to $1 - \mathsf{negl}(\lambda)$, and so the pair $(\mathcal{U}^t, D^t)$ forms a EFID pair.

Unfortunately, this construction has a number of pseudorandom bits dependent on $H(k,s)$. Thus, the EFID pair construction has to have knowledge of the entropy of the one-way puzzle sampler output. This can be done by giving the construction $\Theta(\log \lambda)$ bits of advice, and so instead of a full EFID pair, we get a non-uniform EFID pair.

From Non-uniform EFID Pairs to EFI Pairs. To recap, [KT24] built imbalanced EFID (a stronger version of non-uniform EFID) from one-way puzzles, while our technique only builds non-uniform EFID from one-way puzzles. Note that this is not a fundamental difference, upon observation it is clear that our construction also satisfies the requirements of imbalanced EFID.

However, the reason [KT24] required this stronger notion of non-uniform EFID was because, at the time that work was published, it was unknown how to build combiners for EFI pairs. Recent work (interestingly using similar techniques to [KT24]) has shown how to combine EFI pairs [HKNY23], and so using these techniques EFI pairs follow directly from non-uniform EFID.

2.2 Combiners and Universal Constructions

One major property satisfied by one-way functions is the existence of a universal construction [Lev87]. By this, we mean that there exists a specific construction of a one-way function which is secure if any one-way functions exist.

As shown originally by Levin [Lev87] and formalized in [HKN+05], this useful fact is essentially a corollary of the fact that there exists *robust combiners* for one-way functions. That is, given any two one-way function candidates f and g, there is a construction $h^{f,g}$ such that h is one-way as long as one of f or g is one-way.

The universal one-way function is then defined as follows. Take the first $\log \lambda$ Turing machines and treat them as one-way function candidates. Running the combiner on all these candidates results in a universal one-way function f_U. As long as one-way functions exist, there is a Turing machine with some constant length which acts as a good one-way function. Thus, for all sufficiently large λ, f_U will also be a one-way function.

Since both combiners and universal constructions are highly desirable properties, we would like to investigate whether robust combiners also exist for one-way puzzles. We thus prove the following theorem.

Theorem 2 (Informal Version of Corollary 11). *There exists a robust combiner for one-way puzzles.*

with the following corollary

Corollary 1 (Informal Version of Theorem 26). *There exists a pair of algorithms* $(\mathsf{Samp}_U, \mathsf{Ver}_U)$ *such that as long as one-way puzzles exist,* $(\mathsf{Samp}_U, \mathsf{Ver}_U)$ *is a one-way puzzle.*

Note that it has been shown that combiners and universal constructions exist for quantum primitives which both imply one-way puzzles and are implied by one-way puzzles, namely one-way state generators and EFI pairs respectively [HKNY23]. Thus, this result should not be particularly surprising. However, none of the arguments for constructing combiners for one-way state generators, EFI pairs, or one-way functions translate directly into building combiners for one-way puzzles.

Note that if we know that both candidate one-way puzzles satisfy correctness, then it is easy to construct a combiner. In particular, running both candidate samplers in parallel and having the verification algorithm accept if and only if both candidate verification algorithms accept is enough to ensure that the combined construction satisfy both correctness and security.

However, if we omit the correctness requirement, then it is possible that the "bad" verification algorithm always rejects. In this case, the combiner we defined previously will also not satisfy correctness.

To resolve this issue, we follow the template of [HKNY23] and show that there is a "correctness guaranteeing" procedure for any one-way puzzle. Namely

Theorem 3 (Informal Version of Corollary 9). *Let* (Samp, Ver) *be a one-way puzzle candidate. There exists a construction* (Samp', Ver') *where* Samp', Ver' *depend on* (Samp, Ver) *satisfying the following*

1. *If* (Samp, Ver) *is a one-way puzzle, then so is* (Samp', Ver').
2. *Regardless of whether* (Samp, Ver) *is a one-way puzzle,* (Samp', Ver') *satisfies one-way puzzle correctness.*

If we apply this correctness amplification procedure to the candidate one-way puzzles and then apply the security combiner described earlier, we achieve a robust combiner for one-way puzzles.

The main question remaining is how to actually do this correctness amplification. The natural approach to correctness guaranteeing (which is analogous to the approach used by [HKNY23]) is to have the sampler check whether verification passes on its produced key-puzzle pair. If not, the sampler will output a special symbol $\bot$, on which the verifier will always accept. However, this approach requires that the sampler be able to run the verifier. But for one-way puzzles, the verification algorithm may not be efficient.

Our solution is to defer the checking step to the verification algorithm itself. In particular, we will say that a puzzle is good if the probability that verification passes when it is naturally generated is high. Since our verification algorithm is inefficient, it has the computational resources to check if a given puzzle is good. The key idea, then is that we modify verification to automatically accept any good puzzle.

If the scheme originally satisfied correctness, then all but a negligible fraction of puzzles will be good and so we do not compromise security. Furthermore, since the probability that verification fails on a good puzzle is by definition low, the probability that the modified verification fails will also be low. Note that this style of correctness guaranteeing will only give a guarantee that the correctness error is below some constant (say $1/2$). We can then boost to full correctness through parallel repetition.

A Note on the Definition of One-Way Puzzles. The original definition of one-way puzzles introduced required that the verification procedure be represented by a Turing machine which is guaranteed to halt (i.e. a decider) [KT24]. When defining a robust combiner for use in a universal construction, it is necessary that the combiner work even if one of the candidate verification algorithms does not halt. This makes building a combiner seemingly as difficult as solving the halting problem.

We instead define one-way puzzles so that verification can be any arbitrary function. Note that, because Ver is never actually run, all known constructions using one-way puzzles go through when using this weakened definition. In addition, under our definition, combiners and universal constructions exist. Thus, we believe that this generalized definition is the "right" definition of a one-way puzzle, and that the restriction of verification to halting Turing machines used by [KT24] is unnecessarily restrictive.

2.3 Amplification of One-Way Puzzles

A second desirable property for a central primitive to have is an amplification theorem. In particular, given a one-way function with a weaker security guarantee, it is possible to build a normal one-way function. This makes it significantly easier to construct one-way functions from other primitives as well as produce candidate one-way functions.

Thus, one may wonder whether the same is true for one-way puzzles. That is, given a one-way puzzle with a weakened security guarantee, is it possible to build a normal one-way puzzle? We can also ask the same question of correctness. Given a one-way puzzle with a weakened correctness guarantee, is it possible to build a normal one-way puzzle?

In particular, we define (α, β) one-way puzzles, where α is the correctness error and β the security error. Observe that standard one-way puzzles are simply $(\mathsf{negl}(\lambda), \mathsf{negl}(\lambda))$ one-way puzzles. We show the following

Theorem 4 (Restatement of Theorem 20). *If there exists a $(1 - 1/\mathsf{poly}(\lambda), \mathsf{negl}(\lambda))$ one-way puzzle, then there exists a $(\mathsf{negl}(\lambda), \mathsf{negl}(\lambda))$ one-way puzzle.*

Theorem 5 (Restatement of Theorem 22). *If there exists a $(\mathsf{negl}(\lambda), 1 - 1/\mathsf{poly}(\lambda))$ one-way puzzle, then there exists a $(\mathsf{negl}(\lambda), \mathsf{negl}(\lambda))$ one-way puzzle.*

Amplifying Security. For the purposes of this section, we will refer to a $(\mathsf{negl}(\lambda), 1 - 1/\mathsf{poly}(\lambda))$ one-way puzzle as a weak one-way puzzle. We will also refer to the standard notion of a one-way puzzle as a strong one-way puzzle. The question of security amplification can then be rephrased as "can we build a strong one-way puzzle from any weak one-way puzzle?"

Recently, [BQSY23] showed that parallel repetition amplifies soundness guarantees for any 3 round quantum interactive protocol. At first glace, one might think that this result immediately gives a security amplification theorem for one-way puzzles.

Upon observation, it turns out that the argument of [BQSY23] relies on the assumption that the security game itself can be run efficiently. But the one-way puzzle security game requires running the verification algorithm, which has no guarantees on efficiency. And so the obvious approach to amplifying security falls short in this setting.

But what can we do? Our key observation is that strong one-way puzzles can be built from EFID pairs (which we recall is the classical version of an EFI pair). In addition, [KT24] shows that one-way puzzles can be used to build EFID pairs, and along the way they show that strong one-way puzzles can be used to build a variant of EFID pairs, which we here call a non-uniform EFID pair. Unfortunately, their techniques do not work for weak one-way puzzles, an issue we remedy in Sect. 2.1.

The outline of our argument is to use our improved construction of EFI pairs from one-way puzzles from Sect. 2.1, which shows that we can build non-uniform

EFID pairs from weak one-way puzzles as well. We then show how to build strong one-way puzzles from non-uniform EFID pairs.

Building Strong One-Way Puzzles from Non-uniform EFID. Recall, a non-uniform cryptographic primitive is a cryptographic primitive where the construction takes in a short advice string of length $O(\log \lambda)$. Our construction of strong one-way puzzles from EFID pairs then allows us to build a non-uniform strong one-way puzzle from a non-uniform EFID pair. For each possible advice string s, we can instantiate the non-uniform strong one-way puzzle with s to get a new strong one-way puzzle candidate. For each security parameter, one of these candidates is a strong one-way puzzle. Thus, using a combiner on all of these candidates simultaneously produces a strong one-way puzzle which does not need any advice string.

We remark that in general, if we have a robust combiner for a primitive then we can turn any non-uniform construction of that primitive into its full version.

Amplifying Correctness. To amplify correctness, we observe that our correctness guaranteer will always increase correctness at some cost to security. By carefully tracking this cost and interleaving with security amplification, it is possible to boost to full correctness without hurting security.

2.4 Relationships with Other QCCC Primitives

It has been shown in [KT24] that one-way puzzles can be built from almost all QCCC style primitives. In particular, they show how to build a one-way puzzle from a digital signature, a symmetric encryption protocol, or a commitment scheme. Just as a one-way function can be built from any useful classical primitive, a one-way puzzle can be built from any useful QCCC primitive.

Note that minimality of a primitive is not very hard to achieve. As an example, any primitive which can be built unconditionally is at least as minimal as a one-way function. But, importantly, one-way functions are also *useful*. One-way functions can be used to construct a large class of important cryptographic primitives, often referred to as symmetric key or Minicrypt primitives. In particular, one-way functions can be used to build (classical) digital signatures, symmetric encryption protocols, and commitment schemes. Thus, if we want to treat one-way puzzles as a central primitive for QCCC cryptography, it seems important that one-way puzzles imply at least one more directly useful QCCC primitive.

Unfortunately, existing results in this direction are noticeably weaker. In particular, as far as the authors are aware, the only QCCC primitive for which a construction is known from one-way puzzles is non-uniform EFID pairs [KT24]. Instead, there are *quantum output* implications of one-way puzzles. In particular, it is known how to build commitments with quantum output (and all equivalent primitives) from one-way puzzles [KT24].

2.5 Efficiently Verifiable One-Way Puzzles

The key challenge to using one-way puzzles to build other primitives is that the constructions may not make use of the verification scheme in a black-box manner since the verification scheme is not itself efficient. Thus, to make the problem easier, we consider a variant of one-way puzzles with efficient verification.

A very similar primitive, termed "hard quantum planted problems for QCMA," has been studied before in the context of publicly verifiable deletion [KNY23]. A hard quantum planted problem is essentially an efficiently verifiable one-way puzzle with perfect correctness. Direct observation shows that perfect correctness is unnecessary for any of the applications of hard quantum planted problems for QCMA, and so their results hold for efficiently verifiable one-way puzzles as well. In particular, they show that

Theorem 6 (Theorem 6.2 from [KNY23]). *If there exists an efficiently verifiable one-way puzzle and quantum*

$$Z \in \{SKE, COM, PKE, ABE, QFHE, TRE, WE\},$$

then there exists Z with publicly verifiable deletion.

Their construction requires building a stronger variant of a one-time signature scheme from efficiently verifiable one-way puzzles. In particular

Theorem 7 (Theorem 3.2 from [KNY23]). *If there exists an efficiently verifiable one-way puzzle, then there exists a QCCC one-time signature scheme.*

The construction is essentially just a Lamport signature [Lam79]. As this theorem is not presented with full proof details in [KNY23], for completeness we restate this claim as Theorem 14 and give a full proof.

Since efficiently verifiable one-way puzzles seem more useful than normal one-way puzzles, we might wonder whether they are also minimal. Fortunately, most of the constructions of one-way puzzles from QCCC primitives have efficient verification algorithms. The two notable exceptions are EFID pairs and commitment schemes.

Theorem 8 (Theorems A.4 and A.6 from [KT24] and Theorems 15 and 16 in this paper). *If there exists a QCCC signature scheme, secret key encryption scheme, non-interactive commitment scheme, or pseudodeterministic PRG, then there exists an efficiently verifiable one-way puzzle.*

Applying this theorem to the results of [KNY23] then gives the following two interesting corollaries.

Corollary 2. *If there exists QCCC*

$$Z \in \{SKE, PKE, ABE, QFHE, TRE\}$$

then there exists Z with publicly verifiable deletion.

Corollary 3. *There exists an efficiently verifiable one-way puzzle if and only if there exists a QCCC one-time signature scheme.*

Amplification and Combiners for Efficiently Verifiable One-Way Puzzles. Since efficiently verifiable one-way puzzles seem to be about as minimal for QCCC as one-way puzzles, but have much more powerful applications, we may consider whether efficiently verifiable one-way puzzles should instead be considered a "central" primitive for QCCC cryptography. We then may hope that there exists an amplification theorem and a universal construction for efficiently verifiable one-way puzzles. We show that this is indeed the case.

Theorem 9 (Restatement of Theorem 20). *If there exists a $(1-1/\mathsf{poly}(\lambda), \mathsf{negl}(\lambda))$ efficiently verifiable one-way puzzle, then there exists a $(\mathsf{negl}(\lambda), \mathsf{negl}(\lambda))$ efficiently verifiable one-way puzzle.*

Theorem 10 (Restatement of Theorem 24). *If there exists a $(\mathsf{negl}(\lambda), 1 - 1/\mathsf{poly}(\lambda))$ efficiently verifiable one-way puzzle, then there exists a $(\mathsf{negl}(\lambda), \mathsf{negl}(\lambda))$ efficiently verifiable one-way puzzle.*

Theorem 11 (Informal Version of Corollary 11). *There exists a robust combiner for efficiently verifiable one-way puzzles.*

Corollary 4 (Informal Version of Theorem 25). *There exists a pair of algorithms $(\mathsf{Samp}_U, \mathsf{Ver}_U)$ such that as long as efficiently verifiable one-way puzzles exist, $(\mathsf{Samp}_U, \mathsf{Ver}_U)$ is an efficiently verifiable one-way puzzle.*

Note that most of the barriers to these results go away when the verification algorithm is required to be efficient. Thus, the "naive" constructions described earlier are provably secure for efficiently verifiable one-way puzzles.

Are One-Way Puzzles Equivalent to Efficiently Verifiable One-Way Puzzles? Although the advantage of treating efficiently verifiable one-way puzzles as a "central" QCCC primitive is that they have actual applications in the QCCC setting, this does come at a cost to its "minimality". It is not clear how to build efficiently verifiable one-way puzzles from every primitive known to imply OWPuzz. In particular, constructions are lacking from EFID pairs and commitments.

Thus, we may consider whether or not it even matters whether verification is efficient. Ideally, we would be able to build an efficiently verifiable one-way puzzle from any one-way puzzle. In fact, if we restrict the sampling algorithm to being a classical randomized algorithm, such a claim holds true. Given a classical one-way puzzle, we can build an efficiently verifiable one-way puzzle by replacing the key with the random coins of the sampler. Then, the verifier can simply check whether running the sampler on the randomness given produces the given puzzle.

However, as this approach directly uses the randomness of sampling, it is inherently non-quantum. In fact, it turns out that in the quantum setting, there is a black-box separation.

Theorem 12 (Informal Version of Theorem 19). *There exists a quantum oracle $\mathcal{O}$ relative to which pesudorandom states (and thus one-way puzzles) exist but efficiently verifiable one-way puzzles do not exist.*

This theorem follows from a simple observation. A search-to-decision argument shows that any efficiently verifiable one-way puzzle can be broken using a QCMA oracle. But there exists an oracle relative to which pseudorandom states exist and BQP=QCMA [Kre21]. As pseudorandom states can be used to build one-way puzzles [KT24,MY22b], Theorem 12 follows.

A Barrier Against Length Shrinking for Pseudorandom States. An open question in the literature is whether pseudorandom states with output length $n(\lambda)$ can be built from pseudorandom states with output length $n'(\lambda)$ for any values of n, n' such that $n \neq n' \geq \log n$. However, pseudorandom states with output length $O(\log \lambda)$ can be used to build QCCC pseudodeterministic PRGs, and thus efficiently verifiable one-way puzzles. But our argument gives a black-box separation between efficiently verifiable one-way puzzles and pseudorandom states with output length λ. Thus, we get the following corollary.

Corollary 5 (Informal version of Corollary 8). *There exists a quantum oracle $\mathcal{O}$ relative to which PRSs with output length λ exist but PRSs with output length $c \log \lambda$ (for $c > 12$) do not.*

Note that this observation at its core comes from the simple observation that pseudodeterministic PRGs can be broken with a QCMA oracle, and so this observation is little more than a corollary of the results of [ALY23b,Kre21], and is known in folklore. However, we provide a full formal proof of this statement as a contribution towards the systemization of knowledge in quantum cryptography.

2.6 Random Input OWPuzz

Another natural variant of one-way puzzles we might consider is a one-way puzzle where the key must be sampled uniformly at random, and then the puzzle is sampled from the key. We will call this a random input one-way puzzle. This more closely aligns with the classical notion of one-way functions, and in fact the construction of one-way puzzles from one-way state generators produces a random input one-way puzzle (assuming the key generation for the one-way state generator is uniform) [KT24].

[KT24] left as an open question whether random input one-way puzzles can be built from arbitrary one-way puzzles. Note that this statement does hold classically, since both are equivalent to one-way functions.

We show that these two notions are indeed equivalent

Theorem 13 (Formal Statement and Proof in Full Version). *If there exists a one-way puzzle, then there exists a random input one-way puzzle. If there exists an efficiently verifiable one-way puzzle, then there exists a random input efficiently verifiable one-way puzzle.*

The idea is fairly natural. We simply treat the random input as a one-time pad, and apply it to the original key. We then include the one-time padded key with the original puzzle in the final output.

Note that our amplification lemma for one-way puzzles also produces a random input one-way puzzle, and so also gives an indirect proof of this theorem, although this approach does not hold for efficiently verifiable one-way puzzles.

3 Open Questions

Although we are aware of a few implications, the landscape of QCCC reductions, even those relating to one-way puzzles/efficiently verifiable one-way puzzles, is still fairly unexplored. We list a few interesting questions in this space related to our work

1. Is it possible to build efficiently verifiable one-way puzzles from a QCCC commitment scheme? QCCC commitments and EFID pairs are the two QCCC primitives for which the obvious construction of one-way puzzles does not have an efficient verifier. If the answer to this question is no, then it may be possible to build QCCC commitments from standard one-way puzzles.
2. Are there any useful cryptographic primitives we can construct from one-way puzzles without efficient verification? Due to the black-box separation between one-way puzzles and efficiently verifiable one-way puzzles, it seems like the answer may be no. However, a few primitives (such as EFID pairs and QCCC commitments) fall outside of this separation, and so there is still hope for a construction.
3. Is there a combiner for QCCC EFID pairs? If so, by using the construction of non-uniform EFID from one-way puzzles, we would be able to construct standard EFID from one-way puzzles. Interestingly, there does exist a combiner for both the quantum version and the classical version of this primitive [HKNY23,Lev87,Gol90].
4. Can we build any QCCC primitives besides one-time signatures from efficiently verifiable one-way puzzles, for example secret key encryption or pseudodeterministic PRGs? What about many-time signatures? Although we observe that the known construction of many time signatures from one-way functions uses a pseudorandom function in order to be stateless, so this may necessitate building a QCCC style pseudorandom function [GMR87].

4 Concurrent Work

Two concurrent works [BEM24,CM24] also produced black-box separations of QCCC primitives from linear output pseudorandom states.

[BEM24] shows that if QCCC pseudodeterministic one-way functions exist, then $\mathsf{BQP} \neq \mathsf{QCMA}$. Since by [Kre21], there exists an oracle relative to which linear output pseudorandom states exist and $\mathsf{BQP} = \mathsf{QCMA}$, this gives a black-box separation of pseudodeterministic one-way functions from pseudorandom states. In addition, pseudodeterministic one-way functions can be built from pseudodeterministic PRGs, which in turn can be built from pseudorandom states with logarithmic output length. Thus, [BEM24] gives a black-box barrier against length extension for pseudorandom states.

In comparison, our black-box separation shows that if efficiently verifiable one-way puzzles exist, then BQP ≠ QCMA. It is easy to see that efficiently verifiable one-way puzzles can be built from pseudodeterministic one-way functions, and so the results of [BEM24] follow as a corollary of our Theorem 19.

[CM24] shows that many-time signatures with quantum verification key and classical signature/signing key cannot be built in a black-box manner from pseudorandom states. In particular, they define a novel oracle (using similar techniques to [Kre21]) under which linear output pseudorandom states exist and such many-time signature schemes do not. Since a signature scheme of this type can be built from logarithmic output pseudorandom states [BBO+24], this again gives a black-box barrier against length extension for pseudorandom states. Their result is also interesting since one-time signatures with quantum verification key and classical signature/signing key *can* be built from pseudorandom states [MY22a]. Thus, this gives a black-box separation between one-time and many-time security for such signature schemes.

Note that entirely QCCC signatures (with classical verification key) can be used to build efficiently verifiable one-way puzzles [KT24]. Thus, our Theorem 19 gives a barrier towards building QCCC signatures from pseudorandom states. However, our techniques do not apply when the verification key is quantum, and [CM24]'s solution for this requires significant technical work.

In comparison to both of these results, our black-box separation has the advantage that it is fairly general. Efficiently verifiable one-way puzzles can be built from most QCCC cryptographic primitives (see Theorem 8). And so our separation gives a barrier against building any of these QCCC primitives from pseudorandom states (or inefficiently verifiable one-way puzzles).

5 Preliminaries

5.1 Definitions of QCCC Primitives

As discussed previously this definition of OWPuzz slightly generalizes the notion given in [KT24].

Definition 1. *An (α, β) one way puzzle (OWPuzz) is a pair of a sampling algorithm and a verification function (Samp, Ver) with the following syntax:*

1. *Samp$(1^\lambda) \to (k, s)$ is a uniform QPT algorithm which outputs a pair of classical strings (k, s). We refer to s as the puzzle and k as the key. Without loss of generality, we can assume $k \in \{0, 1\}^\lambda$.*
2. *Ver$(k, s) \to b$ is some (possibly uncomputable) function which takes in a key and puzzle and outputs a bit $b \in \{0, 1\}$.*

satisfying the following properties:

1. *Correctness: For all sufficiently large λ, outputs of the sampler pass verification with overwhelming probability*
$$\Pr_{\mathsf{Samp}(1^\lambda) \to (k,s)}[\mathsf{Ver}(k,s) \to 1] \geq 1 - \alpha$$

2. *Security: Given a puzzle s, it is computationally infeasible to find a key s which verifies. That is, for all non-uniform QPT algorithms $\mathcal{A}$, for all sufficiently large λ,*
$$\Pr_{\mathsf{Samp}(1^\lambda) \to (k,s)}[\mathsf{Ver}(\mathcal{A}(s), s) \to 1] \leq \beta$$

If for all c, (Samp, Ver) is a $(\lambda^{-c}, \lambda^{-c})$ one way puzzle, then we say that (Samp, Ver) is a strong OWPuzz and omit the constants. When unambigious, we will simply say that (Samp, Ver) is a OWPuzz.

Definition 2. *A one-time signature scheme is a set of QPT algorithms (KeyGen, S, V) with the following syntax*

1. $KeyGen(1^\lambda) \to (vk, sk)$ *takes the security parameter as input and ouptuts a signing key sk and a verification key vk*
2. $S(sk, m) \to \sigma$ *takes in the signing key and a message as input, and outputs a signature σ*
3. $V(vk, m, \sigma) \to 0/1$ *takes in a verification key vk, a message m, and a signature σ, and outputs a single bit*

satisfying the following security properties

1. *Correctness: For all m in the message space,*
$$\Pr_{KeyGen(1^\lambda) \to (vk, sk)}[V(vk, m, S(sk, m)) \to 1] \geq 1 - \mathsf{negl}(\lambda)$$

2. *One-time Security: An adversary with the ability to make one signature query can not forge a signature for a different message. More formally, for all $m_0 \neq m_1$ in the message space and for all PPT $\mathcal{A}$,*
$$\Pr_{KeyGen(1^\lambda) \to (vk, sk)}[V(vk, m_1, \mathcal{A}(vk, S(sk, m_0))) \to 1] \leq \mathsf{negl}(\lambda)$$

Definition 3. *An EFID pair is a randomized algorithm $\mathrm{Gen}(1^\lambda, b)$ taking a unary security parameter λ and a classical bit $b \in \{0, 1\}$ which outputs a classical string satisfying the following two properties:*

1. *Statistically far:*
$$\Delta(\mathrm{Gen}(1^\lambda, 0), \mathrm{Gen}(1^\lambda, 1)) \geq 1 - \epsilon$$

2. *Computationally close: For all QPT $\mathcal{A}$ and for all sufficiently large λ, the distributions $\mathrm{Gen}(1^\lambda, 0)$ and $\mathrm{Gen}(1^\lambda, 1)$ are indistinguishable.*

If Gen is a quantum algorithm (with classical output), then we call Gen a quantum EFID pair (or QEFID).

5.2 Complexity

Definition 4. *We say a promise problem $\Pi : \{0,1\}^* \to \{0,1,\perp\}$ is in* Promise QCMA *if there exists a QPT algorithm $\mathcal{V}(x,y)$ and a polynomial p such that:*

1. *Completeness: If $\Pi(x) = 1$, then there exists a $p(|x|)$-bit string y such that*

$$\Pr[\mathcal{V}(x,y) \to 1] \geq \frac{2}{3}$$

2. *Soundness: If $\Pi(x) = 0$, then for all $p(|x|)$-bit strings y,*

$$\Pr[\mathcal{V}(x,y) \to 1] \leq \frac{1}{3}$$

Definition 5. *We say a promise problem $\Pi : \{0,1\}^* \to \{0,1,\perp\}$ is in* Promise QMA *if there exists a QPT algorithm $\mathcal{V}(x,|\phi\rangle)$ and a polynomial p such that:*

1. *Completeness: If $\Pi(x) = 1$, then there exists a $p(|x|)$-qubit state $|\phi\rangle$ such that*

$$\Pr[\mathcal{V}(x,|\phi\rangle) \to 1] \geq \frac{2}{3}$$

2. *Soundness: If $\Pi(x) = 0$, then for all $p(|x|)$-qubit states $|\phi\rangle$,*

$$\Pr[\mathcal{V}(x,|\phi\rangle) \to 1] \leq \frac{1}{3}$$

5.3 Oracles

We define, in the spirit of Kretschmer [Kre21], a query to a single unitary $\mathcal{U}$ to be a single quantum call of either $\mathcal{U}$ or controlled-$\mathcal{U}$. We do not allow queries to $\mathcal{U}^\dagger$. $\mathcal{A}^{\mathcal{U}}(x)$ refers to a quantum algorithm on a classical input x which can make quantum queries to the unitary (or collection of unitaries) $\mathcal{U}$. In terms of computational cost, a single query to $\mathcal{U}_n$ will be charged n units of computation. This allows us to define quantum polynomial-time (QPT) algorithms relative to an oracle $\mathcal{U}$. In particular, a QPT algorithm relative to $\mathcal{U}$ on an input of length ℓ can query $\mathcal{U}_n$ for any $n < \text{poly}(\ell)$.

Also in the style of Kretschmer, we consider versions of PromiseBQP, Promise QCMA, and PromiseQMA augmented with a collection of quantum oracles $\mathcal{U} = \{\mathcal{U}_n\}_{n \in \mathbb{N}}$. We denote these by PromiseBQP$^{\mathcal{U}}$, PromiseQCMA$^{\mathcal{U}}$, and PromiseQMA$^{\mathcal{U}}$ respectively. For PromiseBQP$^{\mathcal{U}}$, the deciding algorithm is allowed to be a QPT algorithm relative to $\mathcal{U}$, and for PromiseQCMA$^{\mathcal{U}}$ and PromiseQMA$^{\mathcal{U}}$, the verifying algorithm is allowed to be a QPT algorithm relative to $\mathcal{U}$.

It is easy to see that in this model, the traditional inequalities still hold. In particular, for any oracle $\mathcal{U}$, PromiseBQP$^{\mathcal{U}} \subseteq$ PromiseQCMA$^{\mathcal{U}} \subseteq$ PromiseQMA$^{\mathcal{U}}$.

We also consider cryptographic primitives in the oracle setting. In this case, we allow the cryptographic algorithm to be a uniform QPT algorithm relative to $\mathcal{U}$, and we consider security against non-uniform QPT algorithms relative to $\mathcal{U}$.

6 Constructions of EV − OWPuzz from QCCC Primitives

In this section we give the results that EV − OWPuzz are equivalent to QCCC one time signatures, and can be constructed from QCCC non-interactive commitments and QPRGs. The proofs are deferred to the full version of this paper.

Theorem 14. *There exists a one-time signature scheme if and only if there exists a EV − OWPuzz.*

[KT24] shows that EV − OWPuzz can be built from one-time signatures even if the signing key or the signature are quantum. Thus, an interesting corollary of Theorem 14 is that QCCC one-time signatures with classical signature, signing and verification keys can be built from one-time signatures where either the signing key or the signature is quantum.

Theorem 15. *If there exists a non-interactive commitment scheme (Com, Rec), then there exists a EV − OWPuzz (Samp, Ver).*

Theorem 16. *If there exists a QPRG G with stretch $\ell(\lambda) \geq 3n(\lambda)$, then there exists a EV − OWPuzz (Samp, Ver).*

7 Efficiently Verifiable One Way Puzzles Can be Broken with a QCMA Oracle

Proposition 1 (From [INN+22, ABOBS22]). *There exists a search-to-decision reduction for PromiseQCMA. Formally, there exists a promise problem $\Pi^* \in$ PromiseQCMA such that for every $\Pi \in$ PromiseQCMA with verifier $\mathcal{V}$, there exists a QPT algorithm $\mathcal{A}^{\Pi^*}$ such that for all x such that $\Pi(x) = 1$,*

$$\Pr[\Pr[\mathcal{V}(\mathcal{A}^\Pi(x), x) \to 1] \geq \frac{2}{3}] \geq \frac{1}{2}$$

Theorem 17. *For every efficiently verifiable one way puzzle (Samp, Ver), there exists a promise problem $\Pi^* \in$ PromiseQCMA and a QPT algorithm $\mathcal{A}^{\Pi^*}$ with oracle access to Π^* which breaks security. That is*

$$\Pr_{\mathsf{Samp}(1^\lambda) \to (k,s)}[\mathsf{Ver}(\mathcal{A}^{\Pi^*}(s), s) \to 1] \geq \frac{1}{\mathsf{poly}(\lambda)}$$

Proof. Let (Samp, Ver) be a EV − OWPuzz. Define Π to be the following promise problem:

1. (yes): s is a yes instance if there exists k such that $\Pr[\mathsf{Ver}(k,s) \to 1] \geq \frac{2}{3}$
2. (no): s is a no instance if for all k, $\Pr[\mathsf{Ver}(k,s) \to 1] < \frac{1}{3}$

It is trivial to see that $\Pi \in$ PromiseQCMA.

Our promise problem Π^* will be the problem from Proposition 1 and our algorithm $\mathcal{A}^{\Pi^*}$ will be the algorithm from Proposition 1 corresponding to Π. In particular, we have that for all s such that there exists a k with $\Pr[\mathsf{Ver}(k, s) \to 1] \geq \frac{2}{3}$, then

$$\Pr[\Pr[\mathsf{Ver}(\mathcal{A}^{\Pi^*}(s), s) \to 1] \geq \frac{2}{3}] \geq \frac{1}{2}$$

In particular, this means that

$$\Pr[\mathsf{Ver}(\mathcal{A}^{\Pi^*}(s), s) \to 1] \geq \frac{1}{3}$$

Correctness states that

$$\Pr_{\mathsf{Samp}(1^\lambda) \to (k,s)}[\mathsf{Ver}(k, s) \to 1] \geq 1 - \mathsf{negl}(\lambda).$$

And so an averaging argument gives us that

$$\Pr_{\mathsf{Samp}(1^\lambda) \to (k,s)}[\Pr[\mathsf{Ver}(k, s) \to 1] \geq \frac{2}{3}] \geq 1 - \mathsf{negl}(\lambda) \geq \frac{1}{2}$$

In particular, s is a yes instance of Π with all but negligible probability.

Putting things together, we get that

$$\Pr_{\mathsf{Samp}(1^\lambda) \to (k,s)}[\mathsf{Ver}(\mathcal{A}^{\Pi^*}(s), s) \to 1] \geq \frac{1}{6}$$

and we are done.

8 A Black-Box Separation Between OWPuzz and EV − OWPuzz

We begin by recalling the very powerful quantum black-box separation theorem by Kretschmer.

Theorem 18 ([Kre21]). *There exists a set of quantum oracles $\mathcal{U}$ such that with probability 1 over $\mathcal{U}$,*

1. *$\mathsf{PromiseBQP}^\mathcal{U} = \mathsf{PromiseQMA}^\mathcal{U}$.*
2. *Relative to $\mathcal{U}$, there exists a PRS family mapping λ bits to λ qubit states.*

First, we observe that all of our theorems are black-box and thus relativize. In particular, we get the following corollaries

Corollary 6. *Let $\mathcal{U}$ be any collection of classical or quantum oracles. For every efficiently verifiable one way puzzle $(\mathsf{Samp}^\mathcal{U}, \mathsf{Ver}^\mathcal{U})$, there exists a promise problem $\Pi \in \mathsf{PromiseQCMA}^\mathcal{U}$ and a QPT algorithm $\mathcal{A}^\Pi$ with oracle access to Π which breaks security. That is*

$$\Pr_{\mathsf{Samp}^\mathcal{U}(1^\lambda) \to (k,s)}[\mathsf{Ver}^\mathcal{U}(\mathcal{A}^\Pi(s), s) \to 1] \geq \frac{1}{\mathsf{poly}(\lambda)}$$

Corollary 7. *Let $\mathcal{U}$ be any collection of classical or quantum oracles. If there exists a QPRG $G^{\mathcal{U}}$ with stretch $\ell(\lambda) \geq 3n(\lambda)$ secure relative to $\mathcal{U}$, then there exists a EV − OWPuzz $(\mathsf{Samp}^{\mathcal{U}}, \mathsf{Ver}^{\mathcal{U}})$ secure relative to $\mathcal{U}$.*

Let us then consider the oracle $\mathcal{U}$ from Theorem 18. We know that relative to $\mathsf{PromiseBQP}^{\mathcal{U}} \subseteq \mathsf{PromiseQCMA}^{\mathcal{U}} \subseteq \mathsf{PromiseQMA}^{\mathcal{U}}$, and we also have $\mathsf{PromiseBQP}^{\mathcal{U}} = \mathsf{PromiseQMA}^{\mathcal{U}}$. Thus, this gives us that $\mathsf{PromiseBQP}^{\mathcal{U}} = \mathsf{Promise\,QCMA}^{\mathcal{U}}$. So Corollary 6 immediately shows that relative to $\mathcal{U}$, there does not exist any EV − OWPuzz.

But it is also known from [KT24,MY22b] that OWPuzz can be built in a black-box manner from PRSs. Thus, we get the following corollary:

Theorem 19. *There exists a set of quantum oracles $\mathcal{U}$ such that with probability 1 over $\mathcal{U}$,*

1. *There does not exist any EV − OWPuzz relative to $\mathcal{U}$.*
2. *There exists a OWPuzz relative to $\mathcal{U}$.*

[ALY23b] shows that PRSs with output length $c \log \lambda$ for $c > 12$ can be used to build QPRGs with triple stretch. Note that this reduction is itself black-box, and so holds relative to any quantum oracle. Applying Corollary 7 then gives the following result

Corollary 8. *There exists a set of quantum oracles $\mathcal{U}$ such that with probability 1 over $\mathcal{U}$, relative to $\mathcal{U}$*

1. *There does not exist any PRS family mapping λ-bits to $c \log \lambda$-qubits for any constant $c > 12$.*
2. *There does exist a PRS family mapping λ-bits to λ-qubits.*

9 OWPuzz Amplification, Combiners, and Universal Constructions

In this section we present security and correctness amplifiers, combiners, and universal constructions for both OWPuzz and EV − OWPuzz. We defer most of the amplification proofs to the full version of this paper and defer the proof of OWPuzz security amplification to the next section. With these results we establish that both primitives are well behaved and have many of the desirable properties of one-way functions.

9.1 Amplification

Theorem 20 (Correctness Amplification for OWPuzz and EV − OWPuzz). *Let $(\mathsf{Samp}, \mathsf{Ver})$ be a (α, β) OWPuzz. Define $(\mathsf{Samp}', \mathsf{Ver}')$ by*

1. $\mathsf{Samp}' = \mathsf{Samp}^{\otimes t}$
2. $\mathsf{Ver}'((k_1, \ldots, k_t), (s_1, \ldots, s_t))$: *output 1 if $\mathsf{Ver}(k_i, s_i)$ for some $i \in [t]$.*

Then (Samp', Ver') is a $(\alpha^t, t\beta)$ OWPuzz.

Remark 1. We note that if Ver is efficient, so is Ver'.

Theorem 21 (Weak Correctness Amplification for OWPuzz). *Let* (Samp, Ver) *be a* (α, β) *OWPuzz. Define* (Samp', Ver') *by*

1. Samp' = Samp
2. Ver'(k, s): If $\Pr_{\mathsf{Samp}(1^\lambda) \to (k', s')}[\mathsf{Ver}(k', s') \to 0 | s' = s] \geq t$, output 1. Otherwise, output Ver(k, s). (The idea here is that if s was sampled in a way that it would not verify honestly then we accept it anyway, otherwise we do normal verification)

Then (Samp', Ver') is a $(t, \alpha/t + \beta)$ OWPuzz.

Remark 2. Note that this construction only holds for standard inefficiently verifiable one-way puzzles, as Ver' is not efficient.

Theorem 22 (Security Amplification for OWP). *If, for some $c > 0$, there exists a* $(\mathsf{negl}(\lambda), 1 - \lambda^{-c})$ *one-way puzzle* (Samp, Ver), *then there exists a strong one-way puzzle.*

We defer the proof of the above theorem to the next section.

Theorem 23 (Weak Correctness Amplification for EV − OWPuzz). *Let* (Samp, Ver) *be a* (α, β) *EV − OWPuzz. Define* (Samp', Ver') *by*

1. Samp'(1^λ): Run Samp$(1^\lambda) \to (k, s)$. If Ver$(k, s) \to 1$, output (k, s). Otherwise, output $(\bot, \bot)$.
2. Ver'(k, s): If $s = \bot$, output 1. Otherwise, output Ver(k, s).

Then (Samp', Ver') is a $(1/4, \alpha + \beta)$ OWPuzz.

Theorem 24 (Security Amplification for EV − OWPuzz). *Let* (Samp, Ver) *be a* (α, β) *EV − OWPuzz. Then* (Samp$^{\otimes t}$, Ver$^{\otimes t}$) *is a* $(t\alpha, \beta^t)$ *EV − OWPuzz.*

Remark 3. The proof of Theorem 4.1 from [BQSY23] requires that the soundness game be efficiently falsifiable. Thus, this same amplification theorem does not hold for OWPuzz with inefficient verification. Amplification of such puzzles is an open question.

9.2 Combiners

Corollary 9. *Let* (Samp, Ver) *be a OWPuzz candidate and define* (Samp', Ver') *to be the constructions from Theorem 21 and Theorem 20 applied in sequence with $t = 1/2$ and $t = \lambda$ respectively. Then if* (Samp, Ver) *is a OWPuzz, so is* (Samp', Ver'). *Furthermore, regardless of whether* (Samp, Ver) *is a OWPuzz,* (Samp', Ver') *satisfies n^{-c} correctness for all c.*

Proof. Let us say that (Samp, Ver) satisfies (α, β) correctness and security. Then (Samp', Ver') satisfies $(2^{-\lambda}, \lambda(\alpha/2 + \beta))$ correctness and security.

Observe that if $\alpha, \beta = \mathsf{negl}(\lambda)$, then $\lambda(\alpha/2 + \beta) = \mathsf{negl}(\lambda)$. Furthermore, no matter what, $2^{-\lambda} = \mathsf{negl}(\lambda)$.

Corollary 10. *Let (Samp, Ver) be a EV − OWPuzz candidate and define (Samp', Ver') to be the constructions from Theorem 23 and Theorem 20 applied in sequence with $t = \lambda$. Then if (Samp, Ver) is a EV − OWPuzz, so is (Samp', Ver'). Furthermore, regardless of whether (Samp, Ver) is a EV − OWPuzz, (Samp', Ver') satisfies n^{-c} correctness for all c.*

Proof. Same argument as before

Corollary 11. *Let $(\mathsf{Samp}_0, \mathsf{Ver}_0)$ and $(\mathsf{Samp}_1, \mathsf{Ver}_1)$ be two OWPuzz candidates. Let $(\mathsf{Samp}'_0, \mathsf{Ver}'_0)$ and $(\mathsf{Samp}'_1, \mathsf{Ver}'_1)$ be the construction from Corollary 9 applied to $(\mathsf{Samp}_0, \mathsf{Ver}_0)$ and $(\mathsf{Samp}_1, \mathsf{Ver}_1)$ respectively. Define $(\widetilde{\mathsf{Samp}}, \widetilde{\mathsf{Ver}})$ by*

1. $\widetilde{\mathsf{Samp}}(1^\lambda)$: Run $\mathsf{Samp}'_0 \to (k_0, s_0)$ and $\mathsf{Samp}'_1 \to (k_1, s_1)$. Output $(k = (k_0, k_1), s = (s_0, s_1))$.
2. $\widetilde{\mathsf{Ver}}((k_0, k_1), (s_0, s_1))$: Output 1 if and only if $\mathsf{Ver}'_0(k_0, s_0) = 1$ and $\mathsf{Ver}'_1(k_1, s_1) = 1$.

Then $(\widetilde{\mathsf{Samp}}, \widetilde{\mathsf{Ver}})$ is a OWPuzz as long as one of $(\mathsf{Samp}_0, \mathsf{Ver}_0)$ or $(\mathsf{Samp}_1, \mathsf{Ver}_1)$ is a OWPuzz.

The same corollary holds for EV − OWPuzz when replacing Corollary 9 with Corollary 10.

Remark 4. Given any polynomial p different OWPuzz candidates $\{(\mathsf{Samp}_i, \mathsf{Ver}_i)\}_{i \in [p]}$, we can use the same idea to build a OWPuzz $(\widetilde{\mathsf{Samp}}, \widetilde{\mathsf{Ver}})$ which is secure as long as one of the candidates is secure. This follows the same logic as above with $\widetilde{\mathsf{Samp}}(1^\lambda) \to ((k_0, ..., k_p), (s_0, ..., s_p))$ and Ver only outputting 1 if all p Ver'_i's output 1.

9.3 Universal Construction

The universal construction of EV follows standard techniques.

Definition 6 (Universal EV − OWPuzz). *A set of uniform algorithms (Samp, Ver) is a universal construction of a EV − OWPuzz if it is a EV − OWPuzz so long as some EV − OWPuzz exists.*

Theorem 25 (Universal EV − OWPuzz). *Define Samp_i as the ith Quantum Turing machine and Ver_j as the jth Quantum Turing machine each of which with an attached alarm clock which will halt the machine after λ^3 steps.*

Define $(\mathsf{Samp}_U, \mathsf{Ver}_U)$ using the construction from Remark 4 for the λ^2 candidates $(\mathsf{Samp}_i, \mathsf{Ver}_j)$ for all $(i, j) \in [\lambda]^2$. If any EV − OWPuzz (Samp, Ver) exists, then $(\mathsf{Samp}_U, \mathsf{Ver}_U)$ is a OWPuzz.

Proof. Using standard padding arguments (see [Lev87,HKNY23]) we can show that if there exists a (α, β) EV − OWPuzz with both Ver and Samp running in time less than λ^c, then there exists a $(\alpha^{(1/c)}, \beta^{(1/c)})$ EV − OWPuzz with Ver′ and Samp′ running in time less than λ^3. If EV − OWPuzz's exist then there exists a (negl, negl)EV − OWPuzz and therefore a (negl, negl)EV − OWPuzz running in time less than λ^3.

If any one-way puzzle exists then for some i, j, $(\mathsf{Samp}_i, \mathsf{Ver}_j)$ will be a one way puzzle with both algorithms running in time less than n^3. Once $\lambda \geq \max(i, j)$ a one way puzzle will be one of the candidates. By Remark 4 we know that $(\mathsf{Samp}_U, \mathsf{Ver}_U)$ will be a OWPuzz.

Theorem 26 (Universal OWPuzz). *Define Samp_i as the ith Quantum Turing machine with an attached alarm clock which will halt the machine after λ^3 steps. Define Ver_i to be the function such that the sum of the correctness and security error of $(\mathsf{Samp}_i, \mathsf{Ver}_i)$ is minimized.*

Define $(\mathsf{Samp}_U)(1^\lambda)$ using the construction from Remark 4 for the λ^2 candidates $(\mathsf{Samp}_i, \mathsf{Ver}_i)$ for all $(i, j) \in [\lambda]^2$. If any OWPuzz $(\mathsf{Samp}, \mathsf{Ver})$ exists, then $(\mathsf{Samp}_U, \mathsf{Ver}_U)$ is a OWPuzz.

Proof. Observe that if there exists a OWPuzz $(\mathsf{Samp}, \mathsf{Ver})$ then when i is such that $\mathsf{Samp}_i = \mathsf{Samp}$, $(\mathsf{Samp}_i, \mathsf{Ver}_i)$ is also a OWPuzz. The rest of the proof follows by the same argument as Theorem 25.

10 OWPuzz Security Amplification

In this section we prove the following theorem:

Theorem 27 (Restatement of Theorem 22). *If, for some $c > 0$, there exists a $(\mathsf{negl}(\lambda), 1 - \lambda^{-c})$ one-way puzzle $(\mathsf{Samp}, \mathsf{Ver})$, then there exists a strong one-way puzzle.*

We do this be showing that weak OWPuzz imply non-uniform EFID pairs, and then show that non-uniform EFID pairs imply strong OWPuzz. The first of these steps serves as a simpler and more general version of the argument presented in [KT24].

10.1 OWPuzzs Imply Non-uniform EFID

Theorem 28. *If there exists a OWPuzz, then there exists a non-uniform EFID pair.*

This argument will follow from adapting the techniques of [VZ12,HRV10]. We recall a number of technical lemmas from these papers, and observe that since these lemmas rely only on quantum friendly black-box techniques, they also hold in the QCCC setting. While we will focus on the non-uniform setting, the results should also hold against uniform adversaries by adapting the arguments of [VZ12,HRV10] in the uniform setting.

We first recall the following definitions used in [VZ12,HRV10] (all of which operate in the non-uniform setting)

Definition 7. *Let X, B be two jointly sampled random variables. We say that B has (t, ϵ) (quantum) pseudoentropy at least k given X if there exists a random variable C jointly sampled with X such that*

1. $H(C|X) \geq k$
2. (X, B) and (X, C) are (t, ϵ)-indistinguishable (by quantum circuits)

When $t = 1/\mathsf{negl}$ and $\epsilon = \mathsf{negl}$ we can omit the t, ϵ and simply say that B has (quantum) pseudoentropy k.

Definition 8. *Let $B^{(i)}$ be a random variable over $[q]$ for each $i \in [m]$. We say that $B = (B^{(1)}, \ldots, B^{(m)})$ has next-block (quantum) pseudoentropy at least k if the random variable $B^{(I)}$ has (quantum) pseudoentropy at least k/m given $B^{(1)}, \ldots, B^{(I-1)}$, for $I \sim [m]$. If $q = 2$, then we will use the term next-bit pseudoentropy.*

Definition 9. *Let $B^{(i)}$ be a random variable for each $i \in [m]$. We say that every block of $B = (B^{(1)}, \ldots, B^{(m)})$ has next-block (quantum) pseudoentropy at least k if for all i, the random variable $B^{(i)}$ has (quantum) pseudoentropy at least k given $B^{(1)}, \ldots, B^{(i-1)}$.*

Definition 10. *For random variables A, B the KL divergence from A to B is defined as*

$$KL(A||B) = \mathop{\mathbb{E}}_{a \sim A} \left[\log \frac{\Pr[A \to a]}{\Pr[B \to a]} \right]$$

Definition 11. *Let X, B be jointly sampled random variables. We say that B is (t, δ) (quantum) KL-hard for sampling given X if for all size-t randomized (quantum) circuits S,*

$$KL(X, B || X, S(X)) > \delta$$

Remark 5. We will also define pseudo-min-entropy to have the same definition as pseudoentropy, but with Shannon entropy replaced with min-entropy. We analogously define next-block pseudo-min-entropy.

OWPuzz Imply Next-Bit Pseudoentropy. We state quantum versions of the corresponding lemmas from [VZ12]

Lemma 1 (Quantum Version of Theorem 3.15 and Lemma 3.6 from [VZ12]). *Let (X, B) be jointly sampled random variables over $\{0, 1\}^n \times [q]$. If B is quantum (t, δ) KL-hard for sampling given X, then for every $\epsilon > 0$, B has quantum (t', ϵ) psuedoentropy at least $H(B|X) + \delta - \epsilon$ given X, for $t' = t^{\Omega(1)}/\mathsf{poly}(n, q, 1/\epsilon)$.*

Proof. The proof is exactly the same as the proofs of Lemma 3.6 and Theorem 3.15 from [VZ12], but with the use of the Min-Max theorem replaced by its quantum equivalent (Theorem 4.1 from [CCL+17]).

Lemma 2 (Quantum Chain Rule for KL-Hardness (Variant of Lemma 4.3 from [VZ12]). *Let Y be a distribution over $\{0,1\}^n$, jointly distributed with Z. If Y is quantum (t, δ) KL-hard for sampling given Z, then Y_I is quantum $(t', \delta/n)$ KL-hard for sampling given $(Z, Y_1, \ldots, Y_{I-1})$, for $I \sim [n]$, $t' = t/O(n)$.*

Proof. Same as Lemma 4.3 from [VZ12].

Theorem 29. *Let $(\mathsf{Samp}, \mathsf{Ver})$ be a (ω, γ)-OWPuzz with puzzle length $m(\lambda)$ secure against all time t adversaries. Then for all $\epsilon > 0$, $\mathsf{Samp} \to (k, s)$ has quantum $(t', \epsilon/m)$ next-bit pseudoentropy at least*

$$H(k, s) + \delta - \epsilon$$

for $t' = t^{\Omega(1)}/\mathsf{poly}(\lambda, 1/\epsilon)$ and

$$\delta = (1-\omega)\log\frac{1-\omega}{\gamma} + \omega\log\frac{\omega}{1-\gamma}$$

Proof. We first observe that k is (t, δ) KL-hard to sample given s. Let S be any time t quantum circuit. We will show that $KL(s, k || s, S(s)) \geq \delta$.

By monotonicity of quantum relative entropy,

$$KL(\mathsf{Ver}(s, k) || \mathsf{Ver}(s, S(s))) \leq KL(s, k || s, S(s))$$

But observe that $\mathsf{Ver}(s, k)$ is a Bernoulli random variable $Bern(p)$ for some $p > 1-\omega$ by correctness. But $\mathsf{Ver}(s, S(s))$ is a Bernoulli random variable $Bern(p')$ for p' the advantage of S in the OWPuzz game. By security of the OWPuzz, $p' \leq \gamma$.

$$KL(\mathsf{Ver}(s, k) || \mathsf{Ver}(s, S(s))) \geq KL(Bern(1-\omega), Bern(\gamma))$$
$$= (1-\omega)\log\tfrac{1-\omega}{\gamma} + \omega\log\tfrac{\omega}{1-\gamma} = \delta.$$

Let $m = \mathsf{poly}(\lambda)$ be the length of k. By Lemma 2, for $I \sim [m]$, k_I is quantum $\left(\frac{t}{O(m)}, \frac{\delta}{m}\right)$ KL-hard for sampling given $(s, k_1, \ldots, k_{I-1})$.

And so by Lemma 1, for every $\epsilon > 0$, k_I has quantum $(t', \epsilon/m)$ pseudoentropy at least $H(k_I | s, k_1, \ldots, k_{I-1}) + \frac{\delta}{m} - \epsilon/m$ given s. But by definition, this means that k has $(t', \epsilon/m)$ next-bit pseudoentropy $m \cdot H(k_I | s, k_1, \ldots, k_{I-1}) + \delta - \epsilon$ given s. But $m \cdot H(k_I | s, k_1, \ldots, k_{I-1}) \geq H(k|s)$, so (k, s) has $(t', \epsilon/m)$ next-bit pseudoentropy $H(s) + H(k|s) + \delta - \epsilon = H(k, s) + \delta - \epsilon$ for $t' = t^{\Omega(1)}/\mathsf{poly}(\lambda, 1/\epsilon)$.

Next-Bit Pseudoentropy Implies Non-uniform EFID. This argument follows the framework of [HRV10]. The argument is nearly identical to the classical case. The primary difference is that instead of lower bounding the length of the resultant string by the length of the input, we instead lower bound the length of the resultant string by the entropy of the input.

Definition 12 (From [KT24]). *A ν^*-non-uniform EFID pair is a QPT algorithm $G_\nu(1^\lambda, b)$ with classical parameter-dependent advice ν. On input a unary security parameter λ and $b \in \{0,1\}$ outputs a classical string such that*

1. For all QPT $\mathcal{A}$ and for all sufficiently large λ, the distributions $G_{\nu^*}(1^\lambda, 0)$ and $G_{\nu^*}(1^\lambda, 1)$ are indistinguishable.
2.
$$\Delta(G_{\nu^*}(1^\lambda, 0), G_{\nu^*}(1^\lambda, 1)) \geq 1 - \epsilon$$

Lemma 3 (Lemma 5.2 from [HRV10]). *For $i \in [m]$, $x^{(1)}, \ldots, x^{(\ell)} \in \mathcal{M}^m$, we define*

$$Equalizer(i, x^{(1)}, \ldots, x^{(\ell)}) := x_i^{(1)}, \ldots, x_m^{(1)}, x^{(2)}, \ldots, x^{(\ell-1)}, x_1^{(\ell)}, \ldots, x_{i-1}^{(\ell)}$$

That is, $Equalizer(i, x^{(1)}, \ldots, x^{(\ell)})$ truncates the first $i-1$ blocks from the first input and the last $m - (i-1)$ blocks from the last input.

Let X be a random variable over $\mathcal{M}^m$ with (t, ϵ) next block quantum pseudoentropy at least k. Let $X^{(1)}, \ldots, X^{(\ell)}$ be ℓ independent and identically distributed copies of X, and let I be uniformly distributed over $[m]$. Define $\widetilde{X} = Equalizer(I, X^{(1)}, \ldots, X^{(\ell)})$. Then every block of $\widetilde{X}$ has $(t - O(\ell \cdot m \cdot \log|\mathcal{M}|), \ell \cdot \epsilon)$ next-block quantum pseudoentropy at least k/m.

Lemma 4 (Lemma 5.3 from [HRV10]). *Let X be a random variable over $\mathcal{M}^m$ where every block of X has (t, ϵ) next-block quantum pseudo-min-entropy at least k. Let X^a refer to a i.i.d. copies of X. For every $\kappa > 0$, X^a has (t', ϵ') next-block quantum pseudo-min-entropy k' where*

1. $t' = t - O(ma \log |\mathcal{M}|)$
2. $\epsilon' = a^2(\epsilon + 2^{-\kappa} + 2^{-ca})$ for a universal constant $c > 0$
3. $k' = ak - O(\log(a|\mathcal{M}|)\sqrt{a\kappa})$

Lemma 5 (Lemma 5.4 from [HRV10]). *There exists an efficient procedure $\mathsf{Ext} \in NC^1$ on input $x \in (\{0,1\}^a)^m$ and $s \in \{0,1\}^a$ which outputs a string of length $y \in \{0,1\}^{a+m(k-k')}$ such that the following holds: Let X be a random variable over $(\{0,1\}^a)^m$ such that every block of X has (t, ϵ) next-bit quantum pseudo-min-entropy k, then for all QPT $\mathcal{A}$ running in time $t - m \cdot a^{O(1)}$*

$$\left| \Pr[\mathcal{A}(\mathsf{Ext}(X, \mathcal{U}_a)) \to 1] - \Pr[\mathcal{A}(\mathcal{U}_{a+m(k-k')}) \to 1] \right| \leq m(\epsilon + 2^{-k'/2})$$

Proof. The reductions for all three of these lemmas from [HRV10] are fully blackbox (in a quantum friendly way), and also hold in the quantum setting.

Lemma 6. *Let X be a random variable with $|X| = m$. If $H(X) \leq m - \delta$ for some $\delta > 0$, then*

$$SD(X, \mathcal{U}_m) \geq \frac{\delta}{2m - \delta} - 2^{-\delta/2}$$

In particular, if $m = O(p(\lambda))$ and $\delta = \Omega(p'(\lambda))$ for some polynomials p and p', then there exists a polynomial q such that

$$SD(X, \mathcal{U}_m) = \Omega\left(\frac{1}{q(\lambda)}\right)$$

We defer the proof to the full version of this paper.

Theorem 30 (Adapted from Theorem 5.5 from [HRV10]). *Let $m(\lambda), \Delta(\lambda)$ be two computable functions such that $\Delta = \Delta(\lambda) \in [1/\text{poly}(\lambda), \lambda]$. Let $\{X\}_{\lambda \in \mathbb{N}}$ be a family of efficiently samplable random variables of length $m(\lambda)$ with next-bit pseudoentropy at least $H(X) + \Delta$. Then there exists a function $\nu^*(\lambda) \leq |X|$ such that there exists a QPT algorithm $D_\nu(1^\lambda)$ outputting a classical string such that*

1. $D_{\nu^*}(1^\lambda) \approx \mathcal{U}$
2. $SD(D_{\nu^*}(1^\lambda), \mathcal{U}) \geq \frac{1}{p(\lambda)}$

for some efficiently computable polynomial p.

The proof of this theorem follows essentially the same lines as the proof from [HRV10], but with all references to the input length replaced by the entropy of X. This gives a distribution indistinguishable from uniform but with less than full entropy. Lemma 6 then gives a bound on the statistical distance. However, this bound is not $1 - \mathsf{negl}$. Fortunately, taking the product distribution amplifies statistical distance, so we simply take the direct product of the construction from [HRV10].

Proof. Without loss of generality, we will assume that the block-length of X is a power of 2 (otherwise, we can just append 0s). We have that for all $c > 0$ and sufficiently large λ, X has $(t = \lambda^c, \epsilon = \lambda^{-c})$ next-bit pseudoentropy $H(X) + \Delta$. We set $\ell := \lceil 2(\nu^* + \Delta + \log m)/\Delta \rceil = \Omega(\nu^*/\Delta)$ in Lemma 3 and get a new random variable $\widetilde{X} = Equalizer(I, X^{(1)}, \ldots, X^{(\ell)})$. We will define

$$D_s(1^\lambda, 1) := \mathsf{Ext}((\widetilde{X})^a, \mathcal{U}_a)$$

using the Ext from Lemma 5 for some value of $a = \mathsf{poly}(\lambda)$ and with output length $d_s := a + m(\ell - 1)(k'_s - \kappa)$ for $k'_s := ak_s - O(\log(a|\mathcal{M}|)\sqrt{a\kappa})$ and $k_s := (s + \Delta)/m$.

Observe that when $\nu = \nu^* = H(X)$, Lemma 3 shows that every bit of $\widetilde{X}$ has $(t - O(\ell m), \ell \epsilon)$ next-bit quantum pseudoentropy at least $k_{\nu^*} = (\nu^* + \Delta)/m$.

Next, Lemma 4 shows that every block of $(\widetilde{X})^a$ has $(t - O(m\ell a), a^2(\epsilon + 2^{-\kappa} + 2^{-\Omega(a)}))$ next-bit quantum pseudo-min-entropy at least $k'_{\nu^*} = ak_{\nu^*} - O(\sqrt{a\kappa} \log a)$.

Finally, Lemma 5 shows that for all QPT $\mathcal{A}$ running in time $t - O(m\ell a^{O(1)}) = t - \mathsf{poly}(\lambda)$,

$$\big|\Pr[\mathcal{A}(D_{\nu^*}(1^\lambda)) \to 1] - \Pr[\mathcal{A}(\mathcal{U}) \to 1]\big| \leq m\ell(a^2(\epsilon + 2^{-\kappa} + 2^{-\Omega(a)}) + 2^{-\kappa/2})$$
$$\leq \mathsf{poly}(\lambda)(\epsilon + 2^{-\kappa/2} + 2^{-\Omega(a)})$$

Setting $\kappa = \lambda/2$ and using the fact that this holds for all $t = n^c, \epsilon = n^{-c}$, we get that $D_{\nu^*}(1^\lambda)$ and $\mathcal{U}_{d_s}$ are indistinguishable.

It just remains to be shown that

$$\Delta(D_{\nu^*}(1^\lambda), \mathcal{U}_{d_s}) \geq \frac{1}{\mathsf{poly}(\lambda)}$$

We will do this by showing that $H(D_{\nu^*}) \leq H(\mathcal{U}_{d_{\nu^*}}) - \Omega(\mathsf{poly}(\lambda)) = d_{\nu^*} - \Omega(\mathsf{poly}(\lambda))$ and then applying Lemma 6.

Observe that when $\nu^* = H(X)$, $H(\tilde{X}) \leq \ell H(X) + \log m$. And so $H(\tilde{X}^a) \leq a(\ell H(X) + \log m)$. It is clear to see that $H(D_{\nu^*}) \leq a(\ell H(X) + \log m) + a$. Let us denote this value by $d' := H(D_{\nu^*})$.

$$\begin{aligned} d_{\nu^*} &= a + m(\ell - 1)(k'_{\nu^*} - \kappa) \\ &= a + m(\ell - 1)(ak_{\nu^*} - O(\sqrt{a\kappa}\log a) - \kappa) \\ &= a + a(\ell H(X) + \log m) + a\ell\Delta - a(\nu^* + \Delta + \log m) - m(\ell-1)(O(\sqrt{a\kappa}\log a) + \kappa) \\ &\geq a + a(\ell H(X) + \log m) + a\ell\Delta/2 - m(\ell-1)(O(\sqrt{a\kappa}\log a) + \kappa) \\ &\geq d' + a\ell\Delta/2 - m(\ell-1)(O(\sqrt{a\kappa}\log a) + \kappa) \\ &\geq d' + a\ell\Delta/4 \\ &= d' + \Omega(as) \\ &= d' + \Omega(\mathsf{poly}(\lambda)) \end{aligned}$$

when

$$a = \Theta\left(\left(\left(\frac{m(\ell-1)}{\Delta\ell}\right)^2 \kappa \log^2\left(\frac{m(\ell-1)\kappa}{\Delta\ell}\right)\right)\right) = \Theta\left(\frac{m^2\kappa\log^2\lambda}{\Delta^2}\right)$$

Lemma 7 (Amplification of Statistical Distance.). Let $SD(X,Y) \geq \delta$. If $q \geq \frac{12t}{\delta^2}$ then $SD(X^q, Y^q) \geq 1 - 2e^{-t}$.

We defer this proof to the full version.

Corollary 12. *Let $\Delta = \Delta(n) \in [1/\mathsf{poly}(n), n]$ and let $\{X\}_{n\in\mathbb{N}}$ be a family of efficiently samplable random variables of length m with next-bit pseudoentropy at least $H(X) + \Delta$. Then there exists a function $\nu^*(\lambda) \leq |X|$ such that there exists a non-uniform ν^*-EFID.*

Proof. Define $G_\nu(1^\lambda, 0)$ to be uniform over $q(\lambda) \cdot d_s$ bits for some $q = \mathsf{poly}(\lambda)$ to be set later. Define $G_\nu(1^\lambda, 1) = D_{\nu^*}(1^\lambda)^{q(\lambda)}$.

Since $D_{\nu^*}(1^\lambda) \approx \mathcal{U}_{d_s}$, $D_{\nu^*}(1^\lambda)^{q(\lambda)} \approx \mathcal{U}_{q(\lambda) \cdot d_s}$.

Since $SD(D_{\nu^*}(1^\lambda), \mathcal{U}_{d_s}) \geq \frac{1}{p(\lambda)}$, if we define $q(\lambda) = 12\lambda p(\lambda)$, then by Lemma 7

$$SD(G_\nu(1^\lambda, 0), G_\nu(1^\lambda, 1)) \geq 1 - 2e^{-\lambda} = 1 - \mathsf{negl}(\lambda)$$

Corollary 13. *If, for some $c > 0$, there exists a $(\mathsf{negl}(\lambda), 1 - \lambda^{-c})$ one-way puzzle $(\mathsf{Samp}, \mathsf{Ver})$, then there exists an ν^*-non-uniform EFID pair.*

Proof. Let $\omega = \mathsf{negl}(\lambda)$ and $\gamma = 1 - \lambda^{-c}$ be the correctness and security parameters of $(\mathsf{Samp}, \mathsf{Ver})$, and let $n(\lambda)$ be the length of the key and let $m(\lambda)$ be the length of the puzzle. For all $t = \mathsf{poly}(\lambda)$, $\epsilon > 0$, by Theorem 29, $\mathsf{Samp} \to (k, s)$ has $(t^{\Omega(1)}/\mathsf{poly}(\lambda, 1/\epsilon), \epsilon/m)$ quantum next-bit pseudoentropy at least $H(k,s) + \delta - \epsilon$ for

$$\delta = (1-\omega)\log\frac{1-\omega}{\gamma} + \omega\log\frac{\omega}{1-\gamma}.$$

But observe,

$$(1-\omega)\log\frac{1-\omega}{\gamma} + \omega\log\frac{\omega}{1-\gamma}$$

$$\geq \frac{1}{2}\log\frac{1}{1-\lambda^{-c}} + (1-\omega)\log(1-\omega) + \omega\log\omega + \omega\log\lambda^c$$

$$\geq \frac{1}{2}\log\frac{1}{1-\lambda^{-c}} - \mathsf{negl}(\lambda) \geq \lambda^{-(c+1)}$$

for all sufficiently large λ.

Thus, for all sufficiently large d such that $n^{-d} \cdot m \leq \lambda^{-(c+1)}/2$, for all $t = \mathrm{poly}(\lambda)$, $\mathsf{Samp} \to (k,s)$ has $(t^{\Omega(1)}/\mathrm{poly}(\lambda, \lambda^d), n^{-d})$ quantum next-bit pseudoentropy at least $H(k,s) + \frac{1}{2}\lambda^{-(c+1)}$. Adjusting the value of t shows us that $\mathsf{Samp} \to (k,s)$ has quantum next-bit pseudoentropy at least $H(k,s) + \frac{1}{2}\lambda^{-(c+1)}$.

By Corollary 12 there exists a ν^*-EFID for $\nu^* \leq m + n$.

Corollary 14. *If, for some $c > 0$, there exists a $(\mathsf{negl}(\lambda), 1 - \lambda^{-c})$ one-way puzzle $(\mathsf{Samp}, \mathsf{Ver})$, then there exists an EFI pair.*

Proof. Prior work shows that there exists a quantum combiner for quantum bit commitments [HKNY23], which are equivalent to EFI pairs [BCQ22]. We observe that this combiner (when composed with the construction of EFI pairs from commitments) operates separately on each security parameter. Thus, given a non-uniform EFID pair, we can apply the combiner from [HKNY23] to the non-uniform construction instantiated with each possible value of the advice. This process maintains security, but produces a quantum output. Thus, this process takes a non-uniform EFID pair and produces an EFI pair.

Since Corollary 13 shows that weak one-way puzzles can be used to build a non-uniform EFID pair, composing that construction with this approach produces an EFI pair from any weak one-way puzzle.

10.2 QEFID Imply OWPuzz

Definition 13 (ν^*-**Non-uniform** OWPuzz). *Let $\nu^*(\lambda)$ be some function. A ν^*-non-uniform one way puzzle (OWPuzz) is a pair of a sampling algorithm and a verification function $(\mathsf{Samp}_\nu, \mathsf{Ver}_\nu)$ taking in advice ν with the following syntax:*

1. *$\mathsf{Samp}_\nu(1^\lambda) \to (k,s)$ is a uniform QPT algorithm which outputs a pair of classical strings (k,s). We refer to s as the puzzle and k as the key. Without loss of generality, we can assume $k \in \{0,1\}^\lambda$.*
2. *$\mathsf{Ver}_\nu(k,s) \to b$ is a function which takes in a key and puzzle and outputs a bit $b \in \{0,1\}$.*

satisfying the following properties:

1. *Correctness: Outputs of the sampler pass verification with overwhelming probability*

$$\Pr_{\mathsf{Samp}_{\nu^*}(1^\lambda) \to (k,s)}[\mathsf{Ver}_{\nu^*}(k,s) \to 1] \geq 1 - \alpha$$

2. Security: Given a puzzle s, it is computationally infeasible to find a key s which verifies. That is, for all non-uniform QPT algorithms $\mathcal{A}$,

$$\Pr_{\mathsf{Samp}_{\nu^*}(1^\lambda) \to (k,s)}[\mathsf{Ver}_{\nu^*}(\mathcal{A}(s), s) \to 1] \leq \beta$$

That is, a non-uniform one-way puzzle is a one-way puzzle for which correctness and security are only guaranteed to hold when given the correct advice.

Lemma 8 (From QEFID to OWPuzz). *If there exists QEFID pair G, then there exists a OWPuzz (Samp, Ver).*

We observe that the same argument also works relative to an advice string, and so we have

Lemma 9 (From Non-uniform QEFID to Non-uniform OWPuzz). *Let $\nu^*(\lambda)$ be some function. If there exists a ν^*-non-uniform QEFID pair G_ν, then there exists a ν^*-non-uniform OWPuzz $(\mathsf{Samp}_\nu, \mathsf{Ver}_\nu)$.*

Lemma 10 (From Non-uniform OWPuzz to OWPuzz). *Let $p(\lambda)$ be some computable polynomial. Let $\nu^*(\lambda)$ be some function satisfying $\nu^*(\lambda) \leq p(\lambda)$. If there exists a ν^*-non-uniform OWPuzz $(\mathsf{Samp}_\nu, \mathsf{Ver}_\nu)$, then there exists a OWPuzz $(\widetilde{\mathsf{Samp}}, \widetilde{\mathsf{Ver}})$.*

Proof. We simply apply the construction from Remark 4 to $(\mathsf{Samp}_1, \mathsf{Ver}_1), \ldots, (\mathsf{Samp}_p, \mathsf{Ver}_p)$. An analogous argument to the proof that this construction is a combiner will give that the resulting $(\widetilde{\mathsf{Samp}}, \widetilde{\mathsf{Ver}})$ is a OWPuzz.

We now have all the pieces to show Theorem 22 that security for OWPuzz can be amplified. First Corollary 13 gives us that weak OWPuzz imply non-uniform QEFID, Then the two lemmas above give us that non-uniform QEFID imply non-uniform OWPuzz which in turn imply strong OWPuzz.

Acknowledgments. We thank Yanyi Liu for insightful discussion. Kai-Min Chung was partially supported by the Air Force Office of Scientific Research under award number FA2386-23-1-4107 and NSTC QC project, under Grant no. NSTC 112-2119-M-001-006. E. Goldin was supported by a National Science Foundation Graduate Research Fellowship.

References

[ABOBS22] Aharonov, D., Ben-Or, M., Brandão, F.G.S.L., Sattath, O.: The pursuit of uniqueness: extending valiant-vazirani theorem to the probabilistic and quantum settings. Quantum **6**, 668 (2022)

[AC01] Adcock, M., Cleve, R.: A quantum Goldreich-Levin theorem with cryptographic applications (2001)

[ACC+22] Austrin, P., Chung, H., Chung, K.-M., Fu, S., Lin, Y.-T., Mahmoody, M.: On the impossibility of key agreements from quantum random oracles. In: Dodis, Y., Shrimpton, T. (eds.) CRYPTO 2022, Part II, pp. 165–194. Springer, Cham (2022). https://doi.org/10.1007/978-3-031-15979-4_6

[ALY23a] Ananth, P., Lin, Y.-T., Yuen, H.: Pseudorandom strings from pseudorandom quantum states. arXiv preprint arXiv:2306.05613 (2023)

[ALY23b] Ananth, P., Lin, Y.-T., Yuen, H.: Pseudorandom strings from pseudorandom quantum states. Cryptology ePrint Archive, Paper 2023/904 (2023. https://eprint.iacr.org/2023/904

[AQY22] Ananth, P. Qian, L., Yuen, H.: Hyptography from pseudorandom quantum states. In: Dodis, Y., Shrimpton, T. (eds.) CRYPTO 2022, pp. 208–236. Springer, Cham (2022)

[BBO+24] Barhoush, M., Behera, A., Ozer, L., Salvail, L., Sattath, O.: Signatures from pseudorandom states via ⊥-prfs (2024)

[BCQ22] Brakerski, Z., Canetti, R., Qian, L.: On the computational hardness needed for quantum cryptography. Cryptology ePrint Archive, Paper 2022/1181 (2022). https://eprint.iacr.org/2022/1181

[BEM24] Bouaziz-Ermann, S., Muguruza, G.: Quantum pseudorandomness cannot be shrunk in a black-box way. Cryptology ePrint Archive, Paper 2024/291 (2024). https://eprint.iacr.org/2024/291

[BQSY23] Bostanci, J., Qian, L., Spooner, N., Yuen, H.: An efficient quantum parallel repetition theorem and applications (2023)

[CCL+17] Chen, Y.-H., Chung, K.-M., Vadhan, S.P., Wu, X., Lai , C.-Y.: Computational notions of quantum min-entropy (2017)

[CGG+23] Cavalar, B., Goldin, E., Gray, M., Hall, P., Liu, Y., Pelecanos, A.: On the computational hardness of quantum one-wayness. arXiv preprint arXiv:2312.08363 (2023)

[CLM23] Chung, K.-M., Lin, Y.-T., Mahmoody, M.: Black-box separations for non-interactive classical commitments in a quantum world. In: Hazay, C., Stam, M. (eds.) EUROCRYPT 2023, pp. 144–172. Springer, Cham (2023). https://doi.org/10.1007/978-3-031-30545-0_6

[CM24] Coladangelo, A., Mutreja, S.: On black-box separations of quantum digital signatures from pseudorandom states (2024)

[GGM86] Goldreich, O., Goldwasser, S., Micali, S.: How to construct random functions. J. ACM **33**(4), 792–807 (1986)

[GL89] Goldreich, O., Levin, L.A.: A hard-core predicate for all one-way functions. In: Proceedings of the Twenty-First Annual ACM Symposium on Theory of Computing, STOC 1989, pp. 25–32. Association for Computing Machinery, New York (1989)

[GMR87] Goldwasser, S., Micali, S., Rivest, R.L.: A digital signature scheme secure against adaptive chosen message attack this research was supported by NSF grant MCS-80-06938, an IBM/MIT faculty development award, and Darpa contract n00014-85-k-0125: extended abstract. In: Johnson, D.S., Nishizeki, T., Nozaki, A., Wilf, H.S. (eds.) Discrete Algorithms and Complexity, pp. 287–310. Academic Press (1987)

[Gol90] Goldreich, O.: A note on computational indistinguishability. Inf. Process. Lett. **34**(6), 277–281 (1990)

[HILL99] HÅstad, J., Impagliazzo, R., Levin, L.A., Luby, M.: A pseudorandom generator from any one-way function. SIAM J. Comput. **28**(4), 1364–1396 (1999)

[HKN+05] Harnik, D., Kilian, J., Naor, M., Reingold, O., Rosen, A.: On robust combiners for oblivious transfer and other primitives. In: Cramer, R. (ed.) EUROCRYPT 2005. LNCS, vol. 3494, pp. 96–113. Springer, Heidelberg (2005). https://doi.org/10.1007/11426639_6

[HKNY23] Hiroka, T., Kitagawa, F., Nishimaki, R., Yamakawa, T.: Robust combiners and universal constructions for quantum cryptography. Cryptology ePrint Archive, Paper 2023/1772 (2023). https://eprint.iacr.org/2023/1772

[HMY23] Hhan, M., Morimae, T., Yamakawa, T.: Quantum public key encryption and commitments from the hardness of detecting superpositions to cryptography (2023)

[HRV10] Haitner, I., Reingold, O., Vadhan, S.: Efficiency improvements in constructing pseudorandom generators from one-way functions. In: Proceedings of the Forty-Second ACM Symposium on Theory of Computing, STOC 2010, pp. 437–446. Association for Computing Machinery, New York (2010)

[IL89] Impagliazzo, R., Luby, M.: One-way functions are essential for complexity based cryptography. In: 30th Annual Symposium on Foundations of Computer Science, pp. 230–235 (1989)

[Imp95] Impagliazzo, R.: A personal view of average-case complexity. In: Proceedings of Structure in Complexity Theory, Tenth Annual IEEE Conference, pp. 134–147 (1995)

[INN+22] Irani, S., Natarajan, A., Nirkhe, C., Rao, S., Yuen, H.: Quantum search-to-decision reductions and the state synthesis problem. Schloss Dagstuhl - Leibniz-Zentrum für Informatik (2022)

[KNY23] Kitagawa, F., Nishimaki, R., Yamakaw, T.: Publicly verifiable deletion from minimal assumptions. Cryptology ePrint Archive, Paper 2023/538 (2023). https://eprint.iacr.org/2023/538

[Kre21] Kretschmer, W.: Quantum pseudorandomness and classical complexity. Schloss Dagstuhl - Leibniz-Zentrum für Informatik (2021)

[KT24] Khurana, D., Tomer, K.: Commitments from quantum one-wayness (2024)

[Lam79] Lamport, L.: Constructing digital signatures from a one way function. Technical Report CSL-98, October 1979. This paper was published by IEEE in the Proceedings of HICSS-43 in January (2010)

[Lev87] Levin, L.A.: One way functions and pseudorandom generators. Combinatorica **7**(4), 357–363 (1987)

[MP23] Mazor, N., Pass, R.: Counting unpredictable bits: a simple PRG from one-way functions. Cryptology ePrint Archive, Paper 2023/1451 (2023). https://eprint.iacr.org/2023/1451

[MY22a] Morimae, T., Yamakawa, T.: One-wayness in quantum cryptography. Cryptology ePrint Archive, Paper 2022/1336 (2022). https://eprint.iacr.org/2022/1336

[MY22b] Morimae, T., Yamakawa, T.: Quantum commitments and signatures without one-way functions. In: Annual International Cryptology Conference, pp. 269–295. Springer (2022). https://doi.org/10.1007/978-3-031-15802-5_10

[Nao91] Naor, M.: Bit commitment using pseudorandomness. J. Cryptol. **4**(2), 151–158 (1991)

[VZ12] Vadhan, S., Zheng, C.J.: Characterizing pseudoentropy and simplifying pseudorandom generator constructions. In: Proceedings of the 44th Annual ACM Symposium on Theory of Computing (STOC 2012), pp. 817–836. ACM (2012)

[Yao82] Yao, A.C.: Theory and application of trapdoor functions. In: 23rd Annual Symposium on Foundations of Computer Science (SFCS 1982), pp. 80–91 (1982)

Threshold Cryptography

Adaptively Secure BLS Threshold Signatures from DDH and co-CDH

Sourav Das[✉] and Ling Ren

University of Illinois at Urbana Champaign, Champaign, USA
{souravd2,renling}@illinois.edu

Abstract. Threshold signatures are one of the most important cryptographic primitives in distributed systems. A popular choice of threshold signature scheme is the BLS threshold signature introduced by Boldyreva (PKC'03). Some attractive properties of Boldyreva's threshold signature are that the signatures are unique and short, the signing process is non-interactive, and the verification process is identical to that of non-threshold BLS. These properties have resulted in its practical adoption in several decentralized systems. However, despite its popularity and wide adoption, up until recently, the Boldyreva scheme has been proven secure only against a static adversary. Very recently, Bacho and Loss (CCS'22) presented the first proof of adaptive security for the Boldyreva scheme, but they have to rely on strong and non-standard assumptions such as the hardness of one-more discrete log (OMDL) and the Algebraic Group Model (AGM). In this paper, we present the first adaptively secure threshold BLS signature scheme that relies on the hardness of DDH and co-CDH in asymmetric pairing groups in the Random Oracle Model (ROM). Our signature scheme also has non-interactive signing, compatibility with non-threshold BLS verification, and practical efficiency like Boldyreva's scheme. These properties make our protocol a suitable candidate for practical adoption with the added benefit of provable adaptive security.

1 Introduction

Threshold signatures schemes [32,33,42] protect the signing key by sharing it among a group of signers so that an adversary must corrupt a threshold number of signers to be able to forge signatures. The increasing demand for decentralized applications has resulted in large-scale adoptions of threshold signature schemes. Many state-of-the-art Byzantine fault tolerant protocols utilize threshold signatures to lower communication costs [6,40,43,55,57,71]. Efforts to standardize threshold cryptosystems are already underway [19].

A popular choice of threshold signature is the BLS signature, introduced by Boldyreva [15] building on the work of Boneh-Lynn-Shacham [16]. Boldyreva's BLS threshold signature scheme is popular because its verification is identical to standard non-threshold BLS signature, its signing process is non-interactive, the signatures are unique and small (a single elliptic curve group element), and the

© International Association for Cryptologic Research 2024
L. Reyzin and D. Stebila (Eds.): CRYPTO 2024, LNCS 14926, pp. 251–284, 2024.
https://doi.org/10.1007/978-3-031-68394-7_9

scheme is very efficient in terms of both computation and communication. These properties have resulted in practical adoptions of Boldyreva's BLS threshold signature for applications in the decentralized setting [1–4].

Static vs. Adaptive Security. However, despite its popularity and wide adoption, until recently, Boldyreva's scheme has been proven secure only against a static adversary. A static adversary must decide the set of signers to corrupt at the start of the protocol. In contrast, an adaptive adversary can decide which signers to corrupt during the execution of the protocol based on its view of the execution. Clearly, an adaptive adversary is a safer and more realistic assumption for the decentralized setting.

Designing an adaptively secure threshold signature scheme (BLS or otherwise) is challenging, let alone keeping it compatible with a non-threshold signature scheme. The generic approach to transforming a statically secure protocol into an adaptive one by guessing the set of parties an adaptive adversary may corrupt incurs an unacceptable exponential (in the number of parties) security loss. Existing adaptively secure threshold signature schemes in the literature have to make major sacrifices such as relying on parties to erase their internal states [23,54], inefficient cryptographic primitives like non-committing encryptions [46,56], or strong and non-standard assumptions such as one more discrete logarithm (OMDL) in the algebraic group model (AGM) [8,28]. To make matters worse, for Boldyreva's variant of BLS signatures in particular, the recent work of Bacho-Loss [8] proves that a strong assumption such as OMDL is necessary.

Our Results. We present an adaptively secure BLS threshold signature scheme. Our scheme retains the attractive properties of Boldyreva's scheme: signing is non-interactive, verification is identical to non-threshold BLS, and the scheme is simple and efficient.

The adaptive security proof of our signature scheme assumes the hardness of the decisional Diffie-Hellman (DDH) problem in a source group and the hardness of the co-computational Diffie-Hellman (co-CDH) problem in asymmetric pairing groups in the random oracle model (ROM). To put things into perspective, note that the standard non-threshold BLS signature assumes hardness of computational Diffie-Hellman (CDH) in pairing groups[1] in the ROM. Thus, our scheme only relies on DDH besides what standard non-threshold BLS signature already relies on. Moreover, if one is content with proving our scheme statically secure, we only need CDH in the ROM, as in the standard BLS signature.

In terms of efficiency, our scheme is only slightly more expensive than the Boldyreva scheme [15]. The signing key of each signer consists of three field elements compared to one in Boldyreva. The threshold public keys consist of n group elements in total, identical to Boldyreva. Here n is the total number of signers. Our per-signer signing cost and partial signature verification cost of the aggregator are also small. We implement our scheme in Go and compare its performance with Boldyreva's scheme. Our evaluation confirms that our scheme adds very small overheads.

---

[1] The standard non-threshold BLS signature scheme can also work with symmetric pairing groups and hence the CDH assumption instead of co-CDH.

We also describe a distributed key generation (DKG) protocol to secret share the signing key of our scheme. Our DKG adds minimal overhead compared to existing DKG schemes.

All of the above properties combined make our scheme a suitable candidate for a drop-in replacement for BLS signature in deployment systems, and a worthwhile trade-off for the added benefit of provable adaptive security at modest performance cost.

Paper Organization. We discuss the related work in §2 and present a technical overview of our scheme in §3. In §4, we describe the required preliminaries. We then describe our threshold signature scheme assuming a trusted party for generating signing keys in §5, and prove its adaptive security in §6. Next, in §7, we describe a DKG protocol that parties can use to generate signing keys in a distributed manner and briefly discuss how we prove the adaptive security with DKG. We analyze the properties of the DKG protocol, and prove the adaptive security of our threshold signature scheme with the DKG in the full version. We discuss the implementation and evaluation details in §8, and conclude with a discussion in §9.

2 Related Works

Threshold signature schemes were first introduced by Desmedt [32]. Since then, numerous threshold signature schemes with various properties have been proposed. Most of the natural and popular threshold signature schemes are proven secure only against a static adversary [10,12,15,22,26,27,32,41,42,45,51,62,65–67]. The difficulty in proving adaptive security usually lies in the reduction algorithm's inability to generate consistent internal states for all parties. As a result, the reduction algorithm needs to know which parties will be corrupt, making the adversary static [10]. We will next review threshold signatures with adaptive security. We classify them into *interactive* and *non-interactive* schemes.

Interactive Threshold Signatures. In an interactive threshold signature, signers interact with each other to compute the signature on a given message. The first adaptively secure threshold signatures were independently described by Canetti et al. [23] and Frankel et al. [36,37]. They prove adaptive security of their threshold signature scheme by introducing the "single inconsistent player" (SIP) technique. In the SIP approach, there exists only one signer whose internal state cannot be consistently revealed to the adversary. Since this inconsistent signer is chosen at random, it is only corrupt with probability less than $1/2$ for $n > 2t$. These schemes also rely on secure erasure.

Lysyanskaya-Peikert [56] and Abe and Fehr [5] use the SIP technique along with expensive cryptographic primitives such as threshold homomorphic encryptions and non-committing encryptions, respectively, to design adaptively secure threshold signatures without relying on erasures. Later works [7,69] extend the SIP technique to Rabin's threshold RSA signature [61] and the Waters [70] signatures. A major downside of all these works is the high signing cost. For every message, signers need to run a protocol similar to a DKG protocol. Concurrently and independently, [9] presents a three-round adaptively secure threshold signature scheme assuming the hardness of DDH.

Non-interactive Threshold Signatures. A non-interactive threshold signature requires each signer to send a single message to sign. Practical, robust, non-interactive threshold signatures were described by Shoup [65] under the RSA assumption and by Katz and Yung [49] assuming the hardness of factoring. Boldyreva [15] presented a non-interactive threshold BLS signature scheme. Until recently, these schemes were proven secure against static adversaries only.

Bacho and Loss [8] recently proved adaptive security for Boldyreva's scheme based on the One More Discrete Logarithm (OMDL) assumption in the Random Oracle Model (ROM) and Algebraic Group Model (AGM). Their method addresses the challenge of revealing internal states of corrupt nodes to the adversary by giving the reduction adversary limited access to discrete logarithm oracle. (This approach has since been extended to the interactive threshold Schnorr signature [28].) Bacho-Loss [8] also proves that reliance on OMDL is necessary for proving Boldyreva's BLS signature adaptively secure. This implies that a new protocol is needed to prove adaptive security under more standard assumptions.

Libert et al., [53] presented a pairing-based, non-interactive threshold signature scheme assuming the hardness of the double-pairing assumption. However, their signature scheme is incompatible with standard BLS signature verification and thus cannot be a drop-in replacement for BLS in deployment systems. The signature size of their scheme is also twice as large as a BLS signature. Very recently, [30,39] also present pairing-based non-interactive threshold signatures with adaptive security. However, their signatures are also incompatible and more than 5× larger than BLS signatures.

3 Technical Overview

We need to introduce several new ideas to design a new BLS threshold signature scheme and prove it adaptively secure. First, we introduce a new way of embedding the co-CDH input into a simulation of our scheme. Since we want our final signature to be a standard BLS signature, and BLS signatures are deterministic, these changes are delicate. Moreover, we embed the co-CDH challenge in such a way that during simulation, it remains indistinguishable from an honest execution of the protocol. This should hold, even if we use a DKG to generate the signing keys. We address this as follows. In our security proof, the reduction adversary can simulate the DKG and the threshold signature scheme to the adversary by faithfully running the protocol on behalf of all but one honest signer, i.e., we work with the single inconsistent party (SIP) technique. Second, we use a new approach to program two random oracles in a correlated way while ensuring that it remains indistinguishable from uniformly random to a computationally bounded adversary. This step is crucial for the reduction adversary to simulate signing queries.

Boneh-Lynn-Sacham (BLS) Signature Scheme [16]. Before we describe our techniques, we briefly recall the non-threshold BLS signature scheme. Let $(\mathbb{G}, \hat{\mathbb{G}}, \mathbb{G}_T)$ be a tuple of prime order pairing groups with scalar field $\mathbb{F}$. Let $\mathcal{M}$ be the finite message space of the signature scheme. Let $g \in \mathbb{G}$ be a uniformly random generator of $\mathbb{G}$ and $\mathsf{H} : \mathcal{M} \to \hat{\mathbb{G}}$ be a hash function modeled as a random oracle. The signing key $\mathsf{sk} = s \in \mathbb{F}$ is a random field element, and $\mathsf{pk} = g^s \in \mathbb{G}$ is the corresponding public verification key. The signature σ on a message m is then $\mathsf{H}(m)^{\mathsf{sk}} \in \hat{\mathbb{G}}$. Any verifier validates a signature σ' on a message m by checking that $e(\mathsf{pk}, \mathsf{H}(m)) = e(g, \sigma')$, where $e : \mathbb{G} \times \hat{\mathbb{G}} \to \mathbb{G}_T$ is the bilinear pairing operation. The BLS signature is proven secure assuming the hardness of CDH in the ROM [16].

Our Core Ideas. We will illustrate our core ideas using a simplified threshold signature scheme, which we do not know how to prove adaptively secure. We describe our final protocol and its adaptive security proof in §5 and §6, respectively.

Let $(\mathbb{G}, \hat{\mathbb{G}}, \mathbb{G}_T)$ be a tuple of prime order asymmetric pairing groups with scalar field $\mathbb{F}$. Let $g, h \in \mathbb{G}$ be two uniformly random generators of $\mathbb{G}$ and $\hat{g}$ be a generator of $\hat{\mathbb{G}}$. As in the non-threshold BLS signature scheme, let $\mathsf{sk} = s \in \mathbb{F}$ be the secret signing key and $\mathsf{pk} = g^s \in \mathbb{G}$ be the public verification key. To get an (n, t) threshold signature scheme, the secret signing key s is then shared among n signers using a degree t polynomial $s(x)$. Additionally, signers also receive a share on a uniformly random polynomial $r(x)$ with the constraint that $r(0) = 0$. Precisely, the signing key of signer i is $\mathsf{sk}_i = (s(i), r(i))$ and the public verification key of signer i is $\mathsf{pk}_i = g^{s(i)} h^{r(i)} \in \mathbb{G}$.

With this initial setup, signers sign any message $m \in \mathcal{M}$, for a finite message space $\mathcal{M}$, as follows. Let $\mathsf{H}_0, \mathsf{H}_1$ be two random oracles where $\mathsf{H}_b : \mathcal{M} \to \hat{\mathbb{G}}$ for $b \in \{0, 1\}$. The partial signature from signer i on a message m is then $\sigma_i = \mathsf{H}_0(m)^{s(i)} \mathsf{H}_1(m)^{r(i)} \in \hat{\mathbb{G}}$. Upon receiving $t+1$ valid partial signatures from a set of signers T, the aggregator computes the threshold signature by interpolating them in the exponent, i.e., it computes the aggregated signature $\sigma = \prod_{i \in T} \sigma_i^{L_i}$ for appropriate Lagrange coefficients L_i. It is easy to see that since $r(0) = 0$, the interpolation yields a standard BLS signature $\sigma = \mathsf{H}_0(m)^s \mathsf{H}_1(m)^0 = \mathsf{H}_0(m)^s$.

An avid reader will note that the partial signatures are no longer verifiable using a pairing check. Indeed, signers in our protocol instead use a Σ-protocol to prove the correctness of their partial signatures.

Naturally, the important question is how this modified BLS threshold signature helps us prove adaptive security. (We reiterate that the goal of this section is to give intuition, and we do not know how to prove this exact scheme adaptively secure.) At a very high level, the additional parameter h, the additional polynomial $r(x)$, and the additional random oracle $\mathsf{H}_1(\cdot)$ provide the reduction adversary with extra avenues to embed the co-CDH input and extract a solution to the co-CDH input from a signature forgery. We will elaborate on this next.

Let $\mathcal{A}_{\text{co-CDH}}$ be the reduction algorithm and $\mathcal{A}$ be the adversary that breaks the unforgeability of our scheme. $\mathcal{A}_{\text{co-CDH}}$ will run our threshold signature scheme with a rigged public key $\mathsf{pk} = g^s h^r \in \mathbb{G}$ with $r \neq 0$. Concretely, we work with $r = 1$, i.e., $\mathsf{pk} = g^s h$, however, any non-zero value of r will also work. $\mathcal{A}_{\text{co-CDH}}$ will carefully interact with $\mathcal{A}$ so that $\mathcal{A}$ does not realize that the public key is rigged. Then, by definition, $\mathcal{A}$ will forge a BLS signature on some message m, i.e., $e(\mathsf{pk}, \mathsf{H}_0(m)) = e(g, \sigma)$. Now given a co-CDH input tuple $(g, \hat{g}, g^a, \hat{g}^a, \hat{g}^b)$, if we set $h = g^a$ and program the random oracle in a way such that $\mathsf{H}_0(m) = \hat{g}^b$, then $\sigma = \hat{g}^{(s+a)b}$. This implies that if $s \in \mathbb{F}$ is known, then we can efficiently compute $\hat{g}^{ab}$ given σ.

Let $s(x), r(x)$ be degree t polynomials for Shamir secret sharing of $s = s(0)$ and $r(0) = 1$. We will discuss in §6 how $\mathcal{A}_{\text{co-CDH}}$ interacts with $\mathcal{A}$ while ensuring that $\mathcal{A}_{\text{co-CDH}}$ knows $s(x)$ and $r(x)$, and $r(0) = 1$. Furthermore, in the full version, we will discuss how $\mathcal{A}_{\text{co-CDH}}$ achieves this even when we use a DKG key to generate the signing keys while relying on just a single inconsistent party. This implies that since $\mathcal{A}_{\text{co-CDH}}$ knows both $s(x), r(x)$, it can reveal the internal state of any party that $\mathcal{A}$ corrupts, except the inconsistent party to $\mathcal{A}$. Unless $\mathcal{A}$ corrupts the inconsistent party, $\mathcal{A}$'s view in a real protocol instance and an instance rigged by $\mathcal{A}_{\text{co-CDH}}$ are computationally indistinguishable.

The final part of our protocol is how $\mathcal{A}_{\text{co-CDH}}$ simulates the signing queries under the rigged public key. Consider a naive approach where we use the signing procedure of Boldyreva's scheme, i.e., the partial signature of signer i is $\mathsf{H}_0(m)^{s(i)}$. Then, the unique aggregated signature is $\sigma = \mathsf{H}_0(m)^s$. However, since $r(0) = 1$, unless $\mathsf{H}_0(m) = 1_{\hat{\mathbb{G}}}$, i.e., the identity of the group $\hat{\mathbb{G}}$, it will always be the case that $e(\mathsf{pk}, \mathsf{H}_0(m)) \neq e(g, \sigma)$, so $\mathcal{A}$ realizes that it is in a rigged instance. This is why we bring in an additional random oracle H_1 and have the partial signatures as $\sigma_i = \mathsf{H}_0(m)^{s(i)} \mathsf{H}_1(m)^{r(i)}$. The final aggregated signature is now $\sigma = \mathsf{H}_0(m)^s \mathsf{H}_1(m)$. If $\mathcal{A}_{\text{co-CDH}}$ programs the two random oracles in a correlated manner, the pairing check $e(\mathsf{pk}, \mathsf{H}_0(m)) = e(g, \sigma)$ will pass. Crucially, the correlated programming of the two random oracles must be undetectable to $\mathcal{A}$. In §6, we will prove this is indeed the case for our final scheme, assuming the hardness of DDH in $\hat{\mathbb{G}}$.

4 Preliminaries

Notations. For any integer a, we use $[a]$ to denote the ordered set $\{1, 2, \ldots, a\}$. For any set S, we use $s \leftarrow_\$ S$ to indicate that s is sampled uniformly randomly from S. We use $|S|$ to denote the size of set S. Throughout the paper, we will use "$\leftarrow$" for probabilistic assignment and "$:=$" for deterministic assignment. We use λ to denote the security parameter. A machine is probabilistic polynomial time (PPT) if it is a probabilistic algorithm that runs in poly(λ) time. We also use $\mathsf{negl}(\lambda)$ to denote functions negligible in λ. We use the terms *party* (resp. *parties*) and *signer* (resp. *signers*) interchangeably.

4.1 Model

We consider a set of n signers denoted by $\{1, 2, \ldots, n\}$. We consider a PPT adversary $\mathcal{A}$ who can corrupt up to $t < n$ out of the n signers. Corrupted signers can deviate arbitrarily from the protocol specification. Note that with $t \geq n/2$, i.e., with a dishonest majority, it is impossible to achieve both unforgeability and guaranteed output delivery [48]. We focus on unforgeability over guaranteed output delivery for the dishonest majority case.

When the signing keys of our signature scheme are generated by a trusted setup, we assume the network is asynchronous. However, for simplicity, we will assume lock-step synchrony for our DKG protocol, i.e., parties execute the protocol in synchronized rounds, and a message sent at the start of a round arrives by the end of that round. Moreover, our DKG assumes an honest majority, i.e., $t < n/2$. Furthermore, during DKG, we let signers access a broadcast channel to send a value to all signers. We can efficiently realize such a broadcast channel by running a Byzantine broadcast protocol [13,34,52,58]. We note that the synchrony assumption is not necessary since asynchronous DKG protocols exist [31,50]. Similarly, we can remove the honest majority assumption using ideas from [25].

4.2 Shamir Secret Sharing, Bilinear Pairing, and Assumptions

Shamir Secret Sharing. The Shamir secret sharing [64] embeds the secret s in the constant term of a polynomial $p(x) = s + a_1 x + a_2 x^2 + \cdots + a_d x^d$, where other coefficients $a_1, \cdots, a_d$ are chosen uniformly randomly from a field $\mathbb{F}$. The i-th share of the secret is $p(i)$, i.e., the polynomial evaluated at i. Given $d+1$ distinct shares, one can efficiently reconstruct the polynomial and the secret s using Lagrange interpolation. Also, s is information-theoretically hidden from an adversary that knows d or fewer shares.

Definition 1 (Bilinear Pairing). *Let $\mathbb{G}, \hat{\mathbb{G}}$ and $\mathbb{G}_T$ be three prime order cyclic groups with scalar field $\mathbb{F}$. Let $g \in \mathbb{G}$ and $\hat{g} \in \hat{\mathbb{G}}$ be generators. A pairing is an efficiently computable function $e : \mathbb{G} \times \hat{\mathbb{G}} \to \mathbb{G}_T$ satisfying the following properties.*

1. *bilinear: For all $u, u' \in \mathbb{G}$ and $\hat{v}, \hat{v}' \in \hat{\mathbb{G}}$ we have*

$$e(u \cdot u', \hat{v}) = e(u, \hat{v}) \cdot e(u', \hat{v}), \quad \text{and} \quad e(u, \hat{v} \cdot \hat{v}') = e(u, \hat{v}) \cdot e(u, \hat{v}')$$

2. *non-degenerate: $g_T := e(g, \hat{g})$ is a generator of $\mathbb{G}_T$.*

We refer to $\mathbb{G}$ and $\hat{\mathbb{G}}$ as the source groups and refer to $\mathbb{G}_T$ as the target group.

We require that the decisional Diffie-Hellman (DDH) assumption holds for $\hat{\mathbb{G}}$ and the co-computational Diffie-Hellman (co-CDH) assumption holds for $(\mathbb{G}, \hat{\mathbb{G}})$.

Assumption 1 (DDH). *Let GGen be a group generation algorithm, that on input 1^λ outputs the description of a prime order group $\hat{\mathbb{G}}$ with scalar field $\mathbb{F}$ of prime order p. The description also contains a generator $\hat{g} \in \hat{\mathbb{G}}$, and a description of the group operation. We say that the decisional Diffie-Hellman (DDH)* *assumption holds relative to* GGen, *if for all PPT adversary* $\mathcal{A}$, *the following advantage is negligible:*

$$\mathsf{Adv}^{\mathsf{DDH}}_{\mathcal{A},\mathsf{GGen}}(\lambda) := \left| \Pr\left[\mathcal{A}(\hat{\mathbb{G}}, \mathbb{F}, p, \hat{g}, \hat{g}^a, \hat{g}^b, \hat{g}^{ab}) = 1 \; \middle| \; \begin{array}{l} (\hat{\mathbb{G}}, \mathbb{F}, p, \hat{g}) \leftarrow \mathsf{GGen}(1^\lambda), \\ a, b \leftarrow_\$ \mathbb{F} \end{array} \right] \right.$$
$$\left. - \Pr\left[\mathcal{A}(\hat{\mathbb{G}}, \mathbb{F}, p, \hat{g}, \hat{g}^a, \hat{g}^b, \hat{g}^c) = 1 \; \middle| \; \begin{array}{l} (\hat{\mathbb{G}}, \mathbb{F}, p, \hat{g}) \leftarrow \mathsf{GGen}(1^\lambda), \\ a, b, c \leftarrow_\$ \mathbb{F} \end{array} \right] \right| = \varepsilon_{\mathsf{DDH}}$$

Assumption 2 (co-CDH). *Let* GGen' *be a group generation algorithm, that on input* 1^λ *outputs the description of prime order groups* $(\mathbb{G}, \hat{\mathbb{G}}, \mathbb{G}_T)$ *with the scalar field* $\mathbb{F}$ *of order* p, *and a bilinear pairing operation* $e : \mathbb{G} \times \hat{\mathbb{G}} \to \mathbb{G}_T$. *The description also contains generators* $(g, \hat{g}) \in (\mathbb{G}, \hat{\mathbb{G}})$, *and a description of the group operation. We say that the co-computational Diffie-Hellman (co-CDH) assumption holds relative to* GGen', *if for all PPT adversary* $\mathcal{A}$, *the following advantage is negligible:*

$$\mathsf{Adv}^{\mathsf{CDH}}_{\mathcal{A},\mathsf{GGen}'}(\lambda) := \Pr\left[\mathcal{A}(\mathbb{G}, \hat{\mathbb{G}}, \mathbb{F}, p, g, \hat{g}, g^a, \hat{g}^b, \hat{g}^b) = \hat{g}^{ab} \right.$$
$$\left. \middle| \; \begin{array}{l} (\mathbb{G}, \hat{\mathbb{G}}, \mathbb{G}_T, \mathbb{F}, p, g, \hat{g}) \leftarrow \mathsf{GGen}'(1^\lambda), \\ a, b \leftarrow_\$ \mathbb{F} \end{array} \right] = \varepsilon_{\mathsf{CDH}}$$

Remark on Pairing Group Types. Looking ahead, the final threshold signatures in our schemes are in $\hat{\mathbb{G}}$, and hence, we require DDH to be hard in $\hat{\mathbb{G}}$. This implies that the pairing groups must be asymmetric, i.e., $\mathbb{G} \neq \hat{\mathbb{G}}$. There are two types of asymmetric pairing groups: type-II and type-III [38]. A type-II pairing group supports one-directional efficient homomorphism. In our context, we can work with a type-II group $(\mathbb{G}, \hat{\mathbb{G}}, \mathbb{G}_T)$ with bilinear pairing operation $e : \mathbb{G} \times \hat{\mathbb{G}} \to \mathbb{G}_T$ that supports an efficient homomorphism $\Phi : \mathbb{G} \to \hat{\mathbb{G}}$, but not the other way around. Note that even with such one-directional efficient homomorphism, DDH can still be hard in $\hat{\mathbb{G}}$. Thus, we can use both type-II and type-III pairing groups for our threshold signature scheme.

4.3 Threshold Signature

In this section, we introduce the syntax and security definitions for threshold signature schemes. We focus on schemes that have non-interactive signing and deterministic verification. Our security definitions are based on those of [17].

Definition 2 (Non-interactive Threshold Signature). *Let* t, n *with* $t < n$ *be natural numbers. A non-interactive* (n, t)-*threshold signature scheme* TS *for a finite message space* $\mathcal{M}$ *is a tuple of polynomial time algorithms* TS = (Setup, KGen, PSign, PVer, Comb, Ver) *defined as follows:*

1. Setup(1^λ) $\to$ pp *takes as input a security parameter and outputs public parameters* pp *(which are given implicitly as input to all other algorithms).*

Game UF-CMA$_{\mathsf{TS}}^{\mathcal{A}}$:	Game RB-CMA$_{\mathsf{TS}}^{\mathcal{A}}$:
1: pp ← Setup(1^λ)	17: pp ← Setup(1^λ)
2: pk, $\{\mathsf{pk}_i, \mathsf{sk}_i\}_{i \in [n]}$ ← KGen(pp)	18: pk, $\{\mathsf{pk}_i, \mathsf{sk}_i\}_{i \in [n]}$ ← KGen(pp)
3: Let $\mathcal{C} := \emptyset, \mathcal{H} := [n]$	19: Let $\mathcal{C} := \emptyset, \mathcal{H} := [n]$
4: inp := pp, pk, $\{\mathsf{pk}_i\}_{i \in [n]}$	20: inp := pp, pk, $\{\mathsf{pk}_i\}_{i \in [n]}$
// $Q[m]$, initially $\{\}$, denotes the set of signers $\mathcal{A}$ queries for the partial signatures on m	// Verification of honest partial signatures are always successful
	21: $i, m \leftarrow \mathcal{A}^{\text{CORR}, \text{PSIG}}(\text{inp})$
	22: $\sigma_i \leftarrow \mathsf{PSign}(\mathsf{sk}_i, m)$
5: $(m, \sigma) \leftarrow \mathcal{A}^{\text{CORR}, \text{PSIG}}(\text{inp})$	23: if $\mathsf{PVer}(\mathsf{pk}_i, m, \sigma_i) \neq 1$:
6: if $|Q[m] \cup \mathcal{C}| \leq t \land \mathsf{Ver}(m, \mathsf{pk}, \sigma) = 1$:	24: return 1
7: return 1	// Combining valid partial signature must yield valid threshold signatures
8: return 0	
	25: $S, m', \{\sigma_i\}_{i \in S} \leftarrow \mathcal{A}^{\text{CORR}, \text{PSIG}}(\text{inp})$
Oracle CORR(i):	26: assert $|S| \geq t + 1$
9: if $\mathcal{C} \geq t$: return ⊥	27: assert $\mathsf{PVer}(\mathsf{pk}_i, m', \sigma_i) = 1, \forall i \in S$
10: $\mathcal{C} := \mathcal{C} \cup \{i\}; \mathcal{H} := \mathcal{H} \setminus \{i\}$	28: $\sigma := \mathsf{Comb}(S, m', \{\mathsf{pk}_i, \sigma_i\}_{i \in S})$
11: return sk_i	29: if $\mathsf{Ver}(\mathsf{pk}, m', \sigma) \neq 1$:
	30: return 1
Oracle PSIG(i, m):	31: return 0
12: if $i \in \mathcal{H}$:	
13: $Q[m] := Q[m] \cup \{i\}$	
14: Let $\sigma_i \leftarrow \mathsf{PSign}(m, \mathsf{sk}_i)$	
15: return σ_i	
16: return ⊥	

Fig. 1. The unforgeability security game UF-CMA$_{\mathsf{TS}}^{\mathcal{A}}$ and the robustness security game RB-CMA$_{\mathsf{TS}}^{\mathcal{A}}$ for a non-interactive (n, t)-threshold signature TS = (Setup, KGen, PSign, Comb, Ver) with an adaptive adversary $\mathcal{A}$.

2. KGen() → pk, $\{\mathsf{pk}_i, \mathsf{sk}_i\}_{i \in [n]}$ outputs a public key pk, a vector of threshold public keys $\{\mathsf{pk}_1, \ldots, \mathsf{pk}_n\}$, and a vector of secret key shares $\{\mathsf{sk}_1, \ldots, \mathsf{sk}_n\}$. The j-th signer receives $(\mathsf{pk}, \{\mathsf{pk}_i\}_{i \in [n]}, \mathsf{sk}_j)$.

3. PSign(sk_i, m) → σ_i takes as input a secret key share sk_i, and a message $m \in \mathcal{M}$. It outputs a signature share σ_i.

4. PVer($\mathsf{pk}_i, m, \sigma_i,$) → $0/1$ takes as input a threshold public key share pk_i, a message m, and a signature share σ_i. It outputs 1 (accept) or 0 (reject).

5. Comb($S, m, \{(\mathsf{pk}_i, \sigma_i)\}_{i \in S}$) → $\sigma/\bot$ takes as input a set S with $|S| \geq t + 1$, a message m, and a set of tuples $(\mathsf{pk}_i, \sigma_i)$ consisting of public keys and signature shares of signers in S. It outputs either a signature σ or $\bot$.

6. Ver(pk, m, σ) → $0/1$ takes as input a public key pk, a message m, and a signature σ. It outputs 1 (accept) or 0 (reject).

We require a non-interactive (n, t)-threshold signature scheme to satisfy *Unforgeability* and *Robustness* properties we describe next.

We formalize the unforgeability property using the UF-CMA$_{\mathsf{TS}}^{\mathcal{A}}$ game in Fig. 1. Let $\mathcal{A}$ be the adversary in the UF-CMA$_{\mathsf{TS}}^{\mathcal{A}}$ game. $\mathcal{A}$ gets as input the public parameters pp, an honestly generated public key pk and threshold public keys

$\{\mathsf{pk}_i\}_{i\in[n]}$. At any point in time, $\mathcal{A}$ can query the partial signature on a message m from any honest signer i by querying the oracle $\mathrm{PSIG}(i,m)$. The game also maintains a list Q to store the subset of parties $\mathcal{A}$ has queried for partial signatures, i.e., for any message m, $Q[m]$ stores the subset of honest signers $\mathcal{A}$ has queried for partial signatures on m. Initially, $Q[m] = \{\}$ for every message m.

$\mathcal{A}$ can corrupt up to t signers throughout the protocol using the CORR oracle. Upon corrupting any party, say party $i \in [n]$, $\mathcal{A}$ learns its signing key sk_i. Our protocol also has the property that the internal state used in all partial signings by a signer is efficiently computable from the signing key of the signer and the public messages sent by the signer. Thus, upon corruption, revealing only the signing key of the signer is sufficient.

Finally, when $\mathcal{A}$ outputs a valid forgery (m^*, σ^*), we say that $\mathcal{A}$ wins if $\mathcal{A}$ queried for partial signatures on m^* from at most $t - |\mathcal{C}|$ signers, i.e., $|Q[m] \cup \mathcal{C}| \leq t$.

With the $\mathsf{UF\text{-}CMA}^{\mathcal{A}}_{\mathsf{TS}}$ game defined in Fig. 1, we define the unforgeability under chosen message attack property as follows.

Definition 3 (Unforgeability Under Chosen Message Attack). *Let* $\mathsf{TS} = (\mathsf{Setup}, \mathsf{KGen}, \mathsf{PSign}, \mathsf{Comb}, \mathsf{Ver})$ *is a* (n,t)*-threshold signature scheme. Consider the game* $\mathsf{UF\text{-}CMA}^{\mathcal{A}}_{\mathsf{TS}}$ *defined in Fig. 1. We say that* TS *is* $\mathsf{UF\text{-}CMA}^{\mathcal{A}}_{\mathsf{TS}}$ *secure, if for all PPT adversaries* $\mathcal{A}$*, the following advantage is negligible, i.e.,*

$$\varepsilon_\sigma := \mathsf{Adv}^{\mathsf{UF\text{-}CMA}}_{\mathcal{A},\mathsf{TS}}(\lambda) := \Pr[\mathsf{UF\text{-}CMA}^{\mathcal{A}}_{\mathsf{TS}}(\lambda) \Rightarrow 1] = \mathsf{negl}(\lambda) \qquad (1)$$

We formalize the robustness property using the $\mathsf{RB\text{-}CMA}^{\mathcal{A}}_{\mathsf{TS}}$ game in Fig. 1. Intuitively, the robustness property ensures that the protocol behaves as expected for honest parties, even in the presence of an adaptive adversary that corrupts up to t parties. More precisely, it says that: (i) PVer should always accept honestly generated partial signatures; and (ii) if we combine $t+1$ valid partial signatures (accepted by PVer) using the Comb algorithm, the output of Comb should be accepted by Ver, except with a negligible probability. The latter requirement ensures that maliciously generated partial signatures cannot prevent an honest aggregator from efficiently computing a threshold signature (except with a negligible probability). Note that $\mathcal{A}$ can generate the partial signatures in an arbitrary manner. Also, looking ahead, our scheme achieves robustness even if $\mathcal{A}$ corrupts all parties.

Definition 4 (Robustness Under Chosen Message Attack). *Let* $\mathsf{TS} = (\mathsf{Setup}, \mathsf{KGen}, \mathsf{PSign}, \mathsf{Comb}, \mathsf{Ver})$ *is a* (t,n)*-threshold signature scheme. Consider the game* $\mathsf{RB\text{-}CMA}^{\mathcal{A}}_{\mathsf{TS}}$ *defined in Fig. 1. We say that* TS *is* $\mathsf{RB\text{-}CMA}^{\mathcal{A}}_{\mathsf{TS}}$ *secure, if for all PPT adversaries* $\mathcal{A}$*, the following advantage is negligible, i.e.,*

$$\mathsf{Adv}^{\mathsf{RB\text{-}CMA}}_{\mathcal{A},\mathsf{TS}}(\lambda) := \Pr[\mathsf{RB\text{-}CMA}^{\mathcal{A}}_{\mathsf{TS}}(\lambda) \Rightarrow 1] = \mathsf{negl}(\lambda) \qquad (2)$$

4.4 Boldyreva's BLS Threshold Signature Scheme [15]

For a security parameter λ, let $(\mathbb{G}, \hat{\mathbb{G}}, \mathbb{G}_T, \mathbb{F}, p, g) \leftarrow \mathsf{GGen}(1^\lambda)$ with bilinear pairing operation $e : \mathbb{G} \times \hat{\mathbb{G}} \to \mathbb{G}_T$. The public parameters of Boldyreva's (n,t)-threshold signature scheme for a message space $\mathcal{M}$ are $(\mathbb{G}, \hat{\mathbb{G}}, \mathbb{F}, p, g, \mathsf{H})$, where

H : $\mathcal{M} \to \hat{\mathbb{G}}$ is a hash function modelled as a random oracle. The signature scheme works as follows:

- KGen() samples a uniformly random polynomial $s(x) \in \mathbb{F}[X]$ of degree t. The signing key of i-th signer is $\mathsf{sk}_i := s(i)$, the public key $\mathsf{pk} := g^{s(0)}$, and the threshold public keys are $\{\mathsf{pk}_i := g^{\mathsf{sk}_i}\}_{i \in [n]}$.
- $\mathsf{PSign}(\mathsf{sk}_i, m)$ computes the partial signature with respect to secret key sk_i as $\sigma_i := \mathsf{H}(m)^{\mathsf{sk}_i} \in \hat{\mathbb{G}}$.
- $\mathsf{PVer}(\mathsf{pk}_i, m, \sigma_i)$ retruns 1 if $e(\mathsf{pk}_i, \mathsf{H}(m)) = e(g, \sigma_i)$, and 0 otherwise.
- $\mathsf{Comb}(S, m, \{(\mathsf{pk}_i, \sigma_i)\})$ first checks that $|S| \geq t+1$ and then runs $\mathsf{PVer}(\mathsf{pk}_i, \sigma_i, m)$ for all $i \in S$. If any of these calls outputs 0, then return $\bot$. Otherwise, return $\sigma := \prod_{i \in S} \sigma_i^{L_{i,S}}$, where $L_{i,S} := \prod_{i \in S}\left(\frac{j}{j-i}\right)$ is the i-th Lagrange coefficient for the set S.
- $\mathsf{Ver}(\mathsf{pk}, m, \sigma)$ returns 1 if $e(\mathsf{pk}, \mathsf{H}(m)) = e(g, \sigma)$, and 0 otherwise.

Boldyreva's scheme is secure in the presence of a *static* adversary assuming hardness of computational Diffie-Hellman assumption in the random oracle model [10,15].

5 Adaptively Secure BLS Threshold Signature

In this section, we will describe our adaptively secure (n, t)-threshold signature scheme assuming that KGen is run by a trusted party.

Setup(1^λ): Let $(\mathbb{G}, \hat{\mathbb{G}}, \mathbb{G}_T, \mathbb{F}, p) \leftarrow \mathsf{GGen}(1^\lambda)$ be pairing groups with scalar field $\mathbb{F}$ of prime order p and bilinear pairing operation $e : \mathbb{G} \times \hat{\mathbb{G}} \to \mathbb{G}_T$. Let $g, h, v \in \mathbb{G}$ are three uniformly random independent generators of $\mathbb{G}$. Let $\mathsf{H}_0, \mathsf{H}_1 : \mathcal{M} \to \hat{\mathbb{G}}$ and $\mathsf{H}_{\mathsf{FS}} : \{0,1\}^* \to \hat{\mathbb{G}}$ be three distinct hash functions modelled as random oracles. The public parameters of our scheme are then $(\mathbb{G}, \hat{\mathbb{G}}, \mathbb{F}, g, h, v, \mathsf{H}_0, \mathsf{H}_1, \mathsf{H}_{\mathsf{FS}})$. As we discuss earlier, we assume that all the algorithms below implicitly takes the public parameters as input.

KGen(): Sample three uniformly random polynomials $s(x), r(x)$ and $u(x)$ of degree t each with the constraint that $r(0) = u(0) = 0$. The signing key of signer i is then $\mathsf{sk}_i := (s(i), r(i), u(i))$. Let $\mathsf{pk} := g^{s(0)}h^{r(0)}v^{u(0)} = g^{s(0)}$ be the public verification key, and $\mathsf{pk}_i := g^{s(i)}h^{r(i)}v^{u(i)}$ be party i's threshold public key.

$\mathsf{PSign}(\mathsf{sk}_i, m)$: The partial signature of signer i on a message m is the tuple (σ_i, π_i), where $\sigma_i := \mathsf{H}_0(m)^{s(i)}\mathsf{H}_1(m)^{r(i)}$, and π_i is a non-interactive zero-knowledge (NIZK) proof of the correctness of σ_i with respect to pk_i. Signer i computes π_i using the Σ-protocol in Fig. 3. We use the Fiat-Shamir heuristic to make the signing phase non-interactive.

$\mathsf{PVer}(\mathsf{pk}_i, m, \sigma_i)$: On input the threshold public key pk_i and the partial signature tuple (σ_i, π_i), and the message m validates σ_i by running the Σ-protocol verifier $\mathcal{V}$, and accepts if and only if $\mathcal{V}$ accepts.

```
Setup(1^λ):
 1: (𝔾, Ĝ, 𝔾_T, 𝔽, p) ← GGen(1^λ) be pairing groups (𝔾, Ĝ, 𝔾_T) of prime order p, scalar field 𝔽 and bilinear pairing operation e : 𝔾 × Ĝ → 𝔾_T.
 2: Let g, h, v ∈ 𝔾 be three uniformly random independent generators of 𝔾.
 3: Let H_0, H_1 : ℳ → Ĝ and H_FS : {0,1}* → 𝔽 be three hash functions modeled as random oracle.
 4: return (𝔾, Ĝ, 𝔽, g, h, v, H_0, H_1, H_FS).
// We assume all algorithms implicitly take the output of Setup as input. We use H_FS in SigmaProve and SigmaVer.

KGen():
 5: Let s(·), r(·), u(·) ←$ 𝔽[x] be three polynomials of degree t with r(0) = u(0) = 0.
 6: Let pk := g^{s(0)} h^{r(0)} v^{u(0)} = g^{s(0)}
 7: for each i ∈ [n] :
 8:     Let sk_i := (s(i), r(i), u(i))
 9:     Let pk_i := g^{s(i)} h^{r(i)} v^{u(i)}
10: return (pk, {pk_i}_{i∈[n]}, sk_j) to signer j for all j ∈ [n]

PSign(sk_i = (s_i, r_i, u_i), m):
11: Let σ_i := H_0(m)^{s_i} H_1(m)^{r_i}
12: Let π_i := SigmaProve(pk_i, m, σ_i, sk_i)
13: return σ_i, π_i

PVer(pk_i, m, (σ_i, π_i)):
14: return SigmaVer(pk_i, m, σ_i, π_i)

Comb(S, m, {(pk_i, (σ_i, π_i))}_{i∈S}):
15: assert |S| ≥ t + 1
16: for each i ∈ S :
17:     assert PVer(pk_i, m, (σ_i, π_i))
18: Let L_{i,S} be the i-th Lagrange coefficients for S
19: return σ := ∏_{i∈S} σ_i^{L_{i,S}}

Ver(pk, m, σ):
21: if e(pk, H_0(m)) = e(g, σ) :
22:     return 1
23: return 0
```

Fig. 2. Adaptively secure (n, t) BLS threshold signature with trusted key generation.

Comb$(S, m, \{(\text{pk}_i, (\sigma_i, \pi_i))\}_{i \in S})$: Upon receiving a set of signers S with $|S| \geq t+1$, a message m, and the corresponding threshold public-key and partial signatures tuples $\{(\text{pk}_i, (\sigma_i, \pi_i))\}_{i \in S}$, first validates each of the partial signature using PVer. If any of these partial signatures verification fails, i.e., returns 0, the Comb algorithm returns $\perp$. Otherwise, the Comb algorithm computes the threshold signature σ as:

$$\sigma := \prod_{i \in T} \sigma_i^{L_{i,S}} \qquad (3)$$

where $L_{i,S}$ is the i-th Lagrange coefficient with respect to the set S.

Ver(pk, m, σ): The verification procedure of our scheme is identical to that of the standard BLS signature: on input the public key pk and the signature σ on a message m, a verifier accepts if $e(\text{pk}, H_0(m)) = e(g, \sigma)$.

Remark. Note that signers do not use $u(i)$ while computing σ_i. It is in the public verification key (and hence used in computing π_i) as an artifact to make our adaptive security proof go through.

Input: $(g, h, v, \mathsf{pk}) \in \mathbb{G}^4$, $(\hat{g}_0, \hat{g}_1) = (\mathsf{H}_0(m), \mathsf{H}_1(m))$ for some $m \in \mathcal{M}$, $\sigma \in \hat{\mathbb{G}}$
Witness: $(s, r, u) \in \mathbb{F}^3$
The prover $\mathcal{P}$ wants to convince the verifier $\mathcal{V}$ that it knows $s, r, u \in \mathbb{F}$ such that $\mathsf{pk} = g^s h^r v^u$ and $\sigma = \hat{g}_0^s \hat{g}_1^r$.
// We assume that both algorithms implicitly take of $g, h, v, \mathsf{H}_0, \mathsf{H}_1$ as input

SigmaProve($\mathsf{pk}, m, \sigma, (s, r, u)$):
1: Let $\hat{g}_0 := \mathsf{H}_0(m)$ and $\hat{g}_1 := \mathsf{H}_1(m)$
2: Sample $a_s, a_r, a_u \leftarrow_\$ \mathbb{F}$. Let $x := g^{a_s} h^{a_r} v^{a_u}$, and $y := \mathsf{H}_0(m)^{a_s} \mathsf{H}_1(m)^{a_r}$.
3: Let $c := \mathsf{H}_{\mathsf{FS}}(x, y, \mathsf{pk}, \sigma, \hat{g}_0, \hat{g}_1)$, for hash function $\mathsf{H}_{\mathsf{FS}} : \{0,1\}^* \to \mathbb{F}$ modeled as a random oracle.
4: Let $z_s := a_s + s \cdot c$, $z_r := a_r + r \cdot c$ and $z_u := a_u + u \cdot c$.
5: **return** $\pi := (x, y, z_s, z_r, z_u)$.

SigmaVer($\mathsf{pk}, m, \sigma, \pi = (x, y, z_s, z_r, z_u)$):
6: Let $\hat{g}_0 := \mathsf{H}_0(m)$ and $\hat{g}_1 := \mathsf{H}_1(m)$
7: Let $c := \mathsf{H}_{\mathsf{FS}}(x, y, \mathsf{pk}, \sigma, \hat{g}_0, \hat{g}_1)$
8: **if** $g^{z_s} h^{z_r} v^{z_u} = x \cdot \mathsf{pk}^c$ and $\hat{g}_0^{z_s} \hat{g}_1^{z_r} = y \cdot \sigma^c$:
9:     **return** 1
10: **return** 0

Fig. 3. Σ-protocol for computing and verifying the correctness proof for partial signatures.

6 Proofs of Adaptive Security

We first analyze the properties of the Σ-protocol in Fig. 3, which we then use to prove the robustness and adaptive security of our threshold signature scheme.

6.1 Properties of the Σ-Protocol

We require the Σ-protocol to satisfy the standard *completeness, knowledge-soundness*, and *zero-knowledge* properties [29]. Briefly, the completeness property guarantees that an honest prover will always be able to convince an honest verifier about true statements. The knowledge soundness property ensures that, for every prover who convinces an honest verifier about a statement with a non-negligible probability, there exists an efficient extractor who interacts with the prover to compute the witness. Finally, the zero-knowledge property ensures that the proof reveals no information other than the statement's truth. We remark that achieving zero-knowledge against honest verifiers is sufficient for our purposes. The completeness of our Σ-protocol is straightforward. The knowledge soundness and honest-verifier zero-knowledge properties also follow from standard Σ-protocol analysis.

Knowledge Soundness. We prove knowledge soundness by extractability. For any PPT prover $\mathcal{P}$, let $\mathcal{E}$ be the extractor. Then $\mathcal{E}$ interacts with $\mathcal{P}$ with two different challenges c and c' on the same first message, to receive two pairs of valid responses (z_s, z_r, z_u) and (z'_s, z'_r, z'_u). Then, we have:

$$g^{z_s-z'_s} h^{z_r-z'_r} v^{z_u-z'_u} = \mathsf{pk}^{c-c'} \quad \text{and} \quad \mathsf{H}_0(m)^{z_s-z'_s} \mathsf{H}_1(m)^{z_r-z'_r} = \sigma^{c-c'}$$

$$\implies s = \frac{z_s - z'_s}{c - c'}; \quad r = \frac{z_r - z'_r}{c - c'}; \quad u = \frac{z_u - z'_u}{c - c'}$$

Let ε_{ext} be the success probability of the extractor $\mathcal{E}$. Then, it follows from the generalized forking lemma [11] that $\varepsilon_{\text{ext}} \geq \varepsilon^2/q_{\text{FS}} - \varepsilon/|\mathbb{F}|$ where ε is the probability that an adversary $\mathcal{A}$ outputs a valid response while making at most q_{FS} random oracle queries to H_{FS}.

Honest Verifier Zero-Knowledge (HVZK). Let $\mathcal{S}$ be the simulator. $\mathcal{S}$ samples uniformly random $(c, z_s, z_r, z_u) \in \mathbb{F}^4$ and computes x and y as

$$x := g^{z_s} h^{z_r} v^{z_u} \cdot \mathsf{pk}^{-c} \quad \text{and} \quad y =: \mathsf{H}_0(m)^{z_s} \mathsf{H}_1(m)^{z_r} \cdot \sigma^{-c} \tag{4}$$

$\mathcal{S}$ then programs the random oracle such that $\mathsf{H}_{\text{FS}}(x, y, \mathsf{pk}, \sigma, m) = c$ and outputs $\pi = (c, z_s, z_r, z_u)$ as the proof. Clearly, the simulated transcript is identically distributed to the real-protocol transcript.

6.2 Robustness

Before we prove robustness of our scheme, we prove the following helper lemma.

Lemma 1. *If any signer i with threshold public key $\mathsf{pk}_i = g^{s(i)} h^{r(i)} v^{u(i)}$ outputs a partial signature σ_i on a message m along with a valid Σ-protocol proof π_i as per Fig. 3, then assuming hardness of discrete logarithm in $\mathbb{G}$, σ_i is well-formed, i.e., $\sigma_i = \mathsf{H}_0(m)^{s(i)} \mathsf{H}_1(m)^{r(i)}$.*

Proof. For valid Σ-protocol proof π_i, let $\mathcal{E}$ be the extractor from §6.1 and let s', r', u' be the extracted witness. We need to prove $(s', r', u') = (s(i), r(i), u(i))$.

For the sake of contradiction, assume this is not the case. Then, we can construct an adversary $\mathcal{A}_{\text{DL}}$ that breaks the discrete logarithm in $\mathbb{G}$ as follows. On input a discrete logarithm instance $(g, y) \in \mathbb{G}^2$, $\mathcal{A}_{\text{DL}}$ samples $\theta \in \{0, 1\}$ and sets either $h = y$ or $v = y$ depending on the value of θ. $\mathcal{A}_{\text{DL}}$ picks the other parameter as g^α for some known uniformly random $\alpha \in \mathbb{F}$. $\mathcal{A}_{\text{DL}}$ next faithfully emulates the trusted key generation with $\mathcal{A}$ with some chosen polynomials $s(\cdot), r(\cdot), v(\cdot)$. $\mathcal{A}_{\text{DL}}$ also faithfully emulates the corruption, partial signature queries, and random oracle queries.

Now $(s', r', u') \neq (s(i), r(i), u(i))$ for any signer i implies that

$$g^{s'-s(i)} h^{r-r(i)} v^{u'-u(i)} = 1_\mathbb{G} \tag{5}$$

where $1_\mathbb{G}$ is the identity element of $\mathbb{G}$.

Say $h = g^{\alpha_h}$ and $v = g^{\alpha_v}$ for some $\alpha_h, \alpha_v \in \mathbb{F}$, and let $\delta_s := s' - s(i)$, $\delta_r := r' - r(i)$, and $\delta_u := u' - u(i)$. Then, Eq. (5), implies that $\delta_s + \delta_r \alpha_h + \delta_u \alpha_v = 0$. If either δ_r or δ_u is non-zero, then we can compute α_h or α_v, respectively, as:

$$\delta_r \neq 0 \implies \alpha_h = (-\delta_s - \alpha_v \delta_u) \cdot \delta_r^{-1}; \quad \delta_u \neq 0 \implies \alpha_v = (-\delta_s - \alpha_h \delta_r) \cdot \delta_u^{-1} \tag{6}$$

Finally, $(\delta_r, \delta_u) = (0,0)$, implies that $\delta_s = 0$. Since $\mathcal{A}_{\mathsf{DL}}$ uses y as either h or v uniformly at random, it implies that if the extractor $\mathcal{E}$ outputs $(s', r', u') \neq (s(i), r(i), u(i))$ with probability $\varepsilon_{\mathsf{ext}}$, then $\mathcal{A}_{\mathsf{DL}}$ outputs the discrete logarithm of y with respect to g, with probability at least $\varepsilon_{\mathsf{ext}}/2$. □

We will now prove that robustness, i.e., any PPT adversary $\mathcal{A}$ wins the RB-CMA$_{\mathsf{TS}}^{\mathcal{A}}$ game in Fig. 1 only with a negligible probability. More formally,

Theorem 3 (Robustness). *The non-interactive (n,t)-threshold signature scheme* TS = (Setup, KGen, PSign, PVer, Comb, Ver) *in Fig. 2 is* RB-CMA$_{\mathsf{TS}}^{\mathcal{A}}$ *secure.*

Proof. There are two possible winning cases for an adversary $\mathcal{A}$ in the RB-CMA$_{\mathsf{TS}}^{\mathcal{A}}$ game: (1) honestly computed partial signatures does not satisfy the validation check PVer (line 23 in the RB-CMA$_{\mathsf{TS}}^{\mathcal{A}}$ game in Fig. 1), and (2) every partial signatures passes PVer but the honestly aggregated full signature does not satisfy the validation check Ver (line 29 in Fig. 1).

Let us first analyze the first winning case. Note that PVer algorithm in our protocol runs the verifier of the Σ-protocol in Fig. 3. Then, the completeness property of the Σ-protocol guarantees that the Σ-protocol verifier always accepts honestly generated proofs. This implies that the winning condition in line 8 in Fig. 1 never occurs for our protocol.

Now let us consider the second winning case. Lemma 1 ensures that assuming hardness of discrete logarithm in $\mathbb{G}$, the aggregator only aggregates well-formed partial signatures. Thus, we get

$$\sigma = \prod_{i \in S} \sigma^{L_{i,S}} = \prod_{i \in S} \mathsf{H}_0(m)^{s(i)L_{i,S}} \mathsf{H}_1(m)^{r(i)L_{i,S}}$$
$$= \mathsf{H}_0(m)^{\sum_{i \in S} s(i)L_{i,S}} \mathsf{H}_1(m)^{\sum_{i \in S} r(i)L_{i,S}} = \mathsf{H}_0(m)^s \mathsf{H}_1(m)^0 = \mathsf{H}_0(m)^s.$$

Note that $\sigma = \mathsf{H}_0(m)^s$ always satisfy the final verification check Ver.

Thus we get that assuming hardness of discrete logarithm in $\mathbb{G}$ any PPT adversary $\mathcal{A}$ wins the RB-CMA$_{\mathsf{TS}}^{\mathcal{A}}$ game only with a negligible probability. □

6.3 Helper Lemmas for Unforgeability

Our unforgeability proof crucially relies on the following lemma from Naor-Reingold [59, Lemma 4.4]. We refer the reader to [59] for its proof.

Lemma 2. (Lemma 4.4 in [59]). *For any security parameter λ, let $(\hat{\mathbb{G}}, \mathbb{F}, p, \hat{g}) \leftarrow \mathsf{GGen}(1^\lambda)$ be a cyclic group of prime order p with scalar field $\mathbb{F}$ and generator $\hat{g} \in \hat{\mathbb{G}}$. For all $q_{\mathsf{H}} \leq \mathsf{poly}(\lambda)$, assuming hardness of decisional Diffie-Hellman (DDH) assumption in $\hat{\mathbb{G}}$, the following two distributions are indistinguishable.*

$$\mathcal{D}_0 := \hat{g}, \hat{g}^\alpha, \{(\hat{g}^{\beta_i}, \hat{g}^{\gamma_i})\}_{i \in [q_{\mathsf{H}}]} \text{ for } \alpha \leftarrow_\$ \mathbb{F} \text{ and } \forall i \in [q_{\mathsf{H}}]\ (\beta_i, \gamma_i) \leftarrow_\$ \mathbb{F}^2 \quad (7)$$

$$\mathcal{D}_1 := \hat{g}, \hat{g}^\alpha, \{(\hat{g}^{\beta_i}, \hat{g}^{\alpha \cdot \beta_i})\}_{i \in [q_{\mathsf{H}}]} \text{ for } \alpha \leftarrow_\$ \mathbb{F} \text{ and } \forall i \in [q_{\mathsf{H}}]\ \beta_i \leftarrow_\$ \mathbb{F} \quad (8)$$

More precisely, if an adversary $\mathcal{A}$ can distinguish between a sample from $\mathcal{D}_0$ and $\mathcal{D}_1$ with probability ε, then $\mathcal{A}$ can break the DDH assumption with probability at least $\varepsilon - 1/|\mathbb{F}|$. This implies $\varepsilon \leq \varepsilon_{\mathsf{DDH}} + 1/|\mathbb{F}|$.

We use the abovementioned lemma to prove the following.

Lemma 3. *For security parameter λ, let $(\hat{\mathbb{G}}, \mathbb{F}, p, \hat{g}) \leftarrow \mathsf{GGen}(1^\lambda)$ be a cyclic group of prime order p with scalar field $\mathbb{F}$ and generator $\hat{g} \in \hat{\mathbb{G}}$. For all $q_\mathsf{H} \leq \mathsf{poly}(\lambda)$ and any fixed $k \in [q_\mathsf{H}]$, let the distribution $\mathcal{D}_{1,k}$ be defined as follows:*

$$\mathcal{D}_{1,k} := g, \{(g^{\beta_i}, g^{\gamma_i})\}_{i \in [q_\mathsf{H}]} \text{ for } \alpha \leftarrow_\$ \mathbb{F} \text{ and } \begin{cases} \forall i \neq k, \ \beta_i \leftarrow_\$ \mathbb{F}, \gamma_i := \alpha \cdot \beta_i \\ i = k, \ (\beta_i, \gamma_i) \leftarrow_\$ \mathbb{F}^2 \end{cases}$$

Then, assuming hardness of DDH in $\hat{\mathbb{G}}$, the distributions $\mathcal{D}_0$ (defined in Lemma 2) and $\mathcal{D}_{1,k}$ are indistinguishable except with probability at most $\varepsilon_\mathsf{DDH} + 1/|\mathbb{F}|$.

Proof. Define $\mathcal{D}_{0,k}$ to be identical to $\mathcal{D}_0$ for notational convenience. For any fixed k, given a sample $(g, g^\alpha, \{(g^{\beta_i}, g^{\gamma_i})\})$ from $\mathcal{D}_\theta$ for either $\theta \in \{0, 1\}$ we can get a sample from $\mathcal{D}_{\theta,k}$ by substituting g^{γ_k} in the given sample with a uniformly random element in $\hat{\mathbb{G}}$ and dropping the term g^α.

6.4 Unforgeability with an Adaptive Adversary

We will prove the unforgeability assuming the hardness of the DDH in $\hat{\mathbb{G}}$ and the hardness of co-CDH in $(\mathbb{G}, \hat{\mathbb{G}})$. Let $\mathcal{A}_\text{co-CDH}$ be the reduction adversary. Upon input a co-CDH instance $(g, \hat{g}, g^a, \hat{g}^a, \hat{g}^b)$, $\mathcal{A}_\text{co-CDH}$ interacts with $\mathcal{A}$ such that when $\mathcal{A}$ forges a signature, $\mathcal{A}_\text{co-CDH}$ uses the forgery to compute $\hat{g}^{ab}$. We summarize $\mathcal{A}_\text{co-CDH}$ interaction with $\mathcal{A}$ in Fig. 4, and describe it next.

Simulating the Public Parameters. On a co-CDH input $(g, \hat{g}, g^a, \hat{g}^a, \hat{g}^b)$, $\mathcal{A}_\text{co-CDH}$ samples $\alpha_v \leftarrow_\$ \mathbb{F}$, sets $h := g^a, v := g^{\alpha_v}$, and sends (g, h, v) to $\mathcal{A}$. $\mathcal{A}_\text{co-CDH}$ provides $\mathcal{A}$ access to the random oracles using lazy programming, i.e., $\mathcal{A}_\text{co-CDH}$ programs random oracles on any input only upon a query.

Simulating the KGen functionality. $\mathcal{A}_\text{co-CDH}$ samples $s, u \leftarrow_\$ \mathbb{F}$ and three uniformly random degree t polynomials $s(\cdot), r(\cdot), u(\cdot) \in \mathbb{F}[x]$, but crucially with the constraints $s(0) = s$, $u(0) = u$, and $r(0) = 1$ for the multiplicative identity 1 in $\mathbb{F}$. $\mathcal{A}_\text{co-CDH}$ then computes the public key and threshold public keys as follows:

$$\mathsf{pk} := g^{s(0)} h^{r(0)} v^{u(0)} = g^s h v^u; \text{ and } \left\{\mathsf{pk}_i := g^{s(i)} h^{r(i)} v^{u(i)}\right\}_{i \in [n]} \tag{9}$$

$\mathcal{A}_\text{co-CDH}$ then sends $\mathsf{pk}, \{\mathsf{pk}_i\}_{i \in [n]}$ to $\mathcal{A}$.

Simulating Corruption Queries. Let $\mathcal{H}$ and $\mathcal{C} = [n] \setminus \mathcal{H}$ be the set of honest and malicious parties, respectively. Anytime during the signing phase, if $\mathcal{A}$ corrupts signer $i \in [n]$, $\mathcal{A}_\text{co-CDH}$ checks whether $|\mathcal{C}| < t$ or not. If the check is successful, $\mathcal{A}_\text{co-CDH}$ faithfully reveals the secret signing key $\mathsf{sk}_i := (s(i), r(i), u(i))$ of signer i, and updates $\mathcal{C} := \mathcal{C} \cup \{i\}$ and $\mathcal{H} := \mathcal{H} \setminus \{i\}$. $\mathcal{A}_\text{co-CDH}$ lets $\mathcal{A}$ only corrupt up to t signers. Otherwise, $\mathcal{A}_\text{co-CDH}$ outputs $\bot$.

Simulating Threshold Signature. $\mathcal{A}_\text{co-CDH}$ simulates the signing queries by programming the random oracles as follows. Let $\alpha = a + \alpha_v u$. Note that H_0 is

Input: co-CDH tuple $(g, g^a, \hat{g}, \hat{g}^a, \hat{g}^b) \in \mathbb{G}^3 \times \hat{\mathbb{G}}$.

KGen simulation:
1. Let $\alpha_v \leftarrow_\$ \mathbb{F}$. Let $h := g^a$ and $v := g^{\alpha_v}$.
2. Let $s, u \leftarrow_\$ \mathbb{F}$. Sample three uniformly random degree t polynomials $s(x), r(x), u(x) \in \mathbb{F}[x]$ with the constraints $s(0) = s$, $u(0) = u$ and $r(0) = 1$. Here 1 is the multiplicative identity element of the field $\mathbb{F}$.
3. Compute $\mathsf{pk} := g^{s(0)} h^{r(0)} v^{u(0)} = g^s h v^u$, and for each $i \in [n]$, $\mathsf{pk}_i := g^{s(i)} h^{r(i)} v^{u(i)}$
4. For each $i \in [n]$, let $\mathsf{sk}_i := (s(i), r(i), u(i))$. Send $\mathsf{pk}, \{\mathsf{pk}_j\}_{j \in [n]}$ to $\mathcal{A}$.

Corruption simulation:
5. Let $\mathcal{H}$ and $\mathcal{C} = [n] \setminus \mathcal{H}$ be the set of honest and malicious parties, respectively.
6. When $\mathcal{A}$ submits a corruption query i, if $|\mathcal{C}| \geq t$, respond with $\perp$. Otherwise, send sk_i to $\mathcal{A}$. Update $\mathcal{H} := \mathcal{H} \setminus \{i\}$ and $\mathcal{C} := \mathcal{C} \cup \{i\}$.

Threshold signature simulation:
7. For each query to H_{FS} on input x, Return $\mathsf{H}_{\mathsf{FS}}(x)$ if $\mathsf{H}_{\mathsf{FS}}(x) \neq \perp$. Otherwise, return $\mathsf{H}_{\mathsf{FS}}(x) := y \leftarrow_\$ \mathbb{F}$.
8. Let $\alpha := a + \alpha_v u$, thus $\hat{g}^\alpha := \hat{g}^a \cdot \hat{g}^{\alpha_v u}$. // $\mathcal{A}_{\text{co-CDH}}$ does not know α.
9. Let q_H be an upper bound on the total number of random oracle queries to H_0 and H_1, combined.
10. Sample $\hat{k} \leftarrow_\$ [q_\mathsf{H}]$.
11. On k-th random oracle query to H_θ for either $\theta \in \{0, 1\}$ on message m_k:
    (a) If $\mathsf{H}_\theta(m_k) \neq \perp$, return $\mathsf{H}_\theta(m_k)$. Otherwise,
    (b) If $k \neq \hat{k}$, program the random oracles as follows and return $\mathsf{H}_\theta(m_k)$.

    $$\mathsf{H}_0(m_k) := \hat{g}^{\beta_k}; \quad \mathsf{H}_1(m_k) := (\hat{g}^\alpha)^{\beta_k} \text{ for } \beta_k \leftarrow_\$ \mathbb{F} \quad (9)$$

    (c) If $k = \hat{k}$, set the random oracles as follows and return $\mathsf{H}_\theta(m_k)$.

    $$\mathsf{H}_0(m_k) := \hat{g}^b; \quad \mathsf{H}_1(m_k) := \hat{g}' \text{ for } \hat{g}' \leftarrow_\$ \hat{\mathbb{G}} \quad (10)$$

12. Let $m_{\hat{k}}$ be the queried message for $k = \hat{k}$. Then, except for message $m_{\hat{k}}$, respond to partial signing queries as per the honest protocol.
13. For message $m_{\hat{k}}$, faithfully respond to up to $t - |\mathcal{C}|$ partial signing queries and abort if $\mathcal{A}$ queries for more partial signatures on $m_{\hat{k}}$.

Compute co-CDH output:
14. When $\mathcal{A}$ outputs a valid forgery $(m_{\hat{k}}, \sigma)$, output $\sigma \cdot (\hat{g}^b)^{-(s + \alpha_v u)}$ as the co-CDH solution.

Fig. 4. $\mathcal{A}_{\text{co-CDH}}$'s interaction with $\mathcal{A}$ to compute the co-CDH solution, when signers use the KGen functionality to setup the signing keys.

always queried on the forged message, at least by $\mathcal{A}_{\text{co-CDH}}$ during the signature verification. Moreover, whenever $\mathcal{A}$ queries H_θ for either $\theta \in \{0, 1\}$ on any message, $\mathcal{A}_{\text{co-CDH}}$ internally queries $\mathsf{H}_{1-\theta}$ on the same message. Let q_H be an upper bound on the number of queries by $\mathcal{A}$ to H_0 and H_1 combined. $\mathcal{A}_{\text{co-CDH}}$ samples $\hat{k} \leftarrow_\$ [q_\mathsf{H}]$. On the k-th random oracle query on message m_k, depending upon the value of k, $\mathcal{A}_{\text{co-CDH}}$ programs the random oracles as follows.

$$k \neq \hat{k} \implies \mathsf{H}_0(m_k) := \hat{g}^{\beta_k}; \quad \mathsf{H}_1(m_k) := \hat{g}^{\alpha \cdot \beta_k} \text{ for } \beta_k \leftarrow_\$ \mathbb{F}$$
$$k = \hat{k} \implies \mathsf{H}_0(m_k) := \hat{g}^b; \quad \mathsf{H}_1(m_k) := \hat{g}' \text{ for } \hat{g}' \leftarrow_\$ \hat{\mathbb{G}}$$

Let $m_{\hat{k}}$ be the queried message for $k = \hat{k}$. Then, except for message $m_{\hat{k}}$, $\mathcal{A}_{\text{co-CDH}}$ always responds to partial signing queries as per the honest protocol. For message $m_{\hat{k}}$, $\mathcal{A}_{\text{co-CDH}}$ faithfully responds to up to $t - |\mathcal{C}|$ partial signing queries and aborts if $\mathcal{A}$ queries for more partial signatures on $m_{\hat{k}}$.

Computing the co-CDH Solution. When $\mathcal{A}$ outputs a valid forgery $(m_{\hat{k}}, \sigma)$, $\mathcal{A}_{\text{co-CDH}}$ uses its knowledge of (s, u) and computes the co-CDH solution as follows:

$$\hat{g}_{\text{cdh}} := \sigma \cdot (\hat{g}^b)^{-b(s + \alpha_v u)} \tag{10}$$

Lemma 4. *If $(m_{\hat{k}}, \sigma)$ is a valid forgery, then $\hat{g}_{\text{cdh}}$ is the valid co-CDH solution.*

Proof. Since $(m_{\hat{k}}, \sigma)$ is a valid forgery, the following holds.

$$e(\mathsf{pk}, \mathsf{H}_0(m_{\hat{k}})) = e(g, \sigma) \implies e(g^s h v^u, \hat{g}^b) = e(g, \sigma) \tag{11}$$

Let $\hat{h} = \hat{g}^a$ and $\hat{v} = \hat{g}^{\alpha_v}$. Then, from Eq. (11), we get that:

$$\sigma = \left(\hat{g}^s \hat{h} \hat{v}^u\right)^b \implies \sigma \cdot \hat{g}^{-b(s + \alpha_v u)} = \hat{h}^b = \hat{g}^{ab} = \hat{g}_{\text{cdh}}$$

□

Next, we illustrate that assuming the hardness of DDH in $\hat{\mathbb{G}}$, if $\mathcal{A}$ forges a signature in the UF-CMA$_{\mathsf{TS}}^{\mathcal{A}}$ game, then $\mathcal{A}$ also forges a signature during its interaction with $\mathcal{A}_{\text{co-CDH}}$, just with a slightly lower probability.

We will illustrate this via a sequence of games. Game $\mathbf{G}_0$ is the real protocol execution, and game $\mathbf{G}_7$ is the interaction of $\mathcal{A}$ with $\mathcal{A}_{\text{co-CDH}}$. Here on, for any game $\mathbf{G}_i$, we will use "$\mathbf{G}_i \Rightarrow 1$" as a shorthand for the event that a PPT adversary $\mathcal{A}$ forges a signature in game $\mathbf{G}_i$.

GAME $\mathbf{G}_0$: This game is the security game UF-CMA$_{\mathsf{TS}}^{\mathcal{A}}$ for our threshold signature scheme, where the game follows the honest protocol. Here, the game provides $\mathcal{A}$ access to any random oracle using the standard lazy simulation technique.

We also make a purely conceptual change to the game. Let (m^*, σ^*) be the forgery. Then, we assume that $\mathcal{A}$ always queries $\mathsf{H}_0(m^*)$ before outputting the forgery. This is without loss of generality and does not change the advantage of $\mathcal{A}$ because one could build a wrapper adversary that internally runs $\mathcal{A}$ but queries $\mathsf{H}_0(m^*)$ before outputting. Then by definition, we have:

$$\mathsf{Adv}_{\mathcal{A},\mathsf{TS}}^{\mathsf{UF-CMA}}(\lambda) = \Pr[\mathbf{G}_0 \Rightarrow 1] = \varepsilon_\sigma.$$

GAME $\mathbf{G}_1$: Let q_H be the upper-bound on the total number of random oracle queries to H_0 and H_1. For each $k \in [q_\mathsf{H}]$, let m_k be the input to the k-th random oracle query. This game is identical to $\mathbf{G}_0$, except that we sample $\hat{k} \leftarrow_\$ [q_\mathsf{H}]$, and the game aborts if the $\mathcal{A}$ forges a message m_k for $k \neq \hat{k}$ or queries for more than $t - |\mathcal{C}|$ partial signatures for $m_{\hat{k}}$. Clearly, if no abort occurs, games $\mathbf{G}_0$ and $\mathbf{G}_1$ are the same. Furthermore, the view of $\mathcal{A}$ is independent of $\hat{k}$. Thus, we get:

$$\Pr[\mathbf{G}_1 \Rightarrow 1] \geq \frac{1}{q_\mathsf{H}} \cdot \Pr[\mathbf{G}_0 \Rightarrow 1] \tag{12}$$

GAME $\mathbf{G}_2$: This game is identical to $\mathbf{G}_1$, except that we sample $\alpha_h, \alpha_v \leftarrow_\$ \mathbb{F}$ and set $h := g^{\alpha_h}$ and $v := g^{\alpha_v}$. Clearly, the view of $\mathcal{A}$ in $\mathbf{G}_1$ is identical to its view in $\mathbf{G}_2$, hence $\Pr[\mathbf{G}_1 \Rightarrow 1] = \Pr[\mathbf{G}_2 \Rightarrow 1]$.

GAME $\mathbf{G}_3$: In this game, we change how we program the random oracles H_0 and H_1. In particular, we program the random oracles $\mathsf{H}_0, \mathsf{H}_1$ in a correlated manner to ensure a distribution identical to how $\mathcal{A}_{\text{co-CDH}}$ programs these random oracles in Fig. 4. The rest of the steps are identical to game $\mathbf{G}_2$.

More specifically, in game $\mathbf{G}_3$, we sample $u \leftarrow_\$ \mathbb{F}$ and let $\alpha := \alpha_h + \alpha_v u$. Then, for the k-th random oracle query, depending upon whether $k = \hat{k}$, we program the random oracles as follows:

$$k \neq \hat{k} \implies \mathsf{H}_0(m_k) := \hat{g}^{\beta_k};\quad \mathsf{H}_1(m_k) := \hat{g}^{\alpha \cdot \beta_k} \text{ for } \beta_k \leftarrow_\$ \mathbb{F} \tag{13}$$

$$k = \hat{k} \implies \mathsf{H}_0(m_k) := \hat{g}^{\beta};\quad \mathsf{H}_1(m_k) := \hat{g}' \text{ for } \hat{g}' \leftarrow_\$ \hat{\mathbb{G}} \tag{14}$$

We next bound the probability $\Pr[\mathbf{G}_3 \Rightarrow 1]$ as follows.

Lemma 5. *Let $\varepsilon_{\mathsf{DDH}}$ be the advantage of breaking DDH in $\hat{\mathbb{G}}$ as defined in Assumption 1, then $|\Pr[\mathbf{G}_2 \Rightarrow 1] - \Pr[\mathbf{G}_3 \Rightarrow 1]| \leq \varepsilon_{\mathsf{DDH}} + 1/|\mathbb{F}|$.*

Proof. Observe that, in game $\mathbf{G}_2$, we program the random oracles H_0 and H_1 with a sample from $\mathcal{D}_0$ defined in Lemma 2. Similarly, in game $\mathbf{G}_3$, we program the random oracles H_0 and H_1 exactly with a sample from the distribution $\mathcal{D}_{1,\hat{k}}$ defined in Lemma 3. Apart from the output of the random oracles H_0 and H_1, the rest of the view is identically distributed in $\mathbf{G}_2$ and $\mathbf{G}_3$. Recall from Lemma 3, assuming hardness of DDH in $\hat{\mathbb{G}}$, samples from distributions $\mathcal{D}_0$ and $\mathcal{D}_{1,\hat{k}}$ are computationally indistinguishable. Thus, we get,

$$|\Pr[\mathbf{G}_2 \Rightarrow 1] - \Pr[\mathbf{G}_3 \Rightarrow 1]| \leq \varepsilon_{\mathsf{DDH}} + \frac{1}{|\mathbb{F}|} \tag{15}$$

GAME $\mathbf{G}_4$: This game is identical to $\mathbf{G}_3$, except that for each honest signer we use simulated NIZK proofs for correctness of partial signatures instead of actual NIZK proofs. Looking ahead, we switch to simulated NIZK proofs in this game to later argue in game $\mathbf{G}_6$ that the NIZK proofs do not reveal any information about the secret signing keys. This is crucial to argue the indistinguishability between game $\mathbf{G}_5$ and $\mathbf{G}_6$.

During the NIZK simulation, the game programs the random oracle H_{FS} on input $(x, y, \mathsf{pk}, \sigma, \hat{g}_0, \hat{g}_1)$ at a choice of its challenge. The game aborts if H_{FS} is already programmed at $(x, y, \mathsf{pk}, \sigma, \hat{g}_0, \hat{g}_1)$. Note that the NIZK protocol we use is perfect honest-verifier zero-knowledge (HVZK). Hence, conditioned on the successful programming of the random oracle H_{FS}, i.e., if the game does not abort, $\mathcal{A}$'s view in games $\mathbf{G}_3$ and $\mathbf{G}_4$ are identically distributed. Next, we will formally analyze the abort probability.

Let E be the event that at least one of our H_{FS} query collides with $\mathcal{A}$'s random oracle query. Then, we have,

$$|\Pr[\mathbf{G}_3 \Rightarrow 1] - \Pr[\mathbf{G}_4 \Rightarrow 1]| = |\Pr[\mathbf{G}_3 \Rightarrow 1|E] - \Pr[\mathbf{G}_4 \Rightarrow 1|E]| \cdot \Pr[E] \leq \Pr[E].$$

Here, we use the fact that $|\Pr[\mathbf{G}_3 \Rightarrow 1|E] - \Pr[\mathbf{G}_4 \Rightarrow 1|E]| \leq 1$ and $\Pr[\mathbf{G}_3 \Rightarrow 1|\neg E] = \Pr[\mathbf{G}_4 = 1|\neg E]$.

We now analyze the probability of event E. For each NIZK simulation, the game needs to program H_{FS} at a input $(x, y, \mathsf{pk}, \sigma, \hat{g}_0, \hat{g}_1)$ for some uniformly random $x, y \leftarrow_\$ \mathbb{G}$. Since $\mathcal{A}$ makes at most q_{FS} queries to the random oracle H_{FS}, the probability that the game aborts during each NIZK simulation is at most $q_{\mathsf{FS}}/|\mathbb{F}|^2$. Since $\mathcal{A}$ makes at most q_s signing queries and we need to simulate at most n partial signatures per signing query, using a simple union bound, we get

$$\Pr[E] \leq \frac{q_{\mathsf{FS}} \cdot q_s \cdot n}{|\mathbb{F}|^2} = \varepsilon_{\mathsf{nizk}}\text{-fail.} \tag{16}$$

Hence, we get $|\Pr[\mathbf{G}_3 \Rightarrow 1] - \Pr[\mathbf{G}_4 \Rightarrow 1]| \leq \varepsilon_{\mathsf{nizk}}$-fail.

GAME $\mathbf{G}_5$: In this game, we change how we sample the signing keys. To illustrate our modification, we will distinguish between the signing key polynomials of game $\mathbf{G}_4$ and $\mathbf{G}_5$. More precisely, let $s_4(x), r_4(x), u_4(x)$ and $s_5(x), r_5(x), u_5(x)$ be the signing key polynomials in game $\mathbf{G}_4$ and game $\mathbf{G}_5$, respectively. Then, in game $\mathbf{G}_5$ we sample the signing key polynomial $s_5(x) := s_4(x) + \alpha$ where $\alpha = \alpha_h + \alpha_v u$. The other two signing key polynomials remain unchanged, i.e., $r_5(x) = r_4(x)$ and $u_5(x) = u_4(x)$.

Observe that for any fixed α, since $s_4(x)$ is a random degree t polynomial, $s_5(x) = s_4(x) + \alpha$ is also a random degree t polynomial. Hence, $\mathcal{A}$'s view in game $\mathbf{G}_4$ is identical to its view in game $\mathbf{G}_5$, and $\Pr[\mathbf{G}_4 \Rightarrow 1] = \Pr[\mathbf{G}_5 \Rightarrow 1]$.

GAME $\mathbf{G}_6$: In this game, we change how we sample the signing keys again. More precisely, we sample signing key polynomials such that $s_6(x) := s_4(x)$, $r_6(x) := r_4(x) + 1$ and $u_6(x) := u_4(x) + u$, for uniformly random $u \in \mathbb{F}$ we use to define $\alpha = \alpha_h + \alpha_v u$.

The indistinguishability between $\mathcal{A}$'s view in game $\mathbf{G}_5$ and game $\mathbf{G}_6$ is another crucial step of our proof.

Lemma 6. $\Pr[\mathbf{G}_5 \Rightarrow 1] = \Pr[\mathbf{G}_6 \Rightarrow 1]$

Proof. Let $\mathsf{pk}_{\mathbf{G}_5}$ and $\mathsf{pk}_{\mathbf{G}_6}$ are the public keys in game $\mathbf{G}_5$ and $\mathbf{G}_6$, respectively. We first prove that $\mathsf{pk}_{\mathbf{G}_5}$ and $\mathsf{pk}_{\mathbf{G}_6}$ are identically distributed. Note that by design, we have $s_6(0) = s_4(0)$, $r_6(0) = 1$, and $u_6(0) = u$. This implies that,

$$\mathsf{pk}_{\mathbf{G}_5} = g^{s_5(0)} h^{r_5(0)} v^{u_5(0)} = g^{s_4(0)+\alpha} = g^{s_4(0)+\alpha_h+\alpha_v u}$$
$$= g^{s_4(0)} h v^u = g^{s_6(0)} h^{r_6(0)} v^{u_6(0)} = \mathsf{pk}_{\mathbf{G}_6}$$

Next, for any signer i, let $\mathsf{pk}_{i,\mathbf{G}_5}$ and $\mathsf{pk}_{i,\mathbf{G}_6}$ be its threshold public keys in game $\mathbf{G}_5$ and $\mathbf{G}_6$, respectively. Then, since $h = g^{\alpha_h}$ and $v = g^{\alpha_v}$, we have:

$$\mathsf{pk}_{i,\mathbf{G}_5} = g^{s_5(i)} h^{r_5(i)} v^{u_5(i)} = g^{s_4(0)+\alpha_h+\alpha_v u} \cdot h^{r_4(i)} \cdot v^{u_4(i)}$$
$$= g^{s_4(i)} \cdot h^{r_4(i)+1} \cdot v^{u_4(i)+u}$$
$$= g^{s_6(i)} \cdot h^{r_6(i)} \cdot v^{u_6(i)} = \mathsf{pk}_{i,\mathbf{G}_6} \tag{17}$$

Similarly, for any signer i, for any message m_k for $k \neq \hat{k}$, let $\sigma_{i,\mathbf{G}_5}$ and $\sigma_{i,\mathbf{G}_6}$ be its partial signatures in $\mathbf{G}_5$ and $\mathbf{G}_6$, respectively. Recall from Eq. (13), for $k \neq \hat{k}$, we have that:

$$H_0(m_k) = \hat{g}^{\beta_k} \quad \text{and} \quad H_1(m_k) = \hat{g}^{\alpha \cdot \beta_k} \text{ for } \alpha = \alpha_h + u\alpha_v \text{ and } \beta_k \leftarrow_\$ \mathbb{F}$$

This implies that,

$$\begin{aligned}
\sigma_{i,\mathbf{G}_5} &= H_0(m_k)^{s_5(i)} H_1(m_k)^{r_5(i)} = H_0(m_k)^{s_4(i)+\alpha} \cdot H_1(m_k)^{r_4(i)} \\
&= g^{\beta_k \cdot (s_4(i)+\alpha)} \cdot g^{\alpha \beta_k r_4(i)} = g^{\beta_k s_4(i)} \cdot g^{\alpha \beta_k (1+r_4(i))} \\
&= g^{\beta_k s_6(i)} \cdot g^{\alpha \beta_k r_6(i)} = H_0(m)^{s(i)} \cdot H_1(m)^{r+r(i)} = \sigma_{i,\mathbf{G}_7}
\end{aligned} \quad (18)$$

Equations (17) and (18) imply that the threshold public keys and the partial signatures are identically distributed in games $\mathbf{G}_5$ and $\mathbf{G}_6$. Moreover, the simulated partial signature correctness NIZK proofs reveal no additional information about the signing keys of the honest signers, except what is revealed by the threshold public keys and the partial signatures.

Hence, it remains to show that the joint view of signing keys of the corrupt signers and the set of partial signatures on the forged message $m_{\hat{k}}$ in games $\mathbf{G}_5$ and $\mathbf{G}_6$ are identically distributed. Let $\mathcal{C}$ be the set of corrupt signers. Let $Q[m_{\hat{k}}] \subset \mathcal{H}$ be the subset of honest signers $\mathcal{A}$ queries for partial signatures on the forged message $m_{\hat{k}}$. We have $|Q(m_{\hat{k}}) \cup \mathcal{C}| \leq t$. Also, let $\hat{g}_0 = H_0(m_{\hat{k}})$ and $\hat{g}_1 = H_1(m_{\hat{k}})$. Then, for any fixed α, let $\mathcal{D}_5$ and $\mathcal{D}_6$ be the views of $\mathcal{A}$ in game $\mathbf{G}_5$ and $\mathbf{G}_6$, respectively, i.e.,

$$\mathcal{D}_5 = \left(\left\{ \hat{g}_0^{s_4(i)+\alpha} \cdot \hat{g}_1^{r_4(i)} \right\}_{i \in Q[m_{\hat{k}}]}, \{s_4(i)+\alpha, \; r_4(i), \; u_4(i)\}_{i \in \mathcal{C}} \right),$$

$$\mathcal{D}_6 = \left(\left\{ \hat{g}_0^{s_4(i)} \cdot \hat{g}_1^{r_4(i)+1} \right\}_{i \in Q[m_{\hat{k}}]}, \{s_4(i), \; r_4(i)+1, \; u_4(i)+u\}_{k \in \mathcal{C}} \right)$$

We argue that $\mathcal{D}_5$ and $\mathcal{D}_6$ are identically distributed based on the following. Consider the following two distributions $\mathcal{D}_{5,t}$ and $\mathcal{D}_{6,t}$ as defined below:

$$\mathcal{D}_{5,t} = \left(\{s_4(i)+\alpha, \; r_4(k), \; u_4(k)\}_{k \in \mathcal{C} \cup Q[m_{\hat{k}}]} \right)$$

$$\mathcal{D}_{6,t} = \left(\{s_4(k), \; r_4(k)+1, \; u_4(k)+u\}_{k \in \mathcal{C} \cup Q[m_{\hat{k}}]} \right)$$

Observe that the distributions $\mathcal{D}_{5,t}$ and $\mathcal{D}_{6,t}$ are Shamir's secret shares of three secrets using independent random polynomials. Since $|\mathcal{C} \cup Q[m_{\hat{k}}]| \leq t$, the perfect secrecy of Shamir's secret sharing implies that $\mathcal{D}_{5,t}$ and $\mathcal{D}_{6,t}$ are identically distributed. Observe that given a sample from either $\mathcal{D}_{5,t}$ or $\mathcal{D}_{6,t}$, one can efficiently compute a sample from $\mathcal{D}_5$ or $\mathcal{D}_6$, respectively. Hence, $\mathcal{D}_5$ and $\mathcal{D}_6$ are also identically distributed. Therefore, $\mathcal{A}$'s view in $\mathbf{G}_5$ and $\mathbf{G}_6$ are identically distributed, and hence $\Pr[\mathbf{G}_5 \Rightarrow 1] = \Pr[\mathbf{G}_6 \Rightarrow 1]$. □

GAME $\mathbf{G}_7$: This game is identical to $\mathbf{G}_6$, except that we use actual NIZK proofs for partial signatures. We switch back to real proofs in this game because

$\mathcal{A}_{\text{co-CDH}}$ in Fig. 4 uses real proofs during its interaction with $\mathcal{A}$. Finally, using an argument similar as in the advantage of $\mathcal{A}$ between $\mathbf{G}_4$ and $\mathbf{G}_5$, we get that:

$$|\Pr[\mathbf{G}_6 \Rightarrow 1] - \Pr[\mathbf{G}_7 \Rightarrow 1]| \leq \varepsilon_{\text{nizk}}\text{-fail}. \tag{19}$$

Observe that, if game $\mathbf{G}_7$ does not abort, then $\mathcal{A}$'s view in game $\mathbf{G}_7$ is identically distributed as its view in its interaction with $\mathcal{A}_{\text{co-CDH}}$, where $\mathcal{A}_{\text{co-CDH}}$ uses (g^a, g^b) from co-CDH input $(g, g^a, g^b, \hat{g}^a)$ as (h, g^β) in game $\mathbf{G}_7$. Additionally, $\mathcal{A}_{\text{co-CDH}}$ uses $\hat{g}^a$ to compute the random oracle outputs in step 11(b) in Fig. 4. Hence, from the above sequence of games, we get that:

$$|\Pr[\mathbf{G}_0 \Rightarrow 1] - \Pr[\mathbf{G}_7 \Rightarrow 1]| \leq \varepsilon_{\text{DDH}} + \frac{1}{|\mathbb{F}|} + 2\varepsilon_{\text{nizk}}\text{-fail} + \left(1 - \frac{1}{q_\mathsf{H}}\right) \cdot \Pr[\mathbf{G}_0 \Rightarrow 1]$$

$$\Rightarrow \Pr[\mathbf{G}_7 \Rightarrow 1] \geq \frac{1}{q_\mathsf{H}} \cdot \varepsilon_\sigma - \varepsilon_{\text{DDH}} - \frac{1}{|\mathbb{F}|} - 2\varepsilon_{\text{nizk}}\text{-fail}. \tag{20}$$

This implies that if adversary $\mathcal{A}$ outputs a forgery in the UF-CMA$_{\text{TS}}^{\mathcal{A}}$ game of our signature scheme (i.e., $\mathbf{G}_0$) with probability ε_σ, then $\mathcal{A}$ outputs a forgery on $m_{\hat{k}}$ during its interaction with $\mathcal{A}_{\text{co-CDH}}$ (i.e., in $\mathbf{G}_7$) with probability at least $\varepsilon_\sigma/q_\mathsf{H} - \varepsilon_{\text{DDH}} - 1/|\mathbb{F}| - 2\varepsilon_{\text{nizk}}\text{-fail}$. Moreover, Lemma 4 implies that $\mathcal{A}_{\text{co-CDH}}$ can efficiently compute the co-CDH solution using the forgery on $m_{\hat{k}}$. Combining all the above, we get our main theorem, as stated below.

Theorem 4 (Adaptively secure BLS threshold signature). *Let λ be the security parameter, and let $(\mathbb{F}, \mathbb{G}, \hat{\mathbb{G}}, \mathbb{G}_T, p) \leftarrow \mathsf{GGen}(1^\lambda)$ be pairing groups of prime order p. For any n, t for $n = \mathsf{poly}(\lambda)$ and $t < n$, assuming hardness of decisional Diffie-Hellman (DDH) in $\hat{\mathbb{G}}$, and hardness of co-computational Diffie-Hellman (co-CDH) in $(\mathbb{G}, \hat{\mathbb{G}})$ in the random oracle model, any PPT adversary making at most q_H random oracle queries to H_0 and H_1 combined, q_FS queries to the random oracle H_FS, and at most q_s signature queries wins the UF-CMA$_{\text{TS}}^{\mathcal{A}}$ game Fig. 1 for our scheme in Fig. 2 with probability at most ε_σ where:*

$$\varepsilon_\sigma \leq q_\mathsf{H} \cdot \left(\varepsilon_{\text{DDH}} + \frac{1}{|\mathbb{F}|} + 2\varepsilon_{\text{nizk}}\text{-fail} + \varepsilon_{\text{CDH}}\right),$$

$\varepsilon_{\text{nizk}}\text{-fail} = (q_\mathsf{FS} \cdot q_s \cdot n)/|\mathbb{F}|^2$, *and ε_{DDH} and ε_{CDH} are the advantages of an adversary running in $T \cdot \mathsf{poly}(\lambda, n)$ time in breaking DDH in $\hat{\mathbb{G}}$ and co-CDH in $(\mathbb{G}, \hat{\mathbb{G}})$, respectively. This implies that ε_σ is negligible, and hence, our threshold signature scheme in §5 is unforgeable.*

Remark. Note that the unforgeability property of our threshold signature scheme does not rely on the *soundness* property of the Σ-protocol signers use to prove the correctness of the partial signatures. We only rely on the knowledge-soundness property to achieve robustness of our scheme (see §6.2).

6.5 Unforgeability with Static Adversary

We now briefly argue that if we are content with proving our signature scheme statically secure, then we only need the hardness of CDH assumption in a pairing group $(\mathbb{G}, \hat{\mathbb{G}})$ in the ROM. For static security, we do not require asymmetric pairing groups. Thus, we will assume $\mathbb{G} = \hat{\mathbb{G}}$ in this analysis, and hence the CDH assumption instead of co-CDH. Moreover, we will only consider the TS-UF-0 threat model from [10]. Our security proof is similar to the static security proof of Boldyreva's scheme. We want to note that assuming the hardness of CDH in the random oracle model, Boldyreva's scheme has only been proven TS-UF-0 secure. We adopt TS-UF-0 for simplicity since static security is not the main focus of the paper.

Let $\mathcal{A}_{\text{static}}$ be the static adversary that breaks the unforgeability of our signature scheme, and let $\mathcal{A}_{\text{CDH}}$ be the CDH adversary. Let $\mathcal{C}$ be the set of signers $\mathcal{A}_{\text{static}}$ corrupts at the beginning of the protocol, and $\mathcal{H} = [n] \setminus \mathcal{C}$ be the set of honest signers. Also, let $\mathcal{S} \subset \mathcal{H}$ be the subset of honest signers $\mathcal{A}_{\text{static}}$ will query for partial signatures on the forged message. By the definition of a static adversary, we require that $|\mathcal{C} \cup \mathcal{S}| \leq t$ and $\mathcal{A}_{\text{static}}$ declare the sets $\mathcal{C}, \mathcal{S}$ to $\mathcal{A}_{\text{CDH}}$. $\mathcal{A}_{\text{CDH}}$ on input a CDH input $(g, g^a, g^b) \in \mathbb{G}^3$ simulates the KGen functionality and the signature scheme with $\mathcal{A}_{\text{static}}$ as follows.

Simulating the KGen functionality. For simplicity, let us assume $|\mathcal{C} \cup \mathcal{S}| = t$. $\mathcal{A}_{\text{CDH}}$ samples $h, v \leftarrow\!\!\!\$ \ \mathbb{G}$. Next, $\mathcal{A}_{\text{CDH}}$ samples two random degree t polynomials $r(x), u(x)$ with the constraint $r(0) = u(0) = 0$. To compute the polynomial $s(x)$, $\mathcal{A}_{\text{static}}$ samples $s(j) \leftarrow\!\!\!\$ \ \mathbb{F}$ for each $j \in \mathcal{C} \cup \mathcal{S}$. $\mathcal{A}_{\text{CDH}}$ sets the public key as $\mathsf{pk} = g^a$ and computes threshold public keys $\{\mathsf{pk}_i\} = \{g^{s(i)} h^{r(i)} v^{u(i)}\}_{i \in [n]}$ using interpolation in the exponent. $\mathcal{A}_{\text{CDH}}$ then sends $\mathsf{pk}, \{\mathsf{pk}_i\}_{i \in [n]}, \{\mathsf{sk}_i\}_{i \in \mathcal{C}}$ to $\mathcal{A}_{\text{static}}$.

Simulating the Signing Queries. Throughout the simulation $\mathcal{A}_{\text{CDH}}$ always faithfully responds to queries to H_1. Note that H_0 is always queried on the forged message, at least by $\mathcal{A}_{\text{CDH}}$ during the signature verification. Let q_H be an upper bound on the number of random oracle queries to H_0, including the query during the signature verification. For static security, the number of queries to H_1 can be unbounded. $\mathcal{A}_{\text{CDH}}$ samples $\hat{k} \leftarrow\!\!\!\$ \ [q_\mathsf{H}]$. On the k-th random oracle query on message m_k, depending upon the value of k, $\mathcal{A}_{\text{CDH}}$ programs the random oracle as follows:

$$k \neq \hat{k} \implies \mathsf{H}_0(m_k) = g^{\beta_k} \text{ for } \beta_k \leftarrow\!\!\!\$ \ \mathbb{F}; \quad \text{and} \quad k = \hat{k} \implies \mathsf{H}_0(m_k) = g^b;$$

Let q_s be the maximum number of signing queries made by $\mathcal{A}_{\text{static}}$. We have $q_s \leq q_\mathsf{H}$. Then, whenever $k \neq \hat{k}$, $\mathcal{A}_{\text{CDH}}$ uses its knowledge of β_k and polynomial $r(\cdot)$ to respond to partial signing queries correctly. Alternatively, when $k = \hat{k}$ and let $m_{\hat{k}}$ be the corresponding message, $\mathcal{A}_{\text{CDH}}$ correctly responds to partial signing queries for each signer $j \in \mathcal{C} \cup \mathcal{S}$, using its knowledge of $s(j)$. If $\mathcal{A}_{\text{static}}$ queries for partial signatures on $m_{\hat{k}}$ from signers not in $\mathcal{C} \cup \mathcal{S}$, $\mathcal{A}_{\text{CDH}}$ aborts.

Now, whenever $\mathcal{A}_{\text{static}}$ outputs a valid forgery $(m_{\hat{k}}, \sigma^*)$, $\mathcal{A}_{\text{CDH}}$ outputs σ^* as the CDH solution. It is easy to see that $\sigma^* = g^{ab}$.

7 Adaptive Security with Distributed Key Generation

In our discussion so far, we proved the adaptive security of our threshold signature scheme, assuming that a trusted party generates the signing keys. In this section, we present a distributed key generation (DKG) protocol that signers can run to set up the signing keys of our threshold signature scheme instead of relying on the trusted KGen. DKG has the following interface.

DKG() : For any (n,t) non-interactive threshold signature scheme TS with $t < n/2$, DKG is an interactive protocol among n parties, which all take some public parameters as inputs. At the end of the protocol, signers output a public key pk, a vector of threshold public keys $\{pk_1, \ldots, pk_n\}$. Each signer i additionally outputs a secret key share sk_i.

As in §5, concretely, at the end of the DKG protocol, each party i outputs $sk_i := (s(i), r(i), u(i))$, threshold public keys $\{pk_j := g^{s(j)} h^{r(j)} v^{u(j)}\}_{j \in [n]}$, and the public verification key $pk := g^{s(0)} h^{r(0)} v^{u(0)}$. Here, $s(\cdot), r(\cdot)$ and $u(\cdot)$ are three degree t polynomials with $r(0) = 0$ and $u(0) = 0$. This implies that $pk := g^{s(0)}$.

7.1 Design of Our DKG Protocol

We design our DKG protocol by augmenting the classic Pedersen DKG protocol, also referred to as the JF-DKG protocol [42]. We pick JF-DKG due to its simplicity and popularity. We believe we can use many other DKG protocols using a similar modification (see our discussion at the end of this section). We summarize our protocol in Fig. 5 and describe it next.

Let $g, h, v \in \mathbb{G}$ be three uniformly random generators of $\mathbb{G}$ with a scalar field $\mathbb{F}$. We will describe our DKG protocol in three phases: *Sharing, Agreement* and *Key Derivation*.

Sharing Phase. During the sharing phase, each party i, as a verifiable secret sharing (VSS) dealer, samples three random degree-t polynomials $s_i(x), r_i(x), u_i(x)$ with $r_i(0) = u_i(0) = 0$ such that

$$s_i(x) := s_{i,0} + s_{i,1} x + \cdots + s_{i,t} x^t$$
$$r_i(x) := r_{i,1} x + \cdots + r_{i,t} x^t \quad \text{and} \quad u_i(x) := u_{i,1} x + \cdots + u_{i,t} x^t$$

Party i then computes a commitment $cm_i \in \mathbb{G}^{t+1}$ to these polynomials

$$cm_i := [g^{s_{i,0}}, g^{s_{i,1}} h^{r_{i,1}} v^{u_{i,1}}, \cdots, g^{s_{i,t}} h^{r_{i,t}} v^{u_{i,t}}] \tag{21}$$

and a proof of knowledge π of discrete logarithm of $cm_i[0] = g^{s_{i,0}}$ with respect to the generator g using the Schnorr identification scheme [63] (steps 2 and 3).

Party i then publishes (step 4), using a broadcast channel, (cm_i, π_i). Intuitively, the proof π_i ensures that the constant terms of $r_i(x)$ and $u_i(x)$ are zero, except with a negligible probability. Also, party i sends each party j, via a private channel, the tuple $(s_i(j), r_i(j), u_i(j))$.

Agreement Phase. The purpose of the agreement phase is for parties to agree on a subset of dealers, also referred to as the qualified set, who correctly participated in the sharing phase. To agree on the qualified set, each party j, upon receiving from dealer i the tuple (s', r', u') (via the private channel) and (cm_i, π_i)

Public parameters: $(g, h, v) \in \mathbb{G}^3, \mathbb{F}$

Sharing phase:
1. Each party i (as a dealer) chooses random polynomials $s_i(x), r_i(x)$ and $u_i(x)$ over $\mathbb{F}$ of degree t each, where

$$s_i(x) := s_{i,0} + s_{i,1}x + \cdots + s_{i,t}x^t$$
$$r_i(x) := r_{i,1}x + \cdots + r_{i,t}x^t \quad \text{and} \quad u_i(x) := u_{i,1}x + \cdots + u_{i,t}x^t$$

2. Party i computes $\mathsf{cm}_i := [g^{s_0}, g^{s_1}h^{r_1}v^{u_1}, \ldots g^{s_t}h^{r_t}v^{u_t}]$.
3. Party i computes π_i, the NIZK proof of knowledge of $s_{i,0}$ with respect to $g^{s_{i,0}}$.
4. Party i broadcasts (cm_i, π_i) to all.
5. Party i privately sends $s_i(j), r_i(j), u_i(j)$ to party j.

Agreement phase:
6. Each party j verifies the shares it receives from other parties by checking for $i = 1, \ldots, n$:

$$g^{s_i(j)} h^{r_i(j)} v^{u_i(j)} = \prod_{k \in [0,t]} \mathsf{cm}_i[k]^{j^k} \qquad (23)$$

7. If the check fails for an index i, party j broadcasts a complaint against P_i
8. Party i (as a dealer) reveals $s_i(j), r_i(j), u_i(j)$ matching eq. (23). If any of the revealed shares fails this equation, party i is disqualified. Let $\mathcal{Q}$ be the set of non-disqualified parties.

Key-derivation phase:
9. The public key pk is computed as $\mathsf{pk} := \prod_{i \in \mathcal{Q}} \mathsf{cm}_i[0]$. The threshold public keys pk_j for each $j \in [n]$ are computed as:

$$\mathsf{pk}_j := \prod_{i \in \mathcal{Q}} \prod_{k \in [0,t]} \mathsf{cm}_i[k]^{j^k} \qquad (24)$$

10. Each party j sets its signing key as $\mathsf{sk}_j := (\sum_{i \in \mathcal{Q}} s_i(j), \sum_{i \in \mathcal{Q}} r_i(j), \sum_{i \in \mathcal{Q}} u_i(j))$.
11. The shared secret key is $s =: \sum_{i \in \mathcal{Q}} s_i$.

Fig. 5. Our DKG protocol which is a modification of the JF-DKG [42].

(via the broadcast channel), accepts them as valid shares if π_i is a valid proof and the following holds:

$$g^{s'} h^{r'} v^{u'} = \prod_{k \in [0,t]} \mathsf{cm}_i[k]^{j^k} \qquad (22)$$

If either of the validation checks fails for any dealer i, the party broadcasts a complaint against the dealer i (step 7). The dealer i then responds to all the complaints against it by publishing the shares of all the complaining parties. All parties then locally validate all the revealed shares for all the complaints. If any dealer i publishes an invalid response to any complaint or does not respond at all, then dealer i is disqualified (step 8). Let $\mathcal{Q}$ be the set of qualified dealers. Note that all honest parties will always be part of $\mathcal{Q}$.

Key-Derivation Phase. With a qualified set $\mathcal{Q}$, the final public key is $\mathsf{pk} = \prod_{i \in \mathcal{Q}} \mathsf{cm}_i[0]$. The threshold public key pk_j of every party j is computed as in Eq. (24). The signing key sk_j of each party j is the sum of the j-th share of all dealers in $\mathcal{Q}$ as shown in step 10 of Fig. 5. Let $s(x), r(x), u(x)$ be the polynomials defined as:

$$s(x) := \sum_{i \in \mathcal{Q}} s_i(x); \qquad r(x) := \sum_{i \in \mathcal{Q}} r_i(x); \qquad u(x) := \sum_{i \in \mathcal{Q}} u_i(x). \qquad (23)$$

Once the DKG protocol finishes, each party i outputs its signing key $\mathsf{sk}_i := (s(i), r(i), u(i))$, the public key $\mathsf{pk} := g^{s(0)} h^{r(0)} v^{u(0)} = g^{s(0)}$, and the threshold public keys $\{\mathsf{pk}_j := g^{s(j)} h^{r(j)} v^{u(j)}\}_{j \in [n]}$.

Using other DKG Protocols. In Fig. 5, we augment the JF-DKG protocol for our signature scheme. Our augmentation techniques are generic and can be used with many existing DKG protocols that follow the same three-phase structure [23, 24, 31, 35, 42, 44, 47, 50, 60]. Specifically, we can augment any such DKG protocol by having each VSS dealer: (i) share two additional zero-polynomials $r(\cdot)$ and $u(\cdot)$; and (ii) publish a NIZK proof π for the correctness of the zero-polynomial. Similarly, each VSS recipient will validate the shares it receives with the updated check in Fig. 5.

Signature Scheme with DKG Our threshold signature scheme with a DKG protocol is identical to Fig. 2, except that signers generate their signing keys by running the DKG protocol in Fig. 5.

7.2 Adaptive Security Analysis with DKG

To ensure robustness of our threshold signature scheme, we require the DKG protocol to satisfy *robustness*. Intuitively, the robustness property states that the keys output by the DKG protocol are well-formed, even in the presence of an adaptive adversary that can corrupt up to t out of n signers. The robustness property ensures that the constant terms of the polynomials $r(x)$ and $u(x)$ are zero. In the full version, we will formalize the robustness property and prove that our DKG ensures robustness, assuming the hardness of discrete logarithm in $\mathbb{G}$.

Next, similar to §6, we will prove unforgeability, assuming the hardness of the DDH in $\hat{\mathbb{G}}$ and the hardness of co-CDH in $(\mathbb{G}, \hat{\mathbb{G}})$. To break the co-CDH assumption, the reduction adversary $\mathcal{A}_{\text{co-CDH}}$ simulates the DKG and threshold signing protocol with the adversary $\mathcal{A}$. Importantly, for this to work, we require the DKG protocol to satisfy the *single inconsistent party (SIP) simulatability* property. Recall that the security proof of our threshold signature used a rigged public key with $r(0) = 1$ and uniformly random $u(0)$. However, with DKG, we do not have a trusted entity to set up the rigged public key. Instead, we will rely on the *single inconsistent party* (SIP) technique [23, 36, 37] to set up a rigged public key. In more detail, we will let one honest party deviate from the specified DKG protocol so that the final DKG output has the rigged with

$r(0) = 1$ and uniformly random $u(0)$ structure we need. For this to go through, we need to ensure that $\mathcal{A}$ cannot distinguish between the real execution of the protocol where all parties follow the DKG protocol and the execution with a single inconsistent party. We capture this by requiring the DKG protocol to satisfy the SIP simulatability property we formally define in in the full version.

In the full-version, we prove that our DKG protocol satisfies the SIP simulatability property. Intuitively, the SIP simulatability of our DKG scheme follows from the fact that for uniformly random $s(x)$, $u(x)$ and non-zero $r(0)$, cm_i for each $i \in \mathcal{H}$ perfectly hides $s(0), r(0)$, and $u(0)$. Given a DKG protocol with the SIP simulatability property, the rest of our security proof is similar to that of §6. We present the full proof in the full version.

8 Implementation and Evaluation

8.1 Evaluation Setup

We implement our threshold signature scheme in Go. Our implementation is publicly available at https://github.com/sourav1547/adaptive-bls. We use the gnark-crypto library [18] for efficient finite field and elliptic curve arithmetic for the BLS12-381 curve. We also use (for both our implementation and the baselines) the multi-exponentiation of group elements using Pippenger's method [14] for efficiency. We evaluate our scheme and baselines on a *t3.2xlarge* Amazon Web Service (AWS) instance with 32 GB RAM, 8 virtual cores, and 2.50 GHz CPU.

Baselines. We implement two variants of Boldyreva's BLS threshold signatures as baselines. The variants differ in how the aggregator validates the partial signatures. The Boldyreva-I variant is the standard variant we describe in §4.4. In Boldyreva-II, along with the partial signatures, signers also attach a Σ-protocol proof attesting to the correctness of the partial signatures. Instead of pairings, the aggregator uses the Σ-protocol proof to check the validity of the partial signatures, resulting in faster verification time. We refer readers to Burdges et al. [20] for more details on Boldyreva-II. For Σ-protocols in both Boldyreva-II and our scheme, we use the standard optimization where the proof omits the first message of the prover and instead includes the Fiat-Shamir challenge [21].

We evaluate the *signing time* and *partial signature verification time* of our scheme. The signing time refers to the time a signer takes to sign a message and compute the associated proofs. The partial signature verification time measures the time the aggregator takes to verify a single partial signature. Note that after partial signature verification, the aggregation time of our threshold signature is identical to the aggregation time of Boldyreva's scheme, but for completeness, we also measure the total *aggregation time*. Our final verification time is identical to Boldyreva's scheme (and standard BLS).

Table 1. Comparison of BLS threshold signatures using BLS12-381 elliptic curve. We assume that public keys are in $\mathbb{G}$ and signatures are in $\hat{\mathbb{G}}$.

Scheme	Partial signing time (in ms)	Partial signature verification time (in ms)	Partial Signature size (in bytes)	Aggregation time for $t=64$ (in ms)
Boldyreva-I	0.81	1.12	96	74.01
Boldyreva-II	1.20	0.76	160	55.43
Ours scheme	3.92	2.16	224	149.52

8.2 Evaluation Results

We report our results in Table 1. Through our evaluation, we seek to illustrate that our scheme only adds a small overhead compared to Boldyreva's scheme [15] to achieve adaptive security.

Signing Time. As expected, the per signer signing time of Boldyreva-II is slightly higher than Boldyreva-I, since a signer in Boldyreva-II also computes the Σ-protocol proof. Similarly, our per signer signing cost is 3.3× higher than Boldyreva-II as our Σ-protocol involves more computation than Boldyreva-II.

Partial Signature Verification Time. The verification time of Boldyreva-II is less than Boldyreva-I, since pairings operations are much slower than group exponentiations. As expected, our partial signature verification time is 2.84× longer than Boldyreva-II due to more expensive Σ-protocol verification. Compared to Boldyreva-I, our partial signature verification is 1.92× slower.

Partial Signature Size. The partial signature size only depends on the underlying elliptic curve group we use. For the BLS12-381 elliptic curve, $\mathbb{F}, \mathbb{G}$ and $\hat{\mathbb{G}}$ elements are 32, 48, and 96 bytes, respectively. The partial signature in Boldyreva-I is a single $\hat{\mathbb{G}}$ element, which is 96 bytes. In Boldyreva-II, the partial signature also consists of a Σ-protocol proof, that, using the standard optimization of including the Fiat-Shamir challenge [21] is $(c, z) \in \mathbb{F}^2$. Hence, the partial signatures in Boldyreva-II are 64 bytes longer compared to Boldyreva-I. Finally, our partial signature includes a Σ-protocol proof $(c, z_s, z_r, z_u) \in \mathbb{F}^4$, and hence in total are 224 bytes long. If we assume that parties are semi-honest, then partial signatures of all three schemes will be identical.

Total Aggregation Time. We measure the total signature aggregation time for $t = 64$. Recall during aggregation, the aggregator, apart from verifying the partial signatures, performs $O(t \log^2 t)$ field operations to compute all the Lagrange coefficients and a multi-exponentiation of width t [68]. Since field operations are orders of magnitude faster than group exponentiations, for moderate values of t such as 64, the partial signature verification costs dominate the total aggregation time. Thus, the aggregation time of all three schemes we evaluate is approximately t times the single partial signature verification time.

Common Case Optimization of Aggregation Time. Note that it is possible to optimize the aggregation time of both the baselines and our scheme in the common case. More specifically, the aggregator can optimistically aggregate the partial signatures without verifying them individually and then verify the aggregated signature. If the final verification is successful, the aggregator outputs the aggregated signature. Otherwise, the aggregator validates the partial signature individually, identifies the invalid ones, discards them, and recomputes the aggregated signature. Moreover, the aggregator discards the partial signatures from the signers who sent invalid partial signatures in all future aggregations. We refer to the latter as the *fall-back* path.

Our evaluation illustrates that with this optimization, the aggregation in the optimistic case is 7.7 ms (in AWS t3.2xlarge machine) for both the baselines and our scheme. Also, the robustness property implies that the aggregator will always identify at least one malicious party in case of the fall-back path and will never blame an honest party. This implies that the aggregator needs to run the fall-back path at most t times in total. Thus, we believe that in long-running system, our added overhead is very minimal.

9 Discussion and Conclusion

In this paper, we presented a new adaptively secure threshold BLS signature scheme and a distributed key generation protocol for it. Our scheme is adaptively secure assuming the hardness of decisional Diffie Hellman (DDH) and co-computational Diffie Hellman assumption (co-CDH) in asymmetric pairing groups in the random oracle model (ROM). The security of our scheme gracefully degenerates: in the presence of a static adversary, our scheme relies only on the hardness of CDH in pairing groups in the ROM, which is the same assumption as in the standard non-threshold BLS signature scheme.

Our scheme maintains the non-interactive signing, compatible verification, and practical efficiency of Boldyreva's BLS threshold signatures. We implemented our scheme in Go, and our evaluation illustrates that it has a small overhead over the Boldyreva scheme.

Future Research Directions. Our scheme only works with type-II and type-III asymmetric pairing groups. This is because the security of our signature scheme assumes the hardness of DDH. Removing the reliance on the DDH assumption on a source group is a fascinating open problem. Another exciting research direction is to extend our ideas to prove the adaptive security of other threshold signature or encryption schemes such as threshold Schnorr, ECDSA, and RSA.

Acknowledgments. We want to thank Dan Boneh for pointing us to the DDH rerandomization in their book and Leonid Reyzin for pointing us to the [59]. We would also like to thank Crypto 2024 and Eurocrypt 2024 reviewers for their helpful suggestions on how to improve the paper presentation. Finally, we thank Amit Agarwal, Renas

Bacho, Julian Loss, Victor Shoup, Alin Tomescu, and Zhoulun Xiang for helpful discussions related to the paper. This work is funded in part by a Chainlink Labs Ph.D. fellowship and the National Science Foundation award #2240976.

References

1. Distributed randomness beacon: Verifiable, unpredictable and unbiased random numbers as a service (2023). https://drand.love/docs/overview/
2. Internet computer: Chain-key cryptography (2023). https://internetcomputer.org/how-it-works/chain-key-technology/
3. Randcast-arpa network (2023). https://docs.arpanetwork.io/randcast
4. Skale network documentation: Distributed key generation (DKG) (2023). https://docs.skale.network/technology/dkg-bls
5. Abe, M., Fehr, S.: Adaptively secure feldman VSS and applications to universally-composable threshold cryptography. In: Franklin, M. (ed.) CRYPTO 2004. LNCS, vol. 3152, pp. 317–334. Springer, Heidelberg (2004). https://doi.org/10.1007/978-3-540-28628-8_20
6. Abraham, I., Malkhi, D., Spiegelman, A.: Asymptotically optimal validated asynchronous byzantine agreement. In: Proceedings of the 2019 ACM Symposium on Principles of Distributed Computing, pp. 337–346 (2019)
7. Almansa, J.F., Damgård, I., Nielsen, J.B.: Simplified threshold RSA with adaptive and proactive security. In: Vaudenay, S. (ed.) EUROCRYPT 2006. LNCS, vol. 4004, pp. 593–611. Springer, Heidelberg (2006). https://doi.org/10.1007/11761679_35
8. Bacho, R., Loss, J.: On the adaptive security of the threshold bls signature scheme. In: Proceedings of the 2022 ACM SIGSAC Conference on Computer and Communications Security, pp. 193–207 (2022)
9. Bacho, R., Loss, J., Tessaro, S., Wagner, B., Zhu, C.: Twinkle: threshold signatures from ddh with full adaptive security. In: Annual International Conference on the Theory and Applications of Cryptographic Techniques, pp. 429–459. Springer (2024). https://doi.org/10.1007/978-3-031-58716-0_15
10. Bellare, M., Crites, E., Komlo, C., Maller, M., Tessaro, S., Zhu, C.: Better than advertised security for non-interactive threshold signatures. In: Annual International Cryptology Conference pp. 517–550. Springer (2022). https://doi.org/10.1007/978-3-031-15985-5_18
11. Bellare, M., Neven, G.: Multi-signatures in the plain public-key model and a general forking lemma. In: Proceedings of the 13th ACM Conference on Computer and Communications Security, pp. 390–399 (2006)
12. Benhamouda, F., Halevi, S., Krawczyk, H., Ma, Y., Rabin, T.: Sprint: high-throughput robust distributed schnorr signatures. In: Annual International Conference on the Theory and Applications of Cryptographic Techniques, pp. 62–91. Springer (2024). https://doi.org/10.1007/978-3-031-58740-5_3
13. Berman, P., Garay, J.A., Perry, K.J.: Bit optimal distributed consensus. In: Computer Science, pp. 313–321. Springer (1992). https://doi.org/10.1007/978-1-4615-3422-8_27
14. Bernstein, D.J., Doumen, J., Lange, T., Oosterwijk, J.-J.: Faster batch forgery identification. In: Galbraith, S., Nandi, M. (eds.) INDOCRYPT 2012. LNCS, vol. 7668, pp. 454–473. Springer, Heidelberg (2012). https://doi.org/10.1007/978-3-642-34931-7_26

15. Boldyreva, A.: Threshold signatures, multisignatures and blind signatures based on the gap-diffie-hellman-group signature scheme. In: Desmedt, Y.G. (ed.) PKC 2003. LNCS, vol. 2567, pp. 31–46. Springer, Heidelberg (2003). https://doi.org/10.1007/3-540-36288-6_3
16. Boneh, D., Lynn, B., Shacham, H.: Short signatures from the weil pairing. In: Boyd, C. (ed.) ASIACRYPT 2001. LNCS, vol. 2248, pp. 514–532. Springer, Heidelberg (2001). https://doi.org/10.1007/3-540-45682-1_30
17. Boneh, D., Shoup, V.: A graduate course in applied cryptography. Draft 0.6 (2023)
18. Botrel, G., Piellard, T., Housni, Y.E., Tabaie, A., Gutoski, G., Kubjas, I.: Consensys/gnark-crypto: v0.9.0 (Jan 2023). https://doi.org/10.5281/zenodo.5815453
19. Brandão, L.T.A.N., Peralta, R.: Nist ir 8214c: First call for multi-party threshold schemes (2023). https://csrc.nist.gov/pubs/ir/8214/c/ipd
20. Burdges, J., Ciobotaru, O., Lavasani, S., Stewart, A.: Efficient aggregatable bls signatures with chaum-pedersen proofs. Cryptology ePrint Archive (2022)
21. Camenisch, J., Stadler, M.: Proof systems for general statements about discrete logarithms. Technical Report/ETH Zurich, Department of Computer Science **260** (1997)
22. Canetti, R., Gennaro, R., Goldfeder, S., Makriyannis, N., Peled, U.: Uc non-interactive, proactive, threshold ecdsa with identifiable aborts. In: Proceedings of the 2020 ACM SIGSAC Conference on Computer and Communications Security, pp. 1769–1787 (2020)
23. Canetti, R., Gennaro, R., Jarecki, S., Krawczyk, H., Rabin, T.: Adaptive security for threshold cryptosystems. In: Wiener, M. (ed.) CRYPTO 1999. LNCS, vol. 1666, pp. 98–116. Springer, Heidelberg (1999). https://doi.org/10.1007/3-540-48405-1_7
24. Canny, J., Sorkin, S.: Practical large-scale distributed key generation. In: Cachin, C., Camenisch, J.L. (eds.) EUROCRYPT 2004. LNCS, vol. 3027, pp. 138–152. Springer, Heidelberg (2004). https://doi.org/10.1007/978-3-540-24676-3_9
25. Chen, Y.H., Lindell, Y.: Feldman's verifiable secret sharing for a dishonest majority. Cryptology ePrint Archive (2024)
26. Chu, H., Gerhart, P., Ruffing, T., Schröder, D.: Practical schnorr threshold signatures without the algebraic group model. In: Annual International Cryptology Conference. Springer (2023). https://doi.org/10.1007/978-3-031-38557-5_24
27. Crites, E., Komlo, C., Maller, M.: How to prove schnorr assuming schnorr: security of multi-and threshold signatures. Cryptology ePrint Archive (2021)
28. Crites, E., Komlo, C., Maller, M.: Fully adaptive schnorr threshold signatures. In: Annual International Cryptology Conference. Springer (2023). https://doi.org/10.1007/978-3-031-38557-5_22
29. Damgård, I.: On σ-protocols. Lecture Notes, University of Aarhus, Department for Computer Science p. 84 (2002)
30. Das, S., Camacho, P., Xiang, Z., Nieto, J., Bünz, B., Ren, L.: Threshold signatures from inner product argument: succinct, weighted, and multi-threshold. In: Proceedings of the 2023 ACM SIGSAC Conference on Computer and Communications Security, pp. 356–370 (2023)
31. Das, S., Yurek, T., Xiang, Z., Miller, A., Kokoris-Kogias, L., Ren, L.: Practical asynchronous distributed key generation. In: 2022 IEEE Symposium on Security and Privacy (SP), pp. 2518–2534. IEEE (2022)
32. Desmedt, Y.: Society and group oriented cryptography: a new concept. In: Pomerance, C. (ed.) CRYPTO 1987. LNCS, vol. 293, pp. 120–127. Springer, Heidelberg (1988). https://doi.org/10.1007/3-540-48184-2_8

33. Desmedt, Y., Frankel, Y.: Threshold cryptosystems. In: Brassard, G. (ed.) CRYPTO 1989. LNCS, vol. 435, pp. 307–315. Springer, New York (1990). https://doi.org/10.1007/0-387-34805-0_28
34. Dolev, D., Strong, H.R.: Authenticated algorithms for byzantine agreement. SIAM J. Comput. **12**(4), 656–666 (1983)
35. Fouque, P.-A., Stern, J.: One round threshold discrete-log key generation without private channels. In: Kim, K. (ed.) PKC 2001. LNCS, vol. 1992, pp. 300–316. Springer, Heidelberg (2001). https://doi.org/10.1007/3-540-44586-2_22
36. Frankel, Y., MacKenzie, P., Yung, M.: Adaptively-secure distributed public-key systems. In: Nešetřil, J. (ed.) ESA 1999. LNCS, vol. 1643, pp. 4–27. Springer, Heidelberg (1999). https://doi.org/10.1007/3-540-48481-7_2
37. Frankel, Y., MacKenzie, P., Yung, M.: Adaptively-secure optimal-resilience proactive RSA. In: Lam, K.-Y., Okamoto, E., Xing, C. (eds.) ASIACRYPT 1999. LNCS, vol. 1716, pp. 180–194. Springer, Heidelberg (1999). https://doi.org/10.1007/978-3-540-48000-6_15
38. Galbraith, S.D., Paterson, K.G., Smart, N.P.: Pairings for cryptographers. Discret. Appl. Math. **156**(16), 3113–3121 (2008)
39. Garg, S., Jain, A., Mukherjee, P., Sinha, R., Wang, M., Zhang, Y.: hints: Threshold signatures with silent setup. In: 2024 IEEE Symposium on Security and Privacy (SP) (2024)
40. Gelashvili, R., Kokoris-Kogias, L., Sonnino, A., Spiegelman, A., Xiang, Z.: Jolteon and ditto: Network-adaptive efficient consensus with asynchronous fallback. In: International conference on financial cryptography and data security. Springer (2022). https://doi.org/10.1007/978-3-031-18283-9_1
41. Gennaro, R., Jarecki, S., Krawczyk, H., Rabin, T.: Robust threshold DSS signatures. In: Maurer, U. (ed.) EUROCRYPT 1996. LNCS, vol. 1070, pp. 354–371. Springer, Heidelberg (1996). https://doi.org/10.1007/3-540-68339-9_31
42. Gennaro, R., Jarecki, S., Krawczyk, H., Rabin, T.: Secure distributed key generation for discrete-log based cryptosystems. J. Cryptol. **20**(1), 51–83 (2007)
43. Gilad, Y., Hemo, R., Micali, S., Vlachos, G., Zeldovich, N.: Algorand: scaling byzantine agreements for cryptocurrencies. In: Proceedings of the 26th Symposium on Operating Systems Principles, pp. 51–68 (2017)
44. Groth, J.: Non-interactive distributed key generation and key resharing. IACR Cryptol. ePrint Arch. **2021**, 339 (2021)
45. Groth, J., Shoup, V.: Fast batched asynchronous distributed key generation. In: Annual International Conference on the Theory and Applications of Cryptographic Techniques. pp. 370–400. Springer (2024). https://doi.org/10.1007/978-3-031-58740-5_13
46. Jarecki, S., Lysyanskaya, A.: Adaptively secure threshold cryptography: introducing concurrency, removing erasures. In: Preneel, B. (ed.) EUROCRYPT 2000. LNCS, vol. 1807, pp. 221–242. Springer, Heidelberg (2000). https://doi.org/10.1007/3-540-45539-6_16
47. Kate, A., Huang, Y., Goldberg, I.: Distributed key generation in the wild. IACR Cryptol. ePrint Arch. **2012**, 377 (2012)
48. Katz, J., Lindell, Y.: Introduction to modern cryptography: principles and protocols. Chapman and hall/CRC (2007)
49. Katz, J., Yung, M.: Threshold cryptosystems based on factoring. In: Zheng, Y. (ed.) ASIACRYPT 2002. LNCS, vol. 2501, pp. 192–205. Springer, Heidelberg (2002). https://doi.org/10.1007/3-540-36178-2_12

50. Kokoris Kogias, E., Malkhi, D., Spiegelman, A.: Asynchronous distributed key generation for computationally-secure randomness, consensus, and threshold signatures. In: Proceedings of the 2020 ACM SIGSAC Conference on Computer and Communications Security, pp. 1751–1767 (2020)
51. Komlo, C., Goldberg, I.: FROST: flexible round-optimized schnorr threshold signatures. In: Dunkelman, O., Jacobson, Jr., M.J., O'Flynn, C. (eds.) SAC 2020. LNCS, vol. 12804, pp. 34–65. Springer, Cham (2021). https://doi.org/10.1007/978-3-030-81652-0_2
52. Lamport, L., Shostak, R., Pease, M.: The byzantine generals problem. ACM Trans. Program. Lang. Syst. **4**(3), 382–401 (1982)
53. Libert, B., Joye, M., Yung, M.: Born and raised distributively: fully distributed non-interactive adaptively-secure threshold signatures with short shares. In: Proceedings of the 2014 ACM Symposium on Principles of Distributed Computing, pp. 303–312 (2014)
54. Libert, B., Yung, M.: Adaptively secure non-interactive threshold cryptosystems. Theoret. Comput. Sci. **478**, 76–100 (2013)
55. Lu, Y., Lu, Z., Tang, Q., Wang, G.: Dumbo-mvba: Optimal multi-valued validated asynchronous byzantine agreement, revisited. In: Proceedings of the 39th Symposium on Principles of Distributed Computing, pp. 129–138 (2020)
56. Lysyanskaya, A., Peikert, C.: Adaptive security in the threshold setting: from cryptosystems to signature schemes. In: Boyd, C. (ed.) ASIACRYPT 2001. LNCS, vol. 2248, pp. 331–350. Springer, Heidelberg (2001). https://doi.org/10.1007/3-540-45682-1_20
57. Miller, A., Xia, Y., Croman, K., Shi, E., Song, D.: The honey badger of bft protocols. In: Proceedings of the 2016 ACM SIGSAC Conference on Computer And Communications Security, pp. 31–42 (2016)
58. Momose, A., Ren, L.: Optimal communication complexity of authenticated byzantine agreement. In: 35th International Symposium on Distributed Computing, DISC 2021. p. 32. Schloss Dagstuhl-Leibniz-Zentrum fur Informatik GmbH, Dagstuhl Publishing (2021)
59. Naor, M., Reingold, O.: Number-theoretic constructions of efficient pseudo-random functions. J. ACM (JACM) **51**(2), 231–262 (2004)
60. Pedersen, T.P.: A threshold cryptosystem without a trusted party. In: Davies, D.W. (ed.) EUROCRYPT 1991. LNCS, vol. 547, pp. 522–526. Springer, Heidelberg (1991). https://doi.org/10.1007/3-540-46416-6_47
61. Rabin, T.: A simplified approach to threshold and proactive RSA. In: Krawczyk, H. (ed.) CRYPTO 1998. LNCS, vol. 1462, pp. 89–104. Springer, Heidelberg (1998). https://doi.org/10.1007/BFb0055722
62. Ruffing, T., Ronge, V., Jin, E., Schneider-Bensch, J., Schröder, D.: Roast: robust asynchronous schnorr threshold signatures. In: Proceedings of the 2022 ACM SIGSAC Conference on Computer and Communications Security, pp. 2551–2564 (2022)
63. Schnorr, C.P.: Efficient identification and signatures for smart cards. In: Brassard, G. (ed.) CRYPTO 1989. LNCS, vol. 435, pp. 239–252. Springer, New York (1990). https://doi.org/10.1007/0-387-34805-0_22
64. Shamir, A.: How to share a secret. Commun. ACM **22**(11), 612–613 (1979)
65. Shoup, V.: Practical threshold signatures. In: Preneel, B. (ed.) EUROCRYPT 2000. LNCS, vol. 1807, pp. 207–220. Springer, Heidelberg (2000). https://doi.org/10.1007/3-540-45539-6_15
66. Shoup, V.: The many faces of schnorr. Cryptology ePrint Archive (2023)

67. Tessaro, S., Zhu, C.: Threshold and multi-signature schemes from linear hash functions. In: Annual International Conference on the Theory and Applications of Cryptographic Techniques, pp. 628–658. Springer (2023). https://doi.org/10.1007/978-3-031-30589-4_22
68. Tomescu, A., et al.: Towards scalable threshold cryptosystems. In: 2020 IEEE Symposium on Security and Privacy (SP), pp. 877–893. IEEE (2020)
69. Wang, Z., Qian, H., Li, Z.: Adaptively secure threshold signature scheme in the standard model. Informatica **20**(4), 591–612 (2009)
70. Waters, B.: Efficient identity-based encryption without random oracles. In: Cramer, R. (ed.) EUROCRYPT 2005. LNCS, vol. 3494, pp. 114–127. Springer, Heidelberg (2005). https://doi.org/10.1007/11426639_7
71. Yin, M., Malkhi, D., Reiter, M.K., Gueta, G.G., Abraham, I.: Hotstuff: Bft consensus with linearity and responsiveness. In: Proceedings of the 2019 ACM Symposium on Principles of Distributed Computing, pp. 347–356. ACM (2019)

Round-Optimal, Fully Secure Distributed Key Generation

Jonathan Katz

Google and University of Maryland, College Park, USA
jkatz@dfns.co, jkatz2@gmail.com

Abstract. Protocols for distributed (threshold) key generation (DKG) in the discrete-logarithm setting have received a tremendous amount of attention in the past few years. Several synchronous DKG protocols have been proposed, but most such protocols are not *fully secure*: they either allow corrupted parties to *bias* the key, or are not *robust* and allow malicious parties to prevent successful generation of a key.

We explore the round complexity of fully secure DKG in the honest-majority setting where it is feasible. We show the impossibility of one-round, statistically unbiased DKG protocols (even if not robust), regardless of any prior setup. On the positive side, we show various round-optimal protocols for fully secure DKG offering tradeoffs in terms of their efficiency, necessary setup, and required assumptions.

1 Introduction

In a $(t+1)$-out-of-n *threshold cryptosystem*, a secret key is shared among n parties such that any collection of $t+1$ honest parties can jointly perform some cryptographic operation, while an adversary compromising up to t parties cannot. There has recently been a significant interest in threshold signing, in particular, motivated by its application to the protection of cryptocurrency wallets as well as other applications such as access control, random beacons, and distributed-protocol design. Research on threshold cryptography has developed threshold protocols for the ECDSA, Schnorr, and BLS signature schemes, as well as protocols for distributed key generation (DKG) [1–3,5,11,12,17,19,22,25,26,30,32,33,38,39,42,43,45,47,49,50,53] in the discrete-logarithm setting that underlies those schemes. Threshold protocols based on this work are being used extensively by companies such as Fireblocks, Dfns, and Coinbase (among others), and there has also been interest in their standardization [10,15].

DKG has been studied in the synchronous [1,5,11,12,17,22,25,26,30,33,39, 43,45,49,50,53] and asynchronous [2,3,19,32,42] settings. Although the asynchronous model may be more appropriate for large-scale protocols with globally distributed parties, the synchronous model is assumed in practice for small-scale

---

This work was done entirely at Dfns. It was not part of my U. Maryland duties.

© International Association for Cryptologic Research 2024
L. Reyzin and D. Stebila (Eds.): CRYPTO 2024, LNCS 14926, pp. 285–316, 2024.
https://doi.org/10.1007/978-3-031-68394-7_10

protocols running in a local network (as is the case for the companies mentioned above). We consider the synchronous model in this paper. As is standard in this setting (an exception is [50]), we assume a broadcast channel and leave open the question of round optimality in point-to-point networks.

We focus here on the round complexity of *fully secure* DKG protocols in the discrete-logarithm setting. Roughly speaking, the goal in this context is for n parties to distributively generate a public key $y = g^x$ (where g is a fixed generator of a cyclic group $\mathbb{G}$) such that the parties hold $(t+1)$-out-of-n secret shares $\{\sigma_i\}$ of the private exponent x. We also ensure that parties can compute public "commitments" $\{g^{\sigma_i}\}$ to each others' shares, as is often required by threshold protocols. "Full security" for a DKG protocol is defined in a simulation-based framework via an appropriate ideal functionality (see below and Sect. 3). A fully secure protocol must, in particular, prevent the adversary from being able to *bias* the generated public key y. It also requires *robustness* (aka *guaranteed output delivery*); namely, the honest parties must always produce correct output, even in the presence of malicious behavior. We assume an honest majority since fully secure DKG protocols are impossible[1] otherwise.

Perhaps surprisingly, there are few explicit constructions of fully secure DKG protocols in the literature [9,26,53], and most existing DKG protocols—even in the honest-majority setting—allow bias (e.g., [22,39]) and/or are not robust (e.g., [30,43]). The most round-efficient explicit construction of a fully secure DKG protocol appears to be the 6-round protocol by Gennaro et al. [26]. One could apply known results [18,28,29] for generic secure multiparty computation (MPC) with guaranteed output delivery in the honest-majority setting to obtain a 3-round DKG protocol assuming a common reference string (CRS), or a 2-round protocol assuming a CRS and a public-key infrastructure (PKI), but the resulting protocols would not be particularly efficient; moreover, they would require strong primitives (like fully homomorphic encryption or indistinguishability obfuscation) and cryptographic assumptions. While round-efficient constructions of computational VSS [6] and verifiable relation sharing [4] are known, these also seem to imply no better than 3-round DKG protocols.

1.1 Our Results

We work in a simulation-based framework and define full security for DKG protocols via a corresponding ideal functionality that (in particular) prevents bias and ensures guaranteed output delivery. We also show in Appendix A several other ideal functionalities for DKG one might consider. Although such simulation-based definitions seem to us the most natural way to define security, several recent works have instead given (different) game-based definitions that are quite complex, somewhat difficult to interpret or compare to one another, and hard to use in a modular fashion when designing threshold protocols based on them.

---

[1] This follows by a reduction from coin tossing to DKG, plus the well-known impossibility result of Cleve [14].

Table 1. Summary of protocols in this paper. Guide to acronyms not defined in the introduction: NIZK = non-interactive zero knowledge proofs, PKE = public-key encryption, OWF = one-way functions. Note that the ROM implies a CRS, which is why we list it as a form of setup.

Protocol	Setup	Rounds	Assumptions	poly(n)?
Π_1	CRS + PKI	2	NIZK + PKE	YES
Π_{CRS}	CRS	2	NIZK + MP-NIKE	NO
Π_{ROM}	ROM + 1-round preprocessing	2	—	NO
Π_1-round	CRS + 2-round preprocessing	1	NIZK + OWF	NO

We hope our definitional treatment, though perhaps obvious to those familiar with MPC, will be useful for future work.

We then consider the round complexity of fully secure DKG in the honest-majority setting. On the negative side, we show in Sect. 4 the impossibility of one-round, *statistically unbiased* DKG, i.e., where the distribution of the public key is statistically close to uniform in an honest execution. Our impossibility result (1) holds even when there is only a single corrupted party; (2) holds regardless of any prior setup or idealized models (like the random-oracle model) used; and (3) gives quantitative bounds on the statistical bias of any one-round DKG protocol. To the best of our knowledge, the impossibility result does not follow from prior work; in particular, existing lower bounds on the round complexity of MPC with guaranteed output delivery [18,24,28,29,48] take advantage of the fact that honest parties have input, and do not seem to extend to the case of no-input functionalities like DKG (Table 1).

On the positive side, we show several constructions of round-optimal fully secure DKG protocols that offer tradeoffs in terms of their computational efficiency, necessary setup, and cryptographic assumptions (cf. Fig. 1):

1. In Sect. 5, we show a framework for constructing 2-round, fully secure DKG protocols assuming a CRS and a PKI. Although the same round complexity could be obtained using prior work on generic MPC, our framework uses weaker cryptographic assumptions and can lead to more-efficient constructions. In particular, we propose a reasonably efficient instantiation of our framework based on the El Gamal and Paillier encryption schemes in the random-oracle model.

2. In Sect. 6, we show a 2-round, fully secure DKG protocol based on a CRS alone. This is particularly interesting since, to the best of our knowledge, such a result does not follow from existing results on generic MPC. One drawback of this construction is that, for $n > 6$, it relies on multiparty non-interactive key exchange (NIKE), something currently known to exist only based on strong assumptions.[2] (We refer to Koppula et al. [44] for a survey of

---

[2] For $n = 3, 4$ the standard decisional Diffie-Hellman assumption suffices, and when $n = 5, 6$ the decisional bilinear Diffie-Hellman assumption can be used.

known results.) It also has $O(\binom{n}{t})$ complexity, and thus technically only solves the problem for a constant number of parties. As such, we view this result as primarily demonstrating the difficulty of proving *impossibility* of 2-round fully secure DKG in the CRS model.

3. We show in Sect. 7 a fully secure protocol in the random-oracle model (ROM) with the following property: After one round of preprocessing (run by the parties themselves), the parties can generate an unbounded number of keys via repeated invocations of a 2-round protocol.[3] A simple modification of the protocol can also be proven adaptively secure. This approach relies on combinatorial techniques from pseudorandom secret sharing [16], and is extremely efficient for small values of n typically used in practice even though its asymptotic complexity is $O(\binom{n}{t})$. We thus believe this protocol is a competitive choice for many real-world applications of DKG.

4. Finally, and somewhat surprisingly given our impossibility result, we show in Sect. 8 a fully secure DKG protocol that requires only a *single* round. This protocol does not violate the impossibility result claimed earlier since it is *not* statistically unbiased. This may itself seem surprising, as the ideal functionality used to define fully secure DKG *is* statistically unbiased (as it chooses a uniform public key). There is no contradiction since this protocol generates a *pseudorandom* (i.e., computationally unbiased) public key.

This protocol relies on a CRS. In addition, similar to the previous protocol, it requires[4] two rounds of preprocessing after which the parties can generate an unbounded number of keys; it also has complexity $O(\binom{n}{t})$.

In work done subsequent to our own, Boneh et al. [8] show a similar (though concretely more efficient) result based on ideas that are similar-in-spirit.

Our proofs of security do not use rewinding, and hence (with appropriate modifications to handle SIDs) are universally composable (in a synchronous model).

We leave as interesting open questions whether there is a two-round, fully secure DKG protocol in the plain model, or whether there is an efficient such protocol in the ROM without preprocessing. As far as we know the first question is open even for sub-optimal corruption threshold $t < n/3$.

2 Background

Notation. We let $\mathbb{G}$ be a cyclic group of prime order q and let $g \in \mathbb{G}$ be a fixed generator. We let $\mathbb{Z}_q$ be the field $\{0, \ldots, q-1\}$ modulo q, and $[k] = \{1, \ldots, k\}$. We

---

[3] Alternately, one can view it as a 3-round protocol in the ROM or a 2-round protocol in the ROM given certain correlated randomness. In practice, however, we believe it would be run in the manner described.

[4] As before, it could alternately be viewed as a 3-round protocol in the CRS model or, if one prefers, as a 1-round protocol given certain correlated randomness.

write "←" for probabilistic assignment and ":=" for deterministic assignment. In particular, if R is a randomized algorithm then $y \leftarrow R(x)$ means that we run R on input x and a uniform random tape to obtain y, whereas $y := R(x; \omega)$ means that we (deterministically) run R on input x and random tape ω to obtain y.

System and Communication Model. We assume n parties $P_1, \ldots, P_n$, at most t of whom are corrupted. We work in the standard synchronous communication model where parties are connected by pairwise private and authenticated channels in addition to a public broadcast channel. We always consider a *rushing* adversary, by which we mean that in each round the corrupted parties receive all messages sent by honest parties in that round before having to send their own messages. In some cases we rely on[5] a public-key infrastructure (PKI), by which we mean that all parties hold the same vector $(\mathsf{pk}_1, \ldots, \mathsf{pk}_n)$ of public keys and each honest party P_i holds the secret key sk_i associated with pk_i. Parties who are corrupted at the outset may generate their public keys in an arbitrary fashion, possibly depending on public keys of the honest parties.

Defining Round Complexity. The round complexity of a protocol execution in the synchronous model is straightforward to define. However, some protocols may run for a different number of rounds in different executions. For some protocols the round complexity is a random variable. In other work, a distinction is made between *optimistic* round complexity (when all parties are honest) and *worst-case* round complexity (which holds for arbitrary adversarial behavior). All the protocols in this paper run for a fixed number of rounds in every execution.

2.1 Cryptographic Building Blocks

Shamir Secret Sharing. We use the standard notion of Shamir secret sharing. To share a secret $x \in \mathbb{Z}_q$ in a $(t+1)$-out-of-n fashion, a dealer chooses uniform coefficients $f_1, \ldots, f_t \in \mathbb{Z}_q$ and forms the polynomial $f(X) := x + \sum_{i=1}^{t} f_i \cdot X^i$; it then defines shares $\{\sigma_i\}_{i=1}^{n}$ by setting $\sigma_i := f(i)$, and distributes σ_i to P_i via a private channel. It is useful to also define $\sigma_0 := f(0) = x$ (though note that σ_0 is not a share that is sent to any party), and we write $\{\sigma_i\}_{i=0}^{n} \leftarrow \mathsf{SS}_t(x)$ to denote the process by which these values are generated. No information about x is revealed by the shares of any t parties, but $x = \sigma_0$ can be reconstructed from the shares of any $t+1$ parties. More generally, it is possible to reconstruct the value of f at any point from its values at any $t+1$ points using Lagrange interpolation. I.e., for any $(t+1)$-size set $S \subset \mathbb{Z}_q$ and any $k \in \mathbb{Z}_q$ it is possible to (publicly) compute coefficients $\{\lambda_{i,k}^{S}\}_{i \in S}$ such that $f(k) = \sum_{i \in S} \lambda_{i,k}^{S} \cdot f(i)$. We denote such interpolation of the value of $f(k)$ from

---

[5] In practice, a PKI is typically assumed; it is anyway necessary for broadcast or could be established using broadcast in a preprocessing phase. Thus, avoiding a PKI is mainly of theoretical interest.

the values $\{f(i)\}_{i\in S}$ by $\mathsf{interpolate}(k, S, \{f(i)\}_{i\in S})$. In particular, when $S \subset [n]$ we have $x = \mathsf{interpolate}(0, S, \{\sigma_i\}_{i\in S})$.

It is a standard fact that interpolation can also be done "in the exponent," i.e., given any $(t+1)$-size set $S \subset \mathbb{Z}_q$, the values $\{g^{f(i)}\}_{i\in S}$, and $k \in \mathbb{Z}_q$, it is possible to compute $g^{f(k)} = \prod_{i\in S} \left(g^{f(i)}\right)^{\lambda_{i,k}^S}$. Overloading notation slightly, we also denote this by $g^{f(k)} = \mathsf{interpolate}(k, S, \{g^{f(i)}\}_{i\in S})$.

Feldman Verifiable Secret Sharing. Feldman's variant of Shamir secret sharing [21] allows parties to verify that they have received shares consistent with a polynomial of the correct degree. We describe a slight variant of the usual scheme that is functionally equivalent. Here, the dealer generates $\{\sigma_i\}_{i=0}^n$ as above, and broadcasts $y_0 := g^{\sigma_0}, \ldots, y_t := g^{\sigma_t}$ (in addition to sending σ_i to P_i via a private channel, as before). We write $(\{y_i\}_{i=0}^t, \{\sigma_i\}_{i=1}^n) \leftarrow \mathsf{FVSS}_t(x)$ to denote the process by which the indicated values are generated. Given the broadcasted information, P_i can check correctness of the share σ_i it received from the dealer by setting $S := \{0,\ldots,t\}$ and then verifying that $g^{\sigma_i} \stackrel{?}{=} \mathsf{interpolate}(i, S, \{y_j\}_{j\in S})$. The behavior of P_i in case verification fails (including the case when P_i does not receive anything from the dealer) is protocol-dependent.

Feldman's scheme leaks the value $y_0 = g^x$, but for our applications this will not be a problem.

CPA-Secure Encryption. We use the standard notion of CPA-security [40] for a public-key encryption scheme defined by algorithms (Gen, Enc, Dec).

Non-interactive Zero-Knowledge (NIZK) Proofs. We rely on a variant of (unbounded) simulation-sound NIZK proofs [20,41]. Let R be an NP relation. A collection of efficient algorithms (GenCRS, $\mathcal{P}$, $\mathcal{V}$, Sim$_1$, Sim$_2$, KE) is an *ID-based simulation-sound NIZK proof system for R* if the following hold:

- **Completeness:** For all $(x, w) \in R$ and all $i \in [n]$,

$$\Pr[\mathsf{crs} \leftarrow \mathsf{GenCRS}; \pi \leftarrow \mathcal{P}(\mathsf{crs}, i, x, w) : \mathcal{V}(\mathsf{crs}, i, x, \pi) = 1] = 1.$$

- **Adaptive, multi-theorem zero knowledge:** For any efficient adversary $\mathcal{A}$, the following is negligible

$$\left| \Pr[\mathsf{crs} \leftarrow \mathsf{GenCRS} : \mathcal{A}^{\mathcal{P}^*(\mathsf{crs},\cdot,\cdot,\cdot)}(\mathsf{crs}) = 1] \right.$$
$$\left. - \Pr[(\mathsf{crs},\mathsf{td}) \leftarrow \mathsf{Sim}_1 : \mathcal{A}^{\mathsf{Sim}_2^*(\mathsf{td},\cdot,\cdot,\cdot)}(\mathsf{crs}) = 1] \right|,$$

where $\mathcal{P}^*(\mathsf{crs}, i, x, w)$ returns $\mathcal{P}(\mathsf{crs}, i, x, w)$ if $(x,w) \in R$ (and $\bot$ otherwise) and $\mathsf{Sim}_2^*(\mathsf{td}, i, x, w)$ returns $\mathsf{Sim}_2(\mathsf{td}, i, x)$ if $(x,w) \in R$ (and $\bot$ otherwise).

- **Unbounded, identity-based simulation soundness:** The standard notion of simulation soundness requires that even if an adversary is given multiple simulated proofs, it cannot generate a new, valid proof for a false statement. This is formalized by requiring that if the adversary outputs a (new) valid proof for a statement x, a knowledge extractor KE can extract a witness corresponding to x. We also bind proofs to identities, and require that an adversary given multiple simulated proofs with respect to one set of identities $\mathcal{H}$ cannot generate a valid proof (whether new or not) for a false statement with respect to any identity outside of $\mathcal{H}$. More formally, the success probability of every efficient adversary $\mathcal{A}$ in the following experiment should be small:
  1. Run $(\mathsf{crs}, \mathsf{td}) \leftarrow \mathsf{Sim}_1$, and choose a uniform bit $b \in \{0,1\}$.
  2. Run $\mathcal{A}(\mathsf{crs})$ to obtain a set $\mathcal{H} \subset [n]$. Then give $\mathcal{A}$ access to two oracles:
     (a) The first oracle takes input (i, x, w) and returns $\bot$ if $(x, w) \notin R$ or $i \notin \mathcal{H}$. Otherwise, it returns $\mathsf{Sim}_2(\mathsf{td}, i, x)$.
     (b) The second oracle takes input (i, x, π) and returns $\bot$ if $i \in \mathcal{H}$ or $\mathcal{V}(\mathsf{crs}, i, x, \pi) = 0$. Otherwise:
       - If $b = 0$ it returns 1.
       - If $b = 1$ it computes $w \leftarrow \mathsf{KE}(\mathsf{td}, i, x, \pi)$ and returns 1 if it holds that $(x, w) \in R$ (and returns $\bot$ otherwise).
  3. $\mathcal{A}$ outputs a guess $b' \in \{0, 1\}$, and succeeds iff $b = b'$.

3 Defining Secure Distributed Key Generation

We use a standard simulation-based notion of security that we briefly summarize below. For self-containment, our definition is for stand-alone security, but it could easily be adapted to the universal composability (UC) framework. (As noted earlier, the security proofs for all our protocols use straight-line simulation, so apply also in the UC setting.) We assume static corruptions.

Fix some n-party DKG protocol Π. A real-world execution of the protocol in the presence of an adversary $\mathcal{A}$ proceeds as follows (note that parties have no initial input):

1. $\mathcal{A}$ specifies a set $\mathcal{C} \subset [n]$ of corrupted parties.
2. The honest parties run Π with the corrupted parties. Honest parties follow the protocol as prescribed, while the actions of the corrupted parties are controlled by $\mathcal{A}$.
3. When an honest party terminates, it outputs the value prescribed by the protocol.
4. The *view* of $\mathcal{A}$ in this execution consists of the randomness used by $\mathcal{A}$, any messages sent to any of the corrupted parties by an honest party, and any messages sent on the broadcast channel by an honest party.

We let $\mathrm{REAL}_{\Pi, \mathcal{A}}$ be the random variable consisting of (1) the identities $\mathcal{C}$ of the corrupted parties, (2) the vector of outputs of the honest parties, and (3) the view of $\mathcal{A}$ at the end of the execution.

Fix an n-party (randomized), no-input functionality $\mathcal{F}$. An ideal execution of $\mathcal{F}$ in the presence of an adversary $\mathcal{S}$ proceeds as follows:

$\mathcal{F}_{\text{KeyGen}}^{t,n}$

Let $\mathcal{C}'$ be an arbitrary set of size t with $\mathcal{C} \subseteq \mathcal{C}' \subset [n]$.

1. Receive $\{\sigma_i\}_{i \in \mathcal{C}}$ from the adversary. (If some σ_i is not sent, set it to 0.)
2. Choose $x \leftarrow \mathbb{Z}_q$ and set $y := g^x$. Choose uniform $\sigma_i \in \mathbb{Z}_q$ for $i \in \mathcal{C}' \setminus \mathcal{C}$.
3. Let f be the polynomial of degree at most t such that $f(0) = x$ and $f(i) = \sigma_i$ for $i \in \mathcal{C}'$. Set $\sigma_i := f(i)$ for $i \in [n] \setminus \mathcal{C}'$.
4. For $i \in [n]$, set $y_i := g^{\sigma_i}$. Let $Y = (y_1, \ldots, y_n)$.
5. For $i \in [n]$, send (y, σ_i, Y) to P_i. Also send (y, Y) to the adversary.

Fig. 1. Ideal functionality for fully secure key generation, parameterized by t, n.

1. $\mathcal{S}$ specifies a set $\mathcal{C} \subset [n]$ of corrupted parties.
2. $\mathcal{S}$ controls what corrupted parties send to $\mathcal{F}$, and observes all values that $\mathcal{F}$ sends to corrupted parties. (Note $\mathcal{F}$ is aware of the set $\mathcal{C}$ of corrupted parties.) $\mathcal{S}$ may also send messages directly to, and receive messages directly from, $\mathcal{F}$. (The effect of those messages depends on $\mathcal{F}$.)
3. An honest party outputs the value sent to it by $\mathcal{F}$.
4. The adversary $\mathcal{S}$ outputs an arbitrary function of its view.

We let IDEAL$_{\mathcal{F},\mathcal{S}}$ be the random variable consisting of (1) the identities $\mathcal{C}$ of the corrupted parties, (2) the vector of outputs of the honest parties, and (3) the output of $\mathcal{S}$.

We say that protocol Π *t-securely realizes* $\mathcal{F}$ if for any efficient adversary $\mathcal{A}$ corrupting at most t parties there is an efficient adversary $\mathcal{S}$ such that no efficient distinguisher D can distinguish REAL$_{\Pi,\mathcal{A}}$ and IDEAL$_{\mathcal{F},\mathcal{S}}$. In the concrete setting we adopt here, one can quantify security by bounding the running times of $\mathcal{A}, \mathcal{S}$, and D as well as the acceptable distinguishing advantage of D. In an asymptotic setting, one would instead provide parties with a security parameter κ as input, and parameterize the random variables REAL$_{\Pi,\mathcal{A}}$ and IDEAL$_{\mathcal{F},\mathcal{S}}$ by κ; security would then require that for any probabilistic polynomial-time (PPT) $\mathcal{A}$ there is a PPT adversary $\mathcal{S}$ such that no PPT distinguisher D (possibly with access to non-uniform auxiliary input) can distinguish REAL$_{\Pi,\mathcal{A}}(\kappa)$ and IDEAL$_{\mathcal{F},\mathcal{S}}(\kappa)$ with advantage that is not negligible (in κ).

Given this definitional framework, we can define security for key-generation protocols by defining an appropriate ideal functionality. In our context, the basic requirement is for the ideal functionality to choose a uniform private key $x \in \mathbb{Z}_q$ and give each party P_i the corresponding public key $y = g^x$ along with P_i's share σ_i in a $(t+1)$-out-of-n sharing of x. Many threshold protocols also require the parties to each hold a vector of "commitments" $Y = (g^{\sigma_1}, \ldots, g^{\sigma_n})$ to the shares of the other parties (such commitments can be used by parties to prove correctness of their actions in a subsequent protocol using the generated key), and this is incorporated in the ideal functionality as well. We ensure robustness by defining the ideal functionality such that it always provides output to the honest parties. These requirements are encapsulated by the ideal functionality

$\mathcal{F}_{\text{KeyGen}}$ shown in Fig. 1 that corresponds to "fully secure" key generation. (A similar functionality was defined by Wikström [53].)

Notes on the Functionality. In the synchronous setting we consider, some form of synchrony is also (implicitly) assumed in the ideal world as well. This means, in particular, that the ideal functionality can identify when the adversary has failed to send some share in step 1, and can proceed accordingly.

$\mathcal{F}_{\text{KeyGen}}^{t,n}$ does not assume the adversary corrupts exactly t parties. In particular, the adversary may corrupt no parties, and in that case (y, Y) is given to the adversary in step 5. (That part of step 5 is redundant if at least one party is corrupted.) Translated to the security of a protocol Π realizing $\mathcal{F}_{\text{KeyGen}}$, this means an adversary who eavesdrops on an execution of Π (but corrupts no parties) may learn the public key y and the parties' commitments Y. This is acceptable, as those values are considered public.

$\mathcal{F}_{\text{KeyGen}}^{t,n}$ assumes a Shamir secret sharing of the private key x for concreteness, but could be modified in the natural way for other secret-sharing schemes, e.g., n-out-of-n additive sharing of x when $t = n-1$. A more subtle aspect of $\mathcal{F}_{\text{KeyGen}}$ is that it allows the adversary to choose the shares of the corrupted parties in step 1; we stress that the remaining shares are still uniform subject to that constraint. One could strengthen the functionality to prevent this (cf. functionality $\widehat{\mathcal{F}}_{\text{KeyGen}}$ in Appendix A), but we are not aware of any (natural[6]) application of key generation where the distinction is important, and weakening the functionality as we have done potentially allows for more-efficient protocols. Alternately, one could consider an even weaker definition where the adversary is allowed to choose its shares *after* learning the public key y. In general, one advantage of working in the simulation-based framework is that it is simple to define other notions of security for key-generation protocols (by giving different ideal functionalities), and very clear what security properties are being added or sacrificed. We provide other examples of alternate ideal functionalities in Appendix A.

The Multi-session Extension of $\mathcal{F}_{\text{KeyGen}}$. When shared state (i.e., setup) is used across multiple executions of a protocol, technically one should show that repeated execution of the protocol securely realizes the *multi-session extension* of the corresponding ideal functionality [13]. We do not formalize this here, but it is not hard to verify that our protocols satisfy this requirement.

4 Impossibility of One-Round DKG Protocols

Here we rule out the existence of one-round *statistically unbiased* DKG protocols, where this means that the public key computed in an honest execution of the protocol is (close to) uniform in $\mathbb{G}$. (We define this more formally below.) We prove this by showing the impossibility of one-round (statistically unbiased) coin tossing, even if only a single party is corrupted. Our result shows that for any

---

[6] It is possible to show contrived scenarios where the difference matters.

one-round coin-tossing protocol it is always possible for some corrupted party to bias the coin. Since the attack does not require the corrupted party to abort, it rules out even weaker notions of coin tossing (and hence DKG) that do not require robustness. Our result also holds regardless of any prior setup the parties have, and holds even in idealized models (e.g., the random-oracle model).

We remark that existing impossibility results for collective coin tossing [7], relying on analyzing the influence of boolean functions [37], could potentially also be used to rule out one-round statistically unbiased DKG protocols. However, a direct application of those results would only show that an *all-powerful* adversary can bias the outcome; our result holds even for *computationally bounded* adversaries. Moreover, we obtain quantitatively stronger bounds on the bias a corrupted party can achieve than what follows from those results.

We now proceed with the details. Let $\mathbb{G}_0, \mathbb{G}_1$ be a balanced partition of $\mathbb{G}$. Given a one-round, n-party DKG protocol Π, we can construct a coin-tossing protocol $\Pi_{\sf ct}$ by having the parties run Π and then output 0 (resp., 1) if the public key is in $\mathbb{G}_0$ (resp., $\mathbb{G}_1$). Let $f_\Pi(r_1,\ldots,r_n)$ denote[7] the output when parties run $\Pi_{\sf ct}$ honestly, each using the randomness indicated.

Definition 1. *DKG protocol Π is* **statistically unbiased** *if*

$$\Pr[f_\Pi(r_1,\ldots,r_n) = 1] = 1/2.$$

If Π uses setup, this should hold for all possible outputs of the setup phase.

(This can be relaxed to require $\Pr[f_\Pi(r_1,\ldots,r_n) = 1] \approx 1/2$, or to hold only with high probability over outputs of setup, but we ignore this for simplicity.)

Theorem 1. *There is no 1-round, statistically unbiased DKG protocol that 1-securely realizes $\mathcal{F}_{\sf KeyGen}^{1,n}$.*

Proof. Let Π be a 1-round DKG protocol. As discussed, Π defines a 1-round coin-tossing protocol $\Pi_{\sf ct}$ (that relies on setup if Π does); if protocol Π 1-securely-realizes $\mathcal{F}_{\sf KeyGen}^{1,n}$, then $\Pi_{\sf ct}$ 1-securely realizes the coin-tossing functionality (with guaranteed output delivery). We write $f(r_1,\ldots,r_n)$ for the output when parties run $\Pi_{\sf ct}$ honestly, each using the indicated randomness.

Consider the following strategy by a corrupted party P_i to bias the outcome of $\Pi_{\sf ct}$ toward a particular bit b. Based on the messages of the other parties and local randomness r_i, compute the output that would result from running $\Pi_{\sf ct}$ honestly using r_i. If the result is b, then run $\Pi_{\sf ct}$ honestly using r_i; otherwise, sample fresh randomness r_i' and run $\Pi_{\sf ct}$ honestly using r_i'. (We are here using the fact that the adversary is *rushing*.) The probability that this strategy results in output b is exactly

$$\Pr[f(r_1,\ldots,r_n) = b]$$
$$+ \Pr\left[f(r_1,\ldots,r_n) = \bar{b} \bigwedge f(r_1,\ldots,r_{i-1},r_i',r_{i+1},\ldots,r_n) = b\right].$$

---

[7] If Π relies on setup, then f depends on any prior setup the parties have (including any oracles to which they have access).

Since $\Pr[f(r_1,\ldots,r_n) = b] = \frac{1}{2}$, this means P_i can bias the outcome toward some bit if

$$\Pr_{r_1,\ldots,r_n,r'_i} [f(r_1,\ldots,r_{i-1},r_i,r_{i+1},\ldots,r_n) \neq f(r_1,\ldots,r_{i-1},r'_i,r_{i+1},\ldots,r_n)] \quad (1)$$

is noticeable. We show this must be the case for some i.

$\Pr[f(r_1,\ldots,r_n) = b] = \frac{1}{2}$ implies $\Pr[f(r_1,\ldots,r_n) \neq f(r'_1,\ldots,r'_n)] = \frac{1}{2}$ as well. Also, note that $f(r_1,\ldots,r_n) \neq f(r'_1,\ldots,r'_n)$ implies

$$\exists i : f(r'_1,\ldots,r'_{i-1},r_i,\ldots,r_n) \neq f(r'_1,\ldots,r'_{i-1},r'_i,r_{i+1},\ldots,r_n).$$

Therefore,

$$\frac{1}{2} = \Pr\left[f(r_1,\ldots,r_n) \neq f(r'_1,\ldots,r'_n)\right]$$

$$\leq \Pr \begin{bmatrix} f(r_1,\ldots,r_n) \neq f(r'_1,r_2,\ldots,r_n) \\ \vee f(r'_1,r_2,\ldots,r_n) \neq f(r'_1,r'_2,r_3,\ldots,r_n) \\ \vdots \\ \vee f(r'_1,\ldots,r'_{n-1},r_n) \neq f(r'_1,\ldots,r'_n) \end{bmatrix}$$

$$\leq \Pr[f(r_1,\ldots,r_n) \neq f(r'_1,r_2,\ldots,r_n)]$$
$$+ \Pr[f(r'_1,r_2,\ldots,r_n) \neq f(r'_1,r'_2,r_3,\ldots,r_n)]$$
$$\vdots$$
$$+ \Pr[f(r'_1,\ldots,r'_{n-1},r_n) \neq f(r'_1,\ldots,r'_n)],$$

which implies that, for some $i \in [n]$,

$$\Pr\left[f(r'_1,\ldots,r'_{i-1},r_i,r_{i+1},\ldots,r_n) \neq f(r'_1,\ldots,r'_{i-1},r'_i,r_{i+1},\ldots,r_n)\right] \geq \frac{1}{2n}.$$

But this exactly shows that (1) is noticeable.

5 Two-Round Protocols in the CRS+PKI Model

In this section we show fully secure, 2-round DKG protocols assuming a PKI and a CRS. We first describe a general framework for constructing 2-round protocols realizing $\mathcal{F}_{\mathsf{KeyGen}}$, and then discuss a concrete instantiation of this framework based on Paillier encryption and efficient zero-knowledge proofs used previously in the context of threshold cryptography [11]. In Sect. 5.3 we show how to realize a stronger DKG functionality, still using only two rounds.

5.1 A General Framework

The starting point of our protocol is the usual approach of having every party act as the dealer in a $(t+1)$-out-of-n secret sharing scheme, and then having the parties homomorphically combine the results. This approach yields a 1-round protocol, in which each party P_i does the following:

1. Choose a uniform value $x_i \in \mathbb{Z}_q$ and compute $\{\sigma_{i,j}\}_{j=0}^n \leftarrow \mathsf{SS}_t(x_i)$.
2. For $j \in [n]$, broadcast $y_{i,j} := g^{\sigma_{i,j}}$ and send $\sigma_{i,j}$ to P_j over a private channel.

Each party P_i computes its share $\sigma_i := \sum_{j \in [n]} \sigma_{j,i}$ and the commitment $y_j := \prod_{k \in [n]} y_{k,j}$ to the share of any party P_j. Letting $S = [t+1]$, parties also compute the public key as $\mathsf{interpolate}(0, S, \{y_j\}_{j \in S})$.

The above description assumes semi-honest behavior. While parties can verify that a party P_i broadcasted consistent information (by checking that the exponents of the $\{y_{i,j}\}_{j=1}^n$ lie on a degree-t polynomial), the protocol does nothing to address a malicious adversary who sends an incorrect share to another party. This can be addressed using two additional rounds: one round in which a party can *complain* about another party who sent it an incorrect share, and a second round for honest parties to respond to complaints.[8] Protocols relying on complaints seem to inherently require at least three rounds.

A natural idea is to have parties use NIZK proofs to publicly prove correct behavior. However, such proofs will be useless for proving correctness of values sent over private channels. (Parties already have the ability to check correctness of values they receive, but now we want parties to additionally be able to check correctness of the values sent to all other parties.) To account for this, we can modify the protocol so that instead of sending shares over (ideal) private channels, parties instead send shares encrypted using a public-key encryption scheme. This requires parties to distribute public encryption keys, which can be done using either an additional round or by assuming a PKI. Using this approach we obtain the 1-round protocol in which each party P_i does:

1. Choose a uniform value $x_i \in \mathbb{Z}_q$ and compute $\{\sigma_{i,j}\}_{j=0}^n \leftarrow \mathsf{SS}_t(x_i)$.
2. For each $j \in [n]$, broadcast $y_{i,j} := g^{\sigma_{i,j}}$ and an encryption of $\sigma_{i,j}$ under the public key of P_j. Additionally, give an NIZK proof of correct behavior.

Parties compute the public key, their shares, and commitments to other parties' shares as before, excluding the contributions from parties whose NZIK proofs fail to verify. (We omit details.) This exactly corresponds to having each party act as a dealer in a *publicly verifiable secret-sharing scheme* (PVSS) [52] (see [27] for a recent survey). Using PVSS (or something similar) in the context of distributed key generation has been proposed in several other works [9, 22, 30, 39]; none of those achieve fully secure DKG with the exception of Boneh and Shoup [9, Section 22.4.2], who achieve it using many more rounds (see below).

NIZK proofs force parties to either behave correctly or (effectively) abort. But they are not enough to make the protocol fully secure! Indeed, in the protocol sketched above a single corrupted party can *bias* the public key by waiting until all other parties have sent their messages, locally running the protocol (honestly) multiple times, and then selecting which messages to send based on the public keys it computes in those executions. (Recall we assume a rushing adversary.) A natural way to address this is to have each party commit to g^{x_i} in the first round,

---

[8] While this addresses the particular problem of incorrect shares, the resulting protocol is not fully secure as it still suffers from the bias problem discussed below.

and then give NIZK proofs relative to that commitment in a second round; this would not fully address the problem, however, since it would still allow an adversary to bias the resulting public key by deciding whether to *abort* (i.e., refuse to open its commitment) in the second round. Boneh and Shoup [9, Section 22.4.2] address this by assuming *simultaneous* broadcast (where all parties act as a sender in a broadcast protocol, but are forced to choose their messages independently), which can in turn be instantiated via a multi-round protocol. It does not seem possible to obtain a 2-round protocol using that approach.

Instead, we modify the protocol so that only encrypted shares—and no $\{y_{i,j}\}$ values—are sent in the first round. Parties still send NIZK proofs of correct behavior as before, and are excluded if their proofs fail to verify. Then, in the second round, each party uses the shares it received from all non-excluded parties to compute appropriate $\{y_{i,j}\}$ values, and then *broadcasts those values along with an NIZK proof that they were computed correctly*. (In fact, it suffices for each party P_i to just broadcast the commitment $y_i = g^{\sigma_i}$ to its final share σ_i.) As intuition for security, note first that because of the NIZK proofs adversarial behavior is effectively limited to aborting. The adversary is unable to bias the key by aborting in the first round because it is unable to compute the key until the second round. On the other hand, aborts in the second round cannot introduce bias since the public key is *fixed* at the end of the first round, in the sense that the same public key y will be computed by the honest parties regardless of what the malicious parties do in the second round. This is because the presence of $t+1$ honest parties ensures that sufficiently many correct commitments will be broadcast to allow the public key to be computed. Simulation is possible due to the NIZK proofs in the second round, which allow the simulator to "force" the final key to any desired value.

We formalize the resulting protocol in Fig. 2. The protocol relies on zero-knowledge proofs for the following NP relations:

$$R_L = \left\{ (\{(\mathsf{pk}_j, c_j)\}_{j \in [n]}, \{(\sigma_j, \omega_j)\}_{j \in [n]}) : \begin{array}{l} \exists \text{ poly. } f \text{ of degree } \leq t \text{ s.t.} \\ \forall j \ f(j) = \sigma_j \wedge c_j := \mathsf{Enc}_{\mathsf{pk}_j}(\sigma_j; \omega_j) \end{array} \right\}$$

$$R_{L'} = \left\{ ((\mathsf{pk}, \{c_j\}_{j \in \mathcal{I}}, y), \mathsf{sk}) : \begin{array}{l} \mathsf{sk} \text{ is a valid secret key corresponding to } \mathsf{pk}; \\ y = g^{\sum_{i \in \mathcal{I}} \mathsf{Dec}_{\mathsf{sk}}(c_i)} \end{array} \right\}.$$

The protocol also relies on public-key encryption having perfect correctness with overwhelming probability for honestly generated keys.

Theorem 2. *Assume* (Gen, Enc) *is a perfectly correct, CPA-secure encryption scheme and* $\mathcal{P}, \mathcal{P}'$ *are identity-based simulation-sound NIZK proof systems for relations* $R_L, R_{L'}$. *Then for* $t < n/2$, *protocol* $\Pi_1^{t,n}$ t-*securely realizes* $\mathcal{F}_{\mathsf{KeyGen}}^{t,n}$.

Proof. We define a simulator $\mathcal{S}$, given black-box access to an adversary $\mathcal{A}$:

Setup: $\mathcal{S}$ runs $\mathcal{A}$ to obtain a set $\mathcal{C}$ of corrupted parties with $|\mathcal{C}| \leq t$. Let $\mathcal{H} := [n]\setminus\mathcal{C}$. Then $\mathcal{S}$ runs $(\mathsf{crs}, \mathsf{td}) \leftarrow \mathsf{Sim}_1$ and $(\mathsf{crs}', \mathsf{td}') \leftarrow \mathsf{Sim}_1'$ and, for $i \in \mathcal{H}$, runs $(\mathsf{pk}_i, \mathsf{sk}_i) \leftarrow \mathsf{Gen}$. It gives $\mathsf{crs}, \mathsf{crs}'$, and $\{\mathsf{pk}_i\}_{i \in \mathcal{H}}$ to $\mathcal{A}$. In return, $\mathcal{A}$ outputs $\{\mathsf{pk}_i\}_{i \in \mathcal{C}}$.

$\Pi_1^{t,n}$

We assume a PKI (with pk_i being the public key of P_i) and a common reference string containing $\mathsf{crs}, \mathsf{crs}'$.

Round 1: Each party P_i does the following:
1. Choose uniform $x_i \in \mathbb{Z}_q$ and compute $\{\sigma_{i,j}\}_{j \in [n]} \leftarrow \mathsf{SS}_t(x_i)$. For $j \in [n]$ choose $\omega_{i,j} \leftarrow \{0,1\}^*$ and compute $c_{i,j} := \mathsf{Enc}_{\mathsf{pk}_j}(\sigma_{i,j}; \omega_{i,j})$.
2. Compute $\pi_i \leftarrow \mathcal{P}(\mathsf{crs}, i, \{(\mathsf{pk}_j, c_{i,j})\}_{j \in [n]}, \{(\sigma_{i,j}, \omega_{i,j})\}_{j \in [n]})$.
3. Broadcast $\{c_{i,j}\}_{j \in [n]}$ and π_i.

Round 2: Let $\mathcal{I} := \{i \in [n] : \mathcal{V}(\mathsf{crs}, i, \{(\mathsf{pk}_j, c_{i,j})\}_{j \in [n]}, \pi_i) = 1\}$. Each party P_i then does:
1. For $j \in \mathcal{I}$, compute $\sigma_{j,i} := \mathsf{Dec}_{\mathsf{sk}_i}(c_{j,i})$. Set $\sigma_i := \sum_{j \in \mathcal{I}} \sigma_{j,i}$ and $y_i := g^{\sigma_i}$.
2. Compute $\pi'_i \leftarrow \mathcal{P}'(\mathsf{crs}', i, (\mathsf{pk}_i, \{c_{j,i}\}_{j \in \mathcal{I}}, y_i), \mathsf{sk}_i)$.
3. Broadcast y_i and π'_i.

Output: Let $\mathcal{I}' := \{i \in \mathcal{I} : \mathcal{V}'(\mathsf{crs}', i, (\mathsf{pk}_i, \{c_{j,i}\}_{j \in \mathcal{I}}, y_i), \pi'_i) = 1\}$. Each party P_i then does:
1. For $j \in \mathcal{I}'$, let y_j be the value broadcast by P_j in round 2.
2. Let $\mathcal{I}''$ be the $t+1$ lowest indices in $\mathcal{I}'$. For $j \in [n] \setminus \mathcal{I}'$, set $y_j := \mathsf{interpolate}(j, \mathcal{I}'', \{y_i\}_{i \in \mathcal{I}''})$. Set $y := \mathsf{interpolate}(0, \mathcal{I}'', \{y_i\}_{i \in \mathcal{I}''})$.
3. Output $(y, \sigma_i, (y_1, \ldots, y_n))$.

Fig. 2. A 2-round DKG protocol in the CRS+PKI model, parameterized by t, n. Relations $R_L, R_{L'}$ associated with $\mathcal{P}, \mathcal{P}'$ are described in the text.

Round 1: To simulate the first round, $\mathcal{S}$ does:
1. For all $i \in \mathcal{H}$ do:
   (a) For $j \in \mathcal{C}$, choose uniform $\sigma_{i,j} \in \mathbb{Z}_q$ and compute $c_{i,j} \leftarrow \mathsf{Enc}_{\mathsf{pk}_j}(\sigma_{i,j})$.
   (b) For $j \in \mathcal{H}$, compute $c_{i,j} \leftarrow \mathsf{Enc}_{\mathsf{pk}_j}(0)$.
   (c) Compute $\pi_i \leftarrow \mathsf{Sim}_2(\mathsf{td}, i, \{(\mathsf{pk}_j, c_{i,j})\}_{j \in [n]})$.
   (d) Give $\{c_{i,j}\}_{j \in [n]}$ and π_i to $\mathcal{A}$ as the message broadcast by P_i.
2. In response, $\mathcal{A}$ sends $\{c_{i,j}\}_{j \in [n]}$ and π_i for all $i \in \mathcal{C}$. (If some corrupted party P_i aborts, it will be anyway be excluded from $\mathcal{C}_\mathcal{I}$ below.)

Let $\mathcal{C}_\mathcal{I} := \{i \in \mathcal{C} : \mathcal{V}(\mathsf{crs}, i, \{(\mathsf{pk}_j, c_{i,j})\}_{j \in [n]}, \pi_i) = 1\}$ and $\mathcal{I} := \mathcal{C}_\mathcal{I} \cup \mathcal{H}$. For $j \in \mathcal{C}_\mathcal{I}$ do:
– For $i \in \mathcal{H}$, compute $\sigma_{j,i} := \mathsf{Dec}_{\mathsf{sk}_i}(c_{j,i})$; then let f_j be the polynomial of degree $\leq t$ with $f_j(i) = \sigma_{j,i}$ for $i \in \mathcal{H}$. (If no such f_j exists, abort.)

For $j \in \mathcal{C}$ compute $\sigma_j := \sum_{i \in \mathcal{H}} \sigma_{i,j} + \sum_{i \in \mathcal{C}_\mathcal{I}} f_i(j)$. Send $\{\sigma_j\}_{j \in \mathcal{C}}$ to $\mathcal{F}_{\mathsf{KeyGen}}^{t,n}$, and receive in return y and $Y = (y_1, \ldots, y_n)$.

Round 2: For $i \in \mathcal{H}$ do:
1. Compute $\pi'_i \leftarrow \mathsf{Sim}'_2(\mathsf{td}', i, (\mathsf{pk}_i, \{c_{j,i}\}_{j \in \mathcal{I}}, y_i))$.
2. Give y_i and π'_i to $\mathcal{A}$ as the message broadcast by P_i.

Output whatever $\mathcal{A}$ outputs.

We show that $\mathsf{REAL}_{\Pi_1^{t,n}, \mathcal{A}}$ is indistinguishable from $\mathsf{IDEAL}_{\mathcal{F}_{\mathsf{KeyGen}}^{t,n}, \mathcal{S}}$ via a sequence of hybrid experiments. We start by explicitly describing an experiment Expt_0 that corresponds to $\mathsf{REAL}_{\Pi_1^{t,n}, \mathcal{A}}$.

Round-Optimal, Fully Secure Distributed Key Generation

Experiment Expt_0. This experiment is defined as follows:

Setup: $\mathcal{A}$ outputs a set $\mathcal{C}$ of corrupted parties; let $\mathcal{H} = [n] \setminus \mathcal{C}$. Run $\mathsf{crs} \leftarrow \mathsf{GenCRS}$ and $\mathsf{crs}' \leftarrow \mathsf{GenCRS}'$ and, for $i \in \mathcal{H}$, run $(\mathsf{pk}_i, \mathsf{sk}_i) \leftarrow \mathsf{Gen}$. Give $\mathsf{crs}, \mathsf{crs}'$, and $\{\mathsf{pk}_i\}_{i \in \mathcal{H}}$ to $\mathcal{A}$, who outputs $\{\mathsf{pk}_i\}_{i \in \mathcal{C}}$.

Round 1: For $i \in \mathcal{H}$ do:
1. Choose $x_i \leftarrow \mathbb{Z}_q$ and compute $\{\sigma_{i,j}\}_{j \in [n]} \leftarrow \mathsf{SS}_t(x_i)$. For all $j \in [n]$, choose $\omega_{i,j} \leftarrow \{0,1\}^*$ and compute $c_{i,j} := \mathsf{Enc}_{\mathsf{pk}_j}(\sigma_{i,j}; \omega_{i,j})$.
2. Compute $\pi_i \leftarrow \mathcal{P}(\mathsf{crs}, i, \{(\mathsf{pk}_j, c_{i,j})\}_{j \in [n]}, (\sigma_{i,j}, \omega_{i,j}))$.

Give $\{c_{i,j}\}_{i \in \mathcal{H}, j \in [n]}$ and $\{\pi_i\}_{i \in \mathcal{H}}$ to $\mathcal{A}$. In response, $\mathcal{A}$ sends $\{c_{i,j}\}_{i \in \mathcal{C}, j \in [n]}$ and $\{\pi_i\}_{i \in \mathcal{C}}$. (If some corrupted party aborts, it will be excluded from $\mathcal{C}_\mathcal{I}$.)

Round 2: Let $\mathcal{C}_\mathcal{I} := \{i \in \mathcal{C} : \mathcal{V}(\mathsf{crs}, i, \{(\mathsf{pk}_j, c_{i,j})\}_{j \in [n]}, \pi_i) = 1\}$ and $\mathcal{I} := \mathcal{C}_\mathcal{I} \cup \mathcal{H}$. For all $i \in \mathcal{H}$ do:
1. For $j \in \mathcal{I}$, compute $\sigma_{j,i} := \mathsf{Dec}_{\mathsf{sk}_i}(c_{j,i})$. Set $\sigma_i := \sum_{j \in \mathcal{I}} \sigma_{j,i}$ and $y_i := g^{\sigma_i}$.
2. Compute $\pi'_i \leftarrow \mathcal{P}'(\mathsf{crs}', i, (\mathsf{pk}_i, \{c_{j,i}\}_{j \in \mathcal{I}}, y_i), \mathsf{sk}_i)$.

Give $\{(y_i, \pi'_i)\}_{i \in \mathcal{H}}$ to $\mathcal{A}$. In response, $\mathcal{A}$ sends $\{(y_i, \pi'_i)\}_{i \in \mathcal{C}_\mathcal{I}}$.

Output: Let $\mathcal{I}' := \{i \in \mathcal{I} : \mathcal{V}'(\mathsf{crs}', i, (\mathsf{pk}_i, \{c_{j,i}\}_{j \in \mathcal{I}}, y_i), \pi'_i) = 1\}$. Then:
1. For $j \in \mathcal{I}'$, let y_j be the corresponding value sent by P_j in round 2.
2. Let $\mathcal{I}''$ be the $t+1$ smallest indices in $\mathcal{I}'$. (Since $\mathcal{H} \subseteq \mathcal{I}'$, such a set $\mathcal{I}''$ must exist.) For $j \in [n] \setminus \mathcal{I}'$, set $y_j := \mathsf{interpolate}(j, \mathcal{I}'', \{y_i\}_{i \in \mathcal{I}''})$. Set $y := \mathsf{interpolate}(0, \mathcal{I}'', \{y_i\}_{i \in \mathcal{I}''})$.

The output of the experiment is[9] $\mathcal{C}, (y, \{\sigma_i\}_{i \in \mathcal{H}}, (y_1, \ldots, y_n))$, and the output of $\mathcal{A}$.

Experiment Expt_1. In this experiment we modify Expt_0 as follows: during setup, we now generate $\mathsf{crs}, \mathsf{crs}'$ (along with $\mathsf{td}, \mathsf{td}'$) using simulators $\mathsf{Sim}_1, \mathsf{Sim}'_1$, respectively. Then, honest parties use Sim_2 in place of $\mathcal{P}$ in round 1, and use Sim'_2 in place of $\mathcal{P}'$ in round 2.

Indistinguishability of this experiment and Expt_0 follows immediately from the zero-knowledge property of $\mathcal{P}, \mathcal{P}'$.

Experiment Expt_2. We modify Expt_1 as follows. Before round 2, for all $j \in \mathcal{C}_\mathcal{I}$ run the knowledge extractor $\mathsf{KE}(\mathsf{td}, j, \{(\mathsf{pk}_i, c_{j,i})\}_{i \in [n]}, \pi_j)$ to obtain $\{\sigma_{j,i}\}_{i \in \mathcal{H}}$; if those values do not lie on a polynomial f_j of degree at most t, abort. (We remark that if $|\mathcal{H}| = t+1$ then an abort can never occur here; however, the check is relevant if $|\mathcal{H}| > t+1$.) Then, in the first step of round 2 do the following for all $i \in \mathcal{H}$: for $j \in \mathcal{C}_\mathcal{I}$, let $\sigma_{j,i}$ be the value extracted; for $j \in \mathcal{H}$, let $\sigma_{j,i}$ be the value chosen in round 1. Then compute $\sigma_i := \sum_{j \in \mathcal{I}} \sigma_{j,i}$ and $y_i := g^{\sigma_i}$ as before.

Indistinguishability of this experiment and Expt_1 follows from simulation soundness of $\mathcal{P}$ and perfect correctness of the encryption scheme.

Experiment Expt_3. Now we modify Expt_2 by changing the first step of round 1 so that for $i, j \in \mathcal{H}$ we compute $c_{i,j}$ as $c_{i,j} \leftarrow \mathsf{Enc}_{\mathsf{pk}_j}(0; \omega_{i,j})$. Indistinguishability of this and Expt_2 follows from CPA-security of the encryption scheme.

---

[9] Technically the output includes the values of y and $(y_1, \ldots, y_n)$ output by each honest party, but it is easy to see that for this experiment those values will be identical.

Experiment Expt_4. Here we revert the change made in Expt_2 by computing $\{\sigma_{j,i}\}_{j\in\mathcal{C}_\mathcal{I}, i\in\mathcal{H}}$ as $\sigma_{j,i} := \mathsf{Dec}_{\mathsf{sk}_i}(c_{j,i})$. (We still abort if for some $j \in \mathcal{C}_\mathcal{I}$ the $\{\sigma_{j,i}\}_{i\in\mathcal{H}}$ do not lie on a polynomial of degree at most t.) As before, indistinguishability of this and the previous experiment follow from simulation soundness of $\mathcal{P}$ and perfect correctness of the encryption scheme.

Experiment Expt_5. We modify Expt_4 in the following way. Let $\mathcal{C}'$ be an arbitrary set of size t with $\mathcal{C} \subseteq \mathcal{C}' \subset [n]$. In the first step of round 1, for each $i \in \mathcal{H}$ and $j \in \mathcal{C}$ choose uniform $\sigma_{i,j} \in \mathbb{Z}_q$. Then before round 2, for each $i \in \mathcal{H}$ do:

1. Choose uniform $x_i \in \mathbb{Z}_q$ and, for $j \in \mathcal{C}' \setminus \mathcal{C}$, choose uniform $\sigma_{i,j} \in \mathbb{Z}_q$.
2. Let f_i be the polynomial of degree at most t with $f_i(0) = x_i$ and $f_i(j) = \sigma_{i,j}$ for $j \in \mathcal{C}'$.
3. For $j \in [n] \setminus \mathcal{C}'$ set $\sigma_{i,j} := f_i(j)$.

The $\{\sigma_{j,i}\}_{i,j\in\mathcal{H}}$ values thus defined are then used in the first step of round 2.

Since all that has changed was to defer from round 1 to round 2 the choice of the $\{x_i\}_{i\in\mathcal{H}}$ (and shares $\{\sigma_{i,j}\}_{i\in\mathcal{H}, j\in\mathcal{C}'\setminus\mathcal{C}}$ that are not used in round 1), information-theoretic security of Shamir secret sharing implies that Expt_5 is perfectly indistinguishable from Expt_4.

Experiment Expt_6. Note that in Expt_5, if the experiment is not aborted by the beginning of round 2 then for all $i \in \mathcal{I}$ a polynomial f_i of degree at most t is defined; moreover, for all $i \in \mathcal{H}$ the value σ_i computed in the first step of round 2 satisfies $\sigma_i = \sum_{j\in\mathcal{I}} f_j(i)$. In Expt_6 we introduce the following step after round 2: for all $i \in \mathcal{C}$, compute $\sigma_i := \sum_{j\in\mathcal{I}} f_j(i)$; then abort if $g^{\sigma_i} \neq y_i$ for some $i \in \mathcal{C} \cap \mathcal{I}'$. The output-determination step is also modified so that, if the experiment has not aborted, we set $y := g^{\sum_{j\in\mathcal{I}} f_j(0)}$ and $y_i := g^{\sum_{j\in\mathcal{I}} f_j(i)}$ for $i \in [n]$.

Simulation soundness of $\mathcal{P}'$ and perfect correctness of the encryption scheme imply that Expt_6 is indistinguishable from Expt_5.

Experiment Expt_7. Observe that in Expt_6 the values $\{\sigma_i\}_{i\in\mathcal{C}}$ can be computed after round 1: this is so even though the polynomials $\{f_i\}_{i\in\mathcal{H}}$ are not yet defined at that point, because the values $\{f_i(j)\}_{i\in\mathcal{H}, j\in\mathcal{C}}$ are defined at that point. With the $\{\sigma_i\}_{i\in\mathcal{C}}$ thus defined, we now modify Expt_6 in the following way: in the first step of round 2, choose uniform $x \in \mathbb{Z}_q$ and for $i \in \mathcal{C}' \setminus \mathcal{C}$ choose uniform $\sigma_i \in \mathbb{Z}_q$; let f be the polynomial of degree at most t with $f(0) = x$ and $f(i) = \sigma_i$ for $i \in \mathcal{C}'$. Then set $\sigma_i := f(i)$ for $i \in \mathcal{H} \setminus \mathcal{C}'$.

It is easy to see that Expt_7 is perfectly indistinguishable from Expt_6, and moreover that Expt_7 is statistically indistinguishable from $\mathrm{IDEAL}_{\mathcal{F}_{\mathsf{KeyGen}}^{t,n}, \mathcal{S}}$. □

5.2 An Instantiation Using Paillier Encryption

We briefly sketch a protocol based on the Paillier (additively homomorphic) encryption scheme that can be viewed as inspired by Π_1. (Several prior works [22,23,35,46] show how to construct PVSS from Paillier encryption, and our construction is similar in that regard.) Each party publishes a Paillier public key; correctness of public keys can be demonstrated with existing NIZK proofs if desired [11]. The CRS also includes a uniform $h \in \mathbb{G}$ that will be used as a public key for the El Gamal encryption scheme. We let $\mathsf{Enc}_{\mathsf{pk}_i}(\cdot)$ denote Paillier encryption using the public key pk_i of P_i, and let $\mathsf{Enc}_h(\cdot)$ denote El Gamal encryption using h. Let $S = \{0\} \cup [t]$. The protocol then proceeds as follows:

Round 1: Each P_i chooses uniform $x_i \in \mathbb{Z}_q$ and computes

$$(\{y_{i,j}\}_{j=0}^t, \{\sigma_{i,j}\}_{j\in[n]}) \leftarrow \mathsf{FVSS}_t(x_i).$$

It then computes $C_{i,j} \leftarrow \mathsf{Enc}_h(y_{i,j})$ for $j \in S$, and $c_{i,j} \leftarrow \mathsf{Enc}_{\mathsf{pk}_j}(\sigma_{i,j})$ for $j \in [n]$. It broadcasts $\{C_{i,j}\}_{j\in S}$ and $\{c_{i,j}\}_{j\in[n]}$. Additionally, for each $j \in [n]$, it broadcasts an NIZK proof (cf. [11]) that the value encrypted in $c_{i,j}$ is equal to the discrete logarithm of the value encrypted in $\mathsf{interpolate}(j, S, \{C_{i,k}\}_{k\in S})$ (where we again overload notation to let $\mathsf{interpolate}$ refer to homomorphic interpolation of El Gamal ciphertexts).

Round 2: Each P_i computes $\mathcal{I}$, σ_i, and y_i analogously to the way those values are computed in Π_1. It then broadcasts y_i with an NIZK proof (cf. [11]) that the discrete logarithm of y_i is equal to the value encrypted by $c_i^* \stackrel{\text{def}}{=} \prod_{j\in\mathcal{I}} c_{j,i}$.

Output determination: Parties compute output as in Π_1.

We leave optimization and implementation of this approach to future work.

5.3 Realizing a Stronger Ideal Functionality

We can adapt our framework to realize the stronger functionality $\widehat{\mathcal{F}}_{\mathsf{KeyGen}}$ (cf. Appendix A), still using only two rounds. Since we view this as primarily of theoretical interest, we only provide a sketch of the details. The main idea is that instead of having the parties each generate shares of their contributions (which are added together to give the private key), the parties now generate *shares of shares* of their contributions. Corrupted parties do not learn their shares of the private key until the second round, by which time they are already committed to the shares they generated and distributed in the first round. The protocol proceeds as follows:

Round 1: Each party P_i does the following: Choose uniform $x_i \in \mathbb{Z}_q$ and compute the first-level sharing $\{\sigma_{i,j}\}_{j\in[n]} \leftarrow \mathsf{SS}_t(x_i)$. Then for $j \in [n]$, compute second-level sharing $\{\sigma_{i,j,k}\}_{k\in[n]} \leftarrow \mathsf{SS}_t(\sigma_{i,j})$. For $k \in [n]$, encrypt the shares $\{\sigma_{i,j,k}\}_{j\in[n]}$ using the public key pk_k and broadcast all the resulting ciphertexts. Also give an NIZK proof of correct behavior.

Round 2: Let $\mathcal{I}$ be the set of parties whose round-1 proofs verify. Each party P_k then does:
1. For $j \in [n]$ do:
   (a) For $i \in \mathcal{I}$, recover $\sigma_{i,j,k}$ by decrypting the corresponding ciphertext. Then compute $\sigma'_{j,k} := \sum_{i\in\mathcal{I}} \sigma_{i,j,k}$.
   (b) Encrypt $\sigma'_{j,k}$ using pk_j, and broadcast the resulting ciphertext along with $y_{j,k} := g^{\sigma'_{j,k}}$. Also give an NIZK proof of correct behavior.

Output determination: Let $\mathcal{I}' \subseteq \mathcal{I}$ be the set of parties whose round-2 proofs verify, and let $\mathcal{I}''$ be the $t+1$ lowest indices in $\mathcal{I}'$. Each P_j then does:
1. For $k \in \mathcal{I}''$, recover $\sigma'_{j,k}$ by decrypting the corresponding ciphertext. Then set $\sigma_j := \mathsf{interpolate}(0, \mathcal{I}'', \{\sigma'_{j,k}\}_{k \in \mathcal{I}''})$.
2. For $i \in [n]$, set $y_i := \mathsf{interpolate}(0, \mathcal{I}'', \{y_{i,k}\}_{k \in \mathcal{I}''})$.
3. Set $y := \mathsf{interpolate}(0, \mathcal{I}'', \{y_i\}_{i \in \mathcal{I}''})$.
4. Output $(y, \sigma_i, (y_1, \ldots, y_n))$.

A proof of the following is similar to the proof of Theorem 2.

Theorem 3. *Assume* (Gen, Enc) *is a perfectly correct, CPA-secure encryption scheme and identity-based simulation-sound NIZK proof systems are used. Then for $t < n/2$, the protocol above t-securely realizes $\widehat{\mathcal{F}}_{\mathsf{KeyGen}}^{t,n}$.*

6 A Two-Round Protocol in the CRS Model

We show here a 2-round fully secure DKG protocol based on a CRS alone. The protocol requires $(t+1)$-party NIKE to tolerate t corrupted parties. We build up to this result by first discussing the case $n = 3, t = 1$, where 2-party NIKE corresponds to Diffie-Hellman key exchange. In that setting, we begin by describing a fully secure 3-party protocol for generating a uniform group element y ("coin tossing"), and then show how to extend it to a full-fledged DKG protocol.

A challenge that arises in the context of coin tossing, as in the case of DKG, is the need to prevent the adversary from biasing the outcome. To obtain a 2-round fully secure protocol, we need to ensure (roughly) that the outcome is determined at the end of the first round regardless of what the corrupted parties do in the second round. At the same time, it must not be possible for the corrupted parties to learn the outcome at the end of the first round, since otherwise they could bias the result then. To prevent such bias in the case of 3-party coin tossing, we use the following idea: in the first round each pair of parties runs an instance of Diffie-Hellman key exchange; in the second round, each party broadcasts the key it shares with each other party (with NIZK proofs used to ensure correctness). The product of all the shared keys is the common output. Of course, a corrupted party may abort in the second round; the crucial observation that ensures robustness, however, is that such an abort by a party P_i does not prevent computation of the key, since the remaining honest parties *on their own* can collectively compute the shared keys P_i was supposed to broadcast. In more detail, the protocol works as follows:

Round 1: Each party P_i does the following: for $j \neq i$, choose $x_{i,j} \leftarrow \mathbb{Z}_q$, set $h_{i,j} := g^{x_{i,j}}$, and broadcast $h_{i,j}$. (If a party fails to broadcast a value, that value is treated as the identity element.)
Round 2: Each party P_i does the following: for $j \neq i$, compute $k_{i,j} := h_{j,i}^{x_{i,j}}$; then broadcast $k_{i,j}$ along with an (identity-based simulation-sound) NIZK proof $\pi_{i,j}$ that $k_{i,j}$ was computed correctly.

Output determination: For each unordered pair $\{i,j\}$, let $k_{\{i,j\}} \in \{k_{i,j}, k_{j,i}\}$ be the value for which the associated round-2 proof is valid. Output $y := k_{\{1,2\}} \cdot k_{\{1,3\}} \cdot k_{\{2,3\}}$.

We provide a brief sketch that this protocol 1-securely realizes the natural (robust) coin-tossing functionality. To do so, we describe an ideal-world adversary $\mathcal{S}$ corresponding to any real-world adversary $\mathcal{A}$, assuming for simplicity that $\mathcal{A}$ corrupts P_1. Adversary $\mathcal{S}$ receives $y \in \mathbb{G}$ from the ideal functionality. It simulates an execution of the protocol with $\mathcal{A}$ by running the first round of the protocol honestly, and computing $k_{\{1,2\}}, k_{\{1,3\}}$. Then $\mathcal{S}$ sets

$$k_{\{2,3\}} := y \cdot k_{\{1,2\}}^{-1} \cdot k_{\{1,3\}}^{-1},$$

and broadcasts $k_{2,3} := k_{3,2} := k_{\{2,3\}}$ plus simulated NIZK proofs in the second round. (It also broadcasts $k_{2,1}, k_{3,1}$ with honestly generated NIZK proofs.)

We can extend this idea to obtain a full-fledged DKG protocol by having the parties use the (shared) random values $k_{\{1,2\}}, k_{\{1,3\}}, k_{\{2,3\}}$ as randomness for an instance of secret sharing that they run in the second round. That is, the value $k_{\{1,2\}}$ will be used by both P_1 and P_2 to derive a secret $x_{\{1,2\}}$ and shares $\{\sigma_{\{1,2\},i}\}$; both parties will broadcast commitments $\{g^{\sigma_{\{1,2\},i}}\}$ to the shares (along with NIZK proofs of correctness) and send the shares to the corresponding parties via private channel. A corrupted party can abort in the second round, but as before this does not matter since at least one party in each pair of parties is guaranteed to be honest.

Generalizing to arbitrary n**.** The protocol can be generalized to arbitrary n and $t < n/2$ assuming the existence of $(t+1)$-party NIKE. This consists of algorithms $(\mathsf{NIKE}_1, \mathsf{NIKE}_2)$ where:

- NIKE_1 is a randomized algorithm that outputs a pair of values $(\mathsf{st}, \mathsf{msg})$.
- NIKE_2 is a deterministic algorithm that takes as input st and $\mathsf{msg}_1, \ldots, \mathsf{msg}_t$ and outputs a value k.

For correctness, we require that if we have $t+1$ independent invocations of NIKE_1 to obtain $(\mathsf{st}_1, \mathsf{msg}_1), \ldots, (\mathsf{st}_{t+1}, \mathsf{msg}_{t+1}) \leftarrow \mathsf{NIKE}_1$, then it holds that

$$\mathsf{NIKE}_2(\mathsf{st}_1, \{\mathsf{msg}_i\}_{i \in [t+1] \setminus \{1\}}) = \cdots = \mathsf{NIKE}_2(\mathsf{st}_{t+1}, \{\mathsf{msg}_i\}_{i \in [t+1] \setminus \{t+1\}}).$$

Security requires that $\mathsf{NIKE}_2(\mathsf{st}_1, \{\mathsf{msg}_i\}_{i \in [t+1] \setminus \{1\}})$ be indistinguishable from a uniform element in the appropriate domain, even given $\{\mathsf{msg}_i\}_{i \in [t+1]}$. For our purposes, we view the key k output by NIKE_2 as a pair $k = (x, \omega) \in \mathbb{Z}_q \times \mathbb{Z}_q^t$.

Note that Diffie-Hellman key exchange (based on the decisional Diffie-Hellman assumption) is a 2-party NIKE, while Joux's protocol [36] (based on the decisional bilinear Diffie-Hellman assumption) gives a 3-party NIKE.

Let $\mathbb{S}_{t+1,n}$ denote the collection of all subsets of $[n]$ of size $t+1$. We can extend the earlier idea to the general case by running $(t+1)$-party key exchange among all sets in $\mathbb{S}_{t+1,n}$; see Fig. 3. (For notational simplicity we assume $\mathsf{FVSS}_t(x)$ outputs commitments to x and all n shares, instead of only commitments to x and the first t shares; one can derive the former from the latter, anyway.)

Theorem 4. Assume $\Pi_{\mathsf{CRS}}^{t,n}$ uses a secure $(t+1)$-party NIKE and an identity-based simulation-sound NIZK proof system. Then for $t < n/2$, the protocol t-securely realizes $\widehat{\mathcal{F}}_{\mathsf{KeyGen}}^{t,n}$.

We defer a proof to the full version of this work. Note that the protocol realizes the stronger functionality $\widehat{\mathcal{F}}_{\mathsf{KeyGen}}$.

7 A Two-Round Protocol Using Preprocessing

Here we show a fully secure DKG protocol that requires one round of preprocessing, following which it is possible to generate an unbounded number of keys via a 2-round protocol. (Alternately, one may view it as a 2-round protocol assuming trusted setup, or as a 3-round protocol with no setup.) A drawback of the protocol in theory is that is has complexity $O(\binom{n}{t})$; for small values of n, t encountered in practice, however, the protocol is extremely efficient.

Our protocol is based on pseudorandom secret sharing (PRSS) [16] (see also [51, Section 19.4]). A non-interactive PRSS-based protocol for sharing a random secret is well known, but to the best of our knowledge it has not been previously observed that (1) it is possible to (easily) add robustness to that protocol, or that (2) robustness is possible even in the absence of a trusted dealer to distribute the initial PRSS shares.

We begin by recalling the non-interactive PRSS-based protocol for sharing a random secret. Let $\mathbb{S}_{n-t,n}$ be the collection of all subsets of $[n]$ of size $n - t$.

$$\Pi_{\mathsf{CRS}}^{t,n}$$

We assume a CRS used for the required NIZK proofs.

Round 1: Each party P_i does the following: for all $S \in \mathbb{S}_{t+1,n}$ such that $i \in S$: run $(\mathsf{st}_{i,S}, \mathsf{msg}_{i,S}) \leftarrow \mathsf{NIKE}_1$ and broadcast $\mathsf{msg}_{i,S}$. If a party fails to broadcast some message, it is treated as some canonical (valid) message.

Round 2: Each party P_i does the following for all $S \in \mathbb{S}_{t+1,n}$ such that $i \in S$:
1. Compute $(x_S, \omega_S) := \mathsf{NIKE}_2(\mathsf{st}_{i,S}, \{\mathsf{msg}_{j,S}\}_{j \in S \setminus \{i\}})$.
2. Compute $(\{y_{i,S,j}\}_{j=0}^n, \{\sigma_{i,S,j}\}_{j \in [n]}) := \mathsf{FVSS}_t(x_S; \omega_S)$, along with an NIZK proof $\pi_{i,S}$ that the values $\{y_{i,S,j}\}_{j=0}^n$ were computed correctly based on $\{\mathsf{msg}_{i,S}\}_{i \in S}$.
3. Broadcast $\{y_{i,S,j}\}_{j=0}^n$ and $\pi_{i,S}$. For $j \in [n]$, send $\sigma_{i,S,j}$ to P_j via private channel.

Output determination: Each party P_i does:
1. For each $S \in \mathbb{S}_{t+1,n}$ do:
  (a) Let $j \in S$ be s.t. P_j broadcasted a valid proof $\pi_{j,S}$, and $g^{\sigma_{j,S,i}} = y_{j,S,i}$. Set $\sigma_{S,i} := \sigma_{j,S,i}$, and $y_{S,k} := y_{j,S,k}$ for $k = 0, \ldots, n$.
2. Set $\sigma_i := \sum_{S \in \mathbb{S}_{t+1,n}} \sigma_{S,i}$, and $y_k := \prod_{S \in \mathbb{S}_{t+1,n}} y_{S,k}$ for $k = 0, \ldots, n$.
3. Output $(y_0, \sigma_i, (y_1, \ldots, y_n))$.

Fig. 3. A 2-round DKG protocol in the CRS model, parameterized by t, n.

For $S \in \mathbb{S}_{n-t,n}$, let $Z_S \in \mathbb{Z}_q[X]$ be the polynomial of degree at most t satisfying $Z_S(0) = 1$ and $Z_S(i) = 0$ for $i \in [n] \setminus S$. (Each Z_S is publicly known.) In an initialization phase a trusted dealer does the following: for every $S \in \mathbb{S}_{n-t,n}$ a uniform key $k_S \in \{0,1\}^\kappa$ is chosen, and each party $i \in S$ is given k_S.

Let $F : \{0,1\}^\kappa \times \{0,1\}^* \to \mathbb{Z}_q$ be a pseudorandom function. The sharing of a secret indexed by a nonce[10] N is done by having each P_i compute its share

$$\sigma_i := \sum_{S \in \mathbb{S}_{n-t,n}\,:\,i \in S} F_{k_S}(N) \cdot Z_S(i). \tag{2}$$

To see that this is a correct $(t+1)$-out-of-n Shamir secret sharing, let f_N be the polynomial

$$f_N(X) \stackrel{\text{def}}{=} \sum_{S \in \mathbb{S}_{n-t,n}} F_{k_S}(N) \cdot Z_S(X) \tag{3}$$

of degree at most t. Then note that for all $i \in [n]$ we have

$$f_N(i) = \sum_{S \in \mathbb{S}_{n-t,n}} F_{k_S}(N) \cdot Z_S(i) = \sum_{S \in \mathbb{S}_{n-t,n}\,:\,i \in S} F_{k_S}(N) \cdot Z_S(i) = \sigma_i.$$

The value x_N being shared is

$$x_N \stackrel{\text{def}}{=} f_N(0) = \sum_{S \in \mathbb{S}_{n-t,n}} F_{k_S}(N) \cdot Z_S(0) = \sum_{S \in \mathbb{S}_{n-t,n}} F_{k_S}(N). \tag{4}$$

Since any set $\mathcal{C} \subset [n]$ of t corrupted parties has no information about $k_{[n]\setminus \mathcal{C}}$, this means that x_N is computationally indistinguishable from a uniform element of $\mathbb{Z}_q$ given the view of the parties in $\mathcal{C}$.

The above protocol is robust because it is non-interactive. But it is not a key-generation protocol since, although it allows the parties to compute a sharing of a secret x, it does not allow them to compute $y \stackrel{\text{def}}{=} g^x$ without further interaction. Moreover, the protocol as described assumes a trusted dealer who sets up the initial keys. We show how to address both these issues.

At a high level, the idea is as follows. During a preprocessing phase, a designated party in each $S \in \mathbb{S}_{n-t,n}$ chooses a uniform key k_S and sends it over a private channel to each party in S. Let $k_{i,S}$ be the key that P_i receives from the designated party P_S for set S. If P_S is corrupted, it may choose k_S nonuniformly; this will not affect security since P_S learns k_S anyway (regardless of how it is chosen). A more serious problem is that P_S might send different keys to different (honest) parties in S; we will see below how the protocol deals with this. One crucial point, however, is that at least one set $S_\mathcal{H} \in \mathbb{S}_{n-t,n}$ contains only honest parties; the key $k_{S_\mathcal{H}}$ for that set will be uniform, unknown to the adversary, and shared correctly among all parties in $S_\mathcal{H}$.

---

[10] The nonce does not need to be random, only non-repeating. It could be a counter, or a session id, or derived in some other agreed-upon fashion by the parties.

The key-generation protocol itself has a simple structure. In the first round, each party P_i computes $\hat{y}_{i,S} := g^{F_{k_{i,S}}(N)}$ for each set S of which they are a member, and broadcasts a "commitment" $h_{i,S} := H(\hat{y}_{i,S})$ to that value, where H is a cryptographic hash function. For each set $S \in \mathbb{S}_{n-t,n}$ there are now two possibilities: either all parties in S broadcasted the same value, which we may simply call h_S, or parties in S broadcasted different values. In the latter case all parties simply exclude the set S from further consideration. Let $\mathcal{I} \subseteq \mathbb{S}_{n-t,n}$ be the collection of non-excluded sets.

In the second round, each party P_i broadcasts $\{\hat{y}_{i,S}\}$ for each $S \in \mathcal{I}$ of which they are a member. Each party then sets $\hat{y}_S$ (for $S \in \mathcal{I}$) equal to any valid preimage of h_S that was broadcast. (We discuss below why such a value is guaranteed to exist.) Parties compute their output as in the non-interactive PRSS scheme described earlier, but now summing only over sets in $\mathcal{I}$. Specifically, P_i computes its share as

$$\sigma_i := \sum_{S \in \mathcal{I} : i \in S} F_{k_{i,S}}(N) \cdot Z_S(i)$$

(compare to (2)), and all parties compute the public key $y := \prod_{S \in \mathcal{I}} \hat{y}_S$ and the commitments $y_j := \prod_{S \in \mathcal{I} : j \in S} \hat{y}_S^{Z_S(j)}$ for all $j \in [n]$. See Fig. 4 for details.

Before discussing security, we briefly sketch correctness. Let $\{\hat{y}_S\}_{S \in \mathcal{I}}$ be the values used by parties to compute the public key and the commitments, and let $x_S \stackrel{\text{def}}{=} \log_g \hat{y}_S$. Then

$$\log_g y_i = \sum_{S \in \mathcal{I} : i \in S} x_S \cdot Z_S(i)$$

(compare to (2)), and so the exponents of the $\{y_j\}_{j \in [n]}$ do indeed lie on the degree-t polynomial $f(X) = \sum_{S \in \mathcal{I}} x_S \cdot Z_S(X)$ (compare to (3)). Moreover, the exponent of the public key y is

$$\log_g y = \sum_{S \in \mathcal{I}} x_S = f(0) \qquad (5)$$

(compare to (4)), as required. As for the shares computed by the (honest) parties, note that for each $S \in \mathcal{I}$ all honest parties in S must have broadcast the same value h_S in round 1; collision-resistance of H thus implies that every honest party P_i in S holds the same value of $F_{k_{i,S}}(N) = \log_g \hat{y}_S = x_S$. Thus, honest parties' shares are consistent with the publicly computed information.

As for security, one crucial property of the protocol is that—as in the protocols from the previous sections—the public key y is *fully determined* at the end of the first round (regardless of the actions of the corrupted parties in the second round), even though it cannot yet be *computed* by the adversary. Roughly, this is because for each set $S \in \mathbb{S}_{n-t,n}$ containing a corrupted party there are two possibilities: either there is agreement in the $\{h_{i,S}\}_{i \in S}$ or not. In the latter case, the effect is simply to exclude S from $\mathcal{I}$. In the former case, collision-resistance of H ensures that the common value h_S cannot be "opened" to conflicting values $\hat{y}_{i,S} \neq \hat{y}_{j,S}$; moreover, the attacker cannot choose to prevent a preimage of h_S

from being revealed since S contains at least one honest party. This shows that the attacker cannot bias the key or prevent it from being computed. Secrecy of the private key holds since $S_\mathcal{H}$ is always in $\mathcal{I}$, and hence the pseudorandom contribution of the key $k_{S_\mathcal{H}}$ used by the set of honest parties is always included in the computation of the private key (cf. (5)).

$$\Pi_{\mathsf{ROM}}^{t,n}$$

Let $H : \mathbb{G} \to \{0,1\}^\kappa$ be a cryptographic hash function.

Preprocessing: For each $S \in \mathbb{S}_{n-t,n}$, the lowest-index party in S chooses a uniform key $k_S \in \{0,1\}^\kappa$ and sends it (over a private channel) to each party P_i, $i \in S$. Each party P_i sets $k_{i,S}$ to the value thus received. If P_i does not receive k_S for some $S \in \mathbb{S}_{n-t,n}$ with $i \in S$, it sets $k_{i,S} := 0$.

Key generation: To generate a key for a nonce N, each party P_i does:

  Round 1: For all $S \in \mathbb{S}_{n-t,n}$ with $i \in S$, compute $\hat{y}_{i,S} := g^{F_{k_{i,S}}(N)}$ and $h_{i,S} := H(\hat{y}_{i,S})$. Then broadcast $\{h_{i,S}\}_{S \in \mathbb{S}_{n-t,n}\,:\,i \in S}$.
  If for some $S \in \mathbb{S}_{n-t,n}$ and $j \in S$, party P_j fails to broadcast $h_{j,S}$, then set $h_{j,S} := \bot$.

  Round 2: Initialize $\mathcal{I} := \emptyset$. Then for each $S \in \mathbb{S}_{n-t,n}$, do:
  If there exists h_S with $h_{j,S} = h_S$ for all $j \in S$, add S to $\mathcal{I}$.
  Broadcast $\{\hat{y}_{i,S}\}_{S \in \mathcal{I}\,:\,i \in S}$.

Output determination: Each party P_i does:
  1. For each $S \in \mathcal{I}$, if some party P_j with $j \in S$ broadcasted $\hat{y}_{j,S}$ with $H(\hat{y}_{j,S}) = h_S$ then set $\hat{y}_S := \hat{y}_{j,S}$.
  2. Set $\sigma_i := \sum_{S \in \mathcal{I}\,:\,i \in S} F_{k_{i,S}}(N) \cdot Z_S(i)$.
  3. For $j \in [n]$ set $y_j := \prod_{S \in \mathcal{I}\,:\,j \in S} \hat{y}_S^{Z_S(j)}$. Set $y := \prod_{S \in \mathcal{I}} \hat{y}_S$.
  4. Output $(y, \sigma_i, (y_1, \ldots, y_n))$.

Fig. 4. A DKG protocol in the ROM, parameterized by t, n.

Theorem 5. *Let F be a pseudorandom function, and model H as a random oracle. Then for $t < n/2$, protocol $\Pi_{\mathsf{ROM}}^{t,n}$ t-securely realizes $\mathcal{F}_{\mathsf{KeyGen}}^{t,n}$.*

Proof. We define a simulator $\mathcal{S}$, given black box access to an adversary $\mathcal{A}$, as follows. (Queries to H, whether by honest parties or by $\mathcal{A}$, are handled in the natural way unless otherwise specified.)

Preprocessing: $\mathcal{S}$ runs $\mathcal{A}$ to obtain a set $\mathcal{C}$ of corrupted parties with $|\mathcal{C}| \leq t$. Let $\mathcal{H} := [n] \setminus \mathcal{C}$ be the set of honest parties. Then:
  - For each $S \in \mathbb{S}_{n-t,n}$ with $S \subseteq \mathcal{H}$, do nothing.
  - For each $S \in \mathbb{S}_{n-t,n}$ with $S \not\subseteq \mathcal{H}$ in which the lowest-indexed party P_i is honest, choose uniform $k_S \in \{0,1\}^\kappa$ and send k_S to all parties in $S \cap \mathcal{C}$ on behalf of P_i. Also set $k_{i,S} := k_S$ for all $i \in S \cap \mathcal{H}$.

– For each $S \in \mathbb{S}_{n-t,n}$ with $S \not\subseteq \mathcal{H}$ in which the lowest-indexed party is corrupted, receive $\{k_{i,S}\}_{i \in S \cap \mathcal{H}}$ from $\mathcal{A}$. Set $k_S := k_{i,S}$ for arbitrary index $i \in S \cap \mathcal{H}$.

Key generation: Let N be the nonce. Then:

Round 1: To simulate the first round, $\mathcal{S}$ does:
- For each $S \in \mathbb{S}_{n-t,n}$ with $S \subseteq \mathcal{H}$: choose uniform $h_S \in \{0,1\}^\kappa$, and for all $i \in S$ broadcast $h_{i,S} := h_S$.
- For each $S \in \mathbb{S}_{n-t,n}$ with $S \not\subseteq \mathcal{H}$, and each $i \in S \cap \mathcal{H}$, run the protocol honestly. (I.e., compute $\hat{y}_{i,S} := g^{F_{k_{i,S}}(N)}$ followed by $h_{i,S} := H(\hat{y}_{i,S})$; then broadcast $h_{i,S}$.)

In response, for $S \in \mathbb{S}_{n-t,n}$ with $S \not\subseteq \mathcal{H}$ and $i \in S \cap \mathcal{C}$, the adversary $\mathcal{A}$ broadcasts $h_{i,S}$. (If $\mathcal{A}$ fails to send some such $h_{i,S}$, then set $h_{i,S} := \perp$.) Initialize $\mathcal{I} := \emptyset$. Then for each $S \in \mathbb{S}_{n-t,n}$ do:

If there exists h_S such that $h_{i,S} = h_S$ for all $i \in S$, add S to $\mathcal{I}$. (Note that $\mathcal{I}$ contains all $S \in \mathbb{S}_{n-t,n}$ with $S \subseteq \mathcal{H}$.)

For all $i \in \mathcal{C}$, compute $\sigma_i := \sum_{S \in \mathcal{I}: i \in S} F_{k_S}(N) \cdot Z_S(i)$. Send $\{\sigma_i\}_{i \in \mathcal{C}}$ to $\mathcal{F}_{\mathsf{KeyGen}}^{t,n}$ and receive in return y and $Y = (y_1, \ldots, y_n)$.

For all $S \in \mathcal{I}$ with $S \not\subseteq \mathcal{H}$, set $\hat{y}_S := g^{F_{k_S}(N)}$. Then choose uniform $\{\hat{y}_S\}_{S \in \mathcal{I}, S \subseteq \mathcal{H}}$ subject to the constraint that $\prod_{S \in \mathcal{I}} \hat{y}_S = y$. Program H so that $H(\hat{y}_S) = h_S$ for each $S \in \mathcal{I}, S \subseteq \mathcal{H}$.

Round 2: For each $i \in \mathcal{H}$, broadcast $\{\hat{y}_S\}_{S \in \mathbb{S}_{n-t,n}: i \in S}$. Output whatever $\mathcal{A}$ outputs.

We show that $\mathsf{REAL}_{\Pi_{\mathsf{ROM}}^{t,n}, \mathcal{A}}$ is indistinguishable from $\mathsf{IDEAL}_{\mathcal{F}_{\mathsf{KeyGen}}^{t,n}, \mathcal{S}}$ via a sequence of hybrid experiments. Key observations we rely on, which follow from the fact that $|\mathcal{C}| \leq t < n/2$, are that (1) every $S \in \mathbb{S}_{n-t,n}$ contains at least one honest party, and (2) there is at least one $S \in \mathbb{S}_{n-t,n}$ containing only honest parties. Let Expt_0 refer to experiment $\mathsf{REAL}_{\Pi_{\mathsf{ROM}}^{t,n}, \mathcal{A}}$.

Experiment Expt_1. In this experiment, modify Expt_0 in the following way. For each $S \in \mathbb{S}_{n-t,n}$ with $S \subseteq \mathcal{H}$, do the following:

– During initialization, do nothing. (In particular, do not choose any key k_S.)
– In round 1 of key generation, choose uniform $\hat{y}_S \in \mathbb{G}$ and then for each $i \in S$ set $\hat{y}_{i,S} := \hat{y}_S$. Run the rest of the protocol honestly.

It follows immediately from the fact that F is a pseudorandom function that Expt_0 and Expt_1 are indistinguishable.

Experiment Expt_2. We now introduce the following modification to Expt_1. For each $S \in \mathbb{S}_{n-t,n}$ with $S \subseteq \mathcal{H}$, do the following during key generation: in round 1, choose uniform $h_S \in \{0,1\}^\kappa$ and set $h_{i,S} := h_S$ for all $i \in S$. Each $i \in S$ broadcasts $\hat{y}_{i,S}$ in round 2 as before, where $\hat{y}_S$ is defined as in Expt_1. Now, however, H is then programmed so that $H(\hat{y}_S) = h_S$.

If H is modeled as a random oracle, the only difference between Expt_2 and Expt_1 occurs if $\mathcal{A}$ ever queries $H(\hat{y}_S)$ for some $S \subseteq \mathcal{H}$ before $\hat{y}_S$ is broadcast in round 2. Since each such $\hat{y}_S$ is uniform in $\mathbb{G}$, the probability of that event is negligible and so Expt_2 and Expt_1 are indistinguishable.

Experiment Expt₃. Now modify the output-determination step of Expt₂ as follows: for each $S \in \mathcal{I}$ with $S \nsubseteq \mathcal{H}$, set $\hat{y}_S = g^{F_{k_{i,S}}(N)}$ for arbitrary $i \in S \cap \mathcal{H}$. Note that an observable difference between Expt₃ and Expt₂ can only possibly occur if for some $S \in \mathbb{S}_{n-t,n}$, $i \in S \cap \mathcal{H}$, and $j \in S \cap \mathcal{C}$, parties P_i, P_j broadcast $h_{i,S} = h_{j,S}$ in round 1 and $\hat{y}_{i,S} \neq \hat{y}_{j,S}$ in round 2 but $H(\hat{y}_{i,S}) = H(\hat{y}_{j,S})$. Collision-resistance of H—which follows when H is modeled as a random oracle—thus implies that Expt₃ and Expt₂ are indistinguishable.

Experiment Expt₄. Now, instead of choosing uniform and independent values $\{\hat{y}_S\}_{S \in \mathbb{S}_{n-t,n}, S \subseteq \mathcal{H}}$, we instead choose a uniform value $y \in \mathbb{G}$ and then choose uniform $\{\hat{y}_S\}_{S \in \mathbb{S}_{n-t,n}, S \subseteq \mathcal{H}}$ subject to the constraint that $\prod_{S \in \mathcal{I}} \hat{y}_S = y$. This is perfectly indistinguishable from Expt₃, and it can be verified that this experiment is identical to $\text{IDEAL}_{\mathcal{F}_{\text{KeyGen}}^{t,n}, \mathcal{S}}$. □

Achieving adaptive security. Assuming secure erasures, it is easy to achieve adaptive security for the above protocol by having each party P_i make a simple change: after computing $\{F_{k_{i,S}}(N)\}_{i \in S}$ in round 1, update all keys by setting $k_{i,S} := H'(k_{i,S})$ for all S with $i \in S$, where $H' : \{0,1\}^\kappa \rightarrow \{0,1\}^\kappa$ is an independent random oracle.

8 A One-Round Protocol Using Preprocessing

We show here that, given certain setup, it is possible to construct a *one*-round fully secure DKG protocol. This does not contradict the impossibility result from Sect. 4 since the protocol we construct will not be statistically unbiased—in fact, it will be a deterministic function of the setup. Such a protocol can still be fully secure if the key is *computationally indistinguishable from uniform* conditioned on the setup given to the corrupted parties, as will be the case in our protocol. (We remark that the protocol in the previous section is not statistically unbiased, either.) As in the previous section, we show that it is possible to generate the appropriate setup in a preprocessing phase run by the parties themselves. Here, however, preprocessing requires two rounds.

The protocol we describe is similar to the protocol in the previous section, and in particular we again rely on non-interactive PRSS. Let $\mathbb{S}_{n-t,n}$ continue to denote the collection of all subsets of $[n]$ of size $n-t$ and, for $S \in \mathbb{S}_{n-t,n}$, let $Z_S \in \mathbb{Z}_q[X]$ be the polynomial of degree at most t satisfying $Z_S(0) = 1$ and $Z_S(i) = 0$ for $i \in [n] \setminus S$. As in the previous protocol, during a preprocessing phase a designated party P_S in each $S \in \mathbb{S}_{n-t,n}$ chooses $k_S \in \{0,1\}^\kappa$ and sends it (over a private channel) to all parties in S. Now, however, P_S additionally broadcasts a commitment com_S to k_S, and sends the decommitment information to all parties in S. (It suffices for the commitment scheme to be computationally hiding and binding. In the CRS model, a statistically binding non-interactive commitment scheme can be constructed from one-way functions.) In the second round of preprocessing, any party in S who does not receive a correct decommitment to com_S broadcasts a complaint; any set S for which there is a complaint is excluded from consideration from then on. Let $\mathcal{I}$ be the collection of non-excluded sets.

$$\Pi_{1\text{-round}}^{t,n}$$

Here we assume a CRS used for the required NIZK proofs; it is possible to remove this assumption (see text).

Preprocessing:
  Round 1: For each $S \in \mathbb{S}_{n-t,n}$, designated party P_S in S chooses uniform $k_S \in \{0,1\}^\kappa$ and $\omega_S \in \{0,1\}^*$, computes $\text{com}_S := \text{Com}(k_S; \omega_S)$, broadcasts com_S, and sends k_S, ω_S by private channel to $\{P_i\}_{i \in S}$.
  Round 2: Each party P_i does the following: for each $S \in \mathbb{S}_{n-t,n}$ with $i \in S$, if P_S did not broadcast com_S or did not send k_S, ω_S to P_i, or if it did but $\text{com}_S \neq \text{Com}(k_S; \omega_S)$, then broadcast $(\text{complaint}, S)$. Let $\mathcal{I} = \{S \in \mathbb{S}_{n-t,n} \mid \text{no party in } S \text{ broadcast } (\text{complaint}, S)\}$.

Key generation: To generate a key for nonce N, each party P_i does:
  Round 1: For each $S \in \mathcal{I}$ with $i \in S$, compute $\hat{y}_{i,S} := g^{F_{k_S}(N)}$. Broadcast $\hat{y}_{i,S}$, along with an NIZK proof $\pi_{i,S}$ that $\hat{y}_{i,S}$ is computed correctly relative to com_S.

Output determination: Each party P_i does:
  1. For each $S \in \mathcal{I}$, if some P_j with $j \in S$ broadcasted $\hat{y}_{j,S}$ along with a valid proof $\pi_{j,S}$ relative to com_S, then set $\hat{y}_S := \hat{y}_{j,S}$.
  2. Set $\sigma_i := \sum_{S \in \mathcal{I}: i \in S} F_{k_S}(N) \cdot Z_S(i)$.
  3. For $j \in [n]$ set $y_j := \prod_{S \in \mathcal{I}: j \in S} \hat{y}_S^{Z_S(j)}$. Set $y := \prod_{S \in \mathcal{I}} \hat{y}_S$.
  4. Output $(y, \sigma_i, (y_1, \ldots, y_n))$.

Fig. 5. A DKG protocol, parameterized by t, n.

Due to the commitment com_S, all honest parties in any set $S \in \mathcal{I}$ hold the same key k_S; we thus write k_S in place of $k_{i,S}$. To generate a key for a nonce N during the key-generation phase, each party P_i simply broadcasts $\hat{y}_{i,S} := g^{F_{k_S}(N)}$ for each set $S \in \mathcal{I}$ to which they belong, plus an NIZK proof of correctness relative to com_S. Let $\hat{y}_S \in \{\hat{y}_{i,S}\}_{i \in S}$ be such that the associated proof verifies; there will always be one such value (since each set S includes at least one honest party) and there cannot be more than one (by soundness of the NIZK proof). As in the previous protocol, all parties then compute the public key $y := \prod_{S \in \mathcal{I}} \hat{y}_S$ and the commitments $y_j := \prod_{S \in \mathcal{I}: j \in S} \hat{y}_S^{Z_S(j)}$ for all $j \in [n]$. See Fig. 5.

Theorem 6. *Let F be a pseudorandom function, and assume $\Pi_{1\text{-round}}^{t,n}$ uses a secure commitment scheme and an identity-based simulation-sound NIZK proof system. Then for $t < n/2$, protocol $\Pi_{1\text{-round}}^{t,n}$ t-securely realizes $\mathcal{F}_{\text{KeyGen}}^{t,n}$.*

It is possible to modify the protocol to work in the plain model while keeping the round complexity (in both the preprocessing and key-generation phases) the same. Specifically, we can avoid assuming a CRS by having the parties generate a suitable CRS as part of preprocessing [31].

Acknowledgments. I thank Chelsea Komlo for inspiring me to think about this problem, for helpful discussions about DKG, and for motivating me to prove the result in Sect. 5.3. I also thank the Crypto 2024 reviewers for their many helpful comments.

A Alternate Ideal Functionalities for Key Generation

As discussed in Sect. 3, one can define different notions of security for distributed key generation by specifying different ideal functionalities. We explore several such possibilities here. We do not claim any particular novelty for any of these functionalities, but hope that having them in one place and following a common format will be useful for researchers pursuing future work in this area.

All functionalities are implicitly parameterized by t and n, though we leave this implicit to reduce notational clutter. We begin by showing in Fig. 6 an alternate ideal functionality $\widehat{\mathcal{F}}_{\mathsf{KeyGen}}$ for fully secure key generation. This functionality is stronger than $\mathcal{F}_{\mathsf{KeyGen}}$ in that it does not give the adversary the ability to choose its own shares. $\widehat{\mathcal{F}}_{\mathsf{KeyGen}}$ is arguably a more natural than $\mathcal{F}_{\mathsf{KeyGen}}$, though—as we have already noted—using the latter does not seem to have any practical disadvantages while potentially allowing for more-efficient protocols.

$\widehat{\mathcal{F}}_{\mathsf{KeyGen}}$

1. Choose $x \leftarrow \mathbb{Z}_q$ and compute $y := g^x$.
2. Compute $\{\sigma_i\}_{i=0}^n \leftarrow \mathsf{SS}_t(x)$. For $i \in [n]$, set $y_i := g^{\sigma_i}$; let $Y = (y_1, \ldots, y_n)$.
3. For $i \in [n]$, send (y, σ_i, Y) to P_i. Also send (y, Y) to the adversary.

Fig. 6. Alternate ideal functionality for fully secure key generation.

One can also consider weaker ideal functionalities. This is essential in the dishonest-majority setting where full security is impossible; it may also be interesting for exploring tradeoffs between efficiency and security even in the honest-majority setting. For simplicity, the remaining functionalities we introduce allow the adversary to choose its own shares; of course, each of the functionalities we consider could also be defined in a way that prevents the attacker from doing so.

In Fig. 7 we consider two non-robust functionalities. The first variant, denoted $\mathcal{F}_{\mathsf{KeyGen}}^{\perp}$, is a "secure-with-abort" version of $\mathcal{F}_{\mathsf{KeyGen}}$ where the adversary can abort the protocol and prevent the honest parties from receiving output. This functionality allows the adversary to make its decision about whether to abort based on the public key returned by the functionality, and hence allows the attacker to bias the public key. We also define $\mathcal{F}_{\mathsf{KeyGen}}^{\perp,\mathsf{fair}}$, a version of the key-generation functionality that also lacks guaranteed output delivery, but forces the adversary to determine whether to abort *independent* of the value of the key. We conjecture that the recent DKG protocol of Komlo et al. [43] realizes $\mathcal{F}_{\mathsf{KeyGen}}^{\perp,\mathsf{fair}}$.

Either of the above functionalities could be augmented to also have "identifiable abort" [34], meaning that some corrupted party is identified in case the

$\mathcal{F}_{\mathsf{KeyGen}}^{\perp}$

Let $\mathcal{C}'$ be an arbitrary set of size t with $\mathcal{C} \subseteq \mathcal{C}' \subset [n]$.

1. Receive $\{\sigma_i\}_{i \in \mathcal{C}}$ from the adversary.
2. Choose $x \leftarrow \mathbb{Z}_q$ and set $y := g^x$. Choose $\sigma_i \leftarrow \mathbb{Z}_q$ for $i \in \mathcal{C}' \setminus \mathcal{C}$.
3. Let f be the polynomial of degree at most t such that $f(0) = x$ and $f(i) = \sigma_i$ for $i \in \mathcal{C}'$. Set $\sigma_i := f(i)$ for $i \in [n] \setminus \mathcal{C}'$.
4. For $i \in [n]$ set $y_i := g^{\sigma_i}$. Let $Y = (y_1, \ldots, y_n)$.
5. Send (y, Y) to the adversary. The adversary responds with either **abort** or **continue**. If the adversary sent with **abort** and $|\mathcal{C}| \geq 1$ then send $\perp$ to all honest parties and stop. Otherwise, for $i \in [n]$ send (y, σ_i, Y) to P_i.

$\mathcal{F}_{\mathsf{KeyGen}}^{\perp,\mathsf{fair}}$

Let $\mathcal{C}'$ be an arbitrary set of size t with $\mathcal{C} \subseteq \mathcal{C}' \subset [n]$.

1. The adversary sends either **abort** or $\{\sigma_i\}_{i \in \mathcal{C}}$. If the adversary sent **abort** and $|\mathcal{C}| \geq 1$ then send $\perp$ to all honest parties and stop.
2. Choose $x \leftarrow \mathbb{Z}_q$ and set $y := g^x$. Choose $\sigma_i \leftarrow \mathbb{Z}_q$ for $i \in \mathcal{C}' \setminus \mathcal{C}$.
3. Let f be the polynomial of degree at most t such that $f(0) = x$ and $f(i) = \sigma_i$ for $i \in \mathcal{C}'$. Set $\sigma_i := f(i)$ for $i \in [n] \setminus \mathcal{C}'$.
4. For $i \in [n]$, set $y_i := g^{\sigma_i}$. Let $Y = (y_1, \ldots, y_n)$.
5. For $i \in [n]$, send (y, σ_i, Y) to P_i. Send (y, Y) to the adversary.

Fig. 7. Non-robust key-generation functionalities.

$\mathcal{F}_{\mathsf{KeyGen}}^{\Delta}$

1. Choose $x' \leftarrow \mathbb{Z}_q$ and compute $y' := g^{x'}$.
2. Send y' to the adversary, and receive $(\Delta, \{\sigma_i\}_{i \in \mathcal{C}})$ in return.
3. If $|\mathcal{C}| \geq 1$ set $x := x' + \Delta$; otherwise, set $x := x'$. Set $y := g^x$.
4. Compute $\{\sigma_i\}_{i=0}^n \leftarrow \mathsf{SS}_t(x)$. For $i \in [n]$, set $y_i := g^{\sigma_i}$; let $Y = (y_1, \ldots, y_n)$.
5. For $i \in [n]$, send (y, σ_i, Y) to P_i. Also send (y, Y) to the adversary.

Fig. 8. Ideal functionality for key generation allowing additive bias.

---

functionality is aborted. This could be done by requiring an adversary who sends an **abort** message to also specify some index $i \in \mathcal{C}$ which would then be sent to all honest parties along with $\perp$.

Finally, in Fig. 8 we consider a DKG functionality $\mathcal{F}_{\mathsf{KeyGen}}^{\Delta}$ that explicitly allows for (a limited type of) adversarial *bias*. (For simplicity, we incorporate robustness but one could also consider weaker versions without it.) Specifically, it allows an adversary who has corrupted at least one party to specify an additive shift Δ that is added to an (unknown) key x'. We conjecture that a non-robust version of this functionality is realized by the DKG protocols of [25, 33], and that the threshold protocols they consider (that they prove to be secure when using those DKG protocols) can be proven secure in the $\mathcal{F}_{\mathsf{KeyGen}}^{\Delta}$-hybrid model.

References

1. Abe, M., Fehr, S.: Adaptively secure Feldman VSS and applications to universally-composable threshold cryptography. In: Franklin, M. (ed.) CRYPTO 2004. LNCS, vol. 3152, pp. 317–334. Springer, Heidelberg (2004). https://doi.org/10.1007/978-3-540-28628-8_20
2. Abraham, I., Jovanovic, P., Maller, M., Meiklejohn, S., Stern, G.: Bingo: adaptivity and asynchrony in verifiable secret sharing and distributed key generation. In: Handschuh, H., Lysyanskaya, A. (eds.) Advances in Cryptology – CRYPTO 2023. CRYPTO 2023. LNCS, vol. 14081. Springer, Cham (2023). https://doi.org/10.1007/978-3-031-38557-5_2
3. Abraham, I., Jovanovic, P., Maller, M., Meiklejohn, S., Stern, G., Tomescu, A.: Reaching consensus for asynchronous distributed key generation. In: 40th Annual ACM Symposium on Principles of Distributed Computing (PODC), pp. 363–373. ACM Press (2021)
4. Applebaum, B., Kachlon, E., Patra, A.: Verifiable relation sharing and multi-verifier zero-knowledge in two rounds: trading NIZKs with honest majority. In: Dodis, Y., Shrimpton, T. (eds.) Advances in Cryptology – CRYPTO 2022. CRYPTO 2022. LNCS, vol. 13510. Springer, Cham (2022). https://doi.org/10.1007/978-3-031-15985-5_2
5. Bacho, R., Loss, J.: On the adaptive security of the threshold BLS signature scheme. In: 29th ACM Conference on Computer and Communications Security (CCS), pp. 193–207. ACM Press (2022)
6. Backes, M., Kate, A., Patra, A.: Computational verifiable secret sharing revisited. In: Lee, D.H., Wang, X. (eds.) ASIACRYPT 2011. LNCS, vol. 7073, pp. 590–609. Springer, Heidelberg (2011). https://doi.org/10.1007/978-3-642-25385-0_32
7. Ben-Or, M., Linial, N.: Collective coin flipping. Adv. Comput. Res. **5**, 91–115 (1989)
8. Boneh, D., Haitner, I., Lindell, Y.: Exponent-VRFs and their applications (2024). https://eprint.iacr.org/2024/397
9. Boneh, D., Shoup, V.: A graduate course in applied cryptography, v. 0.6 (2023). http://toc.cryptobook.us
10. Brandão, L., Peralta, R.: NIST first call for multi-party threshold schemes. Technical report, National Institute of Standards and Technology (2023). Internal Report (IR 8214C ipd). https://doi.org/10.6028/NIST.IR.8214C.ipd
11. Canetti, R., Gennaro, R., Goldfeder, S., Makriyannis, N., Peled, U.: UC non-interactive, proactive, threshold ECDSA with identifiable aborts. In: 27th ACM Conference on Computer and Communications Security (CCS), pp. 1769–1787. ACM Press (2020)
12. Canetti, R., Gennaro, R., Jarecki, S., Krawczyk, H., Rabin, T.: Adaptive security for threshold cryptosystems. In: Wiener, M. (ed.) CRYPTO 1999. LNCS, vol. 1666, pp. 98–116. Springer, Heidelberg (1999). https://doi.org/10.1007/3-540-48405-1_7
13. Canetti, R., Rabin, T.: Universal composition with joint state. In: Boneh, D. (ed.) CRYPTO 2003. LNCS, vol. 2729, pp. 265–281. Springer, Heidelberg (2003). https://doi.org/10.1007/978-3-540-45146-4_16

14. Cleve, R.: Limits on the security of coin flips when half the processors are faulty. In: 18th Annual ACM Symposium on Theory of Computing (STOC), pp. 364–369. ACM Press (1986)
15. Connolly, D., Komlo, C., Goldberg, I., Wood, C.: Two-round threshold Schnorr signatures with FROST (2023). IRTF draft-irtf-cfrg-frost-12. https://datatracker.ietf.org/doc/draft-irtf-cfrg-frost
16. Cramer, R., Damgård, I., Ishai, Y.: Share conversion, pseudorandom secret-sharing and applications to secure computation. In: Kilian, J. (ed.) TCC 2005. LNCS, vol. 3378, pp. 342–362. Springer, Heidelberg (2005). https://doi.org/10.1007/978-3-540-30576-7_19
17. Crites, E., Komlo, C., Maller, M.: How to prove Schnorr assuming Schnorr: Security of multi- and threshold signatures (2021). https://eprint.iacr.org/2021/1375
18. Damgård, I., Magri, B., Ravi, D., Siniscalchi, L., Yakoubov, S.: Broadcast-optimal two round MPC with an honest majority. In: Malkin, T., Peikert, C. (eds.) CRYPTO 2021. LNCS, vol. 12826, pp. 155–184. Springer, Cham (2021). https://doi.org/10.1007/978-3-030-84245-1_6
19. Das, S., Yurek, T., Xiang, Z., Miller, A.K., Kokoris-Kogias, L., Ren, L.: Practical asynchronous distributed key generation. In: IEEE Symposium on Security and Privacy, pp. 2518–2534. IEEE (2022)
20. De Santis, A., Di Crescenzo, G., Ostrovsky, R., Persiano, G., Sahai, A.: Robust non-interactive zero knowledge. In: Kilian, J. (ed.) CRYPTO 2001. LNCS, vol. 2139, pp. 566–598. Springer, Heidelberg (2001). https://doi.org/10.1007/3-540-44647-8_33
21. Feldman, P.: A practical scheme for non-interactive verifiable secret sharing. In: 28th Annual Symposium on Foundations of Computer Science (FOCS), pp. 427–437. IEEE (1987)
22. Fouque, P.-A., Stern, J.: One round threshold discrete-log key generation without private channels. In: Kim, K. (ed.) PKC 2001. LNCS, vol. 1992, pp. 300–316. Springer, Heidelberg (2001). https://doi.org/10.1007/3-540-44586-2_22
23. Gennaro, R., Goldfeder, S.: Fast multiparty threshold ECDSA with fast trustless setup. In: 25th ACM Conference on Computer and Communications Security (CCS), pp. 1179–1194. ACM Press (2018)
24. Gennaro, R., Ishai, Y., Kushilevitz, E., Rabin, T.: On 2-round secure multiparty computation. In: Yung, M. (ed.) CRYPTO 2002. LNCS, vol. 2442, pp. 178–193. Springer, Heidelberg (2002). https://doi.org/10.1007/3-540-45708-9_12
25. Gennaro, R., Jarecki, S., Krawczyk, H., Rabin, T.: Secure applications of Pedersen's distributed key generation protocol. In: Joye, M. (ed.) CT-RSA 2003. LNCS, vol. 2612, pp. 373–390. Springer, Heidelberg (2003). https://doi.org/10.1007/3-540-36563-X_26
26. Gennaro, R., Jarecki, S., Krawczyk, H., Rabin, T.: Secure distributed key generation for discrete-log based cryptosystems. J. Cryptology **20**(1), 51–83 (2007). Preliminary version in Eurocrypt '99
27. Gentry, C., Halevi, S., Lyubashevsky, V.: Practical non-interactive publicly verifiable secret sharing with thousands of parties. In: Dunkelman, O., Dziembowski, S. (eds.) Advances in Cryptology – EUROCRYPT 2022. EUROCRYPT 2022. LNCS, vol. 13275. Springer, Cham (2022). https://doi.org/10.1007/978-3-031-06944-4_16
28. Goel, A., Jain, A., Prabhakaran, M., Raghunath, R.: On communication models and best-achievable security in two-round MPC. In: Nissim, K., Waters, B. (eds.) TCC 2021. LNCS, vol. 13043, pp. 97–128. Springer, Cham (2021). https://doi.org/10.1007/978-3-030-90453-1_4

29. Dov Gordon, S., Liu, F.-H., Shi, E.: Constant-round MPC with fairness and guarantee of output delivery. In: Gennaro, R., Robshaw, M. (eds.) CRYPTO 2015. LNCS, vol. 9216, pp. 63–82. Springer, Heidelberg (2015). https://doi.org/10.1007/978-3-662-48000-7_4
30. Groth, J.: Non-interactive distributed key generation and key resharing (2021). https://eprint.iacr.org/2021/339
31. Groth, J., Ostrovsky, R.: Cryptography in the multi-string model. J. Cryptology **27**(3), 506–543 (2013). https://doi.org/10.1007/s00145-013-9152-y
32. Groth, J., Shoup, V.: Fast batched asynchronous distributed key generation. In: Joye, M., Leander, G. (eds.) Advances in Cryptology – EUROCRYPT 2024. EUROCRYPT 2024. LNCS, vol. 14655. Springer, Cham (2024). https://doi.org/10.1007/978-3-031-58740-5_13
33. Gurkan, K., Jovanovic, P., Maller, M., Meiklejohn, S., Stern, G., Tomescu, A.: Aggregatable distributed key generation. In: Canteaut, A., Standaert, F.-X. (eds.) EUROCRYPT 2021. LNCS, vol. 12696, pp. 147–176. Springer, Cham (2021). https://doi.org/10.1007/978-3-030-77870-5_6
34. Ishai, Y., Ostrovsky, R., Zikas, V.: Secure multi-party computation with identifiable abort. In: Garay, J.A., Gennaro, R. (eds.) CRYPTO 2014. LNCS, vol. 8617, pp. 369–386. Springer, Heidelberg (2014). https://doi.org/10.1007/978-3-662-44381-1_21
35. Jhanwar, M., Venkateswarlu, A., Safavi-Naini, R.: Paillier-based publicly verifiable (non-interactive) secret sharing. Des. Codes Crypt. **73**(2), 529–546 (2014)
36. Joux, A.: A one-round protocol for tripartite Diffie-Hellman. J. Cryptol. **17**(4), 263–276 (2004)
37. Kahn, J., Kalai, G., Linial, N.: The influence of variables on Boolean functions. In: 29th Annual Symposium on Foundations of Computer Science (FOCS), pp. 68–80. IEEE (1988)
38. Kate, A., Huang, Y., Goldberg, I.: Distributed key generation in the wild (2012). https://eprint.iacr.org/2012/377
39. Kate, A., Mangipudi, E., Mukherjee, P., Saleem, H., Thyagarajan, S.: Non-interactive VSS using class groups and application to DKG (2023). https://eprint.iacr.org/2023/451
40. Katz, J., Lindell, Y.: Introduction to Modern Cryptography, 3rd edition. Chapman & Hall/CRC Press (2020)
41. Katz, J., Ostrovsky, R., Rabin, M.O.: Identity-based zero-knowledge. In: Blundo, C., Cimato, S. (eds.) SCN 2004. LNCS, vol. 3352, pp. 180–192. Springer, Heidelberg (2005). https://doi.org/10.1007/978-3-540-30598-9_13
42. Kokoris-Kogias, E., Malkhi, D., Spiegelman, A.: Asynchronous distributed key generation for computationally-secure randomness, consensus, and threshold signatures. In: 27th ACM Conference on Computer and Communications Security (CCS), pp. 1751–1767. ACM Press (2020)
43. Komlo, C., Goldberg, I., Stebila, D.: A formal treatment of distributed key generation, and new constructions (2023). https://eprint.iacr.org/2023/292
44. Koppula, V., Waters, B., Zhandry, M.: Adaptive multiparty NIKE. In: Kiltz, E., Vaikuntanathan, V. (eds.) Theory of Cryptography. TCC 2022. LNCS, vol. 13748. Springer, Cham (2022). https://doi.org/10.1007/978-3-031-22365-5_9
45. Lindell, Y.: Simple three-round multiparty Schnorr signing with full simulatability. Comm. Cryptology **1**(1), 25 (2024). https://eprint.iacr.org/2022/374
46. Lindell, Y., Nof, A.: Fast secure multiparty ECDSA with practical distributed key generation and applications to cryptocurrency custody. In: 25th ACM Conference

on Computer and Communications Security (CCS), pp. 1837–1854. ACM Press (2018)
47. Neji, W., Blibech Sinaoui, K., Ben Rajeb, N.: Distributed key generation protocol with a new complaint management strategy. Secur. Commun. Netw. **9**(17), 4585–4595 (2016)
48. Patra, A., Ravi, D.: On the exact round complexity of secure three-party computation. In: Shacham, H., Boldyreva, A. (eds.) CRYPTO 2018. LNCS, vol. 10992, pp. 425–458. Springer, Cham (2018). https://doi.org/10.1007/978-3-319-96881-0_15
49. Pedersen, T.P.: Non-interactive and information-theoretic secure verifiable secret sharing. In: Feigenbaum, J. (ed.) CRYPTO 1991. LNCS, vol. 576, pp. 129–140. Springer, Heidelberg (1992). https://doi.org/10.1007/3-540-46766-1_9
50. Shrestha, N., Bhat, A., Kate, A., Nayak, K.: Synchronous distributed key generation without broadcasts (2021). https://eprint.iacr.org/2021/1635
51. Smart, N.: Cryptography Made Simple. Springer (2016). https://doi.org/10.1007/978-3-319-21936-3
52. Stadler, M.: Publicly verifiable secret sharing. In: Maurer, U. (ed.) EUROCRYPT 1996. LNCS, vol. 1070, pp. 190–199. Springer, Heidelberg (1996). https://doi.org/10.1007/3-540-68339-9_17
53. Wikström, D.: Universally composable DKG with linear number of exponentiations. In: Blundo, C., Cimato, S. (eds.) SCN 2004. LNCS, vol. 3352, pp. 263–277. Springer, Heidelberg (2005). https://doi.org/10.1007/978-3-540-30598-9_19

Accountability for Misbehavior in Threshold Decryption via Threshold Traitor Tracing

Dan Boneh[✉], Aditi Partap, and Lior Rotem

Stanford University, Stanford, USA
{dabo,aditi712,lrotem}@cs.stanford.edu

Abstract. A t-out-of-n threshold decryption system assigns key shares to n parties so that any t of them can decrypt a well-formed ciphertext. Existing threshold decryption systems are *not secure* when these parties are rational actors: an adversary can offer to pay the parties for their key shares. The problem is that a quorum of t parties, working together, can sell the adversary a decryption key that reveals nothing about the identity of the traitor parties. This provides a risk-free profit for the parties since there is no accountability for their misbehavior—the information they sell to the adversary reveals nothing about their identity. This behavior can result in a complete break in many applications of threshold decryption, such as encrypted mempools, private voting, and sealed-bid auctions.

In this work we propose a solution to this problem. Suppose a quorum of t or more parties construct a decoder algorithm $D(\cdot)$ that takes as input a ciphertext and outputs the corresponding plaintext or $\bot$. They sell D to the adversary. Our threshold decryption systems are equipped with a tracing algorithm that can trace D to members of the quorum that created it. The tracing algorithm is only given blackbox access to D and will identify some members of the misbehaving quorum. The parties can then be held accountable, which may discourage them from selling the decoder D in the first place.

Our starting point is standard (non-threshold) traitor tracing, where n parties each holds a secret key. Every party can decrypt a well-formed ciphertext on its own. However, if a subset of parties $\mathcal{J} \subseteq [n]$ collude to create a pirate decoder $D(\cdot)$ that can decrypt well-formed ciphertexts, then it is possible to trace D to at least one member of $\mathcal{J}$ using only blackbox access to the decoder D.

In this work we develop the theory of traitor tracing for threshold decryption, where now only a subset $\mathcal{J} \subseteq [n]$ of t or more parties can collude to create a pirate decoder $D(\cdot)$. This problem has recently become quite important due to the real-world deployment of threshold decryption in encrypted mempools, as we explain in the paper. While there are several non-threshold traitor tracing schemes that we can leverage, adapting these constructions to the threshold decryption settings requires new cryptographic techniques. We present a number of constructions for traitor tracing for threshold decryption, and note that much work remains to explore the large design space.

1 Introduction

Accountability is needed in many applications of cryptography. In the context of digital signatures, accountability is often needed when using threshold signatures: if a quorum of t-out-of-n parties sign an invalid message, there is a need to identify the misbehaving quorum. An accountable threshold signature scheme is often built from a multisignature scheme [5,7,10,12,15,42,44] where every signature securely identifies the set of signing parties that generated it.

In this paper we develop the concept of accountability for threshold decryption. In a t-of-n threshold decryption scheme, there are n parties, and party i obtains at setup a *secret key share* sk_i. Later, when that party chooses to decrypt a ciphertext c, it uses sk_i to output a *decryption share*. Another party, which we call the *combiner*, collects t decryption shares and uses them to obtain a plaintext m, possibly using a public *combiner key* denoted by pkc.

The concern is that an adversary could offer to buy the secret key shares from some parties. Without accountability, this offer provides a risk-free profit for the parties. Our goal is to ensure that if some parties sell their secret key shares, then it is possible to securely identify those parties—or some subset of them—and hold them accountable. Here we are assuming that a whistleblower, William, reveals the information that the adversary purchased. William wants to ensure that this information securely identifies the guilty parties. We explain below why this is a good framing of the problem.

William might hope that reporting a set of well-formed secret key shares will identify the subset who sold their keys. However, this is clearly insecure. First, for common threshold decryption schemes (such as [9,25,31,55] and many others), a quorum of t parties has enough information to derive the secret key share of every other party. This lets them frame an innocent quorum by giving the adversary key shares that belong to some other parties. Second, only a naive decryption party would give the adversary its decryption key share as is. A more sophisticated set of t parties would jointly generate a "master" key that lets the adversary decrypt, but cannot be traced to anyone.

We will need to defend against both issues raised above. These issues suggest that a sophisticated set of parties will not sell the adversary a simple key. Instead, they will jointly construct a decoder algorithm $D(\cdot)$ that takes as input a ciphertext c and outputs a plaintext m. The challenge is to identify the guilty set of parties using only black-box access to this decoder D. This question is closely related to traitor tracing [27], but in a very different context. Traitor tracing schemes are designed for settings where every party can decrypt a ciphertext *on its own*. Think of a set of DVD players, where every player needs to decrypt an encrypted DVD disk on its own. In our settings, at least t secret key shares are needed to decrypt a ciphertext. As such, this work generalizes the traitor tracing problem to the settings of threshold decryption. We consider two very different situations.

Case 1: A Decoder from a Greater-Than-Threshold Quorum. Suppose that a coalition of f traitors, where $f \geq t$, constructs a decoder algorithm $D(\cdot)$.

They have enough information to construct a decoder that takes as input a ciphertext c and outputs its decryption. Our goal is to trace this decoder to at least one member of the coalition of traitors, possibly using a tracing key tk generated at setup. We give precise definitions in Sect. 3.

A natural starting point to construct such a system is any of the (non-threshold) traitor tracing schemes that are fully collusion resistant. Some such systems are built from pairings [18,33,34,60,61], some are built from lattices [26, 35], and some are built from iO [23], to name a few. We explain in Sect. 3 that adapting these schemes to the threshold settings requires new techniques. In this paper we look at using a fully collusion-resistant scheme due to Boneh and Naor [14] and Billet and Phan [6] (see Sect. 4). This traitor tracing scheme has *constant* size ciphertext and public key. Secret key shares in this scheme are long (quadratic in n), but still quite reasonable when n is at most a few hundreds, as is usually the case in applications of threshold decryption.

Adapting this non-threshold traitor tracing system to the threshold decryption settings requires a new cryptographic primitive we call *Bipartite Threshold Encryption* (technically, Bipartite Threshold KEM, or BT-KEM), as described in Sect. 4.1. We give three constructions for a BT-KEM: a direct (but inefficient) combinatorial construction, an efficient construction with short ciphertexts from DDH, and a further improvement providing short public keys as well, using pairings. These constructions illustrate the added complexity in constructing traitor tracing systems for threshold decryption. Our tracing algorithm works by feeding the decoder D malformed ciphertexts. The decoder will successfully decrypt some ciphertexts and output "fail" on others. We show that this success and failure pattern reveals at least one traitor whose key was used to create D.

We stress that the short ciphertext size in our schemes (four group elements in the pairing scheme) is especially appealing for an encrypted mempool system, such as [4], where ciphertexts are posted on chain. In the full version [16, App. B], we also show how to adapt the recent traitor tracing scheme of Gong, Lou, and Wee [34] to the threshold setting using very different techniques.

Case 2: A Decoder from a Below-Threshold Quorum. We next turn to tracing a decoder D built from a coalition $\mathcal{J}$ of f traitors, where $f < t$. This decoder cannot decrypt a ciphertext on its own and needs to take additional decryption shares as input. In particular, for a ciphertext c the decoder D is invoked as $D(c, d_1, \ldots, d_k)$, where $d_1, \ldots, d_k$ are decryption shares for c from some set of parties $\mathcal{S} \subseteq [n]$ of size $|\mathcal{S}| = k \geq t - f$. We consider two types of decoders:

- A *universal decoder* outputs the correct decryption of a well-formed ciphertext c (with non-negligible probability) whenever $|\mathcal{J} \cup \mathcal{S}| \geq t$. That is, the decoder will decrypt a well-formed c whenever it has enough information to do so. In Sect. 6 we describe a generic tracing procedure for such a decoder, assuming that the threshold decryption scheme is semantically secure. The tracing procedure will output at least one member of the coalition $\mathcal{J}$ that created D.

- An *exact decoder* outputs the correct decryption of a well-formed ciphertext c (with non-negligible probability) only when $|\mathcal{S}| = t - f$ and $|\mathcal{J} \cup \mathcal{S}| = t$. This is a more restrictive decoder that only takes $t - f$ valid decryption shares as input. Tracing is not possible in this case because, without knowledge of $\mathcal{J}$, the tracing algorithm cannot find a set $\mathcal{S}$ such that $|\mathcal{S}| = t-f$ and $|\mathcal{J} \cup \mathcal{S}| = t$. To see why, observe that the number of such sets is only $\binom{n-f}{t-f}$, and this can be a negligible fraction of the total number of subsets of size $t - f$. For example, when $t = n/3$ and $f = t/2$, the fraction is $2^{-\Omega(n)}$. Consequently, we show in Sect. 6 that for a robust threshold decryption scheme, the tracing algorithm can never get the decoder to work (the decoder always outputs $\bot$), and this implies that tracing is impossible.

  Instead, we design in Sect. 6 a *confirmation* algorithm. The algorithm takes as input a suspect coalition $\mathcal{J}^* \subseteq [n]$ and uses blackbox access to the decoder D to convince a verifier that $\mathcal{J}^*$ is the traitor set.

Note that we disallow a decoder D that only works for a constant number of specific sets $\mathcal{S}^*$ where $|\mathcal{J} \cup \mathcal{S}^*| = t$. In this extreme case, neither confirmation nor tracing is possible, by a similar argument as above.

1.1 Motivation

Why study traitor tracing for threshold decryption? First, accountability for threshold decryption is a long-standing and well-motivated question that is interesting in its own right. It comes up naturally in many applications of threshold decryption, such as voting [28] and sealed-bid auctions [53]. In all these applications one wants accountability for parties who sell their secret key shares. Second, this topic has recently become important due to the introduction of encrypted mempools [4] using threshold decryption in multiple blockchain projects [47,56,59]. The goal of an encrypted mempool is to keep the data in a block secret until the block is finalized (posted) on chain. After finalization, the block should become available in the clear so that all the transactions in the block can be executed. Keeping transaction data hidden until the block is finalized is intended to prevent a certain value extraction technique called MEV [2,29,49]. We refer to Rondelet and Kilbourn [50] for a detailed analysis of the benefits and limitations of deploying an encrypted mempool.

Several encrypted mempool designs use identical consensus and decryption committees [1,4]. The idea is that when a validator signs a block, it also releases one decryption share for that block. This way, once two thirds of the validators in the consensus committee sign the block—thereby finalizing it—there are also enough decryption shares to decrypt the block. In particular, the decryption threshold is set to two thirds of the consensus committee.

A critical weakness of this design is that an adversary could bribe members of the consensus committee into creating a decoder D that lets the adversary decrypt blocks *before* they are finalized. This lets the adversary engage in MEV extraction and defeats the purpose of encrypting the mempool in the first place.

Crucially, without the ability to trace the decoder D, this bribe provides a risk-free profit for the validators, so there is no reason for them to refuse the bribe. Traitor tracing for threshold decryption puts the validators at risk of being slashed and may compel them to not engage with the adversary.

A similar problem comes up in other applications of threshold decryption, such as voting [28] and sealed-bid auctions [53]. In the case of a sealed-bid auction, threshold decryption is used to ensure that the bids are decrypted only after all the encrypted bids are submitted. If the decryption parties sell their key shares to the adversary, risk free, then secrecy of the bids is compromised, and the adversary can optimally win every auction.

Why Focus on Tracing a Decoder? So far we focused on tracing a decoder algorithm that can be reset and run multiple times (a stateless decoder). One could argue that a set of t or more traitors might only be willing to provide an anonymous decryption service: the adversary sends a well-formed ciphertext c to the service, the traitors jointly decrypt it, and send back (anonymously) the decryption of c. This will defeat our tracing strategy because the set of traitors can maintain state across different decryption requests. If they ever detect a request to decrypt a malformed ciphertext (which is how tracing often works) they could panic and refuse to answer any more requests. This will defeat tracing algorithms designed to trace stateless algorithms.

We provide two arguments for why tracing a decoder D is a good model to focus on. First, a decryption service is unappealing to an adversary who is trying to decrypt a ciphertext for its own benefit. The problem is that the parties running the decryption service will learn the plaintext before the adversary. They could then front-run the adversary by using the plaintext for their own benefit and cut the adversary off. In other words, in the setting of an encrypted mempool, it is very likely that an adversary will only pay the bribe in exchange for a decoding algorithm that the adversary can run on its own machines.

Our second argument is more technical. In the context of traitor tracing we can model a decryption service as a *stateful* decoder, namely a decoder that maintains state and can modify its behavior based on an earlier sequence of requests. Tracing a stateful decoder is much harder even in the non-threshold settings. Several schemes have been proposed [38,48,57], however these constructions rely on watermarking digital media and cannot be used for encrypting short messages, as in voting, auctions, and encrypted mempools.

1.2 Additional Related Work

Although the literature on traitor tracing is vast, this work is the first to define and construct traitor tracing in the context of threshold decryption. Some (non-threshold) traitor tracing schemes, such as [11,27,40], are designed to trace a pirate decoder that was created by a coalition of bounded size. Schemes that are secure against an arbitrary coalition size are said to be *fully collusion resistant*.

The first fully collision-resistant traitor tracing scheme with a public key, ciphertext, and secret key that are all sublinear in the number n of parties was proposed by Boneh, Sahai, and Waters [18] (see also [22]). Their scheme was based on an assumption over composite order bilinear groups, and enjoyed public key and ciphertext of size $O(\sqrt{n})$ and constant size secret keys. Garg, Kumarasubramanian, Sahai, and Waters [33] subsequently achieved similar parameters using prime order bilinear groups. In [60], Wee constructed a functional encryption scheme for quadratic functions, that can be used to reproduce the result of [33] directly using the framework of [18]. In a recent breakthrough result, Zhandry [61] constructed a pairing-based traitor tracing scheme where the public key, ciphertext, and secret key were all of size $O(n^{1/3})$. His proof of security was in the generic group model [54]. This was later on improved by Gong, Luo, and Wee [34], who got the secret key size down to a constant while relying on standard assumptions over bilinear groups.

There are also traitor-tracing schemes from lattice-based assumptions. The groundbreaking work of Goyal, Koppula, and Waters [35] constructed the first fully collision-resistant traitor tracing scheme directly from lattice-based assumptions. Their construction boasts essentially optimal parameters, where the public key, ciphertext size, and secret keys, all grow poly-logarithmically in n. Their construction was later greatly simplified by Chen et al. [26]. In Sect. 3 we discuss the techniques underlying all these pairing-based and lattice-based schemes in more detail.

Optimal traitor tracing can also be achieved from indistinguishability obfuscation [23]. We believe that this construction lends itself to the threshold decryption setting in a fairly straightforward manner.

Naor and Pinkas studied [43] *threshold traitor tracing*, where the goal is to trace a pirate decoder that successfully decrypts an input ciphertext with some threshold probability. This is unrelated to traitor tracing for threshold decryption.

The recent work of Li et al. [41] also considered accountability for decryption. However, their focus was completely dissimilar to ours, as they considered notions of accountability in the non-threshold setting and hardware-based solutions.

Finally, we mention that Goyal, Song, and Srinivasan [37] and Boneh, Partap and Rotem [17] considered the question of accountability in a secret sharing scheme, where share holders might be willing to sell their shares. Apart from the fact that they consider accountability in secret sharing, whereas we consider threshold decryption, there are two other reasons why their techniques cannot be used for tracing traitors in threshold decryption. First, both works only consider a collusion of less-than-threshold set of corrupt parties. This is inherent, since a set of t parties can simply reconstruct and sell the secret, in which case there is no hope of tracing. Second, both Goyal et al. [37] and Boneh et al. [17] consider a different leakage model than ours. Essentially, in both these works, the leak is modeled as a reconstruction box that takes in additional shares and outputs a secret (there are differences between the two works, which we will not go into here). This is functionally different from a decoder box that has t keys hardcoded in it, and takes in only messages to decrypt, as is the case in this paper. These differences necessitate very different techniques. The reader is referred to [17,37] for further details.

2 Preliminaries

Threshold Decryption Schemes. We begin by defining threshold decryption schemes [30,31]. The definitions we use follow those of Boneh and Shoup [21]. A threshold decryption scheme $\mathcal{E} = (\mathsf{KeyGen}, \mathsf{Enc}, \mathsf{Dec}, \mathsf{Combine})$ is a tuple of four polynomial-time algorithms:

1. $\mathsf{KeyGen}(1^\lambda, n, t) \to (pk, pkc, sk_1, \ldots, sk_n)$ is the probabilistic **key generation algorithm**. It takes in the security parameter $\lambda \in \mathbb{N}$, the number n of decryptors and the threshold t. It outputs a public key pk, a combiner public key pkc, and secret keys $sk_1, \ldots, sk_n$.
2. $\mathsf{Enc}(pk, m) \to c$ is the probabilistic **encryption algorithm**. It takes as input the public key pk and a message m, and it outputs a ciphertext c.
3. $\mathsf{Dec}(sk_i, c) \to d_i$ is the deterministic **decryption algorithm**. It takes in a decryptor's secret key sk_i and a ciphertext c, and its output is a decryption share d_i of c under sk_i.
4. $\mathsf{Combine}(pkc, c, \mathcal{J}, \{d_j\}_{j \in \mathcal{J}}) \to m/\bot$ is the deterministic **combiner algorithm**. Its input is a combiner public key pkc, a ciphertext c, a subset $\mathcal{J}$ of $[n]$, and decryption shares $\{d_j\}_{j \in \mathcal{J}}$. It outputs either a message m or a rejection symbol $\bot$.

Correctness. An honestly generated ciphertext should be correctly decrypted by any subset of t decryptors. Specifically, there exists a negligible function $\mathsf{negl}(\lambda)$ of the security parameter λ, such that, for all $\lambda \in \mathbb{N}$, all $n, t \in \mathbb{N}$, all t-sized subsets $\mathcal{J} \subseteq [n]$, and all messages m in the message space, it holds that

$$\Pr\left[m' = m : \begin{array}{c} (pk, pkc, sk_1, \ldots, sk_n) \xleftarrow{\$} \mathsf{KeyGen}(1^\lambda, n, t) \\ c \xleftarrow{\$} \mathsf{Enc}(pk, m) \\ \forall\, i \in \mathcal{J},\ d_i \leftarrow \mathsf{Dec}(sk_i, c) \\ m' \leftarrow \mathsf{Combine}(pkc, c, \mathcal{J}, \{d_j\}_{j \in \mathcal{J}}) \end{array} \right] \geq 1 - \mathsf{negl}(\lambda).$$

Security. We require that a threshold decryption scheme satisfies the standard notion of **semantic security**. Many applications require the stronger notion of security against chosen-ciphertext attacks (CCA security). We do not consider CCA security in this paper since our focus is the notion of traitor tracing, which seems orthogonal to CCA security (see Sect. 7). The notion of semantic security is captured by the security game in Fig. 1.

Definition 2.1 (Semantic security). *We say that $\mathcal{E}$ satisfies* semantic security *if for every probabilistic polynomial time adversary $\mathcal{A}$, the following function is negligible in λ:*

$$\mathsf{Adv}^{\mathsf{cpa}}_{\mathcal{A}, \mathcal{E}}(\lambda) := |1 - 2 \cdot \Pr[\mathbf{IND\text{-}CPA}_{\mathcal{A}, \mathcal{E}}(\lambda) = 1]|.$$

Experiment IND-CPA$_{\mathcal{A},\mathcal{E}}(\lambda)$

1: $\mathcal{J} \leftarrow \emptyset$
2: $(n, t, \text{state}) \leftarrow \mathcal{A}(1^\lambda)$
3: $(pk, pkc, sk_1, \ldots, sk_n) \xleftarrow{\$} \text{KeyGen}(1^\lambda, n, t)$
4: $(m_0, m_1) \xleftarrow{\$} \mathcal{A}^{\text{corrupt}(\cdot)}(\text{state}, pk, pkc)$
5: $b \xleftarrow{\$} \{0, 1\}$, $c \xleftarrow{\$} \text{Enc}(pk, m_b)$
6: $b' \xleftarrow{\$} \mathcal{A}^{\text{corrupt}(\cdot)}(\text{state}, c)$
7: **if** $|\mathcal{J}| \geq t$ **then return** 0
8: **if** $b' = b$ **then return** 1 **else return** 0

Oracle corrupt(i)

1: **if** $i \notin [n]$ **then return** $\bot$
2: $\mathcal{J} \leftarrow \mathcal{J} \cup \{i\}$
3: **return** sk_i

Fig. 1. The semantic security experiment for a threshold decryption scheme $\mathcal{E}$ and an adversary $\mathcal{A}$.

Robustness. Most scenarios call for a *robust* threshold decryption scheme. By that, we mean that a decryption share d_i can be publicly verified, to make sure that it is indeed a valid decryption share of a ciphertext c, originating from party i. Syntactically, the KeyGen algorithm now outputs an additional verification key vk and the Dec algorithm outputs a robustness proof π_i along with the decryption share d_i. We define an additional algorithm, ShareVf$(pk, vk, c, (d_i, \pi_i), i)$, that takes as input the public key pk, the verification key vk, a cipher text c and a decryption share along with the corresponding robustness proof (d_i, π_i) from party i, and the index i of that party. It outputs 0 or 1, denoting whether (d_i, π_i) is a valid decryption share for c for party i. For correctness, we require that ShareVf outputs 1 for an honestly generated share, i.e. ShareVf$(pk, vk, c, (d_i, \pi_i), i) = 1$ for any $(pk, pkc, sk_1, \ldots, sk_n) \xleftarrow{\$} \text{KeyGen}(1^\lambda, n, t), c \xleftarrow{\$} \text{Enc}(pk, m), (d_i, \pi_i) \leftarrow \text{Dec}(sk_i, c)$ for all values of n, t, m, i. We may sometimes implicitly assume that in a robust scheme, each decryption share d_i encodes the party i from which it originated. For security, we require that the threshold decryption scheme satisfies **decryption consistency**. Informally, it means that an adversary cannot produce two different shares $d_i, \hat{d}_i$ with valid robustness proofs for any party i, and any ciphertext c, even if it is given the secret keys for all parties. This is captured by the security game in Fig. 2.

Definition 2.2 (Robustness). *We say that $\mathcal{E}$ satisfies robustness if, for every probabilistic polynomial time adversary $\mathcal{A}$, the following function is negligible in λ:*

$$\mathsf{Adv}^{\mathrm{dc}}_{\mathcal{A},\mathcal{E}}(\lambda) := \Pr\left[\mathbf{DC}_{\mathcal{A},\mathcal{E}}(\lambda) = 1\right]$$

Experiment $\mathbf{DC}_{\mathcal{A},\mathcal{E}}(\lambda)$

1: $\mathcal{J} \leftarrow \emptyset$
2: $(n, t, \mathsf{state}) \leftarrow \mathcal{A}(1^\lambda)$
3: $(pk, pkc, sk_1, \ldots, sk_n, vk) \xleftarrow{\$} \mathsf{KeyGen}(1^\lambda, n, t)$
4: $(c, (d_i, \pi_i), (\hat{d}_i, \hat{\pi}_i), i) \xleftarrow{\$} \mathcal{A}(\mathsf{state}, pk, pkc, sk_1, \ldots, sk_n, vk)$
5: **if** $d_i \neq \hat{d}_i \wedge \mathsf{ShareVf}(pk, vk, c, (d_i, \pi_i), i) = \mathsf{ShareVf}(pk, vk, c, (\hat{d}_i, \hat{\pi}_i), i) = 1$ **then**
6:    **return** 1
7: **else return** 0

Fig. 2. The security game $\mathbf{DC}_{\mathcal{A},\mathcal{E}}(\lambda)$ capturing robustness for a threshold decryption scheme $\mathcal{E}$ and an adversary $\mathcal{A}$.

Looking ahead, our constructions in Sects. 4 and 5 do not explicitly provide robustness (since this is not the focus of this work), but can be made robust using standard techniques. One of our constructions in Sect. 6 relies on a generic threshold decryption scheme, that is robust as per Definition 2.2 above.

KEM vs. Encryption. In certain parts of the paper, we may find it convenient to work with *threshold key-encapsulation mechanisms (KEMs)* rather than threshold decryption schemes. Syntactically, a threshold KEM is defined by the same algorithms as a threshold decryption scheme, but the **encapsulation algorithm Enc** gets only the public key pk (and no message) as input. It outputs a ciphertext c but also a key k from some key space $\mathcal{K} = \mathcal{K}(\lambda)$ induced by the KEM. Accordingly, Combine outputs a key k' from the key space, rather than a message. Correctness requires that there exists a negligible function $\mathsf{negl}(\lambda)$ of the security parameter, such that, for all $\lambda \in \mathbb{N}$, all $0 < t < n$, and all t-sized subsets $\mathcal{J}$ of $[n]$ it holds that

$$\Pr\left[k' = k \; \middle| \; \begin{array}{c} (pk, pkc, sk_1, \ldots, sk_n) \xleftarrow{\$} \mathsf{KeyGen}(1^\lambda, n, t) \\ (c, k) \xleftarrow{\$} \mathsf{Enc}(pk) \\ d_i \leftarrow \mathsf{Dec}(sk_i, c) \text{ for } i \in \mathcal{J} \\ k' \leftarrow \mathsf{Combine}(pkc, c, \mathcal{J}, \{d_i\}_{i \in \mathcal{J}}) \end{array}\right] \geq 1 - \mathsf{negl}(\lambda).$$

Semantic security is defined similarly to that of threshold decryption with the following changes to the **IND-CPA**$_{\mathcal{A},\mathcal{E}}(\lambda)$ experiment: the adversary $\mathcal{A}$ now does not choose messages (m_0, m_1). Instead, Enc outputs a key k together with c. If $b = 1$, then when $\mathcal{A}$ is given the ciphertext c, it is also given the key k. If $b = 0$, then $\mathcal{A}$ is given a uniformly random key k' in the key space $\mathcal{K}$.

3 Tracing Large Traitor Coalitions

In this section, we define traitor tracing for threshold KEM schemes, in the setting where the number f of corruptions is greater than the threshold t.

A traitor tracing threshold KEM (TTT-KEM for short) is a threshold KEM (recall Sect. 2) with the following modifications:

- KeyGen($1^\lambda, n, t, 1^{1/\epsilon}$) → ($pk, pkc, sk_1, \ldots, sk_n, \boldsymbol{tk}$) now also takes in an error parameter $\epsilon = \epsilon(\lambda)$ and outputs an additional tracing key tk.
- There is an additional PPT **tracing algorithm** Trace that is invoked as $\mathcal{J} \xleftarrow{\$} \mathsf{Trace}^{D(\cdot)}(pk, tk, 1^{1/\epsilon})$. The algorithm takes as input the public key pk, the tracing key tk, and an error bound $\epsilon = \epsilon(\lambda)$. Trace also has oracle access to a "decoder" algorithm D. It outputs a subset $\mathcal{J} \subseteq [n]$.

Informally, if the decoder D, given a ciphertext c, can learn any information about the encapsulated key, then Trace traces D back to a party from the coalition that "manufactured" it. The following definition captures this property using the security experiment in Fig. 3.

Experiment **ExpTrace**$_{\mathcal{A},\mathcal{E},\epsilon}(\lambda)$

1: $\mathcal{J} \leftarrow \emptyset$
2: $(n, t, \mathsf{state}) \leftarrow \mathcal{A}(1^\lambda)$
3: $(pk, pkc, sk_1, \ldots, sk_n, tk) \xleftarrow{\$} \mathsf{KeyGen}(1^\lambda, n, t, 1^{1/\epsilon(\lambda)})$
4: $D \xleftarrow{\$} \mathcal{A}^{\mathsf{corrupt}(\cdot)}(\mathsf{state}, pk, pkc)$ // output a decoder alg. D
5: $\mathcal{J}' \xleftarrow{\$} \mathsf{Trace}^{D(\cdot)}(pk, tk, 1^{1/\epsilon(\lambda)})$ // trace decoder
6: **return** $(pk, D, \mathcal{J}, \mathcal{J}')$

Fig. 3. The tracing experiment for a threshold KEM $\mathcal{E}$ and an adversary $\mathcal{A}$. The corruption oracle corrupt($\cdot$) is defined as in Fig. 1.

Definition 3.1. *Let* $\epsilon = \epsilon(\lambda)$ *and* $\delta = \delta(\lambda)$ *be functions of the security parameter* $\lambda \in \mathbb{N}$. *A traitor-tracing threshold KEM* $\mathcal{E} =$ (KeyGen, Enc, Dec, Combine, Trace) *with key space* $\mathcal{K} = \{\mathcal{K}_\lambda\}$ *is* (ϵ, δ)-*secure if for every* PPT *adversary* $\mathcal{A}$ *and for every* $\lambda \in \mathbb{N}$, *the following two conditions hold*

$$\Pr[\mathsf{GoodTr}] \geq \Pr[\mathsf{GoodDec}] - \delta(\lambda) \quad \text{and} \quad \Pr[\mathsf{BadTr}] \leq \delta(\lambda)$$

where $(pk, D, \mathcal{J}, \mathcal{J}') \xleftarrow{\$} \mathbf{ExpTrace}_{\mathcal{A},\mathcal{E},\epsilon}(\lambda)$ *as defined in Fig. 3. The events* GoodDec, GoodTr, *and* BadTr *are defined as follows:*

- GoodDec *occurs when* $P(D) \geq 1/2 + \epsilon(\lambda)$, *where* $P(D)$ *is defined by*

$$P(D) := \Pr\big[D(c, k_b) = b \ : \ (c, k_0) \xleftarrow{\$} \mathsf{Enc}(pk), \ k_1 \xleftarrow{\$} \mathcal{K}(\lambda), \ b \xleftarrow{\$} \{0,1\}\big].$$

- GoodTr *holds when* $\mathcal{J}' \neq \emptyset$ *and* $\mathcal{J}' \subseteq \mathcal{J}$.
- BadTr *holds when* $\mathcal{J}' \neq \emptyset$ *and* $\mathcal{J}' \not\subseteq \mathcal{J}$.

We say that $\mathcal{E}$ *is secure if there exists a negligible function* $\nu = \nu(\lambda)$ *such that* $\mathcal{E}$ *is* $(1/p, \nu)$-*secure for every polynomial* $p = p(\lambda)$. *For an adversary* $\mathcal{A}$ *and a TTT-KEM scheme* $\mathcal{E}$, *we define*

$$\mathsf{Adv}^{\mathsf{tt}}_{\mathcal{A}_1, \mathcal{TTTE}}(\lambda) := \max\big\{\Pr[\mathsf{GoodDec} = 1] - \Pr[\mathsf{GoodTr} = 1], \ \Pr[\mathsf{BadTr} = 1]\big\}.$$

Semantic security and robustness for TTT-KEM schemes are defined as in Sect. 2, but the adversary is also given the tracing key tk in both experiments. In case the TTT-KEM is robust, then in the **ExpTrace**, the adversary is also given the share verification key vk.

Secret Tracing Key. Note that in our definition of tracing security, the tracing key is kept secret from the adversary. This is because, for our constructions, knowledge of this key can allow the adversary to evade tracing. But, semantic security is preserved even against adversaries with access to this key. We discuss this in more detail in Sect. 7.

On "Thresholdizing" Traitor Tracing Schemes. Definition 3.1 is a strict generalization of standard traitor tracing schemes for non-threshold KEM or public key encryption. In particular, setting the threshold $t = 1$ gives the traitor tracing definition for non-threshold schemes. This suggests that TTT-KEMs are harder to construct than standard traitor tracing schemes.

Existing Approaches for Traitor Tracing. Given the above, a natural avenue to realize the notion of TTT-KEM is to try and "thresholdize" existing traitor tracing schemes. We briefly survey some prominent schemes that might serve as the basis for TTT-KEM constructions:[1] Starting with the work of Boneh, Sahai, and Waters [18] (BSW hereinafter), most efficient constructions of traitor tracing go through variants of a notion called **Private Linear Broadcast Encryption (PLBE)**. Since the work of BSW, there have been many works constructing pairing-based PLBE or variants thereof [22,33,60], constructions of PLBE from lattices [26,35], and a construction from indistinguishability obfuscation [23]. Zhandry [61] recently constructed a pairing-based traitor tracing scheme that deviates from the PLBE framework considerably, but still relies on the general idea of a broadcast system with private revocation.

A completely different approach to traitor tracing was suggested by Boneh and Naor [14] and Billet and Phan [6], utilizing **fingerprinting codes** [19].

---

[1] We focus here on schemes that offer *full* collusion resistance, as in our definition. Other constructions focus on defending against more restricted traitor coalitions whose size is a-priori bounded.

Using such codes, they showed how to construct a traitor tracing scheme with constant-size ciphertexts from any public key encryption scheme. Zhandry [61] observed that by replacing the underlying public-key encryption scheme with an identity-based encryption (IBE) scheme, the public-key size is reduced to constant size.

From Traitor Tracing to TTT-KEM. Converting the above schemes to a TTT-KEM is harder than might first appear. The traditional route of converting a cryptosystem into a threshold variant of itself is by secret-sharing some secret key material among all parties. This approach seems to be at odds with the traitor tracing task: in such transformations, a coalition of $f \geq t$ corrupted parties can typically reconstruct the secret key of all other parties, and hence can also frame any innocent party. More generally, to allow tracing, traitor-tracing schemes need to guarantee some sort of (computational) independence among the parties' keys. This independence needs to be preserved even given more than t secret keys, which seems to go against the traditional thresholdizing via secret-sharing paradigm. Different traitor-tracing schemes employ different algebraic or combinatorial mechanisms to ensure this independence among keys, and so different insights may be necessary in order to convert them into TTT-KEMs. In this paper, we initiate this endeavor by constructing a TTT-KEM starting from a traitor tracing scheme based on fingerprinting codes [6,14]. Future work may do the same for other traitor tracing schemes, such as algebraic PLBE-based schemes, but this will require very different techniques.

Tracing vs. Semantic Security. In the context of *non-threshold* traitor tracing, Zhandry [61] recently observed that any scheme that provides tracing vis-à-vis a definition similar to Definition 3.1, automatically provides semantic security as well. In other words, an adversary that breaks semantic security can be used to break the tracing guarantee. Consider a successful adversary breaking the semantic security of a KEM with an advantage of at least 2ϵ for some non-negligible ϵ. Then the state of this adversary after observing the public key pk can be seen as a decoder. With non-negligible probability, this decoder will have an advantage of at least ϵ in distinguishing real keys from random, and so the event GoodDec occurs with non-negligible probability. However, the semantic security adversary has corrupted no one! Hence, the event GoodTr occurs with probability 0. This breaks the tracing definition.

In the threshold setting, however, this is no longer the case. The reason is that the semantic security adversary *can* corrupt up to $t-1$ parties. Hence, GoodTr can occur with strictly positive probability. As a toy example, say that we have a traitor-tracing threshold KEM $\mathcal{E}$ that satisfies both tracing security and semantic security. Consider a new (flawed) scheme $\mathcal{E}'$ that on threshold t instantiates $\mathcal{E}$ on threshold $t' < t$. $\mathcal{E}'$ inherits the tracing security of $\mathcal{E}$, but it is not semantically secure: an adversary in possession of $t' < t$ keys can decrypt any ciphertext. This shows that for threshold KEM, tracing security does not imply semantic security.

Knowing ϵ in Advance. Note that our definition requires that KeyGen gets a lower bound on the decoder's success probability ϵ. Naor and Pinkas [43] refer to such schemes as "threshold traitor tracing" schemes (not to be confused with our notion of TTT-KEM). The Boneh and Naor traitor tracing scheme is a threshold traitor tracing scheme in this sense, and hence our construction in Sect. 4 will also share the same property. For scenarios in which this assumption may be unwanted, Zhandry [61] presented a general compiler that transforms any threshold traitor tracing scheme to a non-threshold one, without changing the dependency of the scheme's parameters on the number n of parties. His compilation carries over to our setting.

4 Traitor Tracing from Bipartite Threshold KEM

In this section, we construct a traitor tracing threshold KEM scheme. We begin with a brief overview.

Overview of the Construction. The starting point of our construction is the (non-threshold) traitor tracing PKE scheme of Boneh and Naor [14] and Billet and Phan [6]. Their construction relies on a primitive called *fingerprinting codes* [20,58]. A (binary) fingerprinting code is a set of words $\Gamma = \{\bar{w}^{(1)}, \ldots, \bar{w}^{(n)}\}$, where each $\bar{w}^{(j)}$ is an ℓ-bit string. What makes fingerprinting codes special is that they come equipped with a tracing algorithm Trace that has the following functionality. Say that an adversary is in possession of a subset $W \subseteq \Gamma$ of words, and it comes up with a word $\bar{w}$. It can decide on $\bar{w}$ as it pleases but there is a stipulation: $\bar{w}$ has to be constructable by mixing and matching the bits of the words in W. That is, if for some index i, the ith bit of all words in W is 0, then the ith bit of $\bar{w}$ must be 0 as well (and similarly if the ith bit of all words is 1). Call such a word *feasible* for W. The guarantee of fingerprinting codes is that Trace can trace $\bar{w}$ back to least one of the words in W.

Equipped with such a code Γ, Boneh and Naor constructed a traitor tracing scheme from any public key encryption scheme $\mathcal{E}$. The idea is to generate 2ℓ key pairs for $\mathcal{E}$, where ℓ is the length of the words in Γ. The public key consists of all 2ℓ public keys, and can be seen as a matrix with ℓ rows and two columns in which jth row is $(pk_{j,0}, pk_{j,1})$ for $j = 1, \ldots, \ell$. Denote the secret key associated with these public keys by $(sk_{j,0}, sk_{j,1})$. To decide on the secret keys, Boneh and Naor associate the ith party with the ith word in the code, $\bar{w}^{(i)}$. The secret key of party i is then $(sk_{1,w_1^{(i)}}, \ldots, sk_{\ell,w_\ell^{(i)}})$ where $\bar{w}^{(i)} = w_1^{(i)} \ldots w_\ell^{(i)}$. To encrypt a message m, one chooses a random index $j \xleftarrow{\$} [\ell]$, and encrypts m under both $pk_{j,0}$ and $pk_{j,1}$ to obtain to ciphertexts c_0 and c_1. The final ciphertext is $c = (j, c_0, c_1)$. Note that any party with a secret key can decrypt either c_0 or c_1.

Tracing relies on the observation that, thanks to the semantic security of $\mathcal{E}$, a coalition of parties holding only $sk_{j,0}$ cannot distinguish between an honestly generated ciphertext (c_0, c_1) and a ciphertext (c_0, c_1') where c_1 is an encryption to some random message m'. The same goes for a coalition holding only $sk_{j,1}$. This observation can be used to extract a word $\bar{w}^*(D)$ from a pirate decoder

D with the property that $\bar{w}^*(D)$ is feasible for the set of words associated with the corrupted coalition. Hence, we can rely on the tracing algorithm of the fingerprinting code to trace D back to one of the corrupted parties.

Now let us try and extend the approach of Boneh and Naor to the threshold setting. A naive attempt would be to replace the use of the public key encryption $\mathcal{E}$ with a threshold decrpyion scheme. Immediately, we can see that this approach runs into a correctness issue. The problem is this: say that a coalition of t parties wants to decrypt some ciphertext $c = (j, c_0, c_1)$. It may very well be the case that some parties can compute decryption shares for c_0 and others can compute decryption shares for c_1. These decryption shares do not match and hence do not allow the decryption of c.

It turns out that what we need is a new kind of threshold decryption that we call "bipartite threshold decryption". Loosely speaking, we can think of bipartite threshold decryption as having two-sided ciphertexts (c_0, c_1), and each party is given a secret key that can decrypt either c_0 or c_1. Moreover, it should satisfy two seemingly contradicting requirements:

- **One-sided security:** An adversary that holds only keys that can partially decrypt c_0 should not be able to distinguish between an honestly generated ciphertext (c_0, c_1) and a ciphertext (c_0, c_1') where c_1 is an encryption to some random message m' (an analogous condition should hold if the adversary can only partially decrypt c_1). This property, which we call *one-sided security*, is necessary for the tracing argument to go through and it is satisfied by the naive construction above. Informally speaking, one-sided security implies that c_0 and c_1 must be **computationally independent** from the standpoint of such an adversary.
- **Two-sided correctness:** Still, any coalition holding t secret keys must be able to decrypt c to recover the encrypted message. This should hold regardless of how many of these keys can decrypt c_0 and how many can decrypt c_1. This condition, which we call *two-sided correctness*, is necessary for correctness to hold, and it implies that conditioned on the public key, c_0 and c_1 **must be correlated** somehow. This condition *is not met* by the naive construction.

We formally define bipartite encryption in Sect. 4.1, where for convenience, we focus on KEM rather than PKE. The formal definition addresses several technical aspects that are ignored in this informal overview. In Sect. 4.2 we construct a traitor tracing scheme for threshold KEM from such a bipartite threshold KEM and fingerprinting codes and prove its security. In our case, the correlation that must be introduced between the two parts of the ciphertext introduces some subtleties to the security proofs that were not covered in this overview.

In Sect. 5 we show that even though our requirements of bipartite threshold KEM might seem contradictory at first glance, they *can* be constructed and even efficiently. First, we formally define the building blocks for our traitor tracing scheme.

4.1 Building Blocks

Our construction of a traitor tracing threshold KEM, a TTT-KEM, relies on two building blocks: a collusion resistant fingerprinting code [20,58] and a new notion we call a bipartite threshold KEM. We explain each in turn.

Collusion Resistant Fingerprinting Codes. Originally, collusion-resistant fingerprinting codes (or fingerprinting codes for short) were introduced for fingerprinting digital content [20,58] but they have found applications to traitor tracing as well (e.g., [14,27,39]). In order to present fingerprinting codes, we first introduce some notation. A word $\bar{w} \in \{0,1\}^\ell$ is a binary string, and we use w_i to denote the ith letter of $\bar{w}$ for $i = 1, \ldots, \ell$; that is $\bar{w} = w_1 w_2 \ldots w_\ell$. A *noisy word* is a ternary string $\bar{w} \in \{0, 1, \text{'?'}\}^\ell$, and we similarly write $\bar{w} = w_1 w_2 \ldots w_\ell$ where each w_i is in $\{0, 1, \text{'?'}\}$.

Let $W = \{\bar{w}^{(1)}, \ldots, \bar{w}^{(f)}\}$ be a set of words in $\{0,1\}^\ell$. We say that a noisy word $\bar{w}^*$ is feasible for W if for all $i \in [\ell]$, either $w_i = \text{'?'}$ or there is a $j \in [f]$ such that $w_i^* = w_i^{(j)}$. That is, if all the words in W have 0 as their ith bit, then $\bar{w}^*$ must have either 0 or '?' in its ith bit as well (the analogous condition should for 1). For example, if $W = \{00110, 10100\}$, then the words that are feasible for W are $00100, 00110, 10100, 10110$ and any word obtained from any of these four by replacing a subset of the bits with '?'. For a set W of words, the *feasible set* for W, denoted $F(W)$, is the set of all noisy words feasible for W. For $\delta \in [0, 1]$, we say that a word is δ-noisy if at most a δ-fraction of its characters is '?', and for a set W of words we denote $F_\delta(W) = \{\bar{w} \in F(W) : \bar{w} \text{ is } \delta\text{-noisy}\}$.

Formally, a **fingerprinting code** is a pair $\mathcal{C} = (\mathsf{FCGen}, \mathsf{FCTrace})$ of algorithms:

- $\mathsf{FCGen}(1^n, \epsilon, \delta) \to (\Gamma, tk)$ is the probabilistic **code generation algorithm**. It takes in a number $n > 0$ of words, a security parameter ϵ, and a noise bound δ. It outputs a code Γ, which is a set of n words in $\{0,1\}^\ell$, and a tracing key tk. The length ℓ of the code words is a function $\ell = \ell(n, \epsilon, \delta)$ of the code size n, the security parameter ϵ, and the noise bound δ.
- $\mathsf{FCTrace}(\bar{w}^*, tk) \to S$ is the deterministic **tracing algorithm**. It takes as input a noisy word $\bar{w}^*$ and the tracing key tk, and outputs a subset S of $[n]$.

The security property of fingerprinting codes says that if an adversary in possession of a subset $W \subseteq \Gamma$ of codewords generates a δ-noisy word $\bar{w}^*$ which is feasible for W (that is, $\bar{w}^* \in F_\delta(W)$), then $\mathsf{FCTrace}(\bar{w}^*, tk)$ outputs a set S that corresponds to a non-empty subset of W. This is formally captured by the security game in Fig. 4, which is parameterized by n, ϵ, δ, and the subset $\mathcal{I}$ of indices that defines the subset W of words given to the adversary.

Definition 4.1. *A fingerprinting code $\mathcal{C}$ is said to be **fully collusion resistant** if for all algorithms $\mathcal{A}$, all $n > 0$, all $\epsilon \in (0,1]$, all $\delta \in [0,1]$, and all subsets $\mathcal{I} \subseteq [n]$ it holds that*

$$\mathsf{Adv}^{\mathsf{cr}}_{\mathcal{A},\mathcal{C}}(n, \mathcal{I}, \epsilon, \delta) := \Pr[\mathbf{ExpFC}_{\mathcal{A},\mathcal{C}}(n, \mathcal{I}, \epsilon, \delta) = 1] < \epsilon.$$

332   D. Boneh et al.

Experiment ExpFC$_{\mathcal{A},\mathcal{C}}(n, \mathcal{I}, \epsilon, \delta)$

1: $(\Gamma, tk) \xleftarrow{\$} \mathsf{FCGen}(1^n, \epsilon, \delta)$ // write $\Gamma = \{\bar{w}^{(1)}, \ldots, \bar{w}^{(n)}\}$
2: $W \leftarrow \{\bar{w}^{(i)}\}_{i \in \mathcal{I}}$
3: $\bar{w}^* \xleftarrow{\$} \mathcal{A}(W)$
4: **if** $\bar{w}^* \notin F_\delta(W)$ **then return** 0
5: $S \leftarrow \mathsf{FCTrace}(\bar{w}^*, tk)$
6: **if** $S = \emptyset \lor S \not\subseteq \mathcal{I}$ **then return** 1 **else return** 0

Fig. 4. The security experiment for a fingerprinting code $\mathcal{C}$ and an adversary $\mathcal{A}$. The integer n indicates the number of words in the code, the subset $\mathcal{I} \subseteq [n]$ the set of corrupted codewords, the parameter $\epsilon \in [0, 1]$ specifies the desired error bound on the tracing success, and $\delta \in [0, 1]$ the fraction of unknown ('?') locations.

Known Constructions. The fingerprinting codes we use, that allow for tracing even in the presence of a bounded fraction of unknown bits (represented by '?' symbols), are called *robust* fingerprinting codes. These were originally introduced by Boneh and Naor [14], who constructed the first such codes based on Boneh-Shaw codes [19]. Their construction achieved codewords of length $O(n^4 \log(n/\epsilon) \log(1/\epsilon)/(1-\delta)^2)$, where n is the number of words in the code, ϵ is the tracing error, and δ is an upper bound on the fraction of '?' in the noisy word that is given to the tracing algorithm. This was later improved by Nuida [46] and by Boneh, Kiayias, and Montgomery [13]. The latter work is based on Tardos codes [58] and enjoys codewords of length $O((n \log n)^2 \log(n/\epsilon)/(1-\delta))$. This is optimal up to logarithmic factors.

Bipartite Threshold KEM. The second building block that we will use is a new notion that we put forth, called a **bipartite threshold KEM** scheme, or a BT-KEM scheme for short. A BT-KEM scheme is a threshold KEM scheme, where instead of one set of secret keys, there are 2ℓ sets, for a parameter ℓ of the scheme. We think of these keys as arranged in 2ℓ rows, or "positions", and in each position, there are two possible secret keys for each party: a *left* key and a *right* key. Similarly, a ciphertext is now comprised of two parts: a left ciphertext and a right ciphertext. A BT-KEM should satisfy two properties: one-sided security and two-sided correctness.

Formally, A BT-KEM is a tuple (KeyGen, Enc, Dec, Combine) of algorithms with the following syntax:

- KeyGen$(1^\lambda, n, t, \ell) \to (pk, pkc, \{(sk_{1,0}^{(j)}, sk_{1,1}^{(j)}), \ldots, (sk_{n,0}^{(j)}, sk_{n,1}^{(j)})\}_{j \in [\ell]})$ is the probabilistic **key generation algorithm**. It takes in the security parameter $\lambda \in \mathbb{N}$, the number n of decryptors, the threshold t, and a number ℓ of "positions". It outputs a public key pk, a combiner public key pkc, and n secret keys $sk_1, \ldots, sk_n$. Each secret key is made up of 2ℓ keys: $sk_i = \{sk_{i,0}^{(j)}, sk_{i,1}^{(j)}\}_{j \in [\ell]}$

for $i = 1, \ldots, n$. $sk_{i,0}^{(j)}$ is called the left secret key of i at position j and $sk_{i,1}^{(j)}$ is called the right secret key of i at position j.
- $\mathsf{Enc}(pk, j) \to (c_0, c_1, k)$ is the probabilistic **encapsulation algorithm**. It takes as input the public key pk and a position $j \in [\ell]$, and it outputs a ciphertext $c = (c_0, c_1)$ and a key k. c_0 is called the left ciphertext and c_1 is called the right ciphertext.
- $\mathsf{Dec}(j, sk_{i,b}^{(j)}, c = (c_0, c_1)) \to d_i$ is the deterministic **decryption algorithm**. It takes in a decryptor's secret key $sk_{i,b}^{(j)}$—where $i \in [n]$, $j \in [\ell]$, and $b \in \{0, 1\}$—and a ciphertext c, and its output is a decryption share d_i of c under $sk_{i,b}^{(j)}$. To simplify notation, we may assume $sk_{i,b}^{(j)}$ encodes the bit b even if this is not explicitly noted.
- $\mathsf{Combine}(pkc, j, c, \mathcal{J}, \{d_i\}_{i \in \mathcal{J}}) \to k/\bot$ is the deterministic **combiner algorithm**. Its input is a combiner public key pkc, a position $j \in [\ell]$, a ciphertext c, a subset $\mathcal{J}$ of $[n]$, and decryption shares $\{d_i\}_{i \in \mathcal{J}}$. It outputs either a key k or a rejection symbol $\bot$.

Definition 4.2 (correctness). *A BT-KEM scheme $\mathcal{E} = $ (KeyGen, Enc, Dec, Combine) is said to be correct if for every polynomially-bounded functions $n = n(\lambda)$, $t = t(\lambda)$, and $\ell = \ell(\lambda)$ of the security parameter $\lambda \in \mathbb{N}$ the following holds:*
For all $\lambda \in \mathbb{N}$, positions $j \in [\ell]$, subsets $\mathcal{J} \subseteq [n]$ of size $t(\lambda)$, and n-bit strings $s \in \{0, 1\}^n$ it holds that

$$\Pr\left[k = k' : \begin{array}{c} (pk, pkc, \{(sk_{1,0}^{(j)}, sk_{1,1}^{(j)}), \ldots, (sk_{n,0}^{(j)}, sk_{n,1}^{(j)})\}_{j \in [\ell]}) \xleftarrow{\$} \mathsf{KeyGen}(1^\lambda, n, t) \\ (c, k) \xleftarrow{\$} \mathsf{Enc}(pk, j) \\ d_i \leftarrow \mathsf{Dec}(j, sk_{i, s_i}^{(j)}, c) \text{ for } i \in \mathcal{J} \\ k' \leftarrow \mathsf{Combine}(pkc, j, c, \mathcal{J}, \{d_i\}_{i \in \mathcal{J}}) \end{array}\right] = 1.$$

Semantic Security. We require that a BT-KEM scheme satisfies semantic security. Observe that any BT-KEM scheme can be seen as a standard threshold KEM scheme with additional syntactic properties, and so semantic security is already defined in Sect. 2, with the following modifications to the **IND-CPA** security experiment:

- In addition to n and t, the adversary $\mathcal{A}$ also chooses the number ℓ of positions.
- The secret key of party i is made up of all of its 2ℓ secret keys – the left key and the right key of each position. That is,

$$sk_i = ((sk_{i,0}^{(1)}, sk_{i,1}^{(1)}), \ldots, (sk_{i,0}^{(\ell)}, sk_{i,1}^{(\ell)})).$$

- The challenge ciphertext is computed by the challenger by invoking the encapsulation algorithm with respect to a random position in $[\ell]$. That is, the challenger first samples a uniformly random $j \xleftarrow{\$} [\ell]$, and then samples $(c = (c_0, c_1), k) \xleftarrow{\$} \mathsf{Enc}(pk, j)$.

One-Sided Security. In addition, we require that a BT-KEM scheme satisfies "one-sided security" as discussed at the beginning of this section. The security game for one-sided security is given in Fig. 5 and the security notion is formally captured by the following definition.

Definition 4.3. *We say that $\mathcal{E}$ has* one-sided security *if for every probabilistic polynomial time adversary $\mathcal{A}$, the following function is negligible in λ:*

$$\mathsf{Adv}^{\mathrm{oss}}_{\mathcal{A},\mathcal{E}}(\lambda) := \left|2\Pr[\mathbf{ExpBTKEM}_{\mathcal{A},\mathcal{E}}(\lambda) = 1] - 1\right|.$$

Observe that $\mathbf{ExpBTKEM}_{\mathcal{A},\mathcal{E}}(\lambda)$ in Fig. 5 is defined by two cases that are not entirely symmetric. When the adversary chooses $d = 0$, then it receives a key $k^{(0)}$ and a left ciphertext $c_0^{(0)}$ that is consistent with it. Its task is to distinguish between the case in which c_1 given to it is also consistent with $k^{(0)}$ and $c_0^{(0)}$ (that is $c_1 = c_1^{(0)}$), and the case where c_1 is an independent right ciphertext ($c_1 = c_1^{(1)}$). On the other hand, when $d = 1$, the adversary receives a key $k^{(0)}$, and a right ciphertext $c_1^{(1)}$ that is *independent* of this key. Its task is to distinguish between the case in which c_0 is consistent with $k^{(0)}$ (but not with $c_1^{(1)}$; that is $c_0 = c_0^{(0)}$), and the case where c_0 is consistent with $c_1^{(1)}$ (and is independent of $k^{(0)}$; that is $c_0 = c_0^{(1)}$). The reason for the asymmetry between $d = 0$ and $d = 1$ will become apparent in our construction of a traitor tracing threshold KEM from BT-KEM, and its proof of security (Sect. 4.2).

Experiment $\mathbf{ExpBTKEM}_{\mathcal{A},\mathcal{E}}(\lambda)$

1: $(n, t, \ell, u, d, \mathsf{state}) \xleftarrow{\$} \mathcal{A}(1^\lambda)$ // $t \le n$, $u \in [\ell]$, $d \in \{0, 1\}$
2: $(pk, pkc, \{(sk_{1,0}^{(j)}, sk_{1,1}^{(j)}), \ldots, (sk_{n,0}^{(j)}, sk_{n,1}^{(j)})\}_{j \in [\ell]}) \xleftarrow{\$} \mathsf{KeyGen}(1^\lambda, n, t, \ell)$
3: $(c^{(0)} = (c_0^{(0)}, c_1^{(0)}), k^{(0)}) \xleftarrow{\$} \mathsf{Enc}(pk, u)$
4: $(c^{(1)} = (c_0^{(1)}, c_1^{(1)}), k^{(1)}) \xleftarrow{\$} \mathsf{Enc}(pk, u)$
5: $b \xleftarrow{\$} \{0, 1\}$
6: **if** $b = 0$ **then** $c^* \leftarrow (c_0^{(0)}, c_1^{(1)})$ // set c^* to a mixture of $c^{(0)}$ and $c^{(1)}$
7: **if** $b = 1$ **then** $c^* \leftarrow (c_0^{(d)}, c_1^{(d)}) = c^{(d)}$ // set c^* to $c^{(0)}$ or $c^{(1)}$
8: $\vec{sk}_{-u} \leftarrow \{(sk_{1,0}^{(j)}, sk_{1,1}^{(j)}), \ldots, (sk_{n,0}^{(j)}, sk_{n,1}^{(j)})\}_{j \in [\ell] \setminus \{u\}}$
9: $b' \xleftarrow{\$} \mathcal{A}(\mathsf{state}, pk, pkc, c^*, k^{(0)}, \vec{sk}_{-u}, (sk_{1,d}^{(u)}, \ldots, sk_{n,d}^{(u)}))$
10: **return** $(b' = b)$

Fig. 5. The one-sided security experiment for a BT-KEM $\mathcal{E}$ and an adversary $\mathcal{A}$.

4.2 Our Construction of a Traitor Tracing Threshold KEM

Equipped with the above two building blocks, we are now ready to present our construction of a TTT-KEM.

Let $\mathcal{BTE} = (\mathcal{BTE}\text{.KeyGen}, \mathcal{BTE}\text{.Enc}, \mathcal{BTE}\text{.Dec}, \mathcal{BTE}\text{.Combine})$ be a bipartite threshold decryption scheme and let $\mathcal{C} = (\mathcal{C}\text{.FCGen}, \mathcal{C}\text{.FCTrace})$ be a collusion-resistant fingerprinting code. Assume for simplicity that the keys outputted by $\mathcal{BTE}$ are uniformly distributed over its key space $\mathcal{K}$.[2] Our construction uses the following subroutine, TR that takes in a public key pk, an index $j \in [\ell]$, an integer N, and three bits $b_k, b_0, b_1 \in \{0, 1\}$, and has oracle access to a decoder D. The subroutine TR^D is defined as follows:

1. Set $ctr \leftarrow 0$.
2. For $r = 1, \ldots, N$:
   (a) Sample $(c^{(0)} = (c_0^{(0)}, c_1^{(0)}), k^{(0)}) \xleftarrow{\$} \mathcal{BTE}\text{.Enc}(pk, j)$ and $(c^{(1)} = (c_0^{(1)}, c_1^{(1)}), k^{(1)}) \xleftarrow{\$} \mathcal{BTE}\text{.Enc}(pk, j)$.
   (b) Set $c^* \leftarrow (j, c_0^{(b_0)}, c_1^{(b_1)})$.
   (c) Query D on $(c^*, k^{(b_k)})$. If the response is 1, set $ctr \leftarrow ctr + 1$.
3. Return ctr.

Our TTT-KEM scheme, denoted $\mathcal{TTTE}$, is defined in Fig. 6. Tracing is done in two steps. First, the tracing algorithm constructs a word $\bar{w} \in \{0, 1\}^{\ell}$, with the supposed invariant that if the adversary only corrupts parties with left (resp. right) keys in position j, then $w_j = 0$ (resp. $w_j = 1$). Then, it invokes the FCTrace algorithm of the underlying fingerprinting code on $\bar{w}$. Note that there is an asymmetry in the tracing algorithm. To determine whether the adversary has only right keys for a position j (i.e. whether w_j should be 1), we run the decoder with two types of inputs: (a) a random key and a ciphertext valid with respect to this key and (b) a random key with a valid left ciphertext and an invalid (independent) right ciphertext, and check if it can distinguish between them. But the procedure to determine whether to set w_j to 0 is not entirely symmetric. We see if the decoder can distinguish between the following two types of inputs: (a) a random key and invalid left and right ciphertexts, and (b) a random key with a valid left ciphertext and an invalid right ciphertext, i.e. the right ciphertext is invalid in both types of inputs. This asymmetry in the inputs to the decoder for the two cases utilizes the asymmetry in the one-sided security game defined in Fig. 5. The formal argument uses one-sided security to relate the advantage of the adversary in breaking the tracing security of our scheme, to its advantage in breaking the tracing security of an idealized scheme, in which the tracing algorithm depends on the identity of the corrupted parties. The reader is referred to the proof of Theorem 4.4 for more detail.

It is immediate that construction is correct and semantically secure, by the correctness and semantic security of the underlying BT-KEM. The following theorem establishes that it also provides tracing.

---

[2] This assumption will be satisfied by our constructions of BT-KEM schemes. Generally speaking, note that given a BT-KEM scheme not satisfying the assumption, we can always construct a scheme for which this condition *is* satisfied by applying a randomness extractor to the key.

A TTT-KEM scheme $\mathcal{TTTE}$

$\mathcal{TTTE}.\mathsf{KeyGen}(1^\lambda, n, t, 1^{1/\epsilon})$:

1. Set $\delta \leftarrow (1/2 - \epsilon)/(1/2 - 2/\sqrt{\lambda})$ and
   sample a fingerprinting code: $(\Gamma, tk) \xleftarrow{\$} \mathcal{C}.\mathsf{FCGen}(1^n, 2^{-\lambda}, \delta)$.
2. Sample keys for $\mathcal{BTE}$:   // $\ell = \ell(n, \lambda, \epsilon)$ is the word length of the code Γ
   $(pk, pkc, \{(sk_{1,0}^{(j)}, sk_{1,1}^{(j)}), \ldots, (sk_{n,0}^{(j)}, sk_{n,1}^{(j)})\}_{j \in [\ell]}) \xleftarrow{\$} \mathsf{KeyGen}(1^\lambda, n, t, \ell)$.
3. Set $pk' \leftarrow pk$, $pkc' \leftarrow pkc$ and $tk' \leftarrow tk$.
4. For $i = 1, \ldots, n$, set $sk_i' \leftarrow (sk_{i,w_1^{(i)}}^{(1)}, \ldots, sk_{i,w_\ell^{(i)}}^{(\ell)})$
   // $\bar{w}^{(i)}$ is the ith word in the code Γ
5. Return $(pk', pkc', sk_1', \ldots, sk_n', tk')$.

$\mathcal{TTTE}.\mathsf{Enc}(pk)$:

1. Sample $j \xleftarrow{\$} [\ell]$.
2. $(c_0, c_1, k) \xleftarrow{\$} \mathcal{BTE}.\mathsf{Enc}(pk, j)$.
3. Let $c = (j, c_0, c_1)$ and return (c, k).

$\mathcal{TTTE}.\mathsf{Dec}(sk_i, c)$:

1. Parse sk_i as $(sk_{i,w_1^{(i)}}^{(1)}, \ldots, sk_{i,w_\ell^{(i)}}^{(\ell)})$ and c as (j, c_0, c_1).
2. Compute $d_i \leftarrow \mathcal{BTE}.\mathsf{Dec}(j, sk_{i,w_j^{(i)}}^{(j)}, (c_0, c_1))$.
3. Return d_i.

$\mathcal{TTTE}.\mathsf{Combine}(pkc, c, \mathcal{J}, \{d_i\}_{i \in \mathcal{J}})$:

1. Parse c as (j, c_0, c_1) and set $c' \leftarrow (c_0, c_1)$.
2. Compute $k \leftarrow \mathcal{BTE}.\mathsf{Combine}(pkc, j, c', \mathcal{J}, \{d_i\}_{i \in \mathcal{J}})$.
3. Return k.

$\mathcal{TTTE}.\mathsf{Trace}^D(pk, tk, 1^{1/\epsilon})$:

1. Set $N \leftarrow \lambda^2$ and $B \leftarrow \lambda^{3/2}$.
2. For $j = 1, \ldots, \ell$:
   (a) Compute the following:
      − $p_{001} \xleftarrow{\$} \mathsf{TR}^D(pk, j, N, 0, 0, 1)$
         // runs D with a valid left ciphertext and an invalid right ciphertext
      − $p_{100} \xleftarrow{\$} \mathsf{TR}^D(pk, j, N, 1, 0, 0)$
         // runs D with invalid left and right ciphertexts
      − $p_{111} \xleftarrow{\$} \mathsf{TR}^D(pk, j, N, 1, 1, 1)$
         // runs D with valid left and right ciphertexts
   (b) Set $a_0 \leftarrow |p_{001} - p_{100}|$ and $a_1 \leftarrow |p_{001} - p_{111}|$.
   (c) If $a_0 \geq B$, set $w_j \leftarrow 0$. If not, check if $a_1 \geq B$, and if so set $w_j \leftarrow 1$. If both conditions do not hold, set $w_j \leftarrow$ '?'.
3. Run $\mathcal{J} \leftarrow \mathsf{FCGen}.\mathsf{Trace}(tk, \bar{w}^*)$, where $\bar{w}^* \leftarrow w_1 w_2 \ldots w_\ell$.
4. Return $\mathcal{J}$.

Fig. 6. Our TTT-KEM scheme, denoted $\mathcal{TTTE}$, built from a fingerprinting code and a BT-KEM.

Theorem 4.4. *For every probabilistic polynomial time algorithm $\mathcal{A}$ there exists a probabilistic polynomial-time algorithm $\mathcal{B}$ such that*

$$\mathsf{Adv}^{\mathsf{tt}}_{\mathcal{A},\mathcal{TTTE}}(\lambda) \leq 9\ell \cdot 2^{-\lambda/24} + 2\ell\lambda^2 \cdot \mathsf{Adv}^{\mathsf{oss}}_{\mathcal{B},\mathcal{BTE}}(\lambda)$$

for all $\lambda \in \mathbb{N}$, where $\ell = \ell(\lambda, n, \epsilon)$ is the codeword length as defined in the scheme.

We stress that our definition of decoders is much more general than the one originally considered by Boneh and Naor [14]. Whereas they considered tracing decoders that *fully decrypt* with high probability, we consider (in line with more modern definition of traitor tracing) tracing any decoder that can learn any non-trivial information regarding the plaintext (via a semantic security type definition). This on its own poses new technical challenges that require new technical insight in the security proof.

Due to space limitations, the proof of Theorem 4.4 is given in the full version of the paper [16, Sec. 4.2].

5 Constructing Bipartite Threshold KEM

In this section, we construct BT-KEM schemes from various assumptions: the stronger the assumption, the more efficient the BT-KEM construction is, and hence also the resulting TTT-KEM scheme.

Before turning to our efficient constructions, we note that one can fairly easily construct a BT-KEM scheme from any threshold KEM scheme. The construction is rather inefficient, since the keys and the ciphertext scale linearly with the threshold t. We sketch this construction in the full version [16, App. A].

5.1 Constant-Size Ciphertexts from DDH

Although the parameters achieved by the generic construction are non-trivial, it still suffers from long ciphertexts. In this section, we show how to construct a BT-KEM scheme with constant-size ciphertexts by relying on the DDH assumption in cyclic groups. For asymptotic reasoning, we consider a distribution ensemble over such groups. This is formalized by the existence of a group generation algorithm $\mathcal{G}$ that takes the security parameter as input and outputs a triple $(\mathbb{G}, g, p)$, where $\mathbb{G}$ is a description of a group of order p generated by g. The scheme is formally defined in Fig. 7.

Correctness. Let $0 < t < n$ and let $\ell > 0$. Let $\mathcal{J}$ be a subset of size t of $[n]$. Then, for all $j \in [\ell]$, $i \in [n]$, and $\bar{\tau} \in \{0,1\}^n$ it holds that

> **A BT-KEM scheme $\mathcal{BTDDH}$**
>
> **Public parameters:** $(\mathbb{G}, g, p)$ sampled by $\mathcal{G}(1^\lambda)$.
>
> $\mathcal{BTDDH}$.KeyGen$(1^\lambda, n, t, \ell)$:
>
> 1. For $j = 1, \ldots, \ell$ do:
>   (a) Sample $x_j, y_j, z_j \xleftarrow{\$} \mathbb{Z}_p$ and set $X_j \leftarrow g^{x_j}$, $Y_j \leftarrow g^{y_j}$ and $Z_j \leftarrow g^{z_j}$.
>   (b) Sample a Shamir t-out-of-n secret sharing $s_{j,1}, \ldots, s_{j,n}$ of x_j.
>   (c) Set $pk_j \leftarrow (X_j, Y_j, Z_j)$, $sk_{i,0}^{(j)} \leftarrow s_{j,i}/y_j$ and $sk_{i,1}^{(j)} \leftarrow s_{j,i}/z_j$.
> 2. Set $pk \leftarrow (pk_1, \ldots, pk_\ell)$ and $pkc \leftarrow \perp$.
> 3. Return $(pk, pkc, \{(sk_{1,0}^{(j)}, sk_{1,1}^{(j)}), \ldots, (sk_{n,0}^{(j)}, sk_{n,1}^{(j)})\}_{j \in [\ell]})$.
>
> $\mathcal{BTDDH}$.Enc(pk, j):
>
> 1. Parse pk as $(pk_1, \ldots, pk_\ell)$ and pk_j as (X_j, Y_j, Z_j).
> 2. Sample $r \xleftarrow{\$} \mathbb{Z}_p$ and set $k \leftarrow X_j^r$.
> 3. Compute $c_0 \leftarrow Y_j^r$ and $c_1 \leftarrow Z_j^r$ and set $c \leftarrow (c_0, c_1)$.
> 4. Return (c, k).
>
> $\mathcal{BTDDH}$.Dec$(j, sk_{i,b}^{(j)}, c = (c_0, c_1))$:
>
> 1. Compute $d_i \leftarrow c_b^{sk_{i,b}^{(j)}}$. Observe that $d_i = g^{s_{j,i} r}$.
> 2. Return d_i.
>
> $\mathcal{BTDDH}$.Combine$(pkc, j, c, \mathcal{J}, \{d_i\}_{i \in \mathcal{J}})$:
>
> 1. Compute the Lagrange coefficients $(\lambda_i^\mathcal{J})_{i \in \mathcal{J}}$ for the subset $\mathcal{J}$:
> $\lambda_i^\mathcal{J} \leftarrow \prod_{v \in \mathcal{J} \setminus \{i\}} \frac{v}{v-i} \in \mathbb{Z}_p$.
> 2. Compute $k \leftarrow \prod_{i \in \mathcal{J}} d_i^{\lambda_i^\mathcal{J}}$.
> 3. Return k.

Fig. 7. Our BT-KEM in cyclic groups, denoted $\mathcal{BTDDH}$.

$$\prod_{i \in \mathcal{J}} d_i^{\lambda_i^\mathcal{J}} = \prod_{i \in \mathcal{J}, \tau_i = 0} d_i^{\lambda_i^\mathcal{J}} \cdot \prod_{i \in \mathcal{J}, \tau_i = 1} d_i^{\lambda_i^\mathcal{J}}$$

$$= \prod_{i \in \mathcal{J}, \tau_i = 0} (Y_j^r)^{s_{j,i} \lambda_i^\mathcal{J} / y_j} \cdot \prod_{i \in \mathcal{J}, \tau_i = 1} (Z_j^r)^{s_{j,i} \lambda_i^\mathcal{J} / z_j}$$

$$= \prod_{i \in \mathcal{J}, \tau_i = 0} (g^{y_j r})^{s_{j,i} \lambda_i^\mathcal{J} / y_j} \cdot \prod_{i \in \mathcal{J}, \tau_i = 1} (g^{z_j r})^{s_{j,i} \lambda_i^\mathcal{J} / z_j}$$

$$= \prod_{i \in \mathcal{J}} (g^r)^{\lambda_i^\mathcal{J} s_{j,i}} = g^{r \cdot \sum_{i \in \mathcal{J}} \lambda_i^\mathcal{J} s_{j,i}} = g^{x_j r} = X_j^r = k.$$

And so every subset of t parties can decapsulate the correct key k, regardless of how many left keys and how many right keys there are.

One-Sided Security. The one-sided security of the scheme is based on the hardness of the following formulation of the Decisional Diffie-Hellman (DDH) problem relative to $\mathcal{G}$.

Definition 5.1. *Let $\mathcal{G}$ be a group generation algorithm. We say that the Decisional Diffie-Hellman (DDH) problem is hard relative to $\mathcal{G}$ if for every probabilistic polynomial-time algorithm $\mathcal{A}$, the following function*

$$\mathsf{Adv}^{\mathsf{ddh}}_{\mathcal{A},\mathcal{G}}(\lambda) := \left| \Pr\left[\mathcal{A}(\mathbb{G}, p, g, \vec{h}, g^{xy}) = 1\right] - \Pr\left[\mathcal{A}(\mathbb{G}, p, g, \vec{h}, g^{xy'}) = 1\right] \right|$$

is negligible in $\lambda \in \mathbb{N}$, where $(\mathbb{G}, p, g) \xleftarrow{\$} \mathcal{G}(1^\lambda)$ and $\vec{h} = (g^x, g^y, g^{y'})$ for $x, y, y' \xleftarrow{\$} \mathbb{Z}_p$.

Note that this is not the standard formulation of the DDH assumption, but is easily reducible to it.

Theorem 5.2. *For every probabilistic polynomial-time adversary $\mathcal{A}$ there exists a probabilistic polynomial-time adversary $\mathcal{B}$ such that*

$$\mathsf{Adv}^{\mathsf{ddh}}_{\mathcal{B},\mathcal{G}}(\lambda) = \mathsf{Adv}^{\mathsf{oss}}_{\mathcal{A},\mathcal{BTDDH}}(\lambda)$$

for all $\lambda \in \mathbb{N}$.

The proof of Theorem 5.2 can be found in the full version of the paper [16, Sec. 5.1].

Semantic Security. We now argue the semantic security of the scheme, which is also based on the DDH assumption. Here, we rely on the standard formulation of the DDH assumption: given $g^\alpha, g^\beta, g^\gamma$ for $\alpha, \beta \xleftarrow{\$} \mathbb{Z}_p$, it should be hard to distinguish between the case where $\gamma = \alpha\beta$ and γ being uniformly random and independent of (α, β).

Theorem 5.3. *For every probabilistic polynomial-time adversary $\mathcal{A}$ there exists a probabilistic polynomial-time adversary $\mathcal{B}$ such that*

$$\mathsf{Adv}^{\mathsf{ddh}}_{\mathcal{B},\mathcal{G}}(\lambda) = \mathsf{Adv}^{\mathsf{cpa}}_{\mathcal{A},\mathcal{BTDDH}}(\lambda)$$

for all $\lambda \in \mathbb{N}$.

The proof of Theorem 5.3 is in the full version [16].

5.2 Constant-Size Ciphertexts and Public Keys from Pairings

In this section, we show that by relying on pairings, one can obtain a BT-KEM scheme with a constant-size public key, in addition to a constant-size ciphertext.

Formally, we consider a bilinear group generation algorithm $\mathcal{G}$ that takes in the security parameter and outputs a tuple $(\mathbb{G}_1, \mathbb{G}_2, \mathbb{G}_T, e, g_1, g_2, p)$, where $\mathbb{G}_1, \mathbb{G}_2, \mathbb{G}_T$ are descriptions of cyclic groups of order p, where $\mathbb{G}_b$ is generated by g_b for $b = 0, 1$. The function e is an efficiently computable non-degenerate bilinear map from $\mathbb{G}_1 \times \mathbb{G}_2$ to $\mathbb{G}_T$. Though we will present our construction in asymmetric bilinear groups (in which $\mathbb{G}_1$ and $\mathbb{G}_2$ may be different), it remains secure in symmetric groups as well (under the same assumptions in symmetric bilinear groups, when $\mathbb{G}_1 = \mathbb{G}_2$ and $g_1 = g_2$). The construction also uses two hash function $H_1 : \mathbb{N} \to \mathbb{G}_1$ and $H_2 : \mathbb{G}_T \to \{0,1\}^\lambda$. Formally, H_1 and H_2 should depend on the specific bilinear group, but to simplify the notation we fix a single pair of functions H_1, H_2 for all groups.

The scheme is presented in Fig. 8. We next prove correctness and security of this scheme.

Correctness. Let $0 < t < n$ and let $\ell > 0$. As noted in Fig. 8, for a ciphertext with respect to position $j \in [\ell]$, the decryption share d_i of party $i \in [n]$ is $d_i = e(g_1, g_2)^{s_i y z r}$, regardless of whether party i has a left key or a right key for position j. Hence, by the correctness of Lagrange interpolation, it holds that for any subset $\mathcal{J}$ of parties of size at least t, the combined decryption is $e(g_1, g_2)^{\alpha y z r}$, and it's hash is precisely the encapsulated key.

One-Sided Security. We now prove the one-sided security of $\mathcal{BTBF}$. One-sided security follows from the following DDH-like assumption.

Definition 5.4. *Let $\mathcal{G}$ be a bilinear group generation algorithm. We say that the Augmented Decisional Diffie-Hellman problem (ADDH) is hard relative to the source group of $\mathcal{G}$ if for every probabilistic polynomial-time algorithm $\mathcal{A}$ the following function*

$$\mathsf{Adv}^{\mathrm{addh}}_{\mathcal{A},\mathcal{G}}(\lambda) := \left| \begin{array}{l} \Pr\left[\mathcal{A}((\mathbb{G}_1, \mathbb{G}_2, \mathbb{G}_T, e, p), \vec{h}, g_1^{zr+wt}) = 1\right] \\ - \Pr\left[\mathcal{A}((\mathbb{G}_1, \mathbb{G}_2, \mathbb{G}_T, e, p), \vec{h}, g_1^{zr'+wt}) = 1\right] \end{array} \right|$$

is negligible in $\lambda \in \mathbb{N}$, where $(\mathbb{G}_1, \mathbb{G}_2, \mathbb{G}_T, e, g_1, g_2, p) \xleftarrow{\$} \mathcal{G}(1^\lambda)$ and

$$\vec{h} = \left(g_1, g_2, g_1^w, g_1^z, g_1^y, g_1^{yz}, g_1^{yr}, g_1^{wz}, g_2^z, g_2^y, g_2^t, e(g_1, g_2)^{yzr'}\right)$$

for $y, z, w, t, r, r' \xleftarrow{\$} \mathbb{Z}_p$.

The ADDH problem defined above can be seen as a special case of the Uber problem in bilinear groups [8,24]. Also note that there is no trivial zero-test involving the "target element", g_1^{zr+wt} or $g_1^{zr'+wt}$, that can be trivially computed via group operations and the pairing operation from the other input elements, namely the elements in $\vec{h}$. Therefore, the ADDH problem is hard in the generic group model [8,54] and its hardness is reducible to that of the standard discrete log problem in the (decisional) algebraic group model [3,32,51,52].

The following theorem reduces the one-sided security of $\mathcal{BTBF}$ to the hardness of ADDH in the pairing groups.

A BT-KEM scheme $\mathcal{BTBF}$

Public parameters: $(\mathbb{G}_1, \mathbb{G}_2, \mathbb{G}_T, e, g_1, g_2, p)$ sampled by $\mathcal{G}(1^\lambda)$.

$\mathcal{BTBF}$.KeyGen($1^\lambda, n, t, \ell$):

1. Sample $\alpha, y, z \xleftarrow{\$} \mathbb{Z}_p$ and set $X \leftarrow g_1^{\alpha y z}$, $Y \leftarrow g_1^y$, and $Z \leftarrow g_1^z$.
2. The public key is $\mathsf{pk} \leftarrow (X, Y, Z)$ and $pkc \leftarrow \bot$.
3. Sample a Shamir t-out-of-n secret sharing $s_1, \ldots, s_n$ of $\alpha \in \mathbb{Z}_p$.
4. For $i = 1, \ldots, n$ and $j = 1, \ldots, \ell$ set:

$$k_0^{(0)} \leftarrow H_1(j)^{zs_i}, \quad k_1^{(0)} \leftarrow g_2^{zs_i}, \quad \mathsf{sk}_{i,0}^{(j)} \leftarrow (k_0^{(0)}, k_1^{(0)}) \in \mathbb{G}_1 \times \mathbb{G}_2$$
$$k_0^{(1)} \leftarrow H_1(j)^{ys_i}, \quad k_1^{(1)} \leftarrow g_2^{ys_i}, \quad \mathsf{sk}_{i,1}^{(j)} \leftarrow (k_0^{(1)}, k_1^{(1)}) \in \mathbb{G}_1 \times \mathbb{G}_2$$

5. Return $(\mathsf{pk}, pkc, \{(\mathsf{sk}_{1,0}^{(j)}, \mathsf{sk}_{1,1}^{(j)}), \ldots, (\mathsf{sk}_{n,0}^{(j)}, \mathsf{sk}_{n,1}^{(j)})\}_{j \in [\ell]})$.

$\mathcal{BTBF}$.Enc(pk, j):

1. Parse pk as (X, Y, Z).
2. Sample $r, t_0, t_1 \xleftarrow{\$} \mathbb{Z}_p$.
3. Set $W \leftarrow e(X, g_2)^r$ so that $W = e(g_1, g_2)^{\alpha y z r}$.
4. Set $k \leftarrow H_2(W)$.
5. Set

$$u_0 \leftarrow g_2^{t_0}, \quad v_0 \leftarrow Y^r \cdot H_1(j)^{t_0}, \quad c_0 \leftarrow (u_0, v_0) \in \mathbb{G}_2 \times \mathbb{G}_1$$
$$u_1 \leftarrow g_2^{t_1}, \quad v_1 \leftarrow Z^r \cdot H_1(j)^{t_1}, \quad c_1 \leftarrow (u_1, v_1) \in \mathbb{G}_2 \times \mathbb{G}_1$$

Observe that c_0 is an ElGamal encryption of Y^r and c_1 is an ElGamal encryption of Z^r.

6. Set $c \leftarrow (c_0, c_1)$.
7. Return (k, c).

$\mathcal{BTBF}$.Dec($j, \mathsf{sk}_{i,b}^{(j)}, c = (c_0, c_1)$):

1. Parse c_b as (u, v) and $\mathsf{sk}_{i,b}^{(j)}$ as (k_0, k_1).
2. Compute $d_i \leftarrow e(v, k_1)/e(k_0, u)$. Observe that $d_i = e(g_1, g_2)^{s_i y z r}$.
3. Return d_i.

$\mathcal{BTBF}$.Combine($pkc, j, c, \mathcal{J}, \{d_i\}_{i \in \mathcal{J}}$):

1. Compute the Lagrange coefficients $(\lambda_i^{\mathcal{J}})_{i \in \mathcal{J}}$ for the subset $\mathcal{J}$:
$\lambda_i^{\mathcal{J}} \leftarrow \prod_{v \in \mathcal{J} \setminus \{i\}} \frac{v}{v-i} \in \mathbb{Z}_p$.
2. Compute $W \leftarrow \prod_{i \in \mathcal{J}} d_i^{(\lambda_i^{\mathcal{J}})}$ and $k \leftarrow H_2(W)$.
3. Return k.

Fig. 8. Our BT-KEM scheme in pairing groups, denoted $\mathcal{BTBF}$.

Theorem 5.5. *For every probabilistic polynomial-time adversary $\mathcal{A}$ there exists a probabilistic polynomial-time adversary $\mathcal{B}$ such that*

$$\mathsf{Adv}^{\mathsf{oss}}_{\mathcal{A},\mathcal{BTBF}}(\lambda) \leq 2L \cdot \mathsf{Adv}^{\mathsf{addh}}_{\mathcal{B},\mathcal{G}}(\lambda),$$

for all $\lambda \in \mathbb{N}$, where the hash function H_1 is modeled as a random oracle, and $L = L(\lambda)$ is an upper bound on the number of positions ℓ in the scheme.

Theorem 5.5 is proven in the full version of the paper [16].

Semantic Security. We now argue the semantic security of $\mathcal{BTBF}$, relying on the following variant of the Computational Bilinear Diffie-Hellman (CBDH) assumption.

Definition 5.6. *Let $\mathcal{G}$ be a bilinear group generation algorithm. We say that the Augmented Computational Bilinear Diffie-Hellman (ACBDH) problem is hard relative to $\mathcal{G}$ if for every probabilistic polynomial-time algorithm $\mathcal{A}$ the following function*

$$\mathsf{Adv}^{\mathsf{acbdh}}_{\mathcal{A},\mathcal{G}}(\lambda) := \Pr\left[\mathcal{A}((\mathbb{G}_1,\mathbb{G}_2,\mathbb{G}_T,p,g_1,g_2,e),\vec{h}) = e(g_1,g_2)^{\alpha y z r}\right]$$

is negligible in $\lambda \in \mathbb{N}$, where $(\mathbb{G}_1,\mathbb{G}_2,\mathbb{G}_T,p,g_1,g_2,e) \xleftarrow{\$} \mathcal{G}(1^\lambda)$ and

$$\vec{h} = (g_1^y, g_1^z, g_1^{yr}, g_1^{zr}, g_1^{\alpha y z}, g_2^y, g_2^z)$$

for $\alpha, r, z, y, v \xleftarrow{\$} \mathbb{Z}_p$.

The following theorem establishes the semantic security of $\mathcal{BTBF}$.

Theorem 5.7. *For every probabilistic polynomial-time adversary $\mathcal{A}$ there exists a probabilistic polynomial-time adversary $\mathcal{B}$ such that*

$$\mathsf{Adv}^{\mathsf{cpa}}_{\mathcal{A},\mathcal{BTBF}}(\lambda) \leq q_2 \cdot \mathsf{Adv}^{\mathsf{acbdh}}_{\mathcal{B},\mathcal{G}}(\lambda)$$

for all $\lambda \in \mathbb{N}$, when the hash functions H_1, H_2 are modeled as random oracles and $q_2 = q_2(\lambda)$ is a bound on the number of H_2-queries issued by $\mathcal{A}$.

The proof of Theorem 5.7 can be found in the full version of the paper [16].

6 The Case of Small Traitor Coalitions

In this section, we consider the setting in which the traitor coalition is small; namely, there are $f < t$ traitors, where t is the decryption threshold as before. We begin with a brief overview of the challenges that this setting poses and ways to circumvent them. Due to space limitations, formal definitions and constructions for the small traitor coalition case are deferred to the full version of the paper [16]. In this informal discussion, we omit many technical details that can be found in the full version.

In the small coalition setting, we would like to capture the scenario in which the traitor coalition publishes or sells any piece of information that might be useful for decryption by another set of parties. To be as general as possible, we model this information as a decoder D that receives additional decryption shares for some ciphertext c. When the decoder receives enough information to decrypt, it outputs the encrypted message m. The decoder may be tied to a specific ciphertext c and only decrypt this ciphertext, or it may be a general decoder that gets also a ciphertext c as input and tries to decrypt it.[3] We focus on decoders that are tied to a specific ciphertext, but the same problems and solutions arise in both cases. As a concrete example, think of a decoder D that has a ciphertext c and the secret keys of the $f < t$ corrupted parties embedded in it. Whenever it gets $t - f$ decryption shares from *additional* parties as input, it decrypts and outputs the message. If it does not get enough information to decrypt, it outputs $\bot$. Given black-box access to such a decoder, we would like to trace it back to at least one of the corrupted parties.

Unfortunately, if we allow for arbitrary decoders, then for robust schemes (where in particular, shares can be publicly traced to their generating party), efficient tracing becomes hopeless for most choices of f and t. The issue arises already with the simple decoder D described above that has a subset $\mathcal{I}$ of f keys embedded in it, if it is restricted to accept *exactly* $t - f$ shares as input. If it gets more shares than that as input, it refuses to decrypt and outputs $\bot$. Denote this decoder by $D_\mathcal{I}$. Intuitively, to extract any meaningful information from the decoder, we need to make it work; i.e., output something other than $\bot$. Now consider the distribution over decoders that are defined as above, where the subset $\mathcal{I}$ is sampled uniformly at random from all subsets of $[n]$ of size f. In this case, we prove the following lower bound.

Theorem 6.1 (informal). *If the underlying threshold decryption scheme is robust, then for any algorithm $\mathcal{B}$ making at most Q oracle queries to $D_\mathcal{I}$, the probability that $D_\mathcal{I}$ returns anything but $\bot$ is bounded by $\frac{Q}{\binom{n}{f} - Q \cdot \binom{n-(t-f)}{f}}$.*

As an example, consider the setting where $t = n/3$ and $f = t/2$. In this case, the probability of making $D_\mathcal{I}$ output something other than $\bot$ is bounded by $Q \cdot 2^{-\Omega(n)}$. Hence, an exponential number of queries to $D_\mathcal{I}$ are required to even make it work. In the full version [16, App. B], we make this theorem precise and provide a proof.

In light of the above, we explore two restricted classes of decoders that still capture meaningful traitor attacks on the one hand, yet allow for some meaningful notion of accountability on the other hand.

Option I: A decoder that can decrypt, must. The reason the decoder D sketched above was untraceable, was that it could choose to reject any input that

---

[3] Note that in the case where $f \geq t$ it makes no sense to consider decoders that are tied to a specific ciphertext c. This is because when $f \geq t$ the traitor coalition can just decrypt c and publish the underlying message m as the decoder. This "decoder" is trivially untraceable.

consisted of more than $t-f$ shares. A natural question is then what happens if we disallow such behavior on the side of the decoder? Concretely, we consider here a restricted class of decoders: a decoder $D = D(\mathcal{I})$ is associated with some subset $\mathcal{I}$ of corrupted parties, and if the decoder is fed decryption shares from a subset $\mathcal{S}$ of parties, it outputs the correct message whenever $|\mathcal{I} \cup \mathcal{S}| \geq t$. This means that the decoder may output the correct message also on inputs that include up to t, and in particular more than $t-f$, decryption shares. We call such decoders *universal*. Though (unavoidably) restricted, this class of decoders already captures natural forms of information leakage, such as leaking the secret keys of the parties in $\mathcal{I}$ or their decryption shares of a specific ciphertext c (or malformed keys/decryption shares, that still allow decryption).

We show that with this restriction on the decoder, tracing becomes possible. We present a tracing procedure that can be seen as the mirror image of tracing using private linear broadcast encryption [18]. By semantic security, we know that when the decoder D gets no decryption share as input, it should output the correct message with negligible probability. On the other hand, when given any t decryption shares $d_1, \ldots, d_t$ as input, any universal decoder should output the correct message, say with probability 1 (in the full version, we relax this notion and consider probabilistic decoders). This means that there must be some index $i \in [t]$ such that $D(d_1, \ldots, d_i)$ outputs the correct message, but $D(d_1, \ldots, d_{i-1})$ does not. Since D is universal, we may deduce that $\{d_1, \ldots, d_{i-1}\}$ is insufficient information for D to decrypt, but $\{d_1, \ldots, d_i\}$ is. Hence it must be the case that party i is innocent, in the sense that it is not a member of the subset $\mathcal{I}$ of corrupted parties that define the universal decoder $D = D(\mathcal{I})$. Feeding the subsets $\emptyset, \{d_1\}, \{d_1, d_2\}, \ldots, \{d_1, \ldots, d_t\}$ to D one by one, we are guaranteed to find this i. Moreover, we show that by repeating this procedure, we can "exonerate" all innocent parties in $\{1, \ldots, t\}$. The full tracing algorithm is obtained by doing the same for all subsets $\{1, \ldots, t\}, \{t+1, \ldots, 2t\}, \ldots, \{n-t+1, \ldots, n\}$.

Option II: Confirmation Instead of Tracing. The tracing procedure above crucially relied on the fact that the decoder works for inputs consisting of a variable number of decryption shares. More clever decoders might try to avoid detection by insisting that the decoder takes in *exactly* $t-f$ decryption shares as input. This can be done, for example, by hard-coding the traitors' secret keys to the decryption circuit and obfuscating it. By the lower bound result sketched above, in this setting we cannot hope for full-fledged traitor tracing. Instead, we explore the task of *"traitor confirmation"*: given knowledge of the traitor coalition $\mathcal{I}$ that manufactured some decoder D (and possibly some trapdoor information) the task is to create a publicly-verifiable proof that ascertains that this is indeed the set of traitors. Both the prover and the verifier are given black-box access to D. Importantly, a malicious prover should not be able to frame an innocent party for the creation of a decoder D. This should be the case even if the malicious prover gets access to more than t of the parties' secret keys. This is important, for example, to fend against cases in which a coalition creates some decoder D, and at a later stage obtains additional secret keys that it did not possess when manufacturing D. If now this coalition has more than t keys, they could potentially reconstruct the keys of all n parties. Framing an innocent party that did not partake in the creation of D should still be impossible.

Here, too, we consider decoders $D = D(\mathcal{I})$ that are specified by a subset $\mathcal{I}$ of corrupted parties, and must decrypt if they get decryption shares from a disjoint subset of parties $\mathcal{S}$ of size $t-f$ where $f = |\mathcal{I}|$.[4] But now, we do allow the decoder to take in exactly $t-f$ decryption shares as inputs, and refuse to work on more shares than that. We call such decoders *exact decoders*. This is exactly the decoder from the lower bound sketched above. Focusing on confirmation rather than tracing allows us to circumvent the lower bound.

Now say that we have a robust threshold decryption scheme, and want to produce a proof that a subset $\mathcal{I}$ of size $f < t$ is the corrupted subset behind some decoder D for a ciphertext c. The first idea that comes to mind is to include in the proof the decryption shares $\{d_j\}_{j \in [n] \setminus \mathcal{I}}$ of c of all parties outside of $\mathcal{I}$. To verify, one partitions these into $k \approx (n-f)/(t-f)$ subsets $\mathcal{S}_1, \ldots, \mathcal{S}_k$, each of size $t-f$, feeds these to D one by one, and asserts that D outputs the correct message m every time. If $\mathcal{I}$ is indeed the corrupted subset underlying D, then verification will indeed go through. However, there is a problem. This confirmation system is completely insecure and is susceptible to framing! As a small example, consider the case $n = 6$ and $t = 4$, and an adversary that corrupts the subset $\mathcal{I} = \{1, 3, 5\}$ and constructs the decoder $D = D(\{1, 3, 5\})$. This adversary can later claim that the corrupted set of parties is in fact the set $\mathcal{J} = \{1, 4\}$ and as proof gives the decryption shares of the other parties $\pi = \{d_2, d_3, d_5, d_6\}$. Verification will now go through since both $D(d_2, d_3)$ and $D(d_5, d_6)$ have enough information to decrypt. The issue here is that the adversary can lie about the number f of corrupted parties underlying the decoder.

To fix this issue, the verification procedure needs to run a few more checks. For every subset $\mathcal{S}_j$, for every party $i \in \mathcal{S}_j$, and for every party i' in the claimed set of traitors $\mathcal{I}$, verification will run $D((\mathcal{S}_j \setminus \{i\}) \cup \{i'\})$. If this query returns the correct message m, then we will reject the proof as invalid. The intuition behind this check is that if the corrupted subset is actually larger than what is claimed by the adversarially conjured proof, then there is a decryption share by a corrupted party i^* in some $\mathcal{S}_j$. Hence, removing it from $\mathcal{S}_j$ (and replacing it with an element in $\mathcal{I}$ to keep the number of input shares the same) should not affect D's ability to decrypt.

7 Conclusion and Future Directions

This work initiates the study of accountability for threshold decryption schemes, focusing on the notion of traitor tracing for such schemes. To the best of our knowledge, this is the first work to consider this problem, and it gives new definitions and constructions that satisfy them. We strongly believe that this may open an exciting avenue for research, as there are many natural open questions that arise from our work. We present two of them here, in the setting of tracing large traitor coalitions.

---

[4] This restriction is necessary due to a lower bound similar to the one described above.

Thresholdizing Additional Traitor Tracing Schemes. As we explain in Sect. 3, a natural path to constructing a threshold decryption scheme with traitor tracing is by converting existing traitor tracing schemes into their threshold variant. In this work, we make the first step in this effort, showing how to convert the traitor tracing scheme of Boneh and Naor [14] to a threshold decryption scheme that allows for traitor tracing. In the full version [16, App. B], we do the same for the recent traitor tracing scheme of Gong, Lou, and Wee [34]. An interesting open question is to adapt other traitor tracing schemes to the threshold setting. Natural candidates are other schemes based on private linear broadcast encryption (PLBE) from either pairing-based assumptions [22,33,60] or lattice-based assumptions [26,35], as well as the recent construction of Zhandry [61], which takes a different approach for implementing broadcast encryption with private revocation. Extending any of these works to the threshold setting will most likely require very different techniques than the ones we develop in this paper.

Detecting Many Traitors. Our definition of traitor tracing (Sect. 3) requires that the tracing algorithm Trace outputs at least *one* member of the traitor coalition. This is in line with previous definitions for traitor tracing in the non-threshold case. In the non-threshold setting, this is unavoidable: an adversary that corrupts $f > 1$ parties may very well still "use" just one of their secret keys when constructing the decoder. In threshold decryption, however, the decoder must use – in some intuitive sense – the secret keys of at least t parties in order to decrypt, or semantic security is broken. So one may consider a strengthening of our definition that requires that Trace outputs at least t corrupted parties. We observe that there is an inefficient scheme that does satisfy this definition, built from any semantically secure public key encryption $\mathcal{E}$. Consider the trivial threshold decryption scheme, in which each party i has its own secret-public key pair (sk_i, pk_i) and the overall public key is $pk = (pk_1, \ldots, pk_n)$. To encrypt a message m, we secret share m into shares $s_1, \ldots, s_n$ using a t-out-of-n secret sharing scheme, and encrypt the ith share under pk_i to obtain $c_i \xleftarrow{\$} \mathcal{E}.\mathsf{Enc}(pk_i, s_i)$. The final ciphertext is $c = (c_1, \ldots, c_n)$. It is not hard to see that this scheme has a tracing algorithm (à la PLBE) that can find at least t traitors given black-box access to a good decoder. The task is to satisfy this stronger requirement— tracing a decoder to t or more traitors—with an efficient construction. The combinatorial objects underlying most existing efficient traitor tracing constructions (PLBE and fingerprinting codes) are specifically tailored to catch just one traitor, and no more. So extending them to the task of catching t traitors seems to require new ideas, and is a very interesting open question.

Distributed Key Generation. Our definition and constructions consider a central key generation procedure. However, one could also consider a distributed key generation protocol instead, taking place among the n decryptors and a tracing authority. The tracing authority would only learn the information needed to trace the decoder back to a corrupted party, and no more. In particular, in our constructions, the trapdoor information needed for tracing would not allow the tracing authority to break semantic security of the encryption scheme.

CCA Security. Our definitions of semantic security only consider chosen plaintext (CPA) attacks. However, for applications such as auctions or encrypted mempools, it might be important to consider a stronger attack model where the adversary is allowed to see decryptions of arbitrary ciphertexts of its choice, i.e. Chosen Ciphertext attacks. We leave the task of constructing a CCA-secure threshold decryption with traitor tracing as an interesting future direction.

Public Tracing. As mentioned in Sect. 3, our constructions only support private tracing since an adversary can evade tracing if the tracing key gets leaked. Many works on the related notion of traitor tracing construct public tracing schemes (see [36,45] and the references therein), where the tracing key is public. An interesting open question is to adapt the techniques from these works to achieve public tracing in the threshold setting.

Acknowledgments. This work was funded by NSF, DARPA, the Simons Foundation, UBRI, and NTT Research. Opinions, findings, and conclusions or recommendations expressed in this material are those of the authors and do not necessarily reflect the views of DARPA.

References

1. Asayag, A., et al.: Helix: a scalable and fair consensus algorithm resistant to ordering manipulation. Cryptology ePrint Archive, Report 2018/863 (2018). https://eprint.iacr.org/2018/863
2. Babel, K., Daian, P., Kelkar, M., Juels, A.: Clockwork finance: automated analysis of economic security in smart contracts. In: IEEE S&P, pp. 2499–2516. IEEE (2023)
3. Bauer, B., Fuchsbauer, G., Loss, J.: A classification of computational assumptions in the algebraic group model. In: Micciancio, D., Ristenpart, T. (eds.) CRYPTO 2020, Part II. LNCS, vol. 12171, pp. 121–151. Springer, Cham (2020). https://doi.org/10.1007/978-3-030-56880-1_5
4. Bebel, J., Ojha, D.: Ferveo: threshold decryption for mempool privacy in BFT networks. Cryptology ePrint Archive, Report 2022/898 (2022). https://eprint.iacr.org/2022/898
5. Bellare, M., Neven, G.: Multi-signatures in the plain public-key model and a general forking lemma. In: Juels, A., Wright, R.N., De Capitani di Vimercati, S. (eds.) ACM CCS 2006, pp. 390–399. ACM Press, Alexandria, Virginia, USA, 30 October–3 November 2006. https://doi.org/10.1145/1180405.1180453
6. Billet, O., Phan, D.H.: Efficient tracing from collusion secure codes. In: Safavi-Naini, R. (ed.) ICITS 2008. LNCS, vol. 5155, pp. 171–182. Springer, Heidelberg (2008). https://doi.org/10.1007/978-3-540-85093-9_17
7. Boldyreva, A.: Threshold signatures, multisignatures and blind signatures based on the gap-diffie-hellman-group signature scheme. In: Desmedt, Y.G. (ed.) PKC 2003. LNCS, vol. 2567, pp. 31–46. Springer, Heidelberg (2003). https://doi.org/10.1007/3-540-36288-6_3
8. Boneh, D., Boyen, X., Goh, E.-J.: Hierarchical identity based encryption with constant size ciphertext. In: Cramer, R. (ed.) EUROCRYPT 2005. LNCS, vol. 3494, pp. 440–456. Springer, Heidelberg (2005). https://doi.org/10.1007/11426639_26

9. Boneh, D., Boyen, X., Halevi, S.: Chosen ciphertext secure public key threshold encryption without random oracles. In: Pointcheval, D. (ed.) CT-RSA 2006. LNCS, vol. 3860, pp. 226–243. Springer, Heidelberg (2006). https://doi.org/10.1007/11605805_15
10. Boneh, D., Drijvers, M., Neven, G.: Compact multi-signatures for smaller blockchains. In: Peyrin, T., Galbraith, S. (eds.) ASIACRYPT 2018, Part II. LNCS, vol. 11273, pp. 435–464. Springer, Cham (2018). https://doi.org/10.1007/978-3-030-03329-3_15
11. Boneh, D., Franklin, M.: An efficient public key traitor tracing scheme. In: Wiener, M. (ed.) CRYPTO 1999. LNCS, vol. 1666, pp. 338–353. Springer, Heidelberg (1999). https://doi.org/10.1007/3-540-48405-1_22
12. Boneh, D., Gentry, C., Lynn, B., Shacham, H.: Aggregate and encrypted signatures from bilinear maps. In: Biham, E. (ed.) EUROCRYPT 2003. LNCS, vol. 2656, pp. 416–432. Springer, Heidelberg (2003). https://doi.org/10.1007/3-540-39200-9_26
13. Boneh, D., Kiayias, A., Montgomery, H.W.: Robust fingerprinting codes: a near optimal construction. In: Proceedings of the Tenth Annual ACM Workshop on Digital Rights Management. DRM '10, pp. 3–12. Association for Computing Machinery, New York, NY, USA (2010). https://doi.org/10.1145/1866870.1866873
14. Boneh, D., Naor, M.: Traitor tracing with constant size ciphertext. In: Ning, P., Syverson, P.F., Jha, S. (eds.) ACM CCS 2008, pp. 501–510. ACM Press, Alexandria, Virginia, USA, 27–31 October 2008. https://doi.org/10.1145/1455770.1455834
15. Boneh, D., Partap, A., Rotem, L.: Accountable threshold signatures with proactive refresh. Cryptology ePrint Archive, Report 2022/1656 (2022). https://eprint.iacr.org/2022/1656
16. Boneh, D., Partap, A., Rotem, L.: Accountability for misbehavior in threshold decryption via threshold traitor tracing. Cryptology ePrint Archive, Paper 2023/1724 (2023). https://eprint.iacr.org/2023/1724
17. Boneh, D., Partap, A., Rotem, L.: Traceable secret sharing: strong security and efficient constructions. Cryptology ePrint Archive, Report 2024/405 (2024). https://eprint.iacr.org/2024/405. To be published in CRYPTO 2024
18. Boneh, D., Sahai, A., Waters, B.: Fully collusion resistant traitor tracing with short ciphertexts and private keys. In: Vaudenay, S. (ed.) EUROCRYPT 2006. LNCS, vol. 4004, pp. 573–592. Springer, Heidelberg (2006). https://doi.org/10.1007/11761679_34
19. Boneh, D., Shaw, J.: Collusion-secure fingerprinting for digital data (extended abstract). In: Coppersmith, D. (ed.) CRYPTO 1995. LNCS, vol. 963, pp. 452–465. Springer, Heidelberg (1995). https://doi.org/10.1007/3-540-44750-4_36
20. Boneh, D., Shaw, J.: Collusion-secure fingerprinting for digital data. IEEE Trans. Inf. Theory **44**(5), 1897–1905 (1998). https://doi.org/10.1109/18.705568
21. Boneh, D., Shoup, V.: A graduate course in applied cryptography (version 0.6) (2023). cryptobook.us
22. Boneh, D., Waters, B.: A fully collusion resistant broadcast, trace, and revoke system. In: Juels, A., Wright, R.N., De Capitani di Vimercati, S. (eds.) ACM CCS 2006, pp. 211–220. ACM Press, Alexandria, Virginia, USA, 30 October–3 November 2006. https://doi.org/10.1145/1180405.1180432
23. Boneh, D., Zhandry, M.: Multiparty key exchange, efficient traitor tracing, and more from indistinguishability obfuscation. In: Garay, J.A., Gennaro, R. (eds.) CRYPTO 2014, Part I. LNCS, vol. 8616, pp. 480–499. Springer, Heidelberg (2014). https://doi.org/10.1007/978-3-662-44371-2_27

24. Boyen, X.: The uber-assumption family: a unified complexity framework for bilinear groups. In: Galbraith, S.D., Paterson, K.G. (eds.) Pairing 2008. LNCS, vol. 5209, pp. 39–56. Springer, Heidelberg (2008). https://doi.org/10.1007/978-3-540-85538-5_3
25. Canetti, R., Goldwasser, S.: An efficient *threshold* public key cryptosystem secure against adaptive chosen ciphertext attack (extended abstract). In: Stern, J. (ed.) EUROCRYPT 1999. LNCS, vol. 1592, pp. 90–106. Springer, Heidelberg (1999). https://doi.org/10.1007/3-540-48910-X_7
26. Chen, Y., Vaikuntanathan, V., Waters, B., Wee, H., Wichs, D.: Traitor-tracing from LWE made simple and attribute-based. In: Beimel, A., Dziembowski, S. (eds.) TCC 2018, Part II. LNCS, vol. 11240, pp. 341–369. Springer, Cham (2018). https://doi.org/10.1007/978-3-030-03810-6_13
27. Chor, B., Fiat, A., Naor, M.: Tracing traitors. In: Desmedt, Y.G. (ed.) CRYPTO 1994. LNCS, vol. 839, pp. 257–270. Springer, Heidelberg (1994). https://doi.org/10.1007/3-540-48658-5_25
28. Cramer, R., Gennaro, R., Schoenmakers, B.: A secure and optimally efficient multi-authority election scheme. In: Fumy, W. (ed.) EUROCRYPT 1997. LNCS, vol. 1233, pp. 103–118. Springer, Heidelberg (1997). https://doi.org/10.1007/3-540-69053-0_9
29. Daian, P., et al.: Flash boys 2.0: frontrunning in decentralized exchanges, miner extractable value, and consensus instability. In: 2020 IEEE Symposium on Security and Privacy, pp. 910–927. IEEE Computer Society Press, San Francisco, CA, USA, 18–21 May 2020. https://doi.org/10.1109/SP40000.2020.00040
30. Desmedt, Y.: Society and group oriented cryptography: a new concept. In: Pomerance, C. (ed.) CRYPTO 1987. LNCS, vol. 293, pp. 120–127. Springer, Heidelberg (1988). https://doi.org/10.1007/3-540-48184-2_8
31. Desmedt, Y., Frankel, Y.: Threshold cryptosystems. In: Brassard, G. (ed.) CRYPTO 1989. LNCS, vol. 435, pp. 307–315. Springer, New York (1990). https://doi.org/10.1007/0-387-34805-0_28
32. Fuchsbauer, G., Kiltz, E., Loss, J.: The algebraic group model and its applications. In: Shacham, H., Boldyreva, A. (eds.) CRYPTO 2018, Part II. LNCS, vol. 10992, pp. 33–62. Springer, Cham (2018). https://doi.org/10.1007/978-3-319-96881-0_2
33. Garg, S., Kumarasubramanian, A., Sahai, A., Waters, B.: Building efficient fully collusion-resilient traitor tracing and revocation schemes. In: Al-Shaer, E., Keromytis, A.D., Shmatikov, V. (eds.) ACM CCS 2010, pp. 121–130. ACM Press, Chicago, Illinois, USA, 4–8 October 2010. https://doi.org/10.1145/1866307.1866322
34. Gong, J., Luo, J., Wee, H.: Traitor tracing with $N^{1/3}$-size ciphertexts and $O(1)$-size keys from k-Lin. In: Hazay, C., Stam, M. (eds.) EUROCRYPT 2023, Part III. LNCS, vol. 14006, pp. 637–668. Springer, Cham (2023). https://doi.org/10.1007/978-3-031-30620-4_21
35. Goyal, R., Koppula, V., Waters, B.: Collusion resistant traitor tracing from learning with errors. In: Diakonikolas, I., Kempe, D., Henzinger, M. (eds.) 50th ACM STOC, pp. 660–670. ACM Press, Los Angeles, CA, USA, 25–29 June 2018. https://doi.org/10.1145/3188745.3188844
36. Goyal, R., Koppula, V., Waters, B.: New approaches to traitor tracing with embedded identities. In: Hofheinz, D., Rosen, A. (eds.) TCC 2019, Part II. LNCS, vol. 11892, pp. 149–179. Springer, Cham (2019). https://doi.org/10.1007/978-3-030-36033-7_6

37. Goyal, V., Song, Y., Srinivasan, A.: Traceable secret sharing and applications. In: Malkin, T., Peikert, C. (eds.) CRYPTO 2021, Part III. LNCS, vol. 12827, pp. 718–747. Springer, Cham (2021). https://doi.org/10.1007/978-3-030-84252-9_24
38. Kiayias, A., Yung, M.: On crafty pirates and foxy tracers. In: Sander, T. (ed.) DRM 2001. LNCS, vol. 2320, pp. 22–39. Springer, Heidelberg (2002). https://doi.org/10.1007/3-540-47870-1_3
39. Kiayias, A., Yung, M.: Traitor tracing with constant transmission rate. In: Knudsen, L.R. (ed.) EUROCRYPT 2002. LNCS, vol. 2332, pp. 450–465. Springer, Heidelberg (2002). https://doi.org/10.1007/3-540-46035-7_30
40. Kurosawa, K., Desmedt, Y.: Optimum traitor tracing and asymmetric schemes. In: Nyberg, K. (ed.) EUROCRYPT 1998. LNCS, vol. 1403, pp. 145–157. Springer, Heidelberg (1998). https://doi.org/10.1007/BFb0054123
41. Li, R., Li, Y., Wang, Q., Duan, S., Wang, Q., Ryan, M.: Accountable decryption made formal and practical (2023). here
42. Micali, S., Ohta, K., Reyzin, L.: Accountable-subgroup multisignatures: extended abstract. In: Reiter, M.K., Samarati, P. (eds.) ACM CCS 2001, pp. 245–254. ACM Press, Philadelphia, PA, USA, 5–8 November 2001. https://doi.org/10.1145/501983.502017
43. Naor, M., Pinkas, B.: Threshold traitor tracing. In: Krawczyk, H. (ed.) CRYPTO 1998. LNCS, vol. 1462, pp. 502–517. Springer, Heidelberg (1998). https://doi.org/10.1007/BFb0055750
44. Nick, J., Ruffing, T., Seurin, Y.: MuSig2: simple two-round Schnorr multi-signatures. In: Malkin, T., Peikert, C. (eds.) CRYPTO 2021. LNCS, vol. 12825, pp. 189–221. Springer, Cham (2021). https://doi.org/10.1007/978-3-030-84242-0_8
45. Nishimaki, R., Wichs, D., Zhandry, M.: Anonymous traitor tracing: how to embed arbitrary information in a key. In: Fischlin, M., Coron, J.-S. (eds.) EUROCRYPT 2016, Part II. LNCS, vol. 9666, pp. 388–419. Springer, Heidelberg (2016). https://doi.org/10.1007/978-3-662-49896-5_14
46. Nuida, K.: A general conversion method of fingerprint codes to (more) robust fingerprint codes against bit erasure. In: Kurosawa, K. (ed.) ICITS 2009. LNCS, vol. 5973, pp. 194–212. Springer, Heidelberg (2010). https://doi.org/10.1007/978-3-642-14496-7_16
47. Osmosis. link
48. Phan, D.H.: Traitor tracing for stateful pirate decoders with constant ciphertext rate. In: Nguyen, P.Q. (ed.) VIETCRYPT 2006. LNCS, vol. 4341, pp. 354–365. Springer, Heidelberg (2006). https://doi.org/10.1007/11958239_24
49. Qin, K., Zhou, L., Gervais, A.: Quantifying blockchain extractable value: how dark is the forest? In: 2022 IEEE Symposium on Security and Privacy, pp. 198–214. IEEE Computer Society Press, San Francisco, CA, USA, 22–26 May 2022. https://doi.org/10.1109/SP46214.2022.9833734
50. Rondelet, A., Kilbourn, Q.: Threshold encrypted mempools: limitations and considerations (2023). here
51. Rotem, L.: Revisiting the uber assumption in the algebraic group model: fine-grained bounds in hidden-order groups and improved reductions in bilinear groups. In: Dachman-Soled, D. (ed.) 3rd Conference on Information-Theoretic Cryptography (ITC 2022), vol. 230, pp. 13:1–13:13. Schloss Dagstuhl – Leibniz-Zentrum für Informatik, Dagstuhl, Germany (2022). https://doi.org/10.4230/LIPIcs.ITC.2022.13, https://drops.dagstuhl.de/opus/volltexte/2022/16491

52. Rotem, L., Segev, G.: Algebraic distinguishers: from discrete logarithms to decisional Uber assumptions. In: Pass, R., Pietrzak, K. (eds.) TCC 2020, Part III. LNCS, vol. 12552, pp. 366–389. Springer, Cham (2020). https://doi.org/10.1007/978-3-030-64381-2_13
53. Sako, K.: An auction protocol which hides bids of losers. In: Imai, H., Zheng, Y. (eds.) PKC 2000. LNCS, vol. 1751, pp. 422–432. Springer, Heidelberg (2000). https://doi.org/10.1007/978-3-540-46588-1_28
54. Shoup, V.: Lower bounds for discrete logarithms and related problems. In: Fumy, W. (ed.) EUROCRYPT 1997. LNCS, vol. 1233, pp. 256–266. Springer, Heidelberg (1997). https://doi.org/10.1007/3-540-69053-0_18
55. Shoup, V., Gennaro, R.: Securing threshold cryptosystems against chosen ciphertext attack. In: Nyberg, K. (ed.) EUROCRYPT 1998. LNCS, vol. 1403, pp. 1–16. Springer, Heidelberg (1998). https://doi.org/10.1007/BFb0054113
56. Shutter: Preventing front running and malicious MEV on ethereum. link
57. Sirvent, T.: Traitor tracing scheme with constant ciphertext rate against powerful pirates. Cryptology ePrint Archive, Report 2006/383 (2006). https://eprint.iacr.org/2006/383
58. Tardos, G.: Optimal probabilistic fingerprint codes. J. ACM **55**(2) (2008). https://doi.org/10.1145/1346330.1346335, https://doi.org/10.1145/1346330.1346335
59. de Valence, H.: The Penumbra protocol. link
60. Wee, H.: Functional encryption for quadratic functions from k-Lin, revisited. In: Pass, R., Pietrzak, K. (eds.) TCC 2020, Part I. LNCS, vol. 12550, pp. 210–228. Springer, Cham (2020). https://doi.org/10.1007/978-3-030-64375-1_8
61. Zhandry, M.: New techniques for traitor tracing: size $N^{1/3}$ and more from pairings. In: Micciancio, D., Ristenpart, T. (eds.) CRYPTO 2020, Part I. LNCS, vol. 12170, pp. 652–682. Springer, Cham (2020). https://doi.org/10.1007/978-3-030-56784-2_22

Threshold Encryption with Silent Setup

Sanjam Garg[1]($\boxtimes$), Dimitris Kolonelos[2], Guru-Vamsi Policharla[1], and Mingyuan Wang[1]

[1] UC Berkeley, Berkeley, USA
{sanjamg,guruvamsip,mingyuan}@berkeley.edu
[2] IMDEA Software Institute, Universidad Politécnica de Madrid, Madrid, Spain
dimitris.kolonelos@imdea.org

Abstract. We build a concretely efficient threshold encryption scheme where the joint public key of a set of parties is computed as a *deterministic* function of their locally computed public keys, enabling a *silent* setup phase. By eliminating interaction from the setup phase, our scheme immediately enjoys several highly desirable features such as asynchronous setup, multiverse support, and dynamic threshold.

Prior to our work, the only known constructions of threshold encryption with silent setup relied on heavy cryptographic machinery such as indistinguishability Obfuscation or witness encryption for all of NP. Our core technical innovation lies in building a special purpose witness encryption scheme for the statement "at least t parties have signed a given message". Our construction relies on pairings and is proved secure in the Generic Group Model.

Notably, our construction, restricted to the special case of threshold $t = 1$, gives an alternative construction of the (flexible) distributed broadcast encryption from pairings, which has been the central focus of several recent works.

We implement and evaluate our scheme to demonstrate its concrete efficiency. Both encryption and partial decryption are constant time, taking $< 7\,\mathrm{ms}$ and $< 1\,\mathrm{ms}$, respectively. For a committee of 1024 parties, the aggregation of partial decryptions takes $< 200\,\mathrm{ms}$, when all parties provide partial decryptions. The size of each ciphertext is $\approx 8\times$ larger than an ElGamal ciphertext.

1 Introduction

Threshold encryption [28,29] is a fundamental cryptographic primitive that allows an encryptor to generate a *succinct* ciphertext such that it can be decrypted by any threshold t sized subset of n parties, while remaining semantically secure against any coalition of up to $t - 1$ parties. Typically, a threshold encryption system begins with an *interactive* setup phase where a distributed key generation (DKG) protocol is run to establish a public key pair, where the secret key is shared amongst the n parties. Any party can then encrypt a message using the public key and produce a *succinct* ciphertext, of size independent of the number of parties. It is highly desirable for the decryption process to be *non-interactive*, i.e., the parties locally produce partial decryptions of the ciphertext, which can be *publicly* aggregated to recover the message.

Expensive DKG. Although the original notion was proposed over three decades ago, and there has been a long line of research on this topic, virtually all known threshold encryption schemes[1] require a DKG protocol to sample a correlated partial decryption key for each party. While this is theoretically feasible, DKG protocol in practice is quite expensive. For instance, it typically requires high communication/computation complexity [44,73]. Moreover, these theoretical solutions typically assume a synchronous setting. For the more practically-relevant asynchronous setting, despite many efforts [2,21,22,55,56], these costs remains even higher. Moreover, these asynchronous protocols can only tolerate $< 1/3$ fraction of malicious corruptions. Therefore, for many practical applications (refer to Sect. 1.2), it is much desirable if the setup phase of threshold encryption schemes can be made entirely non-interactive.

Multiverse Support. One may also want the ability to add or remove a party from the committee without any additional interaction between the parties. This is particularly useful in practice, where one may want to easily onboard new parties or remove unresponsive members from the committee. This feature is absent is traditional threshold encryption schemes and any changes require (at least a threshold number of) committee members to be online. Instead, it would be highly desirable if a one-time setup could enable, *without any additional interaction*, the setup of all future threshold encryption for different universes (i.e., the multiverse setting introduced for signatures in [4,43]).

Dynamic Threshold. Another desirable property is to allow encrypting parties to choose a different threshold for each ciphertext without the need for repeating the interactive setup. This allows for a flexible tradeoff between security and liveness. For instance, a party can choose a higher threshold if they are willing to tolerate a higher risk of decryption failure (say due to offline parties), in exchange for reducing the trust in the committee. Typically, any new threshold would require parties to engage in a new instance of DKG, and the committee member's secret state will grow with the number of thresholds maintained.

Although there have been prior attempts to achieve the latter two properties, they either require a dedicated trusted party (typically called the Private Key Generator) to generate and pass the secret keys of the users [27,50] or the size of the ciphertext is linear in committee size [24,25]. The only known solution with constant sized ciphertexts uses $i\mathcal{O}$ [67]. In this work, we ask:

Can we realize threshold encryption without an interactive setup phase?

In particular, we want constant-size ciphertexts and non-interactive decryption. Similar questions have been recently asked for threshold signatures [20,43] or threshold encryption restricted to the special case of threshold $t = 1$ (a.k.a.,

---

[1] The only exception we are aware of is [67], which relies on Indistinguishability Obfuscation ($i\mathcal{O}$) [5].

distributed broadcast encryption[2]) [14,37,39,57,77]; however, this question has remained unexplored for threshold encryption.

1.1 Our Contributions

Silent Threshold Encryption. As our first contribution, we propose the notion of silent threshold encryption (STE). In STE, all parties locally sample a public key pair $\{(\mathsf{sk}_i, \mathsf{pk}_i)\}_{i \in [n]}$. These public keys can be *publicly* aggregated in a *deterministic* manner to produce a *succinct* encryption key ek. Importantly, ek is the only information required to encrypt a message. The threshold number of parties required to decrypt a ciphertext can be chosen *at the time of encryption*. As a crucial efficiency requirement, the encryption key ek, the ciphertext ct, and partial decryptions σ_i should all be of constant size. The aggregation time for recovering the message from partial decryptions should be both asymptotically (i.e., linear in the number of parties) and concretely comparable to standard threshold encryption.

STE naturally achieves all of the properties discussed above. It enjoys 1) silent setup – no interaction is required at all, 2) multiverse – a one-time setup that enables all future universe generation, and 3) dynamic threshold – every ciphertext comes with a ciphertext-specific threshold.

We emphasize that, before our work, the only known path to build STE used heavy cryptographic machinery such as indistinguishability Obfuscation ($i\mathcal{O}$) [5] or witness encryption for all NP [40].[3] In fact, various related primitives have been studied in the literature, such as distributed broadcast encryption [14,77] and threshold broadcast encryption [67]. Although some of these works studied a weaker variant of our primitive, all of their constructions require strong assumptions ($i\mathcal{O}$ and witness encryption). We refer the readers to Sect. 1.2 and Sect. 1.3 for more detailed discussions on this. Our work directly gives the first (concretely efficient) construction of this primitive based on pairing-friendly groups, which we discuss next.

A Practical STE Scheme. Our construction assumes a common reference string (CRS), which is similar to the CRS used in the KZG polynomial commitment scheme [53]. We prove the security of our scheme in the generic group model (GGM) [59,71].

Stated simply, our approach starts with committee members sampling a signature key pair $(\mathsf{sk}_i, \mathsf{pk}_i)$ and having them publish pk_i. When encrypting a message, a random ciphertext-specific tag is sampled, which can be viewed as a

---

[2] That is, distributed broadcast encryption can be seen as a setup-free threshold encryption supporting multiverse with threshold $t = 1$.
[3] This is in sharp contrast to threshold signatures with silent setup [20,43], where, theoretically, one could always apply a succinct non-interactive argument of knowledge (SNARK) to obtain a non-black-box solution.

random string. We then build a witness encryption scheme[4] for the following statement: "I have valid signatures under t-out-of-n public keys $\{\mathsf{pk}_i\}_{i \in [n]}$ on the (ciphertext-specific) tag". During decryption, committee members simply sign the tag as their partial decryption, using which, the corresponding ciphertext can be decrypted. The semantic security is guaranteed against any collusion of $< t$ number of parties.

In more detail, the signature scheme we use is a modification of the silent threshold signature scheme recently introduced in [43] (also concurrently [20]). Notably, our modification actually improves the efficiency of the original scheme [43]. In particular, the verification of the aggregated signature does not use any Fiat-Shamir heuristics [34], which is also crucial for our construction.

Arbitrary Threshold in the Asynchronous Setting. In typical threshold encryption schemes, the secret key is first shared using a linear-secret sharing scheme during the interactive setup phase which requires a DKG. In the asynchronous network setting, this limits the maximum corruption threshold to be $t < n/3$. In contrast, our scheme is the first, practical, threshold encryption scheme that can tolerate arbitrary corruption threshold in the asynchronous setting as we completely avoid the DKG and only need a PKI where parties register their public key.

Implementation and Evaluation. We created a Rust crate containing an implementation of our silent-threshold encryption scheme. Our benchmarks reveal that threshold encryption with silent setup is indeed practical. The ciphertext size is 9 group elements (768 bytes), which is only 8× as large as an ElGamal ciphertext. The encryption time is < 7 ms, which is independent of the committee size. For a maximum committee size of 1024 parties, it takes < 28 s for parties to set up their public keys. This is a one-time cost, and our implementation can be optimized further. Partial decryption takes < 1 ms as it requires just one group operation, irrespective of committee size. Finally, given partial decryptions, the message can be recovered in ≈ 200 ms for a committee size of 1024 parties. In large-scale distributed networks where DKGs can be very expensive, thereby limiting committee sizes to small numbers, we argue that our scheme offers a viable path for scaling to large committee sizes.

1.2 Applications

Advanced Encryption Schemes. Our work also provides new constructions and insights into many other advanced encryption primitives. We highlight them next.

---

[4] Throughout our work we slightly abuse the term 'witness encryption(WE)'. As a matter fact, we mostly refer to a relaxed type of WE where semantic security holds even when the witness is only computationally hard to find (in contrast to statistically in the original WE notion [40]).

1. *Distributed Broadcast Encryption.* Broadcast encryption [33] allows encryption to a subset $S \subseteq [n]$ (of parties). The security requirement is that parties can decrypt the message if and only if they belong to the target universe S. Crucially, the ciphertext should be succinct, ideally independent of the set size $|S|$. Traditionally, broadcast encryption considers the setting, where a central trusted party (the Private Key Generator) distributes secret keys for each party. A distributed broadcast encryption (DBE) [14,77], on the other hand, asks for the same functionality, while also demanding a silent setup, without any central trusted party. That is, parties locally sample their secret/public key pairs. For more than a decade, the only constructions of distributed broadcast encryption either relied on indistinguishability obfuscation ($i\mathcal{O}$) [14] or came without formal security arguments [77]. Only very recently, two works showed constructions of this primitive from simpler assumptions [37,57]. Our work provides an alternative solution to this problem. Indeed, distributed broadcast encryption is a special case of threshold encryption with silent setup, where the threshold $t = 1$. [5] In particular, the concrete efficiency of our scheme is comparable to the state-of-the-art [57], which is also based on pairings.

2. *Flexible Broadcast Encryption.* Recently Freitag et al. introduced the notion of Flexible Broadcast Encryption (FBE) [37], which is, in essence, a stronger variant of Distributed Broadcast Encryption (DBE) where users are oblivious of the state of the system at the time of their local keys sampling. In particular, in DBE users keys' are associated with a unique index, typically a counter of the users currently in the system, unlike FBE where keys are statelessly sampled. Freitag et al. showed a construction of FBE from Witness Encryption. Concurrently to our work, Garg et al. [39] showed a compiler to boost any DBE scheme to an FBE, therefore in combination with [57] achieved an FBE from pairings. However their compiler induces an $\omega(\log \lambda)$ overhead on the size of each public key. We show that a slight modification of our STE scheme provides a direct construction of FBE *without any overhead on the size of the public keys*. Therefore, this comprises the first FBE from pairings with $O(1)$ (in group elements) public keys' size. We stress that this is not the focus of our work, but, notably, our techniques allow us to get this highly desired feature for free.

3. *Threshold Broadcast Encryption.* More generally, one may consider a broadcast encryption with threshold $t > 1$. That is, the message can only be decrypted if and only if $\geq t$ parties from the target universe S partially decrypt it. This primitive is studied by several prior works under different names (e.g., dynamic threshold encryption [27] and threshold broadcast encryption [24,50,67]). Note that this notion is slightly weaker than

---

[5] In fact, threshold encryption ($t = 1$) with silent setup is slightly stronger than distributed broadcast encryption in that it decouples the generation of encryption key ek for a universe S and the encryption step. This one-time cost of computing ek could be amortized if one wants to broadcast many messages to the same universe S. In distributed broadcast encryption, this is not necessarily the case.

our notion of *multiverse threshold encryption*.[6] Unlike broadcast encryption, there is no work that realized threshold broadcast encryption with a silent setup – either the size of the ciphertext is linear in $|S|$ [24,25] or they require a trusted setup [27,50], with the only exception being [67] that resorts to $i\mathcal{O}$. Our work is the first one to construct a practical, threshold broadcast encryption with a silent setup.

Mempool Transaction Privacy. In many popular blockchains, including Ethereum (the chain with the largest DeFi liquidity), transactions from users are first submitted to a public mempool from which miners select transactions and create blocks that are to be appended to the blockchain. During the process, miners are free to insert their own transactions before and/or after a user's transactions, thereby allowing them to frontrun/backrun other transactions. This provides users of Decentralized Exchanges with worse prices, hurting the users' experience. This phenomenon was first documented under the umbrella of *Miner Extractable Value* (MEV), [19] with many followup works showing that it is a widespread issue [17,45,52,65,74]. In particular, an estimated 200,000,000 USD were lost on Ethereum in 2021 alone, mostly benefiting miners [62].

Consider another situation where a user discovers a bug in their smart contract that allows any party to drain all of its funds. A natural course of action could be to first *recover* the funds before any other party drains the account. However, when this user submits a transaction to the public mempool, a miner can *copy* this transaction to make themselves the receiver, and bribe other miners/pay higher gas fees to be included before the honest user. Finally, revealing the content of transactions allows miners to selectively censor certain users or certain types of transactions.

By encrypting transactions, the above issues can be mitigated as miners cannot frontrun transactions they have no information about. Encrypted mempools [7,32,54,58,63,68] have been a topic of active research in recent years, but they all require an expensive setup procedure limiting the committee sizes. Our solution completely avoids the setup procedure and is non-interactive, thereby allowing committees to scale even further.

Finally, in many applications, encryption and signatures are often used together – signatures for authentication and encryption for confidentiality. This is, in particular, true in the threshold setting. In blockchain applications, for instance, signatures are used for validating blocks and encryptions are used for the confidentiality of the transactions. Thus, it would be ideal if the same system supports both encryption and signatures. Otherwise, two independent systems need to be implemented. This was done as part of McFly [32], where the threshold signature functionality was augmented to support threshold encryption. However, their system needs a DKG setup. The solution we develop in this work achieves both signatures and encryption in one system without setup.

---

[6] Similar to the case of Distributed Broadcast Encryption, the difference is the decoupling of the encryption key derivation and the encryption step.

1.3 Related Work

Removing DKG from Threshold Crypto. DKG has been a bottleneck for deploying threshold signatures at scale for a long time. For instance, Ethereum 2.0 periodically samples 512 validators to sign on the newly created blocks to reach consensus [1]. Even for this moderate universe size, DKG is too costly that they opt for a multisignature, mainly due to the advantage of having a non-interactive setup. For the purpose of removing DKG, several recent works [20,43,60] gave various solutions to construct threshold signatures with a silent setup.

Note that, even in the silent setup setting where parties sample their key pairs independently, one can always generically apply existing succinct non-interactive arguments (SNARKs) to construct threshold signature schemes. That is, the aggregator will produce a SNARK proof certifying the statement: $\geq t$ parties have signed the message. With the recent rapid development in SNARK literature [38,48], such generic constructions will have small aggregated signatures and extremely fast verification time. The bottleneck, however, lies in proof generation time, which is the signature aggregation time for threshold signature. Therefore, the recent research efforts [20,43,60] can be viewed as designing custom SNARK schemes for signature verification with concretely efficient aggregation time.

Contrary to threshold signatures, removing DKG from threshold encryption is a *significantly more difficult* task. Note that, unlike threshold signature, there are *no generic feasibility solutions*. That is, it is not even clear if there are theoretical solutions regardless of the concrete efficiency. In fact, the only solution for threshold encryption with silent setup in the literature [67] requires $i\mathcal{O}$. As we have already discussed in Sect. 1.2, even for the restricted setting of $t = 1$ and the closely related notion of distributed broadcast encryption, we only recently began to have feasibility solutions [37,57].

Removing Setup from Advanced Encryption. More broadly, many recent works have been trying to remove the trusted setup in different advanced encryption schemes to move to a silent setup setting. In Sect. 1.2, we have already discussed the works [14,37,39,57,77] that construct broadcast encryption with a silent setup (i.e., distributed broadcast encryption). For identity-based encryption (IBE), the work of [41] initiated the study of registration-based encryption (RBE) as an IBE with a silent setup. A long line of works has been trying to construct concretely efficient RBE schemes [18,30,35,42,46,47]. Moreover, several recent works have extended this research effort to other advanced encryption schemes, such as (registered) attribute-based encryption [51,78] and (registered) functional encryption [23,36].

Our work belongs to this line of research, which initiates the removal of setup for the case of threshold encryption.

2 Technical Overview

Our objective is to construct a silent threshold encryption (STE), where parties independently sample their key pair ($\mathsf{sk}_i, \mathsf{pk}_i$). Afterward, a *succinct* encryption key ek can be *deterministically* derived from the public keys $\{\mathsf{pk}_i\}_i$. Given any message msg and a message-specific threshold t, the encryptor can produce a ciphertext $\mathsf{ct} = \mathsf{Enc}(\mathsf{ek}, \mathsf{msg}, t)$. Given any ct, party can locally partial decrypt it as $\sigma_i = \mathsf{Dec}(\mathsf{sk}_i, \mathsf{ct})$. We emphasize that the ciphertext ct and partial decryptions σ_i are also required to be constant-size. Given enough ($\geq t$) partial decryptions, the correct message can be reconstructed.

As we have already discussed, although STE is a natural strengthening of "threshold encryption with an interactive setup" (e.g., DKG), this notion turns out to be remarkably hard to construct (even for $t = 1$). On the other hand, silent threshold signature (STS) [20,43] is relatively easier to construct. Hence, our work starts with the following question.

Can we leverage a silent threshold signature to construct a silent threshold encryption?

Signature-based witness encryption (SWE) [32] is a generic tool for building encryption schemes from signature schemes. It allows the encryptor to encrypt a message with respect to the statement that there is a valid (aggregated) signature under some tag. The security guarantees that one can recover the message if and only if it does hold such a valid signature.

Although this approach conceptually works, many technical challenges remains. We do not know how to construct SWE for an arbitrary signature scheme. [32] only shows how to construct SWE for threshold BLS signatures [13]. In general, (plain) witness encryption for any NP languages typically requires strong assumptions such as $i\mathcal{O}$ [40] or non-standard non-falsifiable (knowledge) lattice assumptions [75,76]. Therefore, to instantiate this conceptual plan, we must overcome the following technical challenges.

1. Construct an *SWE for a* large class *of signatures.*
2. Construct an *STS that falls into this class.*

2.1 Signature-Based Witness Encryption for Linear Verifiable Signature

The starting point of our construction is to realize that one can construct an SWE for any signature scheme whose verification is a *public linear constraint* system. Take BLS signature [13] (refer to Definition 1) as an example, the verification checks if[7]

$$g \circ \sigma \stackrel{?}{=} \mathsf{pk} \circ \mathsf{RO}(\mathsf{tag}).$$

Here, the signature is σ, and everything else is *public*. Crucially, the verification is checking *a linear function* in the signature σ (as in it never computes $\sigma \circ \sigma$). Given such a linear verification, one may witness encrypt a message msg as[8]

$$\mathsf{ct} = (\mathsf{ct}_1, \mathsf{ct}_2) = \Big(\alpha \cdot g, \ \alpha \cdot (\mathsf{pk} \circ \mathsf{RO}(\mathsf{tag})) + \mathsf{msg} \Big),$$

---

[7] Here, RO stands for the random oracle, and ∘ stands for the pairing operation. For simplicity, we present it with symmetric pairing for now, but everything works similarly for asymmetric pairing.

[8] We adopt additive notation for the standard group operation.

where α is a random field element sampled by the encryptor. Given the signature σ, the decryption is done by $\mathsf{ct}_2 - (\mathsf{ct}_1 \circ \sigma)$. An astute reader might realize that this is Boneh-Franklin identity-based encryption [12] from a different perspective.

More generally, one may imagine a more sophisticated signature scheme with a linear verification (in matrix form) as[9]

$$A_{u \times v} \circ \begin{pmatrix} \sigma_1 \\ \sigma_2 \\ \vdots \\ \sigma_v \end{pmatrix} \overset{?}{=} \begin{pmatrix} b_1 \\ b_2 \\ \vdots \\ b_u \end{pmatrix}. \tag{1}$$

In this particular example, the signature consists of v group elements $(\sigma_1, \ldots, \sigma_v)$ and the verification checks u pairing equations. Most crucially, the matrix A and the vector $(b_1, \ldots, b_u)^\mathsf{T}$ are public information given the tag to sign. For such a signature scheme, one may witness encrypt it as

$$\mathsf{ct} = \left((\alpha_1, \ldots, \alpha_u) \cdot A, \ (\alpha_1, \ldots, \alpha_u) \cdot \begin{pmatrix} b_1 \\ b_2 \\ \vdots \\ b_u \end{pmatrix} + \mathsf{msg} \right)$$

$$= \Big((\alpha_1, \ldots, \alpha_u) \cdot A, \ \alpha_1 \cdot b_1 + \cdots + \alpha_u \cdot b_u + \mathsf{msg} \Big).$$

Again, $\alpha_1, \ldots, \alpha_u$ are random field elements sampled by the encryptor. Here, the ciphertext consists of $v + 1$ group elements and, given a valid signature $(\sigma_1, \ldots, \sigma_v)$, one may decrypt is as

$$\mathsf{ct}_{v+1} - \left((\mathsf{ct}_1, \ldots, \mathsf{ct}_v) \circ \begin{pmatrix} \sigma_1 \\ \sigma_2 \\ \vdots \\ \sigma_v \end{pmatrix} \right).$$

We remind the readers that the BLS example above is simply a special case of this general framework with a single group element signature (i.e., $v = 1$) and a single pairing equation verification step (i.e., $u = 1$).

2.2 Silent Threshold Signature with Linear Verification

Now that we have established that one can build a signature-based witness encryption scheme for any signature scheme with a linear verification, our next objective is to build a silent threshold signature that comes with a linear verification. At this point, it is helpful to first recall the silent threshold signature scheme from [43].[10]

---

[9] $A_{u \times v}$ highlights the fact that the dimension of A is $u \times v$.
[10] Although the construction we present here is based on a modification of [43], similar adaptations can be made to [20] to obtain a silent threshold signature with a linear verification scheme as well.

Overview of hinTS [43]. hinTS is a silent threshold signature scheme based on BLS signature. During the silent setup, each party will sample an independent BLS key pair $\{\mathsf{sk}_i, \mathsf{pk}_i = g^{\mathsf{sk}_i}\}$. In the online phase, given a tag to sign, parties simply sign it using the BLS signature. Now, suppose a subset $B \subseteq [n]$ of parties have signed tag, the aggregator will proceed to aggregate the partial signatures as follows. It first shall aggregate the partial signatures $\{\sigma_i\}_{i \in B}$ and public keys $\{\mathsf{pk}_i\}_{i \in B}$ as σ^* and aPK. Furthermore, to ensure unforgeability, the aggregator must prove the honest aggregation of aPK. In particular, the aggregator needs to commit to the vector B[11] and generating two corresponding succinct proofs π_1, π_2.

1. π_1 proves that aPK is the honest aggregation of public keys for parties in B, i.e.,

$$\mathsf{aPK} = (\mathsf{pk}_1, \ldots, \mathsf{pk}_n) \cdot \begin{pmatrix} b_1 \\ \vdots \\ b_n \end{pmatrix}.$$

2. π_2 proves that the committed subset B is an authorized set, i.e., $|B| \geq t$.

The final signature consists of the aggregated public key aPK, the aggregated signature σ^*, the commitment $\mathsf{Com}(B)$, and the two succinct proofs π_1, π_2. Correspondingly, the verification needs to verify the proofs π_1 and π_2 and verify the aggregated signature σ under the aggregated public key aPK.

Recall that our objective is to have a silent threshold signature with linear verification. Is the hinTS verification entirely linear? First, verifying σ^* under aPK is identical to BLS verification, i.e.,

$$g \circ \sigma^* \stackrel{?}{=} \mathsf{aPK} \circ \mathsf{RO}(\mathsf{tag}).$$

Therefore, this part of the verification is linear. To answer whether verifying π_1 and π_2 is linear or not, we need to delve deeper into how $\mathsf{Com}(B), \pi_1, \pi_2$ are generated, which we explain next.

Polynomial Commitment as Vector Commitment. Similar to pairing-based SNARKs, hinTS use KZG polynomial commitment [53] as a succinct vector commitment scheme. That is, for any vector $B = (b_1, b_2, \ldots, b_n)$, it is equivalently treated as a polynomial $B(x)$. [12] The commitment of B is simply the polynomial commitment of $B(x)$, i.e., $[B(\tau)]$, [13] where τ is the trapdoor in the KZG CRS $[\tau], [\tau^2], \ldots, [\tau^n]$.

---

[11] For a set $B \subseteq [n]$, we also think of B as an indicator vector $(b_1, \ldots, b_n) \in \{0,1\}^n$, i.e., $b_i = 1$ if and only if $i \in B$.
[12] For technical reasons, we treat $(b_1, b_2, \ldots, b_n)$ as the evaluation form of the polynomial instead of the coefficient form.
[13] For $x \in \mathbb{F}$, we use $[x]$ to denote group element $x \cdot g$, where g is the generator of the group. Refer to Sect. 3.1.

The Proof π_1. For proving that aPK is the inner product between the vector of public keys and B, hinTS relies on the following polynomial identity (known as generalized sumcheck)[14]

$$\mathsf{SK}(x) \cdot B(x) = \mathsf{aSK} + Q_x(x) \cdot x + Q_Z(x) \cdot Z(x),$$

where $\deg(Q_x)$ is required to be $\leq n-2$. We refer the readers to Lemma 1 for technical details. Given this polynomial identity, the proof consists of the polynomial commitment of $Q_x(x)$ and $Q_Z(x)$, i.e., $\pi_1 = ([Q_x(\tau)], [Q_Z(\tau)])$. Verifying π_1 involves checking the polynomial identity through pairing as

$$[\mathsf{SK}(\tau)] \circ [B(\tau)] \stackrel{?}{=} \mathsf{aPK} \circ [1] + [Q_x(\tau)] \circ [\tau] + [Q_Z(\tau)] \circ [Z(\tau)]. \quad (2)$$

Essentially, this verification step checks that the polynomial identity holds at the random location $x = \tau$. For our purpose, we crucially note that this verification step is linear. In particular, in Eq. 2, the group elements from the signature are *highlighted* and the rest are *public group elements*. Before we move on to π_2, we make a few remarks.

1. Although $[\mathsf{SK}(\tau)]$ is public information, computing this group element involves terms the verifier cannot compute, e.g., $[\mathsf{sk}_1 \cdot \tau]$. Therefore, this scheme crucially relies on each party (holding secret key sk) to also publish $[\mathsf{sk} \cdot \tau], [\mathsf{sk} \cdot \tau^2], \ldots$ [15] Similarly, the aggregator also relies on these additional terms to compute $[Q_x(\tau)]$ and $[Q_Z(\tau)]$.
2. As observed by [43], this proof π_1 is only *weakly sound* in the following sense. If some $[B(\tau)], \mathsf{aPK}, [Q_x(\tau)], [Q_Z(\tau)]$ passes Eq. 2 (for instance, the honest generated proof), the adversary can easily produce other tuples of elements, which will also pass Eq. 2. For instance,

$$[B(\tau)], \mathsf{aPK} + \tau, [Q_x(\tau) - 1], [Q_Z(\tau)].$$

However, this is not an issue in terms of unforgeability since the adversary cannot produce a valid signature σ for the (maliciously computed) aggregated public key (e.g., $\mathsf{aPK} + \tau$ in the above example).
3. We are omitting the fact that one needs to check the degree of Q_x is $\leq n-2$. As we will see shortly, the degree check is again a linear verification.

The Proof π_2. So far, the verification of hinTS is entirely linear. However, verifying π_2 turns out to be tricky. In particular, hinTS checks $B(x)$ is authorized by checking (1) B is a binary vector, (2) the inner product between B and $(1, 1, \ldots, 1)$ is t.[16] While the second condition can be proven similarly as π_1,

---
[14] Here, $\mathsf{SK}(x)$ is the polynomial defined by the vector $(\mathsf{sk}_1, \mathsf{sk}_2, \ldots, \mathsf{sk}_n)$ and $Z(x)$ is the (public) vanishing polynomial.
[15] These are referred to as *hints*, which is why the scheme is coined as hinTS.
[16] By changing $(1, 1, \ldots, 1)$ to some weighted vector $(w_1, \ldots, w_n)$, one naturally constructs a weighted threshold signature.

which supports linear verification, proving (1) turns out to be problematic. In particular, one typically uses the polynomial identity

$$B(x) \cdot (1 - B(x)) = Q(x) \cdot Z(x)$$

to prove that B is binary. As highlighted, this is a *degree-2* check (as in one needs to pair $[B(\tau)]$ with itself), which we do not know how to build a witness encryption for. Moreover, it seems inherent that one needs to check if B is binary; otherwise, the adversary may use $B = (t, 0, 0, \ldots, 0)$ to prove that B is authorized even though B contains only one party. This bottleneck raises the following technical question:

How can we prove that B is authorized using only linear verification?

Degree-check to the rescue. Our key observation for addressing this technical challenge is the following. Even if B is not a binary vector, as long as this vector B has $\geq t$ non-zero coordinates, $\mathsf{aPK} = (\mathsf{pk}_1, \ldots, \mathsf{pk}_n) \cdot (b_1, \ldots, b_n)^\mathsf{T}$ will be the aggregation of *sufficiently many* (i.e., $\geq t$) public keys, which by the security of BLS multisignature, is unforgeable if one does not have $\geq t$ partial signatures.

Now, checking that B has $\geq t$ non-zero coordinates could actually be done by a linear check. In particular, one may check this by running a degree check on $B(x)$. Intuitively, if a *non-zero* polynomial has degree $\leq n - t$, its evaluations will have $\leq n - t$ zeros and, hence, $\geq t$ non-zeros. Now, suppose the CRS is $[\tau], [\tau^2], \ldots, [\tau^n]$, checking if a committed polynomial $B(x)$ has degree $\leq n - t$ simply means, asking the prover to also commit to $\widehat{B}(x) = B(x) \cdot x^t$ and check if

$$[B(\tau)] \circ [\tau^t] \stackrel{?}{=} [\widehat{B}(\tau)] \circ [1].$$

Crucially for us, note that this is again a linear check.

Are we done? One subtlety is that we do require the committed polynomial $B(x)$ to be non-zero, i.e., $[B(\tau)] \neq [0]$. This check is actually non-linear. However, this can be simply fixed by introducing a dummy party P_0 and always requiring $\mathsf{P}_0 \in B$. Proving $\mathsf{P}_0 \in B$ introduces another KZG opening proof, whose verification again conforms to a linear check.

2.3 Putting It Together

We are now ready to put everything together to build our silent threshold encryption. First, the silent threshold signature scheme with a linear verification is summarized as follows. During silent setup phase, each party independently samples sk, pk and publishes pk together with the hints $[\mathsf{sk} \cdot \tau], [\mathsf{sk} \cdot \tau^2], \ldots$ Given a random group elements $[\gamma]$ to sign,[17] parties partially sign it as $[\gamma \cdot \mathsf{sk}]$. The aggregator aggregates these partial signatures into

---

[17] Looking ahead, this element is sampled by the encryptor in the encryption scheme. Therefore, it is not necessary to use a random oracle to sample a random group element as in the signature scheme.

aPK, σ^*, $[B(\tau)]$, $[Q_x(\tau)]$, $[Q_Z(\tau)]$, $[\hat{Q}_x(\tau)]$, $[\hat{B}(\tau)]$, $[Q_0(\tau)]$

which should satisfy the linear verification through the following five pairing equations.

$$[\mathsf{SK}(\tau)]_1 \circ [B(\tau)]_2 = [1]_2 \circ \mathsf{aPK} + [Z(\tau)]_2 \circ [Q_Z(\tau)]_1 + [\tau]_2 \circ [Q_x(\tau)]_1 \quad \text{(Sumcheck)}$$

$$[\tau]_2 \circ [Q_x(\tau)]_1 = [1]_2 \circ [\hat{Q}_x(\tau)]_1 \quad \text{(Degreepscheck)}$$

$$[\gamma]_2 \circ \mathsf{aPK} = [1]_1 \circ \sigma^* \quad \text{(Signature Verification)}$$

$$[\tau^t]_1 \circ [B(\tau)]_2 = [1]_2 \circ [\hat{B}(\tau)]_1 \quad \text{(Degreepscheck)}$$

$$[1]_1 \circ [B(\tau)]_2 = [\tau - 1]_2 \circ [Q_0(\tau)]_1 + 1 \quad \text{(DummyParty)}$$

As a sanity check, note that without introducing the dummy party, the linear system is trivially satisfiable (since all zero is a trivial solution), which means the corresponding signature scheme is trivially forgeable. Given this silent threshold signature scheme, one compiles it into an encryption scheme just as described in Sect. 2.1. In particular, our STS is a signature with $u = 8$ group elements and $v = 5$ pairing check verification.

This sums up our construction on a high level. We next discuss a few more points.

Security. We prove the security of our scheme in the generic group model (GGM) [59,71]. Intuitively, the security of the encryption scheme reduces to the unforgeability of the signature scheme. In GGM, the adversary can distinguish a ciphertext from a random group element if and only if it can derive this element by generic operations. By careful argument, this means that the adversary must be able to find $(\sigma_1, \ldots, \sigma_v)$ that satisfies Eq. 1, which gives us a forgery. One may argue that this cannot happen using similar reasoning as hinTS [43].

Efficiency. In our framework of constructing STE from STS: 1. the encryption key (of STE) is the verification key (of STS); 2. the partial decryption (of STE) is the partial signing (of STS); 3. decryption aggregation (of STE) is the partial signature aggregation (of STS), plus a few more constant-time operations (corresponding to the SWE). Therefore, our scheme inherits the efficiency of the STS scheme of the (modified) hinTS [43]. We provide implementation and evaluation details in Sect. 7.

Extensions. Our basic and CPA-secure scheme is described in Sect. 5. We then proceed to present some extensions to the basic scheme. First, we show that it readily enjoys a multiverse setting. Then we show a simple extension that has CCA2 security. We show that a straightforward variant of our scheme for $t = 1$ serves as a direct Flexible Broadcast Encryption construction with constant-sized public keys. We also discuss how to achieve STE with the highly desirable security properties of Post-Compromise and Forward Security. For the former, we argue that it is a property that we get for free from the Silent Setup setting. For the latter, we discuss how one can rely on a Forward Secure STS (seen as a variant of hinTS) to build a Forward Secure STE. Finally, we also note that our scheme supports a natural feature of *batch decryption*, which could be well-motivated in real-world scenarios. Namely, for a set of ciphertexts encrypted under the same tag, the committee member could send a succinct (i.e., independent of the number of ciphertexts to be decrypted) partial decryption to decrypt all such ciphertext simultaneously.

These extensions are discussed in Sect. 6.

3 Preliminaries

Notation. Throughout this work, we use λ for the security parameter and negl(λ) for a negligible function, i.e., a function that is less than $1/f(\lambda)$ for *any* polynomial f. We use $[n]$ to denote the set $\{1, \ldots, n\}$ and $[a, b]$ (for $a, b \in \mathbb{Z}$ and $a < b$) the set $\{a, a+1, \ldots, b\}$.

3.1 Bilinear Groups

A Bilinear Group $\mathcal{BG}$, generated as $(p, \mathbb{G}_1, \mathbb{G}_2, \mathbb{G}_T, g_1, g_2, e) \leftarrow \mathcal{BG}(1^\lambda)$, is specified by three groups $\mathbb{G}_1, \mathbb{G}_2, \mathbb{G}_T$ (the first two we call 'source groups' and the third 'target group') of prime order $p = 2^{\Theta(\lambda)}$, a bilinear map $e : \mathbb{G}_1 \times \mathbb{G}_2 \to \mathbb{G}_T$ that we call 'pairing' and one random generator g_1, g_2 for each group. We use the *implicit notation*, i.e., $[x]_s := x \cdot g_s$ and more generally $[\boldsymbol{A}]_s$ represents a matrix of the corresponding group elements, for $s \in \{1, 2, t\}$. Also, we denote the group operation additively, $[x]_s + [y]_s = [x+y]_s$, for $s \in \{1, 2, t\}$. By $[x]_1 \circ [y]_2 = [y]_2 \circ [x]_1 = [x \cdot y]_T$, we denote the pairing $e([x]_1, [y]_2)$. We note that the way it is defined '$\circ$' is commutative, for instance $([a]_1, [b]_2)^\intercal \circ ([c]_2, [d]_1)$ is well-defined and gives the outcome $[ac + bd]_T$.

All the algorithms of our constructions implicitly take as input a Bilinear Group generated by $\mathcal{BG}(\lambda)$, even if it is not explicitly stated.

For completeness, we include a definition of BLS signature [13] below.

Definition 1 (BLS Signature). *Let* RO $: \{0,1\}^* \to \mathbb{G}_2$ *be a random oracle. The BLS signature consists of the following algorithms.*

- blsgen*: It samples a random* sk $\leftarrow \mathbb{F}$ *and output a public/secret key pair as* (pk $=$ [sk]$_1$, sk)*.*
- blssign(msg)*: It signs as* $\sigma =$ sk $\cdot \mathcal{H}$(msg)*.*
- blsver(pk, msg, σ)*: It verifies the validity of the signature by* pk $\circ$ RO(msg) $\stackrel{?}{=}$ [1]$_1 \circ \sigma$*.*

3.2 Polynomials over $\mathbb{Z}_p$

Throughout the paper, we use the following notations for polynomials over the field $\mathbb{Z}_p$, defined by the bilinear group. Let $\omega \in \mathbb{Z}_p$ be an ℓ-th primitive root of unity, i.e. $\omega^\ell = 1$ over $\mathbb{Z}_p$. ω generates the multiplicative subgroup of roots of unity $\mathbb{H} = \{\omega, \omega^2, \ldots, \omega^\ell\}$, with $|\mathbb{H}| = \ell$. Let $L_1(x), L_2(x), \ldots, L_\ell(x)$ denote the Lagrange basis polynomial. That is, L_i is the unique degree-$(\ell - 1)$ polynomial defined by: $L_i(\omega^j)$ is 1 when $i = j$ and 0 when $i \neq j$. Let $Z(x) = \prod_{i=1}^{\ell}(x - \omega^i)$ be the vanishing polynomial on $\mathbb{H}$. Since $\mathbb{H}$ is a multiplicative subgroup, $Z(x) = x^\ell - 1$ and $L_i(x) = \frac{\omega^i}{\ell} \cdot \frac{x^\ell - 1}{x - \omega^i}$. Note that $L_i(0) = \frac{1}{\ell}$. Sometimes, we will refer to ω^ℓ as ω_0 and $L_0 = L_\ell$; since $\mathbb{H}$ is cyclic, they are equivalent.

3.3 Generic Group Model

Generic (Bilinear) Group model (GGM). Our security proof is based on the Generic Group Model [59,71]. A 'generic' adversary does not have concrete representations of the elements of the group and can only use generic group operations. This model captures the possible 'algebraic' attacks that an adversary can perform.

In particular, we follow the Maurer's GGM [59], which is extended to Bilinear Groups by [10]. The adversary in GGM makes oracle queries for each generic group operation she wishes to perform and receives a handle for the resulting group element, instead of the actual element itself. We call the party that answers the queries the 'challenger'. The challenger keeps three lists $\boldsymbol{L_1, L_2, L_T}$ of all group elements resulted from the queries of the adversary together with their corresponding handles.

A standard GGM technique in security proofs is the 'symbolic' equivalence. We call 'symbolic' experiment (and symbolic group representation, respectively) the model where the challenger is storing polynomials instead of group elements and performs polynomial operations instead of group operations. The formal variables of the polynomials are the initial elements that the adversary received. For example, a generic adversary to the discrete logarithm problem is initially receiving $[1], [x]$; thus, the formal variables are $1, X$, and then can perform any generic group operation which is going to be symbolically performed by the challenger with the corresponding polynomials in $\mathbb{Z}_p[1, X]$.

Master Theorem. We recall the 'Master Theorem' [10,15] that simplifies the proofs of the hardness of decisional problems.

Theorem 1 (Master theorem [10,15]). *Let $\boldsymbol{L_1} \in \mathbb{Z}_p[X_1, \ldots, X_n]^{\nu_1}$, $\boldsymbol{L_2} \in \mathbb{Z}_p[X_1, \ldots, X_n]^{\nu_2}$, $\boldsymbol{L_3} \in \mathbb{Z}_p[X_1, \ldots, X_n]^{\nu_T}$ be three lists[18] of n-variate polynomials over $\mathbb{Z}_p$ of maximum degree $d_{\boldsymbol{L}_1}, d_{\boldsymbol{L}_2}, d_{\boldsymbol{L}_T}$, respectively. Let $f \in \mathbb{Z}_p[X_1, \ldots, X_n]$ be an n-variate polynomial of degree d_f and denote $d =$*

---
[18] Throughout this section, we will abuse the notation sometimes, treating lists as vectors.

$\max\{d_{L_1}+d_{L_2}, d_{L_T}, d_f\}$, $\nu = \nu_1 + \nu_2 + \nu_3$. If f is independent of (L_1, L_2, L_T), then for any generic adversary $\mathcal{A}$ that makes at most q group oracle queries: where $\mathsf{h}_1, \mathsf{h}_2, \mathsf{h}_T$ denote the corresponding handles, and the probabilities are taken over the choices of $\boldsymbol{x} \leftarrow_\$ (\mathbb{Z}_p)^n$ and $r \leftarrow_\$ \mathbb{Z}_p$.

We have yet to specify what the f-(in)depenence of $\boldsymbol{L} = (L_1, L_2, L_T)$ means. First, define the *completion* [6] of $\boldsymbol{L}$ as

$$C(\boldsymbol{L}) := \{L_1 \otimes L_2\} \cup L_T.$$

Intuitively $\{L_1 \otimes L_2\}$ are all the elements in $\mathbb{G}_T$ that can be computed using pairings. Given this, f-(in)dependence is defined as follows.

Definition 2 *Let the lists of polynomials L_1, L_2, L_T with elements in $\mathbb{Z}_p[X_1, \ldots, X_n]$, the polynomial $f \in \mathbb{Z}_p[X_1, \ldots, X_n]$ and $C(\boldsymbol{L}) = \{g_1(X_1, \ldots, X_n), \ldots, g_D(X_1, \ldots, X_n)\}$. We say that f is dependent on $\boldsymbol{L} = (L_1, L_2, L_T)$ if there exist coefficients $\kappa_i \in \mathbb{Z}_p$ such that:*

$$f(X_1, \ldots, X_n) = \sum_{i=1}^{D} \kappa_i \cdot g_i(X_1, \ldots, X_D).$$

Otherwise, we say that f is independent of $\boldsymbol{L}$.

3.4 Univariate Sumcheck

Our construction relies on a univariate sumcheck protocol [9,66], slightly modified to work for inner products [16]. In particular, we use the following lemma.

Lemma 1 (Univariate Sumcheck [9,66]). *Let $A(x) = \sum_{i=1}^{|\mathbb{H}|} a_i \cdot L_i(x)$, $B(x) = \sum_{i=1}^{|\mathbb{H}|} b_i \cdot L_i(x)$. It holds that*

$$A(x) \cdot B(x) = \frac{\sum_i a_i b_i}{|\mathbb{H}|} + Q_x(x) \cdot x + Q_Z(x) \cdot Z(x),$$

where both Q_x and Q_Z are polynomials with degree $\leq |\mathbb{H}| - 2$ defined as

$$Q_x(x) = \sum_i a_i b_i \frac{L_i(x) - L_i(0)}{x},$$

$$Q_Z(x) = \sum_i a_i b_i \frac{L_i^2(x) - L_i(x)}{Z(x)} + \sum_{i \neq j} a_i b_j \frac{L_i(x) L_j(x)}{Z(x)}$$

We note that the original sumcheck is concretely stated for $b_i = 1$. In our case, we treat general inner products, which is a straightforward generalization (see [16]).

4 Defining Silent Threshold Encryption

This section formally defines the primitive: *silent threshold encryption* (STE). Our formal definition below is inspired by the silent threshold signature definition of [43]. In particular, parties will publish some "hints" together with their public key in a *silent* manner. Given all the hints, a public algorithm will verify the validity of the hints. Furthermore, a *succinct* encryption key will be deterministically computed from the hints.

Definition 3 (STE). *A Silent Threshold Encryption consists of a tuple of algorithms* $\Sigma =$ (Setup, KGen, HintGen, Preprocess, Enc, PartDec, PartVerify, DecAggr) *with the following syntax.*

- CRS $\leftarrow$ Setup($1^\lambda, M$): *On input the security parameter* λ *and an upper bound* M *on the maximum number of users, the* Setup *algorithm outputs a common reference string* CRS.
- (pk, sk) $\leftarrow$ KGen(1^λ): *On input the security parameter* λ, *the* KGen *algorithm outputs a public/secret key pair* (pk, sk).
- $\text{hint}_i \leftarrow$ HintGen(CRS, sk, M, i): *On input the* CRS, *the secret key* sk, *the number of parties* M, *and a position* $i \in [M]$, *the* HintGen *algorithm outputs a hint* hint_i.
- (ak, ek) $\leftarrow$ Preprocess(CRS, $\mathcal{U}$, $\{\text{hint}_i, \text{pk}_i\}_{i \in \mathcal{U}}$): *On input the* CRS, *a universe* $\mathcal{U} \subseteq [M]$, *all pairs* $\{\text{hint}_i, \text{pk}_i\}_{i \in \mathcal{U}}$, *the* Preprocess *algorithm computes an aggregation key* ak *and a encryption key* ek.
- ct $\leftarrow$ Enc(ek, msg, t) : *On input an encryption key* ek, *a message* msg *and a threshold* t, *it outputs a ciphertext* ct.
- $\sigma \leftarrow$ PartDec(sk, ct) : *On input a secret key* sk, *and a ciphertext* ct, PartDec *algorithm outputs a partial decryption* σ.
- 1/0 $\leftarrow$ PartVerify(ct, σ, pk) : *On input a ciphertext* msg, *a partial decryption* σ, *and a public key* pk, *it returns 1 if and only if the partial decryption verifies.*
- msg $\leftarrow$ DecAggr(CRS, ak, ct, $\{\sigma_i\}_{i \in S}$) : *On input the* CRS, *an aggregation key* ak, *and a set of partial decryptions* $\{\sigma_i\}_{i \in S}$, *the* DecAggr *algorithm outputs a message* msg.

Moreover, STE must have the following efficiency requirements:

– *The encryption key* ek *and the ciphertext* ct *should be constant size.*
– *Partial decryption should only take constant time.*

Remark 1 (Silent Setup). We note that HintGen does not take other parties' public keys pk_i's as input. It solely depends on the CRS and, hence, parties can publish ($\text{pk}_i, \text{hint}_i$) in *one shot*. In other words, ($\text{pk}_i, \text{hint}_i$) can be viewed as the (extended) public key of party i.

Remark 2 (Preprocessing). The preprocessing algorithm is only decoupled from encryption and decryption aggregation for efficiency reasons. In terms of functionality and security, it could be equivalently embedded in the Enc and DecAggr algorithms.

This decoupling is helpful in the threshold encryption setting, where a universe $\mathcal{U}$ is generated once, and an encryptor will encrypt with respect to $\mathcal{U}$ repetitively. In this way, the preprocessing cost is *amortized*. In other applications, such as threshold broadcast encryption (see Sect. 1.2), one may equivalently embed processing inside encryption and decryption aggregation.

Due to the complexity of the primitive, we define correctness through a game between a challenger and an adversary. Note that the adversary is computationally unbounded, and the correctness is perfect. Intuitively, we allow the adversary to choose the universe $\mathcal{U}$ and control any number of users in $\mathcal{U}$. Furthermore, the adversary can output the partial decryptions of any party it controls. It is important to note that correctness should hold even for *maliciously generated* public keys, hints, and partial decryptions of users controlled by the adversary. The formal definition of correctness can be found below.

---

1. The challenger runs CRS $\leftarrow$ Setup($1^\lambda, M$) and gives CRS to $\mathcal{A}$.
2. The adversary picks a universe $\mathcal{U}^*$ and a subset Cor of corrupt parties such that Cor $\subseteq \mathcal{U}^*$.
3. For all $i \in \mathcal{U}^* \setminus$ Cor, the public key and hint are sampled honestly $(\mathsf{pk}_i, \mathsf{sk}_i) \leftarrow \mathsf{KGen}(1^\lambda)$ and $\mathsf{hint}_i = \mathsf{HintGen}(\mathsf{CRS}, \mathsf{sk}_i, M, i)$.
4. For all $i \in$ Cor, the adversary returns a (potentially maliciously generated) public key pk_i and hint hint_i to the challenger.
5. The challenger invokes the preprocessing as (ek, ak) $\leftarrow$ Preprocess(CRS, $\mathcal{U}^*$, $\{\mathsf{hint}_i, \mathsf{pk}_i\}_{i \in \mathcal{U}^*}$) and the outputs are given to $\mathcal{A}$.
6. The adversary is given access to the partial decryption oracle of the honest parties, and it picks a message msg and a threshold t.
7. The honest ciphertext is generated ct $\leftarrow$ Enc(ek, msg, t).
8. The adversary prepares the partial decryptions $\{\sigma_i\}_{i \in S_1}$ for some subset of malicious parties $S_1 \subseteq$ Cor. Let $S_1' \subseteq S_1$ be the subset of maliciously generated partial decryptions that *verifies* under PartVerify.
9. The adversary may also request a subset of honest parties $S_2 \subseteq \mathcal{U}^* \setminus$ Cor for partial decryptions, which are returned by computing $\sigma_i \leftarrow$ PartDec(sk_i, ct).
10. If $|S_1' \cup S_2| \geq t$ (i.e., there are sufficiently many *verified* partial decryptions), the challenger computes the aggregated decryption as msg' $\leftarrow$ DecAggr(CRS, ak, ct, $\{\sigma_i\}_{i \in S}$), where $S = S_1' \cup S_2$.
11. The output of this game is 0 if msg $\neq$ msg'.

Fig. 1. Correctness Game

Definition 4 (Correctness). *The STE scheme Σ satisfies correctness if, for any unbounded adversary $\mathcal{A}$ and any $M = \mathsf{poly}(\lambda)$, the output of the correctness game defined in Fig. 1 is 0 with probability 0.*

For the security of STE, we naturally define a semantic security game between a challenger $\mathcal{C}$ and a PPT adversary $\mathcal{A}$. Again, the adversary chooses the target universe $\mathcal{U}^*$ and corrupts any subset of parties, denoted by Cor, in $\mathcal{U}^*$. Later, the adversary also chooses the threshold t (adaptively). For the security to be meaningful, we demand that $t > |\mathsf{Cor}|$; otherwise, $\mathcal{A}$ can trivially win the game.

Definition 5 (Semantic Security). *The STE scheme Σ satisfies semantic security if, for every $M = \mathsf{poly}(\lambda)$ and any adversary PPT $\mathcal{A}$, the output of the game in Fig. 2 is 1 with probability $\leq 1/2 + \mathsf{negl}(\lambda)$.*

---

1. The challenger runs $\mathsf{CRS} \leftarrow \mathsf{Setup}(1^\lambda, M)$ and gives CRS to $\mathcal{A}$.
2. The adversary picks $\mathcal{U}^*$ and a subset of parties to corrupt $\mathsf{Cor} \leftarrow \mathcal{A}(\mathsf{CRS})$.
3. For all honest parties $i \in \mathcal{U}^* \setminus \mathsf{Cor}$, the public key and hint are sampled honestly by the challenger $(\mathsf{pk}_i, \mathsf{sk}_i) \leftarrow \mathsf{KGen}(1^\lambda)$ and $\mathsf{hint}_i = \mathsf{HintGen}(\mathsf{CRS}, \mathsf{sk}_i, M, i)$ and are sent to $\mathcal{A}$.
4. For all $i \in \mathsf{Cor}$, the adversary picks a public key pk_i and the corresponding hint hint_i.
5. The challenger invokes the preprocessing as $(\mathsf{ek}, \mathsf{ak}) \leftarrow \mathsf{Preprocess}(\mathsf{CRS}, \mathcal{U}^*, \{\mathsf{hint}_i, \mathsf{pk}_i\}_{i \in \mathcal{U}^*})$ and the output are given to $\mathcal{A}$.
6. The adversary picks messages $\mathsf{msg}_0, \mathsf{msg}_1$, and a threshold t.
7. The challenger picks a bit $b \leftarrow \{0,1\}$ and generates a ciphertext $\mathsf{ct}^* \leftarrow \mathsf{Enc}(\mathsf{ek}, \mathsf{msg}_b, t)$.
8. The adversary outputs a bit b' and wins the semantic security game if $t > |\mathsf{Cor}|$ and $b' = b$, in which case, the output of the game is 1.

Fig. 2. Security Game

Remark 3. The adversary $\mathcal{A}$ can also corrupt parties outside the target universe $\mathcal{U}^*$. However, they do not play any role as they do not participate in the decryption committee, i.e., their public keys are not taken as input on Enc or DecAggr. For correctness and security, we can ignore them; equivalently, one may consider all parties outside $\mathcal{U}^*$ corrupted.

5 Our Silent Threshold Encryption Construction

This section presents our core contribution: our construction of a silent threshold encryption scheme. First, in Sect. 5.1, we show the description of the construction. Then, Sect. 5.2 presents the analysis of the scheme: its (asymptotic) efficiency, correctness, and security proof.

5.1 Construction

Here, we describe formally our silent threshold encryption scheme. For an intuitive description of the construction, we refer to Sect. 2. As noted there, the core of the construction is a (witness) encryption with respect to a matrix $\boldsymbol{A}$ representing the verification of a threshold signature. To ease the presentation, we explain here where this matrix comes from. Consider the following five pairing equations[19] (recall from Sect. 3 that '$\circ$' is commutative).

1. $[\mathsf{SK}(\tau)]_1 \circ [B(\tau)]_2 = [1]_2 \circ \mathsf{aPK} + [Z(\tau)]_2 \circ [Q_Z(\tau)]_1 + [\tau]_2 \circ [Q_x(\tau)]_1$
2. $[\tau]_2 \circ [Q_x(\tau)]_1 = [1]_2 \circ [\hat{Q}_x(\tau)]_1$
3. $[\gamma]_2 \circ \mathsf{aPK} = [1]_1 \circ \sigma^*$
4. $[\tau^t]_1 \circ [B(\tau)]_2 = [1]_2 \circ [\hat{B}(\tau)]_1$
5. $[1]_1 \circ [B(\tau)]_2 = [\tau - 1]_2 \circ [Q_0(\tau)]_1 + 1$

where $\mathsf{SK}(X) = \sum_{i=1}^{M} \mathsf{sk}_i L_i(X)$. This, essentially, yields a Silent Threshold Signature verification. In particular, this is a variant of hinTS [43].

Intuitively, the first equation is for proving the honest aggregation of aPK by the univariate sumcheck (Lemma 1). The second and fourth equation is for the degree check on Q_x and B. The third equation verifies the aggregated signature σ (for a random tag $[\gamma]_2$) under the aggregated public key aPK. Finally, the fifth equation is for checking that a dummy party is always included in B, so that setting everything to $[0]$ does not give a valid solution.

In matrix form, this can be written as $\boldsymbol{A} \circ \boldsymbol{w} = \boldsymbol{b}$, where

$$\boldsymbol{w} = \left([B(\tau)]_2, -\mathsf{aPK}, [-Q_Z(\tau)]_1, [Q_x(\tau)]_1, [\hat{Q}_x(\tau)]_1, \sigma^*, [\hat{B}(\tau)]_1, [Q_0(\tau)]_1\right)^\top$$

is the aggregated signature. In conclusion, the matrix $\boldsymbol{A}$ comes from the above linear verification. The only difference is that, we can replace $\mathsf{RO}(\mathsf{tag})$ with a random element $[\gamma]_2$ during the encryption.

Henceforth, we will consider that $M + 1$ is a power of 2 and we set the subgroup $\mathbb{H} = \{\omega^0, \omega^1, \ldots, \omega^M\}$ of roots of unity to be such that $|\mathbb{H}| = M + 1$. M is the maximum number of decryptors participating in the system. We reserve an artificial position 0 that always has $\mathsf{sk}_0 = 1$. No actual user is allowed to use 0 as her index. We consider that the artificial user 0 is always in the set of the universe $\mathcal{U}$.

Construction 1 *We present below a formal description of our silent threshold encryption scheme:*

- Setup(1^λ): *Sample* $\tau \leftarrow_\$ \mathbb{Z}_p$ *and output:* [20]

$$\mathsf{CRS} = \left([\tau^1]_1, \ldots, [\tau^{M+1}]_1, [\tau^1]_2, \ldots, [\tau^{M+1}]_2\right).$$

---

[19] The shaded elements are from the signature. The rest are public group elements.
[20] For efficiency, we assume that all algorithms also have direct access to $\{[L_i(\tau)]_{1,2}\}_i$, which can be efficiently computed from $\{[\tau^i]_{1,2}\}$ without knowing τ.

- KGen(1^λ): *Sample $x \leftarrow_\$ \mathbb{Z}_p^*$ and output* pk $= [x]_1$, sk $= x$.
- HintGen(CRS, sk$_i$, i, M): *output*

$$\text{hint}_i = \Bigg([\text{sk}_i L_i(\tau)]_1, [\text{sk}_i(L_i(\tau) - L_i(0))]_1, \left[\text{sk}_i \frac{L_i^2(\tau) - L_i(\tau)}{Z(\tau)} \right]_1,$$

$$\left[\text{sk}_i \frac{L_i(\tau) - L_i(0)}{\tau} \right]_1, \left\{ \left[\text{sk}_i \frac{L_i(\tau) L_j(\tau)}{Z(\tau)} \right]_1 \right\}_{j \in [0, M], j \neq i} \Bigg).$$

- Preprocess(CRS, $\mathcal{U}$, $\{\text{hint}_i, \text{pk}_i\}_{i \in \mathcal{U}}$): *Verify the validity of each hint: for each $i \in \mathcal{U}$ run* isValid(CRS, hint$_i$, pk$_i$) *(*isValid *is defined below) and let $V \subseteq \mathcal{U}$ be the set of the indices with valid hints. Set* sk$_0 = 1$ *and* sk$_i = 0$ *for each $i \notin \mathcal{U}$ outside the universe. Implicitly, set* sk$_i = 0$ *for each $i \notin V$ and for each $i \in [M] \setminus \mathcal{U}$ outside the universe. Output*

$$\text{ak} = \Bigg(V, \{\text{pk}_i\}_{i \in V \cup \{0\}}, \left\{ [\text{sk}_i(L_i(\tau) - L_i(0))]_1 \right\}_{i \in V \cup \{0\}},$$

$$\left\{ \left[\text{sk}_i \frac{L_i^2(\tau) - L_i(\tau)}{Z(\tau)} \right]_1 \right\}_{i \in V \cup \{0\}}, \left\{ \left[\text{sk}_i \frac{L_i(\tau) - L_i(0)}{\tau} \right]_1 \right\}_{i \in V \cup \{0\}},$$

$$\left\{ \left[\sum_{j \in S, j \neq i} \text{sk}_j \frac{L_i(\tau) L_j(\tau)}{Z(\tau)} \right]_1 \right\}_{i \in V \cup \{0\}} \Bigg).$$

$$\text{ek} = \Bigg(\left[\sum_{i \in V} \text{sk}_i L_i(\tau) \right]_1, [Z(\tau)]_2 \Bigg) := (C, Z)$$

- Enc(ek, msg, t): *Sample $[\gamma]_2 \leftarrow_\$ \mathbb{G}_2$, parse* ek $:= (C, Z)$, *set $Z_0 = [\tau - \omega^0]_2$ and set*

$$\boldsymbol{A} = \begin{pmatrix} C & [1]_2 & Z & [\tau]_2 & 0 & 0 & 0 & 0 \\ 0 & 0 & 0 & [\tau]_2 & [1]_2 & 0 & 0 & 0 \\ 0 & [\gamma]_2 & 0 & 0 & 0 & [1]_1 & 0 & 0 \\ [\tau^t]_1 & 0 & 0 & 0 & 0 & 0 & [1]_2 & 0 \\ [1]_1 & 0 & 0 & 0 & 0 & 0 & 0 & Z_0 \end{pmatrix}$$

$$\boldsymbol{b} = ([0]_T, [0]_T, [0]_T, [0]_T, [1]_T)^\top.$$

Notice that each column of $\boldsymbol{A}$ contains elements from the same source group (looking ahead, this is so that the pairing $\boldsymbol{A} \circ \boldsymbol{w}$ can be properly performed.) Sample a vector $\boldsymbol{s} \leftarrow_\$ (\mathbb{Z}_p^*)^5$ and output

$$\text{ct} = \left([\gamma]_2, \boldsymbol{s}^\top \cdot \boldsymbol{A}, \boldsymbol{s}^\top \cdot \boldsymbol{b} + \text{msg} \right).$$

- PartDec(sk, ct): *Parse* ct $:= ([\gamma]_2, \text{ct}_2, \text{ct}_3)$ *and output $\sigma = $ sk $\cdot [\gamma]_2$.*

- PartVerify(ct, σ, pk) : *Parse* ct := $([\gamma]_2, \mathbf{ct}_2, \mathsf{ct}_3)$ *and output* 1 *if and only if* pk $\circ$ $[\gamma]_2 = [1]_1 \circ \sigma$.
- DecAggr(CRS, ak, ct, $\{\sigma_i\}_{i\in S}$) : *Using* ak *compute the subset of indices with valid hints,* $S_v = S \cap V$. *Then proceed as follows:*
  1. *Compute a polynomial* $B(X)$ *by interpolating* 0 *on all* ω_i *with* $i \notin S_v$ *and* 1 *on* ω^0, *i.e., interpolate* B *as* $\{(\omega^0, 1), (\omega^i, 0)_{i \notin S_v}\}$ *and set*

$$B = \left[\sum_{i=0}^{M} B(\omega^i) L_i(\tau)\right]_2$$

  2. *Set* aPK $= \frac{1}{M+1}(\sum_{i \in S_v} B(\omega^i) \mathsf{pk}_i + [1]_1)$.
  3. *Compute polynomials* $Q_x(X)$ *and* $Q_Z(X)$ *such that*

$$\mathsf{SK}(X)B(X) = \frac{\mathsf{aSK}}{M+1} + Q_Z(X)Z(X) + Q_x(X)X$$

where aSK $= \sum_{i=0}^{M} \mathsf{SK}(\omega^i)B(\omega^i) := \sum_{i \in S_v} \mathsf{sk}_i B(\omega^i) + 1$ *(since, by definition, B evaluates to* 0 *outside* S_v *and to* 1 *on* ω^0).
According to Lemma 1 they can be computed as:

$$Q_Z(X) = \sum_{i=0}^{M+1} B(\omega^i)\left(\mathsf{sk}_i \frac{L_i^2(X) - L_i(X)}{Z(X)}\right)$$

$$+ \left(\sum_{i=0}^{M+1} B(\omega^i) \sum_{j=0, j \neq i}^{M+1} \mathsf{sk}_j \frac{L_i(X)L_j(X)}{Z(X)}\right),$$

$$Q_x(X) = \sum_{i=0}^{M+1} B(\omega^i)\left(\mathsf{sk}_i \frac{L_i(X) - L_i(0)}{X}\right).$$

Then using ak *compute* $Q_Z = [Q_Z(\tau)]_1$.
  4. *Compute* $Q_x = [Q_x(\tau)]_1$.
  5. *Compute* $\hat{Q}_x = [Q_x(\tau) \cdot \tau]_1$
  6. *Set* $\sigma^* = \frac{1}{M+1}(\sum_{i \in S_v} B(\omega^i)\sigma_i + \mathsf{ct}_1)$.
  7. *Compute* $\hat{B} = [\tau^t B(\tau)]_1$
  8. *Compute a KZG evaluation at* ω^0, *i.e., compute* $Q_0(X)$ *such that* $B(X) - 1 = Q_0(X)(X - \omega^0)$ *and compute* $Q_0 = [Q_0(\tau)]_1$.

Set $\boldsymbol{w} = \left(B, -\mathsf{aPK}, -Q_Z, -Q_x, \hat{Q}_x, \sigma^*, -\hat{B}, -Q_0\right)^\top$, *parse* ct $= (\mathsf{ct}_1, \mathbf{ct}_2, \mathsf{ct}_3)$ *and output:*

$$\mathsf{msg}^* = \mathsf{ct}_3 - \mathbf{ct}_2 \circ \boldsymbol{w}$$

In order to confirm that hint_i is well-formed in the Preprocess algorithm we use an isValid algorithm which we define as follows.

isValid(CRS, hint_i, pk_i) $\to \{0, 1\}$: parses $\mathsf{hint}_i := (h_1, h_2, h_3, h_4, \{h_{5,j}\}_{j \in [0,M], j \neq i})$ and output 1 iff it holds that:

1. $h_1 \circ [1]_2 = \mathsf{pk}_i \circ [L_i(\tau)]_2$,
2. $h_2 \circ [1]_2 = \mathsf{pk}_i \circ [(L_i(\tau) - L_i(0))]_2$,
3. $h_3 \circ [1]_2 = \mathsf{pk}_i \circ [\frac{L_i^2(\tau) - L_i(\tau)}{Z(\tau)}]_2$,
4. $h_4 \circ [1]_2 = \mathsf{pk}_i \circ [\frac{L_i(\tau) - L_i(0)}{\tau}]_2$,
5. $h_5 \circ [1]_2 = \mathsf{pk}_i \circ [\frac{L_i(\tau)L_j(\tau)}{Z(\tau)}]_2$, for each $j \in [0, M], j \neq i$.

5.2 Analysis

Efficiency. We measure the computational complexity (running times) of our algorithms in group operations. Firstly, if we have CRS as 'powers-of-tau' $[\tau^i]_{1,2}$, it takes $O(M \log M)$ time to compute the 'powers-of-Lagrange' $[L_i(\tau)]_{1,2}$ via DFT. KGen takes $O(1)$ time. HintGen takes $O(M)$ multiplication and additions, respectively. Preprocess for $\mathcal{U}$ is dominated by $O(|\mathcal{U}|^2)$ additions. Enc and PartDec require $O(1)$ multiplications, while PartVerify requires $O(1)$ pairings. Finally, DecAggr require $O(|\mathcal{U}|\mathsf{polylog}|\mathcal{U}|)$ field operations and $O(|\mathcal{U}|)$ group multiplications (see Sect. 7 last paragraph).

For the communication complexity (sizes), we measure in group elements:

- $|\mathsf{CRS}| = (M+1)|\mathbb{G}_1| + (M+1)|\mathbb{G}_2|$,
- $|\mathsf{pk}_i| = 1|\mathbb{G}_1|, |\mathsf{sk}_i| = 1|\mathbb{Z}_p|$,
- $|\mathsf{hint}_i| = (M+3)|\mathbb{G}_1|$,
- $|\mathsf{ak}| = (5|\mathcal{U}|+5)|\mathbb{G}_1|, |\mathsf{ek}| = 1|\mathbb{G}_1| + 1|\mathbb{G}_2|$,
- $|\mathsf{ct}| = 2|\mathbb{G}_1| + 7|\mathbb{G}_2| + 1|\mathbb{G}_T|$,
- $|\sigma_i| = 1|\mathbb{G}_2|$.

Correctness. For correctness, we first show that if the partial decryptions and the malicious keys sent by the adversary pass the verification, then they are well-formed.

- Malicious σ_i: If PartVerify$(\mathsf{ct}, \sigma_i, \mathsf{pk}_i) = 1$ then by definition $\mathsf{pk}_i \circ [\gamma]_2 = [1]_1 \circ \sigma_i$. Since $\mathbb{G}_1$ is cyclic (since it has prime order p), there always exist $\mathsf{sk}_i \in \mathbb{Z}_p$ such that $\mathsf{pk}_i = [\mathsf{sk}_i]_1$ and $y \in \mathbb{Z}_p$ such that $\sigma_i = [y]_2$. Therefore, from the pairing we get that $[y]_T = [\gamma \mathsf{sk}_i]_T$, which means that $y = \gamma \mathsf{sk}_i$, thus $\sigma_i = [\gamma \mathsf{sk}_i]_2$ is well-formed.
- Malicious $\mathsf{pk}_i, \mathsf{hint}_i$: If isValid(CRS, $\mathsf{hint}_i, \mathsf{pk}_i) = 1$ then using the same argument $\mathsf{pk}_i = [\mathsf{sk}_i]$ for some $\mathsf{sk}_i \in \mathbb{G}_1$. Then by applying the five pairing checks and repeating the same line of thought as above it is straightforward to get that $\mathsf{hint}_i = \mathsf{HintGen}(\mathsf{CRS}, \mathsf{sk}_i, i, M)$ is well-formed.

At this point, correctness comes by careful inspection, in essence using the correctness of the univariate sumcheck (Lemma 1).

Security. The semantic security of our construction is summarized as the following Theorem 2. Due to space constraints, we omit the proof and refer the readers to the full version of this work.

Theorem 2. *Construction 1 is a semantically secure Silent Threshold Encryption scheme in the generic group model.*

6 Extensions of the Basic Construction

We present various extensions and implications of our core silent threshold encryption scheme described in Sect. 5.

6.1 Multiverse Silent Threshold Encryption

As described in the introduction, a highly desirable property for a threshold encryption scheme is to be able to support different sets of decryptor committees, i.e., different 'universes', without re-running the setup of the system. This is reminiscent of multiverse threshold signatures [4,43].

We stress that our construction supports *by default* any universe. We specify at the beginning an upper bound on the size of the universe M and then the scheme works for any subset of parties of size $\leq M$. Each user is computing her hint, which is then valid for *every* universe. Then, notice that the Preprocess algorithm takes as input any universe. Crucially, the efficiency of our scheme only scales with the maximum number of universe M, but not the overall number of users participating in the system. For instance, even if we have a million users, if the maximum universe size is 1024, each user only needs to publish hints[21] of size ≤ 1024.

6.2 CCA2 Security

In CCA2 security for threshold encryption [11], the adversary $\mathcal{A}$ is given access to the partial decryption oracle for honest users before and after she receives the challenge ciphertext ct^*. Intuitively, to enhance an STE with CCA2 security, we need to make sure that ct^* is not *indirectly* queried for partial decryption after $\mathcal{A}$ sees it. Of course, for the security definition to be meaningful the adversary cannot query *directly* ct^*.

A bit more formally, the ciphertext $\mathsf{ct} = ([\gamma]_2, \mathbf{ct}_2, \mathsf{ct}_3)$. The partial decryption, nonetheless, is oblivious to $\mathbf{ct}_2, \mathsf{ct}_3$, it solely depends on $[\gamma]_2$. What an adversary can possibly do after receiving the challenge ciphertext $\mathsf{ct}^* = ([\gamma^*]_2, \mathbf{ct}_2^*, \mathsf{ct}_3^*)$ is to query $\mathsf{ct}' = ([\gamma^*]_2, \mathbf{ct}_2', \mathsf{ct}_3')$, which is technically a different ciphertext.

To prevent this and achieve CCA2 security, it suffices to 'bind' together the three parts of the ciphertext. For this, we employ a straight-line simulation-extractable [26,69] tag-based NIZK as was done in [72] for the ElGamal encryption scheme. The NIZK proves knowledge of γ, while the tag contains $\mathbf{ct}_2$ and ct_3. This can be, for instance, a straight-line simulation-extractable Schnorr protocol for $[\gamma]_2$ in the Algebraic Group Model, where we use Fiat-Shamir, and the random oracle additionally takes the $\mathsf{tag} = (\mathbf{ct}_2, \mathsf{ct}_3)$ as input. Then, the ciphertext of the CCA2 secure scheme gets $([\gamma]_2, \mathbf{ct}_2, \mathsf{ct}_3, \pi)$, where π is the NIZK proof. After this appropriate adaptation, it is straightforward for the challenger to simulate partial decryption-oracle queries: She uses the extractor of the NIZK to obtain $[\gamma]_2$ and then computes the partial decryption $\mathsf{sk}_i \cdot [\gamma]_2$ honestly. The

---

[21] The hints can be made independent of the index i as described in Sect. 6.3.

only difference between CPA and CCA security game is the adversary's partial decryption query, once we can simulate these queries, the rest of the proof is similar to CPA security. Since this transformation is a standard technique, we only describe it at a high level.

6.3 Flexible Broadcast (and Threshold) Encryption

Freitag et al. [37] recently introduced the notion of *Flexible Broadcast Encryption* (FBE). This is, essentially, an enhancement of Distributed Broadcast Encryption (DBE) [14,77], i.e., Broadcast Encryption without a central authority (see Sect. 1.2), in which the user does not need to be assigned to a specific index in $i \in [M]$. That is, the public keys of the users are oblivious to any index i. Then, the public keys alone suffice to encrypt and decrypt. [37] provided a construction from general-purpose witness encryption. Then Garg et al. [39] provided a generic compiler for FBE from any DBE, however inducing an $\omega(\log \lambda)$ overhead on the size of the public keys. Here we present a direct FBE construction from Pairings with $O(1)$ keys.

We refer the readers to the full version for a definition of the Flexible Broadcast Encryption.

With a simple modification, our construction can achieve this property, where the public key and the corresponding hints do not depend on any index i. First, we observe that the actual public key already does not depend on the index of the user: $\mathsf{pk} = [\mathsf{sk}]_1$. The hint hint_i, however, depend on the specific index: for instance $[\mathsf{sk}_i L_i(\tau)]_1$ depends on the specific lagrange poynomial L_i. To circumvent this we observe that a 'powers-of-tau' hint $\mathsf{hint}'_i = \{[\mathsf{sk}_i \tau^j]_1\}_{j \in [M+1]}$ is functionally fully equivalent; from hint'_i one can efficiently derive hint_i. Therefore, the modified STE scheme with hint'_i as hints is equivalent, in terms of correctness, with Construction 1. We note that the observation, regarding hint'_i being i-independent and equivalent to hint_i, was already made in [43] in the context of Silent Threshold Signatures.

Our Construction. For completeness, we show our FBE construction below.

- Setup(1^λ): Sample $\tau \leftarrow\!\!\!\$\, \mathbb{Z}_p$ and output:

$$\mathsf{CRS} = \left([\tau^1]_1, \ldots, [\tau^{M+1}]_1, [\tau^1]_2, \ldots, [\tau^{M+1}]_2\right).$$

- KGen(1^λ): Sample $x \leftarrow\!\!\!\$\, \mathbb{Z}_p^*$ and output $\mathsf{pk} = [x]_1$, $\mathsf{sk} = x$.
- HintGen(CRS, sk, M): output

$$\mathsf{hint}_\mathsf{pk} = \left([\mathsf{sk} \cdot \tau]_1, \ldots, [\mathsf{sk} \cdot \tau^{M+1}]_1\right)$$

- Preprocess(CRS, $\{\mathsf{hint}_{\mathsf{pk}_i}, \mathsf{pk}_i\}_{i=1}^k$): Verify the validity of each hint: for each $i \in [k]$ run isValid(CRS, $\mathsf{hint}_{\mathsf{pk}_i}, \mathsf{pk}_i$) (isValid is defined below) and let $V \subseteq [k]$ be the set of the indices with valid hints. Set $\mathsf{sk}_0 = 1$ and $\mathsf{sk}_i = 0$ for each $i \notin V$. Output:

$$\mathsf{dk} = \left(V, \{\mathsf{pk}_i\}_{i \in V \cup \{0\}}, \left\{ [\mathsf{sk}_i(L_i(\tau) - L_i(0))]_1 \right\}_{i \in V \cup \{0\}}, \right.$$
$$\left\{ \left[\mathsf{sk}_i \frac{L_i^2(\tau) - L_i(\tau)}{Z(\tau)} \right]_1 \right\}_{i \in V \cup \{0\}}, \left\{ \left[\mathsf{sk}_i \frac{L_i(\tau) - L_i(0)}{\tau} \right]_1 \right\}_{i \in V \cup \{0\}},$$
$$\left. \left\{ \left[\sum_{j \in S, j \neq i} \mathsf{sk}_j \frac{L_i(\tau) L_j(\tau)}{Z(\tau)} \right]_1 \right\}_{i \in V \cup \{0\}} \right).$$
$$\mathsf{ek} = \left(\left[\sum_{i \in V} \mathsf{sk}_i L_i(\tau) \right]_1, [Z(\tau)]_2 \right) := (C, Z)$$

It is crucial that the above can be computed by having access to $([\mathsf{sk}_i\tau^j]_1)_{j \in [k+1]}$ and $[\mathsf{sk}_i]_1$ (which is contained in $\mathsf{hint}_{\mathsf{pk}} = ([\mathsf{sk}_i\tau^j]_1)_{j \in [M+1]}$ and pk_i respectively). In essence, from $([\mathsf{sk}_i\tau^j]_1)_{j \in [0,k+1]}$ one can efficiently compute any $[\mathsf{sk} \cdot f(\tau)]_1$ for *any* univariate polynomial f of degree at most $k+1$

- $\mathsf{Enc}(\mathsf{ek}, \mathsf{msg})$: Identical to Construction 1 with threshold set to 1.
- $\mathsf{Dec}(\mathsf{dk}, \mathsf{ct}, (j, \mathsf{sk}_j))$: Each user runs $\sigma_j \leftarrow \mathsf{PartDec}(\mathsf{sk}, \mathsf{ct})$ and outputs $\mathsf{msg}^* \leftarrow \mathsf{DecAggr}(\mathsf{CRS}, \mathsf{dk}, \mathsf{ct}, \sigma_j)$, where $\mathsf{DecAggr}$ is defined in Construction 1.

To conclude our FBE construction we define the isValid algorithm as follows:

isValid($\mathsf{CRS}, \mathsf{hint}_{\mathsf{pk}}, \mathsf{pk}$) $\to \{0, 1\}$: parses $\mathsf{hint}_{\mathsf{pk}} := (h_1, \ldots, h_{M+1})$ and output 1 iff it holds that:
1. $h_1 \circ [1]_2 = \mathsf{pk} \circ [\tau]_2$
2. $h_i \circ [1]_2 = h_{i-1} \circ [\tau]_2$, for each $i \in [2, M+1]$

Security. For semantic security, observe that the security proof already uses a modified scheme with 'powers-of-tau' hints in a game-hop, it is essentially $\mathbf{Game}_1$. Therefore, the security of this modification readily follows from that.

Remark 4. We describe our construction in the context of FBE, to stress the implications of our STE scheme to this recently introduced notion. That is we describe it for a threshold of $T = 1$. We note that our construction can be extended in a straightforward way to work for any threshold T. Overall, this yields the first pairing-based Flexible Threshold Encryption scheme.

6.4 Forward and Post-compromise Security

As a final extension, in this subsection, we briefly discuss how we can achieve Threshold Encryption with Silent Setup that additionally supports Forward Security [8] and Post-Compromise Security [61]. These are two highly desirable properties in real-world applications where secret keys can be potentially compromised.

Forward Secure STE. A Threshold Encryption scheme has, informally, Forward Security if a secret key compromise at the present cannot affect old ciphertexts. That is, a leakage of a secret key should not allow one to partially decrypt (sufficiently) old ciphertexts. This, intuitively, requires that users' keys are periodically updated in manner that the new keys cannot decrypt ciphertexts computed with the old keys.

In this section, we informally discuss how we can obtain a Forward Secure STE scheme from Pairings using the techniques we developed for our STE scheme of Sect. 5.

Following our reasoning for STE, if we start from a Pairing-based Threshold Signature scheme that has (1) silent setup, (2) public linear verification (in the pairing operator, '∘'), and additionally has (3) *Forward Security*, we can use our witness encryption methodology to construct an STE with Forward Security.

To this end, we can resort to Pixel [31], a Forward Secure aggregate signature scheme, which is a variant of BLS. The verification equation of an aggregated signature in Pixel is similar to the one of BLS:

$$[\alpha]_2 \circ \mathsf{aPK} + [\alpha_0 + \sum_{j=1}^{t} \alpha_j t_j + \alpha_{\ell+1}\gamma]_1 \circ \sigma_2^* = \sigma_1^* \circ [1]_2$$

where $\sigma^* = (\sigma_1^*, \sigma_2^*) = (\prod_{i=1}^{n} \sigma_{i,1}, \prod_{i=1}^{n} \sigma_{i,2})$ is the aggregated signature of $\sigma_1, \ldots, \sigma_n$, $\{[\alpha]_2, [\alpha_0]_1, \ldots, [\alpha_{\ell+1}]_1\}$ are public group elements, $[\gamma]_1$ is the tag and **t** a public variable specifying the session number of the signature. Crucially the aggregated public key $\mathsf{aPK} = [x_1 + \ldots + x_n]_2$ is identical to the one in the BLS signature. Therefore, one can build a Silent Setup version of Pixel analogously to the STS scheme of BLS, unveiled in the technical overview (see sec. 2.2). The verification of the Silent Setup Pixel would be as follows:

1. $[\mathsf{SK}(\tau)]_1 \circ [B(\tau)]_2 = [1]_2 \circ \mathsf{aPK} + [Z(\tau)]_2 \circ [Q_{\dot{z}}(\tau)]_1 + [\tau]_2 \circ [Q_x(\tau)]_1$
2. $[\tau]_2 \circ [Q_x(\tau)]_1 = [1]_2 \circ [\hat{Q}_x(\tau)]_1$
3. $[\alpha]_2 \circ \mathsf{aPK} + [\alpha_0 + \sum_{j=1}^{t} \alpha_j t_j + \alpha_{\ell+1}\gamma]_1 \circ \sigma_2^* = \sigma_1^* \circ [1]_2$
4. $[\tau^t]_1 \circ [B(\tau)]_2 = [1]_2 \circ [\hat{B}(\tau)]_1$
5. $[1]_1 \circ [B(\tau)]_2 = [\tau - 1]_2 \circ [Q_0(\tau)]_1 + 1$

Finally, we observe that the above is a public linear constraint system, thus from this STS scheme, we can build a Threshold Encryption scheme with Silent Setup that admits Forward Security. The latter property is inherited directly from the forward security of Pixel.

Post-compromise Secure STE. Post-Compromise Security in the context of Threshold Encryption is, essentially, the property that even if a secret key is leaked in a specific time instance, it will become shortly useless in (partially) decrypting ciphertexts. In particular, to achieve this property users' keys should be periodically updated.

We stress that Silent Setup offers a straightforward means to Post-Compromise Security, in comparison to DKG protocols. That is, a party is updating her keys by just locally sampling a new secret and then (deterministically) computing the corresponding public keys and hints. After that, the user posts her updated public key/hint pair, and new ciphertexts can be computed with respect to the updated keys of the user. In contrast, in Threshold Encryption schemes that resort to Distributed Key Generation protocols a new round of interaction between the users should happen in order to update the users' keys.

Batch Decryption. Finally, we observe that our scheme also supports batch decryption of a set of ciphertext encrypted under the same tag. Indeed, if a set of ciphertext is witness-encrypted under the same statement that "at least a threshold number of parties have signed the group element tag". Then each committee member's signature of tag enables the decryption of all such ciphertexts.[22] One can also imagine scenarios where this feature is well-motivated. For example, in the mempool transaction application we discussed, users can encrypt their transactions from the same time period (say, from time t_1 to time t_2) under the same tag (say, tag = $\mathsf{RO}(t_1, t_2)$). Consequently, the committee can send a succinct partial decryption to decrypt all transactions simultaneously as opposed to a per-transaction partial decryption.

7 Implementation and Evaluation

To evaluate the concrete performance of our silent-threshold encryption scheme, we implement our scheme in Rust. We use the arkworks [3] library for implementations of pairing-friendly curves and the associated algebra. Our code can be found at https://anonymous.4open.science/r/silent-threshold-D07D/.

Setup. All of our experiments were run on a 2019 MacBook Pro with a 2.4 GHz Intel Core i9 processor and 16 GB of DDR4 RAM in single-threaded mode.[23] We use BLS12-381 as our pairing-friendly curve. For all experiments, we use a threshold $t = n/2$, where n is the number of parties.

Evaluation. We now evaluate the performance of our STE. In particular, we aim to answer the following questions and provide insights about bottlenecks in different parts of the protocol.

- How long does it take to set up and aggregate public keys? What are their sizes?
- How long does it take to encrypt a message? What is the size of corresponding ciphertexts?
- How long does it take to recover all messages given partial decryptions?

---

[22] Note that the fresh randomness employed in each ciphertext ensures semantics security even if they are witness-encrypted under the same statement.

[23] We note that our scheme can take can full advantage of multi-threaded architectures to achieve a perfect division of work.

Finally, how do the above vary with committee size? Throughout the evaluation, where meaningful, we compare our scheme against the ElGamal encryption scheme to understand the *price* of silent setup.

Key Generation. We note that local key generation cost scales linearly with the number of parties. But our implementation does not preprocess commitments to Lagrange Polynomials, and instead uses the KZG CRS in *coefficient* form. As a result, it runs in quadratic time. Nonetheless, this provides a very crude upperbound on the key generation time. It is only done once per party, and for a large committee of size 1024, it takes less than 28 s, even using our inefficient implementation. We provide the local key generation times for smaller committee sizes in Table 1.

Table 1. Scaling of key generation and reconstruction times with committee size.

Parties	Key Gen. (s)	Decryption (ms)
8	0.007	12.9
32	0.06	20.2
128	0.65	45.5
512	7.87	126.1
1024	27.79	211.0

Encryption. Given an aggregated public key, a constant number of group operations are needed to encrypt a ciphertext. The ciphertext consists of 7 $\mathbb{G}_2$ elements and 2 $\mathbb{G}_1$ elements and a string proportional to the message length, which amounts to 768 bytes ignoring the message size. In comparison to ElGamal, which requires an expensive interactive setup, our ciphertexts are only 12× larger. We observe that it takes < 7 ms to encrypt a message, independent of the committee size. There is a trade-off possible between the size of the public key and ciphertexts by switching the source groups. In this case, the ciphertext size would be 528 bytes, and the encryption would be faster.

Partial Decryption. Here, each party computes one group exponentiation which takes < 1 ms, and the size of each partial decryption is just one $\mathbb{G}_2$ element (96 bytes), which can again be halved by switching the groups. This makes the communication needed for decryption quite small – in fact, identical to ElGamal.

Reconstruction. Any party can publicly recover the message given enough partial decryptions of the ciphertext. The main bottleneck here is the group exponentiations involved in computing various witness elements w, which scale linearly with the number of parties.[24] arkworks provides an implementation

---

[24] Since aggregation takes all partial descriptions as input, its cost inevitably scales with n.

of Pippenger's algorithm [64], which brings the complexity of multi-scalar-multiplications down to $O(n/\log n)$. Even for a committee of size 1024, ciphertexts can be decrypted in close to 200 ms. Indeed, ElGamal only needs one multi-scalar-multiplication of size $O(n)$ for reconstruction and will be more efficient than our scheme.

We note that, when interpolating the polynomial $B(X)$, we are only given evaluations over a subset of the roots of unity, which do not necessarily form a set FFT-friendly evaluation points. Interpolating this polynomial naïvely using Lagrange interpolation, would take $O(n^2)$ *field operations*. This is indeed what we do in our implementation. However, one can speed up this to $O(n \operatorname{polylog}(n))$ using standard techniques for non-FFT friendly evaluation points (see, e.g., [49, 70]). We do not implement this faster version because, for the committee sizes (e.g., 1024) that we benchmark, $O(n^2)$ field operations are still much faster than $O(n)$ group operations. Actually, the interpolation cost is only $< 1\%$ of the total reconstruction time. As a result, it would not meaningfully affect the reported numbers.

Acknowledgments. The first, third, and fourth authors are supported in part by DARPA under Agreement No. HR00112020026, AFOSR Award FA9550-19-1-0200, NSF CNS Award 1936826, and research grants by the Sloan Foundation, Visa Inc, the BAIR Commons Meta Fund, and the Stellar Development Foundation. The third author is also supported by the AI Policy Hub Fellowship from the UC Berkeley Center for Long-Term Cybersecurity. The second author received funding from projects from the European Research Council (ERC) under the European Union's Horizon 2020 research and innovation program under project PICOCRYPT (grant agreement No. 101001283) and from the Spanish Government under projects PRODIGY (TED2021-132464B-I00) and ESPADA (PID2022-142290OB-I00). The last two projects are co-funded by European Union EIE, and NextGenerationEU/PRTR funds.

References

1. Ethereum: Minimal Light Client. https://github.com/ethereum/annotated-spec/blob/master/altair/sync-protocol.md
2. Abraham, I., Jovanovic, P., Maller, M., Meiklejohn, S., Stern, G., Tomescu, A.: Reaching consensus for asynchronous distributed key generation. In: Proceedings of the 2021 ACM Symposium on Principles of Distributed Computing, PODC'21, pp. 363–373, New York, NY, USA (2021). Association for Computing Machinery
3. Arkworks contributors. `arkworks` zksnark ecosystem. https://arkworks.rs (2022)
4. Baird, L., et al.: Threshold signatures in the multiverse. IEEE S&P 2023 (2023). https://eprint.iacr.org/2023/063
5. Barak, B., et al.: On the (Im)possibility of obfuscating programs. In: Kilian, J. (ed.) Advances in Cryptology — CRYPTO 2001, pp. 1–18. Springer, Berlin, Heidelberg (2001). https://doi.org/10.1007/3-540-44647-8_1
6. Barthe, G., Fagerholm, E., Fiore, D., Mitchell, J., Scedrov, A., Schmidt, B.: Automated analysis of cryptographic assumptions in generic group models. J. Cryptol. **32**(2), 324–360 (2018). https://doi.org/10.1007/s00145-018-9302-3

7. Bebel, J., Ojha, D.: Ferveo: Threshold decryption for Mempool privacy in BFT networks. Cryptology ePrint Archive, Report 2022/898 (2022). https://eprint.iacr.org/2022/898
8. Bellare, M., Miner, S.K.: A forward-secure digital signature scheme. In: Wiener, M. (ed.) CRYPTO 1999. LNCS, vol. 1666, pp. 431–448. Springer, Heidelberg (1999). https://doi.org/10.1007/3-540-48405-1_28
9. Ben-Sasson, E., Chiesa, A., Riabzev, M., Spooner, N., Virza, M., Ward, N.P.: Aurora: transparent succinct arguments for R1CS. In: Ishai, Y., Rijmen, V. (eds.) EUROCRYPT 2019. LNCS, vol. 11476, pp. 103–128. Springer, Cham (2019). https://doi.org/10.1007/978-3-030-17653-2_4
10. Boneh, D., Boyen, X., Goh, E.-J.: Hierarchical identity based encryption with constant size ciphertext. In: Cramer, R. (ed.) EUROCRYPT 2005. LNCS, vol. 3494, pp. 440–456. Springer, Heidelberg (2005). https://doi.org/10.1007/11426639_26
11. Boneh, D., Boyen, X., Halevi, S.: Chosen ciphertext secure public key threshold encryption without random oracles. In: Pointcheval, D. (ed.) CT-RSA 2006. LNCS, vol. 3860, pp. 226–243. Springer, Heidelberg (2006). https://doi.org/10.1007/11605805_15
12. Boneh, D., Franklin, M.: Identity-based encryption from the Weil pairing. In: Kilian, J. (ed.) CRYPTO 2001. LNCS, vol. 2139, pp. 213–229. Springer, Heidelberg (2001). https://doi.org/10.1007/3-540-44647-8_13
13. Boneh, D., Lynn, B., Shacham, H.: Short signatures from the Weil pairing. In: Boyd, C. (ed.) ASIACRYPT 2001. LNCS, vol. 2248, pp. 514–532. Springer, Heidelberg (2001). https://doi.org/10.1007/3-540-45682-1_30
14. Boneh, D., Zhandry, M.: Multiparty key exchange, efficient traitor tracing, and more from indistinguishability obfuscation. In: Garay, J.A., Gennaro, R. (eds.) CRYPTO 2014. LNCS, vol. 8616, pp. 480–499. Springer, Heidelberg (2014). https://doi.org/10.1007/978-3-662-44371-2_27
15. Boyen, X.: The uber-assumption family. In: Galbraith, S.D., Paterson, K.G. (eds.) Pairing 2008. LNCS, vol. 5209, pp. 39–56. Springer, Heidelberg (2008). https://doi.org/10.1007/978-3-540-85538-5_3
16. Campanelli, M., Nitulescu, A., Ràfols, C., Zacharakis, A., Zapico, A.: Linear-map vector commitments and their practical applications. In: Agrawal, S., Lin, D., editors, Advances in Cryptology – ASIACRYPT 2022, Part IV, volume 13794 of Lecture Notes in Computer Science, pp. 189–219, Taipei, Taiwan, December 5–9, 2022. Springer, Heidelberg, Germany (2022). https://doi.org/10.1007/978-3-031-22972-5_7
17. Capponi, A., Jia, R., Wang, Y.: The evolution of blockchain: from lit to dark. *arXiv preprint* (2022)
18. Cong, K., Eldefrawy, K., Smart, N.P.: Optimizing registration based encryption. In: Paterson, M.B. (ed.) IMACC 2021. LNCS, vol. 13129, pp. 129–157. Springer, Cham (2021). https://doi.org/10.1007/978-3-030-92641-0_7
19. Daian, P., et al.: Flash boys 2.0: frontrunning in decentralized exchanges, miner extractable value, and consensus instability. In: 2020 IEEE Symposium on Security and Privacy, pp. 910–927, San Francisco, CA, USA, May 18–21, 2020. IEEE Computer Society Press (2020)
20. Das, S., Camacho, P., Xiang, Z., Nieto, J., Bunz, B., Ren, L.: Threshold signatures from inner product argument: succinct, weighted, and multi-threshold. CCS 2023 (2023). https://eprint.iacr.org/2023/598
21. Das, S., Xiang, Z., Ren, L.: Asynchronous data dissemination and its applications. In: Vigna, G., Shi, E., editors, ACM CCS 2021: 28th Conference on Computer

and Communications Security, pp. 2705–2721, Virtual Event, Republic of Korea, November 15–19, 2021. ACM Press (2021)
22. Das, S., Yurek, T., Xiang, Z., Miller, A., Kokoris-Kogias, L., Ren, L.: Practical asynchronous distributed key generation. In: 2022 IEEE Symposium on Security and Privacy (SP), pp. 2518–2534 (2022)
23. Datta, P., Pal, T.: Registration-based functional encryption. Cryptology ePrint Archive (2023)
24. Daza, V., Herranz, J., Morillo, P., Ràfols, C.: CCA2-secure threshold broadcast encryption with shorter ciphertexts. In: Susilo, W., Liu, J.K., Mu, Y. (eds.) Provable Security, pp. 35–50. Springer, Berlin, Heidelberg (2007). https://doi.org/10.1007/978-3-540-75670-5_3
25. Daza, V., Herranz, J., Morillo, P., Ràfols, C.: Ad-hoc threshold broadcast encryption with shorter ciphertexts. Electron. Notes Theor. Comput. Sci. **192**(2), 3–15 (2008)
26. De Santis, A., Di Crescenzo, G., Ostrovsky, R., Persiano, G., Sahai, A.: Robust non-interactive zero knowledge. In: Kilian, J. (ed.) CRYPTO 2001. LNCS, vol. 2139, pp. 566–598. Springer, Heidelberg (2001). https://doi.org/10.1007/3-540-44647-8_33
27. Delerablée, C., Pointcheval, D.: Dynamic threshold public-key encryption. In: Wagner, D. (ed.) CRYPTO 2008. LNCS, vol. 5157, pp. 317–334. Springer, Heidelberg (2008). https://doi.org/10.1007/978-3-540-85174-5_18
28. Desmedt, Y.: Society and group oriented cryptography: a new concept. In: Pomerance, C. (ed.) CRYPTO 1987. LNCS, vol. 293, pp. 120–127. Springer, Heidelberg (1988). https://doi.org/10.1007/3-540-48184-2_8
29. Desmedt, Y., Frankel, Y.: Threshold cryptosystems. In: Brassard, G. (ed.) CRYPTO 1989. LNCS, vol. 435, pp. 307–315. Springer, New York (1990). https://doi.org/10.1007/0-387-34805-0_28
30. Döttling, N., Kolonelos, D., R.W.F. Lai, Lin, C., Malavolta, G., Rahimi, A.: Efficient laconic cryptography from learning with errors. In: Hazay, C., Stam, M., editors, Advances in Cryptology – EUROCRYPT 2023, Part III, volume 14006 of Lecture Notes in Computer Science, pp. 417–446, Lyon, France, April 23–27, 2023. Springer, Heidelberg, Germany (2023). https://doi.org/10.1007/978-3-031-30620-4_14
31. Drijvers, M., Gorbunov, S., Neven, G., Wee, H.: Pixel: multi-signatures for consensus. In: Capkun, S., Roesner, F., editors, USENIX Security 2020: 29th USENIX Security Symposium, pp. 2093–2110. USENIX Association, August 12–14 (2020)
32. Döttling, N., Hanzlik, L., Magri, B., Wohnig, S.: McFly: verifiable encryption to the future made practical. Financial Crypto 2023 (2023). https://eprint.iacr.org/2022/433
33. Fiat, A., Naor, M.: Broadcast Encryption. In: Stinson, D.R. (ed.) Advances in Cryptology — CRYPTO' 93, pp. 480–491. Springer, Berlin, Heidelberg (2001). https://doi.org/10.1007/3-540-48329-2_40
34. Fiat, A., Shamir, A.: How to prove yourself: practical solutions to identification and signature problems. In: Odlyzko, A.M. (ed.) Advances in Cryptology — CRYPTO' 86, pp. 186–194. Springer, Berlin, Heidelberg (2000). https://doi.org/10.1007/3-540-47721-7_12
35. Fiore, D., Kolonelos, D., de Perthuis, P.: Cuckoo commitments: registration-based encryption and key-value map commitments for large spaces. In: Asiacrypt 2023- International Conference on the Theory and Application of Cryptology and Information Security (2023)
36. Francati, D., Friolo, D., Maitra, M., Malavolta, G., Rahimi, A., Venturi, D.: Registered (inner-product) functional encryption. Cryptology ePrint Archive (2023)

37. Freitag, C., Waters, B., Wu, D.J.: How to use (plain) witness encryption: registered ABE, flexible broadcast, and more. CRYPTO 2023 (2023). https://eprint.iacr.org/2023/812
38. Gabizon, A., Williamson, Z.J., Ciobotaru, O.: PLONK: permutations over Lagrange-bases for oecumenical noninteractive arguments of knowledge. Cryptology ePrint Archive, Report 2019/953 (2019). https://eprint.iacr.org/2019/953
39. Garg, R., Lu, G., Waters, B., Wu, D.J.: Realizing flexible broadcast encryption: how to broadcast to a public-key directory. In: Proceedings of the 2023 ACM SIGSAC Conference on Computer and Communications Security, pp. 1093–1107 (2023)
40. Garg, S., Gentry, C., Halevi, S., Raykova, M., Sahai, A., Waters, B.: Candidate indistinguishability obfuscation and functional encryption for all circuits. In: 54th Annual Symposium on Foundations of Computer Science, pp. 40–49, Berkeley, CA, USA, October 26–29, 2013. IEEE Computer Society Press (2013)
41. Garg, S., Hajiabadi, M., Mahmoody, M., Rahimi, A.: Registration-based encryption: removing private-key generator from IBE. In: Beimel, A., Dziembowski, S., editors, TCC 2018: 16th Theory of Cryptography Conference, Part I, vol. 11239 of Lecture Notes in Computer Science, pp. 689–718, Panaji, India, November 11–14, 2018. Springer, Heidelberg, Germany (2018). https://doi.org/10.1007/978-3-030-03807-6_25
42. Garg, S., Hajiabadi, M., Mahmoody, M., Rahimi, A., Sekar, S.: Registration-based encryption from standard assumptions. In: Lin, D., Sako, K. (eds.) PKC 2019. LNCS, vol. 11443, pp. 63–93. Springer, Cham (2019). https://doi.org/10.1007/978-3-030-17259-6_3
43. Garg, S., Jain, A., Mukherjee, P., Sinha, R., Wang, M., Zhang, Y.: Hints: threshold signatures with silent setup. IEEE S&P 2024 (2024). https://eprint.iacr.org/2023/567
44. Gennaro, R., Jarecki, S., Krawczyk, H., Rabin, T.: Secure distributed key generation for discrete-log based cryptosystems. J. Cryptol. **20**, 51–83 (1999)
45. Gervais, A., Karame, G.O., Wüst, K., Glykantzis, V., Ritzdorf, H., Capkun, S.: On the security and performance of proof of work blockchains. In: Proceedings of the 2016 ACM SIGSAC Conference on Computer and Communications Security (2016)
46. Glaeser, N., Kolonelos, D., Malavolta, G., Rahimi, A.: Efficient registration-based encryption. In: Proceedings of the 2023 ACM SIGSAC Conference on Computer and Communications Security, pp. 1065–1079 (2023)
47. Goyal, R., Vusirikala, S.: Verifiable registration-based encryption. In: Micciancio, D., Ristenpart, T. (eds.) CRYPTO 2020. LNCS, vol. 12170, pp. 621–651. Springer, Cham (2020). https://doi.org/10.1007/978-3-030-56784-2_21
48. Groth, J.: On the size of pairing-based non-interactive arguments. In: Fischlin, M., Coron, J.-S. (eds.) EUROCRYPT 2016. LNCS, vol. 9666, pp. 305–326. Springer, Heidelberg (2016). https://doi.org/10.1007/978-3-662-49896-5_11
49. Harvey, D., Van Der Hoeven, J., Lecerf, G.: Faster polynomial multiplication over finite fields. J. ACM (JACM) **63**(6), 1–23 (2017)
50. Herranz, J., Laguillaumie, F., Ràfols, C.: Constant size ciphertexts in threshold attribute-based encryption. In: Nguyen, P.Q., Pointcheval, D. (eds.) PKC 2010. LNCS, vol. 6056, pp. 19–34. Springer, Heidelberg (2010). https://doi.org/10.1007/978-3-642-13013-7_2
51. Hohenberger, S., Lu, G., Waters, B., Wu, D.J.: Registered attribute-based encryption. In: Hazay, C., Stam, M. (eds.) Advances in Cryptology – EUROCRYPT 2023:

42nd Annual International Conference on the Theory and Applications of Cryptographic Techniques, Lyon, France, April 23-27, 2023, Proceedings, Part III, pp. 511–542. Springer Nature Switzerland, Cham (2023). https://doi.org/10.1007/978-3-031-30620-4_17
52. Judmayer, A., Stifter, N., Schindler, P., Weippl, E.R.: Estimating (miner) extractable value is hard, let's go shopping!. IACR Cryptology ePrint Archive (2021)
53. Kate, A., Zaverucha, G.M., Goldberg, I.: Constant-size commitments to polynomials and their applications. In: Abe, M. (ed.) Advances in Cryptology - ASIACRYPT 2010, pp. 177–194. Springer, Berlin, Heidelberg (2010). https://doi.org/10.1007/978-3-642-17373-8_11
54. Kavousi, A., Le, D.V., Jovanovic, P., Danezis, G.: BlindPerm: efficient MEV mitigation with an encrypted mempool and permutation. Cryptology ePrint Archive, Paper 2023/1061 (2023). https://eprint.iacr.org/2023/1061
55. Kogias, E.K., Malkhi, D., Spiegelman, A.: Asynchronous distributed key generation for computationally-secure randomness, consensus, and threshold signatures. New York, NY, USA (2020). Association for Computing Machinery
56. Kokoris-Kogias, E., Malkhi, D., Spiegelman, A.: Asynchronous distributed key generation for computationally-secure randomness, consensus, and threshold signatures. In: Ligatti, J., Ou, X., Katz, J., Vigna, G., editors, ACM CCS 2020: 27th Conference on Computer and Communications Security, pp. 1751–1767, Virtual Event, USA, November 9–13, 2020. ACM Press (2020)
57. Kolonelos, D., Malavolta, G., Wee, H.: Distributed broadcast encryption from bilinear groups. Cryptology ePrint Archive, Paper 2023/874 (2023). https://eprint.iacr.org/2023/874
58. Malkhi, D., Szalachowski, P.: Maximal extractable value (MEV) protection on a DAG (2022)
59. Maurer, U.: Abstract models of computation in cryptography. In: Smart, N.P. (ed.) Cryptography and Coding 2005. LNCS, vol. 3796, pp. 1–12. Springer, Heidelberg (2005). https://doi.org/10.1007/11586821_1
60. Micali, S., Reyzin, L., Vlachos, G., Wahby, R.S., Zeldovich, N.: Compact certificates of collective knowledge. In: 2021 IEEE Symposium on Security and Privacy, pp. 626–641, San Francisco, CA, USA, May 24–27, 2021. IEEE Computer Society Press (2021)
61. Ostrovsky, R., Yung, M.: How to withstand mobile virus attacks (extended abstract). In: Proceedings of the Tenth Annual ACM Symposium on Principles of Distributed Computing, Montreal, Quebec, Canada, August 19-21, 1991, pp. 51–59 (1991)
62. Piet, J., Fairoze, J., Weaver, N.: Extracting Godl [sic] from the salt mines: ethereum miners extracting value (2022)
63. Piet, J., Nair, V., Subramanian, S.: Mevade: an MEV-resistant blockchain design. In: 2023 IEEE International Conference on Blockchain and Cryptocurrency (ICBC), pp. 1–9. IEEE (2023)
64. Pippenger, N.: On the evaluation of powers and monomials. SIAM J. Comput. **9**(2), 230–250 (1980)
65. Qin, K., Zhou, L., Gervais, A.: Quantifying blockchain extractable value: how dark is the forest? ArXiv preprint (2021)
66. Ràfols, C., Zapico, A.: An algebraic framework for universal and updatable SNARKs. In: Malkin, T., Peikert, C. (eds.) Advances in Cryptology – CRYPTO 2021: 41st Annual International Cryptology Conference, CRYPTO 2021, Virtual

Event, August 16–20, 2021, Proceedings, Part I, pp. 774–804. Springer International Publishing, Cham (2021). https://doi.org/10.1007/978-3-030-84242-0_27
67. Reyzin, L., Smith, A., Yakoubov, S.: Turning HATE into LOVE: compact homomorphic ad hoc threshold encryption for scalable MPC. In: Dolev, S., Margalit, O., Pinkas, B., Schwarzmann, A. (eds.) Cyber Security Cryptography and Machine Learning: 5th International Symposium, CSCML 2021, Be'er Sheva, Israel, July 8–9, 2021, Proceedings, pp. 361–378. Springer International Publishing, Cham (2021). https://doi.org/10.1007/978-3-030-78086-9_27
68. Rondelet, A., Kilbourn, Q.: Threshold encrypted mempools: limitations and considerations (2023)
69. Sahai, A.: Non-malleable non-interactive zero knowledge and adaptive chosen-ciphertext security. In: 40th Annual Symposium on Foundations of Computer Science, pp. 543–553, New York, NY, USA, October 17–19, 1999. IEEE Computer Society Press (1999)
70. Schonhage, A.: Schnelle multiplikation grosser zahlen. Computing **7**, 281–292 (1971)
71. Shoup, V.: Lower bounds for discrete logarithms and related problems. In: Fumy, W. (ed.) Advances in Cryptology — EUROCRYPT '97, pp. 256–266. Springer, Berlin, Heidelberg (1997). https://doi.org/10.1007/3-540-69053-0_18
72. Shoup, V., Gennaro, R.: Securing threshold cryptosystems against chosen ciphertext attack. J. Cryptol. **15**(2), 75–96 (2002)
73. Tomescu, A., et al.: Towards scalable threshold cryptosystems. In: 2020 IEEE Symposium on Security and Privacy (SP), pp. 877–893 (2020)
74. Torres, C.F., Camino, R., et al.: Frontrunner jones and the raiders of the dark forest: an empirical study of frontrunning on the ethereum blockchain. In: 30th USENIX Security Symposium (2021)
75. Tsabary, R.: Candidate witness encryption from lattice techniques. In: Dodis, Y., Shrimpton, T. (eds.) Advances in Cryptology – CRYPTO 2022: 42nd Annual International Cryptology Conference, CRYPTO 2022, Santa Barbara, CA, USA, August 15–18, 2022, Proceedings, Part I, pp. 535–559. Springer Nature Switzerland, Cham (2022). https://doi.org/10.1007/978-3-031-15802-5_19
76. Vaikuntanathan, V., Wee, H., Wichs, D.: Witness encryption and Null-IO from evasive LWE. In: Agrawal, S., Lin, D. (eds.) Advances in Cryptology – ASIACRYPT 2022: 28th International Conference on the Theory and Application of Cryptology and Information Security, Taipei, Taiwan, December 5–9, 2022, Proceedings, Part I, pp. 195–221. Springer Nature Switzerland, Cham (2022). https://doi.org/10.1007/978-3-031-22963-3_7
77. Wu, Q., Qin, B., Zhang, L., Domingo-Ferrer, J.: Ad hoc broadcast encryption (poster presentation). In: Al-Shaer, E., Keromytis, A.D., Shmatikov, V., editors, ACM CCS 2010: 17th Conference on Computer and Communications Security, pp. 741–743, Chicago, Illinois, USA, October 4–8, 2010. ACM Press (2010)
78. Zhu, Z., Zhang, K., Gong, J., Qian, H.: Registered ABE via predicate encodings. Cryptology ePrint Archive (2023)

Two-Round Threshold Signature from Algebraic One-More Learning with Errors

Thomas Espitau[1](✉), Shuichi Katsumata[2,3], and Kaoru Takemure[2,3]

[1] PQShield SAS, Paris, France
thomas.espitau@pqshield.com
[2] PQShield, Ltd., Oxford, UK
{shuichi.katsumata,kaoru.takemure}@pqshield.com
[3] AIST, Tokyo, Japan

Abstract. Threshold signatures have recently seen a renewed interest due to applications in cryptocurrency while NIST has released a call for multi-party threshold schemes, with a deadline for submission expected for the first half of 2025. So far, all lattice-based threshold signatures requiring two-rounds or less are based on heavy tools such as (fully) homomorphic encryption (FHE) and homomorphic trapdoor commitments (HTDC). This is not unexpected considering that most efficient two-round signatures from classical assumptions either rely on idealized model such as algebraic group models or on one-more type assumptions, none of which we have a nice analogue in the lattice world.

In this work, we construct the first efficient two-round lattice-based threshold signature without relying on FHE or HTDC. It has an offline-online feature where the first round can be preprocessed without knowing message or the signer sets, effectively making the signing phase non-interactive. The signature size is small and shows great scalability. For example, even for a threshold as large as 1024 signers, we achieve a signature size roughly 11 KB. At the heart of our construction is a new lattice-based assumption called the *algebraic one-more learning with errors* (AOM-MLWE) assumption. We believe this to be a strong inclusion to our lattice toolkits with an independent interest. We establish the selective security of AOM-MLWE based on the standard MLWE and MSIS assumptions, and provide an in depth analysis of its adaptive security, which our threshold signature is based on.

1 Introduction

A T-out-of-N threshold signature [41,42] allows to distribute a secret signing key to N signers, where any set of the $T \leq N$ signers can collaborate to sign a message. Security guarantees that a set of signers less than T cannot produce a valid signature. While threshold signatures have always been a topic of interest, in recent years, it has seen a renewed real-world interest largely due to applications in cryptocurrency, where secure and reliable storage of cryptographic keys

© International Association for Cryptologic Research 2024
L. Reyzin and D. Stebila (Eds.): CRYPTO 2024, LNCS 14926, pp. 387–424, 2024.
https://doi.org/10.1007/978-3-031-68394-7_13

are vital. Such interest has led US agency NIST to release a call for multi-party threshold schemes [78], with a deadline for submission expected for the first half of 2025.

Current State of Post-Quantum Threshold Signature. *Classically* secure threshold signature has approached a high state of maturity with the recent rapid developments. We now have a plethora of efficient solutions, covering many design choices, such as threshold BLS [8,17], threshold ECDSA [27,28,36,37,44,54,69], and threshold Schnorr [10,31,34,65,68].

While development on *post-quantum* threshold signature has been elusive for many years, we have started to see some interesting progress lately. The first *round-optimal* (i.e., one-round) lattice-based threshold signature was by Boneh et al. [18], later optimized by Agrawal, Stehlé, and Yadav [4]. This remained mainly of theoretical interest as they required a threshold fully homomorphic encryption (FHE) to compute a standard (non-thresholdized) signature. Very recently, Gur, Katz, and Silde [62] building on similar ideas, constructed a *two-round* threshold signature based on a threshold linear homomorphic encryption and homomorphic trapdoor commitment (HTDC) [38,60]. They provide a rough estimate claiming a signature size of around 12 KB with 1.5 MB communication per signer for the 3-out-of-5 setting. While this brings the original idea of [18] closer to practice, it does not scale well due to the heavy use of HTDC. In an independent and concurrent work, del Pino et al. [79] constructed a *three-round* threshold signature without relying on any heavy tools such as FHE or HTDC for the first time. As such, [79] has a small signature size of 13 KB with only 40 KB communication per user, achieving a great scalability supporting a threshold T as large as 1024, a parameter range considered by NIST [78].

A Closer Look at Round Complexity. While [79] brings lattice-based threshold signatures to the practical regime, the main drawback is that it requires three rounds. In environments where signers are using network-limited devices or unreliable networks for transmission, multiple rounds may become a performance bottleneck. This is why there is a strong interest in a round-optimal or a so-called *offline-online efficient* two-round protocol [25, Section 5.3.5]. The latter type allows to preprocess the first-round without knowing the set of T signers and the message to be signed, effectively making the online signing phase non-interactive.

In the classical setting, we have efficient solutions for both of these types: threshold BLS [8,17] offers a round-optimal protocol, whereas threshold Schnorr such as FROST and its variants [10,31,65] offer an offline-online efficient two-round protocol. This is in sharp contrast to the post-quantum setting where we currently need heavy tools like FHE or HTDC for threshold signatures offering two rounds or less.

Barriers to 2($\geq$)-Round Lattice Schemes. When we look at how these classical protocols achieve low round complexity, the fundamental barriers in replicating them in the lattice setting becomes clear. First, the round-optimal threshold BLS is based on the BLS signature [21]; a signature scheme using the rich algebraic properties of bilinear maps, something thought to be highly unlikely to be reproducible from lattices. On the other hand, the two-round threshold Schnorr like FROST only requires standard group operations for the construction. Unfortunately, the security proof relies on either the algebraic group model (AGM) [53] or a variant of the one-more discrete logarithm (OM-DL) problem, both of which we do not have nice analogue in the lattice world.[1] Indeed, as exemplified with FHE computation, since lattice operations can be non-algebraic, an idealized model like AGM does not seem to meaningfully capture lattice adversaries. To make matters worse, this does not seem to be just an artifact of the proof technique as a simple adaptation of the classical constructions are known to lead to insecure schemes.

In summary, to construct a lattice-based threshold signature with two rounds or less, we need to develop new techniques not yet in our lattice toolkits. This brings us to the main question of this work:

Can we replicate the classically secure efficient $2(\geq)$-round threshold signatures from lattices?

1.1 Our Contribution

In this work, we construct a new lattice-based offline-online efficient two-round threshold signature. Unlike prior works on lattice-based one or two-round threshold signatures [4,18,62], we do not rely on heavy tools such as FHE or HTDC. At a high level, our scheme is similar to the simple threshold Schnorr protocol FROST [65], one of the most popular classically secure two-round threshold signatures. In fact, it can be viewed as a thresholdized version of Raccoon [80], a lattice-based signature scheme by del Pino et al., submitted to the additional NIST call for proposals [77]. This interchangeability is a desirable property as it allows to seamlessly use our threshold signature in an ecosystem with Raccoon.

At the heart of our construction is a new lattice (falsifiable [56,75]) assumption named the *algebraic one-more module Learning with Errors* (AOM-MLWE) assumption. AOM-MLWE is defined, in spirit, similarly to the algebraic one-more discrete logarithm (AOM-DL) assumption, originally introduced by Nick, Ruffing, and Seurin [76] to establish the security of the multi-signature scheme called MuSig2. AOM-DL is a strictly weaker assumption than the (non-falsifiable and non-algebraic) OM-DL. Informally, in OM-DL, an adversary has access to a very strong oracle that solves the discrete logarithm of any group element of its choice; in contrast, in AOM-DL, an adversary is limited to access this DL solving oracle on an *algebraic* combination of the provided challenge instances.[2] While the distinction may seem insignificant on first sight, it has a large impact in the lattice setting. This extra algebraic restriction on the adversary is the

---

[1] Note that while we have one-more-ISIS [3], an assumption having "one-more" in its name, it is qualitatively quite different from those considered in the classical setting. More discussion can found in the full version.

[2] In more detail, in OM-DL, the adversary is given $g^{\mathbf{a}} := (g^{a_i})_{i \in [Q]}$ as the challenge; can query any $h \in \mathbb{G}$ to the oracle; and receives $\text{dlog}_g(h)$. In contrast, in AOM-DL, the adversary can only query $\mathbf{d} \in \mathbb{Z}_p^Q$ and receives $\langle \mathbf{a}, \mathbf{d} \rangle$, making the oracle efficient.

key allowing us to provide a well-defined and non-trivial definition.[3] We provide more detailed discussions on why a non-algebraic OM-MLWE would be difficult to define and use in the full version.

In more detail, half of our work is devoted to a theoretical and practical analysis of the newly introduced AOM-MLWE assumption. As typical with any lattice-based assumptions, the hardness of AOM-MLWE problem is dictated by many parameters. The most unique restriction to AOM-MLWE is the "allowed" algebraic combinations that an adversary can query to the MLWE solving oracle. Since MLWE secrets are small, there are several trivial queries an adversary can make to break the AOM-MLWE problem with a naive parameter selection. In our work, we pinpoint what these "weak" instances are and analyze the hardness of AOM-MLWE for specific "hard" instances, one of which underlies our threshold signature. Concretely, we first show that a *selective* variant of AOM-MLWE (sel-AOM-MLWE) of these hard instances is as secure as MLWE and MSIS—a variant where the adversary must commit to all the queries at the outset of the security game. We then provide an in-depth cryptanalysis analyzing the effect of an adaptive adversary and heuristically establish that an adaptive adversary is no stronger than a selective adversary.

It is worth noting that we have recently seen a boom in new lattice-based assumptions, used to construct exciting primitives: one-more-ISIS [3], K-R-ISIS [5], BASIS [89], evasive LWE [87,88], only to name a few. While some (variants of the) assumptions can be based on standard lattice-assumptions, many of them are still new and have not undergone scrutiny, both from theory and practical cryptanalysis. Within this landscape, our assumption is in spirit closest to the *adaptive* LWE problem by Quach, Wee, and Wichs [83], used to construct adaptively secure laconic function evaluation schemes and attribute-based encryption schemes [66]. Similarly to AOM-MLWE, while adaptive LWE is heuristically thought to be as hard as LWE, the selective variant is implied by the standard definition of LWE. We view this as one characteristic that differentiates AOM-MLWE from recent assumptions.

The second half of our work is devoted to the construction of our two-round threshold signature. The starting point of our construction is the recent efficient three-round threshold signature by del Pino et al. [79], which is in a bird's eyes view, an analog of the folklore construction of a three-round Schnorr signature using Shamir's secret sharing protocol [85]. Our high level strategy to make it two-round is similar to FROST [65], however, there arise many lattice-related complications. As we explained above, the hardness of AOM-MLWE is dictated by the choice of the parameters, and consequently, our threshold signature must be constructed in a meticulous manner to comply with these restrictions. Along the way, as an independent interest, we resolve one of the open problems stated in [79]. In their construction, they required each signer to maintain a long-term state and to authenticate their views with a standard (non-thresholdized)

---

[3] Note that this is fundamentally different from the AGM where the adversary is restricted to be algebraic. In AOM-MLWE, while the adversary can only make algebraic queries to the MLWE solving oracle, it has otherwise no algebraic restrictions.

signature for unforgeability. Our two-round construction resolves both issues without any overhead.

Lastly, our two-round threshold signatures are *practical* with aggregated signature size roughly 11 KB. Our scheme naturally supports threshold up to 1024 participants, an upper limit of the "large" requirements of NIST preliminary call for threshold [78]. The main overhead is the offline phase where signers must exchange the preprocessing tokens with size a couple of hundreds kilobytes. See Sect. 8.3 for more details.

1.2 Related Works

Other Post-Quantum Threshold Signatures. Bendlin, Krehbiel, and Peikert [14] constructed a threshold signature based on the GPV signature [55]. The protocol relies on generic multi-party computation (MPC) to perform Gaussian sampling. Khaburzaniya et al. [63] recently proposed a threshold signatures from hash-based signatures using STARK. They report a signature of size 170 KB for a threshold of size 1024 signers, with an aggregation time of 4 to 20 s. While there are some isogeny-based threshold signatures [32,40], they only support sequential aggregation and thus requires numerous rounds to aggregate the signature.

Post-Quantum Multi-signatures. Most closest to threshold signatures are multi-signatures. It can be viewed as an N-out-of-N threshold signature where each signers posses an individual signing key, rather than a secret share of one signing key. Unlike threshold signatures, constructing lattice-based multi-signatures has been more fruitful [23,29,38,39,52]. The recent work by Boschini et al. [23] and Chen [29] achieve a two-round protocol with signatures size roughly 100 KB and 30 KB, respectively. While Chen's protocol has smaller signature size, it does not offer offline-online efficiency as Boschnini et al.'s protocol.

Related Lattice Assumptions. We review two lattice-based assumptions that seem most similar to our AOM-MLWE assumption. The one-more-ISIS assumption was introduced by Agrawal et al. [3] to construct a blind signature. While the assumption includes the term "one-more" and is formalized as a one-more style assumption, it is qualitatively quite different from those considered in the classical setting like OM-DL. In essence, the assumption claims that given a lattice trapdoor $\mathbf{T} \in \mathbb{Z}^{m \times m}$ for a random matrix $\mathbf{A} \in \mathbb{Z}_q^{n \times m}$, i.e., $\mathbf{T}$ is short and $\mathbf{AT} = \mathbf{0} \bmod q$, it is difficult to create a lattice trapdoor $\mathbf{T}'$ with a better quality than $\mathbf{T}$. Such notion of "quality" is lattice specific. The *hint* MLWE (Hint-MLWE) assumption was recently introduced by Kim et al. [64]. This assumption claims that the MLWE problem $(\mathbf{A}, \mathbf{As}+\mathbf{e})$ remains hard even given hints $(c_i \cdot \mathbf{s}+\mathbf{z}_i, c_i \cdot \mathbf{e}+\mathbf{z}'_i)_{i \in [Q]}$, where c_i is some random small element and $(\mathbf{z}_i, \mathbf{z}'_i)$ are sampled from a discrete Gaussian distribution. When the samples $(\mathbf{z}_i, \mathbf{z}'_i)$ are super-polynomially larger than $(c_i \cdot \mathbf{s}, c_i \cdot \mathbf{e})$ it is clear that Hint-MLWE is as hard as MLWE. Kim et al. showed that even under milder conditions, Hint-MLWE are as hard as MLWE. While it shares similarity to AOM-MLWE since the adversary receives some information on the MLWE secret, the main difference is that in

AOM-MLWE, the adversary obtains the *exact* value of the *adversarially chosen* inner product of the MLWE secrets.

Further Properties of Threshold Signatures. We consider only the key generation that should be executed by a trusted dealer in this paper. To avoid relying on the trusted dealer, we could use the distributed key generation (DKG), e.g., a lattice-based DKG with respect to a LWE-type verification key [50,62]. We remain the DKG, that can be used for our scheme, and the security analysis of our schemes with a concrete DKG as interesting future works.

Our proposed scheme does not provide a way to detect misbehavior when a resulting signature is invalid. The identifiable abort (IA) is one of the well-known solutions to enable the detection of it. Specifically, participants execute the IA protocol and eventually identify the misbehavior when the signing protocol aborts or the resulting signature is invalid. The robustness is a property that ensures honest users can generate a valid signature, even in the presence of malicious users. Espitau et al. [50] proposed a lattice-based robust threshold signature scheme by constructing verifiable short secret sharing. We also leave the IA protocol for our scheme and robust signing protocol as an important future work.

2 Technical Overview

We provide an overview of our offline-online efficient two-round threshold signature and establish its security based on the AOM-MLWE assumption. We then discuss the hardness of the assumption.

2.1 Two-Round Threshold Signature from AOM-MLWE

We first explain how we arrive at our threshold signature assuming AOM-MLWE is hard.

Base Signature Scheme. We use Lyubashevsky's lattice-based signature scheme [70,71] as our starting point. Let us briefly recall the protocol. Let $\mathbf{A} \in \mathcal{R}_q^{k \times \ell}$ and $\mathbf{t} = \mathbf{A} \cdot \mathbf{s} + \mathbf{e} \in \mathcal{R}_q^k$ for "short" vectors $(\mathbf{s}, \mathbf{e})$. The verification and signing keys are set as $(\mathsf{vk}, \mathsf{sk}) = ((\mathbf{A}, \mathbf{t}), (\mathbf{s}, \mathbf{e}))$. To sign a message M, the signer first constructs a *commitment* $\mathbf{w} = \mathbf{A} \cdot \mathbf{r} + \mathbf{e}'$, where $(\mathbf{r}, \mathbf{e}')$ are "short" vectors sampled from some specific distribution. A *challenge* $c \leftarrow \mathsf{H}(\mathsf{vk}, \mathsf{M}, \mathbf{w})$, followed by a "short" *response* $(\mathbf{z}, \mathbf{z}') := (c \cdot \mathbf{s} + \mathbf{r}, c \cdot \mathbf{e} + \mathbf{e}')$ is then computed. Finally, $(c, \mathbf{z}, \mathbf{z}')$ is the signature. To verify, we check if $(\mathbf{z}, \mathbf{z}')$ are short and that $c = \mathsf{H}(\mathsf{vk}, \mathsf{M}, \mathbf{A} \cdot \mathbf{z} + \mathbf{z}' - c \cdot \mathbf{t})$.

While it is standard to perform rejection sampling [70,71] to make the distribution of the responses independent of the signing key, we rely on noise "flooding" [57]. This allows the signers to never abort and works very well in the interactive setting. This is the approach also taken in recent lattice-based threshold signatures [4,62,79], using the Rényi divergence to granularly control the amount of noise flood required.

$(\mathsf{vk} = (\mathbf{A}, \mathbf{A} \cdot \mathbf{s} + \mathbf{e}), \mathsf{sk} = \mathbf{s})$ with $\mathbf{A} \in \mathcal{R}_q^{k \times \ell}$
Signer i: $\mathsf{sk}_i := (\mathbf{s}_i, \mathbf{e}_i, (\mathsf{seed}_{i,j}, \mathsf{seed}_{j,i})_{j \in \mathsf{SS}}, \mathsf{sk}_{\mathsf{S},i})$ s.t. $\mathbf{s} = \sum_{i \in [\mathsf{SS}]} L_{\mathsf{SS},i} \cdot \mathbf{s}_i$

$(\mathbf{r}_i, \mathbf{e}'_i) \xleftarrow{\$} \mathcal{D}^\ell \times \mathcal{D}^k$
$\mathbf{w}_i := \mathbf{A} \cdot \mathbf{r}_i + \mathbf{e}'_i$
$\mathsf{cmt}_i := \mathsf{H}_{\mathsf{com}}(\mathsf{sid}, \mathsf{SS}, M, \mathbf{w}_i)$
$\mathbf{m}_i := \sum_{j \in \mathsf{SS}} \mathsf{PRF}(\mathsf{seed}_{i,j}, \mathsf{sid})$ $\mathsf{contrib}_{1,i} := (\mathsf{cmt}_i, \mathbf{m}_i)$
$\xrightarrow{}$
$(\mathsf{contrib}_{1,j})_{j \in \mathsf{SS} \setminus \{i\}}$
$\xleftarrow{}$

$\sigma_{\mathsf{S},i} \xleftarrow{\$} \mathsf{S.Sign}(\mathsf{sk}_{\mathsf{S},i}, \mathsf{sid} \| (\mathsf{contrib}_{1,i})_{j \in \mathsf{SS}})$ $\mathsf{contrib}_{2,i} := (\mathbf{w}_j, \sigma_{\mathsf{S},i})$
$\xrightarrow{}$
$(\mathsf{contrib}_{2,j})_{j \in \mathsf{SS} \setminus \{i\}}$
$\xleftarrow{}$

Check hash commitments and signatures
$\mathbf{w} := \sum_{i \in \mathsf{SS}} \mathbf{w}_i$
$c = \mathsf{H}(\mathsf{vk}, M, \mathbf{w})$
$\mathbf{m}_i^* := \sum_{j \in \mathsf{SS}} \mathsf{PRF}(\mathsf{seed}_{j,i}, \mathsf{sid})$
$\mathbf{z}_i = c \cdot L_{\mathsf{SS},i} \cdot \mathbf{s}_i + \mathbf{r}_i + \mathbf{m}_i^*$
$\mathbf{z}'_i = c \cdot \mathbf{e}_i + \mathbf{e}'_i$ $\widehat{\mathsf{sig}}_i := (\mathbf{z}_i, \mathbf{z}'_i)$
$\xrightarrow{}$

Fig. 1. Simplified three-round threshold signature of [79]. $\mathsf{sid} \in \{0,1\}^*$ is a session identifier and $\mathsf{SS} \subseteq [N]$ is the set of active users. The second round is only initiated once signer i obtains $T = |\mathsf{SS}|$ first-round contributions. The final aggregated signature is $(c, \mathbf{z}, \mathbf{z}')$ where $\mathbf{z} := \sum_{j \in \mathsf{SS}} (\mathbf{z}_i - \mathbf{m}_i)$ and $\mathbf{z}' := \sum_{j \in \mathsf{SS}} \mathbf{z}'_i$. By ignoring the highlights in blue, we arrive at an insecure adaptation of a naive threshold Schnorr.

A Naive Extension to a Threshold Signature. One naive way to thresholdize Lyubashevsky's signature is to use Shamir's secret sharing protocol to share the signing key. This is depicted in Fig. 1 (ignoring the blue highlights). The partial signing key $(\mathbf{s}_i)_{i \in [N]}$ satisfy $\mathbf{s} = \sum_{i \in \mathsf{SS}} L_{\mathsf{SS},i} \cdot \mathbf{s}_i$ for any set $\mathsf{SS} \subset [N]$ with $|\mathsf{SS}| = T$, where $L_{\mathsf{SS},i}$ is the Lagrange coefficient. Correctness follows from observing that $\mathbf{z} = \sum_{i \in \mathsf{SS}} \mathbf{z}_i = c \cdot \mathbf{s} + \mathbf{r}$, where $\mathbf{r} := \sum_{i \in \mathsf{SS}} \mathbf{r}_i$. It is worth mentioning that the signers need to perform a hash-and-open with the commitment $\mathbf{w}_i$ to force a malicious signer i^* to prepare its commitment $\mathbf{w}_{i^*}^*$ independently from the honest users' commitments. This is a procedure required for classical three-round schemes as well [13, 33].

Unfortunately, it turns out this naive construction is insecure due to lattice-specific reasons. Since Lagrange coefficients can be arbitrarily large over modulo q, this forces the partial response $\mathbf{z}_i = c^* \cdot \mathbf{s}_i + \mathbf{r}_i$ to be large, where $c^* = c \cdot L_{\mathsf{SS},i}$. Similarly to why Lyubashevsky's signature becomes easily forgeable for large challenge spaces, the partial signing key $\mathbf{s}_i$ can be recovered from such a partial response using a large challenge c^*. While there are several workarounds to overcome large Lagrange coefficients, e.g. [2, 4, 6, 18, 20, 30, 43, 67], they are notorious for being highly impractical and/or non-scalable. For instance, one of the most simple and common approaches [2,18] require the modulus q to grow with at least $O(N!^2)$—even for a small $N = 15$, we would require $q > 2^{80}$.[4]

Three-Round Threshold Signature by del Pino et al. Very recently, del Pino et al. [79] came up with a simple and elegant solution to sidestep this issue. Their idea is to additively *mask* the individual responses by a random vector and devise a way to publicly remove only the sum of the masks. This is depicted in Fig. 1. Each signers additionally share a pair-wise seed for a pseudorandom function (PRF). In the first round, signer i now computes a so-called *row* mask $\mathbf{m}_i := \sum_{j \in \mathsf{SS}} \mathsf{PRF}(\mathsf{seed}_{i,j}, \mathsf{sid})$ and shares it along with the hash commitment cmt_i, where sid is some unique string defined per session. In the third round, it computes a *column* mask $\mathbf{m}_i^* := \sum_{j \in \mathsf{SS}} \mathsf{PRF}(\mathsf{seed}_{j,i}, \mathsf{sid})$ and adds this to the response $\mathbf{z}_i$. Importantly, while the row masks $(\mathbf{m}_i)_{i \in \mathsf{SS}}$ are public, the column masks $(\mathbf{m}_i^*)_{i \in \mathsf{SS}}$ are kept private. Moreover, by construction, we have $\sum_{j \in \mathsf{SS}} \mathbf{m}_j = \sum_{j \in \mathsf{SS}} \mathbf{m}_j^*$. To offset the column masks, we subtract $\sum_{j \in \mathsf{SS}} \mathbf{m}_i$ from $\sum_{j \in \mathsf{SS}} \mathbf{z}_i'$ to arrive at the desired aggregated response $\mathbf{z} = c \cdot \mathbf{s} + \mathbf{r}$.

The key observation to understand the security is that while the individual row masks $(\mathbf{m}_j)_{j \in \mathsf{SS}}$ are known to the adversary, the only knowledge the adversary gains on the column masks $(\mathbf{m}_j^*)_{j \in \mathsf{HS}}$ of honest signers $\mathsf{HS} \subset \mathsf{SS}$ are their sum $\sum_{j \in \mathsf{HS}} \mathbf{m}_j^*$; put differently, $(\mathbf{m}_j^*)_{j \in \mathsf{HS}}$ are distributed randomly, conditioned on their sum being $\sum_{j \in \mathsf{HS}} \mathbf{m}_j^*$. This observation is leveraged to move around the terms $c \cdot L_{\mathsf{SS},i} \cdot \mathbf{s}_i$ included in the partial responses $\mathbf{z}_i$ of the honest signers, effectively allowing the reduction to reconstruct the signing key $\mathbf{s}$ *under the hood* of the adversary's view.

We note that the security proof is easier said than done. The main source of difficulty is that an adversary can adaptively alter the views of the honest signers without being detected. In the context of the above intuition, this means moving the terms $c \cdot L_{\mathsf{SS},i} \cdot \mathbf{s}_i$ around consistently with the adversary's view become very difficult. To this end, [79] requires a standard signature scheme to authenticate the view of each honest signers. Moreover, so as not to sign on the same sid, the signers must remain stateful.

Making it Two-Round. To turn the protocol into a two-round protocol, we collapse the seemingly superfluous second round, consisting of only opening the hash commitment. Recall we required this hash-and-open to prevent a malicious signer i^* from creating a commitment $\mathbf{w}_{i^*}$ affecting the aggregated commitment $\mathbf{w}$. We follow a similar high level approach taken by FROST [65] to prevent this while removing the second round. Our two-round threshold signature is depicted in Fig. 2. In the first round, each signer now generates a list of commitments *in the clear*. In the second round, they use a hash function G modeled as a random oracle to compute a random weight $(\beta_b)_{b \in [\mathsf{rep}]}$ and (locally) set the partial commitment $\mathbf{w}_j$ as $\mathbf{w}_j := \sum_{b \in [\mathsf{rep}]} \beta_b \cdot \mathbf{w}_{j,b}$. Moreover, the row and column masks $(\mathbf{m}_i, \mathbf{m}_i^*)$ are now created in the second round at the same time

---

[4] While Albrecht and Lai [6, Section 3.1] defines the Lagrange interpolating polynomial on specific elements in $\mathcal{R}_q$ to handle the blowup more granularly, the concrete gain is unclear for a general T-out-of-N threshold.

$(\text{vk} = (\mathbf{A}, \mathbf{A} \cdot \mathbf{s} + \mathbf{e}), \text{sk} = \mathbf{s})$ with $\mathbf{A} \in \mathcal{R}_q^{k \times \ell}$
Signer i: $\text{sk}_i := (\mathbf{s}_i, \mathbf{e}_i, (\text{seed}_{i,j}, \text{seed}_{j,i})_{j \in \text{SS}})$ s.t. $\mathbf{s} = \sum_{i \in [\text{SS}]} L_{\text{SS},i} \cdot \mathbf{s}_i$

for $b \in [\text{rep}]$ do
$\quad (\mathbf{r}_{i,b}, \mathbf{e}'_{i,b}) \xleftarrow{\$} \mathcal{D}^\ell \times \mathcal{D}^k$
$\quad \mathbf{w}_{i,b} := \mathbf{A} \cdot \mathbf{r}_{i,b} + \mathbf{e}'_{i,b}$
$\vec{\mathbf{w}}_i := [\mathbf{w}_{i,1} \mid \cdots \mid \mathbf{w}_{i,\text{rep}}]$

$\quad\quad\quad\quad\quad\quad\quad\quad\quad\quad\quad\quad\quad\quad \text{pp}_i := \vec{\mathbf{w}}_i \longrightarrow$
$\quad\quad\quad\quad\quad\quad\quad\quad\quad\quad\quad\quad\quad\quad (\text{pp}_j)_{j \in \text{SS} \setminus \{i\}} \longleftarrow$

$\text{ctnt} := \text{SS} \| \text{M} \| (\vec{\mathbf{w}}_j)_{j \in \text{SS}}$
$(\beta_b)_{b \in [\text{rep}]} := G(\text{vk}, \text{ctnt})$
for $j \in \text{SS}$ do
$\quad \mathbf{w}_j := \sum_{b \in [\text{rep}]} \beta_b \cdot \mathbf{w}_{j,b}$
$\mathbf{w} := \sum_{j \in \text{SS}} \mathbf{w}_j$
$c = H(\text{vk}, M, \mathbf{w})$
$\mathbf{m}_i := \sum_{j \in \text{SS}} \text{PRF}(\text{seed}_{i,j}, \text{ctnt})$
$\mathbf{m}_i^* := \sum_{j \in \text{SS}} \text{PRF}(\text{seed}_{j,i}, \text{ctnt})$
$\mathbf{z}_i = c \cdot L_{\text{SS},i} \cdot \mathbf{s}_i + \sum_{b \in [\text{rep}]} \beta_b \cdot \mathbf{r}_{i,b} + \mathbf{m}_i^*$
$\mathbf{z}'_i = c \cdot \mathbf{e}_i + \sum_{b \in [\text{rep}]} \beta_b \cdot \mathbf{e}'_{i,b}$

$\quad\quad\quad\quad\quad\quad\quad\quad\quad\quad\quad\quad\quad\quad \widehat{\text{sig}}_i := (\mathbf{z}_i, \mathbf{z}'_i, \mathbf{m}_i) \longrightarrow$

Fig. 2. Our simplified offline-online efficient two-round threshold signature. The major differences between the three-round threshold signature in Fig. 1 are highlighted in blue. Concrete values of $\text{rep} \in \mathbb{N}$ and the output of the hash function G is scheme specific, implicitly dictated by the parameters of the underlying AOM-MLWE assumption.

from the PRF evaluated on input $\text{ctnt} = \text{SS} \| \text{M} \| (\vec{\mathbf{w}}_j)_{j \in \text{SS}}$. Importantly, we no longer require a session specific identifier sid as in [79]. Otherwise, it proceeds as before. Notice the first round *pre-processing token* pp_i can be generated without the knowledge of the message or set of signers, making the protocol offline-online efficient.

Before explaining the intuition of the security proof using AOM-MLWE, we note the effect of our modified mask evaluation. While it is a simple modification, including the commitments $(\vec{\mathbf{w}}_j)_{j \in \text{SS}}$ in the PRF effectively "kills two birds with one stone". First of all, the signer no longer needs to maintain a state since a commitment $\vec{\mathbf{w}}_j$ has high min-entropy. That is, as long as the signers are correctly following the protocol, no adversary can trick them to use the same input to the PRF. This removes the need of using a session specific identifier sid. Moreover, we are also able to remove the usage of standard signatures since $\text{PRF}(\text{seed}_{i,j}, \text{ctnt})$ and $\text{PRF}(\text{seed}_{j,i}, \text{ctnt})$ can be viewed as *random MACs* from signer i to j of the fact that i's view is ctnt, which effectively includes all the communication transcript. Noticing the role of signers i and j are symmetric, the random MAC embedded in the partial responses $\mathbf{z}_i$ and $\mathbf{z}_j$ cannot be removed unless both signers agree on the same ctnt. If ctnt agrees, then the reduction can move around the terms $c \cdot L_{\mathsf{SS},i} \cdot \mathbf{s}_i$ as explained prior. Otherwise, the responses remain random from the view of the adversary.

Security Proof with AOM-MLWE. It remains to explain how AOM-MLWE is used to prove security. The reduction is given $\mathbf{A}$, $\mathbf{t}$, and $(\mathbf{w}_{i,b}^{(k)})_{(k,i,b)\in[Q_\mathsf{S}]\times[N]\times[\mathsf{rep}]}$ as the challenge, where $\mathbf{t} = \mathbf{As} + \mathbf{e}$ and $\mathbf{w}_{i,b}^{(k)} = \mathbf{A}\mathbf{r}_{i,b}^{(k)} + \mathbf{e}_{i,b}^{(k)}$. The reduction sets $(\mathbf{A}, \mathbf{t})$ as the verification key and when the adversary invokes signer i on the k-th signing query, the reduction sets the pre-processing token as $\mathsf{pp}_i^{(k)} := \vec{\mathbf{w}}^{(k)} = (\mathbf{w}_{i,1}^{(k)}, \cdots \mathbf{w}_{i,\mathsf{rep}}^{(k)})$. Thanks to the above random MAC technique, we can guarantee the reduction to only be required to simulate partial responses of the form $\mathbf{z}_i = c \cdot \mathbf{s} + \sum_{b\in[\mathsf{rep}]} \beta_b \cdot \mathbf{r}_{i,b}^{(k)} + $ (public vector) or $\mathbf{z}_i = \sum_{b\in[\mathsf{rep}]} \beta_b \cdot \mathbf{r}_{i,b}^{(k)} + $(public vector). Thus the reduction only needs to query the linear combination $(c, 0, \cdots, \beta_1, \cdots, \beta_\mathsf{rep}, \cdots, 0)$ or $(0, 0, \cdots, \beta_1, \cdots, \beta_\mathsf{rep}, \cdots, 0)$ to the MLWE solving oracle to simulate these partial responses.

The technically interesting part is what the reduction does once the adversary outputs a forgery. As typical with any signatures based on identification protocols, by relying on the forking lemma [13,81], we can extract an (approximate) MLWE solution $(\mathbf{s}, \mathbf{e})$ relative to the verification key $\mathbf{t}$.[5] The difference between standard proofs is that the reduction's goal is to break AOM-MLWE, defined by the $\mathsf{rep} \cdot Q_\mathsf{S} \cdot N + 1$ MLWE instances. Observe that in the course of simulating the adversary, the reduction may make up to $2 \cdot Q_\mathsf{S} \cdot N$ queries to the MLWE solving oracle, where the factor 2 comes from running the adversary twice. We then require $\mathsf{rep} \geq 2$ at the minimum to non-trivialize the game as the reduction cannot query more than the number of challenges it receives. It is relatively easy to show that when $\mathsf{rep} \geq 2$, the reduction can (approximately) compute all of $(\mathbf{s}, \mathbf{e})$, $(\mathbf{r}_{i,b}^{(k)}, \mathbf{e}_{i,b}^{(k)})_{(k,i,b)\in[Q_\mathsf{S}]\times[N]\times[\mathsf{rep}]}$ from the partial responses and adversary's forgery, satisfying the winning condition of AOM-MLWE.

The only thing missing from our proof is establishing the hardness of the underlying AOM-MLWE assumption. The above does not yet tell us anything on how we should set $\mathsf{rep} \geq 2$, what the noise distributions should be, or what should the allowable linear combinations to the MLWE solving oracles be.

2.2 Analyzing Hardness of AOM-MLWE

In the classical setting, the hardness of the algebraic one-more discrete logarithm (AOM-DL) problem [76] is easy-to-state and well-established. It is a strictly harder problem than the (non-algebraic) OM-DL problem, already widely believed to be difficult. Indeed, AOM-DL can be shown to be hard in the generic group model (GGM) [73,86].

---

[5] For the attentive readers, since the reduction is playing an interactive game with AOM-MLWE, we must rely on a variant of the forking lemma with oracle access [46].

Theoretical Hardness of AOM-MLWE. The situation vastly changes when looking at the algebraic one-more MLWE (AOM-MLWE) problem. We do not have an already established (non-algebraic) OM-LWE problem to base hardness on or any idealized model such as the GGM to formally argue its hardness. In fact, the problem becomes trivially insecure if we naively define AOM-MLWE. However, this is not unsuspected as MLWE already exhibits a similar phenomenon; one can always set the parameters for MLWE so that it becomes trivially insecure. The added complexity of analyzing AOM-MLWE comes from the need to take into account the extra information an adversary learns by querying the MLWE solving oracle.

Let us give a very simple example. Assume the AOM-MLWE challenge is $\mathbf{A}, (\mathbf{t}_i = \mathbf{A} \cdot \mathbf{s}_i + \mathbf{e}_i)_{i \in [2]}$ such that the secrets have infinity norm smaller than B. Then, the adversary can query the linear combination $(1, B)$ to the MLWE solving oracle $\mathcal{O}_{\mathsf{solve}}$ to obtain $\mathbf{s}_1 + B \cdot \mathbf{s}_2$. If $B \ll q$, then by taking modulo B, the adversary easily recovers $\mathbf{s}_1$ and $\mathbf{s}_2$. Since it solves two MLWE instances with one query, it breaks AOM-MLWE. In Sect. 4, we present less obvious "weak" parameters for which AOM-MLWE admits a more sophisticated attack.

We then turn all our findings on the weak parameters of AOM-MLWE into a constructive argument to establish the hardness of AOM-MLWE. Specifically, we provide several sets of "hard" parameters and prove that the *selective* AOM-MLWE is as hard as the standard MLWE and MSIS problems. Here, selective security means that the adversary must commit to all the linear combinations it queries to oracle $\mathcal{O}_{\mathsf{solve}}$ at the outset of the game. This establishes that to break AOM-MLWE, an adversary must cleverly use $\mathcal{O}_{\mathsf{solve}}$ in an *adaptive* manner. While our result does not formally say anything about the adaptive security of AOM-MLWE, it illustrates that there is nothing fundamentally wrong with the hard parameters. We draw parallel between this situation to the numerous lattice-based primitives only proven selectively secure but are plausibly adaptively secure, e.g. [1,19,58–61]. Considering that most natural selectively secure cryptographic primitives are plausibly adaptively secure, it would be highly interesting to see any attack exploiting the adaptive nature of AOM-MLWE. We leave it as an important theoretical question to bridge selective and adaptive security, often times very easy to establish in the classical setting using idealized models such as GGM.

Practical Hardness of AOM-MLWE. Lastly, we complement our theoretical analysis of AOM-MLWE with practical cryptanalysis. To provide a basic understanding of the techniques introduced, we present another simple attack, this one being purely statistical. Suppose we are allowed $Q - 1$ queries on the challenge $\mathbf{A}, (\mathbf{t}_i = \mathbf{A} \cdot \mathbf{s}_i + \mathbf{e}_i)_{i \in [Q]}$, where all secrets and errors have a norm bounded by B. We request all the $(\mathbf{s}_1 + \mathbf{s}_i, \mathbf{e}_1 + \mathbf{e}_i)_{i \in [2, Q]}$, such that summing them gives us the values of $(Q - 1)\mathbf{s}_1 + \sum_i \mathbf{s}_i$ and $(Q - 1)\mathbf{e}_1 + \sum_i \mathbf{e}_i$. These two equations effectively position $\mathbf{s}_1$ and $\mathbf{e}_1$ within balls of radius $\frac{B}{\sqrt{Q}}$. This estimation is highly precise for large Q, enabling the reconstruction of $\mathbf{s}_1, \mathbf{e}_1$ and derivation of all other values using elementary linear algebra. We demonstrate that this attack can be generalized to provide statistical information on all the secrets and errors of the AOM-MLWE instance. By meticulously analyzing the geometry of generic queries, we can gather enough information to pinpoint the errors and secrets within a specific region of the space. Subsequently, we craft a final MLWE instance to decode these within the identified regions and solve the instance. In the context of our threshold signature schemes, we illustrate that the practical security of forgery, after collecting Q transcripts, is equivalent to solving an MLWE instance with parameters that are $\frac{1}{\sqrt{W \cdot Q}}$ times smaller than for a direct forgery. Here, W is the hamming weight of a challenge polynomial. Integrating this cryptanalysis with state-of-the-art lattice reduction estimation allows us to construct a set of parameters that align with the standard NIST levels I, III, and V.

3 Preliminary

We provide a some backgrounds. See the full version for standard definitions and primitives.

Notations. We use lower (resp. upper) case bold fonts $\mathbf{v}$ (resp. $\mathbf{M}$) for vectors (resp. matrices). We always view vectors in the column form. We use v_i (resp. $\mathbf{m}_i$) to indicate the i-th entry (resp. column) of $\mathbf{v}$ (resp. $\mathbf{M}$). For $(\mathbf{v}, \mathbf{M}) \in \mathcal{R}_q^\ell \times \mathcal{R}_q^{k \times \ell}$, $\mathbf{v}^\top \odot \mathbf{M}$ denotes the column-wise multiplication: $[v_1 \cdot \mathbf{M}_1 \mid \cdots \mid v_\ell \cdot \mathbf{M}_\ell]$. For $\mathbf{M} = [\mathbf{m}_1 \mid \cdots \mid \mathbf{m}_\ell] \in \mathcal{R}_q^{k \times \ell}$, $\|\mathbf{M}\|_2$ denotes $\max_{i \in [\ell]} \|\mathbf{m}_i\|_2$.

Modular Most-Significant Bit Decomposition. Following del Pino et al. [79,80], we perform bit dropping for efficiency purpose. Let $\nu \in \mathbb{N} \setminus \{0\}$. Any integer $x \in \mathbb{Z}$ can be *uniquely* decomposed as:

$$x = 2^\nu \cdot x_\top + x_\perp, \quad (x_\top, x_\perp) \in \mathbb{Z} \times [-2^{\nu-1}, 2^{\nu-1} - 1], \quad (1)$$

which consists essentially in separating the lower-order bits from the higher-order ones. We define the function $\lfloor \cdot \rceil_\nu : \mathbb{Z} \to \mathbb{Z}$ s.t. $\lfloor x \rceil_\nu = \lfloor x/2^\nu \rceil = x_\top$, where $\lfloor \cdot \rceil : \mathbb{R} \mapsto \mathbb{Z}$ denotes the rounding operator. With a slight overload of notation, when $q > 2^\nu$, we extend $\lfloor \cdot \rceil_\nu$ to take inputs in $\mathbb{Z}_q$, in which case, we assume the output is an element in $\mathbb{Z}_{q_\nu}$ where $q_\nu = \lfloor q/2^\nu \rfloor$. Formally, we define:

$$\lfloor \cdot \rceil_\nu : \mathbb{Z}_q \mapsto \mathbb{Z}_{q_\nu} = \mathbb{Z}_{\lfloor q/2^\nu \rfloor} \quad \text{s.t.} \quad \lfloor x \rceil_\nu = \lfloor \bar{x}/2^\nu \rceil \bmod q_\nu = (\bar{x})_\top \bmod q_\nu,$$

where $\bar{x}$ is the so-called canonical unsigned representation of x modulo q. The function $\lfloor \cdot \rceil_\nu$ naturally extends to vectors coefficient-wise. More details can be found in the full version.

3.1 Lattices and Gaussians

For integers $n, q \in \mathbb{N}$ we define the ring $\mathcal{R}$ as $\mathbb{Z}[X]/(X^n + 1)$ and $\mathcal{R}_q$ as $\mathcal{R}/q\mathcal{R}$. For a positive real σ, let $\rho_\sigma(\mathbf{z}) = \exp\left(-\frac{\|\mathbf{z}\|_2}{2\sigma^2}\right)$. The discrete Gaussian distribution over $\mathbb{Z}^n$ and standard deviation σ is defined by its probability distribution function: $\mathcal{D}_{\mathbb{Z}^n, \sigma}(\mathbf{z}) = \frac{\rho_\sigma(\mathbf{z})}{\sum_{\mathbf{z}' \in \mathbb{Z}^n} \rho_\sigma(\mathbf{z}')}$. We may simply note $\mathcal{D}_\sigma$.

We denote $\mathcal{C} \subset \mathcal{R}_q$ as the set of polynomials with $\{-1, 0, 1\}$-coefficient and fixed hamming weight W, i.e., $\{c \in \mathcal{R}_q \mid \|c\|_\infty = 1 \land \|c\|_1 = W\}$. We denote $\mathbb{T} \subset \mathcal{R}_q$ as the set of all signed monomials, i.e., $\{(-1)^b \cdot X^i \mid (b, i) \in \{0, 1\} \times [n]\}$. We have the following guarantee on invertibility of differences of elements in $\mathbb{T}$ (see for example [15]).

Lemma 3.1. *Let n be a power of 2. For any distinct $a, b \in \mathbb{T}$, $(a - b)$ is invertible over $\mathcal{R}_q$ and $2 \cdot (a - b)^{-1} \in \mathcal{R}_q$ is a polynomial with coefficients in $\{-1, 0, 1\}$.*

3.2 Two Round Threshold Signature

A two-round threshold signature scheme consists of the following efficient algorithms. Let N be the number of total signers and T be a reconstruction threshold s.t. $T \leq N$. Also, let SS be a signer set such that $\mathsf{SS} \subseteq [N]$ with size T. Each signer $i \in [N]$ maintains a state st_i to retain a short-lived session specific information. We also define correctness and unforgeability. For the definition of correctness, see the full version.

TS.Setup($1^\lambda, N, T$) → tspar: The setup algorithm takes as input a security parameter 1^λ, the number N of total signers, and a reconstruction threshold $T \leq N$ and outputs a public parameter tspar. We assume tspar includes N and T.

TS.KeyGen(tspar) → (vk, $(\mathsf{sk}_i)_{i \in [N]}$): The key generation algorithm takes as input a public parameter tspar and outputs a verification key vk, and secret key shares $(\mathsf{sk}_i)_{i \in [N]}$. It implicitly sets up an empty state $\mathsf{state}_i := \emptyset$ for all N signers. We assume vk includes tspar.

TS.PP(vk, i, sk_i, st_i) → (pp_i, st_i): The signing algorithm for a pre-processing round takes as input a verification key vk, an index i of a signer, a secret key share sk_i, and a state st_i of the signer i, and outputs a pre-processing token pp_i and an updated state st_i.

TS.Sign(vk, SS, M, i, $(\mathsf{pp}_j)_{j \in \mathsf{SS}}$, sk_i, st_i) → ($\widehat{\mathsf{sig}}_i$, st_i): The signing algorithm takes as input a verification key vk, a signer set SS, a message M, an index $i \in \mathsf{SS}$ of a signer, a tuple of pre-processing tokens $(\mathsf{pp}_j)_{j \in \mathsf{SS}}$, a secret key share sk_i, and a state st_i of the signer i and outputs a partial signature $\widehat{\mathsf{sig}}_i$ and an updated state st_i.

TS.Agg(vk, SS, M, $(\widehat{\mathsf{sig}}_i)_{i \in \mathsf{SS}}$) → sig: The aggregation algorithm takes as input a verification key vk, a signer set SS, a message M, and a tuple of partial signatures $(\widehat{\mathsf{sig}}_i)_{i \in \mathsf{SS}}$ and outputs a signature sig.

TS.Verify(vk, M, sig) → 1 or 0: The verification algorithm takes as input a verification key vk, a message M, and a signature sig, and outputs 1 if sig is valid and 0 otherwise.

Definition 3.1 (Unforgeability). *For a two round threshold signature scheme TS, the advantage of an adversary $\mathcal{A}$ against the unforgeability of TS in the random oracle model is defined as $\mathsf{Adv}^{\mathsf{ts\text{-}uf}}_{\mathsf{TS},\mathcal{A}}(1^\lambda, N, T) = \Pr[\mathsf{Game}^{\mathsf{ts\text{-}uf}}_{\mathsf{TS},\mathcal{A}}(1^\lambda, N, T) = 1]$, where $\mathsf{Game}^{\mathsf{ts\text{-}uf}}_{\mathsf{TS},\mathcal{A}}(1^\lambda, N, T)$ is described in Fig. 3. We say that TS is unforgeable in the random oracle model if, for all $\lambda \in \mathbb{N}$, $N, T \in \mathsf{poly}(\lambda)$ s.t. $T \leq N$, and efficient adversary $\mathcal{A}$, $\mathsf{Adv}^{\mathsf{ts\text{-}uf}}_{\mathsf{TS},\mathcal{A}}(1^\lambda) = \mathsf{negl}(\lambda)$ holds.*

```
Game_{TS,A}^{ts-uf}(1^λ, N, T)                    O_{TS.PP}(i)
 1: Q_M := ∅  // Empty set                         1: req [[i ∈ HS]]
 2: tspar ←$ TS.Setup(1^λ, N, T)                   2: (pp_i, st_i) ←$ TS.PP(vk, i, sk_i, st_i)
 3: (CS, st_A) ←$ A^H(tspar)                       3: return pp_i
 4: req [[CS ⊈ [N]]] ∨ [[|CS| ≥ T]]                ─────────────────────────────────────────
 5: HS := [N]\CS,                                  O_{TS.Sign}(SS, M, i, (pp_j)_{j∈SS})
 6: for i ∈ HS do st_i := ∅                        1: req [[SS ⊆ [N]]] ∧ [[i ∈ HS ∩ SS]]
 7: (vk, (sk_i)_{i∈[N]}) ←$ TS.KeyGen(tspar)       2: ŝig_i ←$ TS.Sign(vk, SS, M, i, (pp_j)_{j∈SS}, sk_i, st_i)
 8: (sig*, M*) ←$ A^{O_{TS.PP}, O_{TS.Sign}, H}(vk, (sk_i)_{i∈CS}, st_A)   3: Q_M := Q_M ∪ {M}
 9: if [[M* ∈ Q_M]] then                           4: return ŝig_i
10:   return 0
11: return TS.Verify(tspar, vk, M*, sig*)
```

Fig. 3. Unforgeability game for a two round threshold signature scheme, where H denotes the random oracle. In the above, the oracles return ⊥ to $\mathcal{A}$ when TS.PP or TS.Sign output ⊥ (i.e., fail to output a pre-processing token or a partial signature).

Remark 3.1 (Q_S-Bounded Scheme). While our construction of threshold signature supports an unbounded polynomially many signing queries, we would require a super-polynomial sized modulus q, making the scheme impractical. To this end, we consider a more fined grained bounded scheme where unforgeability holds against any adversary making at most $Q_S = \text{poly}(\lambda)$ signing queries to $\mathcal{O}_{\text{TS.Sign}}$. As per NIST's 2022 call for additional (post-quantum) signatures [77], we set $Q_S \approx 2^{64}$ for our concrete instantiation. Indeed, this is common practice among practical signatures such as Falcon [82] and Raccoon [80], including the three-round threshold Raccoon [79].

4 Algebraic One-More Module Learning with Errors

We introduce the "Algebraic One-More Module Learning with Errors" (AOM-MLWE) problem, a term coined in reference to the algebraic one-more discrete logarithm (AOM-DL) problem recently introduced by Nick, Ruffing, and Seurin [76]. This problem represents a notably milder variant when compared to the conventional "non-algebraic" one-more challenges encountered in classical contexts, such as the One-More Discrete Logarithm (OM-DL) problem [9,11,12,26]. After presenting AOM-MLWE and discussing the subtleties of the interplay of parameters, we delve into its relationship with the well-established MLWE and MSIS problems. For the interested readers, we include the motivation of considering AOM-MLWE in the full version.

4.1 Definition of AOM-MLWE

An AOM-MLWE adversary is given a set of Q MLWE challenges $(\mathbf{t}_i)_{i \in [Q]} = (\mathbf{A}\mathbf{s}_i + \mathbf{e}_i)_{i \in [Q]}$ and has access to an MLWE solving oracle $Q - 1$ times. Its goal is then to solve Q of the MLWE challenges. The term "algebraic" is employed because when the adversary queries the MLWE solving oracle with a vector $\mathbf{b}$, it must also provide a vector $\mathbf{d}$ that essentially "explains" the vector $\mathbf{b}$, as a proof that the query was made on a linear combination of the challenges. More formally, this requirement is expressed as $\mathbf{b} = \mathbf{Td}$, where $\mathbf{T} = [\mathbf{As}_1 + \mathbf{e}_1 \mid \cdots \mid \mathbf{As}_Q + \mathbf{e}_Q]$, is a matrix representing the set of Q MLWE challenges generated by the challenger.

In particular, the AOM-MLWE problem restricts the adversary to only query the MLWE oracle on a linear combination of the MLWE challenges. Notice that since the challenger knows the corresponding MLWE secrets, it can answer the adversary's queries efficiently, thus making the AOM-MLWE assumption falsifiable.

The algebraic restriction in the Algebraic One-More Module Learning with Errors (AOM-MLWE) problem offers additional advantages. Firstly, it simplifies the cryptanalysis process in comparison to the non-algebraic case, primarily because of the stringent limitations placed on the vector $\mathbf{b}$ that the adversary can query to the MLWE solving oracle. In our subsequent analysis, we demonstrate that the "selective" variant of the AOM-MLWE problem is as hard as solving the standard MLWE and MSIS problems. Importantly, we believe that no such analogous reduction exists in the non-algebraic setting, even when considering the selective scenario. This reduction not only enhances the credibility of the AOM-MLWE problem's hardness but also underscores that the only conceivable approach to weaken its security would be to exploit the adaptiveness.

Definition of **AOM-MLWE**. Formally, the AOM-MLWE problem is defined as follows, supposing we are working over the ring of integer R_q of a number field.

Definition 4.1 (AOM-MLWE). *Let ℓ, k, q, Q be integers and $(\mathcal{D}_i)_{i \in [Q]}$ be a set of probability distributions over R_q with $k \geq \ell$. Let $\mathcal{L}$ denote an efficiently checkable subset of $R_q^{Q \times (Q-1)}$ and $B_{\mathcal{L}}, B_{\mathbf{s}}, B_{\mathbf{e}}$ be integers. The advantage of an adversary $\mathcal{A}$ against the (search) Algebraic One-More Module Learning with Errors* AOM-MLWE$_{q,\ell,k,Q,(\mathcal{D}_i)_{i \in [Q]}, \mathcal{L}, B_{\mathcal{L}}, B_{\mathbf{s}}, B_{\mathbf{e}}}$ *problem is defined as:*

$$\mathsf{Adv}_{\mathcal{A}}^{\mathsf{AOM\text{-}MLWE}}(1^\lambda) = \Pr\left[\mathsf{Game}_{\mathcal{A}}^{\mathsf{AOM\text{-}MLWE}}(1^\lambda, 1^Q) = 1\right],$$

where $\mathsf{Game}_{\mathcal{A}}^{\mathsf{AOM\text{-}MLWE}}$ *is shown in Fig. 4. The* AOM-MLWE$_{q,\ell,k,Q,(\mathcal{D}_i)_{i \in [Q]}, \mathcal{L}, B_{\mathcal{L}}, B_{\mathbf{s}}, B_{\mathbf{e}}}$ *assumption states that any efficient adversary $\mathcal{A}$ has negligible advantage. We also define a* selective *variant of* AOM-MLWE, *denoted as* sel-AOM-MLWE, *whose game is shown in Fig. 4.*

In above, we allow each MLWE samples to come from a different distribution. As we later see, for threshold signatures, we set the first MLWE sample to have smaller noise compared to the other MLWE samples. Moreover, we weaken the winning condition of the adversary so that it only needs to solve an *approximate* MLWE problem. We insist that the adversary wins even if it recovers a solution to the MLWE problem where each MLWE challenge ($\mathbf{t}_i = \mathbf{As}_i + \mathbf{e}_i$) is modified to be $v_i \cdot \mathbf{t}_i$ for a small non-zero $v_i \in R_q$. This relaxation captures a recurrent issue

Game$_\mathcal{A}^{\text{AOM-MLWE}}(1^\lambda, 1^Q)$	$\mathcal{O}_{\text{solve}}(\mathbf{d})$
1: $(\text{ctr}, \mathbf{D}) := (1, \perp)$ // $\mathbf{D}$ is an "empty" matrix	1: if $[\![\mathbf{d} \notin \mathcal{R}_q^Q]\!] \vee [\![\text{ctr} \geq Q]\!]$
2: $\mathbf{A} \xleftarrow{\$} \mathcal{R}_q^{k \times \ell}$	2: return 0
3: for $i \in [Q]$ do	3: $\mathbf{D} \leftarrow [\mathbf{D} \mid \mathbf{d}]$ // Update matrix $\mathbf{D} \in \mathcal{R}_q^{Q \times \text{ctr}}$
4: $(\mathbf{s}_i, \mathbf{e}_i) \xleftarrow{\$} \mathcal{D}_i^\ell \times \mathcal{D}_i^k$	4: $\text{ctr} \leftarrow \text{ctr} + 1$
5: $(\mathbf{S}, \mathbf{E}) := ([\mathbf{s}_1 \mid \cdots \mid \mathbf{s}_Q], [\mathbf{e}_1 \mid \cdots \mid \mathbf{e}_Q])$	5: return $(\mathbf{Sd}, \mathbf{Ed}) \in \mathcal{R}_q^\ell \times \mathcal{R}_q^k$
6: $\mathbf{T} := \mathbf{AS} + \mathbf{E} \in \mathcal{R}_q^{k \times Q}$	Game$_\mathcal{A}^{\text{sel-AOM-MLWE}}(1^\lambda, 1^Q)$
7: $(\mathbf{v}, \widehat{\mathbf{S}}, \widehat{\mathbf{E}}) \xleftarrow{\$} \mathcal{A}^{\mathcal{O}_{\text{solve}}}(\mathbf{A}, \mathbf{T})$	1: $\mathbf{A} \xleftarrow{\$} \mathcal{R}_q^{k \times \ell}$
8: // Check format of output, where $\mathcal{L} \subseteq \mathcal{R}_q^{Q \times (Q-1)}$	2: for $i \in [Q]$ do
9: if $[\![(\mathbf{D}, \mathbf{v}, \widehat{\mathbf{S}}, \widehat{\mathbf{E}}) \in \mathcal{L} \times \mathcal{R}_q^Q \times \mathcal{R}_q^{\ell \times Q} \times \mathcal{R}_q^{k \times Q}]\!]$	3: $(\mathbf{s}_i, \mathbf{e}_i) \xleftarrow{\$} \mathcal{D}_i^\ell \times \mathcal{D}_i^k$
10: // Check size of solution: v_i is the i-th entry of $\mathbf{v}$	4: $(\mathbf{S}, \mathbf{E}) := ([\mathbf{s}_1 \mid \cdots \mid \mathbf{s}_Q], [\mathbf{e}_1 \mid \cdots \mid \mathbf{e}_Q])$
11: if $[\![\forall i \in [Q], 0 < \|v_i\|_2 \leq B_\mathcal{L}$	5: $\mathbf{T} := \mathbf{AS} + \mathbf{E} \in \mathcal{R}_q^{k \times Q}$
12: $\wedge \|\widehat{\mathbf{S}}\|_2 \leq B_\mathbf{s} \wedge \|\widehat{\mathbf{E}}\|_2 \leq B_\mathbf{e}]\!]$	6: $\mathbf{D} \xleftarrow{\$} \mathcal{A}(\mathbf{A})$
13: // Check if it is an *approximate* MLWE solution	7: if $[\![\mathbf{D} \notin \mathcal{L} \subseteq \mathcal{R}_q^{Q \times (Q-1)}]\!]$
14: if $[\![\mathbf{v}^\top \odot \mathbf{T} = \mathbf{A}\widehat{\mathbf{S}} + \widehat{\mathbf{E}}]\!]$	8: return 0
15: return 1	9: $(\mathbf{v}, \widehat{\mathbf{S}}, \widehat{\mathbf{E}}) \xleftarrow{\$} \mathcal{A}(\mathbf{A}, \mathbf{T}, (\mathbf{SD}, \mathbf{ED}))$
16: return 0	10: // Remaining check is identical to Game$_\mathcal{A}^{\text{AOM-MLWE}}$

Fig. 4. The adaptive and selective algebraic one-more MLWE problem. In the selective setting, the adversary $\mathcal{A}$ commits to all the coefficients before observing the MLWE samples. Recall $\odot$ denotes the column-wise multiplication.

in lattice-based identification protocols, Fiat-Shamir based signatures, and zero-knowledge proof systems (see for instance [15,22,46,47] for some discussions). Moreover, we define the assumption to be Q-bounded, that is, any adversary is limited to making at most $Q - 1$ queries to the MLWE solving oracle. If needed we can define a (polynomially) unbounded definition where the game is not quantified by Q.

4.2 Preliminary Discussion on the Hardness of AOM-MLWE

Here, we provide an informal discussion on the hardness of (adaptive) AOM-MLWE under standard assumptions, this section provides insight into why we believe it is hard. We later use these insights to establish the hardness of the *selective* AOM-MLWE problem for well-chosen parameters based on MSIS and MLWE. This informal discussion will also form the basis for the cryptanalysis of the AOM-MLWE problem in Sect. 7.

When AOM-MLWE is Trivially Broken. The AOM-MLWE problem is parameterized by many parameters, of which the space of accepted linear combinations $\mathcal{L} \subseteq \mathcal{R}_q^{Q \times (Q-1)}$ and the distributions $(\mathcal{D}_i)_{i \in [Q]}$ play one of the most fundamental roles. All other parameters such as the size of the MLWE solutions (i.e., $B_\mathbf{s}, B_\mathbf{e}$) and the accepted "slack" $B_\mathcal{L}$ are more standard and can be handled similarly following prior works on lattice-based cryptography. Throughout this section, for simplicity of explanation, assume $\mathcal{L} = \prod_{i \in [Q-1]} \widehat{\mathcal{L}}$ which naturally embeds into $\oplus_{i \in [Q]} \mathcal{R}_q = \mathcal{R}_q^Q$ and allows to consider each column of $\mathcal{L}$ as being included in $\hat{\mathcal{L}}$. Specifically, the vector $\mathbf{d}$ the adversary $\mathcal{A}$ queries to the MLWE solving oracle $\mathcal{O}_{\mathsf{solve}}$ satisfies $\mathbf{d} \in \hat{\mathcal{L}}$.

First Insecure Example: Overstretched Queries and Separation of Secrets. In the scenario where $\mathcal{D}_i = \mathcal{D}$ for all $i \in [Q]$ and $\mathcal{D}$ represents a distribution that generates polynomials with coefficients having an ℓ_∞-norm smaller than $0 < B < \sqrt{q/2}$ and with the additional assumptions that $\mathbf{d} = [1 \mid B \mid \mathbf{0}]^\top \in \mathcal{R}_q^Q$ is within $\hat{\mathcal{L}}$, a non-trivial vulnerability emerges.

The combination of the secrets by $\mathbf{d}$ gives the equation $\mathbf{Sd} = \mathbf{s}_1 + B \cdot \mathbf{s}_2$ (mod q). However, by the assumption on the size of $\mathbf{s}_i$ and B, the magnitude of $\mathbf{Sd}$ is much smaller than q, meaning that this equation actually holds without modular reduction. Then the adversary can easily recover $(\mathbf{s}_1, \mathbf{s}_2)$: we simply have $\mathbf{s}_1 = \mathbf{Sd} \mod B$ precisely corresponding to the original $\mathbf{s}_1$, as the entries of $\mathbf{s}_1$ are all smaller than B. Significantly, in this situation, the adversary can extract two MLWE secrets using just one oracle query to the MLWE solver. This outcome effectively breaches the security of AOM-MLWE and underscores the critical requirement that the size of the MLWE secret and noise must be quite larger than the elements present in $\hat{\mathcal{L}}$.

Second Insecure Example: Anomalously Large Number of Queries and Statistical Recovery. Now assume $\hat{\mathcal{L}} = B_{\infty,1}(0)$ the ℓ_∞ ball of radius 1 and assert that the secrets are independently and uniformly distributed with coefficients bounded by $1 \ll B < q/2$.

While the above attack no longer works as the query vectors $\mathbf{d}$ are too small compared to the size of the secrets and noises, consider an adversary that queries the oracle on input $\mathbf{d}_i \in \mathcal{R}_q^Q$ for $i \in [2:Q]$, where $\mathbf{d}_i = (1, 0, \ldots, 0, 1, 0, \ldots, 0)^T$ is the vector with zero entries except for the 1-st and i-th entries which are set to 1. Hence, the adversary receives tuples of the form $(\mathbf{s}_i^* = \mathbf{s}_1 + \mathbf{s}_i)_{i \in [2:Q]}$ (mod q) and this result is also valid without modular reduction by assumption on B. The attacker can then construct the empirical estimator $\tilde{\mathbf{s}}_1 = \frac{1}{Q-1} \sum_{i=2}^{Q} \mathbf{s}_i^*$ which converges towards its mean value $\mathbf{s}_1$. Quantitatively, this sum will be a random variable centered at $\mathbf{s}_1$ and of standard deviation of order $B/\sqrt{3Q}$. The attacker can then round $\tilde{\mathbf{s}}_1$ to the nearest integer and claim it as the secret $\mathbf{s}_1$. By the Tchebyshev inequality and amplification, this process is correct with probability at least $(1 - \frac{2B^2}{3Q})^n$ for n being the number of coefficients of the secrets. Hence when $Q \geq nB^2$, i.e., the size of the secrets is much smaller than the square root number of oracle queries, a total recovery is possible in linear time. The probability density of the candidate estimator is superposed with the acceptance zone which is the segment of length 1 centered at the secret. This example indicates that the size of the MLWE secret and noise crucially depend on the accepted number of queries Q.

When AOM-MLWE is Plausibly Hard. It is important to highlight that the attacks discussed in the previous examples are, in a sense, statistical in nature. These attacks rely solely on the linear combination of the secrets or the vectors but do not utilize any information about the specific MLWE sample $\mathbf{T} = \mathbf{AS} + \mathbf{E}$. Indeed, when we delve into the assessment of the hardness of the "selective" AOM-MLWE problem, we observe that these statistical attacks represent the sole advantage an adversary possesses compared to MLWE and MSIS. To put it differently, once we configure the parameters in such a way that the aforementioned statistical attacks are no longer viable, the only viable approach to compromise sel-AOM-MLWE is to break MLWE or MSIS. This insight serves as a cornerstone when evaluating the concrete hardness of AOM-MLWE using state-of-the-art cryptanalysis techniques.

In this work, we provide two reductions from MLWE or MSIS to sel-AOM-MLWE. Conceptually, the two reductions embed, in a different way, a single MLWE instance $\mathbf{t}^* \in \mathcal{R}_q^k$ into the Q MLWE instances $\mathbf{T} \in \mathcal{R}_q^{k \times Q}$ provided by the sel-AOM-MLWE game. It is worth noting that in the non-algebraic setting, it is unclear whether even the selective variant is implied by any standard assumptions. We thus believe that there is a fundamental gap between the hardness of the AOM-MLWE problem and its non-algebraic variant and view this indication as an evidence for the hardness of AOM-MLWE.

In the following, we present only one of the reductions, capturing the parameter setting of the threshold signature we construct in Sect. 5. This will be our main focus of cryptanalysis. The second reduction, which we call the "alternative" reduction, captures a parameter setting not used in this work and is presented in the full version.

4.3 MSIS and MLWE Imply Selective AOM-MLWE

In this section, we embed $\mathbf{t}^* = \mathbf{A}\mathbf{s}^* + \mathbf{e}^*$ in one of the columns of $\mathbf{T} = \mathbf{AS} + \mathbf{E}$ and define the accepted linear combinations $\mathcal{L}$ so that $\mathbf{t}^*$ remains a hard MLWE instance even after the adversary obtains the hints $(\mathbf{SD}, \mathbf{ED})$. Without loss of generality, we set the first column $(\mathbf{S}, \mathbf{E})$ to be $(\mathbf{s}^*, \mathbf{e}^*)$. Moreover, for simplicity, we focus on the uniform secret sel-AOM-UMLWE, establishing the hardness of sel-AOM-MLWE.

Remark 4.1 (Invertible Submatrix of $\mathbf{A}$). In this section, we restrict the challenge matrix $\mathbf{A}$ to contain ℓ rows that form an invertible matrix over $\mathcal{R}_q$—we say that $\mathbf{A}$ *contains an invertible submatrix* in the remaining of this work. This condition is easily enforced by resampling $\mathbf{A} \xleftarrow{\$} \mathcal{R}_q^{k \times \ell}$ until an invertible matrix is found, an efficiently computable check using standard linear algebra. For certain choices of $(k, \ell, \mathcal{R}_q)$, this is without loss of generality as $\mathbf{A} \xleftarrow{\$} \mathcal{R}_q^{k \times \ell}$ satisfies this condition with overwhelming probability. In other cases like $k = \ell$ and $\mathcal{R}_q$ a fully-splitting ring, $\mathbf{A}$ is non-invertible with a non-negligible probability (see [24, Appendix A] for details).

This restriction is explicitly used when reducing MSIS to sel-AOM-UMLWE. While this seems like an artifact of our proof technique, we choose to simply enforce this restriction on the sel-AOM-UMLWE problem as this restriction on $\mathbf{A}$ makes the original sel-AOM-UMLWE problem no easier. For consistency, this restriction on $\mathbf{A}$ is enforced in our threshold signature as well. We leave it as an interesting problem to complete the reduction without the invertible submatrix restriction.

Constraints and Parameter Selection. As discussed in the previous section, the parameters for which (selective) AOM-UMLWE is hard needs to be chosen in a meticulous manner. We provide the set of parameters for which we establish hardness of sel-AOM-UMLWE$_{q,\ell,k,Q,(\mathcal{D}_i)_{i\in[Q]},\mathcal{L},B_\mathcal{L},B_e}$. Below, on first glance, the condition on the accepted linear combinations $\mathcal{L} \subseteq \mathcal{R}_q^{Q\times(Q-1)}$ may seem contrived and it is not immediately clear how one sets $\mathcal{L}$ in practice. A concrete example of $\mathcal{L}$ satisfying such constraints is provide in Sect. 4.4. Looking ahead, this is exactly the same $\mathcal{L}$ appearing in the proof of our threshold signature scheme.

Constraints on Parameters. We first define the following intermediate variables that will be used in the proof:

- $\mathcal{D}_1$ is defined as $2 \cdot \mathcal{D}_{\sigma_1} := \{2 \cdot x \mid x \xleftarrow{\$} \mathcal{D}_{\sigma_1}\}$, where $\mathcal{D}_{\sigma_1}$ is a discrete Gaussian distribution $\mathcal{D}_{\sigma_1}$ with width $\sigma_1 > 0$.
- $\mathcal{D}_i$ for $i \in [2:Q]$ is a discrete Gaussian distribution $\mathcal{D}_{\sigma_i}$ with width $\sigma_i > 0$, where we denote $\sigma^* = \min_{i \in [2:Q]} \sigma_i$.
- Accepted linear combinations $\mathcal{L} \subseteq \mathcal{R}_q^{Q\times Q-1}$ satisfy that for any matrix $\mathbf{D} = \begin{bmatrix} \mathbf{d}^\top \\ \underline{\mathbf{D}} \end{bmatrix} \in \mathcal{L}$, where $\mathbf{d}^\top$ is the first row of $\mathbf{D}$, $\underline{\mathbf{D}}$ is invertible over $\mathcal{R}_q$.[6]
- $\gamma_\mathcal{L} > 0$ is a bound w.r.t. $\mathcal{L}$ such that for any element $\mathbf{D} \in \mathcal{L}$ as above, we have $\gamma_\mathcal{L} \geq \|u_i\|_2$ for all $i \in [Q-1]$, where $\mathbf{u} = 2 \cdot \mathbf{d}^\top \underline{\mathbf{D}}^{-1} \in \mathcal{R}_q^{1\times(Q-1)}$, and u_i is the i-th entry of $\mathbf{u}$.[7]
- $\epsilon_{\text{lattice}} = \mathsf{Adv}_\mathcal{B}^{\mathsf{UMLWE}}(1^\lambda) + \mathsf{Adv}_{\mathcal{B}'}^{\mathsf{MSIS}}(1^\lambda) + 2^{-\frac{nk}{10}}$, where n is the dimension of $\mathcal{R}_q$ and $\mathcal{B}$ and $\mathcal{B}'$ are constructed from the adversary $\mathcal{A}$ against the AOM-UMLWE problem.
- The order of the Rényi divergence $\alpha = \frac{\sigma^*}{\gamma_\mathcal{L} \cdot \sigma_1 \cdot n} \cdot \sqrt{\frac{-\log(\epsilon_{\text{lattice}})}{Q \cdot k}} \geq 2$ and $\sigma^* \geq \gamma_\mathcal{L} \cdot \sigma_1 \cdot n \cdot \sqrt{Q \cdot k}$, chosen to minimize the overall advantage advantage, over all possible choices of Rényi's orders.

The above parameters are then set so that our proof of Theorem 4.1 holds, i.e., UMLWE$_{q,\ell,k,\mathcal{D}_{\sigma_1}}$ and MSIS$_{q,\ell+1,k-\ell,B_\mathcal{L}+B_e}$ are hard and $2^{-\frac{nk}{10}} = \mathsf{negl}(\lambda)$.

Candidate Asymptotic Parameters. Finally, we give a set of asymptotic parameters which fit the above constraints. Below it is helpful to keep in mind that the number Q of UMLWE samples and the "quality" $\gamma_\mathcal{L}$ of the accepted linear combinations $\mathcal{L}$ dictate the parameters.

---
[6] This and the following requirements come from the discussion regarding the last insecure example provided in Sect. 4.2.
[7] In general, we can allow $\mathbf{u} = v \cdot \mathbf{d}^\top \underline{\mathbf{D}}^{-1}$ for some fixed small polynomial v and replace the factor 2 in $\mathcal{D}_1$ by v. For simplicity, we use 2 as it is the only case relevant for our later instantiation of threshold signatures.

Definition 4.2 (Parameters Establishing Hardness of sel-AOM-UMLWE).
We denote the set of following asymptotic parameters and conditions along with the restricted accepted linear combinations $\mathcal{L}$ explained above as hard-param.

- $n, \ell, k = \mathsf{poly}(\lambda)$ such that $n \geq \lambda$.
- $\mathbf{A}$ is resampled from $\mathcal{R}_q^{k \times \ell}$ until it contains an invertible submatrix.
- $\mathcal{D}_1 = 2 \cdot \mathcal{D}_{\sigma_1}$ with $\sigma_1 = \sqrt{\ell} \cdot \log n$.
- $\mathcal{D}_i = \mathcal{D}_{\sigma_i}$ for $i \in [2:Q]$ such that $\sigma^* = \min_{i \in [2:Q]} \sigma_i$.
- $\sigma^* = \gamma_\mathcal{L} \cdot \sigma_1 \cdot n \cdot \sqrt{Q \cdot k}$.
- q is the smallest prime larger than $(B_\mathcal{L} + B_\mathbf{e}) \cdot \sqrt{n(k-\ell)} \cdot \log^2(n(k-\ell))$.
- Plugging in σ^*, $\alpha = \sqrt{-\log(\epsilon_{\mathsf{lattice}})}$ which is larger than 2 assuming hardness of UMLWE and MSIS.

Theorem 4.1 (UMLWE *and* MSIS *imply* sel-AOM-UMLWE). *If there exists an adversary $\mathcal{A}$ against the* sel-AOM-UMLWE$_{q,\ell,k,Q,(\mathcal{D}_i)_{i \in [Q]}, \mathcal{L}, B_\mathcal{L}, B_\mathbf{e}}$ *problem, defined with respect to the* hard-param *parameters in Definition 4.2, then we can construct an adversaries $\mathcal{B}$ and $\mathcal{B}'$ against the* UMLWE$_{q,\ell,k,\mathcal{D}_{\sigma_1}}$ *and* MSIS$_{q,\ell+1,k-\ell,B_\mathcal{L}+B_\mathbf{e}}$ *problems such that*

$$\mathsf{Adv}_\mathcal{A}^{\mathsf{sel\text{-}AOM\text{-}UMLWE}}(1^\lambda) \leq \epsilon_{\mathsf{lattice}} \cdot \exp\left(\sqrt{-Q \cdot k \cdot \log(\epsilon_{\mathsf{lattice}})} \cdot \frac{\gamma_\mathcal{L} \cdot \sigma_1 \cdot n}{\sigma^*}\right) + 2^{-\frac{nk}{10}}.$$

where $\epsilon_{\mathsf{lattice}} = \mathsf{Adv}_\mathcal{B}^{\mathsf{UMLWE}}(1^\lambda) + \left(1 + \frac{2n\ell}{q^{n/s}}\right) \cdot \mathsf{Adv}_{\mathcal{B}'}^{\mathsf{MSIS}}(1^\lambda) + 2^{-n}$ *and* Time($\mathcal{B}$), Time($\mathcal{B}'$) $\approx$ Time($\mathcal{A}$). *Concretely, plugging in* hard-param *and assuming the hardness of* UMLWE *and* MSIS*, we have* $\mathsf{Adv}_\mathcal{A}^{\mathsf{sel\text{-}AOM\text{-}UMLWE}}(1^\lambda) = \mathsf{negl}(\lambda)$.

Due to page limitation, the full proof is provided in the full version. We provide an outline of the proof below.

1. Instead of independently and uniformly sampling the $Q - 1$ other secrets $\mathbf{s}_2, \ldots, \mathbf{s}_Q$, our initial transformation involves the challenger first uniformly sampling the answer $\mathbf{W}$ corresponding to $\mathbf{SD}$ and then reverse-engineering the corresponding other $Q-1$ secrets so that $\mathbf{W} = \mathbf{SD}$. Importantly, the first secret $\mathbf{s}_1$ is still uniformly sampled from $\mathcal{R}_q$, independent of $\mathbf{W}$.
2. Similarly, we next wish to retain the first error $\mathbf{e}_1$ as a valid error for UMLWE, answer $\mathbf{ED}$ by some $\mathbf{Y}$ sampled independently of $\mathbf{e}_1$, and then reverse-engineer the $Q - 1$ other noises $\mathbf{e}_2, \ldots, \mathbf{e}_Q$ to keep the view of the adversary consistent. However, unlike the secrets which are uniformly random, the noises must follow a specific discrete Gaussian distribution. To this end, we use Rènyi divergence to carefully argue that this modification cannot be detected with overwhelming probability. This is the key step where we use above restriction on the accepted linear combinations $\mathcal{L}$.
3. Finally, the challenger replaces the construction of the first challenge $\mathbf{As}_1 + \mathbf{e}_1$ with a truly uniform element, which is an indistinguishable transformation according to the UMLWE assumption. We conclude the reduction by constructing a MSIS adversary based on an adversary in our modified game. This final step is where we use the condition that $\mathbf{A}$ contains an invertible submatrix (cf. Remark 4.1).

4.4 Example of Accepted Linear Combination $\mathcal{L} = \mathcal{L}_{\mathsf{TS}}$

Lastly, we provide a concrete example of an accepted linear combinations $\mathcal{L}$ satisfying the constraints in Sect. 4.3. The $\mathcal{L}$ we consider in this section appears in the threshold signature scheme presented in Sect. 5. We define $\mathcal{L}_{\mathsf{TS}} := \mathcal{L}$. More specifically, when we reduce the unforgeability of our threshold signature scheme to the AOM-MLWE problem, the set of vectors the reduction queries to the MLWE solving oracle $\mathcal{O}_{\mathsf{solve}}$ is guaranteed to be in $\mathcal{L}_{\mathsf{TS}}$. Below, $\mathcal{L}_{\mathsf{TS}}$ is defined by two sets $\mathcal{C}$ and $\mathbb{T}$, where $\mathcal{C}$ is the so-called challenge set of the threshold signature scheme consisting of $\{-1, 0, 1\}$-coefficient polynomials with fixed hamming weight $W > 0$ and $\mathbb{T}$ is the set of signed monomials. Recall Sect. 3.1 for their definitions. Formally, $\mathcal{L}_{\mathsf{TS}}$ is defined as follows.

Definition 4.3 (Accepted Linear Combinations $\mathcal{L}_{\mathsf{TS}}$ for Threshold Signature). *Let $\mathcal{C}$ and $\mathbb{T}$ be the sets defined in Sect. 3.1. Let τ and Q' be integers such that $\tau \geq 2$ and set $Q = \tau \cdot Q' + 1$. Let $\mathcal{P}_k$ be the set of permutation matrices of size $k > 0$. Define two sets $\mathcal{C}_{\mathsf{TS}}$ and $\mathcal{B}_{\mathsf{TS}}$ as follows:*

- $\mathcal{C}_{\mathsf{TS}} = \{[c, c', 0, \cdots, 0]^\top \in \mathcal{R}_q^\tau \mid c, c' \in \mathcal{C} \cup \{0\}\}$. *I.e., a set of row vectors where the first two entries are in $\mathcal{C} \cup \{0\}$ and the remaining $\tau - 2$ entries are zero.*

- $\mathcal{B}_{\mathsf{TS}} = \left\{ \begin{bmatrix} 1 & 1 & & & \\ b_1 & b'_1 & & & \\ b_2 & b'_2 & 1 & & \\ \vdots & \vdots & & \ddots & \\ b_{\tau-1} & b'_{\tau-1} & & & 1 \end{bmatrix} \in \mathcal{R}_q^{\tau \times \tau} \;\middle|\; \begin{array}{c} \forall i \in [\tau-1], (b_i, b'_i) \in \mathbb{T}^2 \\ \wedge\; b_1 \neq b'_1 \end{array} \right\}$. *I.e., a set of invertible matrices where the first two columns consist of entries in $\mathbb{T}$, the first two rows are full-rank, and the remaining entries consist an identity matrix of dimension $\tau - 2$.*

Then, define the set of accepted linear combinations $\mathcal{L}_{\mathsf{TS}}$ as follows:

$$\mathcal{L}_{\mathsf{TS}} = \left\{ \begin{bmatrix} 1 & \\ & \mathbf{P}_{\mathsf{row}} \end{bmatrix} \begin{bmatrix} \mathbf{c}_1^\top & \mathbf{c}_2^\top & \cdots & \mathbf{c}_{Q'}^\top \\ \mathbf{B}_1 & & & \\ & \mathbf{B}_2 & & \\ & & \ddots & \\ & & & \mathbf{B}_{Q'} \end{bmatrix} \cdot \mathbf{P}_{\mathsf{column}} \subset \mathcal{R}_q^{Q \times (Q-1)} \;\middle|\; \begin{array}{c} \forall i \in [Q'], (\mathbf{c}_i, \mathbf{B}_i) \in \mathcal{C}_{\mathsf{TS}} \times \mathcal{B}_{\mathsf{TS}}, \\ (\mathbf{P}_{\mathsf{row}}, \mathbf{P}_{\mathsf{column}}) \in \mathcal{P}_{Q-1}^2 \end{array} \right\}.$$

The following shows that $\mathcal{L}_{\mathsf{TS}}$ satisfies the condition required to establish the hardness of sel-AOM-MLWE problem via Theorem 4.1. The proof is provided in the full version.

Lemma 4.1. *The set of accepted linear combinations $\mathcal{L}_{\mathsf{TS}}$ defined in Definition 4.3 satisfies the condition imposed by* hard-param *defined in Definition 4.2, where $\gamma_{\mathcal{L}_{\mathsf{TS}}} = 2 \cdot W \sqrt{n}$.*

Concretely, for any matrix $\mathbf{D} = \begin{bmatrix} \mathbf{d}^\top \\ \underline{\mathbf{D}} \end{bmatrix} \in \mathcal{L}_{\mathsf{TS}}$, where $\mathbf{d}^\top$ is the first row of $\mathbf{D}$, $\underline{\mathbf{D}}$ is invertible over $\mathcal{R}_q$. Moreover, we have $\gamma_{\mathcal{L}_{\mathsf{TS}}} \geq \|u_i\|_2$ for all $i \in [Q-1]$, where $\mathbf{u} = 2 \cdot \mathbf{d}^\top \underline{\mathbf{D}}^{-1} \in \mathcal{R}_q^{1 \times (Q-1)}$ and u_i is the i-th entry of $\mathbf{u}$.

5 Construction of Our 2-Round Threshold Signature

In this section, we present our 2-round threshold signature scheme $\mathsf{TS}_{\text{2-round}}$.

Parameters. For reference, we provide in Table 1 the parameters used in the scheme. Parameters related to the security proof will be provide in Sect. 6.

Table 1. Overview of parameters used in our 2-round threshold signature.

Parameter	Explanation
$\mathcal{R}_q$	Polynomial ring $\mathcal{R}_q = \mathbb{Z}[X]/(q, X^n + 1)$
(k, ℓ)	Dimension of public matrix $\mathbf{A} \in \mathcal{R}_q^{k \times \ell}$
$(\mathcal{D}_t, \sigma_t)$	Gaussian distribution with width σ_t used for the verification key $\mathbf{t}$
$(\mathcal{D}_w, \sigma_w)$	Gaussian distribution with width σ_w used for the commitment $\mathbf{w}$
ν_t	Amount of bit dropping performed on verification key
ν_w	Amount of bit dropping performed on (aggregated) commitment
(q_{ν_t}, q_{ν_w})	Rounded moduli satisfying $(q_{\nu_t}, q_{\nu_w}) := (\lfloor q/2^{\nu_t} \rfloor, \lfloor q/2^{\nu_w} \rfloor) = (\lceil q/2^{\nu_t} \rceil, \lfloor q/2^{\nu_w} \rfloor)$
$\mathbb{T} \subset \mathcal{R}_q$	Set of signed monomials (see Sect. 3)
rep	An integer s.t. $|\mathbb{T}|^{\mathsf{rep}-1} \geq 2^\lambda$
$(\mathcal{C} \subset \mathcal{R}_q, W)$	Challenge set $\{c \in \mathcal{R}_q \mid \|c\|_\infty = 1 \land \|c\|_1 = W\}$ s.t. $|\mathcal{C}| \geq 2^\lambda$
B	Two-norm bound on the signature

Construction. The construction of our 2-round threshold signature $\mathsf{TS}_{\text{2-round}}$ is provide in Fig. 5. Our scheme uses two hash functions modeled as a random oracle in the security proof. $\mathsf{G} : \{0,1\}^* \to \{1\} \times \mathbb{T}^{\mathsf{rep}-1}$ is used to aggregate the *individual* commitments into one commitment; that is, each user outputs rep commitments in the pre-processing phase and G is used to aggregate them. $\mathsf{H} : \{0,1\}^* \to \mathcal{C}$ is used to generate the random challenge polynomial for which the users reply with a response. The proof of correctness is provided in the full version.

In the setup, we resample $\mathbf{A} \xleftarrow{\$} \mathcal{R}_q^{k \times \ell}$ until ℓ of its row consists of an invertible matrix in $\mathcal{R}_q^{\ell \times \ell}$. While we believe this to be an artifact of our current proof, this restriction is used to establish hardness of the sel-AOM-UMLWE (see Sects. 4.3 and 6). Another peculiarity of our construction is that the the verification key $\mathbf{t}$ is generated using $2 \cdot (\mathbf{A} \cdot \mathbf{s} + \mathbf{e})$ rather than the more conventional $\mathbf{A} \cdot \mathbf{s} + \mathbf{e}$. While from an algorithmic point of view, this has almost no impact on the signing and verification algorithms, it is vital when establishing security based on our AOM-MLWE assumption. Specifically, this is used to invoke Lemma 4.1, establishing that the adversary's queries fall into the accepted linear combinations

$\mathcal{L}_{\mathsf{TS}}$ required to argue hardness of AOM-MLWE. It is not clear whether this is an artifact of our proof and we leave it as an interesting problem to remove the factor 2 from our construction.

6 Security of Our 2-Round Threshold Signature

In this section, we prove the unforgeability of our 2-round threshold signature scheme $\mathsf{TS}_{\mathsf{2\text{-}round}}$. We will rely on the hardness of the AOM-MLWE problem with parameters based on those proposed in Sects. 4.3 and 4.4. Before providing the proof of unforgeability, we first give asymptotic parameters for which our scheme is provably secure. A concrete parameter selection along with an efficiency analysis is provided in Sect. 7.

6.1 Asymptotic Parameters

We will first be explicit on how we establish the parameters for the hardness of the AOM-MLWE problem. We begin by chosing the parameters for which the *selective* AOM-UMLWE problem is hard as in Theorem 4.1. We then use the equivalence between sel-AOM-UMLWE and sel-AOM-MLWE, that is proven in the full version. Lastly, as discussed in Sect. 4, we assume that AOM-MLWE is as hard as its selective variant. The final step is the only step for which we do not have a supporting security reduction. Concretely, we rely on the following:

1. Let us define sel-AOM-UMLWE$_{q,\ell,k+\ell,Q,(\mathcal{D}_i)_{i\in[Q]},\mathcal{L}_{\mathsf{TS}},B_{\mathcal{L}_{\mathsf{TS}}},\max\{B_{\mathsf{s}},B_{\mathsf{e}}\}}$, where
   - $Q = \mathsf{rep} \cdot Q_{\mathsf{S}} + 1$,
   - $\mathcal{D}_1 = 2 \cdot \mathcal{D}_{\mathsf{t}}$ and $\mathcal{D}_i = \mathcal{D}_{\mathsf{w}}$ for $i \in [2, \mathsf{rep} \cdot Q_{\mathsf{S}} + 1]$,
   - $\mathcal{L}_{\mathsf{TS}}$ is the accepted linear combinations defined in Definition 4.3,
   - $B_{\mathsf{s}} = 8e^{1/4} \cdot (W^2 \cdot \sigma_{\mathsf{t}} + W \cdot \sigma_{\mathsf{w}}) \cdot \sqrt{n\ell} + 4B$,
   - $B_{\mathcal{L}_{\mathsf{TS}}} = 4\sqrt{W}$,
   - $B_{\mathsf{e}} = (2^{\nu_{\mathsf{w}}+3} + W \cdot 2^{\nu_{\mathsf{t}}+2} + 8e^{1/4} \cdot (W^2 \cdot \sigma_{\mathsf{t}} + W \cdot \sigma_{\mathsf{w}})) \cdot \sqrt{nk} + 4B$.

   By setting the parameters $(q, n, \ell, \mathcal{D}_{\mathsf{t}} = \mathcal{D}_{\sigma_1}, \mathcal{D}_{\mathsf{w}} = \mathcal{D}_{\sigma^*})$ showing up in our 2-round threshold signature scheme (c.f., from Table 1) according to hard-param in Definition 4.2 and setting the set of accepted linear combinations $\mathcal{L}_{\mathsf{TS}}$ according to Definition 4.3, we have $\mathsf{Adv}^{\mathsf{sel\text{-}AOM\text{-}UMLWE}}_{\mathcal{B}_1}(1^\lambda) = \mathsf{negl}(\lambda)$ for any efficient adversary $\mathcal{B}_1$.

2. Let us define sel-AOM-MLWE$_{q,\ell,k,Q,(\mathcal{D}_i)_{i\in[Q]},\mathcal{L}_{\mathsf{TS}},B_{\mathcal{L}_{\mathsf{TS}}},B_{\mathsf{s}},B_{\mathsf{e}}}$ with the same parameters as above. Then, from the equivalence between sel-AOM-UMLWE and sel-AOM-MLWE, assuming the hardness of sel-AOM-UMLWE above, we have $\mathsf{Adv}^{\mathsf{sel\text{-}AOM\text{-}MLWE}}_{\mathcal{B}_2}(1^\lambda) = \mathsf{negl}(\lambda)$ for any efficient adversary $\mathcal{B}_2$.

3. Lastly, let us define AOM-MLWE$_{q,\ell,k,Q,(\mathcal{D}_i)_{i\in[Q]},\mathcal{L}_{\mathsf{TS}},B_{\mathcal{L}_{\mathsf{TS}}},B_{\mathsf{s}},B_{\mathsf{e}}}$ with the same parameters as above. Here, assuming that any adaptive adversary $\mathcal{B}$ against the AOM-MLWE problem can perform no better than a selective adversary $\mathcal{B}_2$ against the sel-AOM-MLWE problem defined above, we have $\mathsf{Adv}^{\mathsf{AOM\text{-}MLWE}}_{\mathcal{B}}(1^\lambda) = \mathsf{negl}(\lambda)$. This is the assumption our 2-round threshold signature is based on.

We set the candidate asymptotic parameters of our construction so that the above constraints are satisfied. An example is provide in the full version.

TS.Setup($1^\lambda, N, T$)	TS.PP(vk, i, sk$_i$, st$_i$)
// Resample until **A** contains invertible submatrix	1: parse (tspar, **t**) ← vk
1: $\mathbf{A} \xleftarrow{\$} \mathcal{R}_q^{k \times \ell}$	2: parse (**A**, N, T) ← tspar
2: tspar := (**A**, N, T)	3: for $b \in [\text{rep}]$ do
3: return tspar	4: $(\mathbf{r}_{i,b}, \mathbf{e}'_{i,b}) \xleftarrow{\$} \mathcal{D}_\mathbf{w}^\ell \times \mathcal{D}_\mathbf{w}^k$
TS.KeyGen(tspar)	5: $\mathbf{w}_{i,b} := \mathbf{A}\mathbf{r}_{i,b} + \mathbf{e}'_{i,b} \in \mathcal{R}_q^k$
1: parse (**A**, N, T) ← tspar	6: $\vec{\mathbf{w}}_i := [\mathbf{w}_{i,1} \mid \cdots \mid \mathbf{w}_{i,\text{rep}}]$
2: (**s**, **e**) $\xleftarrow{\$} \mathcal{D}_\mathbf{t}^\ell \times \mathcal{D}_\mathbf{t}^k$	7: pp$_i$:= $\vec{\mathbf{w}}_i$
3: $\mathbf{t} := \lfloor 2 \cdot (\mathbf{As} + \mathbf{e}) \rceil_{\nu_t} \in \mathcal{R}_{q\nu_t}^k$	8: st$_i$ ← st$_i \cup \{(\vec{\mathbf{w}}_i, (\mathbf{r}_{i,b})_{b \in [\text{rep}]})\}$
4: for $(i, j) \in [N] \times [N]$ do	9: return (pp$_i$, st$_i$)
5: seed$_{i,j} \xleftarrow{\$} \{0,1\}^\lambda$	**TS.Sign(vk, SS, M, i, (pp$_j$)$_{j \in \text{SS}}$, sk$_i$, st$_i$)**
6: $\vec{P} \xleftarrow{\$} \mathcal{R}_q^\ell[X]$ with $\deg(\vec{P}) = T - 1, \vec{P}(0) = 2 \cdot \mathbf{s}$	1: parse $(\mathbf{s}_i, (\text{seed}_{i,j}, \text{seed}_{j,i})_{j \in [N]}) \leftarrow$ sk$_i$
7: $(\mathbf{s}_i)_{i \in [N]} := (\vec{P}(i))_{i \in [N]}$	2: req $[\![\text{SS} \subseteq [N]]\!] \wedge [\![i \in \text{SS}]\!] \wedge [\![(\text{pp}_i, \cdot) \in \text{st}_i]\!]$
8: vk := (tspar, **t**)	3: parse $(\vec{\mathbf{w}}_j)_{j \in \text{SS} \setminus \{i\}} \leftarrow (\text{pp}_j)_{j \in \text{SS}}$
9: $(\text{sk}_i)_{i \in [N]} := \left((\mathbf{s}_i, (\text{seed}_{i,j}, \text{seed}_{j,i})_{j \in [N]})\right)_{i \in [N]}$	4: pick $(\vec{\mathbf{w}}_i, (\mathbf{r}_{i,b})_{b \in [\text{rep}]})$ from st$_i$ with pp$_i = \vec{\mathbf{w}}_i$
10: return (vk, (sk$_i$)$_{i \in [N]}$)	5: ctnt := SS$\|$M$\|(\vec{\mathbf{w}}_j)_{j \in \text{SS}}$
TS.Agg(vk, SS, M, $(\widehat{\text{sig}}_j)_{j \in \text{SS}}$)	6: $(\beta_b)_{b \in [\text{rep}]} := $ G(vk, ctnt) // $\beta_1 = 1, \beta_b \in \mathbb{T}$
1: parse (tspar, **t**) ← vk	7: for $j \in $ SS do
2: parse (**A**, N, T) ← tspar	8: parse $[\mathbf{w}_{j,1} \mid \cdots \mid \mathbf{w}_{j,\text{rep}}] \leftarrow \vec{\mathbf{w}}_j$
3: parse $(\mathbf{w}_j, \mathbf{m}_j, \mathbf{z}_j)_{j \in \text{SS}} \leftarrow (\widehat{\text{sig}}_j)_{j \in \text{SS}}$	9: $\mathbf{w}_j := \sum_{b \in [\text{rep}]} \beta_b \cdot \mathbf{w}_{j,b} \in \mathcal{R}_q^k$
4: $\mathbf{w} := \left\lfloor \sum_{j \in \text{SS}} \mathbf{w}_j \right\rceil_{\nu_\mathbf{w}} \in \mathcal{R}_{q\nu_\mathbf{w}}^k$	10: $\mathbf{w} := \left\lfloor \sum_{j \in \text{SS}} \mathbf{w}_j \right\rceil_{\nu_\mathbf{w}} \in \mathcal{R}_{q\nu_\mathbf{w}}^k$
5: $\mathbf{z} := \sum_{j \in \text{SS}} (\mathbf{z}_j - \mathbf{m}_j) \in \mathcal{R}_q^\ell$	11: $c := $ H(vk, M, **w**) // $c \in \mathcal{C}$
6: $c := $ H(vk, M, **w**)	12: $\mathbf{m}_i := \sum_{j \in \text{SS}} \text{PRF}(\text{seed}_{i,j}, \text{ctnt}) \in \mathcal{R}_q^\ell$
7: $\mathbf{y} := \lfloor \mathbf{Az} - 2^{\nu_t} \cdot c \cdot \mathbf{t} \rceil_{\nu_\mathbf{w}} \in \mathcal{R}_{q\nu_\mathbf{w}}^k$	13: $\mathbf{m}_i^* := \sum_{j \in \text{SS}} \text{PRF}(\text{seed}_{j,i}, \text{ctnt}) \in \mathcal{R}_q^\ell$
8: $\mathbf{h} := \mathbf{w} - \mathbf{y} \in \mathcal{R}_{q\nu_\mathbf{w}}^k$	14: $\mathbf{z}_i := c \cdot L_{\text{SS},i} \cdot \mathbf{s}_i + \sum_{b \in [\text{rep}]} \beta_b \cdot \mathbf{r}_{i,b} + \mathbf{m}_i^* \in \mathcal{R}_q^\ell$
9: return sig := $(c, \mathbf{z}, \mathbf{h})$	15: st$_i$ ← st$_i \setminus \{(\vec{\mathbf{w}}_i, (\mathbf{r}_{i,b})_{b \in [\text{rep}]})\}$
TS.Verify(vk, M, sig)	16: $\widehat{\text{sig}}_i := (\mathbf{w}_i, \mathbf{m}_i, \mathbf{z}_i)$
1: parse $(c, \mathbf{z}, \mathbf{h}) \leftarrow $ sig	17: return $(\widehat{\text{sig}}_i, \text{st}_i)$
2: $c' := $ H(vk, M, $\lfloor \mathbf{Az} - 2^{\nu_t} \cdot c \cdot \mathbf{t} \rceil_{\nu_\mathbf{w}} + \mathbf{h}$)	
3: if $[\![c = c']\!] \wedge [\![\|(\mathbf{z}, 2^{\nu_\mathbf{w}} \cdot \mathbf{h})\|_2 \leq B]\!]$ then	
4: return 1	
5: return 0	

Fig. 5. Our two round threshold signature TS$_{2\text{-round}}$. In the above, $L_{\text{SS},i}$ denotes the Lagrange coefficient of user i in the set SS $\subseteq [N]$. **pick X from Y** denotes the process of picking an element X from the set Y.

6.2 Main Theorem

The following is the main theorem establishing the unforgeability of our 2-round threshold signature scheme. The statement assumes the asymptotic parameter selections in Sect. 6.1.

Theorem 6.1. *The 2-round threshold signature* $\mathsf{TS}_{\text{2-round}}$ *in Fig. 5 is unforgeable under the* $\mathsf{AOM\text{-}MLWE}_{q,\ell,k,Q,(\mathcal{D}_i)_{i\in[Q_\mathsf{G}]},\mathcal{L}_{\mathsf{TS}},\mathcal{B}_{\mathcal{L}_{\mathsf{TS}}},\mathcal{B}_\mathsf{s},\mathcal{B}_\mathsf{e}}$ *assumption and the pseudorandomness of* PRF.

Formally, for any N *and* T *with* $T \leq N$ *and an adversary* $\mathcal{A}$ *against the unforgeability game making at most* Q_H, Q_G, *and* Q_S *queries to the random oracles* H *and* G, *and the signing oracle, respectively, there exists adversaries* $\mathcal{B}$ *and* $\mathcal{B}'$ *against the* $\mathsf{AOM\text{-}MLWE}_{q,\ell,k,Q,(\mathcal{D}_i)_{i\in[Q_\mathsf{G}]},\mathcal{L}_{\mathsf{TS}},\mathcal{B}_{\mathcal{L}_{\mathsf{TS}}},\mathcal{B}_\mathsf{s},\mathcal{B}_\mathsf{e}}$ *problem and pseudorandomness of* PRF *such that*

$$\mathsf{Adv}^{\text{ts-uf}}_{\mathsf{TS},\mathcal{A}}(1^\lambda, N, T) \leq \sqrt{Q_{\mathsf{RO}} \cdot \mathsf{Adv}^{\mathsf{AOM\text{-}MLWE}}_{\mathcal{B}}(1^\lambda)} + N^2 \cdot \mathsf{Adv}^{\mathsf{PRF}}_{\mathcal{B}'}(1^\lambda) + \frac{Q_\mathsf{S}^2}{2^{n-1}} + \mathsf{negl}(\lambda),$$

where $Q_{\mathsf{RO}} = Q_\mathsf{H} + 2Q_\mathsf{G} + 2Q_\mathsf{S} + 1$ *and* $\mathsf{Time}(\mathcal{B}) \approx 2 \cdot \mathsf{Time}(\mathcal{A})$.

Due to page limitation, the full proof is provided in the full version. Below, we provide a proof overview.

Proof Overview The proof consists of two parts. The first half consists of carefully crafting a sequence of games so that the reduction can simulate the game using only knowledge of the signing key sk = **s**, implicitly defined by the partial signing keys $\mathbf{s}_i$ included in the secret key shares sk_i. At a birds eye's view, this is similar to what was done in [79]. At a lower level, as explained in Sect. 2, the difference lies in how we generate the masks $\mathbf{m}_i$ and $\mathbf{m}_i^*$. We no longer rely on session unique identifiers sid $\in \{0,1\}^*$ and standard signatures to explicitly authenticate the signers' views. Instead, we replace sid with ctnt := $\mathsf{SS}||\mathsf{M}||(\vec{\mathbf{w}}_j)_{j\in\mathsf{SS}}$ and the signature by viewing the masks as an implicit MAC on the "message" ctnt. The reduction then consists of a careful book keeping of the signers that have signed with respect to ctnt.

The second half consists of constructing an AOM-MLWE adversary $\mathcal{B}$ using the adversary $\mathcal{A}$ against the unforgeability game. $\mathcal{B}$ is given $\mathbf{T} = \mathbf{AS} + \mathbf{E}$ as the problem instance, where $\mathbf{A} \xleftarrow{\$} \mathcal{R}_q^{k \times \ell}$, $(\mathbf{s}, \mathbf{e}) \xleftarrow{\$} \mathcal{D}_\mathbf{t}^\ell \times \mathcal{D}_\mathbf{t}^k$, $(\widehat{\mathbf{r}}_{i,b}, \widehat{\mathbf{e}}'_{i,b}) \xleftarrow{\$} \mathcal{D}_\mathbf{w}^\ell \times \mathcal{D}_\mathbf{w}^k$ for $(i,b) \in [Q_\mathsf{S}] \times [\mathsf{rep}]$, and $(\mathbf{S}, \mathbf{E}) = \left([2 \cdot \mathbf{s} \mid \widehat{\mathbf{r}}_{1,1} \mid \widehat{\mathbf{r}}_{1,2} \mid \cdots \mid \widehat{\mathbf{r}}_{Q_\mathsf{S},\mathsf{rep}}], [2 \cdot \mathbf{e} \mid \widehat{\mathbf{e}}'_{1,1} \mid \widehat{\mathbf{e}}'_{1,2} \mid \cdots \mid \widehat{\mathbf{e}}'_{Q_\mathsf{S},\mathsf{rep}}]\right) \in \mathcal{R}_q^{\ell \times \mathsf{rep}\cdot Q_\mathsf{S}+1} \times \mathcal{R}_q^{\ell \times \mathsf{rep}\cdot Q_\mathsf{S}+1}$. It embeds the first column $\mathbf{t}_1$ of $\mathbf{T}$ into the verification key $\mathbf{t}$, and the rest is used to simulate the pre-processing token pp_i of the honest signers. Due to the above modification, whenever the reduction needs to simulate a partial response $\mathbf{z}_i$, they will be of the form $\mathbf{z}_i = c \cdot \mathbf{s} + \sum_{b \in [\mathsf{rep}]} \beta_b \cdot \mathbf{r}_{i,b} + (\text{public vector})$ or $\mathbf{z}_i = \sum_{b \in [\mathsf{rep}]} \beta_b \cdot \mathbf{r}_{i,b} + (\text{public vector})$. Thus, it can simulate them by querying the MLWE solving oracle on the respective coefficients (i.e., linear combination). The bulk of the proof consists of checking that the all the queries fall into the accepted linear combinations $\mathcal{L}_{\mathsf{TS}}$, required by the winning condition of the AOM-MLWE problem. This check is non-trivialized by the fact that the adversary is rewound in order to extract from the forgery an MLWE solution with respect to the verification key **t**. □

7 Cryptanalysis of AOM-MLWE

We now turn to the concrete security analysis of the AOM-MLWE problem and go beyond the reductions proposed in Sect. 4. To do so, we aim at giving the sharpest concrete reduction to AOM-MLWE from approx-SVP, which in turns can be solved using lattice reduction algorithms and converted in a bitsec estimate.

7.1 A First Naive Attempt

Let $\mathbf{T} = \mathbf{AS} + \mathbf{E}$ be an AOM-MLWE challenge with $Q-1$ queries available. The first intuition we might have is that from a linear algebra perspective each of the $Q-1$ query removes one degree of freedom in the module rank. Hence since our problem consists in Q independent MLWE instances (or equivalently one big instance in rank $Q\ell$!) we can assume that after the query, the dimension of the resulting linear algebra problem is reduced to $Q - (Q-1) = 1$, that is a single MLWE. We can very easily formalize this intuition by querying first $\mathbf{e}_1, \mathbf{s}_1$, then $\mathbf{e}_2, \mathbf{s}_2$ and so on until $\mathbf{e}_{Q-1}, \mathbf{s}_{Q-1}$. We then solve the remaining instance $\mathbf{As}_Q + \mathbf{e}_Q$ to retrieve $\mathbf{s}_Q$ and $\mathbf{e}_Q$, completing the resolution. One might argue that because of the shape of the query matrices, we cannot query directly the values of $\mathbf{e}_i$ and $\mathbf{s}_i$. However, we can always do so as the challenge space has sufficiently many invertible elements and use basic Gaussian elimination with pivoting to exactly retrieve $Q-1$ of them. However, this attack is *far* from being optimal. We now show that we can diffuse a bit of the final vector in each of the queries so that we can get a statical leak in addition of the sole values, which will make the final instance of MLWE much easier.

7.2 Solving AOM-MLWE with Selective Queries Better than Naively

As we saw in the preliminary discussion of Sect. 4, the query power gives a statistical advantage in breaking the final MLWE instance. The attack we proposed in Sect. 7.1 is fully relying on lattice reduction and completely ignores the subtlety of the choices of the queries. Whereas the attack proposed in Sect. 4.2, we fully break the scheme with only a statistical recovery. For harder set of parameters, we can not do so. We however show that we can combine this statistical information with standard lattice reduction arguments to do better.

7.3 A Simple Example

Let us reuse the attack we already described in Sect. 4.2 and roughly analyze it, as it will give the main intuitions on how the leakage exploitation works.

We use the (selective) queries: $\mathbf{d}_i = (1, \ldots, 0, 1, 0, \ldots, 0)^T$ where the second 1 is in position i, for i ranging from 2 to Q. As in Sect. 4.2, we then get the the sets of $Q-1$ secrets $\mathbf{s}_1 + \mathbf{s}_i$ and noises $\mathbf{e}_1 + \mathbf{e}_i$. Computing the sum of them yields $\tilde{\mathbf{s}}_1 = (Q-1)\mathbf{s}_1 + \eta$ and $\tilde{\mathbf{e}}_1 = (Q-1)\mathbf{e}_1 + \epsilon$ where $(\eta, \epsilon) = \sum_{i=2}^{Q}(\mathbf{s}_i, \mathbf{e}_i)$. As we are working above the smoothing parameter of R—the functional conditions on the standard deviation of the error and secret in our scheme are *orders of magnitude* above even the crudest estimate of the smoothing of this cyclotomic ring—, these two variables are distributed as discrete Gaussians of width multiple by a factor $Q - 1$. For the sake of simplicity, let us assume for a moment that both variables $\tilde{s}_1, \tilde{e}_1$ are both multiple of $Q - 1$. We will see in a minute that we can treat the general case in a similar manner; but for now write $s'_1 = \frac{\tilde{s}_1}{Q-1} = s_1 + \eta'$ and $e'_1 = \frac{\tilde{e}_1}{Q-1} = e_1 + \epsilon'$. Now we can write a new MLWE instance derived from the sample $t_1 = As_1 + e_1$. To do so let expand s_1, e_1 using our approximations:

$$t_1 = As_1 + e_1 = A(s'_1 - \eta') + (e'_1 - \epsilon') = (As'_1 + e'_1) - (A\eta' + \epsilon')$$

Since $As'_1 + e'_1$ is known by the attacker, we can write $\tau := -t_1 + (As'_1 + e'_1) = A\eta' + \epsilon'$. This new instance is now easier than the original one, as the absolute norms of the secret and noise are smaller by a factor $\frac{1}{\sqrt{Q-1}}$.

Remark 7.1. We can directly handle the general case where the divisibility condition $Q - 1 | \tilde{s}_1, \tilde{e}_1$ is not fulfilled. For that it suffices to scale the instance $t = As_1 + e_1$ by the factor $Q - 1$. As such, we will end with a final instance of the shape $(Q - 1) \cdot (A\eta' + \epsilon') \mod q(Q-1)$, where the information/noise ratio are exactly the same as in the specific case presented.

Once s_1, e_1 are recovered from η', ϵ', simply remark that each query result $s_1 + s_i, e_1 + e_i$ yield the *exact* values of s_i, e_i by subtracting s_1, e_1. We then recovered all the secrets and errors, completing the attack.

7.4 The General Case

The generic situation is quite similar but a bit more subtle than this attack. Indeed, we need to accommodate to the specific shape that is imposed on the query matrix. For an AOM-MLWE challenge $T = AS + E$ with $Q - 1$ queries collected in a matrix D. The blueprint of the attack goes as follows:

1. Get the matrices of query answers: $\mathsf{Ans}_s = SD$ and $\mathsf{Ans}_e = ED$.
2. Decompose the Queries and Extraction of e_1: separate the first line of D and perform linear algebra in order to rewrite e_1 as a known target e'_1 plus some *controlled* noise ϵ'. This localizes e_1 in an ellipsoid centered at e'_1 and of known parameters with overwhelming probability. Same goes for s_1 decomposed as s'_1 plus some noise η'.
3. Decode e_1 by yet another MLWE instance: craft the following challenge $\tau := -t_1 + (As'_1 + e'_1) = A\eta' + \epsilon'$. The trick here is that both η' and ϵ' are elliptically distributed, which implies to isotropize the problem to solve it classically. This step induces a distortion of the space which we can quantify finely.
4. Recover η', ϵ' from lattice reduction and use linear algebra to recover s_1, e_1 and subsequently s_i, e_i.

We now turn to these steps in more details.

Setup. Let $\mathbf{T} = \mathbf{AS} + \mathbf{E}$ the AOM-MLWE challenge, with the secret matrix $\mathbf{S} \in \mathcal{R}_q^{\ell \times q}$ and the error matrix $\mathbf{E} \in \mathcal{R}_q^{k \times Q}$. Suppose that the query is encoded in a matrix $\mathbf{D} \in \mathcal{R}_q^{Q \times Q-1}$, so that the challenger returns the matrices of answers $\mathsf{Ans}_s = \mathbf{SD}$ and $\mathsf{Ans}_e = \mathbf{ED}$.

Decomposing the Query and Extraction of $\mathbf{e}_1$. Up to permutation of the rows, let us assume that we can decompose $\mathbf{D}$ as

$$\mathbf{D} = \begin{pmatrix} \mathbf{d}^\dagger \\ \overline{\mathbf{D}} \end{pmatrix} \text{ for a vector } \mathbf{d} \in \mathcal{R}_q^{Q-1} \text{ and } \overline{\mathbf{D}} \in \mathsf{GL}_{Q-1}(\mathcal{R}_q).$$

Similarly, we decompose the errors and secrets by their first columns as: $\mathbf{E} = (\mathbf{e}_1 \,|\, \overline{\mathbf{E}})$ and $\mathbf{S} = (\mathbf{s}_1 \,|\, \overline{\mathbf{S}})$ Using these decompositions, we have by linear algebra:

$$\mathsf{Ans}_s = \mathbf{s}_1 \mathbf{d}^\dagger + \overline{\mathbf{SD}} \quad \text{and} \quad \mathsf{Ans}_e = \mathbf{e}_1 \mathbf{d}^\dagger + \overline{\mathbf{ED}}.$$

We now have explicit dependency on $\mathbf{s}_1$ and $\mathbf{e}_1$, but only through the multiplication by $\mathbf{d}^\dagger$. To make this latter term disappear we use the pseudo-inversion trick: multiplying on the right by $\mathbf{d}$, then dividing by the totally positive element $\mathbf{d}^\dagger \mathbf{d}$ gives:

$$\mathbf{s}_1 = \underbrace{\frac{\mathsf{Ans}_s \mathbf{d}}{\mathbf{d}^\dagger \mathbf{d}}}_{:=\mathbf{s}_1'} - \underbrace{\frac{\overline{\mathbf{SD}} \mathbf{d}}{\mathbf{d}^\dagger \mathbf{d}}}_{:=\eta} \quad \text{and} \quad \mathbf{e}_1 = \underbrace{\frac{\mathsf{Ans}_e \mathbf{d}}{\mathbf{d}^\dagger \mathbf{d}}}_{:=\mathbf{e}_1'} - \underbrace{\frac{\overline{\mathbf{ED}} \mathbf{d}}{\mathbf{d}^\dagger \mathbf{d}}}_{:=\epsilon}. \tag{2}$$

Exploiting the MLWE *Structure with the Leakage.* We now assume—exactly as we did first in the example before—that the vectors $\mathbf{s}_1', \mathbf{e}_1'$ are of integral coefficients. We now have derived a non-trivial *statstical* information: $\mathbf{e}_1$ and $\mathbf{s}_1$ are random variables centered respectively at $\mathbf{e}_1'$ and $\mathbf{s}_1'$ and with covariances $\sigma_e^2 \Sigma^\dagger \Sigma$ and $\sigma_s^2 \Sigma^\dagger \Sigma$ where $\Sigma = \left(\frac{\overline{\mathbf{D}} \mathbf{d}^\dagger}{\mathbf{d}^\dagger \mathbf{d}}\right)$.

This translates directly into a geometric information as we canconstruct a new corresponding MLWE instance corresponding to the decoding of ϵ and η:

$$\tau := \mathbf{t}_1 - (\mathbf{As}_1' + \mathbf{e}_1') = \mathbf{A}\eta + \epsilon.$$

Solving Approximate Elliptic Secret/Noise MLWE. The situation is then syntactically very similar to the previous attack, but this time, the distribution of the resulting secret/error is elliptic instead of spherical. As it is now the case in *all* lattice-based schemes based on structured lattices, we will do a *leap of faith* and assume that the security of MLWE is the same as the security of the lattice problem obtained when descending over $\mathbb{Z}$.

To solve this new instance, we will use a reduction to unique-SVP through so-called distorted-BDD, as done for instance in [35]. The core trick is to first embed the MLWE instance into a module lattice of rank $\ell \cdot n + 1$. Let $\Lambda = \{(\mathbf{x}, \mathbf{y}, w) \,|\, \mathbf{x} + \mathbf{A} \cdot \mathbf{y} - \tau w \equiv 0 \pmod{q}\}$ where $\mathbf{A}$ is overloaded to also denote the anticirculant matrix corresponding to the multiplication endomorphism in

$\mathcal{R}_q^\ell$ by the matrix $\mathbf{A}$. A basis of this lattice is given by

$$\begin{pmatrix} q\mathbf{I}_{\ell n} & 0 & 0 \\ \mathbf{A} & -\mathbf{I}_{kn} & 0 \\ \tau & 0 & \mathbf{I}_n \end{pmatrix}.$$

Now remark that the vector[8] $(\mathbf{e}, \mathbf{s}, 1)$ belong to the lattice Λ, but that any short vector of the shape $(\mathbf{e}', \mathbf{s}', \mathbf{v})$ for small enough $\mathbf{v}$ will also be a solution of the approximate problem, with the relaxation by $\mathbf{v}$. We can be even more precise and remark that with overwhelming probability this vector belongs to the intersection of the ellipsoid defined by the symmetric block-diagonal semi-definite positive matrix S with $\sigma_e \Sigma$, $\sigma_s \Sigma$, and $\mathbf{I}_n$ on its diagonal, that is to say the set $\mathcal{E} = \{\mathbf{x} \in \mathbb{R}^{(k+\ell+1)n} \mid \langle \mathbf{x}, S^{-T}S^{-1}\mathbf{x}\rangle \leq \sqrt{d\ell}\}$.

It then suffices to apply the matrix S^{-1} on Λ to re-isotropize the problem and reduce it to a usual spherical DBDD instance.

Solving the Final approx-SVP Instance. From this point, we can apply lattice reduction on this lattice $\Lambda^* = S^{-1}\Lambda$ to retrieve short vectors. To do so, we rely on the DBKZ algorithm, which achieve the best time/quality trade-offs in the literature. Let us do a very brief recall on the output guarantees of this algorithm.

Modelization of the Output of Reduced Bases. For the sake of clarity in the following explanations, we adopt the "Geometric series assumption" (GSA). This assumption states that the norm of the Gram-Schmidt vectors of a reduced basis decreases with a geometric decay. Specifically, in the context of the self-dual Block Korkine-Zolotarev (DBKZ) reduction algorithm proposed by Micciancio and Walter [74], the GSA can be instantiated as follows. Suppose we have an output basis $(\mathbf{b}_i)_{i \in [n]}$ obtained from the DBKZ algorithm with a block size denoted as β, applied to a lattice Λ of rank n. Then, the following equation holds for the i-th Gram-Schmidt vector $\mathbf{b}_i^*$ of the basis:

$$\|\mathbf{b}_i^*\| = \gamma^{n-2(i-1)} \mathrm{vol}(\Lambda)^{\frac{1}{n}}, \quad \text{where} \quad \gamma_\beta = \left(\frac{(\pi\beta)^{\frac{1}{\beta}} \cdot \beta}{2\pi e}\right)^{\frac{1}{2(\beta-1)}},$$

for $\mathbf{b}_i^*$ being the i-th Gram Schmidt vector of the basis. In particular this implies that the first vector of the output basis is satisfying the relation: $\|\mathbf{b}_1\| \leq \gamma^n \mathrm{vol}(\Lambda)^{\frac{1}{n}}$.

In order to get a finer estimate, when computing the actual figures this analysis can be refined by using the probabilistic simulation of [35] rather than this coarser GSA-based model to determine the BKZ blocksize β for a successful attack. This helps to take into account the well-known *quadratic tail* phenomenon of reduced bases [90].

---

[8] for the sake of notational simplicity, we denote the vectors of the modules $\mathcal{R}_q^\ell$, $\mathcal{R}_q^k$ and their descent over $\mathbb{Z}$ by the same symbol.

Solving uSVP. To retrieve vectors of size comparable to $\|(\mathbf{e}^*, \mathbf{s}^*)\|$, we therefore need to select a blocksize β such that:

$$\sqrt{\frac{\beta}{(k+\ell+1)n}} \|(\mathbf{e}_1, \mathbf{s}_1)\| \leq \gamma_\beta^{(k+\ell+1)n} \mathrm{vol}(\Lambda^*)^{\frac{1}{(k+\ell+1)n}}.$$

Conveniently, during the isotropization step, we rescaled the target secret vector to be normally distributed, so that with overwhelming probability we have $\|(\mathbf{e}^*, \mathbf{s}^*)\| \leq \sqrt{\ell d}$. Further, we also know the volume of Λ^* since by multilinearity of the determinant we get $\mathrm{vol}(\Lambda^*) = \mathrm{vol}(\Lambda) \det(S) = q^{\ell d} \det(S)$. All in all we then seek for the minimal β such that:

$$\sqrt{\beta} \leq \gamma_\beta^{(k+\ell+1)n} \det(S)^{\frac{1}{(k+\ell+1)n}}.$$

8 Parameters Selection

We now turn to parameters selection. Classically for parameter selection of lattice scheme, we rely on the so-called *Core-SVP* methodology to convert lattice reduction blocksize into concrete bitsecurity. We provide a complete overview of this in the full version. The security of our two-round threshold scheme is evaluated against forgery and key recovery/pseudo-randomness of the verification key. We point out that the practical bounds are not directly based on the advantage bounds given in the asymptotic security proof (e.g., we ignore the loss from the forking lemma, we devise a more direct reduction for AOM-MLWE). However we still *do enforce* that all the *functional* constraints between parameters are satisfied. This is common practice when dealing with practical security, as epitomized in the parameter selection process of the NIST standards ML-DSA (Dilithium) [72], FN-DSA(Falcon) [82], or the recent signatures [48,80].

8.1 Direct Forgery Resilience

A direct forgery can be done by reverse-engineering a signature from the verification process. More precisely this amounts to solve the following problem usually referred as the SelfTargetMSIS assumption. Following the methodology of Dilithium [72, §C.3], combined with the *nearest colattice* algorithm for solving CVP gives the condition: $B \leq \min_{\ell n \leq m \leq (k+\ell)n} \left(\gamma^m q^{\frac{kn}{m}} \right)$. Together with the challenge space condition $\binom{n}{W} \cdot 2^W \geq 2^\lambda$. We let the reader refer to appendix more details.

8.2 Breaking Unforgeability

For the second attack, we will follow the security reduction done in Sect. 6, which quantifies the reduction to the AOM-MLWE problem and amounts to perform a key recovery using the maximal number of signature queries to collect as much information as we can. Recall the advantage of the adversary $\mathsf{Adv}^{\mathsf{ts\text{-}uf}}_{\mathsf{TS},\mathcal{A}}(1^\lambda, N, T)$ of our two-round threshold signature in Theorem 6.1, where the $\mathsf{negl}(\lambda)$ term being indeed negligible when the set of relations between coefficients given in Sect. 6 are satisfied. We normalize the cost by the global number of queries, that is to say Q_{RO} when computing the bit-security:

$$\lambda_{\mathrm{REAL}} = \log_2(\mathsf{Time}(\mathcal{A})/\mathsf{Adv}^{\mathsf{ts\text{-}uf}}_{\mathsf{TS},\mathcal{A}}(1^\lambda, N, T)), \qquad (3)$$

where the running time of the adversary satisfies $\mathsf{Time}(\mathcal{A}) \geq Q_{\mathsf{RO}}$. Our goal is then to ensure $\lambda_{\mathrm{REAL}} \leq \lambda + O(1)$. The term in $N^2 \cdot \mathsf{Adv}^{\mathsf{PRF}}_{\mathcal{B}}(1^\lambda)$ is itself exponentially small in λ when normalized by $\mathsf{Time}(\mathcal{A})$ and the term $Q_S 2^{-2\lambda}$ is itself smaller than $2^{-\lambda}$, so that we only care about the first term. As typical with practice oriented schemes (e.g., [16,51,84]), we treat the advantage by ignoring the square root induced by the forking lemma. To do so we rely on the worst case analysis of Sect. 7 to reduce the problem to a single MLWE instance in dimension $d\ell$. In order to evaluate the cost of this remaining MLWE, we need to analyse the shape of the admissible queries in fine-grained way. As this analysis is purely geometrical and quite convoluted, we defer it to the full version. The analysis reveals that, practically speaking, the secret/vectors of the resulting MLWE instance are $\sqrt{WQ_S}$ times smaller than for the original parameters of the AOM-MLWE challenge itself, meaning that an attacker would need to solve an $\mathsf{MLWE}_{n,q,k,\ell,\frac{\sigma}{\sqrt{W \cdot Q_S}}}$ type instance. Hence we seek for a set of parameters which are secure even reduced by this large factor. To do so, we can rely on the extensive literature on the cryptanalysis of MLWE. To our knowledge, the state-of-the-art for estimating the concrete hardness of MLWE is the so-called lattice estimator (https://github.com/malb/lattice-estimator). According to this estimator on our tentative parameters, the best known attacks are the primal uSVP attack by Alkim et al. [7] and the dual/hybrid attack by Espitau et al. [49] all in all combined with the so-called dimension for free trick of [45].

8.3 Parameter Sets

Despite the apparently large number of variables, parameters can be set in a systematic way and we can devise an optimization tool to explore the parameter space and find the signatures with the smallest size/communication complexity while still achieving the desired security guarantees. The result of our exploration are collected in Table 2, targeting NIST level I, III and V of security, with supporting roughly 2^{60} queries of signatures before being endanger. Moreover all of them support a threshold up to 1024 participants, which is the upper limit of the "large" requirements of NIST preliminary call for threshold. It is remarkable that our 2 round signatures are practical with aggregated signature size lower than 11KiB. The main overhead in its use being in the offline phase where signers must exchange the tokens, which are of size a couple of hundreds kilobytes. It is worth highlighting that if we consider a model where the aggregator stores the preprocessing tokens, the individual signers do not need to include $\mathbf{w}_i$ in the partial signature $\widehat{\mathsf{sig}}_i$. In this case, the online communication per user becomes much smaller: 14KB, 19KB, and 22KB for NIST level I, III, and V, respectively.

Table 2. All sizes are given in KB for a maximum T of 1024 and Q_S being upper bounded by 2^{59}. on, off refers to the communication cost *per user* in the online/offline phase. The online cost is written $XX(YY)$ for XX being the size of the optimized version where the tokens are already processed by the aggregator and YY being the naive scheme where the tokens are transmitted at an online phase. The corresponding security is given in bits: Sec F for the forgery and Sec K for the key recovery respectively.

Sec (F/K)	$\lfloor \log q \rfloor$	$\log \sigma_t$	$\log \sigma_w$	ν_t	ν_w	n	ℓ	k	W	$\|vk\|$	$\|Sig\|$	on/usr	off/usr
128 / 146	50	5	34.5	38	38	256	9	11	23	5.5	10.8	14.1 (276)	262
192 / 192	50	10	35	34	38	512	6	7	31	7	14.5	19 (461)	442
256 / 282	51	15	37	35	40	512	7	10	44	9.5	18	22 (853)	831

Acknowledgement. This work has been supported in part by JST CREST Grant Number JPMJCR22M1, JST-AIP Acceleration Research JPMJCR22U5, JSPS KAKENHI Grant Numbers JP22KJ1366.

References

1. Agrawal, S., Boneh, D., Boyen, X.: Efficient lattice (H)IBE in the standard model. In: Gilbert, H. (ed.) EUROCRYPT 2010. LNCS, vol. 6110, pp. 553–572. Springer, Heidelberg (2010). https://doi.org/10.1007/978-3-642-13190-5_28
2. Agrawal, S., Boyen, X., Vaikuntanathan, V., Voulgaris, P., Wee, H.: Functional encryption for threshold functions (or Fuzzy IBE) from lattices. In: Fischlin, M., Buchmann, J., Manulis, M. (eds.) PKC 2012. LNCS, vol. 7293, pp. 280–297. Springer, Heidelberg (2012). https://doi.org/10.1007/978-3-642-30057-8_17
3. Agrawal, S., Kirshanova, E., Stehlé, D., Yadav, A.: Practical, round-optimal lattice-based blind signatures. In: Yin, H., Stavrou, A., Cremers, C., Shi, E. (eds.) ACM CCS 2022. pp. 39–53. ACM Press (2022)https://doi.org/10.1145/3548606.3560650
4. Agrawal, S., Stehlé, D., Yadav, A.: Round-optimal lattice-based threshold signatures, revisited. In: Bojanczyk, M., Merelli, E., Woodruff, D.P. (eds.) ICALP 2022. LIPIcs, vol. 229, pp. 8:1–8:20. Schloss Dagstuhl (2022).https://doi.org/10.4230/LIPIcs.ICALP.2022.8
5. Albrecht, M.R., Cini, V., Lai, R.W.F., Malavolta, G., Thyagarajan, S.A.K.: Lattice-based SNARKs: Publicly verifiable, preprocessing, and recursively composable - (extended abstract). In: Dodis, Y., Shrimpton, T. (eds.) CRYPTO 2022, Part II. LNCS, vol. 13508, pp. 102–132. Springer, Heidelberg (2022). https://doi.org/10.1007/978-3-031-15979-4_4
6. Albrecht, M.R., Lai, R.W.F.: Subtractive sets over cyclotomic rings - limits of Schnorr-like arguments over lattices. In: Malkin, T., Peikert, C. (eds.) CRYPTO 2021, Part II. LNCS, vol. 12826, pp. 519–548. Springer, Heidelberg (2021). https://doi.org/10.1007/978-3-030-84245-1_18
7. Alkim, E., Ducas, L., Pöppelmann, T., Schwabe, P.: Post-quantum key exchange - A new hope. In: Holz, T., Savage, S. (eds.) USENIX Security 2016. pp. 327–343. USENIX Association (Aug 2016)

8. Bacho, R., Loss, J.: On the adaptive security of the threshold BLS signature scheme. In: Yin, H., Stavrou, A., Cremers, C., Shi, E. (eds.) ACM CCS 2022, pp. 193–207. ACM Press (Nov 2022). https://doi.org/10.1145/3548606.3560656
9. Bauer, B., Fuchsbauer, G., Plouviez, A.: The one-more discrete logarithm assumption in the generic group model. In: Tibouchi, M., Wang, H. (eds.) ASIACRYPT 2021. LNCS, vol. 13093, pp. 587–617. Springer, Cham (2021). https://doi.org/10.1007/978-3-030-92068-5_20
10. Bellare, M., Crites, E.C., Komlo, C., Maller, M., Tessaro, S., Zhu, C.: Better than advertised security for non-interactive threshold signatures. In: Dodis, Y., Shrimpton, T. (eds.) CRYPTO 2022, Part IV. LNCS, vol. 13510, pp. 517–550. Springer, Heidelberg (2022). https://doi.org/10.1007/978-3-031-15985-5_18
11. Bellare, M., Namprempre, C., Pointcheval, D., Semanko, M.: The power of RSA inversion oracles and the security of Chaum's RSA-based blind signature scheme. In: Syverson, P. (ed.) FC 2001. LNCS, vol. 2339, pp. 319–338. Springer, Heidelberg (2002). https://doi.org/10.1007/3-540-46088-8_25
12. Bellare, M., Namprempre, C., Pointcheval, D., Semanko, M.: The one-more-RSA-inversion problems and the security of Chaum's blind signature scheme. J. Cryptol. **16**(3), 185–215 (2003). https://doi.org/10.1007/s00145-002-0120-1
13. Bellare, M., Neven, G.: Multi-signatures in the plain public-key model and a general forking lemma. In: Juels, A., Wright, R.N., De Capitani di Vimercati, S. (eds.) ACM CCS 2006, pp. 390–399. ACM Press (Oct / Nov 2006). https://doi.org/10.1145/1180405.1180453
14. Bendlin, R., Krehbiel, S., Peikert, C.: How to share a lattice trapdoor: threshold protocols for signatures and (H)IBE. In: Jacobson, M., Locasto, M., Mohassel, P., Safavi-Naini, R. (eds.) ACNS 2013. LNCS, vol. 7954, pp. 218–236. Springer, Heidelberg (2013). https://doi.org/10.1007/978-3-642-38980-1_14
15. Benhamouda, F., Camenisch, J., Krenn, S., Lyubashevsky, V., Neven, G.: Better zero-knowledge proofs for lattice encryption and their application to group signatures. In: Sarkar, P., Iwata, T. (eds.) ASIACRYPT 2014. LNCS, vol. 8873, pp. 551–572. Springer, Heidelberg (2014). https://doi.org/10.1007/978-3-662-45611-8_29
16. Beullens, W., Kleinjung, T., Vercauteren, F.: CSI-FiSh: efficient isogeny based signatures through class group computations. In: Galbraith, S.D., Moriai, S. (eds.) ASIACRYPT 2019. LNCS, vol. 11921, pp. 227–247. Springer, Cham (2019). https://doi.org/10.1007/978-3-030-34578-5_9
17. Boldyreva, A.: Threshold signatures, multisignatures and blind signatures based on the gap-diffie-hellman-group signature scheme. In: Desmedt, Y.G. (ed.) PKC 2003. LNCS, vol. 2567, pp. 31–46. Springer, Heidelberg (2003). https://doi.org/10.1007/3-540-36288-6_3
18. Boneh, D., et al.: Threshold cryptosystems from threshold fully homomorphic encryption. In: Shacham, H., Boldyreva, A. (eds.) CRYPTO 2018. LNCS, vol. 10991, pp. 565–596. Springer, Cham (2018). https://doi.org/10.1007/978-3-319-96884-1_19
19. Boneh, D., et al.: Fully key-homomorphic encryption, arithmetic circuit abe and compact garbled circuits. In: Nguyen, P.Q., Oswald, E. (eds.) EUROCRYPT 2014. LNCS, vol. 8441, pp. 533–556. Springer, Heidelberg (2014). https://doi.org/10.1007/978-3-642-55220-5_30
20. Boneh, D., Lewi, K., Montgomery, H., Raghunathan, A.: Key homomorphic PRFs and their applications. In: Canetti, R., Garay, J.A. (eds.) CRYPTO 2013. LNCS, vol. 8042, pp. 410–428. Springer, Heidelberg (2013). https://doi.org/10.1007/978-3-642-40041-4_23

21. Bonehé, D., Lynn, B., Shacham, H.: Short signatures from the weil pairing. In: Boyd, C. (ed.) ASIACRYPT 2001. LNCS, vol. 2248, pp. 514–532. Springer, Heidelberg (2001). https://doi.org/10.1007/3-540-45682-1_30
22. Bootle, J., Lyubashevsky, V., Seiler, G.: Algebraic techniques for Short(er) exact lattice-based zero-knowledge proofs. In: Boldyreva, A., Micciancio, D. (eds.) CRYPTO 2019. LNCS, vol. 11692, pp. 176–202. Springer, Cham (2019). https://doi.org/10.1007/978-3-030-26948-7_7
23. Boschini, C., Takahashi, A., Tibouchi, M.: MuSig-L: Lattice-based multi-signature with single-round online phase. In: Dodis, Y., Shrimpton, T. (eds.) CRYPTO 2022, Part II. LNCS, vol. 13508, pp. 276–305. Springer, Heidelberg (2022). https://doi.org/10.1007/978-3-031-15979-4_10
24. Boudgoust, K., Jeudy, C., Roux-Langlois, A., Wen, W.: On the hardness of module learning with errors with short distributions. J. Cryptol. **36**(1), 1 (2023). https://doi.org/10.1007/s00145-022-09441-3
25. Brandão, L., Davidson, M.: Notes on threshold eddsa/schnorr signatures. National Institute of Standards and Technology (2022). https://doi.org/10.6028/NIST.IR.8214B.ipd
26. Bresson, E., Monnerat, J., Vergnaud, D.: Separation results on the "One-More" computational problems. In: Malkin, T. (ed.) CT-RSA 2008. LNCS, vol. 4964, pp. 71–87. Springer, Heidelberg (2008). https://doi.org/10.1007/978-3-540-79263-5_5
27. Canetti, R., Gennaro, R., Goldfeder, S., Makriyannis, N., Peled, U.: UC non-interactive, proactive, threshold ECDSA with identifiable aborts. In: Ligatti, J., Ou, X., Katz, J., Vigna, G. (eds.) ACM CCS 2020, pp. 1769–1787. ACM Press (Nov 2020). https://doi.org/10.1145/3372297.3423367
28. Castagnos, G., Catalano, D., Laguillaumie, F., Savasta, F., Tucker, I.: Bandwidth-efficient threshold EC-DSA. In: Kiayias, A., Kohlweiss, M., Wallden, P., Zikas, V. (eds.) PKC 2020. LNCS, vol. 12111, pp. 266–296. Springer, Cham (2020). https://doi.org/10.1007/978-3-030-45388-6_10
29. Chen, Y.: sfDualMS: Efficient lattice-based two-round multi-signature with trapdoor-free simulation. In: Handschuh, H., Lysyanskaya, A. (eds.) CRYPTO 2023, Part V. LNCS, vol. 14085, pp. 716–747. Springer, Heidelberg (2023). https://doi.org/10.1007/978-3-031-38554-4_23
30. Chowdhury, S., et al.: Efficient threshold FHE with application to real-time systems. Cryptology ePrint Archive, Report 2022/1625 (2022). https://eprint.iacr.org/2022/1625
31. Chu, H., Gerhart, P., Ruffing, T., Schröder, D.: Practical Schnorr threshold signatures without the algebraic group model. In: Handschuh, H., Lysyanskaya, A. (eds.) CRYPTO 2023, Part I. LNCS, vol. 14081, pp. 743–773. Springer, Heidelberg (2023). https://doi.org/10.1007/978-3-031-38557-5_24
32. Cozzo, D., Smart, N.P.: Sashimi: cutting up CSI-FiSh secret keys to produce an actively secure distributed signing protocol. In: Ding, J., Tillich, J.-P. (eds.) PQCrypto 2020. LNCS, vol. 12100, pp. 169–186. Springer, Cham (2020). https://doi.org/10.1007/978-3-030-44223-1_10
33. Crites, E., Komlo, C., Maller, M.: Fully adaptive schnorr threshold signatures. In: Handschuh, H., Lysyanskaya, A. (eds.) Advances in Cryptology - CRYPTO 2023, pp. 678–709. Springer Nature Switzerland, Cham (2023). https://doi.org/10.1007/978-3-031-38557-5_22
34. Crites, E.C., Komlo, C., Maller, M.: Fully adaptive Schnorr threshold signatures. In: Handschuh, H., Lysyanskaya, A. (eds.) CRYPTO 2023, Part I. LNCS, vol. 14081, pp. 678–709. Springer, Heidelberg (2023)https://doi.org/10.1007/978-3-031-38557-5_22

35. Dachman-Soled, D., Ducas, L., Gong, H., Rossi, M.: LWE with side information: attacks and concrete security estimation. In: Micciancio, D., Ristenpart, T. (eds.) CRYPTO 2020. LNCS, vol. 12171, pp. 329–358. Springer, Cham (2020). https://doi.org/10.1007/978-3-030-56880-1_12
36. Dalskov, A., Orlandi, C., Keller, M., Shrishak, K., Shulman, H.: Securing DNSSEC keys via threshold ECDSA from Generic MPC. In: Chen, L., Li, N., Liang, K., Schneider, S. (eds.) ESORICS 2020. LNCS, vol. 12309, pp. 654–673. Springer, Cham (2020). https://doi.org/10.1007/978-3-030-59013-0_32
37. Damgård, I., Jakobsen, T.P., Nielsen, J.B., Pagter, J.I., Østergaard, M.B.: Fast threshold ECDSA with honest majority. In: Galdi, C., Kolesnikov, V. (eds.) SCN 2020. LNCS, vol. 12238, pp. 382–400. Springer, Cham (2020). https://doi.org/10.1007/978-3-030-57990-6_19
38. Damgård, I., Orlandi, C., Takahashi, A., Tibouchi, M.: Two-Round n-out-of-n and multi-signatures and trapdoor commitment from lattices. In: Garay, J.A. (ed.) PKC 2021. LNCS, vol. 12710, pp. 99–130. Springer, Cham (2021). https://doi.org/10.1007/978-3-030-75245-3_5
39. Damgård, I., Orlandi, C., Takahashi, A., Tibouchi, M.: Two-round n-out-of-n and multi-signatures and trapdoor commitment from lattices. J. Cryptol. **35**(2), 14 (2022). https://doi.org/10.1007/s00145-022-09425-3
40. De Feo, L., Meyer, M.: Threshold schemes from isogeny assumptions. In: Kiayias, A., Kohlweiss, M., Wallden, P., Zikas, V. (eds.) PKC 2020. LNCS, vol. 12111, pp. 187–212. Springer, Cham (2020). https://doi.org/10.1007/978-3-030-45388-6_7
41. Desmedt, Y.: Abuses in cryptography and how to fight them. In: Goldwasser, S. (ed.) CRYPTO 1988. LNCS, vol. 403, pp. 375–389. Springer, New York (1990). https://doi.org/10.1007/0-387-34799-2_29
42. Desmedt, Y., Frankel, Y.: Threshold cryptosystems. In: Brassard, G. (ed.) CRYPTO 1989. LNCS, vol. 435, pp. 307–315. Springer, New York (1990). https://doi.org/10.1007/0-387-34805-0_28
43. Devevey, J., Libert, B., Nguyen, K., Peters, T., Yung, M.: Non-interactive CCA2-secure threshold cryptosystems: achieving adaptive security in the standard model without pairings. In: Garay, J.A. (ed.) PKC 2021. LNCS, vol. 12710, pp. 659–690. Springer, Cham (2021). https://doi.org/10.1007/978-3-030-75245-3_24
44. Doerner, J., Kondi, Y., Lee, E., Shelat, A.: Threshold ECDSA from ECDSA assumptions: The multiparty case. In: 2019 IEEE Symposium on Security and Privacy, pp. 1051–1066. IEEE Computer Society Press (May 2019)https://doi.org/10.1109/SP.2019.00024
45. Ducas, L.: Shortest vector from lattice sieving: a few dimensions for free. In: Nielsen, J.B., Rijmen, V. (eds.) EUROCRYPT 2018. LNCS, vol. 10820, pp. 125–145. Springer, Cham (2018). https://doi.org/10.1007/978-3-319-78381-9_5
46. El Kaafarani, A., Katsumata, S.: Attribute-based signatures for unbounded circuits in the rom and efficient instantiations from lattices. In: Abdalla, M., Dahab, R. (eds.) PKC 2018. LNCS, vol. 10770, pp. 89–119. Springer, Cham (2018). https://doi.org/10.1007/978-3-319-76581-5_4
47. Esgin, M.F., Nguyen, N.K., Seiler, G.: Practical exact proofs from lattices: new techniques to exploit fully-splitting rings. In: Moriai, S., Wang, H. (eds.) ASIACRYPT 2020. LNCS, vol. 12492, pp. 259–288. Springer, Cham (2020). https://doi.org/10.1007/978-3-030-64834-3_9
48. Espitau, T., et al.: Mitaka: a simpler, parallelizable, maskable variant of falcon. In: Dunkelman, O., Dziembowski, S. (eds.) EUROCRYPT 2022, Part III. LNCS, vol. 13277, pp. 222–253. Springer, Heidelberg (2022). https://doi.org/10.1007/978-3-031-07082-2_9

49. Espitau, T., Joux, A., Kharchenko, N.: On a dual/hybrid approach to small secret LWE. In: Bhargavan, K., Oswald, E., Prabhakaran, M. (eds.) INDOCRYPT 2020. LNCS, vol. 12578, pp. 440–462. Springer, Cham (2020). https://doi.org/10.1007/978-3-030-65277-7_20
50. Espitau, T., Niot, G., Prest, T.: Flood and submerse: Verifiable short secret sharing and application to robust threshold signatures on lattices (2024), to Appear in CRYPTO 2024
51. Fersch, M., Kiltz, E., Poettering, B.: On the provable security of (EC)DSA signatures. In: Weippl, E.R., Katzenbeisser, S., Kruegel, C., Myers, A.C., Halevi, S. (eds.) ACM CCS 2016, pp. 1651–1662. ACM Press (Oct 2016). https://doi.org/10.1145/2976749.2978413
52. Fleischhacker, N., Simkin, M., Zhang, Z.: Squirrel: Efficient synchronized multi-signatures from lattices. In: Yin, H., Stavrou, A., Cremers, C., Shi, E. (eds.) ACM CCS 2022, pp. 1109–1123. ACM Press (Nov 2022).https://doi.org/10.1145/3548606.3560655
53. Fuchsbauer, G., Kiltz, E., Loss, J.: The algebraic group model and its applications. In: Shacham, H., Boldyreva, A. (eds.) CRYPTO 2018. LNCS, vol. 10992, pp. 33–62. Springer, Cham (2018). https://doi.org/10.1007/978-3-319-96881-0_2
54. Gennaro, R., Goldfeder, S.: Fast multiparty threshold ECDSA with fast trustless setup. In: Lie, D., Mannan, M., Backes, M., Wang, X. (eds.) ACM CCS 2018, pp. 1179–1194. ACM Press (Oct 2018). https://doi.org/10.1145/3243734.3243859
55. Gentry, C., Peikert, C., Vaikuntanathan, V.: Trapdoors for hard lattices and new cryptographic constructions. In: Ladner, R.E., Dwork, C. (eds.) 40th ACM STOC, pp. 197–206. ACM Press (May 2008). https://doi.org/10.1145/1374376.1374407
56. Gentry, C., Wichs, D.: Separating succinct non-interactive arguments from all falsifiable assumptions. In: Fortnow, L., Vadhan, S.P. (eds.) 43rd ACM STOC, pp. 99–108. ACM Press (Jun 2011). https://doi.org/10.1145/1993636.1993651
57. Goldwasser, S., Kalai, Y.T., Peikert, C., Vaikuntanathan, V.: Robustness of the learning with errors assumption. In: Innovations in Computer Science - ICS 2010, Tsinghua University, Beijing, China, 5-7 January 2010. Proceedings, pp. 230–240. Tsinghua University Press (2010)
58. Gorbunov, S., Vaikuntanathan, V., Wee, H.: Attribute-based encryption for circuits. In: Boneh, D., Roughgarden, T., Feigenbaum, J. (eds.) 45th ACM STOC, pp. 545–554. ACM Press (Jun 2013). https://doi.org/10.1145/2488608.2488677
59. Gorbunov, S., Vaikuntanathan, V., Wee, H.: Predicate encryption for circuits from LWE. In: Gennaro, R., Robshaw, M. (eds.) CRYPTO 2015. LNCS, vol. 9216, pp. 503–523. Springer, Heidelberg (2015). https://doi.org/10.1007/978-3-662-48000-7_25
60. Gorbunov, S., Vaikuntanathan, V., Wichs, D.: Leveled fully homomorphic signatures from standard lattices. In: Servedio, R.A., Rubinfeld, R. (eds.) 47th ACM STOC, pp. 469–477. ACM Press (Jun 2015)https://doi.org/10.1145/2746539.2746576
61. Gorbunov, S., Vinayagamurthy, D.: Riding on asymmetry: efficient ABE for branching programs. In: Iwata, T., Cheon, J.H. (eds.) ASIACRYPT 2015. LNCS, vol. 9452, pp. 550–574. Springer, Heidelberg (2015). https://doi.org/10.1007/978-3-662-48797-6_23
62. Gur, K.D., Katz, J., Silde, T.: Two-round threshold lattice signatures from threshold homomorphic encryption (2023). https://eprint.iacr.org/2023/1318, to Appear in PQCrypto 2024. https://eprint.iacr.org/2023/1318

63. Khaburzaniya, I., Chalkias, K., Lewi, K., Malvai, H.: Aggregating and thresholdizing hash-based signatures using STARKs. In: Suga, Y., Sakurai, K., Ding, X., Sako, K. (eds.) ASIACCS 2022, pp. 393–407. ACM Press (May/Jun 2022). https://doi.org/10.1145/3488932.3524128
64. Kim, D., Lee, D., Seo, J., Song, Y.: Toward practical lattice-based proof of knowledge from hint-MLWE. In: Handschuh, H., Lysyanskaya, A. (eds.) CRYPTO 2023, Part V. LNCS, vol. 14085, pp. 549–580. Springer, Heidelberg (2023). https://doi.org/10.1007/978-3-031-38554-4_18
65. Komlo, C., Goldberg, I.: FROST: flexible round-optimized schnorr threshold signatures. In: Dunkelman, O., Jacobson, Jr., M.J., O'Flynn, C. (eds.) SAC 2020. LNCS, vol. 12804, pp. 34–65. Springer, Cham (2021). https://doi.org/10.1007/978-3-030-81652-0_2
66. Li, H., Lin, H., Luo, J.: ABE for circuits with constant-size secret keys and adaptive security. In: Kiltz, E., Vaikuntanathan, V. (eds.) TCC 2022, Part I. LNCS, vol. 13747, pp. 680–710. Springer, Heidelberg (2022)https://doi.org/10.1007/978-3-031-22318-1_24
67. Libert, B., Stehlé, D., Titiu, R.: Adaptively Secure Distributed PRFs from LWE. In: Beimel, A., Dziembowski, S. (eds.) TCC 2018. LNCS, vol. 11240, pp. 391–421. Springer, Cham (2018). https://doi.org/10.1007/978-3-030-03810-6_15
68. Lindell, Y.: Simple three-round multiparty schnorr signing with full simulatability. Cryptology ePrint Archive, Report 2022/374 (2022). https://eprint.iacr.org/2022/374
69. Lindell, Y., Nof, A.: Fast secure multiparty ECDSA with practical distributed key generation and applications to cryptocurrency custody. In: Lie, D., Mannan, M., Backes, M., Wang, X. (eds.) ACM CCS 2018, pp. 1837–1854. ACM Press (Oct 2018). https://doi.org/10.1145/3243734.3243788
70. Lyubashevsky, V.: Fiat-shamir with aborts: applications to lattice and factoring-based signatures. In: Matsui, M. (ed.) ASIACRYPT 2009. LNCS, vol. 5912, pp. 598–616. Springer, Heidelberg (2009). https://doi.org/10.1007/978-3-642-10366-7_35
71. Lyubashevsky, V.: Lattice signatures without trapdoors. In: Pointcheval, D., Johansson, T. (eds.) EUROCRYPT 2012. LNCS, vol. 7237, pp. 738–755. Springer, Heidelberg (2012). https://doi.org/10.1007/978-3-642-29011-4_43
72. Lyubashevsky, V., et al.: CRYSTALS-DILITHIUM. Tech. rep., National Institute of Standards and Technology (2022). https://csrc.nist.gov/Projects/post-quantum-cryptography/selected-algorithms-2022
73. Maurer, U.: Abstract models of computation in cryptography. In: Smart, N.P. (ed.) Cryptography and Coding 2005. LNCS, vol. 3796, pp. 1–12. Springer, Heidelberg (2005). https://doi.org/10.1007/11586821_1
74. Micciancio, D., Walter, M.: Practical, predictable lattice basis reduction. In: Fischlin, M., Coron, J.-S. (eds.) EUROCRYPT 2016. LNCS, vol. 9665, pp. 820–849. Springer, Heidelberg (2016). https://doi.org/10.1007/978-3-662-49890-3_31
75. Naor, M.: On cryptographic assumptions and challenges. In: Boneh, D. (ed.) CRYPTO 2003. LNCS, vol. 2729, pp. 96–109. Springer, Heidelberg (2003). https://doi.org/10.1007/978-3-540-45146-4_6
76. Nick, J., Ruffing, T., Seurin, Y.: MuSig2: simple two-round schnorr multi-signatures. In: Malkin, T., Peikert, C. (eds.) CRYPTO 2021. LNCS, vol. 12825, pp. 189–221. Springer, Cham (2021). https://doi.org/10.1007/978-3-030-84242-0_8
77. NIST: Call for additional digital signature schemes for the post-quantum cryptography standardization process (2022). https://csrc.nist.gov/csrc/media/Projects/pqc-dig-sig/documents/call-for-proposals-dig-sig-sept-2022.pdf

78. Peralta, R., Brandão, L.T.: Nist first call for multi-party threshold schemes. National Institute of Standards and Technology (2023). https://doi.org/10.6028/NIST.IR.8214C.ipd, https://doi.org/10.6028/NIST.IR.8214C.ipd
79. del Pino, R., Katsumata, S., Maller, M., Mouhartem, F., Prest, T., Saarinen, M.J.O.: Threshold raccoon: Practical threshold signatures from standard lattice assumptions (2024), to Appear in EUROCRYPT 2024. https://eprint.iacr.org/2024/184
80. del Pino, R., et al.: Raccoon. Tech. rep., National Institute of Standards and Technology (2023). https://csrc.nist.gov/Projects/pqc-dig-sig/round-1-additional-signatures
81. Pointcheval, D., Stern, J.: Security arguments for digital signatures and blind signatures. J. Cryptol. **13**(3), 361–396 (2000). https://doi.org/10.1007/s001450010003
82. Prest, T., et al.: FALCON. Tech. rep., National Institute of Standards and Technology (2022). https://csrc.nist.gov/Projects/post-quantum-cryptography/selected-algorithms-2022
83. Quach, W., Wee, H., Wichs, D.: Laconic function evaluation and applications. In: Thorup, M. (ed.) 59th FOCS, pp. 859–870. IEEE Computer Society Press (2018). https://doi.org/10.1109/FOCS.2018.00086
84. Schnorr, C.P.: Efficient identification and signatures for smart cards. In: Brassard, G. (ed.) CRYPTO 1989. LNCS, vol. 435, pp. 239–252. Springer, New York (1990). https://doi.org/10.1007/0-387-34805-0_22
85. Shamir, A.: How to share a secret. Commun. ACM **22**(11), 612–613 (1979)
86. Shoup, V.: Lower bounds for discrete logarithms and related problems. In: Fumy, W. (ed.) EUROCRYPT 1997. LNCS, vol. 1233, pp. 256–266. Springer, Heidelberg (1997). https://doi.org/10.1007/3-540-69053-0_18
87. Tsabary, R.: Candidate witness encryption from lattice techniques. In: Dodis, Y., Shrimpton, T. (eds.) CRYPTO 2022, Part I. LNCS, vol. 13507, pp. 535–559. Springer, Heidelberg (2022). https://doi.org/10.1007/978-3-031-15802-5_19
88. Wee, H.: Optimal broadcast encryption and CP-ABE from evasive lattice assumptions. In: Dunkelman, O., Dziembowski, S. (eds.) EUROCRYPT 2022, Part II. LNCS, vol. 13276, pp. 217–241. Springer, Heidelberg (2022). https://doi.org/10.1007/978-3-031-07085-3_8
89. Wee, H., Wu, D.J.: Succinct vector, polynomial, and functional commitments from lattices. In: Hazay, C., Stam, M. (eds.) EUROCRYPT 2023, Part III. LNCS, vol. 14006, pp. 385–416. Springer, Heidelberg (2023). https://doi.org/10.1007/978-3-031-30620-4_13
90. Yu, Y., Ducas, L.: Second order statistical behavior of LLL and BKZ. In: Adams, C., Camenisch, J. (eds.) SAC 2017. LNCS, vol. 10719, pp. 3–22. Springer, Cham (2018). https://doi.org/10.1007/978-3-319-72565-9_1

Flood and Submerse: Distributed Key Generation and Robust Threshold Signature from Lattices

Thomas Espitau[1](✉), Guilhem Niot[1,2], and Thomas Prest[1]

[1] PQShield SAS, Paris, France
thomas@espitau.com
[2] Univ Rennes, CNRS, IRISA, Rennes, France

Abstract. We propose a new framework based on *random submersions*—that is projection over a random subspace blinded by a small Gaussian noise—for constructing verifiable short secret sharing and showcase it to construct efficient threshold lattice-based signatures in the hash-and-sign paradigm, when based on *noise flooding*. This is, to our knowledge, the first hash-and-sign lattice-based threshold signature.

Our threshold signature enjoys the very desirable property of *robustness*, including at key generation. In practice, we are able to construct a robust hash-and-sign threshold signature for threshold and provide a typical parameter set for threshold $T = 16$ and signature size 13kB. Our constructions are provably secure under standard MLWE assumption in the ROM and only require basic primitives as building blocks. In particular, we do not rely on FHE-type schemes.

1 Introduction and State-of-the-Art

1.1 Post-quantum Surge and Multiparty Protocols

The field of post-quantum cryptography has experienced significant growth, underscored by numerous standardization efforts over the past decade. Lattice-based cryptosystems have demonstrated their versatility and efficiency. A key area of development is threshold cryptography, which enables secure collaborative generation of information (e.g., secrets, signatures, encryptions). For example, a T-out-of-N threshold signature scheme [10,11] allows any group of $T \leq N$ participants to jointly sign a message, ensuring that groups with strictly fewer than T members cannot produce a valid signature. The security of these protocols is nuanced, requiring mechanisms to address potential misbehavior of parties—including those acting dishonestly or those who are *honest but curious* [24], merely observing the protocol's execution. These aspects are often referred to as *robustness* properties. While extensively studied in the classical context, the exploration of post-quantum solutions for these issues is relatively recent. Notably, NIST is set to announce a call for proposals on multiparty threshold schemes [7], with submissions expected by the first half of 2025.

1.2 Distributed Key Generation and Verifiable Secret Sharing

Classical DKGs... A core concept in threshold cryptography is *distributed key generation* (DKG). This protocol allows n participants to collaboratively generate a public key while distributing its corresponding secret key among them. Once completed, this setup enables a subset of T or more members to perform operations requiring the secret key, such as decryption or signing, without a central trusted authority.

... from VSS. The subproblem of *secret sharing* extends beyond mere secret distribution to include robustness through verification, allowing any party to verify the secret. This led to the development of *publicly verifiable secret sharing schemes* (pVSS), introduced by Stadler [28], although the initial VSS concept by Chor et al. [8] already incorporated verifiability. Several VSS have been proposed over the years [3,4,22,25], see [3,22] for excellent comparative introductions. These VSS are easily instantiated in the discrete logarithm setting.

Threshold Signatures, Old and New. Robust threshold protocols based on RSA [14] and DSS [13] have been proposed, with most robustness-oriented works employing a reliable broadcast model. More recently, ROAST [27] build over the the FROST [21] proposal and offers a generic framework for enhancing semi-interactive threshold signatures with robustness[1].

Once again with lattices, achieving practical, let alone robust, post-quantum threshold signatures has been challenging. [5] laid a theoretical foundation for robust threshold signatures within the GPV framework [16]. In a higher-level view, by relying on the universal thresholdizer of [6], Agrawal et al. [1] introduced a two-round threshold signature based on threshold fully homomorphic encryption (FHE), achieving robustness through homomorphic signatures. This incurs a high cost. Following this initial attempt, Gur et al. [17] optimized this approach and removed homomorphic signatures, but also lost robustness in the process. They obtain a signature size of 11.5kB and a communication cost per party of 1.5MB for signing. [18] proposed a robust threshold signature scheme based on Fiat-Shamir with aborts, however requiring the participation of all non-corrupted users.

Analogously to the classical setting, it is expected that a VSS with shortness proof such as [15] could be used for concretizing a post-quantum DKG and robust threshold signature scheme. However, adding to the complexity of using zero-knowledge proofs, their current instantiation relies on discrete-log assumptions, and moving it to post-quantum secure assumptions is deemed impractical.

When it comes to constructing post-quantum threshold signature schemes *without robustness*, several works [26,29] managed to have quite efficient instantiations. But, achieving robustness via their mechanisms is deemed highly non-trivial. In short, it seems that we can get *efficient* threshold from lattices at the cost of loosing robustness, or we can get *robust* threshold at the cost of relying on highly inefficient primitives. As such, remains the following interrogation:

---
[1] It requires only a semi-trusted coordinator instead of broadcast channels but necessitating $2(|S| - T) + 3$ asynchronous rounds.

Can we reconcile efficiency and robustness in the post-quantum era, using lattices?

1.3 Our Proposal: Full-Fledged (publicly) V3S, Synchronous DKG and Threshold Signatures from MLWE and MSIS in the ROM

We study and propose a solution for robust (short) secret sharing, turn it into a robust distributed key generation (DKG), and as a byproduct get a lattice-based threshold signature using noise flooding. Before further presentation, we shed light on that all our primitives are underpinned by *standard lattice assumptions* and do not require advanced additional primitives such as (threshold) FHE.

Lattice-Based Verifiable (Short) Secret Sharing Scheme: We propose a "random submersion" technique for secret sharing, enabling the secure generation and distribution of Learning With Errors (LWE) samples. This approach provides a form of zero-knowledge proof to affirm the shortness of these samples, a critical aspect in maintaining both the integrity and confidentiality of secrets in a distributed environment. Our proposal is inspired by [3] for its syntax and challenge sampling, and [15] for its compactness proof, employing Johnson-Lindenstrauss-type projections. We adopt a pragmatic approach for our VSS and prove approximate shortness only, with a small loss factor in the norm proven of about 10. This small loss allows us to improve over the practicality of [15] by removing complex zero-knowledge proofs – which are computationally intensive, and large in size – and the use of classical hardness assumptions in their instantiation.

Robust Distributed Key Generation: Building upon our V3S, we build a *robust* DKG. The protocol is *three-round, synchronous*, and uses a general complaint round to reach a consensus on the trustable parties.

More precisely, we propose a broadcast protocol where each party performs its own verifiable secret sharing via the V3S protocol highlighted above. Next, each party broadcasts its list of trustees, and the (public) intersection of these lists is computed, effectively forming a public clique of mutually trusted parties. Finally, each party aggregates the shares they received from trusted parties, which yields a secret sharing of a jointly generated short secret key, thanks to the linearity of Shamir's secret sharing.

While this solution has a nonnegligible communication cost (as the proofs are sent to every party by every party, it ensures maximal robustness for a minimal number of rounds.

Robust Threshold Signatures: We can adapt this methodology, almost *verbatim*, to construct threshold signatures. This follows from the fact that in the underlying signature scheme[2], the signing algorithm is essentially the key generation procedure with extra steps and slightly different parameters. As a consequence, the robustness of such signatures follows from similar arguments to

---

[2] In our case this scheme is the hash-then-sign scheme Plover, but the same comment would apply to the Fiat-Shamir signature Raccoon.

the ones used for the DKG protocol. Our approach relies on the *noise-flooding* technique to create signatures; here the *flooding* involves linearly concealing secret values with sufficiently large noise and ensuring security by quantifying the residual statistical leakage. Due to its linearity, this method has proven to be very effective in masking-friendly [9,12] and threshold-friendly signatures [1,26]. In our case, it is also very amenable to Shamir's secret sharing.

We instantiate our framework in Pelican – a threshold signature scheme system featuring a 3-round distributed key generation and a 4-round signing protocol.[3] Pelican boasts a signature size of 12.3kB and a communication overhead of 59.8 + 19NkB per participant for a threshold $T = 16$ among N parties. It is noteworthy that, while our framework solely depends on LWE in the ROM, it is sufficiently versatile to accommodate thresholding for both the Fiat-Shamir and Hash-And-Sign paradigms.

While Pelican builds upon the digital signature scheme Plover, we emphasize that our robust threshold signature and distributed key generation constructions are generic and could for instance be applied to the NIST submission Raccoon [9]. We leave this as future work.

Before training to the details and security proofs of all these protocols, we propose a high-level overview of the main technicalities, caveats, and ideas used further.

2 Technical Overview

We now turn to a high-level introduction of our techniques and protocols. Our first contribution is a proposal for a lattice-based verifiable short secret sharing scheme, for which we can control its leakage very precisely, but which is not technically zero-knowledge. From this essential building framework, we show how to extend it to devise a protocol for robust distributed key generation and robust threshold signatures. All of these are secure under *standard* lattice assumptions and *does not* require more advanced primitives such as FHE.

2.1 A Lattice Verifiable Short Secret Sharing Proposal

Many lattice-based cryptographic schemes hinge on variants of the Learning With Errors (LWE) assumption, which is crucially based on the shortness of some secret elements. In particular, in the context of devising a threshold scheme, the verification of this shortness is critical. Addressing this challenge, we introduce a new technique coined *random submersion*. This method enables the secure generation and distribution of an LWE sample, concurrently providing a zero-knowledge proof to confirm the shortness of the sample. It ensures both the integrity and the confidentiality of the secret and we will leverage the technique

---

[3] We continue the "tradition" of naming lattice-based hash-then-sign schemes after birds: Falcon, Eagle, Robin, Plover, etc. Since our scheme relies on random submersions and noise flooding, we named it after the aquatic, diving species *Pelican*.

to ensure the robustness of our threshold scheme in Sect. 5.2. Our technique aims for practicality, and only provides approximate shortness bounds in exchange for a lower communication and computational cost than prior work [15]. *Random submersion* relies on a Johnson-Lindenstrauss type lemma, blinded by a Gaussian noise for confidentiality. This type of lemma was already successfully applied for verifiable secret sharing with approximate shortness – relying on rejection sampling – in [15, Section 3.4], but differs in the distribution of its blindings, which removes the need for rejection sampling and provides tighter shortness proofs.

We present a tweakable framework for securely distributing a small secret vector among N parties, with the provision that a maximum of $T < N/2$ among these parties may be untrustworthy. Our approach revolves on the sharing of secrets that are derived from a Gaussian distribution and also accommodates secret vectors chosen by adversaries, provided these vectors have a norm capped at B. We name our secret sharing technique V3S (Verifiable Short Secret Sharing).

Methodology. The cornerstone of our method is to construct a scheme *as linear as feasible*, to ensure compatibility with lattice-based operations. Our initial step involves defining the most fundamental requirements for our scheme, starting with the secret itself.

1. The secret is represented as a compact vector, which is then distributed linearly into a series of random vectors.
2. The verification of the secret's smallness is achieved through a random linear transformation applied to itself.
3. To prevent excessive leakage of the secret by the output of this transformation, we blind it by incorporating an additive mask within its image space.
4. The choice of the randomness used to construct the transformation shall be verifiable by the parties.

Writing what precedes as an algorithm would yield a blueprint of the following shape, using a Merkle tree to handle the randomness verifiability:

1. The dealer samples an ephemeral Gaussian blinding value $\mathbf{y}$, that will be used within their individual proof to prove the shortness of $\mathbf{x}$ without leaking its value.
2. Then they generate a linear random secret sharing for $\mathbf{x}$ and $\mathbf{y}$ of order T, noted $[\![\mathbf{x}]\!]$ and $[\![\mathbf{y}]\!]$.
3. To generate verifiable randomness, the dealer hashes the shares $[\![\mathbf{x}]\!]_{i\in\{1,\ldots,N\}}$ and $[\![\mathbf{y}]\!]_{i\in\{1,\ldots,N\}}$ into a Merkle tree of hash h. It also produces individual proofs proof_i allowing each party to verify that $[\![\mathbf{x}]\!]_i, [\![\mathbf{y}]\!]_i$ belongs to the tree.
4. It derives a challenge matrix $\mathbf{R} = H(h)$ from a suitable distribution, and computes the value $[\![\mathbf{v}]\!] = \mathbf{R} \cdot [\![\mathbf{x}]\!] + [\![\mathbf{y}]\!]$.
5. The broadcast proof π is $(h, [\![\mathbf{v}]\!])$. Individual proofs are $\pi_i = ([\![\mathbf{y}]\!]_i, \mathsf{proof}_i)$.

Any party i, given its share $[\![\mathbf{x}]\!]_i$ and proofs $\pi = (h, [\![\mathbf{v}]\!])$ and $\pi_i = ([\![\mathbf{y}]\!]_i, \mathsf{proof}_i)$ performs the following verifications:

1. proof_i correctly proves that $[\![\mathbf{x}]\!]_i$ and $[\![\mathbf{y}]\!]_i$ are included in Merkle tree h.
2. Derive $\mathbf{R} = H(h)$ and verify that $[\![\mathbf{v}]\!]_i = \mathbf{R} \cdot [\![\mathbf{x}]\!]_i + [\![\mathbf{y}]\!]_i$.
3. Verify that $\|\mathbf{v}\|$ is smaller than some fixed bound B'.

The reconstruction hinges here on the fact that we can see Shamir's secret sharing as from a Reed-Solomon code, which allows to recover $\mathbf{b}$ even if a set of users behaved dishonestly by the robustness of error correction.

Guaranteeing soundness and correctness. While the verification of the randomness is classical thanks to the Merkle tree, the crux of the shortness proof will lie in the following requirements:

small secret implies small proof—The proof $\mathbf{R} \cdot \mathbf{x} + \mathbf{y}$ must be small—with overwhelming probability—if both $\mathbf{x}$ and $\mathbf{y}$ are small, for instance when Gaussian is drawn.

big secret implies big proof—It must become large if $\|\mathbf{x}\|$ is compromised, that is when it is larger than the desired acceptance bound B.

few collisions—Obviously, for correctness, we can not tolerate too many collisions in the values, so we should not have too many pairs $(\mathbf{x}, \mathbf{y})$ being sent to the same value $\mathbf{R}\mathbf{x} + \mathbf{y} \bmod q$.

This means that from a geometric perspective, we are asking the matrix $\mathbf{R}$ to act as a random *pseudo-isometry* in the mod q hypercube. This is very reminiscent of the Johnson-Lindenstrauss type lemma [19], which has been successfully applied to the modular setting in cryptography in [15]. In the following, we say that such distributions satisfy property G (see Definition 8 for a formal definition).

Adding zero-knowledge. Revealing the pair $(\mathbf{R}, \mathbf{R}\cdot\mathbf{x}+\mathbf{y})$ *leaks* some statistical information on $\mathbf{x}$. However, when the dealer is honest, $\mathbf{y}$ is sampled from a Gaussian distribution of sufficiently large variance with regards to $\|\mathbf{R} \cdot \mathbf{x}\|$, so that this information leakage is very mitigated. More precisely, we can even estimate it when generating an MLWE sample from $\mathbf{x}$: after the secret sharing, parties can additionally sample a matrix $\mathbf{A} \in \mathcal{R}^{k\times\ell}$, and a MLWE sample $\mathbf{A} \cdot \mathbf{x}$. From there we get an instance of the recent "MLWE problem with hint" $\mathbf{R}\cdot\mathbf{x}+\mathbf{y}$, which in turn reduces to an MLWE with a smaller standard deviation.

2.2 A Proposal for Robust Secret Sharing and Robust DKG

From V3S to Distributed Secret Sharing. Consider a scenario where N users aim to collectively generate a secret and each obtains a share of a short vector $\mathbf{s}$ as a secret share. Each user $i \in \{1, \ldots, N\}$ will possess $[\![\mathbf{s}]\!]_i = \mathbf{P}(i)$, where $\mathbf{P}$ is an interpolation polynomial such that $\mathbf{P}(0) = \mathbf{s}$. To achieve this, we require each participant to generate their own share of the global secret and transmit it to all other participants. However, for reasons of robustness and security, direct broadcast of their share is inadvisable, as it would allow any eavesdropper to learn all the shares and, by extension, the secret. Instead, each participant divides their share into smaller shares (termed local shares) and distributes these local shares to others. To ensure each local share between parties i and j remains confidential to them, we assume the existence of symmetric encryption between each pair of parties.

This method alone does not guarantee robustness, nor does it prevent potential dishonesty in the generation of local shares. To address this, our approach involves using a V3S scheme to allow parties to verify the local shares they receive. If a proof of a local share fails – say, if party i detects an incorrect proof from party j – then i broadcasts a complaint against j along with a proof of the error, enabling *all parties* to verify the incorrectness of j's proof to i and exclude j from their list of trusted parties. After addressing these complaints, every honest party knows the other parties that shared a secret honestly, and the correct local shares, allowing them to aggregate the local shares they have received to form their share of the secret. The protocol proceeds as follows:

(V1) **Round 1 (Secret-Share Individual Secret).** Each party i:
  a. Generates a short vector $\mathbf{s}_i$.
  b. Utilizes the V3S *as dealer* to secret-share $\mathbf{s}_i$ and generate a distributed proof of shortness, denoting $[\![\mathbf{s}_i]\!]$ as the secret-sharing and $\pi_{i \to j}$ as the partial proof for j.
  c. For each j, encrypts $[\![\mathbf{s}_i]\!]_j, \pi_{i \to j}$ under a symmetric key known only to i and j.
  d. Broadcasts the encrypted proofs and shares.

(V2) **Round 2 (Verify and Complain).** Each party i:
  a. Decrypts all secret shares $[\![\mathbf{s}_j]\!]_i$ and partial proofs $\pi_{j \to i}$ sent by others.
  b. Only keep secret shares with valid partial V3S proofs. We note valid$_i$ the set of participants j with valid proofs, and complaints$_i$ as those without.
  c. Broadcasts complaints$_i$ along with proof of incorrectness for the partial V3S proofs.

(V3) **Round 3 (Review Complaints).** Each party i:
  a. Receives complaints$_j$ from user j, including "proof of incorrectness".
  b. Removes any user from valid$_i$ if proven invalid by j's complaint.

(V4) **Round 4 (Aggregate Valid Secrets).** Each party i, now with a confirmed list valid$_i$ of valid users:
  a. Aggregates the valid secret shares received: $[\![\mathbf{s}]\!]_i = \sum_{j \in \text{valid}_i} [\![\mathbf{s}_j]\!]_i$, thus forming a secret sharing of $\mathbf{s} = \sum_{j \in \text{valid}_i} \mathbf{s}_j$.

When the protocol ends, when a sufficient number of honest users participate, each honest user i holds a share $[\![\mathbf{s}]\!]_i$ of the aggregated secret $\mathbf{s} = \sum_{j \in \text{valid}_i} \mathbf{s}_j$ Fig. 1.

Turning a V3S into a Robust DKG. Leveraging our robust secret sharing protocol, we can readily derive a robust distributed key generation (DKG) protocol. After all, a secret is essentially comprised of the secret itself and a bit of salt. Our protocol is robust and secure as long as $T \leqslant N/3$ for the final reconstruction.

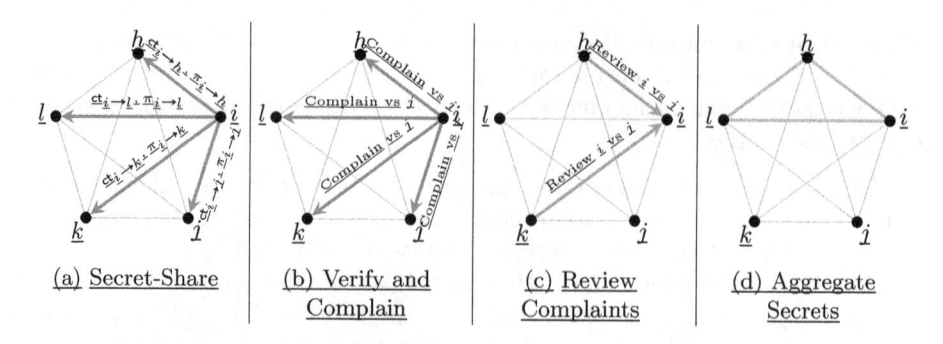

Fig. 1. Our blueprint for secret-sharing a jointly generated short secret $\mathbf{x} = \sum_{i \in \text{honest}} \mathbf{x}_i$. This structured underlies the distributed signing (Figs. 6 and 7) and key generation (Fig. 5) protocols of Pelican.

(a) Secret-Share (b) Verify and Complain (c) Review Complaints (d) Aggregate Secrets

(K1) **Round 1.** Each participant i undertakes the following:
  a. Generate, secret-share, prove, and encrypt the shares and partial proofs of a short secret vector $\mathbf{s}_i$, following the procedure outlined in (V1).
  b. Concurrently, generate an individual salt salt_i and broadcast it.
(K2) **Round 2.** Participant i continues by:
  a. Decrypting and verifying the shares+proofs received, and broadcasting complaints against users who submitted invalid shares/proofs, mirroring the steps in (V2).
(K3) **Round 3.** Participant i proceeds to:
  a. Review the complaints issued by all users, update valid_i accordingly, and compute an aggregate secret share $[\![\mathbf{s}]\!]_i = \sum_{j \in \text{valid}_i} [\![\mathbf{s}_j]\!]_i$, akin to the method described in (V3).
  b. Produce a public salt salt by hashing the salts of all users in valid_i.
  c. Utilize salt to generate a public matrix $\mathbf{A} = [\bar{\mathbf{A}} \; \mathbf{I}]$, which is identical for all honest users. Calculate a partial public key $[\![\mathbf{b}]\!]_i = \mathbf{A} \cdot [\![\mathbf{s}]\!]_i$.
  d. Broadcast the salt salt and the partial public key $[\![\mathbf{b}]\!]_i$.
(K4) **Round 4.** Participant i:
  a. Retrieves the salt from the previous round, and in case of conflicting contributions, employ majority voting.
  b. Reconstructs the secrets using the V3S for a robust reconstruction.

Upon completion, provided a sufficient number of honest users participate, the public key $\mathbf{A}, \mathbf{b} = \mathbf{A} \cdot \mathbf{s}$ can be recovered using the error-correcting features of Reed-Solomon codes/Shamir's secret sharing. Each honest participant i retains a share $[\![\mathbf{s}]\!]_i$ of $\mathbf{s}$. Our DKG is formally described and proven in Sect. 5.1.

2.3 Robust Threshold Lattice-Based Signature

Another application of our robust distributed secret-sharing protocol is threshold signing, wherein the secrets being shared and combined are the shares of the signature itself. Utilizing our technique, we can robustly adapt both signatures in the Hash-and-Sign paradigm and the Fiat-Shamir paradigm. For example, we can develop robust variants of both recent proposals Raccoon and Plover. In this section, we focus on presenting a threshold Hash-and-Sign method based on Plover, marking the first instance of a *robust hash and sign threshold signature* grounded in standard lattice assumptions. We emphasize again the adaptability of our techniques.

Noise-Flooded Hash-and-Sign in a Nutshell. Before delving further into our design, we briefly revisit the concept behind the masking-friendly hash and sign signature Plover. The scheme's core idea is straightforward: within the GPV-like framework, it obviates the need to produce a signature that is zero-knowledge concerning the secret key by employing sufficiently large noise to independently conceal the secret. This approach involves replacing the traditional choice of Gaussian distribution, which relies solely on the (public) lattice and not on the short secret key, with a substantial sum of uniform noise. The leak is mitigated through the Hint-RLWE problem, which encapsulates this scenario: a public RLWE sample accompanied by a leak.

Key Generation. The process initiates by sampling a public polynomial a, derived from a seed. The second component of the public key is essentially an RLWE sample b offset by β, an integer power of two.

Signing Procedure. The procedure begins by hashing the provided message msg to a target polynomial u. It then employs its trapdoor to locate a short pre-image $\mathbf{z} = (z_1, z_2, c_1)$ such that $\mathbf{A} \cdot \mathbf{z} \equiv z_1 + a \cdot z_2 + b \cdot c_1 = u - c_2 \bmod q$ for a short c_2 and $\mathbf{A} \equiv \begin{bmatrix} 1 & a & b \end{bmatrix}$. To prevent the trapdoor's disclosure, a noise vector $\mathbf{p}$ is sampled and added to the pre-image $\mathbf{z}$. The actual signature is z_2, as $z_1 + c_2 = u - a \cdot z_2 - b \cdot c_1$ is recoverable in the verification process.

Verification. The verification commences with the recovery of $z_1' := u - a \cdot z_2 - b \cdot c_1$ (equivalent to $z_1 + c_2$), followed by verifying the shortness of (z_1', z_2). This concise description lays the algorithmic groundwork for our methodology.

Towards Pelican: A Robust Threshold Hash-and-Sign. Now presenting our third application of the technique, we opt for a more condensed exposition. The principal idea remains unchanged from the distributed key generation: signers are tasked with generating and locally sharing their portion of what will become the perturbation vector $\mathbf{p}$ – akin to the noise from Plover, employing the V3S. Upon reaching a consensus on the perturbation share (via a four-round protocol that identifies dishonest participants through a complaint round), each portion of the final signature is derived from the perturbation share, given the linear nature of the Plover signing operations. We propose the following protocol:

(S1) **Round 1.** Each user i performs the following:
  a. Generate, secret-share, prove, and encrypt the shares and partial proofs of a short perturbation vector $\mathbf{p}_i$, akin to (V1).
(S2) **Round 2.** Each user i performs the following:

a. Decrypt and verify the shares and partial proofs received, broadcasting complaints against users who sent invalid shares/proofs, as in (V2). Complaints are also raised if user i fails to receive another user's share.

(S3) **Round 3.** Each user i performs the following:
   a. Review complaints from all users, adjust valid$_i$ accordingly, and compute an aggregate secret share $[\![\mathbf{p}]\!]_i = \sum_{j \in \mathsf{valid}_i} [\![\mathbf{p}_j]\!]_i$, as in (V3).
   b. Compute a partial commitment $[\![w]\!]_i = \mathbf{A} \cdot [\![\mathbf{p}]\!]_i$.
   c. Broadcast valid$_i$ and $[\![w]\!]_i$.

(S4) **Round 4.** Each user i reconstructs $w = \mathbf{A} \cdot \mathbf{p}$ from the shares $[\![w]\!]_i$, derives a salt from w which acts as a source of randomness, and concludes the signature as in the non-threshold scenario. The sole distinction lies in the necessity to calculate shares of $\mathbf{z}$ using the shares $[\![\mathbf{s}]\!]_i$ and $[\![\mathbf{p}]\!]_i$.

At the protocol's conclusion, if a sufficient number of honest users are present, a valid vector $\mathbf{z} = \mathbf{p} + c \cdot \mathbf{s}$ can be assembled using the error-correcting properties of Reed-Solomon codes. Consequently, sig $= (\mathsf{salt}, c, \mathbf{z})$ constitutes a valid signature for the message msg under a Plover public key.

2.4 Some Open Problems and Directions

The protocol we constructed is synchronous as we must wait for each round to be completed, in particular for the complaint round. It is in particular quite easy to perform a forking-like attack web we do not have all complaints.

3 Preliminaries

3.1 Notations

Sets, functions, and distributions. For an integer $N > 0$, we note $[N] = \{0, \ldots, N-1\}$. To denote the *assign* operation, we use $y := f(x)$ when f is deterministic and $y \leftarrow f(x)$ when randomized. When S is a finite set, we note $\mathcal{U}(S)$ the uniform distribution over S, and shorthand $x \xleftarrow{\$} S$ for $x \leftarrow \mathcal{U}(S)$.

Linear algebra. Throughout the work, for a fixed power-of-two n, we note $\mathcal{K} = \mathbb{Q}[x]/(x^n + 1)$ and $\mathcal{R} = \mathbb{Z}[x]/(x^n + 1)$ the associated cyclotomic field and cyclotomic ring. We also note $\mathcal{R}_q = \mathcal{R}/(q\mathcal{R})$. Given $\mathbf{x} \in \mathcal{K}^\ell$, we abusively note $\|\mathbf{x}\|$ the Euclidean norm of the $(n\,\ell)$-dimensional vector of the coefficients of $\mathbf{x}$. By default, vectors are treated as *column* vectors (unless specified otherwise).

Rounding. Let $\beta \in \mathbb{N}, \beta \geq 2$ be a power-of-two. Any integer $x \in \mathbb{Z}$ can be decomposed uniquely as $x = \beta \cdot x_1 + x_2$, where $x_2 \in \{-\beta/2, \ldots, \beta/2 - 1\}$. In this case, $|x_1| \leq \lceil \frac{x}{\beta} \rceil$, where $\lceil \cdot \rceil$ denote rounding up to the nearest integer. For odd q, we note $\mathsf{Decompose}_\beta : \mathbb{Z}_q \to \mathbb{Z} \times \mathbb{Z}$ the function which takes as input $x \in \mathbb{Z}_q$, takes its unique representative in $\bar{x} \in \{-(q-1)/2, \ldots, (q-1)/2\}$, and decomposes $\bar{x} = \beta \cdot x_1 + x_2$ as described above and outputs (x_1, x_2). We extend $\mathsf{Decompose}_\beta$

to polynomials in $\mathbb{Z}_q[x]$, by applying the function to each of its coefficients. For $c \xleftarrow{\$} \mathbb{Z}_q$ and $(c_1, c_2) := \mathsf{Decompose}_\beta(c)$, we have $|c_1| \leq \left\lceil \frac{q-1}{2\beta} \right\rceil$, $\mathbb{E}[c_1] = 0$ and $\mathbb{E}[c_1^2] \leq \frac{M^2-1}{12}$ for $M = 2\left\lceil \frac{q-1}{2\beta} \right\rceil + 1$.

Polynomials. Given a finite commutative ring R, we note $R[x]$ the set of univariate polynomials over R. We also note $R_{<T}[x]$ the subset of polynomials of degree $< T$.

3.2 Distributions

Definition 1 (Discrete Gaussians). *Given a positive definite $\Sigma \in \mathbb{R}^{m \times m}$, we note $\rho_{\sqrt{\Sigma}}$ the Gaussian function defined over $\mathbb{R}^m$ as $\rho_{\sqrt{\Sigma}}(\mathbf{x}) = \exp\left(-\frac{\mathbf{x}^t \cdot \Sigma^{-1} \cdot \mathbf{x}}{2}\right)$.*

The above definition may be extended to $(\Sigma, \mathbf{x}) \in \mathcal{K}^{m \times m} \times \mathcal{K}^m$ by treating Σ as a block-circulant matrix in $\mathbb{R}^{nm \times nm}$ and $\mathbf{x}$ as a vector in $\mathbb{R}^{nm}$.

We may note $\rho_{\sqrt{\Sigma},\mathbf{c}}(\mathbf{x}) = \rho_{\sqrt{\Sigma}}(\mathbf{x} - \mathbf{c})$. When Σ is of the form $\sigma \cdot \mathbf{I}_m$, where $\sigma \in \mathcal{K}^{++}$ and $\mathbf{I}_m$ is the identity matrix, we note $\rho_{\sigma,\mathbf{c}}$ as shorthand for $\rho_{\sqrt{\Sigma},\mathbf{c}}$.

For any countable set $S \subset \mathcal{K}^m$, we note $\rho_{\sqrt{\Sigma},\mathbf{c}}(S) = \sum_{\mathbf{x} \in \mathcal{K}^m} \rho_{\sqrt{\Sigma},\mathbf{c}}(\mathbf{x})$ whenever this sum converges. Finally, when $\rho_{\sqrt{\Sigma},\mathbf{c}}(S)$ converges, the discrete Gaussian distribution $D_{S,\mathbf{c},\sqrt{\Sigma}}$ is defined over S by its probability distribution function:

$$D_{S,\sqrt{\Sigma},\mathbf{c}}(\mathbf{x}) = \frac{\rho_{\sqrt{\Sigma},\mathbf{c}}(\mathbf{x})}{\rho_{\sqrt{\Sigma},\mathbf{c}}(S)}. \tag{1}$$

3.3 Shamir Secret Sharing over Modules

Let $\mathbb{F}$ be a finite field. Given $a \in \mathbb{F}$, $1 \leq T$ and $\mathcal{S} \subseteq \mathbb{F}^*$, a $(T, \mathcal{S})$-sharing of a is obtained by doing the following:

1. Generate $P \in \mathbb{F}_{<T}[x]$ uniformly at random, conditioned to $P(0) = a$.
2. For $s \in \mathcal{S}$, compute $[\![a]\!]_s^P = P(s)$.
3. The output is the indexed tuple $[\![a]\!]_\mathcal{S}^P = ([\![a]\!]_s^P)_{s \in \mathcal{S}}$.

Given $(a, P, \mathcal{S})$, $[\![a]\!]_\mathcal{S}^P$ is uniquely defined. We say that an indexed tuple $[\![a]\!]$ is a valid T-sharing of a if there exists a polynomial $P \in \mathbb{F}_{<T}[x]$ and an evaluation set $\mathcal{S} \subseteq \mathbb{F}^*$ such that $[\![a]\!] = [\![a]\!]_\mathcal{S}^P$. If $|\mathcal{S}| \geq T$, then for any indexed tuple $b = (b_s)_{s \in \mathcal{S}}$ there exists at most a single pair (a, P) such that $b = [\![a]\!]_\mathcal{S}^P$.

When P and/or $\mathcal{S}$ are clear from context, we may omit them and note $[\![a]\!]^P$, $[\![a]\!]_\mathcal{S}$ or $[\![a]\!]$. The set of valid $(T, \mathcal{S})$-sharings is a $\mathbb{F}$-linear space of dimension T. Indeed, given $\lambda, \mu \in \mathbb{F}$:

$$\lambda [\![a]\!]_\mathcal{S}^P + \mu [\![b]\!]_\mathcal{S}^Q = [\![\lambda a]\!]_\mathcal{S}^{\lambda P} + [\![\mu b]\!]_\mathcal{S}^{\mu Q} = [\![\lambda a + \mu b]\!]_\mathcal{S}^{\lambda P + \mu Q} \tag{2}$$

Given a T-sharing $[\![a]\!]_\mathcal{S}$ where $|\mathcal{S}| = T$, we can recover a using Lagrange interpolation. Note that this recovery process is independent of P.

$$a = \sum_{s \in \mathcal{S}} \lambda_{s,\mathcal{S}} [\![a]\!]_s, \quad \text{where} \quad \lambda_{s,\mathcal{S}} = \prod_{s' \in \mathcal{S} \setminus s} \frac{s'}{s' - s}. \tag{3}$$

Generalizations. We can generalize secret-sharing as follows:

- **Composite rings.** We can generalize secret-sharing to any finite commutative ring R. Instead of $\mathcal{S} \subseteq F\backslash\{0\}$, this requires the stronger condition $\{\forall s, s' \in \mathcal{S}, (s - s') \in R^\times\}$, where $R^\times$ is the multiplicative group of invertible elements of R.
  This allows us to secret-share over $\mathbb{Z}_q$, where $q = q_1 \cdot q_2$ and $q_1 < q_2$ are two prime numbers. Over this ring, we can perform secret-sharing for any set $\mathcal{S} \subseteq \{1, \ldots, q_1 - 1\}$.
- **Vectors.** We can perform secret-sharing for vector secrets $\mathbf{a} = (a_i)_{i \in [k]} \in R^k$. This is done by secret-sharing each coefficient independently: $\forall i \in [k]$ we secret-share a_i with a distinct polynomial $P_i(x) = \sum_{j<T} p_{i,j} x^j \in R[x]$.
  If we note $[\![\mathbf{a}]\!]_\mathcal{S} = ([\![\mathbf{a}]\!]_s)_{s \in \mathcal{S}}$ the tuple obtained, and $\mathbf{p}_j = (p_{i,j})_{i \in [k]} \in R^k$, we can see that $\forall s \in \mathcal{S}$, $[\![\mathbf{a}]\!]_s = \sum_{j<T} s^j \cdot \mathbf{p}_j$. Abusing notation, we note $\boldsymbol{P}(x) = \sum_{j<T} x^j \cdot \mathbf{p}_j$ and will refer to $\boldsymbol{P}(x)$ as the interpolation polynomial of $[\![\mathbf{a}]\!]_\mathcal{S}$, which we may also note $[\![\mathbf{a}]\!]_\mathcal{S}^P$. This notation is abusive since R^k is not a ring but a module when $k > 1$, however, it is helpful for our purposes.

The set of polynomials over the module R^k, which we note $R^k[x]$, is a R-module. In particular, operations such as addition and multiplication by a scalar $a \in R$ are well-defined over $R^k[x]$. Given a matrix $\mathbf{M} \in R^{\ell \times k}$, one can check that:

$$\mathbf{M} \cdot [\![\mathbf{a}]\!]_\mathcal{S}^P = [\![\mathbf{M} \cdot \mathbf{a}]\!]_\mathcal{S}^{\mathbf{M} \cdot \boldsymbol{P}} \tag{4}$$

3.4 Hardness Assumptions

We recall the Ring-SIS (RSIS) assumption.

Definition 2 (RSIS). *Let ℓ, q be integers and $B_2 > 0$ be a real number. The advantage $\mathsf{Adv}_\mathcal{A}^{\mathsf{RSIS}}(\kappa)$ of an adversary $\mathcal{A}$ against the Ring Short Integer Solutions problem $\mathsf{RSIS}_{q,\ell,B_2}$ is defined as:*

$$\mathsf{Adv}_\mathcal{A}^{\mathsf{RSIS}}(\kappa) = \Pr\left[\mathbf{a} \xleftarrow{\$} \mathcal{R}_q^\ell, \mathbf{z} \leftarrow \mathcal{A}(\mathbf{a}) : 0 < \|\mathbf{z}\| \leq B_2 \wedge [1\ \mathbf{a}^\top]\, \mathbf{z} = \mathbf{0} \bmod q\right].$$

The $\mathsf{RSIS}_{q,\ell,B_2}$ assumption states that any efficient adversary $\mathcal{A}$ has a negligible advantage $\mathsf{Adv}_\mathcal{A}^{\mathsf{RSIS}}(\kappa)$.

Another assumption of interest is the Hint-MLWE problem which was introduced recently in [20] and enjoys a dimension-preserving reduction to RLWE.

Recall however from the technical overview that our DKG and threshold signatures reveal matricial hints $\mathbf{R} \cdot \mathbf{s} + \mathbf{y}_1$ and $\mathbf{R}' \cdot \mathbf{p} + \mathbf{y}_2$ through the use of our V3S, and then computes combined hints of the form $c \cdot \mathbf{s} + \mathbf{p}$. The Hint-MLWE problem doesn't capture the use of matrices in hints, nor leakage on noises.

The following section thus introduces a generalized variant of Hint-MLWE.

3.5 Generalization of Hint-MLWE

We introduce a generalized version of Hint-MLWE, allowing matrix hints and variable perturbation standard deviations. We call it MatrixHint-MLWE. Although we do not make full use of them in this paper, we believe they are of independent interest. Like Hint-MLWE, MatrixHint-MLWE reduces efficiently to MLWE.

Definition 3 (MatrixHint-MLWE). *Let k, ℓ, q, Q be integers, $\mathcal{D}_{\mathsf{sk}}, (\mathcal{D}_{\mathbf{p}}^{(i)})_{i \in [Q]}$ be probability distributions over $\mathbb{Z}^{k+\ell}$, and $\mathcal{M}$ be a distribution of challenge matrices over $\left(\mathbb{Z}^{n(k+\ell) \times n(k+\ell)}\right)^Q$. The advantage $\mathsf{Adv}_{\mathcal{A}}^{\mathsf{MatrixHint\text{-}MLWE}}(\kappa)$ of an adversary $\mathcal{A}$ against $\mathsf{MatrixHint\text{-}MLWE}_{k,\ell,q,Q,\mathcal{D}_{\mathsf{sk}},(\mathcal{D}_{\mathbf{p}}^{(i)})_i,\mathcal{M}}$—Matrix Hint Module Learning with Errors problem—is defined as:*

$$\left| \Pr\left[1 \leftarrow \mathcal{A}\left(\mathbf{A}, [\mathbf{I}_k \; \mathbf{A}] \cdot \mathbf{s}, (\mathbf{M}_i, \mathbf{z}_i)_{i \in [Q]}\right)\right] - \Pr\left[1 \leftarrow \mathcal{A}\left(\mathbf{A}, \mathbf{u}, (\mathbf{M}_i, \mathbf{z}_i)_{i \in [Q]}\right)\right]\right|,$$

where $(\mathbf{A}, \mathbf{u}) \xleftarrow{\$} \mathcal{R}_q^{k \times \ell} \times \mathcal{R}_q^k$, $\mathbf{s} \leftarrow \mathcal{D}_{\mathsf{sk}}$ and for $i \in [Q]$: $\mathbf{M}_i \leftarrow \mathcal{M}$, $\mathbf{y}_i \leftarrow \mathcal{D}_{\mathbf{p}}^{(i)}$, and $\mathbf{z}_i = \mathbf{M}_i \cdot \mathbf{s} + \mathbf{y}_i$. The $\mathsf{MatrixHint\text{-}MLWE}_{k,\ell,q,Q,\mathcal{D}_{\mathsf{sk}},(\mathcal{D}_{\mathbf{p}}^{(i)})_i,\mathcal{M}}$ assumption states that any efficient adversary $\mathcal{A}$ has a negligible advantage.

Note that in the product $\mathbf{M}_i \cdot \mathbf{s}$, we consider $\mathbf{s}$ as a vector of $n(k + \ell)$ scalars in $\mathbb{Z}$. We can recover the polynomial version of Hint-MLWE by taking $\mathbf{M}_i$ to be a matrix in blocs with negacyclic matrices of size $n \times n$ corresponding to the desired polynomial on the diagonal. We also recover the classical RLWE problem by taking $Q = 0$: $\mathsf{RLWE}_{q,\mathcal{D}_{\mathsf{sk}}} = \mathsf{MatrixHint\text{-}MLWE}_{q,Q=0,\mathcal{D}_{\mathsf{sk}},(\mathcal{D}_{\mathsf{pert}}^{(i)})_i,\mathcal{M}}$.

The spectral norm $s_1(\mathbf{M})$ of a matrix $\mathbf{M}$ is defined as the value $\max_{\mathbf{x} \neq \mathbf{0}} \frac{\|\mathbf{M}\mathbf{x}\|}{\|\mathbf{x}\|}$. We recall that if $\mathbf{M}$ is symmetric, then its spectral norm is also its largest eigenvalue.

Theorem 1 (Hardness of MatrixHint-MLWE). *Let k, ℓ, q, Q, be positive integers, and $\mathcal{M}$ be a distribution over $\mathbb{Z}^{n(k+\ell) \times n(k+\ell) \times Q}$. For $\sigma_{\mathsf{sk}}, (\sigma_y^{(i)})_{i \in [Q]} > 0$, let $\sigma > 0$ be a real number defined as $\frac{1}{\sigma^2} = 2(\frac{1}{\sigma_{\mathsf{sk}}^2} + \sum_{i \in [Q]} \frac{s_1(\mathbf{M}_i^\top \mathbf{M}_i)}{(\sigma_y^{(i)})^2})$. If $\sigma \geq \sqrt{2} \cdot \eta_\varepsilon(\mathbb{Z}^{n(k+\ell)})$ for some $\varepsilon \in (0, 1/2]$, then there exists an efficient reduction from $\mathsf{MLWE}_{k,\ell,q,\sigma}$ to $\mathsf{MatrixHint\text{-}MLWE}_{k,\ell,q,Q,\sigma_{\mathsf{sk}},(\sigma_y^{(i)})_i,\mathcal{M}}$ that reduces the advantage by at most 2ε.*

Note that we recover the Hardness of MatrixHint-MLWE again by taking $\mathbf{M}_i$ equal to a matrix in blocs with the negacyclic matrix of some polynomial γ on the diagonal.

When the distributions $\mathcal{D}_{\mathsf{sk}}$ and $(\mathcal{D}_{\mathbf{p}}^{(i)})_i$ are discrete Gaussians, the proof relies as in [20] on the fact that the distribution of $\mathbf{s}$ conditioned on the values $(\mathbf{M}_i \cdot \mathbf{s} + \mathbf{y}_i)_i$ still follows a discrete Gaussian distribution. We formalize this in Lemma 1 and Theorem 1, which are proven in the full version of this paper.

Lemma 1. *Let $Q > 0$ be an integer, and $\sigma_{\mathsf{sk}}, (\sigma_y^{(i)})_{i \in [Q]}$ be reals > 0. Take $\mathbf{M}_0, \ldots, \mathbf{M}_{Q-1} \in \mathbb{Z}^{n(k+\ell) \times n(k+\ell)}$. We define $\mathbf{\Sigma}_0 := (\frac{1}{\sigma_{\mathsf{sk}}^2} \cdot \mathbf{I} + \sum_{i \in [Q]} \frac{1}{\sigma_{y,i}^2} \cdot \mathbf{M}_i^\top \mathbf{M}_i)^{-1}$. Then the following two distributions over $\mathcal{R} \times \mathbb{Z}^{n(k+\ell) \cdot Q}$ are statistically identical.*

1. $\left\{ (\mathbf{s}, \mathbf{z}_0, ..., \mathbf{z}_{Q-1}) \;\middle|\; \mathbf{s} \leftarrow \mathcal{D}_{\mathbb{Z}^{n(k+\ell)}, \sigma_{\mathsf{sk}}}, \mathbf{y}_i \leftarrow \mathcal{D}_{\mathbb{Z}^{n(k+\ell)}, \sigma_y^{(i)}}, \mathbf{z}_i = \mathbf{M}_i \cdot \mathbf{s} + \mathbf{y}_i \right\}$

2. $\left\{ (\hat{\mathbf{s}}, \mathbf{z}_0, ..., \mathbf{z}_{m-1}) \;\middle|\; \begin{array}{l} \mathbf{s} \leftarrow \mathcal{D}_{\mathbb{Z}^{n(k+\ell)}, \sigma_{\mathsf{sk}}}, \mathbf{y}_i \leftarrow \mathcal{D}_{\mathbb{Z}^{n(k+\ell)}, \sigma_y^{(i)}}, \mathbf{z}_i = \mathbf{M}_i \cdot \mathbf{s} + \mathbf{y}_i, \\ \mathbf{c} = \Sigma_0 \cdot \sum_{i \in [Q]} \frac{1}{(\sigma_y^{(i)})^2} \mathbf{M}_i^\top \mathbf{z}_i, \hat{\mathbf{s}} \leftarrow \mathcal{D}_{\mathbb{Z}^{n(k+\ell)}, \mathbf{c}, \sqrt{\Sigma_0}} \end{array} \right\}$

Lemma 1 actually suffices to prove results in this paper. Intuitively, when $\mathbf{s}$ follows a Gaussian distribution parameterized with Σ_0, we can reexpress it as the sum of an isotropic Gaussian of variance equal to the minimal radius of Σ_0, plus some smaller Gaussian. When $\mathbf{y}$ has sufficiently large deviation, the minimal radius of Σ_0 is close to σ_{sk}^2. This lemma allows us to extract some "good randomness" from the $\mathbf{s}_i$ and perturbations $\mathbf{p}_i$ in Pelican even after revealing hints on them.

Elliptic MatrixHint-MLWE. Interestingly, it is possible to obtain a more general reduction of MatrixHint-MLWE covering the case of leakage on the perturbations. We give a quick introduction to it here, although we decided to not make use of it in our proofs and rather rely on Lemma 1 as it doesn't lead to a substancial gain in parameters in our case.

Theorem 2 (Hardness of Elliptic MatrixHint-MLWE). *Let k, ℓ, Q, q, be positive integers, and $\mathcal{M}$ be a distribution over $\mathbb{Z}^{n(k+\ell) \times n(k+\ell) \times Q}$. For $\Sigma_{\mathsf{sk}}, \Sigma_{y,i}$ symmetric positive definite matrices, vectors $\mathbf{c}_{\mathbf{s}}, (\mathbf{c}_{\mathbf{y}}^{(i)})_i \in \mathbb{Z}^{n(k+\ell)}$. Let $\sigma > 0$ be a real number defined as $\frac{1}{\sigma^2} = 2 \cdot (s_1(\Sigma_{\mathsf{sk}}^{-1}) + \sum_{i \in [Q]} s_1(\mathbf{M}_i^\top \mathbf{M}_i) s_1(\Sigma_{y,i}^{-1}))$. If $\sigma \geq \sqrt{2} \cdot \eta_\varepsilon(\mathbb{Z}^{n(k+\ell)})$ for some $\varepsilon \in (0, 1/2]$, then there exists an efficient reduction from $\mathsf{MLWE}_{k,\ell,q,\sigma}$ to $\mathsf{MatrixHint\text{-}MLWE}_{k,\ell,q,Q,\mathcal{D}_{\mathsf{sk}}:=\mathcal{D}_{\mathbf{c}_{\mathbf{s}}, \sqrt{\Sigma_1}}, (\mathcal{D}_{\mathsf{pert}}^{(i)}:=\mathcal{D}_{\mathbf{c}_i, \sqrt{\Sigma_{y,i}}})_{i \in [Q]}, \mathcal{M}}$ that reduces the advantage by at most 2ε.*

We include a proof overview in the full version of this paper.

In our case, secrets and perturbations are of the form $\mathbf{r} = \sum_i \mathbf{r}_i$, and the reveal of hints $\mathbf{R}_i \cdot \mathbf{r}_i + \mathbf{y}_i$ modifies their distribution. We can see with Lemma 1 that the resulting distribution has covariance matrix:

$$\Sigma_{\mathbf{r}} := \sum_i \left(\frac{1}{\sigma_{\mathbf{r}}^2} \mathbf{I} + \frac{1}{\sigma_{\mathbf{y}}^2} \mathbf{R}_i^\top \mathbf{R}_i \right)^{-1}$$

If B is an overwhelming bound on $s_1(\mathbf{R}_i^\top \mathbf{R}_i)$, then the minimum eigenvalue of $\Sigma_{\mathbf{r}}$ is at least $\sum_i (\frac{1}{\sigma_{\mathbf{r}}^2} + \frac{B}{\sigma_{\mathbf{y}}^2})^{-1}$. When taking such a sum with k elements for both the secret and perturbations, we obtain a reduction to MLWE with σ verifying:

$$\frac{1}{\sigma^2} = 2 \cdot \frac{1}{k} \left(\frac{1}{\sigma_{\mathsf{sk}}^2} + \frac{B}{\sigma_{y,\mathsf{sk}}^2} + \sum_{i \in [Q]} s_1(c_i c_i^*) \cdot \left(\frac{1}{\sigma_{\mathbf{p}}^2} + \frac{B}{\sigma_{y,\mathbf{p}}^2} \right) \right)$$

4 Verifiable Short Secret Sharing

We start with our new proposal for verifiable (short) secret sharing. As presented in Sect. 2.1, we introduce a new *random submersion* technique allowing one to distribute and prove the shortness of a secret among N parties. This shortness is crucial in the context of lattice-based cryptographic schemes based on variants of the Learning With Errors (LWE) assumption, which is based on the shortness of secret elements. Importantly, our technique controls the leakage on the secret and can be leveraged to sample short secrets in threshold schemes, as will be formalized for a threshold robust signature scheme, and a distributed key generation protocol in Sect. 5.

4.1 Security Notions

We first define in Definition 4 the syntax of a verifiable short secret sharing, as well as standard security properties in Definitions 5 and 6.

Definition 4 (Verifiable Short Secret Sharing). *Let $\mathcal{D}_\mathbf{x}$ be a distribution (corresponding to honestly generated secrets), and V be a subset of its support Sec (the acceptable secrets). Let $N > T$ be two nonnegative integers. Assume that we have N parties communicating and yet another distinguished party called dealer. A Verifiable Short Secret Sharing (V3S) is defined as a tuple of functions:*

- V3S.Share$(N, T, \mathbf{x}) \to (\llbracket \mathbf{x} \rrbracket_1, ..., \llbracket \mathbf{x} \rrbracket_N, \pi, \pi_1, ..., \pi_N) \in \mathsf{Sec}^N \times (\{0,1\}^*)^N$, *run by the dealer.*
- V3S.Verify$_i(\llbracket \mathbf{x} \rrbracket_i, \pi, \pi_i) \to$ (true | false): *run by the party i if sufficiently enough parties accept the proof from the dealer, they are guaranteed to have shares from an acceptable secret, i.e. belonging to V.*
- V3S.Reconstruct$(\llbracket \mathbf{x} \rrbracket_{i_1}, ..., \llbracket \mathbf{x} \rrbracket_{i_k}) \to (\mathbf{x} \mid \perp)$: *reconstruct the secret from $k \geqslant T$ shares. Returns $\perp$ in case of failure.*
- V3S.RobustReconstruct$(\llbracket \mathbf{x} \rrbracket_{i_1}, ..., \llbracket \mathbf{x} \rrbracket_{i_k}) \to \mathbf{x}$: *reconstruct the secret from $k \geqslant T$ shares in the presence of up to $(k-T)/2$ invalid shares.*

Definition 5 (V3S Correctness). *A V3S scheme is said to be correct if when V3S.Share() is honestly executed with a secret $\mathbf{x}$ sampled from the honest distribution $\mathcal{D}_\mathbf{x}$, then verification correctly passes for all parties with overwhelming probability, and V3S.Reconstruct() correctly recovers the secret.*

Definition 6 (V3S Soundness). *A V3S scheme is said sound if for any $S \subseteq \{1, ..., N\}$ of cardinal at least T, and any sharing $\llbracket \mathbf{x} \rrbracket$, with corresponding proofs π, π_i, verification will fail with overwhelming probability if either:*

- *shares are inconsistent among S, i.e. reconstructions over shares of S returns $\perp$. Then, at least one party in S will fail verification.*
- *or the secret is invalid, i.e. the secret reconstructed by parties in S does not belong to V. Then verification will fail for at least one party in S.*

This is formalized as requiring any efficient adversary $\mathcal{A}$ to win Game V3S-sound defined in Figure 2 with negligible probability.

```
Game_{V3S-sound}
 1: L_H := ∅
 2: N, T, S ← A()                    ▷ The adversary A chooses a subset S of parties to target
 3: assert{ S ⊂ {1, ..., N} ∧ |S| ⩾ T }     ▷ S must be large enough to allow
    reconstruction
 4: (s_i)_{i∈{1,...,N}}, π, (π_i)_{i∈{1,...,N}} ← A^{H(·)}(N, T, S)   ▷ A produces a T-sharing
    among N parties
 5: if ∀i ∈ S, V3S.Verify(s_i, π, π_i) = false then
 6:     return 0                    ▷ If a party in S fails verification, A loses
 7: x = V3S.Reconstruct((s_i)_{i∈S})
 8: if x = ⊥ then                   ▷ Verification passes but shares are inconsistent in S
 9:     return 1
10: if x ∉ V then                   ▷ Verification passes but the secret is invalid
11:     return 1
12: return 0                        ▷ The sharing chosen by the adversary is valid

H(str, digest)
 1: assert{ str ∈ pp.HashParams }       ▷ Check domain string
 2: if ∃r.(str, digest, r) ∈ L_H then
 3:     return r
 4: else
 5:     Sample r uniformly
 6:     L_H := L_H ∪ {(str, digest, r)}
 7:     return r
```

Fig. 2. Soundness game for a V3S. $\mathcal{A}$ wins if the game V3S-sound returns 1.

We say that a V3S has the fragmentary knowledge property if knowledge of at most $T-1$ shares and proofs leaks only partial information on the secret key, and keeps sufficient entropy. This is formalized with two simulators as follows:

Definition 7 (Computational/Statistical V3S Fragmentary Knowledge). *A V3S has the fragmentary knowledge property if there exists two simulators* $\mathsf{SimProof}(S) \to ((\llbracket \mathbf{x} \rrbracket_i)_{i \in S}, \pi, (\pi_i)_{i \in S})$, *defined for subsets* $S \subset \{1, ..., N\}$ *of cardinality at most* $T-1$, *and* $\mathsf{SimSecret}(\pi, (\pi_i)_{i \in S})$ *such that the output distribution* $(\mathbf{x}, (\llbracket \mathbf{x} \rrbracket_i)_{i \in S}, \pi, (\pi_i)_{i \in S})$ *of the two processes*

- $((\llbracket \mathbf{x} \rrbracket_i)_{i \in S}, \pi, (\pi_i)_{i \in S}) \leftarrow \mathsf{SimProof}(S)$, and $\mathbf{x} \leftarrow \mathsf{SimSecret}(\pi, (\pi_i)_{i \in S})$
- or $\mathbf{x} \leftarrow \mathcal{D}_\mathbf{x}$, $((\llbracket \mathbf{x} \rrbracket_i)_{i \in \{1,...,N\}}, \pi, (\pi_i)_{i \in \{1,...,N\}}) \leftarrow \mathsf{V3S.Share}(N, T, \mathbf{x})$

are (computationally/statistically) indistinguishable. This is formalized as requiring the winning advantage of any efficient adversary $\mathcal{A}$ *to win Game* V3S-fk *defined in Figure 3 to be at a negligible distance from* $1/2$.

```
Game_{V3S-fk^b}, with b ∈ {0,1}
 1: L_H := ∅
 2: N, T, S ← A()                    ▷ The adversary chooses a subset S of parties to target
 3: assert{ S ⊂ {1, ..., N} ∧ |S| = T − 1 }
 4: if b = 0 then
 5:     x ← D_x
 6:     (⟦x⟧_i)_{i∈{1,...,N}}, π, (π_i)_{i∈{1,...,N}} ← V3S.Share(x)    ▷ Honest sharing of x
 7: else
 8:     (⟦x⟧_i)_{i∈{1,...,N}}, π, (π_i)_{i∈{1,...,N}} ← SimProof(S)     ▷ Simulation of the sharing
        transcript
 9:     x ← SimSecret(π, (π_i)_{i∈S})
10: b' ← A^H(x, (⟦x⟧_i)_{i∈S}, π, (π_i)_{i∈S})
11: return b'

H(str, digest)
 1: assert{ str ∈ pp.HashParams }                      ▷ Check domain string
 2: if ∃r.(str, digest, r) ∈ L_H then
 3:     return r
 4: else
 5:     Sample r uniformly
 6:     L_H := L_H ∪ {(str, digest, r)}
 7:     return r
```

Fig. 3. Fragmentary Knowledge game for a VSSS. We consider the distinguishing advantage of an adversary $\mathcal{A}$ between the games with $b = 0$, and $b = 1$.

4.2 Formal Definition of Our VSSS

The protocol drafted in the technical overview translates to pseudo-code quite straightforwardly and is given in Fig. 4. The syntax and formalization are inspired by the recent work of [3], as well as the use of hash functions to commit on secret shares and derive a challenge for verification. We formalize the requirements on the submersion matrices which were hinted in Sect. 2.1.

Definition 8 (Property G). *A distribution of matrices $\mathbf{R}$ is said to satisfy the property G_{p_1,p_2,p_3} if there exists two bounds B, B' such that we have:*

separation *if $(\mathbf{x}, \mathbf{y}) \neq (\mathbf{x}', \mathbf{y}')$, $\Pr_{\mathbf{R} \leftarrow \mathcal{D}_\mathbf{R}}[\mathbf{Rx} + \mathbf{y} \bmod q = \mathbf{Rx}' + \mathbf{y}' \bmod q] = p_1$ with $p_1 = \mathsf{negl}(\kappa)$: the matrices $\mathbf{R}$ send different secrets to different points.*
large norm detection *if $\|\mathbf{x}\| > B$, for any $\mathbf{y}$, $\Pr_{\mathbf{R} \leftarrow \mathcal{D}_\mathbf{R}}[\|\mathbf{Rx} + \mathbf{y} \bmod q\| > B'] = 1 - p_2$ with $p_2 = \mathsf{negl}(\kappa)$: intuitively, if $\mathbf{x}$ is large, we want the challenge to also be large with overwhelming probability.*
honest execution $\Pr_{\mathbf{x} \leftarrow \mathcal{D}^n_{\sigma_x}, \mathbf{y} \leftarrow \mathcal{D}_{\sigma_y}, \mathbf{R} \leftarrow \mathcal{D}_\mathbf{R}}[\|\mathbf{Rx} + \mathbf{y} \bmod q\| \leq B'] = 1 - p_3$ *with $p_3 = \mathsf{negl}(\kappa)$: in case of honest generation of the secret, the challenge is small.*

Assuming this crucial property in the construction, we show that our V3S construction is secure for the notions introduced in Sect. 4.1. We classically work in

---

Algorithm 1 V3S.Share($N, T, \mathbf{x}$)

1: $\mathbf{y} \leftarrow \mathcal{D}_{\sigma_y}^d$; $(r_i)_{i \in \{1,\ldots,N\}} \xleftarrow{\$} \{0,1\}^{N \cdot 2\kappa}$
2: Generate T-out-of-N sharings $[\![\mathbf{x}]\!] = [\![\mathbf{x}]\!]_{\{1,\ldots,N\}}$, $[\![\mathbf{y}]\!] = [\![\mathbf{y}]\!]_{\{1,\ldots,N\}}$ ▷ Section 3.3
3: $h :=$ root of Merkle tree Tree with leaves $\text{leaf}_i = ([\![\mathbf{x}]\!]_i, [\![\mathbf{y}]\!]_i, r_i)$ for $i \in \{1,\ldots,N\}$
4: **for** $i \in \{1,\ldots,N\}$ **do**
5: $\quad\text{proof}_i :=$ co-path of leaf_i in the tree Tree ▷ Proves $([\![\mathbf{x}]\!]_i, [\![\mathbf{y}]\!]_i, r_i)$ is in h
6: $\quad\pi_i := ([\![\mathbf{y}]\!]_i, \text{proof}_i)$
7: $\mathbf{R} := H_\mathbf{R}(h)$ ▷ Hash h to obtain a random matrix from $\mathcal{D}_\mathbf{R}$
8: $[\![\mathbf{v}]\!] := \mathbf{R} \cdot [\![\mathbf{x}]\!] + [\![\mathbf{y}]\!]$ ▷ Johnson-Lindenstrauss
9: $\pi := (h, [\![\mathbf{v}]\!])$ ▷ Challenge polynomial and Merkle tree root
10: **return** $([\![\mathbf{x}]\!], \pi, (\pi_i)_{i \in \{1,\ldots,N\}})$

Algorithm 2 V3S.Verify($[\![\mathbf{x}]\!]_i, \pi, \pi_i$)

1: Parse $\pi := (h, [\![\mathbf{v}]\!])$ and $\pi_i := ([\![\mathbf{y}]\!]_i, r_i, \text{proof}_i)$
2: Recover $\mathbf{v}$ from $[\![\mathbf{v}]\!]$ ▷ See Section 3.3
3: **if** (proof_i is not a valid proof that $([\![\mathbf{x}]\!]_i, [\![\mathbf{y}]\!]_i, r_i)$ is in Tree) **then**
4: $\quad$**return** false
5: $\mathbf{R} := H_\mathbf{R}(h)$
6: **if** ($[\![\mathbf{v}]\!]_i \neq \mathbf{R} \cdot [\![\mathbf{x}]\!]_i + [\![\mathbf{y}]\!]_i) \vee (\|\mathbf{v}\| > B')$ **then**
7: $\quad$**return** false ▷ Check the consistency of shares, and shortness of secret vector
8: **return** true

Algorithm 3 V3S.Reconstruct($[\![\mathbf{x}]\!]_I$), with $|I| \geq T$

1: $J = \{\text{the first } T \text{ indices in } I\}$ ▷ Reconstruct over a set of size T
2: Compute the unique $P \in (\mathbb{Z}_q)_{<T}[X]$ such that $\forall j \in J, P(j) = [\![\mathbf{x}]\!]_j$
3: **if** $\exists i \in I \setminus J$ s.t. $P(i) \neq [\![\mathbf{x}]\!]_i$ **then**
4: $\quad$**return** $\perp$
5: **return** $\mathbf{x} := P(0)$

Algorithm 4 V3S.RobustReconstruct$(([\![\mathbf{x}]\!]_i)_{i \in I})$, with $|I| \geq T$

1: Interpret $([\![x]\!]_i)_{i \in I}$ as a Reed-Solomon codeword of $\begin{cases} \text{block length } T \\ \text{message length } |I| \end{cases}$
2: Run error correction on $([\![\mathbf{x}]\!]_i)_{i \in I}$ ▷ Fixes up to $(|I| - T)/2$ errors
3: **return** V3S.Reconstruct$(([\![\mathbf{x}]\!]_i)_{i \in I})$

Fig. 4. Algorithms for our Verifiable Short Secret Sharing (V3S). Shamir's sharing modulo q is done using standard Lagrange interpolation. Secrets space is $\mathbb{Z}^n$, and matrices $\mathbf{R}$ are sampled in $\mathbb{Z}^{d \times n}$ following distribution $\mathcal{D}_\mathbf{R}$. The support for the honest secrets $\mathbf{x}$ is $\mathcal{D}_\mathbf{x} = \mathcal{D}_{\sigma_x}^n$, and the support for the blinding $\mathbf{y}$ is $\mathcal{D}_{\sigma_y}^d$.

the ROM and assume that hash functions are modeled as random oracles with output size 2κ.

Theorem 3 (Security of V3S in the ROM). *Let Q_H be the maximum number of queries allowed to the random oracle. For the V3S in Fig. 4, taking as set of valid secrets $V = \{\mathbf{x} \mid \|\mathbf{x}\| \leq B\}$, if the distribution of matrices $\mathbf{R}$ satisfies property G_{p_1,p_2,p_3}, then we have:*

- **Correctness** *with probability $1 - p_3$.*
- **Soundness** *with an advantage of at most: $\frac{Q_H^2}{2^{2\kappa-1}} + Q_H \cdot (p_1 + p_2)$*
- **Fragmentary knowledge** *with an advantage of at most $N \cdot \frac{Q_H}{2^{2\kappa}}$, where for a set $|S| = T - 1$ the simulators are defined in Algorithms 5 and 6.*

Algorithm 5 SimProof(S)

1: $\forall i \in S, [\![\mathbf{x}]\!]_i, [\![\mathbf{y}]\!]_i \xleftarrow{\$} \mathbb{Z}_q, r_i \xleftarrow{\$} \{0,1\}^{2\kappa}$
2: Generate Merkle tree h containing $([\![\mathbf{x}]\!]_i, [\![\mathbf{y}]\!]_i, r_i)_{i \in S}$ and complete the hashes of missing shares $j \notin S$ by uniform i.i.d values in $\{0,1\}^{2\kappa}$.
3: Produce proof_i for shares in S.
4: $\mathbf{x}, \mathbf{y} \leftarrow \mathcal{D}_{\sigma_x}^n, \mathcal{D}_{\sigma_y}^d$
5: Compute $[\![v]\!]$ such that:
   - for $i \in S$, $[\![\mathbf{v}]\!]_i = \mathbf{R} \cdot [\![\mathbf{x}]\!]_i + [\![\mathbf{y}]\!]_i$
   - $[\![\mathbf{v}]\!]_0 = \mathbf{R} \cdot \mathbf{x} + \mathbf{y}$
6: **return** $([\![\mathbf{x}]\!]_i)_{i \in S}, \pi = (h, [\![\mathbf{v}]\!]), (\pi_i)_{i \in S} = ([\![\mathbf{y}]\!]_i, r_i, \mathrm{proof}_i)_{i \in S}$

Algorithm 6 SimSecret($\pi \equiv (h, [\![\mathbf{v}]\!]), (\pi_i \equiv ([\![\mathbf{y}]\!]_i, r_i, \mathrm{proof}_i))_{i \in S}$)

1: Compute $\mathbf{R} = H_{\mathbf{R}}(h)$.
2: $\mathbf{c} \equiv \Sigma_0 \cdot \frac{1}{\sigma_y^2} \cdot \mathbf{R}^\top \cdot \mathbf{z}$
3: $\Sigma_0 \equiv \left(\frac{1}{\sigma_x^2} \cdot \mathbf{I} + \frac{1}{\sigma_y^2} \cdot \mathbf{R}^\top \mathbf{R}\right)^{-1}$
4: $\mathbf{z} = [\![\mathbf{v}]\!]_0$.
5: **return** $\mathbf{x} \leftarrow \mathcal{D}_{\mathbb{Z}^n, \mathbf{c}, \sqrt{\Sigma_0}}$

We demonstrate in Sect. 6 how to efficiently construct such a desirable distribution.

The proof of this theorem is quite lengthy and relies on a certain number of hybrids, we let the reader refer to the full version. For completeness purposes, we still give here the main sketch and ideas upon which the proofs are built.

Correctness. V3S.Share() correctly constructs a Shamir's sharing and a corresponding Merkle tree for secure sharing and verification. The V3S.Reconstruct function can accurately reconstruct the original value for any subset of shares of size at least T, and the V3S.Verify() function consistently passes its checks by the *honest execution* property of the distribution of $\mathbf{R}$.

Soundness. The proof employs a hybrid argument approach, consisting of three main steps:
- The first game is the actual soundness game.
- Hybrid$_2$ is a tweak of the soundness game ensuring that the matrix **R** is sampled *after* the shares are chosen, which is the crux for applying *separation and large norm detection properties* of $\mathcal{D}_\mathbf{R}$. This hybrid aims to maintain the integrity of the Merkle tree hashes and the random oracle's programming, penalizing the adversary for any inconsistency or attempts to exploit the hash function's collision or pre-image resistance.
- Hybrid$_3$: modifies the conditions under which an adversary can win, specifically targeting inconsistencies and too large norms in the reconstructed secret during the verification process.
- Probability of Winning: Rely on the *separation and large norm detection* to limit the probability of an adversary's success.

Fragmentary Knowledge. The proof also goes by three hybrids.
- Hybrid$_1$: Adversary observes the real distribution of transcripts, corresponding to $b = 0$ in the V3S-fk game.
- Hybrid$_2$: Introduces uniform random strings in place of the hashes of shares not in set S, arguing the adversary's view changes negligibly if they had not queried these shares (basically, the view of the adversary differs *only if* it did query the random oracle on one of the shares ($[\![\mathbf{x}]\!]_i, [\![\mathbf{y}_i]\!], r_i$) with $i \notin S$ in Hybrid$_1$)
- Hybrid$_3$: Further modifies by replacing shares in S with uniformly random vectors and simulating the adversary's view under $b = 1$. It uses the correctness of the secret sharing and the indistinguishability proved in Lemma 1 to argue the adversary's advantage remains unchanged from Hybrid 2.

4.3 Towards Applications

Our definition of V3S is agnostic to the communication means used. We describe at a high level in this section two generic ways for using our V3S in protocols to obtain different guarantees and cost tradeoffs. Further, we demonstrate concrete usage and security proofs in Sect. 5.

VSSS protocol with detection of malicious behavior. The first protocol we introduce allows us to detect misbehavior during the protocol execution and abort in that case. It requires lightweight communication assumptions, i.e. confidential and authenticated pairwise channels, additionally reliable for correctness when all the parties are honest. However, the counterpart is that as soon as at least one of the parties is dishonest, the protocol may abort with no possibility of recovery. We assume from now on that there are at least T honest parties. The protocol proceeds in several rounds:

1. In the first round, the dealer samples $\mathbf{x} \leftarrow \mathcal{D}_\mathbf{x}$ and runs $([\![\mathbf{x}]\!]_i)_{i\in\{1,...,N\}}, \pi, (\pi_i)_{i\in\{1,...,N\}} \leftarrow$ V3S.Share($\mathbf{x}$). It then sends $([\![\mathbf{x}]\!]_i, \pi, \pi_i)$ to each other party i over the pairwise channel between them.

2. In the second round, everyone checks the data provided by the dealer. They run $b = \text{V3S.Verify}(\llbracket \mathbf{x} \rrbracket_i, \pi, \pi_i)$. After that, they send b to each other party, along with a hash of π to prove they had the same common proof.
3. Finally, each party accepts the sharing only if it receives a positive response from all other parties, along with the same hash as theirs.

From the good properties of our V3S proposal, we can easily show that this protocol has also:

- *correctness*: in case all parties behave honestly, then the protocol terminates and all honest parties accept the sharing.
- *soundness*: in case the dealer sends inconsistent shares to any honest party, or reconstructing to an invalid secret, it will be detected with overwhelming probability and the protocol will abort.
- *fragmentary knowledge*: in case the dealer is honest, and the protocol terminates, the transcript is indistinguishable from the one simulated by the fragmentary knowledge property of our VSSS.

Robust V3S protocol. We propose a second protocol providing guaranteed delivery in case the dealer is honest, and, in case the dealer is dishonest and misbehaves, all honest parties simultaneously abort. This protocol assumes the existence of an *authenticated reliable* (even for corrupted parties) *non-ordered broadcast channel*, and that a majority of the parties are honest.

It works with an IND-CPA symmetric encryption scheme SKE to implement non-repudiable pairwise communication. We assume that pairwise keys $\mathsf{sk}_i^{\mathsf{SKE}}$ are shared prior to the protocol execution to communicate with the dealer, along with a signature $\mathsf{sig}_i = \mathsf{Sign}(\mathsf{sk}, (i, \mathsf{sk}_{i,j}))$ signed by the dealer for a verified reveal of the key. Note, that requirements on these prior steps could be reduced by using non-repudiable and publicly verifiable signcryption. We could then simply assume that their public keys are pre-shared, and the verified reveal can be replaced by proofs that a given ciphertext is invalid, or corresponds to a given message using the non-repudiability property.

Our robust protocol also works in three rounds:

1. The dealer samples $\mathbf{x}$, and runs V3S.Share($\mathbf{x}$). It broadcasts the proof π along with individual encryptions produced with the SKE for each other party of $\llbracket \mathbf{x} \rrbracket_i, \pi_i$.
2. In the second round, each party decrypts the message from the dealer and runs V3S.Verify() on its share. If decryption or verification fails, the party broadcasts a complaint containing the secret key of its communication channel with the dealer $\mathsf{sk}_i^{\mathsf{SKE}}$, along with sig_i.
3. The third round consists of opening and verifying all the complaints. If any of the complaints is valid, it means that the dealer behaved dishonestly, if no complaint is valid, the sharing is valid, and the party can accept it.

In this protocol, we achieve:

- *unframeability:* if the dealer is honest, no corrupted party will be able to make honest parties reject. Indeed, as the signature scheme is unforgeable, only a complaint with the correct SKE key can be produced, and then the message sent by the dealer will be correctly decrypted.
- *accountability:* if the dealer is corrupted, the use of a broadcast channel ensures that all honest parties will receive the same set of complaints and will conclude identically. If they accept the shares, the shares of all honest parties pass verification, which means that the shares are consistent, and the secret is valid.

We could reduce the communication of our protocol by exchanging ciphertexts on pairwise channels instead of broadcasting them. We would then add an extra round after the round of complaints to allow dealers to answer complaints by broadcasting the share of the plaintiff in case there was a complaint.

5 Pelican: A Robust Threshold Signature Scheme

We make the following assumptions in our communication model:

- **Authenticated broadcast.** All contributions by user i are broadcast on a reliable public channel. In addition, they are signed by i and therefore authenticated. Concretely, i has a signing key sk_i and signs all their contributions: $\mathsf{SIG.Sign}(\mathsf{sk}_i, \mathsf{contrib}_j[i])$, where SIG is an UF-CMA standard signature scheme $\mathsf{SIG} = \{\mathsf{Keygen}, \mathsf{Sign}, \mathsf{Verify}\}$.

  These signatures are checked by other parties upon reception, and the contribution is declared invalid if the signature is invalid. For conciseness, this is omitted from the descriptions of the distributed key generation and distributed signing protocols.
- **Signed pairwise keys.** For any ordered pair of users (i,j), i and j share a pairwise symmetric key $\mathsf{K}_{i\to j}$ that has been signed by i. This secret key is used by i to send encrypted data to i using an IND-CPA symmetric key encryption scheme $\mathsf{SKE} = \{\mathsf{Encrypt}, \mathsf{Decrypt}\}$.

  Encrypted messages are sent over the broadcast channel in order to authenticate the sender. When j files a complaint against i, they reveal the $\mathsf{K}_{i\to j}$ along with the signature. This binds i to the data they have sent to j, and in case of misbehavior, revealing $\mathsf{K}_{i\to j}$ allows other parties to acknowledge the misbehavior.

  Concretely, signed pairwise keys can be easily established in a setup phase. It suffices that i generates a KEM ciphertext i encapsulating a KEM symmetric key, and uses this KEM symmetric key to encrypt $\mathsf{K}_{i\to j}$ and a signature $\mathsf{sig}_{i\to j} \leftarrow \mathsf{SIG.Sign}(\mathsf{sk}_i, \{i, j, \mathsf{K}_{i\to j}\})$.

Our protocols are round-based, with one algorithm per round. Rounds are run sequentially and synchronously, with the returned value being posted to the broadcast channel.

5.1 Robust Distributed Key Generation (DKG)

We present a first application of our framework, allowing one to verifiably sample and share a short secret among parties, assuming that 2 out of 3 participants are honest. We apply it to the key generation of Pelican and prove that the resulting scheme remains robust and unforgeable.

In environments where the key generation cannot be entitled to a single trusted entity, it is important to provide the possibility to distribute the key generation process among several actors.

Distributed key generation description. Our Distributed Key Generation was informally presented in Sect. 2.2. We now provide a formal description of its algorithms in Fig. 5. Note that usual rounding techniques on the public key apply. We omit them in our description for simplicity. Introducing rounding only incurs a small loss in the SIS bound B_2, and requires introducing an infinite norm bound on c in the verification procedure.

As our DKG allows the adversary to partly bias the distribution of the secret key, it makes it very complex to define a secrecy notion for our DKG that is independent of the underlying primitive.

While the literature introduced zero-knowledge notions [22] to abstract the unbiased behavior of a DKG, and leverage it in any threshold scheme, this does not easily generalize to our setting where the key generation allows some bias. It would be possible to define a generic notion with several simulators similar to V3S-fk, but we concluded that the added complexity in the proofs was not worth the small gain in generality. Instead, we introduce in Theorem 4 new robustness and unforgeability notions for a signature scheme used in conjunction with a DKG. The unforgeability and robustness of our scheme is stated in Theorem 5 (resp. Theorem 4), which are proven in the full version of this paper.

Definition 9 (Unforgeability and robustness with DKG). *A threshold signature scheme with DKG* (ShareKeygen$_i$)$_{i \in \{1,\ldots,\text{rnd}_{\text{Keygen}}\}}$, (ShareSign$_i$)$_{i \in \{1,\ldots,\text{rnd}_{\text{sig}}\}}$, CombineKey, Combine *is unforgeable (resp. robust) if all probabilistic polynomial-time adversaries $\mathcal{A}$ win the game* Game$_{\text{DKG-TH-UF}}$ *(resp.* Game$_{\text{DKG-TH-RB}}$*), formalized in the full version, with negligible probability.*

Theorem 4. *Consider $\mathcal{K}$ a distribution of keys of the form $\sum_j \mathbf{s}_j$ such that:*

1. *at most $(T-1)$ vectors $\mathbf{s}_j$ have norm bounded by B;*
2. *the other vectors $\mathbf{s}_j$ are sampled from $\mathcal{D}_{\text{sk}}^2$.*

Assume that we have $\|(z_1, z_2, c_1)\| \leq B_2$ with overwhelming probability p for any set valid, $\mathbf{p} = \sum_{j \in \text{valid}} \mathbf{p}_j$ *with (i) at most $T-1$ arbitrary perturbations of norm bounded by B, (ii) the others sampled from Gaussians of standard deviation $\sigma_\mathbf{p}$, and over any distribution of keys $\mathcal{K}$.*

The advantage of any polynomial-time adversary $\mathcal{A}$ in the game DKG-TH-RB, *formalized in the full version, reduces to the robustness of* Pelican *with a small advantage loss. Formally, there exist adversaries $\mathcal{B}_1$ against the* UF-CMA *security*

Algorithm 7 Pelican.ShareKeygen$_1$(state$_i$)

1: **assert**{ state.rnd = $\varnothing$ }; state.rnd = 1
2: salt$_i \xleftarrow{\$} \{0,1\}^\kappa$
3: $\mathbf{s}_i \leftarrow \mathcal{D}_{\sigma_t}^2$
4: $([\![\mathbf{s}_i]\!], \pi_i, (\pi_{i,j})_{j \in \{1,...,N\}}) \leftarrow$ V3S.Share$(N, T, \mathbf{s}_i)$ ▷ Share $[\![\mathbf{s}_i]\!]$ and make proofs
5: **if** {$\exists j$ s.t. V3S.Verify$([\![\mathbf{s}_i]\!]_j, \pi_i, \pi_{i \to j})$ = false} **then** {restart} ▷ Invalid proof
6: **for** $j \in \{1,...,N\}$ **do**
7: $\quad$ pt$_j := ([\![\mathbf{s}_i]\!]_j, \pi_{i,j})$
8: $\quad$ ct$_{i,j} \leftarrow$ SKE.Encrypt(K$_{i \to j}$, pt$_j$) ▷ Encrypt (share, proof) to each party
9: **return** contrib$_1[i]$:= salt$_i, \pi_i, (\text{ct}_{i,j})_{j \in \{1,...,N\}}$

Algorithm 8 Pelican.ShareKeygen$_2$(state$_i$, contrib$_1$)

1: **assert**{ state.rnd = 1 }; state.rnd = 2;
2: complaints$_i := \{\}$
3: **for** ($j \in$ contrib$_1$) **do** ▷ Set of round 1 contributors
4: $\quad$ salt$_j, \pi_j, (\text{ct}_{j \to k})_{k \in \{1,...,N\}}$:= contrib$_1[j]$
5: $\quad [\![\mathbf{s}_j]\!]_i, \pi_{j \to i}$:= SKE.Decrypt(K$_{j \to i}$, ct$_{j \to i}$)
6: $\quad$ **if** (SKE.Decrypt failed) **or** (V3S.Verify$([\![\mathbf{s}_j]\!]_i, \pi_j, \pi_{j \to i})$ = false) **then**
7: $\quad\quad$ complaints$_i[j]$ = {K$_{j \to i}$, sig$_{j \to i}$} ▷ i complains against j
8: valid$_i = \{j \in$ contrib$_1\} \backslash$complaints$_i$
9: state$_i$.session.valid := valid$_i$
10: state$_i$.session.contrib$_1$:= contrib$_1$
11: state$_i$.session.shares := $([\![\mathbf{s}_j]\!]_i)_{j \in \text{valid}_i}$
12: **return** contrib$_2[i]$:= complaints$_i$

Algorithm 9 Pelican.ShareKeygen$_3$(state$_i$, contrib$_2$)

1: **assert**{ state.rnd = 2 }; state.rnd = 3
2: valid$_i$:= state$_i$.session.valid $\cap \{j \in$ contrib$_2\}$
3: **for** $j \in \{1,...,N\}$ **do**
4: $\quad$ **for** $k \in$ complaints$_j$ **do** ▷ Lines 5 to 9 study j's complaint against k
5: $\quad\quad$ {K$_{k \to j}$, sig$_{k \to j}$} := complaints$_j[k]$
6: $\quad\quad$ **if** {SIG.Verify(pk$_k$, sig$_{k \to j}$, $\{k, j,$ K$_{k \to j}\}$) = false} **then** {continue}
7: $\quad\quad [\![\mathbf{s}_k]\!]_j, \pi_{k \to j}$:= SKE.Decrypt(K$_{k \to j}$, ct$_{k \to j}$)
8: $\quad\quad$ **if** (SKE.Decrypt failed) **or** V3S.Verify$([\![\mathbf{s}_k]\!]_j, \pi_k, \pi_{k \to j})$ = false **then**
9: $\quad\quad\quad$ valid$_i$ = valid$_i \backslash \{k\}$ ▷ If j's complaint against k is valid, invalidate j
10: state$_i$.session.salt := $H_{\text{salt}}((\text{salt}_j)_{j \in \text{valid}_i})$
11: $a := H_a(\text{state}_i.\text{session.salt}) \in \mathcal{R}_q$ ▷ Derive the public key $a \in \mathcal{R}_q$ from a seed
12: $[\![\mathbf{s}]\!]_i := \sum_{j \in \text{valid}_i} [\![\mathbf{s}_j]\!]_i$ ▷ $s = \sum_{j \in \text{valid}} s_j$
13: $[\![b]\!]_i := \beta - \begin{bmatrix} 1 & a \end{bmatrix} \cdot [\![\mathbf{s}]\!]_i$
14: Store $[\![\mathbf{s}]\!]_i$ in state$_i$
15: **return** contrib$_3[i]$:= (state$_i$.session.salt, $[\![b]\!]_i$)

Algorithm 10 Pelican.CombineKey(contrib$_3$)

1: Retrieve salt from contrib$_3$ ▷ If contradictory contributions use majority vote
2: $b :=$ V3S.RobustReconstruct($[\![b]\!]_i, ..., [\![b]\!]_N$)
3: **assert**{ $b \neq \bot$ }
4: **return** vk := (salt, b)

Fig. 5. Algorithms for the distributed Keygen. For conciseness, we omit the parsing of (contrib$_i)_{i \in \{1,2,3\}}$ in Algorithms 8 to 10.

of SIG, $\mathcal{B}_2$ against the V3S-sound security of V3S, $\mathcal{B}_3$ against the Leak-TH-RB security of Pelican, with running time $T_{\mathcal{B}_1} \approx T_{\mathcal{B}_2} \approx T_{\mathcal{B}_3} \approx T_{\mathcal{A}}$.

$$\mathsf{Adv}_{\mathcal{A}}^{\mathsf{DKG\text{-}TH\text{-}RB}}(\kappa) \leq N \cdot \mathsf{Adv}_{\mathcal{B}_1}^{\mathsf{UF\text{-}CMA}}(\kappa) + \mathsf{Adv}_{\mathcal{B}_2}^{\mathsf{V3S\text{-}sound}}(\kappa) + \mathsf{Adv}_{\mathcal{B}_3}^{\mathsf{Leak\text{-}TH\text{-}RB}}(\kappa)$$
$$+ N \cdot (1 - \Pr[\text{V3S correctness}])$$

Theorem 5. *Define σ'_{sk} as $\frac{1}{\sigma_{sk}^{\prime 2}} = 2\left(\frac{1}{\sigma_{sk}^2} + \frac{B}{\sigma_y^2}\right)$, with B such that $\Pr\left[s_1(\mathbf{R}^\top \mathbf{R}) \leq B\right]$ with overwhelming probability and $\sigma'_{sk} \geq \sqrt{2}\eta_\varepsilon(\mathbb{Z}^{2n})$.*

The advantage of any polynomial-time adversary $\mathcal{A}$ in the game DKG-TH-UF, formalized in the full version, reduces to the unforgeability of Pelican with a small advantage loss. Formally, there exist adversaries $\mathcal{B}_1$ against the UF-CMA security of SIG, $\mathcal{B}_2$ against the IND-CPA security of SKE, $\mathcal{B}_3$ against the V3S-sound security of V3S, $\mathcal{B}_4$ against the V3S-fk security of V3S, $\mathcal{B}_5$ against the Leak-TH-UF security of Pelican with $\sigma_t = \sigma'_{sk}$, with running time $T_{\mathcal{B}_i} \approx T_{\mathcal{A}}$ for $i \in \{1, ..., 5\}$.

$$\mathsf{Adv}_{\mathcal{A}}^{\mathsf{DKG\text{-}TH\text{-}UF}}(\kappa) \leq N \cdot \mathsf{Adv}_{\mathcal{B}_1}^{\mathsf{UF\text{-}CMA}}(\kappa) + N^2 \cdot \mathsf{Adv}_{\mathcal{B}_2}^{\mathsf{IND\text{-}CPA}}(\kappa) + \mathsf{Adv}_{\mathcal{B}_3}^{\mathsf{V3S\text{-}sound}}(\kappa)$$
$$+ N \cdot \mathsf{Adv}_{\mathcal{B}_4}^{\mathsf{V3S\text{-}fk}}(\kappa) + \mathsf{Adv}_{\mathcal{B}_5}^{\mathsf{Leak\text{-}TH\text{-}UF}}(\kappa)$$
$$+ 4N \cdot \varepsilon + N \cdot \Pr[\text{V3S correctness}]$$

5.2 Robust Distributed Signing Procedure

We present as a second application of our result an efficient lattice-based robust threshold signature based on standard assumptions. It provides additional guarantees over the existing threshold schemes such as threshold Raccoon [26] which provides unforgeability, but no guarantee of termination.

Assuming the existence of an authenticated reliable *broadcast channel*, and that at least 2/3 of the parties are honest, it ensures that the signature protocol will produce a valid signature.

5.2.1 Description of Pelican
Pelican was drafted in the Technical Overview, in Sect. 2.3. It relies on a symmetric encryption scheme SKE, a signature scheme SIG, and a Verifiable Short Secret Sharing V3S.

Our informal description of Pelican easily translates to formal algorithms, described in Figs. 6 and 7.

Robustness of Pelican. The *robustness* property of Pelican lies in its ability to generate signatures even in the presence of malicious signers. We prove it when Pelican is used over a broadcast channel by following the methodology of [22] with successive rounds. The robustness of Pelican is stated in Theorem 6, which is proven in the full version of our paper.

Theorem 6. *Assume that selected parameters are such that we have $\|(z_1, z_2, c_1)\| \leq B_2$ with overwhelming probability p for any set valid, $\mathbf{p} =$*

Algorithm 11 Pelican.ShareSign$_1$(state$_i$, sid, msg)

1: **assert**{ state$_i$.session[sid] does not exist }
2: $\mathbf{p}_i \leftarrow \mathcal{D}_\mathbf{p}^2$
3: $[\![\mathbf{p}_i]\!], \pi_i, (\pi_{i \to j})_{j \in \{1,...,N\}} \leftarrow$ V3S.Share$(N, T, \mathbf{p}_i)$
4: **if** $\exists j$ s.t. V3S.Verify$([\![\mathbf{p}_j]\!], \pi_j, \pi_{j \to i}) =$ false **then**
5:    **restart**   ▷ Restart if the V3S produced an invalid proof
6: **for** $j \in \{1, ..., N\}$ **do**
7:    $\mathsf{ct}_{i \to j} \leftarrow$ SKE.Encrypt$(\mathsf{K}_{i \to j}, ([\![\mathbf{p}_i]\!]_j, \pi_{i \to j}))$
8: state$_i$.session[sid] := {rnd = 1, msg, $[\![\mathbf{p}_i]\!], \varnothing, \varnothing$}
9: **return** contrib$_1[i] := (\pi_i, (\mathsf{ct}_{i \to j})_{j \in \{1,...,N\}})$

Algorithm 12 Pelican.ShareSign$_2$(state$_i$, sid, contrib$_1$)

1: Fetch (rnd, msg) from state$_i$.session[sid]
2: **assert**{ rnd = 1 }
3: complaints$_i$:= {}
4: **for** $(j \in $ contrib$_1)$ **do**
5:    $\pi_j, (\mathsf{ct}_{j \to k})_{k \in \{1,...,N\}} :=$ contrib$_1[j]$
6:    $[\![\mathbf{p}_j]\!]_i, \pi_{j \to i} :=$ SKE.Decrypt$(\mathsf{K}_{j \to i}, \mathsf{ct}_{j \to i})$
7:    **if** (SKE.Decrypt failed) **or** (V3S.Verify$([\![\mathbf{p}_j]\!]_i, \pi_j, \pi_{j \to i}) =$ false) **then**
8:       complaints$_i[j] = \{\mathsf{K}_{j \to i}, \mathsf{sig}_{j \to i}\}$ ▷ j's ciphertext or proof is invalid
9: valid$_i = \{j \in $ contrib$_1\} \setminus$ complaints$_i$
10: state$_i$.session[sid] := {rnd = 2, msg, $([\![\mathbf{p}_j]\!]_i)_{j \in \mathsf{valid}_i}$, valid$_i$, contrib$_1$}
11: **return** contrib$_2[i] :=$ complaints$_i$

Algorithm 13 Pelican.ShareSign$_3$(state$_i$, sid, contrib$_2$)

1: Fetch (rnd, msg, $([\![\mathbf{p}_j]\!]_i)_{j \in \mathsf{valid}_i}$, valid$_i$, contrib$_1$) from state$_i$.session[sid]
2: **assert**{ rnd = 2 }
3: valid$_i :=$ valid$_i \cap \{j \in $ contrib$_2\}$
4: **for** $j \in \{1, ..., N\}$ **do**
5:    **for** $k \in$ complaints$_j$ **do**   ▷ Lines 6 to 11 study j's complaint against k
6:       $\{\mathsf{K}_{k \to j}, \mathsf{sig}_{k \to j}\} :=$ complaints$_j[k]$
7:       **if** SIG.Verify$(\mathsf{pk}_k, \mathsf{sig}_{k \to j}, \{k, j, \mathsf{K}_{k \to j}\}) =$ false **then**   ▷ See Section 5
8:          **continue**
9:       $[\![\mathbf{s}_k]\!]_j, \pi_{k \to j} :=$ SKE.Decrypt$(\mathsf{K}_{k \to j}, \mathsf{ct}_{k \to j})$
10:      **if** (SKE.Decrypt failed) **or** V3S.Verify$([\![\mathbf{p}_k]\!]_j, \pi_k, \pi_{k \to j}) =$ false **then**
11:         valid$_i = $ valid$_i \setminus \{k\}$
12: $[\![\mathbf{p}]\!]_i := \sum_{j \in \mathsf{valid}_i} [\![\mathbf{p}_j]\!]_i$ ▷ $\mathbf{p} = (p_1, p_2)$
13: state$_i$.session[sid] := {3, msg, $([\![\mathbf{p}_j]\!]_i)_{j \in \mathsf{valid}_i}$, valid$_i$, contrib$_1$}
14: **return** contrib$_3[i] := ([\![w]\!]_i := \mathbf{A} \cdot [\![\mathbf{p}]\!]_i)$ ▷ $\mathbf{A} = \begin{bmatrix} 1 & a & b \end{bmatrix}$

Fig. 6. Algorithms for robust threshold signature, part 1/2. For conciseness, we omit the parsing of (contrib$_i)_{i \in \{1,2\}}$ in Algorithms 12 and 13.

Algorithm 14 Pelican.ShareSign$_4$(state$_i$, sid, contrib$_3$)

1: Fetch (rnd, msg, $(\llbracket \mathbf{p}_j \rrbracket_i)_{j \in \text{valid}_i}$, valid$_i$, contrib$_1$) from state$_i$.session[sid]
2: **assert**{ rnd = 3 }
3: Parse contrib$_3$ = $(\llbracket w \rrbracket_j)_j$
4: $w :=$ V3S.RobustReconstruct$((\llbracket w \rrbracket_j)_{j \in \text{valid}_i})$ ▷ $w = \mathbf{A} \cdot \mathbf{p}$, where $\mathbf{p} = \sum_{j \in \text{valid}_i} \mathbf{p}_j$
5: salt := $H_{\text{salt}}(w)$
6: $u := H_u(\text{vk}, \text{salt}, \text{msg}) \in \mathcal{R}_q$ ▷ Hash the message msg to a random $u \in \mathcal{R}_q$
7: $c := u - w$
8: $(c_1, c_2) :=$ Decompose$_\beta(c)$ ▷ Recall $c = \beta \cdot c_1 + c_2$
9: $\llbracket z \rrbracket_i := c_1 \cdot \llbracket s \rrbracket_i + \llbracket p_2 \rrbracket_i$ ▷ Recall $\mathbf{s} = (e, s)$ and $\mathbf{p} = (p_1, p_2)$
10: state$_i$.session[sid] := $\varnothing$
11: **return** contrib$_4[i] = (\text{salt}, \llbracket z \rrbracket_i, c_1)$

Algorithm 15 Pelican.Combine(vk, msg, contrib$_4$)

1: Parse contrib$_4$ = (salt$_j$, $\llbracket z \rrbracket_j$, c_1)$_j$
2: Retrieve salt, c_1 from contrib$_3$ ▷ If contradictory contributions: majority vote
3: $u = H_u(\text{vk}, \text{salt}, \text{msg}) \in \mathcal{R}_q$
4: $z :=$ V3S.RobustReconstruct$((\llbracket z \rrbracket_j)_{j \in \text{contrib}_4})$
5: **return** sig := (salt, z, c_1)

Algorithm 16 Pelican.Verify(vk = (seed, b), msg, sig = (salt, z, c_1))

1: $a := H_a(\text{seed}) \in \mathcal{R}_q$
2: $u := H_u(\text{vk}, \text{salt}, \text{msg}) \in \mathcal{R}_q$
3: $z_2 := z$
4: $z_1 := u - a \cdot z_2 - b \cdot c_1$
5: **return** $\|(z_1, z_2, c_1)\| \leq B_2$

Fig. 7. Algorithms for robust threshold signature, part 2/2. For conciseness, we omit the parsing of (contrib$_i$)$_{i \in \{1,3,4\}}$, vk and sig in Algorithms 14 to 16.

$\sum_{j \in \text{valid}} \mathbf{p}_j$ with (i) at most $T-1$ arbitrary perturbations of norm bounded by B, (ii) the others sampled from Gaussians of standard deviation $\sigma_{\mathbf{p}}$, and over the distribution of keys. Recall that $(z_1, z_2, c_1) = \begin{bmatrix} c_1 \cdot \mathbf{s} + \mathbf{p} \\ c_1 \end{bmatrix} + \begin{bmatrix} c_2 \\ 0 \\ 0 \end{bmatrix}$.

The advantage of any polynomial-time adversary $\mathcal{A}$ making at most Q_s signing queries in the game TH-RB, formalized in the full version, is bounded by

$$N \cdot \text{Adv}_{\mathcal{B}_1}^{\text{UF-CMA}}(\kappa) + \text{Adv}_{\mathcal{B}_2}^{\text{V3S-sound}}(\kappa) + NQ_s \cdot (1 - \Pr[\text{V3S correctness}]) + (1-p)$$

where $\mathcal{B}_1$ is an adversary against the UF-CMA security of SIG, $\mathcal{B}_2$ is an adversary against the V3S-sound security of V3S, with running time $T_{\mathcal{B}_1} \approx T_{\mathcal{B}_2} \approx T_{\mathcal{A}}$.

Unforgeability of Pelican. Importantly, we also want our scheme to remain unforgeable in the presence of dishonest signers. The unforgeability of our scheme is stated in Theorem 7, which is proven in the full version of our paper.

Theorem 7. *Define* $\sigma'_\mathbf{p}$ *as* $\frac{1}{\sigma_\mathbf{p}'^2} = 2\left(\frac{1}{\sigma_\mathbf{p}^2} + \frac{B}{\sigma_\mathbf{y}^2}\right)$, *with* B *such that* $s_1(\mathbf{R}^\top\mathbf{R}) \leqslant B$ *with overwhelming probability and* $\sigma'_\mathbf{p} \geqslant \sqrt{2}\eta_\varepsilon(\mathbb{Z}^{2n})$.

Pelican *is* TH-UF *secure in the random oracle model.*

Formally, let $\mathcal{A}$ *be an adversary against the* TH-UF *security game, formally introduced in the full version, starting at most* Q_s *signing sessions, and making at most* Q_H *random oracles queries.*

Then there exists adversaries $\mathcal{B}_1$ *against the* UF-CMA *security of* SIG, $\mathcal{B}_2$ *against the* IND-CPA *security of* SKE, $\mathcal{B}_3$ *against the* V3S-sound *security of* V3S, $\mathcal{B}_4$ *against the* V3S-fk *security of* V3S, $\mathcal{B}_5$ *against* Hint-RLWE$_{q,Q_{\text{Sign}},\mathcal{D}_{\sigma_t},\mathcal{D}_{\sigma'_\mathbf{p}},\mathcal{C}_1}$, $\mathcal{B}_6$ *against* RLWE$_{q,\mathcal{U}([-B_2/\sqrt{2n},B_2/\sqrt{2n}]^n)^2}$, $\mathcal{B}_7$ *against* RSIS$_{q,2,2B_2}$, *and running time* $T_{\mathcal{B}_i} \approx T_\mathcal{A}$ *for* $i \in \{1,\dots,7\}$, *such that*

$$\mathrm{Adv}_\mathcal{A}^{\text{TH-UF}}(\kappa) \leqslant N \cdot \mathrm{Adv}_{\mathcal{B}_1}^{\text{UF-CMA}}(\kappa) + N^2 \cdot \mathrm{Adv}_{\mathcal{B}_2}^{\text{IND-CPA}}(\kappa) + \mathrm{Adv}_{\mathcal{B}_3}^{\text{V3S-sound}}(\kappa)$$
$$+ Q_s \cdot N \cdot \mathrm{Adv}_{\mathcal{B}_4}^{\text{V3S-fk}}(\kappa) + N \cdot Q_s \cdot (1 - \Pr[\text{V3S } correctness])$$
$$+ \mathrm{Adv}_{\mathcal{B}_5}^{\text{Hint-RLWE}}(\kappa) + Q_H \cdot \mathrm{Adv}_{\mathcal{B}_6}^{\text{RLWE}}(\kappa) + \mathrm{Adv}_{\mathcal{B}_7}^{\text{RSIS}}(\kappa)$$
$$+ \frac{Q_s}{2^{2\kappa}} + 4Q_sN \cdot \varepsilon + Q_s \cdot 2^{-n+2} + p_c$$

for some $p_c \leqslant 2^{-n(2\log_2(2B_2/\sqrt{2n})-\log_2(q))}$.

6 Parameter Selection and Instantiation

We now move on to instantiation of our constructions. The main component required is a proper distribution of matrices $\mathbf{R}$ verifying property G from Definition 8. We chose to leverage matrices $\mathbf{R} \in \{0,\pm1\}^{256\times 2n}$ where each coefficient of $\mathbf{R}$ is 0 with probability $1/2$, and ± 1 with probability $1/4$. They have strong distribution properties, and have been already successfully applied in [15,23]. We note this distribution $\mathcal{D}_\mathbf{R}$. We will rely on Lemmas 2 to 4. Proofs are included in the full version.

Lemma 2 (Large Norm Detection, Lemma 3.2.5 from [23]). *Fix* $n, q \in \mathbb{N}$, *and a bound* $b \leqslant q/(82n)$, *and let* $\mathbf{s} \in [\pm q/2]^{2n}$, *with* $\|\mathbf{s}\|_2 \geqslant b$. *Let* $\mathbf{y} \in [\pm q/2]^{256}$. *Then* $\Pr_{\mathbf{R}\leftarrow\mathcal{D}_\mathbf{R}}\left[\|\mathbf{R}\cdot\mathbf{s}+\mathbf{y} \bmod q\|_2 < \frac{1}{2}b\sqrt{26}\right] < 2^{-128}$.

Lemma 3 (separation). *Fix* $n, q \in \mathbb{N}$, *and* $(\mathbf{s},\mathbf{y}) \neq (\mathbf{s}',\mathbf{y}') \in [\pm q/2]^{2n+256}$. *Then* $\Pr_{\mathbf{R}\leftarrow\mathcal{D}_\mathbf{R}}[\mathbf{R}\cdot\mathbf{s}+\mathbf{y} = \mathbf{R}\cdot\mathbf{s}'+\mathbf{y}' \bmod q] \leqslant 2^{-256}$.

Lemma 4 (small spectral norm). *Fix* $n, q \in \mathbb{N}$ *and* $\mathbf{R} \in \{0,\pm1\}^{256\times 2n}$. $s_1(\mathbf{R}^\top\mathbf{R}) \leqslant 512 \cdot n$. *For fixed values of* n, *we can obtain better average bounds. For* $n = 2048$,

$$\Pr_{\mathbf{R}\leftarrow\mathcal{D}_\mathbf{R}}\left[s_1(\mathbf{R}^\top\mathbf{R}) < 20096\right] \geqslant 1 - 2^{-142}$$

6.1 Reminder: Parameter Selection in Plover

In the (standard) signature scheme Plover, a signature is essentially a pair $(\mathsf{salt}, \mathbf{z} = (z_1, z_2, c_1)^t)$, where $\mathbf{z}$ is of the form:

$$\mathbf{z} = \begin{bmatrix} e \\ s \\ 1 \end{bmatrix} \cdot c_1 + \begin{bmatrix} p_1 \\ p_2 \\ 0 \end{bmatrix} + \begin{bmatrix} c_2 \\ 0 \\ 0 \end{bmatrix}$$

One can see that $\begin{bmatrix} 1 & a & b \end{bmatrix} \cdot \mathbf{z} = H(\mathsf{vk}, \mathsf{salt}, \mathsf{msg})$. Following the analysis of [12, Section 3.5], and assuming $\sigma_{\mathsf{sk}} = \frac{\beta^2}{q\sqrt{2n}}$:

$$\mathbb{E}\left[\|\mathbf{z}\|^2\right] \approx n\left(2\sigma_{\mathsf{p}}^2 + \frac{\beta^2}{12} + \frac{q^2 n}{6\beta^2}\sigma_{\mathsf{sk}}^2\right) \approx 2n\left(\sigma_{\mathsf{p}}^2 + \frac{\beta^2}{12}\right)$$

Following the security reduction of [12], Plover is unforgeable under the $\mathsf{RSIS}_{q,\ell,B_2}$ and $\mathsf{Hint\text{-}RLWE}_{q,Q_{\mathsf{Sign}},\mathcal{D}_{\mathsf{sk}},\mathcal{D}_{\mathsf{p}},\mathcal{C}_1}$ assumptions. In our case, all distributions are Gaussians, so that $\mathsf{Hint\text{-}RLWE}_{q,Q_{\mathsf{Sign}},\sigma_{\mathsf{sk}},\sigma_{\mathsf{p}},\mathcal{C}_1} \geqslant \mathsf{RLWE}_{q,\sigma_{\mathsf{red}}}$, where $\frac{1}{\sigma_{\mathsf{red}}^2} = 2\left(\frac{1}{\sigma_{\mathsf{sk}}^2} + \frac{B_{\mathsf{HRLWE}}}{\sigma_{\mathsf{p}}^2}\right) \approx \frac{2B_{\mathsf{HRLWE}}}{\sigma_{\mathsf{p}}^2}$, where $B_{\mathsf{HRLWE}} \approx \frac{n Q_{\mathsf{Sign}} q^2}{12\beta^2}$, see Lemma 2 in [12]. If $\sigma_{\mathsf{p}} = o(\beta\sqrt{Q_{\mathsf{Sign}}})$, then $\sigma_{\mathsf{sk}} = \omega(\frac{\sigma_{\mathsf{p}}}{\sqrt{B_{\mathsf{HRLWE}}}})$ and therefore $\sigma_{\mathsf{red}} \sim \frac{\sigma_{\mathsf{p}}}{\sqrt{2}\cdot B_{\mathsf{HRLWE}}}$. Fig. 8.

$$\{\mathsf{RLWE}\}\{\mathsf{Hint\text{-}RLWE} \geqslant \mathsf{RLWE}\ (\text{Thm. 1})\}$$

| σ_{red} | $\sqrt{n/6}\cdot(q/\beta)$ | $\sqrt{Q_{\mathsf{Sign}}}$ | q/β |

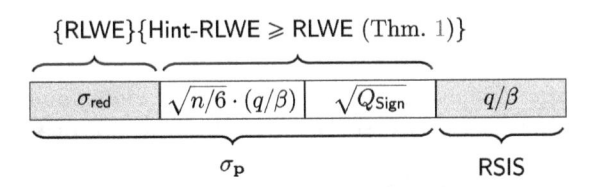

$\underbrace{}_{\sigma_{\mathsf{p}}}\ \underbrace{}_{\mathsf{RSIS}}$

Fig. 8. Constraints on the modulus q in Plover [12]. We represent q in logarithmic scale. Each constraint adds an overhead to the mimimum size of q. As a rule of thumb, dimensions must scale in $\tilde{O}(\log q)$ for security, and as a result the cryptosystem's bitsizes scale in $\tilde{O}((\log q)^2)$.

6.2 Parameter Selection for the Signing Procedure of Pelican

Parameter selection for Pelican is much more involved than for Plover. Note that a parameter set defined for a threshold T also supports any $1 \leqslant T' \leqslant T$ with the same security and verification procedure. We thus limit our analysis to an upper bound T on supported thresholds, while ensuring that Pelican is interchangeable[4]. It is achieved by increasing σ_{sk} and σ_{p} by a factor $\sqrt{T/T'}$. Parameter selection for Pelican can be fairly delicate since we need to balance several (sometimes conflicting) conditions. Therefore we present in Table 1 the relationship between parameters (modulus, dimensions, etc.) and security metrics (RLWE, RSIS, etc.).

---

[4] Interchangeability guarantees that a threshold scheme has static public parameters for any supported threshold and number of parties.

Table 1. Relationship between the parameters of Pelican and the associated security and efficiency metrics. For the cell in the X-th row and Y-th column, we use the symbol ↗ (resp. ↘, resp. ≈) to indicate that increasing the parameter X has a positive (resp. negative, resp. limited) influence on the metric Y. Note that the signature size increases logarithmically in the maximum values of T and Q_{Sign}, but the public key size can be made essentially independent of them using appropriate bit-dropping, see Sect. 6.4.

Parameter	RLWE	{Hint-RLWE ⩾ RLWE}	RSIS	V3S Slack	Public key bitsize	Signature bitsize
q	↘	≈	↗	≈	↘	≈
n	↗	↘	↗	≈	↘	↘
σ_{sk}	↗	≈	≈	≈	↗	≈
$\sigma_{\mathbf{p}}$	↗	↗	↘	≈	≈	↘
q/β	≈	↘	↗	≈	≈	↘
T	≈	↗	↗	↗	≈	↘
Q_{Sign}	≈	↘	≈	≈	≈	↘

Let us fix an upper bound T on supported thresholds. For simplicity, we assume here that the set of signers S satisfies $|S| = 3T$;[5] our analysis is easily extended to other values of $|S|$. For our choice of S, at least $2/3$ of the users are honest, so that the vector $\mathbf{p} = \sum_{i \in S} \mathbf{p}_i$ contains at least $2T$ vectors that are unknown to the set of corrupted users; as a benefit, the Hint-RLWE reduction can support $\sqrt{2T}$ more queries.

The signing procedure of Pelican (Figs. 6 and 7) provides, for each $(\mathbf{p}_i)_{i \in [Q_{\text{Sign}}]}$, a V3S proof which contains $\mathbf{v}_i = \mathbf{R} \cdot \mathbf{p}_i + \mathbf{y}_i$. This has two consequences:

1. The V3S proves a slightly looser bound on the norm of $\mathbf{p}_i$.
2. The pair $(\mathbf{R}_i, \mathbf{v}_i = \mathbf{R} \cdot \mathbf{p}_i + \mathbf{y}_i, i)$ biases the conditional distribution of $\mathbf{p}_i$.

Slack of the V3S. Lemma 2 tells us that $\frac{\sqrt{26}}{2} \|\mathbf{p}_i\| \leq \|\mathbf{v}_i\|$ with overwhelming probability. On the other hand, [23, Lemma 3.2.4] tells us:

$$\|\mathbf{v}_i\| \leq \|\mathbf{R}_i \cdot \mathbf{p} + \mathbf{y}\| \leq \sqrt{337} \cdot \|\mathbf{p}\| + \|\mathbf{y}\|, \tag{5}$$

where τ is a value such that $\mathbb{P}_{\mathbf{x} \leftarrow \mathcal{D}_{\sigma_{\mathbf{p}}}^{256}}[\|\mathbf{x}\| \geq \tau \sigma_{\mathbf{p}} \sqrt{256}] \leq 2^{-128}$, here $\tau \leq 1.4$. If we set $\sigma_{\mathbf{y}} = \sqrt{337} \cdot \sigma_{\mathbf{p}}$ and note $\text{SLACK}_{\text{V3S}} = \tau \sqrt{337} \frac{2}{\sqrt{26}} \approx 10$, our V3S proves:

$$\|\mathbf{p}_i\| \leq \text{SLACK}_{\text{V3S}} \cdot (\sigma_{\mathbf{p}} \sqrt{2n}) \tag{6}$$

There is a gap $\text{SLACK}_{\text{V3S}}$ between the expected norm of $\mathbf{p}_i$, which is $\sigma_{\mathbf{p}} \sqrt{2n}$, and the norm that is actually proven, which is the one in Eq. (6). While $\text{SLACK}_{\text{V3S}}$ is constant due to the lemmas we use, increasing the security parameter κ will also increase $\text{SLACK}_{\text{V3S}}$. In order to have robustness, we need to use the latter

---

[5] If $|S| < 2T$, then we still have unforgeability but the V3S can no longer detect dishonest users. Taking $|S| > 3T$ is also of limited interest since it cannot detect more than $T - 1$ dishonest users.

norm in our verification procedure. In addition, S perturbations $\mathbf{p}_i$ are added in the signature and this needs to be taken into account. Therefore we pick this bound on the norm in the verification procedure:

$$B_2 = |S| \cdot \text{SLACK}_{\text{V3S}} \cdot (\sigma_{\mathbf{p}}\sqrt{2n}) \tag{7}$$

Leakage from the V3S. The pair $(\mathbf{R}_i, \mathbf{v}_i = \mathbf{R}_i \cdot \mathbf{p}_i + \mathbf{y}_i)$ is a hint on the value of $\mathbf{p}_i$. More precisely, Lemma 1 tells us that the conditional distribution of $\mathbf{p}_i$ conditioned on $(\mathbf{R}_i, \mathbf{v}_i)$ follows a (non-spherical) Gaussian $D_{\mathcal{R}^2, \mathbf{c}, \sqrt{\Sigma_0}}$, where:

$$\Sigma_0^{-1} := \sigma_{\mathbf{p}}^{-2} \cdot \mathbf{I} + \sigma_{\mathbf{y}}^{-2} \cdot \mathbf{R}_i^\top \mathbf{R}_i \tag{8}$$

Theorem 7 tells us that we can safely use an isotropic Gaussian from each $\mathbf{p}_i$ of standard deviation $\sigma'_{\mathbf{p}}$ verifying $\frac{1}{\sigma_{\mathbf{p}}^{\prime 2}} = \frac{1}{\sigma_{\mathbf{p}}^2} + \frac{s_1(\mathbf{R}_i^\top \mathbf{R}_i)}{\sigma_y^2}$ (we ignore the factor 2 which could be removed in the proof using Theorem 2).

Recall that according to Lemma 4, for $n = 2048$, we have $s_1(\mathbf{R}_i^\top \mathbf{R}_i) < 20096$ with overwhelming probability. Combining this with Eq. (8) and the fact that $\sigma_{\mathbf{y}} = \sqrt{337} \cdot \sigma_{\mathbf{p}}$, the usable part of perturbations $\mathbf{p}_i$ for $n = 2048$ has a standard deviation $\sigma'_{\mathbf{p}} = \Theta(\sigma_{\mathbf{p}})$ since:

$$\sigma'_{\mathbf{p}} := \left(\sigma_{\mathbf{p}}^{-2} + \sigma_{\mathbf{y}}^{-2} \cdot 20096\right)^{-1/2} \approx \sqrt{\frac{337}{20096}} \cdot \sigma_{\mathbf{p}} \approx \frac{1}{\sqrt{60}} \cdot \sigma_{\mathbf{p}} \tag{9}$$

Reduction from Hint-RLWE *to* RLWE. Hints on the secrets are masked with the sum of the honest perturbations. The resulting perturbation has standard deviation $\sqrt{|\text{honest}|} \cdot \sigma'_{\mathbf{p}}$, where $|\text{honest}| \geq \frac{2}{3}|S| = 2T$. The analysis of Plover thus adapts with $\sigma_{\text{red}} \sim \frac{\sqrt{T} \cdot \sigma'_{\mathbf{p}}}{\sqrt{2} \cdot B_{\text{HRLWE}}}$ (Fig. 9).

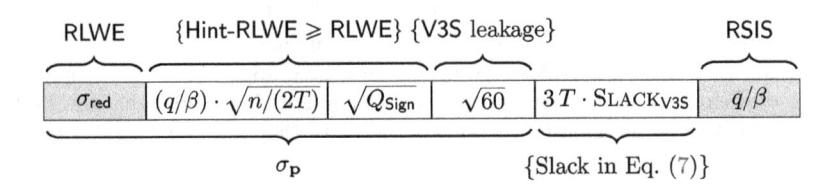

RLWE	{Hint-RLWE ⩾ RLWE}	{V3S leakage}		RSIS
σ_{red}	$(q/\beta) \cdot \sqrt{n/(2T)}$	$\sqrt{Q_{\text{Sign}}}$	$\sqrt{60}$	$3T \cdot \text{SLACK}_{\text{V3S}}$	q/β
	$\sigma_{\mathbf{p}}$			{Slack in Eq. (7)}	

Fig. 9. Constraints on the modulus q in Pelican. We represent q in logarithmic scale. Each constraint adds an overhead to the mimimum size of q.

6.3 Distributed Key Generation

Parameter selection for our DKG is analogous to the signing procedure of Pelican. Similarly, the resulting σ_{sk} usable in the Hint-MLWE reduction after revealing $\mathbf{R}_i \cdot \mathbf{s}_i + \mathbf{y}_i$ is $\sigma'_{\text{sk}} := \frac{\sqrt{2T}}{\sqrt{60}} \sigma_{\text{sk}}$.

However, since σ_p was selected so that $s_1(\mathbf{R}) \cdot \sigma_{sk}$ is negligible compared to σ_p, the norm of $\mathbf{R} \cdot \mathbf{s}$ remains negligible compared to the norm of $\mathbf{p}$ even with the slack of the V3S on the bound on $\|\mathbf{s}\|$, and the norm of the signatures produced by our scheme is not affected by our V3S. Hence, we simply need to ensure that Hint-MLWE remains hard with σ'_{sk}.

6.4 Selected Parameter Sets

We rely on the lattice estimator [2] – an open-source tool available at https://github.com/malb/lattice-estimator – for estimating the concrete hardness of RLWE. We provide three possible parameter sets in Table 2, providing different tradeoffs between security, size, and the maximum supported threshold.

Note that in order to use Lemma 2, we need to fulfill the condition $b \leqslant q/(82n)$. It would be inefficient to increase q in the entire scheme for this, and we instead introduce q_{V3S} a multiple of q, for use during V3S secret sharing. Local shares are later reduced mod q before use in round 3 and 4.

We express the communication cost per party in round 1 as a function of T. It increases linearly with T as our V3S broadcasts an entire sharing. The total communication cost of our protocol hence evolves quadratically T. We recall that the bytesizes of vk and sig are computed as:

$$8 \cdot |\mathsf{vk}| = 2 \cdot \kappa + n \lceil \log_2 q \rceil \tag{10}$$
$$8 \cdot |\mathsf{sig}| \approx 2 \cdot \kappa + n \lceil \log_2(T \cdot \sigma_\mathbf{p}) \rceil + n \lceil \log_2(q/\beta) \rceil \tag{11}$$

This omits the optimization that consists of performing bit-dropping in vk. The formula for $|\mathsf{sig}|$ is approximate since it depends on the exact encoding used for the vector z.

Table 2. Parameter sets for Pelican. We showcase parameter sets for different security levels κ, and value of T. We take $N = 3T$, $q \approx 2^{50}$ and $\sigma_{sk} \approx 2^{20}$. All sizes are in kilobytes (kB). We indicate the core-SVP hardness of Hint-RLWE and RSIS, a metric which ignores several polynomial factors. We also give approximate communication cost per participant in each round of key generation and threshold signature, excluding authentication of broadcast communication. Note that round 4 happens only for signature generation.

κ	n	$\log \beta$	$\lfloor q_{V3S} \rfloor$	T	$\sigma_\mathbf{p}$	Q_{Sign}	$|\mathsf{vk}|$	$|\mathsf{sig}|$	Hint-RLWE C/Q	RSIS C/Q	comm. per party rnd$_1$	rnd$_3$	rnd$_4$
128	2048	43	2^{65}	16	2^{32}	2^{36}	12.8	12.3	113/99	113/99	$56T$	12.8	14
192	4096	43	2^{68}	1024	2^{31}	2^{48}	25.6	26.4	227/199	222/195	$115T$	25.6	28.2
256	4096	45	2^{70}	64	2^{33}	2^{48}	25.6	25.1	251/220	249/219	$119T$	25.6	27.4

References

1. Agrawal, S., Stehlé, D., Yadav, A.: Round-optimal lattice-based threshold signatures, revisited. In: Bojanczyk, M., Merelli, E., Woodruff, D.P. (eds.) ICALP 2022. LIPIcs, vol. 229, pp. 1–20. Schloss Dagstuhl (Jul 2022). https://doi.org/10.4230/LIPIcs.ICALP.2022.8
2. Albrecht, M.R., Player, R., Scott, S.: On the concrete hardness of learning with errors. J. Math. Cryptol. **9**(3), 169–203 (2015). http://www.degruyter.com/view/j/jmc.2015.9.issue-3/jmc-2015-0016/jmc-2015-0016.xml
3. Atapoor, S., Baghery, K., Cozzo, D., Pedersen, R.: VSS from distributed ZK proofs and applications. In: Guo, J., Steinfeld, R. (eds.) Advances in Cryptology – ASIACRYPT 2023: 29th International Conference on the Theory and Application of Cryptology and Information Security, Guangzhou, China, December 4–8, 2023, Proceedings, Part I, pp. 405–440. Springer Nature Singapore, Singapore (2023). https://doi.org/10.1007/978-981-99-8721-4_13
4. Ben-Or, M., Goldwasser, S., Wigderson, A.: Completeness theorems for non-cryptographic fault-tolerant distributed computation (extended abstract). In: 20th ACM STOC, pp. 1–10. ACM Press (May 1988). https://doi.org/10.1145/62212.62213
5. Jacobson, Michael, Locasto, Michael, Mohassel, Payman, Safavi-Naini, Reihaneh (eds.): Applied Cryptography and Network Security: 11th International Conference, ACNS 2013, Banff, AB, Canada, June 25-28, 2013. Proceedings. Springer Berlin Heidelberg, Berlin, Heidelberg (2013)
6. Boneh, D., Gennaro, R., Goldfeder, S., Jain, A., Kim, S., Rasmussen, P.M.R., Sahai, A.: Threshold cryptosystems from threshold fully homomorphic encryption. In: Shacham, H., Boldyreva, A. (eds.) CRYPTO 2018, Part I. LNCS, vol. 10991, pp. 565–596. Springer, Heidelberg (Aug 2018). https://doi.org/10.1007/978-3-319-96884-1_19
7. Brandão, L.T.A.N., Peralta, R.: Nist first call for multi-party threshold schemes. NIST Internal Report (IR) 8214C, National Institute of Standards and Technology (January 2023). https://doi.org/10.6028/NIST.IR.8214C.ipd, https://doi.org/10.6028/NIST.IR.8214C.ipd, initial Public Draft
8. Chor, B., Goldwasser, S., Micali, S., Awerbuch, B.: Verifiable secret sharing and achieving simultaneity in the presence of faults. In: 26th Annual Symposium on Foundations of Computer Science (sfcs 1985), pp. 383–395. IEEE (1985)
9. del Pino, R., Espitau, T., Katsumata, S., Maller, M., Mouhartem, F., Prest, T., Rossi, M., Saarinen, M.: Raccoon. Tech. rep., National Institute of Standards and Technology (2023). https://csrc.nist.gov/Projects/pqc-dig-sig/round-1-additional-signatures.
10. Desmedt, Y.: Abuses in cryptography and how to fight them. In: Goldwasser, S. (ed.) CRYPTO'88, LNCS, vol. 403, pp. 375–389. Springer, Heidelberg (Aug 1990). https://doi.org/10.1007/0-387-34799-2_29
11. Desmedt, Y., Frankel, Y.: Threshold cryptosystems. In: Brassard, G. (ed.) CRYPTO'89. LNCS, vol. 435, pp. 307–315. Springer, Heidelberg (Aug 1990). https://doi.org/10.1007/0-387-34805-0_28
12. Esgin, M., Espitau, T., Niot, G., Prest, T., Sakzad, A., Steinfeld, R.: Plover: Masking-friendly hash-and-sign lattice signatures. In: EUROCRYPT (2024). https://tprest.github.io/pdf/pub/plover.pdf
13. Gennaro, R., Jarecki, S., Krawczyk, H., Rabin, T.: Robust threshold DSS signatures. In: Maurer, U.M. (ed.) EUROCRYPT'96, LNCS, vol. 1070, pp. 354–371. Springer, Heidelberg (May 1996). https://doi.org/10.1007/3-540-68339-9_31

14. Gennaro, R., Rabin, T., Jarecki, S., Krawczyk, H.: Robust and efficient sharing of RSA functions. J. Cryptol. **13**(2), 273–300 (2000). https://doi.org/10.1007/s001459910011
15. Gentry, C., Halevi, S., Lyubashevsky, V.: Practical non-interactive publicly verifiable secret sharing with thousands of parties. In: Dunkelman, O., Dziembowski, S. (eds.) EUROCRYPT 2022, Part I. LNCS, vol. 13275, pp. 458–487. Springer, Heidelberg (May/Jun 2022). https://doi.org/10.1007/978-3-031-06944-4_16
16. Gentry, C., Peikert, C., Vaikuntanathan, V.: Trapdoors for hard lattices and new cryptographic constructions. In: Ladner, R.E., Dwork, C. (eds.) 40th ACM STOC, pp. 197–206. ACM Press (May 2008). https://doi.org/10.1145/1374376.1374407
17. Gur, K.D., Katz, J., Silde, T.: Two-round threshold lattice signatures from threshold homomorphic encryption. Cryptol. ePrint Arch. Paper **2023**, 1318 (2023). https://eprint.iacr.org/2023/1318, https://eprint.iacr.org/2023/1318
18. Ji, Y., Tao, Y., Zhang, R.: Robust (t, n)-threshold lattice signature (2023). https://doi.org/10.2139/ssrn.4588269, http://dx.doi.org/10.2139/ssrn.4588269
19. Johnson, W.B., Lindenstrauss, J., Schechtman, G.: Extensions of Lipschitz maps into Banach spaces. Israel J. Math. **54**(2), 129–138 (1986)
20. Kim, D., Lee, D., Seo, J., Song, Y.: Toward practical lattice-based proof of knowledge from hint-MLWE. In: Handschuh, H., Lysyanskaya, A. (eds.) CRYPTO 2023, Part V. LNCS, vol. 14085, pp. 549–580. Springer, Heidelberg (Aug 2023). https://doi.org/10.1007/978-3-031-38554-4_18
21. Komlo, C., Goldberg, I.: FROST: Flexible round-optimized Schnorr threshold signatures. In: Dunkelman, O., Jr., M.J.J., O'Flynn, C. (eds.) SAC 2020, LNCS, vol. 12804, pp. 34–65. Springer, Heidelberg (Oct 2020). https://doi.org/10.1007/978-3-030-81652-0_2
22. Komlo, C., Goldberg, I., Stebila, D.: A formal treatment of distributed key generation, and new constructions. Cryptol. ePrint Arch. Rep. **2023**, 292 (2023). https://eprint.iacr.org/2023/292
23. Nguyen, N.K.: Lattice-Based Zero-Knowledge Proofs Under a Few Dozen Kilobytes. Ph.D. thesis, ETH Zurich, Zürich, Switzerland (2022). https://doi.org/10.3929/ETHZ-B-000574844, https://hdl.handle.net/20.500.11850/574844
24. Paverd, A., Martin, A., Brown, I.: Modelling and automatically analysing privacy properties for honest-but-curious adversaries
25. Pedersen, T.P.: Non-interactive and information-theoretic secure verifiable secret sharing. In: Feigenbaum, J. (ed.) CRYPTO'91, LNCS, vol. 576, pp. 129–140. Springer, Heidelberg (Aug 1992). https://doi.org/10.1007/3-540-46766-1_9
26. Pino, R.D., Katsumata, S., Maller, M., Mouhartem, F., Prest, T., Saarinen, M.O.: Threshold raccoon: Practical threshold signatures from standard lattice assumptions (2024). https://eprint.iacr.org/2024/184
27. Ruffing, T., Ronge, V., Jin, E., Schneider-Bensch, J., Schröder, D.: ROAST: robust asynchronous schnorr threshold signatures. In: Yin, H., Stavrou, A., Cremers, C., Shi, E. (eds.) ACM CCS 2022, pp. 2551–2564. ACM Press (Nov 2022). https://doi.org/10.1145/3548606.3560583
28. Stadler, M.: Publicly verifiable secret sharing. In: Maurer, U.M. (ed.) EUROCRYPT'96, LNCS, vol. 1070, pp. 190–199. Springer, Heidelberg (May 1996). https://doi.org/10.1007/3-540-68339-9_17
29. Tang, G., Pang, B., Chen, L., Zhang, Z.: Efficient lattice-based threshold signatures with functional interchangeability. IEEE Trans. Inf. Forensics Secur. **18**, 4173–4187 (2023). https://doi.org/10.1109/TIFS.2023.3293408

Adaptively Secure 5 Round Threshold Signatures from MLWE/MSIS and DL with Rewinding

Shuichi Katsumata[1,2](✉), Michael Reichle[3], and Kaoru Takemure[1,2]

[1] PQShield, Ltd., Oxford, UK
`{shuichi.katsumata,kaoru.takemure}@pqshield.com`
[2] AIST, Tokyo, Japan
[3] ETH Zurich, Zurich, Switzerland
`michael.reichle@inf.ethz.ch`

Abstract. T-out-of-N threshold signatures have recently seen a renewed interest, with various types now available, each offering different tradeoffs. However, one property that has remained elusive is *adaptive* security. When we target thresholdizing existing efficient signatures schemes based on the Fiat-Shamir paradigm such as Schnorr, the elusive nature becomes clear. This class of signature schemes typically rely on the forking lemma to prove unforgeability. That is, an adversary is *rewound and run twice* within the security game. Such a proof is at odds with adaptive security, as the reduction must be ready to answer $2(T-1)$ secret key shares in total, implying that it can reconstruct the full secret key. Indeed, prior works either assumed strong idealized models such as the algebraic group model (AGM) or modified the underlying signature scheme so as not to rely on rewinding based proofs.

In this work, we propose a new proof technique to construct adaptively secure threshold signatures for existing rewinding-based Fiat-Shamir signatures. As a result, we obtain the following:

1. The first adaptively secure 5 round lattice-based threshold signature under the MLWE and MSIS assumptions in the ROM. The resulting signature is a standard signature of **Raccoon**, a lattice-based signature scheme by del Pino et al., submitted to the additional NIST call for proposals.

2. The first adaptively secure 5 round threshold signature under the DL assumption in the ROM. The resulting signature is a standard Schnorr signature. To the best of our knowledge, this is the first adaptively secure threshold signature based on DL even assuming stronger models like AGM.

Our work is inspired by the recent statically secure lattice-based 3 round threshold signature by del Pino et al. (Eurocrypt 2024) based on **Raccoon**. While they relied on so-called one-time additive masks to solve lattice specific issues, we notice that these masks can also be a useful tool to achieve adaptive security. At a very high level, we use these masks throughout the signing protocol to carefully control the information the adversary can learn from the signing transcripts. Intuitively, this allows the reduction to return a total of $2(T-1)$ *randomly sampled* secret key shares to the adversary consistently and without being detected, resolving the above paradoxical situation. Lastly, by allowing the parties to maintain a simple state, we can compress our 5 round schemes into 4 rounds.

1 Introduction

A T-out-of-N threshold signature [13,14] allows to distribute a secret key to N parties such that a set of at least T parties can jointly generate a signature with respect to the verification key. In particular, even if an adversary corrupts up to $T-1$ parties, it should not be possible to forge a signature. This ability to distribute trust has seen a renewed interest in the blockchain ecosystem where secure and reliable storage of secret keys are critical. With the increase in real-world interest, governmental bodies such as the US agency NIST has announced a standardization effort for multi-party threshold schemes [29].

In this work, we focus on thresholdizing existing signature schemes based on the Fiat-Shamir paradigm [16], e.g., ECDSA, Schnorr [32], Dilithium [15], Raccoon [31], a wide class of efficient signature schemes that has been a popular target to thresholdize in the literature.

Static vs Adaptive Security. Threshold signatures being a multi-party protocol, we have two choices when defining unforgeability: static and adaptive security. Static security artificially restricts the adversary to commit to all the $T-1$ parties it corrupts at the beginning of the security game. In contrast, adaptive security allows the adversary to arbitrarily corrupt up to $T-1$ parties as the security game progresses. Specifically, it may dynamically choose which party to corrupt even after observing the verification key, partial signatures, and the corrupted secret key shares of the other parties.

Adaptive security captures much more closely the threat model in reality, and as such, the recent call for threshold schemes by NIST [9,29] has put a strong preference on schemes satisfying it. Indeed, there are simple schemes that are statically secure but trivially non-adaptively secure [10], highlighting a fundamental difference in these two security models.

Difficulty of Adaptive Security (in the ROM). While adaptive security is the sought after security requirement, most prior works on threshold signatures have only been proven statically secure. However, this is not a simple lack of interest to prove adaptive security but rather a demonstration of the limit of our current proof technique. Signature schemes based on the Fiat-Shamir paradigm [16] typically rely on the forking lemma [6,16] to prove security in the random oracle model (ROM). At a high level, a proof using the forking lemma proceeds as follows: The reduction embeds a hard problem into the verification key and simulates the security game to the adversary. Once the adversary outputs a forgery, it *rewinds* the adversary and runs it again from some specific point in the security game by programming the random oracle differently. If the adversary outputs a forgery in the second run, the reduction is able to extract the solution to the hard problem using the two forgeries.

Now, consider what happens when we try to use this for adaptive security. The reduction needs to simulate $T-1$ secret key shares of the corrupted parties in the first *and* second run. Since the set of corrupted parties may change after rewinding, the reduction may need to simulate up to $2(T-1)$ secret key shares. However, if a simulator knew T (or more) of the secret key shares, it can generate forgeries without the adversary's help, thus breaking the hard problem on its own. This seemingly contradicts the hardness of the problem, indicating that such a security proof does not work. Here, such an issue does not appear in the static setting since the set of corrupted parties remain unchanged in the two runs.

State-of-the-Art. To overcome this apparent issue, Crites, Komlo, and Maller [12] considered a relaxed form of adaptive security where the adversary is limited to making either $T-1$ static or $(T-1)/2$ adaptive corruptions; the latter implies that the reduction only needs to simulate at most $T-1$ secret key shares in total. In this relaxed model, they proved security of their threshold Schnorr signature (Sparkle) under an interactive algebraic one-more DL (AOM-DL) assumption. More recently, Bacho et al. [3] proposed an adaptive threshold signature (Twinkle) under the DDH assumption. Their novel insight was to base Twinkle on a specific class of signature schemes based on identification protocols that avoided rewinding to prove unforgeability, drawing inspiration from [11,21]. A caveat though is that Twinkle no longer produces Schnorr signatures like Sparkle and requires a signature size that is twice as large.

It is also worth noting that another way to overcome the issue is to assume a stronger idealized model like the algebraic group model (AGM) [17]. Indeed, Crites et al. [12] showed that Sparkle is adaptively secure in the ROM and AGM under the AOM-DL assumption. However, this avenue of research seems quite grim for *post-quantum* threshold signatures like those based on lattices, since no such model is known to exist nor believed to hold in general.

This brings us to our main question of this work:

Can we construct an adaptively secure threshold signature scheme for existing rewinding-based Fiat-Shamir signatures? Moreover, can we base security under the same assumption?

We believe the latter question is also an important point if we were to deploy threshold signatures based on existing signature schemes. For example, an ideal situation would be to prove threshold Schnorr signature under the DL assumption in the ROM, similarly to the non-thresholdized Schnorr signature.

1.1 Our Contribution

We answer the above question affirmatively and propose a new proof technique to construct adaptively secure threshold signatures. As a result, we obtain the following:

Table 1. Comparison of T-out-of-N lattice-based threshold signatures.

Schemes	Adaptive?	Assumptions	Rounds	Model	Corruptions	Stateless session id?
[30]	✗	MLWE + MSIS[†]	3	ROM	$< T$	✗
[2]	✗	AOM-MLWE	2	ROM	$< T$	✓
TRaccoon$_{3\text{-rnd}}^{\text{sel}}$	✗	MLWE + MSIS	3	ROM	$< T$	✓
TRaccoon$_{4\text{-rnd}}^{\text{adp}}$	✓	MLWE + MSIS	4	ROM	$< T$	✗
TRaccoon$_{5\text{-rnd}}^{\text{adp}}$	✓	MLWE + MSIS	5	ROM	$< T$	✓

We omit schemes based on (linearly/fully) homomorphic encryption e.g., [1,8,18]. MLWE and MSIS stand for the module LWE and SIS, respectively. AOM-MLWE stands for the algebraic one-more MLWE. The (✓) in the column "Stateless session id?" indicates that the parties can be stateless. Else (✗), the parties need to store the session id's so as not to reuse them.

†: To be precise, they rely on the hint MLWE and self target MSIS problems, both of which are know to reduce from the MLWE and MSIS problem. The same can be said for our schemes.

1. The first adaptively secure 5 round lattice-based threshold signature under the MLWE and MSIS assumptions in the ROM. The resulting signature is a standard signature of Raccoon [31], a lattice-based signature scheme by del Pino et al., submitted to the additional NIST call for proposals [28]. We can easily make this 4 round by assuming a (non-repeating) unique session identifier sid being broadcast to the signing parties.
2. The first adaptively secure 5 round threshold signature under the DL assumption in the ROM. The resulting signature is a standard Schnorr signature. Making the same assumption as above, we can turn it into a 4 round protocol. We note this is the first adaptively secure threshold signature based on the DL assumption.

As a byproduct of our new proof technique, we also obtain the following lattice-based threshold signature:

3. A selectively secure 3 round lattice-based threshold signature under the MLWE and MSIS assumptions in the ROM. The resulting signature is a standard signature of Raccoon. This improves the very recent work by del Pino et al. [30] in two metrics: it removes the need for a stateful signing algorithm and improves the communication cost. The signature size remains identical to [30].

Importantly, all of our threshold signature is proven secure under the same assumptions and security model (i.e., ROM) as those of the underlying non-thresholdized signature. In addition, none of them require secure state erasures, a requirement often difficult to enforce in practice. We can also preprocess the first round of both of our 5 round threshold signatures, making the online phase four rounds [9, Section 5.3.5]. A comparison of prior related threshold signatures is given in Tables 1 and 2.

Before getting into the technical details, we clarify a downside of Crackle and Snap compared with other threshold Schnorr signatures. In order to prove adaptive security, we do not allow the parties to publish a partial verification key of the form $g^{a_i} \in \mathbb{G}$, where $a_i \in \mathbb{Z}_p$ is the secret key share. This specific partial verification key is typically used to achieve *non-interactive* identifiable abort; a property allowing the parties to non-interactively trace a malicious party in case the threshold signing protocol outputs an invalid signature. We note that static security of Crackle and Snap remains intact even if we publish g^{a_i}. For lattice-based threshold signatures, none of the schemes in Table 1 consider partial verification keys or non-interactive identifiable abort. We refer to Sec. 1.3 in the full version for more discussion on related work.

Table 2. Comparison of T-out-of-N classical Schnorr-like threshold signatures.

Schemes	Adaptive?	Assumptions	Rounds	Model	Corruptions	Stateless session id?
[5,24] (Frost)	✗	AOM-DL	2	ROM	$< T$	✓
[25]	✗	DL	3	ROM	$< T$	✓
[34]	✗	DL	2	ROM	$< T$	✓
[12] (Sparkle)	✗	DL	3	ROM	$< T$	✓
[12] (Sparkle)	✓	AOM-DL	3	ROM	$< T/2$	✓
[12] (Sparkle)	✓	AOM-DL	3	ROM + AGM	$< T$	✓
[3] (Twinkle)	✓	DDH	3	ROM	$< T$	✗
TSchnorr$^{adp}_{4\text{-rnd}}$ (Snap)	✓	DL	4	ROM	$< T$	✗
TSchnorr$^{adp}_{5\text{-rnd}}$ (Crackle)	✓	DL	5	ROM	$< T$	✓

We compare pairing-free Schnorr-like threshold signatures. ($< T/2$)-corruption indicates that adaptive security holds if only at most $T/2$ parties are corrupted. AOM-DL stands for the algebraic one-more DL. The (✓) in the column "Stateless session id?" indicates that the parties can be stateless. Else (✗), the parties need to store the session id's so as not to reuse them.

Technique in a Birds Eye's View. At a technical level, our work is inspired by the recent lattice-based 3 round threshold signature by del Pino et al. [30] based on Raccoon. Their work can be seen as a lattice-based counterpart of the 3 round threshold Schnorr signature Sparkle by Crites et al. [12] but with a unique twist. Due to lattice specific reasons, a natural adaptation of Sparkle to the lattice setting turns out to be insecure as the partial signature leaks too much information on the signing key shares. To overcome this issue, del Pino et al. relied on non-interactively shared *one-time additive masks*. At a high level, this allows each parties to output a *masked* partial signature, where the masks cancel out only when all T partial signatures are combined.

Our main technical contribution is noticing that this one-time additive mask not only solves lattice specific issues but is also a useful technique for achieving adaptive security. Recall that one of the reasons why rewinding proofs were at odds with adaptive security was that a reduction being able to simulate $T - 1$ secret key shares in both of the runs can seemingly reconstruct the full secret key on its own. Specifically, there is no room left to embed a hard problem.

An idea to resolve this paradoxical situation is for the reduction to simply output *random* secret key shares in both runs. Looking through the lens of the adversary, this modification seems undetectable since *within each individual run*, the $T-1$ secret keys are indeed uniformly random when the secret key is being T-out-of-N secret shared. However, such a naive approach does not work as it stands. Throughout the game, an adversary can concurrently interact with the parties and observe the transcripts of any given signing session. Then, once corrupted a party, the adversary can check whether the secret key share is consistent with what it observed; if the secret key share was randomly simulated, this will certainly be detected.

This brings us to our main idea. We use one-time additive masks throughout the protocol to carefully control the information the adversary can learn from the transcripts. When a corruption occurs, we will generate randomness for the one-time additive masks so that it becomes consistent with the random secret key share and the transcript the adversary observed. While the proof strategy is intuitive, constructing a protocol that fits this intuition and proving it is *far* easier said than done. We refer the readers to the next section for a more technical overview. Lastly, while our technique is quite general, we choose not to phrase our scheme abstractly using linear function families (cf., [19,20]) as optimized lattice-based constructions like Raccoon do not neatly fit in this abstraction.

1.2 Technical Overview

We first recall the statically secure 3 round lattice-based threshold signature by del Pino et al. [30]. We then show a simple improvement of their protocol, leading to our stateless 3 round threshold signature $\mathsf{TRaccoon}^{\mathsf{sel}}_{\mathsf{3\text{-}rnd}}$. This scheme is only statically secure but our proof technique forms the basis of the more complex adaptively secure 5 round threshold signature $\mathsf{TRaccoon}^{\mathsf{adp}}_{\mathsf{5\text{-}rnd}}$, which we then explain. While our overview focuses on the lattice setting, it will be clear that it trivially adapts to the classical Schnorr setting.

Lastly, while we try our best to keep the overview self-contained, we encourage the readers to look at [30, Section 2] for an in depth overview on the original threshold signature by del Pino et al.

3 Round Threshold Raccoon by [30]. We recall below a simplified variant of their scheme based on Lyubashevsky's lattice-based signature scheme [26,27]. The NIST submission Raccoon [31] is a variant of Lyubashevsky's (and also Dilithium [15]), that is more susceptible to thresholdization. For the sake of simplicity, we ignore this lattice specific detail in the overview.

The verification key vk is an MLWE instance $(\mathbf{A}, \mathbf{b} = [\mathbf{A} \mid \mathbf{I}] \cdot \mathbf{s}) \in \mathcal{R}_q^{k \times \ell} \times \mathcal{R}_q^k$, where $\mathbf{s} \in \mathcal{R}_q^{\ell+k}$ is a secret short vector.[1] The secret key $\mathbf{s}$ is distributed to each

---

[1] In the main body, we write $\mathbf{b}$ as $\mathbf{As} + \mathbf{e} = [\mathbf{A} \mid \mathbf{I}] \cdot \begin{bmatrix} \mathbf{s} \\ \mathbf{e} \end{bmatrix}$. This reflects the standard optimization [4] performed by Dilithium and Raccoon where we ignore the noise $\mathbf{e}$ and only view the upper $\mathbf{s}$ as the secret key. Since this makes the protocol more complex, we opt using the simplest version in the overview.

party using Shamir's secret sharing [33]. Namely, each party $i \in [N]$ is given s_i such that for any $\mathsf{SS} \subseteq [N]$ and $|\mathsf{SS}| = T$, we have $\mathsf{s} = \sum_{j \in \mathsf{SS}} L_{\mathsf{SS},j} \mathsf{s}_i$ where $(L_{\mathsf{SS},j})_{j \in \mathsf{SS}}$ are the Lagrange coefficients. The novelty of [30] is that, each party i is further distributed a random PRF seed $\vec{\mathsf{seed}}_i = (\mathsf{seed}_{i,j}, \mathsf{seed}_{j,i})_{j \in [N]}$, where parties i and j share seeds $(\mathsf{seed}_{i,j}, \mathsf{seed}_{j,i})$. Lastly, each party i is also assumed to have their own set of keys $(\mathsf{vk}_{\mathsf{S},i}, \mathsf{sk}_{\mathsf{S},i})$ for a standard signature scheme. In summary, the secret key share for party i is $\mathsf{sk}_i = (\mathsf{s}_i, \vec{\mathsf{seed}}_i, \mathsf{sk}_{\mathsf{S},i})$.

To sign on a message M with a signer set SS, it proceeds as follows, where assume sid is a session identifier that has never been used.

Round 1. Signer i samples a commitment $\mathbf{w}_i = [\mathbf{A}|\mathbf{I}] \cdot \mathbf{r}_i \in \mathcal{R}_q^k$ for a short vector $\mathbf{r}_i \in \mathcal{R}_q^{\ell+k}$ and creates a hash commitment $\mathsf{cmt}_i = \mathsf{H}_{\mathsf{com}}(i, \mathbf{w}_i)$. It also computes a so-called *row mask* $\mathbf{m}_i = \sum_{j \in \mathsf{SS}} \mathsf{PRF}(\mathsf{seed}_{i,j}, \mathsf{sid}) \in \mathcal{R}_q^{\ell+k}$ and outputs $(\mathsf{cmt}_i, \mathbf{m}_i)$.

Round 2. Signer i obtains $\mathsf{ctnt} = (\mathsf{cmt}_j, \mathbf{m}_j)_{j \in \mathsf{SS}}$, signs it $\sigma_{\mathsf{S},i} \xleftarrow{\$}$ Sign$(\mathsf{sk}_{\mathsf{S},i}, \mathsf{sid} \| \mathsf{ctnt})$, and outputs the opening $\mathbf{w}_i$ and the signature $\sigma_{\mathsf{S},j}$.

Round 3. Signer i checks that for all $j \in \mathsf{SS}$, the hash commitment cmt_j are opened correctly by signer j, i.e., $\mathsf{cmt}_j = \mathsf{H}_{\mathsf{com}}(j, \mathbf{w}_j)$, and the signature $\sigma_{\mathsf{S},j}$ verifies with respect to $\mathsf{sid} \| \mathsf{ctnt}$ it signed in Round 2. If the check passes, it computes the aggregate commitment $\mathbf{w} = \sum_{j \in \mathsf{SS}} \mathbf{w}_j$. It then computes the challenge $c = \mathsf{H}_c(\mathsf{vk}, \mathsf{M}, \mathbf{w})$, the so-called *column mask* $\mathbf{m}_i^* = \sum_{j \in \mathsf{SS}} \mathsf{PRF}(\mathsf{seed}_{j,i}, \mathsf{sid}) \in \mathcal{R}_q^{\ell+k}$, and outputs the *masked* response $\widetilde{\mathbf{z}}_i = c \cdot L_{\mathsf{SS},i} \cdot \mathbf{s}_i + \mathbf{r}_i - \mathbf{m}_i^* \in \mathcal{R}_q^{\ell+k}$.

Aggregate. Given the transcript $((\mathsf{cmt}_j, \mathbf{m}_j), (\mathbf{w}_j, \sigma_{\mathsf{S},j}), \widetilde{\mathbf{z}}_j)_{j \in \mathsf{SS}}$, it outputs the aggregate signature $\mathsf{sig} = (c, \mathbf{z})$, where $\mathbf{z} = \sum_{j \in \mathsf{SS}} (\widetilde{\mathbf{z}}_j - \mathbf{m}_j)$ and $(\mathbf{w}, c)$ are computed as above.

A signature sig is deemed valid if $c = \mathsf{H}_c(\mathsf{vk}, \mathsf{M}, \mathbf{Az} - c \cdot \mathbf{b})$ and $\mathbf{z}$ is short. Correctness is established by the equality $\sum_{i \in \mathsf{SS}} \mathbf{m}_i = \sum_{i \in \mathsf{SS}} \mathbf{m}_i^*$, i.e., the sum of row masks and column masks are identical. Concretely, we have $\mathbf{z} = c \cdot \sum_{j \in \mathsf{SS}}(L_{\mathsf{SS},i} \cdot \mathbf{s}_i + \mathbf{r}_i) = c \cdot \mathbf{s} + \sum_{j \in \mathsf{SS}} \mathbf{r}_i$. Since $\mathbf{w} = \sum_{j \in \mathsf{SS}} \mathbf{w}_j = [\mathbf{A}|\mathbf{I}] \cdot (\sum_{j \in \mathsf{SS}} \mathbf{r}_j)$, the signature sig is indeed a valid Lyubashevsky's signature.

Intuition of Security Proof. As opposed to classical cryptography, in lattice-based cryptography secrets are "short". Specifically, if parties instead output an unmasked partial response $\widetilde{\mathbf{z}}_i = c \cdot L_{\mathsf{SS},i} \cdot \mathbf{s}_i + \mathbf{r}_i \in \mathcal{R}_q^{\ell+k}$, there is a concrete attack on the scheme as the Lagrange coefficient $L_{\mathsf{SS},i}$ can arbitrarily amplify the size of the secret key share $\mathbf{s}_i$ (see [30, Section 2] for the details). This is where the mask plays a critical role. Due to the pseudorandomness of the PRF, the masks are distributed uniformly random conditioned on the sum of row masks and column masks being identical. Informally, this implies that the partial response only leaks information of the final aggregate signature $\mathbf{z} = c \cdot \mathbf{s} + \sum_{j \in \mathsf{SS}} \mathbf{r}_i$. Turning this around, the partial response can be simulated only by using the full secret key $\mathbf{s}$. From a reductionist's point of view, this allows us to invoke honest-verifier zero-knowledge (HVZK) with respect to the verification key vk to simulate the signature $\mathsf{sig} = (c, \mathbf{z})$, followed by programming the random oracle so that $\mathsf{H}_c(\mathsf{vk}, \mathsf{M}, \mathbf{Az} - c \cdot \mathbf{b}) = c$.

While the intuition is clear, the concrete proof contains subtleties. First of all, the above argument hinges on the pseudorandomness of the PRF, and in particular, if the same input sid is used to derive the masks, the scheme becomes insecure. This is where del Pino et al. [30] assumes the parties to maintain state of all the sid it signed. Furthermore, when we stated that the partial response only leaks information of the final aggregate signature $\mathbf{z} = c \cdot \mathbf{s} + \sum_{j \in \mathsf{SS}} \mathbf{r}_i$, we implicitly used the fact that all the parties agree on the *same* challenge c in Round 3. As an example of how things can go wrong, assume a malicious party 3 invokes honest parties 1 and 2 on the same sid and provides them $(\mathsf{cmt}_1, \mathsf{cmt}_2, \mathsf{cmt}_3)$ and $(\mathsf{cmt}_1, \mathsf{cmt}_2, \mathsf{cmt}'_3)$, respectively, in Round 2, where cmt_3 and cmt'_3 open to different commitments. Then, since the aggregate commitment differs, parties 1 and 2 will derive different challenges in Round 3. However, since the masks are only defined via sid, they will cancel out when combining the partial responses, and in particular, the adversary learns $c_1 \cdot L_{\mathsf{S},1} \cdot \mathbf{s}_1 + c_2 \cdot L_{\mathsf{S},2} \cdot \mathbf{s}_2 + \sum_{j \in [2]} \mathbf{r}_j$ for $c_1 \neq c_2$. Again, this leads to concrete attacks.[2] Thus, to thwart such an attack, del Pino et al. [30] requires the parties to sign their entire view sid∥ctnt in Round 2. This effectively enforces that if all parties with sid finished Round 3, then they must have used the same unique challenge c. Piecing these arguments together, we can formally invoke HVZK to complete the above proof intuition.

A Simple Tweak and a New Proof. Looking at the prior construction (and security proof) closely, it can be checked that there is no need to compute the masks in different rounds. In particular, the row and column masks can be generated together in Round 3. We also remove the signature in Round 2 and consider the following simplified 3-round threshold signature $\mathsf{TRaccoon}^{\mathsf{sel}}_{\mathsf{3\text{-}rnd}}$.

Round 1. Signer i samples a commitment $\mathbf{w}_i = [\mathbf{A}|\mathbf{I}] \cdot \mathbf{r}_i \in \mathcal{R}_q^k$ for a short vector $\mathbf{r}_i \in \mathcal{R}_q^{\ell+k}$ and outputs a hash commitment $\mathsf{cmt}_i = \mathsf{H}_{\mathsf{com}}(i, \mathbf{w}_i)$.
Round 2. Signer i obtains $\mathsf{ctnt}_\mathbf{w} = (\mathsf{cmt}_j)_{j \in \mathsf{SS}}$ and outputs the opening $\mathbf{w}_i$.
Round 3. Signer i checks that for all $j \in \mathsf{SS}$, the hash commitment cmt_j are opened correctly by signer j, i.e., $\mathsf{cmt}_j = \mathsf{H}_{\mathsf{com}}(j, \mathbf{w}_j)$. If the check passes, it computes the aggregate commitment $\mathbf{w} = \sum_{j \in \mathsf{SS}} \mathbf{w}_j$ and sets $\mathsf{ctnt}_\mathbf{z} = (\mathsf{cmt}_j, \mathbf{w}_j)_{j \in \mathsf{SS}}$. It then computes the challenge $c = \mathsf{H}_c(\mathsf{vk}, \mathsf{M}, \mathbf{w})$, a *zero-share* mask $\boldsymbol{\Delta}_i = \sum_{j \in \mathsf{SS}} (\mathsf{PRF}(\mathsf{seed}_{i,j}, \mathsf{ctnt}_\mathbf{z}) - \mathsf{PRF}(\mathsf{seed}_{j,i}, \mathsf{ctnt}_\mathbf{z})) \in \mathcal{R}_q^{\ell+k}$, and outputs the masked response $\widetilde{\mathbf{z}}_i = c \cdot L_{\mathsf{SS},i} \cdot \mathbf{s}_i + \mathbf{r}_i + \boldsymbol{\Delta}_i \in \mathcal{R}_q^{\ell+k}$.[3]

---

[2] For those knowledgeable in classical threshold signatures like Sparkle and Twinkle, we note that such an attack cannot be used to break unforgeability. This is because unlike in the lattice setting, we can invoke HVZK with respect to the *partial* verification key, i.e., the partial response can be simulated individually. In the lattice setting, the unmasked partial response leaks too much information on the secret key share and thus HVZK must be applied to the full secret key..

[3] In the actual construction, we include the signer set SS and message M in $\mathsf{ctnt}_\mathbf{z}$, as otherwise, it opens the door to ROS attacks [7]. We gloss over this detail in the overview for simplicity as it can be handled using standard methods.

Aggregate. Given the transcript $(\mathsf{cmt}_j, \mathbf{w}_j, \widetilde{\mathbf{z}}_j)_{j \in \mathsf{SS}}$, it outputs the aggregate signature $\mathsf{sig} = (c, \mathbf{z})$, where $\mathbf{z} = \sum_{j \in \mathsf{SS}} \widetilde{\mathbf{z}}_j$ and $(\mathbf{w}, c)$ are computed as above.

The verification algorithm is defined identically as before, where correctness follows immediately by the equality $\sum_{j \in \mathsf{SS}} \mathbf{\Delta}_j = \mathbf{0}$. Notice that this modification allows to remove the state since an honest party i is now guaranteed to always invoke the PRF on a distinct input; this is an immediate implication of including $\mathbf{w}_i$ in the input $\mathsf{ctnt_z}$.

The most important part though, is whether the scheme remains secure even if we remove the standard signature in Round 2. As a sanity check, let us observe that the aforementioned attack will not work. Consider an adversary invoking parties 1 and 2 on different Round 2 hash commitments $(\mathsf{cmt}_1, \mathsf{cmt}_2, \mathsf{cmt}_3)$ and $(\mathsf{cmt}_1, \mathsf{cmt}_2, \mathsf{cmt}_3')$, respectively. In our modified scheme, since both parties now compute a mask using different PRF inputs in Round 3, the masks no longer cancel out. Specifically, the adversary learns nothing by combining the partial response as it will compute to $\sum_{j \in [2]} (c_j \cdot \mathsf{L}_{\mathsf{S},j} \cdot \mathbf{s}_j + \mathbf{r}_j + \mathbf{\Delta}_j)$ for $\sum_{j \in [2]} \mathbf{\Delta}_j \neq \mathbf{0}$. Let us now formalize this below.

The key argument in the security proof of del Pino et al. [30] was enforcing all parties with sid in Round 2, eventually finishing Round 3, to satisfy two properties: (i) the masks they use in Round 3 must be computed from the same PRF input and (ii) they must all be using the same unique challenge c. The first property guaranteed the equality $\sum_{i \in \mathsf{SS}} \mathbf{m}_i = \sum_{i \in \mathsf{SS}} \mathbf{m}_i^*$ and this held by virtue since the masks were computed only using sid. The second property guaranteed that the partial responses leak no more information than the final signature $\mathbf{z} = c \cdot \mathbf{s} + \sum_{j \in \mathsf{SS}} \mathbf{r}_i$. This was enforced by using standard signatures.

Translating their key argument to our scheme, we have to enforce the same two properties as above but now with respect to all parties with $\mathsf{ctnt_w}$ in Round 2, eventually finishing Round 3. We show that these two properties combined allows us to invoke HVZK *before* Round 3 as desired. To prove the properties, we use the fact that $\mathsf{ctnt_w} = (\mathsf{cmt}_j)_{j \in \mathsf{SS}}$ is a set of binding hash commitments, i.e., cmt_j can only be uniquely opened to a commitment $\mathbf{w}_j$. Using this, we can guarantee that there is only a unique $\mathsf{ctnt_z}$ in Round 3 that can lead from $\mathsf{ctnt_w}$ in Round 2, enforcing the first property. Moreover, using the same argument, there can only be one aggregate commitment $\mathbf{w} = \sum_{j \in \mathsf{SS}} \mathbf{w}_j$ in Round 3, enforcing the second property. It is worth noting that a similar argument appears in Bacho et al. [3], where they notice a slight gap in the security proof of Sparkle [12]. They use a technical argument called *equivalence classes* to enforce the second property. Our proof is inherently more involved than theirs as we must also enforce the first property, stemming from the fact that we have to invoke HVZK on the full verification key vk (see also Footnote 2). Piecing the arguments together, we conclude static security of $\mathsf{TRaccoon}_{\text{3-rnd}}^{\text{sel}}$.

Why Adaptive Security Fails. As briefly explained in the previous section, to resolve the paradoxical situation, a natural proof strategy for adaptive security is for the reduction to simply output a random secret key share $\mathbf{s}_i \xleftarrow{\$} \mathcal{R}_q^{\ell+k}$. However, it is clear that such a proof strategy fails for $\mathsf{TRaccoon}_{\text{3-rnd}}^{\text{sel}}$. Once party i is corrupted, the adversary obtains $\mathsf{sk}_i = (\mathbf{s}_i, \vec{\mathsf{seed}}_i)$. Using $\vec{\mathsf{seed}}_i$, it can unmask the masked response $\widetilde{\mathbf{z}}_i$ and further recover the commitment randomness $\mathbf{r}_i = \widetilde{\mathbf{z}}_i - c \cdot L_{\mathsf{SS},i} \cdot \mathbf{s}_i - \mathbf{\Delta}_i$. From this, it can check if the commitment $\mathbf{w}_i$ equals $[\mathbf{A}|\mathbf{I}]\cdot\mathbf{r}_i$. If $\mathbf{s}_i$ was sampled uniformly, this equality will clearly not hold, rendering the simulation to be distinguishable from the real security game.

This example illustrates another difficulty of adaptive security. We have seen that if the adversary obtains sk_i, it can recover the randomness $\mathbf{r}_i$ used to generate the commitment $\mathbf{w}_i$. Let us consider the following situation: the adversary invokes all the parties up to Round 2 and obtains $(\mathbf{w}_j)_{j\in\mathsf{SS}}$. Assume the adversary corrupts half of the parties $\mathcal{Q} \subset \mathsf{SS}$ in the first run. The reduction then rewinds the adversary, and assume it corrupts the other half of the parties $\mathsf{SS} \setminus \mathcal{Q}$ in the second run. For this to work, the reduction must be ready to answer all the commitment randomness $(\mathbf{r}_j)_{j\in\mathsf{SS}}$. However, once again, this leaves the reduction no space to embed its hard problem! Indeed, if the reduction tries to invoke HVZK, there is no place to embed the simulated commitment $\mathbf{w}$.

More Masking Solves the Problem. Our key insight to solve the above problem is to add another layer of masking to the commitments $\mathbf{w}_i$, and moreover, to generate the mask using a random oracle $\mathsf{H}_{\mathsf{mask}}$ as opposed to using a PRF. The following is our 4-round threshold signature $\mathsf{TRaccoon}^{\mathsf{adp}}_{\text{4-rnd}}$, where we again assume each party has their own set of keys for a standard signature scheme and assume an unused sid is provided to the parties.

Round 1. Signer i samples a commitment $\mathbf{w}_i = [\mathbf{A}|\mathbf{I}] \cdot \mathbf{r}_i \in \mathcal{R}_q^k$ for a short vector $\mathbf{r}_i \in \mathcal{R}_q^{\ell+k}$ and computes a zero-share mask $\widetilde{\mathbf{\Delta}}_i = \sum_{j\in\mathsf{SS}}(\mathsf{H}_{\mathsf{mask}}(\mathsf{seed}_{i,j}, \mathsf{sid}) - \mathsf{H}_{\mathsf{mask}}(\mathsf{seed}_{j,i}, \mathsf{sid})) \in \mathcal{R}_q^k$. It then computes a *masked* commitment $\widetilde{\mathbf{w}}_i = \mathbf{w}_i + \widetilde{\mathbf{\Delta}}_i$ and outputs a hash commitment $\mathsf{cmt}_i = \mathsf{H}_{\mathsf{com}}(i, \widetilde{\mathbf{w}}_i)$.
Round 2. Signer i obtains $\mathsf{ctnt}_{\mathbf{w}} = (\mathsf{cmt}_j)_{j\in\mathsf{SS}}$ and outputs a signature $\sigma_{\mathsf{S},i} \xleftarrow{\$} \mathsf{Sign}(\mathsf{sk}_{\mathsf{S},i}, \mathsf{sid}\|\mathsf{ctnt}_{\mathbf{w}})$.
Round 3. Signer checks that for all $j \in \mathsf{SS}$ the signature $\sigma_{\mathsf{S},j}$ verifies with respect to $\mathsf{sid}\|\mathsf{ctnt}_{\mathbf{w}}$ it signed in Round 2. If so, it outputs the opening $\widetilde{\mathbf{w}}_i$.
Round 4. Signer i checks that for all $j \in \mathsf{SS}$, the hash commitment cmt_j are opened correctly by signer j, i.e., $\mathsf{cmt}_j = \mathsf{H}_{\mathsf{com}}(j, \widetilde{\mathbf{w}}_j)$. If the check passes, it computes the aggregate commitment $\mathbf{w} = \sum_{j\in\mathsf{SS}} \widetilde{\mathbf{w}}_j$ and sets $\mathsf{ctnt}_{\mathbf{z}} = \mathsf{sid}\|(\mathsf{cmt}_j, \widetilde{\mathbf{w}}_j)_{j\in\mathsf{SS}}$. It then computes the challenge $c = \mathsf{H}_c(\mathsf{vk}, \mathsf{M}, \mathbf{w})$, a zero-share mask $\mathbf{\Delta}_i = \sum_{j\in\mathsf{SS}} (\mathsf{H}_{\mathsf{mask}}(\mathsf{seed}_{i,j}, \mathsf{ctnt}_{\mathbf{z}}) - \mathsf{H}_{\mathsf{mask}}(\mathsf{seed}_{j,i}, \mathsf{ctnt}_{\mathbf{z}})) \in \mathcal{R}_q^{\ell+k}$, and outputs the masked response $\widetilde{\mathbf{z}}_i = c \cdot L_{\mathsf{SS},i} \cdot \mathbf{s}_i + \mathbf{r}_i + \mathbf{\Delta}_i \in \mathcal{R}_q^{\ell+k}$.

The aggregation algorithm is defined identically as in $\mathsf{TRaccoon}^{\mathsf{sel}}_{\text{3-rnd}}$. Correctness holds by observing that the aggregate commitment $\mathbf{w}$ adds up to the same value as before using the fact $\sum_{j\in\mathsf{SS}} \widetilde{\mathbf{\Delta}}_j = \mathbf{0}$.

While it is not immediately clear why this scheme can be proven adaptively secure, it will be informative to see why the previously explained distinguishing attack no longer works. First, observe that before the adversary corrupts any party, the individual commitments $\widetilde{\mathbf{w}}_j$ and partial responses $\widetilde{\mathbf{z}}_j$ are distributed uniformly random thanks to the two masks $\widetilde{\mathbf{\Delta}}_j$ and $\mathbf{\Delta}_j$, conditioned on the resulting signature $\mathsf{sig} = (c, \mathbf{z})$ being valid. That is, $c = \mathsf{H}_c(\mathsf{vk}, \mathsf{M}, \mathbf{w})$ and $\mathbf{w} = \mathbf{A}\mathbf{z} - c \cdot \mathbf{b}$ where $\mathbf{w} = \sum_{j \in \mathsf{SS}} \widetilde{\mathbf{w}}_j$ and $\mathbf{z} = \sum_{j \in \mathsf{SS}} \widetilde{\mathbf{z}}_j$. Now, assume party i is corrupted. Then, the reduction first samples a random secret key share $\mathbf{s}_i \xleftarrow{\$} \mathcal{R}_q^{\ell+k}$ and a random commitment randomness $\mathbf{r}_i$. It then computes a *fake* commitment $\mathbf{w}_i = [\mathbf{A}|\mathbf{I}] \cdot \mathbf{r}_i$ and a *fake* response $\mathbf{z}_i = c \cdot L_{\mathsf{SS},i} \cdot \mathbf{s}_i + \mathbf{r}_i$. It further programs the random oracle $\mathsf{H}_{\mathsf{mask}}$ so that the two masks $(\vec{\boldsymbol{\Delta}}_i, \boldsymbol{\Delta}_i)$ compute to $(\widetilde{\mathbf{w}}_j - \mathbf{w}_j, \widetilde{\mathbf{z}}_j - \mathbf{z}_j)$. This is where we require to generate the masks using a random oracle as opposed to using a PRF. Lastly, the reduction outputs $\mathsf{sk}_i = (\mathbf{s}_i, \overrightarrow{\mathsf{seed}}_i, \mathsf{sk}_{\mathsf{S},i})$ to the adversary. Due to the way we program the masks, sk_i is consistent with $(\widetilde{\mathbf{w}}_i, \widetilde{\mathbf{z}}_i)$ observed by the adversary. It is worth noting that no secure state erasure is necessary since we can simulate all the randomness to the adversary.

The above reduction strategy tells us, at least intuitively, that the entire transcript only leaks the information on the full signature $\mathsf{sig} = (c, \mathbf{z})$. Turning this intuition into a formal proof consists the main technical contribution of our work. In particular, the above reduction only concerns how to randomly answer the adversary's corruption query, and tells us nothing about how to embed a hard problem in the reduction. As in the static setting, the goal will be to simulate sig by invoking HVZK with respect to the verification key vk through a careful chain of technical arguments.

At a very high level, our proof consists of three steps. We first enforce all parties with sid in Round2, eventually arriving at Round 3, to agree on the same $\mathsf{cnt}_\mathbf{w}$ (call this property (i)). This allows us to argue that every masked commitment $\widetilde{\mathbf{w}}_i$ except for the last one is uniform random. To prove property (i), we use a similar argument to del Pino et al. [30], relying on the masks generated with sid and standard signatures $\sigma_{\mathsf{S},i}$. We next enforce all parties with $\mathsf{cnt}_\mathbf{w}$ in Round 3, eventually finishing Round 4, to satisfy two additional properties: (ii) the masks $\boldsymbol{\Delta}_j$ they use in Round 4 must be computed from the same $\mathsf{H}_{\mathsf{mask}}$ input and (iii) they must all be using the same unique challenge c. This allows us to argue that every masked response $\widetilde{\mathbf{z}}_i$ except for the last one is uniform random and that the aggregated response $\mathbf{z}$ can be expressed using the fully secret key $\mathbf{s}$, as opposed to using the secret key shares. To prove properties (ii) and (iii), we use a similar argument to our $\mathsf{TRaccoon}^{\mathsf{sel}}_{\mathsf{3\text{-}rnd}}$. The final step consists of carefully gluing these properties (i), (ii), and (iii) together to show that we can consistently embed $(\mathbf{w}, c, \mathbf{z})$ simulated by HVZK.

We emphasize that the above is a major simplification of our proof. The simplification arises when we loosely used the term "every masked commitment $\widetilde{\mathbf{w}}_i$ (and masked response $\widetilde{\mathbf{z}}_i$) *except the last one* is uniform random". Since the adversary is adaptive, the last masked commitment and response are not known in advance to the reduction. To make matters worse, we have to consider situations where the last commitment is $\widetilde{\mathbf{w}}_i$ while the last response is $\widetilde{\mathbf{z}}_j$ for a different party $i \neq j$. This highly non-trivializes the final step of consistently embedding $(\mathbf{w}, c, \mathbf{z})$ into the security game. We provide a more detailed proof overview in Sect. 4.3.

Removing States with One More Round. Our 4-round threshold signature $\mathsf{TRaccoon}_{\text{4-rnd}}^{\text{adp}}$ required to maintain state so that the same sid is never reused. We remove this restriction and construct a stateless scheme by adding one more round, resulting in our 5-round threshold signature $\mathsf{TRaccoon}_{\text{5-rnd}}^{\text{adp}}$. The idea is very simple: In the first round, each party i broadcasts a random string str_i. The parties then set $\mathsf{sid} = (\mathsf{str}_j)_{j \in \mathsf{SS}}$ and proceeds as in $\mathsf{TRaccoon}_{\text{4-rnd}}^{\text{adp}}$. The main observation is that since sid contains a uniform random string str_i sampled by party i, it is guaranteed to be distinct from prior sid's. Since the first round can be performed without knowing the signer set SS or the message M, it can be preprocessed, making the online phase of $\mathsf{TRaccoon}_{\text{5-rnd}}^{\text{adp}}$ 4-round.

2 Preliminary

We provide some backgrounds. Standard definitions and primitives are provided in Sect. 2 and App. A in the full version.

Notations. We use lower (resp. upper) case bold fonts $\mathbf{v}$ (resp. $\mathbf{M}$) for vectors (resp. matrices). We always view vectors in the column form. We use v_i (resp. $\mathbf{m}_i$) to indicate the i-th entry (resp. column) of $\mathbf{v}$ (resp. $\mathbf{M}$). We denote by $\mathcal{U}_S$ the uniform distribution over some set S. We write $x \sim D$ if a random variable x follows the distribution D.

2.1 Threshold Signatures

We define R round threshold signatures. Let N be the number of total signers and T be a reconstruction threshold s.t. $T \leq N$. Also, let SS be a signer set such that $\mathsf{SS} \subseteq [N]$ with size T. Each signer $i \in [N]$ maintains a state st_i to retain short-lived session specific information.

$\mathsf{Setup}(1^\lambda, N, T) \to \mathsf{tspar}$: The setup algorithm takes as input a security parameter 1^λ, the number N of total signers, and a reconstruction threshold $T \leq N$ and outputs a public parameter tspar. We assume tspar includes N and T.

$\mathsf{KeyGen}(\mathsf{tspar}) \to (\mathsf{vk}, (\mathsf{sk}_i)_{i \in [N]})$: The key generation algorithm takes as input a public parameter tspar and outputs a verification key vk, and secret key shares $(\mathsf{sk}_i)_{i \in [N]}$. It implicitly sets up an empty state $\mathsf{st}_i := \emptyset$ for all N signers. We assume vk includes tspar.

$\mathsf{Sign} = (\mathsf{Sign}_1, \cdots, \mathsf{Sign}_R, \mathsf{Agg})$: The signing algorithms for the signing protocol of R round threshold signatures consist the following $(R+1)$ algorithms.

$\mathsf{Sign}_r(\mathsf{vk}, \mathsf{SS}, \mathsf{M}, i, (\mathsf{pm}_{r-1,j})_{j \in \mathsf{SS}}, \mathsf{sk}_i, \mathsf{st}_i) \to (\mathsf{pm}_{r,i}, \mathsf{st}_i)$: The signing algorithm for the rth round for $r \in [R]$ takes as input a verification key vk, a signer set SS, a message M, an index i of a signer, a tuple of protocol messages of the $(r-1)$th round $(\mathsf{pm}_{r-1,j})_{j \in \mathsf{SS}}$, a secret key share sk_i, and a state st_i of the signer i and outputs a protocol message $\mathsf{pm}_{r,i}$ for the second round and an updated state st_i. Note that $\mathsf{pm}_{0,j}$ is $\perp$ for all $j \in \mathsf{SS}$. If the round r can be executed before deciding SS and/or M, Sign_r does not take as input them.

$\mathsf{Agg}(\mathsf{vk}, \mathsf{SS}, \mathsf{M}, (\mathsf{pm}_{r,i})_{r \in [R], i \in \mathsf{SS}}) \to \mathsf{sig}$: The aggregation algorithm takes as input a verification key vk, a signer set SS, a message M, and a tuple of protocol messages $(\mathsf{pm}_{r,i})_{r \in [R], i \in \mathsf{SS}}$ and outputs a signature sig.

$\mathsf{Verify}(\mathsf{vk}, \mathsf{M}, \mathsf{sig}) \to 1$ or 0: The verification algorithm takes as input a verification key vk, a message M, and a signature sig, and outputs 1 if sig is valid and 0 otherwise.

We consider the standard definition of correctness of threshold signature schemes. We provide the formal definition of the correctness in Sect. 2.2 in the full version. Below, we provide the intuition of unforgeability under both static and adaptive corruptions.

Selective Security. In the selective setting, an adversary $\mathcal{A}$ determines the set CS of users to be corrupted at the beginning of the security game (after obtaining the parameters tspar). After this, it is not allowed to corrupt more honest users during the game. The challenger executes the key generation after CS is determined. It then provides $\mathcal{A}$ with the verification key and secret key shares of corrupted users as input. It also provides access to signing oracles for each round. In the end, $\mathcal{A}$ outputs a signature-message pair $(\mathsf{sig}^*, \mathsf{M}^*)$ that constitutes the forgery. The adversary $\mathcal{A}$ wins the game if $(\mathsf{sig}^*, \mathsf{M}^*)$ is deemed *non-trivial*. We refer to App. A.1.1 in the full version for a formal definition based on [12].

Adaptive Security. We briefly explain the adaptive security of threshold signature schemes. Adaptive security is defined as selective security, except that an adversary is allowed to corrupt up to $T-1$ signers at any time via a corruption oracle $\mathcal{O}_{\mathsf{Corrupt}}$. The oracle $\mathcal{O}_{\mathsf{Corrupt}}$ receives an index i of a honest signer and returns the secret key share sk_i and the state st_i of the signer to be corrupted. We refer to Sec. 2.2.2 in the full version for a formal definition.

In this paper, we consider a stronger notion of security that better captures attacks in real-world scenarios, such as those considered in [5]. Roughly, we allow the signer to query the forgery's message M^* up to $T-1$ times in the last round. Also, we also consider a security model with stateful session identifier for our adaptive secure 4 round threshold signatures. We refer to Sect. 2.2 and App. 1 in the full version for details.

2.2 Linear Secret Sharing

We recall the *linear Shamir secret sharing* scheme [33]. Let $N < q$ be an integer such that for distinct $i, j \in [N]$, $(i - j)$ is invertible over $\mathbb{Z}_q$. Let $S \subseteq [N]$ be a set of cardinality at least T. Let $s \in \mathcal{R}_q$ be a secret to be shared, $P \in \mathcal{R}_q[X]$ a degree $T-1$ polynomial such that $P(0) = s$. Given any set of evaluation points $E = \{(i, y_i)\}_{i \in S}$ such that $y_i = P(i)$ for all $i \in S$, we note that $s = \sum_{i \in S} L_{S,i} \cdot y_i$, where $L_{S,i} := \prod_{j \in S \setminus \{i\}} \frac{-j}{i-j}$ is the Lagrange coefficient. The notations naturally extend to secrets that are in vector form. With a slight abuse of notation, we say $\vec{P} \in \mathcal{R}_q^\ell[X]$ is of degree $T-1$ if each entry of $\vec{P}$ is a degree $T-1$ polynomial. Moreover, $\vec{P}(x)$ denotes the evaluation of each entry of $\vec{P}$ on the point x.

2.3 Lattices, Gaussians, and Rounding

For integers $n, q \in \mathbb{N}$ we define the ring $\mathcal{R}$ as $\mathbb{Z}[X]/(X^n + 1)$ and $\mathcal{R}_q$ as $\mathcal{R}/q\mathcal{R}$. For a positive real σ, let $\rho_\sigma(\mathbf{z}) = \exp\left(-\frac{\|\mathbf{z}\|_2}{2\sigma^2}\right)$. The discrete Gaussian distribution over $\mathbb{Z}^n$ and standard deviation σ is defined by its probability distribution function: $\mathcal{D}_{S,\sigma}(\mathbf{z}) = \frac{\rho_\sigma(\mathbf{z})}{\sum_{\mathbf{z}' \in \mathbb{Z}^n} \rho_\sigma(\mathbf{z}')}$. We may simply note $\mathcal{D}_\sigma$.

Similarly to [30, 31], we rely on *rounding* for efficiency purpose. Below, we provide a minimal preparation and omit the formal treatment to App. B.2 in the full version. For a positive integer q and ν such that $q > 2^\nu$, we define $q_\nu = \lfloor q/2^\nu \rfloor$. We then define the rounding function as $\lfloor \cdot \rceil_\nu : \mathbb{Z}_q \mapsto \mathbb{Z}_{q_\nu}$ s.t. $\lfloor x \rceil_\nu = \lfloor \bar{x}/2^\nu \rceil + q_\nu \mathbb{Z}$, where $\bar{x} \in [0, 1, \cdots, q-1]$ denotes the canonical unsigned representation (or the so-called *lift*) of $x \in \mathbb{Z}_q$. The function $\lfloor \cdot \rceil_\nu$ naturally extends to vectors coefficient-wise.

2.4 Hardness Assumptions

Here, we explain two lattice-based assumption, the *hint* MLWE (Hint-MLWE) and *self-target* MSIS (SelfTargetMSIS) assumptions. For detail on lattice-related and DL-related hardness assumptions, see Sec. 2.5, App. A.3, and App. A.4 in the full version.

We rely on two lattice-based assumptions: the *hint* MLWE (Hint-MLWE) and *self-target* MSIS (SelfTargetMSIS) assumptions. Both assumptions are reduced from the standard MLWE and MSIS assumptions, and in particular, are merely useful intermediate assumptions to aid the security proof (see App. B.3 in the full version, for the formal statements). They have been used by the three-round selective threshold Raccoon by del Pino et al. [30]. We refer to the full version for a formal definitions and sketch them below.

The Hint-MLWE problem, introduced in [23], is defined similarly to MLWE, except that the adversary also obtains some *noisy leakage* of the MLWE secrets. This is useful when invoking honest-verifier zero-knowledge, which unlike in the group setting, is not perfectly indistinguishable from the real transcript. The Hint-MLWE problem is known to be as hard as MLWE for the parameter settings we are interested in. Roughly, the adversary is asked to distinguish whether $\mathbf{b} = \mathbf{A} \cdot \mathbf{s} + \mathbf{e}$ or $\mathbf{b} \xleftarrow{\$} \mathcal{R}_q^k$ given

$$(\mathbf{A}, \mathbf{b}, (c_i, \mathbf{z}_i, \mathbf{z}'_i)_{i \in [Q]}),$$

where $(\mathbf{A}, \mathbf{s}, \mathbf{e}) \leftarrow \mathcal{R}_q^{k \times \ell} \times \mathcal{D}^\ell \times \mathcal{D}^k$, $c_i \leftarrow \mathcal{C}$ for $i \in [Q]$, and $(\mathbf{z}_i, \mathbf{z}'_i) = (c_i \cdot \mathbf{s} + \mathbf{r}_i, c_i \cdot \mathbf{e} + \mathbf{e}'_i)$ where $(\mathbf{r}_i, \mathbf{e}'_i) \leftarrow \mathcal{G}^\ell \times \mathcal{G}^k$ for $i \in [Q]$.

The *self-target* MSIS (SelfTargetMSIS) problem [15, 22] is a variant of the standard MSIS problem, where the problem is defined relative to some hash function modeled as a random oracle. Using the forking lemma [6, 16], it is easily shown to be equivalent to the MSIS problem (see App. B.3 in the full version). This has also been used by the signature scheme Dilithium [15], recently selected by NIST for standardisation. Roughly, given $\mathbf{A} \xleftarrow{\$} \mathcal{R}_q^{k \times \ell}$ and oracle access to H, the adversary is asked to output $(\mathbf{z}, \mathsf{M}) \in \mathcal{R}_q^{\ell+k} \times \{0,1\}^{2\lambda}$ s.t.

$$\left(\mathbf{z} = \begin{bmatrix} c \\ \mathbf{z}' \end{bmatrix} \right) \wedge \mathsf{H}\left([\mathbf{A} \mid \mathbf{I}] \cdot \mathbf{z}, \mathsf{M} \right) = c \wedge \mathbf{z} \text{ is "small"}$$

3 Construction of Our 3-Round Threshold Raccoon

In this section, we present our 3-round threshold signature scheme $\mathsf{TRaccoon}_{\text{3-rnd}}^{\text{sel}}$, a thresholdized version of the NIST submission Raccoon by del Pino et al. [31]. We show that $\mathsf{TRaccoon}_{\text{3-rnd}}^{\text{sel}}$ is selectively secure under the Hint-MLWE and SelfTargetMSIS assumptions. Our protocol is only a slight adaptation of the 3-round threshold Raccoon by del Pino et al. [30], and notably, the hardness assumptions and the concrete parameters we rely on are exactly the same as theirs. The main novelty is the new security analysis due to the modification in the scheme.

3.1 Parameters and Preparations

For reference, we provide the parameters of $\mathsf{TRaccoon}_{\text{3-rnd}}^{\text{sel}}$ in Table 3. Our protocol relies on the same parameters as those by del Pino et al. [30, Section 7.1]. For completeness, we provide a candidate parameter selection in App. D in the full version.

Table 3. Overview of parameters used in $\mathsf{TRaccoon}_{\text{3-rnd}}^{\text{sel}}$, $\mathsf{TRaccoon}_{\text{4-rnd}}^{\text{adp}}$, and $\mathsf{TRaccoon}_{\text{5-rnd}}^{\text{adp}}$.

Parameter	Explanation
$\mathcal{R}_q$	Polynomial ring $\mathcal{R}_q = \mathbb{Z}[X]/(q, X^n+1)$
(k, ℓ)	Dimension of public matrix $\mathbf{A} \in \mathcal{R}_q^{k \times \ell}$
$(\mathcal{D}_\mathbf{t}, \sigma_\mathbf{t})$	Gaussian distribution with width $\sigma_\mathbf{t}$ used for the verification key $\mathbf{t}$
$(\mathcal{D}_\mathbf{w}, \sigma_\mathbf{w})$	Gaussian distribution with width $\sigma_\mathbf{w}$ used for the commitment $\mathbf{w}$
$\nu_\mathbf{t}$	Amount of bit dropping performed on verification key
$\nu_\mathbf{w}$	Amount of bit dropping performed on (aggregated) commitment
$(q_{\nu_\mathbf{t}}, q_{\nu_\mathbf{w}})$	Rounded moduli satisfying $(q_{\nu_\mathbf{t}}, q_{\nu_\mathbf{w}}) := (\lfloor q/2^{\nu_\mathbf{t}} \rfloor, \lfloor q/2^{\nu_\mathbf{w}} \rfloor) = (\lceil q/2^{\nu_\mathbf{t}} \rceil, \lceil q/2^{\nu_\mathbf{w}} \rceil)$
$(\mathcal{C} \subset \mathcal{R}_q, W)$	Challenge set $\{c \in \mathcal{R}_q \mid \|c\|_\infty = 1 \wedge \|c\|_1 = W\}$ s.t. $|\mathcal{C}| \geq 2^\lambda$
B	Two-norm bound on the signature

We also prepare a helper algorithm called *zero share* (ZeroShare) to simplify the presentation of the protocol. While the underlying property of ZeroShare has been implicitly used in prior threshold signatures based on Raccoon [2,30][4],

---

[4] To be precise, the way del Pino et al. [30] implements the ZeroShare algorithm is slightly different from our abstraction. However, this is a superficial difference and our formalization allows for a slightly better communication cost as we remove broadcasting one element in $\mathcal{R}_q^\ell$.

we make this explicit. We believe this abstraction fosters a more intuitive understanding of our protocol, particularly for our adaptively secure 5-round variant. Concretely, each user is given a tuple of random strings of the form $\vec{\mathsf{seed}}_i = (\mathsf{seed}_{i,j}, \mathsf{seed}_{j,i})_{j \in [N]}$ at the setup. For any set $\mathsf{SS} \subseteq [N]$, we denote $\vec{\mathsf{seed}}_i[\mathsf{SS}]$ as the tuple $(\mathsf{seed}_{i,j}, \mathsf{seed}_{j,i})_{j \in \mathsf{SS}}$. The helper algorithm ZeroShare is defined with respect to a random oracle $\mathsf{H}_{\mathsf{mask}}$ with range $\mathcal{R}_q^\ell$. For any $\vec{\mathsf{seed}}_i[\mathsf{SS}]$ and string $x \in \{0,1\}^*$, it is defined as follows:

$$\mathsf{ZeroShare}(\vec{\mathsf{seed}}_i[\mathsf{SS}], x) := \sum_{j \in \mathsf{SS} \setminus \{i\}} (\mathsf{H}_{\mathsf{mask}}(\mathsf{seed}_{j,i}, x) - \mathsf{H}_{\mathsf{mask}}(\mathsf{seed}_{i,j}, x)).$$

Looking ahead, we use $\boldsymbol{\Delta}_i := \mathsf{ZeroShare}(\vec{\mathsf{seed}}_i[\mathsf{SS}], x)$ to mask the response $\mathbf{z}_i \in \mathcal{R}_q^\ell$. We will extensively use the following easy to check fact:

$$\sum_{i \in \mathsf{SS}} \mathsf{ZeroShare}(\vec{\mathsf{seed}}_i[\mathsf{SS}], x) = \sum_{i \in \mathsf{SS}} \boldsymbol{\Delta}_i = \mathbf{0}. \qquad (1)$$

Moreover, observe that from an adversary without knowledge of $(\vec{\mathsf{seed}}_i[\mathsf{SS}])_{i \in \mathsf{SS}}$, each $\boldsymbol{\Delta}_i$ is distributed uniformly over $\mathcal{R}_q^\ell$ conditioned on their sum being $\mathbf{0}$. In the remainder of the document, we may call $\boldsymbol{\Delta}_i$ as a mask or zero share interchangeably.

3.2 Construction

The construction of our 3-round threshold signature $\mathsf{TRaccoon}_{\text{3-rnd}}^{\text{sel}}$ is provide in full detail in Sect. 3.2 in the full version. We give an overview of the protocol below. Our scheme uses three hash functions modeled as a random oracle in the security proof. $\mathsf{H}_{\mathsf{com}} : \{0,1\}^* \to \{0,1\}^{2\lambda}$ is used to generate the hash commitment. $\mathsf{H}_c : \{0,1\}^* \to \mathcal{C}$ is used to generate the random challenge polynomial for which the users reply with a response. $\mathsf{H}_{\mathsf{mask}} : \{0,1\}^* \to \mathcal{R}_q^\ell$ is used to generate the random vectors to mask the individual response.

The setup algorithm outputs system parameters $\mathsf{tspar} = (\mathbf{A}, N, T)$ for some random $\mathbf{A} \xleftarrow{\$} \mathcal{R}_q^{k \times \ell}$. The verification key is tspar and a (rounded) MLWE instance $\mathbf{t} = \lfloor \mathbf{As} + \mathbf{e} \rceil_{\nu_t} \in \mathcal{R}_{q_{\nu_t}}^k$. The secret keys are of the form $\mathsf{sk}_i = (\mathbf{s}_i, \vec{\mathsf{seed}}_i)$, where $\mathbf{s}_i$ is a share of $\mathbf{s}$ and $\vec{\mathsf{seed}}_i$ are seeds for ZeroShare. Importantly, the verification key and the verification algorithm are identical to Raccoon [31]. The signing protocol proceeds in 3 rounds as follows:

Round 1. Signer i samples a commitment $\mathbf{w}_i := \mathbf{Ar}_i + \mathbf{e}_i'$, where $(\mathbf{r}_i, \mathbf{e}_i') \xleftarrow{\$} \mathcal{D}_\mathbf{w}^\ell \times \mathcal{D}_\mathbf{w}^k$, and outputs a hash commitment $\mathsf{cmt}_i := \mathsf{H}_{\mathsf{com}}(i, \mathbf{w}_i)$.
Round 2. Signer i obtains the hash commitments $(\mathsf{cmt}_j)_{j \in \mathsf{SS}}$ and opens cmt_i by sending $\mathbf{w}_i$.
Round 3. Signer i checks that for all $j \in \mathsf{SS}$, the hash commitments cmt_j are opened correctly by signer j, i.e., $\mathsf{cmt}_j = \mathsf{H}_{\mathsf{com}}(j, \mathbf{w}_j)$. If the check passes, it computes the aggregate commitment $\mathbf{w} := \lfloor \sum_{j \in \mathsf{SS}} \mathbf{w}_j \rceil_{\nu_\mathbf{w}}$, else it aborts.

Then, it sets $\mathsf{cntt_z} := \mathsf{SS}||\mathsf{M}||(\mathsf{cmt}_j, \mathbf{w}_j)_{j \in \mathsf{SS}}$, computes the challenge $c := \mathsf{H}_c(\mathsf{vk}, \mathsf{M}, \mathbf{w})$ and outputs the *masked* response $\widetilde{\mathbf{z}}_i := c \cdot L_{\mathsf{SS},i} \cdot \mathbf{s}_i + \mathbf{r}_i + \boldsymbol{\Delta}_i$, where $\boldsymbol{\Delta}_i := \mathsf{ZeroShare}(\vec{\mathsf{seed}}_i[\mathsf{SS}], \mathsf{cntt_z}) \in \mathcal{R}_q^\ell$ and $L_{\mathsf{SS},i}$ is the Lagrange coefficient.

The aggregate algorithm computes the response $\mathbf{z} := \sum_{j \in \mathsf{SS}} \widetilde{\mathbf{z}}_j$, $\mathbf{y} := \lfloor \mathbf{Az} - 2^{\nu_t} \cdot c \cdot \mathbf{t} \rceil_{\nu_w}$, hint $\mathbf{h} := \mathbf{w} - \mathbf{y}$, and outputs $\mathsf{sig} = (c, \mathbf{z}, \mathbf{h})$, where $\mathbf{w}$ and c are computed as above. Importantly, the final signature is a valid Raccoon signature. While it looks quite complicating on first glance, the hint $\mathbf{h}$ and multiplying of $c \cdot \mathbf{t}$ by 2^{ν_w} are simply there to compensate for the error induced by the rounding in the verification key $\mathbf{t}$ and the aggregate commitment $\mathbf{w}$. Specifically, these are simply used for optimization purpose, inherited by Raccoon [31], and will not appear for instance in the threshold Schnorr signatures (cf. Sec. 7 in full version).

3.3 Correctness and Selective Security

Correctness. The proof of correctness is almost identical to those provided in del Pino et al. [30, Lemma 7.1] as we use the same parameters. The only difference between their protocol and ours is how the shares are generated. By using Eq. (1) and using the correctness of the Shamir secret sharing scheme, the response can be written as follows:

$$\mathbf{z} := \sum_{j \in \mathsf{SS}} \widetilde{\mathbf{z}}_j = \sum_{j \in \mathsf{SS}} c \cdot L_{\mathsf{SS},i} \cdot \mathbf{s}_i + \mathbf{r}_i + \boldsymbol{\Delta}_i = c \cdot \mathbf{s} + \sum_{j \in \mathsf{SS}} \mathbf{r}_i$$

Since this is exactly the same as those computed in [30], correctness is satisfied under the same parameters as theirs.

Selective Security. Due to the proof being quite long and involved, we provide a proof overview of our 3-round threshold signature $\mathsf{TRaccoon}_{\text{3-rnd}}^{\text{sel}}$ here. Our scheme achieves selective security under the same assumptions to the selectively secure three round scheme [30] without using signature schemes. Below, we state the simplified main theorem statement of this section establishing the security of $\mathsf{TRaccoon}_{\text{3-rnd}}^{\text{sel}}$. For the formal main theorem, security proof, and for which the following theorem holds are provided in Theorem 4.1, App. E.1, and App. D in the full version, respectively.

Theorem 1 (simplified). *The 3-round threshold signature $\mathsf{TRaccoon}_{\text{3-rnd}}^{\text{sel}}$ is selectively secure under the* Hint-MLWE *and* SelfTargetMSIS *assumptions.*

Proof Overview. Let us provide the proof overview. Our strategy is to use a hybrid argument to transition to a game, where the challenger simulates the signing oracles without the secret key shares $(\mathbf{s}_i)_{i \in \mathsf{HS}}$. We then embed an SelfTargetMSIS problem into the verification key and extract a solution from the forgery. We denote by $\mathcal{A}$ the adversary, and by sHS (resp. sCS) the subset of honest users sHS = SS ∩ HS (resp. corrupt users sCS = SS ∩ CS) queried to the signing oracle. We describe the hybrids below.

Game_1 to Game_3: *postpone sampling* $\mathbf{w}_i$. In Game_1 to Game_3, the challenger delays sampling $\mathbf{w}_i$ until the 2nd round. Instead of committing to $\mathbf{w}_i$ in $\mathcal{O}_{\text{Sign}_1}$, the challenger samples a random $\text{cmt}_i \xleftarrow{\$} \{0,1\}^{2\lambda}$. In $\mathcal{O}_{\text{Sign}_2}$, it samples $\mathbf{w}_i = \mathbf{A}\mathbf{r}_i + \mathbf{e}'_i$ as before and programs H_{com} such that $\text{cmt}_i = \mathsf{H}_{\text{com}}(\mathbf{w}_i, i)$. Also, the challenger aborts in case there is a collision in H_{com} and prepares some tables for bookkeeping in $\mathcal{O}_{\text{Sign}_2}$. In more detail:

Game_1: This game is identical to the real game.

Game_2 : In this game, the challenger outputs a fresh $\text{cmt}_i \xleftarrow{\$} \{0,1\}^{2\lambda}$ in $\mathcal{O}_{\text{Sign}_1}$ and delays sampling $\mathbf{w}_i$ until $\mathcal{O}_{\text{Sign}_2}$, where H_{com} is programmed such that $\text{cmt}_i = \mathsf{H}_{\text{com}}(\mathbf{w}_i, i)$. Since $\mathbf{w}_i$ has high min-entropy, this change is unnoticeable.

Game_3: In this game, the challenger aborts if there is a collision in H_{com}. Note that the output of H_{com} is of bit-size 2λ, so we can conclude that the abort probability is negligible by a birthday bound argument.

Game_4: In this game, the challenger introduces tables UnOpenedHS and SumComRnd in $\mathcal{O}_{\text{Sign}_2}$, indexed by $\text{ctnt}_\mathbf{w} := \text{SS}\|\text{M}\|(\text{cmt}_j)_{j \in \text{SS}}$. Note that $\text{ctnt}_\mathbf{w}$ represents the signer's view in $\mathcal{O}_{\text{Sign}_2}$. None of these tables are accessed, so the view of $\mathcal{A}$ remains identical, but we describe their meaning below. If $\text{UnOpenedHS}[\text{ctnt}_\mathbf{w}] \neq \bot$, then some honest user started round 2 with $\text{ctnt}_\mathbf{w}$ and $\text{UnOpenedHS}[\text{ctnt}_\mathbf{w}] = \widetilde{\text{sHS}}_\mathbf{w}$ stores the set of honest users $\widetilde{\text{sHS}}_\mathbf{w}$ that have not passed round 2 with $\text{ctnt}_\mathbf{w}$. The table $\text{SumComRnd}[\text{ctnt}_\mathbf{w}]$ stores the sum of the commitment $\mathbf{w}_i$'s randomness $\mathbf{r}_i$ of honest users $i \in \text{sHS} \setminus \widetilde{\text{sHS}}_\mathbf{w}$, i.e., honest users that have opened their commitment cmt_i via $\mathcal{O}_{\text{Sign}_2}$ with respect to $\text{ctnt}_\mathbf{w}$.

Before proceeding, let us remark that the adversary cannot invoke $\mathcal{O}_{\text{Sign}_2}$ (resp. $\mathcal{O}_{\text{Sign}_3}$) twice with the same value $\text{ctnt}_\mathbf{w}$ for a honest user $i \in \text{sHS}$ except with negligible probability. This is because user i samples cmt_i with high min-entropy in $\mathcal{O}_{\text{Sign}_1}$ at random and cmt_i is part of $\text{ctnt}_\mathbf{w}$. In some sense, this notion of uniqueness of $\text{ctnt}_\mathbf{w}$ is a core reason we can omit the requirement of a unique session identifier (which was required in [30]). This is captured in the following remark.

Remark 1. The adversary cannot invoke $\mathcal{O}_{\text{Sign}_2}$ (resp. $\mathcal{O}_{\text{Sign}_3}$) twice with the same value $\text{ctnt}_\mathbf{w}$.

Game_5 to Game_9: *sample* $\widetilde{\mathbf{z}}_i$ *at random*. In Game_5 to Game_9, the challenger transitions to a game where $\widetilde{\mathbf{z}}_i \xleftarrow{\$} \mathcal{R}_q^\ell$ is sampled at random. Roughly, this is possible because $\widetilde{\mathbf{z}}_i = \mathbf{z}_i + \mathbf{\Delta}_i$ is masked by $\mathbf{\Delta}_i = \text{ZeroShare}(\text{seed}_i[\text{SS}], \text{ctnt}_\mathbf{z})$. Note that not all responses $\widetilde{\mathbf{z}}_i$ are random in the view of $\mathcal{A}$: the last mask $\mathbf{\Delta}_i$ is fully determined by $(\mathbf{\Delta}_j)_{j \in \text{SS} \setminus \{i\}}$ since all masks sum up to $\mathbf{0}$ (cf. Eq. (1)). Thus, when i is the last user to sign with respect to $\text{ctnt}_\mathbf{w}$, then the response $\widetilde{\mathbf{z}}_i$ is setup *consistently* in $\mathcal{O}_{\text{Sign}_3}$, i.e., it respects the constraint $\mathbf{\Delta}_i = -\sum_{j \in \text{SS} \setminus \{i\}} \mathbf{\Delta}_j$.

Note that while in the protocol, the value $\mathsf{ctnt_z}$ serves as input to ZeroShare, the value $\mathsf{ctnt_w}$ uniquely defines $\mathsf{ctnt_z}$ implicitly due to the binding of the hash commitments. This allows us to interchange $\mathsf{ctnt_w}$ and $\mathsf{ctnt_z}$ within the security proof when analyzing the distribution of $\boldsymbol{\Delta}_i$.

Also, observe that if the views of honest users $\mathsf{ctnt_w}$ were distinct in round 2, then the value $\mathsf{ctnt_z}$ is distinct in round 3, so all $\boldsymbol{\Delta}_i$ are distributed at random. This observation is the core reason we can simulate later: if the view $\mathsf{ctnt_w}$ is identical amongst honest users in round 2, then we can invoke HVZK with respect to the verification key $\mathbf{t}$ and program H_c accordingly. If the view is distinct in round 2, then the reduction cannot simulate, but since all responses in round 3 are random, this is not required. Our proof structure handles this by only sampling $\widetilde{\mathbf{z}}_i$ consistently if i is the last user in round 3 with respect to $\mathsf{ctnt_w}$. Below, we show that the last masked response is distributed as follows:

$$\widetilde{\mathbf{z}}_i := c \cdot \mathbf{s} - c \sum_{j \in \mathsf{sCS}} L_{\mathsf{SS},j} \cdot \mathbf{s}_j + \mathsf{SumComRnd}[\mathsf{ctnt_w}] - \sum_{j \in \mathsf{sHS} \setminus \{i\}} \widetilde{\mathbf{z}}_j - \sum_{j \in \mathsf{sCS}} \boldsymbol{\Delta}_j, \quad (2)$$

where $\widetilde{\mathbf{z}}_j$ is the masked response of user i with $\mathsf{ctnt_w}$. Recall that $\mathsf{SumComRnd}[\mathsf{ctnt_w}] = \sum_{j \in \mathsf{sHS}} \mathbf{r}_j$ stores the sum of the honest commitment $\mathbf{w}_j$'s randomness.

Game$_5$: In this game, the challenger introduces tables $\mathsf{UnSignedHS}, \mathsf{Mask_z}$ and $\mathsf{MaskedResp}$ indexed by $\mathsf{ctnt_w}$. None of the tables impact the view of $\mathcal{A}$ but we detail their meaning. If $\mathsf{UnSignedHS}[\mathsf{ctnt_w}] \neq \bot$, then it stores the set of honest users $\widetilde{\mathsf{sHS_z}}$ that have not passed round 3 with $\mathsf{ctnt_w}$. The tables $\mathsf{Mask_z}[\mathsf{ctnt_w}, i]$ and $\mathsf{MaskedResp}[\mathsf{ctnt_w}, i]$ store the mask $\boldsymbol{\Delta}_i$ and the masked response $\widetilde{\mathbf{z}}_i$ of user i in $\mathcal{O}_{\mathsf{Sign}_3}$ with $\mathsf{ctnt_w}$.

Game$_6$: In this game, we expand the definition of ZeroShare in $\mathcal{O}_{\mathsf{Sign}_3}$. The challenger samples partial masks $\mathbf{m}_{i,j} = \mathsf{H}_{\mathsf{mask}}(\mathsf{seed}_{i,j}, \mathsf{ctnt_z})$ and $\mathbf{m}_{j,i} = \mathsf{H}_{\mathsf{mask}}(\mathsf{seed}_{j,i}, \mathsf{ctnt_z})$ for $j \in \mathsf{SS} \setminus \{i\}$, then sets $\boldsymbol{\Delta}_i = \sum_{j \in \mathsf{SS} \setminus \{i\}} (\mathbf{m}_{j,i} - \mathbf{m}_{i,j})$. This change is purely conceptual.

Game$_7$: In this game, the challenger samples the partial masks $\mathbf{m}_{i,j}$ and $\mathbf{m}_{j,i}$ at random for $j \in \widetilde{\mathsf{sHS_z}} \setminus \{i\}$ (and programs $\mathsf{H}_{\mathsf{mask}}$ accordingly). Both games are identically distributed in the view of $\mathcal{A}$ because seeds $\mathsf{seed}_{i,j}$ and $\mathsf{seed}_{j,i}$ are hidden from $\mathcal{A}$ and the partial masks have not yet been evaluated for users in $j \in \widetilde{\mathsf{sHS_z}}$. In the detailed proof, we argue this formally via Remark 1.

Game$_8$: In this game, the challenger samples the mask $\boldsymbol{\Delta}_i \xleftarrow{\$} \mathcal{R}_q^\ell$ in $\mathcal{O}_{\mathsf{Sign}_3}$, except if $\widetilde{\mathsf{sHS_z}} = \{i\}$, i.e., user i is the last signer with respect to $\mathsf{ctnt_w}$. If i is the last signer, it sets

$$\boldsymbol{\Delta}_i = - \sum_{j \in \mathsf{sHS} \setminus \{i\}} \mathsf{Mask_z}[\mathsf{ctnt_w}, j] - \sum_{j \in \mathsf{sCS}} \boldsymbol{\Delta}_j. \quad (3)$$

Both games are identically distributed because: (1) If i is not the last signer for $\mathsf{ctnt_w}$, then $\widetilde{\mathsf{sHS_z}} \setminus \{i\}$ contains at least another honest signer j, so $\mathbf{m}_{i,j}$ and $\mathbf{m}_{j,i}$ are sampled at random from the previous game. in particular, $\boldsymbol{\Delta}_i =

$\sum_{j \in \mathsf{SS} \setminus \{i\}} (\mathbf{m}_{j,i} - \mathbf{m}_{i,j})$ is distributed uniform random over $\mathcal{R}_q^\ell$. (2) If i is the last signer for $\mathsf{ctnt_w}$, then all partial masks are fully determined. Since we have that $\sum_{j \in \mathsf{SS}} \Delta_j = \mathbf{0}$ (cf. Eq. (1)), we can reorder the expression to obtain Eq. (3) via the identity $\mathsf{Mask_z}[\mathsf{ctnt_w}, j] = \Delta_j$. Lastly, note that the masked response for each signer i is still defined as in the real game:

$$\widetilde{\mathbf{z}}_i := c \cdot L_{\mathsf{SS},i} \cdot \mathbf{s}_i + \mathbf{r}_i + \Delta_i. \tag{4}$$

Game_9: In this game, the challenger aborts if in $\mathcal{O}_{\mathsf{Sign}_3}$ the value of challenge c is not unique amongst invocations with $\mathsf{ctnt_w}$. The view of $\mathcal{A}$ remains identical conditioned on no abort. Note that the hash commitments $(\mathsf{cmt}_j)_{j \in \mathsf{SS}}$ in $\mathsf{ctnt_w}$ fix the commitments $\mathbf{w}_i$ due to binding. Since $c = \mathsf{H}_c(\mathsf{vk}, \mathsf{M}, \mathbf{w})$, where $\mathbf{w} := \lfloor \sum_{j \in \mathsf{SS}} \mathbf{w}_j \rceil_{\nu_\mathbf{w}}$, the value of c is fixed by $\mathsf{ctnt_w}$ and the abort probability is negligible.

Game_{10}: In this game, the challenger instead samples $\widetilde{\mathbf{z}}_i \xleftarrow{\$} \mathcal{R}_q^\ell$ in $\mathcal{O}_{\mathsf{Sign}_3}$, except if $\widetilde{\mathsf{sHS}}_\mathbf{z} = \{i\}$. If $\widetilde{\mathsf{sHS}}_\mathbf{z} = \{i\}$, then it sets $\widetilde{\mathbf{z}}_i$ according to Eq. (2). We can show that Game_{10} and Game_9 are identically distributed by looking at an intermediate game $\mathsf{Game}_{9,*}$, where instead of sampling $\Delta_i \xleftarrow{\$} \mathcal{R}_q^\ell$, we sample $\Delta_i^* \xleftarrow{\$} \mathcal{R}_q^\ell$ and set $\Delta_i := \Delta_i^* - (c \cdot L_{\mathsf{SS},i} \cdot \mathbf{s}_i + \mathbf{r}_i)$. This intermediate game is identically distributed to Game_9 as both Δ_i and Δ_i^* are uniform random. Also, observe that in $\mathsf{Game}_{9,*}$, we have that $\widetilde{\mathbf{z}}_i = \Delta_i^*$ if $\widetilde{\mathsf{sHS}}_\mathbf{z} \neq \{i\}$ due to Eq. (4), and $\widetilde{\mathbf{z}}_i$ as in Eq. (2) otherwise. To see the latter, first substitute $\mathsf{Mask_z}[\mathsf{ctnt_w}, j] = \Delta_j = \widetilde{\mathbf{z}}_j - (c \cdot L_{\mathsf{SS},j} \cdot \mathbf{s}_j + \mathbf{r}_j)$ for all $j \in \mathsf{sHS} \setminus \{i\}$ in Eq. (3), then substitute the resulting identity for Δ_i in the identity of $\widetilde{\mathbf{z}}_i$ in Eq. (4). Finally, using the equality $\mathbf{s} = \sum_{j \in \mathsf{SS}} L_{\mathsf{SS},j} \cdot \mathbf{s}_j$ yields Eq. (2). We point out that for the last step, it is crucial that the value c is identical for all users in round 3 with $\mathsf{ctnt_w}$. This is guaranteed by the abort condition added in the previous game.

Game_{11} *to* Game_{14}: *Invoke HVZK.* In games Game_{11} to Game_{14}, we invoke HVZK to simulate the commitment $\mathbf{w}_i$ for the last signer i in round 2 with respect to the verification key $\mathbf{t}$. This later allows to compute the response $\widetilde{\mathbf{z}}_h$ of the last signer h in round 3 without secret key $\mathbf{s}$. At the end of Game_{14}, the challenger no longer requires the secret key $\mathbf{s}$ to simulate the signing oracles.

Game_{11}: In this game, the challenger chooses a random challenge $c \xleftarrow{\$} \mathcal{C}$ before sampling the commitment $\mathbf{w}_i$ for the last signer i in round 2 with $\mathsf{ctnt_w}$. Before outputting $\mathbf{w}_i$, the challenger retrieves the other commitments $\mathbf{w}_j$ for $j \in \mathsf{SS} \setminus \{i\}$ from cmt_j by searching through all the random oracle queries made to $\mathsf{H}_{\mathsf{com}}$. If $\mathbf{w}_j$ are found, it programs H_c such that $\mathsf{H}_c(\mathsf{vk}, \mathsf{M}, \mathbf{w}) = c$, where $\mathbf{w} = \lfloor \sum_{j \in \mathsf{SS}} \mathbf{w}_j \rceil_{\nu_\mathbf{w}}$. Further, the challenger aborts if some $\mathbf{w}_j$ was not found in round 2, but $\mathcal{O}_{\mathsf{Sign}_3}$ is invoked for all honest users with $\mathsf{ctnt_w}$.

Note that since $\mathbf{w}_i$ has high min-entropy, H_c was never queried with $(\mathsf{vk}, \mathsf{M}, \mathbf{w})$ before it is programmed, so the view of $\mathcal{A}$ is identically distributed. Let us analyze the probability of an abort. Since the challenger checks in $\mathcal{O}_{\mathsf{Sign}_3}$ whether each $\mathbf{w}_j$ is committed in cmt_j, the adversary must have found a preimage for cmt_j between the last call to $\mathcal{O}_{\mathsf{Sign}_2}$ with $\mathsf{ctnt_w}$ and the first call to $\mathcal{O}_{\mathsf{Sign}_3}$ with $\mathsf{ctnt_w}$. This happens with negligible probability.

Game$_{12}$: In this game, the challenger invokes HVZK with respect to the verification key $\mathbf{t}$ to simulate the commitment $\mathbf{w}_i$ of the last honest signer i in round 2, and computes the response $\widetilde{\mathbf{z}}_h$ of the last honest user h in round 3 in a different manner. Note that the last signers in round $\mathcal{O}_{\mathsf{Sign}_2}$ and $\mathcal{O}_{\mathsf{Sign}_3}$ are not required to be the same, i.e., it can be that $h \neq i$. In more detail, in $\mathcal{O}_{\mathsf{Sign}_2}$ if $\widetilde{\mathsf{sHS}}_\mathbf{w} = \{i\}$, after sampling the challenge c, the challenger simulates the commitment-response pair $(\mathbf{w}_i, \mathbf{z}_*)$, where $\mathbf{z}_* = c \cdot \mathbf{s} + \mathbf{r}_i$. Also, $\mathbf{r}_i$ is *not* added to $\mathsf{SumComRnd}[\mathsf{ctnt_w}]$. Instead, the challenger computes the last honest response, i.e., if $\widetilde{\mathsf{sHS}}_\mathbf{z} = \{h\}$ in $\mathcal{O}_{\mathsf{Sign}_3}$, via the simulated response $\mathbf{z}_*$

$$\widetilde{\mathbf{z}}_h := \mathbf{z}_* - c \sum_{j \in \mathsf{sCS}} L_{\mathsf{SS},j} \cdot \mathbf{s}_j + \mathsf{SumComRnd}[\mathsf{ctnt_w}] - \sum_{j \in \mathsf{sHS} \setminus \{h\}} \widetilde{\mathbf{z}}_j - \sum_{j \in \mathsf{sCS}} \mathbf{\Delta}_j,$$

where the simulated response is chosen as above.

The above identity for $\widetilde{\mathbf{z}}_h$ is obtained by rewriting Eq. (2) using $\mathbf{z}_* = c \cdot \mathbf{s} + \mathbf{r}_i$. Note that it is crucial that the challenge c—precomputed when the last user i opens its commitment in round 2 to define $\mathbf{z}_*$—must be identical to the challenge c in round 3 for the last user h. This is guaranteed by the abort condition in the previous game.

Game$_{13}$: In this game, the challenger replaces $\mathbf{t}$ in the verification key with $\mathbf{t} := \left[\widehat{\mathbf{t}}\right]_{\nu_t} \in \mathcal{R}_{q_{\nu_t}}^k$, where $\widehat{\mathbf{t}} \xleftarrow{\$} \mathcal{R}_q^k$. Also, when setting up the secret key shares, it samples $\mathbf{s}_i$ for $j \in \mathsf{CS}$ at random, and omits the honest secret key share in $\mathsf{vk}_i = (\bot, \vec{\mathsf{seed}}_i)$ for $j \in \mathsf{HS}$.

Observe that the challenger in Game$_{11}$ uses the secret key $\mathbf{s}$ only when computing the simulated response $\mathbf{z}_* = c \cdot \mathbf{s} + \mathbf{r}_i$ in $\mathcal{O}_{\mathsf{Sign}_2}$ for a challenge c randomly chosen by the challenger. Under Hint-MLWE, Game$_{12}$ and Game$_{13}$ are indistinguishable. Note that simulated responses $\mathbf{z}_*$ correspond to the provided hints in Hint-MLWE.

Reduction from SelfTargetMSIS. In Game$_{13}$, the challenger no longer requires the secret key $\mathbf{s}$ to run the game. When considering the same unforgeability notion as [30], the rest of the proof is identical to theirs. We refer to Sect. 4.1 in the full version for details on the proof with respect to the stronger definition.

4 Construction of Our 5-Round Threshold Raccoon

In this section, we present our 5-round threshold signature scheme $\mathsf{TRaccoon}_{\text{5-rnd}}^{\mathsf{adp}}$. We prove that $\mathsf{TRaccoon}_{\text{5-rnd}}^{\mathsf{adp}}$ is adaptive secure under the Hint-MLWE and SelfTargetMSIS assumptions.

4.1 Parameters and Preparations

The used parameters are identical to $\text{TRaccoon}_{\text{3-rnd}}^{\text{sel}}$ (cf. Sect. 3) and the threshold protocol by del Pino et al. [30]. We refer the readers to Table 3 for the parameters. Moreover, the correctness and security proof relies on the same parameter selection as well.

As in $\text{TRaccoon}_{\text{3-rnd}}^{\text{sel}}$, we rely on masking via the helper algorithm ZeroShare. The definition is identical, except that we assume that H_{mask} outputs vectors over $\mathcal{R}_q^k$ and $\mathcal{R}_q^\ell$ when the first bit of the input x is 0 and 1, respectively. Looking ahead, we use ZeroShare to mask the commitment $\mathbf{w}_i \in \mathcal{R}_q^k$ and response $\mathbf{z}_i \in \mathcal{R}_q^\ell$. Note that Eq. (1) still holds (i.e., $\sum_{i \in \text{SS}} \text{ZeroShare}(\vec{\text{seed}}_i[\text{SS}], x) = \mathbf{0}$) with this minor modification.

In addition, we also require an EUF-CMA secure signature scheme $\text{S} = (\text{KeyGen}_\text{S}, \text{Sign}_\text{S}, \text{Verify}_\text{S})$. Looking ahead, we use S in the security proof to ensure that the view of all honest users is consistent in the round where the commitment cmt_i is revealed.

4.2 Construction

We present the construction of our 5-round threshold signature $\text{TRaccoon}_{\text{5-rnd}}^{\text{adp}}$. Below, we give an overview. Our scheme uses three hash functions modeled as a random oracle in the security proof. $\text{H}_{\text{com}} : \{0,1\}^* \to \{0,1\}^{2\lambda}$ is used to generate the hash commitment. $\text{H}_c : \{0,1\}^* \to \mathcal{C}$ is used to generate the random challenge polynomial for which the users reply with a response. $\text{H}_{\text{mask}} : \{0,1\}^* \to \mathcal{R}_q^k \cup \mathcal{R}_q^\ell$ is used to generate the random vectors to mask the individual commitment or response via ZeroShare.

The setup algorithm outputs system parameters $\text{tspar} = (\mathbf{A}, N, T)$ for some random $\mathbf{A} \xleftarrow{\$} \mathcal{R}_q^{k \times \ell}$. The public key is identical to a Raccoon public key $\text{vk} = (\text{tspar}, \mathbf{t})$ with Raccoon secret key $\mathbf{s}$, and the secret keys are of the form $\text{sk}_i = (\mathbf{s}_i, (\text{vk}_{\text{S},j})_{j \in [N]}, \text{sk}_{\text{S},i}, \vec{\text{seed}}_i)$, where $\mathbf{s}_i$ is a share of $\mathbf{s}$, $(\text{vk}_{\text{S},j})_{j \in [N]}$ are S verification keys with secret keys $(\text{sk}_{\text{S},j})_{j \in [N]}$, and $\vec{\text{seed}}_i$ are seeds for ZeroShare. Verification is identical to Raccoon verification. The signing protocol proceeds in 5 rounds and is described in Fig. 1.

Let us highlight the main differences to our 3-round selective threshold signature $\text{TRaccoon}_{\text{3-rnd}}^{\text{sel}}$ from Sect. 3. These changes are made to prove adaptive security. We provide some intuition for our choices.

<u>Masking the Commitments.</u> In $\text{TRaccoon}_{\text{3-rnd}}^{\text{sel}}$, the signer sends the commitments $\mathbf{w}_i$ in clear. In security proof, one $\mathbf{w}_i$ per session is simulated via HVZK. In that case, the reduction does *not* know its randomness $\mathbf{r}_i$ and $\mathbf{e}'_i$. But in the adaptive setting, the adversary $\mathcal{A}$ is allowed to corrupt honest users after $\mathbf{w}_i$ is output. Then, we have to provide the randomness $(\mathbf{r}_i, \mathbf{e}'_i)$ to $\mathcal{A}$, so the reduction fails in the adaptive setting.

In $\text{TRaccoon}_{\text{5-rnd}}^{\text{adp}}$, the signer masks the commitment $\mathbf{w}_i$ with a fresh mask $\widetilde{\boldsymbol{\Delta}}_i = \text{ZeroShare}(\vec{\text{seed}}_i[\text{SS}], \text{cnt}_\mathbf{w})$ and sends $\widetilde{\mathbf{w}}_i = \mathbf{w}_i + \widetilde{\boldsymbol{\Delta}}_i$ instead of $\mathbf{w}_i$, where

$\mathsf{ctnt}_\mathsf{w} = 0\|\mathsf{SS}\|(\mathsf{str}_j)_{j \in \mathsf{SS}}$. Here, str_j are random strings exchanged in the additional initial round. Note that the entropy of str_i ensures that each mask $\widetilde{\boldsymbol{\Delta}}_i$ is random in each signing session[5]. With our modification, the values $(\widetilde{\mathbf{w}}_j)_{j \in \mathsf{SS}}$ output in round 4 only reveal the sum $\mathbf{w} = \left\lfloor \sum_{j \in \mathsf{SS}} \mathbf{w}_i \right\rceil_{\nu_\mathsf{w}}$. This allows the reduction to simulate a single commitment $\mathbf{w}_*$ via HVZK and sample the other commitments $\mathbf{w}_j = \mathbf{A} \cdot \mathbf{r}_j + \mathbf{e}'_j$ honestly with known $(\mathbf{r}_j, \mathbf{e}'_j)$ for honest users. When some user i is corrupted, we can choose a honest commitment $\mathbf{w}_j$ and program $\mathsf{H}_{\mathsf{mask}}$ in such a way that $\widetilde{\mathbf{w}}_i = \mathbf{w}_j + \widetilde{\boldsymbol{\Delta}}_i$. Since at most $T-1$ honest users are corrupted, we never have to reveal the randomness of the simulated $\mathbf{w}_*$. Formalizing this vague argument is a core technical challenge in the security proof.

Authenticating the Views. In $\mathsf{TRaccoon}^{\mathsf{sel}}_{\mathsf{3\text{-}rnd}}$, the security proof crucially relies on the fact that ctnt_w in round 2 fixes the value of ctnt_z used in round 3. The security proof of $\mathsf{TRaccoon}^{\mathsf{adp}}_{\mathsf{5\text{-}rnd}}$ also requires this to hold, but here, ctnt_w does not contain the commitments $(\mathsf{cmt}_j)_{j \in \mathsf{SS}}$. Thus, ctnt_w itself does not determine ctnt_z yet. Instead, we ensure that for each ctnt_w, there is a unique ctnt_z in round 5 via signature-based authentication of the views in round 4.

Reducing the Number of Rounds. We provide a stateful 4 round Raccoon threshold signature $\mathsf{TRaccoon}^{\mathsf{adp}}_{\mathsf{4\text{-}rnd}}$, obtained by a simple modification of $\mathsf{TRaccoon}^{\mathsf{adp}}_{\mathsf{5\text{-}rnd}}$. Roughly, we replace $(\mathsf{str}_j)_{j \in \mathsf{SS}}$ with a unique session identifier sid and omit the first round. If sid is never reused, we can show adaptive security. We refer to the full version for details.

4.3 Correctness and Adaptive Security

Correctness. Correctness follows as in Sect. 3.3, as the only difference between $\mathsf{TRaccoon}^{\mathsf{sel}}_{\mathsf{3\text{-}rnd}}$ and $\mathsf{TRaccoon}^{\mathsf{adp}}_{\mathsf{5\text{-}rnd}}$ is that the commitment $\mathbf{w}$ is computed in a different manner and the additional signature verification step. By using Eq. (1), the commitment $\mathbf{w}$ can be rewritten as

$$\mathbf{w} = \left\lfloor \sum_{j \in \mathsf{SS}} \widetilde{\mathbf{w}}_i \right\rceil_{\nu_\mathsf{w}} = \left\lfloor \sum_{j \in \mathsf{SS}} \mathbf{w}_i + \widetilde{\boldsymbol{\Delta}}_i \right\rceil_{\nu_\mathsf{w}} = \left\lfloor \sum_{j \in \mathsf{SS}} \mathbf{w}_i \right\rceil_{\nu_\mathsf{w}}.$$

This is exactly how $\mathbf{w}$ is computed in $\mathsf{TRaccoon}^{\mathsf{adp}}_{\mathsf{3\text{-}rnd}}$. Also, by correctness of the signature scheme S, the signatures $\sigma_{\mathsf{S},i}$ on M_S verify correctly in Sign_4 when computed as in Sign_3.

Adaptive Security. We provide the proof overview of our 5-round threshold signature $\mathsf{TRaccoon}^{\mathsf{adp}}_{\mathsf{5\text{-}rnd}}$. We emphasize that $\mathsf{TRaccoon}^{\mathsf{adp}}_{\mathsf{5\text{-}rnd}}$ achieves adaptive security under the same assumption as the Raccoon [31] signature scheme. The

---

[5] More concretely, it is guaranteed that ZeroShare is never invoked more than once with the same input ctnt_w for each honest user. This allows the reduction to program $\mathsf{H}_{\mathsf{mask}}$ freely in the security proof.

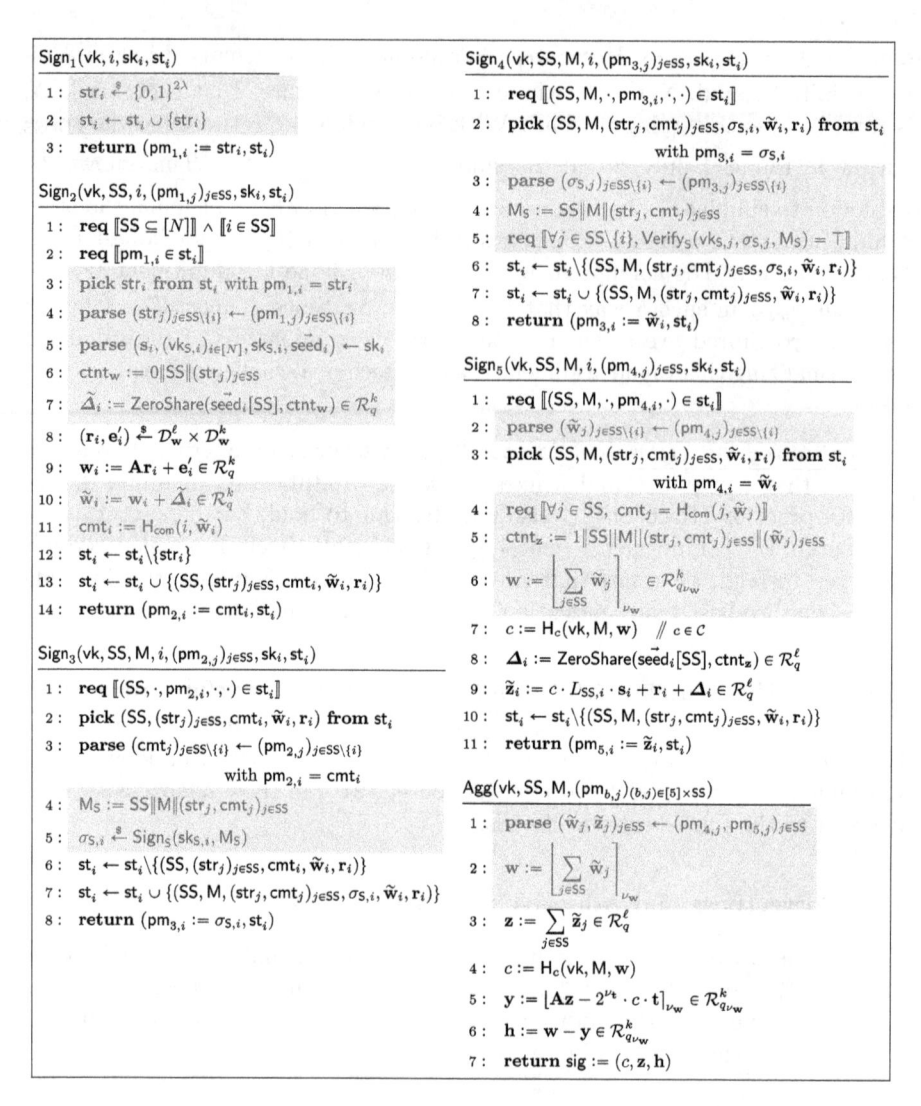

```
Sign₁(vk, i, skᵢ, stᵢ)
─────────────────────────────
1 :  strᵢ ←$ {0,1}^{2λ}
2 :  stᵢ ← stᵢ ∪ {strᵢ}
3 :  return (pm₁,ᵢ := strᵢ, stᵢ)

Sign₂(vk, SS, i, (pm₁,ⱼ)ⱼ∈SS, skᵢ, stᵢ)
─────────────────────────────
1 :  req [SS ⊆ [N]] ∧ [i ∈ SS]
2 :  req [pm₁,ᵢ ∈ stᵢ]
3 :  pick strᵢ from stᵢ with pm₁,ᵢ = strᵢ
4 :  parse (strⱼ)ⱼ∈SS\{i} ← (pm₁,ⱼ)ⱼ∈SS\{i}
5 :  parse (sᵢ, (vkS,ᵢ)ᵢ∈[N], skS,ᵢ, seedᵢ) ← skᵢ
6 :  cntt_w := 0‖SS‖(strⱼ)ⱼ∈SS
7 :  Δ̃ᵢ := ZeroShare(seedᵢ[SS], cntt_w) ∈ R_q^k
8 :  (rᵢ, e'ᵢ) ←$ D_w^ℓ × D_w^k
9 :  wᵢ := Arᵢ + e'ᵢ ∈ R_q^k
10:  w̃ᵢ := wᵢ + Δ̃ᵢ ∈ R_q^k
11:  cmtᵢ := H_com(i, w̃ᵢ)
12:  stᵢ ← stᵢ\{strᵢ}
13:  stᵢ ← stᵢ ∪ {(SS, (strⱼ)ⱼ∈SS, cmtᵢ, w̃ᵢ, rᵢ)}
14:  return (pm₂,ᵢ := cmtᵢ, stᵢ)

Sign₃(vk, SS, M, i, (pm₂,ⱼ)ⱼ∈SS, skᵢ, stᵢ)
─────────────────────────────
1 :  req [(SS, ·, pm₂,ᵢ, ·, ·) ∈ stᵢ]
2 :  pick (SS, (strⱼ)ⱼ∈SS, cmtᵢ, w̃ᵢ, rᵢ) from stᵢ
3 :  parse (cmtⱼ)ⱼ∈SS\{i} ← (pm₂,ⱼ)ⱼ∈SS\{i}
        with pm₂,ᵢ = cmtᵢ
4 :  M_S := SS‖M‖(strⱼ, cmtⱼ)ⱼ∈SS
5 :  σ_S,ᵢ ←$ Sign_S(sk_S,ᵢ, M_S)
6 :  stᵢ ← stᵢ\{(SS, (strⱼ)ⱼ∈SS, cmtᵢ, w̃ᵢ, rᵢ)}
7 :  stᵢ ← stᵢ ∪ {(SS, M, (strⱼ, cmtⱼ)ⱼ∈SS, σ_S,ᵢ, w̃ᵢ, rᵢ)}
8 :  return (pm₃,ᵢ := σ_S,ᵢ, stᵢ)

Sign₄(vk, SS, M, i, (pm₃,ⱼ)ⱼ∈SS, skᵢ, stᵢ)
─────────────────────────────
1 :  req [(SS, M, ·, pm₃,ᵢ, ·, ·) ∈ stᵢ]
2 :  pick (SS, M, (strⱼ, cmtⱼ)ⱼ∈SS, σ_S,ᵢ, w̃ᵢ, rᵢ) from stᵢ
        with pm₃,ᵢ = σ_S,ᵢ
3 :  parse (σ_S,ⱼ)ⱼ∈SS\{i} ← (pm₃,ⱼ)ⱼ∈SS\{i}
4 :  M_S := SS‖M‖(strⱼ, cmtⱼ)ⱼ∈SS
5 :  req [∀j ∈ SS\{i}, Verify_S(vk_S,ⱼ, σ_S,ⱼ, M_S) = ⊤]
6 :  stᵢ ← stᵢ\{(SS, M, (strⱼ, cmtⱼ)ⱼ∈SS, σ_S,ᵢ, w̃ᵢ, rᵢ)}
7 :  stᵢ ← stᵢ ∪ {(SS, M, (strⱼ, cmtⱼ)ⱼ∈SS, w̃ᵢ, rᵢ)}
8 :  return (pm₃,ᵢ := w̃ᵢ, stᵢ)

Sign₅(vk, SS, M, i, (pm₄,ⱼ)ⱼ∈SS, skᵢ, stᵢ)
─────────────────────────────
1 :  req [(SS, M, ·, pm₄,ᵢ, ·) ∈ stᵢ]
2 :  parse (w̃ⱼ)ⱼ∈SS\{i} ← (pm₄,ⱼ)ⱼ∈SS\{i}
3 :  pick (SS, M, (strⱼ, cmtⱼ)ⱼ∈SS, w̃ᵢ, rᵢ) from stᵢ
        with pm₄,ᵢ = w̃ᵢ
4 :  req [∀j ∈ SS, cmtⱼ = H_com(j, w̃ⱼ)]
5 :  cntt_x := 1‖SS‖M‖(strⱼ, cmtⱼ)ⱼ∈SS‖(w̃ⱼ)ⱼ∈SS
6 :  w := ⌊∑_{j∈SS} w̃ⱼ⌉_{ν_w} ∈ R_{q_{ν_w}}^k
7 :  c := H_c(vk, M, w)   // c ∈ C
8 :  Δᵢ := ZeroShare(seedᵢ[SS], cntt_x) ∈ R_q^ℓ
9 :  z̃ᵢ := c · L_{SS,i} · sᵢ + rᵢ + Δᵢ ∈ R_q^ℓ
10:  stᵢ ← stᵢ\{(SS, M, (strⱼ, cmtⱼ)ⱼ∈SS, w̃ᵢ, rᵢ)}
11:  return (pm₅,ᵢ := z̃ᵢ, stᵢ)

Agg(vk, SS, M, (pm_{b,j})_{(b,j)∈[5]×SS})
─────────────────────────────
1 :  parse (w̃ⱼ, z̃ⱼ)ⱼ∈SS ← (pm₄,ⱼ, pm₅,ⱼ)ⱼ∈SS
2 :  w := ⌊∑_{j∈SS} w̃ⱼ⌉_{ν_w}
3 :  z := ∑_{j∈SS} z̃ⱼ ∈ R_q^ℓ
4 :  c := H_c(vk, M, w)
5 :  y := ⌊Az - 2^{ν_t} · c · t⌉_{ν_w} ∈ R_{q_{ν_w}}^k
6 :  h := w - y ∈ R_{q_{ν_w}}^k
7 :  return sig := (c, z, h)
```

Fig. 1. The Signing protocol of our five round threshold signature TRaccoon$_{\text{5-rnd}}^{\text{adp}}$. In the above, $L_{SS,i}$ denotes the Lagrange coefficient of user i in the set $SS \subseteq [N]$ (see Sect. 2.2 for the definition). **pick X from Y** denotes the process of picking an element X from the set Y. The differences to TRaccoon$_{\text{3-rnd}}^{\text{sel}}$ are highlighted in blue (except changes with respect to the signer states).

formal security proof and the parameters for which the following theorem hold are provided in App. E.2 and App. D in the full version, respectively. Below, we state the main theorem establishing adaptive security of TRaccoon$_{\text{5-rnd}}^{\text{adp}}$.

Theorem 2 (simplified). *The 5-round threshold signature* TRaccoon$_{\text{5-rnd}}^{\text{adp}}$ *is adaptive secure under the* Hint-MLWE *and* SelfTargetMSIS *assumptions.*

Proof Overview. Let us provide the proof overview. As in the proof of TRaccoon$_{3\text{-rnd}}^{\text{sel}}$, our strategy is to use a hybrid argument to transition to a game, where the challenger simulates the signing oracles without the secret key s. We then embed an SelfTargetMSIS problem into the verification key and extract a solution from the forgery. The core difference to the security proof of TRaccoon$_{3\text{-rnd}}^{\text{sel}}$ is that the challenger provides a corruption oracle to the adversary $\mathcal{A}$. This means we have to setup the signer states st_i in accordance with the adversaries view when user i is corrupted. As before, we denote by sHS (resp. sCS) the subset of honest users sHS = SS∩HS (resp. corrupt users sCS = SS∩CS) queried to the signing or corruption oracle. We describe the hybrids below. Since the proof is involved, the arguments and hybrids are simplified for the sake of readability. We encourage the reader to first look at the proof overview for TRaccoon$_{3\text{-rnd}}^{\text{sel}}$ in Sect. 3.3 since the techniques are related—but simpler in the selective setting.

Game$_1$ to Game$_5$: In Game$_1$ to Game$_5$, the challenger delays sampling $\widetilde{\mathbf{w}}_i$ until the 4th round or when a user is corrupted. That is, the challenger outputs a random $\text{cmt}_i \xleftarrow{\$} \{0,1\}^{2\lambda}$ in $\mathcal{O}_{\text{Sign}_2}$. In $\mathcal{O}_{\text{Sign}_4}$, it samples $\mathbf{w}_i = \mathbf{A}\mathbf{r}_i + \mathbf{e}'_i$ and sets $\widetilde{\mathbf{w}}_i = \mathbf{w}_i + \widetilde{\boldsymbol{\Delta}}_i$. Then, it programs H_{com} such that $\text{cmt}_i = \mathsf{H}_{\text{com}}(\mathbf{w}_i, i)$ and outputs $\widetilde{\mathbf{w}}_i$. This is also done if i is corrupted for all signer states before round 4. Further, the challenger aborts in case there is a collision in H_{com} and ensures that all sampled str_i are unique.

Game$_1$: This game is identical to the real game.
Game$_2$: In this game, the challenger aborts in $\mathcal{O}_{\text{Sign}_1}$ if str_i was previously sampled. The abort probability is negligible because str_i has high min-entropy.
Game$_3$: In this game, the challenger outputs a fresh $\text{cmt}_i \xleftarrow{\$} \{0,1\}^{2\lambda}$ in $\mathcal{O}_{\text{Sign}_2}$. The preimage for cmt_i is computed either in $\mathcal{O}_{\text{Sign}_4}$ or $\mathcal{O}_{\text{Corrupt}}$ as described above. Since $\mathbf{w}_i$ has high min-entropy, this change is not noticable.
Game$_4$: In this game, the challenger aborts if there is a collision in H_{com}. We can show with as birthday bound argument that this happens with negligible probability.
Game$_5$: In this game, the challenger aborts if it the adversary invokes $\mathcal{O}_{\text{Sign}_4}$ but it did not sign M_S in $\mathcal{O}_{\text{Sign}_3}$ for all honest users. Under EUF-CMA security of S, this happens with negligible probability.

Before we proceed, let us discuss the implication of Game$_5$. Roughly, M_S corresponds to the view of each honest user in round 4 before the commitments are opened. The consistency check ensures that $\mathcal{O}_{\text{Sign}_5}$ is not invoked unless all honest users share an identical view in round 4 with respect to $\text{cnt}_\mathbf{w}$ *before* their commitments are opened. This is essential for simulation later.

Note that as in the selective proof of TRaccoon$_{3\text{-rnd}}^{\text{sel}}$, the adversary cannot invoke each signing oracle twice with the same value $\text{cnt}_\mathbf{w}$ for a honest user $i \in$ sHS except with negligible probability. Here, this is because user i samples str_i with high min-entropy in $\mathcal{O}_{\text{Sign}_1}$ at random and str_i is part of $\text{cnt}_\mathbf{w}$. This is captured in the following remark.

Game₆ to Game₁₁: In Game₆ to Game₁₁, the challenger transitions to a game where $\widetilde{\mathbf{w}}_j \xleftarrow{\$} \mathcal{R}_q^k$ is sampled at random, except the last revealed commitment $\widetilde{\mathbf{w}}_i$ is sampled *consistently*. Note that the adversary $\mathcal{A}$ can request the opening $\widetilde{\mathbf{w}}_i$ of hash commitment cmt_i either via a call to $\mathcal{O}_{\text{Sign}_4}$ by following the protocol *or* via a corruption query[6]. Again, consistently means that $\widetilde{\mathbf{w}}_i$ respects the constraint $\widetilde{\boldsymbol{\Delta}}_i = -\sum_{j \in \text{SS} \setminus \{i\}} \widetilde{\boldsymbol{\Delta}}_j$. Below, we show that the last masked commitment $\widetilde{\mathbf{w}}_i$ is distributed as follows:

$$\widetilde{\mathbf{w}}_i = \text{SumCom}[\text{cnt}_\mathbf{w}] - \sum_{j \in \text{sCS}} \widetilde{\boldsymbol{\Delta}}_j - \sum_{j \in \text{sHS} \setminus \{i\}} \widetilde{\mathbf{w}}_j, \qquad (5)$$

where $\widetilde{\mathbf{w}}_j$ is the masked commitment of user i with $\text{cnt}_\mathbf{w}$ and $\text{SumCom}[\text{cnt}_\mathbf{w}] = \sum_{j \in \text{sHS}} \mathbf{w}_j$ stores the sum of the honest commitments $(\mathbf{w}_j)_{j \in \text{sHS}}$. Further, since all $\widetilde{\mathbf{w}}_j$ but the last are random, the challenger can delay sampling the honest commitments $(\mathbf{w}_j)_{j \in \text{sHS}}$ until the last signer opens its commitment cmt_i. Also, observe that the protocol messages $(\widetilde{\mathbf{w}}_j)_{j \in \text{sHS}}$ of round 4 reveal only the sum of the commitments $\mathbf{w}_j$ but *not* their attribution to users, i.e., which user sampled which commitment $\mathbf{w}_j$. Thus, when the last cmt_i is opened to $\widetilde{\mathbf{w}}_i$, the challenger generates $|\text{sHS}|$-many honest commitments at once, stores them in $\text{UnUsedCom}[\text{cnt}_\mathbf{w}] = \{\widetilde{\mathbf{w}}_j\}_{j \in \text{SS}}$ and their sum in $\text{SumCom}[\text{cnt}_\mathbf{w}]$. The challenger then carefully attributes commitments from the set $\text{UnUsedCom}[\text{cnt}_\mathbf{w}]$ in round 5 or when a user between round 4 and 5 is corrupted. In the latter case, the reduction also programs the oracle H_{mask} so that the users state is consistent with the choice. Finally, the challenger also sets up a table $\text{SumComRnd}[\text{cnt}_\mathbf{w}] = \sum_{j \in \text{sHS}} \mathbf{r}_j$ that the sum of the honest commitments $\mathbf{w}_j$'s randomness for later.

Game₆ : In this game, we introduce some tables InitializeOpen, UnOpenedHS, $\text{Mask}_\mathbf{w}$ and MaskedCom indexed by $\text{cnt}_\mathbf{w}$. None of the tables impact the view of $\mathcal{A}$ but we detail their meaning. If $\text{InitializeOpen}[\text{cnt}_\mathbf{w}] \neq \bot$, then $\text{UnOpenedHS}[\text{cnt}_\mathbf{w}] = \widetilde{\text{sHS}}_\mathbf{w}$ stores the set of honest users $\widetilde{\text{sHS}}_\mathbf{w}$ that have not passed round 4 with $\text{cnt}_\mathbf{w}$, i.e., the hash commitment cmt_i is not yet opened. The tables $\text{Mask}_\mathbf{w}[\text{cnt}_\mathbf{w}, i]$ and $\text{MaskedCom}[\text{cnt}_\mathbf{w}, i]$ store the mask $\widetilde{\boldsymbol{\Delta}}_i$ and masked commitment $\widetilde{\mathbf{w}}_i$ of user i in $\mathcal{O}_{\text{Sign}_4}$ with $\text{cnt}_\mathbf{w}$, respectively.

Game₇: In this game, we expand the definition of ZeroShare in $\mathcal{O}_{\text{Sign}_4}$ and $\mathcal{O}_{\text{Corrupt}}$. The challenger samples partial masks $\widetilde{\mathbf{m}}_{i,j} = \mathsf{H}_{\text{mask}}(\text{seed}_{i,j}, \text{cnt}_\mathbf{w})$ and $\widetilde{\mathbf{m}}_{j,i} = \mathsf{H}_{\text{mask}}(\text{seed}_{j,i}, \text{cnt}_\mathbf{w})$ for $j \in \text{SS} \setminus \{i\}$, then sets $\boldsymbol{\Delta}_i = \sum_{j \in \text{SS} \setminus \{i\}} (\widetilde{\mathbf{m}}_{j,i} - \widetilde{\mathbf{m}}_{i,j})$. This change is purely conceptual.

Game₈: In this game, the challenger samples the partial masks $\widetilde{\mathbf{m}}_{i,j}$ and $\widetilde{\mathbf{m}}_{j,i}$ at random for $j \in \widetilde{\text{sHS}}_\mathbf{w} \setminus \{i\}$ (and programs H_{mask} accordingly). Both games are identically distributed in the view of $\mathcal{A}$ because seeds $\text{seed}_{i,j}$ and $\text{seed}_{j,i}$ are hidden from $\mathcal{A}$ and the partial masks have not yet been evaluated for users in $j \in \widetilde{\text{sHS}}_\mathbf{w}$.

---

[6] The challenger identifies that user i is the last user to open cmt_i via $\widetilde{\text{sHS}}_\mathbf{w} = \{i\}$ in $\mathcal{O}_{\text{Sign}_4}$ or $\mathcal{O}_{\text{Corrupt}}$, where $\widetilde{\text{sHS}}_\mathbf{w}$ is introduced in Game₆.

Game$_9$: In this game, the challenger samples the mask $\widetilde{\boldsymbol{\Delta}}_i \xleftarrow{\$} \mathcal{R}_q^k$ in $\mathcal{O}_{\mathsf{Sign}_4}$ and $\mathcal{O}_{\mathsf{Corrupt}}$, except if $\widetilde{\mathsf{sHS}}_{\mathsf{w}} = \{i\}$, i.e., user i is the last to open its cmt_i with respect to $\mathsf{ctnt}_{\mathsf{w}}$. If i is the last signer to open cmt_i, it sets

$$\widetilde{\boldsymbol{\Delta}}_i = - \sum_{j \in \mathsf{sHS}\setminus\{i\}} \mathsf{Mask}_{\mathsf{w}}[\mathsf{ctnt}_{\mathsf{w}}, j] - \sum_{j \in \mathsf{sCS}} \widetilde{\boldsymbol{\Delta}}_j. \qquad (6)$$

Note that when user i is corrupted, it also obtains $\vec{\mathsf{seed}}_i$. Since we sample the masks $\widetilde{\boldsymbol{\Delta}}_i$ *without* consulting the oracle $\mathsf{H}_{\mathsf{mask}}$ in this game, the challenger needs to ensure that $\mathsf{H}_{\mathsf{mask}}$ respects the identity

$$\widetilde{\boldsymbol{\Delta}}_i = \sum_{j \in \mathsf{SS}\setminus\{i\}} (\mathsf{H}_{\mathsf{mask}}(\mathsf{seed}_{j,i}, \mathsf{ctnt}_{\mathsf{w}}) - \mathsf{H}_{\mathsf{mask}}(\mathsf{seed}_{i,j}, \mathsf{ctnt}_{\mathsf{w}}))$$

when user i is corrupted. It does so via an additional helper algorithm ProgramZeroShare that sets up $\mathsf{H}_{\mathsf{mask}}$ in accordance with $\widetilde{\boldsymbol{\Delta}}_i$ stored in $\mathsf{Mask}_{\mathsf{w}}[\mathsf{ctnt}_{\mathsf{w}}, i]$. We refer to the formal proof in the full version.

Both games are identically distributed because: (1) If i is not the last signer for $\mathsf{ctnt}_{\mathsf{w}}$ in $\mathcal{O}_{\mathsf{Sign}_4}$ or $\mathcal{O}_{\mathsf{Corrupt}}$, then $\widetilde{\mathsf{sHS}}_{\mathsf{w}} \setminus \{i\}$ contains at least another honest signer j, so $\widetilde{\mathsf{m}}_{i,j}$ and $\widetilde{\mathsf{m}}_{j,i}$ are sampled at random from the previous game. In particular, $\widetilde{\boldsymbol{\Delta}}_i = \sum_{j \in \mathsf{SS}\setminus\{i\}} (\widetilde{\mathsf{m}}_{j,i} - \widetilde{\mathsf{m}}_{i,j})$ is distributed uniform random over $\mathcal{R}_q^k$. (2) If i is the last signer for $\mathsf{ctnt}_{\mathsf{w}}$, then all partial masks are fully determined and it holds that $\sum_{j \in \mathsf{SS}} \widetilde{\boldsymbol{\Delta}}_j = \boldsymbol{0}$. The latter yields Eq. (6) via the identity $\mathsf{Mask}_{\mathsf{z}}[\mathsf{ctnt}_{\mathsf{w}}, j] = \boldsymbol{\Delta}_j$. Note that the masked commitment for each signer i is still defined as in the real game:

$$\widetilde{\mathbf{w}}_i := \mathbf{w}_i + \widetilde{\boldsymbol{\Delta}}_i. \qquad (7)$$

Game$_{10}$: In this game, the challenger samples the masked commitment $\widetilde{\mathbf{w}}_i \xleftarrow{\$} \mathcal{R}_q^k$ at random when cmt_i is opened, except if $\widetilde{\mathsf{sHS}}_{\mathsf{w}} = \{i\}$, then it sets $\widetilde{\mathbf{w}}_i$ according to Eq. (5) consistently. Also, it manages tables $\mathsf{SumCom}[\mathsf{ctnt}_{\mathsf{w}}] = \sum_{j \in \mathsf{sHS}} \mathbf{w}_j$ and $\mathsf{SumComRnd}[\mathsf{ctnt}_{\mathsf{w}}] = \sum_{j \in \mathsf{sHS}} \mathbf{r}_j$ that store the sum of commitments $\mathbf{w}_j$ and $\mathbf{w}_j$'s randomenes $\mathbf{r}_j$, respectively. Also, the table $\mathsf{Mask}_{\mathsf{w}}[\mathsf{ctnt}_{\mathsf{w}}, i] := \widetilde{\mathbf{w}}_j - \mathbf{w}_i$ is initialized via $\mathsf{MaskedCom}[\mathsf{ctnt}_{\mathsf{w}}, i] = \widetilde{\mathbf{w}}_j$ only when a user is corrupted. This is required to setup $\mathsf{H}_{\mathsf{mask}}$ consistently when a user is corrupted, but not in $\mathcal{O}_{\mathsf{Sign}_4}$ anymore.

We can show that Game$_{10}$ and Game$_9$ are identically distributed by looking at an intermediate game Game$_{9,*}$, where instead of sampling $\widetilde{\boldsymbol{\Delta}}_i \xleftarrow{\$} \mathcal{R}_q^k$, we sample $\widetilde{\boldsymbol{\Delta}}_i^* \xleftarrow{\$} \mathcal{R}_q^k$ and set $\widetilde{\boldsymbol{\Delta}}_i := \widetilde{\boldsymbol{\Delta}}_i^* - \mathbf{w}_i$. This intermediate game is identically distributed to Game$_9$ as both $\widetilde{\boldsymbol{\Delta}}_i$ and $\widetilde{\boldsymbol{\Delta}}_i^*$ are uniform random. Also, observe that in Game$_{9,*}$, we have that $\widetilde{\mathbf{w}}_i = \widetilde{\boldsymbol{\Delta}}_i^*$ if $\widetilde{\mathsf{sHS}}_{\mathsf{w}} \neq \{i\}$ due to Eq. (7), and $\widetilde{\mathbf{w}}_i$ as in Eq. (5) otherwise. To see the latter, first substitute $\mathsf{Mask}_{\mathsf{w}}[\mathsf{ctnt}_{\mathsf{w}}, j] = \widetilde{\mathbf{w}}_j - \mathbf{w}_i$ for all $j \in \mathsf{sHS} \setminus \{i\}$ in Eq. (6), then substitute the resulting identity for $\widetilde{\boldsymbol{\Delta}}_i$ in the identity of $\widetilde{\mathbf{w}}_i$ in Eq. (7).

Game$_{11}$: In this game, the challenger samples the honest commitments $\mathbf{w}_j$ in round 4 when the last cmt$_i$ is opened to $\widetilde{\mathbf{w}}_i$. That is, if $\widetilde{\mathsf{sHS}}_\mathbf{w} \neq \{i\}$ in $\mathcal{O}_{\mathsf{Sign}_4}$, the challenger outputs random masked commitments $\widetilde{\mathbf{w}}_i \xleftarrow{\$} \mathcal{R}_q^k$ as before but does *not* sample $\mathbf{w}_i$ yet. Only when the last commitment cmt$_i$ is opened (either via a corruption or $\mathcal{O}_{\mathsf{Sign}_4}$ query), the challenger generates $|\mathsf{sHS}|$-many honest commitments at once and stores them in $\mathsf{UnUsedCom}[\mathsf{cnt}_\mathbf{w}] = \{\mathbf{w}_j\}_{j \in [|\mathsf{sHS}|]}$. Also, tables $\mathsf{SumCom}[\mathsf{cnt}_\mathbf{w}] = \sum_{j \in [|\mathsf{sHS}|]} \mathbf{w}_j$ and $\mathsf{SumComRnd}[\mathsf{cnt}_\mathbf{w}] = \sum_{j \in [|\mathsf{sHS}|]} \mathbf{r}_j$ are initialized, where $\mathbf{r}_j$ is $\mathbf{w}_j$'s randomness. In round 5 or when a user i is corrupted between round 4 and 5, then the challenger chooses one of the commitments $\mathbf{w}_i$ from the set $\mathsf{UnUsedCom}[\mathsf{cnt}_\mathbf{w}]$ and removes it from the set. In the latter case, the reduction also sets $\mathsf{Mask}_\mathbf{w}[\mathsf{cnt}_\mathbf{w}, i] = \widetilde{\mathbf{w}}_i - \mathbf{w}_i$ and programs the oracle $\mathsf{H}_{\mathsf{mask}}$ via $\mathsf{ProgramZeroShare}$ for consistency.

We can show that Game$_{10}$ and Game$_{11}$ are identically distributed. For this, observe that the protocol messages $(\widetilde{\mathbf{w}}_j)_{j \in \mathsf{sHS}}$ of round 4 reveal only the sum of the commitments $\mathbf{w}_j$ but *not* their attribution to users, *i.e.*, which user sampled which commitment $\mathbf{w}_j$. For now, this attribution is leaked implicitly in round 5 (since the challenger uses $\mathbf{r}_i$ in the computation of the masked response $\widetilde{\mathbf{z}}_i$) or explicitly when a user is corrupted. In those cases, since the challenger chooses a fresh commitment via $\mathsf{UnUsedCom}[\mathsf{cnt}_\mathbf{w}]$, the view of adversary $\mathcal{A}$ remains consistent.

This key step allows us to later simulate one of the commitments and attribute non-simulated honest commitments $\mathbf{w}_j$ to users *on-the-fly* in corruption queries.

Game$_{12}$ to Game$_{17}$: In Game$_{12}$ to Game$_{17}$, the challenger transitions to a game where $\widetilde{\mathbf{z}}_i \xleftarrow{\$} \mathcal{R}_q^\ell$ is sampled at random, except that the last response $\widetilde{\mathbf{z}}_i$ with $\mathsf{cnt}_\mathbf{w}$ is setup consistently, *i.e.*, it respects the constraint $\mathbf{\Delta}_i = -\sum_{j \in \mathsf{SS} \setminus \{i\}} \mathbf{\Delta}_j$. Again, adversary $\mathcal{A}$ can obtain this response either via $\mathcal{O}_{\mathsf{Sign}_5}$ or $\mathcal{O}_{\mathsf{Corrupt}}$. While in the protocol, the value $\mathsf{cnt}_\mathbf{z}$ serves as input to $\mathsf{ZeroShare}$, we can show that the value $\mathsf{cnt}_\mathbf{w}$ uniquely determines $\mathsf{cnt}_\mathbf{z}$ in round 5. This allows us to interchange $\mathsf{cnt}_\mathbf{w}$ and $\mathsf{cnt}_\mathbf{z}$ within the security proof when analyzing the distribution of $\mathbf{\Delta}_i$. We can show that the last masked response is distributed as follows:

$$\widetilde{\mathbf{z}}_i := c \cdot \mathbf{s} - c \sum_{j \in \mathsf{sCS}} L_{\mathsf{SS},j} \cdot \mathbf{s}_j + \mathsf{SumComRnd}[\mathsf{cnt}_\mathbf{w}] - \sum_{j \in \mathsf{sHS} \setminus \{i\}} \widetilde{\mathbf{z}}_j - \sum_{j \in \mathsf{sCS}} \mathbf{\Delta}_j, \quad (8)$$

where $\widetilde{\mathbf{z}}_j$ is the masked response of user i with $\mathsf{cnt}_\mathbf{w}$. Recall that $\mathsf{SumComRnd}[\mathsf{cnt}_\mathbf{w}] = \sum_{j \in [|\mathsf{sHS}|]} \mathbf{r}_j$ stores the sum of the honest commitment $\mathbf{w}_j$'s randomness.

The transition to Game$_{17}$ is similar to the transition from Game$_5$ to Game$_{10}$ in the proof of TRaccoon$_{\text{3-rnd}}^{\text{sel}}$. A crucial difference is that $\mathsf{cnt}_\mathbf{w}$ does *not* contain the commitments $(\mathsf{cmt}_j)_{j \in \mathsf{SS}}$ here. The authentication of the signer views in round 4 via the signatures $\sigma_{\mathsf{S},i}$ on M_S binds $\mathsf{cnt}_\mathbf{w}$ to a unique set of commitments $(\mathsf{cmt}_j)_{j \in \mathsf{SS}}$. This allows us to argue that $\mathsf{cnt}_\mathbf{z}$—and thus the challenge c—in round 5 is identical for all honest users. The identity in Eq. (8) follows as in the selective proof of $\mathsf{TRaccoon}_{\text{3-rnd}}^{\text{sel}}$, but due to the corruption oracle, we also need to ensure that $\mathsf{H}_{\mathsf{mask}}$ is consistent with the masks $\widetilde{\boldsymbol{\Delta}}_i$. This can be ensured via ProgramZeroShare as above.

Finally, note that since $\mathbf{r}_i$ is not required anymore in $\mathcal{O}_{\mathsf{Sign}_5}$, the challenger can exclusively attribute commitments from $\mathsf{UnUsedCom}[\mathsf{cnt}_{\mathbf{w}}]$ to users during corruption.

Game$_{18}$ to Game$_{20}$: *Invoke HVZK* In games Game$_{18}$ to Game$_{20}$, we invoke HVZK with respect to the verification key $\mathbf{t}$ to simulate one of the honest commitments in $\mathsf{UnUsedCom}[\mathsf{cnt}_{\mathbf{w}}]$ when the last commitment cmt_i with $\mathsf{cnt}_{\mathbf{w}}$ is opened. This later allows to compute the response $\widetilde{\mathbf{z}}_h$ of the last signer h in round 5 without secret key $\mathbf{s}$. At the end of Game$_{20}$, the challenger no longer requires the secret key $\mathbf{s}$ to simulate the signing oracles.

Game$_{18}$: In this game, the challenger chooses a random challenge $c \xleftarrow{\$} \mathcal{C}$ before sampling the honest commitments $\{\mathbf{w}_j\}_{j \in |\mathsf{sHS}|}$ for $\mathsf{UnUsedCom}[\mathsf{cnt}_{\mathbf{w}}]$ if $\widetilde{\mathsf{sHS}}_{\mathbf{w}} = \{i\}$ in $\mathcal{O}_{\mathsf{Sign}_4}$ or $\mathcal{O}_{\mathsf{Corrupt}}$. Before outputting $\widetilde{\mathbf{w}}_i$ or the state st_i, the challenger retrieves the corrupt commitments $\mathbf{w}_j$ for $j \in \mathsf{CS}$ from cmt_j by searching through all the random oracle queries made to $\mathsf{H}_{\mathsf{com}}$. If all $\mathbf{w}_j$ are found, it programs H_c such that $\mathsf{H}_c(\mathsf{vk}, M, \mathbf{w}) = c$, where $\mathbf{w} = \left\lfloor \mathsf{SumCom}[\mathsf{cnt}_{\mathbf{w}}] + \sum_{j \in \mathsf{CS}} \mathbf{w}_j \right\rceil_{\nu_{\mathbf{w}}}$. Further, the challenger aborts if some $\mathbf{w}_j$ was not found in round 4 or $\mathcal{O}_{\mathsf{Corrupt}}$ with $\widetilde{\mathsf{sHS}}_{\mathbf{w}} = \{i\}$, but $\mathcal{O}_{\mathsf{Sign}_5}$ is invoked with $\mathsf{cnt}_{\mathbf{w}}$.

Since $|\mathsf{sHS}| \geq 1$ and $\mathbf{w}_j$ has high min-entropy, H_c was never queried with $(\mathsf{vk}, M, \mathbf{w})$ before it is programmed, so the view of $\mathcal{A}$ is identically distributed. Since the challenger checks in $\mathcal{O}_{\mathsf{Sign}_5}$ whether each $\widetilde{\mathbf{w}}_j$ is committed in cmt_j, the adversary must have found a preimage for all cmt_j. This happens with negligible probability. To argue the above, we use that due to signature-based authentication, we know that $\mathsf{cnt}_{\mathbf{w}}$ fixes $(\mathsf{cmt}_j)_{j \in \mathsf{SS}}$ implicitly and for $j \in \mathsf{sHS}$, the hash commitments cmt_j are honest.

Game$_{19}$: In this game, the challenger invokes HVZK with respect to the verification key $\mathbf{t}$ to simulate one of the commitments $(\mathbf{w}_j)_{j \in |\mathsf{sHS}|}$ when setting up $\mathsf{UnUsedCom}[\mathsf{cnt}_{\mathbf{w}}]$, and computes the consistent response $\widetilde{\mathbf{z}}_h$ for $\mathsf{cnt}_{\mathbf{w}}$ in a different manner. In more detail, if $\widetilde{\mathsf{sHS}}_{\mathbf{w}} = \{i\}$ in $\mathcal{O}_{\mathsf{Corrupt}}$ or $\mathcal{O}_{\mathsf{Sign}_4}$, after sampling the challenge c, the challenger simulates the commitment-response pair $(\mathbf{w}_*, \mathbf{z}_*)$, where $\mathbf{z}_* = c \cdot \mathbf{s} + \mathbf{r}_*$. The commitment $\mathbf{w}_*$ is added to $\mathsf{SumCom}[\mathsf{cnt}_{\mathbf{w}}]$ but *not* stored in $\mathsf{UnUsedCom}[\mathsf{cnt}_{\mathbf{w}}]$ to avoid attributing it to a user in $\mathcal{O}_{\mathsf{Corrupt}}$. Also, $\mathbf{r}_*$ is *not* added to $\mathsf{SumComRnd}[\mathsf{cnt}_{\mathbf{w}}]$. Instead, the challenger computes the last consistent response $\widetilde{\mathbf{z}}_h$, i.e., if $\widetilde{\mathsf{sHS}}_{\mathbf{z}} = \{i\}$ in $\mathcal{O}_{\mathsf{Sign}_5}$ or $\mathcal{O}_{\mathsf{Corrupt}}$, via the simulated response $\mathbf{z}_*$ as follows:

$$\widetilde{\mathbf{z}}_h := \mathbf{z}_* - c \sum_{j \in \mathsf{sCS}} L_{\mathsf{SS},j} \cdot \mathbf{s}_j + \mathsf{SumComRnd}[\mathsf{cnt}_{\mathbf{w}}] - \sum_{j \in \mathsf{sHS} \setminus \{h\}} \widetilde{\mathbf{z}}_j - \sum_{j \in \mathsf{sCS}} \boldsymbol{\Delta}_j.$$

The above identity for $\widetilde{\mathbf{z}}_h$ is obtained by rewriting Eq. (8) using $\mathbf{z}_* = c \cdot \mathbf{s} + \mathbf{r}_*$. Note that it is crucial that the challenge c—precomputed when the last user

i opens its commitment to define $\mathbf{z}_*$—must be identical to the challenge c in Eq. (8). This is guaranteed by the abort condition in the previous game. Also, note that since at least one user $i \in \mathsf{sHS}$ remains uncorrupted, so we never have to attribute the simulated commitment to a user.

Game$_{20}$: In this game, the challenger replaces $\mathbf{t}$ in the verification key with $\mathbf{t} := \left[\hat{\mathbf{t}}\right]_{\nu_t} \in \mathcal{R}_{q_{\nu_t}}^k$, where $\hat{\mathbf{t}} \xleftarrow{\$} \mathcal{R}_q^k$. Also, when a user i is corrupted, it samples $\mathbf{s}_i$ at random.

Observe that the challenger in Game$_{19}$ uses the secret key $\mathbf{s}$ only when computing the simulated response $\mathbf{z}_* = c \cdot \mathbf{s} + \mathbf{r}_i$. Under Hint-MLWE, Game$_{19}$ and Game$_{20}$ are indistinguishable. Note that simulated responses $\mathbf{z}_*$ correspond to the provided hints in Hint-MLWE.

Reduction from SelfTargetMSIS. In Game$_{20}$, the challenger can simulate the signing oracles without knowing $\mathbf{s}$. At this point, we can construct an adversary against SelfTargetMSIS as in selective proof of TRaccoon$_{\text{3-rnd}}^{\text{sel}}$. We omit details.

5 Construction of Our 5-Round Threshold Schnorr

We briefly present our 5-round threshold signature scheme TSchnorr$_{\text{5-rnd}}^{\text{adp}}$. It is proven adaptively secure under the DL assumption. We refer to Sec. 7 in the full version for details.

Preparations. Let $\mathbb{G}$ be a group of prime order p with generator G. We again use the helper algorithm ZeroShare defined with respect to $\mathsf{H}_{\mathsf{mask}}$. Here, we assume that $\mathsf{H}_{\mathsf{mask}}$ outputs vectors over $\mathbb{G}$ and $\mathbb{Z}_p$ when the first bit of input x is 0 and 1, respectively. We still require an EUF-CMA secure signature scheme.

Construction. Essentially, we obtain TSchnorr$_{\text{5-rnd}}^{\text{adp}}$ from TRaccoon$_{\text{5-rnd}}^{\text{adp}}$ by replacing the Raccoon-related elements with their Schnorr-counterparts:

- We replace the matrix $\mathbf{A}$ in tspar with $(\mathbb{G}, p, G)$, and the verification key with (tspar, X), where $X = x \cdot G$ and $x \xleftarrow{\$} \mathbb{Z}_p$ is a Schnorr public and secret key, respectively. Also, x is shared into partial secrets $(x_i)_{i \in [N]}$ as before.
- We replace verification with the classical Schnorr verification.
- In Sign$_2$, we replace the Raccoon commitments $\mathbf{w}_i = \mathbf{A}\mathbf{r}_i + \mathbf{e}_i'$ with Schnorr commitments $R_i = r_i \cdot G$, where $r_i \xleftarrow{\$} \mathbb{Z}_p$. The commitments are masked via $\widetilde{R}_i = R_i + \widetilde{\Delta}_i$ as before. Again, cmt$_i$ commits to $\widetilde{R}_i$.
- In Sign$_5$, we still sum up the masked commitments $\widetilde{R}_i$ to obtain an aggregated commitment $R = \sum_{j \in \mathsf{SS}} \widetilde{R}_j$. Also, the masked response is computed as before via $\widetilde{z}_i := c \cdot L_{\mathsf{SS},i} \cdot x_i + r_i + \Delta_i$, except that $\widetilde{z}_i \in \mathbb{Z}_p$.

Acknowledgement. This work has been supported in part by JST CREST Grant Number JPMJCR22M1, JST-AIP Acceleration Research JPMJCR22U5, JSPS KAKENHI Grant Numbers JP22KJ1366.

References

1. Agrawal, S., Stehlé, D., Yadav, A.: Round-optimal lattice-based threshold signatures, revisited. In: Bojanczyk, M., Merelli, E., Woodruff, D.P. (eds.) ICALP 2022. LIPIcs, vol. 229, pp. 8:1–8:20. Schloss Dagstuhl (2022). https://doi.org/10.4230/LIPIcs.ICALP.2022.8
2. Anonymous: Two-round threshold signature from algebraic one-more learning with errors (2024). Submitted to CRYPTO 2024
3. Bacho, R., Loss, J., Tessaro, S., Wagner, B., Zhu, C.: Twinkle: threshold signatures from DDH with full adaptive security (2024). To Appear in EUROCRYPT 2024. https://eprint.iacr.org/2023/1482
4. Bai, S., Galbraith, S.D.: An improved compression technique for signatures based on learning with errors. In: Benaloh, J. (ed.) CT-RSA 2014. LNCS, vol. 8366, pp. 28–47. Springer, Cham (2014). https://doi.org/10.1007/978-3-319-04852-9_2
5. Bellare, M., Crites, E.C., Komlo, C., Maller, M., Tessaro, S., Zhu, C.: Better than advertised security for non-interactive threshold signatures. In: Dodis, Y., Shrimpton, T. (eds.) CRYPTO 2022, Part IV. LNCS, vol. 13510, pp. 517–550. Springer, Heidelberg (2022). https://doi.org/10.1007/978-3-031-15985-5_18
6. Bellare, M., Neven, G.: Multi-signatures in the plain public-key model and a general forking lemma. In: Juels, A., Wright, R.N., De Capitani di Vimercati, S. (eds.) ACM CCS 2006, pp. 390–399. ACM Press (2006). https://doi.org/10.1145/1180405.1180453
7. Benhamouda, F., Lepoint, T., Loss, J., Orrù, M., Raykova, M.: On the (in)security of ROS. In: Canteaut, A., Standaert, F.-X. (eds.) EUROCRYPT 2021, Part I. LNCS, vol. 12696, pp. 33–53. Springer, Cham (2021). https://doi.org/10.1007/978-3-030-77870-5_2
8. Boneh, D., et al.: Threshold cryptosystems from threshold fully homomorphic encryption. In: Shacham, H., Boldyreva, A. (eds.) CRYPTO 2018, Part I. LNCS, vol. 10991, pp. 565–596. Springer, Cham (2018). https://doi.org/10.1007/978-3-319-96884-1_19
9. Brandão, L., Davidson, M.: Notes on threshold eddsa/schnorr signatures. National Institute of Standards and Technology (2022). https://doi.org/10.6028/NIST.IR.8214B.ipd
10. Canetti, R., Feige, U., Goldreich, O., Naor, M.: Adaptively secure multi-party computation. In: 28th ACM STOC, pp. 639–648. ACM Press (1996). https://doi.org/10.1145/237814.238015
11. Chevallier-Mames, B.: An efficient CDH-based signature scheme with a tight security reduction. In: Shoup, V. (ed.) CRYPTO 2005. LNCS, vol. 3621, pp. 511–526. Springer, Heidelberg (2005). https://doi.org/10.1007/11535218_31
12. Crites, E.C., Komlo, C., Maller, M.: Fully adaptive Schnorr threshold signatures. In: Handschuh, H., Lysyanskaya, A. (eds.) CRYPTO 2023, Part I. LNCS, vol. 14081, pp. 678–709. Springer, Heidelberg (2023). https://doi.org/10.1007/978-3-031-38557-5_22
13. Desmedt, Y.: Abuses in cryptography and how to fight them. In: Goldwasser, S. (ed.) CRYPTO 1988. LNCS, vol. 403, pp. 375–389. Springer, New York (1990). https://doi.org/10.1007/0-387-34799-2_29
14. Desmedt, Y., Frankel, Y.: Threshold cryptosystems. In: Brassard, G. (ed.) CRYPTO 1989. LNCS, vol. 435, pp. 307–315. Springer, New York (1990). https://doi.org/10.1007/0-387-34805-0_28

15. Ducas, L., et al.: CRYSTALS-Dilithium: a lattice-based digital signature scheme. IACR TCHES **2018**(1), 238–268 (2018). https://doi.org/10.13154/tches.v2018.i1.238-268. https://tches.iacr.org/index.php/TCHES/article/view/839
16. Fiat, A., Shamir, A.: How to prove yourself: practical solutions to identification and signature problems. In: Odlyzko, A.M. (ed.) CRYPTO 1986. LNCS, vol. 263, pp. 186–194. Springer, Heidelberg (1987). https://doi.org/10.1007/3-540-47721-7_12
17. Fuchsbauer, G., Kiltz, E., Loss, J.: The algebraic group model and its applications. In: Shacham, H., Boldyreva, A. (eds.) CRYPTO 2018, Part II. LNCS, vol. 10992, pp. 33–62. Springer, Cham (2018). https://doi.org/10.1007/978-3-319-96881-0_2
18. Gur, K.D., Katz, J., Silde, T.: Two-round threshold lattice signatures from threshold homomorphic encryption. Cryptology ePrint Archive, Paper 2023/1318 (2023). https://eprint.iacr.org/2023/1318. https://eprint.iacr.org/2023/1318
19. Hauck, E., Kiltz, E., Loss, J.: A modular treatment of blind signatures from identification schemes. In: Ishai, Y., Rijmen, V. (eds.) EUROCRYPT 2019, Part III. LNCS, vol. 11478, pp. 345–375. Springer, Cham (2019). https://doi.org/10.1007/978-3-030-17659-4_12
20. Hauck, E., Kiltz, E., Loss, J., Nguyen, N.K.: Lattice-based blind signatures, revisited. In: Micciancio, D., Ristenpart, T. (eds.) CRYPTO 2020, Part II. LNCS, vol. 12171, pp. 500–529. Springer, Cham (2020). https://doi.org/10.1007/978-3-030-56880-1_18
21. Kiltz, E., Loss, J., Pan, J.: Tightly-secure signatures from five-move identification protocols. In: Takagi, T., Peyrin, T. (eds.) ASIACRYPT 2017, Part III. LNCS, vol. 10626, pp. 68–94. Springer, Cham (2017). https://doi.org/10.1007/978-3-319-70700-6_3
22. Kiltz, E., Lyubashevsky, V., Schaffner, C.: A concrete treatment of fiat-shamir signatures in the quantum random-oracle model. In: Nielsen, J.B., Rijmen, V. (eds.) EUROCRYPT 2018, Part III. LNCS, vol. 10822, pp. 552–586. Springer, Cham (2018). https://doi.org/10.1007/978-3-319-78372-7_18
23. Kim, D., Lee, D., Seo, J., Song, Y.: Toward practical lattice-based proof of knowledge from hint-MLWE. In: Handschuh, H., Lysyanskaya, A. (eds.) CRYPTO 2023. LNCS, vol. 14085, pp. 549–580. Springer, Cham (2023). https://doi.org/10.1007/978-3-031-38554-4_18
24. Komlo, C., Goldberg, I.: FROST: flexible round-optimized schnorr threshold signatures. In: Dunkelman, O., Jacobson, Jr., M.J., O'Flynn, C. (eds.) SAC 2020. LNCS, vol. 12804, pp. 34–65. Springer, Cham (2021). https://doi.org/10.1007/978-3-030-81652-0_2
25. Lindell, Y.: Simple three-round multiparty schnorr signing with full simulatability. Cryptology ePrint Archive, Report 2022/374 (2022). https://eprint.iacr.org/2022/374
26. Lyubashevsky, V.: Fiat-Shamir with aborts: applications to lattice and factoring-based signatures. In: Matsui, M. (ed.) ASIACRYPT 2009. LNCS, vol. 5912, pp. 598–616. Springer, Heidelberg (2009). https://doi.org/10.1007/978-3-642-10366-7_35
27. Lyubashevsky, V.: Lattice signatures without trapdoors. In: Pointcheval, D., Johansson, T. (eds.) EUROCRYPT 2012. LNCS, vol. 7237, pp. 738–755. Springer, Heidelberg (2012). https://doi.org/10.1007/978-3-642-29011-4_43
28. NIST: Call for additional digital signature schemes for the post-quantum cryptography standardization process (2022). https://csrc.nist.gov/csrc/media/Projects/pqc-dig-sig/documents/call-for-proposals-dig-sig-sept-2022.pdf

29. Peralta, R., Brandão, L.T.: NIST first call for multi-party threshold schemes. National Institute of Standards and Technology (2023). https://doi.org/10.6028/NIST.IR.8214C.ipd, https://doi.org/10.6028/NIST.IR.8214C.ipd
30. del Pino, R., Katsumata, S., Maller, M., Mouhartem, F., Prest, T., Saarinen, M.J.O.: Threshold raccoon: practical threshold signatures from standard lattice assumptions (2024). To Appear in EUROCRYPT 2024. htttps://eprint.iacr.org/2024/184
31. del Pino, R., et al.: Raccoon. Technical report, National Institute of Standards and Technology (2023). https://csrc.nist.gov/Projects/pqc-dig-sig/round-1-additional-signatures
32. Schnorr, C.P.: Efficient signature generation by smart cards. J. Cryptol. **4**(3), 161–174 (1991). https://doi.org/10.1007/BF00196725
33. Shamir, A.: How to share a secret. Commun. ACM **22**(11), 612–613 (1979). https://doi.org/10.1145/359168.359176
34. Tessaro, S., Zhu, C.: Threshold and multi-signature schemes from linear hash functions. In: Hazay, C., Stam, M. (eds.) EUROCRYPT 2023, Part V. LNCS, vol. 14008, pp. 628–658. Springer, Heidelberg (2023). https://doi.org/10.1007/978-3-031-30589-4_22

Author Index

A
Ananth, Prabhanjan 3

B
Bartusek, James 184
Behera, Amit 3
Boneh, Dan 317

C
Chung, Kai-Min 215

D
Das, Sourav 251

E
Espitau, Thomas 387, 425

G
Garg, Sanjam 352
Goldin, Eli 215
Gray, Matthew 215

K
Katsumata, Shuichi 387, 459
Katz, Jonathan 285
Kitagawa, Fuyuki 93
Kolonelos, Dimitris 352

L
Li, Longcheng 152
Li, Qian 152
Li, Xingjian 152
Liu, Qipeng 152

M
Malavolta, Giulio 126
Morimae, Tomoyuki 59, 93

N
Nehoran, Barak 59
Niot, Guilhem 425
Nishimaki, Ryo 93

P
Partap, Aditi 317
Policharla, Guru-Vamsi 352
Prest, Thomas 425

Q
Qian, Luowen 38

R
Raizes, Justin 184
Reichle, Michael 459
Ren, Ling 251
Rotem, Lior 317

T
Takemure, Kaoru 387, 459

W
Walter, Michael 126
Wang, Mingyuan 352

Y
Yamakawa, Takashi 59, 93

© International Association for Cryptologic Research 2024
L. Reyzin and D. Stebila (Eds.): CRYPTO 2024, LNCS 14926, p. 493, 2024.
https://doi.org/10.1007/978-3-031-68394-7

Printed in the USA
CPSIA information can be obtained
at www.ICGtesting.com
CBHW071919030924
13955CB00010B/873

9 783031 683930